THE JOHNS HOPKINS
MEDICAL HANDBOOK

THE
JOHNS HOPKINS
MEDICAL
HANDBOOK

*The 100 Major Medical
Disorders of People Over
the Age of 50*

PLUS A DIRECTORY
TO THE LEADING TEACHING HOSPITALS,
RESEARCH ORGANIZATIONS, TREATMENT
CENTERS, AND SUPPORT GROUPS

Medical Editors
Simeon Margolis, M.D., Ph.D.
Hamilton Moses III, M.D.

Prepared by the Editors of
The Johns Hopkins Medical Letter
HEALTH AFTER 50

PUBLISHED BY
REBUS, INC. NEW YORK

DISTRIBUTED BY RANDOM HOUSE, INC.

THE JOHNS HOPKINS MEDICAL LETTER
HEALTH AFTER 50

THE JOHNS HOPKINS MEDICAL HANDBOOK *is the definitive home medical reference for adults, from America's top research hospital.*

THE JOHNS HOPKINS MEDICAL LETTER HEALTH AFTER 50, *our monthly, eight-page newsletter, provides the same kind of timely information for everyone concerned with taking control of his or her own health and medical care, using clear, nontechnical language that is easy to understand. And, it comes from the century-old tradition of Johns Hopkins excellence. For information on how to order this unique newsletter, write to Medletter Associates, Inc., Department 1102, 632 Broadway, New York, New York 10012.*

For information about permission to reproduce selections from this book, write to Permissions, Medletter Associates, Inc., 632 Broadway, New York, New York 10012.

Library of Congress Cataloging-in-Publication Data
The Johns Hopkins medical handbook : the 100 major medical disorders of people over the age of 50 : plus a directory to the leading teaching hospitals, research organizations, treatment centers, and support groups / prepared by the editors of the Johns Hopkins Medical Letter, Health after 50.
p.   cm.
Includes index.
ISBN 0-929661-04-4
1. Geriatrics—Handbooks, manuals, etc. 2. Aged—Diseases—Handbooks, manuals, etc. 3. Medical care—United States—Directories. I. Johns Hopkins medical letter health after 50. [DNLM: 1. Delivery of Health Care—directories. 2. Disease—in middle age—handbooks. 3. Disease—in old age—handbooks. WB 39J65]
RC952.55.J64 1992
616'.0084'4—dc20
DNLM/DC
for Library of Congress   92-15420
                                                 CIP

Printed in the United States of America
10 9 8 7 6 5 4 3 2 1
Distributed by Random House, Inc.

The Johns Hopkins Medical Handbook

CHARLES L. MEE, JR
Editorial Director

BRENDA SAVARD
Managing Editor

JUDITH HENRY
Art Director

EVAN HANSEN
ERIN KELLY
Associate Editors

KARIN MARTIN
Associate Designer

MARILYN FLAIG
Indexer

CARNEY W. MIMMS III
Directory Database Programmer

RODNEY FRIEDMAN
Editor and Publisher

BARBARA MAXWELL O'NEILL
Associate Publisher

Johns Hopkins Medical Books
are published under the auspices of
The Johns Hopkins Medical Letter
HEALTH AFTER 50.

RODNEY FRIEDMAN
Editor and Publisher

CHARLES L. MEE, JR
Editorial Director

MARY CROWLEY
Executive Editor

BETTE PONACK ALBERT, M.D.
Medical Editor

EVAN HANSEN
Managing Editor

TOM R. DAMRAUER
JANE MARGARETTEN, R.N.
Medical Researchers

BARBARA MAXWELL O'NEILL
Associate Publisher

The following organizations have cooperated with Johns Hopkins in providing material for this Handbook:

THE AMERICAN ACADEMY OF DERMATOLOGY

THE AMERICAN ACADEMY OF OPHTHALMOLOGY

THE AMERICAN ACADEMY OF OTOLARYNGOLOGY

THE AMERICAN COLLEGE OF OBSTETRICIANS AND GYNECOLOGISTS

THE AMERICAN DIABETES ASSOCIATION

THE AMERICAN HEART ASSOCIATION

THE AMERICAN LIVER FOUNDATION

THE AMERICAN LUNG ASSOCIATION

THE AMERICAN PSYCHIATRIC ASSOCIATION

THE AMERICAN SLEEP DISORDERS ASSOCIATION

THE ARTHRITIS FOUNDATION

THE NATIONAL CANCER INSTITUTE

THE NATIONAL INSTITUTE OF ARTHRITIS AND MUSCULOSKELETAL AND SKIN DISEASES

THE NATIONAL INSTITUTE OF DENTAL RESEARCH

THE NATIONAL INSTITUTE OF DIABETES AND DIGESTIVE AND KIDNEY DISEASES

THE NATIONAL INSTITUTE OF NEUROLOGICAL DISORDERS AND STROKE

THE NATIONAL INSTITUTE ON AGING

THE NATIONAL KIDNEY FOUNDATION

THE THYROID FOUNDATION OF AMERICA

THE WARREN GRANT MAGNUSON CLINICAL CENTER

CONTENTS

INTRODUCTION

The Johns Hopkins Medical Handbook is intended to provide a compendium of the 100 major medical disorders of people over the age of 50—along with a directory to the American medical care system. It has been prepared with the cooperation of some of the leading medical societies and health information organizations in the United States and we are honored to have them associated with us in this endeavor.

While many medical encyclopedias are available to the general public, none specifically addresses the major health concerns of people over 50, and none has a directory like this one.

The entries are taken from the most recent publications prepared for the general public by the organizations listed on page seven. Each of these organizations has subjected its material to an extensive review process by physicians who are recognized authorities in their fields. We then asked our specialists at Johns Hopkins to give the texts an additional review. They have added further comments and explanations about the text; these are identified in the Handbook by either the "Hopkins dome" symbol or the signature "The Editors."

The purpose of this handbook, as of any handbook, is to provide a ready-reference source of available knowledge rather than to report the most recent advances in the field. Of course, the information presented here is not meant to substitute for the advice of your own physician.

We believe, however, that the entries in the Handbook will help you gain a familiarity with the vocabulary of the disorder that concerns you, provide you with helpful and detailed explanations of the basics, and serve as a good starting point for further conversations with your physicians or with health care organizations—such as those listed in the Directory—that can provide additional information and assistance. We expect, in this way, that the Handbook will prove to be a valuable asset to you in taking control of your own health and medical care.

The Editors

Cancer

OVERVIEW

Cancer is really a group of diseases. There are more than 100 different types of cancer, however they all are a disease of some of the body's cells.

Healthy cells that make up the body's tissues grow, divide, and replace themselves in an orderly way. This process keeps the body in good repair. Sometimes, however, normal cells lose their ability to limit and direct their growth. They divide too rapidly and grow without any order. Too much tissue is produced and tumors begin to form. Tumors can be either benign or malignant.

Benign tumors are not cancer. They do not spread to other parts of the body and they are seldom a threat to life. Often, benign tumors can be removed by surgery, and they are not likely to return.

Malignant tumors are cancer. They can invade and destroy nearby tissue and organs. Cancer cells also can spread, or metastasize, to other parts of the body, and form new tumors.

Because cancer can spread, it is important for the doctor to find out as early as possible if a tumor is present and if it is cancer. As soon as a diagnosis is made, treatment can begin.

SIGNS AND SYMPTOMS OF CANCER

Cancer and other illnesses often cause a number of problems you can watch for. The most common warning signs of cancer are:

- **C**hange in bowel or bladder habits
- **A** sore that does not heal
- **U**nusual bleeding or discharge
- **T**hickening or lump in the breast or elsewhere
- **I**ndigestion or difficulty swallowing
- **O**bvious change in a wart or mole
- **N**agging cough or hoarseness

These signs and symptoms can be caused by cancer or by a number of other problems. They are not a sure sign of cancer. However, it is important to see a doctor if any problem lasts as long as two weeks. Don't wait for symptoms to become painful; pain is not an early sign of cancer.

EARLY DETECTION

Any illness should be diagnosed and treated as early as possible, but this is especially important for cancer. The earlier cancer is detected and treated, the better a person's chances for a full recovery.

Besides being alert to symptoms of cancer, both women and men should have regular physical exams. Early detection of some cancers is possible with tests for individuals who have no symptoms of disease. Even before symptoms appear, a doctor may be able to detect cancers of the colon, rectum, mouth, skin, breast, cervix, prostate, and testicles.

Exams for Both Women and Men

Colon and rectum. Regular medical exams are important for early detection of cancer of the colon and rectum. To check the rectal area, the doctor inserts a gloved finger into the rectum and gently feels for any bumps.

Beginning at age 50, each person should have an annual test to see if there is blood in the stool. Blood in the stool may be caused by colon cancer, but it also can come from other conditions. Further tests are needed to make a definite diagnosis. Every three to five years after a person reaches 50, the doctor should use an instrument, such as a sigmoidoscope, to look at the patient's rectum and colon.

Mouth. It also is important to check regularly for signs of cancer of the mouth. Tissue changes in the mouth that might signal the early beginnings of cancer can be seen and felt easily. A dentist should perform a thorough exam of a patient's mouth at regular visits. In addition, each month you should examine your own mouth using a mirror. Look for changes in the color of the gums, lips, or cheeks, as well as scabs, cracks, sores, swelling, bleeding, or thickenings in any area of the mouth. Finding these or other problems in the mouth does not always mean that cancer is present, but all problems should be checked by a doctor or a dentist.

Skin. Skin cancer is the most common type of cancer in the United States. You should check yourself regularly for new growths or other changes in the skin. Any changes should be reported to the doctor without delay. Doctors should also look at the skin during routine medical exams.

Exams for Women

Breast. All women should have their breasts examined regularly by a doctor to check for any unusual changes, such as a lump or thickening. In addition, women should learn how to perform breast self-examination (BSE) and should do BSE each month. BSE is best done a few days after the menstrual period has ended, when the breasts are least likely to be swollen or tender. After menopause, a woman should choose the same day each month for BSE. This examination is especially important for women over 40 because the risk of breast cancer increases with age. (See Benign Breast Conditions, page 408.)

If a woman finds a lump or notices a change in her breast, she should see her doctor. About 80 percent of all breast lumps are not cancer, but only a doctor can make a definite diagnosis.

A mammogram, an x-ray of the breast, can show a tumor or change in the breast that is too small to be felt—even by a doctor's careful exam. Beginning at age 40, a woman should have a mammogram every one to two years. When a woman reaches 50, she should have a mammogram every year.

Cervix. Most cases of cervical cancer could be prevented if all women had regular pelvic exams and Pap tests. In a pelvic exam, the doctor feels the uterus, vagina, ovaries, fallopian tubes, bladder, and rectum for any abnormality in their size or shape. The Pap test can detect abnormal cells in and around the cervix. For this test, a sample of cells is collected from the upper vagina and cervix with a cotton swab or a wooden scraper and placed on a glass slide for examination under a microscope.

Women should start having annual Pap tests when they turn 18 or soon after they become sexually active. If a woman has had three or more normal annual Pap tests, the test may be done less frequently, based on the advice of her doctor.

Exams for Men

Prostate. A digital rectal examination is the most reliable way for a doctor to detect early prostate cancer. This exam should be part of the annual medical checkup for all men over 40. The doctor may be able to feel an irregular or unusually firm area in the prostate that might mean that a tumor is present.

Testicles. Most testicular cancers are found by men themselves. Men can detect changes in their testicles by doing testicular self-examination (TSE) each month. This simple exam is best done during or after a warm shower or bath when the scrotum is relaxed and changes are easy to feel. If TSE reveals a lump or other problem (especially enlargement of the testicles, unusual tenderness, pain, or a feeling of heaviness), a man should see his doctor. An exam of the testicles by the doctor should also be part of a man's routine annual medical checkup.

DIAGNOSING CANCER

When symptoms suggest that a person might have cancer, the doctor asks about the patient's medical history and does a complete exam. In addition to checking the general signs of health (temperature, pulse, blood pressure, and so on), the doctor usually does several other tests.

The most common way that doctors explore what's happening inside the body is with x-rays. In addition to standard x-rays, like those used to look inside the chest or to check for broken bones, special x-rays may be used to diagnose cancers and other diseases. One of these, the CT (computed tomography) scan, uses a computer to produce a cross-sectional picture of the body on a screen. Doctors also use angiograms to see if there are blockages or abnormal placement of blood vessels, which may mean that a tumor is present.

Another diagnostic test uses radioactive isotopes to find abnormal growths. In these tests, the patient swallows or is injected with a mild radioactive material. Special equipment then tracks the radioactive material, allowing doctors to locate tumors.

Ultrasound is another way to view the inside of the body. In this exam, high-frequency sound waves, which cannot be heard by humans, are directed toward a particular part of the body. These waves echo or bounce off the tissue and organs, and the echo makes pictures on a screen. Tumors produce different echoes than normal tissues, making it possible to see any abnormal growths.

Sometimes special tests are done to measure substances (tumor markers) that may increase in the blood of a person with cancer. (These same tests may be used later on to find out how the patient is responding to treatment.)

These and other diagnostic tests, including a variety of laboratory tests (such as blood and urine tests), may reveal a tumor. However, the only way to make a definite diagnosis of cancer is by a biopsy. For this test, the whole tumor or a piece of it is removed and examined under a microscope to check for cancer cells.

When cancer is diagnosed, the doctor also needs to know the stage of the disease. Staging tests tell whether the cancer has spread from its primary site, or starting point, to other parts of the body. Knowing the stage of a cancer helps the doctor plan the best treatment.

TREATING CANCER

Partly because of advances in research, more people are recovering from cancer now than ever before, and new ways to treat the disease are being discovered. Today, nearly half of all cancer patients are being cured because of earlier diagnosis and improved treatment methods.

Treatment Planning

The doctor develops a treatment plan that fits the patient's medical history, age and general health, and the extent and type of cancer. Before starting treatment, the patient may want a second doctor to review the diagnosis and treatment plan. If so, there are a number of ways to get a second opinion.

- The doctor can discuss the patient's case with others who specialize in treating a particular type of cancer. Names of doctors are available from the NCI (National Cancer Institute) computer system known as PDQ (Physician Data Query). This system contains up-to-date treatment information for more than 80 types of cancer.
- Patients can get the names of doctors to consult about their treatment plans from the local medical society, a nearby medical school, or the *Directory of Medical Specialists*, a book available in many libraries.
- The Cancer Information Service, at 1-800-4-CANCER, also may be able to help patients locate doctors to consult for a second opinion.

Informed Consent

When treatment is recommended, most health care facilities require patients to sign a form stating their willingness to proceed. This is to certify that the patient understands what procedures will be done and has agreed to have them performed.

Before agreeing to any treatment, you should ask your doctor for information about:

- The recommended procedure
- Its purpose
- Risks and side effects associated with it
- Likely consequences with and without treatment
- Other available treatments
- Advantages and disadvantages of one treatment over another.

You are likely to discover that your concerns about treatment will decrease as your understanding of cancer and how it is treated increases.

Methods of Treating Cancer

Ways to treat cancer include: surgery, radiation therapy, chemotherapy, hormone therapy, and biological therapy. The doctor may use one method or a combination of them. The choice of treatment depends on the type of cancer, the location of the tumor, the stage (extent) of the cancer, the patient's age and general health, and a number of other individual factors. A doctor considers all of these items when choosing the best treatment for each patient. In some cases, the patient may be referred to specialists in the different kinds of cancer treatment.

Because cancer can spread, the treatments used against it are very powerful. It is rarely possible to limit the effects of cancer treatment so that only cancer cells are destroyed. Normal, healthy cells may be damaged at the same time. For this reason, patients may have unpleasant side effects. Doctors try to plan treatment to keep side effects to a minimum. Fortunately, most side effects are temporary and go away after treatment ends.

In the following sections, you will find more information about the different types of treatment for cancer.

Surgery. For many types of cancer, surgery is recommended. Surgery is a local treatment that removes the tumor and any nearby tissue that may contain cancer cells. Sometimes, healthy tissue may also have to be removed from around the tumor to help keep the cancer from spreading.

When cancer cells spread, they can travel through the bloodstream or the lymphatic system. This system carries lymph fluid through the body, and it can carry cancer cells as well. Therefore, during surgery doctors often remove lymph nodes that are near the tumor to see if they contain cancer cells.

Surgery can cause some side effects, depending on the type of operation, the general health of the patient, and other factors. During the first few days after surgery, patients often have soreness in the wound area. Because some nerves may be cut during surgery, patients also may have some numbness or tingling in the area. These problems usually go away within a few weeks, although some numbness may be permanent. Patients also may feel tired or weak for a while. It takes time to recover from an operation, especially from major surgery, and this time differs from patient to patient.

Radiation therapy. In radiation therapy (also called x-ray therapy, radiotherapy, cobalt treatment, or irradiation), high-energy rays are used to damage cancer cells so they are unable to grow and multiply. Like surgery, radiation therapy is a local treatment; it affects only the cells in the treated area. (For some cancers, like leukemia and lymphoma, the whole body may be radiated.)

Radiation therapy may be used before surgery to shrink the tumor or after surgery to destroy any cancer cells that may remain in the area.

The two most common types of radiation therapy are external radiation therapy and radiation implants.

In external radiation therapy, a machine directs high-energy rays at the cancer. Patients usually receive these treatments five days a week for several weeks as outpatients (they don't stay in the hospital). Patients who receive external radiation therapy are not radioactive during or after treatment.

Sometimes it is best to put cancer-killing rays as close as possible to the tumor. By using a radiation implant, the doctor can give a higher dose of radiation than is possible with external therapy while sparing most of the healthy tissue around it. For patients having a radiation implant, a small container of radioactive material is placed in the body cavity or directly into the cancer. While the implant is in place, most patients stay in the hospital. The radioactive material in the implant may transmit rays into the area around the patient, so visits and contact with these patients are limited during treatment. Once the implant is removed, no radioactive material remains in the patient. There is no danger to patients or visitors.

Even though radiation therapy is directed only to the area where treatment is needed, it can cause side effects. Most of the side effects that occur, although unpleasant, are not permanent. The most common side effects of radiation therapy are unusual tiredness and skin reactions (such as rashes or red areas) in the area being treated. Radiation therapy also may cause a decrease in the number of white blood cells, which help to protect the body against infection. The type and degree of side effects depend on the area of the body that is being treated.

Chemotherapy. Treatment with anticancer drugs, called chemotherapy, is used to destroy cancer cells by disrupting their ability to grow and multiply. There are many different drugs used to treat cancer, and they are given to patients in different ways: some are given by mouth; others work better when they are injected into a muscle, a vein, or an artery. Some of these drugs are given in cycles—a treatment period, followed by a rest period, then another treatment period, and so on.

Regardless of how it is given, chemotherapy finds its way into the bloodstream and is carried all through the body. Because chemotherapy can act on cells throughout the body, it is called systemic treatment.

Depending on the specific drugs the doctor orders, most patients take their chemotherapy as outpatients at a hospital, at the doctor's office, or at home. Sometimes it may be necessary to stay in the hospital so the effects of treatment can be watched.

Chemotherapy works mainly on cancer cells, but it also affects other rapidly growing cells, including hair cells and cells that line the digestive tract. As a result, patients may have side effects such as hair loss, nausea, and vomiting. Most anticancer drugs also affect the bone marrow, decreasing its ability to produce blood cells. Therefore, some chemotherapy patients may have a higher risk of getting an infection. The type and degree of side effects depend on the drugs being given, the dosage, the patient's age and general health, and other factors.

Hormone therapy. Some types of cancer depend on hormones for their growth. For this reason, doctors may recommend therapy that prevents cancer cells from getting the hormones they need to grow. This treatment may include the use of drugs to block the body's production of hormones or surgery to remove hormone-producing organs. Hormone therapy is most often used to treat cancers of the breast, prostate, kidney, and uterus. Commonly used drugs include tamoxifen (for cancer of the breast), DES or diethylstilbestrol (for breast and prostate cancers), and Megace (for kidney and uterine cancers).

Hormone therapy can cause a number of side effects, depending on the specific drug or surgical procedure. Patients may have nausea and vomiting, swelling, or weight gain. In some cases, the treatment interferes with the body's production or use of hormones. For example, women taking tamoxifen may have some symptoms of menopause, such as hot flashes.

Biological therapy. Biological therapy (sometimes called immunotherapy) is a new area of cancer treatment. Scientists have identified a number of natural and man-made substances that can boost, direct, or restore the body's immune system. One form of biological therapy uses monoclonal antibodies, substances that can locate cancer cells and bind to them. Another uses interferon, a substance that stimulates the body's immune system to fight cancer cells. A third uses interleukin-2, a protein that regulates cell growth. Other types of biological therapy are under study also.

Nutrition for Cancer Patients

Eating can be difficult for many cancer patients. Often they have no appetite. Or, the taste of food may change; for example, food—especially meat—may taste bitter or like metal. Also, many patients are weak following treatment and are unable to cook for themselves. Still others feel depressed and have little interest in food.

For whatever reason it occurs, loss of appetite can be a serious problem. Researchers are learning that patients who eat well may be better able to withstand the side effects of treatment. Therefore, nutrition is an important part of each patient's treatment plan, especially having enough protein in the diet to build and repair tissues. Eating well also means getting enough calories to prevent weight loss. Many patients have found that eating several small meals throughout the day works better than eating three large meals.

Doctors, nurses, and dietitians can explain the side effects of cancer treatment and can suggest ways to deal with them.

ADJUSTING TO THE DISEASE

When people have cancer, life can change for them and for the people who care about them. These changes in daily life can be difficult to handle. When a person finds out he or she has cancer, a number of different and sometimes confusing emotions may appear.

At times, cancer patients and family members may feel depressed, angry, or frightened. At other times, feelings may vary from hope to despair or from courage to fear. These are normal reactions for people dealing with a major change in their lives. Patients usually are better able to cope with their emotions if they can talk openly about their illness and their feelings with family members and friends.

Concerns about the future, as well as about tests, treatment, a hospital stay, or medical bills are common. Talking to doctors, nurses, or other members of the health care team may help to ease fear and confusion. Patients can take an active part in decisions about their medical care by asking questions about their disease and its treatment. Patients and family members often find it helpful to write down questions for the doctor as they think of them. Taking notes during visits to the doctor also can help them remember what was talked about. Patients should ask their doctor to repeat or fully explain anything that is not clear.

Most patients have important questions to ask about cancer, and their doctor is the best person to provide answers. They usually want to know what kind of cancer they have, how it can be treated, and how successful the treatment is likely to be. The following are some other questions that patients and family members might want to ask the doctor.

- What are the benefits of treatment?
- What are the risks and side effects of treatment?
- Is it possible to keep working?
- Will changes in normal activities be required?
- How often are checkups needed?
- How much will the treatment cost?

Many cancer patients become concerned,

especially after surgery, that the changes to their bodies will affect how they look and how others will react to them. They may worry that they can no longer hold a job or care for their family. Concerns about sexuality also can be upsetting.

The patient's doctor is the best person to give advice about working or limiting other activities, but it may be hard to talk to the doctor about feelings and other very personal matters. Many patients find it helpful to talk with others who are facing similar problems. This kind of help is available through cancer-related support groups. If the emotional problems of the patient or family become too hard to handle, a mental health counselor may be able to help.

Living with any serious disease can be difficult. The public library is a good source for books and articles on cancer.

SUPPORT FOR CANCER PATIENTS

Adapting to the changes that come from having cancer is easier for both patients and their families when they get helpful information and support services. Often, the social services office at the hospital can suggest agencies that will help with rehabilitation, emotional support, financial aid, transportation, or home care. Also, the American Cancer Society (ACS) provides patient services and education. Local offices of the ACS are listed in the telephone book under American Cancer Society, Inc.

Information about other resources and services is available through the Cancer Information Service, at 1-800-4-CANCER.

WHAT THE FUTURE HOLDS

There are more than 5 million Americans living today who have had some type of cancer. The outlook for each patient depends on the type of cancer and the stage of the disease, as well as the patient's age, general health, response to treatment, and other factors. Re-

searchers are working to find better ways to treat cancer, and the chances of recovering are improving.

Doctors usually talk about "surviving" cancer, or they may use the term "remission" rather than "cure." Even though many patients recover completely, doctors use these terms because cancer may show up again at a later time. The doctor will want to watch the cancer patient closely to be sure that the cancer has not returned. For most forms of cancer, five years without symptoms is when a patient is considered "cured."

It is natural to be concerned about the future. Patients often use statistics they have heard about to figure out their own chances of being cured. However, statistics describe averages based on many, many people. No two cancer patients are alike. Only a patient's doctor knows enough about that person's case to discuss the course of the disease.

CANCER RESEARCH

Scientists at hospitals and medical centers across the country are studying the causes, prevention, diagnosis, and treatment of cancer.

Causes and Prevention of Cancer

Doctors can seldom explain why one person gets cancer and another doesn't. It is clear, however, that cancer is not caused by an injury, such as a bump or bruise, to the body. And cancer is not contagious. No one can "catch" cancer from another person.

Researchers study patterns of cancer in the U.S. population to find out why some people are more likely to develop certain cancers and what things in our surroundings and lifestyles may cause cancer. From these studies, we know that people of all ages get cancer, but it is more common in middle-aged and elderly people. According to present rates, 73 million Americans who are alive today will eventually develop cancer; this is about 30 percent of the population. Over the years, cancer will occur in approximately three out of every four families.

Overall, the number of new cases of cancer is decreasing among women and increasing in men, with the rate for black men going up faster than for white men. Lung cancer is the leading cause of cancer-related deaths in men; breast cancer and lung cancer are the leading causes for women.

Many experts believe that people get cancer through repeated and long-term contact with cancer-causing agents, called carcinogens. Some people are more sensitive to carcinogens than others and, therefore, are more likely to get cancer. Scientists believe that most cancers are caused in two steps by two kinds of agents: initiators and promoters.

Initiators start the damage to a cell that can lead to cancer. For example, cigarette smoking has been shown to be an initiator.

Promoters usually do not cause cancer by themselves. They change cells already damaged by an initiator from normal to cancer cells. For example, studies show that alcohol promotes the development of cancer in the mouth when combined with an initiator, such as tobacco.

Scientists have also discovered many risk factors that increase our chances of getting cancer. About 80 percent of all cancers may be related to the things we eat, drink, and smoke, as well as the environment and work place. Other risk factors, such as genetics, are unavoidable.

🔬 Recent research studies have demonstrated that cancer, unlike the classic hereditary diseases, often involves changes in several genes. Bert Vogelstein and colleagues from the Johns Hopkins School of Medicine, as well as research groups at other institutions, have shown that colon cancer appears to develop as a result of a sequence of gene mutations. Some of these mutations activate genes that stimulate the process of carcinogenesis (oncogenes), while others inactivate genes that normally suppress tumor development (tumor suppressor genes). The same mechanisms may be active in other common solid tumors, such as breast and lung cancer. These advances in the understanding of the molecular biology of cancer will certainly accelerate research efforts not only to identify people at substantial risk for cancer but also to develop agents that will prevent cancer from occurring in the first place (chemoprevention).

Risks You Can Avoid

By choosing a lifestyle that avoids certain risks, you can help protect yourself from developing cancer. Many cancers are linked to factors that you can control.

Tobacco. Smoking and using tobacco in any form has been directly linked to cancer. Overall, smoking causes 30 percent of all cancer deaths. The risk of developing lung cancer is 10 times greater for smokers than for nonsmokers. The amount of risk from smoking depends on the number and type of cigarettes you smoke, how long you have been smoking, and how deeply you inhale. Smokers are also more likely to develop cancers of the mouth, throat, esophagus, pancreas, and bladder. And now there is emerging evidence that smoking can also cause cancer of the stomach and cervix.

The use of "smokeless" tobacco (chewing tobacco and oral snuff) increases the risk of cancer of the mouth and pharynx. Once you quit smoking or using smokeless tobacco, your risk of developing cancer begins to decrease right away.

Diet. What you eat may affect your chances of developing cancer. Scientists think there is a link between a high-fat diet and some cancers, particularly those of the breast, colon, endometrium, and prostate. Obesity is thought to be linked with increased death rates for cancers of the prostate, pancreas, breast, and ovary. Still other studies point to an increased risk of getting stomach cancer for those who frequently eat pickled, cured, and smoked foods. The NCI believes that eating a well-balanced diet can reduce the risk of getting cancer. Americans should eat more high-fiber foods (such as whole-grain cereals and fruits and vegetables) and less fatty foods.

Sunlight. Repeated exposure to sunlight increases the risk of skin cancer, especially if you have fair skin or freckle easily. In fact, ultraviolet radiation from the sun is the main cause of skin cancer, which is the most common cancer in the United States. Ultraviolet rays are strongest from 11 a.m. to 2 p.m. during the summer, so that is when risk is greatest. Protective clothing, such as a hat and long sleeves, can help block out the sun's harmful rays. You can also use sunscreens to help protect yourself. Sunscreens with a number 15 on the label means most of the sun's harmful rays will be blocked out.

Alcohol. Drinking large amounts of alcohol (one or two drinks a day is considered moderate) is associated with cancers of the mouth, throat, esophagus, and liver. People who smoke cigarettes and drink alcohol have an especially high risk of getting cancers of the mouth and esophagus.

X-rays. Large doses of radiation increase cancer risk. Although individual x-rays expose you to very little radiation, repeated exposure can be harmful. Therefore, it is a good idea to avoid unnecessary x-rays. It's best to talk about the need for each x-ray with your doctor or dentist. If you do need an x-ray, ask if shields can be used to protect other parts of your body.

Industrial agents and chemicals. Being exposed to some industrial agents or chemicals increases cancer risk. Industrial agents cause damage by acting alone or together with another cancer-causing agent found in the workplace or with cigarette smoke. For example, inhaling asbestos fibers increases the risk of lung disease and cancer. This risk is especially high for workers who smoke. You should follow work and safety rules to avoid coming in contact with such dangerous materials.

Being exposed to large amounts of household solvent cleaners, cleaning fluids, and paint thinners should be avoided. Some chemicals are especially dangerous if inhaled in high concentrations, particularly in areas that are not well ventilated. In addition, inhaling or swallowing lawn and garden chemicals increases cancer risk. Follow label instructions carefully when using pesticides, fungicides, and other chemicals. Such chemicals should not come in contact with toys or other household items.

Hormones. Taking estrogen to relieve menopausal symptoms (such as hot flashes) has been associated with higher-than-average rates of cancer of the uterus. Numerous studies also have examined the relationship between oral contraceptives (the pill) and a variety of female cancers. Recent studies report that taking the pill does not increase a woman's chance of getting breast cancer. Also, pill users appear to have a lower-than-average risk of cancers of the endometrium and ovary. However, some researchers believe that there may be a higher risk of cancer of the cervix among pill users. Women taking hormones (either estrogens or oral contraceptives) should discuss the benefits and risks with their doctor.

Unavoidable Risks

Certain risk factors for cancer cannot be controlled, but people at high risk can help protect themselves by getting regular checkups. The following groups have a higher-than-average risk of developing cancer.

• Individuals who have close relatives with melanoma or cancer of the breast or colon. A small number of these cancers tends to occur more often in some families. If a close relative has been affected by one of these cancers, you should tell your doctor and be sure to have regular checkups to detect early problems.

- Persons who have had x-ray treatment to the head or neck when they were children or young adults. Exposure to these x-ray treatments may result in thyroid tumors, which have been associated with radiation given for an enlarged thymus gland, enlarged tonsils and adenoids, whooping cough, ringworm of the scalp, acne, and other head and neck conditions. Most thyroid tumors are not cancer. If thyroid cancer does develop, it usually can be cured. If you have had such x-rays, you should have a doctor examine your throat and neck every one or two years.
- Daughters and sons whose mothers took a drug called diethylstilbestrol (DES) to prevent miscarriages while they were pregnant with them. DES and some similar drugs given to mothers during pregnancy have been linked to certain unusual tissue formations in the vagina and cervix of their daughters. DES also has caused a rare type of vaginal and cervical cancer in a small number of exposed daughters. Women who took DES and DES-type drugs during pregnancy may themselves have a moderately increased risk of developing breast cancer. DES-exposed daughters and mothers should have examinations at least once a year that include pelvic and breast exams and Pap tests.

No link with cancer due to DES exposure before birth has been found in boys and men. However, there may be an increase in certain reproductive and urinary system problems in DES-exposed sons, who should also be examined regularly by a doctor.

Advances in Treatment

Improved methods of treating cancer have helped to increase survival rates for cancer patients. The National Cancer Institute supports numerous studies to develop and improve all forms of cancer therapy. These studies range from experiments on cells in the laboratory, to those using animals, to others that include large numbers of cancer patients in clinical trials.

Clinical trials are done with the cooperation of cancer patients and are designed to answer scientific questions and to find out if a promising new treatment is both safe and effective. Patients who take part in research make an important contribution to medical science and may have the first chance to benefit from improved treatment methods. Cancer patients who are considering participating in a clinical trial should discuss their interest with their doctor.

Doctors can learn about clinical trials by using PDQ (Physician Data Query), a computerized system developed by the NCI. To obtain information from PDQ, doctors can use an office computer or the services of a medical library. Most Cancer Information Service (CIS) offices provide PDQ searches to physicians and can tell doctors how to use the system. Information about current research also is available to patients through the CIS.

The National Cancer Institute

BLADDER CANCER

The bladder is a hollow organ in the lower abdomen that stores urine. The kidneys filter waste from the blood and produce urine, which enters the bladder through two tubes called ureters. Urine leaves the bladder through another tube, the urethra. In women, the urethra is a short tube that opens just in front of the vagina. In men, it is longer, passing through the prostate gland and then through the penis.

Most bladder cancers develop in the inside lining of the bladder. The cancer often looks like a small mushroom attached to the bladder wall. It may also be called a papillary tumor. Often, more than one tumor is present.

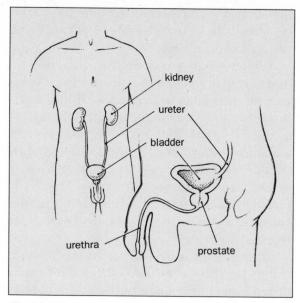 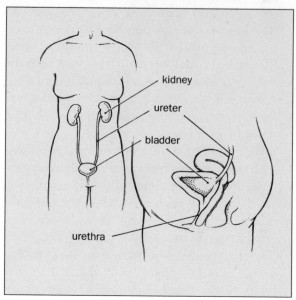

The bladder (essentially the same in both men and women) holds urine, which descends from the kidneys, until it is ready to be excreted. Cancer in the bladder originates in the cells that line the organ.

SYMPTOMS

The most common warning sign of bladder cancer is blood in the urine. Depending on the amount of blood present, the color of the urine can turn faintly rusty to deep red. Pain during urination can also be a sign of bladder cancer. A need to urinate often or urgently may be another warning sign. Often, bladder tumors cause no symptoms.

When symptoms do occur, they are not sure signs of cancer. They may also be caused by infections, benign tumors, bladder stones, or other problems. It is important to see a doctor to find out the cause of the symptoms. Any illness should be diagnosed and treated as early as possible.

DIAGNOSIS

To diagnose bladder cancer, the doctor will take the patient's medical history and do a complete physical exam. Sometimes, the doctor can feel a large tumor during a rectal or vaginal exam. In addition, urine samples are checked under the microscope to see whether any cancer cells are present.

Often, the doctor wants the patient to have an x-ray called an intravenous pyelogram (IVP). This test lets the doctor see the kidneys, ureters, and bladder on an x-ray. An IVP normally causes little discomfort, although a few patients have nausea, dizziness, or pain from the procedure.

The doctor may also look directly into the bladder with an instrument called a cystoscope. In this test, a thin, lighted tube is inserted into the bladder through the urethra. If the doctor sees any abnormal areas, samples of tissue can be removed through the cystoscope. This is called a biopsy. A pathologist examines the tissue under a microscope to see whether cancer cells are present. A biopsy is needed to make a definite diagnosis of bladder cancer.

TREATMENT

Treatment for bladder cancer depends on a number of factors. Among these are how quickly the cancer is growing; the number, size, and location of the tumors; whether the cancer has spread to other organs; and the patient's age and general health. The doctor will develop a treatment plan to fit each patient's needs. (See also Treatment Planning, page 16.)

Staging

Before treatment begins, it is important for the doctor to know exactly where the cancer is located and whether it has spread from its original location. Staging procedures include a complete physical exam and additional blood tests and scans.

The doctor may want the patient to have a CT scan. A CT scan is a series of x-rays put together by a computer to form a three-dimensional picture. Ultrasound is a procedure that creates pictures of the inside of the body using high-frequency sound waves. The echoes make an image on a video screen that is much like a television. Sometimes the doctor asks for magnetic resonance imaging (MRI). In this scan, a cross-sectional image (like a CT scan) is produced on a screen with the use of a powerful magnet instead of x-rays.

Methods of Treatment

Transurethral resection (TUR). Early (superficial) bladder cancer (in which the tumors are found on the surface of the bladder wall) generally can be treated using the cystoscope in a procedure called transurethral resection. The cystoscope can remove all or part of a tumor or destroy it with an electric current.

When several tumors are present in the bladder or when there is a risk that the cancer will recur, TUR may be followed by treatment with drugs. The doctor may put a solution containing the bacillus Calmette-Guerin (BCG), a form of biological therapy, directly into the bladder. Chemotherapy (anticancer drugs) may also be put directly into the bladder.

Radiation therapy (also called radiotherapy) may be needed when the cancer cannot be removed with TUR because it involves a larger area of the bladder. X-rays destroy the ability of cancer cells to grow and multiply. Internal radiation therapy, with the radioactive material placed in the bladder, may be combined with external radiation, which comes from a machine located outside the body.

For internal radiation therapy, radioactive material is inserted into the bladder through the cystoscope. This puts cancer-killing rays as close as possible to the site of the cancer while sparing most of the healthy tissues around it. The patient stays in the hospital for this treatment for between four and seven days.

For external radiation treatments, the patient goes to the hospital or clinic each day. Usually, treatments are given five days a week for five to six weeks. This schedule helps to protect normal tissue by spreading out the total dose of radiation.

Surgery. When the cancer involves much of the surface of the bladder or has grown into the bladder wall, standard treatment is to remove the entire bladder. This surgery is called a radical cystectomy. In this operation, the surgeon removes the bladder as well as nearby organs. In women, this operation includes removing the uterus, fallopian tubes, ovaries, and part of the vagina. In men, the prostate and seminal vesicles are removed. Research is under way to find treatments that spare the bladder.

Chemotherapy. When cancer involves the pelvis or has spread to other parts of the body, the doctor may suggest chemotherapy, the use of anticancer drugs that travel through the bloodstream to reach cancer cells in all parts of the body. Drugs used to treat cancer may be given in different ways: some are given by mouth; others are injected into a muscle or a blood vessel. Chemotherapy is usually given in cycles—a treatment period, followed by a rest period, then another treatment period, and so on.

The patient usually receives chemotherapy as an outpatient at the hospital, at the doctor's office, or at home. Sometimes the patient may need to stay in the hospital for a short while.

Side Effects of Treatment

The methods used to treat bladder cancer are very powerful. It is hard to limit the effects of treatment so that only cancer cells are destroyed; healthy tissue may also be damaged. That's why treatment may cause unpleasant side effects. Side effects depend on the type of treatment used and on the part of the body being treated.

When the bladder is removed, the patient needs a new way to store and pass urine. Various methods are used. In one, the surgeon uses a piece of the person's small intestine to form a new pipeline. The ureters are attached to one end, and the other end is brought out through an opening in the wall of the abdomen. This new opening is called a stoma. (It is also called an ostomy or a urostomy.) A flat bag fits over the stoma to collect urine, and it is held in place with a special adhesive. A specially trained nurse or enterostomal therapist will show the patient how to care for the ostomy.

A newer method uses part of the small intestine to make a new storage pouch (called a continent reservoir) inside the body. The urine collects there and does not empty into a bag. Instead, the patient learns to use a tube (catheter) to drain the urine through a stoma. Other methods are being developed that connect a pouch made from the small intestine to a remaining part of the urethra. When this procedure is possible, a stoma and bag are not necessary because urine leaves the body through the urethra.

Radical cystectomy causes infertility in both men and women. This operation also can lead to sexual problems. In the past, nearly all men were impotent after this procedure, but improvements in surgery have made it possible to prevent this in many men. In women, the vagina may be narrower or shallower, and intercourse may be difficult.

During radiation therapy, patients may become very tired as the treatment continues. Resting as much as possible is important. Radiation treatment to the lower abdomen may cause nausea, vomiting, or diarrhea. Usually, the doctor can suggest certain foods or medications to ease these problems. Radiation therapy can also cause problems with fertility and can make sexual intercourse uncomfortable.

Chemotherapy causes side effects because it damages not only cancer cells but other rapidly growing cells as well. The side effects of chemotherapy depend on the specific drugs that are given. In addition, each patient reacts differently. Chemotherapy commonly affects blood-forming cells and cells that line the digestive tract. As a result, patients may have side effects such as lowered resistance to infection, loss of appetite, nausea and vomiting, less energy, and mouth sores. They may also lose their hair. These are short-term side effects that usually end after treatment stops. When drugs are put directly into the bladder, these side effects may be limited. However, it is common for the bladder to be irritated.

To help withstand the side effects of treatment, it is important that patients maintain good nutrition (see Nutrition for Cancer Patients, page 19).

FOLLOW-UP CARE

Regular follow-up exams are very important after treatment for bladder cancer. The doctor will need to check the bladder with a cystoscope and remove any superficial tumors that may have recurred. The doctor also checks for cancer cells in the urine and may suggest a chest x-ray, an IVP, or other tests.

The doctor will continue to watch the patient for several years, because bladder tumors can come back. If the cancer does recur, it is important for the doctor to detect it right away so additional treatment can be started.

LIVING WITH CANCER

The diagnosis of bladder cancer can change the lives of cancer patients and the people who care about them. These changes in daily life can be difficult to handle. (See Adjusting to the Disease, page 19, and Support for Cancer Patients, page 20.)

WHAT THE FUTURE HOLDS

Each year, more than 47,000 Americans will find out they have bladder cancer. The outlook for patients diagnosed with early bladder cancer is very good. The chances of recovery from more advanced bladder cancer are improving as researchers continue to look for better ways to treat this disease.

The National Cancer Institute

BREAST CANCER

The breasts are organs that produce milk. Each breast has 15 to 20 sections, called lobes, that are arranged like the petals of a daisy. Each lobe has many smaller lobules, which end in dozens of tiny milk-producing bulbs or glands. The lobes, lobules, and bulbs are all linked by thin tubes called ducts. These ducts lead to the nipple in the center of a dark area of skin, called the areola. Fat fills the spaces between the other parts of the breast. Muscles cover the ribs and lie under the breast, but they are not part of the breast.

EARLY DETECTION

Women's breasts come in many sizes and shapes. And each woman's breasts change during her life because of age, the monthly menstrual cycle, pregnancy, menopause, or taking birth control pills or other hormones.

It is important to find breast cancer as early as possible. If cancer is found early, there are choices for treatment. With prompt treatment, the outlook is good. The National Cancer Institute encourages women to take an active role in the early detection of breast cancer by:

- Practicing monthly breast self-examination (BSE)
- Having a yearly breast exam
- Getting a routine mammogram after age 40

Women are often confused about what their breasts are supposed to feel like. It is normal for the breasts to feel lumpy and uneven. Sometimes the breasts are swollen and tender, especially right before a woman's menstrual period. By doing monthly BSE, women learn what's normal for their own breasts, and they are more likely to find anything unusual that might be a warning sign of cancer. Any changes should be reported to the doctor. (See page 413 for an easy-to-follow BSE guide.)

The second step of early detection is for a woman to have her breasts checked regularly by her doctor.

Mammograms (x-rays of the breast) can find many breast cancers before they can be felt. Mammography, together with a breast exam by a health professional, can reduce the

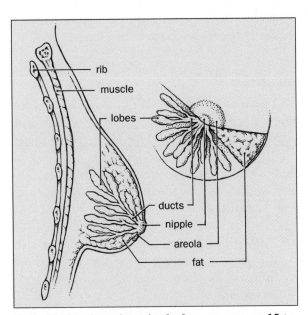

rib
muscle
lobes
ducts
nipple
areola
fat

Embedded in fatty tissue in the breast are some 15 to 20 lobes, each containing dozens of milk-producing glands. The glands are where breast cancer originates.

27

number of deaths from breast cancer. Starting at age 40, a woman should have a mammogram every one to two years. When she reaches 50, she should have a mammogram every year.

SYMPTOMS

Breast cancer can cause many symptoms. Some warning signs to watch for include:

- A lump or thickening in the breast or under the arm
- A change in the size or shape of the breast
- Discharge from the nipple
- A change in the color or feel of the skin of the breast or areola (such as dimpling, puckering, or scaliness)

Pain is usually not an early warning sign of breast cancer. However, a woman should see her doctor if she notices any changes in her breasts. Changes may be caused by cancer or by other less serious problems. Only a doctor can tell for sure.

Early diagnosis is very important because breast cancer can be treated best before it has spread. The earlier breast cancer is found and treated, the better a woman's chances for complete recovery.

DIAGNOSIS

To diagnose breast cancer, a woman's doctor does a careful physical exam and asks her about her personal and family medical history. In addition to checking general signs of health (temperature, pulse, blood pressure, and so on), the doctor may do one or more of these exams.

- *Palpation.* By carefully feeling the breast, the doctor can tell a lot about a breast lump—its size, its texture, and whether it is movable.
- *Aspiration.* The doctor may use a thin needle to remove fluid or a small amount of tissue from a breast lump. This may

show whether the lump is a fluid-filled cyst (not cancer) or a solid mass (which may or may not be cancer).

- *Mammography.* X-rays of the breast can give the doctor important information about a breast lump. Also, a mammogram can show tumors too small to be felt.
- *Other tests.* Sometimes the doctor orders other tests, called imaging techniques, along with mammography. However, at this time, these tests are not reliable enough to be used alone.

  Ultrasound is a test that sends high-frequency sound waves, which cannot be heard by humans, into the breast. The pattern of echoes is shown on a monitor, like a TV screen. This is sometimes called a sonogram. Thermography is a test that measures and records heat patterns in the breast. Diaphanography is an exam that is done by shining a bright light through the breast.
- *Biopsy.* A biopsy is surgery to take out part or all of a lump or suspicious area. The tissue is examined under a microscope by a pathologist. A biopsy is the only sure way to know whether cancer is present.

  A woman who is going to have a biopsy has an important choice to make. She can decide that, if cancer is found, she will have surgery at the same time as the biopsy (a one-step procedure). Or, she can decide to have just a biopsy and, if it shows cancer, have treatment within the next few weeks (a two-step procedure). This short delay gives a woman time to find out about her treatment choices, to get a second opinion, and to prepare for her stay in the hospital. Studies show that a brief delay between biopsy and treatment does not reduce the chances for successful treatment. Many doctors and patients prefer the two-step procedure and it is the most common approach.
- *Hormone receptor tests.* If the biopsy shows that cancer is present, laboratory

tests called estrogen and progesterone receptor tests are usually done on the cancer cells. These tests can tell whether hormones promote the growth of the cancer. This information helps the doctor decide whether hormone treatment is likely to be useful. Hormone receptor tests are done at the time of biopsy because the tissue needed for the test may be hard to get later on.

Four out of five breast lumps are not cancer. If a woman has a fluid-filled cyst, it most likely can be drained by fine needle aspiration. If the lump is a benign tumor, it often can be removed by surgery with no further problems. Some lumps may not need any treatment, but the doctor may want to check the woman regularly.

If the biopsy shows that the lump is cancer, other special laboratory tests may be done on the tissue to learn more about the cancer. Also, the woman will have other tests to find out whether the cancer has spread from the breast to other parts of her body. The doctor usually orders chest x-rays and blood tests. Because breast cancer may spread to the bones, liver, lungs, or brain, the doctor may also order special exams to check these areas.

These tests help the doctor tell the extent, or stage, of the disease. Doctors use this staging system for breast cancer.

- *Carcinoma in situ* is very early breast cancer. Cancer is found in a local area and in only a few layers of cells.
- *Stage I* means the tumor is no larger than 2 centimeters (cm)—about an inch—and has not spread beyond the breast.
- *Stage II* means the tumor is from 2 to 5 cm—about 1 to 2 inches—and/or has spread to the lymph nodes under the arm.
- *Stage III* means the cancer is larger than 5 cm—about 2 inches. It involves more of the underarm lymph nodes, and/or it has spread to other lymph nodes or to other tissues near the breast.

- *Stage IV* means the cancer has spread to other organs of the body, most often the bones, liver, lungs, or brain.

TREATMENT

Treatment depends on the type of breast cancer and how far it has spread, as well as on a woman's age, menopausal status, and general health. The doctor will develop a treatment plan to fit a woman's individual needs. (See also Treatment Planning, page 16.)

Methods of Treatment

Breast cancer is treated with surgery, radiation therapy, chemotherapy, and hormone therapy. The doctor may use just one method or combine them, depending on the patient's needs. In some cases, the patient may be referred to other doctors who specialize in the different kinds of cancer treatment.

Surgery is the most common treatment. The surgeon removes the tumor in the breast and, usually, the lymph nodes under the arm. The lymph nodes are removed because they filter the lymph that flows through the breast and other parts of the body, and they are one of the first places where breast cancer spreads. Cancer cells in the lymph nodes mean that there may be cancer elsewhere in the body.

Radiation therapy (also called radiotherapy) uses high-powered rays to damage cancer cells and stop them from growing. Like surgery, radiation therapy is a local treatment; it affects only the cells in the treated area. Radiation may come from an x-ray machine outside the body (external radiation). It can also come from radioactive materials placed directly in the breast through thin plastic tubes (implant radiation). Sometimes both are used.

The patient goes to the hospital or clinic each day for external radiation treatments. Usually treatments are given five days a week for five to six weeks. At the end of that time, an extra "boost" of radiation is usually given to the tumor site. The boost may be either external or internal (using an implant). Patients usually stay in the hospital for a short time for implant radiation.

Chemotherapy uses drugs to kill cancer cells. The doctor may use just one drug or a combination. Chemotherapy may be given by mouth or by injection into a muscle or vein. The drugs enter the bloodstream and travel through the body. Chemotherapy is given in cycles: a treatment period followed by a rest period, then another treatment, and so on. This type of treatment is called systemic therapy.

Depending on which drugs are given, most patients have chemotherapy as an outpatient at the hospital, at the doctor's office, or at home. Sometimes the patient may need to stay in the hospital for a short while.

Hormone therapy is used to keep cancer cells from getting the hormones they need to grow. This treatment may include the use of drugs that change the way hormones work, or surgery that removes organs such as the ovaries that make hormones. Hormone therapy can act on cells all over the body.

Treatment Choices

Breast cancer is very treatable. The choice of treatment depends on the stage of the cancer (whether it is just in the breast or has spread to other places), the type of breast cancer, and certain characteristics of the cancer cells (such as how fast they are growing). The patient's age, menopausal status, and general health are also important. Decisions about treatment are also based on the experience of the doctor and the desires of the patient.

The following are the different types of surgery used to treat breast cancer.

Modified radical mastectomy removes the breast, the lymph nodes under the arm, and the lining over the chest muscles (but leaves the muscles). This is the most common surgery for breast cancer.

Lumpectomy removes just the breast lump and is followed by radiation therapy. Most surgeons also remove the lymph nodes under the arm.

Total or simple mastectomy removes just the breast. Sometimes the underarm lymph nodes closest to the breast also are removed.

Partial or segmental mastectomy removes the tumor, some of the normal breast tissue around it, and the lining over the chest muscle below the tumor. Usually some of the underarm lymph nodes are removed. In most cases, radiation therapy follows the surgery.

Radical mastectomy (also called the Halsted radical mastectomy) removes the breast, chest muscles, all of the lymph nodes under the arm, and some additional fat and skin. This operation was the standard for many years. It is still used on occasion, but for most patients less extensive surgery is just as effective.

Patients with carcinoma in situ (noninvasive breast cancer) may have a mastectomy or breast-sparing surgery. As with other breast cancers, the type of surgery is based on many factors. Also, depending on the specific type of breast cancer involved, the lymph nodes may be removed, and radiation therapy may be advised.

The treatment choices for early stage breast cancer (stage I and stage II) include limited surgery (such as lumpectomy or partial mastectomy) followed by radiation therapy, or a mastectomy. The lymph nodes under the arm are also removed. The type of surgery depends on the size and location of the tumor, the type of cancer, the age and general health of the woman, and the size of her breast.

In addition, chemotherapy or hormone therapy should be considered after primary treatment for patients with early stage breast cancer. This additional treatment is called adjuvant therapy. It is used to prevent a recurrence by killing undetected cells that may remain in the body. The choice between chemotherapy or hormone therapy depends on the patient's age, menopausal status, hormone receptor status, and other factors.

Women may also consider having plastic surgery to rebuild the breast after surgery.

Patients with stage III breast cancer usually have both local and systemic treatment. The local treatment may be mastectomy and/or radiation therapy. Chemotherapy and/or hormone therapy are also used.

Women who have stage IV breast cancer receive chemotherapy and/or hormone therapy. They may also have limited surgery or radiation therapy to control the tumor in the breast. Radiation may also be useful to treat breast cancer that has spread to specific parts of the body.

If breast cancer returns, treatment depends on the location and extent of the recurrent cancer, the patient's menopausal status and general health, and her response to her initial therapy. If the disease reappears in the breast area, treatment usually is surgery or radiation. Also, some type of systemic therapy is recommended. If the disease develops in other parts of the body, patients are likely to have chemotherapy and/or hormone therapy; some patients also may be helped by radiation therapy or surgery.

Side Effects of Treatment

The methods used to treat breast cancer are very powerful. It is hard to limit the effects of cancer treatment so that only cancer cells are destroyed; normal, healthy tissue may also be damaged. That's why treatment often causes unpleasant side effects. Side effects depend on the type of treatment used and on the part of the body being treated.

Removal of a breast can cause a woman's weight to shift and be out of balance—especially if a woman has large breasts. It can also cause discomfort in her neck and back. Also, surgery can cause the skin in the breast area to be tight and the muscles of the arm and shoulder to feel stiff. With a radical mastectomy, a woman may have some permanent loss of strength, but for most women, reduced strength and limited movement are temporary. The doctor, nurse, or physical therapist can recommend exercises to help a woman regain movement and strength.

Because nerves are cut during surgery, patients may have numbness and tingling in the chest, underarm, shoulder, and arm. These problems usually go away within a few weeks, but some numbness may be permanent.

Removing the lymph nodes under the arm slows the flow of lymph. In some women, lymph builds up in the arm and hand and causes swelling (lymphedema). Also, it is harder for the body to fight infection after the lymph nodes have been removed, and women need to protect the arm or hand on the treated side from injury—for the rest of their lives.

During radiation therapy, patients may become very tired as treatment continues. Resting as much as possible is important. Skin reactions in the breast area, such as redness or dryness, are common. Good skin care is important at this time. The patient should not use lotions or creams on the skin without the doctor's advice. Following radiation therapy, the treated breast may be firmer and somewhat larger or smaller than before.

The side effects of chemotherapy depend on the drugs that are given. In addition, each person reacts differently. Chemotherapy affects rapidly growing cells, such as blood-forming cells and those that line the digestive tract. As a result, the patient may have side effects such as a lower resistance to infection, less energy, loss of appetite, nausea, vomiting, or mouth sores. She may also lose her hair. These are short-term side effects; they usually end after treatment stops. Women taking chemotherapy often have the symptoms of menopause (hot flashes, vaginal dryness, pain during intercourse, and irregular periods). Chemotherapy can also cause long-term side effects such as infertility.

Hormone therapy can cause a number of side effects, depending on the specific drug or surgical procedure, but they usually are not severe. When treatment interferes with the body's production or use of estrogen, the patient may have some of the symptoms of menopause, such as hot flashes, interrupted periods, and vaginal dryness.

To help withstand the side effects of treatment, it is important that patients maintain good nutrition (see Nutrition for Cancer Patients, page 19).

Recovering from Treatment

Recovery from treatment is important for every breast cancer patient. Recovery will be different for each woman, depending on the extent of the disease and the treatment she receives.

Exercising after surgery can help a woman regain motion and strength in her arm and shoulder. It can also reduce pain and stiffness in her neck and back. Carefully planned exercises should be started as soon as the doctor says the woman is ready, often within a day or so after surgery.

At first, exercises are gentle and can even be done in bed. Gradually, the exercises are more active, and regular exercise should become a part of a woman's normal activities. (Women who have a mastectomy and immediate breast reconstruction have different exercise needs that the doctor will explain.)

Lymphedema after surgery can be reduced or prevented with exercises and by resting with the arm propped up on a pillow. If lymphedema becomes a problem later on, the woman should tell her doctor, who may suggest other exercises. Some women with lymphedema wear an elastic sleeve or use an elastic cuff to improve lymph circulation. Other approaches—including medication, a low-salt diet, or a machine that compresses the arm—may be suggested by the doctor.

After a mastectomy, some women choose to wear a breast form (prosthesis). Others have breast reconstruction. Each choice has its pros and cons, and what is right for one woman may not be right for another. What's important is that nearly all breast cancer patients have a choice. It may be helpful to talk with a plastic surgeon before the mastectomy is done, but reconstruction is still possible years later.

FOLLOW-UP CARE

Regular follow-up exams are very important after breast cancer. The doctor will continue to check the patient closely to be sure that the cancer has not returned. Checkups usually include exams of the chest, underarm, and neck. From time to time, the patient will have a complete physical exam, blood and urine tests, a mammogram, and other x-rays. The doctor sometimes orders scans (special x-rays) and other tests, too.

A woman who has had breast cancer should check both the treated area and her other breast each month. She should report any changes to her doctor right away. Also, she should tell her doctor about other physical problems if they come up, such as pain, loss of appetite or weight, changes in menstrual periods, unusual or lasting digestive problems, coughing or hoarseness, headaches, dizziness, or blurred vision. These problems may be a sign that the cancer has returned, but they can also be signs of many other problems. Only the doctor can tell for sure.

LIVING WITH CANCER

The diagnosis of breast cancer can change a woman's life and the lives of those close to her. These changes can be difficult to handle.

(See Adjusting to the Disease, page 19, and Support for Cancer Patients, page 20.)

WHAT THE FUTURE HOLDS

Each year, more than 142,000 American women will find out they have breast cancer. Because researchers are finding better ways to detect and treat breast cancer, the chances of recovery keep improving.

The National Cancer Institute

CERVICAL CANCER

The uterus (womb) is a hollow, pear-shaped organ located in a woman's lower abdomen between the bladder and the rectum. The narrow, lower portion of the uterus is called the cervix. The cervix opens into the vagina (birth canal), which leads to the outside of the body.

DYSPLASIA AND CANCER OF THE CERVIX

In some women, the cells in the cervix may go through a series of changes. Normal, healthy cells may become abnormal (a condition known as dysplasia). Dysplasia is not cancer, although it may develop into very early cancer of the cervix. It is a variation in the size, shape, and number of cervical cells. Dysplastic cells have the same general appearance under the microscope as cancer cells; however, dysplastic cells do not invade nearby healthy tissues. Dysplasia is classified as mild, moderate, or severe, depending on how abnormal the cells appear under the microscope. This condition develops most often in women between the ages of 25 and 35, but it can appear in other age groups as well.

Very early cancer of the cervix (also called carcinoma in situ) involves only the top layer of cervical cells and does not invade deeper

layers of cervical tissue for many months, perhaps years. It is the earliest form of cervical cancer that can be detected. Although very early cancer of the cervix develops most often in women between the ages of 30 and 40, it can occur in younger and older women.

Invasive cervical cancer is cancer that has spread deeper into the cervix and/or to nearby tissues or organs. It occurs most often in women between the ages of 40 and 60.

EARLY DETECTION

Most cases of invasive cervical cancer could be prevented if all women had pelvic exams and Pap smears regularly. A pelvic exam is a physical examination of the uterus, vagina, ovaries, fallopian tubes, bladder, and rectum. The doctor feels these organs for any abnormality in their shape or size. During a pelvic exam, a speculum is used to widen the opening of the vagina so that the doctor can see the upper part of the vagina and the cervix.

The Pap smear is a simple, painless test to detect abnormal cells in and around the

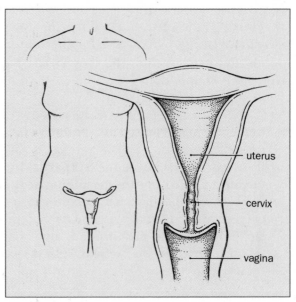

The cervix, at the end of the vaginal canal, marks the opening to the uterus. Cervical cancer is the most common cancer of the female reproductive system.

cervix. The best time to have a Pap smear is two weeks after the first day of the last menstrual period.

A Pap smear can be done in a doctor's office, clinic, or hospital. The doctor collects a sample of cells from the cervix and upper vagina with a wooden scraper, cotton swab, or cervical brush and places the sample on a glass slide. The slide is sent to a medical laboratory for evaluation.

The results of the Pap smear are classified 1 through 5. Class 1 is normal and class 5 is cancer. A new way to report Pap smears was recommended in 1989. This method, called the "Bethesda system," describes infections and other precancerous cell changes in a way that will improve the accuracy and quality of diagnosis.

All women who are 18 or older or who have had sexual intercourse should have annual checkups including a pelvic exam and a Pap smear. After a woman has had three or more normal annual Pap smears, the exam may be done less often, as her doctor advises. Women who are at increased risk of developing cancer of the cervix may need to be examined more often.

The need for a Pap smear following a hysterectomy (surgery to remove the uterus) depends on the reasons for the surgery and the type of procedure done.

- If the hysterectomy was a treatment for cancer, regular Pap smears should be continued.
- If the cervix was not removed (partial hysterectomy), Pap smears are still needed.
- For women who have had the uterus and cervix removed (total hysterectomy), regular pelvic exams are needed, and Pap smears every three to five years may be recommended.

Women who were exposed to the drug DES (diethylstilbestrol) before birth should have a pelvic exam and a Pap smear at least once a year, starting at age 14 or when they begin menstruating, whichever is earlier.

SYMPTOMS

Dysplasia and early cervical cancer seldom cause symptoms. They can only be detected by a pelvic exam and a Pap smear. Symptoms generally do not appear until cervical cancer becomes invasive. The most common symptom of cancer of the cervix is abnormal bleeding. Bleeding may start and stop between regular menstrual periods, or it may occur after sexual intercourse, douching, or a pelvic exam. Menstrual bleeding may last longer and be heavier than usual. Increased vaginal discharge is another symptom of cancer of the cervix. Pain is not an early warning sign of the disease.

These symptoms are not sure signs of cancer; however, it is important for a woman to see her doctor if any symptom lasts longer than two weeks. Any illness should be diagnosed and treated as early as possible. Early diagnosis is especially important for cancer of the cervix.

DIAGNOSIS

If the pelvic exam or the Pap smear shows any abnormality, the doctor will do more tests to find out what the problem is. When a vaginal infection is the suspected cause of an abnormal Pap smear, the doctor will treat the infection and then repeat the Pap smear. If an infection is not the reason for the abnormal Pap smear, the doctor may remove a small amount of tissue for further evaluation (biopsy).

The doctor may use a number of procedures to pinpoint areas that should be biopsied. These tests usually are done in the doctor's office. In the Schiller test, an iodine solution is applied to the cervix. Healthy cells turn brown; abnormal cells turn white or yellow. In another procedure, the doctor may use an instrument much like a microscope (called a colposcope) to look at the cervix.

Small samples of abnormal tissue are taken for further examination.

In some cases, the doctor must remove larger samples of tissue to make a diagnosis. These samples are obtained most often by conization (cone biopsy) or dilatation and curettage (D and C). In a conization, the doctor removes a cone-shaped piece of tissue from the cervix and cervical canal. In a D and C, the doctor dilates (widens) the cervix and inserts a curette (a small spoon-shaped instrument) to scrape tissue from the cervical canal and the lining of the uterus. A brief hospital stay may be needed for these procedures.

If a woman has cervical cancer, it is important to find out whether the disease has spread from the cervix to other parts of the body. Staging procedures include a thorough physical exam that is done under anesthesia, as well as blood and urine tests and a chest x-ray. For some patients, special x-rays are needed. For example, in computed tomography (also called CT scan), a series of x-rays is taken of various sections of the abdomen. Doctors also may use ultrasound to view the inside of the body. In this procedure, high-frequency sound waves that cannot be heard echo off tissues and organs, and the echoes produced can be seen on a screen, much like a television. Healthy tissues and tumors produce different echoes.

Because cancer of the cervix can spread to the bladder, colon, and rectum, the doctor may ask for special exams of those areas, too.

TREATING DYSPLASIA

How dysplasia is treated depends on its severity. Mild dysplasia may not require any treatment, but it should be checked regularly for any changes. Moderate dysplasia usually is treated by cryosurgery (freezing) or cauterization (burning). These methods destroy abnormal areas of the cervix without harming surrounding healthy tissues. Conization is the usual treatment for severe dysplasia.

Recently, lasers have been used to treat dysplasia. The laser uses a powerful beam of light to destroy abnormal cells, leaving the normal cells underneath unharmed.

TREATING CANCER OF THE CERVIX

The doctor considers a number of factors to determine the best treatment for cervical cancer. Among these factors are the extent of the disease, as well as the age and general health of the woman.

Treatment may involve surgery, radiation therapy, or chemotherapy. Surgery may remove only a small area of abnormal tissue, or it may remove the cervix, uterus, and other nearby tissues. Radiation therapy (also called x-ray therapy, radiotherapy, or irradiation) uses high-energy rays to kill cancer cells. Radiation may be given from a machine located outside the body (external radiation therapy) or from radioactive material placed inside the body (internal radiation therapy). Chemotherapy is the use of anticancer drugs to treat cancer. Sometimes, a combination of these methods is used. The doctor develops a treatment plan to fit a woman's individual needs. (See also Treatment Planning, page 16.)

Very Early Cancer of the Cervix

Treatment for very early cervical cancer depends on the age of the woman and on the preferences of the patient and her doctor. Treatment may involve cryosurgery, cauterization, conization, laser treatment, or hysterectomy. Conization is the usual treatment for young women who wish to have children. Most women who do not want to have additional children are treated with total hysterectomy (removal of the cervix and uterus).

Invasive Cervical Cancer

Treatment for invasive cancer of the cervix depends on the extent of the disease. Patients whose cancer has invaded only the cervix and those whose disease has extended into the tissues next to the cervix or to the upper vagina can be treated effectively with either surgery or radiation therapy. Surgery may be a total hysterectomy (removal of the cervix and uterus) or a radical hysterectomy (removal of the cervix, uterus, upper vagina, and the lymph nodes in the area). Both external and internal radiation therapy can be used to treat invasive cervical cancer.

Patients with cancer that has spread to the pelvis, to the lower part of the vagina, or to the ureters are treated with radiation therapy alone. Again, both external and internal radiation therapy can be used.

Patients with cervical cancer that has spread to the bladder, rectum, or distant parts of the body may receive chemotherapy in addition to surgery or radiation therapy. Chemotherapy also is used to treat patients whose disease recurs following treatment with surgery or radiation therapy.

Side Effects of Treatment

The treatments used against cancer must be very powerful. It is rarely possible to limit the effects of treatment so that only cancer cells are destroyed. Normal, healthy cells may be damaged at the same time. That's why cancer treatment often causes side effects.

Hysterectomy is major surgery. After the operation, the hospital stay usually lasts about one week. For several days after surgery, patients may have problems emptying their bladder and having normal bowel movements. The lower abdomen will be sore. Normal activities, including sexual intercourse, usually can be resumed in four to eight weeks.

Women who have had their uterus removed no longer have menstrual periods. When the ovaries are not removed, women do not go through menopause (change of life) because their ovaries still produce hormones. If the ovaries are removed or damaged by radiation therapy, menopause will occur. Hot flashes or other symptoms of menopause caused by treatment may be more severe than those from a natural menopause.

Sexual desire and the ability to have intercourse usually are not affected by hysterectomy. However, many women have an emotionally difficult time after a hysterectomy. They may have feelings of deep loss because they are no longer able to become pregnant.

Radiation therapy destroys the ability of cells to grow and divide. Both normal and diseased cells are affected, but most normal cells are able to recover quickly. Patients usually receive external radiation therapy as an outpatient. Treatments are given five days a week for several weeks. This schedule helps to protect healthy tissues by spreading out the total dose of radiation. Weekend rest breaks allow the normal cells to repair themselves.

Internal radiation therapy puts cancer-killing rays as close as possible to the site of the cancer while sparing most of the healthy tissues around it. This type of radiation therapy requires a short hospital stay. A radiation implant, a capsule containing radioactive material, is inserted through the vagina into the cervix and uterus. The implant usually is left in place for two or three days.

During radiation therapy, patients may notice a number of side effects, which usually disappear when treatment is completed. Patients may be unusually tired, and they may have skin reactions (redness or dryness) in the area being treated. It is important to rest as much as possible and to treat the skin gently. Patients also may have diarrhea and frequent and uncomfortable urination. Patients can expect to stop menstruating and may have other symptoms of menopause. Treatment can cause dryness, itching, or burning in the vagina. Intercourse may be painful, and some women are advised not to have intercourse at this time. Most women can resume sexual activity within a few weeks after treatment ends.

The anticancer drugs used in chemotherapy travel through the bloodstream to almost every part of the body. Drugs used to treat cancer may be given to patients in different ways: some are given by mouth; others are injected into a muscle, a vein, or an artery. Chemotherapy is most often given in cycles—a treatment period, followed by a rest period, then another treatment period, and so on.

Depending on the drugs that are used, the patient may need to stay in the hospital for a few days so that the effects of the drugs can be watched. Sometimes, the patient may receive treatment at the hospital clinic, at the doctor's office, or at home.

The side effects of chemotherapy depend on the drugs given and the individual response of the patient. Chemotherapy commonly affects hair cells, blood-forming cells, and cells lining the digestive tract. As a result, patients may have side effects such as hair loss, lowered resistance to infection, loss of appetite, nausea, or vomiting. Chemotherapy can cause menstrual periods to become irregular or to stop; it can also cause infertility. Most side effects end after treatment is stopped.

To help withstand the side effects of treatment, it is important that patients maintain good nutrition (see Nutrition for Cancer Patients, page 19).

FOLLOW-UP CARE

Regular follow-up exams are very important for any woman who has been treated for dysplasia or cancer of the cervix. The doctor will want to watch the patient closely for several years to be sure that the abnormal tissue has been completely destroyed. Generally, regular follow-up examinations include a pelvic exam, a Pap smear, and other laboratory tests.

LIVING WITH CANCER

When people have cancer, life can change for them and for the people who care about them. These changes in daily life can be difficult to handle. (See Adjusting to the Disease, page 19, and Support for Cancer Patients, page 20.)

WHAT THE FUTURE HOLDS

There are more than 5 million Americans living today who have had some type of cancer. Many are women who have had cancer of the cervix. The outlook for women with dysplasia and very early cancer of the cervix is excellent; nearly all patients with these conditions can be cured. Researchers continue to look for better ways to treat invasive cancer, and the chances of controlling this disease are improving every day.

The National Cancer Institute

COLORECTAL CANCER

The lowest portion of the digestive system is the colon. It is also called the large bowel, or large intestine. The colon is the last 5 to 6 feet of the intestine. The last 8 to 10 inches of the colon is the rectum. After food is digested, solid wastes move through the colon and rectum to the anus, where they are passed out of the body.

SYMPTOMS

When an illness affects the colon or rectum, a number of symptoms may appear. The ones listed here are warning signs of a possible problem.

- Diarrhea or constipation
- Blood in or on the stool (either bright red or very dark in color)
- Stools that are narrower than usual
- General stomach discomfort (bloating, fullness, cramps)
- Frequent gas pains
- A feeling that the bowel doesn't empty completely
- Loss of weight with no known reason
- Constant tiredness

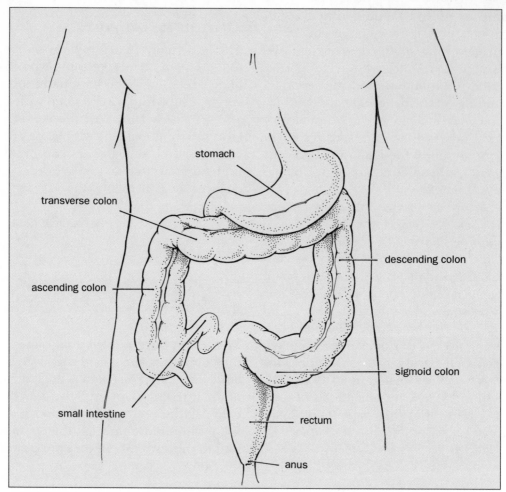

About 75 percent of all colorectal cancers and polyps occur in the rectum or in the sigmoid portion of the colon—the segments easiest to examine and treat.

These symptoms can be caused by a number of problems—such as the flu, ulcers, an inflamed colon, or cancer. It is important to see a doctor if any of these symptoms lasts as long as two weeks. Any illness should be diagnosed and treated as soon as possible, and this is especially true for cancer of the colon and rectum.

DIAGNOSIS

When a person's symptoms suggest that there might be cancer in the colon or rectum, the doctor will ask about the patient's medical history and will conduct a complete exam. In addition to checking the general signs of health

(temperature, pulse, blood pressure, and so on), the doctor usually does several other exams.

To check the rectal area, the doctor inserts a lubricated, gloved finger into the rectum and gently feels for any bumps.

The doctor may also do a "procto" to look at the rectum and the lower end of the colon. For this exam, a thin, lighted instrument called a sigmoidoscope is inserted into the rectum. Some of these scopes are rigid; others are flexible, allowing the doctor to see higher up in the colon. About 50 percent of colon and rectal cancers can be found with the procto exam.

After these first steps, the doctor may order some lab tests and other exams. The doctor may ask the patient for a stool sample to find out if there is blood in the stool. For this test, the patient places a small amount of stool (called a "smear") on a plastic slide or piece of special paper. The sample is then sent to a lab to be examined.

Sometimes the doctor wants to see the entire length of the colon. For this exam, the doctor uses a colonoscope, which is a thin, flexible tube with a light at the end. If an abnormal growth is found, the doctor will remove a small sample for examination in the lab. This procedure is called a biopsy. In many cases, the doctor can use the colonoscope to remove the whole growth. A biopsy is the only sure way to know if the tumor is cancer.

The doctor may also ask for a "lower GI series" or "barium enema." This is an x-ray of the colon that is taken after a thick solution of barium is pumped into the bowel through an enema tube. The barium shows an outline of the colon on the x-ray. It helps the doctor see tumors or other suspicious areas that were not found in other tests.

If a tumor is benign, it most likely can be removed with no further problems. However, if the tumor is cancer, the doctor may want to start planning further diagnostic tests or treatment.

TREATMENT

Treatment Planning

The first step in treatment usually is finding out the stage of the cancer. Staging tests show whether the disease has spread from its starting point in the colon or rectum to other parts of the body. Staging is very important because it helps the doctor plan the best treatment.

During staging, the doctor will often order x-rays or other scans of the lungs, liver, kidneys, and bladder. Sometimes a special blood test (the CEA assay) is done to measure substances that may increase in the blood of a person with colon or rectal cancer. (This same test may be used later on to find out how the patient is responding to treatment.)

The doctor will develop a treatment plan to fit the patient's medical history, age and general health, and the extent and location of the cancer. (See also Treatment Planning, page 16.)

Methods of Treating Cancer

There are three main ways to treat cancer of the colon and rectum: surgery, radiation therapy, and chemotherapy. Another method, called immunotherapy, is now being studied in clinical trials. The doctor may use just one method or combine them. The decision is based on the patient's individual needs. In some cases, the patient may be referred to specialists in the different kinds of cancer treatment.

Surgery. The standard treatment for most colon and rectal cancers is surgery. The kind of operation will depend mostly on the location and size of the tumor.

The surgeon may be able to remove only the part of the bowel that contains the cancer and then join the healthy sections together. This operation is called a bowel resection. Often, it is all that is needed.

During surgery, the lymph nodes near the tumor are also removed. One of the ways that cancer spreads through the body is by way of the lymph system. The surgeon removes the lymph nodes to check if cancer cells are present in them. This information is important in planning future treatment.

If the cancer is blocking the bowel, a procedure called a colostomy may be needed. For this surgery, the cancerous bowel is removed and the surgeon creates an opening in the abdomen (called a stoma) for the body's wastes to be removed, bypassing the lower colon and rectum. A colostomy may be temporary or permanent.

A temporary colostomy is done to let the lower colon and rectum heal. When the area has healed, a second operation is done to close the stoma. Normal bowel functions are regained.

A permanent colostomy is needed when the entire lower rectum is removed. Only about 15 percent of patients with colorectal cancer need a permanent colostomy.

After surgery for a colostomy, a special bag called an appliance is attached to the stoma to collect waste matter. The appliance does not show under most clothing. While in the hospital, the patient may see an enterostomal therapist, a trained health care worker who teaches patients with a colostomy how to care for the stoma and appliance.

Radiation therapy. In radiation therapy (also called x-ray therapy, radiotherapy, cobalt treatment, or irradiation), high-energy rays are used to stop the cancer cells from growing and multiplying. Radiation therapy is sometimes used before surgery to shrink the tumor. More often, it is used after surgery to destroy any cancer cells that may remain, or to relieve pain. Radiation therapy is given in hospitals, clinics, or private offices. Most patients can have radiation therapy as outpatients.

Chemotherapy. The use of drugs to treat cancer is called chemotherapy. Adjuvant therapy is the use of drugs following primary treatment if there is reason to suspect that cancer cells remain in the body after surgery or radiation therapy. Anticancer drugs may also be used when there are signs that the cancer has spread.

The various kinds of drugs used to treat cancer are given to patients in different ways: by mouth, or by injection into a muscle, an artery, or a vein. The drugs travel through the bloodstream to almost every area of the body.

Depending on which drugs are used, the patient may need to stay in the hospital for a few days so that the effects of the drugs can be watched. From then on, the patient may be given chemotherapy as an outpatient, or at home. Chemotherapy is most often given in cycles—a treatment period, followed by a rest period, then another treatment, and so on.

Side Effects of Treatment

Because cancer can spread, the treatments used against this disease must be powerful. It is rarely possible to limit the effects of radiation or chemotherapy so that only cancer cells are destroyed. Some healthy cells may be damaged at the same time. For this reason, patients may have unpleasant side effects.

Patients having radiation therapy may have skin reactions (redness or dryness) in the area being treated, and they may be unusually tired. In addition, patients may have diarrhea, nausea, or vomiting. Radiation to any part of the pelvic area may also cause side effects in the reproductive organs (such as infertility or impotence).

The side effects of chemotherapy depend on the drugs that are given and the response of the patient. Chemotherapy commonly affects hair cells, blood-forming cells, and the cells lining the digestive tract. Patients may have side effects such as hair loss, lowered blood counts, nausea, or vomiting. Most side effects end after the treatment is over. To help withstand the side effects of treatment, it is important that patients maintain good nutrition (see Nutrition for Cancer Patients, page 19).

LIVING WITH CANCER

When people have cancer, life can change for them and for the people who care about them. These changes can be difficult to handle. (See Adjusting to the Disease, page 19, and Support for Cancer Patients, page 20.)

WHAT THE FUTURE HOLDS

There are more than 5 million Americans living today who have had some type of cancer. Many of them have had cancer of the colon or rectum. Because researchers have found better ways to detect and treat these cancers, the chances of recovering are improving.

The National Cancer Institute

HODGKIN'S DISEASE

Hodgkin's disease is a type of lymphoma. Lymphomas are cancers that develop in the lymphatic system, part of the body's circulatory system. The job of the lymphatic system is to help fight diseases and infection.

The lymphatic system is made up of a network of thin tubes that branch, like blood vessels, into all the tissues of the body. Lymphatic vessels carry lymph, a colorless, watery fluid that contains infection-fighting cells called lymphocytes. Along this network of vessels are groups of small, bean-shaped organs called lymph nodes that filter the lymph fluid as it passes through the nodes. Clusters of lymph nodes are found in the underarm, groin, neck, and abdomen.

Other parts of the lymphatic system are the spleen, thymus gland, tonsils, and bone marrow.

Like all types of cancer, Hodgkin's disease affects the body's cells. Healthy cells grow, divide, and replace themselves in an orderly manner. This process keeps the body in good repair. In Hodgkin's disease, cells in the lymphatic system begin growing abnormally, and if left untreated, spread to other organs. As the disease progresses, the number of normal lymphocytes is reduced—leaving the body with fewer cells to fight infection.

Hodgkin's disease is rare. It makes up only 1 percent of all cases of cancer in this country. It is most often seen in young people aged 15 to 34 and in people over the age of 55.

SYMPTOMS

The most common symptom of Hodgkin's disease is a painless swelling in the lymph nodes in the neck, underarm, or groin. Other symptoms may include fevers, night sweats, tiredness, weight loss, or itching skin. However, these symptoms are not sure signs of cancer. They may also be caused by many common illnesses, such as the flu or other infections. But it is important to see a doctor if any of these symptoms lasts longer than two weeks. Any illness should be diagnosed and treated as early as possible, and this is especially true of Hodgkin's disease.

DIAGNOSIS

If Hodgkin's disease is suspected, the doctor will ask about the patient's medical history

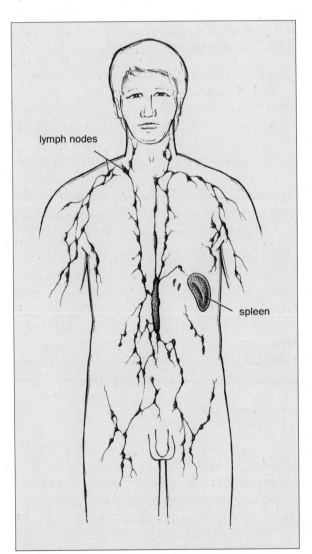

Hodgkin's disease causes swelling in the glands or nodes of the lymphatic system, located throughout the body. The spleen is actually a large lymph gland.

and will conduct a thorough physical exam. Blood tests and x-rays of the chest, bones, liver, and spleen will also be done.

Tissue from an enlarged lymph node will be removed. This is known as a biopsy. It is the only sure way to tell if cancer is present. A pathologist will look at the tissue under the microscope for Reed-Sternberg cells, abnormal cells usually found with Hodgkin's disease. When Hodgkin's disease is diagnosed, the doctor needs to know the stage, or extent, of the disease. Knowing the stage is very important for planning treatment. The stage indicates where the disease has spread and how much tissue is affected. In staging, the doctor checks:

- The number and location of affected lymph nodes
- Whether the affected lymph nodes are above, below, or on both sides of the diaphragm (the thin muscle under the lungs and heart that separates the chest from the abdomen)
- Whether the disease has spread to the bone marrow or to places outside the lymphatic system, such as the liver

In staging, the doctor usually orders several tests, including biopsies of the lymph nodes, liver, and bone marrow. Many patients have lymphangiograms, x-rays of the lymphatic system using a special dye to outline the lymph nodes and vessels. Another test is computed tomography (also called CT scan), a series of x-rays of various cross-sections of the body.

TREATMENT

Treatment decisions for Hodgkin's disease are complex. Before starting treatment, the patient might want another doctor to review the diagnosis and treatment plan. (See also Treatment Planning, page 16.)

Methods of Treatment

Treatment for Hodgkin's disease usually includes radiation therapy or chemotherapy. Sometimes, both are given. Treatment decisions are made depending on the stage of disease, its location in the body, which symptoms are present, and the general health and age of the patient. Often, patients are referred to doctors or medical centers that specialize in the different treatments of Hodgkin's disease.

For early stages of Hodgkin's disease, radiation therapy is usually used. Radiation therapy (also called x-ray therapy, radiotherapy, or irradiation) uses high-energy rays to damage cancer cells and stop their growth. Radiation treatment is generally given in a hospital or clinic. Most often, patients receive radiation therapy five days a week for several weeks as outpatients. Weekend rest periods allow time for healthy cells to repair themselves.

Chemotherapy is used in more advanced stages of Hodgkin's disease. Chemotherapy is the use of drugs to kill cancer cells. To treat Hodgkin's disease, the doctor prescribes a combination of drugs that work together. The drugs may be given in different ways: some by mouth; others injected into an artery, vein, or muscle. The drugs travel through the bloodstream to almost every part of the body. Chemotherapy is usually given in cycles, a treatment period followed by a rest period, then another treatment period, and so on.

Side Effects of Treatment

The methods used to treat Hodgkin's disease are very powerful. That's why the treatment often causes side effects—both short-term and permanent. Side effects depend on the type of treatment and on the part of the body being treated.

During radiation therapy, patients may become unusually tired as therapy continues. Resting as much as possible is important. Skin reactions (redness or dryness) in the area being treated are also common. Patients should be gentle with the treated area of skin. Lotions and creams should not be used without the doctor's advice. When the chest is treated, patients may have a dry, sore throat, and may have trouble swallowing. Sometimes, they have shortness of breath or a dry cough. Radiation treatment to the lower abdomen may cause nausea, vomiting, or diarrhea. Some patients have tingling or numbness in their arms, legs, and lower back. These side effects gradually disappear when treatment is over.

The side effects of chemotherapy depend on the drugs given and the individual response of the patient. Chemotherapy commonly affects hair cells, blood-forming cells, and cells that line the digestive tract. As a result, patients may have side effects such as hair loss, lowered resistance to infection, loss of appetite, nausea and vomiting, and mouth sores. These side effects usually end after chemotherapy is finished.

To help withstand the side effects of treatment, it is important that patients maintain good nutrition (see Nutrition for Cancer Patients, page 19).

Treatment for Hodgkin's disease can cause fertility problems. Women's menstrual periods may stop. Periods are more likely to return in younger women. In men, both Hodgkin's disease and its treatment can affect fertility. Younger men are more likely to regain their fertility. Sperm banking before treatment may be an option for some men.

FOLLOW-UP CARE

Regular follow-up exams are very important for anyone who has been treated for Hodgkin's disease. The doctor will continue to watch the patient closely for several years. Generally, checkups include a careful physical exam, x-rays, blood tests, and other laboratory tests.

Patients treated for Hodgkin's disease have an increased risk of developing other types of cancer later in life, especially leukemia. Patients should follow their doctor's recommendations on health care and checkups. Having regular checkups allows problems to be detected and treated promptly if they should arise.

LIVING WITH CANCER

When people have cancer, life can change for them and for the people who care about them. These changes in daily life can be difficult to handle. (See Adjusting to the Disease, page 19, and Support for Cancer Patients, page 20.)

WHAT THE FUTURE HOLDS

More than 5 million Americans living today have had some type of cancer. Thirty years ago, few patients with Hodgkin's disease recovered from their illness. Now, because of modern radiation therapy and combination chemotherapy, more than 75 percent of all newly diagnosed Hodgkin's disease patients are curable. The chances for recovery continue to improve as scientists find new and more effective treatments.   *The National Cancer Institute*

KIDNEY CANCER

The kidneys are part of the urinary tract. They are a pair of organs found just above the waist on each side of the spine.

The kidneys remove waste products from the blood and produce urine. As blood flows through the kidneys, they filter waste products, chemicals, and unneeded water from the blood. Urine collects in the middle of each kidney, an area called the renal pelvis. Urine then drains from the kidney through a long tube, the ureter, to the bladder, where it is stored.

The kidneys also make substances that help control blood pressure and regulate the formation of red blood cells.

TYPES OF KIDNEY CANCER

In adults, most kidney cancers develop in the tissues that filter blood and produce urine.

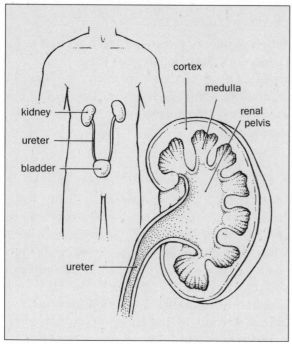

The kidneys eliminate wastes, chemicals, and excess water from the blood and produce urine. Tumors of the kidney tend to form on its top outer edge.

This type of cancer is called renal cell cancer. Cancer of the renal pelvis is called transitional cell carcinoma. This disease is very much like the type of cancer that occurs in the bladder, and is often treated like bladder cancer.

SYMPTOMS

The most common symptom of kidney cancer is blood in the urine. In some cases, a person can actually see the blood. It may be present one day and not the next. Also, traces of blood may be found in urinalysis, a urine test done as part of a regular medical checkup.

Another symptom of kidney cancer is a lump or mass that can be felt in the kidney area. The tumor may cause a dull ache or pain in the back or side. Less often, signs of a kidney tumor include high blood pressure or an abnormal number of red blood cells.

Symptoms may develop suddenly. However, as with other types of cancer, kidney cancer can cause a general feeling of poor health. People with this disease may feel tired, lose their appetite, and lose weight. Some have a fever that comes and goes.

These symptoms may be caused by cancer or by other, less serious problems such as an infection or a fluid-filled cyst. Only a doctor can tell for sure.

DIAGNOSIS

To diagnose kidney cancer, the doctor asks about the patient's personal and family medical history and does a complete physical exam. In addition to checking temperature, pulse, blood pressure, and other general signs of health, the doctor usually orders blood and urine tests and may do one or more of the following exams. (If the doctor thinks the patient might have transitional cell carcinoma, other tests may be used.)

- *An IVP (intravenous pyelogram)* is a test that lets the doctor see the kidneys, ureters, and bladder on x-rays. The x-rays are taken after an injection of dye that shows up on the x-ray film.
- *A CT scan* is another x-ray procedure that gives detailed pictures of cross-sections of the body. The pictures are created by a computer.
- *Ultrasound* is a test that sends high-frequency sound waves, which cannot be heard by humans, into the kidney. The pattern of echoes produced by these waves creates a picture called a sonogram. Healthy tissues, cysts, and tumors produce different echoes.
- *An arteriogram* is a series of x-rays of blood vessels. Dye is injected into a large blood vessel through a narrow tube called a catheter. X-rays show the dye as it moves through the network of smaller blood vessels around and in the kidney.
- *MRI (magnetic resonance imaging)* uses a very strong magnet linked to a computer

to create pictures of cross-sections of the kidney.

- *A nephrotomogram* is a series of x-rays of cross-sections of the kidney. The x-rays are taken from several angles before and after injection of a dye that outlines the kidney.

If these tests suggest that a tumor is present, the doctor may confirm the diagnosis with a biopsy. A thin needle is inserted into the tumor to withdraw a sample of tissue. The tissue is examined under a microscope by a pathologist to check for cancer cells.

When a diagnosis of kidney cancer is made, the doctor needs to know the extent, or stage, of the disease. Because kidney cancer may spread to the bones, lungs, liver, or brain, staging procedures may include special x-rays and tests to check these organs.

TREATMENT

Treatment for kidney cancer depends on the location and size of the tumor and whether the cancer has spread to other organs. The doctor also considers the person's age and general health to develop a treatment plan to fit the patient's needs. (See also Treatment Planning, page 16.)

Treatment Methods

Kidney cancer is treated with surgery, embolization, radiation therapy, hormone therapy, biological therapy, or chemotherapy. The doctor may use just one treatment method or combine them, depending on the patient's needs. In many cases, the patient is referred to doctors who specialize in different kinds of cancer treatment. Sometimes, several specialists work together as a team.

Surgery. Most kidney cancer patients have surgery, an operation called nephrectomy. In some cases, the surgeon removes the whole kidney or just the part of the kidney that contains the tumor. More often, the surgeon removes the whole kidney along with the adrenal gland and the fat around the kidney. Also, nearby lymph nodes may be removed because they are one of the first places where kidney cancer spreads. Finding cancer cells in the lymph nodes means there may be cancer elsewhere in the body.

Embolization. In embolization, a substance is injected to clog the renal blood vessels. The tumor shrinks because it does not get the blood supply it needs to grow. In some cases, embolization makes surgery easier. When surgery is not possible, this treatment may help reduce pain and bleeding.

Radiation therapy (also called radiotherapy) uses high-powered rays to damage cancer cells and stop them from growing. Radiation therapy may be used to shrink a tumor before surgery or to kill cancer cells that may remain in the body after surgery. For patients who cannot have surgery, radiation therapy may be used instead. Also, radiation may be used to treat kidney cancer that has spread to the bones or other parts of the body.

The radiation comes from a large machine. The patient receives radiation therapy five days a week for five to six weeks. This schedule helps protect normal tissue by spreading out the total dose of radiation. The patient doesn't need to stay in the hospital for radiation therapy.

Surgery, embolization, and radiation therapy are forms of local therapy. They affect only the cells in the treated area. Hormone therapy, biological therapy, and chemotherapy are types of systemic therapy. The substances travel through the bloodstream and affect cells all over the body.

Hormone therapy. Some kidney cancers may be treated with hormones to control the growth of cancer cells. Some hormones are taken by mouth; others are given by injection. Patients do not need to be in the hospital for their treatment. This kind of treatment helps

45

a small number of patients with advanced kidney cancer, especially when the disease has spread to the lungs.

Biological therapy is a new way of treating kidney cancer. This treatment attempts to improve the way the body's immune system fights disease.

Interleukin-2 and interferon are two forms of biological therapy being studied to treat advanced kidney cancer. Doctors are also exploring the benefits of using biological therapy after surgery for early stage kidney cancer. This additional treatment is called adjuvant therapy. Doctors are trying to find out whether adjuvant biological therapy can prevent the cancer from recurring by killing undetected cancer cells that may remain in the body.

Most patients having biological therapy must stay in the hospital so that the effects of their treatment can be watched.

Chemotherapy uses drugs to kill cancer cells. Chemotherapy has not been very effective against kidney cancer, but researchers are studying new drugs and new drug combinations that may prove to be useful.

Side Effects of Treatment

The methods used to treat kidney cancer are very powerful. It is hard to limit the effects of treatment so that only cancer cells are destroyed; healthy cells may also be damaged. That's why treatment often causes unpleasant side effects. Side effects depend on the type of treatment and the part of the body being treated.

Nephrectomy is major surgery. For a few days after the operation, most patients need medicine to relieve pain. Discomfort may make it difficult to breathe deeply, and patients have to do special coughing and breathing exercises to help keep their lungs clear. Patients may need IV (intravenous) feedings and fluids for several days before and after the operation. Nurses will keep track of the amount of fluid

the patient takes in and the amount of urine produced. The remaining kidney takes over the work of the one that was removed.

Embolization can cause pain, fever, nausea, or vomiting. These problems are treated with medicine. Often, patients also need intravenous fluids.

During radiation therapy, the patient may become very tired as the treatment continues. Resting as much as possible is important. Skin reactions (redness or dryness) in the treated area are also common, and the skin should be protected from the sun. Good skin care is important at this time, but the patient should not use any lotion or cream on the skin without the doctor's advice. Radiation therapy may cause nausea, vomiting, and diarrhea. Usually, the doctor can suggest certain foods and medicines to ease these problems.

The side effects of hormone therapy are usually mild. Progesterone is the hormone most often used to treat kidney cancer. Drugs containing progesterone generally cause few side effects, though some patients may retain fluid and gain weight.

The side effects caused by biological therapies vary with the type of treatment. Often, these treatments cause flulike symptoms such as chills, fever, muscle aches, weakness, loss of appetite, nausea, vomiting, and diarrhea. Sometimes patients get a rash with dry, itching skin. Patients often feel very tired after treatment. In addition, interleukin-2 can cause the patient to retain fluid. These problems can be severe, and most patients need to stay in the hospital during treatment.

To help withstand the side effects of treatment, it is important that patients maintain good nutrition (see Nutrition for Cancer Patients, page 19).

FOLLOW-UP CARE

Regular follow-up is very important after treatment for kidney cancer. The doctor will continue to check the patient closely to be sure that the cancer has not returned. Check-ups may include exams, chest x-rays, and lab tests. The doctor sometimes orders scans (special x-rays) and other tests, too.

LIVING WITH CANCER

The diagnosis of kidney cancer can change the lives of cancer patients and the people who care about them. These changes can be difficult to handle. (See Adjusting to the Disease, page 19, and Support for Cancer Patients, page 20.)

WHAT THE FUTURE HOLDS

Scientists at hospitals and medical centers all across the country are studying this disease. They are trying to learn what causes kidney cancer and how to prevent it. They also are looking for better ways to diagnose and treat it.

The National Cancer Institute

LEUKEMIA

Leukemia is a generalized disorder of blood cell production in which abnormal white blood cells accumulate in the blood and bone marrow. In lymphocytic leukemia, these white cells are lymphocytes, produced in the lymph nodes. Myelocytic leukemia (also known as granulocytic or myelogenous leukemia) affects the granulocytes, white blood cells produced in the bone marrow. Both lymphocytic and myelocytic leukemia occur as acute (fast-growing) or chronic (slow-growing) diseases.

Leukemia, like other cancers, is a disease of the body's cells. Cells of different shapes and functions make up various parts of the body: the skin, heart, lungs, bones, and so forth. All cells reproduce themselves by dividing. Normal growth and repair of body tissues take place in this orderly manner.

When cell division is not orderly, abnormal growth takes place. In leukemia, among the tiny cells which make up the blood are blast cells, or immature cells, instead of normal cells.

To understand the nature of leukemia, it is necessary to know about function and composition of the blood. It supplies food, oxygen, hormones, and other chemicals the body's cells must have to function properly. The blood transports these substances to and from storage centers, helps in the removal of waste products, and is also one of the body's most effective defenses against infection.

To carry out these and other important functions, the blood contains many components, each with a specific task. Those that are involved in leukemia are red cells, platelets, and white cells.

The red blood cells, along with the platelets and certain of the white blood cells, are formed primarily in the bone marrow and are then released into the bloodstream as they become mature. The bone marrow, a spongy meshwork of tissue which fills up the cavities of the bones, is important in leukemia because this is where the disease seems to begin.

The red cells, or erythrocytes, carry the oxygen necessary for life to all the various organs and tissues of the body. Each of these cells contains a small amount of a compound called hemoglobin, which is capable of taking up oxygen as the blood passes through the lungs, and releasing it in the tissues.

The bone marrow contains certain tiny disc-shaped cells, called platelets, that break off and circulate in the blood. Platelets are necessary for the prevention of abnormal bleeding.

The third group of elements in the blood consists of the white blood cells, or leukocytes. The two types of white cells are the granulocytes (sometimes referred to as neutrophils), and the lymphocytes. These cells play a major role in the body's defense against disease-producing bacteria, viruses, and fungi.

The neutrophils are able to rid the body of

harmful bacteria and other foreign particles by engulfing and destroying them. The number of these white cells in the blood varies greatly and can increase quite rapidly when needed to combat infection. Once an infection is overcome, the number of neutrophils in the blood usually returns to normal.

The lymphocytes act in a different way to maintain good health. When the body is invaded by viruses or bacteria, the lymphocytes and other specialized cells respond by producing antibodies. These are substances which react with the infectious agent so that it is ultimately destroyed and removed from the body. Because each antibody is generally effective against only one type of bacterium or virus, different ones must be produced to combat each infectious agent.

SYMPTOMS

Symptoms of acute lymphocytic leukemia and acute myelocytic leukemia are varied and can progress rapidly. The lymph nodes, spleen, and liver become infiltrated with white blood cells and may be enlarged. Other common symptoms are bone pain, paleness, tendency to bleed or bruise easily, and frequent infections.

Chronic myelocytic leukemia is also known as chronic granulocytic leukemia, chronic myeloid leukemia, chronic myelogenous leukemia, or chronic myelosis.

The patient most often seeks medical treatment because of increasing fatigue or weight loss. There may be a sense of fullness or heaviness under the left ribs, and the doctor may discover a mass in the abdomen. Less frequently, the complaints result from anemia, abnormal perspiration, fever, bleeding, pain in the spleen, or an attack of gout. Sometimes the discovery of the disease may be accidental, in the course of routine clinical or laboratory examinations.

Chronic lymphocytic leukemia usually occurs in older people and develops slowly. In fact, symptoms are entirely absent in some cases, and the disease discovered accidentally when a patient is examined for another complaint. When symptoms do occur, they may be a general feeling of ill health, fatigue, lack of energy, fever, loss of appetite and weight, or night sweats. Enlarged lymph nodes in the neck or groin may be noticed in some patients. Some may show signs of anemia or infections.

DIAGNOSIS

Leukemia can be diagnosed only by microscopic examination of the blood and the bone marrow. If leukemia cells are present in these tissues, they can be identified and the diagnosis made.

The blood test may show low hemoglobin, low white cell levels, and a low platelet level. Blast cells (immature cells) also may be present in the blood.

Because these findings suggest the diagnosis of leukemia, a bone marrow biopsy may be done. A sample of bone marrow is obtained by inserting a needle into the bone and withdrawing a tiny amount of tissue. The bone marrow is examined under the microscope by a pathologist. A pathologist is a physician who interprets and diagnoses the changes caused by disease in body tissues. The bone marrow biopsy establishes the specific type of leukemia, which is essential in determining the best form of treatment. It also is used as a way of checking on the progress of therapy.

When a diagnosis of leukemia is confirmed, it is best for you to begin treatment in a hospital that has an expert staff and resources to apply all forms of effective treatment right from the beginning.

TREATMENT

Your doctor will consider a number of factors in determining the best treatment for you. Among these are your medical history, your general health, the type of leukemia you have, and the extent of your disease. Your treatment must be tailored to your individual needs. (See also Treatment Planning, page 16.)

Acute myelocytic leukemia and acute lymphocytic leukemia are treated with various combinations of drugs, or chemotherapy. Chemotherapy (treatment with anticancer drugs) kills cancer cells. Your physician must maintain a delicate balance of enough drugs to kill cancer cells without destroying too many healthy ones.

Some anticancer drugs may make you feel sick for a while, but your doctor tries to work out a treatment schedule that disrupts your daily routine as little as possible. The length and frequency of drug treatments depend on a number of factors. These include your type of leukemia, the kind of anticancer drugs prescribed, how long it takes you to respond to the treatment, and how well you tolerate any side effects.

Therapy to the central nervous system may also be added to your regular treatment program. Combinations of drugs are then used in maintenance of remission.

A remission is a temporary—and potentially permanent—arrest of leukemia. When a complete remission occurs, there is a complete return to a state of normal good health: the symptoms disappear, the physical findings become normal, and abnormal cells are no longer found in the bone marrow and blood. Sometimes the remission is only partial and one or more of the signs of leukemia may not completely disappear. Examination of the blood at frequent intervals and of the bone marrow from time to time enables your doctor to follow the course of your disease and to select the proper dosage of the appropriate drugs.

Sometimes leukemic cells accumulate in the brain. Here, due to unique properties of the blood vessel walls that prevent certain substances from passing from the blood to the central nervous system, the leukemic cells may be relatively safe from attack by anticancer drugs.

Patients are now being treated before central nervous system symptoms appear with drugs administered directly into the spinal fluid, and in some cases with radiation therapy to the brain as well.

Chronic myelocytic leukemia often can be controlled at the beginning by a variety of treatments. One or more anticancer drugs often are administered. Irradiation with x-rays or radioactive phosphorus may benefit some patients. After a few weeks the patient often goes into remission and can resume his normal activities.

When a patient relapses, the abnormalities reappear and are similar to those seen in acute leukemias. Infections and hemorrhaging are frequent and may be severe. The methods for treatment are the same as those for the acute leukemias during this stage of the disease.

Chronic lymphocytic leukemia may be left untreated when there are no symptoms and few or no abnormal physical signs. Patients may live normal lives with the disease for a number of years. However, the patient should be examined at regular intervals.

When the disease becomes active, one or more anticancer drugs may be of value. Radiation therapy also may be given in some cases.

SUPPORTIVE CARE

Other problems in treating leukemia are the result of drug side effects as well as leukemia itself. Both drugs and leukemia damage the bone marrow and impair the patient's ability to produce two important blood elements. These elements are platelets that prevent bleeding, and white blood cells that help control bacterial and fungal infections.

Transfusions of blood platelets have proved effective in preventing or stopping hemorrhage. A supply of platelets from a donor can be obtained by a technique known as plateletpheresis, in which platelets are removed from normal whole blood by centrifu-

49

gation. Because the red cells are returned promptly, the donor may be able to give platelets as frequently as twice a week for periods up to three months. (In contrast, donors can give whole blood only once every six to eight weeks.) Plateletpheresis enables a single adult donor—often another family member—to provide the major portion of the platelets required by the patient.

The use of platelet transfusions has reduced the occurrence of hemorrhage during the last decade, making it possible to use effective anticancer drugs even though they depress platelet production.

However, patients may become resistant to platelets obtained from persons of different platelet types. When this occurs, the donated platelets are rapidly destroyed, and the patient is again in danger from hemorrhage. Fortunately, platelets can be typed according to a histocompatibility system (HL-A). HL-A matched platelets often survive normally in patients who have become resistant to non-matched platelets. HL-A typing can thus frequently identify a suitable donor. Platelets obtained from the patient himself (while he is in remission) can be frozen and reinfused into the patient during relapse. Such platelets are often effective when the patient is resistant to platelets from available donors.

The success achieved with platelet transfusion prompted scientists to attempt granulocyte (white cell) replacement for treatment of infection in leukemia patients. Granulocyte transfusions can be given with beneficial effects to some patients with bacterial infections, but it has been difficult to obtain these cells in adequate amounts from normal blood donations.

To increase the availability of granulocytes, a special centrifuge can be used to separate granulocytes from the other blood elements, which are then returned to the donor. It is now possible, using this continuous-flow centrifuge, to obtain as many granulocytes from one normal donor at one sitting as are contained in 30 to 40 units of blood collected by standard methods. A suitable donor can effectively support the granulocyte levels of otherwise granulocytopenic patients (patients with a deficiency of granulocytes in the blood) for several weeks.

Another approach to controlling infection in leukemia patients is the use of relatively germ-free environments plus decontamination procedures, to reduce the degree of contact with bacteria and thus the risk of infection. Germ-free laminar air-flow rooms have been developed by the National Cancer Institute and are under study at the Institute and at several other major cancer centers assisted by Institute funds. The occurrence of severe infection has been diminished significantly by the use of these isolation systems.

Also, newly developed antibiotics have been of value in the treatment of bacterial infections. A search is under way for antibiotics more effective against certain resistant bacteria, fungi, and viruses.

LIVING WITH CANCER

When people have cancer, life can change for them and for the people who care about them. These changes in daily life can be difficult to handle. (See Adjusting to the Disease, page 19, and Support for Cancer Patients, page 20.)

The National Cancer Institute

LUNG CANCER

The lungs, a major part of the respiratory system, are a pair of cone-shaped organs made up of pinkish-gray, spongy tissue. They occupy most of the chest cavity and are separated from each other by the mediastinum, which is an area in the chest containing the heart, trachea (windpipe), esophagus, and lymph nodes. The right lung has three sections, called lobes, and is a little larger than the left lung, which has only two lobes. The lungs exchange gases between the body and the air. They remove carbon dioxide, a waste product of the body's cells, and take in oxygen, which is necessary for cells to live and carry out normal activities.

Air enters the body through the nose and mouth and travels down the throat, through the larynx (voice box), and into the lungs through tubes called bronchi. One bronchus goes to the right lung and one to the left lung. The bronchi divide into smaller and smaller tubes called bronchioles, which end in tiny air sacs called alveoli.

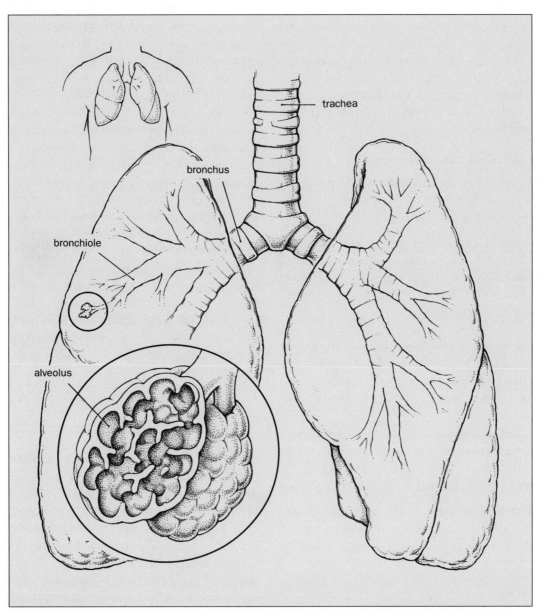

The trachea divides into two bronchi, one in each lung. These branch out into bronchioles and culminate in tiny air sacs, or alveoli. The most common type of lung cancer begins in the bronchi.

TYPES OF LUNG CANCER

Lung cancers are generally divided into two types: small cell lung cancer and nonsmall cell lung cancer. The tumor cells of each type grow and spread differently, and they are treated differently.

Small Cell Lung Cancer

Small cell lung cancer is sometimes called oat cell cancer because the cancer cells look like oats when they are viewed under a microscope. This type of lung cancer makes up about 20 to 25 percent of all cases. It is a rapidly growing cancer that spreads very early to other organs. It is generally found in people who are heavy smokers.

Nonsmall Cell Lung Cancer

There are three main kinds of nonsmall cell lung cancer, and they are named for the type of cells found in the cancer.

Epidermoid carcinoma, which is also called squamous cell carcinoma, makes up about 33 percent of all lung cancer cases. (Carcinoma is a cancer that begins in the lining or covering tissues of an organ.)

This type of lung cancer often begins in the bronchi and may remain in the chest without spreading for longer periods than the other types. Epidermoid carcinoma is the most common type of lung cancer.

Adenocarcinoma accounts for about 25 percent of all lung cancers. It often grows along the outer edges of the lungs and under the tissue lining the bronchi.

Large cell carcinomas make up about 16 percent of all lung cancer cases. These cancers are found most often in the smaller bronchi.

SYMPTOMS

Lung cancer may cause a number of symptoms. A cough is one of the more common symptoms and is likely to occur when a tumor grows and blocks an air passage. Another symptom is chest pain, which feels like a constant ache that may or may not be related to coughing. Other symptoms may include shortness of breath, repeated pneumonia or bronchitis, coughing up blood, hoarseness, or swelling of the neck and face.

In addition, there may be symptoms that do not seem to be at all related to the lungs. These may be caused by the spread of lung cancer to other parts of the body. Depending on which organs are affected, symptoms can include headache, weakness, pain, bone fractures, bleeding, or blood clots.

Sometimes symptoms may be caused by hormones that are produced by lung cancer cells. For example, certain lung cancer cells produce a hormone that causes a sharp drop in the level of salt (sodium) in the body. A decrease in sodium level can produce many symptoms, including confusion and sometimes even coma. Like all cancers, lung cancer can also cause fatigue, loss of appetite, and loss of weight.

These symptoms may be caused by a number of problems. They are not a sure sign of cancer. However, it is important to see a doctor if any of these symptoms lasts as long as two weeks. Any illness should be diagnosed and treated as early as possible, and this is especially true for cancers.

DIAGNOSIS

If lung cancer is suspected, a patient undergoes a series of tests to confirm whether cancer is present. Once cancer is diagnosed, doctors do more tests to learn if the disease has spread. This process is called staging.

When symptoms suggest that there might be cancer growing in the lungs, the first step for all patients is a complete physical examination. This includes telling about any health problems, work history, and anything else that might be important in learning the cause of the symptoms. The physical examination is usually followed by chest x-rays. Next, the doctor may want to collect cells from the lungs so that they can be examined under a microscope. This is important because it is the only sure way to know if cancer is present and, if it is, to identify the type of lung cancer. Doctors may collect cells by biopsy using a needle, surgery, or other methods.

In addition to chest x-rays, the patient may have other x-ray tests. For example, a lung tomogram is a series of x-rays of sections of the lung. In computed tomography (CT scans), a computer helps produce the pictures. The CT scan is useful in finding out if the tumor has spread from the lung to other parts of the chest or to more distant organs such as the brain or liver.

A test called bronchoscopy permits the doctor to see the breathing passages through a thin, hollow, lighted tube. The tube is inserted through the patient's nose or mouth into the lung. The doctor can collect cells from the bronchial walls or snip small pieces of tissue for study under the microscope. This test generally is done in a hospital. The patient, who is given a local anesthetic and is awake during the test, usually can go home a few hours later.

A new procedure, used to collect cells that are hard to reach with the bronchoscope, is needle aspiration biopsy guided by fluoroscopy. Fluoroscopy is an x-ray test that uses a television screen so that internal organs, such as the heart, can be viewed while they are in motion. Using the picture on the screen as a guide, the doctor inserts a needle into the tumor to withdraw cells for examination.

The doctor may use a test called mediastinoscopy to learn if cancer cells have spread to lymph nodes in the mediastinum. This test requires an incision in the chest, so the patient is given a general anesthetic. Mediastinotomy is similar to mediastinoscopy, except the incision is made in another part of the chest.

Doctors also may perform scans to locate lung cancer cells that may have spread to the brain, bone, or liver. In these tests, a substance that is mildly radioactive is injected into the blood, and a machine then scans the body to measure radiation and detect abnormal areas.

TREATMENT

Treatment for lung cancer depends on the type of cancer cells, the location of the tumor, and the stage of the cancer (whether it is just in the lungs or it has spread to other organs). After diagnosis and staging, the doctor develops a treatment plan to fit the type and location of the cancer as well as the patient's medical history and general health. (See also Treatment Planning, page 16.)

There are three basic ways to treat lung cancer: surgery, radiation therapy, and chemotherapy. The type of surgery that the doctor recommends depends on the size and location of the tumor. Radiation therapy (also called x-ray therapy, radiotherapy, or irradiation) uses high-energy rays to kill cancer cells. The use of anticancer drugs to treat cancer is called chemotherapy. Sometimes, a combination of these methods is used.

Small Cell Lung Cancer

Small cell lung cancer spreads quickly to distant parts of the body. Often these second tumors cannot be found by routine tests. Thus, treatment with surgery or radiation therapy to the chest usually is not effective in controlling small cell lung cancer.

Patients with small cell lung cancer are commonly treated with a combination of several anticancer drugs or with anticancer drugs plus radiation to the chest. The radiation is directed to the original (primary) tumor in the lungs, while chemotherapy is used to reach tumors in other parts of the body.

Nonsmall Cell Lung Cancer

Patients with nonsmall cell lung cancer generally can be divided into three groups. The

53

first group includes patients whose cancer is only in the lung and whose tumor can be removed by surgery. An operation that removes only a small part of the lung is called a wedge resection. When an entire lobe of the lung is removed, the procedure is called a lobectomy. Pneumonectomy is the removal of the entire lung. Radiation therapy may be used to treat patients in this group who cannot have surgery because of other medical problems.

The second group is nonsmall cell lung cancer patients whose cancer has spread to nearby tissue or lymph nodes. The usual treatment for these patients is radiation therapy to the chest. This treatment is sometimes combined with other forms of treatment, especially surgery.

The third group includes patients whose cancer has spread to distant parts of the body. Radiation therapy and chemotherapy are used to shrink the cancer and to relieve symptoms.

Side Effects of Treatment

Because cancer can spread rapidly and threaten life, the treatments used against this disease must be very powerful. It is rarely possible to limit the effects of cancer treatment so that only cancer cells are destroyed; normal, healthy cells may be damaged at the same time. For this reason, many patients experience unpleasant side effects while they are having cancer treatments. Doctors try to plan treatments to keep such side effects to a minimum. Most side effects end soon after treatment.

Surgery. Certain problems can occur following surgery to remove cancer in the lungs. For example, blood loss during an operation on the chest may be greater than blood loss during other types of surgery. Other complications are caused by damage to or removal of lung tissue. In such cases, patients may have difficulty breathing and sometimes can become drowsy.

Radiation at high levels destroys the ability of cells to grow and divide. Both normal cells and cancer cells are affected, but most normal cells are able to recover quickly. Radiation therapy is usually given five days a week for several weeks. This schedule helps to protect healthy tissues by spreading out the total dose of radiation and by giving rest breaks so that normal cells can recover. During radiation therapy, the side effects that patients notice most often are unusual tiredness, painful swallowing, and skin reactions in the area being treated.

Chemotherapy. Drugs used to treat cancer are given to patients in different ways: some are given by mouth; others are injected into a muscle, a vein, or an artery. The anticancer drugs travel through the bloodstream to almost every part of the body, helping to stop the growth of cancer cells. Chemotherapy is most often given in cycles—a treatment period, followed by an "off" or "rest" period, then another treatment period, and so on.

Depending on which drugs the doctor orders, the patient may need to stay in the hospital for a few days so that the drugs' effects on the body can be watched. Sometimes, the patient may receive treatments as an outpatient at the hospital, at the doctor's office, or at home.

Chemotherapy affects not only cancer cells but also other rapidly growing cells, such as blood cells, hair cells, and cells that line the digestive tract. As a result, the patient may have side effects such as anemia, an increased risk of infection or bleeding, hair loss, nausea, and vomiting. Fatigue also may occur during treatment with anticancer drugs.

To help withstand the side effects of treatment, it is important that patients maintain good nutrition (see Nutrition for Cancer Patients, page 19).

LIVING WITH CANCER

When people have cancer, life can change for them and for the people who care about them. Changes in daily life can be difficult to handle.

(See Adjusting to the Disease, page 19, and Support for Cancer Patients, page 20.)

WHAT THE FUTURE HOLDS

The outlook for a person with lung cancer depends on the type of cancer, the stage of the disease, and the patient's age, general health, and response to treatment. Researchers are working to find better ways to diagnose and treat lung cancer, and the chances of controlling the disease are improving every day.

The National Cancer Institute

MULTIPLE MYELOMA

Multiple myeloma is a cancer of the plasma cells, one type of white blood cell found in the bone marrow, the soft, spongelike material in the center of the bone. These plasma cells (also called plasmacytes) normally produce antibodies for the body's immune system to use as defense weapons against infection and to attack invading viruses and bacteria.

Normally cells grow in an orderly, controlled pattern. As normal cells wear out, new ones are produced. Just enough new cells grow to replace the old ones. Cells of each part of your body such as your bones, skin, and heart differ in shape and function. Each type of cell is designed to do a particular job in a particular organ.

Sometimes plasma cells may start to grow and multiply in an abnormal manner forming malignant tumors (cancer). When this occurs, the cancer cells may form abnormal proteins or excess amounts of normal immunoglobulins or antibodies that pour into the bloodstream interfering with the body's functions.

When the normal plasma cells stop producing antibodies, the body loses resistance to infection. As a result, the patient may possibly develop other diseases such as pneumonia or kidney infections.

SYMPTOMS

The first signs of myeloma are usually bone pains, especially in the back. As more plasma cells grow in the bone marrow, the pain may become more severe and constant, and may shift to the back, ribs, neck, and pelvic areas.

Another symptom of myeloma may be anemia and fatigue. This can result from cancerous plasma cells displacing the red blood cells. The bone marrow also may make fewer platelets, the tiny cells in the blood that make blood clot. As a result, the patient may have bleeding gums, frequent nosebleeds, or other abnormal bleeding.

Other signs may include unexplained fractures or cracks of the bones, painful swellings on the ribs, or kidney problems. There also may be painful pressure on the spinal cord or loss of weight.

DIAGNOSIS

Laboratory and x-ray tests are necessary to diagnose multiple myeloma. Diagnosis may be tentative at first because some symptoms may be the same as those caused by rheumatoid arthritis or other problems.

- *Laboratory tests of blood and urine* show if there is growth of cancerous plasma cells accompanied by destruction of normal tissue. These tests can detect certain protein products of cancer cells. Concentrations of these myeloma or Bence-Jones proteins (named after the physician who first described them) are a clinical indication of myeloma.
- *Aspiration or biopsy of the bone marrow* can detect increased numbers of cancerous plasma cells. For an aspiration, your doctor numbs an area, usually in the pelvis or breastbone by injecting an anesthetic.

Then he inserts a special needle into the marrow to withdraw a small amount for examination under a microscope. In a biopsy, a larger needle is used, and a small fragment of bone is also removed from the pelvic site for analysis, to check on the spread of cancer to the bone. The doctor who examines the tissue is a pathologist, a physician who interprets and diagnoses the changes caused by disease in body tissue. The biopsy is used to confirm or rule out a diagnosis of cancer.

- ***X-rays of the skeletal system*** may be taken to observe whether any portions of bone have been destroyed or damaged.
- ***Other laboratory tests*** that may be run as part of a full and careful diagnosis include tests of calcium, uric acid, creatinine, and a complete blood count. Each of these tests can indicate problems and abnormalities associated with the disease.

When a diagnosis of cancer is confirmed, it is best for you to begin treatment in a hospital that has an expert staff and resources to apply all forms of effective treatment right from the beginning.

TREATMENT

Your doctor will consider a number of factors in determining the best treatment for you. Among these are your medical history, your general health, and the type and location of the cancer or cancers you have. Your treatment must be tailored to your individual needs. (See also Treatment Planning, page 16.)

Chemotherapy (treatment with anticancer drugs) is available to your physician in treating multiple myeloma. Anticancer drugs kill cancer cells. Because the drugs can act on normal cells as well as cancerous ones, your physician must maintain a delicate balance of enough drugs to kill cancer cells without destroying too many healthy ones.

Some anticancer drugs may make you feel sick for a while, but your doctor tries to work out a treatment schedule that disrupts your daily routine as little as possible. The length and frequency of drug treatments depend on a number of factors. These include the kind of anticancer drugs prescribed, how long it takes you to respond to treatment, and how well you tolerate any side effects.

Radiation therapy may be used for a few minutes each day, usually on specific places of the back and neck. This can relieve pain and help repair bone damage.

The basic principle of radiation therapy is to focus the beam of radiation at doses that will destroy the cancer with minimal damage to surrounding normal tissue. Radiation therapy uses x-rays, cobalt, or other sources of ionizing radiation.

The tumor cells usually decrease in number at a rapid rate during the first few months of treatment, and the patient may go into remission. A remission is a temporary—and potentially permanent—arrest of the myeloma. When a complete remission occurs, there is a complete return to a state of normal good health: the symptoms disappear, the physical findings become normal, and abnormal cells are no longer found in the bone marrow and blood. Sometimes the remission is only partial, and one or more signs of myeloma may not disappear completely. Examination of the blood, urine, and bone marrow at regular intervals enables the doctor to follow the course of the disease and to select the proper dosage of the appropriate anticancer drugs.

LIVING WITH CANCER

When people have cancer, life can change for them and for the people who care about them. Changes in daily life can be difficult to handle. (See Adjusting to the Disease, page 19, and Support for Cancer Patients, page 20.)

The National Cancer Institute

NON-HODGKIN'S LYMPHOMAS

Lymphoma is a general term for cancers that develop in the lymphatic system. They account for about 4 percent of all cases of cancer in this country.

The most common type of lymphoma is called Hodgkin's disease. All other lymphomas are grouped together and are called non-Hodgkin's lymphomas.

The lymphatic system is part of the body's immune defense system. Its job is to help fight diseases and infection. The lymphatic system is made up of a network of thin tubes that branch, like blood vessels, into all the tissues of the body.

Lymphatic vessels carry lymph, a colorless, watery fluid that contains infection-fighting cells called lymphocytes. Along this network of vessels are groups of small, bean-shaped organs called lymph nodes. Clusters of lymph nodes are found in the underarm, groin, neck, chest, and abdomen.

Other parts of the lymphatic system are the spleen, thymus gland, tonsils, and bone marrow. Lymphatic tissue is also found in other parts of the body, including the stomach, intestines, and skin.

Like all types of cancer, lymphomas are diseases of the body's cells. Healthy cells grow, divide, and replace themselves in an orderly manner. This process keeps the body in good repair.

In the non-Hodgkin's lymphomas, cells in the lymphatic system begin growing abnormally. They divide too rapidly and grow without any order. Too much tissue is formed, and tumors may begin to grow.

If left untreated, lymphoma can spread to other organs of the body. The number of normal lymphocytes is reduced as lymphoma progresses—leaving the body with fewer cells to fight infection.

SYMPTOMS

The most common symptom of non-Hodgkin's lymphomas is a painless swelling in the lymph nodes in the neck, underarm, or groin. Other symptoms may include fevers, night sweats, tiredness, weight loss, itching, and reddened patches on the skin. Sometimes there is nausea, vomiting, or abdominal pain.

These symptoms are not sure signs of cancer, however. They may also be caused by many common illnesses, such as the flu or other infections. But it is important to see a doctor if any of these symptoms lasts longer than two weeks. Any illness should be diagnosed and treated as early as possible.

DIAGNOSIS

The doctor will ask about the patient's medical history and will conduct a thorough physical exam. The only sure way to tell whether cancer is present is with a biopsy. Tissue from an enlarged lymph node will be removed. By examining these tissues under the microscope, a pathologist can identify the cancer cells and tell whether the lymphoma is the kind that usually grows slowly or rapidly.

There are at least 10 types of non-Hodgkin's lymphomas. Often, they are grouped into three categories by how fast they grow: low grade (slow growing), intermediate grade, and high grade (rapidly growing).

When lymphoma is diagnosed, the doctor needs to know what kind it is and the stage, or extent, of the disease. This information is very important for planning treatment. The stage indicates where the disease has spread and how much tissue is affected. Blood tests and x-rays of the chest, bones, liver, and spleen are done. The doctor also checks:

- The number and location of affected lymph nodes
- Whether the affected lymph nodes are above, below, or on both sides of the diaphragm (the thin muscle under the lungs

and heart that separates the chest from the abdomen)

- Whether the disease has spread to the bone marrow or organs outside the lymphatic system, such as the liver

In staging, the doctor usually orders several other special tests, including additional biopsies of the lymph nodes, bone marrow, and other sites. Most patients have lymphangiograms, x-rays of the lymphatic system using a special dye to outline the lymph nodes and vessels. The doctor may also want the patient to have a CT scan. A CT scan is a series of x-rays put together by a computer to form three-dimensional pictures of various sections of the body. Ultrasound may also be used. This test allows doctors to view internal organs by creating pictures from echoes of high-frequency sound waves.

TREATMENT

Treatment decisions for non-Hodgkin's lymphomas are complex. Before starting treatment, the patient might want a specialist who treats lymphomas to review the diagnosis and treatment plan. (See also Treatment Planning, page 16.)

Methods of Treatment

Treatment planning takes into account the type of lymphoma, the stage of disease, whether it is likely to grow slowly or rapidly, and the general health and age of the patient.

For low-grade lymphomas that usually grow very slowly and cause few symptoms, the doctor may decide to wait until the disease shows signs of spreading before starting treatment.

Treatment for intermediate or high-grade lymphomas usually involves chemotherapy, with or without radiation therapy. In addition, surgery may be needed to remove a large tumor. Often, patients are referred to medical centers that specialize in treating lymphomas.

Chemotherapy is the use of drugs to kill cancer cells. Chemotherapy for non-Hodgkin's lymphomas usually is a combination of several drugs. Some drugs are given by mouth; others are injected into a blood vessel or muscle. The drugs travel through the bloodstream to almost every part of the body. Chemotherapy is usually given in cycles, a treatment period followed by a rest period, then another treatment period, and so on.

Radiation therapy (also called x-ray therapy, radiotherapy, or irradiation) uses high-energy rays to damage cancer cells and stop their growth. Radiation therapy is generally given in the outpatient department of a hospital or clinic. Most often, patients receive radiation therapy five days a week for five to six weeks. Weekend rest periods allow time for healthy cells to repair themselves.

Side Effects of Treatment

The methods used to treat lymphomas are very powerful. That's why treatment often causes side effects. Fortunately, most side effects are temporary.

The side effects of chemotherapy depend on the drugs given and the individual response of the patient. Chemotherapy commonly affects rapidly growing cells, such as blood-forming cells and cells that line the digestive tract. As a result, patients may have side effects such as lowered resistance to infection, loss of appetite, nausea and vomiting, and mouth sores. They may also lose their hair. These side effects usually end after chemotherapy is finished.

During radiation therapy, patients may notice a number of side effects. They may become unusually tired as the treatment continues. Resting as much as possible is important. Skin reactions (redness or dryness) in the area being treated are also common. Patients should be gentle with the treated area of skin. Lotions and creams should not be used without the doctor's advice. When the chest and neck area is treated, patients may have a dry, sore throat, and may have some trouble swallowing. Sometimes, they have shortness of breath or a dry cough. Radiation therapy to the abdomen may cause nausea, vomiting, or diarrhea. Some patients may have tingling or numbness in their arms, legs, and lower back. These side effects gradually disappear when treatment is over.

To help withstand the side effects of treatment, it is important that patients maintain good nutrition (see Nutrition for Cancer Patients, page 19).

FOLLOW-UP CARE

Regular follow-up exams are very important for anyone who has been treated for non-Hodgkin's lymphoma. Most relapses occur in the first two years after therapy. Patients who have a relapse can be treated successfully.

Generally, checkups include a careful physical exam, x-rays, blood tests, and other laboratory tests. Patients should follow their doctor's recommendations on health care and checkups. Having regular checkups allows problems to be detected and treated promptly if they should arise.

LIVING WITH CANCER

When people have cancer, life can change for them and for the people who care about them. These changes in daily life can be difficult to handle. (See Adjusting to the Disease, page 19, and Support for Cancer Patients, page 20.)

WHAT THE FUTURE HOLDS

More than 5 million Americans living today have had some type of cancer. Thirty years ago, few patients recovered from non-Hodgkin's lymphoma. Because of advances in combination chemotherapy and radiation therapy, about half of all non-Hodgkin's lymphoma patients now survive. As scientists find new and more effective treatments, the chances for recovery continue to improve.

The National Cancer Institute

ORAL CANCERS

The oral cavity (which most often is called the mouth) has many parts. It includes the lips, inner cheeks, gums, teeth, jaw, tongue, floor of the mouth, and hard palate (roof of the mouth). The soft palate, pharynx (upper part of the throat), and tonsils are at the back of the mouth. Salivary glands throughout the oral cavity make saliva, which keeps the mouth moist and helps digest food.

Cancer may develop in any part of the oral cavity. Most frequently, it is found on the lips, the lining of the cheeks, the gums, and the floor of the mouth. The tongue, the area directly behind the wisdom teeth, the pharynx, and the tonsils are other common sites. Cancers of the hard palate and the soft palate are less common.

SYMPTOMS

More than 90 percent of all oral cancers are found in people over the age of 45, but oral cancer can occur at any age. Individuals can spot symptoms by doing a monthly oral self-exam.

This exam should include a check for these symptoms, which are some of the warning signs of oral cancer.

- A sore in the mouth that bleeds easily and does not heal
- A lump or thickening in the cheek that can be felt with the tongue
- A white or red patch on the gums, tongue, or lining of the mouth
- Soreness or a feeling that something is caught in the throat
- Difficulty chewing or swallowing
- Difficulty moving the jaw or tongue

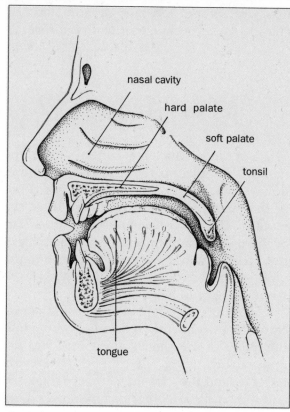

nasal cavity

hard palate

soft palate

tonsil

tongue

Cancer may develop anywhere within the oral cavity. Oral cancers are rare among people under 40; they are most likely to develop in those over 60.

- Numbness of the tongue or other areas of the mouth
- Swelling of the jaw that causes dentures to fit poorly or become uncomfortable

These symptoms are not sure signs of cancer. They can also be caused by many other conditions. However, it is important to see a dentist or doctor if any of these problems lasts more than two weeks. Pain is usually not a symptom of oral cancer.

DIAGNOSIS

To diagnose oral cancer, a dentist or doctor carefully checks the mouth for lumps, swelling, or abnormal-looking areas.

When a problem is found, a biopsy is the only sure way to know whether cancer is present. Usually, an oral surgeon removes part or all of a lump or abnormal-looking area. A pathologist examines the tissue under a microscope to see whether cancer cells are present and, if so, what type they are. Almost all oral cancers are squamous cell carcinomas (cancers that begin in the flat, scalelike cells that line the oral cavity).

When oral cancer is found, the doctor needs to know whether it has spread. This process is called staging. Staging generally includes dental x-rays and x-rays of the head and chest. The doctor feels the lymph nodes in the front and back of the neck to check for swelling or other changes. Sometimes, the doctor uses an endoscope, a flexible, lighted instrument, to look for tumors in the throat.

The doctor may also want the patient to have a CT scan. A CT scan is a series of x-rays put together by a computer to form a detailed picture. Ultrasound is another scan that creates pictures of the inside of the body. High-frequency sound waves, which cannot be heard by humans, are bounced off organs and tissue. Their echoes make an image on a video screen that is much like a television screen. Sometimes the doctor asks for magnetic resonance imaging (MRI). In this scan, a cross-sectional image (like a CT scan) is produced with a powerful magnet instead of radiation.

TREATMENT

Treatment for oral cancer depends on the size, location, and extent (stage) of the disease. The doctor also takes into account the patient's age and general health. Treatment may be surgery, radiation therapy, or a combination of the two. Treatment may cause changes in a patient's appearance and may lead to problems with chewing, swallowing, or talking. For these important reasons, the patient and the doctor should carefully review treatment choices. (See also Treatment Planning, page 16.)

Methods of Treatment

Patients with oral cancer may be treated by a team of specialists. The medical team may include an oral surgeon; ear, nose, and throat surgeon; medical oncologist; radiation therapist; plastic surgeon; prosthodontist; dietitian; and speech therapist.

Surgery. Most patients with oral cancer have surgery to remove the tumor in the mouth. If there is evidence that the cancer may have spread, the surgeon may remove lymph nodes in the neck. The surgeon will attempt to take out only cancerous lymph nodes and a small amount of tissue close to them. If the disease involves muscles and other tissues in the neck, the operation may be more extensive.

Radiation therapy (also called radiotherapy) uses high-energy rays to destroy the cancer cells' ability to grow and multiply. Radiation therapy may be used instead of surgery for small tumors in the mouth. Patients with larger tumors may need both surgery and radiation.

The radiation may be given before or after surgery. Before surgery, radiation helps shrink the tumor so that it can be removed. Radiation after surgery is used to destroy cancer cells that may remain. The radiation may come from a machine outside the body (external radiation), or the doctor may put materials that give off radiation into the tissues of the mouth (implant radiation).

Usually, a patient gets external radiation in an outpatient department of the hospital or clinic five days a week for several weeks. This schedule helps protect healthy tissues by spreading out the total dose of radiation.

Implant radiation puts cancer-killing rays as close as possible to the tumor. A small capsule containing radioactive material is placed into the tissues of the mouth or put directly into the tumor. Generally, an implant is left in place for several days, and the patient needs to stay in the hospital. To keep from moving the implant, the patient is put on a special liquid diet given in small portions through a tiny straw. The patient gets most nutrition and fluids during the treatment period through an intravenous (IV) tube in a vein.

Sometimes an implant is left in place permanently. It loses a little radiation each day. The patient stays in the hospital while the radiation is most active. After a few days, the patient can go home, because the amount of radiation left in the implant is not dangerous.

Chemotherapy uses drugs to kill cancer cells. To date, chemotherapy has not been very effective in treating oral cancers. Researchers are still looking for effective drugs or drug combinations to treat oral cancers.

Side Effects of Treatment

Treatments for oral cancers may injure healthy tissues of the mouth. Therefore, it is important for patients to have a dental checkup and any needed dental work done before cancer treatment begins.

The methods used to treat oral cancers are very powerful. It is hard to limit the effects of cancer treatment so that only cancer cells are destroyed; normal, healthy tissue also may be damaged.

Surgery and radiation therapy often cause side effects—some are short-term, others are permanent. Surgery to remove small tumors in the oral cavity usually does not cause any major problems. For a larger tumor, however, the surgeon may need to remove parts of the pharynx, palate, or jaw. Such surgery is likely to change the patient's ability to chew, swallow, or speak. The patient may also look different. If surgery affects the nerves in the bottom lip, the patient may have difficulty controlling the lip and may drool.

After surgery, the patient's face may be swollen. This swelling usually goes away within a few weeks. However, if the lymphatic system has been damaged, lymph may collect in the tissues and swelling may last for a long time.

Radiation to the mouth reduces the amount of saliva. The mouth may be very dry. The saliva becomes thicker and contains more acid than is normal. Some patients use special sprays (artificial saliva) to help relieve dryness. Iced beverages, special chewing gum, and frequent rinsing also can help keep the mouth moist. Because the saliva is thicker, food remains in contact with the teeth longer, allowing tooth decay to start. Also, because the tissues in the mouth are tender during treatment, many patients are unable to floss or brush their teeth thoroughly. But good mouth care is very important. Using a very soft child's toothbrush or a special toothbrush with a soft, spongy tip can make mouth care easier. A salt and baking soda mouthwash can help keep the mouth fresh and protect the teeth from decay. The doctor may suggest rinsing with a fluoride solution to prevent cavities.

Some patients are able to wear their dentures during radiation therapy. However, because the gums shrink during radiation treatment, dentures may not fit properly. After treatment is over, a patient may need to have dentures refitted or replaced. Radiation therapy can also cause mouth sores that heal slowly. Dentures should not be worn until the sores have healed.

During radiation therapy, patients may become very tired as treatment continues. Resting as much as possible is important. During treatment, the skin may become red or dry. Good skin care is important at this time. The patient should not use lotions or creams on the skin without the doctor's advice. Men may lose all or part of their beard, but facial hair generally grows back after treatment is done. Usually, men shave with an electric razor to prevent cuts that may lead to infections.

Weight loss can be a serious problem for patients being treated for oral cancer. Patients who eat well may be better able to withstand the side effects of their treatment. So, nutrition is an important part of the treatment plan.

Doctors may suggest a number of ways for patients to get enough calories and protein. In many cases, it helps to have food and beverages in very small amounts. Many patients find that eating several small meals and snacks during the day works better than trying to have three large meals.

Often, patients find it easier to eat soft, bland foods that have been moistened with sauces or with gravies. Puddings, high-protein milkshakes, and homemade eggnogs are nourishing and easy to swallow. It may be helpful to prepare other foods in a blender as well. The doctor may also suggest special liquid dietary supplements for patients who cannot chew solid food.

The side effects that patients have during cancer treatment vary for each person. Doctors try to plan treatments to keep problems to a minimum. They may even be different from one treatment to the next.

Doctors, nurses, and dietitians can explain to the patient the side effects that can occur with cancer treatment and can suggest ways to deal with them.

REHABILITATION

Rehabilitation is a very important part of treatment for patients with oral cancer. The goals of rehabilitation will depend on the treatment a patient has received. The medical team makes every effort to help the patient return to normal activities as soon as possible.

Sometimes, a patient needs plastic surgery to rebuild the bones or tissues of the mouth. If this is not possible, a prosthodontist may be able to make an artificial dental and/or facial part (prosthesis). Patients may need special training to use these devices.

Speech therapy generally begins as soon as possible for a patient who has trouble talking. Often, a speech therapist visits the patient in the hospital to plan therapy and teach speech exercises. Speech therapy usually continues after the patient returns home.

FOLLOW-UP CARE

Regular follow-up exams are very important for anyone who has been treated for oral cancer. The physician and dentist watch the patient closely to check the healing process and to be sure the cancer has not returned.

The patient may need to see a dietitian if weight loss or eating problems continue. Most doctors tell their oral cancer patients to stop using tobacco and alcohol to reduce the risk that a new cancer will develop in the mouth.

LIVING WITH CANCER

When people have cancer, life can change for them and for the people who care about them. Changes in daily life can be difficult to handle. (See Adjusting to the Disease, page 19, and Support for Cancer Patients, page 20.)

WHAT THE FUTURE HOLDS

Researchers continue to look for better ways to diagnose and treat oral cancers. This type of cancer can be cured if it is found and treated at an early stage, and the possibility of controlling advanced disease is improving.

The National Cancer Institute

OVARIAN CANCER

The ovaries are located in the pelvis, one on each side of the uterus. Each of these female reproductive organs is the size and shape of an almond. During each monthly menstrual cycle, one ovary releases an egg. The egg travels through a fallopian tube to the uterus.

The ovaries are also the body's main source of female hormones (estrogen and progesterone). These hormones control the development of female body characteristics, such as the breasts, body shape, and body hair. These hormones also regulate the menstrual cycle and pregnancy.

EARLY DETECTION

Most cases of ovarian cancer are found in women over the age of 50, but this disease can also occur in younger women. Women who have regular pelvic exams may increase their chance that, if ovarian cancer develops, it will be found at an early stage.

SYMPTOMS

Ovarian cancer is hard to find because cancer that is limited to the ovary usually does not cause symptoms. A tumor in the ovary can grow for some time before it causes pressure, pain, or other problems. Even when symptoms appear, they may be so vague that they are ignored.

The most common symptoms of ovarian cancer are swelling, bloating, or discomfort in the lower abdomen. The disease may cause a loss of appetite and a feeling of fullness, even after a light meal. Other symptoms may include gas, indigestion, nausea, and weight loss. As the tumor grows, it may press on nearby organs such as the bowel and bladder, causing constipation and frequent urination.

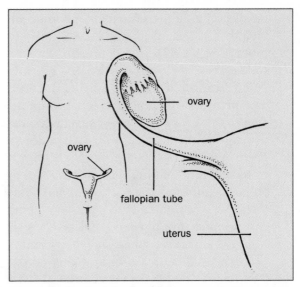

The abdominal cavity is spacious enough that ovarian tumors can often grow for quite some time before they produce any symptoms.

Ovarian cancer that has spread to other parts of the abdomen may cause fluid to build up in the abdomen (ascites) and result in swelling and discomfort. Less often, bleeding from the vagina can be a symptom of ovarian cancer.

These symptoms may be caused by cancer or by other, less serious conditions. Only a doctor can tell for sure. Any illness should be diagnosed and treated as early as possible.

DIAGNOSIS

To diagnose ovarian cancer, the doctor asks about the woman's personal and family medical history and does a physical exam, including a pelvic exam. The doctor will feel the vagina, rectum, and lower abdomen for masses or growths. A Pap smear (a common test for cancer of the cervix) may be done as part of the regular exam, but it is not a reliable way to diagnose ovarian cancer.

The doctor may also order some of the tests described here.

- *Ultrasound* is a test that sends high-frequency sound waves, which cannot be heard by humans, into the ovaries. The pattern of echoes produced by these sound waves creates a picture called a sonogram. Healthy tissues, fluid-filled cysts, and tumors produce different echoes.
- *CT scan* is an x-ray procedure that gives detailed pictures of cross-sections of the body. The pictures are created by a computer.
- *Lower GI series or barium enema* is a series of x-rays of the lower bowel. The patient is given an enema containing a solution called barium that highlights the bowel on an x-ray and may show abnormal areas caused by ovarian cancer.
- *Intravenous pyelogram (IVP)* is a test in which x-rays are taken of the kidneys, ureters, and bladder after an injection of a dye that highlights these organs.

The only sure way to know whether cancer is present is for a pathologist to examine a sample of tumor tissue under the microscope. To obtain the tissue, the surgeon removes the entire affected ovary. The surgeon must remove the entire ovary because, if the problem is cancer, cutting through the outer layer of the ovary can cause spread of the disease.

If the pathologist finds cancer, the surgeon nearly always removes the second ovary, the uterus, and the fallopian tubes. The surgeon will also take samples of nearby lymph nodes (biopsy), the diaphragm, and fluid from the abdomen to see whether the cancer has spread. This process is called staging. Careful surgical staging is needed to tell the extent of the cancer so that follow-up treatment can be planned.

TREATMENT

Treatment for ovarian cancer depends on a number of factors. Among these are the type of tumor, how fast it is growing, and the extent (stage) of the disease. The doctor also takes into account the woman's age and her general health to develop a treatment plan to fit each woman's individual needs. (See also Treatment Planning, page 16.)

Treatment Methods

Ovarian cancer may be treated with surgery, chemotherapy, or radiation therapy. The doctor may use just one method or combine them. In some cases, the woman may be referred to doctors who specialize in the different kinds of cancer treatment.

Surgery is part of the treatment for almost all patients with ovarian cancer.

Chemotherapy—the use of drugs to kill cancer cells—is generally given when there are signs that the cancer has spread or when the entire tumor cannot be removed at the time of surgery.

Radiation therapy may be used in addition to surgery to kill cancer cells that may remain in the pelvic area.

Surgery for ovarian cancer includes removal of the ovaries, uterus, and fallopian tubes.

However, if a woman has a very early, slow-growing tumor and wants to be able to have a child, the doctor may decide to remove only the affected ovary. If the cancer has spread to other organs in the abdomen, doctors try to remove as much of the cancer as possible. This leaves a smaller amount to be treated by chemotherapy and/or radiation therapy.

Chemotherapy for ovarian cancer uses a combination of several drugs. Chemotherapy is usually given in cycles: a treatment period followed by a rest period, then another treatment and rest period, and so on. Chemotherapy is called systemic therapy because the drugs travel all through the body in the bloodstream.

Most women receive chemotherapy as an outpatient at the hospital, at the doctor's office, or at home. Depending on which drugs are used or how they are given, however, a patient may need to stay in the hospital for a short while.

Radiation therapy (also called radiotherapy) uses high-energy rays to damage cancer cells and stop them from growing. Like surgery, radiation therapy is local therapy; it affects only the cells in the treated area. The patient goes to the hospital or clinic each day for radiation treatments. Usually, treatments are given five days a week for five to six weeks.

Another type of radiation therapy is intraperitoneal radiation. It may be used to put radioactive material as close as possible to the cancer. Radioactive liquid is placed directly into the pelvis and abdomen through a thin tube. The patient's position is changed frequently to allow the liquid to coat all the organs in the abdomen and pelvis. A short hospital stay may be necessary for this treatment. Sometimes, both types of radiation are used.

Doctors also are currently studying the use of intraperitoneal chemotherapy. This new approach places anticancer drugs directly in the abdomen and pelvis through a thin tube. As in intraperitoneal radiation treatment, the woman's position is changed frequently to allow the drugs to spread throughout the abdomen and pelvis. In this way, more of the drugs reach the cancer directly.

Another new type of treatment is biological therapy. This cancer treatment uses natural and laboratory-made substances to stimulate or restore the body's immune system so it can fight disease more effectively. This treatment is being studied in patients with recurrent or advanced ovarian cancer to learn if it is effective against this disease.

Side Effects of Treatment

The methods used to treat ovarian cancer are very powerful. It is hard to limit the effects of treatment so that only cancer cells are destroyed; healthy cells may also be damaged. That's why treatment often causes side effects. Side effects depend on the type of treatment used and on the part of the body being treated.

Surgery for ovarian cancer is a major operation. A woman usually is in the hospital for about a week after the operation. Drugs may be given to relieve pain and to prevent or treat infection. For several days after surgery, a woman may have problems emptying her bladder and having normal bowel movements. Doctors generally advise patients not to have sexual intercourse for about six to eight weeks after surgery.

When the ovaries are removed, a woman's natural source of hormones is lost and menopause starts immediately. When menopause occurs because of surgery, the symptoms (such as hot flashes) are more severe than when menopause happens naturally. Although estrogen replacement therapy, sometimes called ERT, may be prescribed for many women during natural menopause to ease these symptoms, it is not used for women with ovarian cancer. (See also Menopause, page 415.)

The side effects of chemotherapy depend on the drugs that are given. Also, each woman reacts differently. Chemotherapy usually affects rapidly growing cells, such as blood-forming cells and those that line the digestive tract.

One result is that a woman may have decreased blood counts that lower her resistance to infection. She also may have other side effects such as less energy, loss of appetite, nausea, vomiting, and mouth sores. She also may lose her hair. Some women receiving chemotherapy for ovarian cancer will have ringing in the ears or hearing loss. They also may develop numbness or tingling in their fingers, toes, or face.

During radiation therapy, a woman will have a loss of energy as the treatment continues, especially in the last weeks of treatment. Resting as much as possible is important. Mild skin reactions (redness or dryness) in the treated area are also common, especially if she has had chemotherapy. Good skin care is important at this time, but a woman should not use any lotion or cream on the skin without her doctor's advice.

Radiation treatment to the lower abdomen may cause nausea, vomiting, diarrhea, or urinary discomfort. Usually the doctor can suggest diet changes or medications to ease these problems.

Radiation therapy can cause vaginal dryness and interfere with intercourse. Some women are advised not to have intercourse during treatment. If the surgery has healed, most women are able to resume sexual activity a few weeks after radiation treatment ends.

To help withstand the side effects of treatment, it is important that patients maintain good nutrition (see Nutrition for Cancer Patients, page 19).

FOLLOW-UP CARE

Regular follow-up is very important after treatment for ovarian cancer. The doctor will continue to check a woman closely to be sure that the cancer has not returned.

Regular checkups include a pelvic exam and laboratory tests. Doctors often recommend a "second-look" laparotomy. This operation, done after one year of chemotherapy, allows the doctor to examine the abdominal area directly and take tissue samples to see whether the treatment has been successful. If cancer is found, chemotherapy will be continued. If no cancer is found, therapy will usually be stopped.

Women treated for ovarian cancer may have an increased risk of developing leukemia and other types of cancer later in life. They should carefully follow their doctor's advice on health care and checkups.

Regular checkups are important for women treated for ovarian cancer because cancer may recur.

LIVING WITH CANCER

The diagnosis of ovarian cancer can change a woman's life and the lives of the people who care about her. These changes can be difficult to handle. (See Adjusting to the Disease, page 19, and Support for Cancer Patients, page 20.)

WHAT THE FUTURE HOLDS

Scientists at hospitals and medical centers all across the country are studying ovarian cancer. They are trying to learn what causes this disease and how to prevent it. They also are looking for better ways to diagnose and treat it.

The National Cancer Institute

PANCREATIC CANCER

The pancreas is a spongy, tube-shaped organ about six inches long. It is located in the back of the abdomen, behind the stomach. The head of the pancreas is on the right side of the abdomen. It is connected to the duodenum,

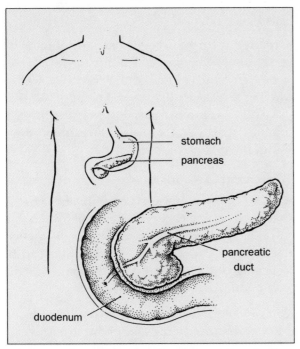

The pancreas secretes digestive enzymes into the duodenum, and makes insulin and glucagon, hormones essential in maintaining blood sugar levels.

the upper end of the small intestine. The narrow end of the pancreas, called the tail, extends to the left side of the body.

The pancreas makes pancreatic juices and hormones, including insulin. Pancreatic juices, also called enzymes, help digest food in the small intestine. Insulin controls the amount of sugar in the blood. Both enzymes and hormones are needed to keep the body working right.

As pancreatic juices are made, they flow into the main pancreatic duct. This duct joins the common bile duct, which connects the pancreas to the liver and the gallbladder. The common bile duct, which carries bile (a fluid that helps digest fat), connects to the small intestine near the stomach.

SYMPTOMS

Pancreatic cancer has been called a "silent" disease because early pancreatic cancer usual-

ly does not cause symptoms. If the tumor blocks the common bile duct and bile cannot pass into the digestive system, the skin and whites of the eyes may become yellow, and the urine may become darker. This condition is called jaundice.

As the cancer grows and spreads, pain often develops in the upper abdomen and sometimes spreads to the back. The pain may become worse after the person eats or lies down. Cancer of the pancreas can also cause nausea, loss of appetite, weight loss, and weakness.

A rare type of pancreatic cancer, called islet cell cancer, begins in the cells of the pancreas that produce insulin and other hormones. Islet cells are also called the islets of Langerhans. Islet cell cancer can cause the pancreas to make too much insulin or hormones. When this happens, the patient may feel weak or dizzy and may have chills, muscle spasms, or diarrhea.

These symptoms may be caused by cancer or by other less serious problems. Only a doctor can tell for sure.

DIAGNOSIS

To diagnose pancreatic cancer, the doctor does a complete physical exam and asks about the patient's personal and family medical history. In addition to checking general signs of health (temperature, pulse, blood pressure, and so on), the doctor usually orders blood, urine, and stool tests.

The doctor may also ask for a "barium swallow" or "upper GI series." For this test, the patient drinks a barium solution before x-rays of the upper digestive system are taken. The barium shows an outline of the pancreas on the x-rays.

The doctor may order other tests such as:

• *An angiogram*, a special x-ray of the blood vessels.

• *CT scans*, x-rays that give detailed pictures

of a cross-section of the pancreas. These pictures are created by a computer.

- *Ultrasound* to view the pancreas. In this procedure, an instrument that sends out high-frequency sound waves, which cannot be heard, is passed over the abdomen. The sound waves echo off the pancreas. The echoes form a picture on a screen that looks like a television.

- *ERCP (endoscopic retrograde cholangio-pancreatogram)*, a special x-ray of the common bile duct. For this test, a long, flexible tube (endoscope) is passed down the patient's throat through the stomach and into the small intestine. A dye is injected into the common bile duct, and x-rays are taken. The doctor can also look through the endoscope and take tissue samples.

A biopsy is the only sure way for the doctor to know whether cancer is present.

In a biopsy, the doctor removes some tissue from the pancreas. It is examined under a microscope by a pathologist, who checks for cancer cells.

One way to remove tissue is with a long needle that is passed through the skin into the pancreas. This is called a needle biopsy. Doctors use x-rays or ultrasound to guide the placement of the needle.

Another type of biopsy is a brush biopsy. This is done during the ERCP. The doctor inserts a very small brush through the endoscope into the bile duct to rub off cells to examine under a microscope.

Sometimes an operation called a laparotomy may be needed. During this operation, the doctor can look at organs in the abdomen and can remove tissue. The laparotomy helps the doctor determine the stage, or extent, of the disease. Knowing the stage helps the doctor plan treatment.

Tissue samples that are obtained with one kind of biopsy may not give a clear diagnosis, and the biopsy may need to be repeated using a different method.

TREATMENT

Treatment for pancreatic cancer depends on a number of factors. Among these are the type, size, and extent of the tumor as well as the patient's age and general health. The doctor will develop a treatment plan to fit each patient's needs. (See also Treatment Planning, page 16.)

Treatment Methods

Cancer of the pancreas is curable only when it is found in its earliest stages, before it has spread. Otherwise, it is very difficult to cure. However, it can be treated, symptoms can be relieved, and the quality of the patient's life can be improved.

Surgery. Pancreatic cancer is treated with surgery, radiation therapy, or chemotherapy. Researchers are also studying biological therapy to see whether it can be helpful in treating this disease. Sometimes several methods are used, and the patient is referred to doctors who specialize in different kinds of cancer treatment.

Surgery may be done to remove all or part of the pancreas. Sometimes it is also necessary to remove a portion of the stomach, the duodenum, and other nearby tissues. This operation is called a Whipple procedure. In cases where the cancer in the pancreas cannot be removed, the surgeon may be able to create a bypass around the common bile duct or the duodenum if either is blocked.

Radiation therapy (also called radiotherapy) uses high-powered rays to damage cancer cells and stop them from growing. Radiation is usually given five days a week for five or six weeks. This schedule helps to protect normal tissue by spreading out the total dose of radiation. Weekend rests give normal cells time to heal. The patient doesn't need to stay in the hospital for radiation therapy.

Radiation is also being studied as a way to kill cancer cells that remain in the area after surgery. In addition, radiation therapy can help relieve pain or digestive problems when the common bile duct or duodenum is blocked.

Chemotherapy uses drugs to kill cancer cells. The doctor may use just one drug or a combination. Chemotherapy may be given by mouth or by injection into a muscle or vein. The drugs enter the bloodstream and travel through the body. Chemotherapy is usually given in cycles: a treatment period followed by a rest period, then another treatment period, and so on.

Side Effects of Treatment

The methods used to treat pancreatic cancer are very powerful. It is hard to limit the effects of treatment so that only cancer cells are destroyed; healthy tissue may also be damaged. That's why treatment often causes unpleasant side effects. Side effects depend on the type of treatment used and on the part of the body being treated.

Surgery for cancer of the pancreas is a major operation. While in the hospital, the patient will need special medications and may be fed only liquids. During recovery from surgery, the patient's diet and weight will be checked carefully.

During radiation therapy, the patient may become very tired as the treatment continues. Resting as much as possible is important. Skin reactions (redness or dryness) in the treated area are also common. Good skin care is important at this time, but the patient should not use any lotions or creams on the skin without the doctor's advice. Radiation therapy to the upper abdomen may cause nausea and vomiting. Usually, the doctor can suggest certain diet changes or medications to ease these problems.

The side effects of chemotherapy depend on the drugs that are given. In addition, each person reacts differently. Chemotherapy affects rapidly growing cells, such as blood-forming cells, those that line the digestive tract, and those in the skin and hair. As a result, patients may have side effects such as lower resistance to infection, less energy, loss of appetite, nausea, vomiting, or mouth sores. Patients may also lose their hair.

To help withstand the side effects of treatment, it is important that patients maintain good nutrition (see Nutrition for Cancer Patients, page 19).

In addition, treatment for cancer of the pancreas may interfere with production of insulin and pancreatic juices. The patient must take medicines to replace these; otherwise the levels of blood sugar may be wrong and digestion may be affected. Even so, taking these medicines can often upset digestion. This is why the doctor must stay in close touch with the patient to change the dose and watch the patient's diet. Careful planning and checkups are important to help the patient avoid weight loss and the weakness and lack of energy caused by poor nutrition.

Patients and family members are often afraid that cancer will cause pain. Cancer patients do not always have pain, but if it does occur, there are many ways to relieve or reduce it. It is important for the patient to let the doctor know about pain, because uncontrolled pain can cause loss of sleep and poor appetite. These problems can make it difficult for the patient to respond to treatment.

LIVING WITH CANCER

The diagnosis of pancreatic cancer can change the lives of cancer patients and the people who care about them. These changes in daily life can be difficult to handle. (See Adjusting to the Disease, page 19, and Support for Cancer Patients, page 20.)

WHAT THE FUTURE HOLDS

Scientists at hospitals and medical centers all across the country are studying pancreatic cancer. They are trying to learn what causes this disease and how to prevent it. They are also looking for better ways to diagnose and treat it.

The National Cancer Institute

PROSTATE CANCER

The prostate, one of the male sex glands, is located below the bladder and above the rectum. About the size of a walnut, the prostate surrounds the first inch or so of the urethra, the tube that carries urine from the bladder. The prostate produces semen, the thick fluid that carries sperm from the testicles. Normal functioning of the prostate gland depends on the male hormone testosterone, which is made by the testicles.

SYMPTOMS

Often, there are no symptoms in the earliest stages of prostate cancer. When symptoms do occur, they may include some of the following problems.

- Need to urinate frequently, especially at night
- Difficulty starting urination or holding back urine
- Inability to urinate
- Weak or interrupted flow of urine
- Painful or burning urination
- Blood in the urine
- Painful ejaculation
- Continuing pain in the lower back, hips, or upper thighs

These symptoms may by caused by prostate cancer, by benign prostate conditions, or by other problems. It is important to have any of these symptoms checked by a doctor to find out what the problem is.

Benign conditions of the prostate include infections, prostate stones, and enlargement of the prostate (known as benign prostatic hyperplasia or benign prostatic hypertrophy, or BPH). More than half of all men in the United States over the age of 50 suffer from BPH, which occurs when the prostate swells and pushes against the urethra and the bladder,

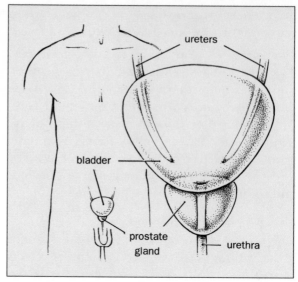

The prostate is just beneath the bladder, surrounding the urethra. Prostate enlargement, common in men over 50, is usually unrelated to prostate cancer.

blocking the flow of urine. (See also Prostate Enlargement, page 398.)

DIAGNOSIS

A rectal exam is the first step in diagnosing prostate cancer. Using a gloved finger to examine inside the rectal area, the doctor may be able to feel a hard lump or growth in the prostate. By doing a rectal exam, the doctor can detect cancer long before symptoms develop. This exam should be part of a regular checkup for all men over the age of 40.

If the doctor finds suspicious, hard, or lumpy areas in the prostate, additional tests (including x-rays, blood tests, and urine tests) are needed. Depending on the test results, the patient may be referred to a urologist, a specialist in diseases of the urinary system. The urologist may do more tests and may provide necessary treatment.

A biopsy is the only sure way to tell whether cancer is present. In a biopsy, a sample of prostate tissue is removed and examined under the microscope by a pathologist, a doctor who specializes in diagnosing disease. Tissue usually is removed from the prostate with a needle that is placed directly into the prostate gland (fine needle aspiration). Sometimes, the doctor operates to remove the entire prostate.

STAGING

If a biopsy shows that cancer is present, other tests are needed to learn if the disease has spread beyond the prostate gland. This procedure, called staging, helps the doctor choose the best treatment.

- *A chest x-ray* may be taken to see if cancer has spread to the lungs.
- *An intravenous pyelogram (IVP)* is a test in which x-rays are taken of the kidneys, ureters, and bladder after an injection of a dye that shows up on x-ray film.
- *A bone scan* can show if cancer has spread to the bones. A small amount of a radioactive substance is injected into the patient and collects in areas of abnormal bone growth. An instrument called a scanner pinpoints these areas and records them on x-ray film.
- *A number of laboratory tests* help define the extent of prostate cancer. One of these is a blood test that measures the level of a chemical called prostatic acid phosphatase (PAP). In a large percentage of prostate cancer patients, PAP may rise above normal when cancer has spread beyond the prostate. Another blood test measures the level of a protein called prostate specific antigen (PSA), which also goes up in men with prostate cancer and other diseases of the prostate.
- *Transrectal ultrasound, computed tomography (CT scan), and magnetic resonance imaging (MRI scan)* also may be used to determine the stage of prostate cancer. Transrectal ultrasound detects cancer by using sound waves, which are produced by an instrument that is inserted into the rectum. The waves bounce off the prostate, and the

pattern of the echoes made by the waves is converted by a computer into a picture. A CT scan is an x-ray procedure that uses a computer to produce a picture of a cross-section of the body. An MRI scan also shows a cross-section of the body, but this procedure uses magnetic fields instead of x-rays.

These tests help the doctor determine the extent of the disease. One staging system divides prostate cancer into the following stages.

- *Stage A.* The tumor cannot be detected by any routine tests, but it has been found during surgery for another disorder of the prostate.
- *Stage B.* The tumor can be felt by rectal exam, but it has not spread beyond the prostate gland.
- *Stage C.* Cancer has spread beyond the prostate to nearby tissues.
- *Stage D.* Cancer has spread to the pelvic lymph nodes or to distant parts of the body, most commonly to the bones.

TREATMENT

Treatment for prostate cancer depends on the man's medical history, his age and general health, and the stage of the disease. Prostate cancer often can be cured when it is found in an early stage. Even when the disease is widespread, prostate cancer responds well to treatment. The doctor develops a treatment plan that fits each man's individual needs. (See also Treatment Planning, page 16.)

Methods of Treatment

Surgery, radiation therapy, and hormone therapy are often used to treat prostate cancer. Sometimes, patients receive a combination of these treatments.

Surgery. If surgery is recommended, the type of operation depends on the size of the tumor and its location. Patients with benign prostate disease or very small cancers may have an operation called a transurethral resection (TUR). In a TUR, a special instrument is inserted through the penis to remove the tumor. In perineal surgery, an incision is made between the scrotum and anus to remove the prostate gland. In a retropubic prostatectomy, the incision is made in the abdomen, and the prostate and nearby lymph nodes are removed at the same time.

Radiation therapy (also called x-ray therapy, irradiation, or radiotherapy) uses high-energy rays to kill cancer cells. Radiation may be given from a machine located outside the body (external radiation therapy), or a radioactive substance may be placed directly into the tumor (interstitial radiation therapy). Sometimes, a combination of these methods is used.

Radiation therapy destroys the ability of cells to grow and divide. Both healthy and diseased cells are affected, but most healthy cells recover quickly. External radiation therapy usually is given five days a week for several weeks. This schedule helps to protect healthy tissues by spreading out the total dose of radiation. Weekend rest breaks allow healthy cells to repair themselves. In interstitial radiation therapy, a radioactive substance is implanted through needles placed in the prostate. A brief hospital stay may be needed for this procedure.

Hormone therapy. Hormones occur naturally in the body; their purpose is to control the activity of specific cells or organs. Because prostate cancer uses the male sex hormones to grow, blocking the production of male hormones or giving female hormones may control the disease.

One form of hormone therapy involves the removal of the testicles, an operation called orchiectomy. This surgery eliminates a major source of the male hormone testosterone, thereby stopping the growth of cancer cells that need this hormone. Another type of hormone therapy uses the female hormone estrogen. Diethylstilbestrol (DES), Estinyl, and TACE are estrogens that may be prescribed.

Another approach involves the use of luteinizing hormone-releasing hormone agonists (or LHRH agonists). Sex hormones in men and women are controlled by LHRH. When given in large amounts for long periods of time, LHRH agonists (drugs similar to LHRH) stop the production of the male hormone testosterone. Leuprolide is an LHRH agonist that may be prescribed along with flutamide, another type of hormone treatment.

Some men with stage A prostate cancer may not be treated for their disease, but they should have regular follow-up exams. Other patients with stage A disease may be treated with surgery to remove the prostate or with radiation therapy. These treatments can cure patients whose disease has not spread beyond the prostate.

Either surgery or radiation therapy may be used to treat patients with stage B prostate cancer. Patients with stage C disease may be treated with surgery and/or radiation therapy. For patients who have stage D prostate cancer, treatment depends on whether the cancer has spread only to nearby lymph nodes or to distant parts of the body. Hormone therapy is often recommended for these patients, although generally doctors delay this treatment until symptoms such as bone pain or bladder problems occur. For patients with advanced cancer who do not respond to hormone therapy, doctors may recommend chemotherapy (treatment with anticancer drugs).

Side Effects of Treatment

Because prostate cancer can spread, the treatments used against this disease must be very powerful. It is rarely possible to limit the effects of cancer treatment so that only cancer cells are destroyed; normal, healthy tissue may be damaged at the same time. For this reason, patients may experience unpleasant side effects.

Treatment for prostate cancer raises many questions about a man's ability to remain sexually active. For some men, changes, including impotence, may be temporary; for others, these problems may be permanent. Sometimes sexual problems may be emotional as well as physical. Patients should talk with their doctor about the possible sexual side effects of treatment.

Surgery. Following prostate surgery using older methods, urinary incontinence and impotence were common. However, after new nerve-sparing surgery to remove the prostate, these side effects have become less common.

Radiation Therapy. During radiation therapy, patients may notice a number of side effects, which usually disappear when treatment ends. For example, patients may have skin reactions (redness, dryness, or moistness) in the area being treated, and they may feel unusually tired. Patients also may have diarrhea and frequent and uncomfortable urination. Some patients are impotent after radiation therapy. This side effect is seen less often in patients who have interstitial radiation therapy.

Hormone therapy also may cause side effects. Female hormones, such as estrogen, may cause breast tenderness and enlargement, nausea, vomiting, and water retention. High doses of estrogens also increase the risk of heart problems. For this reason, doctors keep careful watch on patients receiving hormones and may recommend a lower dose if symptoms occur. Sexual problems commonly caused by hormone therapy include loss of sexual desire and impotence.

Anticancer drugs travel through the bloodstream to almost every area of the body. The side effects of chemotherapy depend on the drugs given and the response of the individual patient. Chemotherapy commonly affects hair cells, blood-forming cells, and cells lining the digestive tract. As a result, patients may have side effects such as hair loss, lowered blood counts, nausea, or vomiting. Most side effects end after the treatment is over.

To help withstand the side effects of treatment, it is important that patients maintain good nutrition (see Nutrition for Cancer Patients, page 19).

FOLLOW-UP CARE

Regular follow-up exams are very important for any man who has been treated for prostate cancer. The doctor will want to watch the patient closely to be sure that the cancer has not returned. In general, follow-up exams include x-rays, scans, blood and urine tests, and other laboratory tests.

LIVING WITH CANCER

When people have cancer, life can change for them and for the people who care about them. These changes in daily life can be difficult to handle. (See Adjusting to the Disease, page 19, and Support for Cancer Patients, page 20.)

WHAT THE FUTURE HOLDS

There are more than 5 million Americans living today who have had some type of cancer. Many are men who have had cancer of the prostate. The outlook for men with early prostate cancer is good; many of them can be cured. The chances of controlling advanced disease are likely to improve as researchers continue to look for better ways to treat this disease.

The National Cancer Institute

SKIN CANCER

The skin is the body's outer covering. It protects us against heat and light, injury, and infection. It regulates body temperature and stores water, fat, and vitamin D. Weighing about six pounds, the skin is the body's largest organ. It is made up of two main layers: the outer epidermis and the inner dermis.

The epidermis (outer layer of skin) is mostly made up of flat, scalelike cells called squamous cells. Under the squamous cells are round cells called basal cells. The deepest part of the epidermis also contains melanocytes. These cells produce melanin, which gives the skin its color.

The dermis (inner layer of skin) contains blood and lymph vessels, hair follicles, and glands. These glands produce sweat, which helps regulate body temperature, and sebum, an oily substance that helps keep the skin from drying out. Sweat and sebum reach the skin's surface through tiny openings called pores.

TYPES OF SKIN CANCER

The two most common kinds of skin cancer are basal cell carcinoma and squamous cell carcinoma.

Basal cell carcinoma accounts for more than 90 percent of all skin cancers in the United States. It is a slow-growing cancer that seldom spreads to other parts of the body. Squamous cell carcinoma also rarely spreads, but it does so more often than basal cell carcinoma. However, it is important that skin cancers are found and treated early because they can invade and destroy nearby tissue.

Basal cell carcinoma and squamous cell carcinoma are sometimes called non-melanoma skin cancer. Another type of cancer that

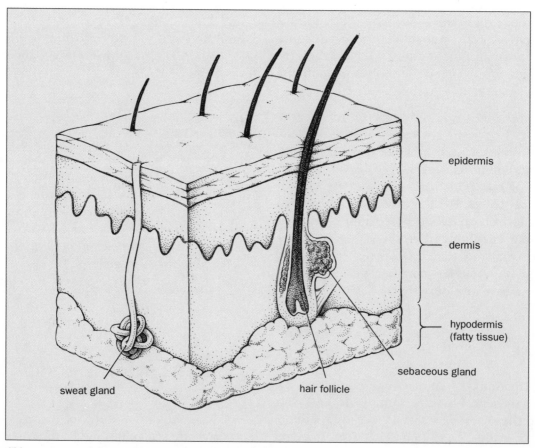

epidermis

dermis

hypodermis (fatty tissue)

sebaceous gland

sweat gland

hair follicle

Skin cancers originate almost exclusively in the uppermost layer of skin, the epidermis. Within this layer are melanocytes and the basal and squamous cells.

occurs in the skin is melanoma, which begins in the melanocytes.

CAUSE AND PREVENTION

Skin cancer is the most common type of cancer in the United States. According to present estimates, 40 to 50 percent of Americans who live to age 65 will have skin cancer at least once.

Several risk factors increase the chance of getting skin cancer. Ultraviolet (UV) radiation from the sun is the main cause of skin cancer. Artificial sources of UV radiation, such as sunlamps and tanning booths, can also cause skin cancer. Although anyone can get skin cancer, the risk is greatest for people who have fair skin that freckles easily—often those with red or blond hair and blue or light-colored eyes.

The risk of developing skin cancer is also affected by where a person lives. People who live in areas that get high levels of UV radiation from the sun are more likely to get skin cancer. In the United States, for example, skin cancer is more common in Texas than it is in Minnesota, where the sun is not as strong. Worldwide, the highest rates of skin cancer are found in South Africa and Australia, areas that receive high amounts of UV radiation.

In addition, skin cancer is related to lifetime exposure to UV radiation. Most skin cancers appear after age 50, but the sun's damaging effects begin at an early age. Therefore, protection should start in childhood to prevent skin cancer later in life.

Protective clothing, such as sun hats and long sleeves, can block out the sun's harmful rays. Also, lotions that contain sunscreens can protect the skin. Sunscreens often contain PABA (para-aminobenzoic acid) and are rated in strength according to an SPF (sun protection factor), which ranges from 2 to 15 or higher. The higher the number on the label, the greater the protection a sunscreen provides, meaning more of the sun's harmful rays will be blocked out.

Scientists are trying to determine whether the chance of getting skin cancer can be reduced by eating foods rich in vitamin A and a precursor of vitamin A called beta-carotene.

SYMPTOMS

The most common warning sign of skin cancer is a change on the skin, especially a new growth or a sore that doesn't heal. Skin cancer has many different appearances. For example, it may start as a small, smooth, shiny, pale, or waxy lump. Or, the cancer can appear as a firm red lump. Sometimes, the lump bleeds or develops a crust. Skin cancer can also start as a flat, red spot that is rough, dry, or scaly. Pain is not a sign of skin cancer.

Both basal and squamous cell cancers are found mainly on areas of the skin that are exposed to the sun. However, skin cancer can occur anywhere.

Another condition that can affect the skin is actinic keratosis, which appears as rough, red or brown, scaly patches on the skin. Because actinic keratosis sometimes develops into squamous cell cancer, it is known as a precancerous condition. Like skin cancer, it usually appears on sun-exposed areas but can be found elsewhere.

Changes in the skin are not sure signs of cancer; however, it is important to see a doctor if any symptom lasts longer than two weeks.

HOW TO DO A SKIN SELF-EXAM

You can improve your chances of finding skin cancer promptly by performing a simple skin self-examination each month.

The best time to do a skin self-examination is after a shower or bath. A skin self-exam should be done in a well-lighted room with a full-length mirror and a hand-held mirror. It's best to begin by learning where birthmarks, moles, and blemishes are located and what they usually look like. Anything new—a change in the size, texture, or color of a mole, or a sore that does not heal—should be noted.

Check all areas of the skin, including the back, scalp, buttocks, and genital area.

(1) Look at the front and back of your body in the mirror, then raise your arms and look at the left and right sides.

(2) Bend your elbows and look carefully at the palms, the forearms, including the undersides, and the upper arms.

(3) Examine the back and front of the legs. Also look between the buttocks and around the genital area.

(4) Sit and closely examine the feet, including the soles and the spaces between the toes.

(5) Look at the neck and scalp (the area of the head covered by hair). You may want to use a comb or a blow dryer to move hair so that you can see better.

By checking your skin each month, you will become familiar with what is normal. (See also Mole Inspection—Learning Your ABCD's, page 393.) If you find anything unusual, see your doctor right away. Remember, the earlier skin cancer is found, the better the chance for cure.

DETECTION AND DIAGNOSIS

Detection

The cure rate for skin cancer could be 100 percent if all skin cancers were brought to a doctor's attention before they had a chance to spread. Therefore, people should check themselves regularly for new growths or other changes in the skin. Any new, colored growths or any changes in growths that are already present should be reported to the doctor without delay. Doctors should also look at the skin during routine physical exams. Persons who have already had skin cancer should be sure to have regular exams so that the doctor can check the skin—both the treated areas and other places where cancer may develop.

Diagnosis

Basal cell carcinoma and squamous cell carcinoma are generally diagnosed and treated in the same way. When an area of skin does not look normal, the doctor may remove all or part of the growth. This is called a biopsy. To check for cancer cells, the tissue is examined under a microscope by a pathologist or a dermatologist. A biopsy is the only sure way to tell if the problem is cancer.

Doctors generally divide skin cancer into two stages: local (affecting only the skin) or metastatic (spreading beyond the skin). Because skin cancer rarely spreads, a biopsy often is the only test needed to determine the stage. In cases where the growth is very large or has been present for a long time, the doctor will carefully check the lymph nodes in the area. In addition, the patient may need to have additional tests, such as special x-rays, to find out whether the cancer has spread to other parts of the body. Knowing the stage of a skin cancer helps the doctor plan the best treatment.

TREATMENT

Treatment Planning

Before starting treatment, the patient might want a second doctor, such as a dermatologist or a plastic surgeon, to review the diagnosis and planned treatment.

Treatment for skin cancer may involve surgery, radiation therapy, or cryosurgery. Sometimes, a combination of these methods is used. The doctor considers a number of factors to determine the best treatment for skin cancer, such as the location of the cancer, its size, and whether or not the cancer has spread beyond the skin.

The doctor's main objective is to destroy the cancer completely while causing as little scarring as possible.

Surgery

Most skin cancers can be removed quickly and easily by surgery. Sometimes, the cancer is completely removed at the time of biopsy, and no further treatment is needed.

To remove small skin cancers, doctors

commonly use a special type of surgery called curettage. After a local anesthetic numbs the area, the cancer is scooped out with a curette, an instrument with a sharp, spoon-shaped end. Then, the area is generally treated by electrodesiccation. An electric current from a special machine is used to control bleeding and kill any cancer cells remaining around the edge of the wound.

Mohs' technique is a special type of surgery used for skin cancer. It is especially helpful for treating skin cancer in cases where the shape and depth of the tumor are hard to determine. In addition, this method is used to treat skin cancers that have recurred. The cancer is shaved off one thin layer of skin at a time until the entire tumor is removed. This method should be used only by doctors who are specially trained in this type of surgery.

Sometimes, when a large cancer is removed, a skin graft may be needed. For this procedure, the doctor takes a piece of skin from another part of the body to replace the skin that was removed.

Surgery that is performed for the removal of skin cancers, with or without skin grafts, may cause scars.

Cryosurgery

Extreme cold may be used to treat precancerous skin conditions, such as actinic keratosis, as well as skin cancers. In cryosurgery, liquid nitrogen is applied to the growth to freeze and kill the abnormal cells. After the area thaws, the dead tissue falls off. More than one freezing may be needed to remove the growth completely. Cryosurgery does not require anesthesia, but patients may experience pain after treatment. A white scar may form in the treated area.

Radiation Therapy

Skin cancer responds well to radiation therapy (also called x-ray therapy, radiotherapy, or irradiation), which uses high-energy rays to kill cancer cells. This treatment is used for cancers that occur in areas that are hard to treat with surgery. For example, radiation therapy might be used to treat skin cancers of the eyelid, the tip of the nose, and the ear. Several treatments may be needed to remove all of the cancer cells. During radiation therapy, patients may notice skin reactions, such as rashes or redness, in the area that is being treated. Changes in skin color and/or texture may develop, becoming more noticeable many years later.

Topical Chemotherapy

Topical chemotherapy is the use of anticancer drugs in a cream or lotion applied to the skin surface. Actinic keratosis can be treated effectively with the anticancer drug fluorouracil (also called 5-FU). The 5-FU cream or lotion is applied daily for several weeks. Intense inflammation is common during treatment, but scars usually do not occur.

Follow-up Therapy

Even though most patients with skin cancer are cured, this type of cancer is the one most likely to recur. That's why it's so important for patients to continue to examine themselves regularly, to visit their doctor for regular checkups, and to follow their doctor's instructions on how to reduce their risk of developing skin cancer again.

LIVING WITH CANCER

When people have cancer, life can change for them and for the people who care about them. These changes in daily life can be difficult to handle. (See Adjusting to the Disease, page 19, and Support for Cancer Patients, page 20.)

WHAT THE FUTURE HOLDS

Skin cancer has a better prognosis, or outcome, than most other types of cancer; it is curable in over 95 percent of cases.

The National Cancer Institute

STOMACH CANCER

The stomach is the chamber located between the end of the esophagus and the beginning of the small intestine. Digestion of food begins in the stomach.

SYMPTOMS

The first symptoms of stomach cancer are much like those of other digestive illnesses: persistent indigestion, a feeling of bloated discomfort after eating, slight nausea, loss of appetite, heartburn, and sometimes mild stomach pain. Later symptoms may be blood in the stool (either red or black in color), vomiting, weight loss, and pain.

DIAGNOSIS

To determine whether your symptoms are caused by stomach cancer or some other con-

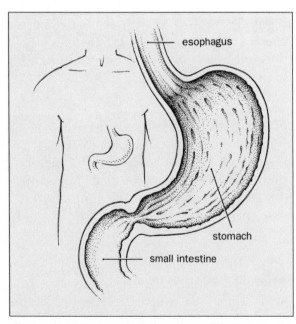

Contractions in the stomach, along with its enzymes and acid, promote digestion. Stomach cancer usually starts as an ulcer in the lining of the stomach.

dition, samples of your blood, stomach fluid, and stool are tested. The presence of anemia and lack of acid in the stomach are conditions often found in patients who have stomach cancer. Blood in the stool can be an indication of cancer in the gastrointestinal tract, including the stomach.

An x-ray examination of your stomach also aids the doctor in making a diagnosis. For this examination, you are asked to drink a liquid containing barium sulfate, a substance that makes parts of your body more visible in x-ray pictures. Using an x-ray machine called a fluoroscope, the doctor can observe the flow of barium sulfate into your stomach and see the outline of the stomach when it is filled. Regular x-ray pictures also may be taken of your stomach from several different angles. The doctor can recognize an abnormality on the outline of the stomach seen with the fluoroscope and in the x-ray pictures.

In some cases the doctor needs to examine the stomach with an instrument passed through the mouth and esophagus. A sedative or an anesthetic may be given before this kind of examination so it is not too uncomfortable.

One instrument that may be used is a flexible tube with a light and a series of mirrors that enable the doctor to see and photograph the inside of the stomach. If a growth is detected, a small sample of the tissue can be removed through the instrument. The sample can then be examined with a microscope to determine whether it is cancerous. The removal and microscopic examination of a tissue sample is called a biopsy.

Other instruments sometimes employed are a suction tube and a very small brush to collect cells shed by the lining of the stomach. If the material collected contains cancer cells, they can be identified under a microscope.

When a diagnosis of cancer is confirmed, it is best for you to begin treatment in a hospital that has an expert staff and resources to apply all forms of effective treatment right from the beginning.

TREATMENT

Your doctor will consider a number of factors in determining the best treatment for you. Among these are your medical history, your general health, and the type and location of the cancer or cancers you have. Your treatment must be tailored to your individual needs. (See also Treatment Planning, page 16.)

Treatment for stomach cancer is generally prompt removal of the tumor by surgery. This may require removing part or all of the stomach. Any post-operative difficulties in digestion can usually be prevented by eating several small meals a day rather than three large ones and by adhering to a low-sugar diet, high in protein and fat.

If the stomach cancer has started to spread, the surgeon may be able to stop the spread by removing the affected parts of neighboring organs, such as the spleen or pancreas. In recent years, advances in surgical techniques and medical care have made extensive surgery possible for persons who were previously considered too old or infirm for this treatment. Today, surgeons have the help of highly competent teams of nurses, therapists, technicians, and other professionals to support patients throughout their post-operative period.

If all of the cancer present in the body cannot be removed by surgery, chemotherapy (treatment with anticancer drugs) may be given. Anticancer drugs enter the bloodstream and circulate through the body to attack cancer in any location. Because the drugs act on normal cells as well as cancerous ones, your physician must maintain a delicate balance of enough drugs to kill cancer cells without destroying too many healthy ones.

Radiation therapy plays a limited role in the treatment of stomach cancer. The main reason is that radiation doses strong enough to destroy these cancer cells could seriously damage the surrounding healthy tissue.

LIVING WITH CANCER

When people have cancer, life can change for them and for the people who care about them. These changes in daily life can be difficult to handle. (See Adjusting to the Disease, page 19, and Support for Cancer Patients, page 20.)

WHAT THE FUTURE HOLDS

Although the causes of stomach cancer, like most cancers, remain unknown, new research findings may suggest ways to prevent the disease. At the same time, the trend toward improved diagnosis and treatment provides hope that more patients with this disease will be treated effectively.

The National Cancer Institute

UTERINE CANCER

The uterus (womb) is a hollow, pear-shaped organ located in a woman's lower abdomen between the bladder and the rectum. The narrow, lower portion of the uterus is the cervix; the broader, upper part is the corpus. The corpus is made up of two layers of tissue: the inner layer of the uterus (endometrium) and the outer layer of the corpus (myometrium). Because most uterine cancer develops in the endometrium, cancer of the uterus also is called endometrial cancer.

Several types of benign tumors occur in the uterus. In some cases, these growths do not need to be treated. Sometimes, however, benign tumors must be removed by surgery. Once removed, these tumors are not likely to return.

Fibroids are benign tumors in the uterus that are found most often in women over 35 years of age. While single fibroid tumors occur, multiple tumors are more common.

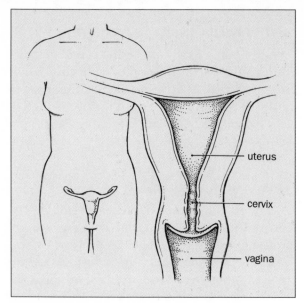

After menopause, the lining of the uterus thins and menstruation ceases. At this time of life, the risk of uterine cancer increases significantly.

uterus

cervix

vagina

Symptoms of fibroids depend on the size and location of the tumors and may include irregular bleeding, vaginal discharge, and frequent urination. When fibroids press against nearby organs and cause pain, surgery may be recommended. Frequently, however, fibroids do not cause symptoms and do not need to be treated, although they should be checked often. When a woman stops having menstrual periods (menopause), fibroids may become smaller, and sometimes they disappear.

Another benign condition of the uterus is endometriosis. In this condition, tissue that looks and acts like endometrial tissue begins to grow in unusual places, such as on the surface of the ovaries, on the outside of the uterus, and in other tissues in the abdomen. Endometriosis is most common in women in their 30s and 40s. This condition causes painful menstrual periods and abnormal bleeding; sometimes, it can cause infertility. Some patients with endometriosis are treated with medication, and some are treated by surgery.

Hyperplasia is an increase in the number of normal cells lining the uterus. Although this condition is not cancer, it may develop into cancer in some women. The most common symptoms of hyperplasia are heavy menstrual periods and bleeding between periods. Treatment depends on the extent of the condition (mild, moderate, or severe) and on the age of the patient. Young women usually are treated with female hormones, and the endometrial tissue is checked often. Hyperplasia in women near or after menopause may be treated with hormones if the condition is not severe. Surgery to remove the uterus is the usual treatment for severe cases.

SYMPTOMS

Abnormal bleeding after menopause is the most common symptom of cancer of the uterus. Bleeding may begin as a watery, blood-streaked discharge. Later, the discharge may contain more blood.

Cancer of the uterus does not often occur before menopause, but it does occur around the time menopause begins. The reappearance of bleeding should not be considered simply part of menopause; it should always be checked by a doctor.

Abnormal bleeding is not always a sign of cancer. It is important for a woman to see her doctor, however, because that is the only way to find out what the problem is. Any illness should be diagnosed and treated as soon as possible, but early diagnosis is especially important for cancer of the uterus.

DIAGNOSIS

When symptoms suggest uterine cancer, the doctor will ask a woman about her medical history and will conduct a thorough exam. In addition to checking general signs of health (temperature, pulse, blood pressure, and so on), the doctor usually performs one of the following exams.

• *Pelvic exam.* The doctor thoroughly examines the uterus, vagina, ovaries, bladder, and rectum (pelvic exam). The doctor feels these organs for any abnormality in their shape or size. A speculum is used to widen the opening of the vagina so that the doctor can look at the upper portion of the vagina and the cervix.

- *Biopsy*. For a biopsy the doctor surgically removes a small amount of suspicious-looking uterine tissue, which is examined under a microscope by a pathologist.
- *D and C*. In a D and C, the doctor dilates (widens) the cervix and inserts a curette (a small spoon-shaped instrument) to remove pieces of the lining of the uterus. A sample of the uterine lining also can be removed by applying suction through a slender tube (called suction curettage). The tissue is examined for evidence of cancer.
- *Pap test*. The Pap test is often used to detect cancer of the cervix. While it is sometimes done for cancer of the uterus, it is not a reliable test for uterine cancer because it cannot always detect abnormal cells from the endometrium.

If cancer cells are found, doctors use other tests to find out whether the disease has spread from the uterus to other parts of the body. These procedures include blood tests and a chest x-ray. For some patients, special x-rays are needed. For example, computed tomography (also called CT scan), is used to take a series of x-rays of various sections of the abdomen. Doctors may also use ultrasound to view organs inside the body. In this procedure, high-frequency sound waves are bounced off internal organs, and the echoes can be seen on a screen that resembles a television. Patients also may have special exams of the bladder, colon, and rectum.

TREATMENT

The doctor considers a number of factors to determine the best treatment for cancer of the uterus. Among these factors are the stage of the disease, the growth rate of the cancer, and the age and general health of the woman. The doctor develops a treatment plan to fit a woman's individual needs. (See also Treatment Planning, page 16.)

Methods of Treatment

Surgery, radiation therapy, hormone therapy, or chemotherapy may be used to treat uterine cancer. Radiation therapy (also called x-ray therapy, radiotherapy, or irradiation) uses high-energy rays to kill cancer cells. Radiation may be given from a machine located outside the body (external radiation therapy), or radioactive material may be placed inside the body (internal radiation therapy). In hormone therapy, female hormones are used to stop the growth of cancer cells. Chemotherapy is the use of drugs to treat cancer. Often, a combination of these methods is used. In some cases, the patient is referred to specialists in the different kinds of cancer treatment.

In its early stages, cancer of the uterus usually is treated with surgery. The uterus and cervix are removed (hysterectomy), as well as the ovaries and fallopian tubes (salpingo-oophorectomy). Some doctors recommend radiation therapy before surgery to shrink the cancer. Others prefer to evaluate the patient carefully during surgery and recommend radiation therapy after surgery for patients whose tumors appear likely to recur. A combination of external and internal radiation therapy often is used. If the cancer has spread extensively or has recurred after treatment, the doctor may recommend a female hormone (progesterone) or chemotherapy.

Side Effects of Treatment

The treatments used against uterine cancer must be very powerful. It is rarely possible to limit the effects of cancer treatment so that only cancer cells are destroyed. Normal, healthy cells may be damaged at the same time. That's why the treatment often causes side effects.

Surgery. Hysterectomy is major surgery. After the operation, the hospital stay usually lasts about one week. For several days after surgery, patients may have problems emptying their bladder and having normal bowel movements. The lower abdomen will be sore. Normal activities, including sexual intercourse, usually can be resumed in four to eight weeks.

Women who have their uterus removed no longer have menstrual periods. When the ovaries are not removed, women do not have symptoms of menopause (change of life) because their ovaries still produce hormones. If the ovaries are removed or damaged by radiation therapy, menopause will occur. Hot flashes or other symptoms of menopause caused by treatment may be more severe than those from a natural menopause. (See also Menopause, page 415.) Sexual desire and the ability to have intercourse usually are not affected by hysterectomy. However, many women have an emotionally difficult time after a hysterectomy. They may have feelings of deep emotional loss because they are no longer able to become pregnant.

Radiation therapy destroys the ability of cells to grow and divide. Both normal and diseased cells are affected, but most normal cells are able to recover quickly. Patients usually receive external radiation therapy as an outpatient. Treatments are given five days a week for several weeks. This schedule helps to protect healthy tissues by spreading out the total dose of radiation. Weekend rest breaks allow the normal cells to repair themselves.

Internal radiation therapy puts the radiation as close as possible to the site of the cancer, while sparing most of the healthy tissues around it. This therapy requires a short hospital stay. A radiation implant, a capsule of radioactive material, is inserted through the vagina into the uterus. The implant usually is left in place two or three days.

During radiation therapy, patients may notice a number of side effects, which usually disappear when treatment is completed. Patients may have skin reactions (redness or dryness) in the area being treated, and they may be unusually tired. Some may have diarrhea and frequent and uncomfortable urination. Treatment can also cause dryness, itching, and burning in the vagina. Intercourse may be painful, and some women are advised not to have intercourse at this time. Most women can resume sexual activity within a few weeks after treatment ends.

Hormone therapy. Hormones occur naturally in the body; their purpose is to regulate the growth of specific cells or organs. In cancer treatment, hormones are sometimes used to stop the growth of cancer cells. Hormones travel through the bloodstream to all parts of the body, affecting cancer cells far from the original tumor. Hormone therapy causes few side effects.

Chemotherapy. Anticancer drugs also travel through the bloodstream to almost every area of the body. Drugs used to treat cancer may be given in different ways: some are given by mouth; others are injected into a muscle, a vein, or an artery. Chemotherapy is most often given in cycles—a treatment period, followed by a rest period, then another treatment period, and so on.

Depending on the drugs that the doctor orders, the patient may need to stay in the hospital for a few days so that the effects of the drugs can be watched. Often, the patient receives treatment as an outpatient at the hospital, at a clinic, at the doctor's office, or at home.

The side effects of chemotherapy depend on the drugs given and the individual response of the patient. Chemotherapy commonly affects hair cells, blood-forming cells, and cells lining the digestive tract. As a result, patients may have side effects such as hair loss, lowered blood counts, nausea, or vomiting. Most side effects end after treatment is stopped.

To help withstand the side effects of treatment, it is important that patients maintain good nutrition (see Nutrition for Cancer Patients, page 19).

FOLLOW-UP CARE

Regular follow-up exams are very important for any woman who has been treated for cancer of the uterus. The doctor will want to watch the patient closely for several years to be sure that the cancer has not returned. In general, follow-up examinations include a regular pelvic exam, a chest x-ray, and other laboratory tests.

LIVING WITH CANCER

When people have cancer, life can change for them and for the people who care about them. These changes in daily life can be difficult to handle. (See Adjusting to the Disease, page 19, and Support for Cancer Patients, page 20.)

WHAT THE FUTURE HOLDS

There are more than 5 million Americans living today who have had some type of cancer. Many are women who have had cancer of the uterus. The outlook for women with very early cancer of the uterus is excellent; nearly all patients with this condition can be cured. The chances of controlling advanced disease are improving as researchers continue to look for better ways to treat this disease.

The National Cancer Institute

83

The Blood

The average adult possesses a total quantity of about 10 pints of blood. The heart normally circulates all 10 pints once every minute when we're at rest—and up to four times a minute when we exercise. The blood's duties are many. Its primary job is to supply all the cells in the body with nutrients harvested from the digestive system and oxygen drawn in through the lungs. Even as it completes this task, the blood becomes useful in another way, by picking up and taking away the cells' waste products. The carbon dioxide formed when cells burn oxygen is returned, via the bloodstream, to the tiny air sacs in the lungs, where it is then spirited away in an exhaled breath. Other toxins and chemical by-products are transported to the kidneys and liver to be filtered out and excreted.

The blood also plays a crucial role in the immune system, with specific blood cells that fight infection. When we are injured, bleeding helps wash dirt and microbes away from the site of the wound, after which a complex mechanism takes over that prompts blood clotting and scab formation (to prevent us from losing too much blood) and initiates the healing process.

The circulatory system also carries hormones and other chemical messengers throughout the body to permit its remotest areas to communicate with each other and coordinate their functions. The blood helps regulate body temperature somewhat as well, by dissipating excess heat produced in the muscles—explaining the familiar sanguine flush we experience during vigorous activity. Conversely, when the air temperature is cold, blood moves away from the extremities and rushes toward the vital organs to keep them warm—which we notice as our fingertips and toes suffer the initial brunt of the chill.

About half of the blood is made up of blood cells; the other half is plasma, the fluid portion of the blood. There are three basic types of blood cells: red cells, white cells, and platelets.

The red cells (erythrocytes) are the most plentiful of all. It is these cells that exchange fresh oxygen for the carbon dioxide exhaust. Red cells contain hemoglobin, a special iron-based protein that binds readily with oxygen when oxygen concentration is high, as it is in the lungs—but releases oxygen just as readily when oxygen concentration is low, as it is in body tissues.

The unique doughnutlike shape of the red blood cell is perfectly suited to its function. It has relatively great overall surface area, which allows maximal absorption of both oxygen and carbon dioxide gases, yet its thinness and small quotient of internal mass make the cell pliable enough to squeeze through minuscule blood vessels without rupturing. Abnormalities in the red blood cells result in the various types of anemia and other disorders.

The white cells (leukocytes) are broken down into several major types (granulocytes, monocytes, and lymphocytes), but all share a common purpose: to fight disease. Some of these cells literally seek out, engulf, and destroy invading bacteria. Other white cells produce antibodies, which form during a disease (such as measles or mononucleosis) and stay in the bloodstream long afterward to prevent a second attack. Sometimes the immune system goes awry, forming antibodies against our own body cells. This can result in autoimmune diseases such as rheumatoid arthritis.

Platelets (thrombocytes), the smallest of the blood cells, along with a number of clotting proteins in the blood, are responsible for the clotting mechanism. Clotting begins within seconds after a cut to the skin. The platelets move to the cut site, where they become sticky and begin to clump together, making a plug in the injured blood vessel and minimizing blood loss. But clots are not always a good thing; when they form in a major blood vessel, they can lead to heart attacks and strokes. So the system also has complex controls to prevent or dissolve unnecessary clots. A careful balance is essential. Abnormalities in the platelets or clotting proteins can result in the tendency to bleed too much (hemophilia, for example); when the balance is tipped the other way, dangerous clots are inclined to form (thrombosis).

Plasma is everything that's left over if you take away all the various cells. It is a yellowish liquid, 95 percent water, with a salt content closely approximating that of seawater. Adrift in the plasma are all of the blood cells, as well as proteins, hormones, sugars, minerals, and fats, including cholesterol.

Since blood interacts with almost every organ, diseases or malfunctions anywhere in the body are frequently reflected by changes in the blood. For this reason, blood tests are among the most fundamental and informative elements in making a medical diagnosis. The most routine test, the complete blood count (CBC), determines the number of each type of blood cell in a given volume of blood, and then examines the cells for any abnormalities in structure or function. The hemoglobin or "hematocrit value" of a CBC measures the quantity of red blood cells; a "differential count" compares the relative numbers of the various white cells. Certain diseases have a direct and predictable effect on the chemical content of the blood. For example, diabetes is indicated by elevated levels of glucose; many types of liver disease result in high levels of a compound called bilirubin. Mild cases of anemia, in fact, usually produce little or no symptoms and are generally discovered only when a doctor obtains a complete blood count.   *The Editors*

VITAMIN AND MINERAL DEFICIENCY ANEMIAS

If you are feeling fatigued, and believe the ads about "tired blood," you might think that taking an iron supplement will cure iron deficiency anemia and pep you right up. In truth, however, most fatigue is not related to tired blood; most anemia comes on without any noticeable symptoms at all; and most anemia in older adults is not due to low iron intake, but is caused by slow intestinal bleeding.

Anemia is one of the most common disorders among older adults. It is usually discovered not by reporting symptoms to a doctor, but rather by the complete blood count your doctor periodically orders. Indeed, screening for anemia is one of the important reasons for doing a complete blood count.

Anemia is not a normal consequence of aging, as had been thought until recently. Nor is anemia itself a disease; it is instead a manifestation of any one of a number of different disorders or diseases that affect your red blood cells—ranging from iron deficiency anemia to the less common types, such as hemolytic and aplastic anemia. All the anemias have different origins, and different treatments. We focus here on the three most common, which have their origin in vitamin or mineral deficiencies.

IRON DEFICIENCY ANEMIA

Iron deficiency anemia arises from too little iron in your body to make sufficient hemoglobin. Most of the blood cells of your body, including the red blood cells that perform the crucial task of picking up oxygen in your lungs and taking it throughout your system, are produced in the marrow that lies within certain bones.

The principal component of these red blood cells, the substance that enables them to transport oxygen, is a special protein, hemoglobin—and a necessary component of hemoglobin is iron. A decrease in the quality or quantity of hemoglobin, or in the number of red blood cells themselves, results in a reduced oxygen-carrying capacity in your blood—which is to say, in anemia (from the Greek, meaning "a lack of blood").

By far the most frequent cause of iron deficiency anemia among older adults is excessive blood loss, which takes iron from the body faster than it can be replaced. This is usually the result of slow, persistent bleeding from any number of intestinal lesions—for example, an ulcer, polyps, or cancer.

The frequent use of aspirin, ibuprofen, or other nonsteroidal anti-inflammatory drugs (NSAIDs) can also result in chronic blood loss from irritation of the stomach lining. Bleeding from the intestines, when severe, generally shows up as black tarry stools, or even frankly bloody stools; most commonly, however, the bleeding is very slow and not readily apparent (so-called "occult blood").

It is possible, too, that iron deficiency anemia can be caused by too little iron in your diet—though this is very unusual, except among menstruating women whose diets have a limited iron content. Most iron in red blood cells is recycled to make new red blood cells—and the amount of iron lost in the recycling process is so minuscule (just 1 mg a day for men, 2 mg for menstruating women) that most diets easily compensate for the loss, except in those on severe weight-loss plans and impoverished people who have little variety of food sources. (Because your body only absorbs 10 percent of the iron you consume, you need to have 10 mg of iron per day—an amount easily provided by a balanced diet of about 1,700 calories.)

Another possible cause of this type of anemia is an inability of the digestive system to absorb iron—most often because part of the stomach or intestine has been removed surgically. But this, too, is uncommon. Again, the most common cause of iron deficiency anemia is slow bleeding.

As you might imagine, the symptoms of iron deficiency anemia—when and if they do appear—are paleness (because it is the pigmented red cells flowing near the skin that produce the pinkness of your complexion), a feeling of weakness (because oxygen is required to use energy), and fatigue. In more severe cases, there can also be shortness of breath, heart palpitations, and an increased heart rate, especially during exertion (as the heart tries to compensate for the lack of oxygen in the system by pumping out more blood), and even chest pains (not totally because the blood flow is impeded, as in coronary artery disease, but because the blood can't carry sufficient oxygen to the heart).

Certain nutritional anemias may manifest as a sore tongue or tiny cracks at the corners of your mouth.

But you should not, under any circumstances, attempt to treat yourself if you feel "anemic." Adding iron-rich foods or multivita-

ANALGESICS AND ANEMIA

Both aspirin and the other nonsteroidal anti-inflammatory drugs (such as Motrin, Nalfon, Ponstel, and Naprosyn) share not only therapeutic effects—painkilling and reduction of inflammation in joints and muscles—but also a propensity toward some unwanted side effects. Chief among these is irritation of the lining of the stomach (gastritis). This effect is so common that evidence of some small amount of blood is found in the stool of as many as 70 percent of users. It is for this reason that these drugs are stopped for at least three days before the stool is checked for occult blood due to ulcers or tumors in the gastrointestinal tract.

To lessen stomach irritation, these medicines may be taken with food or an antacid (one containing magnesium and aluminum hydroxide is best). Unless your doctor has specifically told you to take aspirin and an NSAID together, it is best to avoid this combination, since it greatly increases the risk of irritation and possible bleeding. And be sure to tell your doctor if you are taking over-the-counter NSAIDs on a regular basis, as this could be very significant when trying to diagnose the origin of an iron deficiency anemia.

TAKING IRON SUPPLEMENTS

If your doctor prescribes iron supplements, ask your druggist for the cheapest generic available. Coated, time-release, or combination pills cost much more and may actually impede the iron's absorption into your system.

• Take your iron pill with at least eight ounces of fluid.

• Take it between meals to maximize iron absorption; but, if it causes stomach upset, take the pill with food or right after a meal.

• If you take iron in liquid form, mix it with water or fruit juice and drink it through a straw so that it doesn't stain your teeth. (If you do get stains, brush your teeth with baking soda or 3 percent hydrogen peroxide.)

• If you miss a dose, skip it; don't double-dose.

• Keep your medicine out of reach of children. As few as three or four adult iron tablets can cause serious poisoning in young children.

• Don't store iron tablets in a bathroom medicine chest, as heat or moisture may cause the medicine to break down. Keep them in a cool, dry place.

• While you are taking iron, consume the following foods in only very small amounts, and then only an hour before or two hours after your iron tablet: tea, coffee, cheese, eggs, ice cream, and milk, because they decrease absorption; and whole-grain breads and cereals, because they are already iron-fortified.

• Check with your doctor if you have any of the more common side effects of iron supplements (constipation, diarrhea, heartburn), particularly if you experience nausea or vomiting.

• If you are taking a long-acting or enteric-coated iron tablet, such as Enseals or Fero-Gradumet, and your stools do not turn black, check with your doctor, since the tablets may not be breaking down properly. If your stools are black and tarry, and are accompanied by cramps, soreness, or sharp pains in the stomach, or red streaks in the stool, check with your doctor at once, since this may indicate gastrointestinal bleeding.

• Do not take iron supplements for more than six months without checking back with your doctor.

---

mins with iron to your diet, or taking Geritol, is almost certainly just a way of ignoring the problem. Taking iron supplements may not address the underlying condition (such as an ulcer or a cancer) that is causing the anemia.

VITAMIN B-12 DEFICIENCY

Vitamin B-12 deficiency, or pernicious anemia, most often occurs among older adults. Except among strict vegetarians, or those who have had certain forms of digestive-tract surgery, B-12 deficiency is the result of an impaired ability of the digestive tract to absorb the B-12 that is a normal part of your diet.

For some reason, the condition occurs more often in fair-haired older people of northern European descent.

Vitamin B-12 is essential for the production of red blood cells; if it is deficient in your system, the production of red blood cells declines. Vitamin B-12 is vital also to the maintenance of the nervous system, so a B-12 deficiency produces not only the usual symptoms of anemia, but also leads to damage of the brain and spinal cord—which can show up in numbness and tingling in the hands and feet, a disturbed sense of balance with a change in walking gait, and mental disturbances such as confusion, personality changes, and depression. Because so much B-12 is stored in the liver, it can take a long time for a deficiency to develop.

If you have a close relative who has had pernicious anemia, your risk of having it yourself is increased. You ought to inform your physician and be certain to have the appropriate blood tests.

The disorder is commonly called pernicious anemia because it used to be untreatable, though today it can almost always be effectively treated.

Current treatment usually consists of a life-long regimen of monthly B-12 injections. Neither diet nor any oral supplement can help, since the underlying problem is nonabsorption of B-12 from the gastrointestinal tract. If the deficiency is caught and treated promptly, you should recover completely.

FOLIC ACID DEFICIENCY

Folic acid deficiency is usually caused by an inadequate intake of folic acid, a vitamin mainly supplied by the fresh green leafy vegetables, mushrooms, lima beans, and kidney beans in your diet. Since the body cannot store folic acid, a dietary deficiency will ordinarily show up in only a few weeks as anemia, because folic acid, like B-12, is essential in the production of red blood cells.

Folic acid deficiency may occur among older people who have, for whatever reason, a poor diet. It is particularly common among heavy alcohol drinkers.

This form of anemia is simple to treat with folic acid tablets for a short period of time—followed by an attentiveness to including a range of green vegetables in your diet.

Treatment may be less simple if the deficiency results from an inability to absorb folic acid in the digestive tract—though this is less common. *The Editors*

SICKLE CELL ANEMIA

Sickle cell anemia is a worldwide health problem, affecting many races, countries, and ethnic groups. The World Health Organization estimates that each year more than 250,000 babies are born worldwide with this inherited blood cell disorder, which causes red blood cells to elongate and clog arteries. Chronic pain and life-threatening infections may re-

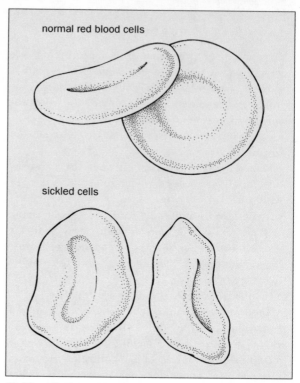

normal red blood cells

sickled cells

Sickle cell disease alters the shape of a red blood cell, so that it breaks down prematurely, functions inefficiently, and can clog tiny blood vessels.

sult from the illness. About one in 400 black newborns in the United States has sickle cell anemia, but the disease is also prevalent in many Spanish-speaking regions of the world, such as South America, Cuba, Central America, and among the Hispanic community in the United States. People in Mediterranean countries—Turkey, Greece, and Italy—also have the illness. And many people, including one in 12 black Americans, carry the sickle cell trait—meaning they can pass the defect onto offspring, although their own health remains excellent.

CAUSES

What exactly causes sickle cell anemia and how did it spread to so many different parts of the world? The answer lies in a curious coincidence. It turns out that anyone who carries the inherited trait for sickle cell anemia, but does not have the actual illness, is protected against the severe form of malaria. So in countries that had a problem with malaria, children born with sickle cell trait survived. Instead, they grew up, had their own children, and passed the gene for sickle cell anemia on to these offspring. As populations migrated, the sickle cell trait and sickle cell anemia moved throughout the world.

One theory proposes that sickle cell anemia originated in Africa and, through the slave trade, spread to South America, North America, and Europe.

Another theory suggests that sickle cell anemia began in the Middle East and then spread from there.

Although we don't know for sure where sickle cell anemia began, scientists have identified four separate types of genetic mutations related to the illness, each associated with a different geographic area—Senegal, Benin, Central Africa, and the Middle East. This information excites geneticists and anthropologists because it allows them to trace the migration of populations depending on which sickle cell mutation they carry. And medically, identifying which type of mutation a person has can be critical to treatment, because the severity of disease appears to vary with the type of mutation.

To understand the causes of sickle cell anemia, we must focus attention on a special molecule found in red blood cells. That molecule, called hemoglobin, takes oxygen from the lungs and transports it to other parts of the body. Hemoglobin's oxygen-carrying ability is essential for living, but a structural defect in the pigmented molecule can wreak havoc in the blood cell.

Hemoglobin contains four chains or strings of amino acids—the compounds that make up proteins. Two of the amino acid chains are known as alpha chains, and two are called beta chains. In normal hemoglobin, the amino acid in the sixth position on the beta chains is glutamic acid. But in people with sickle cell anemia, that sixth position is occupied by another amino acid, valine, instead. This single amino acid substitution has some devastating consequences.

After releasing oxygen, hemoglobin molecules that contain the beta chain defect stick to one another instead of staying separate, forming long, rigid rods or tubules inside red blood cells. The rods cause the normally smooth, doughnut-shaped red blood cells to take on a sickle or curved shape and to lose their vital ability to deform and squeeze through tiny blood vessels. The sickled cells, which become stiff and sticky, clog small blood vessels, depriving tissue from receiving an adequate blood supply. Most of the problems associated with sickle cell anemia stem from this blockage.

SYMPTOMS

Pain caused by the blockage of sickled red blood is the most common symptom of sickle cell anemia, and it can occur unpredictably in any organ or joint of the body—wherever and whenever a blood clot develops. And as with any of the complications of the disease, the frequency and amount of pain varies widely. Some patients experience painful episodes only once a year, some may have as many as 15 to 20 episodes annually.

These painful, disruptive events can be so severe that the patient may require hospitalization for five to seven days to receive intravenous fluids and narcotic painkillers. Right now, we can control the pain, but we can't stop an episode, or even identify when it may be likely to happen.

The sickle cell clots can be life-threatening, depending on where it occurs. For example, in the brain a clot may cause a stroke, leading to paralysis or death. Blood transfusions may be required every three to four weeks for an extended period to avoid recurrence of clots in the brain. Other clots may damage such vital organs as the heart, kidney, lungs, liver, or eyes.

Complicating matters further, the pain associated with a clot can mimic symptoms of several other diseases, making sickle cell disease difficult to diagnose. Joint pain in sickle cell patients resembles that of arthritis, and pain in the intestines might be confused with appendicitis. A sickle-cell-induced clot in the skin can cause ulcers, a condition that may also cause the diagnosis to be missed from the underlying sickle cell problem.

As patients get older, it becomes more difficult for their heart to function normally. Lung clots may also make them more prone to pneumonia or chronic lung disease. Gallstones are common in this illness and may require surgical removal. Another particularly serious problem is the eyes. Many patients with sickle cell anemia have jaundice, causing their eyes to look yellow due to the rapid breakdown of red blood cells. But much more severe is damage to the retina, the onion-skin-thin tissue that acts as the eye's version of photographic film. Containing thousands of tiny sensors that convert light into electrical information for the brain, the retina can severely deteriorate if it is not adequately nourished by the tiny arteries and veins which crisscross it. Blindness may result from sickle cell blockage in the retina. Because of the seriousness of this, ophthalmologists should start examining children's eyes at age five.

As they mature, children with sickle cell anemia develop problems in the growth of their long bones, such as those in the spinal column or hip. Blood supply to the hip is barely adequate even in healthy people, so that patients with sickle cell disease and its associated blockage can be especially vulnerable to hip problems. In severe cases, structural damage may require replacement with a prosthesis, or artificial device. Just as serious can be damage to the spinal column, which may compress and cause severe pain.

It's important to emphasize that not all patients have every complication, and that the severity of symptoms has wide variation. Sickle cell anemia can even affect two brothers in dramatically different ways, even though they grew up in the same environment and have a similar genetic makeup.

One symptom that does affect most people who have the disease is the disorder for which the disease is named—anemia, or a lack of red blood cells.

Anemia occurs because sickled red blood cells last only 10 to 20 days in the bloodstream, rather than the normal 120-day lifetime. The sickled red blood cells are removed faster from the circulation than the bone marrow can produce them.

GENETICS AND SICKLE CELL ANEMIA

There is a big distinction between someone with the sickle cell trait and someone who has the disease. To understand this bit of genetics, it's important to note that about 400 types of hemoglobin exist.

Because the gene for sickling disease is recessive, a child must inherit it from both parents in order to develop the full-blown illness. Similarly, if a child inherits sickled hemoglobin from one parent, and another type of hemoglobin, called hemoglobin C, from the other parent, that child develops a variation of sickle cell disease known as SC disease. (Some other variations of sickle cell anemia exist, depending on differences in the types of hemoglobin inherited from each parent.)

But if a child receives sickle hemoglobin from one parent and healthy hemoglobin from the other, that child has sickle cell trait. That child does not develop sickled cells unless subjected to extreme environmental stress. The child then goes on to live a normal life. But that person does carry the sickle trait, meaning he or she has the ability to pass the sickle gene onto offspring.

SOME MISCONCEPTIONS

One in 12 blacks in the United States has the sickle cell trait (not the disease), and many other races and nationalities also carry the genetic defect. In the past, many people with the trait felt they should not marry or have children, for fear the children might develop the disease. In fact, there were even laws passed in this country requiring black couples to have a sickle cell test before they married. And if they did carry the trait, they were often counseled not to have children. This was never an acceptable approach. People who think they may carry the sickle trait may be tested for it if they so wish. Professionals may give counseling if asked, but the ultimate decision to have children is up to the parents, as it is for any genetic disease.

There are several other misconceptions about sickle cell anemia. One is that the illness is contagious; most people now realize that this is not so.

Another misunderstanding is that sickle cell anemia patients rarely live past the age of 20; in fact, many people with the disease are in their forties, fifties, and sixties.

The Warren Grant Magnuson Clinical Center

The Brain and Nervous System

It takes 100 billion neurons—amounting to about three pounds of matter—to comprise a human brain. A flow of electrical impulses across the neurons that make up the brain, the spinal cord, and the extensive network of nerves that branch out to the most remote places of the body is the basis of all of our talents and personality, our thoughts and emotions, our memories and dreams.

It is this continuous transmission of nerve impulses that gives human behavior its vast complexity. The nervous system handles the vital primary tasks of regulating our metabolism, body temperature, and respiration—even as it also enables us to learn, remember, and draw sophisticated inferences about all that we experience.

Understanding the biological function of the components of the nervous system helps us understand our behavior. At the base of the brain is the brainstem, connecting the spinal cord to the brain. The spinal cord is a conduit for all nerve signals between the brain and body, and it handles a great deal of the body's reflexes. The brainstem manages basic life-support—breathing, heart function, and sleep cycles. Above the brainstem at the back of the skull is the cerebellum. It controls coordination, balance, and posture.

Above the cerebellum is the group of structures known as the limbic system. This part of the brain, which we share in common with all other mammals, provides us with primal urges and powerful emotions crucial for self-preservation: rage, terror, hunger, and sexual desire. The limbic system's direct connections with some of the higher brain faculties allow us both to cogitate upon what we feel emotionally, as well as have emotional reactions to that which we think about. The four major components of the limbic system are the amygdala, the hippocampus, the hypothalamus, and the thalamus. The almond-shaped amygdala, which plays a role in the emotions, especially aggression, is the basic pathway into the limbic system for nerve impulses. The hippocampus is an information processor, matching new data against those already stored in the brain. It therefore is one of the structures absolutely critical in the process of ascribing meaning to the symbols and events of our lives. The hypothalamus, integral to our moods, regulates food intake, internal water balance, and reproductive cycles. It generally acts as a liaison between the brain and the rest of the body, initiating the release of at least seven different hormones to the pituitary (or master) gland, which in turn releases other hormones into the bloodstream that influence growth, aging, and all aspects of reproduction. The thalamus, located near the center of the brain, processes all the senses except smell. It takes the incoming sensory signals and, like a switchboard, sends them to the appropriate region in the brain for interpretation.

Surrounding these evolutionarily older, more primitive, brain structures is the cerebrum, which in humans constitutes the largest portion of the brain. It's here that electrical nerve impulses are transformed into im-

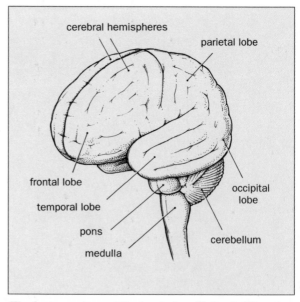

The lower regions of the brain handle basic life-support, while sophisticated interpretation of sensory data occurs in the lobes of the cerebral hemispheres.

ages, symbols, and ideas. It's here that sonnets, melodies, contraptions, and schemes are invented. The outer surface of the cerebrum, known as the cortex, with its convoluted folds of gray matter, gives the brain its familiar appearance. The cortex is the seat of conscious thought, perception, and integration of all sensory input.

A unique feature of the human brain is that the cerebral cortex is divided into two halves, or hemispheres, each with its own set of particular abilities. The right hemisphere specializes in matters of spatial relationships, color perception, visualization, and musical aptitude. For this, the right brain is often thought of as the creative, intuitive, or artistic side of the brain. The left brain is generally more adept at handling analytical tasks, such as mathematical calculation and logical reasoning. The left brain also has particular regions that seem to be dedicated to highly specific tasks such as understanding words or generating speech (so it, too, is creative in its own right). The two hemispheres are connected by a thick neural cable called the corpus callosum.

As we age, neurons die off at a rate of nearly 20 million per year. Surprisingly, this degeneration generally has no significant bearing on our "crystallized" intelligence—that is, our vocabulary, knowledge of specific details and general information, and the ability to comprehend abstract ideas. Thus, years of accumulated knowledge and experience do confer a certain undeniable wisdom. Only "fluid" intelligence—or the amount of new information we're able to master at one time and the speed at which we process information—diminishes with normal aging. So while you may know as much as you ever did, it might take a bit longer to summon up information from your memory bank. But healthy people in their seventies have essentially the same rates of blood flow and oxygen consumption in their brains (about 20 percent of the body's total consumption, despite the brain's fairly small size) as their 20-year-old counterparts; functional mental capacity is hardly altered throughout the course of adulthood.

Thus the onset of senility or general mental deterioration is in no way a natural or inevitable part of aging. It is true that certain areas of the nervous system fare better than others as neurons die off: In the cerebellum and brainstem region, little or no loss of neurons occurs with age, whereas the cortex—the thinking portion of the brain—can lose upwards of 50,000 neurons a day. Nature prepares us for this, however, by endowing us at birth with millions of extra or "redundant" neurons; as some die, others remain to preserve our memories and abilities. It's only in cases of head injury, side effects from drugs, diseases such as Alzheimer's or stroke, or degeneration due to malnutrition or alcoholism that the nervous system suffers damage and displays the more severe mental problems associated with aging.

The Editors

DEMENTIA

Dementia—more accurately, the dementias—are brain diseases that result in the progressive loss of mental faculties, often beginning with memory, learning, attention, and judgment. While some types of dementia are curable, the most common dementing illnesses are not. In time, an unrelenting dementia will erode all aspects of thought, feeling, and behavior, and lead to death.

It is important to realize that demented persons are not insane in the sense of suffering a psychiatric disorder. They become—as the word "dementia" literally means—deprived of mind, deprived of the use of parts of the brain associated with a range of intellectual skills and activities unique to human beings.

Contrary to what many people think, dementing disorders are not the fate that awaits us all with aging. In the United States an estimated 5 percent of the population 65 or over is severely demented. Another 10 percent may be mildly to moderately impaired. That means that 85 percent of the elderly are not demented.

But there is an association of dementia with aging, and because Americans are living longer, the numbers affected will increase. There are now 2 million people in the United States 65 or over who are severely impaired intellectually.

Still another smaller group of adults succumbs to dementing illnesses earlier in life. Over half of these presenile dementias are due to Alzheimer's disease, a progressive dementia. Neurologists now agree that over half the dementias occurring among the elderly—disorders called senile dementia, or chronic organic brain syndrome—are actually cases of disease of the Alzheimer type but beginning at a later stage of life.

THE POWER OF WORDS

Words like "presenile," "senile," and "senility" help perpetuate the myth that aging means mental decline: The words are derived from a Latin root that simply means "to grow old." In Greek and Roman times people so dreaded the infirmities of old age that they regarded aging itself as a disease. Too many people today still hold such beliefs, and it is only as the proportion of older people in the population has risen—and become more vocal—that the myths are beginning to fade. Today neuroscientists know there are age-related changes in the brain, but the changes do not seriously affect mental vigor. Moreover, there are so many examples of intelligence and creativity among the elderly that the belief that getting old means getting senile is simply not true.

Negative feelings about aging, compounded with the fear and shame so often associated with brain disease, have made it difficult for laymen and health professionals to deal with problems posed by the dementias.

THE PSEUDODEMENTIAS

Neurologists seeing patients with suspected dementia work by a process of elimination: They review the roster of true dementing disorders as well as all the ailments that can masquerade as dementia ("pseudodementias").

Depression

High among the disorders that can simulate dementia are depression and manic-depression. (See also Mental Health, page 429.) Depressed individuals are frequently passive and unresponsive. They may appear confused, slow, and forgetful. In manic-depression, the individual may experience mood swings between depression and mania—the latter an excited state in which a person feels powerful and often acts recklessly or foolishly.

People experiencing a dementing illness may also act irrationally and appear excited. They may also be depressed—either as part of the disease process itself or as a reaction to their failing mental powers.

In sorting out depression from dementia the physician may find that depressed individuals have had earlier bouts of depression along with symptoms of insomnia, fatigue, or loss of appetite. In contrast, a person in the early stages of dementia often singles out a memory problem, or difficulties in arithmetic, as the trouble. The onset of a progressive dementia like Alzheimer's disease is also likely to be slow and insidious, while depressions usually develop more quickly.

Sometimes an older person who appears passive, slow, or confused may have recently lost a spouse or close friend and is suffering what is called a reactive depression. It is not unusual for the mourner to seem distracted, speaking and acting as if the dead person were still alive, for example.

In other cases a person who appears withdrawn or absent-minded may be reacting to the diminished circumstances of life, the loss of income and influence, for example. Loneliness and a disappointment with fate or with the state of society may be added burdens. Such a person's prevailing mood has been described as "existential sadness"—a mood that might benefit from sensitive human contact and rewarding activity, but not one that should be considered either mental or physical illness.

Drug Reactions

Rivaling depression as a major factor complicating the diagnosis of dementia are reactions to drugs. Often—especially in older adults—people are taking more than one drug for chronic conditions: "water" pills (diuretics) to control high blood pressure, sedatives for sleeplessness, tranquilizers for "nerves"—in addition to aspirin, laxatives, other over-the-counter drugs, and alcohol.

It is wise to assume that all drugs are powerful; all drugs have side effects, and most drugs interact: In combination, two or more drugs may be more powerful than each taken alone.

What makes drug use a particularly vexing problem in older people are age-related changes in metabolism. Both the liver and the kidneys may be less efficient in clearing the body of drugs, and along with a general slowing of metabolism, a drug may persist in the body longer than in a younger person. Often, too, the dosage appropriate for a 25-year-old is much too strong for a 60-year-old. Some physicians routinely wean a patient off all medications when confronted with mental symptoms.

Chemical Imbalances

The brain makes a high demand on nutrients, and poor eating habits or problems in food absorption can seriously affect the brain. Again the problems can be worse in older people who may be inactive, have little appetite, and often skimp on food. Interestingly, mental symptoms may appear before physical ones. Pernicious anemia, for example, is a blood disorder caused by impaired ability to use one of the B vitamins. In older people the first symptoms may be irritability or depression. Inadequate thyroid hormone can result in apathy, depression, or dementia. Hypoglycemia—a condition in which there is not enough sugar in the bloodstream—can give rise to confusion or personality change. Too little or too much sodium or calcium can also trigger disturbing mental changes. Tests can determine whether any of these imbalances are present.

Heart and Lung Problems

Just as the brain demands high-quality nutrition, it also requires a high level of oxygen. Chronic lung disease can lead to an oxygen shortage that can starve brain cells and lead to the symptoms of dementia. If the heart is not pumping efficiently, if there are disturbances in heart rhythm, malfunctioning heart valves, or other indications of heart disease, the brain may suffer.

All of these "pseudodementias" are treatable, and if the brain has not suffered permanent damage, the dementing symptoms should abate.

Other potentially reversible dementias may be caused by brain swelling (hydrocephalus), meningitis, brain tumor, head injury, certain hereditary disorders, and poisoning by lead, mercury, or by exposure to carbon monoxide, some pesticides, and industrial pollutants. Chronic alcoholism can also seriously impair mental faculties, notably memory for recent events. Some investigators think that alcohol in itself may cause irreparable brain damage, but the memory deficit appears to be related to the chronic drinker's inadequate diet—specifically, thiamine (vitamin B-1) deficiency.

THE TRUE DEMENTIAS

Once the pseudodementias have been eliminated, the physician faced with a patient with failing mental powers will suspect circulatory problems or primary brain disease to be the cause.

Alzheimer's Disease and Infarct Dementia

Next to Alzheimer's disease (see page 101), the leading cause of dementia in aging is obstruction to blood flow in the brain. Most commonly, a blood clot will clog a blood vessel, or a vessel may burst, hemorrhaging into a part of the brain. If a major vessel is involved, the symptoms are sudden, dramatic, and sometimes fatal—the consequences of a major stroke. A small stroke may go unnoticed, however, or result in specific symptoms—a slurring of speech, perhaps, or a numbness in one hand. The evidence of a brain blood vessel (cerebrovascular) accident shows up as a small mass of coagulating blood and dead tissue called an infarct. If the number of infarcts increases over time, the chances are that the individual will experience progressive mental and physical decline.

Multi-infarct dementia is now the preferred term for mental deterioration due to blood vessel disease in the brain. It replaces the old-fashioned and inaccurate "hardening of the arteries of the brain."

Multi-infarct dementia is now thought to account for between 12 and 20 percent of dementia in the elderly; another 16 to 20 percent of dementia patients have both infarcts and Alzheimer's disease.

It is usually not difficult to distinguish between the two most common dementias. Persons with infarct dementia often have a history of high blood pressure, vascular disease, or previous stroke. Infarcts are also the result of events that may occur months or years apart. Thus the dementia progresses in stepwise fashion in contrast to the steady decline seen in Alzheimer's disease. Since the infarct is usually limited to one part of the brain, the symptoms, too, are limited; they may affect only one side of the body or involve a specific faculty like language. Neurologists call these "local" or "focal" symptoms, as opposed to the "global" symptoms seen in Alzheimer's disease.

Other Causes of Progressive Dementia

The remaining causes of progressive dementia are less usual nervous system diseases. While each disorder alone affects a relatively small number of people, the group as a whole accounts for over a million patients with progressive and dementing brain disease in America today.

Multiple sclerosis. Among the better known neurological diseases is multiple sclerosis, a disorder characterized by destruction of the insulating material covering nerve fibers. Usually the disease progresses through a series of acute episodes and partial recoveries. In time, both mental and physical deterioration can occur.

Parkinson's disease. Tremor and difficulty in originating voluntary movements are the hallmarks of Parkinson's disease (see page 149), a disorder which strikes older adults. Drugs can relieve symptoms, but do not halt the progression of the disease. Symptoms of dementia may appear in severe or advanced cases.

Huntington's disease. Children with a parent who has Huntington's disease stand a 50 percent chance of inheriting this relentless dementing disease. Symptoms usually appear in early middle age and can include personality change, mental decline, psychotic symptoms, and a movement disturbance. Restlessness and facial tics may progress to severe uncontrollable flailing of head, limbs, and trunk. At the same time, mental capacity can deteriorate to dementia.

Pick's disease. Symptoms of Pick's disease are

very similar to those of Alzheimer's disease, but the disease is associated with different changes in brain tissue.

Creutzfeldt-Jakob disease. Infectious agents are recognized as the culprits in a growing number of progressive dementias. In Creutzfeldt-Jakob disease, the infectious agent is an unusual virus that may lie dormant in the body for years (hence it is called a "slow" virus). When activated, the virus produces a rapidly progressive dementia along with muscle spasms and changes in gait.

Each of these "true" dementias has inspired new research into causes and cures. In each case, too, active voluntary organizations have mobilized efforts to educate the public and come to the aid of patients and families.

SENSITIVE CARING

From the moment of diagnosis of dementia to the end of life, patients and families are subjected to pressures and strains that rarely let up. If there is a genetic component, the effect of the doctor's pronouncement of the diagnosis can be even more devastating. Sons and daughters, sisters and brothers, fear they themselves may one day succumb to the same remorseless symptoms.

In conditions like Alzheimer's disease, it is often the spouse alone who is left to do the caring—at a time of life when he or she may be elderly and in diminished health. The role is truly exhausting: "It's like a 36-hour day," as one man described it.

More often than not, the husband or wife of a patient will have assumed the burden of responsibility before the patient was diagnosed, quietly covering up for mental failings. After the diagnosis is made, there may be a period in which the loyal spouse and other family members deny the severity of the symptoms. The patient is really not so bad, they say, not as bad as someone else with a similar disorder.

Increasingly, health care professionals are acknowledging that all dementing diseases are family afflictions; patients need family support and flexibility in care—at home, in the community, and finally, if necessary, in a hospital or nursing facility. The voluntary health organizations concerned with dementing disorders understand this, and through their programs of advice and information come to the psychological and practical aid of families. Often they catalogue community resources, offer nursing care tips, and direct families to programs designed for patients with chronic neurological disorders.

While it is important for patients with dementia to relearn old skills and to socialize, it is equally important that family members have time off—respite from around-the-clock nursing demands. Most families want to keep their ailing relatives at home as long as possible. But they need the support of community resources to provide respite facilities—places where a patient can go for brief stays. And they need practical guidance in caring for the patient at home.

Some excellent books have been published to help patients and families cope. Among them are a guide entitled *The 36-Hour Day,* published by The Johns Hopkins University Press, and a manual prepared by the Dementia Research Program group at Burke Rehabilitation Center.

The National Institute of Neurological Disorders and Stroke

ALZHEIMER'S DISEASE

Alzheimer's disease is the term used to describe a dementing disorder marked by certain brain changes, regardless of the age of onset. Alzheimer's disease is not a normal part of aging—it is not something that inevitably happens in later life. Rather, it is one of the dementing disorders, a group of brain diseases that lead to the loss of mental and physical functions. The disorder, whose cause is unknown, affects a small but significant percentage of older Americans.

A very small minority of Alzheimer's patients are under 50 years of age. Most are over 65. Alzheimer's disease is the exception, rather than the rule, in old age. Only about 5 percent of older people are afflicted by Alzheimer's disease or a related dementia.

Although Alzheimer's disease is not curable or reversible, there are ways to alleviate symptoms and suffering and to assist families. Not every person with this illness is better off in a nursing home. Many thousands of patients—especially those in the early stages of the disease—are cared for by their families.

Indeed, one of the most important aspects of medical management is family education and family support services. When, or whether, to transfer a patient to a nursing home is a decision that must be carefully determined by the family.

RISK FACTORS

Some investigators, describing a family pattern of Alzheimer's disease, suggest that heredity may influence its development. A genetic basis, at least with a small subgroup of families where the disease has more frequently occurred, has been identified through the discovery in these families of a genetic marker on chromosome 21.

At the same time, data indicate that the likelihood that a close relative (sibling, child, or parent) of an afflicted individual will develop Alzheimer's disease is low. In most cases, such an individual's risk is only slightly higher than that of someone in the general population, where the lifetime risk is below 1 percent. And, of course, many disorders have a genetic potential that is never expressed—

that is, despite being at risk for a certain illness, one might go through life without ever developing any symptom of the disease. In other instances, a genetic potential for a certain disorder may be released only if it is triggered by other risk factors.

There have been a few reports of a possible association between serious head injuries and the later onset of Alzheimer's disease, but otherwise no other risk factors have been unequivocally identified for Alzheimer's disease.

GENERAL SYMPTOMS

The onset of Alzheimer's disease is usually very slow and gradual, seldom occurring before age 65. Over time, however, it follows a progressively more serious course. Among the symptoms that typically develop, none is unique to Alzheimer's disease at its various stages. It is therefore essential for suspicious changes to be thoroughly evaluated before they become inappropriately or negligently labeled Alzheimer's disease.

The Early Signs

Problems of memory, particularly recent or short-term memory, are common early in the course of the disease. For example, the individual may, on repeated occasions, forget to turn off the iron or may not recall which of the morning's medicines were taken. Mild personality changes, such as less spontaneity or a sense of apathy and a tendency to withdraw from social interactions, occur early in the illness.

As the disease progresses, problems in abstract thinking or in intellectual functioning develop. The individual may begin to have trouble with figures when working on bills, with understanding what is being read, or with organizing the day's work. Further disturbances in behavior and appearance may also be seen at this point, such as agitation, irritability, quarrelsomeness, and diminishing ability to dress appropriately.

The Later Signs

Later in the course of the disorder, the affected individuals may become confused or disoriented about what month or year it is and be unable to describe accurately where they live or to name correctly a place being visited. Eventually they may wander, be unable to engage in conversation, seem inattentive and erratic in mood, appear uncooperative, lose bladder and bowel control, and, in extreme cases, become totally incapable of caring for themselves if the final stage is reached. Death then follows, perhaps from pneumonia or some other problem that occurs in severely deteriorated states of health. The average course of the disease from onset to death is about 10 to 15 years, but it may range from under 2 to over 20 years. Those who develop the disorder later in life may die from other illnesses (such as heart disease) before Alzheimer's disease reaches its final and most serious stage.

Living with the Symptoms

Though the changes just described represent the general range of symptoms for Alzheimer's disease, the specific problems, along with the rate and severity of decline, can vary considerably with different individuals. Indeed, most persons with Alzheimer's disease can function at a reasonable level and remain at home far into the course of the disorder. Moreover, throughout much of the course of the illness individuals maintain the capacity for giving and receiving love, for sharing warm interpersonal relationships, and for participating in a variety of meaningful activities with family and friends.

The reaction of an individual to the illness—his or her capacity to cope with it—also varies, depending on such factors as lifelong personality patterns and the nature and severity of stress in the immediate environment.

Depression, severe uneasiness, and paranoia or delusions may accompany or result from Alzheimer's disease, but they can often be alleviated by appropriate treatments. Although there is no cure for the disease, treatments are available to alleviate many of the symptoms which cause suffering.

DIAGNOSING ALZHEIMER'S DISEASE

Abnormal Brain Tissue Findings

Microscopic brain tissue changes have been described in Alzheimer's disease since Alois Alzheimer first reported them in 1906. These are the plaques and tangles—senile or neuritic plaques (degenerating nerve cells combined with a form of protein called amyloid) and neurofibrillary tangles (nerve cell malformations). The brains of Alzheimer's disease patients of all ages reveal these findings on autopsy examination.

Computed tomography (CT scan) changes become more evident as the disease progresses—not necessarily early on. Thus a CT scan that is performed in the first stages of the disease cannot in itself be used to make a definitive diagnosis of Alzheimer's disease; its value is in helping to establish whether certain disorders (some reversible) that mimic Alzheimer's disease are present. Later on, CT scans often reveal changes characteristic of Alzheimer's disease, namely an atrophied (shrunken) brain with widened sulci (tissue indentations) and enlarged cerebral ventricles (fluid chambers).

Several new types of instrumentation are enabling researchers to learn even more about the brain. Both positron emission tomography (PET scan) and SPECT (single photon emission computed tomography) can map regional cerebral blood flow, metabolic activity, and distribution of specific receptors, as well as integrity of the blood-brain barrier. These procedures may reveal abnormalities characteristic of Alzheimer's disease. Another method, magnetic resonance imaging (MRI), probes the brain by examining the interaction of the magnetic properties of atoms with an external magnetic field. MRI provides both structural and chemical information and distinguishes moving blood from static brain tissue.

As research on Alzheimer's disease progresses, scientists are describing other abnormal anatomical and chemical changes associated with the disease. These include nerve cell degeneration in the brain's nucleus basalis of Meynert and reduced levels of the neurotransmitter acetylcholine in the brains of Alzheimer's disease victims. But from a practical standpoint, the "classical" plaque and tangle changes seen at autopsy typically suffice for a diagnosis of Alzheimer's disease based on brain tissue changes. In fact, it is only through the study of brain tissue from a person who was thought to have Alzheimer's disease that a definitive diagnosis of the disorder can be made.

Clinical Features of Alzheimer's Disease

The "clinical" features of Alzheimer's disease, as opposed to the "tissue" changes, are threefold: (1) dementia—significant loss of intellectual abilities such as memory capacity, severe enough to interfere with social or occupational functioning; (2) insidious onset of symptoms—subtly progressive and irreversible course with documented deterioration over time; and (3) exclusion of all other specific causes of dementia by history, physical examination, laboratory tests, psychometric, and other studies.

Diagnosis By Exclusion

Based on these criteria, the clinical diagnosis of Alzheimer's disease has been referred to as "a diagnosis by exclusion," and one that can only be made in the face of clinical deterioration over time. There is no specific clinical test or finding that is unique to Alzheimer's disease. Hence, all disorders that can bring on similar symptoms must be systematically excluded or "ruled out." This explains why diagnostic workups of individuals where the question of Alzheimer's disease has been

raised can be so frustrating to patient and family alike; they are not told that Alzheimer's disease has been specifically diagnosed, but that other possible diagnoses have been dismissed, leaving Alzheimer's disease as the likely diagnosis by the process of elimination.

Scientists hope to develop one day a specific test for Alzheimer's disease, based on a specific laboratory or genetic finding ("marker"). Some think that the results from genetic research may lead to a diagnostic marker for certain persons evaluated for Alzheimer's disease. Many scientists are working at developing other tests or procedures that may someday identify living persons with the disorder, perhaps even early in its course before behavioral changes become evident. Still, a specific diagnostic marker for Alzheimer's disease is not yet available.

Meanwhile, Alzheimer's disease is the most overdiagnosed and misdiagnosed disorder of mental functioning in older adults. Part of the problem is that many other disorders show symptoms that resemble those of Alzheimer's disease. The crucial difference, though, is that many of these disorders—unlike Alzheimer's disease—may be stopped, reversed, or cured with appropriate treatment. But first they must be identified, not dismissed as Alzheimer's disease or senility.

Organic mental disorders. Conditions that affect the brain and result in intellectual, behavioral, and psychological dysfunction are referred to as "organic mental disorders." These disorders represent a broad grouping of diseases and include Alzheimer's disease. Organic mental disorders that can cause clinical problems like those of Alzheimer's disease, but which might be reversible or controlled with proper diagnosis and treatment, include the following.

• ***Side Effects of Medications.*** Unusual reactions to medications, too much or too little of prescribed medications, combinations of medications which, when taken together, cause adverse side effects.

- *Substance abuse.* Abuse of legal and/or illegal drugs, alcohol abuse.
- *Metabolic disorders.* Thyroid problems, nutritional deficiencies, anemias, etc.
- *Circulatory disorders.* Heart problems, strokes, etc.
- *Neurological disorders.* Normal-pressure hydrocephalus, multiple sclerosis, etc.
- *Infections.* Especially viral or fungal infections of the brain.
- *Trauma.* Injuries to the head.
- *Toxic factors.* Carbon monoxide, methyl alcohol, etc.
- *Tumors.* Any type within the skull—whether originating or metastasizing there.

Other disorders. In addition to organic mental disorders resulting from these diverse causes, other forms of mental dysfunction or mental health problems can also be confused with Alzheimer's disease. For example, a severe form of depression, referred to as "pseudodementia," can cause problems with memory and concentration that initially may be indistinguishable from early symptoms of Alzheimer's disease. But pseudodementia, like depression in general, can be reversed. Other psychiatric problems can similarly masquerade as Alzheimer's disease, and, like depression, respond to treatment.

Of course, not all memory changes or complaints in later life signal Alzheimer's disease or mental disorder. Many memory changes are only temporary, such as those that occur with bereavement or any stressful situation that makes it difficult to concentrate. In fact, older people are often accused or accuse themselves of memory changes which are not really taking place. If a person in his thirties misplaces keys or a wallet, forgets the name of a neighbor, or calls one sibling by another's name, nobody gives it a second thought. But

the same normal forgetfulness for people in their seventies may raise unjustifiable concern. On the other hand, serious memory difficulties should not be dismissed as an unavoidable part of normal aging.

Since rigorous studies on intelligence in later life show that healthy people who stay intellectually active maintain a sharp mind throughout the life cycle, noticeable decline in older adults that interferes with functioning should be clinically explored for an underlying problem.

Comprehensive Clinical Evaluation

Because of the many other disorders that can be confused with Alzheimer's disease, a comprehensive clinical evaluation is essential to arrive at a correct diagnosis of symptoms that look like those of Alzheimer's disease. Such an assessment should include at least three major components: (1) a thorough general medical workup, (2) a neurological examination, and (3) a psychiatric evaluation that may include psychological or psychometric testing. The family physician can be consulted regarding the best way to obtain the necessary examinations.

TREATMENT

Two critical crossroads reached in the approach to treatment for Alzheimer's disease were: (1) the recognition of Alzheimer's disease as a disorder distinct from the normal aging process; and (2) the realization that, in developing therapeutic and social interventions for a major illness or disability, the concept of care can be as important as the concept of cure.

Moreover, in addition to the symptoms of Alzheimer's disease mentioned earlier, other symptoms and aggravating factors may compound the problem. Patient, environmental, and family stresses can converge to exaggerate patient dysfunction and family burden

NORMAL MEMORY CHANGES IN THE AGING BRAIN

As we age, we forget, or grope momentarily to recall—and then fear the possibility of Alzheimer's disease. And yet, there are many possible causes of forgetfulness and disorientation other than Alzheimer's. Some are relatively insignificant, and some are reversible.

Recent studies show that healthy older people are, in fact, only fractionally slower than healthy younger people in most tests of mental agility—and that the differences that do exist may have little or no practical importance. For example, it may take a 70-year-old man a quarter of a second longer, on average, than a 30-year-old man to identify a familiar object presented in a picture. Whether that slight lag is a result of deteriorating mental agility or a need to sort through a larger store of memories to locate the right answer, the importance of the delay is negligible for the majority of people.

Other tests have shown that while some of our mental abilities slow down with age, other mental abilities become enhanced. Being able to draw upon experience does improve judgment—we indeed tend to become wiser as we become older. And, although the brain is at its maximum weight (and contains its maximum number of neurons) at age 20, and thereafter gradually decreases, the intellect does not simply grow to its full splendor by the age of 20 and then begin inevitably to degenerate. While older people have fewer brain cells than younger people, many of the younger people's brain cells are redundant; their loss over the years does not necessarily cause diminished brain function, since other cells take over for those that are lost. There is mounting evidence, too, that the brain retains its capacity for new growth in its nerve cells, as well as for new learning, as it ages.

In general, studies conducted by the National Institute on Aging have shown that 15 to 20 percent of older people have no detectable changes in mental function from youth to old age; the changes that are found in healthy people as they age are small. If you feel you are having trouble with your memory, you should consult your physician about it. For most of those over 50 who fail to do well on tests of mental agility, the impediment is not aging but illness, impairment due to the effects of alcohol, side effects of medications, or depression. While none of these is benign, all are potentially reversible.

Tips to Improve Your Memory
The common causes of ordinary memory troubles include anxiety, fatigue, stress, grief, and mild depression. In addition, an illness, isolation, habitual inactivity, chronic illness that becomes preoccupying, limitations of vision or hearing, and excessive use of alcohol can all induce memory loss. Some of these factors might interfere with taking information in to begin with; others, with retaining or retrieving memories. Using your memory—reading, playing chess, doing crossword puzzles, playing bridge—will help keep your memory fit. And so will these specific tips:

• Make mental pictures of tasks, numbers, names, words, thoughts, or whatever it is that you want to remember.

• Talk about it: Working over material in a conversation helps implant it in your memory.

• Eliminate distractions, background noise, and other things competing for your attention when you are trying to take something in.

• Don't waste your attentiveness trying to retain things a mere piece of paper can retain. Keep lists and a daily calendar.

• Take occasional breaks to rest and refresh your mind, especially when you are trying to learn something new.

• Remember that it's okay to forget.

The Editors

during the clinical course of Alzheimer's disease. Identifying these stresses and making appropriate changes can provide the foundation for more effective treatment and fewer everyday problems.

In the Alzheimer's disease patient, depression or delusions can aggravate dysfunction. These problems, which emerge during the course of the disorder in some individuals with Alzheimer's disease, compound memory impairment; they make the affected individual do worse than would be expected from the dementia alone—causing clinical conditions referred to as "excess disability" states. Depression by itself can mimic dementia, as in pseudodementia. When combined with dementia, depression exacts yet greater incapacity and suffering in the Alzheimer's disease patient.

Depression in the Alzheimer's patient can usually be lessened or relieved by treatment. Indeed, this highlights one of the truly extraordinary phenomena that can be observed in Alzheimer's disease: By alleviating an excess disability state, actual clinical improvement can result—even though the underlying pathological process is advancing. In other words, at a given point in time, the patient's symptoms can be reduced, suffering lowered, capacity to cope buttressed, with family burden eased as a further result. These are traditional goals of treatment for all illnesses.

The patient's immediate environment can similarly interfere with coping, adding to the level of impairment. Modifying the surroundings can reduce stresses imposed by environmental factors. There is the matter of safety, as in the need to protect the person from wandering toward a stairway and subsequently falling. There is the matter of lowering the individual's frustration level, such as by placing different cues in the immediate environment to combat memory loss and to reduce resulting stress and disorganization. There is the matter of finding the most protective but least restrictive setting for care which at some point may involve a move away from home to a nursing home or other care facility well equipped to deal with those who have Alzheimer's disease.

Relieving Stress on the Family

Stress on the family can take a toll on patient and care giver alike. Care givers are usually family members—either spouses or children—and are preponderantly wives and daughters. As time passes and the burden mounts, it not only places the mental health of family care givers at risk, it also diminishes their ability to provide care to the Alzheimer's disease patient. Hence, assistance to the family as a whole must be considered.

As the disease progresses, families experience increasing anxiety and pain at seeing unsettling changes in a loved one, and they commonly feel guilt over not being able to do enough. The prevalence of reactive depression among family members in this situation is disturbingly high—care givers are chronically stressed and are much more likely to suffer from depression than the average person. If care givers have been forced to retire from positions outside the home, they feel progressively more isolated and no longer productive members of society.

Support Through Interventions

The likelihood, intensity, and duration of depression among care givers can all be lowered through available interventions. For example, to the extent that family members can offer emotional support to each other and perhaps seek professional consultation, they will be better prepared to help their loved one manage the illness and to recognize the limits of what they themselves can reasonably do.

Since the components of the problem vary, so too should the focus, nature, and sources of interventions. Interventions should focus on the patient's symptoms, the affected individual's everyday environment, and the family support system. Specific interventions can involve support from the family, the help of a homemaker or other aide in the home, employment of behavioral therapies, and the use of medication.

The sources for interventions can range from family support groups such as those available through the Alzheimer's Association (AA), to professional consultations for the patient and family with a mental health specialist, to a variety of community programs such as day or respite care.

Though Alzheimer's disease cannot at present be cured, reversed, or stopped in its progression, much can be done to help both the patient and the family live through the course of the illness with greater dignity and less discomfort. Toward this goal, appropriate clinical interventions and community services should be vigorously sought.

The National Institute of Mental Health

CHRONIC PAIN

Rare is the person who has not experienced some beyond-belief episode of pain and misery. Mercifully, relief finally came. With treatment, or with the body's healing powers alone, you got better and the pain went away. Doctors call that kind of pain "acute" pain. It is a normal sensation triggered in the nervous system to alert you to possible injury and the need to take care of yourself.

Chronic pain is different. Chronic pain persists. Fiendishly, uselessly, pain signals keep firing in the nervous system for weeks, months, even years. There may have been an initial mishap—a sprained back, a serious infection—from which you've long since recovered. There may be an ongoing cause of pain—arthritis, cancer, ear infection. But some people suffer chronic pain in the absence of any past injury or evidence of body damage.

Whatever the matter may be, chronic pain is real, unremitting, and demoralizing.

THE TERRIBLE TRIAD

Pain of such proportions overwhelms all other symptoms and becomes "the" problem. People so afflicted often cannot work. Their appetite falls off. Physical activity of any kind is exhausting and may aggravate the pain. Soon the person becomes the victim of a vicious circle in which total preoccupation with pain leads to irritability and depression. The sufferer can't sleep at night and the next day's weariness compounds the problem—leading to more irritability, depression, and pain. Specialists call that unhappy state the "terrible triad" of suffering, sleeplessness, and sadness, a calamity that is as hard on the family as it is on the victim.

The urge to do something—anything—to stop the pain makes some patients drug dependent, drives others to undergo repeated operations or, worse, resort to questionable practitioners who promise quick and permanent "cures."

Many chronic pain conditions affect older adults. Arthritis, cancer, angina—the chest-binding, breath-catching spasms of pain associated with coronary artery disease—commonly take their greatest toll among the middle-aged and elderly. Tic douloureux (trigeminal neuralgia) is a recurrent, stabbing facial pain that is rare among young adults. But ask any resident of housing for retired persons if there are any tic sufferers around and you are certain to hear of cases. So the fact that Americans are living longer contributes to a widespread and growing concern about pain. Neuroscientists share that concern.

At a time when people are living longer and painful conditions abound, neuroscientists have made landmark discoveries that are leading to a better understanding of pain and more effective treatments.

SOUNDING THE PAIN ALARM

Part of the inspiration for the new groups has come from a deeper understanding of pain made possible by advances in research techniques. Not long ago neuroscientists debated whether pain was a separate sense at all, supplied with its own nerve cells and brain centers like the senses of hearing or taste or touch. Maybe you hurt, the scientists reasoned, because nerve endings sensitive to touch are pressed very hard. To some extent, that is true: Some nerve fibers in your skin will be stimulated by a painful pinch as well as a gentle touch. But neuroscientists now know that there are many small nerve cells with extremely fine nerve fibers that are excited exclusively by intense, potentially harmful stimulation. Scientists call the nerve cells "nociceptors," from the word "noxious," meaning physically harmful or destructive.

Some nociceptors sound off to several kinds of painful stimulation—a hammer blow that hits your thumb instead of a nail; a drop of acid; a flaming match. Other nociceptors are more selective. They are excited by a pinprick but ignore painful heat or chemical stimulation. It's as though nature had sprinkled your skin and your insides with a variety of pain-sensitive cells, not only to report what kind of damage you're experiencing, but to make sure the message gets through on at least one channel.

BROADCASTING THE NEWS

That same dispersion of forces continues once pain messages reach the central nervous system. Suppose you touch a hot stove. Some incoming pain signals are immediately routed to nerve cells that signal muscles to contract, so you pull your hand back. That streamlined pathway is a reflex, one of many protective circuits wired into your nervous system at birth.

Meanwhile the message informing you that you've touched the stove travels along other pathways to higher centers in the brain. One path is an express route that reports the facts: where it hurts; how bad it is; whether the pain is sharp or burning. Other pain pathways plod along more slowly, the nerve fibers branching to make connections with many nerve cells (neurons) en route. Scientists think that these more meandering pathways act as warning systems alerting you of impending damage and in other ways filling out

the pain picture. All the pathways combined contribute to the emotional impact of pain— whether you feel frightened, anxious, angry, annoyed. Experts called those feelings the "suffering" component of pain.

Still other branches of the pain news network are alerting another major division of the nervous system, the autonomic nervous system. That division handles the body's vital functions like breathing, blood flow, pulse rate, digestion, and elimination. Pain can sound a general alarm in that system, causing you to sweat or stop digesting your food, increasing your pulse rate and blood pressure, dilating the pupils of your eye, and signaling the release of hormones like epinephrine (adrenaline). Epinephrine aids and abets all those responses as well as triggering the release of sugar stored in the liver to provide an extra boost of energy in an emergency.

CENSORING THE NEWS

Obviously, not every source of pain creates a full-blown emergency with adrenaline-surging, sweat-pouring, pulse-racing responses. Moreover, observers are well aware of times and places when excruciating pain is ignored. Think of the quarterback's ability to finish a game oblivious of a torn ligament, or a fakir sitting on a bed of spikes. One of the foremost pioneers in pain research adds his own personal tale, too, of the time he landed a salmon after a long and hearty struggle, only then to discover the deep blood-dripping gash on his leg.

Acknowledging such events, neuroscientists have long suspected that there are built-in nervous system mechanisms that can block pain messages.

Now it seems that just as there is more than one way to spread the news of pain, there is more than one way to censor the news. These control systems involve pathways that come down from the brain to prevent pain signals from getting through.

THE GATE THEORY OF PAIN

Interestingly, a pair of Canadian and English investigators speculated that such pain-suppressing pathways must exist when they devised a new "gate theory of pain" in the mid-sixties. Their idea was that when pain signals first reach the nervous system, they excite activity in a group of small neurons that form a kind of pain "pool." When the total activity of these neurons reaches a certain minimal level, a hypothetical "gate" opens up that allows the pain signals to be sent to higher brain centers. But nearby neurons in contact with the pain cells can suppress activity in the pain pool so that the gate stays closed. The gate-closing cells include large neurons that are stimulated by nonpainful touching or pressing of your skin. The gate could also be closed from above, by brain cells activating a descending pathway to block pain.

The theory explained such everyday behavior as scratching a scab, or rubbing a sprained ankle: the scratching and rubbing excite just those nerve cells sensitive to touch and pressure that can suppress the pain pool cells. The scientists conjectured that brain-based pain control systems were activated when people behaved heroically—ignoring pain in order to finish a football game, or to help a more severely wounded soldier on the battlefield.

The gate theory aroused both interest and controversy when it was first announced. Most importantly, it stimulated research to find the conjectured pathways and mechanisms. Pain studies got an added boost when investigators made the surprising discovery that the brain itself produces chemicals that can control pain.

The landmark discovery of the pain-suppressing chemicals came about because scientists in Aberdeen, Scotland, and at the Johns Hopkins University Hospital in Baltimore were curious about how morphine and other opium-derived painkillers, or analgesics, work.

For some time neuroscientists had known that chemicals were important in conducting nerve signals (small bursts of electric current) from cell to cell. In order for the signal from one cell to reach the next in line, the first cell secretes a chemical "neurotransmitter" from the tip of a long fiber that extends from the cell body. The transmitter molecules cross the gap separating the two cells and attach to special receptor sites on the neighboring cell surface. Some neurotransmitters excite the second cell—allowing it to generate an electrical signal. Others inhibit the second cell—preventing it from generating a signal.

When investigators in Scotland and at Johns Hopkins injected morphine into experimental animals, they found that the morphine molecules fitted snugly into receptors on certain brain and spinal cord neurons. Why, the scientists wondered, should the human brain—the product of millions of years of evolution—come equipped with receptors for a man-made drug? Perhaps there were naturally occurring brain chemicals that behaved exactly like morphine.

THE BRAIN'S OWN OPIATES

Both groups of scientists found not just one pain-suppressing chemical in the brain, but a whole family of such proteins. The Aberdeen investigators called the smaller members of the family "enkephalins" (meaning "in the head"). In time, the larger proteins were isolated and called "endorphins," meaning "the morphine within." The term endorphins is now often used to describe the group as a whole.

The discovery of the endorphins lent weight to the general concept of the gate theory. Endorphins released from brain nerve cells might inhibit spinal cord pain cells through pathways descending from the brain to the spinal cord. Endorphins might also be activated when you rub or scratch your itching skin or aching joints. Laboratory experiments subsequently confirmed that painful stimulation led to the release of endorphins from nerve cells. Some of these chemicals then turned up in cerebrospinal fluid, the liquid that circulates in the spinal cord and brain. Laced with endorphins, the fluid could bring a soothing balm to quiet nerve cells.

A NEW LOOK AT PAIN TREATMENTS

Further evidence that endorphins figure importantly in pain control comes from a new look at some of the oldest and newest pain treatments. The new look frequently involves the use of a drug that prevents endorphins and morphine from working. Injections of this drug, naloxone, can result in a return of pain which had been relieved by morphine and certain other treatments. But, interestingly, some pain treatments are not affected by naloxone: Their success in controlling pain apparently does not depend on endorphins. Thus nature has provided us with more than one means of achieving pain relief.

Acupuncture

Probably no therapy for pain has stirred more controversy in recent years than acupuncture, the 2,000-year-old Chinese technique of inserting fine needles under the skin at selected points in the body. The needles are agitated by the practitioner to produce pain relief, which some individuals report lasts for hours, or even days. Does acupuncture really work? Opinion is divided. Many specialists agree that patients report benefit when the needles are placed near where it hurts, not at the body points indicated on traditional Chinese acupuncture charts. The case for acupuncture has been made by investigators who argue that local needling of the skin excites endorphin systems of pain control. Wiring the needles to stimulate nerve endings electrically (electroacupuncture) also activates endorphin systems, they believe. Further, some experiments have shown that there are higher

levels of endorphins in cerebrospinal fluid following acupuncture.

Those same investigators note that naloxone injections can block pain relief produced by acupuncture. Others have not been able to repeat those findings. Skeptics also cite long-term studies of chronic pain patients that showed no lasting benefit from acupuncture treatments. Current opinion is that more controlled trials are needed to define which pain conditions might be helped by acupuncture and which patients are most likely to benefit.

Local Electrical Stimulation

Applying brief pulses of electricity to nerve endings under the skin, a procedure called transcutaneous electrical nerve stimulation (TENS), yields excellent pain relief in some chronic pain patients. The stimulation works best when applied to the skin near where the pain is felt and where other sensibilities like touch or pressure have not been damaged. Both the frequency and voltage of the electrical stimulation are important in obtaining pain relief.

Brain Stimulation

Another electrical method for controlling pain, especially the widespread and severe pain of advanced cancer, is through surgically implanted electrodes in the brain. The patient determines when and how much stimulation is needed by operating an external transmitter that beams electronic signals to a receiver under the skin that is connected to the electrodes. The brain sites where the electrodes are placed are areas known to be rich in opiate receptors and in endorphin-containing cells or fibers. Stimulation-produced analgesia (SPA) is a costly procedure that involves the risk of brain surgery. However, patients who have used this technique report that their pain "seems to melt away." The pain relief is also remarkably specific: The other senses remain intact, and there is no mental confusion or cloudiness as with opiate drugs.

The National Institute of Neurological Disorders and Stroke (NINDS) is currently supporting research on how SPA works and is also investigating problems of tolerance: Pain may return after repeated stimulation.

Placebo Effects

For years, doctors have known that a harmless sugar pill or an injection of salt water can make many a patient feel better—even after major surgery. The placebo effect, as it has been called, has been thought to be due to suggestion, distraction, the patient's optimism that something is being done, or the desire to please the doctor ("placebo" means "I will please" in Latin).

Now experiments suggest that the placebo effect may be neurochemical, and that people who respond to a placebo for pain relief—a remarkably consistent 35 percent in any experiment using placebos—are able to tap into their brain's endorphin systems. To evaluate it, two NINDS- and NIDR (National Institute of Dental Research)-supported investigators at the University of California at San Francisco designed an ingenious experiment. They asked adults scheduled for wisdom teeth removal to volunteer in a pain experiment. Following surgery, some patients were given morphine, some naloxone, and some a placebo. As expected, about a third of those given the placebo reported pain relief. The investigators then gave these people naloxone. All reported a return of pain.

How people who benefit from placebos gain access to pain control systems in the brain is not known. Scientists cannot even predict whether someone who responds to a placebo in one situation will respond in another. The San Francisco investigators suspect that stress may be a factor. Patients who are very anxious or under stress are more likely to react to a placebo for pain than those who are more calm, cool, and collected. But dental surgery itself may be sufficiently stressful to trigger the release of endorphins—with or without the effects of placebo. For that reason, many specialists believe further studies are indicated to analyze the placebo effect.

As research continues to reveal the role of endorphins in the brain, neuroscientists have been able to draw more detailed brain maps of the areas and pathways important in pain perception and control. They have even found new members of the endorphin family: dynorphin, the newest endorphin, is reported to be 10 times more potent a painkiller than morphine.

At the same time, clinical investigators have tested chronic pain patients and found that they often have lower-than-normal levels of endorphins in their spinal fluid. If you could just boost their stores with man-made endorphins, perhaps the problems of chronic pain patients could be solved.

Not so easy. Some endorphins are quickly broken down after release from nerve cells. Other endorphins are longer lasting, but there are problems in manufacturing the compounds in quantity and getting them into the right places in the brain or spinal cord. In a few promising studies, clinical investigators have injected an endorphin called beta-endorphin under the membranes surrounding the spinal cord. Patients reported excellent pain relief lasting for many hours. Morphine compounds injected in the same area are similarly effective in producing long-lasting pain relief.

But spinal cord injections or other techniques designed to raise the level of endorphins circulating in the brain require surgery and hospitalization. And even if less drastic means of getting endorphins into the nervous system could be found, they are probably not the ideal answer to chronic pain. Endorphins are also involved in other nervous system activities such as controlling blood flow. Increasing the amount of endorphins might have undesirable effects on these other body activities. Endorphins also appear to share with morphine a potential for addiction or tolerance.

Meanwhile, chemists are synthesizing new analgesics and discovering painkilling virtues in drugs not normally prescribed for pain. Much of the drug research is aimed at developing nonnarcotic painkillers. The motivation for the research is not only to avoid introducing potentially addictive drugs on the market, but is based on the observation that narcotic drugs are simply not effective in treating a variety of chronic pain conditions. Developments in nondrug treatments are also progressing, ranging from new surgical techniques to physical and psychological therapies, including exercise, hypnosis, and biofeedback.

NEW AND OLD DRUGS FOR PAIN

When you complain of headache or low back pain and the doctor says take two aspirins every four hours and stay in bed, you may think your pain is being dismissed lightly. Not at all.

Aspirin

One of the most universally used medications, aspirin is an excellent painkiller. Scientists still cannot explain all the ways aspirin works, but they do know that it interferes with pain signals where they usually originate, at the nociceptive nerve endings outside the brain and spinal cord: peripheral nerves. Aspirin also inhibits the production of chemicals manufactured in the blood to promote blood clotting and wound healing: prostaglandins. Unfortunately, prostaglandins, released from cells at the site of injury, are pain-causing substances. They actually sensitize nerve endings, making them—and you—feel more pain. Along with increasing the blood supply to the area, the chemicals contribute to inflammation—the pain, heat, redness, and swelling of tissue damage.

Some investigators now think that the continued release of pain-causing substances in chronic pain conditions may lead to long-term nervous system changes in some patients that make them hypersensitive to pain. People suffering such "hyperalgesia" can cry out in pain at the gentlest touch, or even when a soft breeze blows over the affected area. In addition to the prostaglandins, blister fluid and certain insect and snake venoms also contain pain-causing substances. Presumably these chemicals alert you to the need for care—a fine reaction in an emergency, but not in chronic pain.

Prescription Painkillers

There are several prescription drugs that usually can provide stronger pain relief than aspirin. These drugs include the opiate-related compounds codeine, propoxyphene (Darvon), morphine, and meperidine (Demerol). All these drugs have some potential for abuse, and may have unpleasant and even harmful side effects. In combination with other medications or alcohol, some can be dangerous. Used wisely, however, they are important recruits in the chemical fight against pain.

In the search for effective analgesics, physicians have discovered pain-relieving benefits from drugs not normally prescribed for pain. Certain antidepressants as well as antiepileptic drugs are used to treat several particularly severe pain conditions, notably the pain of shingles and of facial neuralgias like tic douloureux.

Antidepressants

Interestingly, pain patients who benefit from antidepressants report pain relief before any uplift in mood. Pain specialists think that the antidepressant works because it increases the supply of a naturally produced neurotransmitter, serotonin. (Doctors have long associated decreased amounts of serotonin with severe depression.) But now scientists have evidence that cells using serotonin are also an integral part of a pain-controlling pathway that starts with endorphin-rich nerve cells high up in the brain and ends with inhibition of pain-conducting nerve cells lower in the brain or spinal cord. Antidepressant drugs have been used successfully in treating the excruciating pain that can follow an attack of shingles.

Antiepileptic Drugs

Antiepileptic drugs have been used successfully in treating tic douloureux, the riveting attacks of facial pain that affect older adults. The rationale for the use of the antiepileptic drugs (principally carbamazepine—Tegretol) does not involve the endorphin system. It is based on the theory that a healthy nervous system depends on a proper balance of incoming and outgoing nerve signals. Tic and other facial pains or neuralgias are thought to result from damage to facial nerves. That means that the normal flow of messages to and from the brain is disturbed. The nervous system may react by becoming hypersensitive: It may create its own powerful discharge of nerve signals, as though screaming to the outside world, "Why aren't you contacting me?" Antiepileptic drugs—used to quiet the excessive brain discharges associated with epileptic seizures—quiet the distress signals associated with tic and may relieve pain that way.

PSYCHOLOGICAL METHODS

Psychological treatment for pain can range from psychoanalysis and other forms of psychotherapy to relaxation training, meditation, hypnosis, biofeedback, or behavior modification.

The philosophy common to all these varied psychological approaches is the belief that patients can do something on their own to control their pain.

That something may mean changing attitudes, feelings, or behaviors associated with pain, or understanding how unconscious forces and past events have contributed to the present painful predicament.

Psychotherapy

Freud was celebrated for demonstrating that for some individuals physical pain symbolizes real or imagined emotional hurts. He also noted that some individuals develop pain or paralysis as a form of self-punishment for what they consider to be past sins or bad behavior. Sometimes, too, pain may be a way of punishing others. This doesn't mean that the pain is any less real; it does mean that some pain patients may benefit from psychoanalysis or individual or group psychotherapy to gain insights into the meaning of their pain.

Relaxation and Meditation Therapies

These forms of training enable people to relax tense muscles, reduce anxiety, and alter mental state. Both physical and mental tension can make any pain worse, and in conditions such as headache or back pain, tension may be at the root of the problem. Meditation, which aims at producing a state of relaxed but alert awareness, is sometimes combined with therapies that encourage people to think of pain as something remote and apart from them. The methods promote a sense of detachment so that the patient thinks of the pain as confined to a particular body part over which he or she has marvelous control. The approach may be particularly helpful when pain is associated with fear and dread, as in cancer.

Hypnosis

No longer considered magic, hypnosis is a technique in which an individual's susceptibility to suggestion is heightened. Normal volunteers who prove to be excellent subjects for hypnosis often report a marked reduction or obliteration of experimentally induced pain, such as that produced by a mild electric shock. The hypnotic state does not lower the volunteer's heart rate, respiration, or other autonomic responses. These physical reactions show the expected increases normally associated with painful stimulation.

The role of hypnosis in treating chronic pain patients is uncertain. Some studies have shown that 15 to 20 percent of hypnotizable patients with moderate to severe pain can achieve total relief with hypnosis. Other studies have reported that hypnosis reduces anxiety and depression. By lowering the burden of emotional suffering, pain may become more bearable.

Biofeedback

Some individuals can learn voluntary control over certain body activities if they are provided with information about how the system is working—how fast their heart is beating, how tense are their head or neck muscles, how cold are their hands. The information is usually supplied through visual or auditory cues that code the body activity in some obvious way—a louder sound meaning an increase in muscle tension, for example. How people use this "biofeedback" to learn control is not understood, but some masters of the art report that imagery helps: They may think of a warm tropical beach, for example, when they want to raise the temperature of their hands. Biofeedback may be a logical approach in pain conditions that involve tense muscles, like tension headache or low back pain. But results are mixed.

Behavior Modification

This psychological technique (sometimes called operant conditioning) is aimed at changing habits, behaviors, and attitudes that can develop in chronic pain patients. Some patients become dependent, anxious, and homebound—if not bedridden. For some, too, chronic pain may be a welcome friend, relieving them of the boredom of a dull job or the burden of family responsibilities. These psychological rewards—sometimes combined with financial gains from compensation payments or insurance—work against improvements in the patient's condition, and can encourage increased drug dependency, re-

peated surgery, and multiple doctor and clinic visits.

There is no question that the patient feels pain. The hope of behavior modification is that pain relief can be obtained from a program aimed at changing the individual's lifestyle. The program begins with a complete assessment of the painful condition and a thorough explanation of how the program works. It is essential to enlist the full cooperation of both the patient and family members. The treatment is aimed at reducing pain medication and increasing mobility and independence through a graduated program of exercise, diet, and other activities. The patient is rewarded for positive efforts with praise and attention. Rewards are withheld when the patient retreats into negative attitudes or demanding and dependent behavior.

How effective are any of these psychological treatments? Are some superior to others? Who is most likely to benefit? Do the benefits last? The answers are not yet in hand. Patient selection and patient cooperation are all-important. Analysis of individuals who have improved dramatically with one or another of these approaches is helping to pinpoint what factors are likely to lead to successful treatment.

SURGERY TO RELIEVE PAIN

Surgery is often considered the court of last resort for pain: When all else fails, cut the nerve endings. Surgery can bring about instant, almost magical release from pain. But surgery may also destroy other sensations as well, or, inadvertently, become the source of new pain. Further, relief is not necessarily permanent. After six months or a year, pain may return.

For all those reasons, the decision for surgery must always involve a careful weighing of the patient's condition and the outlook for the future. If surgery can mean the difference between a pain-wracked existence ending in death versus a pain-free time in which to compose one's life and see friends and family, then surgery is clearly a humane and compassionate choice.

There are a variety of operations to relieve pain. The most common is cordotomy: severing the nerve fibers on one or both sides of the spinal cord that travel the express routes to the brain. Cordotomy affects the sense of temperature as well as pain, since the fibers travel together in the express route.

Besides cordotomy, surgery within the brain or spinal cord to relieve pain includes severing connections at major junctions in pain pathways, such as at the places where pain fibers cross from one side of the cord to the other, or destroying parts of important relay stations in the brain like the thalamus, an egg-shaped cluster of nerve cells near the center of the brain.

In addition, surgeons sometimes can relieve pain by destroying nerve fibers or their parent cell bodies outside the brain or spinal cord. A case in point is the destruction of sympathetic nerves (a part of the autonomic nervous system) to relieve the severe pain that sometimes follows a penetrating wound from a sharp instrument or bullet.

When pain affects the upper extremities, or is widespread, the surgeon has fewer options and surgery may not be as effective. Still, skilled neurosurgeons have achieved excellent results with upper spinal cord or brain surgery to treat severe intractable pain. These procedures may employ chemicals or use heat or freezing treatments to destroy tissue, as well as the more traditional use of the scalpel.

Recently, Harvard Medical School surgeons reported success with a new brain operation called cingulotomy to relieve intractable pain in patients with severe psychiatric problems. The nerve fibers destroyed are part of a pathway important in emotions and motivation. The surgery appears to eliminate the discomfort and suffering the patient feels, but does not interfere with other mental faculties such as thinking and memory.

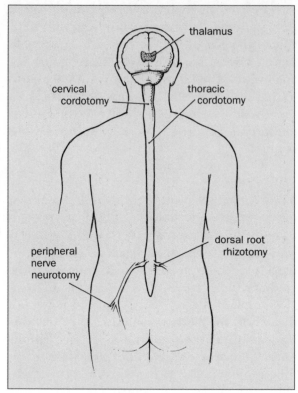

As a last resort for the relief of chronic pain, neurosurgeons can sever nerve fibers at various sites in the brain, along the spinal cord, or in peripheral nerves.

Prior to operating, physicians can often test the effectiveness of surgery by using anesthetic drugs to block nerves temporarily. In some chronic pain conditions—like the pain from a penetrating wound—these temporary blocks can in themselves be beneficial, promoting repair of nerve damage.

How do these current treatments apply to the more common chronic pain conditions? What follows is a brief survey of major pain disorders and the treatments most in use today.

THE MAJOR PAINS

Headache

Tension headache, involving continued contractions of head and neck muscles, is one of the most common forms of headache. The other common variety is the vascular headache involving changes in the pressure of blood vessels serving the head. Migraine headaches are of the vascular type, associated with throbbing pain on one side of the head. Genetic factors play a role in determining who will be a victim of migraine, but many other factors are important as well. A major difficulty in treating migraine headache is that changes occur throughout the course of the headache. Blood vessels may first constrict and then dilate. Changing levels of neurotransmitters have also been noted. While a number of drugs can relieve migraine pain, their usefulness often depends on when they are taken. Some are only effective if taken at the onset.

Drugs are also the most common treatment for tension headache, although attempts to use biofeedback to control muscle tension have had some success. Physical methods such as heat or cold applications often provide additional if only temporary relief.

Low Back Pain

The combination of aspirin, bed rest, and modest amounts of a muscle relaxant are usually prescribed for the first-time low back pain patient. At the initial examination, the physician will also note if the patient is overweight or works at an occupation such as truck-driving or a desk job that offers little opportunity for exercise.

Some authorities believe that low back pain is particularly prevalent in Western society because of the combination of overweight, bad posture (made worse if there is added weight up front), and infrequent exercise. Not surprisingly, then, when the patient begins to feel better, the suggestion is made to take off pounds and take on physical exercise. In some cases, a full neurological examination may be necessary, including an x-ray of the spinal cord called a myelogram, to see if there may be a ruptured disc or other source of pressure on the cord or nerve roots.

Sometimes x-rays will show a disc problem which can be helped by surgery. But neither the myelogram nor disc surgery is foolproof. Milder analgesics (aspirin or stronger non-narcotic medications) and electrical stimulation—using TENS or implanted brain electrodes—can be very effective. What is not effective is long-term use of the muscle-relaxant tranquilizers. Many specialists are convinced that chronic use of these drugs is detrimental to the back patient, adding to depression and increasing pain. Massage or manipulative therapy are used by some clinicians but, other than individual patient reports, their usefulness is still undocumented.

Cancer Pain

The pain of cancer can result from the pressure of a growing tumor or the infiltration of tumor cells into other organs. Or the pain can come about as the result of radiation or chemotherapy. These treatments can cause fluid accumulation and swelling (edema), irritate or destroy healthy tissue causing pain and inflammation, and possibly sensitize nerve endings.

Ideally, the treatment for cancer pain is to remove the cancerous tissue. When that is not possible, pain can be treated by any or all of the currently available therapies: electrical stimulation, psychological methods, surgery, and strong painkillers.

Arthritis Pain

Arthritis is a general descriptive term meaning an affliction of the joints. The two most common forms are osteoarthritis that typically affects the fingers and may spread to important weight-bearing joints in the spine or hips, and rheumatoid arthritis, an inflammatory joint disease associated with swelling, congestion, and thickening of the soft tissue around joints. Recently, a distinguished panel of pain experts commenting on arthritis reported that "in all probability aspirin remains the most widely used . . . and important drug

PERIPHERAL NEUROPATHY

Peripheral neuropathy (or neuritis) is a deterioration in the functioning of the nerves that carry messages between the central nervous system and the extremities. It is caused by damage or irritation to the myelin sheaths that protect most nerves, or damage to the axons themselves (the conducting fibers of the nerve). Most commonly, the disorder is brought on by chronic intoxications such as by alcohol, metabolic disorders such as diabetes mellitus, or in association with cancer, inflammatory disorders such as lupus, or by certain vitamin deficiencies. Quite often, even after thorough diagnostic evaluations, a specific cause cannot be found. Peripheral neuropathy can result in numbness, tingling, pain, the loss of muscle strength and reflexes, and muscle atrophy. Those with peripheral neuropathy may have a history of clumsiness or other vague sensations. Because the onset is usually gradual, people affected by peripheral neuropathy will often try to compensate by overusing other muscles; but, when the disorder is caused by an infection or chronic alcohol intoxication, the onset is usually rapid. If the cause of the disorder can be identified and eliminated before irreversible damage has been done to nerve cells, further progression of the neuropathy can be prevented. Once significant nerve damage has occurred, no specific therapeutic measures can repair the damage or eliminate the symptoms.

The Editors

. . . although it may cause serious side effects." In the 1950s, the steroid drugs were introduced and hailed as lifesavers—important anti-inflammatory agents modeled after the body's own chemicals produced in the adrenal glands. But the long-term use of steroids has serious consequences, among them the lowering of resistance to infection, hemorrhaging, and facial puffiness—producing the so-called "moon face."

Besides aspirin, current treatments for arthritis include several nonsteroid anti-inflammatory drugs (NSAIDs) like indomethacin and ibuprofen.

But these drugs, too, may have serious side effects. TENS and acupuncture have been tried with mixed results. In cases where tissue has been destroyed, surgery to replace a diseased joint with an artificial part has been very successful. The "total hip replacement" operation is an example.

Arthritis is best treated early, say the experts. A modest program of drugs combined with exercise can do much to restore full function and forestall long-term degenerative changes. Exercise in warm water is especially good since the water is both relaxing and provides buoyancy that makes exercises easier to perform. Physical treatments with warm or cold compresses are helpful sources of temporary pain relief.

Neurogenic Pain

The most difficult pains to treat are those that result from damage to the peripheral nerves or to the central nervous system itself. We have mentioned tic douloureux and shingles as examples of extraordinarily searing pain, along with several drugs that can help. In addition, tic sufferers can benefit from surgery to destroy the nerve cells that supply pain-sensation fibers to the face. "Thermocoagulation"—which uses heat supplied by an electrical current to destroy nerve cells—has the advantage that pain fibers are more sensitive to the treatment resulting in less destruction of other sensations (touch and temperature).

Sometimes specialists treating tic find that certain blood vessels in the brain lie near the group of nerve cells supplying sensory fibers to the face, exerting pressure that causes pain. The surgical insertion of a small sponge between the blood vessels and the nerve cells can relieve the pressure and eliminate pain.

Among other notoriously painful neurogenic disorders is pain from an amputated or paralyzed limb—so-called "phantom" pain—that affects up to 10 percent of amputees and paraplegia patients. Various combinations of antidepressants and weak narcotics like Darvon are sometimes effective. Surgery, too, is occasionally successful. Many experts now think that the electrical stimulating techniques hold the greatest promise for relieving these pains.

Psychogenic Pain

Some cases of pain are not due to past disease or injury, nor is there any detectable sign of damage inside or outside the nervous system. Such pain may benefit from any of the psychological pain therapies listed earlier. It is also possible that some new methods used to diagnose pain may be useful. One method gaining in popularity is thermography, which measures the temperature of surface tissue as a reflection of blood flow. A color-coded "thermogram" of a person with a headache or other painful condition often shows an altered blood supply to the painful area, appearing as a darker or lighter shade than the surrounding areas or the corresponding part on the other side of the body. Thus an abnormal thermogram in a patient who complains of pain in the absence of any other evidence may provide a valuable clue that can lead to a diagnosis and treatment.

WHERE TO GO FOR HELP

People with chronic pain have usually seen a family doctor and several other specialists as well. Eventually, they are referred to neurologists, orthopedists, or neurosurgeons. The patient/doctor relationship is extremely important in dealing with chronic pain. Both patients and family members should seek out knowledgeable specialists who neither dismiss nor indulge the patient; physicians who understand full well how pain has come to dominate the patient's life and the lives of everyone else in the family.

Many specialists today refer chronic pain patients to pain clinics for treatment. Over 800 such clinics have opened their doors in the United States since a world leader in pain therapy established a pain clinic at the University of Washington in Seattle in 1960.

Pain clinics differ in their approaches. Generally speaking, clinics employ a group of specialists who review each patient's medical history and conduct further tests when necessary. If the applicant is admitted, the clinic staff designs a personal treatment program that may include individual and group psychotherapy, exercise, diet, ice massage for pain (especially before bedtime), electrical stimulation techniques, and the use of a variety of analgesic but nonnarcotic drugs. The aim is to reduce pain medication and so improve the patient's pain problem that, when he or she leaves the hospital, it is with the prospect of resuming more normal activities with a minimal requirement for analgesics and a positive self-image.

Contrary to what many people think, pain clinic patients are not malingerers or hypochondriacs. They are men and women of all ages, education, and social background, suffering a wide variety of painful conditions. Patients with low back pain are frequent, and so are people with the complications of diabetes, stroke, brain trauma, headache, arthritis, or any of the rarer pain conditions. The majority of patients participate for two or three weeks and usually report substantial improvement at discharge. One young man who had suffered painful chest injury as a result of a factory accident said he literally "felt taller" after his pain clinic experience. Follow-up at three- and six-month intervals, and at lengthier intervals thereafter, is an essential part of the program, both to evaluate the long-term effectiveness of treatment and to initiate a further course of treatment or counseling if necessary.

The National Institute of Neurological Disorders and Stroke

HEADACHE

An estimated 40 million Americans experience chronic headaches. For at least half of these people, the problem is severe and sometimes disabling. It can also be costly: headache sufferers make over 8 million visits a year to doctors' offices. Migraine victims alone lose over 64 million workdays because of headache pain.

WHY DOES IT HURT?

What hurts when you have a headache? Several areas of the head can hurt, including a network of nerves which extends over the scalp and certain nerves in the face, mouth, and throat. Also sensitive to pain, because they contain delicate nerve fibers, are the muscles of the head and blood vessels found along the surface and at the base of the brain.

The bones of the skull and tissues of the brain itself, however, never hurt, because they lack pain-sensitive nerve fibers.

The ends of these pain-sensitive nerves, called nociceptors, can be stimulated by stress, muscular tension, dilated blood vessels, and other triggers of headache. Once stimulated, a nociceptor sends a message up the length of the nerve fiber to the nerve cells in the brain, signaling that a part of the body hurts. The message is determined by the location of the nociceptor. A person who suddenly realizes "My toe hurts," is responding to nociceptors in the foot that have been stimulated by the stubbing of a toe.

A number of chemicals help transmit pain-related information to the brain. Some of these chemicals are natural painkilling proteins called endorphins, Greek for "the morphine within." One theory suggests that people who suffer from severe headache and other types of chronic pain have lower levels of endorphins than people who are generally pain free.

WHEN TO SEE A PHYSICIAN

Not all headaches require medical attention. Some result from missed meals or occasional muscle tension and are easily remedied. But some types of headache are signals of more serious disorders such as head injury and call for prompt medical care. These include:

- Sudden, severe headache
- Headache associated with convulsions
- Headache accompanied by confusion or loss of consciousness
- Headache following a blow on the head
- Headache associated with pain in the eye or ear
- Persistent headache in a person who was previously headache free
- Headache associated with fever
- Headache which interferes with normal life

A headache sufferer usually seeks help from a family practitioner. If the problem is not relieved by standard treatments, the patient may then be referred to a specialist— perhaps an internist or a neurologist. Additional referrals may be made to psychologists.

DIAGNOSING A HEADACHE

Diagnosing a headache is like playing Twenty Questions. Experts agree that a detailed question-and-answer session with a patient can often produce enough information for a diagnosis. Many types of headaches have clear-cut symptoms which fall into an easily recognizable pattern.

Patients may be asked: How often do you have headaches? Where is the pain? How long do the headaches last? When did you first develop headaches?

The patient's sleep habits and family and work situations may also be probed.

Most physicians will also obtain a full medical history from the patient, inquiring about past head trauma or surgery and about the use of medications.

A blood test may be ordered to screen for thyroid disease, anemia, or infections which might cause a headache.

X-rays may be taken to rule out the possibility of a brain tumor or blood clot.

A test called an electroencephalogram (EEG) may be given to measure brain activity. EEGs can indicate a malfunction in the brain, but they cannot usually pinpoint a problem that might be causing a headache.

A physician may suggest that a patient with unusual headaches undergo a computed tomography (CT) scan. The CT scan produces images of the brain that show variations in the density of different types of tissue. The scan enables the physician to distinguish, for example, between a bleeding blood vessel in the brain and a brain tumor. The CT scan is an important diagnostic tool in cases of headache associated with brain lesions or other serious disease. Experts generally agree, however, that this sophisticated and expensive technology is not required to diagnose simple or periodic headache.

An eye exam is usually performed to check for weakness in the eye muscle or unequal pupil size. Both of these symptoms are evidence of an aneurysm—an abnormal ballooning of a blood vessel. A physician who suspects that a headache patient has an aneurysm may also order an angiogram. In this test, a special fluid which can be seen on an x-ray is injected into the patient and carried in the bloodstream to the brain to reveal any abnormalities in the blood vessels there.

Thermography, an experimental technique for diagnosing headache, promises to become a useful clinical tool. In thermography, an infrared camera converts skin temperature into a color picture or thermogram with different degrees of heat appearing as different colors. Skin temperature is affected primarily by blood flow. Research scientists have found that thermograms of headache patients show strikingly different heat patterns from those of people who never or rarely get headaches.

A physician analyzes the results of all these diagnostic tests along with a patient's medical history in order to arrive at a diagnosis.

Headaches are diagnosed as:

- Vascular
- Muscle contraction
- Traction
- Inflammatory

Vascular headaches—a group that includes the well-known migraine—are so named because they are thought to involve abnormal function of the brain's blood vessels or vascular system. Muscle-contraction headaches appear to involve the tightening or tensing of facial and neck muscles. Traction and inflammatory headaches are symptoms of other disorders, ranging from stroke to sinus infection. Some people have more than one type of headache.

MIGRAINE HEADACHES

The most common type of vascular headache is migraine. Migraine headaches are usually characterized by severe pain on one or both sides of the head, an upset stomach, and at times disturbed vision.

Symptoms of Migraine

Sensitivity to light is a standard symptom of the two most prevalent types of migraine-caused headache: classic and common. The major difference between the two types is the appearance of neurological symptoms 10 to 30 minutes before a classic migraine attack. These symptoms are called an aura. The person may see flashing lights or zigzag lines, or may temporarily lose vision. Other classic symptoms include speech difficulty, weakness of an arm or leg, tingling of the face or hands, and confusion.

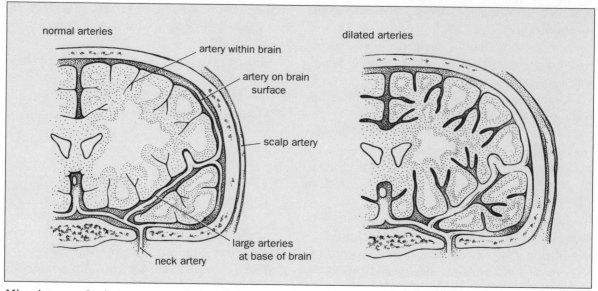

Migraines may begin as a spasm in arteries at the base of the brain, reducing its blood supply. The brain's arteries then dilate to meet its energy needs—but this triggers a release of pain-causing chemicals.

The pain of a classic migraine headache is described as intense, throbbing, or pounding and is felt in the forehead, temple, ear, jaw, or around the eye. Classic migraine starts on one side of the head but may eventually spread to the other side. An attack lasts one to two pain-wracked days.

The common migraine—a term that reflects the disorder's greater occurrence in the general population—is not preceded by an aura. But some people experience a variety of vague symptoms beforehand, including mental fuzziness, mood changes, fatigue, and unusual retention of fluids. During the headache phase of a common migraine, a person may have diarrhea and increased urination, as well as nausea and vomiting. Common migraine pain can last three or four days.

Both classic and common migraine can strike as often as several times a week, or as rarely as once every few years.

Both types can occur at any time. Some people, however, experience migraines at predictable times—near the days of menstruation or every Saturday morning after a stressful week of work.

The Migraine Process

Research scientists are unclear about the precise cause of migraine headaches. There seems to be general agreement, however, that a key element is blood flow changes in the brain. People who get migraine headaches appear to have blood vessels that overreact to various triggers.

Scientists have devised one theory of migraine which explains these blood flow changes and also certain biochemical changes that may be involved in the headache process. According to this theory, the nervous system responds to a trigger such as stress by creating a spasm in the nerve-rich arteries at the base of the brain. The spasm closes down or constricts several arteries supplying blood to the brain, including the scalp artery and the carotid or neck arteries.

As these arteries constrict, the flow of blood to the brain is reduced. At the same time, blood-clotting particles called platelets clump together—a process which is believed to release a chemical called serotonin. Serotonin acts as a powerful constrictor of arteries, further reducing the blood supply to the brain.

Reduced blood flow decreases the brain's supply of oxygen. Symptoms signaling a headache, such as distorted vision or speech, may then result, similar to symptoms of stroke.

Reacting to the reduced oxygen supply, certain arteries within the brain open wider to meet the brain's energy needs. This widening or dilation spreads, finally affecting the neck and scalp arteries. The dilation of these arteries triggers the release of pain-producing substances called prostaglandins from various tissues and blood cells. Chemicals which cause inflammation and swelling, and substances which increase sensitivity to pain are also released. The circulation of these chemicals and the dilation of the scalp arteries stimulate the pain-sensitive nociceptors. The result, according to this theory: a throbbing pain in the head.

Women and Migraine

Although boys and girls seem to be equally affected by migraine, the condition is more common in adult women than in men. Both sexes may develop migraine in infancy, but most often the disorder begins between the ages of five and 35.

The relationship between female hormones and migraine is still unclear. Women may have "menstrual migraine"—headaches around the time of their menstrual period—which may disappear during pregnancy. Other women develop migraine for the first time when they are pregnant. Some are first affected after menopause.

The effect of oral contraceptives on headaches is perplexing. Scientists report that some migrainous women who take birth control pills experience more frequent and severe attacks. However, a small percentage of women have fewer and less severe migraine headaches when they take birth control pills. And normal women who do not suffer from headaches may develop migraines as a side effect when they use oral contraceptives. Investigators around the world are studying hormonal changes in migrainous women in the hope of identifying the specific ways these naturally occurring chemicals cause headaches.

Triggers of Headache

The existence of a migraine personality is a controversial theory which suggests that migraine patients are compulsive, rigid, and perfectionistic. Most scientists believe, however, that not all migraine patients have these traits and that not all individuals with these personality characteristics have migraine.

Rather than focusing on character traits, says one headache specialist, it would be better to view people who get migraines as having an inherited abnormality in the regulation of blood vessels. Many sufferers have a family history of migraine, but the exact hereditary nature of this condition is still unknown.

"It's like a cocked gun with a hair trigger," explains the headache specialist. "A person is born with a potential for migraine and the headache is triggered by things that are really not so terrible."

These triggers include stress and other normal emotions, as well as biological and environmental conditions. Fatigue, glaring or flickering lights, the weather, and even certain foods can set off migraine. It may seem hard to believe that eating such seemingly harmless foods as yogurt, nuts, and lima beans can result in a painful migraine headache. However, some scientists believe that these foods and several others contain chemical substances such as tyramine which constrict arteries—the first step of the migraine process. Other scientists believe that foods cause headaches by setting off an allergic reaction in susceptible people.

While a food-triggered migraine usually occurs soon after eating, other triggers may not cause immediate pain. Scientists report that people can develop migraine not only during a period of stress but also afterwards when their vascular systems are still reacting.

The "Preacher Monday-Morning Headache" is named for those clergymen who get migraines a day after the stress of delivering a Sunday sermon. Migraines that wake people up in the middle of the night are also believed to result from a delayed reaction to stress.

Other Forms of Migraine

In addition to classic and common, migraine headache can take several other forms.

Hemiplegic migraine patients have temporary paralysis on one side of the body, a condition known as hemiplegia. Some people may experience vision problems and vertigo—a feeling that the world is spinning. These symptoms begin 10 to 90 minutes before the onset of headache pain.

Ophthalmoplegic migraine is characterized by pain around the eye and is associated with a droopy eyelid, double vision, and other sight problems.

Basilar artery migraine involves a disturbance of a major brain artery. Preheadache symptoms include vertigo, double vision, and poor muscular coordination. This type of migraine occurs primarily in adolescent and young adult women and is often associated with the menstrual cycle.

Benign exertional headache is brought on by running, lifting, coughing, sneezing, or bending. The headache begins at the onset of activity, and pain rarely lasts more than several minutes.

Status migrainosus is a rare and severe type of migraine that can last 72 hours or longer. The pain and nausea are so intense that people who have this type of headache must be hospitalized. The use of certain drugs can trigger status migrainosus. Neurologists report that many of their status migrainosus patients were depressed and anxious before they experienced headache attacks.

Headache-free migraine is characterized by such migraine symptoms as visual problems, nausea, vomiting, constipation, or diarrhea. Patients, however, do not experience head pain. Headache specialists have suggested that unexplained pain in a particular part of the body, fever, and dizziness could also be possible types of headache-free migraine.

Treating Migraine Headache

During the Stone Age, pieces of a headache sufferer's skull were cut away with flint instruments to relieve pain. Another unpleasant remedy used in the British Isles around the ninth century involved drinking "the juice of elderseed, cow's brain, and goat's dung dissolved in vinegar." Fortunately, today's headache patients are spared such drastic measures.

Drug therapy, biofeedback training, stress reduction, and elimination of certain foods from the diet are the most common methods of preventing and controlling migraine and other vascular headaches. Regular exercise, such as swimming or vigorous walking, can also reduce the frequency and severity of migraine headaches.

During a migraine headache, temporary relief can sometimes be obtained by using cold packs or by pressing on the bulging artery found in front of the ear on the painful side of the head.

Drug therapy. There are two ways to approach the treatment of migraine headache with drugs: prevent the attacks, or relieve symptoms after the headache occurs.

For infrequent migraine, drugs can be taken at the first sign of a headache in order to stop it or to at least ease the pain. People who get occasional mild migraine may benefit by taking aspirin or acetaminophen at the start of an attack. Aspirin raises a person's tolerance to pain and also discourages clumping of blood platelets. Small amounts of caffeine may be useful if taken in the early stages of migraine. But for most migraine sufferers who get moderate to severe headaches, and for all cluster patients, stronger drugs may be necessary to control the pain.

One of the most commonly used drugs for the relief of classic and common migraine symptoms is ergotamine tartrate, a vasoconstrictor which helps counteract the painful dilation stage of the headache. For optimal benefit, the drug is taken during the early stages of an attack.

If a migraine has been in progress for about an hour and has passed into the final throbbing stage, ergotamine tartrate will probably not help.

Because ergotamine tartrate can cause nausea and vomiting, it may be combined with antinausea drugs. Research scientists caution that ergotamine tartrate should not be taken in excess or by people who have angina pectoris, severe hypertension, or vascular, liver, or kidney disease. Patients who are unable to take ergotamine tartrate may benefit from other drugs that constrict dilated blood vessels or help reduce blood vessel inflammation.

For headaches that occur three or more times a month, preventive treatment is usually recommended. Drugs used to prevent classic and common migraine include methysergide maleate, which counteracts blood vessel constriction, propranolol, which stops blood vessel dilation, and amitriptyline, an antidepressant.

In a study of propranolol, amitriptyline, and biofeedback conducted by the Houston Headache Clinic, scientists found that migraine patients improved most on a combination of propranolol and biofeedback. Patients who had mixed migraine and muscle-contraction headaches received the greatest benefit from a combination of propranolol, amitriptyline, and biofeedback.

Another recent study showed that propranolol may continue to prevent migraine headaches even after patients have stopped taking the drug. The scientists who conducted the study speculate that long-term therapy with propranolol may have a lasting effect on blood vessels, training them to react less than usual to the triggers of migraine.

Antidepressants called MAO inhibitors also prevent migraine. These drugs block an enzyme called monoamine oxidase which normally helps nerve cells absorb the artery-constricting chemical, serotonin.

MAO inhibitors can have potentially serious side effects—particularly if taken while ingesting foods or beverages that contain tyramine, a substance that closes down arteries.

Several new drugs for the prevention of migraine have been developed in recent years, including papaverine hydrochloride, which produces blood vessel dilation, and cyproheptadine, which counteracts serotonin.

All these antimigraine drugs can have adverse side effects. But they are relatively safe when used carefully. To avoid long-term side effects of preventive medications, headache specialists advise patients to reduce the dosage of these drugs and then to stop taking them as soon as possible.

Biofeedback and relaxation training. Drug therapy for migraine is often combined with biofeedback and relaxation training. Biofeedback is a space-age word for a technique that can give people better control over such body function indicators as blood pressure, heart rate, temperature, muscle tension, and brain waves. Thermal biofeedback allows a patient to consciously raise hand temperature. Some patients who are able to increase hand temperature can reduce the number and intensity of migraines. The mechanism of this hand-warming effect is being studied by research scientists.

"To succeed in biofeedback," says a headache specialist, "you must be able to concentrate and you must be motivated to get well."

A patient learning thermal biofeedback wears a device which transmits the temperature of an index finger or hand to a monitor.

While the patient tries to warm his hands, the monitor provides feedback either on a gauge that shows the temperature reading or by emitting a sound or beep that increases in intensity as the temperature increases. The patient is not told how to raise hand temperature, but is given suggestions such as, "Imagine that your hands feel very warm and heavy." "I have a good imagination," says one headache sufferer who traded in her medication for thermal biofeedback. The technique decreased the number and severity of headaches she experienced.

In another type of biofeedback called electromyographic or EMG training, the patient learns to control muscle tension in the face, neck, and shoulders.

Either kind of biofeedback may be combined with relaxation training, during which patients learn to relax the mind and body.

Biofeedback can be practiced at home with a portable monitor. But the ultimate goal of treatment is to wean the patient from the machine. The patient can then use biofeedback anywhere at the first sign of a headache.

The antimigraine diet. Scientists estimate that a small percentage of migraine sufferers will benefit from a treatment program focused solely on eliminating headache-provoking foods and beverages.

Other migraine patients may be helped by a diet to prevent low blood sugar. Low blood sugar, or hypoglycemia, can cause dilation of the blood vessels in the head. This condition can occur after a period without food: overnight, for example, or when a meal is skipped. People who wake up in the morning with a headache may be reacting to the low blood sugar caused by the lack of food overnight.

Treatment for headaches caused by low blood sugar consists of scheduling smaller, more frequent meals for the patient. A special diet designed to stabilize the body's sugar-regulating system is sometimes recommended.

For the same reason, many specialists also recommend that migraine patients avoid oversleeping on weekends. Sleeping late can change the body's normal blood sugar level and lead to a headache.

OTHER VASCULAR HEADACHES

After migraine, the most common type of vascular headache is the toxic headache produced by fever. Pneumonia, measles, mumps, and tonsillitis are among the diseases that can cause severe toxic vascular headaches. Toxic headaches can also result from the presence of foreign chemicals in the body. Other kinds of vascular headaches include "clusters," which cause repeated episodes of intense pain, and headaches resulting from a rise in blood pressure.

Chemical Culprits

Repeated exposure to nitrite compounds can result in a dull, pounding headache that may be accompanied by a flushed face. Nitrite, which dilates blood vessels, is found in such products as heart medicine and dynamite. Hot dogs and other meats containing sodium nitrite can also cause headaches.

"Chinese restaurant headache" can occur when a susceptible individual eats foods prepared with monosodium glutamate (MSG)—a staple in many Oriental kitchens. Soy sauce, meat tenderizer, and a variety of packaged foods contain this chemical which is touted as a flavor enhancer.

Vascular headache can also result from exposure to poisons, even common household varieties like insecticides, carbon tetrachloride, and lead. Anyone who has contact with lead batteries or lead-glazed pottery may develop headaches.

Painters, printmakers, and other artists may experience headaches after exposure to art materials that contain chemicals called solvents. Solvents, like benzene, are found in turpentine, spray adhesives, rubber cement, and inks.

Drugs such as amphetamines can cause headaches as a side effect. Another type of drug-related headache occurs during withdrawal from long-term therapy with the antimigraine drug ergotamine tartrate.

Jokes are often made about alcohol hangovers but the headache associated with "the morning after" is no laughing matter. Fortunately, there are several suggested remedies for the pain, including ergotamine tartrate. The hangover headache may also be reduced by taking honey, which speeds alcohol metabolism, or caffeine, a constrictor of dilated arteries. Caffeine, however, can cause headaches as well as cure them. Heavy coffee drinkers often get headaches when they try to break the caffeine habit.

Cluster Headaches

Cluster headaches, named for their repeated occurrence in groups or clusters, begin as a minor pain around one eye, eventually spreading to that side of the face. The pain quickly intensifies, compelling the victim to pace the floor or rock in a chair. "You can't lie down, you're fidgety," explains a cluster patient. "The pain is unbearable." Other symptoms include a stuffed and runny nose and a droopy eyelid over a red and tearing eye.

Cluster headaches last between 30 and 45 minutes. But the relief people feel at the end of an attack is usually mixed with dread as they await a recurrence. Clusters can strike several times a day or night for several weeks or months. Then, mysteriously, they may disappear for months or years. Many people have cluster bouts during the spring and fall. At their worst, chronic cluster headaches can last continuously for years.

Cluster attacks can strike at any age but usually start between the ages of 20 and 40. Unlike migraine, cluster headaches are more common in men and do not run in families. Research scientists have observed certain physical similarities among people who experience cluster headache. The typical cluster patient is a tall, muscular man with a rugged facial appearance and a square, jutting, or dimpled chin. The texture of his coarse skin resembles an orange peel. Women who get clusters may also have this type of skin.

Studies of cluster patients show that they are likely to have hazel eyes and that they tend to be heavy smokers and drinkers. Paradoxically, both nicotine, which constricts arteries, and alcohol, which dilates them, trigger cluster headaches. The exact connection between these substances and cluster attacks is not known.

Despite a cluster headache's distinguishing characteristics, its relative infrequency and similarity to such disorders as sinusitis can lead to misdiagnosis. Some cluster patients have had tooth extractions, sinus surgery, or psychiatric treatment in a futile effort to cure their pain.

Research studies have turned up several clues as to the cause of cluster headache, but no answers. One clue is found in the thermograms of untreated cluster patients, which show a "cold spot" of reduced blood flow above the eye.

The sudden start and brief duration of cluster headaches can make them difficult to treat. By the time medicine is absorbed into the body, the attack is often over. However, research scientists have identified several effective drugs for these headaches. The antimigraine drug ergotamine tartrate can subdue a cluster, if taken at the first sign of an attack. Injections of dihydroergotamine, a form of ergotamine tartrate, are sometimes used to treat clusters.

Some cluster patients can prevent attacks by taking propranolol or methysergide. Investigators have also discovered that mild solutions of cocaine hydrochloride applied inside the nose can quickly stop cluster headaches in most patients. This treatment may work because it both blocks pain impulses and it constricts blood vessels.

Another option that works for some cluster patients is rapid inhalation of pure oxygen through a mask for 5 to 15 minutes. The oxygen seems to ease the pain of cluster headache by reducing blood flow to the brain.

In chronic cases of cluster headache, certain facial nerves may be surgically cut or destroyed to provide relief. These procedures have had limited success. Some cluster patients have had facial nerves cut only to have them regenerate years later.

Painful Pressure

Chronic high blood pressure can cause headache, as can rapid rises in blood pressure like those experienced during anger, vigorous exercise, or sexual excitement.

The severe "orgasmic headache" occurs right before orgasm and is believed to be a vascular type. Since sudden rupture of a cerebral blood vessel can also occur during orgasm, this type of headache should be promptly evaluated by a doctor.

MUSCLE-CONTRACTION HEADACHES

It's 5:00 p.m. and your boss has just asked you to prepare a 20-page briefing paper. Due date: tomorrow. You're angry and tired and the more you think about the assignment, the tenser you become. Your teeth clench, your brow wrinkles, and soon you have a splitting tension headache.

Tension headache is named not only for the role of stress in triggering the pain, but also for the contraction of neck, face, and scalp muscles brought on by stressful events. Tension headache is a severe but temporary form of muscle-contraction headache. The pain is mild to moderate and feels like pressure is being applied to the head or neck. The headache usually disappears after the period of stress is over.

Chronic muscle-contraction headaches, by contrast, can last for weeks, months, and sometimes years. The pain of these headaches is often described as a tight band around the head or a feeling that the head and neck are in a cast. "It feels like somebody is tightening a giant vise around my head," says one patient. The pain is steady, and is usually felt on both sides of the head. Chronic muscle-contraction headaches can cause a sore scalp—even combing one's hair can be painful.

Causes

Many scientists believe that the primary cause of the pain of muscle-contraction headache is sustained muscle tension. Other studies suggest that restricted blood flow may cause or contribute to the pain.

Occasionally, muscle-contraction headaches will be accompanied by nausea, vomiting, and blurred vision, but there is no preheadache syndrome as with migraine. Muscle-contraction headaches have not been linked to hormones or foods, as has migraine, nor is there a strong hereditary connection.

Research has shown that for many people, chronic muscle-contraction headaches are caused by depression and anxiety. These people tend to get their headaches in the early morning or evening when conflicts in the office or home are anticipated.

Emotional factors are not the only triggers of muscle-contraction headaches. Certain physical postures—such as holding one's chin down while reading—can lead to head and neck pain. Tensing head and neck muscles during sexual excitement can also cause headache. So can prolonged writing under poor light, or holding a phone between the shoulder and ear, or even gum-chewing.

More serious problems that can cause muscle-contraction headaches include degenerative arthritis of the neck and temporomandibular joint dysfunction, or TMJ. TMJ is a disorder of the joint between the temporal bone (above the ear) and the mandible or lower jaw bone. The disorder results from poor bite and jaw clenching.

Treatment

Treatment for muscle-contraction headache varies. The first consideration is to treat any specific disorder or disease that may be causing the headache. For example, arthritis of the neck is treated with anti-inflammatory medication and temporomandibular joint dysfunction may be helped by corrective devices for the mouth and jaw.

Acute tension headaches not associated with a disease are treated with muscle relaxants and analgesics like aspirin and acetaminophen. Stronger analgesics, such as propoxyphene and codeine, are sometimes prescribed. As prolonged use of these drugs can lead to dependence, patients taking them should have periodic medical checkups and follow their physicians' instructions carefully.

Nondrug therapy for chronic muscle-contraction headaches includes biofeedback, relaxation training, and counseling. A technique called "cognitive restructuring" teaches people to change their attitudes and responses to stress. Patients might be encouraged, for example, to imagine that they are coping successfully with a stressful situation. In "progressive relaxation therapy," patients are taught to first tense and then relax individual muscle groups. Finally, the patient tries to relax his or her whole body. Many people imagine a peaceful scene—such as lying on the beach or by a beautiful lake. "Passive relaxation" does not involve tensing of muscles. Instead, patients are encouraged to focus on different muscles, suggesting that they relax. Some people might think to themselves, "Relax" or "My muscles feel warm."

People with chronic muscle-contraction headaches may also be helped by taking antidepressants or MAO inhibitors. Mixed muscle-contraction and migraine headaches are sometimes treated with barbiturate compounds, which slow down nerve function in the brain and spinal cord.

People who suffer infrequent muscle-con-traction headaches may benefit from a hot shower or moist heat applied to the back of the neck. Cervical collars are sometimes recommended as an aid to good posture. Physical therapy, massage, and gentle exercise of the neck may also be helpful.

WHEN HEADACHE IS A WARNING

Like other types of pain, headaches can serve as warning signals of more serious disorders. This is particularly true for headaches caused by traction or inflammation.

Traction headaches can occur if pain-sensitive parts of the head are pulled, stretched, or displaced, as, for example, when eye muscles are tensed in order to compensate for eyestrain.

Headaches caused by inflammation include those related to meningitis as well as those resulting from diseases of the sinuses, spine, neck, ears, and teeth. Ear and tooth infections and glaucoma can cause headaches. In oral and dental disorders, headache is experienced as pain throughout the entire head, including the face.

Traction and inflammatory headaches are treated by curing the underlying problem. This may involve surgery, antibiotics, or other drugs.

Characteristics of the various types of traction and inflammatory headaches vary by the disorder.

Brain Tumor

Brain tumors are diagnosed in about 11,000 people every year. As they grow, these tumors sometimes cause headache by pushing on the outer layer of nerve tissue that covers the brain or by pressing against pain-sensitive blood vessel walls. Headache resulting from a brain tumor may be periodic or continuous. Typically, it feels like a strong pressure is being applied to the head. The pain is relieved when the tumor is destroyed by surgery, radiation, or chemotherapy.

Stroke

Headache may accompany several conditions that can lead to stroke, including hypertension or high blood pressure, arteriosclerosis, and heart disease. Headaches are also associated with completed stroke, the latter occurs when brain cells die from lack of sufficient oxygen.

Many stroke-related headaches can be prevented by careful management of the patient's condition through diet, exercise, and medication.

Mild to moderate headaches are associated with so-called "little strokes," or transient ischemic attacks (TIAs), which result from a temporary lack of blood supply to the brain. The head pain occurs near the clot or lesion that blocks blood flow.

The similarity between migraine and symptoms of TIA can cause problems in diagnosis. The rare person under age 40 who suffers a TIA may be misdiagnosed as having migraine; similarly, TIA-prone older patients who suffer migraine may be misdiagnosed as having stroke-related headaches.

Spinal Tap

About one-fourth of the people who undergo a lumbar puncture or spinal tap develop a headache. Many scientists believe these headaches result from leakage of the cerebrospinal fluid that flows through pain-sensitive membranes around the brain and down to the spinal cord. The fluid, they suggest, drains through the tiny hole created by the spinal tap needle, causing the membranes to rub painfully against the bony skull. Since headache pain occurs only when the patient stands up, the "cure" is to remain lying down until the headache runs its course—anywhere from a few hours to several days.

Head Trauma

Headaches may develop after a blow to the head, either immediately or months later.

There is little relationship between the severity of the trauma and the intensity of headache pain. One cause of trauma headache is scar formation in the scalp. Another is ruptured blood vessels which result in an accumulation of blood called a hematoma. This mass of blood can displace brain tissue and cause headaches as well as weakness, confusion, memory loss, and seizures. Hematomas can be drained in order to produce rapid relief of symptoms.

Arteritis and Meningitis

Arteritis, an inflammation of certain arteries in the head, primarily affects people over age 50. Symptoms include throbbing headache, fever, and loss of appetite. Some patients experience blurring or loss of vision. Prompt treatment with corticosteroid drugs helps to relieve symptoms.

Headaches are also caused by infections of meninges, the brain's outer covering, and phlebitis, a vein inflammation.

Tic Douloureux

Tic douloureux, or trigeminal neuralgia, results from a disorder of the trigeminal nerve. This nerve supplies the face, teeth, mouth, and nasal cavity with feeling and also enables the mouth muscles to chew. Symptoms are headache and intense facial pain that comes in short, excruciating jabs set off by the slightest touch to or movement of trigger points in the face or mouth. People with tic douloureux often fear brushing their teeth or chewing on the side of the mouth that is affected. Many tic douloureux patients are controlled with drugs, including carbamazepine. Patients who do not respond to drugs may be helped by surgery on the trigeminal nerve.

Sinus Infection

In a condition called acute sinusitis, a viral or bacterial infection of the upper respiratory tract spreads to the membrane which lines the sinus cavities. When one or all four of these

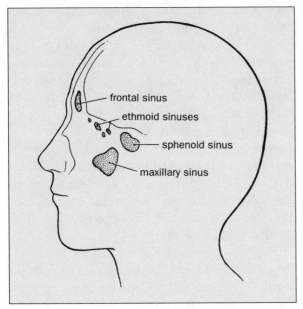

Acute sinusitis headaches can occur when one or more of the four sinus cavities fill with fluid resulting from bacterial or viral infections.

cavities are filled with bacterial or viral fluid, they become inflamed, causing pain and sometimes headache. Treatment of acute sinusitis includes antibiotics, analgesics, and decongestants.

Chronic sinusitis may be caused by an allergy to such irritants as dust, ragweed, animal hair, and smoke. Research scientists disagree about whether chronic sinusitis triggers headache.

RESEARCH INTERVENES

Modern methods of diagnosis and treatment enable physicians and psychologists today to help about 90 percent of chronic headache patients, according to the director of a major U.S. headache clinic.

These methods are based on years of scientific research. New research should lead to even more advanced techniques of headache management.

The National Institute of Neurological Disorders and Stroke

BRAIN TUMORS

The brain is a special organ, special in the cells that compose it, in its position in the head, and in its relation to the rest of the body. When a tumor grows in the brain, doctors have to consider not only the nature of the tumor, but its relation to the brain's distinctive features.

THE NATURE OF THE BRAIN

First and foremost among those features is that the brain is the organ of thought, emotion, and behavior. The idea that a mass of abnormal tissue could encroach on that domain, undermining the mental faculties that make us human and ultimately threatening life itself, is what terrifies most people when they hear the words "brain tumor." Yet some brain tumors can be removed completely at surgery leaving no neurological damage. Even advanced cancers growing deep inside the brain are being tackled today by new treatments that have saved or at least prolonged lives, while preserving the integrity of those lives.

Experts can also point to other features of the brain that offer some reason for hope. Tumors are generally classified as benign—if the tumor cells look much like ordinary cells and the tumor is confined to one place—or malignant, if the tumor cells look very disordered and the tumor can spread (metastasize) to other parts of the body. (Strictly speaking, the word "cancer" applies only to malignant growths.)

Tumors that originate in the brain—primary brain tumors—may be either benign or malignant. Surprisingly, while malignant brain tumor cells can spread throughout the brain, only rarely do they spread to other parts of the body. That means that once you destroy a brain cancer, you need not worry that some cells may have escaped to seed tumors elsewhere in the body.

Another fact that startles many people is that brain tumor tissue almost never consists of the fundamental working cells of the brain—the nerve cells (neurons). Once mature, these nerve cells no longer divide and multiply. Instead, it is the surrounding and supporting cells of the brain that occasionally get out of control. Thus a brain tumor that is diagnosed and treated early may do little or no damage to essential brain matter—the neurons and their circuits that underlie every act of mental life and behavior.

CONFUSING SYMPTOMS

There are "ifs." Brain tumors are not always easy to diagnose. The symptoms can vary widely according to the brain area affected. If a tumor grows in the temporal lobe on the left side of the brain, for example, it may affect speech and memory, or alter mood and emotional state. Such symptoms might suggest mental illness or psychological problems, rather than a brain tumor. If a tumor lies near the cerebellum, an area at the back of the brain important in the control of movement, there may be early symptoms of dizziness and lack of coordination. Tumors growing on or around the major nerves supplying the ears or eyes may lead to symptoms of hearing loss, headaches, or visual problems, thus diverting attention from the brain as the source of trouble.

On the other hand, some brain tumors may produce few symptoms. Parts of the frontal lobes, for example, are presumed to play a role in thinking and other higher mental activities. Yet tumors can sometimes cause considerable tissue damage in these areas with little effect on a person's behavior.

Once a tumor is found, still another "if" centers on its location in relation to surrounding tissue. The brain is one of the most protected organs in the body. It is wrapped in the tough outer coverings of the meninges, bathed in shock-absorbing and nutrient liquid—the cerebrospinal fluid—and armored by the strong bones of the skull.

If a tumor lies near the skull bones or close to major blood vessels or channels circulating cerebrospinal fluid, it need not grow very large before it blocks blood or cerebrospinal fluid circulation and causes increased pressure inside the skull. Or, if the tumor is discovered deep inside the brain, surgery to remove it may be risky, with too great a chance of damaging vital brain centers. Ironically, the distinction between benign and malignant blurs in such cases. If a benign tumor is inaccessible, it can be fatal.

Neurosurgeons who treat brain tumor patients are well aware of the ironies of the condition. They can all tell stories of exceptional survivals as well as tragic deaths. Scientists who have made research on brain tumors their specialty are particularly concerned that the public understand the complex problems posed by brain tumors as well as the growing efforts to solve those problems.

WHO DEVELOPS A BRAIN TUMOR

The chances of developing a primary malignant brain tumor are relatively rare—about one in 22,000. Such cancers account for less than 2 percent of all cancers diagnosed in the United States every year. That is still an impressively large number—11,000 brain cancers annually.

At least twice as many patients have secondary brain cancers, the result of cancer metastasizing to the brain from other sites in the body, principally from the breast, lung, or kidney.

Brain tumors affect children as well as adults. Indeed, primary tumors of the brain or spinal cord (the central nervous system) are the most common tumors of childhood after the leukemias. The peak for brain tumors in children is between the ages of six and nine. Childhood brain tumors generally differ in location and cellular makeup from

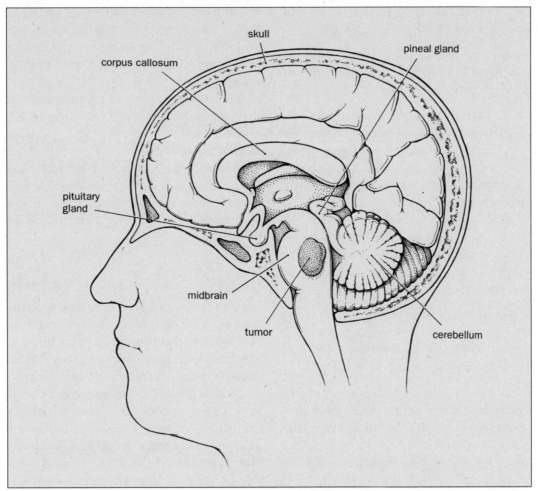

Surgery to remove this tumor in the midbrain would be a risky procedure, since the tumor is surrounded by vital brain centers. A tumor located nearer to the skull, however, might be removed with little noticeable damage to brain function.

adult tumors, differences thought to reflect a still growing and developing nervous system. Adult brain tumors are most common between the ages of 40 and 60, with men affected slightly more than women.

Why primary brain tumors occur remains a mystery. Tumor sleuths have considered the vast array of environmental and genetic factors that have been linked to cancers in other parts of the body, but in the case of brain tumors there are no clear-cut associations. The recent finding of a slightly higher than normal occurrence of brain tumors in workers at certain petrochemical plants is interesting,

but the cases are too few for scientists to come to firm conclusions. There are also a few families in the United States where cancer, including brain cancer, occurs frequently. Some genetic factor could possibly account for these families' high cancer prevalence—perhaps some defect in the body's immune system. Again, more detailed genetic and biochemical studies are needed.

DIAGNOSING BRAIN TUMORS

Clearly not every headache, dizzy spell, or visual disturbance is a sign of brain tumor. And while symptoms can vary widely, specialists pay particular attention to certain signs.

Progressive unrelenting symptoms. Whatever they may be, the symptoms never let up and they get worse over time.

Headache. Given the tight confines of the head, a growing tumor sooner or later will create pressure or swelling that affects tissues in the head, producing severe headache. Often the patient reports that the headache is worse upon first waking in the morning. Interestingly, brain tissue itself is normally insensitive to pain. But the meningeal layers, blood vessel walls, and the tissues lining the cavities of the brain and skull are rich in nerve endings sensitive to pain.

Visual complaints. Double vision, blurring, or other visual symptoms may occur as a result of increased pressure on the optic nerve or the blood vessels supplying the retina.

Motor signs. Some patients report weakness or numbness in their arms and legs. Sometimes reflexes (like the familiar knee jerk reflex) are very strong. In the case of spinal cord tumors, patients may experience a growing loss of sensation below a certain level in the trunk, or increasing difficulty in moving limbs.

Seizures. The onset of seizures or convulsions in a patient who has not been in an accident, been ill with fever, or suffered some other injury or illness is "presumptive evidence of a brain tumor until proven otherwise," says one leading authority.

To confirm the diagnosis, neurologists and neurosurgeons can conduct a battery of tests including simple x-rays of the head, standard brain-wave recordings (the electroencephalogram or EEG), analysis of cerebrospinal fluid, and so on. Their principal diagnostic aid today, however, is the CT scan, the technique that produces a computerized three-dimensional x-ray image of the brain. The CT scan is highly accurate, detecting the presence of a tumor mass in 90 to 95 percent of cases—even when that mass is no larger than half an inch across.

The CT scan can not only indicate the presence of a tumor, but will pin down its location in the brain. At this point the specialist may call for an arteriogram: an x-ray that will outline the arteries supplying blood to the tumor. Some tumors are richly endowed with blood vessels; others are less so. Thus the arteriogram provides another clue to the kind of brain tumor.

THE NEXT STEP: SURGERY

Surgery is the first line of attack against brain tumors. How extensive the operation will be depends on the tumor size and location and whether the tumor cells are concentrated in a mass or spread throughout the brain.

Some of the tissue removed at brain surgery is always reserved for pathological analysis. Studies of this "biopsy" material indicate whether the tumor is benign or malignant. Malignant tumor tissue removed at surgery is also being used in promising research studies aimed at improving treatment—even predicting which treatments will be successful.

Observers examining samples of brain tissue microscopically can tell what kinds of cells make up a tumor, and whether the cells are benign or malignant. Benign cells resemble normal cells of the tissue in question. Malignant cells lose more and more of their distinctive trademarks and acquire the classic characteristics of cancer: large or multiple nuclei, abnormal numbers of chromosomes, and changes in the cell's surface membrane. These changes seem to help very malignant cells to invade and take root in other tissues more easily. The extent of these changes permits classifying tumor cells by degree of malignancy from Grade I, benign, to Grade IV, the most advanced stage of malignancy.

TUMOR VARIETIES

Most brain tumors are gliomas, derived from the glial cells that support the neurons of the brain. Gliomas can be either benign or malignant. Unfortunately, one of the most malignant gliomas—the glioblastoma multiforme—is also the most common brain tumor. In all, gliomas account for 43 percent of primary brain cancers. Glial tumors are further described in terms of the type of glial cell they contain.

Astrocytomas. Star-shaped cells called astrocytes are the cells affected in a large subgroup of gliomas. Benign cerebellar astrocytomas are common childhood tumors. With today's tools and techniques, these tumors are often completely removable surgically. They are one of the recent success stories in tumor treatment.

Medulloblastomas. The root "blast" refers to a cell in an early stage of development. Medulloblasts are immature cells that may develop into either neurons or glial cells. Medulloblastomas are malignant tumors found in the rear of the brain. They typically occur in youngsters under 12 and account for a small percentage of all brain tumors.

Ependymomas. The cells that line the hollow cavities of the brain—ependymal cells—also give rise to a small percentage of brain tumors. These "ependymomas" tend to be benign.

Other gliomas are composed of other varieties of glial cells, such as those that produce the fatty insulating material (myelin) that surrounds many nerve fibers in the brain.

The second major group of primary brain tumors are those made up of covering cells.

Meningiomas. Tumors of the meninges (the membrane coverings of the brain and spinal cord) are usually benign, and account for some 15 percent of all brain tumors.

Schwannomas. These tumors arise from the Schwann cells that form the fatty sheath that envelops nerve fibers in the body. One such tumor develops in relation to the nerve of hearing, the acoustic nerve. Acoustic nerve tumors, called acoustic neuromas, are benign tumors which, if detected early, can be completely removed without loss of hearing or other nervous system damage.

Other kinds of tumors may involve cells in or near the pituitary gland at the base of the brain, or the pineal gland, deep in the center of the brain. In rare instances a brain tumor will develop from types of nerve cells.

SURGERY PLUS

In the case of a benign accessible brain tumor, surgery may be the beginning and end of treatment: The tumor is completely removed and the patient resumes activities with little likelihood of recurrence. If the tumor is malignant, it may not be possible to remove it completely. In that case, or if a tumor is large or difficult to reach, treatment will include radiation and chemotherapy. Radiation is sometimes used before surgery in the hope of reducing tumor size.

Today, an increasing number of tumors formerly considered inoperable can be tackled surgically. Microsurgery—the use of an operating microscope—has played an important role in that development. But often it is a combination of great technical skill and an ingenious strategy for getting at the tumor that has led to surgical success.

A few neurosurgeons are currently using high-frequency sound waves (ultrasound) and laser beams to destroy brain tumors. In one laser technique, for example, the surgeon uses an operating microscope and aims the laser beam at the center of the tumor, using the high-intensity rays to burn out the tissue. The exact position of the tumor is calculated by a computer that translates CT scan images into a set of coordinates referable to a framework set up around the patient's head. Time will tell whether such techniques will improve the success rate for tumor treatment.

Radiation usually begins within a week or two after surgery and continues for six weeks. Among recent refinements in radiation therapy are the use of drugs that make tumor tissue more sensitive to radioactive bombardment, and new radioactive sources that provide more powerful rays or charged particles that can be sharply focused on the tumor.

Chemotherapy, the other major weapon in the attack on brain tumors, has also benefited from refinements and advances. The principal brain tumor-killing drugs in use today go by the initials BCNU and CCNU, both chemically known as nitrosoureas. These drugs pass readily into the brain when given by mouth or injected into the bloodstream. Many drugs are prevented from reaching brain cells by an elaborate meshwork of fine blood vessels and cells—the blood-brain barrier—that filters blood reaching the brain.

The combined treatment of brain cancers with better drugs and radiotherapy, along with surgical techniques aimed at removing as much tumor tissue as possible, has meant longer survival times and richer lives for brain cancer patients. Further improvements in these traditional forms of treatment can be expected in the years ahead. In addition, scientists are developing new therapies based on promising laboratory studies.

The National Institute of Neurological Disorders and Stroke

DIZZINESS

Most of us can remember feeling dizzy—after a roller coaster ride, maybe, or when looking down from a tall building, or when, as children, we would step off a spinning merry-go-round. Even superbly conditioned astronauts have had temporary trouble with dizziness while in space. In these situations, dizziness arises naturally from unusual changes that disrupt our normal feeling of stability.

But dizziness can also be a sign that there is a disturbance or a disease in the system that helps people maintain balance. This system is coordinated by the brain, which reacts to nerve impulses from the ears, the eyes, the neck and limb muscles, and the joints of the arms and legs. If any of these areas fail to function normally or if the brain fails to coordinate the many nerve impulses it receives, a person may feel dizzy. The feeling of dizziness varies from person to person and, to some extent, according to its cause; it can include a feeling of unsteadiness, imbalance, or even spinning.

Disease-related dizziness, whether it takes the form of unsteadiness or spinning, is fairly common in the older population. Today, both older and younger people with serious dizziness problems can be helped by a variety of techniques—from medication to surgery to balancing exercises. Such techniques have been developed and improved by scientists studying dizziness.

A DELICATE BALANCING ACT

To understand what goes wrong when we feel dizzy, we need to know about the vestibular system by which we keep a sense of balance amid all our daily twisting and turning, starting and stopping, jumping, falling, rolling, and bending.

The Vestibular System

The vestibular system is located in the inner ear and contains the following structures: vestibular labyrinth, semicircular canals, vestibule, utricle, and saccule. These structures work in tandem with the vestibular areas of the brain to help us maintain balance.

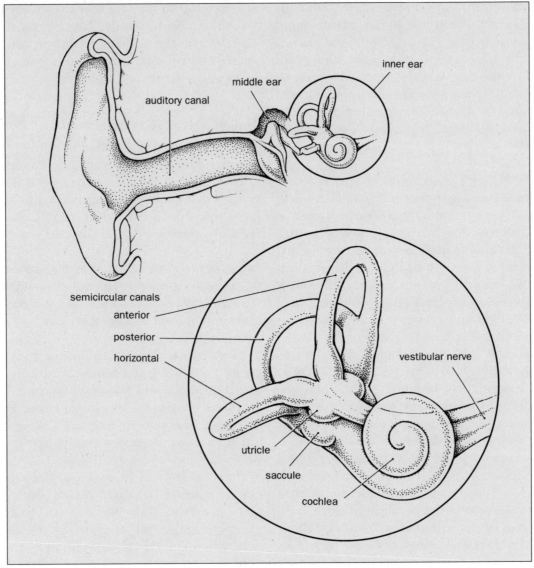

The semicircular canals and vestibule of the inner ear contain a fluid called endolymph that moves in response to head movement, triggering nerve signals to the brain that help maintain balance.

The vestibular labyrinth is located behind the eardrum. The labyrinth's most striking feature is a group of three semicircular canals or tubes that arise from a common base. At the base of the canals is a rounded chamber called the vestibule. The three canals and the vestibule are hollow and contain a fluid called endolymph which moves in response to head movement.

Within the vestibule and the semicircular canals are patches of special nerve cells called hair cells. Hair cells are also found in two fluid-filled sacs, the utricle and saccule, located within the vestibule. These cells are aptly named: rows of thin, flexible, hairlike fibers project from them into the endolymph.

Also located in the inner ear are tiny calcium stones called otoconia. When you move your head or stand up, the hair cells are bent by the weight of the otoconia or movement of the endolymph. The bending of the hair cells transmits an electrical signal about head movement to the brain. This signal travels from the inner ear to the brain along the eighth cranial nerve—the nerve involved in balance and hearing. The brain recognizes the signal as a particular movement of the head and is able to use this information to help maintain balance.

The Senses

The senses are also important in determining balance. Sensory input from the eyes as well as from the muscles and joints is sent to the brain, alerting us that the path we are following bends to the right or that our head is tilted as we bend to pick up a dime. The brain interprets this information—along with cues from the vestibular system—and adjusts the muscles so that balance is maintained.

Dizziness can occur when sensory information is distorted. Some people feel dizzy at great heights, for instance, partly because they cannot focus on nearby objects to stabilize themselves. When one is on the ground, it is normal to sway slightly while standing. A person maintains balance by adjusting the body's position to something close by. But when someone is standing high up, objects are too far away to use to adjust balance. The result can be confusion, insecurity, and dizziness, which is sometimes resolved by sitting down.

Some scientists believe that motion sickness, a malady that affects sea, car, and even space travelers, occurs when the brain receives conflicting sensory information about the body's motion and position. For example, when someone reads while riding in a car, the inner ear senses the movement of the vehicle, but the eyes gaze steadily on the book that is not moving. The resulting sensory conflict may lead to the typical symptoms of motion sickness: dizziness, nausea, vomiting, and sweating.

Another form of dizziness occurs when we turn around in a circle quickly several times and then stop suddenly. Turning moves the endolymph. The moving endolymph tells us we are still rotating but our other senses say we've stopped. We feel dizzy.

DIAGNOSING THE PROBLEM

The dizziness one feels after spinning around in a circle usually goes away quickly and does not require a medical evaluation. But when symptoms appear to be caused by an underlying physical problem, the prudent person will see a physician for diagnostic tests.

According to a study supported by the National Institute of Neurological Disorders and Stroke (NINDS), a thorough examination can reveal the underlying cause of dizziness in about 90 percent of cases.

A person experiencing dizziness may first go to a general practitioner or family physician; between 5 and 10 percent of initial visits to these physicians involve a complaint of dizziness. The patient may then be referred either to an ear specialist (otologist) or a nervous system specialist (neurologist).

The patient will be asked to describe the exact nature of the dizziness, to give a complete history of its occurrence, and to list any other symptoms or medical problems. Patients give many descriptions of dizziness—depending to some extent on its cause. Common complaints are light-headedness, a feeling of impending faint, a hallucination of movement or motion, or a loss of balance without any strange feelings in the head. Some people also report they have vertigo—a form of dizziness in which one's surroundings appear to be spinning uncontrollably or one feels the sensation of spinning.

The physician will try to determine what components of a patient's nervous system are out of kilter, looking first for changes in blood pressure, heart rhythm, or vision—all of which may contribute to the complaints.

Sometimes dizziness is associated with an ear disorder. The patient may have loss of hearing, discomfort from loud sounds, or constant noise in the ear, a disorder known as tinnitus (see Hearing Loss, page 213). The physician will also look for other neurological symptoms: difficulty in swallowing or talking, for example, or double vision.

TESTS AND SCANS

After the initial history-taking and physical examination, the physician may deliberately try to make the patient feel dizzy. The patient may be asked to repeat actions or movements that generally cause dizziness: to walk in one direction and then turn quickly in the opposite direction, or to hyperventilate by breathing deeply for three minutes.

In another test, the patient sits upright on an examining table. The physician tilts the patient's head back and turns it partway to one side, then gently but quickly pushes the patient backward to a lying-down position. The reaction to this procedure varies according to the cause of dizziness. Patients with benign positional vertigo may experience vertigo plus nystagmus: rapid, uncontrollable back-and-forth movements of the eyes.

Caloric test. One widely used procedure, called the caloric test, involves electronic monitoring of the patient's eye movements while one ear at a time is irrigated with warm water or warm air and then with cold water or cold air. This double stimulus causes the endolymph to move in a way similar to that produced by rotation of the head. If the labyrinth is working normally, nystagmus should result. A missing nystagmus reaction is a strong argument that the balance organs are not acting correctly.

NINDS-supported scientists at the Johns Hopkins University in Baltimore observed that not all patients can tolerate the traditional caloric test. Some become sick when the ear is irrigated with the standard amount of water or air before physicians can measure their eye movements. So the scientists are designing a method of conducting the test more gradually by slowly adjusting the amount of water or air reaching the inner ear. Their goal is to reduce patient discomfort while allowing the test to proceed.

Some patients who cannot tolerate the caloric test are given a rotatory test. In this procedure, the patient sits in a rotating chair, head tilted slightly forward. The chair spins rapidly in one direction, then stops abruptly. Depending on the cause of dizziness, the patient may experience vertigo after this rotation.

In one variation of this test, the chair is placed in a tent of striped cloth. As the chair rotates, electrodes record movements of the patient's eyes in response to the stripes. The physician evaluates these eye movements, a form of nystagmus, to determine if the patient has a disorder of the balance system.

Hearing test. Because disorders of balance are often accompanied by hearing loss, the physician may order a hearing test.

Brain-wave test. Hearing loss and associated dizziness could also be due to damaged nerve cells in the brainstem, where the hearing and balance nerve relays signals to the brain. To detect a malfunction, the physician may order a kind of computerized brain-wave study called a brainstem auditory evoked response test. In this procedure, electrodes are attached to several places on the surface of the patient's scalp and a sound is transmitted to the patient's ear. The electrodes then measure the time it takes the nerve signals generated by the sound to travel from the ear to the brainstem.

CT scan. If there is reason to suspect that the dizziness could stem from a tumor or cyst, the patient may undergo a computed tomography (CT) scan. In a CT scan, x-ray pictures are taken of the brain from several different angles. These images are then combined by a computer to give a detailed view that may reveal the damaging growth.

Psychological test. Sometimes anxiety and emotional upset cause a person to feel dizzy. Certain patients may be asked to take a psychological test, to try to find out whether the dizziness is caused or intensified by emotional stress.

The many tests administered by a physician will usually point to a cause for the patient's dizziness.

Disorders responsible for dizziness can be categorized as:

- *Peripheral vestibular disorders,* or those involving a disturbance in the labyrinth
- *Central vestibular disorders,* or those resulting from a problem in the brain or its connecting nerves
- *Systemic disorders,* or those originating in nerves or organs outside the head

CONFUSED SIGNALS

When someone has vertigo but does not experience faintness or difficulty in walking, the cause is probably a peripheral vestibular disorder. In these conditions, nerve cells in the inner ear send confusing information about body movement to the brain.

Ménière's Disease

A well-known cause of vertigo is the peripheral vestibular disorder known as Ménière's disease. First identified in 1861 by Prosper Ménière, a French physician, the disease is thought to be caused by too much endolymph in the semicircular canals and vestibule. Some scientists think that the excess endolymph may affect the hair cells so that they do not work correctly. This explanation, however, is still under study.

The vertigo of Ménière's disease comes and goes without an apparent cause; it may be made worse by a change in position and reduced by being still.

In addition to vertigo, patients have hearing loss and tinnitus. Hearing loss is usually restricted at first to one ear and is often severe. Patients sometimes feel "fullness" or discomfort in the ear, and diagnostic testing may show unusual sensitivity to increasingly loud sounds. In 10 to 20 percent of patients, hearing loss and tinnitus eventually occur in the second ear.

Ménière's disease patients may undergo electronystagmography, an electrical recording of the caloric test, to determine if their labyrinth is working normally.

Attacks of Ménière's disease may occur several times a month or year and last from a few minutes to many hours. Some patients experience a spontaneous disappearance of symptoms while others may have attacks for years.

Treatment of Ménière's disease includes such drugs as meclizine hydrochloride and the tranquilizer diazepam to reduce the feeling of intense motion during vertigo. To control the buildup of endolymph, the patient may also take a diuretic, a drug that reduces fluid production. A low-salt diet—which reduces water retention—is claimed to be an effective treatment of Ménière's disease.

When these measures fail to help, surgery may be considered. In shunt surgery, part of the inner ear is drained to reestablish normal inner ear fluid or endolymph pressure. In another operation, called vestibular nerve section, surgeons expose and cut the vestibular part of the eighth nerve. Both vestibular nerve section and shunt surgery commonly relieve the dizziness of Ménière's disease without affecting hearing.

A more drastic operation, labyrinthectomy, involves total destruction of the inner ear. This procedure is usually successful in eliminating dizziness but causes total loss of hearing in the operated ear—an important consideration since the second ear may one day be affected.

Positional Vertigo

People with benign positional vertigo experience vertigo after a position change. One patient, named Barbara, noticed the first sign of this disorder one morning when she got up out of bed. She felt the room spinning. Frightened, she quickly returned to bed and lay down. After about 30 seconds the vertigo passed. Fearing a stroke, Barbara went to the emergency room of a hospital for a medical evaluation, which failed to show a problem. She had no symptoms for several days, then the problem returned. At this point, Barbara was referred to an otoneurologist, a physician who specializes in the ear and related parts of the nervous system.

Like Barbara, most patients with benign positional vertigo are extremely worried about their symptoms. But the patients usually feel less threatened once the disorder is diagnosed.

The cause of benign positional vertigo is not known, although some patients may recall an incident of head injury. The condition can strike at any adult age with attacks occurring periodically throughout a person's life.

In one type of treatment, the patient practices the position that provokes dizziness until the balance system eventually adapts. Rarely, a physician will prescribe medication to prevent attacks.

Vestibular Neuronitis

In this common vestibular disorder, the patient has severe vertigo. Jack experienced his first attack of this problem at 2 a.m. when he rolled over in bed and suddenly felt the room spinning violently. He started vomiting but couldn't stand up; finally, he managed to crawl to the bathroom. When he returned to bed, he lay very still—the only way to stop the vertigo. Three days later, he was able to walk without experiencing vertigo, but he still felt unsteady. Gradually, over the next several weeks, Jack's balance improved, but it was a year before he was entirely without symptoms.

Unlike Ménière's disease, vestibular neuronitis is not associated with hearing loss. Patients with vestibular neuronitis first experience an acute attack of severe vertigo lasting for hours or days, just as Jack did, with loss of balance sometimes lasting for weeks or months. About half of those who have a single attack have further episodes over a period of months to years.

The cause of vestibular neuronitis is uncertain. Since the first attack often occurs after a viral illness, some scientists believe the disorder is caused by a viral infection of the nerve.

Other Labyrinth Problems

Inner ear problems with resulting dizziness can also be caused by certain antibiotics used to fight life-threatening bacterial infections. Probably the best-known agent of this group is streptomycin. Problems usually arise when high doses of these drugs are taken for a long time, but some patients experience symptoms after short treatment with low doses, especially if they have impaired kidneys.

The first symptoms of damage to the inner ear caused by medication are usually hearing loss, tinnitus, or unsteadiness while walking. Stopping the antibiotic can usually halt further damage to the balance mechanism, but this is not always possible: the medicine may have to be continued to treat a life-threatening infection. Patients sometimes adapt to the inner ear damage that may occur after prolonged use of these antibiotics and recover their balance.

Balance can also be affected by a cholesteatoma, a clump of cells from the eardrum that grow into the middle ear and accumulate there. These growths are thought to result from repeated infections such as recurrent otitis media. If unchecked, a cholesteatoma can enlarge and threaten the inner ear. But if the growth is detected early, it can be surgically removed.

BRAIN AND NERVE DAMAGE

The vestibular nerve carries signals from the inner ear to the brainstem. If either the nerve or the brainstem is damaged, information about position and movement may be blocked or incorrectly processed, leading to dizziness.

Conditions in which dizziness results from damage to the brainstem or its associated nerves are referred to as "central causes of dizziness."

Acoustic Neuroma

One central cause of dizziness is a tumor called an acoustic neuroma. Although the most common sign of this growth is hearing loss followed by tinnitus, some patients also experience dizziness.

An acoustic neuroma usually occurs in the internal auditory canal, the bony channel through which the vestibular nerve passes as it leaves the inner ear. The growing tumor presses on the nerve, sending false messages about position and movement to the brain.

The hearing nerve running alongside the vestibular nerve can also be compressed by the acoustic neuroma, with resulting tinnitus and hearing loss. Or the tumor may press on other nearby nerves, producing numbness or weakness of the face. If the neuroma is allowed to grow, it will eventually reach the brain and may affect the function of other cranial nerves.

Computed tomography has revolutionized the detection of acoustic neuromas. If an early diagnosis is made, a surgeon can remove the tumor. The patient usually regains balance.

Stroke

Dizziness may be a sign of a "small stroke" or transient ischemic attack (TIA) in the brainstem. TIAs, which result from a temporary lack of blood supply to the brain, may also cause transient numbness, tingling, or weakness in a limb or on one side of the face. Other signs include temporary blindness and difficulty with speech. These symptoms are warning signs: one should see a physician immediately for treatment. If a TIA is ignored, a major stroke may follow.

SYSTEMIC DISEASES: UNDERLYING ILLNESS

Dizziness can be a symptom of diseases affecting body parts other than the brain and central nervous system. Systemic conditions like anemia or high blood pressure decrease oxygen supplies to the brain; a physician eliminates the resulting dizziness by treating the underlying systemic illness.

Damaged Sensory Nerves

We maintain balance by adjusting to information transmitted along sensory nerves from sensors in the eyes, muscles, and joints to the spinal cord or brain. When these sensory nerves are damaged by systemic disease, dizziness may result.

Multiple sensory deficits, a systemic disease, is believed by some physicians to be the chief cause of vaguely described dizziness in the aged population. In this disorder, several senses or sensory nerves are damaged. The result: faulty balance.

People with diabetes, which can damage nerves affecting vision and touch, may develop multiple sensory deficits. So can patients with arthritis or cataracts, both of which distort how sensory information reaches the brain.

The first step in treating multiple sensory deficits is to eliminate symptoms of specific disorders. Permanent contact lenses can improve vision in cataract patients, for example, and medication or surgery may ease pain and stiffness related to arthritis.

Symptoms of damaged sensory nerves may be relieved by a collar to eliminate extreme head motion, balancing exercises to help compensate for sensory losses, or a cane to aid balance. Some patients are helped by the drug methylphenidate, which can increase awareness of remaining sensations.

Systemic neurological disorders such as multiple sclerosis, Alzheimer's disease, Parkinson's disease, or Creutzfeldt-Jakob disease may also cause dizziness, primarily during walking. However, dizziness is rarely the sole symptom of these nervous system diseases.

Low Blood Pressure

One common systemic disease causing dizziness is postural or orthostatic hypotension. In this disease, the heart does not move the blood with enough force to supply the brain adequately.

Symptoms include sudden feelings of faintness, light-headedness, or dizziness when standing up quickly.

Because the muscles in aging blood vessels are weak and the arteries inadequate in helping convey blood to the head, older people are particularly susceptible to this condition. Older persons who do not sit or lie down at the first sensation of dizziness may actually lose consciousness.

People who have undetected anemia or those who are taking diuretics to eliminate excess water from their body and reduce high blood pressure are also at risk of developing postural hypotension.

A physician can easily diagnose postural hypotension: the patient's blood pressure is measured before standing abruptly and immediately afterward. Treatment is designed to eliminate dizziness by reducing the patient's blood volume.

A Secondary Symptom

Dizziness may also be a secondary symptom in many other diseases. Faintness accompanied by occasional loss of consciousness can be due to low blood sugar, especially when the faint feeling persists after the patient lies down.

A common cause of mild dizziness—the kind described as light-headedness—is medicine. A number of major prescription drugs may produce light-headedness as a side effect.

Two types of drugs that can cause this problem are sedatives, which are taken to induce sleep, and tranquilizers, which are used to calm anxiety.

WHEN ANXIETY STRIKES

Tranquilizers may cause a type of dizziness referred to as light-headedness—but so may anxiety. Cynthia becomes light-headed under a variety of stressful circumstances. The light-headedness sometimes is accompanied by heart palpitations and panic. She can produce these symptoms at will by breathing rapidly and deeply for a few minutes.

Cynthia's light-headedness is due to hyperventilation: rapid, prolonged deep breathing or occasional deep sighing that upsets the oxygen and carbon dioxide balance in the blood. The episodes are typically brief and often associated with tingling and numbness in the fingers and around the mouth. Hyperventilation is triggered by anxiety or depression in about 60 percent of dizziness patients.

Once made aware of the source of the symptoms, a patient can avoid hyperventilation or abort attacks by breath-holding or breathing into a paper bag to restore a correct balance of oxygen and carbon dioxide. If hyperventilation is due to anxiety, psychological counseling may be recommended.

Some patients who report dizziness may be suffering from a psychiatric disorder. Generally these persons will say that they experience light-headedness or difficulty concentrating; they may also describe panic states when in crowded places. Tests of such patients reveal that the inner ear is working correctly. Treatment may include counseling.

The National Institute of
Neurological Disorders and Stroke

EPILEPSY

Convulsion, seizure, fit, falling sickness—the English language is rich in words that capture the stark drama of a severe epileptic attack. There are many forms of epilepsy, each with characteristic signs and symptoms.

FORMS OF EPILEPSY

The victim cries out, falls to the floor unconscious, the limbs twitch, saliva bubbles at the mouth. Bladder control may be lost. Within minutes the attack is over. The victim comes to, exhausted, dazed, embarrassed. That is the picture most people have in mind when they hear the word "epilepsy." But that type of seizure—the grand mal attack—is only one form of epilepsy.

Take Lisa, for example. She is an intelligent 15-year-old high school student with long dark hair and lashes to match. Lisa has suffered from absence seizures (sometimes called petit mal epilepsy) for some time. In an absence seizure, there is a momentary lapse in consciousness. Lisa is briefly "out of it." But there is no dramatic fall. Sometimes there may be purposeless movements—an arm jerk, for example—but in Lisa's case there is no noticeable symptom, not even the blink of an eye. Immediately following the seizure, Lisa can resume whatever she was doing. But her attacks happen so often—several hundred times a day—that she cannot concentrate in school and is in danger of failing her sophomore year. Moreover, she is so frightened and ashamed of the attacks that she won't tell her friends what is wrong.

In still a third form of the disorder, commonly called psychomotor epilepsy, the patient may laugh, talk strangely, walk around in circles, or make other automatic movements like lip-smacking or chewing. On rare occasions, the victim may strike out at walls or furniture as though angry or afraid. These attacks are also brief. Upon recovery, the individual will be confused and have no memory of what happened.

The strange symptoms and sometimes bizarre behavior of patients with epilepsy have contributed to age-old superstitions and prejudice. As long ago as 400 B.C., Hippocrates repeated the popular folklore that epilepsy was a visitation of the gods—a "sacred disease." He had the wisdom to question folklore, however. Hippocrates suspected that epilepsy was a disorder of the brain. And he was right.

Causes and Effects

Nowadays, scientists know that epilepsy is not a disease with a single cause. Rather, it is a set of symptoms associated with abnormal nerve cell activity in the brain.

Normally, each nerve cell (neuron) generates small bursts of electrical impulses. The impulses, moving from neuron to neuron, and communicating with the body's muscles, sense organs, and glands, underlie all human behavior—our thoughts, feelings, actions. The pattern of activity has been likened to tiny flashes of light flicking on and off in the brain, weaving a constantly changing pattern on an "enchanted loom."

In epilepsy the pattern of nerve cell activity is disturbed. Instead of small bursts of electrical impulses, a group of nerve cells fires a storm of strong bursts like a platoon of soldiers all firing at once. Moreover, the firing comes with machine-gun rapidity.

Whereas normal nerve cells generate electrical impulses up to 80 times a second, an epileptic neuron can fire at rates of 500 times a second, disturbing the normal activity of the brain.

If the abnormal activity is confined to only a part of the brain, the seizure is described as partial, and the area of the brain involved is called the epileptic focus. Partial seizures sometimes affect the temporal lobes at the sides of the brain near the ears. Nerve centers there are associated with speech and hearing, with emotions and memory, and so disturbances in this part of the brain can account for the odd movements (automatisms) and behavior of psychomotor seizures.

In contrast, generalized seizures affect the whole brain, resulting in the unconsciousness, convulsions, and subsequent amnesia of a grand mal seizure. Similarly, seizures in absence epilepsy are generalized, with lapses of consciousness and occasional automatisms, but without convulsions. Sometimes what begins as a partial seizure can develop into a generalized seizure if the abnormal cell behavior spreads throughout the brain.

Classifications

The epilepsies are classified into subtypes within the broad categories of partial and generalized seizures. These divisions, and the more accurate descriptive terms neurologists prefer—generalized tonic-clonic seizure instead of grand mal; absence instead of petit mal; complex partial seizure instead of psychomotor seizure—mark important advances in understanding and controlling epilepsy. The more precise classifications of seizures enable physicians to devise better treatments. The good news is that seizures can be successfully controlled in over half the patients with epilepsy through daily medication with antiepileptic drugs.

History

The story of the ongoing conquest of epilepsy is closely bound up with the history of neurology. Epilepsy is the second most prevalent neurological disorder in the United States (following stroke). Over 2 million Americans at present have epilepsy: one out of a 100 persons. A century ago conditions were far worse. Not only were there few treatments, but epileptic patients were regarded as undesirables whose condition might be contagious. Many patients were placed in hospitals or institutions "for epileptics only." Faced with the

---

INTERNATIONAL CLASSIFICATION OF EPILEPTIC SEIZURES

Generalized Seizures
- **Tonic-clonic (grand mal)**
- **Absence (petit mal)**
- **Infantile spasms**
- **Other (myoclonic seizures, akinetic seizures, undetermined, etc.)**

Partial Seizures
- **Simple partial seizures (e.g., disturbances in movement only)**
- **Complex partial seizures (psychomotor, other)**
- **Secondarily generalized seizures**

(This is a condensed form of the new internationally accepted descriptive terms and classifications of epileptic seizures.)

---

challenge of so many suffering souls, pioneering neurologists of the 19th century turned their attention to the disorder and began the search for causes and cures that continues in the present.

DIAGNOSING EPILEPSY

Two steps are vital in screening and treating patients with suspected epilepsy. One, obvious but nontrivial, is a confirmation of the diagnosis. The second is a precise description of the pattern of seizures: their type or types, frequency, and duration.

Sometimes a child has a convulsion during the course of illness with high fever. Sometimes an adult has a seizure in reaction to anesthesia or a strong drug. Neither individual can be said to have epilepsy unless seizures recur in the absence of the original triggering event.

Sometimes patients with certain forms of mental illness show behavior that mimics a complex partial seizure. Other individuals with psychological problems may suffer seizures, even what appear to be generalized tonic-clonic attacks, but their brain cells show no abnormal activity. These "psychogenic" seizures indicate that the patient has serious problems such as the need for attention, dependency, or the avoidance of stress, but the condition is not epilepsy.

In making a diagnosis of epilepsy, physicians are guided by some general rules-of-thumb. Three-fourths of all patients with epilepsy have their first attacks before the age of 18. Usually a parent will bring a child to the family doctor and describe the symptoms, helpfully noting when seizures occur and how long they last. While this information is enormously useful, the most secure confirmation of the diagnosis can only come from observation of a seizure together with electrical recordings that show the abnormal brain cell activity. These recordings are the familiar wavy line tracings of the electroencephalogram (EEG) obtained from electrodes placed on the surface of the patient's head.

Many cases of epilepsy develop for no known reason. Sometimes the disorder runs in families, as in absence epilepsy which always has its onset in children or young people. On the whole, however, genetic factors are considered to play a secondary role, as contributing or predisposing factors to epilepsy rather than a primary cause. Epilepsy can occur as a complication of infection, head injury, or other conditions affecting the brain. Epilepsy may also be associated with cerebral palsy, mental retardation, or rarer neurological conditions such as tuberous sclerosis. For these reasons the examining physician will always make an exhaustive search for underlying causes.

A CT scan—a computerized x-ray image of the brain—may show up a tumor or cyst, for example, or reveal excess fluid in the brain—hydrocephalus. If these conditions can be treated successfully, the seizures may stop. A lumbar puncture, in which cerebrospinal fluid is withdrawn from the spinal cord, may reveal the presence of infection or other abnormalities. In any case, a thorough medical history of the patient, including details of birth and the health of other family members will be taken, and a battery of physical, mental, and neurological tests will be conducted.

The Unique Pattern

Every epileptic patient is unique in the symptoms, frequency, duration, and type (or types) of seizures he or she experiences. It is essential to describe the seizure pattern in detail because it is on that basis that the physician will determine treatment. Drugs used to treat epilepsy are selected according to the type of seizure the patient experiences. Other forms of treatment, such as surgery, may be appropriate for carefully selected patients with particular forms of epilepsy.

Some patients, particularly ones with complex partial seizures, experience a distinctive warning sign before a seizure, called an aura. The aura is itself a form of partial seizure, but one in which the patient retains awareness. Sometimes the warning sign may be a peculiar odor, a feeling in the pit of the stomach, or a sound. One neurologist describes a patient who was an ardent race track gambler. The man invariably heard the roar of the crowd followed by the name of the favorite in the race just before falling unconscious. Another patient heard rock music. Because patients retain consciousness during the aura, they occasionally may be able to learn methods of warding off the more severe attack.

Drugs are the answer for the majority of patients whose seizures can be controlled. The sizable gains that have been made in recent years can be chalked up to the availability of more and better drugs administered in doses suited to the individual patient.

Taking the Seizure's Measure

In 1966, the National Institute of Neurological Disorders and Stroke (NINDS) began a research program of intensive long-term EEG monitoring of epilepsy patients. Electrodes placed on the patient's head transmit brain wave data to nearby recording equipment. At the same time a television camera provides both full-length and head views of the patient as he or she sits, lies, eats, or sleeps over the course of the day. The video image is displayed on a screen along with the brain wave recordings so that observers can simultaneously compare the EEG tracings with the patient's behavior. The recording sessions are six hours long and continue daily over a period of months.

Intensive monitoring has led to an extensive library of invaluable data on epilepsy and has paid off for many a patient whose seizures had been intractable—impossible to control. Often such patients experience seizures that are difficult to classify—a complex partial seizure that looks like an absence spell, for example, or vice versa. Interestingly, in some patients intensive monitoring shows up occasional abnormalities in the EEG between seizures. The technique also reveals that many epileptic patients experience psychogenic seizures some of the time. Sometimes, too, the EEG shows an epileptiform pattern but the patient shows no outward signs of a seizure.

Refinements in technology have made it possible to free the patient from the hospital setting and still conduct long-term EEG monitoring. The brain wave signals are detected by electrodes fitted into headgear that the patient wears. The signals are then amplified and converted to electronic signals stored on a tape recorder cassette that the patient also wears while moving about at home or work. Automated analysis of EEG data is also an improvement in technology, allowing reliable data to be derived from the recordings without an observer having to study the tapes hour after hour.

TREATMENT

Knowledge of the types of seizures a patient suffers paves the way for effective treatment.

Drugs

There are now 16 antiepileptic drugs on the market. Some work on several different types of seizure. Others, especially some of the new drugs, are suited to specific types of epilepsy.

The history of drugs in the treatment of epilepsy is a spotty one. The first effective antiepileptic drugs were bromides, introduced by an astute English physician, Sir Charles Locock, in 1857. He noted that the bromides had a sedative effect and seemed to reduce seizures in some patients. Over 50 years later came phenobarbital, introduced as a sedative in 1912. Phenobarbital and related compounds quickly proved superior to the bromides in controlling seizures, and side effects were less severe. Surprisingly these early drugs were useful in treating the most severe form of epilepsy—grand mal—as well as partial seizures. They had no effect on absence epilepsy.

The next advances waited until the 1930s and 1940s when the pharmaceutical industry began to grow rapidly and scientists developed ways of testing the anticonvulsant properties of drugs in experimental animals. Phenytoin (Dilantin) was introduced in 1938 and remains a drug of major importance in treating grand mal and partial seizures. Other drugs were introduced in the fifties and sixties, but by the late sixties and seventies there was a marked decline in new drug research. Amendments to the food and drug laws in 1962 required that new drugs had to be proven to be effective as well as safe. The new rules plus the opinion that the market for new antiepileptic drugs was too small to warrant the investment in time or money discouraged antiepileptic drug research as a commercial enterprise.

Tailoring the Dosage

Even when the neurologist is armed with an accurate picture of a patient's seizures, the drugs prescribed may not work. The seizures may be too varied and too frequent; the drugs may simply not help particular individuals, or side effects may be too toxic. Sometimes the problem is one of dosage, however, or of finding the right combination of drugs administered in the right proportion at the right time of day. For these reasons, patients with intractable seizures who undergo long-term EEG monitoring also have frequent blood samples taken to measure the amount of drug circulating in the bloodstream. At the beginning of the study, a patient may be weaned off all medication. Then drugs may be introduced gradually, increasing the amounts or changing the medication to arrive at the ideal treatment: dosages sufficient to control seizures with a minimum of side effects. Similar studies to devise the best medication program are highly recommended for all epilepsy patients.

Surgery

Surgery to remove an epileptic focus in the brain is sometimes successful in preventing seizures in patients whose epilepsy cannot be controlled by drugs. In deciding which patients may benefit, surgeons will consider the location of the brain area involved and its importance in everyday behavior. Neurosurgeons will avoid operating in areas of the brain that will interfere with speech, language, hearing, or other major faculties.

Occasionally, surgery is performed to sever the connections between the two halves of the brain, the cerebral hemispheres. Such surgery can prevent the spread of abnormal discharges from one side of the brain to the other. Usually, such drastic surgery has little effect on behavior. Patients go about their normal activities as usual. It was only when research scientists began to set up experiments that deliberately studied what each half of the brain contributed to behavior that they discovered that the hemispheres were not like Siamese twins, identical in every way. While there is considerable similarity in structure, each hemisphere has special abilities and makes its own contribution to how a person sees, feels, or acts in the world. This is another instance of how concern for epilepsy has opened the door to new and fascinating discoveries about the nervous system.

Diet

In addition to drugs and surgery, treatment for epilepsy has also included special diets and new psychological approaches. Some years ago it was discovered that a diet rich in fats and low in carbohydrates led to a condition in the body called ketosis that benefits some epilepsy patients. Unfortunately, most people hate the diet. It makes them feel sick and they lose weight.

Biofeedback

One psychological approach to treating epilepsy involves training patients in methods that might allow them to control their brain waves. In the experimental technique called biofeedback, patients learn to correlate brain cell activity with visual images or sounds that are provided. They try to modify the sights or sounds and in this way alter the electrical activity in the brain. Biofeedback appears to help some patients, but how or why it does so remain tantalizing questions.

Recognizing the Patient's Multiple Needs

Sometimes people with epilepsy achieve complete control of seizures in the hospital only to have frequent seizures when they return home. The problem may be failure to take medication. Antiepileptic drugs are strong and can have unwanted side effects such as drowsiness, nausea, or other unpleasantness. One antiepileptic drug has a tendency to increase appetite. Many patients gain weight when taking it—enough to discourage use of the drug.

When a patient is at home, there are other factors that may increase the chances of having seizures. The normal pressures of everyday living may create stresses that can trigger seizures. On the other hand, the patient who cannot drive a car or suffers occasional seizures at work may feel rejected, depressed, angry, or frustrated—often a combination of emotional states that can lower the threshold for seizures.

Recent findings about patients monitored at home point up the relations between mental states and seizure activity. In one study it was noted that patients with absence seizures tended to have more seizures at times when they were bored or idle, not when they were fully occupied or interested in some activity. Seizure activity also tended to increase during family discussions of their problem, or even when donning the headgear and cassette and thus being reminded of their condition.

Doctors and others who work closely with patients know that the problems the individual with epilepsy faces do not end with medication. The psychological, social, vocational, and emotional needs of patients—and those close to them—are equally important.

The National Institute of
Neurological Disorders and Stroke

PARKINSON'S DISEASE

Before 1817, what we now know as Parkinson's disease was just one of a number of similar disorders of movement. Then a British doctor, James Parkinson, published a paper on what he called "shaking palsy." In it, he described the major symptoms of the disease that would later bear his name.

Dr. Parkinson's observations allowed the disease to be studied as a special illness for the first time. During the next century, scientists defined its distribution, symptoms, and onset, and the prospects for recovery. But most important, in the early 1960s they identified the fundamental brain defect that is the hallmark

of the disease. This information led to the first effective treatment for parkinsonism and suggested ways of devising new and more effective therapies.

A DISEASE OF LATER LIFE

Very few persons with Parkinson's disease develop serious symptoms before age 40. The great majority of cases are diagnosed between ages 60 and 70, so that the average age of parkinsonian patients is 65 years. In one community studied, the frequency of the disease in those above 50 increased markedly with age. The increasing number of older persons in the United States, therefore, would seem to foreshadow an increase in the number of people who will develop parkinsonism.

Both men and women appear to be equally affected. There are now perhaps 500,000 people with the disease in the United States, but this number is not exact since many cases are not severe enough to need treatment.

Among many populations in the world, there is wide variation in the occurrence of Parkinson's disease. Some scientists believe that high disease rates in certain populations might be due to an increased genetic susceptibility; but other research findings suggest that heredity may not play a major role in determining who gets the disease. A National Institute of Neurological Disorders and Stroke (NINDS) study of over 40 Parkinson's disease patients who had an identical twin uncovered only one case in which the twin also had the disease. This and other findings lend support to the likelihood that an environmental factor, rather than heredity, causes parkinsonism—an idea that is now being investigated.

EARLY SYMPTOMS

The first signs of Parkinson's disease may appear to be simply part of the normal aging process: a little shakiness, some difficulty in rising from a deep, comfortable chair. This is especially true since most symptoms of Parkinson's are first noticed when persons are in their sixties.

But the signs very gradually become more pronounced and extensive. The shaking, or tremor, that affects about two-thirds of parkinsonian patients begins to interfere with daily activities. It may be more difficult to hold utensils steady when eating. A newspaper may shake enough to make it hard to read.

The shaking may become worse when the patient is relaxed. This is characteristic of Parkinson's. A few seconds after the hands are rested on a table, for instance, the shaking is most pronounced.

Although tremor is usually the most obvious early sign of Parkinson's disease, a more distressing problem to the patient is the symptom known as bradykinesia— the gradual loss of spontaneous movement. A person with Parkinson's may sit in one position for a long time without moving. Or the patient may find it difficult to start walking.

Bradykinesia may lead to the loss of facial expression. This is not a sign of an emotional problem, but a loss of activity in the nerves that control the facial muscles. The link between emotions and facial expressions is instinctive: Expressions don't require conscious thought. In Parkinson's, a patient may have natural emotional responses, and not be aware that his or her face is not showing those feelings.

A parkinsonian patient may also have flat, expressionless speech. About half of Parkinson's disease patients experience such problems as loss of volume, difficulty beginning to speak, or inability to speak clearly. Again, these are not emotional problems, but a loss of normally spontaneous activity of the nerves and muscles.

A third characteristic of Parkinson's disease is rigidity. This symptom may not be as obvious to patients as is tremor. They may be aware only of a certain amount of stiffness when they move their arms or legs. But if another person tells a patient to relax and then tries to move the patient's arm, the movements will be ratchetlike: resistance, followed by a quick, short movement, then rigidity again. The result is a series of short, jerky motions, as though the arm is being moved by a gear.

A major principle in the body is that all muscles have an opposing muscle. Movement is possible not just because one muscle becomes more active, but because the opposing muscle relaxes. It may be a disturbance of this dynamic balance that causes rigidity.

Parkinsonian patients may also experience other motor problems. For instance, the posture may become stooped with the shoulders bent forward. When the person is standing at rest, the arms may not hang down in the normal way, but may bend upward from the elbow.

Telltale Signs

To an experienced neurologist, the diagnosis of Parkinson's disease is usually obvious. Shakiness is part of several other diseases, but the special quality of the parkinsonian tremor— that it becomes worse after a few seconds of resting the hand—is very characteristic. By the time the patient has decided to seek medical help, other symptoms are usually also present. The neurologist can put the tremor together with the lack of spontaneous facial expression, flat speech, and the patient's unusual stillness while sitting, and arrive at a fairly certain diagnosis. Peculiar handwriting, which becomes smaller and more cramped after the first few written words, is also a strong clue.

The ability to make a diagnosis almost solely on the basis of clinical signs is fortunate, since there are no sophisticated tests for Parkinson's disease. In about 10 percent of the suspected cases of this illness, there may be some hesitation about making a diagnosis at the first visit. But with time the telltale signs of parkinsonism almost always appear.

AS THE DISEASE WORSENS

Without treatment, Parkinson's disease becomes progressively more severe and disabling. But different patients experience different rates of disease progression. It is generally agreed, however, that with current treatments, many parkinsonian patients enjoy a normal life span.

The course of the disease is variable. With time, patients whose symptoms appeared only on one side of the body may have movement problems on the other side as well. On the other hand, cases of one-sided parkinsonism with no further development of movement problems are well known.

The patient may also begin to experience certain annoying problems, such as drooling. This comes from the difficulty in swallowing due to decreased function of the throat muscles. This swallowing problem can also make eating difficult, and can lead to choking if the patient is not careful. To some extent, the patient can control this problem by eating slowly and swallowing often.

There may also be overproduction of the normal oily coating of the skin, a condition called seborrhea. Its cause is poorly understood. The condition is not dangerous, but does require extra care.

Movement Problems

The more serious symptoms of advanced Parkinson's disease are aggravations of the movement problems, such as a severe loss of the sense of balance, sometimes compounded by loss of the normal armswing that we all use to maintain our walking rhythm. The short steps characteristic of a parkinsonian patient's walk are an attempt to compensate for lost stability.

With a failing sense of balance, the parkinsonian patient may develop a slight forward lean. This leaning causes a shift in the body's center of gravity, and the patient may take a series of quick, small steps forward to "catch up" with the changed gravity center. This stepping forward is the symptom referred to as festination. Another problem—a backward lean—may also appear. When bumped from the front or when starting to walk, patients with this problem have a tendency to step backwards. This is known as retropulsion, and usually accompanies only fairly advanced disease. When either one of these symptoms appears, the use of lifts on shoes or a tripod cane can be helpful.

Late in the course of Parkinson's disease, the patient's loss of spontaneous movements may worsen. When severe, such bradykinesia results in periods when the person is completely unable to start movements. These "frozen states" are known as akinesia. This loss of voluntary movement affects walking most dramatically.

A peculiar feature of these frozen states is that they may be triggered by situations or objects, such as an open doorway or a line drawn on the floor. Or patients may "freeze" when caught in crowds. Since this difficulty is partly psychological, personal support can be of considerable help. A hand or arm quietly offered to a parkinsonian patient experiencing akinesia can be all he or she needs to get going again. On the other hand, if a companion becomes agitated or obviously embarrassed by the patient's condition, the frozen state may get worse.

Dementia

It is important to remember that most patients with Parkinson's disease continue to think clearly. Late in the course of the illness, some patients do suffer loss of mental skills. They may become forgetful, have trouble calculating or counting money, and may lose their way when going between familiar places. These are symptoms of dementia. How many parkinsonian patients undergo these losses is not clear, but it is interesting that James Parkinson did not include dementia in his original description of the disease.

Depression

Parkinsonian patients may also feel depressed. Some neurologists have suggested that depression is a result of the disease process, but this idea is still controversial. Another possibility is that the depression is simply "a realistic reaction to a progressive, crippling illness," as one clinician expressed it.

Complications of Confinement

Parkinsonism symptoms themselves are not fatal. Patients most often die of an illness acquired while confined to bed during the latter stages of the disease. Loss of muscle tone makes coughing difficult, so the lungs are not effectively cleared and the patient becomes susceptible to pneumonia. Lying in bed also makes the patient susceptible to blood clots in the legs that can travel to the lungs and be fatal. Another problem is urinary tract infections, which can spread to the blood. Clearly, good nursing care of the bedridden parkinsonian patient is important.

BRAIN CHANGES

In the early 1960s, research scientists were excited to discover several changes in specific areas of brains taken from deceased Parkinson's disease patients. These observations led to an important insight into the basis for Parkinson's disease: Parkinson patients cannot control their movements because of a deficiency in the part of the brain that produces smooth, directed muscle activity.

The scientists saw that certain pigmented nerve cells were lost from a region of the brain known as the basal ganglia, which appears to be responsible for the dynamic balance of opposing muscles mentioned earlier. This loss of nerve cells (or neurons) occurred in patients with long-standing Parkinson's disease, and was most evident in the substantia nigra ("black substance," so called because the cells in this area are dark), a part of the basal ganglia thought to adjust nerve signals passing to the muscles from the command centers of the brain.

In addition, all regions of the basal ganglia were deficient in a normal brain substance called dopamine, a chemical messenger that transmits signals from one nerve cell to another. Dopamine is made by the pigmented cells of the substantia nigra, the same neurons that are greatly reduced in parkinsonism. Since these cells send fibers throughout the basal ganglia, much like a tree sending out roots, loss of cells from the substantia nigra lowers the supply of dopamine in nearby areas as well.

Without dopamine, the nerve cells in the basal ganglia are like a team of astronauts with no radios in their spacesuits—they are ready for action but they can't communicate. As a result the nerve cells can't cooperate to fine-tune the signals flowing to the muscles.

This conclusion is supported by experiments in animals showing that dopamine loss in the brain leads to abnormal movement. An even more convincing observation is that the extent of loss of dopamine nerve cells found

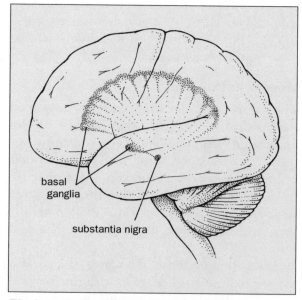

The loss of nerve cells from the brain's substantia nigra region is thought to be responsible for the symptoms of parkinsonism.

at autopsy is related to the severity of patients' symptoms, especially akinesia and tremor.

CAUSES OF PARKINSON'S DISEASE

In a small number of parkinsonism cases, a specific cause can be identified. Carbon monoxide and manganese poisoning may produce parkinsonism, as can certain drugs used to treat psychiatric illness. Parkinsonism caused by psychiatric drugs disappears when the drugs are withdrawn.

But the vast majority of cases of parkinsonism are "idiopathic," meaning that no cause is known. Even the finding that specific nerve cells are lost in the brains of parkinsonian patients has not led scientists to the cause of the disease.

Brain research has provided one important clue, however. Even persons who die early in the course of Parkinson's disease have advanced damage to their dopamine-containing nerve cells. This implies that the disease is the result of a gradual decay process that starts long before symptoms appear. So the search for the first event in the course of Parkinson's disease must involve persons in their forties, thirties, or earlier, when the unseen stages of the disease probably begin.

TREATMENT

Therapy for Parkinson's disease has involved both surgery and drug treatment. Many patients also benefit from exercises, which may provide added strength to help combat movement problems.

The only operation that has been of value for Parkinson's disease was a procedure called cryothalamotomy, or "destruction of the thalamus by cold." In the most successful form of this procedure, a probe cooled with liquid nitrogen was placed into a part of the brain called the thalamus. Guided by a framework around the patient's head, the probe touched only very specific areas of the brain. Nerve cells in these areas were destroyed by the supercooled metal tip of the probe.

This operation successfully stopped the tremor in many patients. Unfortunately, it did little to help the rigidity and loss of spontaneous movement that are the more disabling symptoms of Parkinson's disease.

Cryothalamotomy had another drawback. When performed on both sides of the thalamus (which was necessary to stop tremor on both sides of the body), the surgery itself could produce neurologic damage. Today, with the development of effective drug therapies, cryothalamotomy is seldom performed except in severe cases of unstoppable tremor or movement disorder.

DRUG THERAPY

After James Parkinson clearly delineated the illness that bears his name, many chemicals were tested against it. These included fish-poison bark, strychnine, arsenic, and turpentine. It is not surprising that several classes of drugs were found that had at least some mild benefit for parkinsonian patients. Extracts from the belladonna plant, for example, were used against Parkinson's disease until the 1940s. But effective control of all symptoms was not possible until the drug levodopa was introduced in the 1960s.

Levodopa

The success of levodopa—sometimes called L-dopa—in treating the symptoms of Parkinson's disease has been one of the triumphs of modern research. After dopamine nerve pathways were shown to be depleted in persons with parkinsonian symptoms, several scientists tried to restore normal function by administering levodopa, a natural brain chemical that nerve cells can use to make dopamine. (Dopamine itself could not be given because it does not enter the brain.)

In initial studies, levodopa caused many patients to vomit. But in 1967 a New York neurologist showed that starting with small doses and slowly increasing the dosage overcame this problem. When doctors were able to gradually give higher doses of levodopa, their patients' conditions improved greatly.

Both rigidity and tremor were greatly reduced. But most important, levodopa reduced the most disabling symptom of the disease, bradykinesia, the difficulty in starting movements. No previous medication had controlled this problem.

Still, in the first few years of levodopa use, little more than half of the patients improved. In the other patients, side effects made it impossible to give a high enough dose to reduce the symptoms. Besides nausea, patients experienced movements called dyskinesias, which are undirected involuntary movements. Some also suffered heart problems and others had dangerous drops in blood pressure.

The next major advance was the development of drugs that stopped levodopa from changing to dopamine before it reached the brain. These drugs, called extracerebral decarboxylase inhibitors, include carbidopa and benserazide. When levodopa is kept from changing before it reaches the brain, nausea is reduced. Low blood pressure and heart problems are also avoided. With a decarboxylase inhibitor, many patients can reduce the number of levodopa pills they need, and full doses of levodopa can be reached in weeks instead of months. Carbidopa or benserazide is now combined with levodopa in most medicines.

With today's levodopa treatment, symptoms are reduced in about three of every four parkinsonian patients. The patients also remain independent longer, and many live out a normal life span.

In some cases, however, patients experience involuntary movements from the levodopa treatment, and others have mental symptoms. Reducing the dosage sometimes lowers these side effects. But this means that the doctor must be very skilled in adjusting the levodopa amount to improve symptoms while avoiding bad effects. The doctor must also be aware that certain drugs given for other illnesses can defeat the effect of levodopa.

Eventually, however, the benefits of levodopa may wear off. In about half of the patients with Parkinson's disease, several troubling problems are likely to appear suddenly after three to five years of successful levodopa control.

One of these problems is called the "on-off" reaction. The patient may alternate between dyskinesia (uncontrolled movements) and akinesia (lack of movement), switching back and forth between these states every few seconds or minutes. A second problem is "end-of-dose akinesia," or the quick return of parkinsonian symptoms three to four hours after taking a dose of levodopa.

Some doctors think that these problems are due to the relentless advance of parkinsonism. But not all agree. One doctor who treats parkinsonian patients determined how long each benefited from levodopa therapy. If the reduced effectiveness of levodopa is due to progression of the disease, then the patients who had less severe symptoms at the start of treatment should have been helped by levodopa longer. But this was not so. Instead, he found that patients who took the highest doses of levodopa lost the benefit of the drug soonest. He suggested that giving high doses of levodopa may lower its effectiveness.

This theory is by no means proven. But it has led to two possible methods of prolonging the period of levodopa's effectiveness.

The first is to begin treatment with less powerful drugs, reserving levodopa for the more advanced stages of the disease. When levodopa is started, frequent small doses are given.

Other Drugs

One class of drugs used first is anticholinergic agents. These were the main treatment for Parkinson's disease from the early 1940s until the introduction of levodopa. Among the most common anticholinergic drugs are trihexyphenidyl (Artane), benztropine mesylate (Cogentin), and biperiden (Akineton). They are helpful against tremor and rigidity, but do not affect bradykinesia. Antihistamines such as diphenhydramine (Benadryl) are weaker anticholinergic agents.

Another drug that could be used for early parkinsonism is amantadine hydrochloride (Symmetrel), which was first used to treat and prevent respiratory virus infections. Amantadine also produces modest improvement in tremor and rigidity, plus some reduction of bradykinesia.

The Drug Holiday

A second method for coping with the problems of continued levodopa therapy is the so-called drug holiday. This is a period of three to seven days or more during which the patient is hospitalized and taken off levodopa completely. This hospitalization may be preceded by a period of gradually decreasing doses of levodopa at home. Hospitalized patients must be watched closely, especially if their disease has progressed to the point of affecting their breathing muscles. During the drug-free period, some patients participate in physical, occupational, and speech therapy programs to reduce the hazards of stopping the medication.

A number of doctors have had success with the drug holiday. They find that many patients can resume levodopa therapy without on-off problems or end-of-dose akinesia. Some patients can even benefit from lower doses than they were taking before the drug holiday. This method is still being tested.

PHYSICAL THERAPY

Besides drug treatment, many doctors prescribe muscle-strengthening exercises for their parkinsonian patients. These include exercises for speaking, swallowing, and overall muscle tone.

Exercise will not stop disease progression, but may provide a stronger body so that the patient may be less disabled by movement problems. Exercise can also improve the emotional well-being of parkinsonian patients.

As one doctor puts it, "I include physical therapy with a professional therapist as a standard part of my prescription. You are not doing anything fundamental to the disease, but you are bringing the patient's motor function to an optimal level."

SUPPORT AND UNDERSTANDING

One of the most damaging aspects of Parkinson's disease is its demoralizing effect. The patient's world is completely changed. Emotional support and understanding are needed to encourage the patient to remain as active as possible.

Parkinson's disease can also separate patients from their families. "This disease puts a terrible strain on families," says one neurologist who has treated many parkinsonian patients. One problem is that normal family relationships are changed and traditional expectations are turned upside-down.

A man used to supporting his family for years may find that he can no longer do his job. "I have to work two jobs to support us and pay for John's medical bills," said the wife of a parkinsonian patient. While the wife is working the daughter must stay home to watch her partially disabled dad. These limitations and demands can create resentment in even the most closely knit families.

One older woman who lived alone after her husband died refused to accept the limitations of her Parkinson's disease. "I've had a terrible time with her," said her adult daughter. The patient refused to accept help even though her disease progressed and she fell and broke a hip. After some time in a nursing home, she is returning to her house, but still wants to live alone. Naturally this causes the daughter intense worry.

This situation may not be uncommon. One doctor believes that falling has replaced pneumonia as the greatest danger to parkinsonian patients. Levodopa therapy allows patients to walk around but does not completely reverse their impaired balance. If they are not cautious, they can easily fall.

For patients and their families, support groups can be a great help. At meetings, people learn ways of dealing with their problems. But, more important, they can talk to other people who understand the difficulties they are having.

Such an outlet can be important in relieving the frustrations that both patients and families feel. Parkinsonian patients can do many things for themselves, but they are often very slow. When a patient goes to a store or for a walk, the companion should not try to hurry the impaired person along. Even eating or speaking can be better managed if other people don't become impatient.

Another problem faced by families is the suspicion that a person with parkinsonism is "faking it." They may think, "Why is he so capable sometimes and so helpless at other times?" Talking with support groups will show that this is a normal feature of the disease.

These groups can also help members learn about financial and support services. The parkinsonian patient with advanced disease may need custodial care, and support groups can help the family decide which options best suit its financial and personal situation.

The National Institute of
Neurological Disorders and Stroke

SHINGLES

When the itchy red spots of childhood chicken pox disappear and the child goes back to school, the battle with infection seems won. But for all too many of us this triumph of the body's immune system over a virus is only temporary. The virus has not been destroyed, but lies low, ready to strike again later in life. This second eruption of the chicken pox virus is the disease called shingles.

"I was having exams at college and I got a rash in a band around my waist. I first thought it was chicken pox, but I'd had that years before and instead of itching, this time the spots were very painful," recalls a young woman who had shingles in her twenties.

The young woman's memory was correct. She had had chicken pox as a child. You cannot develop shingles unless you have had an earlier bout of chicken pox. The woman was also typical in her symptoms: Shingles is often more painful than it is itchy. Her age was unusual, however. While young people do develop shingles, the disease most often strikes in later years. About 10 percent of normal adults can be expected to get shingles during their lifetime, usually after age 50. The incidence increases with age so that shingles is 10 times more likely to occur in adults over 60 than in children under 10. The chances of developing shingles are greatest for individuals whose immune systems are weakened.

REVEALING SYMPTOMS

The first sign of shingles is often pain in or under the skin. The individual may also feel ill with fever or headache. After several days, a rash of small fluid-filled blisters appears on reddened skin.

The blisters, or lesions, are usually limited to a band spanning one side of the trunk or clustered on one side of the face. This striking pattern gives the disease its name: "Shingles" comes from "cingulum," the Latin word for belt or girdle. Similarly, the medical term for the disease, "zoster," is the Greek word for girdle.

More importantly, the distribution of the shingles spots is a telltale clue to where the chicken pox virus has been hiding for all the

The assumption is that the chicken pox viruses that weren't wiped out in the original battle were able to leave the skin blisters and travel in the nervous system. There the viruses settled down in an inactive form inside nerve cells (neurons) that lie in clusters adjacent to the spinal cord and brain. These neurons are called sensory cells because they relay information to the brain about what your body is sensing: whether your skin feels hot or cold, whether you've been touched or feel pain. Comparable nerve cell clusters in the head relay information about pain, temperature, or touch in that area, as well as information about what you're seeing, hearing, tasting, or smelling.

The Second Time Around

When the chicken pox virus reactivates, the virus moves down the long nerve fibers that extend from the sensory cell bodies to the skin. There the viruses multiply and the telltale rash erupts. Now the nervous system is deeply involved, however, and the symptoms are often more complex and severe than those of childhood chicken pox. People with "optical" shingles (where the virus has invaded an ophthalmic nerve) may suffer painful eye inflammations that leave them temporarily blind. Infections of facial nerves can lead to paralysis or excruciating pain. People with lesions on the torso may feel spasms of pain at the gentlest touch or breeze.

The Aftermath

For the majority of normally healthy individuals, the second bout with the chicken pox virus is almost always a second triumph of the body's immune system. The shingles attack may last longer than chicken pox, and you may need medication for pain, but in most cases the body has the inner resources to fight back. The lesions heal and the pain subsides within three to five weeks.

There are exceptions. Sometimes, particularly in older people, the pain and other

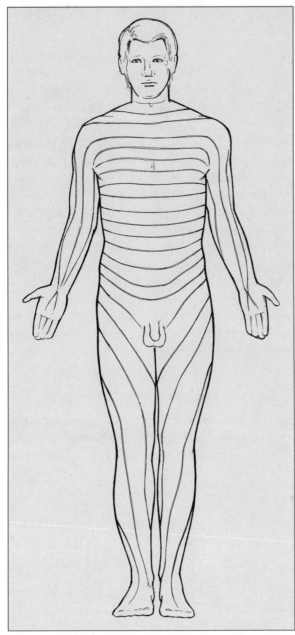

The lines mark the areas of skin served by individual brain or spinal nerves. When shingles strikes, the rash is confined to one of these narrow bands.

years following the initial infection. Scientists now know that the shingles lesions correspond to the area of skin supplied by one of the major nerves that exits from the brain or spinal cord.

symptoms persist long after the rash is healed. It is important to realize that these individuals no longer have shingles: Their infection is over. Instead, they are suffering a neurological disorder, the result of damage to the nervous system.

Investigators think that the virus attack has led to scarring or other lesions affecting the sensory cells and associated nerves. If the eye is involved, the damage from shingles can lead to blindness.

In other cases facial paralysis, headache, and persistent pain are the aftermath. Possibly because the nerve cells conveying pain sensations are hardest hit, or are exquisitely sensitized by the virus attack, pain is the principal complication of shingles. This pain, called postherpetic neuralgia, is among the most devastating known to mankind—the kind of pain that leads to insomnia, weight loss, depression, and that total preoccupation with unrelenting torment that characterizes the chronic pain sufferer.

Even in such severe cases, however, the paralysis, headaches, and pain generally subside, although it may take time. As one elderly sufferer recalls: "The worst thing was that the pain went on for months and months. Another bad part was reflecting on the 60 years since I had the chicken pox. Am I only a culture medium for viruses, for heaven's sake?"

Postherpetic neuralgia may be a nightmare, but it is not life-threatening. Doctors treating the pain currently employ a variety of medications. They generally avoid the powerful narcotic pain relievers in favor of newer nonaddictive but potent painkillers. Studies have also shown that some anticonvulsant drugs used to treat epilepsy, such as carbamazepine (Tegretol) are sometimes effective in relieving postherpetic neuralgia. Antidepressants can help, also. In addition to their effects on mood, the antidepressants appear to relieve pain. Some doctors report that patients occasionally benefit from some of the more controversial treatments for pain, such

as acupuncture and electrical stimulation of nerve endings.

A threat to immunosuppressed patients. People with leukemia, Hodgkin's disease, or other cancers are often treated by drugs or radiation to destroy cancerous tissue. Unfortunately these treatments also damage cells of the immune system that normally fight invading organisms. Patients with kidney or other organ diseases who receive organ transplants are also vulnerable to shingles. These patients are given drugs that suppress the immune system to prevent the body from rejecting the foreign tissue. Should any of these patients contract shingles, there is a real danger that the disease will spread throughout the body, reaching vital organs like the lungs. If unchecked, such disseminated shingles can lead to death from viral pneumonia or secondary bacterial infection.

THE LATENT VIRUS

The virus responsible for shingles and chicken pox belongs to the herpes group of viruses. The group includes the virus that causes cold

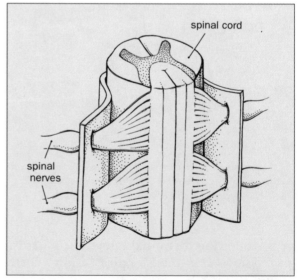

The shingles virus can hide, dormant, inside spinal nerves near the spinal cord or brain, then reactivate and travel along the nerve, out to the skin.

sores, fever blisters, mononucleosis, and genital herpes—a sexually transmitted disease. Like the shingles-causing virus, many herpes viruses can take refuge in the nervous system after an individual has suffered an initial infection. The virus may remain latent for years, then travel down nerve cell fibers to cause a renewed infection.

Scientists call the chicken pox/shingles-causing agent the VZ virus, short for varicella-zoster. "Varicella" is a Latin word meaning "little pox" to distinguish the virus from smallpox, the scourge that once disfigured or killed its victims. (The word "chicken" conveys the same idea of weakness or mildness as in "chicken-hearted.") Like many viruses, the varicella-zoster virus looks as though it were designed by a mathematician. It is a microscopic sphere encasing a 20-sided geometric figure called an icosahedron. Inside the icosahedron is the genetic material of the virus, deoxyribonucleic acid (DNA). When activated, the virus reproduces inside the nucleus of an infected cell. It acquires its spherical wrapping as it buds through the nuclear membrane.

As early as 1909, a German scientist suspected that the viruses causing chicken pox and shingles were one and the same. In the 1920s and 1930s, the case was strengthened. In an experiment, children were inoculated with fluid from the lesions of patients with shingles. Within two weeks about half the children came down with chicken pox. Finally, in 1958, detailed analyses of the viruses taken from patients with either chicken pox or shingles confirmed that the viruses were identical.

Note what that means: A person with shingles can communicate chicken pox to a susceptible individual. But the opposite is not true: A person with chicken pox cannot communicate shingles to someone else. You must already harbor the virus in your nervous system before shingles can develop. "It's a clever virus," notes a National Institute of Neurological Disorders and Stroke (NINDS) virologist. "It doesn't kill its host, but lives for a long time

ON CATCHING CHICKEN POX— BUT NOT CATCHING SHINGLES

Chicken pox is a highly contagious disease. Most of us catch it during childhood because the virus can be spread through air as well as through contact with the rash. The infection begins in the upper respiratory tract where the virus reproduces over a period of 15 days or more (the incubation period). The virus then spreads to the bloodstream and migrates to the skin, giving rise to the familiar rash.

In contrast, you can't catch shingles. You must already have had a case of chicken pox and harbor the virus in your nervous system. When activated, the virus travels down nerves to your skin causing the painful shingles rash. In shingles, the virus does not normally spread to the bloodstream or lungs, so the virus is not shed in air. Because the shingles rash contains active virus particles, however, a person who has never had chicken pox can contract chicken pox by exposure to the shingles rash.

in a suppressed state. And it can reactivate, given the opportunity," he adds.

RESEARCH CHALLENGES

Shingles imposes two immediate challenges to medical research. The first is to develop drugs to fight the disease and to prevent complications. The second challenge is to understand the disease well enough to prevent it, especially in people known to be at high risk.

Developing Antiviral Drugs

Only recently have scientists succeeded in developing antiviral drugs. In 1975, there were virtually no virus-fighting drugs available. Progress has been impressive since then and now there are several antiviral agents in clinical use, with more on the way.

Understanding the Virus

The second major challenge to investigators is to protect susceptible patients from a shingles attack. To do that, scientists will need to know much more about the VZ virus, especially how it remains latent in the body for so long, and what induces it to become active again.

What keeps the VZ virus quiet during its long latency? Probably the immune system, scientists think. A healthy immune system protects against all kinds of diseases, but people with depressed immunity are vulnerable to many illnesses, and have a high incidence of shingles. Even among normal individuals, temporary depression of the immune system because of stress, a cold, and even sunburn, may be associated with an attack of shingles.

Antibodies, one of the immune system's major defense mechanisms against infection, are not very helpful against shingles. Studies have shown that patients with shingles produce VZ antibodies: They just don't check the infection. Similarly, injections of antibody-rich blood serum do not prevent the dissemination of shingles in cancer patients or others whose immune systems are depressed. (This is in contrast to the protection conferred by the serum when given to newborns with chicken pox.)

The components of the immune system that do appear to combat shingles are two types of white blood cell: the T lymphocyte, and a scavenger cell called a macrophage. Scientists are trying to find ways of boosting the activity of these cells—especially in patients at high risk for severe or disseminated shingles.

The National Institute of Neurological
Disorders and Stroke

Dental and Oral Disorders

A healthy smile is a bonus at any age. Too often older people—especially those who wear dentures or false teeth—feel they no longer need dental checkups. Because the idea of preventive dental care dates back to the 1950s, many people over age 65 have not grown up with the idea of preventive care of the teeth.

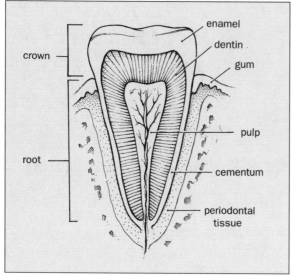

Each tooth consists of a crown and a root. Hard enamel surrounds the dentin, which in turn protects the softer pulp, containing nerves and blood vessels.

TOOTH DECAY

Tooth decay is not just a disease of children; it can continue throughout life as long as natural teeth are in the mouth. Tooth decay is caused by bacteria that normally live in the mouth. The bacteria stick to teeth and form a sticky, colorless film called dental plaque. The bacteria in plaque, which live on sugars, produce decay-causing acids that dissolve minerals in the tooth surfaces. In the presence of gum disease, tooth decay can develop on the exposed roots of the teeth.

Research has shown that adding fluoride to the water supply is the best and least costly way to prevent tooth decay. Just as with children, fluoride is important for adult teeth. In addition to drinking fluoridated water, the use of fluoride toothpastes and mouth rinses can add protection. Fluoride mouth rinses are available in two different strengths, one for daily use, one for weekly use. Daily fluoride rinses can be bought without prescription. Your dentist or dental hygienist may give you regular fluoride treatments or prescribe a fluoride gel or mouth rinse for use at home.

The National Institute on Aging

PERIODONTAL DISEASE

Periodontal disease is a gradual and progressive destructive process that threatens the gums and other supporting structures of the teeth. In the most common form of periodontal disease—called gingivitis—the gums become inflamed and tend to bleed easily. Gingivitis can be controlled with thorough, frequent plaque removal, but if left untreated, it may progress to periodontitis, a more serious state of periodontal disease. In periodontitis, infected pockets may form between the teeth and the gums, and later the bone supporting the teeth may be destroyed. When this happens, perfectly healthy teeth become loosened and can ultimately be lost.

WHO IS AFFECTED BY PERIODONTAL DISEASE?

Everyone is susceptible. At least three out of four of us will probably have some periodontal destruction in our lifetime. A recent National Survey of Adult Oral Health revealed that 77 percent of employed adults aged 18 to 65 and 95 percent of the seniors surveyed had some periodontal attachment loss—a major sign of periodontal destruction.

WHAT CAUSES PERIODONTAL DISEASE?

Often, periodontal disease results from poor oral hygiene. Masses of bacteria adhere to teeth and gums in a sticky film called dental plaque. Food particles, especially sweets, nourish the bacteria and cause them to secrete acids, enzymes, and other harmful substances that irritate soft tissues in the mouth and destroy bone. When plaque is not removed on a regular basis, the microbial attack is constant. Plaque can spread to hard-to-reach spots between the teeth and under the gums, making its removal difficult.

Other factors which can contribute to periodontal conditions include accumulated deposits of tartar or calculus, poor nutrition, hereditary lack of resistance, and imbalances in the body's system from various diseases—such as diabetes—or from pregnancy. Harmful habits such as using tobacco products and clenching and grinding the teeth can worsen periodontal disease.

Gingivitis

Gingivitis is an early stage of periodontal dis-ease and is commonly seen in both youths and adults. The gums are aggravated by bacterial plaque and become inflamed—turning red and swelling around one or more of the teeth. Eventually, the redness and swelling become more pronounced, and the gums tend to bleed easily. Bleeding as a result of brushing or flossing is one of the earliest signs of gum disease. The gums may or may not be tender and sensitive, and there may be no warning initially that the disease is present. However, if gingivitis is not controlled, the inflammation can spread to underlying tissues that support the teeth. This causes a more severe condition called periodontitis, which involves bone destruction.

Periodontitis

Periodontitis is a more serious form of periodontal disease, which occurs in three phases—early, moderate, and advanced. In the early phase, accumulated plaque hardens and extends from the gum line down along the tooth root. The gums gradually pull away from the affected teeth, causing gaps or "pockets" to develop. In the moderate phase, gums are red and swollen and bleed easily. As the gums de-

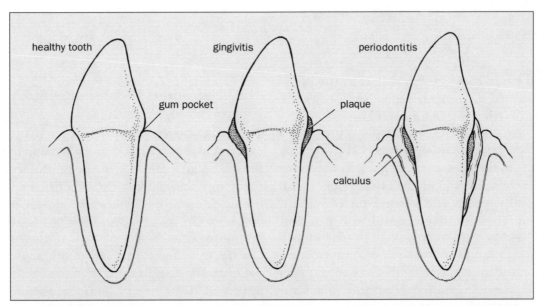

With gingivitis, plaque builds up and aggravates the gums. As gum disease advances, gums gradually pull away from affected teeth, and underlying tissue and bone are destroyed (periodontitis).

COSMETIC DENTAL OPTIONS

Tobacco, coffee, tea, and foods such as berries can permanently stain tooth surfaces; antibiotics such as tetracycline, certain illnesses and injuries, and excessive fluoride can stain teeth internally. Commercially available tooth whiteners, such as Pearl Drops polish, are not the answer, as these tend to be abrasive.

However, there are dental techniques that can safely give you a brighter smile. Your dentist will be able to diagnose and treat your problem. Unfortunately, none of the services described below is cheap, and because they are primarily cosmetic, very few insurance policies will cover them.

• *Bleaching*. For teeth that are stained internally, bleaching may help. A simple, painless, in-office procedure, bleaching is the most thorough way to whiten teeth, and it causes no side effects. The inside of the mouth is shielded with latex so that only the teeth are exposed, and a chemical bleaching agent is applied. A special light beam activates the process. Two to ten visits (usually lasting less than an hour each) may be necessary to achieve desired results.

• *Bonding*. For chips, cracks, or conspicuous gaps between the teeth, as well as severe stains, bonding may be the answer. With this method, an acid-etch solution is used to roughen the tooth surface and make it easier for the gluelike bonding agent to stick to the tooth. Over this, a malleable plastic resin is applied to reshape the tooth, fill in gaps or chips, or cover stains. Finally, the bonded surface is polished smooth. The procedure is usually performed in one visit (unless many teeth are being worked on). Bonding is fine for cosmetic reconstruction of teeth and can also be used for small fillings on front teeth, or, in some cases, even substitute for crowns on molars—but the materials used are never as strong as actual teeth, and therefore may require periodic replacement (usually about every five years).

• *Laminate Veneers*. Made of porcelain or a special resin, laminate veneers are thin shells affixed directly to the tooth. Impressions of your teeth are taken and the veneers are custom made to match the color and shape of your natural teeth. As with bonding, the tooth surface is first etched, followed by the application of a resin that holds the veneer in place.

• *Crowns*. When the structure of the tooth is weakened by previous fillings, veneers may not be the best choice. It may be better to cover the entire tooth with a metal and/or porcelain crown. The whole tooth is reduced in size, an impression is made, and a dental laboratory fabricates the crown, which is then cemented to the tooth.

The Editors

tach further, bacteria that collect in the pockets produce toxins which may begin to erode the underlying soft tissues and bone.

By the advanced stage of periodontal disease, the gums may have receded to expose tooth root surfaces, or deep pockets may have formed between the teeth. These pockets collect food particles and germs which cause infection. They are likely to fill with pus and cause bad breath. At this stage of periodontitis, more than 50 percent of the supporting bone has disintegrated and many of the special fibers which fasten the teeth to bone have been destroyed. As a result, teeth loosen and may eventually fall out.

Acute Necrotizing Ulcerative Gingivitis (ANUG)

This is a less common form of gingivitis. Also called Vincent's infection or trench mouth, this bacterial infection causes painful sores on the gums and makes eating difficult. ANUG usually develops in times of severe stress. Smokers are more susceptible to the disease than nonsmokers. ANUG is one of the "opportunistic infections" that frequently strike AIDS patients. Dentists find that removal of the bacteria and dead tissues, good nutrition, rest, careful brushing and flossing, and sometimes treatment with an antibiotic usually manage to control this type of periodontal disease.

Because many of the symptoms of periodontal disease can occur without any discomfort, you might not be aware that it is developing. Your dentist can detect the disease in its early stages, so it is important to have regular checkups to prevent the unnecessary worsening of periodontal disease.

WHAT CAN BE DONE

Controlling bacteria is the key to prevention of periodontal disease. In its early stages, periodontal disease is completely reversible. Even when some disease has already developed, dentists find that many patients respond well to a plaque removal program. Within a week or so, the inflammation usually subsides, and the swollen gums shrink and grow firm. After a few weeks, loose teeth may become more stable. Although the active disease process can be stopped in a short time, tissues that have been lost will not grow back except in unusual circumstances. However, if you remove plaque regularly, you can usually avoid gum inflammation and the development of pockets.

Brushing is an important step in plaque removal. It should be done carefully, not too vigorously, with a soft nylon brush with rounded ends on its bristles.

Use dental floss to remove bacteria from between the teeth where most pockets begin, but be careful not to let the floss cut the gum tissue. Getting under the small collars of gum tissue around the teeth, especially at the back and between the teeth, takes time and care. Ask your dentist or dental hygienist to show you how to get at some of the harder-to-reach spots.

Occasionally you will want to check on how well you are removing the plaque. Since early bacterial film is colorless, a disclosing solution containing vegetable coloring may be applied to the teeth and gums. It will stain any remaining plaque and show you which areas you have missed. Just brush and floss these areas more carefully. Finally, rinse the mouth well.

Done at least daily, careful cleaning will help protect your teeth and gums from bacterial diseases. When you make your regular visits to the dentist, any calculus that may have accumulated can be removed, and a thorough oral examination will reveal spots requiring special attention. Your dentist can also check your gums to see if they bleed easily or if there has been any detachment of gum tissue from the teeth. An antimicrobial mouth rinse also may be prescribed to help control harmful bacteria in your mouth.

And even if you wear dentures, it is still important to observe proper cleaning techniques to protect your gums and dentures. (See Dentures and Dental Implants, pages 166–167.)

The National Institute of Dental Research

DRY MOUTH (XEROSTOMIA)

Do you feel the need to moisten your mouth frequently? Does your mouth feel dry at mealtime? Do you have less saliva than you once did? Do you have difficulty swallowing? Do you have trouble eating dry foods such as crackers or toast? If you answer "yes" to these questions, you may be one of many people who suffer from dry mouth, or xerostomia.

Although xerostomia is not a disease in itself, it is a symptom of certain diseases. Dry mouth also is a common side effect of some medications and medical treatments. Most cases of dry mouth are caused by failure of the salivary glands to function properly. But some people have the sensation of a dry mouth even though their salivary glands are normal.

Dry mouth is a significant health problem because it can affect nutrition and psychological well-being, while also contributing to tooth decay and other mouth infections. Dry

DENTURES AND DENTAL IMPLANTS

Dentures

While fluoridation and improved dental treatment have allowed most people under the age of 35 to avoid a good deal of tooth decay as well as future periodontal disease, their parents and grandparents have not been so lucky.

Full or partial dentures are the rule rather than the exception if you are over 60. Almost half of those in this age group have none of their natural teeth and many more are missing at least some. Because dentures are subject to many of the same problems as natural teeth, they need as much care.

Brushing and soaking are the mainstays of denture care. They not only keep your dentures looking good but also prevent the accumulation of plaque—a gummy film consisting of saliva and bacteria that is one of the main culprits in tooth and gum decay. Built-up plaque that remains on your dentures will be pressed directly against your mouth while you are wearing them, which can lead to sores, infections, pain, or even bone loss. Brushing actively removes most visible plaque and food debris. Soaking gets rid of plaque microorganisms that might still cling to your dentures after brushing; it also helps remove stains, and reduces odors.

There is a plethora of commercial products available to help you with your denture care. However, you can substitute items that you probably already have at home for many of these products, and there are also some denture-care products that dentists do not advise using at all. Just what you choose to use is largely a matter of personal preference, but consult your dentist first to ask for any particular recommendations. Here's a basic rundown of what you will—and won't—need.

• *Brushes*. You can use a regular soft-bristled toothbrush, but special denture brushes are recommended, as their bristles are designed to mold to the shape of dentures. There are also special brushes for partial dentures that are designed to clean the clasps that attach to your natural teeth—a spot particularly prone to plaque build-up. Avoid stiff-bristled brushes; they can damage the plastic parts of dentures.

• *Cleansers*. Regular toothpaste won't do for cleaning your dentures; it's too abrasive and can damage the acrylic that most dentures are made of. Look for one of the special denture pastes that carries the approval seal of the American Dental Association's Council on Dental Materials, Instruments, and Equipment. However, plain hand-soap, mild dishwashing liquid, or baking soda will also do a good job. Don't use a household cleaner or bleach.

• *Soaking solutions*. When your dentures aren't in your mouth, they should be soaking to keep them from drying out. Cool water will do the job (hot water can warp them), but for extra cleaning power you can buy a commercially prepared solution or can make a solution yourself by mixing one tablespoon of vinegar with eight ounces of water. If you have any manual difficulties, such as arthritis, that make it hard to brush your dentures, it's particularly important that you use one of these cleaning solutions. Renew solu-

mouth also may signal more serious problems in the body. If you have a dry mouth, you should be seen by a dentist or physician to determine the cause of the symptom.

WHY IS SALIVA IMPORTANT?

Saliva has many important functions in the body. Each person needs saliva to:

• Limit the growth of bacteria that cause tooth decay and other oral infections.

• Preserve teeth by bathing them with protective minerals that allow early cavities to remineralize and heal.

• Lubricate the soft tissues lining the mouth to keep them pliable and make speaking and chewing easier.

• Dissolve foods and allow us to experience their sweet, sour, salty, and bitter tastes.

• Assist digestion by providing enzymes that break down food.

• Lubricate food so that it can be easily swallowed.

tion daily, as both the solution and the cup can be reservoirs for growth of microorganisms.

• *Adhesives*. Denture adhesives are widely marketed as the answer to loose dentures. Your dentures may feel loose when you first get them just because you're not used to them; this sensation should soon go away by itself. Dentures that gradually start to feel loose are usually a sign that the shape of the gum or supporting bone is undergoing changes, and that your dentures need to be relined or rebased. Sometimes, a small amount of powder-type adhesive is advisable to aid retention: Consult your dentist to determine when this is appropriate. Need of increasing amounts of adhesive is a sign of an ill-fitting denture. Aided by adhesives, long-term use of poorly fitted dentures can cause such severe mouth problems that it can even interfere with your ability to wear dentures at all.

• *Reliners and repair kits*. Avoid both of these. Most dentures periodically need to be relined or adjusted because of normal changes in your mouth. This takes sophisticated dental know-how, and trying to do it yourself can end up causing severe mouth problems. Likewise, let a dentist repair a cracked or chipped denture; do-it-yourself kits can damage the denture, and some of the glues in these kits even contain chemicals that can harm your mouth as well as the dentures.

Just because you have dentures to care for—and only have some or none of your natural teeth—doesn't mean you can neglect caring for those teeth that remain, or your gums and other parts of your mouth. Every day, you should remove plaque from your mouth by brushing your gums, tongue, and the roof of your mouth with a soft-bristled brush (but not a denture brush), or rubbing them firmly with a piece of damp gauze. Brush and floss remaining teeth as recommended and get professional dental care at regular intervals.

Dental Implants

Now there may be an alternative to removable dentures and fixed bridges: dental implants.

Unlike replacements that rely on remaining natural teeth for support, a dental implant consists of a crown or bridge of metal or some other material fixed to the underlying bone. Once implanted, the teeth can't be removed by the wearer, who treats them like natural teeth and can reasonably expect them to last for a decade or more.

For many wearers, dental implants are more convenient, comfortable, and stable than dentures. However, not everybody is a good candidate for dental implants. Any medical condition, such as diabetes, that might make healing difficult would rule out the surgical procedure.

The success of a dental implant depends on you as well as your dentist. Careful brushing and flossing to remove bacteria-laden plaque are vital to achieving and maintaining the seal between the gum tissue and the implant. You may need to use an antibacterial mouthwash and tiny brushes that fit in the gaps between your teeth as well. *The Editors*

• Cleanse the teeth and soft tissues of food particles.

WHAT CAUSES DRY MOUTH?

Changes in Salivary Gland Function

Dry mouth can be caused by changes in salivary gland function, brought on by the following situations.

Medications. Over 400 commonly used drugs list dry mouth as a side effect. The main culprits are the antihypertensives (for high blood pressure) and antidepressants. Both are prescribed for millions of Americans. Painkillers, tranquilizers, diuretics, and even over-the-counter antihistamines also can decrease saliva.

Cancer treatment. Radiation therapy can permanently damage salivary glands if they are in the field of radiation. Chemotherapy can change the composition of saliva, creating a sensation of dry mouth.

Diseases. Sjögren's syndrome is an autoimmune disorder whose symptoms include dry mouth and dry eyes. Some Sjögren's patients also have a connective tissue disorder, most commonly rheumatoid arthritis or systemic lupus erythematosus.

Other conditions. Bone marrow transplants, endocrine disorders, nutritional deficiencies, anxiety, mental stress, and depression can cause a dry mouth.

Changes Not Related to Salivary Gland Function

Dry mouth can also be caused by certain changes not related to salivary glands, such as those that follow.

Nerve damage. Trauma to the head and neck area from surgery or wounds can damage the nerves that supply sensation to the mouth. While the salivary glands may be left intact, they cannot function normally without the nerves that signal them to produce saliva.

Altered perception. Conditions like Alzheimer's disease or stroke may change the ability to perceive oral sensations.

DOES AGING CAUSE DRY MOUTH?

Until recently dry mouth was regarded as a normal part of aging. Researchers now know that healthy older adults do not produce less saliva. When older people do experience dry mouth, it is because they suffer from diseases that cause the condition or they take medications that produce dry mouth as a side effect.

WHAT HAPPENS WHEN YOU HAVE DRY MOUTH?

Dry mouth caused by malfunctioning salivary glands is associated with changes in saliva. The flow of saliva can decrease. Or the composition of saliva can change.

Patients with dry mouth experience vary-ing degrees of discomfort. Some people feel a dry or burning sensation in their mouth. A dry mouth may affect their ability to chew, taste, swallow, and speak. Changes in saliva also can affect oral and dental health. Severe cases of dry mouth can result in cracking of the lips, slits at the corners of the mouth, changes in the surface of the tongue, rampant tooth decay, ulceration of the mouth's linings, and infection.

IS RELIEF AVAILABLE?

Although there is no single way to treat dry mouth, there are a number of steps you can take to relieve the sense of dryness. The following suggestions will not correct the underlying cause of xerostomia, but may help you feel more comfortable.

- Take frequent sips of water or drinks without sugar. Pause often while speaking to sip some liquid. Avoid caffeine-containing coffee, tea, and soft drinks.
- Drink frequently while eating. This will make chewing and swallowing easier and may increase the taste of foods.
- Keep a glass of water by your bed for dryness during the night or upon awakening.
- Chew sugarless gum. The chewing may help produce more saliva.
- Eat sugarless mints or hard sugarless candies, but let them dissolve in your mouth. Cinnamon and mint are often the most effective.
- Place a small piece of lemon rind or a cherry pit in your mouth. The sucking action helps stimulate saliva.
- Avoid tobacco and alcohol.
- Avoid spicy, salty, and highly acidic foods that may irritate the mouth.
- Ask your dentist about using artificial salivas to help lubricate the mouth.
- Use a humidifier, particularly at night.

The National Institute of Dental Research

The Digestive System

OVERVIEW

The digestive system is a series of hollow organs joined in a long, twisting tube from the mouth to the anus. Inside this tube is a lining called the mucosa. In the mouth, stomach, and small intestine, the mucosa contains tiny glands that produce juices to help digest food.

There are also two solid digestive organs, the liver and the pancreas, which produce juices that reach the intestine through small tubes. In addition, parts of other organ systems (for instance, nerves and blood) play a major role in the digestive system.

When we eat such things as bread, meat, and vegetables, they are not in a form that the body can use as nourishment. Our food and

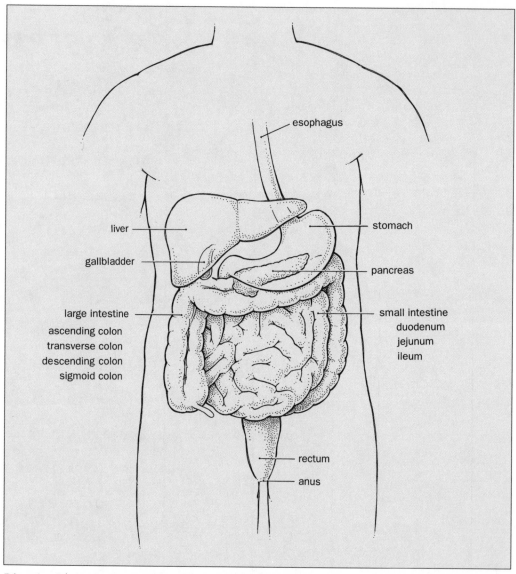

esophagus

liver

gallbladder

stomach

pancreas

large intestine
ascending colon
transverse colon
descending colon
sigmoid colon

small intestine
duodenum
jejunum
ileum

rectum

anus

Digestion begins in the mouth, and progresses through the esophagus, stomach, and intestines. The liver, gallbladder, and pancreas aid by contributing digestive enzymes.

drink must be changed into smaller molecules of nutrients before they can be absorbed into the blood and carried to cells throughout the body. Digestion is the process by which food and drink are broken down into their smallest parts so that the body can use them to build and nourish cells and to provide energy.

HOW FOOD IS DIGESTED

Digestion involves the mixing of food, its movement through the digestive tract, and chemical breakdown of the large molecules of food into smaller molecules. Digestion begins in the mouth, when we chew and swallow, and is completed in the small intestine. The chemical process varies somewhat for different kinds of food.

Movement of Food Through the System

The large, hollow organs of the digestive system contain muscle that enables their walls to move. The movement of organ walls can propel food and liquid and can also mix the contents within each organ. Typical movement of the esophagus, stomach, and intestine is called peristalsis. The action of peristalsis looks like an ocean wave moving through the muscle: the muscle of the organ produces a narrowing and then propels the narrowed portion slowly down the length of the organ. These waves of narrowing push the food and fluid in front of them through each hollow organ.

The first major muscle movement of digestion occurs when food or liquid is swallowed. Although we are able to start swallowing by choice, once the swallow begins, it becomes involuntary and proceeds under the control of the nerves.

The esophagus is the organ into which the swallowed food is pushed. It connects the throat above with the stomach below. At the junction of the esophagus and stomach, there is a ringlike valve closing the passage between the two organs. However, as the food approaches the closed ring, the surrounding muscles relax and allow the food to pass.

The food then enters the stomach, which has three mechanical tasks to do. First, the stomach must store the swallowed food and liquid. This requires the muscle of the upper part of the stomach to relax and accept large volumes of swallowed material. The second job is to mix up the food, liquid, and digestive juice produced by the stomach. The lower part of the stomach mixes these materials by its muscle action. The third task of the stomach is to empty its contents slowly into the small intestine.

Several factors affect emptying of the stomach, including the nature of the food (mainly its fat and protein content) and the degree of muscle action of the emptying stomach and the next organ to receive the stomach contents (the small intestine).

As the food is digested in the small intestine and dissolved into the juices from the pancreas, liver, and intestine, the contents of the intestine are mixed and pushed forward to allow further digestion.

Finally, all of the digested nutrients are absorbed through the intestinal walls. The waste products of this process include the undigested parts of the food, known as fiber, and the older cells that have been shed from the mucosa. These materials are propelled into the colon, where they remain, usually for a day or two, until the feces are expelled by a bowel movement.

Production of Digestive Juices

Glands of the digestive system are crucial to the process of digestion. They produce both the juices that break down the food and the hormones that help to control the process.

The glands that act first are in the mouth—the salivary glands. Saliva produced by these glands contains an enzyme that begins to digest the starch from food into smaller molecules.

The next set of digestive glands is in the

stomach lining. They produce stomach acid and an enzyme that digests protein. One of the unsolved puzzles of the digestive system is why the acid juice of the stomach does not dissolve the tissue of the stomach itself. In most people, the stomach mucosa is able to resist the juice, although food and other tissues of the body cannot.

After the stomach empties the food and its juice into the small intestine, the juices of two other digestive organs mix with the food to continue the process of digestion. One of these organs is the pancreas. It produces a juice that contains a wide array of enzymes to break down the carbohydrates, fat, and protein in our food. Other enzymes active in the process come from glands in the wall of the intestine or are even a part of that wall.

The liver produces yet another digestive juice—bile. The bile is stored between meals in the gallbladder. At mealtime, it is squeezed out of the gallbladder into the bile ducts to reach the intestine and mix with the fat in our food. The bile acids dissolve the fat into the watery contents of the intestine, much like detergents in dishwater that dissolve grease from a frying pan. After the fat is dissolved, it is digested by enzymes from the pancreas and the lining of the intestine.

Absorption and Transport of Nutrients

Digested molecules of food, as well as water and minerals from the diet, are absorbed from the cavity of the upper small intestine. The absorbed materials cross the mucosa into the blood, mainly, and are carried off in the bloodstream to other parts of the body for storage or for further chemical change. As noted above, this part of the process varies with different types of nutrients.

Carbohydrates. An average American adult eats about half a pound of carbohydrate each day. Our most common and least costly foods contain mostly carbohydrate. Examples are bread, potatoes, pastries, candy, soft drinks, rice, spaghetti, fruits, and vegetables. Many of these foods contain both starch, which can be digested, and fiber (sometimes called roughage), which the body cannot digest.

The digestible carbohydrates are broken into simpler molecules by enzymes in the saliva, in juice produced by the pancreas, and in the lining of the small intestine. Starch is digested in two steps: First, an enzyme in the saliva and pancreatic juice breaks the starch into molecules called maltose; then an enzyme in the lining of the small intestine (maltase) splits the maltose into glucose molecules that can be absorbed into the blood. Glucose is carried through the bloodstream to the liver, where it is stored or used to provide energy for the work of the body.

Table sugar is another carbohydrate that must be digested to be useful. An enzyme in the lining of the small intestine digests table sugar into glucose and fructose, each of which can be absorbed from the intestinal cavity into the blood. Milk contains yet another type of sugar, lactose, which is changed into absorbable molecules by an enzyme called lactase, also found in the intestinal lining.

Protein. Foods such as meat, eggs, and beans consist of giant molecules of protein that must be digested by enzymes before they can be used to build and repair body tissues. An enzyme in the juice of the stomach starts the digestion of swallowed protein. Further digestion of the protein is completed in the small intestine. Here, several enzymes from the pancreatic juice and the lining of the intestine carry out the breakdown of huge protein molecules into small molecules called amino acids. These small molecules can be absorbed from the hollow of the small intestine into the blood and then be carried to all parts of the body to build the walls and other parts of cells.

Fats. Fat molecules are a rich source of energy for the body. The first step in the digestion of a fat such as butter is to dissolve it into the watery content of the intestinal cavity. The bile acids produced by the liver act as natural detergents to dissolve fat in water and allow the enzymes to break the large fat molecules into smaller molecules, some of which are fatty acids and cholesterol. The bile acids combine with the fatty acids and cholesterol and help these molecules to move into the cells of the mucosa. In these cells the small molecules are formed back into large molecules, most of which pass into vessels (called lymphatics) near the intestine. These small vessels carry the re-formed fat to the veins of the chest, and the blood carries the fat to storage depots in different parts of the body.

Vitamins. Another vital part of our food that is absorbed from the small intestine is the class of chemicals we call vitamins. There are two different types of vitamins, classified by the fluid in which they can be dissolved: water-soluble vitamins (all the B vitamins and vitamin C) and fat-soluble vitamins (vitamins A, D, and K).

Water and salt. Most of the material absorbed from the cavity of the small intestine is water in which salt is dissolved. The salt and water come from the food and liquid we swallow and the juices secreted by the many digestive glands. In a healthy adult, more than a gallon of water containing over an ounce of salt is absorbed from the intestine every 24 hours.

HOW DIGESTION IS CONTROLLED

Hormone Regulators

A fascinating feature of the digestive system is that it contains its own regulators. The major hormones that control the functions of the digestive system are produced and released by cells in the mucosa of the stomach and small intestine. These hormones are released into the blood of the digestive tract, travel back to the heart and through the arteries, and return to the digestive system, where they stimulate the digestive juices and cause organ movement.

The hormones that control digestion are gastrin, secretin, and cholecystokinin (CCK).

- *Gastrin* causes the stomach to produce an acid for dissolving and digesting some foods. It is also necessary for the normal growth of the lining of the stomach, small intestine, and colon.
- *Secretin* causes the pancreas to send out a digestive juice that is rich in bicarbonate. It stimulates the stomach to produce pepsin, an enzyme that digests protein, and it also stimulates the liver to produce bile.
- *CCK* causes the pancreas to grow and to produce the enzymes of pancreatic juice, and it causes the gallbladder to empty.

Nerve Regulators

Two types of nerves help to control the action of the digestive system.

Extrinsic (outside) nerves come to the digestive organs from the unconscious part of the brain or from the spinal cord. They release a chemical called acetylcholine and another called adrenalin.

Acetylcholine causes the muscle of the digestive organs to squeeze with more force and increase the "push" of food and juice through the digestive tract. Acetylcholine also causes the stomach and pancreas to produce more digestive juice. Adrenalin relaxes the muscle of the stomach and intestine and decreases the flow of blood to these organs.

Even more important, though, are the intrinsic (inside) nerves, which make up a very dense network embedded in the walls of the esophagus, stomach, small intestine, and colon. The intrinsic nerves are triggered to act when the walls of the hollow organs are stretched by food. They release many different substances that speed up or delay the movement of food and the production of juices by the digestive organs.

The National Institute of Diabetes and Digestive and Kidney Diseases

HEARTBURN

People experience heartburn in a variety of forms. Usually heartburn is a burning chest pain located behind the breastbone. Often there is a sensation of food coming back into the mouth, accompanied by an acid or bitter taste. Typically, heartburn occurs after meals and is a common source of complaints of indigestion. Fried or fatty foods, tomato products, citrus fruits and juices, chocolate, and coffee often cause heartburn. Usually the burning-type chest pain lasts for many minutes—sometimes as long as two hours—and often is worse when the sufferer is lying flat or bending over. Heartburn is usually described as a burning sensation, although it may not be considered painful by some people. In addition, heartburn is neither brought on by exercise nor relieved with rest; most people obtain relief by standing upright or by taking an antacid.

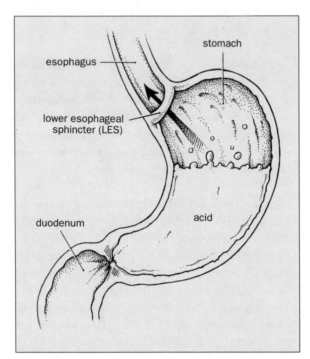

A weak lower esophageal sphincter (LES) or inappropriate relaxation of the LES allows stomach acid to escape into the esophagus, causing heartburn.

HOW COMMON IS HEARTBURN?

Approximately 10 percent of the U.S. population suffers daily from heartburn, and at least one-third of otherwise normal individuals have this symptom occasionally.

Although heartburn is a common malady in our society, it is rarely life-threatening. It can, however, limit an individual's daily activities and productivity. With proper understanding of the causes of heartburn and a rational approach to treatment, most people will find relief.

WHAT CAUSES HEARTBURN?

The esophagus is the tubelike structure that connects the mouth to the stomach. At the point where the esophagus joins the stomach, the esophagus is kept closed by a specialized muscle called the lower esophageal sphincter (LES). This muscle is important because the pressure in the stomach is normally higher than that in the esophagus. The muscle of the LES relaxes after swallowing to allow passage of food into the stomach, but then it quickly closes once again.

Does Heartburn Equal Acid Reflux?

Mainly, yes, since backwash of stomach contents into the esophagus, commonly called reflux, occurs when the LES muscle is very weak or, more commonly, when it inappropriately relaxes. The reflux tends to be worse after big meals and when one lies down at night. The refluxed fluid irritates the esophageal lining.

The occurrence and severity of heartburn depend on LES dysfunction, but they are also affected by the type and amount of fluid brought up from the stomach, by the clearing action of the esophagus, by the neutralizing action of saliva, and by other factors. Although heartburn is the most common manifestation of acid reflux, it is important to recognize that other, more serious problems can result from chronic reflux. Some of these complications such as esophageal bleeding, ulcers, or stricture may require more vigorous treatment.

Is Heartburn Caused by Hiatal Hernia?

For many years, heartburn seemed to be a result of hiatal hernia. It is now known that small hiatal hernias are common and usually innocent.

Hiatal hernia is a condition in which a portion of the stomach slides up through the diaphragm and occupies a place in the chest cavity. In fact, the majority of people past the age of 50 have evidence of a hiatal hernia after certain maneuvers during x-ray examination. Heartburn is not caused by such a hernia but, rather, results from the incompetent valve described earlier.

WHAT CAN BE DONE ABOUT HEARTBURN?

First of all, any chest pain (even burning) requires a medical evaluation. Chest pain is rarely caused by acid reflux. Other causes such as heart disease must be considered.

If acid reflux is suspected, certain specific steps may prevent symptoms of heartburn. Avoiding foods that cause symptoms may be of benefit (fried and fatty foods, tomato products, citrus fruits and juices, chocolate, and coffee are among those often causing symptoms). Although no studies proving that such modification relieves heartburn have been conducted, many physicians note that patients improve after they remove certain foods from their diets. In addition, decreasing the size or volume of a meal consumed can be helpful. Being overweight often contributes to symptoms, and many people find relief when their weight is below a certain point.

Cigarette smoking has been shown to decrease LES pressure dramatically. Therefore, reducing (or, preferably, stopping) smoking can be an important component of treatment.

Elevating the head of the bed on six-inch blocks reduces heartburn by allowing the effect of gravity to minimize reflux of stomach contents into the esophagus at night. Antacids taken on a regular basis will neutralize the stomach acid and stop heartburn. Many patients have discovered that nonprescription antacids provide temporary or partial relief. Antacid combined with a foaming agent such as alginic acid can help some patients. These compounds are believed to form a foam barrier on the top of the gastric pool.

⚠ **Take liquid antacids (Maalox or Mylanta II, for example) whenever heartburn occurs, especially after meals or at bedtime. Avoid Tums and Bisodol, since calcium-containing preparations will increase the secretion of stomach acid.**

It should be recognized that there can be side effects from long-term use of antacids. These effects can include diarrhea, altered calcium metabolism, and magnesium retention. Magnesium retention can be serious for patients with kidney disease. As with other symptoms, if prolonged use of nonprescription antacids becomes necessary, a physician should be consulted.

WHAT IF SYMPTOMS PERSIST?

People with severe acid reflux or with symptoms unresponsive to the measures described above may need more complete diagnostic evaluation.

Tests and Procedures

Usually an upper gastrointestinal (GI) series will be performed during the early phase of evaluation. An upper GI series is a special x-ray test that shows the esophagus, stomach, and duodenum. While this test provides limited information about possible acid reflux, it is performed to rule out other possible diagnoses such as peptic ulcer or to rule out complications such as esophageal ulcer.

A variety of tests and procedures is currently used to evaluate further the patient with heartburn. It is fair to say that the ideal test has not been developed and that no test is 100 percent accurate.

Endoscopy is an important procedure in heartburn patients. By looking through a small tube placed into the esophagus, the physician may see inflammation of the tissue lining the esophagus (esophagitis).

Biopsy (removal of a small sample of tissue) of the lining of the esophagus may be helpful if the findings of the endoscopy are negative or questionable.

The Bernstein test (dripping a mild acid through a tube placed in the midesophagus) is often performed as part of a complete evaluation. This test attempts to confirm that the symptoms are produced by contact of acid with the esophageal lining.

Pressure measurements of the esophagus (esophageal manometric studies) occasionally help identify critically low pressure in the LES.

For those patients in whom the diagnosis is difficult to make, many doctors find it helpful to measure acid levels inside the esophagus (pH testing). Newer techniques of long-term pH monitoring are improving diagnostic capability in this area.

WHAT MEDICAL THERAPIES ARE AVAILABLE?

Once the diagnosis of acid reflux has been confirmed, the physician may prescribe one of a number of new medications available to treat this problem. The most exciting of these new drugs are cimetidine and ranitidine, which suppress gastric acid secretion. Many studies have indicated that these drugs are effective in the short-term treatment of acute reflux symptoms.

Other approaches to medical therapy include the use of drugs to increase the LES pressure. This increase can be accomplished with either bethanechol or metoclopramide.

Both of these drugs have been shown experimentally to be effective in treating heartburn.

CAN HEARTBURN REQUIRE SURGERY?

A few people may need surgery because of poor response to medical treatment. Surgical procedures intended to produce an effective LES have been developed in recent years. However, surgery should not be considered until all other measures have been tried.

WHAT ARE THE COMPLICATIONS OF LONG-TERM HEARTBURN?

Although heartburn itself does not cause complications, the acid reflux with which it is associated can occasionally result in serious complications. Gastrointestinal blood loss from damage to the esophagus can cause anemia, which occasionally may be severe. Scarring of the lower esophagus may result in narrowing of the opening of the esophagus (stricture), which can seriously interfere with swallowing. Reflux may be a cause of recurrent wheezing and other lung symptoms.

CURRENT AND FUTURE RESEARCH

During the past decade, research into the mechanisms and therapy of heartburn in both animals and humans has been quite active. The newer therapeutic approaches discussed above represent some of the results of these research efforts.

The National Institute of Diabetes and
Digestive and Kidney Diseases

HIATAL HERNIA

A hernia is a protrusion of an organ through a wall of a cavity in which it is enclosed. In the case of a hiatal hernia, a portion of the stomach protrudes through a teardrop-shaped hole in the diaphragm where the esophagus and the stomach join.

Hiatal hernias may develop in people of all ages and both sexes, although it is considered to be a condition of middle age. In fact, the majority of otherwise normal people past the age of 50 have small hiatal hernias.

CAUSES

The most frequent known cause of hiatal hernia is an increased pressure in the abdominal cavity produced by coughing, vomiting, straining at stool, or sudden physical exertion. Pregnancy, obesity, or excess fluid in the abdomen also contribute to causing this condition.

HIATAL HERNIAS AND HEARTBURN

For many years, many people, including some doctors, thought that heartburn was a result of having a hiatal hernia.

It is now known that small hiatal hernias are common and usually harmless. While heartburn is sometimes associated with hiatal hernia, it is not caused by it.

Heartburn occurs when the sphincter located at the junction of the esophagus and the stomach (called the LES) either relaxes inappropriately or is very weak. This allows the highly acidic contents of the stomach to back up into the esophagus. The backwash of stomach contents, known as reflux, irritates the lining of the esophagus and causes heartburn.

TREATMENT

Most hiatal hernias do not need treatment. However, if the hernia is in danger of becoming strangulated (constricted in such a way as to cut off the blood supply) or is complicated by esophagitis (inflammation of the esophagus), treatment becomes necessary. To prevent strangulation, your doctor may perform surgery to reduce the size of the hernia.

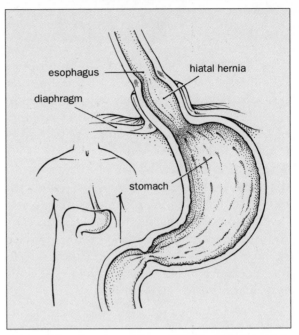

A hiatal hernia occurs when a portion of the stomach slides upward into the chest cavity, through the hiatus, or opening, of the diaphragm.

Treatment of esophagitis is necessary to prevent ulcers from forming in the lining of the esophagus. When these sores heal, they can leave scars that make it difficult or impossible to swallow. In some people, long-term esophagitis may result in Barrett's esophagus, a condition thought to be a precursor of cancer. Most cases of esophagitis respond to antacids, weight reduction, and a common-sense approach to eating, drinking, and other lifestyle habits.

Remember, if prolonged use of antacids becomes necessary, see your doctor. Long-term use of antacids can produce side effects like diarrhea, altered calcium metabolism, and magnesium retention.

If the esophagitis persists, your doctor may perform surgery to restore the stomach to its proper position and strengthen the area around the opening.

The National Institute of Diabetes and Digestive and Kidney Diseases

PEPTIC ULCER

A peptic ulcer is an ulcer of the lining of either the stomach or the first part of the small intestine below the stomach called the duodenum. Peptic ulcers occur only in those regions of the gastrointestinal tract that are bathed by digestive juices secreted by the stomach. These juices contain hydrochloric acid and a digestive enzyme called pepsin—hence the name "peptic" ulcer. Peptic ulcers that appear in the stomach are called gastric ulcers, and those that occur in the duodenum are called duodenal ulcers. In the United States, duodenal ulcers are more common than gastric ulcers. The reverse is true in Japan.

WHO GETS ULCERS

Approximately 1 out of every 10 Americans will have a peptic ulcer sometime during his or her life. Each year, over 46,000 operations

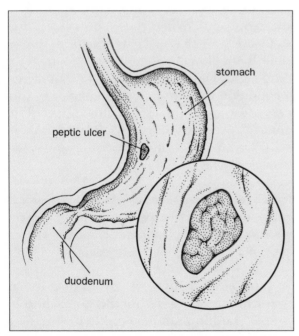

Peptic ulcers can occur anywhere in the lining of the stomach or duodenum. They may break through the lining, resulting in a perforated ulcer.

for peptic ulcer disease are performed, and over 7,000 people in the United States die from complications associated with ulcers.

Although ulcers can occur at any age, they are rare among children and only slightly more common in teenagers. Duodenal ulcers usually first appear in people during their twenties or thirties, while gastric ulcers are more likely to develop among people who are in their forties or older.

Heredity also is a factor in the incidence of peptic ulcer disease. A person's risk for getting an ulcer is increased threefold if any of his or her blood relatives have ulcers. A person has a greater chance of getting a duodenal ulcer if the relative has a duodenal ulcer. Similarly, a gastric ulcer is more likely to occur in a person whose parent or sibling has a gastric ulcer.

Contrary to popular beliefs, there is limited evidence to show that a person's occupation or socioeconomic status has any effect on causing ulcers. However, the incidence of duodenal ulcers in men is about twice that in women, while the occurrence of gastric ulcers is about equal in both sexes.

CAUSES

In a healthy person, there is a balance between factors that cause ulcers and factors that prevent ulcers. Most important among these factors are (1) the amount of acid and pepsin the stomach secretes, especially the former, and (2) the ability of the lining of the stomach and duodenum to resist the erosive action of the acid and pepsin. Sometimes, however, this balance can be upset and may lead to the development of an ulcer.

Most people with duodenal ulcers and some people with gastric ulcers secrete excess amounts of pepsin and acid. High levels of these digestive juices can overcome the lining defenses of the stomach or the duodenal wall and can cause an ulcer.

On the other hand, some ulcer patients se-

HELICOBACTER PYLORI

Infection with the bacteria Helicobacter pylori increases the likelihood of developing an ulcer. That's the conclusion of a study recently conducted in Canada that shows that children in the same family tend to infect one another with Helicobacter pylori, which has been shown previously to be associated with ulcers. Just how Helicobacter pylori damages the stomach lining has not been completely explained; it may be that the bacteria is merely an opportunistic invader of already damaged tissue. In any case, it has been shown in several studies that eliminating the bacteria leads to the prolonged healing of ulcers.   *The Editors*

crete normal amounts of gastric acid. Instead, their ulcer may be caused by a decreased resistance of the lining of the stomach or duodenum. This weakness can leave the lining of the digestive tract unable to tolerate the normal amounts of gastric acid that the stomach secretes.

Environmental Factors

Although a variety of popular beliefs have associated numerous factors with peptic ulcers, only a few have been found to play a role in causing ulcers.

Smoking. A considerable amount of scientific evidence has shown that cigarette smoking not only doubles a person's chances of getting an ulcer, but it also tends to slow the healing process of an existing ulcer. In addition, recent research findings indicate that smoking is an important factor in causing ulcer recurrence. People who stop smoking have a lower rate of recurrent ulcers regardless of what medication they may take. In fact, recent research has shown that the chances of an ulcer healing and staying healed are better if a patient quits smoking and takes no medication than if the patient continues to smoke and receives drug treatment.

Aspirin. Persons who use aspirin regularly over long periods of time, such as some arthritis patients, have an increased chance of developing a gastric ulcer. Researchers have found that aspirin and similar nonsteroidal anti-inflammatory drugs (NSAIDs) inhibit the stomach's production of a substance called prostaglandins. Prostaglandins may act to protect the lining of the stomach from injury by a wide variety of chemical agents, including the stomach's own acid secretions. In most cases, however, these ulcers disappear once the damaging drugs are stopped.

Caffeine. Coffee, tea, cola drinks, and other foods that contain caffeine can stimulate acid secretion in the digestive tract and, in turn, may aggravate the pain of an existing ulcer. However, the role of caffeine products in contributing to the development of ulcers is unknown. The level of acid secretion induced by decaffeinated coffee is the same as with regular coffee. Therefore, substances other than caffeine are present in coffee that stimulate gastric activity.

Diet. No convincing evidence shows that certain diets can cause ulcers or that certain diets can heal ulcers and keep them healed. A diet may help to relieve the pain or indigestion of an existing ulcer, but it will not prevent an ulcer from forming.

Many foods that initially neutralize acid in the stomach also may stimulate additional acid secretion. In fact, research has shown that milk, which was a mainstay in the diets of ulcer patients, actually can be a potent stimulant of gastric acid secretion.

Alcohol. One of the most popular myths about peptic ulcers is that people who drink alcohol are more likely to get an ulcer. The truth is that even those people who are moderate to heavy users of alcohol do not have an increased chance of developing an ulcer. Although alcohol often was thought to be a stimulant of stomach acid secretion, numerous studies have failed to establish such a relationship between acid secretion and concentrated alcoholic drinks.

Stress

Although stress may aggravate the pain or indigestion associated with an ulcer, scientists have not yet been able to determine whether stress is an important factor in causing ulcers. Stress is difficult to measure, because people react differently to similar circumstances. A situation that may cause stress in one person may have no effect on someone else.

So far, there is no convincing proof that people who have high-pressure jobs or who experience a great deal of tension in their lives are more likely to develop ulcers. However, some ulcer patients may be less able to tolerate large amounts of stress or tension. Consequently, these people may believe that their ulcer pain increases or "acts up" when they are confronted with a stressful situation.

Regardless of the level of effect that stress may have on a patient's ulcer, it is a good idea for the patient and his or her physician to work together to identify and then try to reduce or remove stressful factors in the patient's life.

Physical stress, however, is associated with an increase in ulcer incidence. Thus, burns, surgery, and other trauma often require rigorous treatment of acidity.

SYMPTOMS

The most common symptom of a duodenal ulcer is a gnawing or burning pain in the abdomen between the navel and lower end of the breastbone. The pain most often occurs between meals and in the early hours of the morning, when the stomach may increase its acid secretion.

The pain, which can last a few minutes to a few hours, usually is relieved by eating food or taking antacids. Unfortunately, these symptoms are not always specific enough to diagnose an ulcer. Some people may have an ulcer with little or no pain, while others may have an unrelated disorder that causes similar symptoms. Frequently, a physician will conduct more extensive tests to verify the presence of an ulcer.

DIAGNOSIS

When a patient describes symptoms similar to those just mentioned, a physician usually suspects a peptic ulcer. The most common procedure for detecting an ulcer is an x-ray. With this technique, the physician may have the patient swallow a solution containing barium sulfate, a substance that helps to create a sharp silhouette of the digestive tract on x-ray film. If an ulcer is present, a pool of barium liquid may fill the ulcer crater and usually appear in x-ray pictures of the stomach and the duodenum.

Sometimes, an ulcer may not be revealed in an x-ray study. If this happens, the doctor can use an alternative method of detecting ulcers with an instrument called a fiber optic endoscope. This device is a flexible tube containing two bundles of flexible glass fibers that can be passed through a patient's mouth and esophagus and into the stomach and duodenum. One small bundle of fibers is used to conduct light, which illuminates the inner surfaces of the digestive tract. The other bundle lets the physician view the lighted area to look for signs of an ulcer.

TREATMENT

Most treatments for ulcers attempt to reduce stomach acid concentration to allow an ulcer to heal more quickly.

Antacids

Antacids are medications that can offer temporary relief from ulcer pain by neutralizing hydrochloric acid in the stomach. There are many commercially available antacids on the market, and a physician usually can find one for a patient that is not unpleasant to take.

Drugs

Several prescription drugs can successfully relieve pain and promote ulcer healing.

Cimetidine (Tagamet) reduces the amount of acid the stomach secretes by stopping the stomach's response to histamine. (In addition to hay fever and other allergic reactions, histamine also plays a role in gastric acid secretion.) Cimetidine works by blocking the action of the histamine II receptors in the stomach. These receptors are different from the histamine I receptors that are involved with allergies.

Ranitidine (Zantac) also inhibits stomach acid secretion by blocking histamine action at the site of the histamine II receptors. However, ranitidine does not have some of the side effects associated with cimetidine.

Sucralfate (Carafate) has been approved by the Food and Drug Administration (FDA) for short-term (up to eight weeks) treatment of duodenal ulcers. Unlike cimetidine or ranitidine, sucralfate may act directly on an ulcer site by coating the ulcer and protecting the area from further damage by gastric acid.

Surgery

In the vast majority of cases, the drugs just mentioned are successful in healing ulcers. However, some patients may not respond to this type of treatment. In these cases, surgery may be required to correct the problem.

Antrectomy. One type of surgery is known as an antrectomy. This operation involves removing a lower portion of the stomach called the antrum. The antrum is the part of the stomach that produces gastrin, which is the hormone that stimulates the stomach to secrete digestive juices. Sometimes a surgeon may also remove an adjacent part of the stomach that actually secretes pepsin and acid.

Vagotomy. Another type of operation, called a vagotomy, involves cutting the vagus nerve, which connects the brain to the stomach. There are several variations of a vagotomy, depending on where the vagus nerve is cut. The newest and most refined variation of this operation is called a selective vagotomy. This procedure concentrates on cutting only those parts of the vagus nerve that go to the acid-secreting cells in the stomach wall. The operation is designed to avoid those parts of the vagus nerve that influence the motility involved in stomach

NEW DRUG TREATMENTS FOR ULCERS

- *Misoprostol* (Cytotec) is a relatively new drug that is especially effective against NSAID-induced gastric ulcers and is often prescribed for those who must continue to take NSAIDs. It does, however, cause diarrhea in some patients.
- *Omeprazole* (Losec) is a powerful new drug that completely inhibits acid secretion and heals ulcers quickly. But it is reserved for short-term therapy of serious ulcers, since it has been shown to induce a specific type of cancer in animals if administered long term.
- *Bismuth and antibiotics* (bismuth salts, such as those found in Pepto-Bismol, and such antibiotics as amoxicillin and tetracycline) in combination have been used to attack the bacteria known as Helicobacter pylori. The therapy remains experimental, however, until it is confirmed by additional studies and the proper dosage level for the antibiotics can be established (otherwise, the treatment could result in the development of a dangerous resistance of other bacteria to the antibiotics used). Some physicians hope that eliminating Helicobacter pylori with bismuth and antibiotics will become "the" treatment for ulcers, making all other medications obsolete—but that hope remains to be realized. *The Editors*

emptying. This type of surgery has the lowest incidence of side effects, but it is the least effective in keeping ulcers healed.

These operations are usually successful in healing ulcers. However, ulcer surgery sometimes can result in serious complications, which may have long-term effects and which may be more debilitating than the original ulcer disease. Thus, a patient should consult his or her physician and thoroughly consider the possible side effects of an operation before undergoing surgery.

COMPLICATIONS

In addition to pain, ulcer patients may sometimes experience serious complications if their ulcer is left untreated.

Bleeding

As an ulcer erodes into the muscular portion of the gastric or duodenal wall, it can erode into blood vessels and cause bleeding into the digestive tract. If the damaged blood vessels are small, the blood may seep out slowly, and over a long period of time, the patient can gradually become anemic. On the other hand, if the damaged blood vessel is large, bleeding into the intestinal tract is more rapid and can be very dangerous. The patient may feel faint, vomit blood, or collapse suddenly. With some bleeding ulcers, the stool may become a tarry black color due to the digested blood it contains. Without prompt medical attention, often including blood transfusions and surgery, the patient may bleed to death.

Perforation

Sometimes an ulcer will erode all the way through the wall of the stomach or duodenum. If this happens, partially digested food and bacteria from the digestive tract can spill into the sterile abdominal cavity and cause peritonitis, an inflammation of the abdominal cavity and wall. A perforated ulcer, which can cause sudden, severe pain, usually requires hospitalization and corrective surgery.

Narrowing and Obstruction

Ulcers that occur in the duodenum or in the narrow section where the stomach connects to the duodenum can cause spasms of the adjacent muscles and swelling of surrounding tissue. This swelling can cause the intestinal opening to become narrowed or closed off completely. Such an obstruction can prevent food from leaving the stomach and entering the intestinal tract. A patient may vomit the contents of the stomach and, if the condition continues, lose weight and develop other problems. Again, surgery may be necessary to correct this problem.

RECURRENCE

Peptic ulcer disease is a chronic relapsing disorder. About 50 percent of ulcer patients experience another episode within one to two years after the previous ulcer has healed. The longer a person goes without a recurrence, the greater the likelihood that an ulcer will return. The underlying cause of ulcers is still unknown, but researchers believe that peptic ulcer disease is a group of disorders, all of which share the same symptom—an ulceration of the lining of the stomach or duodenum.

The FDA has approved cimetidine (Tagamet) for long-term maintenance therapy to prevent recurrent ulcers. The drug, if taken regularly, can be successful and has exhibited a very low incidence of side effects. It also provides an effective alternative to surgery for those patients with severe cases of peptic ulcers who are at a high risk for surgery or who prefer not to have an operation. However, the protection that the drug gives is lost when the treatment is stopped.

CAN AN ULCER LEAD TO CANCER?

Although there is little evidence that a peptic ulcer ever develops into cancer, there can be ulceration in a stomach cancer. Because stomach cancer can ulcerate or exhibit some symptoms that are similar to those of a peptic ulcer, it is important to establish promptly whether the ulceration is truly a peptic ulcer or an ulcer with cancer. Cancer of the duodenum is very rare, so there is little chance of cancer being the cause of a duodenal ulcer.

ARE PEPTIC ULCERS AND ULCERATIVE COLITIS RELATED?

No, they are entirely different diseases. Ulcerative colitis is an inflammatory condition of the colon and rectum, the lowermost portions of the intestines. Although many small ulcers develop in the colon in ulcerative colitis, the basic cause and treatment of these two disorders are very different.

The National Institute of Diabetes and Digestive and Kidney Diseases

acute form occurs suddenly and may be a severe, life-threatening illness with many complications. Usually, the patient recovers completely. If injury to the pancreas continues, such as when a patient persists in drinking alcohol, a chronic form of the disease may develop, bringing severe pain and reduced functioning of the pancreas that affects digestion and causes weight loss.

ACUTE PANCREATITIS

An estimated 50,000 to 80,000 cases of acute pancreatitis occur in the United States each year. This disease occurs when the pancreas suddenly becomes inflamed and then gets better. Some patients have more than one attack but recover fully after each one. Most cases of acute pancreatitis are caused either by alcohol abuse or by gallstones. Other causes may be use of prescribed drugs, trauma or surgery to the abdomen, or abnormalities of the pancreas or

PANCREATITIS

The pancreas is a large gland behind the stomach and close to the duodenum. The pancreas secretes powerful digestive enzymes that enter the small intestine through a duct. These enzymes help in digesting fats, proteins, and carbohydrates. The pancreas also releases the hormones insulin and glucagon into the bloodstream. These hormones play an important part in metabolizing sugar.

Pancreatitis is a rare disease in which the pancreas becomes inflamed. Damage to the gland occurs when digestive enzymes are activated and begin attacking the pancreas. In severe cases, there may be bleeding into the gland, serious tissue damage, infection, and cysts. Enzymes and toxins may enter the bloodstream and seriously injure organs, such as the heart, lungs, and kidneys.

There are two forms of pancreatitis. The

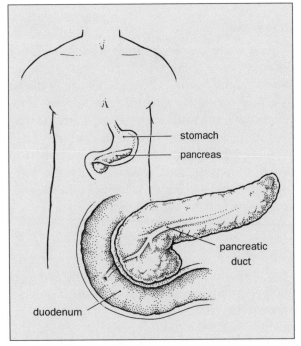

Pancreatitis, or inflammation of the pancreas, activates the pancreas's own digestive enzymes, and the organ begins to attack itself.

intestine. In rare cases, the disease may result from infections, such as mumps. In about 15 percent of cases, the cause is unknown.

Symptoms

Acute pancreatitis usually begins with pain in the upper abdomen that may last for a few days. The pain is often severe. It may be constant pain, just in the abdomen, or it may reach to the back and other areas. The pain may be sudden and intense, or it may begin as a mild pain that is aggravated by eating and slowly grows worse. The abdomen may be swollen and very tender. Other symptoms may include nausea, vomiting, fever, and an increased pulse rate. The person often feels and looks very sick.

About 20 percent of cases are severe. The patient may become dehydrated and have low blood pressure. Sometimes the patient's heart, lungs, or kidneys fail. In the most severe cases, bleeding can occur in the pancreas, leading to shock and sometimes death.

Diagnosis

During acute attacks, high levels of amylase (a digestive enzyme formed in the pancreas) are found in the blood. Changes also may occur in blood levels of calcium, magnesium, sodium, potassium, and bicarbonate. Patients may have high amounts of sugar and lipids (fats) in their blood too. These changes help the doctor diagnose pancreatitis. After the pancreas recovers, blood levels of these substances usually return to normal.

Treatment

The treatment a patient receives depends on how bad the attack is. Unless complications occur, acute pancreatitis usually gets better on its own so treatment is supportive in most cases. Usually the patient goes into the hospital. The doctor prescribes fluids by vein to restore blood volume. The kidneys and lungs may be treated to prevent failure of those organs. Other problems, such as cysts in the pancreas, may need treatment too.

Sometimes a patient cannot control vomiting and needs to have a tube through the nose to the stomach to remove fluid and air. In mild cases, the patient may not have food for three or four days but is given fluids and pain relievers by vein. An acute attack usually lasts only a few days, unless the ducts are blocked by gallstones. In severe cases, the patient may be fed through the veins for three to six weeks while the pancreas slowly heals. Antibiotics may be given if signs of infection arise.

Surgery may be needed if complications such as infection, cysts, or bleeding occur. Attacks caused by gallstones may require removal of the gallbladder or surgery of the bile duct. Surgery is sometimes needed for the doctor to be able to exclude other abdominal problems that can simulate pancreatitis or to treat acute pancreatitis. When there is severe injury with death of tissue, an operation may be done to remove the dead tissue.

After all signs of acute pancreatitis are gone, the doctor will determine the cause and try to prevent future attacks. In some patients the cause of the attack is clear, but in others further tests need to be done.

What If the Patient Has Gallstones?

Ultrasound is used to detect gallstones and sometimes can provide the doctor with an idea of how severe the pancreatitis is. When gallstones are found, surgery is usually needed to remove them. When they are removed depends on how severe the pancreatitis is. If it is mild, the gallstones often can be removed within a week or so. In more severe cases, the patient may wait a month or more, until he improves, before the stones are removed. The CT (computed tomography) scan also may be used to find out what is happening in and around the pancreas and how severe the problem is. This is important information that the doctor needs to determine when to remove the gallstones.

After the gallstones are removed and inflammation subsides, the pancreas usually returns to normal. Before patients leave the hospital, they are advised not to drink alcohol and not to eat large meals.

CHRONIC PANCREATITIS

Chronic pancreatitis usually follows many years of alcohol abuse. It may develop after only one acute attack, especially if there is damage to the ducts of the pancreas. In the early stages, the doctor cannot always tell whether the patient has acute or chronic disease. The symptoms may be the same. Damage to the pancreas from drinking alcohol may cause no symptoms for many years, and then the patient suddenly has an attack of pancreatitis. In more than 90 percent of adult patients, chronic pancreatitis appears to be caused by alcoholism. This is more common in men than women and often develops between 30 and 40 years of age. In other cases, pancreatitis may be inherited. Scientists do not know why the inherited form occurs. Patients with chronic pancreatitis tend to have three kinds of problems: pain, malabsorption of food leading to weight loss, or diabetes.

Some patients do not have any pain, but most do. Pain may be constant in the back and abdomen, and for some patients, the pain attacks are disabling. In some cases, the abdominal pain goes away as the condition advances. Doctors think this happens because pancreatic enzymes are no longer being made by the pancreas.

Patients with this disease often lose weight, even when their appetite and eating habits are normal. This occurs because the body does not secrete enough pancreatic enzymes to break down food, so nutrients are not absorbed normally. Poor digestion leads to loss of fat, protein, and sugar into the stool. Diabetes may also develop at this stage if the insulin-producing cells of the pancreas (islet cells) have been damaged.

Diagnosis

Diagnosis may be difficult but is aided by a number of new techniques. Pancreatic function tests help the physician decide if the pancreas still can make enough digestive enzymes. The doctor can see abnormalities in the pancreas using several techniques (ultrasonic imaging, endoscopic retrograde cholangio-pancreatography [ERCP], and the CT scan). In more advanced stages of the disease, when diabetes and malabsorption (a problem due to lack of enzymes) occur, the doctor can use a number of blood, urine, and stool tests to help in the diagnosis of chronic pancreatitis and to monitor the progression of the disorder.

Treatment

The doctor treats chronic pancreatitis by relieving pain and managing the nutritional and metabolic problems. The patient can reduce the amount of fat and protein lost in stools by cutting back on dietary fat and taking pills containing pancreatic enzymes. This will result in better nutrition and weight gain. Sometimes insulin or other drugs must be given to control the patient's blood sugar.

In some cases, surgery is needed to relieve pain by draining an enlarged pancreatic duct. Sometimes, part or most of the pancreas is removed in an attempt to relieve chronic pain.

Patients must stop drinking, adhere to their prescribed diets, and take the proper medications in order to have fewer and milder attacks.

*The National Institute of Diabetes and
Digestive and Kidney Diseases*

CIRRHOSIS OF THE LIVER

Many people think that cirrhosis is a disease. Cirrhosis is really what happens to the liver as a result of disease. Your liver weighs about three pounds and is the largest organ in your body. It is located in the upper right side of your abdomen, below the ribs. When chronic diseases cause the liver to become permanently injured and scarred, the condition is called cirrhosis.

The scar tissue that forms in cirrhosis harms the structure of the liver, blocking the flow of blood through the organ. The loss of normal liver tissue slows the processing of nutrients, hormones, drugs, and toxins by the liver. Also slowed is production of proteins and other substances made by the liver.

Cirrhosis is the seventh leading cause of death by disease. About 25,000 people die from cirrhosis each year. There also is a great toll in terms of human suffering, hospital costs, and work loss by people with cirrhosis.

CAUSES

Cirrhosis has many causes. In the United States, chronic alcoholism is the most common cause. Cirrhosis also may result from chronic

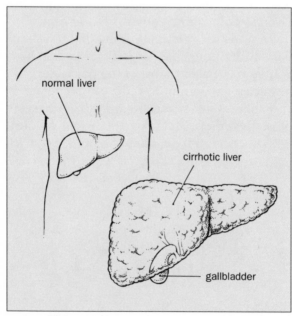

In a cirrhotic liver, healthy cells die and are replaced by scar tissue. Initially, the liver enlarges; in end-stage cirrhosis, the liver shrivels.

viral hepatitis (types B, C, and D). Liver injury that results in cirrhosis also may be caused by a number of inherited diseases such as cystic fibrosis, alpha-1 antitrypsin deficiency, hemochromatosis, Wilson's disease, galactosemia, and glycogen storage diseases.

Two inherited disorders result in the abnormal storage of metals in the liver leading to tissue damage and cirrhosis. People with Wilson's disease store too much copper in their livers, brains, kidneys, and in the corneas of their eyes. In another disorder, known as hemochromatosis, too much iron is absorbed, and the excess iron is deposited in the liver and in other organs, such as the pancreas, skin, intestinal lining, heart, and endocrine glands.

If a person's bile duct becomes blocked, this also may cause cirrhosis. The bile ducts carry bile formed in the liver to the intestines, where the bile helps in the digestion of fat.

In adults, the bile ducts may become inflamed, blocked, and scarred due to another liver disease, primary biliary cirrhosis. Another type of biliary cirrhosis also may occur after a patient has gallbladder surgery in which the bile ducts are injured or tied off.

Other, less common, causes of cirrhosis are severe reactions to prescribed drugs, prolonged exposure to environmental toxins, and repeated bouts of heart failure with liver congestion.

SYMPTOMS

People with cirrhosis often have few symptoms at first. The two major problems that eventually cause symptoms are loss of functioning liver cells and distortion of the liver caused by scarring. The person may experience fatigue, weakness, and exhaustion. Loss of appetite is usual, often with nausea and weight loss.

As liver function declines, less protein is made by the organ. For example, less of the protein albumin is made, which results in water accumulating in the legs (edema) or abdomen (ascites). A decrease in proteins needed for blood clotting makes it easy for the person to bruise or to bleed.

In the later stages of cirrhosis, jaundice (yellow skin) may occur, caused by the buildup of bile pigment that is passed by the liver into the intestines. Some people with cirrhosis experience intense itching due to bile products that are deposited in the skin. Gallstones often form in persons with cirrhosis because not enough bile reaches the gallbladder.

The liver of a person with cirrhosis also has trouble removing toxins, which may build up in the blood. These toxins can dull mental function and lead to personality changes and even coma (encephalopathy). Early signs of toxin accumulation in the brain may include neglect of personal appearance, unresponsiveness, forgetfulness, trouble concentrating, or changes in sleeping habits.

Drugs taken are usually filtered out by the liver, and this cleansing process also is slowed down by cirrhosis. The liver does not remove the drugs from the blood at the usual rate, so the drugs act longer than expected, building up in the body. People with cirrhosis often are very sensitive to medications and their side effects.

A serious problem for people with cirrhosis is pressure on blood vessels that flow through the liver. Normally, blood from the intestines and spleen is pumped to the liver through the portal vein. But in cirrhosis, this normal flow of blood is slowed, building pressure in the portal vein (portal hypertension). This blocks the normal flow of blood, causing the spleen to enlarge. So blood from the intestines tries to find a way around the liver through new vessels.

Some of these new blood vessels become quite large and are called "varices." These vessels may form in the stomach and esophagus (the tube that connects the mouth with the stomach). They have thin walls and carry high pressure. There is great danger that they may break, causing a serious bleeding problem in the upper stomach or esophagus. If this happens, the patient's life is in danger, and the doctor must act quickly to stop the bleeding.

DIAGNOSIS

The doctor often can diagnose cirrhosis from the patient's symptoms and from laboratory tests. During a physical exam, for instance, the doctor could notice a change in how your liver feels or how large it is. If the doctor suspects cirrhosis, you will be given blood tests. The purpose of these tests is to find out if liver disease is present. In some cases, other tests that take pictures of the liver are performed such as the computed tomography (CT) scan, ultrasound, and the radioisotope liver/spleen scan.

The doctor may decide to confirm the diagnosis by putting a needle through the skin (biopsy) to take a sample of tissue from the liver. In some cases, cirrhosis is diagnosed during surgery when the doctor is able to see the entire liver. The liver also can be inspected through a laparoscope, a viewing device that is inserted through a tiny incision made in the abdomen.

TREATMENT

Treatment of cirrhosis is aimed at stopping or delaying its progress, minimizing the damage to liver cells, and reducing complications. In alcoholic cirrhosis, for instance, the person must stop drinking alcohol to halt progression of the disease. If a person has hepatitis, the doctor may administer steroids or antiviral drugs to reduce liver cell injury.

Medications may be given to control the symptoms of cirrhosis, such as itching. Edema and ascites (fluid retention) are treated by reducing salt in the diet. Drugs called diuretics are used to remove excess fluid and to prevent edema from recurring. Diet and drug therapies can help to improve the altered mental function that cirrhosis can cause. For instance, decreasing dietary protein results in less toxin formation in the digestive tract. Laxatives such as lactulose may be given to help absorb toxins and speed their removal from the intestines.

The two main problems in cirrhosis are liver failure, when liver cells just stop working, and the bleeding caused by portal hypertension. The doctor may prescribe blood pressure medication, such as a beta blocker, to treat the portal hypertension. If the patient bleeds from the varices of the stomach or esophagus, the doctor can inject these veins with a sclerosing agent administered through a flexible tube (endoscope) that is inserted through the mouth and esophagus. In critical cases, the patient may be given a liver transplant or another surgery (such as a portacaval shunt) that is sometimes used to relieve the pressure in the portal vein and varices.

Patients with cirrhosis often live healthy lives for many years. Even when complications develop, they can be treated. Many patients with cirrhosis have undergone successful liver transplantation.

The National Institute of Diabetes and Digestive and Kidney Diseases

VIRAL HEPATITIS

Viral hepatitis is the most common of the serious contagious diseases caused by several viruses that attack the liver. About 70,000 cases are reported to the Centers for Disease Control each year, but this represents only a fraction of the cases occurring in this country.

Hepatitis means inflammation of the liver, usually producing swelling and tenderness and sometimes permanent damage to the liver. Hepatitis may also be caused by nonviral substances such as alcohol, chemicals, and drugs. These types of hepatitis are known respectively as alcoholic, toxic, and drug-induced hepatitis.

TYPES OF VIRAL HEPATITIS

At least five types of viral hepatitis are currently known, each caused by a different identified virus.

- *Hepatitis A,* formerly called infectious hepatitis, is most common in children in developing countries, but is being seen more frequently in adults in the western world.
- *Hepatitis B,* formerly called serum hepatitis, is the most serious form of hepatitis, with over 300 million carriers in the world and an estimated 1 million in the United States.
- *Hepatitis C,* formerly called non-A, non-B hepatitis, is now the most common cause of hepatitis after blood transfusion. More than 1 percent of Americans are carriers of the virus.
- *Hepatitis D,* formerly called delta hepatitis, is found mainly in intravenous drug users who are carriers of the hepatitis B virus which is necessary for the hepatitis D virus to spread.
- *Hepatitis E,* formerly called enteric or epidemic non-A, non-B hepatitis, resembles hepatitis A, but is caused by a different virus commonly found in the Indian Ocean area.
- *Other viruses,* especially members of the herpes virus family, including the cold sore virus, chicken pox virus, infectious mononucleosis virus, and others, can affect the liver as well as other organs they infect. This is particularly true when the immune system is impaired.

HOW THE INFECTION IS SPREAD

Hepatitis A and E viruses are excreted or shed in feces. Direct contact with an infected person's feces or indirect fecal contamination of food, the water supply, raw shellfish, hands, and utensils may result in sufficient amounts of virus entering the mouth to cause infections.

Hepatitis B is spread from mother to child at birth or soon after birth, through sexual contact, blood transfusions, or contaminated needles. Almost a quarter of the cases may result from unknown sources in the general population. In families the virus can be spread from adults to children.

Hepatitis C is spread directly from one person to another via blood or needles. While sexual transmission and mother-to-child spread may occur, the transmission of this disease is not clearly understood.

Hepatitis D is spread mainly by needles and blood. Hepatitis D infects only individuals infected with hepatitis B and may be transmitted by carriers of hepatitis D and B.

SYMPTOMS

The most common symptoms are fatigue, mild fever, muscle or joint aches, nausea, vomiting, loss of appetite, vague abdominal pain, and sometimes diarrhea.

Many cases go undiagnosed because the symptoms are suggestive of a flulike illness or may be very mild or absent.

A minority of patients notice dark urine and light-colored stools, followed by jaundice in which the skin and whites of the eyes appear yellow. (Most individuals with viral hepatitis do not develop jaundice.) Itching of the skin may be present. With the onset of jaundice, other symptoms tend to subside. Some people may lose five to ten pounds during the illness.

QUESTIONS FREQUENTLY ASKED

Can I get hepatitis again? Yes, because there are five or more hepatitis viruses, you can ac-

quire different ones at different times. You will not be infected by the same virus as each produces its own immunity after the virus disappears. However, sometimes the viruses of B, C, and D hepatitis remain in the body forever. They can cause flare-ups of hepatitis that look like new disease.

What is a carrier and how can I tell if I am one? A carrier is a person who has hepatitis B, C, or D in his or her blood even after all symptoms (except fatigue) have disappeared. Because the virus is present in the blood, it can be transmitted to others. Hepatitis A does not have a carrier state. The hepatitis B carrier can be recognized by a simple and specific blood test. Some of the carriers are contagious and others are not; this too can be determined by a simple blood test. A test for the hepatitis C carrier has been developed. Prior to transfusion, all blood is now tested for abnormality of the liver function and for hepatitis B and C viruses. These tests have reduced the rate of the post-transfusion hepatitis C by about 50 percent. Blood banks notify donors if they have found such abnormalities. Hepatitis D can be detected by a simple blood test for antibody to the virus and by a positive test for hepatitis B; both must be positive to be sure that the hepatitis D virus is present. Testing for hepatitis E is being developed but is not yet available.

What should I do if I have been exposed to or suspect that I have hepatitis? Consult your physician who will examine you and order blood tests to confirm the diagnosis, identify the specific type of hepatitis, and advise you about diet and activity. Your contacts should be notified about your infection and the need for gamma (immune) globulin and vaccination.

Should I see a specialist if I have hepatitis? Most physicians can care for a patient with an ordinary case of viral hepatitis. However, referral to a specialist in diseases of the liver (hepatologist, gastroenterologist) may be necessary if the disease appears to be unusually severe or complications are recognized.

Is hospitalization necessary? In most cases, no. Some patients are hospitalized if neither liquids nor food can be tolerated or if the disease is unusually severe or complications arise.

Are there medications for viral hepatitis? Until recently there has been no way to treat hepatitis B viral infection. Interferon alpha-2b produces a remission of the disease in 30 percent of those with chronic hepatitis B and 25 percent of those infected with chronic hepatitis C. Only 10 percent of hepatitis B cases are cleared of the virus.

This is a very encouraging first step, leading the way to more effective treatments.

If I take medicine for other purposes, can I continue to do so? Medications taken regularly should be reviewed by a physician and a decision made regarding their continuation. Because the liver plays a key role in processing drugs and this function may be impaired in the patient with hepatitis, medications are usually withheld unless they are essential for the treatment of other problems.

Can I exercise while I have hepatitis? Vigorous exercise during the acute stage of the disease should be discouraged. Light or moderate exercise may be undertaken as symptoms subside.

Must I stay in bed? Restriction to bed is not necessary for patients with viral hepatitis. A good general rule is: "If you feel well, get up, but if you do not, take it easy."

How great is the risk of hepatitis to me and my family? Spread within the family can occur with hepatitis A, B, or E. Prompt diagnosis and appropriate precautions with gamma globulin or vaccination are important for those who are exposed.

Do I need a special diet or vitamins? A nutritious, well-balanced diet with additional calorie-rich fluids (soft drinks, fruit juices) is normally sufficient during the illness. Since many patients describe a reduction in appetite and an increase in nausea as the day progresses, a hearty breakfast is often the best tolerated meal of the day. Multiple small snacks between meals are encouraged if large meals cause problems. Vitamin supplements have no clear value if a balanced diet can be eaten.

Must I give up alcohol? All alcoholic beverages should be avoided during the acute phase of the disease since metabolism of the alcohol stresses the already sick liver. (Modest alcohol consumption later in the convalescent phase or after recovery is not harmful.)

Should I avoid sexual activity? Sexual activity does not seem to affect the disease or recovery. However, your partner may be at risk of acquiring the infection, especially of hepatitis B.

Do dishes and clothing of the patient need special care? Hot water and soap or detergent is sufficient for cleaning dishes or clothing of patients with hepatitis A or E. Special care must be taken if anything has blood on it when the patient has hepatitis B or C. Dishes, utensils, and clothing do not harbor the hepatitis B or C virus.

Can I prepare meals? If you have hepatitis A or E, you should not prepare meals or handle food to be eaten by others. However, you were especially contagious before the symptoms of hepatitis were recognized and you may have already transmitted the infection or exposed others unknowingly.

If you have hepatitis B, C, or D, limitations on food handling are not necessary.

How long does the illness last? The onset is often abrupt and recovery occurs in a few weeks to a month or two. The contagious period lasts two to three weeks. With hepatitis B, the onset is more gradual and the course is longer. Over 80 percent of patients recover within six months, another 10 percent after two years, while 5 to 10 percent either develop chronic hepatitis or become carriers. The onset of hepatitis C is often not recognized and the disease becomes apparent months to years after infection. More than half of the patients who are infected by blood transfusions will develop chronic hepatitis with fluctuating symptoms and laboratory test results. Hepatitis D coinfection with hepatitis B acts as though it were very serious hepatitis B but recovery after a few months is usual. Hepatitis D concurrent infection in a hepatitis B carrier looks like a flare-up of hepatitis B and symptoms may become lifelong. The symptoms of hepatitis E are like those of hepatitis A, although the period of illness may be as long as several months.

How long should I continue to see a doctor?
You should continue to see your doctor until blood tests indicate the illness is clearly over. Abnormalities in the blood tests that persist beyond six months must be carefully evaluated since they may indicate the development of chronic infections.

What are the complications of hepatitis?
Fortunately, most people recover completely from hepatitis A, B, D, and E. Mild flare-ups may occur over a period of several months. Each flare-up is usually less severe than the initial attack and a relapse does not necessarily indicate that complete recovery will not take place.

About one patient in 1,000 dies of hepatitis A, one in 100 of acute hepatitis B, and somewhere in between for hepatitis C. The mortality rate of hepatitis D and B is higher than for hepatitis B alone. Not enough is yet known about hepatitis E.

About 5 percent of patients with hepatitis B and more than 50 percent of patients with hepatitis C develop chronic liver disease which may be mild and slowly progressive, or may be serious and rapidly lead to cirrhosis. The terms "chronic persistent" and "chronic

aggressive" have been used for these two varieties, but we now know that the degree of activity varies with time and in different places in the liver at the same time. Cirrhosis is the final state of scarring which develops in chronic hepatitis. To determine how much scarring is present or how rapidly it may be progressing, a liver biopsy is usually necessary. Predicting who will develop chronic liver disease is not possible at the time of acute hepatitis. Identification of those at risk and methods to prevent these consequences are the subjects of ongoing research.

Is the spread of hepatitis preventable? Adequate sanitation and good personal hygiene will reduce the spread of hepatitis A and E. Water should be boiled prior to its use if any question of safety exists. Similarly, in areas where sanitation is questionable, food should be cooked well and fruits peeled. Washing hands, cleaning utensils, bedding, and clothing with soap and water is necessary for those involved in treating patients, especially in the first couple of weeks of illness.

Those planning to travel to areas where hepatitis A is widespread are advised to take immune globulin before leaving. Its protection is effective for three to four months.

To prevent spread of hepatitis B, avoid exposure to infectious blood or body fluids. Do not have intimate contact, share razors, scissors, nail files, toothbrushes, or needles. If any risk is present, you should receive immune globulin and vaccine as soon as possible.

Blood banks are hard at work to insure the safety of the blood supply. Hepatitis B from transfusion has been largely prevented and hepatitis C has been reduced, with prospects of even further reduction soon. Sharing needles with anyone should be avoided. Dentists, doctors, nurses, laboratory technicians, and others who may draw blood, perform surgical procedures, or handle sharp instruments used on hepatitis patients or carriers must be informed so that adequate precautions can be taken.

Family members and other intimate contacts must be advised to seek medical advice about immune globulin shots or vaccination.

Are there vaccines and can the disease be prevented? A vaccine for hepatitis A is currently under development but it will be many years before testing in humans begins. Several vaccines are presently being tested, but none is yet available.

Several vaccines are available to prevent hepatitis B. They are all safe and effective and they seem to prevent infection if started within a few days of exposure. The usual vaccination schedule used in the United States is two injections a month apart followed by a third injection six months after the first one. Hepatitis B immune globulin may also prevent infection after exposure but it must be given within 48 hours to be useful. Since both vaccination and immune globulin are expensive, rapid confirmation of the diagnosis of hepatitis B is needed. Hepatitis D is prevented by preventing hepatitis B. No vaccine or immune globulin is yet available for hepatitis C or E.

Does hepatitis cause cancer? A high incidence of liver cancer is found in some African and Asian countries where there are many hepatitis B carriers and appears to be related to the chronic hepatitis B carrier state. Research on this relationship is being actively pursued.

The number of cases of liver cancer in patients with chronic hepatitis C is increasing, but whether the cancer rate will ever be as high as with hepatitis B is unknown. About 15 percent of hepatitis B carriers in the Orient are at risk of developing liver cancer, but the rate seems to be considerably lower in the United States.

Is hepatitis related to AIDS? Any relation between AIDS and hepatitis is coincidental. Male homosexuals and intravenous drug users who are at high risk for infection with the human immunodeficiency virus (HIV), the cause of AIDS, are at equally high risk for infection with the hepatitis B virus.

ADVANCES IN RESEARCH

Tremendous advances through research have been made in the field of viral hepatitis within the past decade. These all have followed identification of the specific viruses that cause diseases and will result in development of vaccines that eventually will prevent the one million new cases of viral hepatitis occurring in children and adults each year in the United States.

Vaccination eventually will lead to the prevention of liver cancer found in chronic carriers of some of the viruses.

Recent research has discovered a laboratory method of detecting hepatitis C. This will lead to further reductions in hepatitis after blood transfusions. It will also enable better monitoring of treatment.

Research is also being carried out on drugs that have the potential for eradicating some of these viruses and for improving treament of chronic hepatitis.

The American Liver Foundation

GALLSTONES

This year, over 1 million people will discover that they have gallstones. They will join an estimated 25 million Americans, over 10 percent of the population, who already have gallstones or other gallbladder disorders.

Anyone is a potential candidate for gallstone disease, but women are particularly vulnerable. In fact, women between the ages of 20 and 60 are three times more likely to develop gallstones than are men.

Although anyone in the general popula-

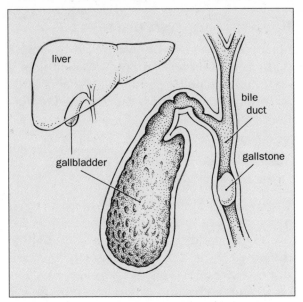

Gallstones may remain in the gallbladder, or pass painlessly through the bile duct. Problems generally occur only when stones get trapped in the bile duct.

tion can develop gallstones, there are several groups who are at higher risk, including the following.

- Women who are overweight
- Women who have been pregnant
- Women who have used oral menopausal estrogen therapy or oral contraceptives
- Those who have recently lost weight
- Those who are of American Indian ancestry

Even though gallstones are more common in females at a younger age, by the age of 60, almost 10 percent of all men, as well as 20 percent of women, have gallstones.

We are just beginning to learn some of the answers to fundamental questions, such as what causes gallstones to form and what are the relative roles of the liver and gallbladder in stone formation. We still do not know why some people develop gallstones and others do not. But researchers are working to find answers to these questions.

WHAT IS THE GALLBLADDER AND WHAT DOES IT DO?

The gallbladder is a small pear-shaped organ that averages three to six inches in length. It is tucked under the liver and is connected to the liver and intestine by small tubes called bile ducts. Bile—a greenish-brown fluid that is essential to the digestion of fatty foods—is produced by the liver and secreted into the gallbladder. The gallbladder serves as a receptacle for the concentration and storage of bile.

WHAT ARE GALLSTONES?

Gallstones are lumps of solid material that form in the gallbladder. They may be as small as tiny specks, or in extreme cases, as large as the gallbladder. The vast majority, however, are small, less than 20 mm, or about 1 inch. There are two major types of gallstones.

- *Cholesterol gallstones,* composed mainly of cholesterol, account for approximately 80 percent of all cases diagnosed in the United States.
- *Pigment gallstones,* composed mainly of calcium salts of bile pigments and other compounds, account for the remaining 20 percent.

Since most patients have cholesterol gallstones, they may be candidates for nonsurgical treatment. Gallstone type is important since only patients with cholesterol gallstones are candidates for nonsurgical treatments.

DO GALLSTONES ALWAYS CAUSE PROBLEMS?

In many patients, gallstones remain "silent" or asymptomatic and cause few serious problems. However, the longer gallstones are present, the more likely they are to cause complications. The chance that a silent gallstone will cause discomfort is about 3 percent per year in any patient. Thus, in 20 years, the majority of patients who have asymptomatic gallstones will develop symptoms. Once symptoms arise, they persist. And, when problems occur in older people, they can be much more difficult to treat, especially if the person has other medical problems.

As gallstones grow larger, they may block the outlet of the gallbladder and begin to cause serious disorder. Blockage can progress from gradual or occasional obstruction of the outlet, causing inflammation of the gallbladder (chronic cholecystitis), to total obstruction, causing acute inflammation of the gallbladder (cholecystitis), a condition which requires surgical treatment.

Other complications may result when gallstones block the common bile duct which leads to the intestine. There can be infection of the bile ducts (acute cholangitis) which causes chills and fever. Bile pigments may accumulate in the blood, causing jaundice, a yellow discoloration of the skin and eyes. Acute inflammation of the pancreas (pancreatitis) may occur. If the bile duct remains blocked for a long period of time, liver damage occurs, leading to liver failure and death. Rarely, large gallstones move into the small intestine and cause obstruction near the junction of the small and large intestine.

WHAT ARE THE SIGNS AND SYMPTOMS OF GALLSTONES?

Many people have gallstones, but do not have any symptoms. When symptoms are evident, a person with gallstones may experience the following.

- Severe and steady pain in the upper abdomen, which can spread to the chest, shoulders, or back, and is sometimes mistaken for the symptoms of a heart attack
- Indigestion, nausea, or vomiting
- Severe abdominal pain and tenderness in the right side of the abdomen when the gallbladder is inflamed
- Jaundice, chills, and fever when gallstones block the passage of bile

HOW ARE GALLSTONES DIAGNOSED?

Most gallstones can be discovered by simple, painless techniques. Patients who complain of abdominal pain or gastrointestinal distress are often given specific tests designed to diagnose gallstones.

X-ray. Often, an ordinary x-ray of the abdomen will detect gallstones. However, such gallstones are rich in calcium.

Ultrasound. This is a more sensitive technique that produces an image or photograph of the gallbladder and bile ducts, and allows the physician to determine if any type of gallstone is present. This is the most common screening technique since no radiation is used.

Cholecystography is a test that requires the patient to swallow pills containing dyes. The dye passes from the bloodstream into the bile, and outlines the gallbladder so gallstones can be detected by x-rays.

More complicated procedures are required when gallstones in the bile ducts are suspected.

ERCP (endoscopic retrograde cholangiopancreatography). For this procedure a flexible tube is passed through the small intestine into the bile duct; dye is injected into the bile ducts and an x-ray is taken.

PTC (percutaneous transhepatic cholangiography). In this technique a thin needle is passed through the abdomen into the duct network of the liver. Then dye is injected and an x-ray is taken.

HOW CAN GALLSTONES BE TREATED?

The gallbladder is an important organ, but is not essential for life. Many patients with gallstones—or complications resulting from gallstones—have had their gallbladders surgically

LAPAROSCOPIC CHOLECYSTECTOMY

For more than 100 years, cholecystectomy was performed by making a surgical incision in the upper abdomen. In the past few years a new technique for gallbladder removal, laparoscopic cholecystectomy, has been developed. This new method employs four small incisions, which patients tolerate very easily. Following laparoscopic cholecystectomy, most patients are observed in the hospital for one night and return to their usual activities within one week. Cholecystectomy, by either technique, has the advantage over other alternatives of essentially eliminating the chance of recurrent gallstone problems. *The Editors*

removed safely. The operation is called a cholecystectomy and is among the most common surgical procedures in the world. More than 500,000 are performed in the United States each year. Surgical risk increases as patients age and when the patient has other illnesses.

If the gallbladder is removed, the bile then flows directly from the liver to the small intestine. There may be little or no effect on digestion. For some patients, however, gallbladder removal may not relieve the symptoms of gas, pain, bloating, or nausea.

An oral medication, ursodiol, dissolves cholesterol gallstones and represents a safe and effective alternative to gallbladder surgery for some patients. Ursodiol is a naturally occurring bile acid which lowers the amount of cholesterol in the bile and slowly dissolves gallstones within 6 to 24 months in carefully selected patients, depending on the size of the stones.

⚠ A major problem with ursodiol treatment is the high incidence of recurrent stones, up to 70 percent, especially in elderly patients.

People who have cholesterol gallstones and in whom there is no obstruction of the flow of bile into and out of the gallbladder may be candidates for treatment with ursodiol. It may be of particular interest for people who are high-risk surgery patients, and for those who wish to avoid surgery. Small stones composed entirely of cholesterol respond especially well to treatment with ursodiol. The drug is extremely well tolerated with only rare instances of mild, transient diarrhea reported.

Another alternative to surgery, being explored on a research basis, is shock wave lithotripsy.

⚠ Only a small proportion of patients are good candidates for shock wave lithotripsy. Moreover, the cost-effectiveness of this treatment has been questioned, and the FDA has not approved this treatment of gallstones in the United States.

Shock wave lithotripsy is a new technique which uses external sound waves to fragment gallstones into small pieces. The pieces are then dissolved by ursodiol taken orally, although some stones will pass spontaneously.

The American Liver Foundation

INFLAMMATORY BOWEL DISEASE

The intestines, sometimes called the bowel, can be injured in many different ways. The bowel may be infected by a wide variety of viruses, bacteria, or parasites. It may be damaged by chemical poisoning, radiation exposure, surgery, physical injury, or disturbances of its blood supply. Any of the above may cause acute or chronic inflammation.

In addition, there are other, mysterious diseases that attack the bowel wall, causing chronic intestinal inflammation and bringing misery and disability to hundreds of thousands of people throughout the world. These bewildering and stubborn illnesses of unknown cause are called inflammatory bowel disease (IBD).

WHAT IS IBD?

Inflammatory bowel disease is a name given to a group of chronic digestive diseases of the small and large intestines. Your doctor may refer to your particular condition by any one of several terms including colitis, proctitis, enteritis, and ileitis.

Most often, doctors divide IBD into two groups: ulcerative colitis and Crohn's disease.

Ulcerative colitis causes ulcers and inflammation of the lining (mucosa) of the colon (large intestine). It almost always involves the rectum and usually causes a bloody diarrhea.

Crohn's disease is an inflammation that extends into the deeper layers of the intestinal wall. The disease either is limited to one or more segments of the small intestine (30 percent), usually the ileum (ileitis), or involves both the ileum and the colon (ileocolitis) (50 percent). In the remaining 20 percent, Crohn's disease is confined to the colon (Crohn's colitis). Sometimes, inflammation may also affect the mouth, esophagus (gullet), stomach, duodenum, appendix, or anus.

Both ulcerative colitis and Crohn's disease are chronic conditions and may recur over a lifetime. On the other hand, many people will have long periods—sometimes years—when they will be free of symptoms. Unfortunately, doctors cannot predict with certainty when the disease will go into remission or when the symptoms will return.

SYMPTOMS

The most common symptoms of IBD are diarrhea and abdominal pain. Ulcerative colitis usually causes rectal bleeding as well. Crohn's disease also may cause rectal bleeding, but less often than does ulcerative colitis. In either disease, inflammation, fever, and bleeding may be serious and persistent, leading to weight loss and anemia (low red blood cell count).

CAUSES

There are many theories about what causes IBD, but none has been proven. The current leading theory suggests that some agent, possibly a virus or an atypical bacterium, interacts with the body's own immune defense system to trigger an inflammatory reaction in the intestinal wall. Although there is much scientific evidence that patients with IBD have abnormalities of the immune system, doctors do not know whether these abnormalities are a cause or a result of the disease. Doctors do believe, however, that there is little basis for the idea that Crohn's disease and ulcerative colitis are caused by emotional distress or are the product of an unhappy childhood.

HOW COMMON IS IBD?

It is estimated that between 1 and 2 million Americans suffer from IBD. Men and women are affected about equally. Some people seem to be more likely targets for these diseases. For instance, IBD seems to be more common among Jews than non-Jews and more prevalent among whites than blacks, Orientals, Hispanics, or Native Americans, although no population group is immune from attack. Also, the number of people who get Crohn's disease has been increasing steadily over the last several decades. The incidence has, in the past, been highest in North America, the British Isles, and northwestern Europe and Scandinavia. In recent years, an increase in frequency has been observed in developing nations throughout the rest of the world. Doctors cannot yet explain why these changes are occurring.

DOES IBD RUN IN FAMILIES?

About 25 percent of people with Crohn's disease or ulcerative colitis have a blood relative with some form of IBD, most often a brother or sister, and sometimes a parent or child. Studies have not yet answered the question of whether this tendency is due primarily to heredity or to environment.

DIAGNOSIS

Ulcerative colitis is usually relatively easy for the doctor to recognize. If bloody diarrhea is what caused you to go to the doctor's office, the doctor will probably examine your rectum with an instrument called a proctoscope or sigmoidoscope. In many cases, the doctor will obtain a culture of the stool and order a barium enema x-ray.

Crohn's disease is not so easily diagnosed because the symptoms are not always so dramatic, and because the affected part of the intestine may not be within the easy reach of a sigmoidoscope. However, if you have experienced chronic abdominal pain, diarrhea, fever, weight loss, and anemia, the doctor will examine you for signs of Crohn's disease. The diagnosis can almost always be established by a good medical history and a thorough x-ray examination of the digestive tract, including an upper gastrointestinal (GI) series, a careful small bowel study, and a barium enema.

CAN IBD BE CURED?

No medicine has yet been found to cure Crohn's disease or ulcerative colitis, but several drugs are helpful in controlling the disease processes and symptoms. Your doctor will work with you to find which treatments will work best for you.

Abdominal cramps and diarrhea may be alleviated by drugs. The drug sulfasalazine often lessens the inflammation. More serious cases may require cortisone-related medication.

Some cases of IBD have improved with certain very potent anti-infective agents or with drugs that suppress the body's immune system. These are relatively new treatments for IBD and, because they sometimes produce severe reactions, they are not used routinely. It is very important that you take only those medications your doctor has prescribed for you.

CAN DIET CONTROL IBD?

No special diet has been proven effective for preventing IBD or helping most IBD patients.

Some patients find their symptoms are made worse by milk, alcohol, hot spices, or roughage. But there are no hard and fast rules for the majority of IBD patients. Let your common sense tell you if you need to avoid any foods that seem to make your symptoms worse.

Maintaining good general nutrition and adequate caloric intake is far more important than emphasizing or avoiding any particular food. Also, large doses of vitamins are useless and may even produce harmful side effects.

Your doctor may recommend nutritional supplements. Special high-calorie liquid formulas are sometimes used for this purpose. A small number of patients may need periods of intravenous feeding, a procedure called total parenteral nutrition (TPN) or hyperalimentation. These techniques can help patients who temporarily need extra nutrition, those whose bowels need to rest, or those whose bowels cannot absorb enough nourishment from food taken by mouth. Such techniques are not in themselves a cure for the disease.

SURGERY AND ULCERATIVE COLITIS

Surgery can cure ulcerative colitis. Although most patients cope effectively with this disease for many years, about one-third will eventually require the removal of the colon. In the standard form of this operation the entire colon and rectum are removed. A small opening (stoma) is made in the front of the abdominal wall and the tip of the lower small intestine (ileum) is then brought through. The stoma is fitted with a pouch to collect waste products. This external opening to the intestine is called an ileostomy.

Cosmetically more appealing options to this standard procedure have recently been developed, but they are controversial because they are more often prone to complications. One such procedure is called a continent ileostomy. In this operation, a pouch is created out of the ileum inside the wall of the lower abdomen. The pouch is emptied regularly through a valve on the outside of the abdomen and a small tube.

In an even newer operation, ileoanal anastomosis, only the diseased inner lining of the rectum is removed, leaving the outer muscle coats of the rectum intact. The ileum is then inserted inside the rectum (a procedure sometimes called a "pull-through") and attached just above the anus. Because the rectal muscles are left intact, stool can be passed normally.

Your doctor will explain the possibilities and recommend which form of surgery is best for you. The most important thing to remember, however, is that removal of the colon and rectum provides a total and permanent cure for ulcerative colitis, regardless of the type of procedure performed.

SURGERY AND CROHN'S DISEASE

Crohn's disease can be helped by surgery, but it cannot be cured by surgery. The inflammation tends to return in areas of the intestine immediately next to the area that has been removed. Even so, about two-thirds of Crohn's disease patients require surgery, either to provide relief from chronic disability or to correct specific complications. Unfortunately, neither the continent ileostomy nor the ileoanal anastomosis can be used in Crohn's disease patients because of the likelihood of recurrence of the disease.

COMPLICATIONS

Most people with IBD never suffer from any complications, but some do.

Ulcerative colitis. Dangerous complications may arise when severe ulcerative colitis is progressing rapidly, with ulceration extending deep into the bowel wall. In such cases, paralysis and distention of the colon (toxic dilatation), bleeding, perforation, or peritonitis (inflammation of the lining of the abdominal cavity) may occur. These uncommon problems often require surgery.

If the disease is sufficiently widespread throughout the colon, and lasts for many years, patients with ulcerative colitis may be at increased risk of cancer of the colon or rectum. Since these cancers have a more favorable outcome when caught in the early stages, patients should see their doctors for regular colon examinations.

Crohn's disease affects deeper layers of the bowel wall than those affected by ulcerative colitis. It often involves the small intestine but frequently spares the rectum. For these reasons, frank rectal bleeding is less common in Crohn's disease than in ulcerative colitis. Because of the tendency of Crohn's disease to thicken the bowel wall with swelling and fibrous scar tissue, intestinal obstruction or "blockage" is the principal complication of long-standing cases.

Crohn's disease may also cause deep ulcer tracts to burrow all the way through the bowel wall into surrounding tissues, into adjacent segments of intestine, or into other nearby organs such as the urinary bladder or vagina. These abnormal tunnels or passageways between the inflamed intestine and adjoining tissues are called fistulas. They are a common complication of Crohn's disease and are often associated with pockets of infection or abscesses.

The anus and rectum are particularly susceptible to these problems in Crohn's disease, so that complicated fistulas or abscesses in this region are often a hallmark of the diagnosis. Fistulas can sometimes be treated with medication, but in many cases they must be drained surgically.

In addition to the damage IBD produces in and around the intestine, there are other complications that may affect more distant parts of the body. These systemic complications include various forms of arthritis, skin problems, inflammation in the eyes or mouth, kidney stones, gallstones, or other diseases of the liver and biliary system. Some of these problems respond to the same treatment as the intestinal symptoms of IBD, but others require separate management.

QUESTIONS FOR THE FUTURE

There are many questions about IBD that scientists have yet to answer. What is the cause of IBD? Why does it run in families? How does it spread or produce complications? What is the best treatment? These and other questions are being studied. Researchers are improving methods of diagnosis, identifying ways to detect early colorectal cancer, and developing newer, safer, and more effective medical and surgical therapies.

The National Institute of Diabetes and Digestive and Kidney Diseases

IRRITABLE BOWEL SYNDROME

Irritable bowel syndrome, or IBS, is a chronic disorder of the colon. Its cause and cure are as yet unknown. Doctors call it a functional disorder because there is no sign of disease when the colon is examined by x-ray or other diagnostic methods. However, IBS causes a variety of symptoms including lower abdominal pain, gas, bloating, constipation or diarrhea, or alternating constipation and diarrhea.

Through the years, IBS has been called by many names—mucous colitis, spastic colon, colitis, spastic bowel, and functional bowel disease. Most of these terms are inaccurate.

Colitis, for instance, means inflammation of the colon. IBS, on the other hand, causes no inflammation and should never be confused with the more serious ulcerative colitis.

Though IBS can cause a great deal of discomfort, it is not serious and does not lead to any serious disease. With attention to proper diet, stress management, and sometimes medication prescribed by their physician, most people with IBS can keep their symptoms under control.

SYMPTOMS

It is important to remember that normal bowel function varies widely from person to person. Doctors generally agree that normal bowel function ranges from three stools a day to three each week. A normal movement is one that is formed but not hard, contains no blood, and is passed without cramps or pain.

People with IBS, on the other hand, usually have some combination of constipation and diarrhea as well as pain, gas, and abdominal bloating. Most people with IBS have episodes of lower abdominal pain and constipation, sometimes followed by diarrhea. Others may have pain and mild constipation and no diarrhea. The rarest form of the disorder is severe, painless diarrhea. People in this group may have watery bowel movements after breakfast almost every day. These may be followed by episodes of diarrhea after other meals, following stressful events, or for no apparent reason. Although IBS is usually a mild annoyance, for some people it can be disabling. Patients in the latter group may be afraid to go to dinner parties, seek employment, or travel on public transportation.

CAUSES

Because doctors have been unable to pinpoint its organic cause, IBS often has been considered to be caused by emotional conflict or stress. While stress may certainly be a factor, recent studies indicate that other factors may be involved.

Most IBS symptoms are related to an abnormal motility (movement) pattern of the colon. The colon connects the small intestine with the anus. Approximately 6 feet long, the colon has two major functions: it absorbs water and salts from digestive products that enter from the small intestine. Two liters of liquid matter enter the colon from the small intestine each day. This material may remain there for several days until most of the fluid and salts are absorbed back into the body. The stool then passes through the colon by a delicate pattern of movements to the rectum where it is stored until a bowel movement occurs.

Movements of the colon are controlled by nerves and hormones and by electrical activity in the colon muscle. The electrical activity serves as a "pacemaker" similar to the mechanism that controls heart function. Movements of the colon propel the contents slowly back and forth, but mainly toward the rectum. Segments of the colon also contract periodically to promote the absorption of water from feces.

In people who have IBS, the muscle of the lower portion of the colon contracts abnormally. An abnormal contraction—or spasm—may be related to episodes of crampy pain. Sometimes the spasm delays the passage of stool, leading to constipation. At other times, the spasm leads to more rapid passage of feces and the result is diarrhea.

DIAGNOSIS

IBS is a diagnosis that doctors reach after more serious organic diseases have been excluded. This process is necessary because IBS offers doctors no signposts to help identify the disorder. A complete medical history that includes a careful description of symptoms, a physical examination, and specific laboratory tests will be done. Also, your doctor will probably order some diagnostic tests such as x-rays or endoscopy to eliminate organic causes of your symptoms. Unless your symptoms change, you will not need to undergo these tests again.

HOW DIET AND STRESS AFFECT IBS

The potential for abnormal function of the colon is always present in people with IBS, but something must trigger it to cause symptoms. The factors that seem to be the most likely culprits are diet and emotional stress. Many people note that their symptoms occur following a meal or when they are under stress. Why this happens, no one is sure, but scientists have some clues. Eating causes contractions of the colon. Normally, this response may cause an urge to have a bowel movement within 30 to 60 minutes after a meal. In people with IBS, the exaggerated reflex can lead to cramps and sometimes diarrhea.

The strength of the response is directly related to the number of calories in a meal, and especially the amount of fat in a meal. Fat, in any form (animal or vegetable), is the strongest stimulus of colonic contractions after a meal. Fat is primarily found in meat, especially bacon and sausage; poultry skin; dairy products including milk, cream, cheese, and butter; vegetable oils; margarines; shortenings; and nondairy whipped toppings.

Stress also stimulates colonic spasm in people with IBS. This process is not clearly understood, but scientists point out that the colon is partially controlled by the nervous system. Mental health counseling is sometimes helpful for alleviating the symptoms due to IBS. However, doctors are quick to note that this does not mean IBS is the result of a personality disorder. IBS is at least partially a disorder of colon motility.

HOW A PROPER DIET HELPS IBS

For many people, eating the proper diet helps lessen IBS symptoms. Before considering a change in diet, you should note whether any particular foods seem to cause distress and then discuss them with your physician. If dairy products cause your symptoms to flare up, try decreasing the amount consumed at any one time. Yogurt can also be a satisfactory substitute. Dairy products are important sources of calcium and other nutrients which the body needs and should not be avoided entirely, unless absolutely necessary.

Dietary fiber, present in whole grain breads and cereals and in fruits and vegetables, also has been shown to be helpful in lessening IBS symptoms. Your doctor should be consulted prior to using an over-the-counter fiber supplement. High-fiber diets keep the colon mildly distended, which helps to prevent spasms from developing. Some forms of fiber also keep water in the stools, thereby preventing hard, difficult-to-pass stools from forming. Doctors usually recommend that you eat just enough fiber so that soft, easily passed, painless bowel movements are produced. High-fiber diets may cause gas and bloating; however, over time these symptoms may dissipate as the digestive tract becomes used to the increased fiber intake.

Large meals may also cause cramping and diarrhea in some people suffering from IBS. Therefore, eating smaller meals more frequently, or eating smaller portions of foods at mealtimes, especially if the foods are low in fat and rich in carbohydrates and protein, may also help to alleviate symptoms. Foods high in carbohydrates and low in fat include pastas, rice, breads, cereals, fruits and vegetables, etc., while those high in protein and low in fat include chicken and turkey without the skin, lean meats, most fish, low-fat dairy products such as skim milk and low-fat cheeses.

DRUGS FOR RELIEF OF IBS SYMPTOMS

No consensus exists among doctors about the drugs to be used in IBS. Some doctors prescribe a combination of antispasmodic drugs and tranquilizers and these may relieve symptoms. Other physicians feel that, first, they

should reassure patients and discuss means of controlling stress-inducing factors in their life situations. The variable nature of the disorder makes it difficult to conduct a well-designed clinical trial, which would help to establish the best form of treatment for IBS.

CONNECTION BETWEEN IBS AND MORE SERIOUS PROBLEMS

IBS has not been shown to lead to any serious, organic diseases. There is no link between IBS and inflammatory bowel diseases such as Crohn's disease or ulcerative colitis. IBS does not lead to cancer. Some doctors think that there may be a connection between IBS and the later development of diverticulosis. Diverticulosis, a condition in which small outpouchings (diverticula) form in the wall of the colon, is very common in people over 60. However, the relationship between diverticulosis and IBS is not proven.

The major concerns in drug therapy of IBS are drug dependency and the effects the disorder can have on lifestyle. In an effort to regulate colonic activity or minimize stress, some patients become dependent on laxatives or tranquilizers. If this becomes the case, doctors generally try to withdraw the drugs slowly.

A few patients have a more severe form of the disorder and the fear of pain and diarrhea may cause them to withdraw from normal activities. In such cases, doctors may recommend mental health counseling.

The National Institute of Diabetes and Digestive and Kidney Diseases

DIVERTICULOSIS AND DIVERTICULITIS

Diverticulosis is a condition in which outpouchings form in the walls of the intestines. These pouches, known as diverticula, are about the size of large peas. They form in weakened areas of the bowels, most often in the lower part of the colon (large bowel).

SYMPTOMS

Most people with diverticula do not have any symptoms from them. They may never know they have the condition. Some people feel tenderness over the affected area or muscle spasms in the abdomen. Pains may be felt on the lower left side of the abdomen or, less often, in the middle or on the right side.

While the diverticula themselves do not cause symptoms, complications such as bleeding and infection may occur. Bleeding is an uncommon symptom and is usually not severe. Sometimes the pouches become infected and inflamed, a more serious condition known as diverticulitis. When inflammation is present, there may be fever and an increased white blood cell count, as well as acute abdominal pain. Diverticulitis also may result in large abscesses (infected areas of pus), bowel blockage, or breaks and leaks through the bowel wall.

DIAGNOSIS

Often diverticulosis is unsuspected and is discovered by an x-ray or intestinal examination done for an unrelated reason. The doctor may see the diverticula through a flexible tube (colonoscope) that is inserted through the anus. Through this scope, the diverticula may be seen as dark passages leading out of the normal colon wall. The doctor also may do a barium enema, an x-ray that reveals the outpouchings in the walls of the colon.

If rectal bleeding occurs, the doctor may take a special x-ray (angiography). In this procedure, dye is injected into an artery that goes to the colon, so that the site of the bleeding problem can be located. Diverticulitis may be diagnosed when a patient has pain and tenderness in the lower abdomen with disturbed bowel function and fever.

HOW COMMON ARE THESE DISORDERS?

Diverticulosis is very common, especially in older people. Studies show that about 10 percent of people over the age of 40 have diver-

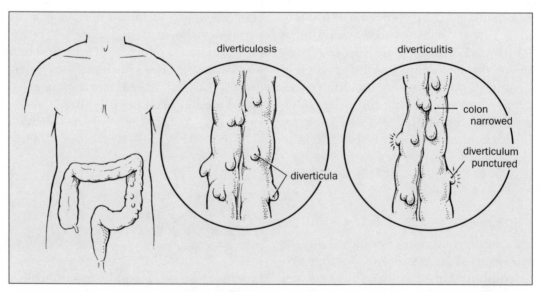

In diverticulosis, small pouches (diverticula) form in weakened areas in the wall of the colon. Should these become infected or inflamed (diverticulitis), serious problems can set in.

ticulosis, and nearly half of people over age 60 have it. But among those who are found to have diverticula, only about 20 percent develop diverticulitis, and of those, only a small number have very serious or life-threatening complications.

WHAT CAUSES DIVERTICULA TO FORM?

No one knows for sure why the pouches form. Scientists think they may be due to increased pressure inside the colon due to muscle spasms or straining.

The sacs might form when increased pressure acts on soft spots along the bowel wall, especially if the person has constipation problems or uses laxatives too often.

HOW SERIOUS ARE THESE DISORDERS?

For most people, diverticulosis is not a problem. Diverticulitis, on the other hand, is a problem, sometimes a serious one. For instance, when one of the sacs (a diverticulum) becomes infected and inflamed, bacteria enter small tears in the surface of the bowel. This leads to small abscesses. Such an infection may remain localized and go away within a few days.

In rare cases, the infection spreads and breaks through the wall of the colon causing peritonitis (infection of the abdominal cavity) or abscesses in the abdomen. Such infections are very serious and can lead to death unless treated without delay.

TREATMENT

If you have diverticulosis with no symptoms, no treatment is needed. Some doctors advise eating a special high-fiber diet and avoiding certain foods. Laxatives and enemas should not be used regularly. Patients with diverticulitis may be hospitalized and treated with bed rest, pain relievers, antibiotics, fluids given by vein, and watchful care.

SURGERY

The vast majority of patients will recover from diverticulitis without surgery. Sometimes patients need surgery to drain an abscess that has resulted from a ruptured diverticulum and to remove that portion of the colon. Surgery is reserved for patients with very severe or multiple attacks. In those cases, the involved segment of colon can be removed and the colon rejoined.

In some cases, the two ends of the colon cannot be rejoined right away, so more than one operation is needed. For instance, an operation may be performed to drain an abscess and remove diseased colon, and a second operation done to rejoin the colon. In this case, the surgeon must connect the colon to a surgically created hole on the body's surface (colostomy) until a second operation can be done to reconnect the colon.

The delay between operations may be only a few weeks, or it might be several months if the patient needs time to overcome infection and build up strength. In rare cases, three operations are needed: the first to drain an abscess, the second to remove part of the colon, and the third to rejoin the bowel.

DIET

If you have diverticulosis with no symptoms, you don't need treatment, but it is a good idea to watch your diet. The diet some doctors recommend is the same kind that is healthy for most people—eat more foods high in fiber. A fiber-rich diet helps prevent constipation and promotes a healthy digestive tract. Fiber-rich foods include whole-grain cereals and breads, fruits, and vegetables. A fiber-rich diet is also thought to help prevent diverticula from forming. Remember, diverticula usually cause no problems at all, so a diagnosis of diverticulosis should not be a serious concern.

The National Institute of Diabetes and Digestive and Kidney Diseases

CONSTIPATION

Constipation is defined as the infrequent and difficult passage of stool. The frequency of bowel movements among normal, healthy people varies greatly, ranging from three movements a day to three a week. As a rule, if more than three days pass without a bowel movement, the intestinal contents may harden and a person may have difficulty or even pain during elimination. Stool may harden and be painful to pass, however, even after shorter intervals between bowel movements.

COMMON MISCONCEPTIONS

Many false beliefs exist concerning "proper" bowel habits. One of these is that you must have a bowel movement every day in order to be normal. This is absolutely incorrect. Another common fallacy is that wastes stored in the body are absorbed and are dangerous to health or shorten the life span. These misconceptions have led to a marked overuse and abuse of laxatives. Every year, Americans spend $225 million on laxatives. Many are not needed and some are harmful.

CAUSES

First of all, it should be understood that constipation is a symptom, not a disease. Like a fever, it can be caused by many different conditions. Most people have experienced an occasional brief bout of constipation that has corrected itself with diet and time. The following is a list of some of the most common causes.

- *Imaginary constipation.* This situation is very common and results from misconceptions about what is normal and what is not. If recognized early enough, this type of constipation can be "cured" simply by informing the sufferer that the frequency of his or her bowel movements is normal.
- *Irritable bowel syndrome (IBS).* Also known as "spastic colon," IBS is one of the most common causes of constipation in the United States. Some people develop spasms of the colon which delay the speed with which the contents of the intestine move through the digestive tract and lead to constipation.
- *Bad bowel habits.* A person can initiate a cycle of constipation by ignoring the urge to defecate. Some people do this to avoid using public toilets, others because they are "too busy." After a period of time a person may stop feeling the urge. This leads to progressive constipation.
- *Laxative abuse.* People who habitually take laxatives become dependent upon them. They may require increasing dosages until, finally, the intestine becomes insensitive and fails to work properly.
- *Travel.* People often experience constipation when traveling long distances. Why this is so is not known but may relate to changes in lifestyle, schedule, diet, and drinking water.
- *Hormonal (gland) disturbances.* Certain hormonal disturbances, such as an underactive thyroid, can produce constipation.
- *Pregnancy.* It is well known that pregnancy can cause constipation. The basis may be partly mechanical, in that the pressure of the heavy womb compresses the intestine, and may be partly hormonal due to changes in the glands of the body during pregnancy.
- *Fissures and hemorrhoids.* Painful conditions of the anus can produce a spasm of the anal sphincter, which can aggravate constipation.
- *Other diseases.* A large number of diseases that affect the body tissues (such as scleroderma or lupus) and certain neurological or muscular diseases (such as multiple sclerosis, Parkinson's disease, and stroke) can be responsible for constipation.

- **Loss of body salts.** The loss of body salts through the kidneys or through vomiting or diarrhea can cause constipation.
- **Mechanical compression.** Scarring, inflammation around diverticula, tumors, and cancer can produce mechanical compression of the intestines and can result in constipation.
- **Nerve damage.** Injuries to the spinal cord and tumors pressing on the spinal cord may produce constipation by affecting the nerves that lead to the intestine.
- **Medications.** A large number of medications can cause constipation. These include pain medications (especially narcotics), antacids that contain aluminum, antispasmodic drugs, antidepressant drugs, tranquilizers, iron supplements, and anticonvulsants (for epilepsy).
- **Poor diet.** A factor in the development of constipation may be the shift away from high-fiber foods (vegetables, fruits, whole grains) to foods that are high in animal fats (meats, dairy products, eggs) and refined sugar (rich desserts and other sweets) but low in fiber. Some studies have suggested that high-fiber diets result in larger stools, more frequent bowel movements, and therefore less constipation.

CAUSES OF CONSTIPATION IN OLDER PEOPLE

Older people are five times more likely than younger people to report problems with constipation. Poor diet, insufficient intake of fluids, lack of exercise, the use of certain drugs to treat other conditions, and poor bowel habits can all result in constipation. Experts agree, however, that too often older people become overly concerned with having a bowel movement and that constipation is frequently an imaginary ailment.

Diet and dietary habits can play a role in developing constipation. Lack of interest in eating—a problem common to many single or widowed older people—may lead to heavy use of convenience foods, which tend to be low in fiber. In addition, loss of teeth may force older people to choose soft, processed foods, which also tend to be low in fiber.

Older people sometimes cut back on fluids, especially if they are not eating regular or balanced meals. Water and other fluids add bulk to stools, making bowel movements softer and easier to pass.

Prolonged bed rest, for example, after an accident or during an illness, and lack of exercise may contribute to constipation. Also, drugs prescribed for other conditions (for example, certain antidepressants, antacids containing aluminum or calcium, antihistamines, diuretics, and antiparkinsonism drugs) can produce constipation in some people.

The preoccupation with bowel movements sometimes leads older people to depend heavily on laxatives. This is not only unnecessary, but it can be habit-forming. The bowel begins to rely on laxatives to bring on defecation and, over time, the natural mechanisms fail to work without the help of drugs. Habitual use of enemas also can lead to a loss of normal function.

DIAGNOSTIC TESTS

In some people, constipation may be caused by abnormalities or obstructions of the digestive system. A doctor can perform a series of tests to determine if constipation is the symptom of an underlying (and often treatable) disorder.

In addition to routine blood, urine, and stool tests, a "procto" examination (proctoscopy) may help detect problems in the rectum and lower colon. In this procedure, which can be done in the doctor's office, the doctor inserts a hollow metal tube through which he or she examines the rectum. To inspect the sigmoid or the entire colon, the doctor may perform a colonoscopy. Colonoscopy is a procedure that uses a flexible, lighted instrument that can follow the twists and turns of the intestine. A barium enema x-ray will provide similar information. If bleeding occurs, a double-contrast barium enema is preferred. Other highly specialized techniques are available for measuring pressures and movements within the colon and its sphincters, but these are used only in unusual cases.

IS CONSTIPATION SERIOUS?

Although it may be extremely bothersome, constipation itself is usually not serious. However, it may signal (and be the only noticeable symptom of) an underlying serious disorder such as cancer. Also, constipation itself can lead to complications such as hemorrhoids caused by extreme straining or fissures (splits in the lining at the anal opening) caused by the hard stool stretching the sphincters. Bleeding can occur from either of these two sources and appears as bright red streaks on the surface of the stool. Fissures may be quite painful and can aggravate the constipation that originally caused them. Fecal impactions tend to occur in the very young and in the elderly and may be accompanied by a loss of control of stool, with liquid stool flowing around the hard impaction.

Occasionally straining causes a small amount of intestinal lining to push out from the rectal opening. This condition is known as a rectal prolapse and may lead to secretion of mucus that may stain underpants.

WHEN SHOULD MEDICAL ATTENTION BE SOUGHT?

You should notify your doctor when symptoms are severe, last longer than three weeks, or are disabling, or when any complications occur. The doctor should be told whenever there is a significant and prolonged change of your usual bowel habits.

TREATMENT

Prevention is the best treatment. The first step is to understand that normal frequency varies widely, from three movements a day to three a week. It is important to know what is normal for you so that you can avoid developing a laxative habit by treating constipation that does not really exist.

If a laxative habit does exist, substitute milder laxatives for stronger ones, and then gradually withdraw the milder ones.

If an underlying disorder is causing constipation, treatment should be directed toward the specific cause. For example, if an underactive thyroid is causing constipation, thyroid extract may help.

Instead of relying upon laxatives and enemas, eat a well-balanced diet that includes unprocessed bran, whole wheat bread, and prunes and prune juice. Bowel habits are also important; set aside sufficient time after breakfast or dinner or after morning coffee to allow for undisturbed visits to the toilet. And never ignore the urge to defecate.

To stimulate intestinal activity, drink plenty of fluids and exercise regularly. Special exercises may be necessary to tone up lax abdominal muscles.

If it becomes necessary to take laxatives or suppositories, they should not be used for

---

THE DIFFERENT CLASSES OF LAXATIVES

• *Stimulant or irritant laxatives* cause rhythmic contractions in the small or large intestine.
• *Osmotic laxatives* cause water to secrete into the colon.
• *Stool softeners or wetting agents* provide moisture to the stool and prevent excessive dehydration.
• *Bulk agents* hold onto water and make the stool softer.
• *Lubricants* tend to soften the stool and make it slip down the intestine more easily.

longer than two or three weeks without the advice of a doctor. Different laxatives act on different portions of the intestine. For example, some stimulate the small intestine, whereas others stimulate the colon. Consult the box on the previous page for an explanation of the different classes of laxatives.

Different types of constipation require different medications, depending upon the underlying cause. Remember, your doctor is best qualified to determine when a laxative is needed and which type is best.

Above all, it is necessary to recognize that a successful treatment program requires persistent effort and time. Constipation does not come on overnight and it is not reasonable to expect that it can be relieved overnight.

The National Institute of Diabetes and
Digestive and Kidney Diseases

DIARRHEA

"The trots," which goes by many other names, polite and impolite, is not funny. Fortunately, it's usually a self-limited ailment—that is, it gets better in a day or two by itself. Diarrhea is the result of the loss of too much water with the stool.

Normally, fluids in the digestive tract are mostly reabsorbed through the intestinal walls, so that fecal matter solidifies as it travels onward. If something interferes with the effectiveness of that process, you'll pass excess fluid as you defecate. (This is why severe diarrhea dehydrates you—and dehydration is its most serious result.)

Drugs for diarrhea work by decreasing water in the stool one of three ways: slowing intestinal motility, increasing reabsorption of fluid through the intestinal wall, or decreasing the amount of material secreted by the intestine.

Diarrhea can have many different causes; most are inconsequential, but a few must be taken seriously.

"NONSPECIFIC" DIARRHEA

The most common kind by far, nonspecific diarrhea appears and disappears so fast that the cause (generally viruses or bacteria) never gets definitively diagnosed, hence the term nonspecific. Stomach flu or the "bug that's going around" are terms commonly applied to nonspecific diarrhea.

Symptoms are frequent, watery bowel movements, excess gas, and stomach cramps.

If you have appointments to keep and work to do, you may want to take something. Since most of the standard drugstore remedies won't help, your best bet may be Imodium (the brand name for loperamide). Until recently a prescription drug only, liquid Imodium A-D has now been approved for over-the-counter (OTC) sale.

Altering your diet temporarily may help too. Avoid milk and dairy products, alcohol, and caffeine. Drink water, juices, broth, and other clear liquids to make up for fluid loss.

The box on the following page evaluates drugs for diarrhea. You may be surprised to see that some "standard" remedies are no longer recommended at all. Whether you take medicine or not, diarrhea lasting more than 48 hours, fever above 101 degrees Fahrenheit, severe cramping, blood in your stool, or light-headedness or dizziness (indicating dehydration) are signals to see a doctor. Frequently recurring diarrhea may be the symptom of more serious bowel disorders and needs prompt medical attention.

TRAVELER'S DIARRHEA

Sometimes dubbed "Montezuma's Revenge," traveler's diarrhea strikes after eating or drinking something contaminated with E. coli or other types of fecal bacteria. It can be serious and debilitating.

DRUGS FOR DIARRHEA— OTC AND PRESCRIPTION

Product	Comment
Acceptable	
IMODIUM A-D (*loperamide*)	Liquid. Side effects uncommon.
IMODIUM (*loperamide*)*	Capsules. Stronger dose than OTC liquid. For nonspecific as well as chronic diarrhea.
LOMOTIL (*diphenoxylate hydrochloride*)*	Tablets. May cause dry mouth.
PEPTO BISMOL (*bismuth subsalicylate*)	Reduces number of bowel movements, but no effect on other symptoms. Contains aspirinlike substance that may produce side effects. May temporarily turn the stool black.
Not recommended	
PARAGORIC† (*tincture of opium*)	Slows intestinal contraction. Prolonged use can cause chronic constipation. (Used only for chronic diarrhea, under doctor's supervision.)
KAOPECTATE (*attapulgite*)	Ineffective.
RHEABAN (*attapulgite*)	Ineffective.
DONNAGEL (*kaolin, pectin and atropinelike substances*)	Ineffective. May cause such side effects as blurred vision or dry mouth.

* available by prescription only
† availability varies from state to state

MEDICATION-INDUCED DIARRHEA

If you've just started a new medication, don't rule it out as a cause of sudden diarrhea. Certain antibiotics, heart drugs, and high blood pressure medications can cause diarrhea. So can many OTC drugs, such as antacids with magnesium (Maalox, for example), and of course, laxatives. So can large amounts of sorbitol, xylitol, and mannitol (sweeteners used in vitamins, diet foods, and sugar-free chewing gum). Stop using any product you suspect, unless it's a prescription drug. In that case, consult your doctor at once.　　*The Editors*

HEMORRHOIDS

Hemorrhoids are swollen veins. Each of us has veins around the anus that tend to stretch under pressure, somewhat like varicose veins in the legs. When these veins swell, we call them "hemorrhoids." One set of veins is inside the rectum (internal), and another is under the skin around the anus (external).

Hemorrhoids also are known as "piles." As a rule, they do not cause pain or bleeding. Problems can occur, however, when these veins become swollen because pressure is raised in them. Increased pressure may result from straining to move the bowels, from sitting too long on the toilet, or from other factors such as pregnancy, obesity, or liver disease.

SYMPTOMS

The only sign you may notice from internal hemorrhoids is bright red blood on the toilet paper or in the toilet bowl.

Sometimes, however, these veins stretch, and may even fall down (prolapse) through the anus to outside the body (protruding hemorrhoids). When this happens, the vein may become irritated and painful.

The set of veins around the anus causes problems when blood clots form in them, and they become large and painful. (These are called thrombosed external hemorrhoids.) You may notice bleeding and a tender lump on the edge of the anus. Bleeding starts when the swollen veins are scratched or broken by straining or rubbing. People who have external hemorrhoids may feel itching at the anus too. This might result from draining mucus and irritation caused by too much rubbing or cleaning of the anus.

A COMMON PROBLEM

Hemorrhoidal problems are very common in men and in women. About half of people have hemorrhoids to some extent by the age of 50. Many people have bleeding from hemorrhoids sometimes, but most often the bleeding is not serious. Women may begin to have problems during pregnancy. The pressure of the fetus in the abdomen, as well as hormonal changes, causes hemorrhoidal veins to enlarge. These veins also are placed under severe pressure during the birth of the baby.

For most women, however, such hemorrhoids are a temporary problem.

THE IMPORTANCE OF DIET AND HYGIENE

Often all that is needed to reduce symptoms is to include more fiber in your diet to soften the stool. Eat more fresh fruits, leafy vegetables, whole-grain breads and cereals (especially bran). Drinking six to eight glasses of fluid (not alcohol) each day will also help. Softer stools make it easier to empty the bowels and lessen pressure on the veins.

Bathe the anus gently after a bowel movement, using soft, moist toilet paper (or a commercial moist pad). Avoid a lot of wiping. If necessary, use the shower as an alternative to wiping. After bathing, dry the anus gently.

WHEN TO SEE THE DOCTOR

It is a good idea to see your doctor any time you see bleeding from the anus. This is important to make sure you don't have cancer or some other disease of the digestive system. You will need an examination of your anus

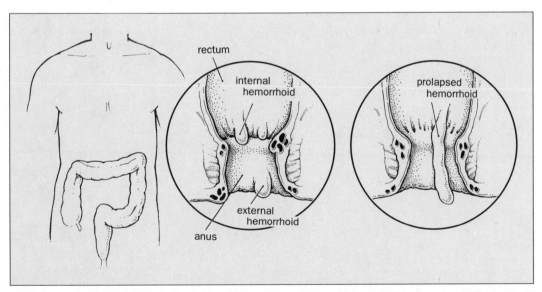

Internal hemorrhoids occur in the veins of the rectum; external hemorrhoids, in veins of the anus. A prolapsed hemorrhoid results when an internal hemorrhoid protrudes outward, through the anus.

and rectum and possibly further examination of the bowel. If the doctor finds hemorrhoids, you may be advised to change your diet or to use a laxative that provides fiber and softens the stool. Your doctor might only recommend ice, warm soaks (sitz bath), or rest in bed.

TREATMENT

If you know you are having pain from hemorrhoids, you might try putting cold packs on the anus, followed by a sitz bath, three or four times a day. To protect against irritation, cleanse the anus carefully and apply zinc oxide paste (or powder) or petroleum jelly to the area. Medicated suppositories also are available at the drugstore. Any of these home treatments may relieve the symptoms, and no other treatment may be needed. If symptoms persist, see your doctor.

In some cases, internal hemorrhoids that have fallen outside of the anus (prolapsed), or that bleed too much, must be removed. Your doctor may be able to remove them during an outpatient visit to his office or to the hospital.

A number of methods besides the usual surgery with a scalpel can be used to remove or reduce the size of hemorrhoids. The surgeon may decide to use a technique in which a rubber band is put around the base of the hemorrhoid. The band cuts off circulation, and the hemorrhoid withers away within a few days. This technique is used only for internal hemorrhoids. Sometimes a chemical is injected around the vein to shrink the hemorrhoid.

Other methods include the use of freezing, electrical or laser heat, or infrared light to destroy the hemorrhoidal tissue.

PREVENTION

The best way to prevent the problem is to pass your bowel movements as soon as possible after the urge occurs. Also, don't sit on the toilet too long. This is the only time that the anus truly relaxes, allowing the veins there to fill with blood. The longer you sit, the longer pressure is put on the hemorrhoids. To avoid constipation, be active. Move around, walk, exercise to help move the stools through your body. Also, adding fiber to your diet reduces straining by helping to produce stools that are softer and easier to pass.

Remember, hemorrhoids usually do not pose a danger to your health. In most cases, hemorrhoidal symptoms will go away naturally within a few days.

The National Institute of Diabetes and Digestive and Kidney Diseases

The Ears, Nose, and Throat

In medicine, the ears, nose, and throat are traditionally treated as a single, integrated system. This is because all three parts overlap in terms of function, structure, and nerve supply. A disorder in any one of the areas may manifest in the other two. So often, for example, a cold that starts off as only a runny nose leads to an earache or a sore throat. Or perhaps you're on an airplane and the change in altitude creates an uncomfortable sensation of pressure in your ears. You discover that a simple swallow—opening up the throat—is all it takes to clear the discomfort in your ears.

The specialty dealing with the ears, nose, and throat—and how they are interrelated—is called otolaryngology; the specialist (usually a surgeon) is called an otolaryngologist or, more simply, an ENT (for ear, nose, and throat) doctor.

THE EARS

Each ear is divided into three distinct sections: outer, middle, and inner ear.

The outer ear consists of the visible, external folds of cartilage, and the canal that leads into the middle ear. If you lost the external cartilage due to an accident, your hearing would not be affected very much. This portion of the ear—the shape of which is unique to each individual and does not change throughout life—is only a rudimentary funnel for sound. It offers some physical protection, but in its absence, sounds still reach the eardrum through the canal of the outer ear. This canal is lined with short hairs and thousands of wax-generating glands. The wax and hair help to stop dust, dirt, small insects—anything that might infiltrate the ear—from reaching the middle ear. The outer ear also modifies the air that reaches the deeper parts of the ear, so that the ear's internal temperature and humidity levels are nearly always constant, regardless of the climate outside.

The middle ear begins where the outer ear ends: at the eardrum, or tympanic mem-

brane. Also in the middle ear are the three smallest bones in the body: the hammer (malleus), the anvil (incus), and the stirrup (stapes). These bones amplify and conduct sound signals to the inner ear.

The inner ear consists of two essential parts: the cochlea and the semicircular canals. The cochlea converts sounds into electrical nerve impulses which can then be sent, via the auditory nerve, to the brain, where they are interpreted. The semicircular canals are responsible for maintaining our sense of balance. The inner ear, containing as many circuits as a city telephone system, is one of the most complex and delicate parts of the body. Fortunately—situated deep within the hard skull and surrounded by a fluid cushion—the inner ear is also one of the best-protected parts of the body.

THE NOSE

The nose provides critical information about our immediate surroundings: warning us of a fire while it is still only smouldering; letting us know when it's time to throw out the leftovers that could result in food poisoning; or simply adding to our appreciation of a garden in full bloom. The sense of taste, in fact, is deeply reliant upon the sense of smell. When the olfactory senses fail (as occurs with a bad cold), you lose about 80 percent of your ability to discern flavors.

In addition to olfaction, the nose is the main conduit for respiration, and it filters the approximately 500 cubic feet of air we breathe every day. The hairs that line the nostrils block airborne pollen, dust, or grit from getting into the lungs; when such particles are especially irritating, the sneeze reflex is triggered, ejecting the offending matter at speeds upwards of 200 miles per hour. The membranes that line the nasal passages secrete mucus that continually cleans and lubricates the region. Mucus not only physically surrounds foreign material, but it contains a substance called lysozyme that chemically destroys bacteria. The nose also warms and humidifies air coming into the lungs.

Beyond these functions, your nose also gives your voice extra richness and resonance, without which you'd sound as if you were always "holding your nose" when you talk. The four sets of sinus cavities are simply air-filled spaces within certain bones of the face. The sinuses allow these bones to be lighter in weight and they too give the voice resonance. Each of the sinuses is lined with a mucus membrane that is integrally connected to the mucus membranes of the throat and, in particular, the nose.

THE THROAT

The throat (pharynx) is the passageway that brings food and drink to the digestive system, as well as air to and from the lungs. It also conducts air through the vocal cords (larynx), allowing us to speak and sing.

The approximately five-inch-long pharynx, a muscular tube lined with a mucus membrane, has the crucial task of handling traffic flow between its two divisions: the trachea (windpipe) and the esophagus (food passage). Without constant automatic regulation, food would enter the lungs and air would enter the stomach. But, when we swallow, a small flap of skin called the epiglottis acts as a safety valve, closing over the top of the larynx to seal off the windpipe. Muscles at the top of the throat help push food down along the esophagus. At the end of the swallow, the epiglottis relaxes again so that breathing can resume.

Sometimes—usually when we're eating too fast or are talking or laughing as we eat—the process doesn't work quite right and food may get stuck at the entrance of the windpipe. Typically, this will trigger powerful choking and coughing to dislodge the blockage. If not, the more aggressive Heimlich maneuver might be necessary.   *The Editors*

HEARING LOSS

Human hearing depends on a series of mechanical and electrical events that enable sound waves in air to be converted to electrical impulses carried by nerves to the brain.

Sound itself is a form of energy. Suppose you snap your fingers. The snap generates a force that presses against the molecules of air surrounding your fingertips.

The molecules are pushed out a short distance in all directions, crowding into space occupied by other air molecules so that a densely packed shell of air molecules forms. That shell—sound experts call it a "shell of compression"—in turn presses against other air molecules nearby so that they too are pushed out to form a second, slightly larger shell of compression, which in turn nudges a third layer of air, and so on.

Meanwhile, the air around your fingertips has become less dense as a result of those first molecules being pushed out. A partial vacuum is created by this "rarefied" air, and the molecules that moved out now rush back to fill that vacuum. Their return creates a second partial vacuum in their wake, which the molecules of the second shell rush back and fill. And so it goes.

Thus, the original sound energy that was generated when you snapped your finger moves through the air on a "wave" which is really a succession of shells of compression and rarefaction created by molecules moving back and forth—vibrating.

The number of shells of compression that pass a given point every second determines the frequency of the sound, measured in cycles per second (cps) or hertz (Hz). Human beings interpret frequency as pitch: the greater the frequency, the higher the pitch. How far the molecules move back and forth as they vibrate is a measure of the energy or intensity of sound. Human beings interpret sound intensity as loudness.

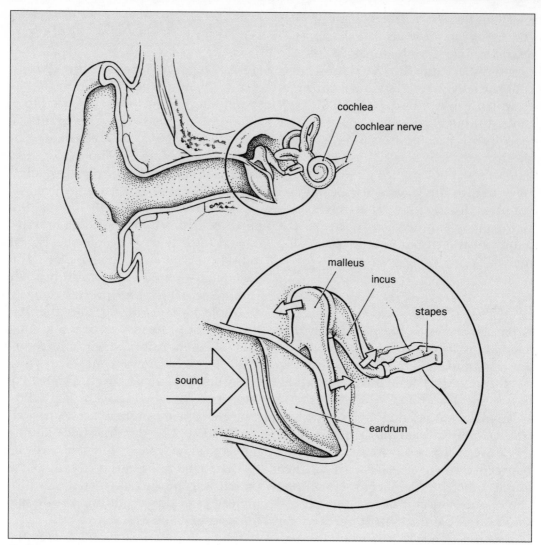

As we age, the bones of the middle ear (malleus, incus, and stapes) may move more stiffly, the ear-drum may thicken, and conduction problems in the cochlea may occur—all leading to hearing loss.

Our ears are sensitive to only certain ranges of frequency and intensity. Healthy young adults can hear notes as low as 20 Hz—lower than the lowest notes of a bass fiddle—as well as sounds at 20,000 Hz, beyond the upper reaches of a flute. The intensity range to which our ears respond is enormous. When sound is just audible—the threshold level of hearing—the force of sound waves acting on the ear is about 140 million times smaller than the force needed to lift a one-ounce weight.

At the other extreme, human ears can respond—painfully—to sonic booms, explosions, or the noise of jackhammers breaking up city streets.

Because the ear can respond to such enormous ranges of sound energy, intensity is measured in ratios. That is the basis of the decibel (dB) scale. A sound 10 times more intense than another at the same frequency differs from it by 10 dB; a sound 100 times more intense differs by 20 dB. The decibel scale is usually set at an arbitrary zero level (0 dB), which does not mean the absence of sound, but the average threshold level of hearing of healthy young adults. On that basis, a whisper is about 20 dB, and normal conversation about 60 dB. The noise of a jet taking off is on the order of 160 dB—10 quadrillion times the zero level!

TUNING IN

Understanding these fundamentals of sound explains a lot of what goes on—and what can go wrong—with the hearing process. Initially the job of the ears is to pick up sound waves and conduct them accurately to the inner ear. That the ears can manage this task with great skill and efficiency is due in part to the design of the outer and middle ear.

When sound waves enter the ear, they travel for an inch or so down a narrow tube, the external auditory canal, before striking the delicate, skin-covered tympanic membrane, or eardrum. The drum is shaped like a broad flat cone about one-half inch across and less than one-fiftieth inch thick. The drum vibrates in tune with the sound waves striking it and transmits the vibrations accurately to three tiny bones in the middle ear, the ossicles. These bones—the malleus, the incus, and the stapes—amplify the vibrations so that the waves can pass on to the inner ear.

It's not hard to understand why specialists find the ear a stunning example of design as well as a challenge for study. For the ear's high-fidelity equipment is miniaturized. The ossicles are the smallest bones in the human body; they fit into a cavity the size of a string bean seed that has been carved out of the temporal bone of the human skull.

Two other features of the middle ear are important. One is that the compartment connects to the throat by a narrow canal with collapsible walls, the eustachian tube. When you swallow, the eustachian tube opens so that air pressure in the middle ear and throat is equalized. That mechanism protects your middle ear from harmful pressure differences that can occur in a fast-rising elevator, for example, or on takeoff and landing in an airplane. The second important middle ear feature is also protective. Muscles attached to the ossicles automatically contract in response to loud noises. These automatic reflexes by the muscles may prevent strong sound pressures from damaging the delicate structures of the inner ear.

To summarize, when the eardrum and middle ear bones are working properly, sound waves striking the drum are faithfully conducted across the middle ear and boosted in energy. The energy boost helps prepare sound waves that have been traveling in air for the more resistant watery medium of their next stop: a fluid-filled bony shell in the inner ear called the cochlea.

CONDUCTIVE PROBLEMS

A variety of problems can affect hearing before sound reaches the cochlea. Because these early stages in the hearing process are concerned with picking up and conducting sound signals, specialists refer to the hearing impairments involved as conductive problems. The following are among the most common problems.

External Blockage

Sometimes there is a buildup of wax in the ears or the introduction of a foreign object. Sometimes a bug crawls in. These are obvious plugs that partially block sound. The removal of impacted wax and foreign objects is best left to experts to avoid the possibility of damaging the eardrum.

Perforated Eardrum

A hole or a tear in the eardrum can occur as a result of injury, sudden pressure change, or infection. Ear specialists can repair or completely rebuild the eardrum using the latest techniques of microsurgery.

Genetic and Congenital Abnormalities

Malformations of the outer and middle ear sometimes occur in connection with hereditary disease or as a result of injuries and illnesses that affect a baby before or around the time of birth. Surgery can sometimes correct these problems.

Otitis Media

By far the most prevalent cause of conductive impairments is a common middle ear disease, otitis media. The problem can occur at any age but is particularly prevalent in children. An estimated two-thirds of preschoolers have at least one episode. The reason that children are so vulnerable may be that their eustachian tubes are shorter and positioned more horizontally than in adults. Infectious agents causing colds or other upper respiratory disease can easily spread to the middle ear. At the same time, mucus, pus, or other fluids accumulating in the middle ear tend not to drain off. Thus the middle ear can become inflamed, swollen, fluid-filled, and painful—the classic symptoms of otitis media that can result in temporary and sometimes permanent hearing impairment. Thanks to today's medications, most middle ear infections can be cleared up with no lasting damage.

Otosclerosis

An example of a hereditary hearing problem that develops in adults is otosclerosis, a condition in which there is an overgrowth of bone in the middle ear. Usually the tiny stirrup-shaped stapes bone is the most affected and becomes fixed in place, impeding sound conduction. Otosclerosis can often be remedied by surgery to remove the excess bone and replace all or part of the stapes with an artificial part. Those who have undergone successful surgery describe the results as miraculous. "I was completely deaf before the operation," one woman said. "As soon as I woke up, I could hear again!"

Presbycusis

Specialists have coined the word presbycusis—literally, old hearing—to describe hearing impairments that occur in aging. While presbycusis is primarily associated with changes in the inner ear and brain, conductive impairments may also occur. The bones of the middle ear may become stiff, for example, or the eardrum thicker and less flexible. Both those changes may reflect a less rich blood supply to the ear as a result of heart disease, high blood pressure, or other circulatory problems in older people.

Conductive impairments can be detected in the course of an ear examination that includes a variety of diagnostic tests.

FROM EAR TO BRAIN

When sound vibrates the three middle ear bones, the last in line, the stapes, presses against a membrane called the oval window. This membrane is fitted into a thin shell of bone that encloses all the inner ear structures. About an inch down from the oval window, the bone spirals to form the snail-shaped cochlea, another ministructure less than one-half inch across at its base, rising a mere one-quarter inch to its tip.

The cochlea is composed of three fluid-filled compartments. The center and smallest compartment is a duct of soft tissue that contains the organ of hearing, called the organ of Corti, after the Italian scientist who first described it. Like the retina of the eye, the organ of Corti contains special cells called sensory receptors that take incoming energy—light in case of the eye, sound for the ear—and transform that energy into electrical signals. The ear cells that do the transforming are called hair cells because the cell tops are fringed with fine hairs that stick up into the fluid filling the duct. The hair cells are sandwiched between two membranes: one membrane rests lightly on the hair tips; the other forms the floor or base of the duct, and so is called the basilar membrane.

Research had led to greater understanding of how the organ of Corti works and to a Nobel prize for the investigator who contributed significantly to that understanding, Georg von Békésy. Put very simply, when the stapes kicks in the oval window, the fluid in the cochlea is stirred and sets the basilar membrane moving in a very special way: Sounds of high frequency cause the greatest movements of the membrane under hair cells at the base of the cochlea, agitating the tips of the cells' protruding hairs. Sounds of middle frequency cause maximum movements of the membrane further toward the center of the cochlea, while sounds of lowest frequencies cause peak membrane movements near the top of the cochlea.

The movements of the hairs cause changes inside the cells that lead to the production of electrical signals. These signals excite nearby nerve cells whose long fibers—some 30,000 in each ear—spiral out from the cochlea to form the eighth, or auditory nerve, which goes from the ear to the brain.

Soon after entering the brain, eighth nerve fibers contact nerve cells in the first of many nerve centers concerned with hearing. Ultimately the auditory signals reach the cortex, the outermost covering of the brain. The cortex contains centers associated with interpreting speech and music, with thinking, memory, learning, and other higher mental faculties.

HEARING PROBLEMS HIGHER UP

Hearing impairments that result from damage to the sensory apparatus (the hair cells and other parts of the inner ear) or to the eighth nerve and auditory centers higher up in the brain (the neural apparatus) are often lumped together as "sensorineural" problems. Included among these are the following.

Hearing Loss at Birth

Some 4,000 infants are born deaf every year in the United States. Close to half those cases are due to hereditary disorders.

Hereditary Hearing Loss

It is important to realize that hereditary conditions not only can result in deafness at birth, but also account for a variety of hearing impairments occurring later. Hereditary disorders can affect the outer and middle ear, as in otosclerosis, but generally involve damage to the cochlea or higher nerve centers. Because there are so many kinds of hereditary disorders, with different risks of inheritance, couples with a history of deafness on either side of the family should consult genetic counselors for information.

Trauma-Induced Problems

A severe blow to the head, an accident, stroke, brain hemorrhage, or other trauma that affects the ear or any of the auditory pathways and brain centers will obviously take its toll on hearing ability.

Tumors

Patients with eighth nerve tumors—called acoustic neuromas—may complain of hearing loss in one or both ears, headaches, dizziness, ringing in the ear (called tinnitus), or numbness over the face. Such symptoms deserve prompt attention. If an eighth nerve tumor is detected early, surgery to remove the tumor can be completely successful, leaving no hearing or other impairment. Tumors diagnosed at later stages may have grown large enough to be life-threatening, or their surgical removal may result in hearing loss, disturbances in the sense of balance (also located in the inner ear), loss of sensation in the face, or facial paralysis.

Acoustic neuromas can occur for no known reason, but can also arise as a result of a hereditary disease called neurofibromatosis.

Noise Damage

Brief exposures to high-intensity sound can cause a temporary but reversible hearing loss. However, continued exposure to loud noise means trouble. Eventually the hair cells sustain permanent damage, resulting in gradual hearing loss.

During the early days of industrialization nobody doubted that the din surrounding boilermakers, hydraulic press operators, or steel mill workers rendered their hearing less than perfect. Nowadays specialists are concerned that the everyday sounds of our highly technological society are also wilting our hair cells. Think of the power mowers and chain saws, the disposals, stereo sets, dishwashers, and food processors we live with—and the sounds of airplanes, motorcycles, city and highway traffic, fire and emergency trucks. Think too of joggers wearing earphones or young people at rock concerts or disco clubs, and you have the reason so many hearing specialists are worried.

Drug-Induced Hearing Loss

Drugs as common as aspirin, the antibiotics streptomycin or neomycin, and certain of the diuretics used to treat high blood pressure can damage the hair cells or other vital parts of the inner ear. Anyone who, while under medication, has a sudden change in hearing, or experiences dizziness or ringing in the ears (tinnitus), or has other problems with hearing or balance should report the symptoms to a physician at once. Often changes in the prescription can eliminate the symptoms and prevent permanent damage to the ear.

Certain powerful anticancer drugs may also damage hearing.

Tinnitus

Many people have experienced one or more occasions when they felt a ringing or buzzing in the ears or inside the head. But a surprising number of people, especially in middle age or later years, complain of a constant ringing in the head for no known reason. In some cases the symptoms may be unnoticed if a person is busy at work, talking, or otherwise distracted. For other people, however, the unpleasant sounds are present during every waking hour, interfering with all activities. In the most severe cases tinnitus even interrupts sleep. The hapless victim is tormented by an incessant internal siren sounding off. The psychological effects on a person can be devastating.

Presbycusis

Changes associated with aging are responsible for the majority of hearing impairments in adults. Many people in their forties and fifties experience a decline in sensitivity to high frequencies. The decline is gradual and progressive so that by their sixties and seventies as many as 25 percent of the elderly are noticeably impaired. However, investigators are beginning to question whether "aging factors" per se are at fault. There are cultures in the world—the Mabaan people of the African Sudan, for example—where presbycusis doesn't exist. Both men and women have excellent hearing in old age. The environment of the Mabaans is exceptionally quiet by Western standards. Further, the Mabaans do not suffer from heart disease, high blood pressure, ulcers, or asthma. They lead relatively stress-free lives. No conclusions can yet be drawn, except that presbycusis is clearly not an inevitable result of aging.

Many experts now think that lifelong exposure to noise, as well as the high prevalence of heart disease, high blood pressure, and other blood vessel disorders increase the odds of hearing loss in later years.

In addition, some hereditary predisposition may be involved. As one investigator puts it, "Some of us may simply be programmed to suffer a decline and fall of our hair cells or our auditory neurons starting at a particular age—as young as the twenties and thirties in some people." Further, the decline may be selective. The hair cells and inner ear structures may be healthy in some older individuals so that they can pass a hearing test for pure tones with flying colors. Yet those same people may have trouble understanding speech, especially under trying conditions. Experts suspect that the listener's confusion is associated with tissue damage or loss of nerve cells in the brain where centers for speech perception and discrimination are located.

DETECTING HEARING LOSS

In the case of a simple infection or impacted wax, the diagnosis and treatment of a hearing problem may begin and end in the family doctor's office. More complicated cases call for the expertise of the otologist. He or she will conduct a thorough ear examination, note the patient's medical history, and inquire about hearing problems affecting other members of the family. Certain blood tests or other laboratory analyses may be necessary, as well as standard hearing tests. The specialist may also want x-rays of the head or the computerized x-ray images of the brain called CT scans.

Hearing tests are usually conducted by audiologists, professionals educated in the science of hearing and in the battery of tests used to assess and analyze hearing impairment. Audiologists also provide counseling and nonmedical rehabilitation for the hearing impaired, such as lipreading and hearing aid evaluation.

Persons undergoing audiological testing sit in a small soundproof room. The examination usually includes tests to determine how well the eardrum and middle ear bones conduct sound. These tests depend on inserting a snug-fitting probe with wires attached into the external canal of the ear. Then air pressure between the probe tip and the eardrum is varied at the same time that a tone is sounded through the probe tip. A machine analyzes the movements of the drum and middle ear bones, printing out the results on a graph, which is called the "tympanogram."

The probe can also be used to check the acoustic reflex to loud noise. The tympanogram and acoustic reflex tests take only a few minutes. Since the tests depend on automatic responses of the auditory system, they can be used to test hearing in infants and others who cannot respond voluntarily.

The audiologist then measures the patient's thresholds for two-syllable words and for pure tones in a range from 250 Hz to 8,000 Hz. The patient wears headphones and indicates when he or she can just barely detect sounds as the decibel level is varied. The graph that plots sound frequency against decibel level is the audiogram. The audiologist also measures the ability to discriminate speech by having the individual repeat one-syllable words. The audiologist may conduct further tests to determine the nature of the hearing loss. These tests may involve manipulations of pure tones and noises or the use of tape recordings that introduce distortions into voice or sound signals.

AN EEG FOR HEARING

In the past decade investigators have developed ways of recording the electrical activity of brain centers associated with hearing. Electrodes are attached to the top of the head and at each side, near the ear. The individual wears earphones and sits quietly in a soundproof room listening to clicks at different intensities. A computer analyzes the nerve cell activity in response to the clicks and displays the brain wave pattern on a video screen. Audiologists know the normal shape of the waves and the time it takes for nerve signals to move from center to center along the auditory pathways. Delays in the appearance of certain waves or changes in their pattern help localize the problem. Because the brain cells recorded lie in the brainstem—a core of brain tissue located below the cortex—the brain wave recording is called the auditory brainstem response. Like tympanometry, the auditory brainstem response test is automatic and so can be used to study hearing in infants. However, the test takes up to an hour and the subject must remain stationary and quiet.

The results of medical and audiological examinations may indicate a problem that can be helped by surgery, medication, or a hearing aid. Sometimes preventive measures are urged. Adults with middle ear infections are cautioned to avoid flying; workers who are beginning to show noise-induced hearing losses are advised to transfer to less noisy departments or at least wear ear protection. Often, however, the hearing loss is long-standing and irreparable. In those instances there is no instant remedy or miraculous cure. But there are important things that can be done.

HEARING AIDS

A hearing aid amplifies sound. The aid provides the extra power to boost sound so that it can stimulate the cochlear cells. Hearing aids can benefit anyone, as long as some hearing remains. How well hearing aids work is another matter. Their effectiveness depends not only on the design of the aid (is it a quiet, high-quality, easy-to-maintain instrument?), but also on how well the aid matches the individual's needs.

Present-day aids are a far cry from the ear trumpets used generations ago. A modern aid is lightweight, battery-operated, and miniaturized. It can be molded to fit inside the ear, worn behind the ear, or fitted into eyeglasses.

Many individuals with hearing impairments become sensitive to amplified sound. This does not mean they cannot wear a hearing aid; it does mean that the aid must accommodate their sensitivities. Some investigators now suspect that hard-of-hearing people occasionally retain "islands of hearing"—frequency ranges where sound is still perceived at near

to normal levels. Such individuals might find the amplification provided by hearing aids uncomfortable. Scientists at Louisiana State University in New Orleans are currently investigating islands of hearing in hearing-impaired people to see how common the phenomenon is, and whether special aids making use of these frequencies could be designed to enable individuals to understand speech.

But no matter how well designed and appropriate to the wearer's hearing impairment, the chances of the aid benefiting the user largely depend on attitude and motivation. It is important to realize that adjustments in the aid have to be made and all wearers go through a period of learning and adaptation. In short, the recommendation and fitting of a hearing aid is not the end of an audiological examination, but the beginning of a new way of life. Follow-up in the first few weeks, proper maintenance, and periodic checkups to see how the human ear and aid are both doing are a necessary part of the process.

At the same time, a person can learn simple skills to enhance the usefulness of an aid. Speech reading (lipreading) is one. Most people already possess this skill to a remarkable degree. If you think you are not a speech reader, consider the times you have watched a TV movie where sound was not quite synchronized with lip movement.

*The National Institute of
Neurological Disorders and Stroke*

SINUSITIS

Every year over one and a half billion dollars worth of "sinus" medicine is purchased in America for the symptoms of sinus disease (i.e., stuffy nose, congestion, headache, and nasal drainage). Everyone has sinuses, which begin as pea-size pouches extending outward from the inside of the nose into the bones of

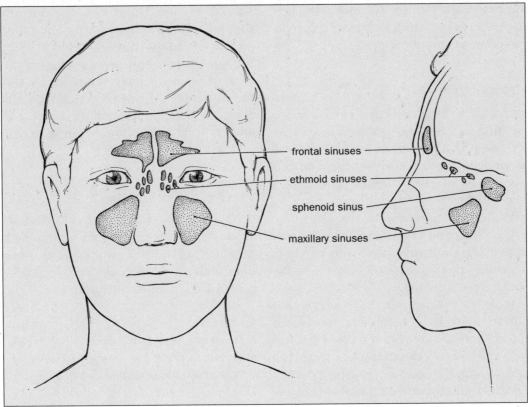

There are four sets of sinus cavities. The maxillary sinuses—the largest—account for most sinus problems in adults. Pain occurs when the thin drainage channels become blocked.

the face and skull. They expand and grow through childhood into young adulthood. They are air pockets, cavities that are lined with the same kind of membranes that line the nose, and they are connected to the inside of the nose through small openings about the size of a pencil lead.

WHAT DO SINUSES DO?

Sinuses are part of the nasal air and membrane system that produces mucus. Normally, the nose and sinuses produce between a pint and a quart of mucus and secretions per day. This mucus passes into and through the nose, sweeping and washing the membranes, picking up dust particles, bacteria, and other air pollutants along the way. The mucus then flows backward into the throat where it is swal-

lowed, down into the stomach where acids destroy any dangerous bacteria. Most people do not notice this mucus flow because it is just a normal bodily function.

WHAT IS POST-NASAL DRIP?

When the nasal passages are irritated by allergies, air pollution, smoke, or viral infections (such as a cold), then the nose and sinus membranes secrete more than the normal amount of mucus. This will be a clear, watery, and profuse mucus that is supposed to wash away the irritation or allergy. This is the most common type of post-nasal drip. Another form of post-nasal drip is mucus that is thick and sticky. This occurs when the air is too dry and the nose membranes cannot produce enough moisture to put into the mucus for it to flow easily. Bacterial infections also produce a thick, sticky mucus with pus in it, turning it a yellow or green color.

WHAT IS SINUSITIS?

The suffix "-itis" is a medical term for infection or inflammation, so "sinusitis" is an infection or inflammation of the sinuses. A typical case of acute sinusitis begins with a cold or flu or an allergy attack that causes swelling of the nasal membranes and increased watery mucous production. The membranes can become so swollen that the tiny openings from the sinuses become blocked. When mucus and air cannot flow easily between the nose and sinuses, abnormal pressures occur in the sinuses, and mucus can build up in them. This creates a pressure-pain in the forehead or face, between and behind the eyes, or in the cheeks and upper teeth, depending on which sinuses are involved.

A blocked sinus cavity filled with mucus becomes a fine place for bacteria to grow. When a person's cold lasts more than the typical week or so, and when his mucus turns yellow/green or develops a bad odor or taste, then a bacterial infection has probably taken over. The pressure and pain in the face and forehead can be quite severe in acute bacterial sinusitis. Chronic sinusitis occurs when the sinus opening is blocked for an extended period. Headaches are less prominent in chronic sinusitis, but congestion and unpleasant nasal secretions usually persist. Also, fleshy growths known as polyps can develop as an exaggerated form of inflammatory swelling of the membranes.

Some cases of sinusitis are brought on by infections in the upper teeth that extend into the sinuses.

IS SINUSITIS DANGEROUS?

Most cases of sinusitis respond promptly to medical treatment and are not serious. It should be noted, however, that an infection that is in the sinus is also very close to the eye and to the brain. But extension of a sinus infection to the eye or brain is rare.

Furthermore, it is not healthy for the lungs to have infected mucus dripping down from infected sinuses. Bronchitis, chronic cough, and asthma are often aggravated, or even brought on, by sinusitis.

WHAT IS A SINUS HEADACHE?

A headache in the face, cheeks, forehead, or around the eyes that comes on during a cold, or when the nose is congested and runny or filled with mucus, is probably a sinus headache: one caused by sinus infection.

Another kind of sinus headache is the one that occurs in the sinus areas during descent (landing) in an airplane, especially if you have a cold or active allergy (this is called a vacuum headache).

Unfortunately, there are many other causes of headaches that can be confused with sinusitis. For example, migraine and other forms of vascular or tension headaches also give pain in the forehead and around the eyes, and they may even cause a slight stuffy-runny nose. But they are more likely to come and go away in a day or so without a physician's treatment, whereas sinusitis usually gives a headache that lasts for days or weeks until it is treated with antibiotics.

Furthermore, intermittent headaches that cause nausea and vomiting are more typical of a migraine-type headache than sinusitis.

Severe, frequent, or prolonged headaches deserve a visit to a physician for diagnosis and treatment. (See also Headache, page 120.)

WHO GETS SINUS TROUBLE?

Actually, anyone can catch a sinus infection, but certain groups of people, such as the following, are more likely to develop sinusitis.

- *People with allergies.* An allergy attack, like a cold, causes swelling in the nasal membranes that will block the sinus openings, obstruct the mucous drainage, and predispose to infection.
- *People with deformities of the nose* that impair good breathing and proper drainage. Examples are a crooked nose or a deviated septum (the structure between the nostrils that divides the inside of the nose into right and left sides).
- *People who are frequently exposed to infection.* School teachers and health workers are especially susceptible.
- *People who smoke.* Tobacco smoke, nicotine, and other pollutants impair the natural resistance to infection.

WHAT WILL A DOCTOR DO FOR YOUR SINUSES?

Your physician will ask you questions about your breathing, the nature of your nasal mucus, and the circumstances (time of day or seasons) that give you symptoms. Be prepared to explain your headaches: When and how often they occur; how long they last; and if they are associated with nausea, vomiting, vision changes, or nasal congestion. An otolaryngologist-head and neck surgeon is the kind of physician who will especially examine your ears, nose, mouth, teeth, and throat with particular attention to the appearance of your nasal membranes and secretions. He or she will check for deformities of your nose that impair breathing and for tenderness over your sinuses. X-rays of your sinuses might be needed.

Treatment will depend on the diagnosis that your physician establishes. Infections may require either antibiotics or surgery or sometimes both. Acute sinusitis most likely will improve on medication, but chronic sinusitis more often requires surgery. If your symptoms are due to allergy, migraine, or some other disease that mimics sinusitis, your doctor will have alternative treatment plans.

WHAT CAN YOU DO FOR YOUR OWN SINUSES?

Manage your allergies if you have them. Use a humidifier when you have a cold, and sleep with the head of your bed elevated. This promotes sinus drainage. Decongestants can also be helpful, but they contain chemicals that act like adrenaline and are dangerous for persons with high blood pressure, irregular heart rhythms, heart disease, or glaucoma. They are also like stimulants that can produce sleeplessness. You should consult your physician before you use these medications.

Avoid air pollutants that irritate the nose, especially tobacco smoke.

Live by good health practices that include a balanced diet and regular exercise.

Minimize exposure to persons with known infections, if possible, and practice sanitary health habits when you must be around them (such as hand washing and avoidance of shared towels, napkins, and eating utensils).

A large variety of nonprescription medications are sold as sinus remedies, but it is folly to try them before a proper diagnosis is established. The best advice you can ever get, of course, is what is given to you by your physician who evaluates your own special symptoms and examines your own nose and sinuses.

*The American Academy of Otolaryngology—
Head and Neck Surgery*

SMELL AND TASTE DISORDERS

One study estimates that more than two million Americans have smell and taste disorders. Another estimate suggests that more than 200,000 people visit a physician for a smell or taste problem each year, while many more smell and taste disturbances go unreported.

A person with a faulty sense of smell and taste is deprived of an early warning system that most of us take for granted. Smell and taste alert us to fires, poisonous fumes, leaking gas, and spoiled foods. Loss of the sense of smell may also be a sign of sinus disease, growths in the nasal passages, or, in rare circumstances, brain tumors. Because an intact sense of smell and taste is required in some professions, chefs and firemen, among others, may be subject to serious economic hardship.

HOW DO SMELL AND TASTE WORK?

Smell and taste belong to our chemical sensing system, or chemosensation. The complicated processes of smelling and tasting begin when molecules released by the substances around us stimulate special nerve cells in the nose, mouth, or throat. These cells transmit messages to the brain, where specific smells or tastes are identified.

Olfactory (smell nerve) cells are stimulated by the odors around us—the fragrance from a rose, the smell of bread baking. These nerve cells are found in a tiny patch of tissue high up in the nose, and they connect directly to the brain.

Taste cells react to food or drink mixed with saliva and are clustered in the taste buds of the mouth and throat. Many of the small bumps that can be seen on the tongue contain taste buds. These surface cells send taste information to nearby nerve fibers, which send messages to the brain.

Cells governing our senses of taste and smell are the only cells in the nervous system that are replaced when they become old or damaged. Scientists are examining this phenomenon while studying ways to replace other damaged nerve cells.

A third chemosensory mechanism, called the common chemical sense, contributes to our senses of smell and taste. In this system, thousands of free nerve endings—especially on the moist surfaces of the eyes, nose, mouth, and throat—identify sensations like the sting of ammonia, the coolness of menthol, and the "heat" of chili peppers.

We can commonly identify four basic taste sensations: sweet, sour, bitter, and salty. Certain combinations of these tastes—along with texture, temperature, odor, and the sensations from the common chemical sense—produce a flavor. It is flavor that lets us know whether we are eating peanuts or caviar.

Many flavors are recognized mainly through the sense of smell. If you hold your nose while eating chocolate, for example, you will have trouble identifying the chocolate flavor—even though you can distinguish the food's sweetness or bitterness. This is because the familiar flavor of chocolate is sensed largely by odor. So is the well-known flavor of coffee. This is why a person who wishes to fully savor a delicious flavor (i.e., an expert chef testing his own creation) will exhale through his nose after each swallow.

CAUSES OF SMELL AND TASTE DISORDERS

The predominant problem is a natural decline in smelling ability that typically occurs after age 60. Scientists have found that the sense of smell is most accurate between the ages of 30 and 60 years. It begins to decline after age 60, and a large proportion of elderly persons have lost their smelling ability. Women of all ages are generally more accurate than men in identifying odors.

Some people are born with a poor sense of smell or taste, but most patients develop them after an injury or illness. Upper respiratory infections are blamed for some losses, and injury to the head can also cause smell or taste problems.

Loss of smell and taste may result from polyps in the nasal or sinus cavities, hormonal disturbances, or dental problems. They can also be caused by prolonged exposure to certain chemicals such as insecticides and by some medicines.

Tobacco smoking is the most concentrated form of pollution that most people will ever be exposed to. It certainly impairs a person's ability to identify odors and diminishes the sense of taste.

Many patients who receive radiation therapy for cancers of the head and neck later complain of lost smell and taste. They can also be lost in the course of some diseases of the nervous system.

Patients who have lost their larynx or voice box commonly complain of poor ability to smell and taste. This emphasizes the contribution of air flow through the nose for these two functions.

DIAGNOSIS

The extent of loss of smell or taste can be tested with a measurement of the lowest concentration of a chemical that a person can accurately detect and recognize. A patient may also be asked to compare the smells or tastes of different chemicals, the intensities of smells or tastes of different chemicals, or how the intensities of smells or tastes grow when a chemical's concentration is increased.

Scientists have developed an easily administered scratch-and-sniff test to evaluate the sense of smell. A person scratches pieces of treated paper to release different odors, sniffs them, and tries to identify each odor from a list of possibilities.

In taste testing, the patient reacts to different chemical concentrations. This may involve a simple sip-spit-and-rinse test, or chemicals may be applied directly to specific areas of the tongue.

TREATMENT

Sometimes a medication causes a smell or taste disorder, and improvement occurs when that medicine is stopped or changed.

Although certain medications can cause chemosensory problems, others—particularly antiallergy drugs—seem to improve the senses of taste and smell.

Some patients—notably those with serious respiratory infections or seasonal allergies—regain their smell or taste simply by waiting for their illness to run its course.

In many cases, nasal obstructions such as polyps can be removed to restore airflow to the receptor area and can correct the loss of smell and taste. Occasionally, chemosenses return to normal just as spontaneously as they disappeared.

WHAT YOU CAN DO

If you experience a smell or taste problem, try to identify and record the circumstances surrounding it. When did you first become aware of it? Did you have a cold or flu then? Did you have a head injury? Were you exposed to air pollutants, pollens, danders, or dust to which you might be allergic? Is this a recurring problem? Does it come in any special season, like hayfever time?

Bring all this information with you when you visit a physician who deals with diseases of the nose and throat. Also be prepared to tell him about your general health and any medications you are taking. Proper diagnosis by a trained professional can provide reassurance that your illness is not imaginary. You may even be surprised by the results. For example, what you may think is a taste problem could actually be a smell problem, because much of what you think you taste you really smell.

Diagnosis may also lead to treatment of an underlying cause for the disturbance.

Many types of smell and taste disorders are reversible, but if yours is not, it is important for you to remember that you are not alone. Thousands of other patients have faced the same situation.

The American Academy of Otolaryngology—
Head and Neck Surgery

SORE THROAT

Sore throat is one of the most common of medical complaints. As many as 1 out of every 10 Americans develops a "strep throat" every year, and 40 million adults will see a doctor for it.

CAUSES

Sore throat is one symptom of an array of different medical disorders.

Infections cause the majority of sore throats, and these are the sore throats that are contagious (can be passed from one person to another). Infections are caused by either viruses (such as the flu, the common cold, or mononucleosis) or bacteria (such as strep, mycoplasma, or hemophilus).

The most important difference between viruses and bacteria is that bacteria respond well to antibiotic treatment, but viruses do not.

Viruses

Most viral sore throats accompany the flu or a cold. When a stuffy-runny nose, sneezing, and generalized aches and pains accompany the sore throat, it is probably caused by one of the hundreds of known viruses. These are highly contagious and cause epidemics in a community, especially in the winter. The body cures itself of a viral infection by building antibodies that destroy the virus, a process that takes about a week.

Sore throats accompany other viral infections such as measles, chicken pox, whooping cough, and croup. Canker sores and fever blisters in the throat also can be very painful.

Infectious mononucleosis. One special viral infection takes much longer than a week to be cured: infectious mononucleosis or "mono." This virus lodges in the lymph system, causing massive enlargement of the tonsils (with white patches on their surface) and swollen glands in the neck, armpits, and groin. It creates a severely sore throat, sometimes causes serious difficulties breathing, and can affect the liver, leading to jaundice (yellow skin and eyes). It also causes extreme fatigue that can last six weeks or more.

Since mono can be transmitted by saliva, it has been nicknamed the "kissing disease." However, it can also be transmitted from mouth-to-hand to hand-to-mouth or by the sharing of towels and eating utensils.

Bacteria

Strep throat is an infection caused by a particular strain of streptococcus bacteria. This infection can also cause damage to the heart valves (rheumatic fever) and kidneys (nephritis). Streptococcal infections can also cause scarlet fever, tonsillitis, pneumonia, sinusitis, and ear infections.

Because of these possible complications, a strep throat should be treated with an antibiotic. Strep infections usually cause a longer-lasting sore throat than a cold or the flu. But strep is not always easy to detect by examination, and a throat culture may be needed.

A newly developed strep test detects a streptococcal infection in about 15 minutes, instead of the 24 hours or more required for a culture to grow. These tests, when positive, influence the physician to prescribe antibiotics. However, strep tests and cultures might not detect a number of other bacteria that can also cause severe sore throats that deserve antibiotic treatment. For example, severe and chronic cases of tonsillitis or tonsillar abscess may be culture negative; similarly, negative cultures are seen with diphtheria, and infections from oral sexual contacts will escape detection with strep culture tests.

Tonsillitis is an infection of the lumpy tissues on each side of the throat toward the back of the tongue. In the first two to three years of childhood, these tissues catch infections, sampling the child's environment to help develop his immunities (antibodies). Healthy tonsils do not remain infected, however, and frequent sore throats from tonsillitis suggest the infection is not fully eliminated between episodes. A recent study has shown that patients who suffer from frequently recurrent episodes of tonsillitis (such as three to four episodes each year for several years) were healthier after their tonsils were surgically removed.

Infections in the nose and sinuses can also cause sore throats because mucus from the nose drains down into the throat and carries the infection with it.

Epiglottitis. The most dangerous throat infection is epiglottitis, caused by bacteria that infect a portion of the larynx (voice box) and cause swelling that closes the airway. This infection is an emergency condition that requires prompt medical attention. Suspect it when swallowing is extremely painful (causing drooling), when speech is muffled and when breathing becomes difficult. A strep culture may miss this infection and be negative.

Allergy

Hayfever and allergy sufferers can get an irritated throat during an allergy attack the same way they get a stuffy, itchy nose, sneezing, and post-nasal drip. The same pollens and molds that irritate the nose when they are inhaled also may irritate the throat. People allergic to cat and dog danders can suffer an irritated throat when they are around such animals. A very common allergy is house dust, and it is a special problem in the winter when a heating system blows dust throughout the house.

Irritation

Dry heat. During the cold winter months, dry heat may create a recurring, mild sore throat with a parched feeling, especially in the mornings. This often responds to humidification of bedroom air and increased liquid intake. Patients with a chronic stuffy nose, causing mouth breathing, also suffer with a dry throat. These patients need examination and treatment of the nose.

Regurgitation of stomach acids. An occasional cause of morning sore throat is regurgitation of stomach acids up into the back of the throat where they are extremely irritating. This can be avoided if you tilt your bed frame so that the head is elevated four to six inches higher than the foot. You should also avoid eating and drinking for one to two hours before retiring. You might find antacids helpful. If these fail, see your doctor.

Industrial pollutants and chemicals in the air can irritate the nose and throat, but by far the most common and pervasive air pollutant is tobacco smoke. It cannot be tolerated by many persons who are either allergic or oversensitive to its contents. Other irritants include smokeless tobacco, alcoholic beverages, and spicy foods.

Voice strain. A person who strains his voice (yelling at a sports event, for example) gets a sore throat not only from muscle strain, but also from the rough treatment of his throat membranes. Well-trained, experienced public speakers and singers learn not to abuse their throats and voices in this way. They produce loud voices by taking deep breaths and using their chest and abdominal muscles more than their throat muscles.

Tumors

Tumors of the throat, tongue, and larynx (voice box) are usually (but not always) associated with the long-time use of tobacco and alcohol. A sore throat and difficult swallowing—sometimes with pain radiating to the ear—may be symptoms of such a tumor. More often the sore throat is so mild or so chronic that it is hardly noticed. Other important symptoms include hoarseness, a lump in the neck, unexplained weight loss, and/or spitting up blood in the saliva or phlegm.

The diagnosis will require examination by a physician with special training in diseases of the ears, nose, throat, head, and neck. Special mirrors or telescopic instruments will be used to see the suspicious areas of the throat.

HOW YOU CAN TREAT A MILD SORE THROAT

A mild sore throat associated with cold or flu symptoms can be made more comfortable with the following remedies.

- Increase your liquid intake (warm tea with honey is a favorite home remedy)
- Use a steamer or humidifier in your bedroom
- Gargle with warm salt water several times daily: one-quarter teaspoon salt to one-half cup water
- Take mild pain relievers such as acetaminophen (Tylenol, Datril, Tempra), ibuprofen (Advil), etc.
- Take nonprescription throat lozenges

WHEN TO SEEK A DOCTOR'S TREATMENT

Whenever a sore throat is severe, persists longer than the usual five-to-seven-day duration of a cold or flu, and is not associated with an avoidable allergy or irritation, you should seek medical attention.

The following signs and symptoms should alert you to see your physician.

- Severe and prolonged sore throat
- Difficulty breathing
- Difficulty swallowing
- Difficulty opening the mouth
- Joint pains
- Earache
- Rash
- Fever (over 101 degrees)
- Blood in saliva or phlegm
- Frequently recurring sore throat
- Lump in the neck
- Hoarseness lasting over two weeks

Antibiotics

Antibiotics are drugs that kill or impair bacteria. Penicillin or erythromycin are prescribed when the physician suspects streptococcal or other bacterial infection that will respond to them. However, a number of bacterial throat infections do not respond to penicillin, but require other categories of antibiotics. Antibiotics do not cure viral infections, but viruses do lower the patient's resistance to bacterial infections. When such a combined infection occurs, antibiotics may be needed.

When an antibiotic is prescribed, it should be taken—as the physician directs—for the full course (usually 10 days). Otherwise, the infection will probably be suppressed rather than eliminated, and it can return.

Throat Culture

A strep culture tests only for the presence of streptococcal infections. Many other infections, both bacterial and viral, will yield negative cultures and sometimes so does a streptococcal infection. Therefore, when your culture is negative, your physician will base the treatment on the severity of your symptoms and the appearance of your throat. Do not discontinue your medications unless your physician instructs you to do so.

Should Other Family Members Be Treated or Cultured?

When strep throat is proven by test or culture, many experts advise treating other family members, because streptococcal infections are so highly contagious. Others recommend treating only those with sore throats and culturing the others. So be sure you tell your physician how other family members are feeling. Practice good sanitary habits. Avoid close physical contact and the sharing of napkins, towels, and utensils with the infected person. Hand washing makes good sense.

The American Academy of Otolaryngology—
Head and Neck Surgery

CHAPTER 7

The Endocrine System

The endocrine system is a complex network of glands that secrete hormones, which travel through the bloodstream to regulate the function of nearly all the organs and tissues of the body. The glands that make up the endocrine system (pituitary, thyroid, parathyroid, adrenal, islet cells of the pancreas, and ovaries or testes) secrete hormones to regulate growth, sexual function, the body's fluid and salt balance, glucose metabolism, and a wide array of other functions.

Because of the complex interactions among various hormones—and between the endocrine system and the nervous system— many facets of the endocrine system are not fully understood. What is clear, however, is that the minuscule amounts of hormones that are released into the bloodstream ordinarily work so smoothly as to go unnoticed; but when the system malfunctions—usually when too much or too little of a particular hormone is secreted, or when an organ or tissue does not respond to the hormone efficiently—the results can be dramatic and even fatal. For example, malfunctions of the pituitary gland in a child can produce a giant or a dwarf. And a malfunction of the pancreas, which secretes insulin into the bloodstream to regulate the way the body converts sugar into energy, or an inability of the body to respond to the insulin that is secreted, precipitates diabetes.

The Editors

DIABETES MELLITUS

OVERVIEW

Diabetes is a disease that affects the way the body uses food. It causes sugar levels in the blood to be too high.

Normally, during digestion, the body changes sugars, starches, and other foods into a form of sugar called glucose. Then the blood carries this glucose to cells throughout the body. There, with the help of insulin (a hormone), glucose is changed into quick energy for immediate use by the cells or is stored for future needs. (Insulin is made in the beta cells of the pancreas, a small organ that lies behind the stomach.) This process of turning food into energy is crucial, because the body depends on food for every action, from pumping blood and thinking to running and jumping.

In diabetes, something goes wrong with the normal process of turning food into energy. Food is changed into glucose readily enough, but there is a problem with insulin. In one type of diabetes, the pancreas cannot make insulin. In another type, the body makes some insulin but either makes too little or has trouble using the insulin (or both). When insulin is absent or ineffective, the glucose in the bloodstream cannot be used by the cells to make energy. Instead, glucose collects in the blood, eventually leading to the high sugar levels that are the hallmark of untreated diabetes.

Types of Diabetes

The two main types of diabetes are insulin-dependent and noninsulin-dependent.

Insulin-dependent (type I) diabetes used to be called juvenile-onset diabetes because it occurs most often in children and young adults. But the name was changed after doctors realized it could occur at any age. In this form of diabetes, the pancreas stops making insulin or makes only a tiny amount. Insulin is necessary to life, so the hormone must be injected every day.

Noninsulin-dependent (type II) diabetes used to be called maturity-onset diabetes because it occurs most often in adults. In noninsulin-dependent diabetes, the pancreas produces some insulin but it is not used effectively.

There are other kinds of diabetes, but these are less common.

Gestational diabetes is high blood sugar that first occurs during pregnancy. It usually disappears after the birth of the baby, although nearly 50 percent of these women develop diabetes (usually noninsulin-dependent) within 5 to 10 years.

Secondary diabetes is the type caused by damage to the pancreas from chemicals, certain medicines, or diseases of the pancreas (such as cancer) or other glands.

Impaired glucose tolerance used to be called latent, chemical, or borderline diabetes but is no longer considered to be a form of diabetes. If you have this diagnosis, it means that your blood sugar falls between "normal" and "diabetic" levels. People with impaired glucose tolerance have an increased risk of developing diabetes.

The Warning Signs

The following symptoms are typical. However, some people with noninsulin-dependent diabetes have symptoms so mild that they go unnoticed.

- ***Insulin-dependent symptoms*** (usually occur suddenly): frequent urination; excessive thirst; extreme hunger; extreme weight loss; irritability; weakness and fatigue; nausea and vomiting.
- ***Noninsulin-dependent symptoms*** (usually occur less suddenly): any of the insulin-dependent symptoms; recurring or hard-to-heal skin, gum, or bladder infections; drowsiness; blurred vision; tingling or numbness in hands or feet; itching.

Causes

The causes of diabetes are still a mystery. But researchers believe that the tendency for diabetes is present at birth.

In insulin-dependent diabetes, any of several different viral infections and a process called autoimmunity are believed to trigger diabetes. In the autoimmune process, the body's defense system attacks its own cells: in insulin-dependent diabetes, the insulin-producing "beta" cells in the pancreas. Note: Although viruses may help to cause some cases of insulin-dependent diabetes, diabetes itself is not catching.

In people prone to noninsulin-dependent diabetes, being overweight can cause diabetes, because excess fat prevents insulin from working properly.

Prevention and Treatment

So far, insulin-dependent diabetes cannot be prevented, although researchers are working on many promising approaches. Noninsulin-dependent diabetes can often be prevented by maintaining normal body weight and keeping physically fit throughout life.

A major aim of treatment is to control blood sugar levels, which means keeping them in the normal range. Research suggests that tight control can help prevent or delay long-term diabetic complications.

Insulin-dependent diabetes is treated with daily insulin injections, regular exercise, and a balanced meal plan that limits sugar. Your meal plan will be tailored to your individual needs and is likely to include three meals and two or three snacks a day. You will generally have to eat these meals and snacks at set times each day to properly balance insulin, which is also given at fixed times. (Insulin lowers blood sugar, and food raises it. To control diabetes, you need to balance these effects.)

Noninsulin-dependent diabetes is treated with an individualized diet plan that restricts calories. If you are overweight, you need to slim down. Treatment also includes restricting sugar and following an exercise plan. These steps should improve your body's ability to use its insulin. If diet and exercise alone do not control blood sugar, prescribed pills or insulin may be needed. They do not take the place of diet and exercise, however.

Testing

Two types of tests are used to monitor blood sugar levels: blood tests and urine tests. Blood tests, done by pricking the finger for a drop of blood, are recommended by most doctors because they give the exact amount of blood sugar at any given moment. Urine test readings are a crude indication of blood sugar, and are much less direct and much less precise. People with insulin-dependent diabetes are often advised to test sugar levels two to four times a day, before and after meals. People with noninsulin-dependent diabetes may be able to test less often.

Tests that measure ketones in the urine are also important. Ketones are acids that collect in the blood and urine when the body uses fat (instead of glucose) for energy. Ketones in the urine are a sign that diabetes is poorly controlled and that prompt attention is needed. Always test for ketones when you are ill or under great stress, the times when diabetes is likely to go out of control.

Be sure to record the results of all your self-tests. These records are useful guides for adjusting food, medicine, or exercise when blood sugar is too high or low.

Another important test, done by a doctor every three to six months, is a "glycohemoglobin" test. This measures the average blood sugar level over the past 30 to 60 days.

Problems to Handle Promptly

Hypoglycemia, low blood sugar, is sometimes called an insulin reaction or insulin shock. It can occur suddenly in people using insulin if too little food is eaten, if a meal is delayed, or if extra exercise is done. It is less common in people whose diabetes is treated with pills, but it can occur. Low blood sugar must be treated quickly, with sugar or sugary foods because, untreated, hypoglycemia can lead to unconsciousness.

The typical symptoms include feeling cold, clammy, nervous, shaky, weak, or very hungry. Some people become pale, get headaches, or act strangely. If a person becomes unconscious, glucagon, a hormone (available by prescription) that raises blood sugar, must be injected.

Hyperglycemia, or high blood sugar, occurs when too much food is eaten or not enough insulin is taken. Illness and emotional stress can also cause high blood sugar. The warning signs are large amounts of sugar in the urine and blood. You may also urinate often, be very thirsty, and feel nauseated. Treat high blood sugar with the help of your doctor.

Ketoacidosis, or diabetic coma, may accompany high blood sugar. It develops when insulin and blood sugar are so out of balance that ketones accumulate in the blood. High levels of ketones are poisonous. Fortunately, ketoacidosis, which develops over several hours or days, can usually be avoided if diabetes is brought under control at the first signs of high blood sugar or ketones in the urine. (Call the doctor for instructions.) In addition to high blood and urine sugar tests and high ketone levels, the symptoms include dry mouth, great thirst, loss of appetite, excessive urination, dry and flushed skin, labored breathing, fruity-smelling breath, and possibly vomiting, abdominal pain, and unconsciousness. Ketoacidosis is most likely to occur in people with insulin-dependent diabetes.

Anyone with diabetes should wear a medical I.D. necklace or bracelet stating the type of treatment they use, in case of emergencies.

Long-Term Health Problems

Diabetic complications are usually caused by changes in the blood vessels and nerves. Unfortunately, they can include eye and kidney disease, heart attack, numbness or pain in the legs, foot infections leading to gangrene, and stroke. Fortunately, however, treatments continue to improve. Also, many researchers now believe that keeping blood sugar levels tightly controlled from the moment of diagnosis can help to prevent complications.

INSULIN-DEPENDENT DIABETES

Insulin-dependent diabetes is a disease that affects the way your body uses food. Insulin-dependent diabetes is also called type I diabetes or insulin-dependent diabetes mellitus (IDDM, for short).

Type I diabetes starts when your body stops making insulin or makes only a tiny amount. Your body needs insulin to use food for energy. Without insulin, your body cannot control blood levels of sugar. And without insulin, you would die. So people with type I diabetes give themselves at least one shot of insulin every day. Type I diabetes usually strikes children and young adults. But it can occur at any age. It used to be called juvenile-onset diabetes. About 1 million Americans have this type of diabetes. That is about 10 percent of all Americans with diabetes.

Why Insulin Must Be Injected

You must inject insulin under the skin—in the fat—for it to work. You cannot take insulin in a pill. The juices in your stomach would destroy the insulin before it could work. Scientists are looking for new ways to give insulin. But today, shots are the only method.

Symptoms of Type I Diabetes

Type I diabetes often appears suddenly, and you should watch for the following symptoms.

- Frequent urination
- Extreme hunger
- Extreme thirst
- Extreme weight loss
- Weakness and tiredness
- Feeling edgy and having mood changes
- Feeling sick to your stomach and vomiting

Causes

We do not know exactly what causes diabetes. We do know that people inherit a tendency to get diabetes. But not all people who have this tendency will get the disease. Other things such as illnesses must also come into play for diabetes to begin.

Diabetes is not like a cold. Your friends and family cannot catch it from you.

Living with Type I Diabetes

People with type I diabetes can live happy, healthy lives. The key is to follow your diabetes treatment plan. The goal of this plan is to keep your blood sugar level as close to normal as possible (good blood sugar control). Your treatment plan will probably include:

Insulin, which lowers blood sugar. Your health care practitioner will prescribe how much and when to take insulin and what kinds.

Food, which raises blood sugar. Most people with type I diabetes have a meal plan. A registered dietitian makes a plan for you. It tells you how much food you can eat and when to eat it. Most people have three meals and at least two snacks every day. Your meal plan can have foods you enjoy.

Exercise, which lowers blood sugar. Like insulin, exercise also helps your body to use blood sugar. So exercise will probably be prescribed for you. Your health care practitioner can help you fit exercise safely into your daily routine.

Blood and urine testing. Testing your blood lets you know if your blood sugar level is high, low, or near normal. The tests are simple. You prick your finger to get a drop of blood. A nurse-educator can teach you how to do this test and use the test results.

You may need to test your urine for ketones. Ketones in the urine may mean that your diabetes is not under good control. A nurse-educator can teach you how to test ketones.

Problems

Type I diabetes can cause problems that you should be prepared for. There are three key problems.

Hypoglycemia, or low blood sugar; sometimes called an insulin reaction. This occurs when your blood sugar drops too low. You correct this problem by eating some sugar—such as three glucose tablets, one-half cup of fruit juice, or five or six pieces of hard candy. Your health care practitioner will teach you the signs of hypoglycemia and show you how to treat it.

Hyperglycemia, or high blood sugar. This occurs when your blood sugar is too high. It can be a sign that diabetes is not well controlled. Your health care practitioner will explain the signs and symptoms and the best way to treat hyperglycemia.

Ketoacidosis, or diabetic coma. This is very serious. Discuss its signs with your health care practitioner.

NONINSULIN-DEPENDENT DIABETES

Noninsulin-dependent diabetes is a disease that affects the way your body uses food. Non-insulin-dependent diabetes is also called type II diabetes or insulin-dependent diabetes mellitus (NIDDM, for short).

Type II diabetes used to be called maturity-onset diabetes because most people who get it are over 40. The most common type of diabetes, it affects about 11 million Americans. Nine out of ten cases of diabetes are type II. Most of the people who get type II diabetes are overweight.

When you have type II diabetes, your body does not make enough insulin. Or, your body still makes insulin but can't use it. Without enough insulin, your body cannot move blood sugar into the cells. Sugar builds up in the bloodstream. High blood levels of sugar can cause problems.

Medical experts do not know the exact cause of type II diabetes. They do know type II diabetes runs in families. A person can inherit a tendency to get type II diabetes. But it usually takes another factor such as obesity to bring on the disease.

Signs and Symptoms of Type II Diabetes

Type II diabetes often develops slowly. Most people who get it have increased thirst and an increased need to urinate. Many also feel edgy, tired, and sick to their stomach. Some people have an increased appetite, but they lose weight. Other signs and symptoms include the following.

- Repeated or hard-to-heal infections of the skin, gums, vagina, or bladder
- Blurred vision
- Tingling or loss of feeling in the hands or feet
- Dry, itchy skin

These symptoms can be so mild that you don't notice them. Older people may confuse these symptoms with signs of aging and may not go to their health care practitioner. Half of all Americans who have diabetes may not know it.

Living with Type II Diabetes

People with diabetes can live happy, healthy lives. The key is to follow a diabetes treatment plan. The goal of this plan is to keep blood sugar levels as close to normal as possible (good blood sugar control).

Your first step is to see your health care practitioner. He or she will prescribe a daily treatment plan. The plan should include a healthy diet and regular exercise. You can often control type II diabetes with diet and exercise—alone. But some people also need medicine—either diabetes pills or insulin shots. Many people find their diabetes gets better when they follow their treatment plan.

For people who have type II diabetes, losing weight is important. Losing weight helps some overweight people to bring their blood sugars into the normal range. People who have a tendency to get type II diabetes can avoid it by losing weight or not becoming overweight. (The health care practitioner may allow some people who are overweight to stop their medication—if they lose weight and follow a good meal plan.)

Your health care practitioner may also want

you to test your blood sugar levels regularly. Testing will let you know if your diabetes is in control. Be sure to ask how to do these tests.

⚠ **You can help control your diabetes if you follow your physician's treatment plan, and follow a healthy diet, control your weight, exercise regularly, have regular checkups, and do not smoke.**

HYPERGLYCEMIA

Hyperglycemia is the technical term for high blood sugar. High blood sugar happens when the body has too little, or not enough insulin, or when the body can't use insulin properly.

A number of things can cause hyperglycemia. For example, if you have type I (insulin-dependent) diabetes, you may not have given yourself enough insulin. If you have type II (noninsulin-dependent) diabetes, your body may have enough insulin, but is not as effective as it should be. Or the problem could be that you ate more than planned or exercised less than planned. The stress of an illness, such as a cold or flu, could also be the cause. Other stresses, such as family conflicts, could also cause hyperglycemia.

Symptoms

The symptoms of hyperglycemia include frequent urination and increased thirst.

Blood Sugar Levels

Part of keeping your diabetes in control is testing your blood sugar often. Ask your doctor how often you should test and what your blood sugar levels should be.

⚠ **Hyperglycemia is defined as a blood sugar above 120 milligrams per deciliter (mg/dl) of blood. Moderate degrees of hyperglycemia (that is, 120 to 220 mg/dl) need to be carefully monitored, but may not require immediate treatment.**

Testing your blood and then treating high blood sugar early will help you avoid the other symptoms of hyperglycemia.

It's important to treat hyperglycemia as soon as you detect it. If you fail to treat hyperglycemia, a condition called ketoacidosis (diabetic coma) could occur. Ketoacidosis develops when your body doesn't have enough insulin. Without insulin, your body can't use glucose for fuel. So, your body breaks down fats to use for energy.

⚠ **People with type II diabetes do not develop ketoacidosis; but they are susceptible to the syndrome of hyperosmolar nonketotic coma (see page 238).**

When your body breaks down fats, waste products called ketones are produced. Your body cannot tolerate large amounts of ketones, and will try to get rid of them through the urine. Unfortunately, the body cannot release all the ketones and they build up in your blood. This can lead to ketoacidosis. Ketoacidosis is life-threatening and needs immediate treatment. Symptoms include shortness of breath, breath that smells fruity, nausea and vomiting, and a very dry mouth. Talk to your doctor about how to handle this condition.

Treatment

Oftentimes, you can lower your blood sugar level by exercising. However, if your blood sugar is above 240 mg/dl, check your urine for ketones. If you have ketones, do not exercise. Exercising when ketones are present may make your blood sugar level go even higher. You'll need to work with your doctor to find the safest way for you to lower your blood sugar level.

Cutting down on the amount of food you eat might also help. Work with your dietitian to make changes in your meal plan. If exercise and changes in your diet don't work, your doctor may change the amount of your medication or insulin, or the timing of when you take it.

Prevention

Your best bet is to practice good diabetes control. The trick is learning to detect and treat hyperglycemia early—before it can get worse.

235

HYPOGLYCEMIA

Hypoglycemia is the technical term for low blood sugar. It is often called an insulin reaction. An insulin reaction can be caused by a number of things. You may have taken too much insulin, eaten too little food or not eaten on time, or exercised too much.

Symptoms

The symptoms of hypoglycemia include the following.

- Shakiness
- Dizziness
- Sweating
- Hunger
- Headache
- Pale skin color
- Sudden moodiness or behavior changes, such as crying for no apparent reason
- Clumsy or jerky movements
- Difficulty paying attention or confusion
- Tingling sensations around the mouth

Blood Sugar Levels

Part of keeping diabetes in control is testing your blood sugar often. Ask your doctor how often you should test and what your blood sugar levels should be. The results from testing your blood will tell you when your blood sugar is low and that you need to treat it. You should test your blood sugar level according to the schedule you work out with your doctor. More importantly, though, you should test your blood whenever you feel an insulin reaction coming on. After you test and see that your blood sugar level is low, you should treat this condition quickly.

If you feel a reaction coming on but cannot test, it's best to treat the reaction rather than wait. Remember this simple rule: When in doubt, treat.

Treatment

The quickest way to raise your blood sugar is with some form of sugar, such as three glucose tablets (you can buy these at the drug store), one-half cup of fruit juice, or five or six pieces of hard candy. Ask your health care professional or dietitian to list foods that you can use to treat an insulin reaction. And then, be sure you always have at least one type of sugar with you.

Once you have tested your blood and treated your reaction, wait 15 or 20 minutes and test your blood again. If your blood sugar is still low and your symptoms don't go away, repeat the treatment. After you feel better, be sure to eat your regular meals and snacks as planned to keep your blood sugar level up.

It's important to treat hypoglycemia quickly because it can get worse and you could pass out. If you pass out, you will need immediate treatment, such as an injection of glucagon or emergency treatment in a hospital.

Glucagon raises blood sugar. It is injected like insulin. Ask your doctor to prescribe it for you and tell you how to use it. You need to tell people around you (such as family members and co-workers) how and when to inject glucagon should you ever need it. If glucagon is not available, you should be taken to the nearest hospital emergency room for treatment. If you need immediate medical assistance or an ambulance, someone should call the emergency number in your area (such as 911) for help. It's a good idea to post emergency numbers by the telephone.

If you pass out, people should inject glucagon and call for emergency help. They should not inject insulin; give you food or fluids; or put their hands in your mouth.

Prevention

Good diabetes control is the best way we know to prevent hypoglycemia. The trick is to learn to recognize the symptoms of an insulin reaction. This way, you can treat low blood sugar before it gets worse.

BLOOD TESTING

Blood testing is one of the main tools you have to keep your diabetes in control. Testing lets you know what your blood sugar level is at any one time.

This information will help you decide what adjustments to make in your diabetes control plan. For example: After exercising, you feel shaky and sweaty. Do you feel this way because you've exercised, or because your blood sugar is low? If your blood test shows that your glucose is low, then you know you need to eat a fast-acting sugar. If your blood test is normal, then you know you are shaky and sweaty because you exercised. Then you won't eat anything extra, which could cause your blood sugar to be high later.

How to Test Your Blood

There are two ways you can test your blood. In both tests, you first need to prick your finger with a special needle called a lancet to get a drop of blood. You then place the drop of blood on a test strip. The steps you follow to do your blood test will depend on what brand of test strip you use or what brand of meter you use. Ask your doctor or nurse-educator to explain the testing process that you need to follow.

In one method, you wait for the test strip to change colors. (The glucose in your blood causes the change.) You then match the color of the strip to a color chart, which is usually on the test strip container. The colors represent ranges of glucose levels, such as 60 to 90. If your test strip color matches 60, then your blood sugar is 60. If it falls between the 60 and 90 color, then it is recorded as 75.

In the second method, you place the test strip in a blood glucose meter. A meter is a small computerized machine that "reads" your test strip. Your blood glucose level is printed on a digital screen (like that on a pocket calculator).

Meters may provide more accurate blood glucose readings than matching the test strip colors to a chart. This is because the meter gives you an exact number so you don't have to guess at the number. It is important that you follow the test directions exactly. Not following the test directions may give you false results.

Recording the Results

Be sure to write down your blood test results. These records will help you and your doctor make adjustments in your diabetes control plan. If your blood glucose levels are frequently higher or lower than normal, you should contact your doctor.

Getting in the habit of testing may be hard at first. But as you get used to it, you'll find that blood testing makes keeping your diabetes in control a lot easier.

KETOACIDOSIS

Ketoacidosis is a serious condition that can lead to diabetic coma and even death. Ketoacidosis may happen to people with insulin-dependent (type I) diabetes.

Ketoacidosis does not occur in people with noninsulin-dependent (type II) diabetes. But some people—especially older people—with type II diabetes may experience a different serious condition. It's called hyperosmolar nonketotic coma.

Ketoacidosis means dangerously high levels of ketones. Ketones are acids that build up in the blood. They appear in the urine when your body doesn't have enough insulin. Ketones can poison the body. They are a warning sign that your diabetes is out of control or that you are getting sick.

Treatment for ketoacidosis usually takes place in the hospital. But you can help prevent ketoacidosis by learning to recognize the warning signs and testing your urine and blood regularly.

HYPEROSMOLAR NONKETOTIC COMA

People with type II diabetes are at risk for hyperosmolar nonketotic coma (HNKC)—a change in body chemistry that can occur when there is a progressive rise in blood sugar coupled with an inability to drink enough water to keep up with the dramatic loss of fluid that accompanies the excretion of excessive sugar through the kidneys. The condition is usually brought on by the stress of another illness. Commonly, for example, an elderly diabetic patient may suffer a stroke, or come down with pneumonia that simultaneously elevates blood sugar and makes it difficult to maintain an adequate fluid intake. The patient experiences no nausea or vomiting or other symptom that might alert him to the need for medical help, and thus simply slips into a coma. For this reason, it is crucial for those with even a moderate degree of diabetes to drink a generous amount of water during any illness.   *The Editors*

Warning Signs

Ketoacidosis usually develops slowly. But when vomiting occurs, this life-threatening condition can develop in a few hours.

The first symptoms are:

- Thirst or a very dry mouth
- Frequent urination
- High blood sugar levels
- High levels of ketones in the urine

Later symptoms include:

- Constantly feeling tired
- Dry or flushed skin
- Nausea, vomiting, or abdominal pain (Vomiting can be caused by many illnesses, not just ketoacidosis. If vomiting continues for more than two hours, contact your health care practitioner.)
- A hard time breathing (short, deep breaths)
- Fruity odor on breath
- A hard time paying attention, or confusion

Ketoacidosis is dangerous and serious. If you have any of the above symptoms, contact your health care practitioner immediately, or go to the nearest emergency room of your local hospital.

Detecting Ketones

A simple urine test can detect ketones. Urine testing is very easy. You use a test strip, like a blood-testing strip, and watch what color it becomes when wet with urine. The color will mean trace (very small), small, moderate, or large amounts of ketones, as shown on the test strip container. Some test strip containers use pluses (+) to show level of ketones.

Your health care practitioner can show you how to test for ketones. Different brands have different procedures, so always read the directions. Many experts advise to check your urine for ketones when your blood sugar is more than 240 mg/dl.

When you are ill (when you have a cold or the flu, for example), test for ketones every four to six hours. And test every four to six hours when your blood sugar is more than 240 mg/dl.

Also, test for ketones when you have any symptoms of ketoacidosis.

Higher-Than-Normal Keytone Levels

If your health care practitioner has not told you what levels of ketones are dangerous, then call when you find moderate amounts after more than one test. Often, your health care practitioner can tell you what to do over the phone.

Call your health care practitioner at once if:

- Your urine tests show large amounts of ketones
- Your urine tests show large amounts of ketones and your blood sugar level is high
- You have vomited more than twice in four hours and your urine tests show large amounts of ketones

Do not exercise when your urine tests show ketones and your blood sugar is high. High levels of ketones and high blood sugars can mean your diabetes is out of control. Check with your health care practitioner about how to handle this situation.

Causes of Ketoacidosis

Ketones mean your body is burning fat to get energy. Moderate or large amounts of ketones in your urine are dangerous. They upset the chemical balance of the blood.

Commonly, the flu, a cold, or other infections may sometimes bring on ketoacidosis.

The following are three basic reasons for moderate or large amounts of ketones in the urine.

Not getting enough insulin. Maybe you did not inject enough insulin. Or your body could need more insulin than usual because of illness. If there is not enough insulin, your body begins to break down body fat for energy.

Not enough food. When people are sick, they often do not feel like eating. Then, high ketones may result. High ketones may also occur when someone misses a meal.

An insulin reaction (low blood sugar). When blood sugar levels fall too low, the body must use fat to get energy. If testing shows high ketones in the morning, the person may have had an insulin reaction while asleep.

DIABETES COMPLICATIONS: AN OVERVIEW

Diabetes complications are medical problems that occur more often in people with diabetes than in people without diabetes. Changes in the blood vessels or the nerves are often the causes of diabetes complications.

Vascular disease. Some people with diabetes may be at greater risk for changes in large blood vessels. This complication is called vascular disease. It starts when the linings of the blood vessels get thicker. Then, blood has a hard time flowing through the narrowed vessel. As a result, the blood cannot carry nutrients to your body's many organs. Heart disease or stroke can result.

Small blood vessel disease. Damage to small blood vessels can occur in the eyes and the kidneys of people with diabetes. At first, there may be no outward symptoms. But damage to blood vessels can lead to blindness and kidney disease.

Nerve damage, or neuropathy. Most often, nerve damage affects the feet and legs. Serious problems can occur in people who have nerve and blood vessel damage in the legs or feet. These people may not feel a blister or a small cut on the foot. The blister or cut may become infected, which may sometimes lead to amputation.

Diabetics are especially susceptible to bacterial and fungal infections of many sorts—including skin infection, urinary tract infections, vaginitis, mouth infections such as thrush and gum disease, and infections of wounds. Moreover, infections significantly increase the need for insulin. As a result, anyone with diabetes should be alert to treating even minor cuts and blisters so they do not develop into major complications.

Who Gets Diabetes Complications

No one can tell who will have diabetes complications. But experts think that keeping blood sugar levels close to normal helps to prevent or delay trouble.

High levels of sugar in the blood over time (poorly controlled diabetes) may speed the onset of complications.

Good control of blood sugar may help delay some complications.

Some people try hard to control their blood sugars. But they still may have a complication. Experts aren't sure why this happens. But even if you do have complications, there is hope. So be sure to see your health care practitioner regularly.

What You Can Do to Avoid Diabetes Complications

First, get regular checkups. You may not know that you have a complication. But your health care practitioner can spot trouble long before symptoms appear. Finding problems early is the best way to keep complications from getting serious.

Keep your appointments with your health care practitioner—even if you are feeling fine. This includes your eye doctor and any other specialists you may need to see.

Also be aware of the following warning signs of trouble.

- Vision problems (blurriness, spots)
- Tiredness or pale skin color
- Obesity (more than 20 pounds overweight)
- Numbness or tingling feelings in hands or feet
- Repeated infections or slow healing of wounds
- Chest pain
- Vaginal itching
- Constant headaches (This may be a symptom of high blood pressure.)

If you have one or more of these symptoms, be sure to let your health care practitioner know.

And practice good diabetes control. Taking care of your health makes medical sense.

- Keep blood sugar levels close to normal (control diabetes)
- Control your weight
- Eat a healthy, well-balanced diet
- Get regular exercise
- Have regular checkups
- Check your feet every day for minor cuts or blisters. Show them to your health care practitioner.
- Do not smoke

If you have high blood pressure or high blood cholesterol, follow the medical advice you have been given.

HEART AND BLOOD VESSEL COMPLICATIONS

People with diabetes are more likely to have heart disease—and have it at an earlier age—than people without diabetes. That's because diabetes may damage blood vessels.

Blood vessels bring blood to the organs and cells of our body. There are two kinds of blood vessels: large vessels and small vessels. Large vessels carry blood from the heart to the organs, such as the liver or kidneys. Small blood vessels carry blood to the body's cells. Diabetes may lead to damage of both large blood vessels and small blood vessels.

Large Blood Vessels

Sometimes, large blood vessels of the heart or legs become blocked or damaged. When this happens, heart disease or leg problems can result.

The heart. When blood vessels of the heart become blocked or damaged, the heart does not get enough blood. Heart disease can result. This is called cardiovascular disease or coronary (heart) disease.

All diabetics are at increased risk for heart disease. Your risk is even greater if you have high blood pressure, high cholesterol levels, and/or you smoke.

The warning signs of heart disease are chest pain, shortness of breath, swollen ankles, and/or irregular heartbeat. If you have any of these symptoms, talk with your health care practitioner.

The legs. Blood vessels in the legs can also be blocked or damaged. This is called peripheral arterial disease.

You may feel weak and have pain and cramping in the legs when walking, but not when standing or sitting. Other symptoms include cold feet and loss of hair on the feet or legs. Your feet may become red when they dangle (for example, when you are sitting on a table and your feet hang over the edge). Your health care practitioner can check for symptoms during your regular office visit. Be sure to tell your health care practitioner if you have any of these problems.

The brain. People who have diabetes are also at increased risk for stroke. Many have hypertension, a major risk factor for stroke. Atherosclerosis occurs at an earlier age among people with diabetes than among others, and advances more rapidly, even in the face of good control of blood sugar levels. Roughly two-thirds of all strokes are caused by a blood clot that completely blocks an artery that has already been narrowed by atherosclerotic plaque.

The symptoms of a stroke usually occur within minutes or hours of the event, although they can sometimes progress over several days. Some strokes cause symptoms that are scarcely noticeable. Others, depending on their location and severity, may cause headache, dizziness and disorientation, vomiting, burning or tingling sensations, some disturbance in your visual field, slurred speech or a loss of speech, difficulty swallowing, and paralysis. If paralysis occurs, most often one side of the body is affected, but sometimes only an arm or a leg. Severe strokes may cause loss of consciousness, coma, or death—or, among survivors, enduring physical or mental handicaps.

Small Blood Vessels

Diabetes can affect the small blood vessels in the eyes and kidneys of some people with the condition.

The eyes. Blood from a broken or leaky blood vessel can affect vision and can even lead to blindness.

You may notice sudden changes in vision, such as blurriness, dark spots, or loss of some vision. Or you may not know that small blood vessels in the eye have been damaged. That's why it's important to go regularly to your health care practitioner. Report any changes in your sight. Don't take chances with your eyes! If you do have a serious problem, early treatment and good care could save your sight.

The kidneys. Small blood vessels in the kidneys can be blocked or damaged. This can lead to kidney disease. Damage to the kidneys usually happens slowly, without notice, over many years.

It's hard for you to know when blood vessels in your kidneys have been damaged. At first, the damage may be very small. That's why it's important to visit your health care practitioner. He or she can check for symptoms of kidney damage during your regular office visits.

EYE COMPLICATIONS

All people with diabetes need to know that the disease can harm their eyesight. If you have diabetes, you must see your eye doctor regularly. Many eye problems are minor and can be easily treated. But some eye problems may be serious and might lead to blindness.

Report any changes in your sight to your doctor. Don't take chances with your eyes! If you do have a serious problem, early treatment and good care could save your sight.

Causes of Eye Problems in People with Diabetes

Experts do not know exactly how diabetes harms the eyes. They also can't predict who will have problems and who will not. But many experts think that high blood sugar levels over time (poorly controlled diabetes) can cause the small blood vessels in the eye to weaken, become leaky, or burst.

People who take insulin have a greater chance of having eye problems than people who do not take insulin.

Diabetic Retinopathy

Diabetic retinopathy affects the retina of the eye. The retina is the area inside the eyeball that records images of objects and sends information about these images to the brain. There are two types of retinopathy.

Background retinopathy is more common. Background retinopathy occurs in about half of all people with diabetes after they have had diabetes for 10 to 15 years. This kind of retinopathy is often mild and does not affect vision. If retinopathy gets worse, the retina may swell. This is called macular edema. Macular edema does affect vision. It is a common cause of decreased vision in people with diabetes. If found early enough, macular edema can be treated. Background retinopathy may develop into the second, more serious type, called proliferative retinopathy.

Proliferative Retinopathy. This type of retinopathy can cause blindness. But most people with diabetes never have this disease. It affects the fluid-filled center of the eye, called the vitreous. Tiny blood vessels grow and push into the vitreous. They may break and the retina may swell, or they can cause bleeding. This may lead to blindness.

Treatment

An operation called vitrectomy can help restore sight for people who have bleeding in the vitreous. And laser surgery has been helpful in slowing the development of proliferative retinopathy. Laser surgery can prevent further bleeding, and is proven effective at reducing visual loss in patients with macular edema.

But the key to preventing eye damage is regular checkups with your eye doctor. Retinopathy comes quietly. At first, you may not know that you have the disease. An eye exam is the best way to find retinopathy early. Then laser treatments can begin to control the disease.

Good control of blood sugar levels, a good diet, and good eye care may all help prevent retinopathy. Background retinopathy may simply require better diabetes control.

Make sure your blood pressure is not too high. People with diabetes and high blood pressure can have a lot more problems. Avoid too much salt and heavy lifting.

Other Types of Eye Problems

A common eye problem related to diabetes is blurred vision. People with noninsulin-dependent (type II) diabetes or insulin-dependent (type I) diabetes may have blurry vision when their diabetes is out of control. When diabetes is brought under control, the blurriness often goes away.

People with diabetes may get cataracts earlier than people without diabetes. Cataract is when the lens of the eye becomes cloudy. Most often, cataracts can be removed with outpatient surgery.

Glaucoma is more common in people with diabetes. Glaucoma means the pressure inside the eye is increased. Your eye doctor will check for glaucoma at your regular visits. If you have glaucoma, your eye doctor will advise treatment.

KIDNEY COMPLICATONS

Kidneys help to keep us alive. They take out harmful wastes and chemicals from the blood. These wastes leave the body in urine. Each kidney is made up of tiny blood vessels that act as filters. When these filters work well, they help keep waste products in our blood at a low level.

Kidney disease called diabetic nephropathy develops over several years. Over time, high blood sugar levels may cause blood vessel changes in some people with diabetes. These changes can harm the tiny vessels in the kidneys. Then the filters cannot take out wastes from the blood.

Who Is at Risk

Most people who have kidney disease from diabetes have had diabetes for at least 10 to 15 years. The disease comes on so slowly that many people do not know they have it. The first sign is often protein in the urine. Your health care practitioner can check for protein with a urine dipstick at your office visit. If you have protein in the urine, you may need more tests to check for kidney damage.

Other symptoms of kidney problems are swelling of the feet and ankles, feeling tired, and pale skin color.

Normal aging also can affect your kidneys. Adults with diabetes need to have more tests for kidney disease then younger people.

High blood pressure and frequent urinary tract infections can also affect the kidneys. If you have diabetes and either of these conditions, your health care practitioner should check how your kidneys are working.

Treatment

If your health care practitioner finds kidney damage, he or she will make changes in your treatment plan. Lowering blood pressure, cutting salt intake, and better control of your blood sugar levels may help to slow the progress of kidney disease. Stopping smoking also helps.

⚠ Making certain to lower blood pressure is essential to slowing the progress of kidney disease. There is growing evidence, too, that reducing your dietary intake of protein helps to slow the progression of kidney damage.

If kidney failure occurs, you will need to have treatments using an artificial kidney. This is called kidney dialysis, or hemodialysis. In one kind of dialysis, blood passes from the body through a dialysis machine. Then the clean blood returns to the body. Another kind of kidney dialysis sends fluids to the stomach area. The special fluid takes out wastes from the blood. This is called peritoneal dialysis. (See also Dialysis, page 309.)

Kidney transplants may free some people from kidney dialysis. But transplant surgery does have some risk. Also, some people may not be a candidate for a transplant because of age or other health problems.

NERVE COMPLICATONS

Neuropathy is damage to the nerves. Both people with insulin-dependent (type I) and noninsulin-dependent (type II) diabetes can get neuropathy. Neuropathy affects nerves that connect the spinal cord to muscles, skin, blood vessels, and organs. Although neuropathy can affect many parts of the body, it most often affects the feet and the legs.

The longer you have had diabetes, the higher your risk for getting neuropathy. Young people do not usually have it. But people who get diabetes as adults may have neuropathy soon after diagnosis.

Symptoms

The most common symptoms of neuropathy are numbness, tingling, weakness, burning, or pain. These sensations often start in the fingers or toes and move up the arms or legs. The pain is usually worse at night. It may ease in the morning.

Symptoms of neuropathy depend on which nerves are affected. If the nerves of the leg muscles are affected, the result may be difficulty walking. Damage to other nerves may result in frequent diarrhea or constipation, difficult urination, bladder infections, impotence, or poor balance.

Dangers of Neuropathy

Neuropathy can cause numbness or loss of feeling. You may not feel pain, heat, cold, or pressure. This can be dangerous. You might feel no pain when the feet are injured, frozen, or burned. Or a stone in the shoe could cause a blister or ulcer. This could lead to serious foot problems.

Infections can be very serious in people with diabetes. So even minor problems, such as a blister on a heel, need prompt attention.

People with diabetes may also have poor circulation from narrowed blood vessels. Poor circulation and the numbness of neuropathy can be especially dangerous. An injury you don't notice may cause infection, gangrene, or even amputation.

Treatment

Today there are no cures for neuropathy. But health care practitioners may prescribe drugs to treat pain, depression, and the loss of sleep that neuropathy often brings. Good diabetes control seems to be the best bet in controlling symptoms of neuropathy.

If you have neuropathy, your health care practitioner may refer you to a podiatrist (a foot specialist). A podiatrist can help with nail problems, foot infections, calluses, ulcers, and other problems you may have with your feet.

Losing excess weight may also help. And there is hope for the future. New drugs are being tested for the treatment of neuropathy.

COMPLICATIONS: IMPOTENCE

Impotence means that a man's penis doesn't get or stay hard enough for sex. He can't have or keep an erection. (See also Impotence, page 396.)

Men with diabetes become impotent more often than other men. But not all men with diabetes become impotent. Even if you have diabetes and become impotent, it does not mean that diabetes is the cause.

Causes

There are many causes of impotence. Some causes, such as diabetes, can be physical. But there are also many psychological causes. Men with diabetes may become impotent from psychological causes, too.

In impotence caused by diabetes, the nerves that cause an erection may be damaged. Impotence can be one symptom of nerve damage.

Another cause of impotence in men with diabetes is called penile artery blockage. This occurs when blood vessels in the penis are damaged.

Some drugs can cause impotence. For example, drugs prescribed for colds, stomachaches, ulcers, depression, high blood pressure, epilepsy, and pain all may cause impotence. (But do not stop taking any medicine unless your health care practitioner agrees.) Injury, illness, lack of male hormones, and alcoholism are also causes of impotence.

Impotence can be related to feelings. Feelings of fear, anxiety, or anger may cause impotence. In fact, some men who have had a heart attack become impotent—not because of the heart attack, but because they are afraid of having another heart attack during sex. (A heart attack during sex does not often happen.)

Tiredness and stress can also be causes of impotence.

Treatment

There are many treatments for impotence. If you have had an experience with impotence, talk with your health care practitioner.

Your health care practitioner will first try to find out if the impotence is physical or psychological. If the cause is psychological, your health care practitioner may suggest you go to a counselor who can help you.

Your impotence may be related to your diabetes. But only your health care practitioner can find the cause of the problem. If your diabetes has been poorly controlled, the impotence may leave when you bring blood sugar levels down to near normal levels. If the nerves of the penis have been damaged, surgery may restore them. And for some blood vessel problems, drug injections into the penis can help increase blood flow.

In some cases, surgical implants in the penis may be the answer. There are different kinds of implants. One kind stays semihard all the time. Another kind inflates when you are ready to have sex.

Vacuum tumescence is another treatment

for impotence. A container is put over the penis. Then a pump takes out the air. This causes an erection. Some men prefer this to implants.

Prevention

Sometimes the fear that they will become impotent causes men with diabetes to become impotent. If you are afraid of impotence, talk with your health care practitioner.

Experts agree that keeping your blood sugar levels near normal is the best way to avoid any diabetes complication. This includes nerve or blood vessel problems that can cause impotence.

Avoid heavy drinking and do not smoke. Alcoholism itself may cause impotence. And smoking may cause problems with blood flow. So if you smoke, stop.

Remember: impotence does not mean an end to your sex life. You can still enjoy sex.

FOOT CARE

Some people with diabetes may have nerve damage and/or poor circulation in the legs and feet They may not feel a little cut or a blister. Later, the cut or blister could become infected, leading to gangrene. If not treated, amputation is sometimes needed to save the rest of the foot or leg.

If you have any cut, scrape, or break in the skin of your foot, keep the area clean and dry. Use adhesive tape bandages with care. When you pull off the tape, do not tear the skin. If you notice redness or heat from a cut or blister, tell your health care practitioner immediately.

Diabetes can also cause changes in the skin of your feet. At times your feet may become very dry. The skin may peel and crack. Proper treatment for dry, scaly feet is easy. After bathing, dry your feet. Rub on a thin coating of petroleum jelly or hand cream. Do not put the jellies or creams between your toes.

People with diabetes—like anyone—can suffer from common foot problems, such as ingrown toenails or plantar warts. You should go to your health care practitioner or podiatrist if you have any of the following.

- *Ingrown toenails.* Your toe can be red, tender, painful, and swollen.
- *Plantar warts.* These are viral infections on the sole of the foot. They can be painful. Your health care professional can treat these.
- *Puncture wounds* (stepping on a nail, for example). These are always serious and should be treated quickly.

Protecting Your Feet

You can take steps to protect your feet. Follow these tips for good foot care.

- Visit your health care practitioner regularly. Be sure that your feet are examined at each visit. Taking off your shoes and socks is a good reminder to your health care practitioner.
- Wash your feet every day. Dry them carefully, especially between the toes.
- Check your feet and between your toes every day. Look for blisters, cuts, and scratches.
- If you have a foot infection, report it quickly to your health care practitioner.
- Before you put your shoes on, check for pebbles or other objects inside the shoe that could hurt your feet.
- Before bathing, use your finger or elbow—not your feet—to check the temperature of the water.
- Be careful with hot water bottles, heating pads, or electric blankets. Burns may occur without your feeling them.
- Never walk barefoot.
- Do not cut corns and calluses yourself. Let your health care practitioner cut them.
- Be careful when you trim your toenails. Cut nails straight across.
- Wear shoes that fit your feet and that feel comfortable.

- Change your socks every day. Socks or nylons should be even and smooth. Socks that are mended or bumpy can put extra pressure on feet.

If your feet become numb or start to burn or tingle, be sure to check with your health care practitioner.

NUTRITION

Nutrition means eating well-balanced meals. Nutrition, along with exercise and medications (insulin or oral diabetes pills), is important for good diabetes control.

People with diabetes have the same nutritional needs as anyone else. Regular, well-balanced meals may help to improve their overall health. Eating healthy foods in the right amounts and keeping weight under control may help diabetes management.

⚠ **The following dietary tips offer good general guidelines for a diet if you have diabetes, but every person with diabetes needs a specific meal plan tailored to his or her individual needs by a diabetes specialist or dietician.**

Which Foods Are Healthy?

No single food will supply all the nutrients your body needs, so good nutrition means eating a variety of foods.

Food is divided into four main groups: (1) fruits and vegetables (oranges, apples, bananas, carrots, and spinach); (2) whole grains, cereals, and bread (wheat, rice, oats, bran, and barley); (3) dairy products (whole or skim milk, cream, and yogurt); and (4) meats, fish, poultry, eggs, dried beans, and nuts. It's important to eat foods from each group every day. By doing that, you will make sure that your body has all the nutrients it needs.

The main nutrients in food are carbohydrates, proteins, fats, vitamins, and minerals. Nutrients help your body work right.

Carbohydrates give you energy. Healthy choices are dried beans, peas, and lentils; whole grain breads, cereals, and crackers; and fruits and vegetables.

Protein is necessary for growth and provides a good back-up supply of energy. Healthy choices include lean meats and low-fat dairy products.

Foods high in fiber are healthy, too. Fiber comes from plants and may help to lower blood sugar and blood fat levels. Foods high in fiber include bran cereals, cooked beans and peas, whole grain bread, fruits, and vegetables.

Which Foods Are Unhealthy?

Fat is a nutrient, and you need some fat in your diet. But too much fat isn't good for anyone. And it can be very harmful to people with diabetes.

Too much fat or cholesterol may increase the chances of heart disease and/or hardening of the arteries. People with diabetes have a greater risk of developing these diseases than those without diabetes. So, it is very important that you limit the fat in your diet.

Fat is found in many foods. Red meat, dairy products (whole milk, cream, cheese, and ice cream), egg yolks, butter, salad dressings, vegetable oils, and many desserts are high in fat. To cut down on fat and cholesterol:

- Choose lean cuts of meat and remove extra fat.
- Eat more fish and poultry (without the skin).
- Use diet margarine instead of butter.
- Drink low-fat or skim milk.
- Limit the number of eggs you eat to three or four a week and choose liver only now and then.

Too much salt may worsen high blood pressure. Many foods contain salt. Sometimes you can taste it (as in pickles or bacon). But there is also "hidden" salt in many foods, such as cheeses, salad dressings, and canned soups.

When using salt or fat, remember: a little goes a long way.

People with diabetes should eat less sugar. Foods high in sugar include desserts such as frosted cake and pie; sugary breakfast foods; table sugar, honey, and syrup. One 12-ounce can of regular soft drink has nine teaspoons of sugar.

Finally, good advice is to stay away from alcohol. If you like an alcoholic drink now and then, ask your dietitian for advice.

Setting Up a Meal Plan

You and your dietitian should work together to design a meal plan that's right for you, and includes foods that you enjoy. A diabetes meal plan is a guide that tells you how much and what kinds of food you can choose to eat at meals and snack times. A good meal plan should fit in with your schedule and eating habits. The right meal plan will also help keep your weight where it should be. Whether you need to lose weight, gain weight, or stay where you are, your meal plan can help.

EXERCISE

Exercise, along with good nutrition and medications (insulin or oral diabetes pills), is important for good diabetes control.

Exercise benefits everyone. It is especially good for people with diabetes. Exercise can be almost any activity you enjoy: walking, bicycling, swimming, jogging, hiking, tennis, or golf.

Exercise usually lowers blood sugar. That helps your body use its food supply better. Also, exercise may help insulin work better. And, if you are overweight, exercise—plus careful attention to diet—can help take off extra pounds.

Exercise is important in many other ways. It improves the flow of blood through the small blood vessels and increases your heart's pumping power. The right exercise program may make you look and feel better.

Your health care practitioner can help you decide what kinds of exercise—and how much exercise—are best suited to your needs. If your blood sugar control is poor, do not exercise. Get medical advice first. If you have retinopathy (diabetic eye disease) or blood vessel problems, see your health care practitioner before you start exercising.

Exercise has value only if it's done regularly. People with diabetes should exercise at least several days a week.

Exercise and Insulin-Dependent Diabetes

Before starting any exercise program, check with your health care practitioner. Your activity must be planned to fit in with your meal plan and with the action times of your insulin.

It's a good idea to eat before you exercise. As a rule, a high-carbohydrate snack is good before mild to moderate exercise (walking, cycling, or golf). Such a snack could be one-half of a peanut butter sandwich or two cheese crackers.

If you plan on doing a heavier exercise for more than an hour (aerobics, running, squash, or handball, for example), you may want to eat an extra amount of carbohydrate, such as a few additional crackers.

Snacks are important before exercising. Without eating before you exercise, you could have too much insulin and too little sugar in your blood. This would cause an insulin reaction. A reaction might make you feel faint, sweaty, dizzy, or confused.

An insulin reaction can occur while you exercise or several hours after exercise, even up to 12 hours later. If you feel one coming on while exercising, stop. Drink some orange juice, a nondiet soft drink, or take some form of sugar immediately. You need to treat an insulin reaction as soon as you feel it coming on. Don't wait, otherwise it could become worse. When you exercise, you should bring along some hard candy or sugar packets to eat, just in case. They will raise your blood sugar level.

If you play a team sport such as baseball or basketball, you should let someone know you have diabetes and teach them how to help you, if needed. If you like running or cycling, do it with a friend or family member. If you can't find anyone to go with you, let someone know where you are going and when you will be back.

With regular exercise, you will need to test your blood sugar more often.

Exercise and Noninsulin-Dependent Diabetes

Almost nine out of ten people with type II diabetes are overweight. Most often, they are also past age 40. In many cases, type II diabetes can be controlled through diet and exercise alone. For these reasons, exercise is a very important part of the control plan for those with type II diabetes.

Exercise burns calories, which your body would otherwise store as extra weight. And because exercise also helps lower blood sugar levels, exercise can help your diabetes control.

Starting an Exercise Program

The first step is to check with your health care practitioner. Together, you can decide how much and which kinds of exercise are best suited for you.

SICK-DAY CARE

The common cold, the flu, and other illnesses can present special problems when you have diabetes. The physical stress of illness can raise blood sugar. And loss of appetite or vomiting can affect diabetes control. You may not be able to prevent catching a cold. But you can help prevent a minor illness from becoming a big problem by being prepared—before you become sick.

How Do You Prepare for an Illness?

You need to have a sick-day plan of action. Your health care practitioner can help you make up the plan. It should include instructions for the following:

• When to call the health care practitioner
• Blood sugar and urine ketone testing
• Foods and fluids to take during your illness
• Medication changes

Remember: Only your health care practitioner knows when to change your insulin, diabetes pills, or diet.

When Do You Call the Health Care Practitioner?

You should call the health care practitioner if you have:

• An illness that does not improve after one or two days
• Diarrhea or vomiting for over six hours
• Moderate to large amounts of ketones in the urine
• High blood sugar readings (Your sick-day plan should list the exact limits.)
• Sleepiness that is not normal for you
• Doubt about what you need to do for the illness
• Stomach or chest pain, difficulty breathing, or a very dry mouth. If you have any of these symptoms, call your health care practitioner immediately.

Should You Test More Often?

When you first think that you are sick, test your blood sugar. Be prepared to follow your sick-day plan. You should also test your urine for ketones.

People with insulin-dependent (type I) diabetes should check blood sugar and urine ketones every four hours. Some people may need to check more often.

People with noninsulin-dependent (type II) diabetes should check blood sugar at least four times a day (usually before each meal and at bedtime). They should check for urine ketones if the blood sugar is more than 240 mg/dl.

Should You Stop Taking Diabetes Medication?

No. Do not stop taking your insulin or diabetes pills. Even if you cannot eat, your body needs the medication that's been prescribed for you.

If you take insulin, take your usual dose. You may need to take more rapid-acting (regular) insulin. Check with your health care practitioner.

If you take diabetes pills, take them if you can. Sometimes on sick days, you may need to take insulin. Check with your health care practitioner.

How Do You Stick to a Meal Plan?

Sometimes during illness, sticking to your meal plan is a problem. When you are sick, you may not feel like eating. You may find it hard to eat some foods on your regular meal plan. That's why you need a list of foods and liquids for sick days.

Drinking plenty of fluids during sick days is important. There is no set rule for how much extra fluid to drink. About four to six ounces every 30 to 60 minutes is reasonable. These extra fluids should not have calories—drink water, diet soft drinks, tea without sugar, for example.

Eating is important, too. If you can't eat your regular foods, replace them with sugar-containing liquids or soft foods. For example, one-half cup apple juice, one-half cup orange juice, one-half cup fruit-flavored yogurt, or six crackers are good choices.

If you are so sick that you keep throwing up fluids, call your health care practitioner immediately.

Can Sick-Day Medications Affect Diabetes?

Yes. If you are sick, you may be taking drugs other than those for diabetes alone. Many cough syrups and cough drops have sugar. Some cold remedies may raise your blood sugar. Be sure to read the labels on any non-prescription drugs you use. Before you use a nonprescription drug, check with your health care practitioner or pharmacist. They can help you choose safe nonprescription medications.

The American Diabetes Association

OBESITY

Obesity is one of the most written about, most discussed, and least understood public health problems facing our nation. An enormous amount of misinformation, myth, and unsuccessful medical management surrounds this serious medical problem.

CAUSES

At the simplest level, obesity is the result of eating more calories in food than required by the body. Many potential causes for this exist, and therefore physicians think of this disorder not as a single disease but as several different conditions that have the symptom of overweight in common.

Several factors appear to influence the prevalence of obesity in the American population. While excess body weight can affect people of all ages, obesity increases in prevalence with increasing age, peaking in middle age. Obesity is common throughout all segments of our society, but it appears to have a particular relationship to socioeconomic status. The lower the socioeconomic status, the greater the prevalence of obesity. Similarly, as the level of education decreases, the prevalence of obesity increases. Obesity among blacks in this country, particularly among black women, appears to be greater in proportion to population than obesity among whites. These socioeconomic trends, however, do not apply to individuals at or below the poverty level; these individuals have a low incidence of obesity.

Genetic factors appear to be important in obesity although their exact nature or role is not well understood at present. Obesity tends to run in families, a fact which reflects, at least in part, the genetic or hereditary basis for obesity. But, environmental, lifestyle factors such as attitudes and practices regarding eating, and physical activity also are important determinants of obesity. Thus, it is probable that both genetic and environmental factors contribute to the development and perpetuation of obesity, and it is often very difficult to separate these two factors in a given individual.

HEALTH CONSEQUENCES

Obesity is associated with serious and significant negative health consequences. For example, obesity appears to be associated with serious consequences for the quality and length of life.

In adults, the mortality rate for obese individuals exceeds the expected death rate for other individuals in that age group, especially for individuals who are more than 30 percent above standard body weight as defined by the Metropolitan Life Insurance Company's 1959 height-weight table. Individuals who are overweight by less than 30 percent are also at increased risk for mortality.

A person does not need to be massively overweight to face an increased risk of death; even a moderate or mild degree of overweight can increase the risk of mortality at each age group.

In large part, this appears to be related to the fact that the obese individual is prone to a greater variety of serious and life-threatening diseases than is the nonobese person.

Diabetes Mellitus

The obese individual runs a greater risk of developing diabetes mellitus than the nonobese person. The chance of developing diabetes may be two or three times greater for the obese person. The health consequences of diabetes are so serious and widespread that public health experts view the increase in obesity with alarm.

Researchers do not fully understand the mechanism whereby obesity increases the risk of developing diabetes. Information from several laboratories, in this country and abroad, suggests that obesity somehow interferes with the action of insulin. In addition, in some obese individuals there appears to be a decreased ability of the pancreas to secrete sufficient amounts of insulin into the blood. As a consequence of insufficient insulin action, the body's regulation of glucose (sugar) metabolism may be abnormal and the blood glucose level may become elevated. A blood test, urinalysis, or glucose tolerance test can detect excessive amounts of glucose in the blood.

If the obese individual with diabetes and an abnormal glucose metabolism loses weight by losing body fat, insulin's ability to regulate glucose metabolism improves, the blood insulin level returns to or toward normal and the blood glucose concentration decreases. Moreover, the symptoms of diabetes often disappear.

Heart Disease

The obese individual also runs an increased risk of developing a variety of cardiac diseases. The most serious of these conditions, atherosclerotic heart disease, can lead to heart attacks. Although the reason for the increased risk of heart disease associated with obesity is not known with certainty, researchers believe that one explanation is that obesity tends to raise blood fat levels. The obese individual is at substantially greater risk of having higher levels of triglyceride (a molecule carrying three fatty acids) and cholesterol in the blood than the nonobese individual. Both triglyceride and cholesterol have been implicated as factors in causing heart attacks. Obesity, especially when associated with diabetes, may also lower the level of a particular lipoprotein that appears to be protective against coronary heart disease. With weight loss and reduction of body fat, the levels of triglyceride and of cholesterol in the blood decrease.

High Blood Pressure

Additional factors probably contribute to the relationship between obesity and heart disease. The obese person is, for example, predisposed to high blood pressure. Although not a disease in itself, high blood pressure contributes to vascular disease and degenerative diseases of the liver and kidney. As with diabetes and plasma fats, blood pressure usually improves with loss of weight and body fat.

Other Consequences

Obesity affects the individual in many other ways. It places severe stress on the internal organs, the musculoskeletal system, the digestive tract, and the psychological state of the obese person.

Obese individuals often find that they are outcasts in our society. They may encounter discrimination in employment as well as daily living situations. This treatment generates emotional stress, an important health consequence of obesity.

WHAT IS OBESITY?

Obesity is an excessive increase in body fat. In man and in animals, fat in the body is stored primarily in specific cells (adipose or fat cells) in the adipose (fat) tissue.

Microscopic examination shows that a fat cell is very different in appearance from other cells. Most cells contain a large amount of cytoplasm, with the cell nucleus near the center of the cell. Fat constitutes almost the entire area of the adipose cell, and the cytoplasm and nucleus are displaced. Thus, fat, in the form of triglyceride, is the major component of the adipose cell.

In the nonobese adult male, approximately 10 to 15 percent of the total body weight is fat. In the nonobese woman, fat may constitute up to 20 percent of total body weight. If fat comprises more than 20 percent of the total body weight, the individual is obese.

At the present time, there is no practical or simple way to determine the amount of a person's body weight which is fat. This measurement cannot be determined by a physician in his office with any accuracy. Only a sophisticated laboratory has equipment capable of measuring the fat/body weight ratio. Thus, people have developed alternative ways to assess obesity.

The most common index of obesity is body weight. Several "standard tables" exist which provide recommended body weight in relation to height and body frame.

If an individual weighs more than the "ideal" or "average" weight for his or her age, height, and body frame, as shown in any of the standard tables, he or she is overweight. An individual who is more than 15 to 20 percent overweight is considered to be definitely obese. Obesity may also, and probably does, exist in individuals who are 5 to 15 percent over the ideal or average body weights shown in the standard tables.

There are difficulties, however, in determining obesity from any "standard" weight-height tables. For example, of two men with the same weight and height, one may be obese, and the other not. Both may weigh 225 pounds and be six feet tall; one man is an athlete and his weight is due to increased muscle mass, while the weight of the second man, in poor physical condition, is due to an increased amount of fat. Both of these men would be classified as overweight according to any of the standard tables, but only one is obese, because obesity is an increase in body fat and not an increase in muscle.

ADIPOSE TISSUE AND ENERGY

In man the adipose tissue (fat) has a very important function; it serves as the principal energy storage organ of the body. Energy is

LOSING WEIGHT AND KEEPING IT OFF

The trick to weight loss is not so much how to lose the weight (many different diets will help achieve that), but how to keep it off. Thirty-four million Americans, including close to a third of all those over 50, are overweight—putting themselves at increased risk for diabetes, heart disease, and even some forms of cancer. At any given time, about 25 percent of all men and half of all women are trying to lose weight—but most of them will subsequently regain what they lost. Not only is "rebound" weight gain demoralizing, it also can change metabolism so that it becomes even harder to lose regained weight. And, while losing weight lowers blood pressure and cholesterol levels, some studies have shown that rebound weight gain can more than offset these positive benefits.

A recent survey, published in the *American Journal of Clinical Nutrition*, examined differences between women who keep weight off, and those who lose it only to gain it back again. (While the survey included women only, rebound weight gain is a problem for men as well.) The researchers interviewed 108 women, most of them middle-aged: 30 "maintainers" (women who were formerly obese, or more than 20 percent above desired weight, who had lost weight and kept it off); 44 "relapsers" (obese women who had lost weight but regained it); and 34 "controls" (women who had never been obese). All were asked about their weight history and childhood eating patterns; about their current eating patterns; if they felt supported by others in their weight-loss endeavors; if they drank alcohol or smoked; if they ate in response to emotional issues; if they had recently been under stress. The results showed sharp differences between maintainers and relapsers. The strategies used by the successful dieters, summa-rized as follows, are excellent guidelines for anyone wanting to keep excess weight off.

•*Exercise regularly.* Staying active was the primary difference separating maintainers from relapsers. Close to 90 percent of maintainers and 82 percent of controls exercised regularly—at least three times a week for at least 30 minutes a session—to stay at their desired weight; only 36 percent of relapsers were regular exercisers, but even they exercised less frequently and strenuously.

•*Eat a healthful diet, but don't deprive yourself.* Maintainers ate an improved diet consisting of less fat and sugar and more fruits and vegetables, and they cooked in a more healthful way (restricting fried foods). However, they occasionally allowed themselves favorite foods so that they didn't feel deprived. Ultimately, they developed new eating habits. In contrast, relapsers resorted to appetite suppressants, fasting, or extremely restrictive diets for weight loss—all of which enhance feelings of deprivation and do not foster eating habits that can be sustained for the long haul.

•*Feel good about your body.* Relapsers were, overall, unhappy with their bodies: More than 70 percent saw themselves as heavy or ugly. In contrast, 86 percent of maintainers and 94 percent of controls saw themselves as thin or of average weight.

•*Actively confront problems.* Most of the women questioned were currently tackling a stressful or troubling issue, but the problem-solving methods differed between the groups. Relapsers were more likely to try to escape from dealing with problems by eating, sleeping more, or wishing the problem would go away. Maintainers and controls were more likely to seek social support from friends or professional help, actively confront the problem, and try to solve it.   *The Editors*

measured in calories. Adipose tissue is the caloric reservoir of the body.

When the amount of energy provided by the calories in the ingested food is equal to the amount of energy needed by the body to perform all of its vital functions plus any additional physical activity, the individual is said to be in energy balance. In this situation the person will maintain the amount of adipose tissue and body weight at a constant level. When the amount of energy provided by the calories in the ingested food is less than the amount of energy needed by the body, the individual is said to be in negative energy balance. In this situation the adipose tissue will be broken down to provide the energy needed by the body, this tissue will decrease in size, and the individual will lose body weight. When energy intake in food is greater than the amount needed by the body, the person will increase the amount of adipose tissue, that is, will become fatter, and will increase in weight.

In an obese person the caloric intake is consistently greater than the amount the body needs to maintain its vital functions and to perform daily activities. The excess calories go to fat. Since the individual is in positive energy balance, the body weight increases and body fat increases, expanding the adipose tissue.

At rest, an adult man requires about 1,200 to 1,500 calories a day to maintain his vital functions. If the person is doing something other than lying at rest, such as working or walking, his energy requirements will rise. In order to maintain his body weight and energy balance, he will have to ingest perhaps 2,000 calories a day. If he does, his body weight remains stable, whereas if he ingests less, his body weight decreases. If he ingests more calories than he expends in his activities, the excess calories are converted to triglyceride and stored in the adipose tissue. Vigorous physical activity, such as exercise, will raise energy requirements even more and caloric requirements will increase. The same principles governing energy balance and body weight just described still apply, however.

The same principles apply to women, although the energy requirements of men and women do differ slightly. A woman at rest requires approximately 1,000 calories to 1,300 calories a day, on the average. When she is active she will require more calories to maintain her weight. Of course, if she ingests more than she needs, she will store the excess in adipose tissue and will gain fat and weight.

Energy requirements at rest and during activity will vary from person to person. People have different rates of basal metabolism; therefore people have slightly different caloric needs. In addition, some people's bodies are physiologically more efficient than others at extracting and utilizing the energy within foodstuffs. One must tailor a nutritional assessment and caloric intake plan to each person individually. Although there is at present no definitive or conclusive data to support the view that subtle differences in the ability to extract or utilize calories cause obesity, recent research may suggest that such differences might contribute to the development or perpetuation of the obese state in some individuals. On the other hand, there is a real need for continued research on whether such metabolic differences between individuals can be causative factors in obesity.

OPPORTUNITIES FOR CHANGE

Overeating seems to be endemic to the American adult population. Our society is oriented toward eating. Food advertisements are persuasive. Fast food restaurants and automats are everywhere; buildings contain canteens, often on every floor. Although it will be very difficult to effect, Americans will have to change their lifestyle—their beliefs, attitudes, and practices regarding eating and exercise—if we are to solve the problem of obesity.

Lack of exercise, the other major factor in adult obesity, applies to most men and women in our society. American adults tend to participate in physical activities as spectators rather than as participants. Again, only a fundamental change in lifestyle can alter the pattern.

The Warren Grant Magnuson Clinical Center

THYROID DISEASE

The thyroid, a small, butterfly-shaped organ located just over the windpipe, secretes the hormone thyroxine, which regulates the growth and development of virtually all of the body's tissues. Thyroxine increases the rate at which chemical reactions occur in the body. If the thyroid gland is either overactive (hyperthyroid) or underactive (hypothyroid), it can create problems. *The Editors*

HYPERTHYROIDISM

Hyperthyroidism is common among elderly individuals; several health reports suggest a prevalence of from 0.5 to 2.5 percent. Approximately 15 percent of all thyrotoxic pa-

tients are over the age of 60. In many cases the symptoms are typical and include nervousness, palpitations, sweating, tremors, and weight loss. However, often the most striking characteristic of hyperthyroidism in older patients is the paucity of symptoms which they describe. In fact, many patients seem to be healthy. They frequently do not have enlarged thyroids, do not complain of heat intolerance, and rather than the usual picture of weight loss despite an increased appetite, older patients may lose their desire for food.

As long ago as 1931, the famous Dr. Frank

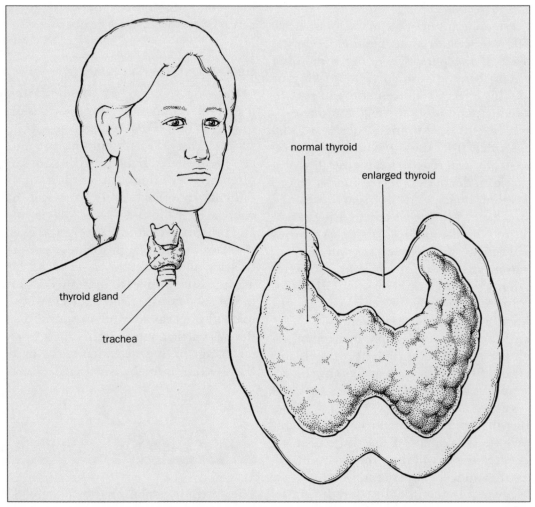

normal thyroid

enlarged thyroid

thyroid gland

trachea

Hyperthyroidism can cause the butterfly-shaped thyroid gland to enlarge. Surgery is rarely warranted, unless the thyroid becomes so large that it interferes with breathing or swallowing.

Lahey called attention to a form of thyrotoxicosis (hyperthyroidism) in which nervous hyperactivity was replaced by lethargy as the dominant clinical feature. These patients looked tired, disinterested, and did not react well to stress. Dr. Lahey found that they usually did not have the typical eye findings of eyelid retraction, staring, or protrusion of the eyeballs, did not have enlarged thyroids, and often had normal rather than rapid heart rates. He described these patients as having "apathetic hyperthyroidism," a term that is still used today.

Therefore, it is apparent that hyperthyroidism can be easily overlooked for many reasons. The presenting features may not conform to the usual findings. The symptoms that do occur often are attributed to the aging process, and weight loss in the absence of other typical symptoms is often attributed to depression or a hidden cancer.

Thus, physicians must consider the possibility of hyperthyroidism in patients who complain of a great variety of symptoms, including shortness of breath, palpitations, nervousness, weakness, constipation, loss of appetite, as well as those who seem to be emotionally ill. Fortunately, those patients whose problems are caused by hyperthyroidism can usually be identified by means of simple and inexpensive blood tests.

Diagnosis

The techniques used by physicians to diagnose hyperthyroidism in elderly patients are usually simple and similar to those employed in younger patients. Blood tests reveal high serum concentrations of thyroid hormones, and a radioactive iodine uptake test and thyroid scan picture tell whether the entire thyroid is overactive or whether there are one or more hyperfunctioning nodules present instead.

Treatment

Treatment of hyperthyroidism is similar for patients of any age, though at times physicians make minor alterations because of the presence of other conditions.

The treatment of choice is almost always radioactive iodine because of the safety and simplicity of its administration. It is taken by mouth. By damaging the thyroid tissue, this treatment begins to slow the thyroid gland's output of thyroid hormone after about a month. The radioiodine effect is completed in from three to six months. After the thyroid levels return to normal, usually they only need to be rechecked once or twice a year after the first six months. Almost all patients develop hypothyroidism (underactive thyroid) after radioiodine. It usually occurs within the first year after treatment, but it can develop at any time.

About 40 percent of patients become hypothyroid within a year after radioactive iodine treatment. Among the others, 3 percent develop hypothyroidism each year.

This makes lifelong monitoring of thyroid function mandatory.

Surgical removal of overactive thyroid nodules (or most of the gland if the entire thyroid is overactive) offers an alternative treatment for hyperthyroidism. Surgery is rarely needed, however, unless the thyroid is so very large as to cause difficulty breathing or swallowing due to pressure on the windpipe or esophagus.

A physician may choose to slow down an overactive thyroid by using an antithyroid drug such as propylthiouracil (PTU) or methimazole (Tapazole). These drugs block the utilization of iodine by the thyroid gland. Since iodine is necessary for the manufacture of thyroid hormone, hormone levels begin to fall in ten days to two weeks and may become normal after just four to six weeks of such therapy. Usually, these drugs only control the thyroid as long as the patient takes them and recurrent hyperthyroidism will be experienced by most patients (up to 75 percent) when they stop the medications.

Moreover, since these drugs may cause side effects, including fever, hives, and white blood cell destruction, they are rarely used in older individuals.

Special uses for antithyroid drugs in elderly patients. In spite of the disadvantages just mentioned, there are important roles for antithyroid drugs in elderly hyperthyroid patients. They are usually employed to reduce thyroid function in individuals who are to have their overactive thyroid or nodule surgically removed. Preliminary control with PTU or methimazole, with iodine drops added in the last few days to reduce the vascularity of the gland, makes the thyroid operation safer and easier for the surgeon to perform.

Antithyroid drugs may also be used before radioactive iodine treatment, especially if the patient has hyperthyroidism complicated by other medical problems such as an irregular heart rhythm or chest pain (angina). This is because radioiodine treatment is occasionally followed by temporary further increases in thyroid hormone levels, presumably due to stored hormone leaking out of the damaged thyroid gland. While a young individual may not be affected by this, an older patient with a serious heart condition might experience complications from even a temporary mild increase in thyroid hormone levels. Pre-treatment with antithyroid drugs will prevent this from happening.

In addition, physicians usually reduce symptoms and rapid pulse to safe levels by prescribing one of the beta adrenergic blocking drugs (Inderal, Corgard, Tenormin, Lopressor). These drugs block the action of circulating thyroid hormone on body tissues. Radioiodine can then be administered safely despite a possible temporary worsening of the thyroid condition.

In summary, although hyperthyroidism is often more difficult to diagnose because its presentation in an elderly patient may be subtle or somewhat unusual, once suspected, the diagnosis is simple to confirm. Radioiodine is the easiest and safest form of treatment.

HYPOTHYROIDISM

Hypothyroidism is often more difficult to recognize and more common than hyperthyroidism in the elderly. The earliest sign of a failing thyroid is an increase in the blood level of thyroid stimulating hormone (TSH). TSH, a hormone produced by the pituitary gland, stimulates the thyroid to manufacture thyroid hormones. When thyroid function declines, the pituitary responds by increasing its production of TSH.

Large population studies have shown that as many as one woman in every ten over the age of 50 has a blood level of TSH that is above normal. Although most of these individuals have no symptoms and have thyroid hormone blood levels within the broad normal range, all have the beginnings of hypothyroidism. They should be carefully followed so that treatment with thyroid hormone can be given if overt hypothyroidism develops.

Symptoms May Mimic Aging Process

The symptoms of hypothyroidism in the elderly are unfortunately very easy to mistake for "normal aging." Therefore, elderly individuals who gradually become hypothyroid may see a variety of specialists because of the various symptoms they may have. These include mental confusion, depression, hoarseness, dry skin, deafness, muscle cramps, numbness and weakness of the hands, unsteadiness of gait, anemia, and constipation. It is easy to see why such vague and nonspecific symptoms can often be attributed to the aging process.

Associated Disorders Suggest Need for Thyroid Screening

Physicians are aware that although hypothyroidism in its many forms is common among elderly patients, it is extremely difficult to recognize by physical examination alone.

There are clues which can lead physicians to test for hypothyroidism in certain individuals within an elderly population. These include premature graying of the hair, protrusion of the eyeballs (known as exophthalmos), the juvenile type of diabetes requiring treatment with insulin, rheumatoid arthritis, pernicious anemia (caused by lack of vitamin B-12), harmless white skin spots known as vitiligo, and patchy hair loss known as alopecia areata.

The presence of these and certain other medical problems in either the patient or a close relative increase the likelihood that that particular individual will develop thyroid failure. By taking a careful family history, physicians can identify the people with the greatest risk for thyroid failure and perform thyroid testing, even in the absence of physical evidence of hypothyroidism.

Diagnosis

Fortunately, the laboratory tests required for the diagnosis of hypothyroidism are simple, inexpensive, and the same as those used in younger patients. A single blood sample is obtained to measure the concentration of the thyroid hormone thyroxine (T4) and the pituitary thyroid stimulating hormone (TSH). Those with obvious evidence of thyroid failure usually show both a decrease in T4 and an increase in TSH. Some patients who are just beginning to experience thyroid failure may only show an increase in TSH.

Who Needs Treatment?

Those patients with obvious thyroid failure require treatment. It is not clear, however, whether individuals with only an increased TSH need treatment with thyroid hormone, too. One long-term follow-up study suggested that approximately 5 percent of patients with a high TSH progress to true hypothyroidism each year. This suggests that patients who feel well and have only a high TSH should be retested every year to be sure that they are not becoming hypothyroid.

⚠ Thyroid replacement is often started when a further reduction in thyroid function is highly likely, such as in those who were treated with radioactive iodine, or when the LDL cholesterol is elevated.

On the other hand, some patients who have only mild TSH elevations actually feel better when they take enough thyroid hormone each day to normalize the TSH level. In a recent study some patients were given real thyroid medication, while others received a placebo tablet identical in appearance to the thyroid pill; neither the doctor nor the patient knew who was taking the thyroid medication. The results showed that thyroid hormone did improve symptoms of fatigue, constipation, and poor energy in some people with only an elevated TSH level. This has led some physicians to recommend a trial of thyroid hormone in every patient who has an increased blood level of TSH.

Dosage of Thyroid Hormone

Treatment of hypothyroidism should be instituted with extreme care in elderly patients. Most have had this condition for many years without obvious symptoms, and most do not feel particularly sick. Furthermore, their requirements for thyroid hormone are usually not very great. The hypothyroid condition slows the chemical reactions within the body so that thyroid hormone is used up more slowly than normal. Thus, it is possible to overdose a patient quite easily if too much thyroid hormone is administered, especially early in the course of treatment.

Therefore, most physicians recommend starting treatment with as little as 25 mcg of thyroxine (T4) per day, increasing the dose of medication by 25 mcg each month until the blood level of TSH falls into the normal range. In patients with heart disease, even lower initial doses and a more gradual increase in medication may be necessary.

Long-term follow-up of all patients is essential. Thyroid function may continue to decline, and, therefore, yearly blood tests for T4 and TSH are necessary.

Choice of Thyroid Hormone Preparation

The choice of the thyroid hormone preparation is extremely important for the well-being of elderly patients. Some generic brands of thyroid hormone tablets lack reliability with regard to the amount of thyroxine in each tablet. An unexpected increase in the amount of hormone taken could have serious consequences for an elderly patient who has heart trouble.

THYROID NODULES

As with younger patients, thyroid nodules are common among older people, while thyroid cancers are not. If an older person is found to have a nodule (lump) within the thyroid gland, every effort should be made to determine the nature of the nodule without having to subject the individual to removal of the nodule in a thyroid operation. Most such nodules may be left alone if thyroid blood levels are normal and if a thyroid scan picture shows that the nodule is functioning normally.

If a nodule shows no evidence of function on a thyroid scan, a sample of the nodule can be obtained by a simple procedure called a fine needle biopsy. Subsequent microscopic examination of the tissue will exclude cancer in the majority of individuals, and surgery may be avoided.

Only those few individuals who are found to have thyroid cancer in the biopsy material or in whom the tissue sample is not adequate to exclude cancer need to have their nodules removed surgically. Fortunately, surgery is neither difficult nor a health risk for most older patients, and recovery following surgery tends to be rapid and complete.

SUMMARY

It is apparent that thyroid disorders have no age limits. When they occur in elderly individuals, they may be difficult to diagnose, require special attention to gradual and careful treatment, and require lifelong follow-up settings where access to medical care may not be easy. By educating patients and those that care for them, thyroid problems will be recognized earlier and treated with a greater safety.

The Thyroid Foundation of America

The Eyes

The eye is an incredibly complex organ—particularly considering its compact size of about one inch in diameter. Like a camera, the eye has a single lens that focuses objects in the world around us, and projects an image of those objects—upside down and in miniature—onto the retina, the light-sensitive region at the back of the eyeball that processes the incoming image. But the eye is far more advanced than any camera.

The movement of the eye is controlled by six muscles attached to the eye's tough outer membrane, which is known as the sclera. (The sclera is the part you see as the "white" of your eye.) These muscles work to move both eyes simultaneously, keeping them centered on the same field of view, to provide a stereoscopic, three-dimensional image.

A layer of clear tissue called the cornea covers the lens, the pupil, and the iris (the pigmented disc that gives the eye its color). The cornea protects these delicate structures and its rounded shape helps to bend light rays through to the eye's lens. In fact, the cornea provides about two-thirds of the eye's total focusing ability. Behind the cornea is a fluid-filled space known as the anterior chamber. The fluid, called the aqueous humor, constantly flows through the anterior chamber and other parts of the inner eye, carrying nutrients and washing away wastes. If the flow of the aqueous humor becomes blocked for any reason, pressure may build up and damage the fragile structures of the inner eye. If high eye pressure leads to damage inside the eye, the patient is said to have glaucoma.

Directly behind the anterior chamber is the iris. (People with brown eyes, incidentally, have the same pigments in the iris as people with blue or green eyes; they just have more of them. Albinos have none; their eyes appear pink from the blood vessels underlying the transparent tissue.) The pupil is the opening at the center of the iris that allows light to enter the eye. Muscles controlling the iris cause the pupil to change size to adjust to the amount of incoming light, much like the aperture of a camera.

Behind the iris and pupil is the lens, enclosed in a capsule and held in place by a network of fibers. The lens is pliant and changes shape in order to focus on an image clearly.

As we age, the lens of the eye loses its elasticity. Consequently, by around age 40, we begin to find that it is harder to focus on nearby objects. This gradual farsightedness is known as presbyopia, meaning "old eye," and it affects everyone eventually.

For many people, age may also bring about cataracts, which occur when the normally crystal-clear lens gradually becomes opaque.

Behind the lens is the largest portion of the eye—a large round chamber filled with a gelatinous clear fluid called the vitreous humor. Tiny bits of unattached cellular material may drift around in the vitreous humor, resulting in "floaters," the phenomenon whereby you see little spots or strings moving across your field of vision. Floaters are generally just a harmless occasional nuisance, but tend to occur more frequently as we age, especially among nearsighted people.

At the back of the eyeball lies the retina, the complex ten-layered structure that processes the light images projected through the cornea and lens. The retina has two distinct types of photosensitive cells—rods and cones—which transform light signals into electrical nerve impulses to be sent to the brain. Rods, which outnumber cones 20 to 1, perceive the world in black and white. The cones perceive color. They require more light to function properly than the rods, which explains why colors appear as shades of gray in faint light, even if shapes seem perfectly distinguishable.

At the center of the retina is the macula, which provides the most acute vision. If this portion of the retina begins to deteriorate (macular degeneration), central sight and the ability to read or do any kind of work requiring keen vision is greatly jeopardized.

Connected to the retina at the rear of the eyeball is the optic nerve. It conducts electro-chemical nerve impulses from the eye to the visual cortex in the rear of the brain, where these signals are then interpreted and trans-formed into meaningful pictures, shapes, symbols, and cues.

People over 50 should have their eyes ex-amined at least every two years by an ophthal-mologist. This is because many important eye diseases, such as glaucoma, cataract, and mac-ular degeneration, increase in prevalence in older adults. As presbyopia initially progress-es, you may need new glasses fairly often. But for most people, by around the age of 65, the eye's lens has lost most of its elasticity; thus, vi-sion stabilizes and the need for new glasses ta-pers off sharply. *The Editors*

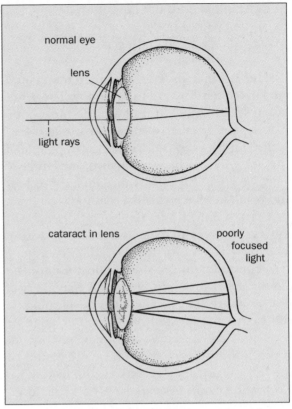

A normal, clear lens allows light to pass through un-obstructed. When a cataract forms, light diffuses in the clouded lens, resulting in blurred vision.*

CATARACT

A cataract is a clouding of the normally clear and transparent lens of the eye. It is not a tumor or a new growth of skin or tissue over the eye, but a fogging of the lens itself. When a cataract develops, the lens becomes cloudy like a frosted window and may cause a painless blurring of vision.

The lens, located behind the pupil, focus-es light on the retina at the back of the eye to produce a sharp image. When a cataract forms, the lens can become so opaque and unclear that light cannot easily be transmitted to the retina. Often, however, a cataract covers only a small part of the lens and if sight is not greatly impaired, there is no need to remove the cataract. If a large portion of the lens be-comes cloudy, sight can be partially or com-pletely lost until the cataract is removed.

There are many misconceptions about cataracts. For instance, cataracts do not spread from eye to eye, though they may de-velop in both eyes at the same time. A cataract is not a film visible on the outside of the eye. Nor is it caused from overuse of the eyes or made worse by use of the eye. Cataracts rarely develop in a matter of months. They usually develop gradually over many years. Finally, cataracts are not related to cancer. Nor does having a cataract mean a person will be per-manently blind.

CAUSES AND SYMPTOMS

There are many types of cataracts. Most are caused by a change in the chemical composi-tion of the lens resulting in a loss of lens trans-parency. These changes can be caused by the following factors.

• Aging
• Eye injuries

- Certain diseases and conditions of the eye and body
- Hereditary or birth defects

The normal process of aging may cause the lens to harden and turn cloudy. These are called senile cataracts and are the most common type. They can occur as early as age 40.

Eye injuries can cause cataracts in people of any age. A hard blow, puncture, cut, intense heat, or chemical burn can damage the lens and result in what is called a traumatic cataract.

Certain infections, drugs, or diseases of the eye such as diabetes can also cause the lens to cloud and form a secondary cataract.

Depending on the size and location of the cloudy areas in a lens, a person may or may not be aware that a cataract is developing. If the cataract is located on the outer edge of the lens, no change in vision may be noticed. If the cloudiness is located near the center of the lens, it usually interferes with clear sight. Common symptoms experienced with developing cataracts include the following.

- Blurred or double vision
- Sensitivity to light and glare which may make driving difficult
- Less vivid perception of color
- Frequent eyeglass prescription changes

As the cataract grows worse, stronger glasses no longer improve sight. It may help to hold objects nearer the eye for reading and close-up work. The pupil, which normally appears black, may undergo noticeable color changes and appear to be yellowish or white.

DETECTION AND DIAGNOSIS

Usually cataracts cannot be viewed from the outside of the eye without proper instruments. If blurred vision or other symptoms are noticed, an ophthalmologist should be visited as soon as possible for a comprehensive medical eye examination.

The ophthalmologist examines the eye with a variety of instruments to determine the type, size, and location of the cataract. The interior of the eye is also viewed with an instrument called an ophthalmoscope to determine if there are any other eye disorders contributing to the blurred vision.

TREATMENT

When cataracts cause enough loss of sight to interfere with a person's work, hobbies, or lifestyle, it is probably time to remove them. Depending on individual needs, the patient and the ophthalmologist decide together when removal is necessary.

Surgery

Surgery, which can be performed under general or local anesthesia and often on an outpatient basis, is the only effective way to remove the cloudy lens from the eye. Cataracts cannot be removed with a laser (an intense beam of light energy). Ophthalmologic laser surgery can, however, be used later to open part of the lens membrane (capsule) if it becomes cloudy after cataract surgery.

Though rapidly changing technology and ongoing research have improved the treatment of cataracts in recent years, eye drops, ointments, pills, special diets, or eye exercises have not been proven to dissolve or reduce a cataract.

Lens replacement. Once the cloudy, natural lens of the eye is removed, the patient needs a substitute lens to focus the eye. Medical advances have provided the following new ways to restore vision after the lens is removed.

- *Intraocular lenses (IOLs).* These permanent lenses are implanted inside the eye during the cataract surgery.
- *Hard or soft contact lenses,* which can be worn all day but are taken out at night.
- *Special extended-wear soft contact lenses,* which are appropriate for longer wear.

• **Cataract glasses.** These are thinner and lighter than they used to be but are still thicker than most ordinary glasses.

Although the intraocular lens is by far the most popular choice, there are advantages and disadvantages to each type of lens replacement. An ophthalmologist helps the patient decide which lens or combination of lenses is best suited to their lifestyle and eye health.

Fortunately, cataract surgery is highly successful and over 90 percent of patients who undergo surgery regain useful vision. It is important to understand that complications during or after surgery can occur. As with any surgery, a good result cannot be guaranteed.

LOSS OF SIGHT IS LARGELY PREVENTABLE

If you notice any cataract symptoms, consult an ophthalmologist as soon as possible. Since cataracts most often form as a result of aging, individuals over the age of 40 with a family history of cataracts should have their eyes checked periodically.

There is no known preventive measure for cataracts, but modern cataract surgery is highly effective and permanent vision loss is usually preventable. Once diagnosed, mild cataracts can be watched to see if they progress. If vision loss due to a cataract is interfering with your daily activities, there is usually no reason to delay surgical treatment. Fortunately, a cataract patient no longer needs to become nearly blind before cataracts can be removed.

The American Academy of Ophthalmology

GLAUCOMA

Glaucoma is an eye disease which is one of the leading causes of blindness in the United States. Two out of every 100 people over the age of 35 have their vision threatened by this disease. Yet when diagnosed early, blindness from glaucoma is almost always preventable.

When we look at an object, the image is carried from the retina to the brain by the nerve of sight (the optic nerve). This nerve is like an electric cable. It contains a million wires, each carrying a message to the brain, which join together to provide side vision, as well as sharp, central reading vision. Glaucoma can produce damage to these wires, causing blind spots in areas of vision to develop. People seldom notice these blind areas in the side vision until considerable optic nerve damage has occurred. If the entire nerve is destroyed, blindness results. Fortunately, this rarely occurs if glaucoma is diagnosed and treated before major damage has taken place.

The key to preventing optic nerve damage or blindness from glaucoma is early diagnosis and treatment. Many doctors can test for glaucoma as part of a periodic physical examination. An ophthalmologist is the medical doctor who is specifically trained to perform this examination and treat this condition. Medical eye examinations from an ophthalmologist are

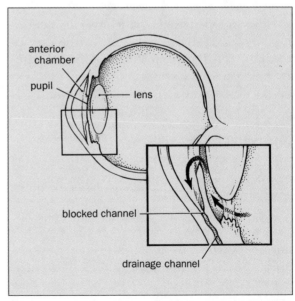

Normally, aqueous humor flows continually through the structures of the inner eye. In glaucoma, this flow is blocked, so that pressure builds up within the eye.

the best defense against glaucoma. For this reason, adults should see an ophthalmologist for periodic eye examinations.

CAUSES AND SYMPTOMS

A clear, transparent liquid called the aqueous humor flows through the inner eye continuously. This inner flow can be compared to a sink with the faucet turned on all the time. If the drainpipe gets clogged, water collects in the sink. If the drainage system of the eye gets similarly blocked, the fluid pressure within the inner eye is increased and can cause damage to the optic nerve.

Blockage of these drainpipes can occur in four ways.

Chronic Open-Angle Glaucoma

Most commonly, the drainpipe can become smaller with age, clogged by deposits which build up slowly. This partial blockage causes a gradual increase of pressure within the eye. This is known as chronic open-angle glaucoma because it develops slowly over a period of time. Most adult glaucoma patients have this type of glaucoma.

Chronic open-angle glaucoma can steal vision so quietly that the patient is unaware of trouble until the optic nerve is badly damaged. Because no symptoms occur, the best way to diagnose this form of glaucoma is by periodic medical eye examination.

Congenital Glaucoma

The drainpipe may have been incorrectly manufactured.

This type of defect is seen in congenital glaucoma, where the drainage openings are abnormal from birth. Since an infant's eye has more elasticity than an adult's when pressure inside the eye is increased, the easily stretchable eye may enlarge. The front of the eye may become cloudy like fog on a windshield. The infant may be sensitive to light and tear excessively. This is a rare condition.

Acute Angle-Closure Glaucoma

A sheet of paper may float near the drain, suddenly drop over the opening, close up the drainage area, and block all outflow. In the eye, the iris may act like the sheet of paper and press up against the drainage area and close it off. Fluid backs up and increases eye pressure rapidly. Such a sudden, complete blockage of fluid flowing out of the eye results in acute angle-closure glaucoma.

Blurred vision, severe pain, rainbow haloes around lights, nausea, and vomiting should bring the patient quickly to an eye physician. Unless this condition is relieved promptly, blindness can result in a day or two.

Secondary Glaucoma

Other conditions, including hemorrhages, tumors, and inflammations, can sometimes block outflow channels in the eye. This may increase inner eye pressure and lead to secondary glaucoma.

DETECTION AND DIAGNOSIS

Early diagnosis can be made by your ophthalmologist in the course of a periodic eye examination. During the painless examination, the eye physician will determine the pressure of the eye. This is only part of the examination for glaucoma. Using an instrument called an ophthalmoscope, the ophthalmologist will examine the back of your eye to see if the optic nerve is healthy and that no damage is occurring. Sometimes, side vision will be tested for shrinkage or blind spots. If necessary, still other tests may be done.

On occasion, a patient will be found to have an eye pressure over the normal range, but no evidence of damage from glaucoma. Some people seem to tolerate high eye pressures without ever developing loss of vision. However, in these cases it is important for the ophthalmologist to consider additional causes which may add to a person's risk of developing damage from glaucoma. A history of glaucoma in the family or general health problems such as diabetes, hardening of the arteries, or anemia are examples of risk factors. African-American patients are also at an increased risk for glaucoma.

The ophthalmologist must weigh all of these factors before deciding whether a patient needs treatment for glaucoma, or whether the patient should be monitored closely as a glaucoma suspect since the risk of developing glaucoma is higher than normal.

TREATMENT

Glaucoma is usually controlled with eye drops given two to four times a day or by pills given in various combinations. These medications act to decrease eye pressure either by assisting flow of fluid out of the eye or by decreasing the amount of fluid entering the eye. To be effective, these medications must be taken regularly and continuously.

Patients with any type of glaucoma need periodic examination. Glaucoma sometimes gets worse (or better) without the patient being aware of it; as a result, treatment may need to be changed after a while.

As a rule, damage caused by glaucoma cannot be reversed. Eye drops, pills, and surgery are used to prevent further damage from occurring, and to preserve existing vision.

However, treatment may occasionally result in unwanted side effects. Some eye drops may sting, redden the eye, and cause blurring or occasional headaches. Such side effects usually disappear after a few weeks. Though rare, other drops may affect pulse, heartbeat, and breathing. Pills sometimes cause tingling of fingers and toes, drowsiness, loss of appetite, bowel irregularities, and occasional kidney stone formation. They are usually prescribed only when absolutely necessary. You should notify your ophthalmologist immediately if there is a question of possible side effects.

GLAUCOMA AND YOU

Control of glaucoma by drugs can only be effective if patients adhere to the treatment schedule prescribed by their ophthalmologists. The treatment team is made up of both you and your doctor. Medication should never be stopped without first consulting your ophthalmologist. It is always important to inform all the physicians you visit about the eye medications you are using. Remember, it is your vision, and you must do your part in maintaining it.

If medications are poorly tolerated or not effective in controlling glaucoma, surgery may become necessary. In some cases, almost painless surgery without an incision can be done with the laser beam. In other cases, a cut in the eye to form a drainage canal is necessary. Complications such as cataract or infection may occur. Fortunately, serious complications of modern glaucoma surgery are rare. In most cases, recommended surgery is safer than permitting continuing loss of the optic nerve from glaucoma.

WHO TREATS GLAUCOMA

An ophthalmologist is the medical doctor (M.D. or osteopath) who is educated, trained, and licensed to provide total care of the eyes, including the diagnosis and treatment of the many different types of glaucoma. Total eye care includes performing comprehensive medical eye examinations, prescribing corrective lenses, diagnosing diseases and disorders of the eye, and using the appropriate medical and surgical procedures necessary for their treatment. Only an ophthalmologist can provide total eye care.

LOSS OF VISION IS LARGELY PREVENTABLE

If you are over age 40, you should have your eyes checked for glaucoma every two to four years. If you are African-American and over age 20, you are at greater risk for glaucoma and should have your eyes checked every three to five years. Your ophthalmologist should be consulted whenever there is any decrease in vision or recurrent pain, or when any of the other symptoms discussed here are present. When diagnosed promptly, eye pressure can be brought under control and future glaucoma attacks can be prevented.

The American Academy of Ophthalmology

MACULAR DEGENERATION

As the eye looks straight ahead, the macula is the point of the retina upon which the light rays meet as they are focused by the cornea and the lens of the eye. Similar to the film in a camera, the retina receives the images that come through the cameralike lens. If the macula is damaged, the central part of the images are blocked as if a blurred area had been placed in the center of the picture. The images around the blurred area may be clearly visible.

Macular degeneration is damage or breakdown of the macula. The eye still sees objects to the side, since side, or peripheral, vision is usually not affected. For this reason, macular

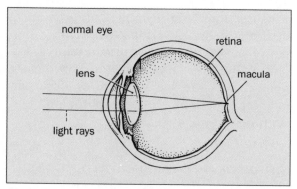

The macula is the part of the retina that distinguishes fine detail. An abnormal growth of blood vessels and scarring causes macular degeneration.

degeneration alone does not result in total blindness. However, it can make reading or close work difficult or impossible without the use of special low vision optical aids.

The retina is the delicate layer of tissue that lines the inside wall of the back of the eye. The macula is a very small area in the center of the retina. In size, the macula is about the same as this capital O. This small area is responsible for our central straight-ahead sight used for reading and other fine tasks.

Although macular degeneration most often occurs in older people, aging alone does not always result in central visual loss. Nevertheless, macular degeneration is the leading cause of impairment of reading and fine close-up vision in the United States.

CAUSES

Involutional macular degeneration. This is the most common form of macular degeneration. It accounts for 70 percent of all cases, and is associated with aging. It is caused by a breakdown or thinning of the tissues in the macula.

Exudative macular degeneration. About 10 percent of macular degeneration falls into a category called exudative macular degeneration. Normally, the macula is protected by a thin tissue that separates it from very fine blood vessels nourishing the back of the eye. Sometimes these blood vessels break or leak and cause scar tissue to form. This often leads to the growth of new abnormal blood vessels in the scar tissue. These newly formed vessels are especially fragile. They rupture easily and may leak. Blood and leaking fluid destroy the macula and cause further scarring. Vision becomes distorted and blurred, and dense scar tissue blocks out central vision to a severe degree.

Other types of macular degeneration are inherited, may occur in juveniles (juvenile macular degeneration), and are not associated with the aging process. Occasionally, injury, infection, or inflammation may also damage the delicate tissue of the macula.

SYMPTOMS

If only one eye is affected, macular degeneration is hardly noticeable in the beginning stages, particularly when the other eye is normal. This condition often involves one eye at a time, so it may be some time before a patient notices visual problems.

Macular degeneration can cause different symptoms in different people. Sometimes only one eye loses vision while the other eye continues to see well for many years. If both eyes are affected, however, reading and close-up work may become extremely difficult. Macular degeneration alone does not cause total blindness. Since side vision is usually unaffected, most people can take care of themselves quite well.

Color vision may become dim and these other visual symptoms can develop due to macular degeneration.

- Words on a page look blurred.
- Straight lines look distorted and, in some cases, the center of vision looks more distorted than the rest of the scene.
- A dark or empty area appears in the center of vision.

DETECTION AND DIAGNOSIS

Many patients do not realize they have a macular problem until blurred vision becomes obvious. Your ophthalmologist can detect macular degeneration in the early stages. The ophthalmologist examines the macula carefully by viewing it with an instrument called an ophthalmoscope to see if damage is present.

The examination will usually include a few more tests.

- *A grid test,* in which the patient is asked to look at a test page (similar to graph paper), will be used to check for the extent of sight loss spots.
- *A color vision test* will reveal whether a patient can discern color differences, and additional tests will help to discover conditions that may be causing deterioration of the macula.
- *A fluorescein angiogram* sometimes is done. The ophthalmologist injects a dye into the patient's arm, and then takes photos of the retina and macula. The dye helps to clarify any blood vessel abnormality that might be present.

Macular degeneration can be detected and diagnosed early by an ophthalmologist if periodic eye examinations are part of health care. Early detection is important since people may not realize their vision is impaired. Having your eyes checked is especially appropriate if other family members have a history of retinal problems. For patients with macular degeneration, early diagnosis by an ophthalmologist may prevent further damage or aid the individual in making a visual adjustment with low vision aids.

MEDICAL AND SURGICAL TREATMENT

There is no cure for the most common involutional form of macular degeneration. However, ophthalmologic laser surgery has been used to retard the spread of the less common exudative form, but only if this treatment is applied in the very early stages of the condition. In this treatment, a focused intense beam of laser light is used to seal off leaking membranes and destroy new blood vessels. This reduces further loss of vision from progressive scarring of the macula and the surrounding retina.

OPTICAL AIDS AND LIGHTING

Low vision optical aids often improve vision for people with macular degeneration. Many

THE BEST SUNGLASSES

A few years ago, a team of researchers from Johns Hopkins conducted a study involving over 800 fishermen from the Chesapeake Bay area, and found that the incidence of cataracts in this group was three times greater than the average. The likely culprit: the invisible but damaging ultraviolet (UV) radiation in the sun's rays. Further research, including a large-scale international study, has since confirmed these findings. Recently, upon re-analyzing the data, the team also discovered some evidence that the wavelengths of visible sunlight that we see as blue light may hasten macular degeneration (deterioration of the central portion of the retina), the fastest growing cause of legal blindness among older Americans.

Fortunately, sunglasses provide simple and effective protection from these hazards, with no risk of side effects. Unfortunately, some marketers have hoped to parlay such research into profit, and are offering sunglasses that provide UV and blue-light protection at prices often approaching or even exceeding $100 a pair. But experts say protecting your eyes need not cost you an arm and a leg.

Dr. Sheila West, associate professor of ophthalmology at Johns Hopkins, and a specialist in light toxicity and the epidemiology of macular degeneration, as well as a co-author of the Chesapeake Bay study, points out that while the research does suggest a correlation between blue light and retinal damage, it would be premature to base any edicts on these findings. "For one thing, the study turned up only eight cases of macular degeneration. How can you make any precise claims from that? Our research is only very preliminary, and mainly indicates the need for further research." And even if the research did indicate that everyone should wear UV and blue-light blocking sunglasses, a high price tag alone in no way ensures the best protection. In fact, when Dr. West and her team tested dozens of pairs of glasses for overall effectiveness against UV and blue light, the very best turned out to be a pair that one of the researchers had received free in a promotion at a Baltimore Orioles game. Put simply: "Wearing sunglasses is prudent and can do no harm," says Dr. West. "But spending one or two hundred dollars is throwing your money away." You should be able to find a perfectly adequate pair for under $20. If the price tag is not a reliable criterion for choosing the best sunglasses, then what factors should you consider?

Adequate UV Protection/The ANSI Label

Many makers (even of very inexpensive brands) voluntarily label their glasses in accord with American National Standard Institute (ANSI) guidelines for UV protection, which fall into three categories: cosmetic, general purpose, and special purpose.

• *Cosmetic glasses* block at least 70 percent of UVB radiation (the particular wavelengths associated with cataracts); 20 percent of UVA rays (the longer wavelengths of UV, also possibly harmful to the eyes, though probably less so than UVB); and 60 percent of

different types of magnifying devices are available. Spectacles, hand or stand magnifiers, telescopes, and closed circuit television for viewing objects are some of the available resources. Aids are either prescribed by your ophthalmologist or by referral to a low vision specialist or center.

Bright illumination properly directed for reading and close work is often beneficial. Special lamps can also be helpful. Books, newspapers, and other items available in large print offer further help.

A patient with macular degeneration can be helped. Fortunately, visual aids are available to assist many patients in leading a comfortable and relatively normal life. With these devices and proper motivation, people with visual loss can often read, do modified close-up work, and continue to take care of themselves.

If you are over age 50, or if your family has a history of retinal problems, you should have your eyes checked periodically for signs of eye problems like macular degeneration. Early detection and subsequent treatment, if indicated, may help prevent additional visual loss.

The American Academy of Ophthalmology

light from the visible portion of the spectrum. These usually lightly tinted lenses are recommended for everyday, around-town wear, when constant harsh light isn't a problem.

• *General-purpose glasses* have medium to dark lenses that block at least 95 percent of UVB rays, 60 percent of UVA, and 60 to 90 percent of visible light. These are good for most outdoor activities, such as driving or playing tennis. Most sunglasses, whether they say so or not, fall into this category (even many pairs costing under $5).

• *Special-purpose sunglasses* must block 99 percent of UVB, 60 percent of UVA, and 97 percent of visible light. They tend to be very dark, and are advised for extremely bright conditions, such as you might find on ski slopes or tropical beaches.

Color

Gray and green lenses distort colors least. You can get greater protection from blue light with reddish, orange, or amber lenses. Glasses that promise 100 percent blockage of blue light are fine, but may be quite expensive, and some people who try them complain of headaches.

Darkness

One common misconception about sunglasses is that darker lenses necessarily mean greater protection. Even clear lenses can provide total UV protection if specially pretreated, while some dark ones might offer significantly less. Again, check for ANSI labels.

The most important thing is that you see well out of your glasses; they should be neither too dark nor too light. Gradient lenses are good for driving since they have less tint at the bottom, enabling you to see the dashboard better.

Size and Fit

The frames should be large enough to keep light out from around all sides. Glasses that slip down your nose even half an inch allow about 20 percent of unfiltered sunlight to reach your eyes. Wraparound styles, popular among skiers, are a good safeguard against this. Make sure the frames don't interfere with your peripheral vision.

Gimmicks

Don't let them fool you. Some companies claim that their glasses improve the clarity of your vision (only prescription lenses can do that); some sell their glasses with vitamin supplement packets that are supposed to restore or protect your vision. Such ploys are grossly misleading.

You might, however, want to consult an ophthalmologist if your job or hobby finds you outside for hours at a stretch, or if you are fair-skinned and have blue or green eyes, or are elderly—especially if you've had cataract surgery or are taking a drug (such as tetracycline) that may increase your sensitivity to ultraviolet light. If you fall into one of these high-risk groups, consider buying special-purpose sunglasses.

The Editors

REFRACTIVE ERRORS

To see clearly, light rays pass through the eye and are focused on the retina that lines the back wall of the eye. The cornea, which is the clear front window of the eye, and the lens inside the eye are responsible for bending, or refracting, light rays so that they focus properly. The retina receives the picture formed by the light rays and sends the image to the brain through the optic nerve.

Myopia (nearsightedness), hyperopia (farsightedness), and astigmatism (distorted vision) are caused by differences in the length or the shape of the eye. Presbyopia (aging eye) occurs when the lens inside the eye loses its focusing ability for near vision.

These conditions are referred to as refractive errors because the shape of the eye affects the way the eye refracts, or bends, light and focuses it on the retina.

It is usual for refractive errors to occur within a certain range. Outside of this range, the error is considered high, as in high myopia or high hyperopia. Other medical prob-

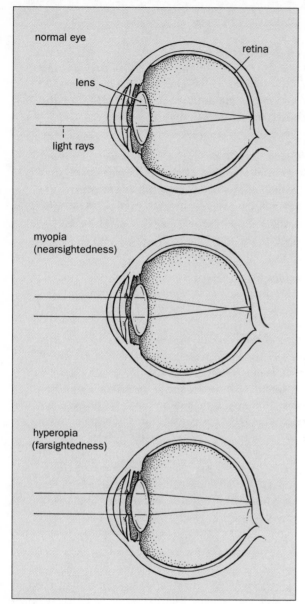

In a normal eye, light focuses precisely on the retina. In nearsightedness, light focuses short of the retina; in farsightedness, beyond the retina.

MYOPIA

Myopia is the medical word for nearsightedness, a condition in which the eyes can see objects that are close but are unable to see distant objects clearly. The word myopia comes from a Greek word for "closed eyes" because people with this condition often squint their eyes to see better in the distance.

Most commonly, myopia is an inherited trait that often becomes evident in children at about eight to twelve years of age. Typically, the condition increases as the body grows during teenage years before leveling off in adulthood.

The major factor influencing nearsightedness is heredity or a family history of nearsightedness. Few factors other than heredity influence nearsightedness. Reading too much, using eyes in dim light, or deficiencies in nutrition do not cause or affect myopia.

Usually myopia is the result of a lengthened eyeball. The eye becomes more oval than round, and because of this increased length, it is impossible for the lens to change its shape sufficiently to focus light from distant objects clearly on the retina. Rarely, myopia can also be caused by a change in the curvature of the cornea or a change in the shape of the lens in the eye.

Nearly everyone with myopia has what is called simple myopia, which increases as the body grows. Although myopia increases, it is the result of normal growth changes. As a child's body grows during adolescence, there are often changes in the length of the eye requiring new eyeglasses as frequently as every six months, much like getting larger shoes to fit growing feet. Myopia may progress rapidly for several years and then change very little thereafter. Between the ages of 20 to 40, there is usually very little change, although an adult form of myopia may occur in the early twenties.

Treatment

Myopia is best treated with eyeglasses or contact lenses. The lenses do not reverse the con-

lems within the eye occur more often when the refractive error is in the high range.

The major symptoms of refractive errors are decreased vision, eye discomfort, or eye strain. They are entirely correctable with the appropriate glasses or contact lenses.

dition but they compensate for the longer shape of the eye by refracting, or bending, light rays to focus on the retina.

There is no scientific evidence that wearing contact lenses or doing eye exercises can stop the progression of myopia. Although some individuals have been fitted with a series of hard contact lenses in a process called orthokeratology, improvement of sight is temporary. After the use of the lenses is discontinued, the cornea returns to its original shape and myopia returns.

Medical treatment for myopia with the use of special drops (atropine) and bifocal glasses has been studied in recent years and appears to be effective in some cases.

Surgical treatment for myopia is now being studied by the federal government. So-called refractive surgery has a number of forms, the most common being a procedure called radial keratotomy. In this surgical procedure, a number of pie-shaped incisions are made into the cornea. As a result, scars are created and these cause the cornea to change its shape. The amount of change is not completely predictable, and long-term results of this surgery are still unclear.

Most ophthalmologists feel that eyes with simple myopia are best treated with glasses or contact lenses. Those who have myopia should have yearly vision tests.

PATHOLOGIC MYOPIA

Pathologic myopia is a rare form of myopia which may cause sight loss that cannot be corrected by glasses or contact lenses. The condition is usually inherited and may progress rapidly, causing the retina to tear and detach from the back of the eye.

Frequent medical eye examinations by an ophthalmologist are needed to watch for signs of these changes. Although pathologic myopia may cause impairment of vision, new methods of treatment usually prevent this condition from resulting in blindness.

HYPEROPIA

Hyperopia is the medical term for farsightedness. In this condition, the eyeball is usually shorter than normal (opposite from myopia, where the eye is often too long). This shortness makes it difficult for the lens to focus light from close-up objects clearly on the retina. Rarely, a flattening of the cornea or thinning of the lens in front of the eye may also cause farsightedness.

Treatment

Hyperopia is most often corrected with the use of glasses or contact lenses.

ASTIGMATISM

Astigmatism is most often caused by distortion or an irregularity of the cornea, the front surface of the eye. For normal, undistorted vision, the cornea should be smooth and equally curved in all directions. When an individual has astigmatism, the cornea is warped and it curves more in one direction than in the other. In other words, the cornea is shaped more like a football than a basketball. The effect of astigmatism is to change vision similar to that seen when looking at a mirror with a wavy surface, like the funhouse mirrors that make you seem too tall or too wide or too thin.

Astigmatism is usually inherited, may be present at birth, and frequently remains unchanged throughout life. Small amounts of astigmatism are very common and often do not require correction with glasses or contact lenses.

Treatment

Correction of astigmatism is not difficult if the distortion proceeds in a regular or straight line across the cornea. In such instances, a similar wave can be ordered as a prescription in the glasses to neutralize or offset the distortion of the cornea. In some instances, however, such as a scar following an injury to the eye, the distortion of the cornea may be irregular. So-called irregular astigmatism is more difficult to correct and often can be improved only by making a totally new surface on the cornea. This may be accomplished either by applying a hard contact lens, or by performing a corneal transplant, which involves removing the old scarred cornea and replacing it with donated tissue.

Normally, the blur from astigmatism is corrected with glasses or contact lenses. Hard or gas-permeable contact lenses improve astigmatism better than soft contact lenses, but special soft contact lenses which correct astigmatism are sometimes helpful. If the amount of astigmatism is very large, glasses that correct the condition may cause some distortion of side vision. Very large amounts of astigmatism are not easily corrected with a contact lens either, since the lens may wobble on the wavy surface of the cornea. In such instances, a special contact lens, called a toric lens, may be ground with a curve in the back surface to stabilize the lens on the cornea.

PRESBYOPIA

As people become older and experience more difficulty in focusing their eyes for close objects, glasses are necessary for reading and close-up work. This condition is called presbyopia (aging eyes).

Most people are not bothered by farsightedness until after the age of 40, when the lens of the eye loses some of its flexibility and cannot focus sharply on near objects. Presbyopia is an inevitable companion of middle age.

Treatment

Presbyopia is usually corrected with reading glasses. No treatment including diet or exercise is known to either increase or decrease its progress. Bifocal or trifocal lenses may be prescribed for persons with presbyopia who have other errors of refraction such as myopia, hyperopia, or astigmatism.

HEADACHES

Headaches are only rarely due to refractive errors. If the headache comes after prolonged use of the eyes and is relieved by resting the eyes, it may indicate a refractive error; however, the vast majority of headaches have no relation to a need for corrective lenses.

The American Academy of Ophthalmology

AMAUROSIS FUGAX

A temporary blockage of blood supply to the eye, called amaurosis fugax or fleeting blindness, can cause a temporary loss of vision in one eye. This sometimes appears like a curtain descending over all or part of your vision in that eye and may last for seconds or several hours. This is a sign of carotid artery disease.

WHAT IS THE CAROTID ARTERY?

The two carotid arteries are the main arteries in the neck which supply blood to the eyes and the brain. One carotid artery supplies the right side, while the other serves the left. Because the eye and the brain share the same source of blood supply, blockages or conditions of the carotid artery can affect either or both organs.

WHAT HAPPENS WHEN THE CAROTID ARTERY IS BLOCKED?

When the large or small branches of the carotid artery are blocked, the brain is deprived of blood and a stroke may result. Depending on the part of the brain involved and the size of the area deprived of its blood supply, the effects of a stroke may be slight or devastating. Severe effects can include paralysis of one side of the body and loss of speech. If the part of the brain having to do with vision is involved, a stroke can lead to loss of side vision. When the ophthalmic artery (the first main branch of the internal carotid artery) or its branch (the central retinal artery) is blocked, a sudden, near-total loss of vision usually occurs. The mechanism of damage is the same in the brain and the eye. Cells die if they are deprived of blood for too long.

IS THIS DAMAGE PERMANENT?

Not everyone who suffers a blocked blood supply to the eye or the brain has permanent damage. A temporary blockage of blood supply to the brain, called a transient ischemic attack (TIA), may result in muscle weakness on one side of the face or numbness of an arm or leg which only lasts about an hour.

Both amaurosis fugax and transient ischemic attacks are possible warnings of a serious problem involving the brain's blood supply. They should be reported to an ophthalmologist, who may recommend further tests.

ARE THERE OTHER SIGNS OF CAROTID ARTERY DISEASE?

As part of a routine eye exam, the ophthalmologist may dilate the pupil to examine the retina at the back of the eye. During this procedure, conditions which could indicate an increased risk of stroke may sometimes be discovered.

For instance, when the carotid artery becomes gradually blocked with fat and calcium deposits, the first signs can appear in the eye, providing critical clues to a life-threatening reduction of circulation to the brain.

If a plaque is found during a routine eye exam, further evaluation may be indicated. Other plaques from the carotid artery may break off, block the brain's blood supply, and cause a stroke.

WHAT FURTHER TESTS OR TREATMENTS MAY BE NEEDED?

Ultrasound may be helpful to measure the flow of blood through the arteries. When a more accurate view of the arteries is required, a special x-ray test called an angiogram or angiography may be ordered. Angiography involves injecting an iodine-containing dye into the artery and taking pictures of the blood flowing into the brain. If an abnormality is found, surgery may be recommended to correct the blockage. The most common operation is an endarterectomy, in which the blockage on the inner wall of the artery is removed.

The American Academy of Ophthalmology

FLOATERS AND FLASHES

The small specks, bugs, or clouds that you may sometimes see moving in your field of vision are called floaters. They are frequently visible when looking at a plain background, such as a blank wall or blue sky. These visual phenomena have been described for centuries; the an-

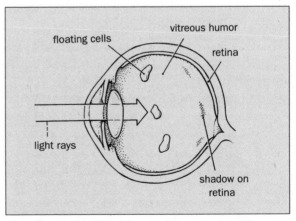

Tiny clumps of protein, or "floaters," may drift around in the vitreous humor, and often create little shadows on the retina.

cient Romans called them "muscae volitantes" or "flying flies," since they can appear like small flies moving around in the air. Floaters are actually tiny clumps of gel or cellular debris within the vitreous, the clear jellylike fluid that fills the inside cavity of the eye. Although these objects appear to be in front of the eye, they are actually floating in the fluid inside the eye and cast their shadows on the retina (the light-sensing inner layer of the eye).

WHAT CAUSES FLOATERS?

The vitreous gel degenerates in middle age, often forming microscopic clumps or strands within the eye. Vitreous shrinkage or condensation is called posterior vitreous detachment, and is a common cause of floaters. It also occurs frequently in nearsighted people or in those who have undergone cataract operations or YAG laser surgery. Occasionally, floaters result from inflammation within the eye or from crystal-like deposits which form in the vitreous gel.

The appearance of floaters, whether in the form of little dots, circles, lines, clouds, or cobwebs, may be alarming, especially if they develop suddenly. However, they are usually nothing to be concerned about, and simply result from the normal aging process.

ARE FLOATERS EVER SERIOUS?

The vitreous covers the retinal surface. Occasionally the retina can become torn when degenerating vitreous gel pulls away. This causes a small amount of bleeding in the eye which may appear as a group of new floaters. A torn retina can be serious if it develops into a retinal detachment.

If you experience any sudden onset of many new floaters or flashes of light, this should be promptly evaluated by your medical eye doctor. Additional symptoms, especially loss of peripheral or side vision, require repeat ophthalmic examination.

WHAT CAN BE DONE ABOUT FLOATERS?

Floaters may interfere with clear vision, often when reading, and can be quite annoying. Although there is no treatment or cure for most floaters, they usually diminish over time. You can take simple steps to temporarily move them from your sight. If a floater appears directly in your line of vision, try moving your eye around. The inside fluid may swirl and allow the floater to move out of the way. We are most used to moving our eyes side to side, but looking up and down will cause different currents within the eye and may be more effective in getting the floaters out of the way.

WHAT CAUSES LIGHT FLASHES?

When the vitreous gel which fills the inside of the eye rubs or pulls on the retina, it sometimes produces the illusion of flashing lights or lightning streaks. You may have experienced this same sensation if you have ever been hit in the eye and seen stars. The flashes of light may appear off and on for weeks or months. This commonly occurs as we age and is usually not cause for worry. On rare occasions, however, light flashes accompany a large number of new floaters and even a partial loss or shadowing of side vision. If this happens, prompt examination by a medical eye doctor is important to determine if a torn retina or retinal detachment has occurred.

Flashes of light appearing as jagged lines or heat waves, often lasting 10 to 20 minutes and present in both eyes, are likely to be migraine caused by a spasm of blood vessels in the brain. If a headache follows, it is called a migraine headache. However, these lines or heat waves usually occur without a subsequent headache. In this case, the light flashes are referred to as ophthalmic migraine, or migraine without headache. As with floaters, if you experience the abrupt onset of many light flashes, you should be examined by an ophthalmologist.

The American Academy of Ophthalmology

The Heart and Blood Vessels

The circulatory system is the network of elastic tubes through which blood flows as it carries oxygen and nutrients to all parts of the body. It includes the heart, lungs, arteries, arterioles (small arteries), and capillaries (minute blood vessels). It also includes venules (small veins) and veins, the blood vessels through which blood flows as it returns to the heart and lungs.

The circulating blood brings oxygen and nutrients to all the organs and tissues of the body, including the heart itself. It also picks up waste products from the body's cells. These waste products are eliminated as they're filtered through the kidneys, liver, and lungs.

The normal heart is a strong, muscular pump a little larger than a fist. It pumps blood continuously through the circulatory system. Each day the average heart "beats" (or expands and contracts) 100,000 times and pumps about 2,000 gallons of blood. In a 70-year lifetime, an average human heart beats more than 2.5 billion times.

The heart has four chambers. The upper two are the atria; the lower two, the ventricles. Blood is pumped through them, aided by four valves that open and close to allow blood to flow in only one direction when the heart contracts (beats).

The four heart valves are: (1) the tricuspid valve, located between the right atrium and right ventricle; (2) the pulmonary (pulmonic) valve, between the right ventricle and the pulmonary artery; (3) the mitral valve, between the left atrium and left ventricle; and (4) the aortic valve, between the left ventricle and the aorta. Each valve has a set of flaps (also called leaflets or cusps). The mitral valve has two flaps; the others have three. Under normal conditions, the valves permit blood to flow in only one direction. Blood flow occurs only when there's a difference in pressure across the valves that causes them to open.

The heart pumps blood to the lungs and to all the body's tissues by a sequence of highly organized contractions of its four chambers. The heart works as follows:

The right atrium receives blood from the veins. This blood carries little oxygen and lots of carbon dioxide, because it's returning from the body's tissues, where much of the oxygen was removed and the carbon dioxide added. Ve-

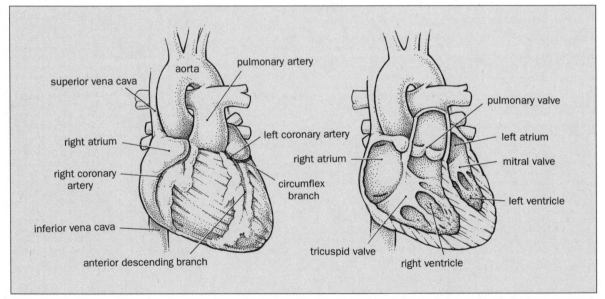

The heart (here in exterior and cut-away views) actually consists of two separate pumps. The right ventricle delivers blood to the lungs to be oxygenated; the left ventricle pumps this blood out to the body.

AORTIC STENOSIS

Aortic stenosis is a narrowing of the aortic valve opening, which causes the left ventricle of the heart to work harder to overcome the resistance of the narrowed passageway. This added workload can cause irremediable damage to the left ventricle and lead to left ventricular failure.

Aortic stenosis can be present without symptoms, and so it may be first detected as a heart murmur on a routine physical examination. But, because the narrowing of the valve opening causes the amount of blood pumped from the heart to be inadequate to meet the needs of the body—especially the needs of the brain—it may result in such symptoms as fatigue, fainting, shortness of breath, and angina. Sudden cardiac death may occur.

More common in men than women, aortic stenosis can be caused by rheumatic fever or a congenital defect. Among older people, however, it is most often caused by deposits of calcium on a previously normal aortic valve, a phenomenon associated with the aging process. If there are significant symptoms, surgery may be required. With recent techniques of valve replacement surgery, the outlook is generally good if stenosis is relieved before extensive damage is done to the left ventricle.

The Editors

nous blood is darker in color than arterial blood because of the difference in dissolved gases.

While the heart is relaxed, venous blood flows through the open tricuspid valve to fill the right ventricle. An electrical signal starts the heartbeat by causing the atria to contract. This contraction "tops off" the filling of the ventricle. Shortly after the atrium contracts, the right ventricle contracts. As this occurs, the tricuspid valve closes and the partially deoxygenated blood is pumped through the pulmonary valve, into the pulmonary artery, and on to the lungs. In the lungs the blood gives up its carbon dioxide and gets oxygen before returning to the left atrium. This newly oxygenated blood is bright red.

At the same time the chambers of the right heart contract, the left atrium contracts, topping off the flow of oxygenated blood through the mitral valve and into the left ventricle. Then a split second later the left ventricle contracts, pumping blood through the aortic valve, into the aorta, and on to the body's tissues.

For the heart to function properly, the four chambers must beat in an organized manner. This is governed by the electrical impulse. A chamber of the heart contracts when an electrical impulse or signal moves across it. Such a signal starts in a small bundle of highly specialized cells located in the right atrium—the sinoatrial node (SA node). A discharge from this natural "pacemaker" causes the heart to beat. This pacemaker generates electrical impulses at a given rate, but emotional reactions and hormonal factors can affect its rate of discharge. This allows the heart rate to respond to varying demands.

The electrical impulses generated by the SA node move throughout the right and left atrium, causing the muscle cells to contract. Shortly after both atria have contracted, the electrical signal travels down specialized fibers throughout the ventricles. The path of the signal causes the ventricles to contract together in a wringing motion, squeezing blood from them. The route of this electrical impulse is specific and produces the coordinated sequential contraction of the heart's four chambers that's necessary for the heart to function properly.

ATHEROSCLEROSIS

Arteriosclerosis is a general term for the thickening and hardening of arteries. Some hardening of arteries normally occurs when

ABDOMINAL ANEURYSM

An aneurysm—an egg-shaped ballooning out of a weakened wall of an artery—can occur in any artery in the body. It is most common, however, in the lower aorta, the main blood vessel that carries blood from the heart into the arteries of the legs. Although aneurysms can be caused by disease or injury or a congenital defect in the arterial wall, abdominal aneurysms are most often the result of atherosclerosis, and they occur most commonly among men over the age of 60. They frequently develop without symptoms, although in their advanced stage they may cause lower back pain. More often, they are found on routine examination.

Aneurysms usually grow slowly, at the rate of one-eighth to one-fourth inch a year. Although aneurysms of any size may burst—and so cause rapid hemorrhaging and death—the larger the aneurysm, the more likely it is to rupture. If your physician discovers an aneurysm, he may well decide simply to monitor its progress if you are not suffering any pain, and the aneurysm is not too large. But if the aneurysm is causing pain, is larger than 6 cm, or is rapidly increasing in size, surgery is called for. During surgery, the damaged artery is replaced by a synthetic vessel. The risk of elective surgery for such aneurysms is small, while less than half of those survive the surgery if they are operated on after the aneurysm ruptures. *The Editors*

(2) formation of a blood clot (thrombus) on the plaque's surface. If either of these occurs and blocks the entire artery, a heart attack or stroke may result.

Atherosclerosis affects large and medium-sized arteries. The type of artery and where the plaque develops varies with the individual.

Atherosclerosis is a slow, progressive disease that may start in childhood. In some people this disease progresses rapidly in their third decade; in others it doesn't become threatening until they're in their 50s or 60s.

HOW ATHEROSCLEROSIS STARTS

The development of atherosclerosis is a complex process. Precisely how atherosclerosis begins or what causes it isn't known, but several theories have been proposed.

Many scientists believe atherosclerosis begins because the innermost layer of the artery (endothelium) becomes damaged. As a result, over time fats, cholesterol, fibrin, platelets, cellular debris, and calcium are deposited in the artery wall. Gradually these substances build up and eventually narrow and block the artery, similar to scale forming on the insides of pipes.

Three of the possible causes of damage to the arterial wall are: (1) elevated levels of cholesterol and triglyceride in the blood, (2) high blood pressure, and (3) cigarette smoking. Cigarette smoking particularly aggravates and accelerates the development of atherosclerosis in the coronary arteries, aorta, and arteries of the legs.

Once cells in the artery wall are damaged, they may separate from the wall, exposing the tissue (collagen, smooth muscle, and other tissue) underneath. Initially, platelets (elements in the blood that help form blood clots) stick to the collagen, which ultimately leads to the formation of plaque. Over time atherosclerosis increases, reducing the diameter of the artery. Eventually a blood clot may form at the site of damage, blocking the

people grow older. Atherosclerosis, a type of arteriosclerosis, comes from the Greek word "athero" (meaning gruel or paste) and "sclerosis" (hardness).

It's characterized by deposits of fatty substances, cholesterol, cellular waste products, calcium, and fibrin (a clotting material in the blood) in the inner lining of an artery. The resulting buildup is called plaque.

Plaque may partially or totally block the blood's flow through an artery. Two things that can happen where plaque occurs are: (1) bleeding (hemorrhage) into the plaque, or

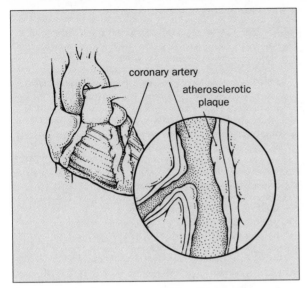

Coronary arteries narrow and harden as atherosclerotic plaque builds up inside them. Ultimately, blockage of these arteries may cause a heart attack.

artery and stopping the normal flow of blood.

Scientists are studying other ways in which platelets may play a role in atherosclerosis. For example, they're involved in forming a group of substances called prostaglandins, one of which may damage arteries. They also contain a substance called "platelet growth factor," which can stimulate the growth of smooth muscle cells. These cells are normally present in the artery wall, but their abnormal growth and proliferation is believed to be one of the earliest events in the development of atherosclerosis.

One of the more recent theories suggests that plasma lipoproteins are trapped within the artery wall. When this happens and they increasingly accumulate, they oxidize, which leads to "modified" lipoproteins that are rapidly taken up by smooth muscle cells. This, in turn, leads to the formation of foam cells and the development of a fatty streak.

WHAT IS CHOLESTEROL?

Cholesterol is a soft, fatlike substance found in all the body's cells. It's used to form cell membranes, certain hormones, and other necessary substances.

People get cholesterol in two ways. The body—primarily the liver—produces varying amounts, usually about 1,000 mg a day. An additional 400 to 500 mg or more can come directly from foods. Foods from animals, especially egg yolks, meat, fish, poultry, and whole milk dairy products, contain it; foods from plants don't. Typically the body makes all the cholesterol it needs, so it's not something that people need to consume to maintain their health.

Besides being present in human tissues, cholesterol is also found in the bloodstream. The blood transports it to and from various parts of the body. Hypercholesterolemia is the term for high levels of cholesterol in the blood.

How Cholesterol Is Carried in the Blood

Cholesterol and other fats can't dissolve in blood and must be transported by special "carriers" called lipoproteins, which are created by the liver. Lipoproteins are made of proteins, cholesterol, and triglycerides (fats made by the body or gotten from foods).

The process starts when cholesterol and fats in food go to the intestine to be digested and absorbed. Chylomicrons (fatty particles containing mainly triglycerides, but also cholesterol, phospholipids, and protein) are produced in the intestinal wall. When the chylomicrons enter the bloodstream, they contact binding sites on capillaries. Many of their triglycerides break down and pass into (primarily fat and muscle) tissues where they're stored or used to produce energy. The remainder of the chylomicron (the "chylomicron remnant"), now richer in cholesterol, continues in circulation until it reaches the liver and is absorbed.

The liver then produces very-low-density lipoprotein (VLDL), the largest type of lipoprotein. VLDL carries triglycerides made in the liver from fatty acids, carbohydrates, alcohol, and some cholesterol. VLDL is released into the bloodstream and, like chylomicrons, is transported to tissue capillaries where the triglycerides are broken down and either used for energy or stored by muscle or fat cells.

After VLDL releases its triglycerides, what remains is a "VLDL remnant" called intermediate-density lipoprotein (IDL). Some IDL is removed from circulation by the liver; the rest is transformed into low-density lipoprotein (LDL).

LDL is the major cholesterol carrier in the blood; about 60 to 80 percent of the body's cholesterol is carried by LDL. Some of this cholesterol circulating in the bloodstream is used by tissues to build cells, some is returned to the liver; but if there's too much LDL cholesterol circulating in the blood, cholesterol may also be deposited in artery walls causing plaques and atherosclerosis. The tendency for high levels of LDL to produce arterial deposits is why LDL is often called "bad" cholesterol and why lower levels of LDL reflect a reduced risk of heart disease.

Another type of lipoprotein is high-density lipoprotein (HDL). HDL is a flat, disklike particle produced primarily in the liver and intestines and released into the bloodstream. As VLDL and chylomicron particles release their triglycerides into the body's cells, fragments containing proteins, fats, and cholesterol break away. It's thought that HDL picks up the cholesterol and brings it back to the liver for reprocessing or excretion. Some researchers believe HDL may also remove excess cholesterol from fat-sated cells, possibly even those in artery walls. Because HDL clears cholesterol out of the system and high levels of it are associated with a decreased risk of heart disease, HDL is often called "good" cholesterol.

The levels of HDL and LDL in the blood are measured in order to evaluate the risk of atherosclerosis.

HDL and Triglyceride Levels

As a rule, women have higher HDL levels than men. The female sex hormone estrogen tends to raise HDL, which may help to explain why premenopausal women are usually protected from developing heart disease. Estrogen production is highest during the childbearing years.

Triglyceride levels normally range from about 50 to 250 mg/dl, depending on age and sex. As people tend to get older (or fatter or both), their triglyceride and cholesterol levels tend to rise. Women also tend to have higher triglyceride levels. An elevated blood triglyceride level and lower HDL is often accompanied by an increase in LDL and total cholesterol.

Several clinical studies have shown that an unusually large number of people with coronary heart disease also have high levels of triglycerides in the blood (hypertriglyceridemia). However, some people with this problem seem remarkably free from atherosclerosis. Thus elevated triglycerides, which are often measured along with HDL and LDL, may not directly cause atherosclerosis but may accompany other abnormalities that speed its development.

RECENT PROGRESS IN RESEARCH

Research aimed at finding ways to prevent or reverse atherosclerosis is now being done. One of the most promising areas of research is in finding ways to control elevated levels of cholesterol and other fats in the blood.

Three recent advances have been especially dramatic. One is the discovery of cell-surface receptors for LDL by 1985 Nobel laureates Drs. Joseph Goldstein and Michael Brown. These receptors bind LDL circulating through the bloodstream, allowing the LDL and its cholesterol to enter cells. Research has shown that when the amount of cholesterol within cells builds up, the number of these receptors on cell surfaces is reduced and blood levels of LDL increase. This can lead to more cholesterol being available for deposit in artery walls.

Another recent research finding has resulted from the Coronary Primary Prevention Trial (CPPT). It showed that lowering a high level of blood cholesterol reduces deaths from heart attack.

A final important advance in recent years has been the development of a new class of cholesterol-lowering drugs. These compounds either block the synthesis of cholesterol by the body's cells, or force its elimination by preventing its absorption from the intestine.

Of course, many fundamental questions remain. Medical scientists are continuing to search for answers by studying life at its most basic level—the cell.

Even though much more work needs to be done, scientists have found some answers. For instance, they've found a definite relationship between the amount of cholesterol in the bloodstream and coronary artery disease (blockage of the arteries supplying blood to the heart muscle itself). A large body of scientific evidence shows that a diet high in saturated fats and cholesterol can raise blood cholesterol levels and thereby contribute to atherosclerosis.

That's why the American Heart Association recommends that healthy adults eat foods low in saturated fats and cholesterol. Eating a proper diet helps reduce the risk of high blood cholesterol and thus the risk of heart attack.

The American Heart Association

HIGH BLOOD PRESSURE

Blood pressure is the force created by the heart as it pushes blood into the arteries and through the circulatory system.

When the heart pumps, it causes the blood to flow through the arteries into the arterioles (small arteries). The walls of the arterioles can contract or expand, altering both the amount of blood flow and the resistance to blood flow. Expansion of the arterioles allows increased blood flow and reduces the resistance to the flow. Contraction of the arterioles has the opposite effect. Hence, regulation of the size of the arterioles plays an important role in regulating blood flow and determining blood pressure. If the arterioles remain constricted, they can create a condition of hypertension or high blood pressure.

HOW BLOOD PRESSURE IS MEASURED

Blood pressure is measured by a quick, painless test using a medical instrument called a sphygmomanometer. A rubber cuff is wrapped around a person's upper arm and inflated. When the cuff is inflated, it compresses a large artery in the arm, momentarily stopping the flow of blood.

Next, air in the cuff is released, and the person measuring the blood pressure listens with a stethoscope. When the blood starts to pulse through the artery, it makes a sound; sounds continue to be heard until pressure in the artery exceeds the pressure in the cuff.

While the person listens and watches the sphygmomanometer gauge, he or she records two measurements. The systolic pressure is the pressure of the blood flow when the heart beats (the pressure when the first sound is heard). The diastolic pressure is the pressure between heartbeats (the pressure when the last sound is heard). Blood pressure is measured in millimeters of mercury, which is abbreviated mm Hg.

A typical blood pressure reading for an adult might be 127/78 mm Hg, although readings vary depending on age and other factors. (Normal blood pressure is defined by a range of values, so don't be alarmed if your own reading is somewhat higher or lower.) The first, larger number is the systolic pressure; the second is the diastolic pressure.

The important point is that the harder it is for blood to flow, the higher the numbers will be.

WHAT IS HIGH BLOOD PRESSURE?

Medical scientists have determined a norm for blood pressure after studying the blood pressure of many people over many years. When blood pressure exceeds this upper limit for extended periods, high blood pressure (or hypertension) exists.

High blood pressure in adults is defined as a systolic pressure greater than or equal to 140 mm Hg and/or a diastolic pressure greater than or equal to 90 mm Hg.

Why High Blood Pressure Is Bad

Elevated blood pressure indicates that the heart is working harder than normal, thereby putting both the heart and the arteries under a greater strain. This may contribute to heart attacks, strokes, kidney failure, and atherosclerosis.

If high blood pressure isn't treated, the heart may have to work progressively harder to pump enough blood and oxygen to the body's organs and tissues to meet their needs.

When the heart is forced to work harder than normal for an extended time, it tends to enlarge. A slightly enlarged heart may function well, but one that's significantly enlarged has a hard time adequately meeting the demands put on it.

Arteries and arterioles also suffer the effects of elevated blood pressure. Over time they become scarred, hardened, and less elastic. This may occur as people age, but elevated blood pressure speeds this process, probably because hypertension accelerates atherosclerosis.

Arterial damage is bad because hardened or narrowed arteries may be unable to supply the amount of blood the body's organs need. And if the body's organs don't get enough oxygen and nutrients, they can't function properly. There's also the risk that a blood clot may lodge in an artery narrowed by atherosclerosis, depriving part of the body of its normal blood supply. The heart, brain, and kidneys are particularly susceptible to damage by high blood pressure.

Why Mortality from High Blood Pressure Seems So Low

Mortality figures for high blood pressure are deceptive. Many people die from heart attacks and strokes caused by high blood pressure. These deaths aren't listed as deaths from hypertension: instead, they're listed as deaths from heart attack and stroke.

The result is that high blood pressure may not seem as dangerous as it really is. Because of the disguised mortality figures and, more importantly, because it's possible to have high blood pressure for years without knowing it, this disease has earned a reputation as a "silent killer." It's not a disease to take lightly!

CAUSES OF HIGH BLOOD PRESSURE

In 90 to 95 percent of the cases of high blood pressure, the cause is unknown. (This type of high blood pressure is called "essential hypertension.") Fortunately, even though scientists don't fully understand the causes of high blood pressure, they have developed drugs that are effective over the long term in treating this disease.

In the remaining cases, high blood pressure is a symptom of a recognizable underlying problem such as a kidney abnormality, tumor of the adrenal gland, or congenital defect of the aorta. When the root cause is corrected, blood pressure usually returns to normal. This type of high blood pressure is called "secondary hypertension."

WHAT CAN BE DONE

Many medications (known as antihypertensives) are available to lower high blood pressure. Some, called diuretics, rid the body of excess fluids and salt (sodium). Others, called beta blockers, reduce the heart rate and the heart's output of blood.

Another class of antihypertensives is called "sympathetic nerve inhibitors." Sympathetic nerves go from the brain to all parts of the body, including the arteries. They can cause the arteries to constrict or narrow, thereby raising blood pressure. This class of drugs reduces blood pressure by inhibiting these nerves from constricting blood vessels.

Yet another group of drugs is the vasodilators. These can cause the muscle in the walls of the blood vessels (especially the arteries) to relax, allowing the artery to dilate (widen).

Two relatively new classes of drugs used to treat high blood pressure are the angiotensin converting enzyme (ACE) inhibitors and the calcium antagonists (calcium channel blockers).

The ACE inhibitors interfere with the body's production of angiotensin, a chemical that causes the arteries to constrict. The calcium antagonists can reduce the heart rate and relax blood vessels.

In most cases these drugs lower blood pressure, but quite often people respond very differently to these medications. Thus most patients must go through a trial period to find out which medications are most effective while causing the fewest side effects.

The most important points for people with high blood pressure to remember are to: (1) follow their doctor's instructions and (2) stay on their medication.

Dietary and lifestyle changes also may help control high blood pressure. Some people with mild hypertension can lower their blood pressure by reducing sodium in their diet. Excessive alcohol intake (more than two ounces daily) raises blood pressure in some people and should be restricted. Blood pressure also returns to normal in many obese people when they lose weight. Increasing physical activity can reduce blood pressure in some people, too. Before drugs are prescribed, these methods to control blood pressure are often recommended for people with only mildly elevated blood pressure.

FACTORS CONTRIBUTING TO HIGH BLOOD PRESSURE

Because medical science doesn't understand the causes of most cases of high blood pressure, it's hard to say how to prevent it. Still, several factors may contribute to it. Being overweight or using excessive salt are two avoidable factors.

Age is one risk factor that can't be changed. Generally speaking, the older people get, the more likely they are to develop high blood pressure.

Heredity is another factor. People whose parents have high blood pressure are more likely to develop it than those whose parents don't. African-Americans are also more likely to have high blood pressure than whites.

The incidence of high blood pressure isn't directly related to a person's sex. However, doctors usually keep a close watch on a woman's blood pressure during pregnancy or if she's taking oral contraceptives. Some women who have never had high blood pressure develop it during pregnancy. Similarly, a woman taking oral contraceptives is more likely to develop high blood pressure if she's overweight, has had high blood pressure during pregnancy, has a family history of high blood pressure, or has mild kidney disease.

The American Heart Association

HEART ATTACK AND ANGINA

WHAT IS A HEART ATTACK?

Heart attacks result from blood vessel disease in the heart. Coronary heart disease (CHD), sometimes referred to as coronary artery disease (CAD), are more general names for heart attack (and angina).

A heart attack, or myocardial infarction, occurs when the blood supply to part of the

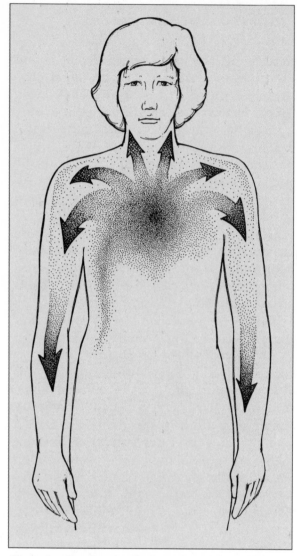

The pain of angina (radiating outward from the heart) typically comes on with exertion and, unlike the pain of a heart attack, subsides shortly with rest.

heart muscle itself (the myocardium) is severely reduced or stopped. This occurs when one of the coronary arteries (the arteries that supply blood to the heart muscle) is blocked by an obstruction, often plaque due to atherosclerosis. A heart attack also can be caused by a blood clot lodged in a coronary artery. Such an event is sometimes called a coronary thrombosis or coronary occlusion.

If the blood supply is cut off drastically or

for a long time, muscle cells suffer irreversible injury and die. Disability or death can result, depending on how much heart muscle is damaged.

Sometimes a coronary artery temporarily contracts or goes into spasm. When this happens, the artery narrows and blood flow to part of the heart muscle decreases or even stops. What causes a spasm is unclear, but it can occur in normal blood vessels as well as vessels partially blocked by atherosclerosis. If a spasm is severe, a heart attack may result.

WHAT IS ANGINA?

A heart attack isn't the only result of coronary artery disease. Chest pain called angina pectoris also can occur. Angina is a symptom of a condition called myocardial ischemia, which occurs when the heart muscle (myocardium) doesn't get as much blood (hence as much oxygen) as it needs for a given level of work. Lack of blood supply is called ischemia.

Angina pectoris can occur when blood circulation to the heart is sufficient for normal needs but inadequate when the heart's needs increase, such as during physical exertion or emotional excitement. Running to catch a bus, for example, could trigger an attack of angina while walking to a bus stop might not. Some people, such as those with a coronary artery spasm, may have angina when they're resting. Angina can be a sign warning that someone is at risk of heart attack.

WHAT IS SILENT ISCHEMIA?

Some people have ischemia without pain. As many as 3 to 4 million Americans may have ischemic episodes without knowing it. These people have silent ischemia. They may have a heart attack with no prior warning. People with angina also may have undiagnosed episodes of silent ischemia. Various tests, such as an exercise test or a 24-hour portable monitor of the electrocardiogram (Holter monitor), are used to diagnose silent ischemia.

WHAT IS COLLATERAL CIRCULATON?

Collateral circulation involves small arteries that connect two larger coronary arteries or different segments of the same artery. They provide an alternate route for blood flow to the heart muscle. Everyone has collateral vessels, at least in microscopic form. These vessels aren't open under normal conditions but grow and enlarge in some people with coronary heart disease. When a collateral vessel enlarges, it lets blood flow from an open artery to either an adjacent artery or further downstream on the same artery. Myocardial ischemia stimulates collateral vessels, so they can form a kind of "detour" around a blockage, providing alternate routes of blood flow.

Research has shown that while everyone has collateral vessels, they don't open and become available in all people. Some people have available collaterals; others don't. People who have open collateral vessels are lucky, because collateral vessels help protect heart muscle from tissue death if the normal blood supply is cut off.

HOW ANGINA IS TREATED

Angina pectoris can be treated with drugs that affect (1) the supply of blood to the heart muscle or (2) the heart's demand for oxygen. Some drugs, called coronary vasodilators, cause blood vessels to relax. When this happens, the opening inside the vessels (the lumen) gets bigger. Then blood flow improves, allowing more oxygen and nutrients to reach the heart muscle. Nitroglycerin is the drug most often used. It relaxes the veins (reducing the amount of blood returning to the heart and thus lessening the work of pumping) and the coronary arteries (increasing the blood supply to the heart).

Alternatively, the heart's demand for oxygen can also be modified. For example, a drug can be prescribed to reduce blood pressure and thus reduce the heart's workload and need for oxygen. Drugs that slow the heart rate achieve a similar effect.

Invasive techniques that improve the blood supply to the heart also may be used. One technique is percutaneous transluminal coronary angioplasty (PTCA), also known as angioplasty or balloon angioplasty. Another procedure is coronary artery bypass graft surgery. Before performing either of these procedures, a doctor must find the blocked part of the coronary arteries. This is done using coronary arteriography, which is done during a procedure called cardiac catheterization. In this procedure a doctor guides a thin plastic tube (a catheter) through an artery in the arm or leg and into the coronary arteries. Then the doctor injects a liquid dye visible in x-rays through the catheter. High-speed x-ray movies record the course of the liquid as it flows through the arteries. Obstructions in the arteries can be identified by tracing the liquid's flow.

Some newer diagnostic procedures are available to evaluate how well the heart works. These tests may be done before or after a heart attack. Some of these tests are still relatively experimental and are limited to larger medical centers.

PTCA is a procedure designed to dilate (widen or expand) narrowed coronary arteries. In it a doctor inserts a catheter into an artery in an arm or a leg and guides it to an obstructed coronary artery. Then a second catheter with a balloon tip is passed inside the first, and the balloon tip is inflated at the arterial blockage. This compresses the plaque, enlarging the inner diameter of the blood vessel so blood can flow more easily. Then the balloon is deflated and the catheters withdrawn.

In about 25 percent of the people who have had PTCA, the dilated part of the coronary artery renarrows. This usually occurs within the first six months. Then a doctor must decide whether to repeat the operation or if open-heart surgery is a better choice.

In coronary artery bypass graft surgery, surgeons take a blood vessel from another part of the body (usually the leg or from inside the chest wall) and construct a detour around the blocked part of a coronary artery. One end of the vessel is attached above the blockage; the other, to the coronary artery just beyond the blocked area. This restores blood supply to the heart muscle.

People with angina should also modify their controllable risk factors. This means they must not smoke, and should control their blood pressure and make sure their diet doesn't contribute to atherosclerosis or obesity.

SYMPTOMS OF A HEART ATTACK

Sometimes the first indications of a heart attack come as warning signals. The actual diagnosis of a heart attack must be made by a physician who has studied the results of several tests. Besides reviewing a patient's complete medical history and giving a physical examination, a doctor will use an electrocardiogram (ECG or EKG) to discover any abnormalities caused by damage to the heart. Sometimes a blood test is used to detect abnormal levels of certain enzymes in the bloodstream.

HOW A HEART ATTACK IS TREATED

When a heart attack occurs, it's critical to recognize the signals and respond immediately. About half of all heart attack victims wait two hours or longer before deciding to get help. This reduces their chance of survival, because most heart attack victims who die do so within two hours of when the signals begin. Time is critical. Anyone experiencing the warning signals of a heart attack should be taken immediately to the nearest hospital with 24-hour emergency cardiac care. People who become unconscious before reaching the emergency room may receive emergency cardiopulmonary resuscitation (CPR).

Most communities have an emergency cardiac care system that can quickly respond to an emergency. This prompt care for heart attack victims dramatically reduces damage to the heart. In fact, 80 percent of heart attack survivors can return to work within three months. Prompt care for heart attack victims isn't the only reason so many people recover so quickly, but it's an important one.

The importance of time cannot be over-

NEW CARDIAC IMAGING TESTS

Radionuclide Imaging. This includes such tests as perfusion imaging, MUGA (Multi-Gated Acquisition) scan, or acute infarct scintigraphy. These tests involve injecting substances called radionuclides into the bloodstream. Computer-generated pictures can then find them in the heart. These tests show how well the heart muscle is supplied with blood, how well the heart's chambers are functioning, or identify a part of the heart damaged by heart attack.

Magnetic Resonance Imaging (MRI). This test uses powerful magnets to look inside the body. Computer-generated pictures can image the heart muscle, identify damage from a heart attack, diagnose certain congenital heart defects, and evaluate disease of larger blood vessels such as the aorta.

Contrast Echo and Doppler Echo. Echocardiography uses sound waves to evaluate the size, shape, and motion of the heart. The sound waves bounce back from the various structures of the heart, and a computer translates those waves into a two-dimensional image of a beating heart. With contrast echo, a radio-opaque substance is injected into the bloodstream, so that blood flow through the heart moving materials, such as blood, so that the velocity and direction of blood flow can be precisely measured.

Digital Cardiac Angiography, Digital Subtraction Angiography (DCA or DSA). This test uses a modified form of imaging that records pictures of the heart and its blood vessels by computer.

The Editors

HEART ATTACK—SIGNALS AND ACTION

Know the Warning Signals of a Heart Attack:
• Uncomfortable pressure, fullness, squeezing, or pain in the center of the chest that lasts more than a few minutes
• Pain spreading to the shoulders, neck, or arms
• Chest discomfort with lightheadedness, fainting, sweating, nausea, or shortness of breath

Not all these warning signs occur in every heart attack. If some start to occur, however, don't wait. Get help immediately. Delay can be deadly!

Know What to Do in an Emergency:
• Find out (in advance) which area hospitals have 24-hour emergency cardiac care
• Know which hospital or medical facility is nearest your home and office, and tell your family and friends to call this facility in an emergency
• Keep a list of emergency rescue service numbers next to the telephone and in your pocket, wallet, or purse

• If you have chest discomfort that lasts ten minutes or more, call the emergency rescue service
• If you can get to a hospital faster by going yourself and not waiting for an ambulance, have someone drive you there

Be a Heart Saver
• If you're with someone experiencing the signs of a heart attack—and the warning signs last more than a few minutes—act immediately
• Expect a "denial." It's normal for someone with chest discomfort to deny the possibility of something as serious as a heart attack. Don't take "no" for an answer. Insist on taking prompt action.
• Call the emergency service, or
• Get to the nearest hospital emergency room that offers 24-hour emergency cardiac care
• Give CPR (mouth-to-mouth breathing and chest compression) if it's necessary and you're properly trained

emphasized. When a coronary artery gets blocked, the heart muscle doesn't die instantaneously—damage increases the longer an artery remains blocked.

If a victim gets to an emergency room fast enough, a technique called reperfusion therapy (or thrombolysis) sometimes can be performed. It involves injecting a thrombolytic (clot-dissolving) agent, such as streptokinase, urokinase, or TPA (tissue plasminogen activator), to dissolve a clot in a coronary artery and restore some blood flow. These drugs must be used within a few (usually one to three) hours of a heart attack. The sooner a drug is used, the more effective it's likely to be.

In the weeks following a heart attack, either PTCA or coronary artery bypass surgery may be performed to improve the blood supply to the heart muscle.

Once part of the heart muscle dies, its function can't be restored. Function may be restored to areas with decreased blood flow, however.

REDUCING THE CHANCE OF A HEART ATTACK

Many scientific studies show that certain characteristics increase the risk of coronary heart disease. These are called risk factors. The three major modifiable risk factors are high blood pressure, high blood cholesterol, and cigarette smoking. Other contributing risk factors are diabetes mellitus, obesity, and physical inactivity.

The American Heart Association strongly urges Americans to control their modifiable risk factors. Also, people with angina should take episodes of chest pain seriously and see their doctor before their atherosclerosis leads to a heart attack.

WHAT ARE ARRHYTHMIAS?

Arrhythmias (or dysrhythmias) are heartbeat irregularities. Normally the heartbeat originates in the right atrium when a specialized group of cells (the sinoatrial, or sinus, node

MONITORING YOUR HEARTBEAT

Electrocardiogram. A person's heartbeat is regulated by the heart's own natural "pacemaker": a wave of electricity that passes through your heart from the sinoatrial node (a small cluster of specialized cells in the right atrium of the heart) down to the ventricles. And, because the body's tissues are good conductors of electricity, these electrical impulses can be detected by placing electrical sensors at various points on your skin.

The impulses are picked up by an electrocardiograph, which produces a printed record—an electrocardiogram (ECG or EKG). The electrical pattern of the ECG can reveal abnormalities of heart rhythm, damage to heart muscle from a previous heart attack, an insufficient blood flow to the heart muscle (possibly because of atherosclerosis), an inflammation of the membrane around the heart (pericarditis) or of the heart muscle itself (myocarditis). And all of this information about the inner workings of the heart can be obtained with an easy, painless, noninvasive test.

An ECG is commonly taken in a physician's office with the patient lying down (a "resting" ECG); but if your physician wants to see how your heart responds when it is subjected to added work, he is likely to recommend a stress test.

Stress Test. An exercise ECG, or "stress test," is most often performed while you walk on a treadmill. As you walk for 10 or 15 minutes, your physician will gradually increase the speed and incline of the treadmill to see how your heart responds to the increasing demands placed on it. Although designed to place a strenuous demand on your cardiovascular system, in order to reveal any coronary heart disease, the test itself is safe when it is performed under the supervision of a physician.

Walking ECG, or Holter Monitor. If your physician wants to evaluate your heart's response to the ordinary stresses of your daily life—rather than the artificial stress of the treadmill—he may ask you to wear a Holter monitor for 24 hours. A Holter monitor is a miniature electrocardiograph; its recording device, which is the size of an instant camera, attaches to your belt; and its tiny electrodes remain in place on your chest through a 24-hour cycle to record your ECG as you work, eat, sleep, and play. *The Editors*

---

or "pacemaker" of the heart) sends an electrical signal. This signal spreads throughout the atria and to the atrioventricular (AV) node. The AV node connects to a group of specialized conducting fibers in the ventricles. The impulse travels down these specialized fibers to all parts of the ventricles. This particular route must be followed to ensure the heart pumps adequately and properly.

As the electrical impulse moves through the heart, the heart contracts. This normally occurs 60 to 100 times a minute; each contraction represents one heartbeat. The atria contract a fraction of a second before the ventricles, which lets them empty their blood into the ventricles before the ventricles contract.

Under certain conditions almost all heart tissue is capable of starting a heartbeat. In other words, another part of the heart can become the pacemaker. An arrhythmia occurs when the heart's natural pacemaker develops an abnormal rate or rhythm, when the normal conduction pathway is interrupted, or when another part of the heart takes over as pacemaker. Arrhythmias cause the heart to pump less effectively.

Heartbeat irregularities can produce either unusual slowing or rapid beating of the heart. Excessive slowing of the heartbeat (bradycardia) can cause fatigue, dizziness, lightheadedness, fainting, or near-fainting spells. These symptoms due to slow heart beating can be readily corrected with an implantable electronic pacemaker.

Rapid heart beating (tachycardia) can produce symptoms of palpitations, rapid heart action, dizziness, lightheadedness, fainting, or near fainting if the heart beats too fast to circulate blood effectively. It may be either regular or irregular in rhythm. When rapid heart

🔔 Most people experience an occasional change in the regular beating of their heart and feel a fluttering in the chest, or a speeding up of their heartbeat, or a bout of dizziness or breathlessness. And for most people with such symptoms, these arrhythmias are harmless. In some people, however, especially if such episodes persist or become worse, the arrhythmias may be associated with heart disease. Only a physician will be able to distinguish with certainty between those arrhythmias that are serious and those that are not, so you should report any changes in the regular beating of your heart to your doctor.

beating arises in the ventricles (called ventricular tachycardia), a life-threatening situation can arise. The most serious cardiac rhythm disturbance is called ventricular fibrillation where the lower chambers are quivering and the heart cannot pump any blood. Immediate collapse and sudden death follows unless medical help is immediately provided.

If recognized in time, ventricular tachycardia and ventricular fibrillation can be converted into normal rhythm with electrical shock. Rapid heart beating can be controlled with medications by identifying or destroying the focus of rhythm disturbances. These days one effective way of correcting these life-threatening rhythms is by using an electronic implantable device called an implantable defibrillator.

WHAT IS SUDDEN DEATH?

Sudden death is a death that occurs unexpectedly and instantaneously or shortly after the onset of symptoms. The most common underlying reason for patients to die suddenly is cardiovascular disease, in particular coronary artery disease.

Sudden cardiac death (SCD) is usually due to rapid onset of ventricular tachycardia/ventricular fibrillation. About one-fourth of all

ARTIFICIAL PACEMAKER

If your heart's own natural electrical pacemaker fails to work properly—if your heart beats too quickly or slowly, or erratically—your physician may recommend an artificial pacemaker. An artificial pacemaker is a small, battery-powered, implanted device that produces does) that travel from your heart's atria down through the ventricles. Some of the newer pacemakers have two wires, or "leads"; one goes to the heart's right upper chamber, or right atrium, and one to the right lower chamber, or right ventricle. This allows the upper and lower chambers to retain their normal pattern of sequential contraction and relaxation and helps the ventricles to fill properly. Some pacemakers even cause the heart rate to increase, as it naturally would, in response to exercise or stress.

As with any such device, an artificial pacemaker needs some care. A minor surgical procedure is required to replace batteries when they wear down; but most people with pacemakers can take part in all the normal activities for a person of their age. *The Editors*

cases of SCD are caused by acute lack of blood flow, which results in new muscle damage. The new muscle damage is called a heart attack or myocardial infarction. In the remaining cases of SCD, there's evidence of previous muscle damage but no evidence of new muscle death. Arrhythmias such as ventricular tachycardia leading to ventricular fibrillation are thought to cause SCD in these people.

If someone may be experiencing ventricular fibrillation, seek help immediately. This problem can be corrected with a defibrillator, which gives an immediate shock to the heart. This must be done in three to four minutes from the start of fibrillation unless blood flow is maintained through cardiopulmonary resuscitation. Survivors of SCD must have all causes (myocardial ischemia, arrhythmia, etc.) corrected to prevent future episodes.

RISK FACTORS FOR HEART DISEASE

Extensive clinical and statistical studies have identified several factors that increase the risk of heart attack and stroke. These risk factors can be grouped into two classifications: (1) major risk factors and (2) contributing risk factors.

Major risk factors are those that medical research has shown to be definitely associated with a significant increase in the risk of cardiovascular disease. The major risk factors for heart attack that cannot be changed are heredity (inherited traits), male sex, and increasing age. The major risk factors that result from modifiable lifestyle habits are cigarette smoking, high blood pressure, and elevated blood cholesterol.

Contributing risk factors are those associated with increased risk of cardiovascular disease, but their significance and prevalence haven't yet been precisely determined. These include diabetes, obesity, and physical inactivity. Stress may also be a contributing factor.

The more risk factors a person has, the greater the chance of developing heart disease.

Major Risk Factors That Can't Be Changed

Heredity. A tendency toward heart disease or atherosclerosis seems to be hereditary. That means children of parents with cardiovascular disease are more likely to develop it themselves. Race is a consideration, too. African-Americans have moderate hypertension twice as often as whites and severe hypertension three times as often. Consequently, their risk of heart disease is greater.

Male sex. Men have a greater risk of heart attack than women, and they have attacks earlier in life. Even after menopause, when women's death rate from heart disease increases, it's not as great as men's.

Increasing age. Fifty-five percent of all heart attack victims are age 65 or older; of those who die, about four out of five are over 65. At older ages, women who have heart attacks are twice as likely as men to die from them within a few weeks.

Major Risk Factors That Can Be Changed

Cigarette smoking. Smokers' risk of heart attack is more than twice that of nonsmokers. In fact, cigarette smoking is the biggest risk factor for sudden cardiac death; smokers have two to four times the risk of nonsmokers. Smokers who have a heart attack are more likely to die and die suddenly (within an hour) than nonsmokers.

Smoking is also the biggest risk factor for peripheral vascular disease (narrowing of blood vessels carrying blood to leg and arm muscles). In fact, this condition is almost exclusively confined to smokers. Smokers with peripheral vascular disease are also more likely to develop gangrene and require leg amputation. Benefits from corrective surgery are also reduced when patients continue to smoke.

When people stop smoking, regardless of how long or how much they have smoked, their risk of heart disease rapidly declines. Ten years after quitting, the risk of death from heart disease for people who smoked a pack a day or less is almost the same as for people who never smoked.

High blood pressure. High blood pressure usually has no specific symptoms and no early warning signs. It's truly a "silent killer." But a simple, quick, painless test can detect it.

High blood pressure increases the heart's workload, causing the heart to enlarge and weaken over time. It also increases the risk of stroke, heart attack, kidney failure, and congestive heart failure. When high blood pressure exists with obesity, smoking, high blood cholesterol levels, or diabetes, the risk of heart attack or stroke increases several times.

As a rule, blood pressure tends to increase with age. Men have a greater risk of high blood pressure than women until age 55, when men's and women's risk is approximately equal. Women age 65 and older are more likely to develop high blood pressure than men. More than half of all women over 55 have high blood pressure, and more than two-thirds of the women over age 65 do.

People with high blood pressure should work with their doctor to control it. Eating a proper diet, losing weight, exercising regularly, restricting salt (sodium) intake, and following a program of medication may all be prescribed to lower blood pressure and keep it within healthy limits.

Blood cholesterol levels. The risk of coronary heart disease rises as blood cholesterol levels increase. When other risk factors (such as high blood pressure and smoking) are present, this risk increases even more. A person's cholesterol level is also affected by age, sex, heredity, and diet.

Based on large population studies, blood cholesterol concentrations below 200 mg/dl (milligrams per deciliter) in adults seem to indicate a relatively low risk of coronary heart disease. A level of 240 mg/dl and over approximately doubles the risk; more than 27 percent of the U.S. population falls into this category. Blood cholesterol values from 200 to 239 mg/dl indicate moderate and increasing risk. Estimates are that 102.7 million Americans have blood cholesterol values over 200 mg/dl, and about 48.7 million Americans have levels of 240 or above.

Blood cholesterol and triglyceride levels should be measured at least once every five years in healthy adults. People with cholesterol levels greater than 200 mg/dl should have a second cholesterol test in one to eight weeks to confirm the first test's results. If the second test's results are within 30 mg/dl of the first result, the results are averaged. If there's more than a 30 mg/dl difference, a third test should be done and the results of all the tests averaged. If the result is from 200 to 239 mg/dl and the person has coronary heart disease or a family history of premature CHD, measuring lipoproteins is warranted.

A certain amount of cholesterol in the body is necessary to build cell membranes, etc. However, the liver produces enough cholesterol to meet these needs. That's why diet is important. A diet high in saturated fat and cholesterol tends to raise blood cholesterol; a diet low in saturated fat and cholesterol usually means lower levels of blood cholesterol. On the whole, Americans should reduce the amount of fat and cholesterol in their diet.

By watching their diet, people with low levels of blood cholesterol will help minimize the tendency for cholesterol levels to rise with age. People with higher levels of blood cholesterol will benefit even more. First, controlling their diet will help reduce their blood cholesterol levels. Second, if drugs are still needed to reduce blood cholesterol, the diet will improve their effectiveness.

Other Contributing Risk Factors

Diabetes. Diabetes is the inability of the body to metabolize or use glucose (sugar) properly. It appears most often in middle age and among overweight people. In a mild form, it can go undetected for many years. Besides increasing the risks of kidney disease, blindness, and nerve and blood vessel damage, diabetes also seriously increases the risk of developing cardiovascular disease. In fact, more than 80 percent of people with diabetes die of some form of heart or blood vessel disease. Part of the reason for this increase is that diabetes affects cholesterol and triglyceride levels.

When diabetes is detected, a doctor may prescribe changes in eating habits, weight control and exercise programs, and even drugs (if necessary) to keep it in check. Despite the different measures that may be taken to control glucose levels, as a contributing risk factor for heart disease, diabetes cannot be changed.

Obesity. People who are more than 30 percent over their ideal body weight (obese) are more likely to develop heart disease and stroke even if they have no other risk factors. Obesity is unhealthy because excess weight increases the strain on the heart. It's linked with coronary heart disease mainly because it influences blood pressure and blood cholesterol and can lead to diabetes.

Recent evidence indicates that how fat is distributed on the body may affect the risk of coronary heart disease. A waist/hip ratio greater than 1.0 for men indicates a significantly increased risk. For women it's 0.8. This means that a man's waist measurement should not exceed his hip measurement, and a woman's waist measurement should not be more than 80 percent of her hip measurement.

Physical inactivity. Physical inactivity can lead to several changes that are risk factors for heart disease. When lack of exercise is combined with overeating, excess weight and increased blood cholesterol levels can result—and these unquestionably contribute to the risk of heart disease. Middle-aged or older people who are sedentary should seek medical advice before they start or significantly increase their physical activity.

Stress. It's almost impossible to define and measure someone's level of emotional stress. There's no way to measure the psychological impact of different experiences. All people feel stress, but they feel it in different amounts and react in different ways. Life would be dull without stress, but excessive amounts of stress over a long time may create health problems in some people.

Some scientists have noted a relationship between coronary heart disease risk and a person's life stress, behavior habits, and socioeconomic status. These factors may affect established risk factors. For example, people under stress may start smoking or smoke more than they otherwise would.

The contributing risk factors just discussed may not be as significant as high blood pressure, smoking, or high blood cholesterol in their impact on heart disease. Still, they're important and shouldn't be ignored.

The American Heart Association

STROKE

Stroke is a form of cardiovascular disease that affects the arteries of the central nervous system. A stroke occurs when a blood vessel bringing oxygen and nutrients to the brain bursts or is clogged by a blood clot or some other particle. Because of this rupture or blockage, part of the brain doesn't get the flow of blood it needs. Deprived of oxygen, nerve cells in the affected area of the brain can't function and die within minutes. And when nerve cells can't function, the part of the body controlled by these cells can't function either. The devastating effects of stroke are permanent because dead brain cells aren't replaced.

TYPES OF STROKE

There are four main types of stroke: two caused by clots, and two by hemorrhage. Cerebral thrombosis and cerebral embolism are by far the most common, accounting for about 70 to 80 percent of all strokes. They're caused by clots that plug an artery. Cerebral and subarachnoid hemorrhages are caused by ruptured blood vessels. They have a much higher fatality rate than strokes caused by clots.

Cerebral thrombosis is the most common type of stroke. It occurs when a blood clot (thrombus) forms and blocks blood flow in an artery bringing blood to part of the brain. Blood clots usually form in arteries damaged by atherosclerosis.

One identifying feature of cerebral thrombotic strokes is that they usually occur at night or first thing in the morning, when blood pressure is low. Another is that very often they're preceded by a transient ischemic attack, also called a TIA or "mini-stroke."

Cerebral embolism accounts for from 5 to 14 percent of all strokes. This type of stroke occurs when a wandering clot (an embolus) or some other particle forms in a blood vessel away from the brain, usually in the heart. The clot is carried by the bloodstream until it lodges in an artery leading to or in the brain, blocking the flow of blood.

The most common cause of these emboli is blood clots that form during atrial fibrillation, a disorder found in close to 2 million Americans. In atrial fibrillation the two small upper chambers of the heart, the atria, quiver instead of beating effectively. Blood isn't pumped completely out of them when the heart beats, allowing the blood to pool and clot. About 15 percent of strokes occur in people with atrial fibrillation.

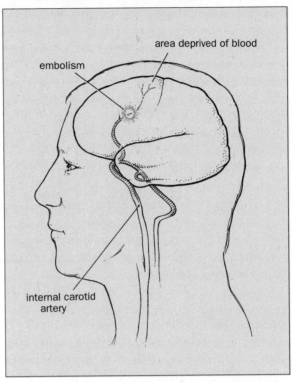

The two carotid arteries are the main bloodlines from heart to brain. In one kind of stroke, a cerebral embolism, or blood clot, blocks an artery to the brain.

🔺 Atrial fibrillation can be brought on by hyperthyroidism, pulmonary embolus, congestive heart failure, acute heart attack, and other types of long-standing heart disease. Its sudden onset presents as palpitations or angina. The first line of treatment is drug therapy to bring the heart rhythm back to normal. If the fibrillation is of recent onset, and drugs do not bring it under control, a physician will use an electrical shock to the heart to reverse it (defibrillation). Since chronic atrial fibrillation may be associated with emboli that may cause a stroke, anticoagulants, or other drugs that will inhibit platelet aggregation, are often given as a prophylactic.

Subarachnoid hemorrhage occurs when a blood vessel on the surface of the brain ruptures and bleeds into the space between the brain and the skull (but not into the brain itself). Subarachnoid hemorrhages account for about 7 percent of all strokes.

Cerebral hemorrhage occurs when a defective artery in the brain bursts, flooding surrounding tissue with blood. About 10 percent of all strokes result from cerebral hemorrhages.

Hemorrhage, or bleeding, from an artery in the brain can be caused by a head injury or a burst aneurysm.

Aneurysms are blood-filled pouches that balloon out from weak spots in the artery wall. They're often caused or aggravated by high blood pressure. Aneurysms aren't always dangerous, but if one bursts in the brain, a stroke results.

When a cerebral or subarachnoid hemorrhage occurs, the loss of a constant blood supply means some brain cells can no longer function. Another problem is that accumulated blood from the burst artery may pressure surrounding brain tissue and interfere with how the brain functions. Severe or mild symptoms can result, depending on the amount of pressure.

The amount of bleeding determines the severity of cerebral hemorrhages. In 50 percent of the cases, people with cerebral hemorrhages die of increased pressure on their brains. Those who live, however, tend to recover much more than those who have had strokes caused by a clot. The reason is that when a blood vessel is blocked, part of the brain dies—and the brain doesn't regenerate. But when a blood vessel in the brain bursts, pressure from the blood compresses part of the brain. If the person survives, gradually the pressure diminishes and the brain may return to its former state.

EFFECTS OF STROKE

Strokes affect different people in different ways, depending on the type of stroke and the area of the brain affected. Brain damage from a stroke can affect the senses, speech and the ability to understand speech, behavioral patterns, thought patterns, and memory. Paralysis on one side of the body is common. Stroke can also cause depression, as victims think they're now less than "whole."

Stroke often causes people to lose feeling in an arm or a leg, or suffer diminished sight in one eye. The loss of feeling or visual field results in a loss of awareness, so stroke victims may forget or ignore their weaker side, a problem called "neglect." As a result, they may ignore items put on their affected side, have trouble reading, or dress only one side of their bodies and think they're completely dressed. Bumping into furniture or door jambs is also common.

A stroke can also affect seeing, touching, moving, and thinking, so a person's perception of everyday objects may be changed. Stroke victims may not be able to recognize and understand familiar objects the way they did before. When vision is affected, objects may look closer or farther away than they really are, causing spills at the table or collisions when walking.

Usually stroke doesn't cause hearing loss, although people may have problems understanding speech. They also may have trouble verbalizing what they're thinking. This is called aphasia. Aphasia affects the ability to talk, listen, read, and write. It usually occurs when a stroke weakens the right side of the body.

A related problem is that a stroke can affect muscles used in talking (those in the tongue, palate, and lips), and speech can be slowed, slurred, or distorted. Stroke victims thus can be hard to understand. This is called dysarthria and may require the help of a speech pathologist. Chewing and swallowing food also can be a problem. One or both sides of the mouth can lack feeling, increasing the risk of choking.

Finally, a stroke can affect the ability to think clearly. Planning and carrying out even simple activities may be hard. Stroke victims may not know how to start a task, confuse the sequence of logical steps in tasks, or forget how to do tasks they've done many times before.

RISK FACTORS FOR STROKE

When stroke occurs, there can be severe losses in mental and bodily functions—if not death. That's why preventing stroke is so important. The best way to prevent a stroke from occurring is to reduce the risk factors for stroke.

Some factors that increase the risk of stroke are genetically determined. Others are a function of natural processes. Still others result from a person's lifestyle. Factors resulting from heredity or natural processes can't be changed, but environmental factors can be modified with a doctor's help.

Risk Factors That Can Be Treated

Five partly controllable risk factors are: (1) high blood pressure, (2) heart disease, (3) cigarette smoking, (4) high red blood cell count, and (5) transient ischemic attacks.

STROKE—SIGNALS AND ACTION

Know the Warning Signals of Stroke:
• Sudden weakness or numbness of the face, arm, or leg on one side of the body
• Sudden dimness or loss of vision, particularly in only one eye
• Loss of speech, or trouble talking or understanding speech
• Sudden severe headaches with no apparent cause
• Unexplained dizziness, unsteadiness, or sudden falls, especially along with any of the previous symptoms

If you notice one or more of these signs, don't wait. See a doctor right away!

About 10 percent of strokes are preceded by "little strokes" (transient ischemic attacks, or TIAs). However, of those who've had one or more TIAs, about 36 percent will later have a stroke. In fact, a person who's had one or more TIAs is 9.5 times more likely to have a stroke than someone of the same age and sex who hasn't. Thus TIAs are extremely important stroke warning signs.

TIAs are more useful for predicting if a stroke will occur rather than when one will happen. They can occur days, weeks, or even months before a major stroke. In about 50 percent of the cases, the stroke occurs within one year of the TIA; in about 20 percent of the cases, within one month.

TIAs occur when a blood clot temporarily clogs an artery, and part of the brain doesn't get the blood it needs. The symptoms occur rapidly and last a relatively short time. More than 75 percent of TIAs last less than five minutes. The average is about a minute, although some can last several hours. By definition, TIAs can last up to—but not over—24 hours, although this is very unusual. Unlike stroke, when a TIA is over, people return to normal.

The usual TIA symptoms are very similar to those of stroke. They are: (1) temporary weakness, clumsiness, or loss of feeling in an arm, a leg, or the side of the face on one side of the body (or some combination thereof); (2) temporary dimness or loss of vision, particularly in one eye (also often in combination with other symptoms); (3) temporary loss of speech or difficulty in speaking or difficulty in understanding speech, particularly with a right-side weakness. Sometimes dizziness, double vision, and staggering also occur. The short duration of these symptoms and lack of permanent damage is the main distinction between TIA and stroke.

Although TIAs signal only about 10 percent of strokes, they're very strong predictors of stroke risk. Don't ignore them! Get medical attention immediately. A doctor should determine if a TIA or stroke has occurred, or if it's another medical problem with similar symptoms (seizure, fainting, migraine, or general medical or cardiac condition). Prompt medical or surgical attention to these symptoms could prevent a fatal or disabling stroke from occurring.

High blood pressure. Hypertension is the most important risk factor for stroke. In fact, stroke risk varies directly with blood pressure. What makes high blood pressure even more significant is that it afflicts almost one in three American adults. That's why everyone should have their blood pressure checked regularly. Controlling high blood pressure reduces the risk of stroke significantly; often blood pressure can be controlled simply by eating a healthier diet and maintaining proper weight. Drugs to control blood pressure are also available. Many people think the reason the death rate from stroke has declined over the past decade is due to better control of high blood pressure.

Heart disease. A diseased heart increases the risk of stroke. Independent of blood pressure, people with heart problems have more than twice the risk of stroke than people with normally functioning hearts.

The three major controllable risk factors for heart attacks are cigarette smoking, elevated blood cholesterol, and high blood pressure. Controlling these reduces the risk of heart disease and thus the risk of stroke.

Cigarette smoking. In recent years studies have shown cigarette smoking to be an important risk factor for stroke. Smoking produces a number of effects damaging to the cardiovascular system. Nicotine in tobacco smoke increases a person's blood pressure. Carbon monoxide gets in the blood, reducing the amount of oxygen the blood can supply to the body. Cigarette smoking also causes the platelets in the blood to become sticky and cluster, shortens platelet survival, decreases clotting time, and increases blood thickness.

High red blood cell count. A marked, or even moderate, increase in the red blood cell count is a risk factor for stroke. The reason is that increased red blood cells thicken the blood and make clots more likely. This problem is treatable by removing blood or administering "blood thinners."

Transient ischemic attacks (TIAs). Only about 10 percent of strokes are preceded by TIAs. Nevertheless, TIAs are extremely important; they're strong predictors of stroke. TIAs are usually treated with drugs that inhibit clots from forming.

Risk Factors That Can't Be Changed

Seven risk factors for stroke can't be changed. These are: (1) age, (2) sex, (3) race, (4) diabetes mellitus, (5) prior stroke, (6) heredity, and (7) asymptomatic carotid bruit.

Age. Incidence of stroke is strongly related to age. In fact, for people over 55 years old, the incidence of stroke more than doubles in each successive decade. This doesn't mean elderly people are the only ones to suffer strokes; about 28 percent of stroke victims in a given year are less than 65 years old. Older people do have a much greater stroke risk than younger people. The risk of stroke in people aged 65 to 74 is about one percent a year. If they have had a TIA, it increases from 5 percent a year to 8 percent a year.

Sex. The incidence of stroke is about 19 percent higher for men than women. For people under age 65, the difference is greater still.

Race. African-Americans have a much greater risk of death and disability from stroke than whites. This may be because African-Americans have a greater incidence of high blood pressure.

Diabetes mellitus. Although diabetes is treatable, the fact that a person has it still makes it much more likely that he or she will suffer a stroke. This is even more true for women than for men. Many times diabetics also have hypertension, increasing their risk of stroke even more.

Prior stroke. The risk of stroke for someone who's already had one is many times that of someone who has not.

Heredity. Stroke risk is greater for people who have a family history of stroke.

Asymptomatic carotid bruit. A bruit is an abnormal sound heard when a stethoscope is placed over an artery (in this case, the carotid artery, which is in the neck). Carotid bruit clearly indicates increased stroke risk. However, a bruit mainly indicates atherosclerosis; it doesn't necessarily mean the carotid artery will become clogged and a stroke will result.

Other, less well documented, risk factors include: (1) geographic area, (2) season and climate, and (3) socioeconomic factors.

Geographic location. Strokes are more common in the southeastern United States (the so-called "Stroke Belt") than in other areas. The stroke belt states are Alabama, Arkansas, Georgia, Indiana, Kentucky, Louisiana, Mississippi, North Carolina, South Carolina, Tennessee, and Virginia.

Season and climate. Stroke deaths occur more often during periods of extreme temperatures.

Socioeconomic factors. There's some evidence that strokes are more likely to occur among poor people than more affluent people.

Other Risk Factors

Besides the risk factors listed, other (controllable) factors indirectly increase stroke risk. These include: (1) elevated blood cholesterol and lipids, (2) excessive alcohol intake, (3) physical inactivity, and (4) obesity. These are secondary risk factors, because they affect the risk of stroke indirectly by increasing the risk of heart disease (which is a primary risk factor for stroke).

Finally, it's worth noting that some rather low-level risk factors—when combined with certain other risk factors—become extremely significant. Taking oral contraceptives and smoking cigarettes, for example, increases the risk of stroke considerably. More to the point, the 10 percent of the population in whom one-third of all strokes occur have a set of five risk factors: (1) high blood pressure, (2) elevated blood cholesterol levels, (3) abnormal glucose tolerance, (4) cigarette smoking, and (5) left ventricular hypertrophy (the overdevelopment of the left side of the heart). People who have all these factors should be given close medical supervision.

DIAGNOSING STROKE

When someone has shown symptoms of a TIA or stroke, one of the first steps a doctor must take is to gather data to make a diagnosis. He or she will take a careful history of the events that have occurred as well as a general medical history for diabetes, hypertension, heart and blood vessel disease, and other neurological diseases.

Measuring blood pressure in both arms, testing the pulse, checking the heart, listening for bruits over the neck and collarbone, checking the eyes, and giving a neurological exam are all standard practices.

A doctor might use many different tests in a neurological exam. For example, doctors may test patients' level of consciousness, orientation, memory, and emotional control. Some doctors test patients by having them stand motionless with feet together, arms outstretched, and eyes closed; testing for facial paresis (paralysis) by having patients bare their gums and stick out their tongues is also sometimes done. Hearing might be tested by rubbing the thumb and forefinger together about 12 inches from the ear. Having patients read newsprint using one eye at a time is a test of vision; visual fields can be tested by having a person cover one eye and look into the doctor's opposite eye. (The doctor will then bring a thumb or small object from the side and ask the patient to signal when it becomes visible.) The perception of pain and light touch, muscular strength, and deep tendon reflexes are also commonly tested.

Different doctors use different tests: the tests listed here are only examples of what might be done.

After these basic tests, many people will need laboratory tests showing a complete blood count, blood sugar, urea, and electrolytes. Some people may even be given an electrocardiogram.

TESTS THAT REVEAL A STROKE

Identifying stroke warning signals is one way to diagnose a stroke. But proper diagnosis doesn't stop there. Other tests may be run because the symptoms may not necessarily result from a stroke. For example, a brain tumor can produce similar symptoms. A doctor must eliminate other possibilities before making a diagnosis.

Remarkable advances in modern technology now make it possible to examine how the brain looks, functions, and gets its blood supply. These tests can outline the affected part of the brain and help define the problem. Most of these newer tests are safe and painless and can be undergone as an outpatient.

These tests fall into three categories. Tests

that image the brain make pictures that look similar to ordinary x-rays. Tests that measure the electrical activity of the brain give useful information about how it's functioning and pinpoint areas where it's functioning abnormally. Finally, blood flow tests measure flow and detect blockages in blood vessels. They're useful in revealing areas of significant atherosclerosis in carotid arteries. A doctor must decide on a case-by-case basis whether such tests will be useful, and if so, which ones to use.

What Are Some Imaging Tests?

The computed tomography scan (or CT scan) may be the most well known imaging test. In computed tomography, the person's head is put in an apparatus resembling a beauty shop hair dryer and taped to avoid movement that might ruin the picture. CT scanning takes from 20 minutes to an hour to complete.

Magnetic resonance imaging (MRI) scanning is another imaging test. It uses a giant magnet to generate an image. MRI is similar to a CT scan but requires a different machine and takes longer.

Radionuclide angiography (nuclear brain scan) is a third imaging test. In it, radioactive compounds are injected into a vein in the arm, and a machine similar to a Geiger counter creates a map showing their uptake into different parts of the head. The pictures, rather than showing the brain's structure, show how it functions. This test can detect blocked blood vessels and areas where the brain is damaged.

What Tests Show the Brain's Electrical Activity?

Two basic tests show the electrical activity of the brain: an electroencephalogram (EEG) and an evoked response test.

An electroencephalogram involves putting small metal disks (electrodes) on a person's scalp to pick up electrical impulses transmitted and received by brain cells. A machine equipped with pens transcribes this activity onto large pieces of paper.

An evoked responses test measures how the brain handles different sensory stimuli. They can detect abnormal areas of the brain. A doctor evokes a visual response by flashing a light or checkerboard pattern in front of a patient. For auditory evoked responses, a doctor makes a sound in one of the patient's ears; for bodily evoked responses, one of the nerves in an arm or a leg is electrically stimulated.

What Tests Show Blood Flow?

This category has the greatest variety of tests.

The Doppler ultrasound test is performed to detect blockages in the carotid artery. In it, a gel is put on the neck or eyelids, then a technologist puts a pencil-like probe into the gel and listens to blood flowing in the carotid artery.

Carotid phonoangiography is a test in which a sensitive microphone is put on the neck over the carotid artery and a technologist listens for a bruit. (A bruit is the sound created by turbulent blood flow as it passes through a partially blocked artery.)

Ocular plethysmography (OPG) is a test in which anesthetizing drops are put into the eyes, and then small plastic cups similar to contact lenses are positioned on the eyes to detect pulses or measure pressure in the eyes.

The cerebral blood flow test (inhalation method) measures how much oxygen dissolved in the blood supply reaches different areas of the brain. A person is told to lie flat on a table, then a cap containing detectors is secured over the head. Then the person starts breathing through a mask containing air mixed with a small amount of radioactive xenon. This test lasts 30 minutes to an hour.

Digital subtraction angiography (DSA) gives an image of the major blood vessels to the brain. It lets a doctor know if there are any blockages, how severe they are, and what can be done about them. In this test, dye is injected into a vein in the arm, and an x-ray machine quickly takes a series of pictures of the head and neck.

TREATMENT AND REHABILITATION

How Are Strokes Treated?

Surgery, drugs, acute hospital care, and rehabilitation are all accepted ways to treat stroke.

When a neck artery has become blocked, surgery might be used to remove the buildup of atherosclerotic plaque. This is called carotid endarterectomy.

Drugs may be used when a blood vessel has been blocked or blood clots are a problem. They can help prevent new clots from forming or prevent an existing clot from getting bigger.

Sometimes treating a stroke means treating the heart, because various forms of heart disease can contribute to the risk of stroke. For example, damaged heart valves may need to be surgically treated or treated with anti-clotting drugs to reduce the chance of clots forming around them. If clots form, there's a chance they could travel to the brain and cause a stroke.

Can Stroke Victims Be Rehabilitated?

Besides being the third leading cause of death in the United States, stroke is a major cause of disability. Many stroke survivors are left with mental and physical disabilities and receive expensive, time-consuming, and intensive rehabilitation to try to increase their independence.

Spontaneous recovery in the first 30 days following a stroke probably accounts for most gains in functional ability. Nevertheless, rehabilitation is important. To a large degree, successful rehabilitation depends on the extent of brain damage, the person's attitude, the rehabilitation team's skill, and the cooperation of family and friends. People with the least impairment are likely to benefit the most, but even when improvement is slight, rehabilita-

tion may still mean the difference between institutionalization and a return home.

The goal of rehabilitation is to reduce dependence and improve physical ability. Often old skills have been lost and new ones are needed.

Rehabilitation begins early as nurses and other hospital personnel work to prevent such secondary complications as stiff joints, bedsores, and pneumonia. These can result from being confined to bed for a long time.

The role of the person's family in rehabilitation is also significant. A caring, able spouse can be one of the most important positive factors in rehabilitation. The knowledge of family members also matters a great deal. Family members need to understand what the stroke victim has undergone and how disabilities can affect the person. The situation will be easier to handle if the family knows what to expect and how to handle problems that arise after the person leaves the hospital.

For a stroke victim, the goal of rehabilitation is to be as independent and productive as possible, given the limitations resulting from the stroke. *The American Heart Association*

CONGESTIVE HEART FAILURE

Congestive heart failure is a condition that occurs because the heart muscle is damaged or overworked. This can result from high blood pressure, a heart attack, atherosclerosis, a congenital heart defect, muscle disease (called cardiomyopathy), rheumatic fever, or high blood pressure in the lungs resulting from lung disease. Because it's damaged, the heart lacks the strength to keep blood circulating normally throughout the body. The "failing" heart keeps working but doesn't work as efficiently as it should.

What happens next? As blood flow out of

the heart slows, blood returning to the heart through the veins backs up, causing congestion in the tissues. Often swelling (edema) results, most commonly in the legs and ankles, but possibly in other parts of the body as well. Sometimes fluid collects in the lungs and interferes with breathing, causing shortness of breath, especially when a person is lying down.

Heart failure also affects the ability of the kidneys to dispose of sodium and water. The retained water increases the edema.

DIAGNOSIS AND TREATMENT

The most common signs of congestive heart failure are swollen legs or ankles or difficulty breathing. Another symptom is weight gain because of accumulating fluid.

Congestive heart failure usually requires a treatment program of rest, proper diet, modified daily activities, and drugs such as digitalis, diuretics, and vasodilators.

The various drugs used to treat congestive heart failure perform different functions. Digitalis increases the pumping action of the heart, while diuretics help the body eliminate excess salt and water. Vasodilators expand blood vessels and decrease resistance, allowing blood to flow more easily and making the heart's work easier.

When a specific cause of congestive heart failure is discovered, it should be treated or, if possible, corrected. For example, in some cases congestive heart failure can be treated by treating high blood pressure or by surgically replacing abnormal heart valves. Most cases of congestive heart failure are treatable. With proper medical supervision, people with heart failure don't have to become invalids.

WHAT ABOUT HEART TRANSPLANTS?

Sometimes the heart is irreversibly damaged by long-lasting heart disease. People with long-term heart failure that doesn't respond to all available treatment may be candidates for heart (cardiac) transplants. People with various forms of cardiomyopathy (acute or chronic disease of the heart muscle) are also possible heart transplant candidates. When the heart can no longer adequately function and a person is at risk of dying, a heart transplant may be indicated. Cardiac transplantation is recognized as a proven procedure in appropriately selected patients. It should be done only in medical centers staffed by teams skilled in transplantation techniques.

The American Heart Association

PERIPHERAL VASCULAR DISEASE

It's a wonderful case of the hair of the dog that bit you: The treatment for intermittent claudication (muscle pain in one or both legs that is brought on by walking) is, usually, more walking. Intermittent claudication is a symptom of peripheral vascular disease—a narrowing of the arteries in the arms and legs due to the buildup of atherosclerotic (fatty) plaque—and in 70 percent of patients, it is the only symptom.

In those with peripheral vascular disease, exercise brings on pain because the blood flow through the narrowed arteries is insufficient to provide the muscles with enough oxygen to meet the increased demands of exercise; the oxygen deficit causes muscle cramping. For some people this pain might begin after walking only a block, for others it might be close to a mile—but for anyone with intermittent claudication, the pain consistently begins at the same distance (occasionally it will only be brought on by walking uphill). A minute or two of rest brings relief. The pain is usually in the calf muscles, but it can also occur in the buttocks, hips, feet, or thighs, depending on where the arterial narrowing is. Increased exercise helps, in part, by enlarging collateral vessels ("side streets" around the main blocked artery in the leg). There is also some evidence that exercise might actually reduce some of the plaque buildup in the artery itself and can lead to better coordination of muscles.

Atherosclerosis is a process that affects the whole body; the same narrowing that causes intermittent claudication causes angina—heart pain that is brought on by exercise and relieved by rest. Angina is the cardinal symptom of narrowed coronary arteries, and 60 percent of those with intermittent claudication also have coronary artery disease. However, unlike angina (which can progress to an actual heart attack), intermittent claudication is not usually dangerous in and of itself. While patients often fear that their problems might lead to loss of a limb, this is highly unlikely. Excluding diabetics and smokers, who are at higher risk for progression of the condition, only about 10 percent ever require surgery, and only about 2 percent actually need amputation—and even these rates can be reduced with proper care.

Dr. Bruce Perler, a Johns Hopkins vascular surgeon, says, "Intermittent claudication is a fairly benign symptom that poses no immediate or even long-term danger. Patients should be cautious if surgery or other treatments such as laser angioplasty are recommended for symptoms that only appear with exercise. In the vast majority, lifestyle changes are the only treatment required." Smokers are counseled to quit, since tobacco causes constriction of peripheral veins and arteries, and all patients are advised to begin a walking training program and, if overweight, lose weight (the walking will help with the weight loss).

One recent study, reported in the *Journal of Vascular Surgery*, shows the significant difference a walking program can make. Fifty-six patients with varying degrees of intermittent claudication were enrolled in a six-month supervised walking training program consisting of three one-hour sessions a week, walking on

WALKING AWAY THE PAIN

If you have muscle pain brought on by walking, see your doctor before starting an exercise program (there are other conditions that may mimic peripheral vascular disease but require different treatments). The following tips should help you increase the distance you can walk without pain:

• Spend several minutes stretching before you walk, and walk on level ground.

• When walking, note how far you can go before pain starts (the initial claudication distance). Continue from this point until pain becomes so severe that you have to stop.

• Rest for a few minutes until pain subsides, then resume walking.

• Repeat this pattern for 40 to 60 minutes.

• Try to walk at least four times a week. In inclement weather, walk in a mall or other indoor space.

• Keep track of initial claudication distances and the stopping distances. Both should increase within a few weeks.

• If you have heart disease, check with your physician about how much you should walk. Even if you don't have a history of heart disease but experience chest pain, shortness of breath, or rapid heartbeat while walking, stop and call your doctor.

an indoor track. Patients were instructed to walk at speeds that caused some discomfort (but not severe pain), and to slow down or stop when the pain became severe. By the end of the training period, patients had, on average, more than doubled the distance they could walk without stopping. Some 84 percent of those who completed the program were able to walk more than 1.25 miles after three months of training; 70 percent could walk almost two miles or more, at an average speed of about 3.5 mph. Furthermore, 20 out of 22 patients who were retested a year later had maintained a good walking ability.

The Editors

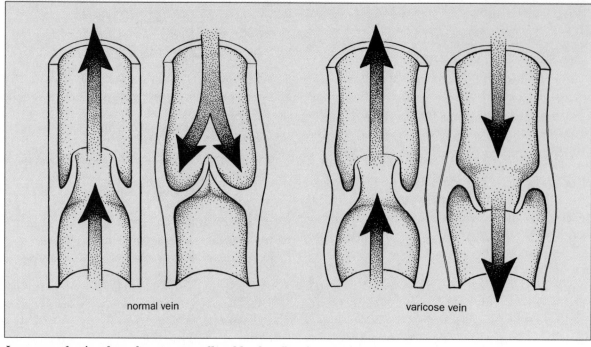

normal vein

varicose vein

In a normal vein, the valve opens to allow blood to flow in one direction, then closes securely to prevent backflow in the opposite direction. A varicose vein occurs when these valves fail.

VARICOSE VEINS

Our prehistoric ancestors' innovation of walking upright may have helped us create civilization, but it also put a lot of stress on our legs—particularly on their thin-walled veins. Blood is pumped under pressure out of the heart into arteries, and gravity helps it reach its destination in the lower extremities. But the return trip through the veins—against gravity—is not so easy. By the time blood has traveled through the tiniest arteries, through the capillaries, and into the tiniest veins, the force provided by the heart is exhausted. Veins must rely on the surrounding skeletal muscles to push and squeeze blood through as they flex.

Valves along the interior of veins permit blood to flow in one direction only. When we stand upright, these valves have to bear the weight of a long column of blood—perhaps more than we are evolutionarily equipped to

handle. Sometimes the load becomes too great and the valves fail, allowing blood to flow backwards and accumulate in one spot, causing the vein to balloon outward. The result: the telltale knotted clusters of swollen blood vessels known as varicose veins.

WHO IS AT RISK?

It's impossible to say just who will develop varicose veins, and when, but there seem to be several contributing factors:

Sex. Women are four times more likely than men to have varicose veins. During pregnancy, heightened hormone levels weaken vein walls and lead to the failure of the valves. Similarly, for women already genetically predisposed to varicosity, the hormones in birth control pills seem to promote it.

Genetics. People of Irish and German descent seem to have a predisposition to varicosities. And indeed, it's not uncommon for a

TIPS FOR PREVENTING VARICOSE VEINS

- Avoid standing or sitting for long periods.
- Put your feet up above hip level periodically during the day. This facilitates blood flow out of the veins, back to the heart.
- Maintain proper weight—excess pounds are a strain.
- Avoid repeated heavy lifting, or straining at stool. These activities induce backflow of blood in the veins.
- Don't smoke. A possible correlation has been found between smoking and incidence of varicose veins.
- Don't wear tight shoes, garters, belts, or other restrictive clothing.
- Exercise. Action in the calf muscles staves off pooling of blood and improves circulation in the lower leg. Regular aerobic exercise will also help keep weight down.

daughter to develop varicose veins identical to her mother's.

Sedentary lifestyle. The large calf muscles are sometimes called the "peripheral heart," as their motion serves to pump blood back up through the veins. Long periods of inactivity stifle this pumping action, and allow blood to pool in the veins and cause them to swell.

Age. As veins and skin lose their elasticity, the veins become more susceptible to varicosity.

ARE THEY DANGEROUS?

Usually varicose veins pose more risk to your vanity than your health. However, they may cause swelling in the calf, dull pain (particularly after standing for long periods), itching, and even skin ulcers due to poor circulation. Although rare, phlebitis (inflammation of the vein), often in association with a blood clot, can occur. Such clots cause local pain, but rarely, if ever, travel to the heart or lungs.

Thrombophlebitis (or, simply, phlebitis) is a condition that involves the inflammation of a vein or veins and the formation of blood clots in the veins. It may occur either in the superficial veins you can readily see near the surface of the skin or in the veins deep within the legs (or, less commonly, the arms). Superficial phlebitis does not usually lead to serious complications, although deep-vein phlebitis can lead to a pulmonary embolism. Most commonly, phlebitis is caused by prolonged bed rest—after an operation, for example—or even by prolonged sitting during an automobile or airplane trip. Superficial phlebitis can usually be treated with bed rest, elevation of the affected limb, heat, and the use of an anti-inflammatory drug. Deep-vein phlebitis is often treated with an anticoagulant drug and the use of antiembolism stockings, and hospitalization is often necessary.

TREATMENT OPTIONS

Fortunately, varicose veins can be safely remedied. Currently, there are two methods: surgery and sclerotherapy—and sometimes a combination of both is used for optimal cosmetic results. Surgery, the more drastic of the two, is being increasingly done on an outpatient basis. In most cases, a branch of the main saphenous vein, which runs down the inside of the thigh and calf, causes most of the backwards flow. These branches can be disconnected surgically, so that blood is forced to flow through veins with good valves. Only under exceptional circumstances, where the main vein itself lacks valves, is "vein stripping" (closing off the whole vein) done, because the saphenous vein is the best one to use for a graft in heart bypass procedures, should this ever become necessary. In sclerotherapy, a chemical solution is injected into the vein to kill the cells lining it. This turns the vein into a useless but innocuous fibrous cord. After either surgery or sclerotherapy, blood reroutes itself into the healthy veins of the leg, lessening the pressure on the veins with broken valves. This, in turn, makes the varicose vein less noticeable. *The Editors*

The Kidneys and Urinary Tract

OVERVIEW

Kidneys perform crucial functions which affect all parts of the body. Many other organs in our body depend upon the kidneys to function normally. The kidneys perform complex operations which keep the rest of the body in balance. But when the kidneys become damaged by disease, the other organs are adversely affected as well.

Kidney problems can range from a minor urinary tract infection to progressive kidney failure. Scientific advances over the past three decades have improved our ability to diagnose and treat those who suffer from kidney disorders.

Even when the kidneys no longer function, treatments such as dialysis and transplantation have brought hope and literally new life to hundreds of thousands of people.

Medical scientists continue to learn more about the function and structure of the kidneys and the diseases that affect them. There

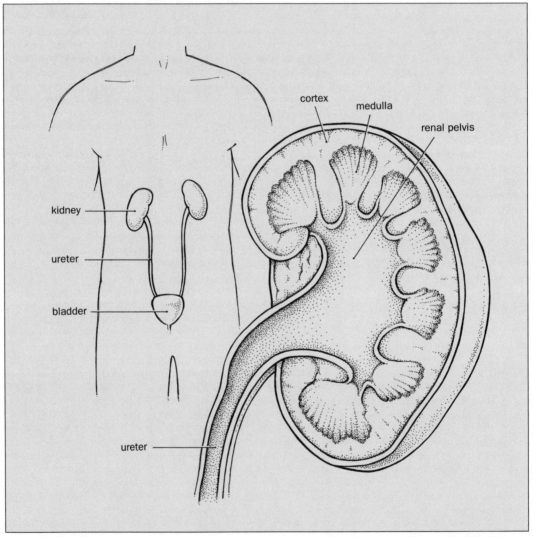

The kidneys are located in the back of the abdomen, one on each side, just above the waist. They produce urine, which flows down the ureters to the bladder, where it is stored until excretion.

is still much to learn and a need for continued support of research.

WHY THE KIDNEYS ARE SO IMPORTANT

A major function of the kidneys is to remove waste products and excess fluid from the body. These waste products and excess fluid are removed through the urine. The production of urine involves highly complex steps of excretion and reabsorption. This process is necessary to maintain a stable balance of body chemicals.

The critical regulation of the body's salt, potassium, and acid content is performed by the kidneys. The kidneys also produce hormones and vitamins which affect the function of other organs. For example, a hormone produced by the kidneys stimulates red blood cell production. In addition, other hormones produced by the kidneys help regulate blood pressure, and others help control calcium metabolism.

Moreover, the kidneys are powerful chemical factories that perform the following functions: remove waste products from the body; balance the body's fluids; release hormones which regulate blood pressure; synthesize the vitamins which control growth; control the production of red blood cells.

LOCATION AND FUNCTION OF THE KIDNEYS

There are two kidneys, each about the size of a fist, located on either side of the spine at the lowest level of the rib cage. Each kidney contains about one million functioning units called nephrons. A nephron consists of a filtering unit of tiny blood vessels called a glomerulus attached to a tubule. When blood enters the glomerulus, it is filtered and the remaining fluid then passes along the tubule. In the tubule, chemicals and water are either added to or removed from this filtered fluid according to the body's needs, the final product being the urine we excrete.

The kidneys perform their life-sustaining job of filtering and returning to the bloodstream about 200 quarts of fluid every 24 hours. (Approximately two quarts are eliminated from the body in the form of urine, and about 198 quarts are retained in the body.) The urine we excrete has been stored in the bladder for approximately one to eight hours.

TYPES AND CAUSES OF KIDNEY DISEASE

Kidney disease usually affects both kidneys. If the kidneys' ability to remove and regulate water and chemicals is seriously damaged by disease, waste products and excess fluid build up, causing severe swelling and symptoms of uremia (kidney failure). There are many different types and causes of kidney disease, and these can be characterized as either hereditary, congenital, or acquired.

Hereditary Disorders

Hereditary disorders can be transmitted to both males and females and generally produce clinical symptoms from teenage years to adulthood. The most prevalent hereditary kidney condition is polycystic kidney disease. Other hereditary conditions include Alport's syndrome, hereditary nephritis, primary hyperoxaluria, and cystinuria.

Congenital Disease

Congenital disease usually involves some malformation of the genitourinary tract, usually leading to some type of obstruction which subsequently produces infection and/or destruction of kidney tissue. The destruction can eventually progress to chronic kidney failure.

Acquired Kidney Diseases

These diseases are very numerous, the general term being nephritis (meaning inflammation of the kidney). The most common type of nephritis is glomerulonephritis, and again this has many causes.

Kidney stones are very common, and when they pass, the pain can be extremely severe in

DIALYSIS TREATMENTS

There are many patients who have been on chronic dialysis treatment since the time it first became widely available in the 1960s.

The total life expectancy remains unknown, but some dialysis patients may approach normal life spans. However, some patients do not tolerate dialysis well and have many complications.

Hemodialysis

In hemodialysis, an artificial kidney (hemodialyzer) is used to remove waste products from the blood and restore the body's chemical balance. In order to get the patient's blood to the artificial kidney, it is necessary to make an access to the patient's blood vessels. This requires surgery on an arm or a leg. The surgical procedure connects an artery to a vein underneath the skin. The joining of an artery to a vein creates an enlarged vessel known as a fistula. Once healing occurs, two needles are placed, one in the artery side and one in the vein side of the fistula. Plastic tubing attached to the needles connects the patient to the artificial kidney. The patient is now ready to begin treatment.

How Does the Artificial Kidney Work?

The artificial kidney has two compartments, one for the patient's blood and one for a cleaning solution called dialysate. A thin porous membrane separates these compartments. Blood cells, protein, and other important substances in the blood remain in their compartment because they are too large to pass through the holes of the membrane. Smaller waste products in the blood, such as urea and creatinine, and excess water pass through the membrane and are washed away. Needed substances such as calcium or dextrose (sugar) can be added to the dialysate and can move from the dialysate through the membrane into the patient's blood.

How Long Does It Take and How Often Is It Necessary?

The time required for each hemodialysis treatment is determined by the patient's amount of remaining kidney function, fluid weight gain between treatments, and the buildup of harmful chemicals between treatments. On the average, each hemodialysis treatment lasts approximately three to four hours and is usually necessary three times per week.

---

your side and back. Stone formation can be an inherited disorder, secondary to a malformation and/or infection in the kidney, or can occur without any prior problem. The pain can appear suddenly, occur in waves, and disappear just as rapidly when the stone is passed.

Evaluation by your doctor can reveal a cause for the kidney stone formation in about one-third of patients who have their first stone.

When kidney stones get stuck in the kidney and ureter (and cannot pass), a new form of shock wave treatment has been used to destroy the stone. This treatment is called extracorporeal shock wave lithotripsy.

Nephrotic syndrome refers to a large protein loss in the urine, frequently in association with low blood protein (albumin) levels, an elevated blood cholesterol, and severe retention of body fluid causing swelling (edema). This disease can be a primary disorder of the kidney or secondary to an illness affecting many parts of the body (for example, diabetes mellitus).

Long-standing high blood pressure (hypertension) can cause kidney disease itself or be a result of a kidney disorder. Uncontrolled high blood pressure can accelerate the natural course of any underlying kidney disease.

Drugs and toxins. Years of heavy use of headache compounds can slowly produce kidney failure. Certain other medications, toxins, pesticides, and "street" drugs (i.e., heroin) can also produce kidney damage.

TREATING KIDNEY DISEASE

Unfortunately, many kidney diseases are still of unknown cause. Some of the kidney diseases noted above can be successfully treated and others progress to advanced kidney fail-

A new treatment called high-flux, or short-time dialysis, is being used in some units. This form of hemodialysis can decrease dialysis time. The exact time is determined by the person's body size, blood chemistry, food intake, and urine output. It is important to stress that high-flux dialysis is not for everyone and is not available everywhere. If treatment is available, the doctor will determine whether it is suitable for the patient.

Peritoneal Dialysis

In this type of dialysis, the patient's blood is cleaned within the body. The blood stays in the blood vessels which line the patient's own abdominal (peritoneal) space. The lining of the space acts like the membrane in the artificial kidney.

A plastic tube called a catheter is surgically placed into the patient's abdomen to create an access. During the treatment, the patient's peritoneal cavity is slowly filled with dialysate through the catheter. As in hemodialysis, an exchange of waste products and chemical balancing takes place. Once a cycle (exchange) has been completed, the used dialysate is drained from the peritoneal cavity through the catheter, and discarded; the process is then repeated.

The following are the different types of peritoneal dialysis.

• *Continuous Ambulatory Peritoneal Dialysis (CAPD).* This is the only type of peritoneal dialysis that is done without the use of machines. Patients perform this procedure themselves, usually four or five times a day at home and at work. The patient drains a bag of dialysate into his or her peritoneal cavity by way of the catheter. The dialysate remains there for about four to five hours. After an exchange is complete, the patient drains the used dialysate back into the bag. The patient then repeats the procedure using a new bag of dialysate. While the dialysate remains inside the peritoneal cavity, the patient can go about daily activities.

• *Continuous Cycling Peritoneal Dialysis (CCPD).* This is usually done at home using a cycling machine. The process is identical to CAPD except the cycle periods are usually one and a half hours and are performed several times a night, as the patient sleeps.

ure, requiring dialysis and/or transplantation. For example, kidney infections and kidney stones can often be successfully treated. Chronic inflammation of the glomerulus (called glomerulonephritis) is the most common kidney disease which slowly progresses to kidney failure.

TREATING ADVANCED KIDNEY FAILURE

Research is now being considered on the effect of special diets in slowing or halting progressive kidney failure, especially if the problem is approached early.

Treatments to slow the progress of kidney failure hold promise for the future. When these therapies are no longer successful, there are now several ways by which chronic, irreversible kidney failure can be treated, and often more than one type of treatment is suitable for any one person. These methods are listed below.

Dialysis

Treatment with hemodialysis (the artificial kidney) may be performed at a dialysis unit or at home. Hemodialysis treatments are usually performed in three separate sessions per week.

Peritoneal dialysis is generally done daily at home. Continuous cycling peritoneal dialysis requires the use of a machine while continuous ambulatory peritoneal dialysis does not.

Transplantation

Finally, there has been increasing success with kidney transplantation. In some cases, the kidney may come from a relative who donates one of his or her own kidneys to the patient. Kidney transplantation from cadaveric donors, however, is more common in the United States. Under these circumstances, individuals who have died have donated their kidneys for potential transplantation.

THE WARNING SIGNS OF KIDNEY DISEASE

Although many forms of kidney disease do not produce symptoms until late in the course of the disease, there are six warning signs of kidney diseases.

- Burning or difficulty during urination
- An increase in the frequency of urination
- Passage of bloody urine
- Puffiness around the eyes, swelling of the hands and feet
- Pain in the small of back just below the ribs
- High blood pressure

The National Kidney Foundation

URINARY TRACT INFECTIONS

The urinary tract is a vital, finely balanced system whose task is to extract and dispose of the body's liquid wastes. Infections of the urinary tract are among the most common in the human body—so common that only respiratory infections occur more often. Each year, patients with symptoms of a urinary tract infection (UTI) account for 5 million visits to a doctor's office. Among women, UTIs are especially troublesome; it is estimated that up to 20 percent of women develop a UTI sometime in their lives.

The urinary system, made up of the kidneys, ureters, bladder, and urethra, eliminates liquid waste products and helps maintain a stable balance of salts and other dissolved substances in the blood. The key players in the system are the kidneys, a pair of purplish-brown organs located below the ribs toward the middle of the back. These highly complex organs remove liquid waste material from the bloodstream in the form of urine and produce a hormone that regulates the formation of red blood cells. Two narrow tubes called ureters carry urine from the kidneys to the bladder, a triangle-shaped chamber in the lower abdomen. Urine is stored in the bladder and emptied through another passageway, the urethra.

CAUSES

Normal urine is sterile. It contains fluids, salts, and waste products, but it is free of microorganisms such as bacteria, viruses, or fungi. An infection occurs when microorganisms, usually bacteria from the digestive tract, ad-

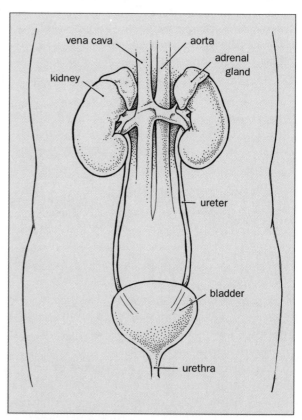

Urinary tract infections are often confined to the urethra (urethritis), but may involve the bladder (cystitis) or kidneys (pyelonephritis).

here to the opening of the urethra and begin to multiply. Most infections can be traced to one type of colon bacteria, called Escherichia coli (E. coli).

Recently, microorganisms called Chlamydia and Mycoplasma have been found to cause urinary tract infections in both men and women, but these tend to remain limited to the urethra and genital system. Unlike the majority of UTIs, infections caused by these two microbes are sexually transmitted, are not detected by standard culturing methods, and require treatment of both sexual partners.

As they reproduce, bacteria colonize the urethra. An infection that is limited to the urethra is called urethritis. Often the bacteria migrate from the urethra to the bladder, causing cystitis (a bladder infection). It is important to treat the infection promptly, before bacteria that invade the lower urinary tract have a chance to travel upward, causing a kidney infection (pyelonephritis) and possibly kidney damage.

The urinary system is structured in a way that helps guard against infection. For instance, the ureters normally prevent the backup of urine toward the kidneys, and the flow of urine from the bladder helps wash harmful bacteria out of the body. In men, the prostate gland produces secretions that kill or inhibit infection-causing bacteria. In both sexes, various immune defenses also play a role in keeping infection at bay. Despite these and other safeguards, infections still occur.

RISK FACTORS

Some people are more prone to getting a urinary infection than others.

Abnormalities of the urinary tract that obstruct or slow the flow of urine makes it easier for bacteria to grow. When the urine does not empty freely, it may stagnate in the bladder.

A stone in the kidney or any part of the urinary tract can form such a blockage, creating the conditions for a UTI.

In men, an enlarged prostate gland can obstruct urine flow and make infection difficult to treat.

Catheters. One of the most common sources of urinary infection is catheters, or tubes, that have been placed in the bladder. Patients who cannot void, are unconscious, or critically ill, often need a catheter that remains in place for a period of time.

Because of the risk that bacteria inhabiting the catheter can enter and infect the bladder, hospital staff take special care to prevent the catheter from becoming contaminated. Also, physicians try to remove the catheter as soon as possible.

Some patients, especially the elderly or those with diseases of the nervous system who lose bladder control, may require a catheter for life.

Diabetes mellitus. People who have diabetes mellitus have a higher risk of a UTI because of changes of the immune system. Any disorder that involves suppression of the immune system sets the stage for urinary infection.

WOMEN AND UTI

The rate of UTIs in females gradually increases as they age. Scientists are not sure why women have more urinary infections than men. One factor may be that in women the urethra is short, allowing easy migration of bacteria to the bladder. Also, a woman's urethral opening is near sources of bacteria from the anus and vagina. For many women, sexual intercourse seems to precipitate an infection. The reasons for this association are unclear, but some doctors think that, in women predisposed to vaginal colonization of bacteria, intercourse may propel bacteria into the urethra.

Yet another factor is the method of birth control. According to several studies, women who use the diaphragm are more likely to develop a UTI than women who use other forms of contraception.

Recurrent Infections

UTIs are a recurrent problem for many women, also for reasons that are poorly understood. In the vast majority of cases, the new infection stems from a strain or type of bacteria that is different from the infection that preceded it. (Even when several infections in a row are traced to E. coli, there are usually slight differences in the bacteria, indicating that each infection was caused by a distinct strain.) Researchers at Tulane University in New Orleans suggest that one factor behind recurrent UTIs may be the ability of bacteria to adhere to the mucous tissue of the urinary tract. Another may be that local immune responses in some women are less effective in preventing the growth of bacteria.

SYMPTOMS

Not everyone with a urinary tract infection has symptoms, but most people get at least some. Such symptoms include a frequent urge to urinate and a painful, burning feeling during urination. It is not unusual to feel bad all over—tired, shaky, washed out—and to feel pain even when not urinating. Often, women feel an uncomfortable pressure above the pubic bone, and some men experience a fullness in the rectum.

It is common for a person with a urinary infection to complain that, despite the urge to urinate, only a small amount of urine is passed. The urine itself may appear milky or cloudy—even reddish if blood is present.

A fever may indicate that the infection has reached the kidneys. Other symptoms of a kidney infection include pain in the back or side below the ribs, nausea, or vomiting.

DIAGNOSIS

Urine tests. A urinary infection can easily be diagnosed by testing a sample of urine for the presence of pus and bacteria. A "clean catch" urine sample is obtained by washing the genital area and collecting a "midstream" sample of urine in a sterile container. (This method of collecting a urine sample helps prevent bacteria around the genital area from contaminating the urine and confusing the test results.) Usually, the sample is sent to a laboratory, although some doctors' offices are equipped to do the testing on site. First, the urine is examined for white and red blood cells and bacteria in a test called urinalysis. The bacteria then are grown in a culture and tested against various antibiotics to determine which drug most effectively destroys the bacteria. This step is called a sensitivity test.

Some microbes, like Chlamydia and Mycoplasma, require special bacterial cultures in order to be detected. A doctor should suspect one of these infections if the patient has symptoms of a UTI and has pus in the urine, but a laboratory culture fails to grow any bacteria.

Intravenous pyelogram. When a patient has a persistent infection—one that does not clear up with appropriate treatment and is traced to the same strain of bacteria—the doctor orders an intravenous pyelogram (IVP). This examination gives x-ray images of the bladder, kidneys, and ureters. An opaque dye visible on x-ray film is injected into a vein, and a series of x-rays are taken. The film shows an outline of the urinary tract, revealing even small changes in the contours of these organs that might contribute to infection.

Some doctors may also recommend an IVP for women patients who have five or more infections in a year. (As stated before, most recurring infections are caused by a different strain or type of bacteria.)

Another test that may be useful for patients with recurring infections is a cystoscopy. A cystoscope is an instrument made of a hollow tube with several lenses and a light source, which allows the doctor to see the inside of the bladder.

TREATMENT

Urinary tract infections are treated with antibacterial drugs. The choice of drug and length of treatment depends on the patient's history and the urine tests that identify the offending bacteria. The sensitivity test is especially useful in helping the doctor select the most effective drug.

Antibiotics

Uncomplicated infections. Several clinical trials have shown that an uncomplicated infection in women can be cured with one or two days of treatment. However, many physicians prefer to have their patients take antibiotics for a longer period (e.g., 7 to 14 days) to ensure that the infection has been cured.

Single-dose treatment is not recommended for certain groups of patients, for example, those who have delayed treatment or have signs of bacterial invasion of tissue, patients with diabetes or structural abnormalities, or men who have infections in the prostate gland. Lengthier treatment is also needed by patients with infections caused by Mycoplasma or Chlamydia, who are usually treated with tetracycline, trimethoprim/sulfamethoxazole (TMP/SMZ), or doxycycline.

A follow-up urinalysis helps to confirm that the urinary tract is infection-free. It is important to take the full course of treatment, even after symptoms disappear.

Severe infections. Severely ill patients with kidney infections may be hospitalized until they are able to take fluids and needed drugs on their own. The consensus among physicians is that kidney infections require several weeks of antibiotic therapy. A recent clinical trial at the University of Washington found that two-week therapy with TMP/SMZ was as effective as six weeks of treatment with the same drug in women with "uncomplicated" kidney infections. (Uncomplicated infections are those in which there is no underlying obstruction or nervous system disorder. In such cases, kidney infections rarely lead to kidney damage or kidney failure unless they go untreated.) Moreover, the research showed that two-week TMP/SMZ treatment was more effective and better tolerated than either two- or six-week treatment with ampicillin.

Additional Measures

Various drugs are available to relieve the pain of a UTI. A heating pad or a warm bath may help. Physicians have different opinions on the importance of drinking extra fluids, but most suggest that drinking plenty of water helps cleanse the urinary tract of harmful bacteria. Others feel that increasing fluid intake is unnecessary because the infection is so quickly cured by antibiotics. For the time being, it is best to avoid irritants like coffee, alcohol, and spicy foods. (And one of the kindest favors a smoker can do for his or her bladder is to quit smoking. Smoking is the most important known risk factor for bladder cancer.)

Preventive Therapy for Women

About four out of five women who have a UTI get another one within 18 months. Many women have them even more frequently. Women who have frequent recurrences (e.g., three or more a year) may benefit from preventive therapy. Doctors use several approaches to manage these patients after the most recent infection has been eradicated.

Antibiotics. One of the most common approaches is for the patient to take low doses of an antibiotic daily for six months or longer. (If taken at bedtime, the drug remains in the bladder longer and may be more effective.)

Another is to take a single dose of an antibiotic after sexual intercourse. Even after long-term treatment, however, some women continue to have recurrent infections.

Other measures. Many doctors suggest steps that a woman can take on her own to avoid an infection.

- Drink plenty of water every day (some doctors suggest drinking cranberry juice, which in large amounts inhibits the growth of some bacteria by acidifying the urine).
- Don't put off urinating when you feel the need.
- Wipe from front to back to prevent bacteria around the anus from entering the vagina or urethra.
- Cleanse the genital area before sexual intercourse.
- Empty the bladder shortly before and after sexual intercourse.
- Avoid using feminine hygiene sprays and scented douches.

Complicated Infections

In both sexes, curing "complicated" infections—those involving an obstruction of urine or disorder of the nervous system—depends on finding and correcting the underlying problem, sometimes with surgery. If the root cause is not treated effectively, this group of patients is at risk of kidney damage. Also, such infections tend to arise from a wider range of bacteria, and occasionally from more than one organism at a time, so choosing the best antibiotic therapy can be more complex.

As discussed earlier, UTIs are unusual in men. When they do occur, it is likely that the patient has some kind of obstruction—for example, a urinary stone or enlarged prostate—or recently had a medical procedure involving a catheter. The first step is to identify the infecting organism and the drugs to which it is sensitive. Usually, doctors recommend lengthier therapy in men than in women, in part to prevent infection of the prostate gland. When infection does involve the prostate (prostatitis), it is harder to cure because antibacterial drugs are unable to penetrate prostatic tissue very well. For this reason, men with prostatitis often need long-term treatment with a carefully selected antibiotic.

The National Institute of Diabetes and
Digestive and Kidney Diseases

KIDNEY STONES

A kidney stone is a hard mass that occurs when certain chemicals in the urine form crystals that stick together. These crystals may grow into a stone ranging in size from a grain of sand to a golf ball. Small stones pass out of the body with the urine. However, larger stones may block the flow of urine or irritate the lining of the urinary tract.

Most stones start to form in the kidney. Some may travel to other parts of the urinary tract, such as the ureter or bladder, and grow there.

The majority of kidney stones (70 to 80 percent) contain mainly calcium oxalate crystals. Stones sometimes injure kidneys and reduce their function by causing an infection or obstruction.

More than a million cases of kidney stones are diagnosed in the United States each year. Kidney stones affect mainly young and middle-aged adults. They are a significant cause of hospital stays and loss of work. Stones are more common in men; four out of five patients with stones are men. Since stones tend to recur, even after they are passed or removed, successful treatment depends on finding out what causes the stones.

CAUSES

The reasons are not always clear as to why some people form stones and others do not. Normally, urine contains chemicals that prevent crystals from forming. However, these do not seem to work for everyone. There is evidence that the following factors contribute to stone formation in susceptible people.

- Drinking too little fluid
- Chronic urinary tract infections
- Misuse of certain medications
- Blockage of the urinary tract

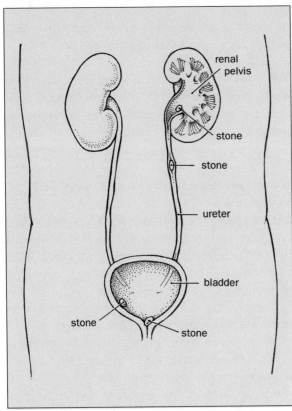

Stones can form in the kidney and may cause substantial pain when they become lodged along the urinary tract. Most kidney stones pass spontaneously

- Limited activity for several weeks or more
- Certain genetic and metabolic diseases

Scientists do not generally believe that eating any specific foods causes stones. However, in susceptible people, certain foods may promote formation of stones. For example, some persons may have a metabolic disorder (called absorptive hypercalciuria), which causes too much calcium to be absorbed from the foods they eat. This results in a high level of calcium in the urine, which may cause calcium oxalate crystals to form.

SYMPTOMS

Some people have no symptoms, but most have at least some of the following symptoms.

- Severe pain (usually starts suddenly in the kidneys or in the lower abdomen and may move to the groin; pain may last for minutes or hours followed by periods of relief)
- Nausea and vomiting
- Burning and frequent urge to urinate
- Fever, chills, and weakness (may mean that an infection is present)
- Cloudy or foul-smelling urine (also associated with infection)
- Blood in the urine
- Blocked flow of urine

Many of these symptoms may be associated with other kidney and urinary tract disorders. A complete medical evaluation is needed to confirm the presence of a stone.

DIAGNOSIS

X-rays can usually identify the presence of stones. Specialized x-ray techniques (sometimes using dye injections) or sound waves may be used to identify more accurately the size and location of the stones and to test kidney function. Blood and urine tests may be done to find out what is causing the stone and to help the doctor to plan the best treatment. Patients are asked about their diet, use of medications, lifestyle, and family background to learn other factors that may contribute to their stone problem. "Silent" stones, those not causing symptoms, usually are found during x-ray examination of the abdomen for other reasons.

TREATMENT

Nonsurgical Methods

Most stones can be treated with increased fluid intake, changes in diet, and medication. About 90 percent of stones will pass by themselves within three to six weeks. Certain types of stones—uric acid and cystine stones, for example—sometimes may be dissolved using medications. Currently, calcium-containing stones (the most common type in the United States) cannot be dissolved. Stones should always be removed when infection, obstruction, or kidney damage are present.

Surgical Methods

When stones must be removed, several different methods are available. The best method for you depends on the size, location, and type of stone. Your doctor will help you to decide on the best treatment after careful medical evaluation, x-rays, and other tests.

Conventional open surgery currently is used in only 5 percent of cases. It may be necessary when internal scarring or blockage are present or when other methods fail. Occasionally, kidney function is so seriously damaged and infection is so severe that the surgeon may decide to remove the entire kidney after making sure the other kidney functions well. One kidney is enough to do the work of removing wastes to keep the body healthy.

Alternate techniques. Stones are treated with simpler methods whenever possible because of the shorter hospital stays and recovery time. Some stones are removed by passing a telescopic instrument into the bladder or ureter to pull the stones out or to break them into small fragments with sound waves or laser beams. Similarly, a telescopic instrument may be inserted directly into the kidney through a slit made in the patient's side. The surgeon then removes the stone whole or breaks it down into small fragments with sound waves, high-energy shock waves, or other methods. When stones are broken down, the fragments pass within a few weeks.

Extracorporeal shock wave lithotripsy. The newest method of stone removal is called extracorporeal shock wave lithotripsy. In this technique, stones are broken down into small fragments by high-energy shock waves, which are focused on the stone from a source outside the body. The patient is positioned in a water bath or on top of a water-filled cushion during the treatment. Again, the stone fragments are passed within a few weeks.

This technique has greatly reduced the costs and recovery time involved in treating kidney stones. However, the long-term effects of the treatment are still being studied.

PREVENTION

If left untreated, many patients who have kidney stones tend to get more stones even after a stone passes or is removed. Treatments that can prevent stones from forming are possible in many cases. Strong evidence suggests that a high fluid intake may decrease the risk of stones. In addition, once the cause of the stone is found, medications or changes in diet may be used to help prevent new stones.

In general, a specific medicine is used only if high fluid intake and diet therapy cannot prevent the patient's stones. The type of medicine used is based on blood and urine tests. Normally, your doctor will collect samples of your urine over a 24-hour period on one or more occasions on your normal diet and fluid intake.

Today, scientific progress has brought about a better understanding of the causes of stone disease, and treatment is far more effective. With newer treatments such as extracorporeal shock wave lithotripsy, much of the suffering of stone surgery has been eliminated. However, some causes of stone formation are still unclear. Further study is necessary to provide a better understanding of these processes.   *The National Kidney Foundation*

GLOMERULONEPHRITIS

Glomerulonephritis is the term used to describe a group of kidney diseases where the filtering part of the kidney (glomerulus) is inflamed. Sometimes the name is shortened to nephritis.

TYPES OF GLOMERULONEPHRITIS

Acute glomerulonephritis (acute nephritis). With acute glomerulonephritis, there is a tendency for spontaneous recovery.

Chronic glomerulonephritis (chronic nephritis). In this form of the disease, progressive damage of kidney tissue occurs. Signs of the disease may include protein and blood in the urine and usually high blood pressure. Chronic glomerulonephritis is the most common cause of chronic kidney failure leading to end-stage renal disease (ESRD).

Rapidly progressive glomerulonephritis (RPGN). RPGN leads to kidney failure fairly quickly. This disease is of unknown cause, is irreversible, can appear suddenly, and is characterized by a decrease in urine output.

SYMPTOMS AND SIGNS

Acute Glomerulonephritis

Acute glomerulonephritis is usually a disease of children, but can occur at any age. Males have the disease more frequently than females. About 10 days after the start of an infection of the throat or skin, the patient will frequently note a fall in the urine output and the urine looks "smoky or rusty" (often described as coffee or cola colored). There can be burning upon urination. Fluid retention is common, typically involving the face, eyelids, and hands. This is most notable in the morning when rising. Shortness of breath and coughing can occur because of fluid congestion in the lungs. High blood pressure is common. Although many or all of these symptoms and signs can occur, it is important to understand that these can vary.

In addition, systemic and hereditary diseases have symptoms and signs which are similar to acute glomerulonephritis. The diseases in this category include systemic lupus erythematosus, Henoch-Schonlein purpura, many types of vasculitis, and Goodpasture's disease. However, these diseases generally do not improve and treatment is needed.

Other kidney diseases of unknown cause may also have qualities which are similar to acute glomerulonephritis. These diseases are called membrano-proliferative glomerulonephritis, IgA nephropathy, and focal and segmental glomerulonephritis. In general, these diseases do not show improvement either on their own or with treatment.

Chronic Glomerulonephritis

The wide variety of diseases that fit in the category of chronic glomerulonephritis generally have a longer course. They have lengthy periods without revealing any symptoms. During this time, there is progressive damage of kidney tissue.

In the early stages, frequently the only findings are an abnormal urinalysis (for example, red blood cells, white blood cells, and protein in the urine). High blood pressure can be found, especially when there is a decrease in kidney function for the first time. As the disease progresses, there is swelling of the

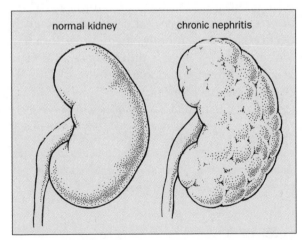

normal kidney   chronic nephritis

Chronic nephritis destroys kidney tissue in addition to damaging the ability of existing kidney tissue to function properly.

legs (edema) and persistent high blood pressure. High blood pressure is often difficult to treat. The following signs of chronic kidney failure (uremia) are noted when there is a severe loss of kidney function.

- Loss of appetite
- Nausea and vomiting
- Extreme fatigue, even after a night's sleep, and a severe loss of energy
- Difficulty sleeping
- Itching and dry skin
- Muscle cramps, especially at night

CAUSES

Acute Glomerulonephritis

Patients with acute glomerulonephritis often have evidence of a recent infection. The most common infection causing glomerulonephritis is a streptococcal infection of the throat or skin. Other serious bacterial and viral infections may also be associated with acute glomerulonephritis.

Chronic Glomerulonephritis

There are many causes for the general term of chronic glomerulonephritis. A wide variety of diseases affecting the glomerulus have a common picture. There is usually a prolonged course, often with years of no symptoms, while progressive scarring of the kidney is silently occurring. Occasionally, an acute glomerulonephritis can have a quiet phase after the original illness and appear many years later as chronic glomerulonephritis.

Many different causes of nephrotic syndrome can sometimes lead to the damaging process of chronic glomerulonephritis, especially when the nephrotic syndrome does not respond to treatment.

DIAGNOSIS

The signs and symptoms noted previously are the first clues to the diagnosis.

Laboratory tests. In acute glomerulonephritis, blood tests can indicate a recent streptococcal infection. Other forms of glomerulonephritis can be detected by special blood tests that show the type of damage occurring in the kidney without learning the exact cause of the injury. Also, cultures of the throat, skin, or other known areas of local infection can identify the bacteria which is causing the problem. Examination of the urine can show the presence of blood, protein, and other elements. Other blood tests which point out inflammation in the kidney can show how much kidney function is lost.

Kidney biopsy. Often it is necessary to do a kidney biopsy (removal of a tiny piece of tissue by a special needle). This is done under local anesthesia to establish the exact diagnosis and determine the short- and long-term outlook for the patient. Sometimes the biopsy is necessary for the doctor to plan the best possible treatment for the patient.

TREATMENT

Acute Glomerulonephritis

There is no specific treatment for acute glomerulonephritis. This illness will usually heal completely within 3 to 12 months after onset. With both acute and chronic glomerulonephritis, it is important to treat high blood pressure. Uncontrolled high blood pressure can lead to a rapid decrease in kidney function. Diuretics often are used to control excess retention of body fluid.

Chronic Glomerulonephritis

In chronic glomerulonephritis, steroids and other drugs have been used. However, most often this treatment is not successful in treating the cause of chronic glomerulonephritis. A special blood-filtering process called plasmapheresis has been used in special types of glomerulonephritis, and at times, there have been very good results with this treatment.

Restricting protein, salt, and sometimes potassium in the diet may be a major part in the conservative treatment used by your doctor. A dietitian can help you with this part of your care.

PREVENTION

Acute Glomerulonephritis

It is not possible to prevent acute glomerulonephritis except with good skin hygiene. Keeping the skin clean will decrease the chances of getting a potentially serious skin infection. There is no good way to prevent getting strep throat. Antibodies will not prevent acute glomerulonephritis, even when used quickly to treat documented infection.

Chronic Glomerulonephritis

Since chronic glomerulonephritis represents a wide variety of diseases, there is no way to prevent getting the disease.

NEPHROTIC SYNDROME (NEPHROSIS)

Nephrotic syndrome (sometimes called nephrosis) is a term used to describe a condition where there is heavy loss of protein in the urine, usually in association with a low protein level in the blood, an increase in the blood cholesterol level, and the retention of fluid (edema). Nephrotic syndrome can be a primary kidney disease or a complication of a systemic illness.

Treatment

In some forms of nephrotic syndrome, treatment with medicines such as corticosteroids will significantly reduce the amount of protein lost in the urine. In other types of nephrotic syndrome, corticosteroids have not been shown to help. In these cases, treatment consists of diuretics to control swelling and high blood pressure.

The National Kidney Foundation

The Lungs and Respiratory System

OVERVIEW

The respiratory system, including the lungs, brings air into the body. The oxygen in the air travels from the lungs through the bloodstream to the cells in all parts of the body. The cells use the oxygen as fuel and give off carbon dioxide as a waste gas. This waste gas is carried by the bloodstream back to the lungs to be eliminated or exhaled. The lungs accomplish this vital process—called gas exchange—using an automatic and quickly adjusting control system.

In addition to gas exchange, the lungs and the other parts of the respiratory system have important jobs to do related to breathing. These include:

- Bringing inhaled air to the proper body temperature.
- Moisturizing the inhaled air for necessary humidity.
- Protecting the body from harmful substances by coughing, sneezing, filtering, or swallowing them, or by alerting the body through the sense of smell.
- Defending the lungs with (1) cilia, microscopic hairs along the air passages; (2) phlegm (mucus or sputum)—a moving carpet of phlegm collects dirt and germs inhaled into the lungs and moves them out to be coughed up or swallowed; (3) macrophages, scavenger cells in the lungs that literally eat up dirt and germs invading the lungs.

THE WARNING SIGNS OF LUNG DISEASE

The most frequent warning signs of lung disease are listed here. If you are experiencing any of these symptoms, discuss them with your doctor as soon as possible.

Chronic cough. Any cough that has lasted a month is chronic. This is an important early symptom indicating something is wrong with your breathing system, regardless of your age.

Shortness of breath. Shortness of breath that continues after a brief rest following normal exercise, or comes after little or no exertion, is not normal. Labored or difficult breathing, the feeling that it is hard to draw air into your lungs or breathe it out, is also a warning sign.

Chronic phlegm production. Phlegm, or sputum, is produced by the lungs as a defense response to infection or irritants. If your phlegm or mucus production has lasted a month, this could be an indication of an underlying problem.

Wheezing. Noisy breathing or wheezing is a sign that something unusual is blocking the airways of your lungs or making the airways too narrow.

Coughing up blood (hemoptysis). If you are coughing up blood, the blood may be coming from your lungs or upper respiratory tract.

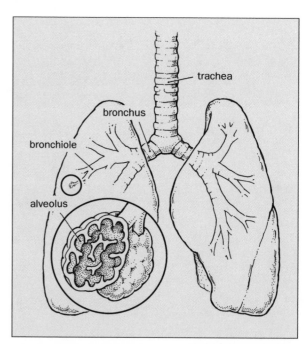

The trachea divides into two bronchi, one leading into each lung. These branch out further into the bronchioles and culminate in tiny air sacs, or alveoli.

Whatever the source of the blood, it signals the onset of a health problem.

Frequent chest colds. If you have more than two colds a year, or if one lasts more than two weeks, you may have an underlying disorder.

WHAT THE SYMPTOMS MEAN

Experts agree that your lungs are not healthy if you have any of these symptoms. You must have them checked out by your doctor. If you wait for symptoms to become severe, you have already lost valuable treatment time. Taking care of mild symptoms can actually be to your advantage.

Even if you have only one of the symptoms of lung disease—chronic cough, shortness of breath or difficult breathing, phlegm, wheezing, or frequent chest colds—you should see your doctor. Most lung conditions can be helped by treatment and can even be reversed if caught early.

DIAGNOSING LUNG DISEASE

Your doctor will usually use very simple tests to determine if you have a lung disease. He or she will take a medical history and give you a complete physical examination. Your examination may include some simple laboratory tests like a chest x-ray, blood tests, a phlegm (sputum) examination, and a pulmonary function test, which is a painless procedure that shows the doctor how well your lungs work when you breathe. Exercise testing may also be done to examine the body's response to exertion or physical activity.

Health authorities advise a tuberculosis (TB) skin test for various groups of people, including all persons who are HIV-positive, meaning that they have tested positive for the human immunodeficiency virus that causes AIDS. Since the TB test reaction may be misleading in AIDS, a chest x-ray and complete physical exam may be recommended even if the tuberculin test is negative. Based on information gathered through these quick and basic tests, your doctor will decide which lung disease, if any, exists. Then appropriate treatment can be started.

COMMON LUNG HAZARDS

Any substance that is breathed in affects what happens to the lungs. Many of these substances can be hazardous and threaten the lungs' ability to work properly. Such hazards may include the following.

Cigarette smoking. The major cause of chronic obstructive pulmonary disease and lung cancer is cigarette smoking. When someone inhales cigarette smoke, irritating gases and particles cause one of the lungs' defenses—the cilia—to slow down. Even one puff on a cigarette slows the cilia, weakening the lungs' ability to defend themselves against infections. Cigarette smoke can cause air passages to close up and make breathing more difficult. It causes chronic inflammation or swelling in the lungs, leading to chronic bronchitis. And cigarette smoke changes the enzyme balance of the lungs, leading to destruction of lung tissue that occurs in emphysema. Macrophages—scavenger cells in the lungs—are also impaired.

Triggers of asthma. Asthma, the temporary blocking of the small passages of the lungs, has many possible triggers and can be life-threatening. Infections, lung irritants, cold weather, allergies, overexertion, excitement, inherited factors, even workplace chemicals and other irritants, play a part in this disease.

Tuberculosis (TB). Tuberculosis is caused by a bacterium spread by the coughing or sneezing of a person who has active TB germs in his or her phlegm (sputum). Most people who develop TB today were infected years ago when the disease was widespread.

Years or decades later, if the natural defense systems of people's bodies begin to weaken, the barriers they built up around the germs begin to crumble, and the TB germs escape and multiply. Such waiting-to-attack infection can become real illness when a person's defenses are weakened by HIV (human immunodeficiency virus) infection or other chronic illnesses such as cancer.

Occupational hazards. Substances you breathe at work can cause lung trouble, too. Workers who are exposed to occupational hazards in the air—dusts like those from coal, silica, asbestos, or raw cotton and metal fumes or chemical vapors—can develop lung disease, including occupational asthma.

Virus, fungus, bacterium (other than TB). Hundreds of germs like these are carried in the air at all times. If they are inhaled into the lungs, the germs can cause colds, influenza, pneumonia, and other respiratory infections. When these germs lodge in your lungs, your breathing patterns can be disrupted, and you can become ill. Some of these illnesses can be prevented with vaccination.

Air pollution. Particles and gases in the air can be a source of lung irritation. Do whatever you can to reduce your exposure to air pollution. Refer to radio or television weather reports or your local newspaper for information about air quality. On days when the ozone (smog) level is unhealthy, restrict your physical activity to early morning or evening because smog is increased in sunlight. When pollution levels are dangerous, limit activities as necessary. People with chronic heart and lung disease should remain indoors.

PROTECTING YOUR LUNGS AND PREVENTING LUNG DISEASE

Controlling and preventing lung disease needs everyone's attention. Learn to recognize the symptoms of lung disease, such as those previously described. If you have any of these symptoms, get medical attention as soon as possible.

Everyone needs to protect their lungs by observing the following measures.

- *Don't smoke.* Quitting smoking is the best protection you can give your lungs and reduces your risk of lung disease.
- *Be honest.* Understand that chronic cough, shortness of breath, and other lung symptoms are not normal.
- *Take action.* Bring any lung disease symptom to your doctor's attention early. Then follow the doctor's advice.
- *Avoid lung hazards.* Secondhand cigarette smoke, air pollution, and lung hazards at work can cause some lung diseases.
- *Think about prevention.* Lung diseases like influenza (flu) and pneumococcal pneumonia can be prevented with vaccination. Get immunized if you are in a high risk group, which includes people over 65 or anyone with a chronic health problem such as heart disease, lung disease, and diabetes. Remember—early detection of lung disease is the key to prompt and successful treatment.

The American Lung Association

ASTHMA

Asthma is a lung disease that causes breathing problems for nearly 10 million Americans. These problems usually happen in "episodes," also called "attacks."

Asthma is usually a chronic problem—that is, people who have asthma live with it every day, often for their whole lives.

Asthma is serious, and it can be life-threatening if not properly managed. However, with proper management most people with asthma can live normal, productive lives.

Signs of asthma may include: a chronic cough at rest or after exercise, shortness of breath, wheezing and/or tightness in the chest. If you or a loved one have any of these signs, see a doctor for proper diagnosis and treatment.

People with asthma and their families need to know how to recognize the early warning signs of asthma attacks, and must know how to manage asthma on a continuous basis. They must work in partnership with a physician and other health care providers to determine which medicines and other treatments can best help them to control the disease.

AN INCREASING PROBLEM

Studies have shown that since the early 1970s, the prevalence of asthma—that is, the total number of people with asthma—has been increasing in the United States and other countries, as has the number of hospitalizations and deaths related to asthma. Nearly 10 million Americans are reported to have asthma, and experts suggest that many other people have the disease but have not yet been diagnosed and treated.

Experts are unsure why these increases have happened. Several factors have been suggested, such as increasing exposure to infections and other "triggers" of the tightening and inflammation of the airways that happen with asthma, such as air pollution; inadequate use of regular, ongoing treatment for asthma which uses up-to-date medical regimens; and the quality of the air we breathe outdoors and indoors.

WHO GETS ASTHMA

Anyone can get asthma. People of all races and nationalities. The rich and the poor. And at any age.

Of the nearly 10 million Americans diagnosed as having asthma, approximately 3 million are under the age of 18, while approximately 7 million are adults. Some adults may have had asthma all their lives, but others may have gotten it for the first time as grownups.

Children sometimes seem to outgrow their asthma, but it may return later in life.

Approximately the same number of men and women have asthma, but under the age of 20 the prevalence rates are higher among males than females. African-Americans have had slightly higher rates than whites (4.4 percent compared to 4 percent of whites). The asthma death rate for African-Americans has also been consistently higher.

Asthma seems to run in families. However, that doesn't mean that the child of someone with asthma is certain to have it, too.

AN ASTHMA ATTACK

Researchers have learned that an asthma episode or attack is not as simple as people once thought. Years ago, doctors thought that an asthma attack was a single event—contraction of the muscle layer in the airways that temporarily narrowed the passages through which a person breathes. Today, they have learned that an asthma attack is more complicated.

Progression of the Attack

An asthma attack typically occurs when an allergen or irritant affects the lungs. A person may feel a tightness in the chest, or experience slight wheezing, coughing, restlessness or difficulty in trying to sleep, or trouble breathing. The passageways that let air into the lungs constrict (narrow). It's hard for the person to breathe air in and even harder to breathe the stale air out.

The cells that line the air passages begin to secrete more mucus than normal, and the mucus is very thick and sticky, so it tends to clog the air passages. And, because the air passages are irritated, they tend to swell, just as skin swells when you get a scrape. All these problems—the constricted air passages, the mucus, and the swelling—make it difficult for the person with asthma to breathe. As breathing becomes more difficult, the air going in and out of the lungs may make a wheezing or whistling sound, and the person may also cough up or spit up mucus.

Severity of the Attack

Asthma attacks can be mild or severe. They may begin suddenly or they may take a long time, even days, to develop. Mild episodes are more common, and the airways open up again in a few minutes or hours. However, some asthma episodes last longer and some are very serious and need immediate medical attention. In a severe attack, the person may become breathless and have difficulty talking. The neck muscles may become tight with each breath in. The lips and nail beds may have a grayish or bluish color. The person may exhibit chest retractions (chest skin sucked in).

Late Phase of the Attack

People with asthma are taught by their doctors to take medication to prevent an attack or to help them if an attack occurs. In severe attacks, they need to get emergency care.

Even though an asthma attack may subside, changes may be taking place in the airways that may lead to prolonging the episode or to a second wave of distress. This second wave—or "late phase" of the attack—is often more severe than the initial attack and potentially more dangerous.

Inflammation is the hallmark of the second wave, and it causes further narrowing of the air passages. The asthma victim may find it even harder to breathe during this second wave or late phase of the attack than during the first.

It is this late-phase attack, which may last a day or even longer unless it is treated effectively, that leads to most hospitalizations for asthma.

This late-phase part of the attack makes lungs more sensitive to other triggers that may set off an asthma attack. This unusual sensitivity may last for days or even for weeks after the initial attack.

CONTROLLING ASTHMA

Asthma treatment today aims to prevent asthma attacks, as well as stop an attack once it has started. People who see a doctor only when they have an asthma emergency may be missing out on new ways to prevent asthma attacks from happening. New drugs that work safely in low doses help to keep airways open. These drugs have helped millions of people manage their asthma.

Education. Medical care by a doctor is essential, but it is also important that people with asthma and their families keep up to date on the many things they can learn to do to better manage asthma.

At the heart of successful treatment of asthma is a caring and educated partnership in which the person with asthma, the doctor, and the family work together to "co-manage" and control the disease. By taking advantage of improved medical treatments and behavioral techniques, asthma's impact on most patients and their families can be lightened.

Diagnosis. Successful control of asthma starts with diagnosis. This usually includes a detailed medical history, a detailed physical examination, and various laboratory tests that can include: lung-function tests involving spirometry (an instrument you blow into to measure the air taken into and out of the lungs) and possibly peak flow monitoring (another measure of lung function); a chest x-ray; and possibly some blood and allergy tests.

Treatment. Once a diagnosis of asthma is made, the medical treatment can begin. It includes the doctor choosing and monitoring the most effective medications at the proper dosages for a particular patient. Treatment may include medications that are taken daily and also medications that are used only if an asthma attack occurs.

Through the care of a doctor who is experienced in treating asthma, supplemented by asthma health education programs, people can learn how to handle an attack if one should occur. Treatment must take a long-term approach, because asthma really doesn't just go away by itself.

MEDICATIONS

As already noted, current treatments for asthma are aimed at preventing, as well as stopping asthma attacks. Several different types of medicines are used in asthma treatment, and these are sold under many brand names. Asthma medicines also come in many different forms, including sprays, pills, powders, liquids, and injections. The doctor determines which medicines and which forms are appropriate for each person.

Corticosteroids (different from the anabolic steroids that are controversial because of use by athletes) may be prescribed to reduce the inflammation that accompanies an asthma attack and the overreactive state of airways. When used in aerosol form, side effects are minimized.

Bronchodilators are medicines that relax the muscles in the airway walls and help open the airways. Bronchodilators may be taken orally (as pills or a liquid) or they may be inhaled. Some bronchodilators can also be given by injection to treat a severe attack.

Cromolyn is a medicine that is used to prevent asthma episodes by lessening the lungs' response to many asthma triggers. It is not useful in treating an attack once it has started. It is taken by an inhaler.

Allergy shots. Some allergy-prone patients may benefit from hyposensitization treatment or "allergy shots."

ASTHMA TRIGGERS

Asthma attacks probably do not occur spontaneously, although the "triggers" frequently can-

---

ASTHMA TRIGGERS ABOUND

Everyday life is filled with the allergens and other precipitating factors that can kick off an attack.
- **Allergic reactions: pollens, feathers, molds, animals, some foods, house dust**
- **Infections: common cold, influenza**
- **Emotional stress and excitement**
- **Vigorous exercise**
- **Cold air**
- **Occupational dusts and vapors: plastics, grains, metals, wood**
- **Air pollution: cigarette smoke, ozone, sulfur dioxide, auto exhaust**
- **Sleep (nocturnal asthma)**
- **Household products: paint, cleaners, sprays**
- **Drugs: aspirin, heart medications**

---

not be identified. The range of these triggers is enormous, from viral infections to allergies, to irritating gases and particles in the air.

Identifying and controlling triggers can help lessen the frequency and severity of attacks. Your doctor and your local American Lung Association can provide helpful advice.

SPECIAL ISSUES

Occupational (on-the-job) exposures, such as dusts or chemicals, can be serious problems. People with asthma also must take their medications as prescribed, even if they feel well. However, it is important to note that feeling the need to take more medication than prescribed is a danger sign and a reason to get help. People with asthma must also know the early warning signs of an asthma attack and act promptly. If the attack does not respond to treatment, they should get medical attention immediately.

Two other important issues are exercise and smoking. Most people with asthma can participate in regular exercise with minimal difficulties, provided their asthma is under control. Exercise-induced asthma can occur, but many people with asthma are advised by their doctor to take appropriate medication prior to exercise to prevent an attack. Short-duration activities and certain types of exercise may prove less likely to cause asthma symptoms.

Smoking makes asthma worse. People with asthma must be encouraged and helped to quit smoking for the sake of their health. Breathing secondhand smoke can trigger asthma symptoms. Smoke-free environments can help prevent asthma attacks.

The American Lung Association

CHRONIC BRONCHITIS

Bronchitis is an inflammation of the lining of the bronchial tubes. These tubes, the bronchi, connect the windpipe with the lungs. When the bronchi are inflamed and/or infected, less air is able to flow to and from the lungs and a heavy mucus or phlegm is coughed up. This is bronchitis.

Many people suffer a brief attack of acute bronchitis with cough and mucus production when they have severe colds. Acute bronchitis is usually not associated with fever.

Chronic bronchitis is defined by the presence of a mucus-producing cough most days of the month, three months of a year for two successive years without other underlying disease to explain the cough. It may precede or accompany pulmonary emphysema.

CAUSES

Cigarette smoking is by far the most common cause of chronic bronchitis. The bronchial tubes of people with chronic bronchitis may also have been irritated initially by bacterial or viral infections. Air pollution and industrial dusts are also causes of chronic bronchitis.

Once the bronchial tubes have been irritated over a long period of time, excessive mucus is produced constantly, the lining of the bronchial tubes becomes thickened, an irritating cough develops, air flow may be hampered, and the lungs are endangered. The bronchial tubes then make an ideal breeding place for infections.

WHO GETS CHRONIC BRONCHITIS

Chronic bronchitis is estimated to affect over 5 percent of the population of the United States. Cough and mucus production are more common among men than women, which is also true of cigarette smoking. Chronic bronchitis symptoms are also more common among people over 40 than younger individuals.

No matter what their occupation or lifestyle, people who smoke cigarettes are those most likely to develop chronic bronchitis. But workers with certain jobs, especially those involving high concentrations of dust

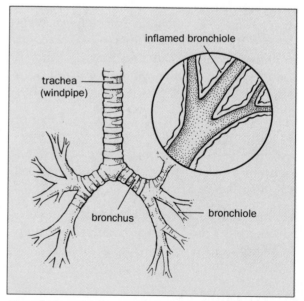

Chronic bronchitis, marked by recurrent inflammation of the lining of the bronchi or bronchioles, may narrow and obstruct the airways.

and irritating fumes, are also at high risk of developing this disease. Higher rates of chronic bronchitis are found among coal miners, grain handlers, metal molders, and other workers exposed to dust. Chronic bronchitis symptoms worsen when atmospheric concentrations of sulfur dioxide and other air pollutants increase. These symptoms are intensified when individuals also smoke.

COMPLICATIONS

Chronic bronchitis is often neglected by individuals until it is in an advanced state, because people mistakenly believe that the disease is not life-threatening. By the time a patient goes to his or her doctor, the lungs have frequently been seriously injured. Then the patient may be in danger of developing serious respiratory problems or heart failure.

HOW CHRONIC BRONCHITIS ATTACKS

Chronic bronchitis doesn't strike suddenly. After a winter cold seems cured, an individual may continue to cough and produce large amounts of mucus for several weeks. Since people who get chronic bronchitis are often smokers, the cough is usually dismissed as only "smoker's cough." As time goes on, colds become more damaging to the lungs. Coughing and bringing up phlegm last longer after each cold.

Without realizing it, one begins to take this coughing and mucus production as a matter of course. Soon they are present all the time—before colds, during colds, after colds, all year round. Generally, the cough is worse in the morning and in damp, cold weather. An ounce or more of yellow mucus may be brought up each day.

TREATMENT

The treatment of chronic bronchitis is primarily aimed at reducing irritation in the bronchial tubes. The discovery of antibiotic drugs has been helpful in treating acute infection associated with chronic bronchitis. However, most people with chronic bronchitis do not need to take antibiotics continually.

Bronchodilator drugs may be prescribed to help relax and open up air passages in the lungs, if there is a tendency for these to close up. These drugs may be inhaled as aerosol sprays or taken orally.

Eliminating irritants. To effectively control chronic bronchitis, it is necessary to eliminate sources of irritation and infection in the nose, throat, mouth, sinuses, and bronchial tubes. This means an individual must avoid polluted air and dusty working conditions and give up smoking. Your local American Lung Association office can suggest methods to help you quit smoking.

If the person with chronic bronchitis is exposed to dust and fumes at work, the doctor may suggest changing to another job or changing the work environment. All persons with chronic bronchitis must develop and follow a plan for a healthy lifestyle. Improving one's general health also increases the body's resistance to infections.

WHAT YOU SHOULD DO IF YOU HAVE CHRONIC BRONCHITIS

A good health plan for any person with chronic bronchitis should include the following rules.

- See your doctor at the beginning of any cold or respiratory infection.
- Don't smoke!
- Follow a nutritious, well-balanced diet, and maintain your ideal body weight.
- Get regular exercise daily, without tiring yourself too much.
- Ask your doctor about whether you should get vaccinated against influenza and pneumococcal pneumonia.

- Avoid exposure to colds and influenza at home or in public, and avoid respiratory irritants such as secondhand smoke, dust, and other air pollutants.

The American Lung Association

EMPHYSEMA

Emphysema is a condition in which there is overinflation of structures in the lungs known as alveoli or air sacs. This overinflation results from a breakdown of the walls of the alveoli, which causes a decrease in respiratory function (the way the lungs work) and often, breathlessness. Early symptoms of emphysema include shortness of breath and cough.

HOW SERIOUS IS EMPHYSEMA?

Emphysema is a widespread disease of the lungs. It is estimated that 70,000 to 100,000 Americans living today were born with a deficiency of a protein known as alpha 1-antitrypsin (AAT) which can lead to an inherited form of emphysema.

Emphysema ranks ninth among chronic conditions that contribute to a person's lack of activity. Over 42 percent of individuals with emphysema report that their daily activities have been limited in some way by the disease.

Many of the people with emphysema are older men, but the condition is increasing among women. Males with emphysema outnumber females by 64 percent.

CAUSES

It is known from scientific research that the normal lung has a remarkable balance between two classes of chemicals with opposing action. The lung also has a system of elastic fibers. The fibers allow the lungs to expand and contract. When the chemical balance is altered, the lungs lose the ability to protect themselves against the destruction of these elastic fibers. This is what happens in emphysema.

There are a number of reasons this chemical imbalance occurs. Smoking is responsible for 82 percent of chronic lung disease, including emphysema. Exposure to air pollution is one suspected cause. Irritating fumes and dusts on the job also are thought to be a factor.

A small number of people with emphysema have a rare inherited form of the disease called "alpha 1-antitrypsin (AAT) deficiency-related emphysema," or early onset emphysema. This form of disease is caused by an inherited lack of the protective protein called AAT.

HOW EMPHYSEMA DEVELOPS

Emphysema begins with the destruction of air sacs (alveoli) in the lungs where oxygen from the air is exchanged for carbon dioxide in the blood. The walls of the air sacs are thin and fragile. Damage to the air sacs is irreversible and results in permanent "holes" in the tissues of the lower lungs. As air sacs are destroyed, the lungs are able to transfer less and less oxygen to the bloodstream, causing shortness of breath. The lungs also lose their elasticity. The patient experiences great difficulty exhaling.

Damage to alveoli is permanent. Alveoli that have burst may fuse with one another, resulting in fewer, larger—and exceedingly less-efficient—air sacs.

Emphysema doesn't develop suddenly—it comes on very gradually. Years of exposure to the irritation of cigarette smoke usually precede the development of emphysema.

A person may initially visit the doctor because he or she has begun to feel short of breath during activity or exercise. As the disease progresses, a brief walk can be enough to bring on difficulty in breathing. Some people may have had chronic bronchitis before developing emphysema.

TREATMENT

Doctors can help persons with emphysema live more comfortably with their disease. The goal of treatment is to provide relief of symptoms and prevent progression of the disease with a minimum of side effects. The doctor's advice and treatment may include:

Quitting smoking. The single most important factor for maintaining healthy lungs.

Bronchodilator drugs (prescription drugs that relax and open up air passages in the lungs) may be prescribed to treat emphysema if there is a tendency toward airway constriction or tightening. These drugs may be inhaled as aerosol sprays or taken orally.

Antibiotics, if you have a bacterial infection, such as pneumococcal pneumonia.

Exercise, including breathing exercises to strengthen the muscles used in breathing as part of a pulmonary rehabilitation program to condition the rest of the body.

Treatment with alpha 1-proteinase inhibitor (A1PI). This applies only if a person has AAT deficiency-related emphysema. AlPI is not recommended for those who develop emphysema as a result of cigarette smoking or other environmental factors.

Lung transplantation. Some recent reports have been encouraging. Experience at this point in time is limited.

PREVENTION

Continuing research is being done to find answers to many questions about emphysema, especially about the best ways to prevent the disease.

Researchers know that quitting smoking can prevent the occurrence and decrease the progression of emphysema. Other environmental controls can also help prevent the disease from occurring.

If an individual has emphysema, the doctor will work hard to prevent the disease from getting worse by keeping the patient healthy and clear of any infection. The patient can participate in this prevention effort by following these general health guidelines.

See your doctor at the first sign of symptoms. Emphysema is a serious disease. It damages your lungs, and it can damage your heart.

Don't smoke. A majority of those who get emphysema are smokers. Continued smoking makes emphysema worse, especially for those who have AAT deficiency, the inherited form of emphysema.

Maintain overall good health habits, which include proper nutrition, adequate sleep, and regular exercise to build up your stamina and resistance to infections.

Reduce your exposure to air pollution, which may aggravate symptoms of emphysema. Refer to radio or television weather reports or your local newspaper for information about air quality. On days when the ozone (smog) level is unhealthy, restrict your activity to early morning or evening. When pollution levels are dangerous, remain indoors and stay as comfortable as possible.

Consult your doctor at the start of any cold or respiratory infection because infection can make your emphysema symptoms worse. Ask about getting vaccinated against influenza and pneumococcal pneumonia.

The American Lung Association

PNEUMONIA

Pneumonia is a serious infection or inflammation of your lungs. The air sacs in the lungs fill with pus, and other liquid. Oxygen has trouble reaching your blood. If there is too little oxygen in your blood, your body cells can't work properly—and may die. Lobar pneumonia affects a section (lobe) of a lung. Bronchial pneumonia (or bronchopneumonia) affects patches throughout both lungs.

Until 1936, pneumonia was the number-one cause of death in the United States. Then antibiotics brought it under control. Now this deadly enemy is making a comeback, in part because some bacteria can resist antibiotics. Pneumonia and influenza combined have ranked as the sixth leading cause of death since 1979.

CAUSES

Pneumonia is not a single disease. It can have over 30 different causes.

There are four main causes of pneumonia: bacteria, viruses, mycoplasmas, and others, such as pneumocystis.

BACTERIAL PNEUMONIA

Bacterial pneumonia can attack anyone from infants through the very old. Alcoholics, the debilitated, postoperative patients, people with respiratory diseases or viral infections, and people who are immunocompromised are particularly vulnerable.

The pneumococcus is the most common cause of bacterial pneumonia. It is the only form of pneumonia for which a vaccine is available.

How It Strikes

Pneumonia bacteria are present in some healthy throats. When body defenses are weakened in some way—by illness, old age,

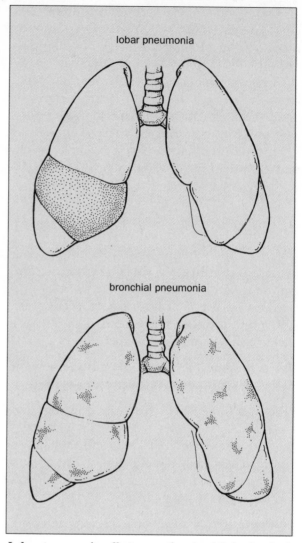

Lobar pneumonia affects a section (or lobe) of a single lung; bronchial pneumonia affects patches throughout both lungs.

malnutrition, general debility, impaired immunity—the bacteria can multiply and do serious damage. Usually when a person's resistance is lowered, bacteria work their way into the lungs and inflame the air sacs. The tissue of part of a lobe of the lung, an entire lobe, or even most of the lung's five lobes becomes completely filled with liquid matter. (This is called "consolidation.") The infection quickly spreads through the bloodstream and the whole body is invaded.

Symptoms

The onset of bacterial pneumonia can vary from gradual to sudden.

The patient may experience symptoms such as shaking chills, chattering, severe chest pain, and a cough that produces rust-colored or greenish sputum. Temperature often shoots up as high as 105. The patient sweats profusely, and his breathing and pulse rate increase rapidly. From lack of oxygen in the blood, the lips and nailbeds may have a bluish cast. A person's mental state may be clouded or delirious.

VIRAL PNEUMONIA

Half of all pneumonias are believed to be of viral origin. More and more viruses are being identified as the cause of respiratory infection, and though most attack the upper respiratory tract, some produce pneumonia. Most of these pneumonias are patchy and self-limiting, but primary influenza virus may be severe and occasionally fatal. The virus invades the lungs and multiplies, but there are almost no physical signs of lung tissue becoming filled with fluid. It finds most of its victims among those who have pre-existing heart or pulmonary illness.

Symptoms

The initial symptoms of viral pneumonia are those of influenza: fever, a dry cough, headache, muscle pain, and weakness. Within 12 to 36 hours, there is increasing breathlessness, then the cough becomes worse and produces a scant amount of bloody sputum.

There is a high fever and there may be blueness of lips. In the final stage of the illness, the patient experiences unbearable air hunger and breathlessness.

Other viral pneumonias are complicated by an invasion of bacteria, along with all the typical symptoms that normally accompany bacterial pneumonia.

MYCOPLASMA PNEUMONIA

Because of its symptoms and physical signs, and because the course of the illness differed strikingly from those of classic pneumococcal pneumonia, mycoplasma pneumonia was once believed to be caused by one or more undiscovered viruses and was called "primary atypical pneumonia."

Identified during World War II, mycoplasmas are the smallest free-living agents of disease in man, unclassified as to whether bacteria or viruses, but having characteristics of both. They generally cause a mild and widespread pneumonia. It affects all age groups, occurring most frequently in older children and young adults. The death rate is low, even in untreated cases.

Symptoms

The most prominent symptom of mycoplasma pneumonia is a cough that tends to come in violent paroxysms, but produces only sparse whitish sputum. Chilly sensations and fever are early symptoms, and some patients experience nausea or vomiting. The patient's heartbeat is often slow, and in some extreme cases he may suffer from breathlessness and have a bluish cast to his lips and nailbeds.

OTHER KINDS OF PNEUMONIA

Pneumocystis carinii pneumonia (PCP) is caused by an organism long thought of as a parasite but now believed to be a fungus. PCP is the first sign of illness in more than half of all persons with AIDS, and perhaps 80 percent (four out of five) will develop it sooner or later. It can be successfully treated in many cases. It may recur a few months later, but treatment can help in preventing or delaying its recurrence.

Many of the less common pneumonias have a high death toll and are occurring more often. Various special pneumonias are caused by the inhalation of food, liquid, gases, dust, or a foreign body, by fungi, or by a bronchial obstruction such as a tumor. Rickettsia (also considered something between viruses and bacteria) cause Rocky Mountain spotted fever, Q fever, typhus, and psittacosis—diseases that involve the lungs to a greater or lesser extent. Tuberculosis pneumonia is an overwhelming lung infection and extremely dangerous unless treated early.

TREATMENT

If you develop pneumonia, your chances of prompt recovery are greatest under certain conditions: if you're young, if your pneumonia was caught early, if your defenses against disease are working well, if the infection hasn't spread, and if you're not suffering from other illness.

Antibiotics. In the young and healthy, prompt treatment with antibiotics can cure bacterial and mycoplasma pneumonia, and a certain percentage of rickettsia cases. There is no effective treatment yet for viral pneumonia.

The drug or drugs used are determined by the germ causing the pneumonia and the judgment of the physician. After the body temperature returns to normal, medication must be continued according to a physician's instructions—otherwise the pneumonia may recur. Relapses can be far more serious than the first attack.

Supportive treatment. Besides antibiotics, patients are given supportive treatment: proper diet, oxygen to relieve breathlessness and bluish cast to lips, medication to ease chest pain, and in the case of mycoplasma, some relief from the violent cough—anything that can produce and maintain in the patient the best possible conditions for recovery.

RECOVERING FROM PNEUMONIA

The vigorous young person may lead a normal life within a week of his recovery from pneumonia. For the middle-aged, however, weeks may elapse before they regain their accustomed strength, vigor, and feeling of well-being. A person should not be discouraged from returning to work or carrying out usual activities, but must be warned to expect some difficulties. Adequate rest is important to maintain progress toward full recovery and to avoid relapse.

PREVENTION

Because pneumonia is a common complication of influenza (flu), getting a flu shot every fall is good pneumonia prevention.

A vaccine is also available to help fight pneumococcal pneumonia—one type of bacterial pneumonia. Your doctor can help you decide if you—or a member of your family—needs the vaccine against pneumococcal pneumonia. It is usually given only to people at high risk of getting the disease and its life-threatening complications. Ask your doctor if you should be vaccinated. The greatest risk of pneumococcal pneumonia usually is among people who:

- Have chronic illnesses such as lung disease, heart disease, kidney disorders, sickle cell anemia, or diabetes
- Are recovering from severe illness
- Are in nursing homes or other chronic care facilities
- Are age 65 or older

The vaccine is generally given only once. Ask your doctor about revaccination recommendations.

Since pneumonia often follows ordinary respiratory infections, the most important preventive measure is for a person to be alert to any symptoms of respiratory trouble that linger more than a few days. Good health habits—proper diet and hygiene, plentiful rest, regular exercise, etc.—increase resistance to all respiratory illnesses. Such habits also help promote fast recovery if the illnesses do occur.

IF YOU HAVE SYMPTOMS OF PNEUMONIA

Even though pneumonia can be satisfactorily treated, it is an extremely serious illness. If you think you have symptoms of pneumonia, you should:

- Call your doctor immediately. Even with the many effective antibiotics, early diagnosis and treatment are important.
- Follow your doctor's advice. If he says you should be in the hospital, go there. If he says you may stay at home if you stay in bed, be sure you stay in bed.
- To prevent recurrence of pneumonia—continue to take the medicine your doctor prescribes until he says you may stop.

The American Lung Association

INFLUENZA

Influenza is a contagious disease caused by a virus. A virus is a germ that is very small. Influenza viruses infect many parts of the body, including the lungs. When someone who has the flu sneezes, coughs, or even talks, the flu virus is expelled into the air and may be inhaled by anyone close by. Flu may be transmitted by direct hand contact.

WHAT HAPPENS WHEN YOU GET THE FLU?

When flu strikes the lungs, the lining of the respiratory tract is damaged. The tissues become swollen and inflamed. Fortunately, the damage is rarely permanent. The tissues usually heal within two weeks.

Influenza is often called a respiratory disease, but it affects the whole body. The victim usually becomes acutely ill with fever, chills,

weakness, loss of appetite, and aching of the head, back, arms, and legs. The flu sufferer may also have a sore throat and a dry cough, nausea, and burning eyes.

The fever mounts quickly—temperature may rise to 104 degrees—but after two or three days, it usually subsides. The patient is often left exhausted for days afterwards.

IS FLU CONSIDERED SERIOUS?

For those who are healthy, influenza is typically a moderately severe illness. Most people are back on their feet within a week. For people who are not healthy or well to begin with, influenza can be very severe and even fatal. The symptoms described above have a greater impact on these persons. In addition, complications can occur.

Most of these complications are bacterial infections, since the body can be so weakened by influenza that its defenses against bacteria are low. Bacterial pneumonia is the most common complication. But the sinuses and inner ears may become inflamed and painful.

WHO GETS THE FLU?

Anyone can get the flu—especially when it is widespread in the community. In a flu epidemic year, from 20 to 50 percent of those not immunized may contract influenza.

People who are not healthy or well to begin with are particularly susceptible to the complications that can follow. These people are known as "high risk." For anyone at high risk, influenza is a very serious illness. You may be at high risk if you have any of the following conditions.

- Chronic lung disease such as asthma, emphysema, chronic bronchitis, bronchiectasis, tuberculosis, or cystic fibrosis
- Heart disease
- Chronic kidney disease
- Diabetes or other chronic metabolic disorder

335

- Severe anemia
- Depressed immunity resulting from diseases or treatments

Additional high-risk features include the following.

- Residing in a nursing home or other chronic care facility
- Being over 65 years of age

A physician, nurse, or other provider of care to high-risk persons should be immunized to protect high-risk patients.

HOW ARE FLU AND COMPLICATONS PREVENTED?

Influenza can be prevented when a person receives the current influenza vaccine. This vaccine is made each year so that the vaccine can contain influenza viruses that are expected to cause illness that year.

The viruses in the vaccine are killed or inactivated so that someone vaccinated cannot get influenza from the vaccine. Instead the person vaccinated develops protection in his or her body in the form of substances called antibodies.

The amount of antibodies in the body is greatest one or two months after vaccination and then gradually declines. For that reason and because the influenza viruses usually change each year, a high-risk person should be vaccinated each fall with the new vaccine. November is the best time to get your flu shot. Such a yearly vaccination has been found to be about 75 percent effective in preventing flu. It also may very well reduce the severity of flu and be lifesaving in vaccinated persons.

A drug called amantadine also can be used to help prevent flu. It is discussed later in the section on treatment.

WHAT ABOUT REACTIONS TO THE VACCINE?

Most people have little or no reaction to the influenza vaccine.

One in four might have a swollen, red, tender area where the vaccination was given.

A much smaller number might also develop a slight fever within 24 hours. They may have chills or a headache, or feel a little sick. People who already have a respiratory disease may find their symptoms worsened. Usually none of these reactions lasts for more than a couple of days.

In addition, adverse reactions to the vaccine, perhaps allergic in nature, have been observed in some people. These could be due to an egg protein allergy, since the egg in which the virus is grown cannot be completely extracted. These people should be vaccinated only if their own physician believes it necessary and if the vaccine is given under close observation by a physician.

WHO SHOULD BE VACCINATED?

People at high risk should be vaccinated yearly against flu. In addition, those who provide care to high-risk patients should be vaccinated.

If you are not in a high-risk group, ask your doctor if you need the vaccine.

CAN YOU HAVE A RECURRENCE OF THE FLU?

A person can have influenza more than once because the virus that causes influenza may belong to one of three different flu virus families, A, B, or C. Influenza A and influenza B are the major families.

Within each flu virus family are many viral strains, like so many brothers and sisters. Both A and B have strains that cause illnesses of varying severity. But the influenza A family has more virulent strains than the B family.

If you have the flu, your body responds by developing antibodies. The following year, a new family member or a member of another family may appear. Your antibodies are less effective or ineffective against this unfamiliar strain. If you are exposed to it, you may come down with flu again.

HOW ARE FLU AND COMPLICATIONS TREATED?

For uncomplicated flu, your doctor will probably tell you to stay in bed at home as long as the sickness is severe—and perhaps for about two days after the fever is gone.

The drug called amantadine is useful for treating someone who develops influenza A, particularly if it is given as soon as possible after the onset of flu. Amantadine also can be used as a preventive, but for prevention it must be taken daily as long as flu cases continue to occur in a community. Your doctor would have to decide whether to use amantadine either for prevention or treatment. If it is used for treating an early case of flu, it may shorten this illness and reduce the severity. Amantadine works only against influenza A viruses and should be used only if influenza A is suspected.

Amantadine sometimes causes side effects such as difficulty in sleeping, tremulousness, or depression; these are usually mild and often go away even when the medicine is continued.

The treatment of nonbacterial complications varies with the illness. If you should develop a bacterial complication, however, your doctor can give you an antibiotic.

WHY IS FLU MORE PREVALENT IN SOME YEARS THAN IN OTHERS?

Every 10 years or so, a flu virus strain appears that is dramatically different from the other members of its family. When this major change occurs, a worldwide epidemic—called a pandemic—almost inevitably follows. Few people have antibodies that are effective against the new virus.

One such virus caused the 1918 flu epidemic that swept the world and left in its wake more than 20 million dead. Fear of a similar outbreak in the fall of 1976 inspired a mass vaccination effort. Fortunately, no epidemic developed. *The American Lung Association*

337

The Muscles and Bones

In the course of our lives, our muscles and bones change significantly. The newborn has 350 bones—nearly 150 more than the typical adult. As we grow up, certain bones (most notably those in the skull and lower spinal column) fuse together. So by about age 25, the normal complement of bones is 206—although an extra vertebra or pair of ribs is not uncommon.

Throughout our young life, the bones build and strengthen. Young individuals typically enjoy a relatively calcium-rich diet, and this large surplus of calcium is stored almost exclusively in the bones. As this occurs, the bones become more dense and solid, a process known as ossification. By about age 35, ossification is complete, and the bones are as hard—and as strong—as they will ever be.

In the ensuing years, people begin to ingest less calcium than they need. The bones are mined for their stores of calcium, resulting in a net loss of this important mineral. Over the decades, bones consequently become weaker: more porous, brittle, and subject to fractures.

Between the bones are joints. Ligaments are the tough fibrous cords that hold one bone to another. Cushioning the site where two bones meet is a rubbery layer of cartilage—a natural shock absorber. A fluid-filled sac, the synovial membrane, surrounds the joint. Within this capsule is the synovial fluid, a slippery lubricant that enables the surfaces of the joint to move against one another practically friction-free. Outside of the synovial membrane is the bursa, which secretes a lubricant that facilitates the movement of muscles across bones or over other muscles.

After years of strenuous use, the joints naturally begin to break down. Especially vulnerable are the joints that bear the most weight—the hips and knees. Other common sites for joint problems are the hands, wrists, feet, and lower back. By age 60, most people have at least some signs of joint problems.

The skeletal muscles—that is, the ones surrounding the bones and joints—are affected by age as well. Overall muscle mass decreases as a matter of course; this is only compounded by the fact that we tend to be less active when we're older, which further encourages muscles to atrophy. Moreover, the resilient fibers of the skeletal muscles are gradually replaced in later years by connective tissue (a process called fibrosis). The usurping connective tissue is certainly strong, but it lacks the elasticity and the power to contract that muscle tissues have.

Changes in the muscles, joints, and bones are inevitable, but whether or not they cause aggravating symptoms or impinge upon activities once taken for granted is another issue. Some people remain hearty and active into their nineties. Others are not as fortunate. It's only when mobility is lost or movement becomes painful that we start to feel truly old.

A number of therapies—ranging from massage to exercises to medication to surgery—can minimize, halt, or sometimes reverse the effects of aging on the musculoskeletal system. There are a variety of specialists to consult, depending on the disorder. An orthopedic surgeon specializes in problems affecting the body parts involved with movement: ligaments, tendons, muscles, and, especially, the bones. A rheumatologist specializes in arthritis and other problems particular to the joints. A physiatrist is a medical doctor whose practice concentrates on physical medicine and rehabilitation. Physical therapists are not M.D.s, but are licensed practitioners who design individual exercise regimens and other therapies to restore mobility and reduce pain.   *The Editors*

BACK PAIN

Back pain is one of the most common health problems in the United States, yet its cause is generally unknown. It is estimated that 50 to 80 percent of adults have had back pain at some time. In fact, it is one of the leading causes of disability and time lost from work. In addition, it costs the public $16 billion to pay for treating back pain each year.

IS THERE ONLY ONE KIND OF BACK PAIN?

You may be thinking that all back pain is the same. Actually, everyone's back pain is differ-

ent. For some people, back pain means a "sore back" or a mild backache. Other people may have severe pain. Mild pain is pain that is bothersome, aching, and sore. Severe pain is pain that hurts all the time, even when resting; it is very painful.

Most doctors refer to back pain as acute or chronic. You may have heard these terms before, but if you would like more information,

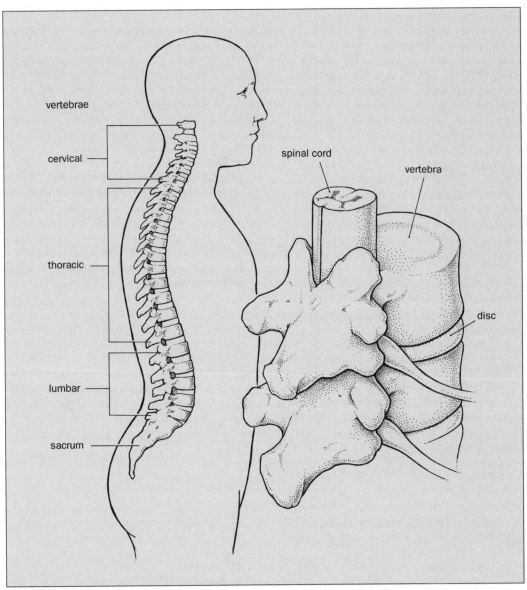

The spinal cord is protected by 7 cervical (neck), 12 thoracic (chest), and 5 lumbar (lower back) vertebrae. Degeneration of the discs of cartilage between these bones can lead to back problems.

see the following definitions (10 percent of all back pain is classified somewhere between these two categories).

Acute back pain (1) usually lasts a few days or 6 to 12 weeks; (2) may be mild or severe; (3) may occasionally be caused by an accident or injury; (4) about 80 percent of all back pain is acute.

Chronic back pain (1) usually lasts more than three months; (2) may be mild or severe; (3) may be related to other illnesses you have; (4) about 10 percent of all back pain is chronic.

WHAT CAUSES BACK PAIN?

Why do you suppose the back is a common target for injury or pain? Let's take a look at your back to help you better understand how problems could occur.

Structure of the Back

Your back is held upright by muscles attached to the backbone. Doctors often call the backbone a spine, spinal column, or vertebral column. The backbone isn't actually one long bone, but 24 separate bones called vertebrae. These 24 vertebrae are stacked, one on top of another, to form the backbone.

Where two vertebrae or bones fit against one another is called a joint. Joints make it possible for you to move and turn in many different directions. You may wonder what keeps joints and bones from rubbing against each other and wearing out. Located between each vertebra are discs made of a soft, elastic material called cartilage. These discs act as cushions, or shock absorbers, much like the shock absorbers in your car. Their main job is to protect the joints from wearing out. Joints also contain a slippery substance called synovial fluid, which keeps them moving smoothly.

The largest and most important nerve in your body is the spinal cord. It runs through a hole in each vertebra in your spine, much like a piece of string through a beaded necklace. It branches off into many smaller nerves.

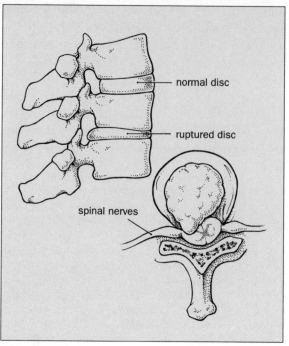

The most severe back pain can occur when a disc ruptures, subjecting the roots of spinal nerves to undue pressure.

These nerves carry messages from your brain to your legs, arms, back, and all other parts of your body. At times, a message might signal pain or discomfort. The pain signal is an important one, because pain tells you that some part of your body needs attention.

Your backbone, with all its parts, cannot hold itself upright. It needs strong muscles, ligaments, and tendons for support. Muscles help you move and hold your bones together. Ligaments stretch from one bone to another to hold bones together. Tendons, on the other hand, fasten bones to nearby muscles.

Possible Problems

With so many parts, can you see how easy it is for back problems to occur? Anything that puts pressure on your back muscles or nerves can cause pain. Any illness or damage to your spine can also cause pain. Although the cause of most back pain is unknown, possible causes are: ruptured intervertebral disc, physical or emotional stress, injury or accident, arthritis, other illness.

In addition, certain factors seem to aggravate back pain, such as: being overweight, having poor posture, lacking proper exercise.

Let's look at each of these problems to see how they can cause back pain.

Ruptured Intervertebral Disc

This may be the most painful, yet easiest condition to identify. A ruptured or herniated disc is one that bulges and extends into the spinal canal, pressing on the nerve roots. This causes the nerve roots to become irritated. On occasion, a ruptured disc can occur after bending over and lifting. However, it usually occurs for no apparent reason.

A ruptured disc may cause back pain and muscle spasms, but a more common symptom is sciatic pain. This is severe pain spreading down one leg and often into the foot. Sometimes it is the only symptom of a ruptured disc.

A ruptured disc can generally be detected by a physical examination alone. Occasionally, a myelogram, CT scan, or magnetic resonance imaging (MRI) are necessary to confirm the diagnosis and determine if surgery is necessary. Treatment includes bed rest, traction, heat, muscle relaxants, and/or weight reduction. Surgery is rarely used, but may be required if pain is prolonged and severe.

Injuries and Accidents

Have you ever moved a piece of furniture that didn't seem too heavy, only to feel pain in your back the next day? Have you ever stretched for something that was just a little out of your reach, and felt a twinge in your back? Many back injuries are caused by an unexpected twist or sudden motion. This usually results in muscle strain.

Back pain from a severe blow or fall may require immediate medical attention. A person with a severe back injury should not be moved until medical help arrives. (Any movement could cause further damage.)

Fortunately, most of us have not experienced back injury from a blow or fall. These injuries could cause fractures in the spinal column, accompanied by tenderness over the fractured vertebrae. There may also be muscle spasms at the fracture. Back movement will be limited. Pain is usually immediate, although it may not occur for days. Spinal fractures are more common in older women with osteoporosis.

Injuries can also damage the spinal cord and nerves. Be especially concerned about any pain that travels down one or both legs. This could be a sign of nerve damage. However, paralysis as a result of low back injury is extremely rare.

With either an injury or accident, severe muscle spasms usually last 48 to 72 hours. They are generally followed by days or weeks of less severe pain. It usually takes two to four weeks to heal completely from a mild back injury. It could take up to six to 12 weeks if there are strained ligaments or if the strain is more severe. Severe back injury from a fall or accident may require hospitalization and a longer recovery period.

Arthritis

Arthritis means joint inflammation ("arthr" means joint and "itis" means inflammation). Joint inflammation can cause the area surrounding the joints to become warm, red, painful, and swollen.

There are over 100 kinds of arthritis. Some forms of arthritis cause aches and pains near and around the joints, but not in the joints themselves. Sometimes arthritis affects the muscles, tendons, ligaments, and other parts of the body. Certain forms of arthritis, such as the following, can cause back pain.

Ankylosing spondylitis. This form of arthritis causes the joints in the spine to become stiff and swollen. With time, stiff joints can grow together (fuse). The most common symptoms are pain and stiffness in the hip and low back, which continue for more than three months. Ankylosing spondylitis is most common in men ages 20 to 40.

Osteoarthritis. This form of arthritis breaks down the soft, elastic material (cartilage) that cushions the spinal joints and other joints in the body. Low back pain can be aggravated when osteoarthritis affects the hips or the knees. Osteoarthritis can also directly affect the spine, which may cause back pain. However, back pain is more commonly associated with osteoarthritis of the hips and knees.

Osteoporosis. This is a type of bone disorder which causes bones to become thin and weak. Fragile bones such as these can break more easily, especially bones in the spinal column.

Rheumatoid arthritis. This form of arthritis causes any joints to become stiff, painful, and swollen. It can affect the neck and, more rarely, the joints in the lower back.

Polymyalgia rheumatica (PMR). This form of arthritis causes muscle pain, aching, and stiffness in the neck and shoulders, low back, thighs, and hips. It can last a few months or many years. Most people experience severe stiffness in the morning.

Paget's disease. This is a type of bone disorder. The bones most commonly affected are in the low back, pelvis, tailbone, skull, and long bones of the legs. It is slightly more common in men than in women. It often begins between 50 to 70 years of age.

Back pain may be a symptom, but most often there are no obvious symptoms. Paget's disease is usually discovered on an x-ray or bone scan done for reasons other than pain.

Fibrositis. Most people with fibrositis experience pain and stiffness around joints, muscles, tendons, and ligaments. The pain can last for weeks, months, or years. It can vary from day to day. Oftentimes, the symptoms go away by themselves. This condition is usually related to stress, sleep problems, or depression. It occurs most often in women ages 20 to 50.

Other Illnesses

A few people have back pain because of other illnesses or problems in their spine, such as those that follow.

Spinal stenosis. In spinal stenosis the spinal canal narrows. This squeezes the back nerves, putting pressure on them. It is this pressure that causes the back pain. Numbness, pain, and weakness in the legs can also occur. The most common symptom of spinal stenosis is pain that gets worse while walking and is relieved by sitting down. Spinal stenosis more commonly occurs in older adults who already have osteoarthritis and advanced disc disease.

Other Conditions

Back pain can also be a symptom of:

- Prostate trouble in men
- Problems associated with reproductive organs in women
- Kidney diseases, such as an infection or kidney stone
- Diseases of the intestines or pancreas, such as cancer or an obstruction
- Metastatic cancer which has spread to the spine
- Multiple myeloma, a form of cancer involving the bone and bone marrow
- Curvature of the spine
- Rarely, tumor on the spinal cord

Factors Aggravating Back Pain

Back pain can be aggravated by such factors as stress, overweight, poor posture, and lack of exercise.

We all react to stress in different ways. Some of us feel tired, sleep poorly, overeat, or feel irritable. There are also many different physical signs of stress. For example, some people clench their jaw. Other people tighten their neck and shoulders. Still others get a headache or upset stomach when tense.

Many people tighten their back muscles

when they are worried or tense. This can make existing back problems worse. Take a minute now to think about what happens in your own body when you worry or get tense. Do you think stress is affecting your back?

Think about the extra pounds people carry every day due to overweight. This puts added pressure and strain on the back and stomach muscles, causing muscles to stretch and weaken. Weak back and stomach muscles cannot support the back properly. Poor posture can shift your body out of balance. This forces only a few muscles and joints to do all the work. Without proper exercise, muscles become weak and tire easily. Exercise is needed to keep backs strong and limber.

Can you see how all of these factors might aggravate back pain? They also make it more likely for back problems to develop.

WHO GETS BACK PAIN

Anyone can have back pain. In fact, 10 percent of all Americans have back pain in a given year. Back pain can occur at any age in both men and women. However, it may occur slightly more in women beginning at middle age, probably due to osteoporosis.

DIAGNOSIS

It is often difficult for doctors to pinpoint the exact cause of back pain, because there are so many possible causes. If the cause is unclear, your family doctor may suggest you see a rheumatologist (a doctor who specializes in arthritis), orthopedist, neurosurgeon, neurologist, or other medical specialist for diagnosis.

If your back pain is accompanied by any of the following, make an appointment to see a doctor today: (1) back pain that is still there after six weeks of home treatment; (2) weakness or numbness in one or both of your legs; (3) pain going down one leg below the knee; (4) back pain from a fall or injury; (5) back pain accompanied by fever without flulike aches.

Medical History

Your doctor will first ask you a number of questions such as those that follow.

The most common questions doctors ask about back pain are: (1) What are your symptoms—that is, what aches or pains do you have? (2) Exactly where is the pain? (3) Where is the pain the strongest? (4) When did the pain begin? How long have you had it? (5) Did something specific cause your back pain such as an accident or injury? (6) What home treatments have you used? (7) Were you under any additional stress when the pain began? (8) Do you have any other health problems? (9) What kind of work do you do? (10) What types of recreational activities do you do?

Think about these ahead of time so you can answer them easily. You may also have questions you'd like to ask the doctor. As you think of questions at home, jot them down and take them to the appointment. You are more likely to ask questions if you have a written list with you.

Physical Exam

Next, your doctor will give you a physical exam. During the exam, the doctor may perform any of the following: observe your muscles and joints; ask you to sit and lie down; ask you to move your back in different positions; observe and feel the area of most pain; check to see if other areas of your body are tender or painful (such as the kidneys, intestines, or other organs).

If the doctor can identify the likely cause of your back pain at this point, no further tests will be needed.

Special Tests

If the doctor needs more specific information, he or she may ask you to have one or more of the following tests.

X-ray. Studies show that in most cases x-rays are not necessary at the first visit, but should

345

only be taken if the pain does not improve. X-rays may or may not be helpful in determining the cause of back pain. In certain cases, x-rays might show the doctor if the pain is due to: an injury in one or more of the back bones; a tumor in the spine; a deformity in the spine; ankylosing spondylitis.

CT (computed tomography) scan. Most people with low back pain do not need a CT scan. This is a special machine that takes an x-ray scan of the area. The information from the scan is then sent into a computer. The computer can display images of the area on a TV-like screen, or store them for permanent record. A CT scan gives the doctor a three-dimensional view of the back. It is particularly useful in determining if there is a ruptured disc. Other conditions that may be detected by using a CT scan are spinal stenosis, tumors, and infections of the spinal cord.

Myelogram. A myelogram may be ordered to detect problems such as spinal stenosis or spinal cord tumors. If back surgery is being considered, many neurosurgeons will require a myelogram beforehand.

During a myelogram, an injection is given into the spinal canal. It contains a special material (called contrast medium). X-rays will then be taken of the area. The contrast medium can make problem areas more visible on the x-ray.

MRI (magnetic resonance imaging). MRI is a relatively new test. It produces very clear images of the skeletal system. Unlike many other tests, the MRI does not use x-rays or radioactive dyes. It is very useful in getting clearer images of soft tissues such as muscles, cartilage, ligaments, tendons, and blood vessels, in addition to bone structure. It can be very expensive.

Bone scan. Occasionally bone scans are done to look for damage or tumors in the bones themselves. However, back pain is rarely due to diseases of the bones.

During a bone scan, you will be asked to take a very small amount of radioactive material. A special radioactive detecting machine will then be used to scan the area of concern.

Blood tests. If your doctor orders blood tests for you, a laboratory technician will carefully draw a small amount of blood from your arm, which will be tested in the laboratory. Any one of the following blood tests may be ordered.

- Erythrocyte sedimentation rate ("sed rate")
- Hematocrit and hemoglobin
- White blood cell count
- HLA B-27 test
- Chemical profile (SMAC)

Your doctor may order other blood tests. Ask him or her to explain the tests to you.

TREATMENT

Many back problems go away in a matter of days or weeks and do not come back. However, the longer back problems last, the more likely they are to come back again. Doctors generally prescribe one or more of the treatments listed below.

For some back conditions, the doctor may refer you to another specialist such as an orthopedist, rheumatologist, physiatrist, physical or occupational therapist, psychologist, psychiatrist, or surgeon.

The most common treatments for back pain are: rest; heat and cold; proper exercise; posture training; weight control; stress management and relaxation exercises; TENS devices; medications; surgery.

Remember, the best treatment for your problem depends on you and the type of back pain you have.

Rest

The first treatment doctors usually recommend for acute back pain is bed rest. Different people require different amounts of rest.

Usually two days staying in bed, except to go to the bathroom, will be enough to ease your back pain. You may want to ask the doctor if special pillows or devices are necessary. Sometimes, these aids give additional support to your neck, back, or feet.

Heat and Cold

Many people have found that hot and cold treatments help relieve back pain. You might try both to find out which works best for you.

Heat relaxes muscles and soothes painful areas. There are many ways to apply heat: Some people like hot showers or baths, while others prefer using heat lamps, heating pads, or warm compresses. If you have arthritis, heating your muscles first might make it easier for you to do back exercises. Be sure not to fall asleep while using heat.

Cold has a numbing effect. This often helps relieve pain. You might try one of these methods for applying cold: an ice bag; a slush pack (freezer bag containing three cups of water and one cup denatured alcohol—place in freezer until slush forms); a large ice cube used to massage the area; a bag of frozen vegetables (peas work best).

Be sure not to leave ice on after the skin becomes numb. This could lead to local frostbite. Do not use cold if you are especially sensitive to cold or have decreased circulation or sensation.

Exercise

For many people, the key to a healthy back is proper exercise. Some exercises are designed to strengthen your back and stomach muscles, while other exercises will keep you totally fit. There are even exercises to improve your posture. The right kind of exercise program may help keep your back problem under control. It can make it easier for you to continue doing your daily activities. You may need to temporarily refrain from strenuous exercise if it aggravates your back pain. Ask your doctor and physical therapist which exercises you can do to relieve back pain, stay fit, and prevent reinjury.

Posture and Shoes

If poor posture is a factor, then posture training may help relieve your back pain. During posture training, an occupational or physical therapist will teach you healthier ways to sit, stand, sleep, and lift objects. The following are some of the techniques recommended for good posture.

When sitting. Sit in a firm chair with arm rests to relieve pressure in your back and shoulders. Keep your upper back straight and shoulders relaxed. Flatten your lower back. You can do this by tightening your stomach and buttocks. Some people are more comfortable sitting with the back of the chair at a 15- to 20-degree angle. Keep your knees slightly higher than your hips. Use a footstool or book under your feet if necessary. Keep your feet flat on the floor or other surface.

When standing. Stand with weight equal on both feet. Avoid locking your knees. Ease tension in your back by placing one foot on a footstool. If you stand for long periods of time, wear flat or low-heeled shoes. Keep your back straight by tightening your stomach muscles and buttocks.

When sleeping. Lie on your side with your knees bent. If more comfortable, place a pillow between your knees. Use a firm mattress.

When lifting and carrying objects. When bending down to lift an object, bend with your knees instead of your back. Hold the object close to you. Straighten your legs to lift the object. Get help with an object that is too heavy.

The type of shoes you wear can also affect your posture. High heels may put more stress on your lower back. You might find it more comfortable to wear low or flat heels. The heels should be strong enough to give your feet support and prevent your legs from getting tired.

Weight Loss

Don't be surprised if your doctor recommends weight loss as one way of reducing your back pain and improving your general health. The best way to lose weight is with a balanced diet along with regular exercise. Be sure to avoid fad diets or fast weight loss programs. These can be harmful and cause new problems for you, instead of solving old ones.

Stress Management and Relaxation

Every day of our lives is filled with some kind of stress. It is a part of daily living. In fact, any situation can cause stress such as work, personal relationships, raising children, paying bills, the death of a loved one, or a new experience. Even very happy occasions such as a family wedding, birth of a new baby, or family vacation can be stressful.

Since we cannot remove everyday problems from our lives, the key to controlling stress is changing how we react to daily living.

Let's look at the following example of two different reactions to everyday problems.

Bob, for example, drives to work every day in heavy traffic. When the traffic slows to a crawl, or someone cuts him off, he becomes extremely upset. By the time he gets to work or gets home at night, his body is tense, and he's often tired and irritable.

On the other hand, Susan, who drives to work in the same traffic, reacts quite differently. Time on the road before work gives her the opportunity to have a few extra sips of coffee before work and to listen to her favorite radio station. The drive home gives her a chance to unwind from the job, and to think about vacation plans, work ideas, or family activities. Because she drives defensively she seldom gets upset when someone cuts in front of her.

Take a minute now to think about how you react to everyday events. What methods do you have for relaxing and releasing tension from daily stress?

Tips for managing stress. First, learn to relax. There are many ways to relax and relieve stress, without using drugs or alcohol, or without spending a lot of money, such as:

- Take a warm bath.
- Take 10 to 15 minutes to sit quietly and breathe deeply.
- Get involved in your favorite hobby or learn a new hobby.
- Start an exercise program.
- Take a short nap.
- Find a comfortable place for light reading.
- Meet a friend for a walk or a chat.
- Eat regular meals and take time to enjoy them.
- Plan fun activities with your family or friends.
- Do something nice for yourself.
- Learn relaxation techniques and set aside time to practice them.
- Take a stress management class.
- Learn to accept what you cannot change instead of feeling constantly frustrated.
- Try laughing instead of taking things too seriously.
- Learn to manage your time effectively.
- Get professional help with problems or stresses that continue to bother you.

TENS (Transcutaneous Electrical Nerve Stimulation)

TENS is a small battery-operated device used to stimulate nerves and block pain. If you use a TENS device, it should not hurt. It may cause a tingling or vibrating sensation. When the unit is turned on, electrical signals are sent to the nerves in that area. These signals tend to block the pain. Check with your doctor to find out if a TENS unit would work for you. A physical therapist can show you the proper way to use it. You might consider trying it out a few times before buying your own unit.

Do not use a TENS unit if you have a cardiac pacemaker or a heart problem.

Medications

Many times medication is not necessary. However, if your back pain is not relieved using other forms of treatment, your doctor can prescribe the proper medications. The medication chosen depends on the back pain. For example, there are medications called analgesics which can relieve pain. Other medications, called muscle relaxants, are prescribed to relax tight muscles.

If your back pain is due to arthritis, your doctor can give you medication that will reduce inflammation, as well as relieve your back pain. The most common medications prescribed are called nonsteroidal anti-inflammatory drugs (NSAIDs). This means they are not cortisonelike drugs and they can reduce inflammation. Aspirin is one NSAID. More often, NSAID medications which cause less stomach distress are prescribed.

By working together, you and your doctor can find the medication that gives you the most relief. Let the doctor know if it is working as expected. You'll need to learn the side effects of the medications you are taking. Tell your doctor if you experience any. Learn all you can about your medications by asking your doctor or pharmacist questions such as:

- What will the medication do?
- How long will it take before I see results?
- What is the name of the medication? Is there a generic brand?
- Are there side effects I should know about?
- How should I take the medication (i.e., before or after meals, with or without food)?
- What time of day and how often should I take the medication?
- What should I do if I forget to take a dose at the specified time?

Let your doctor know if you are taking other medications. This is very important, since sometimes certain medications cannot be taken together.

Surgery

Very few people with back pain need surgery. Most people can be treated successfully with rest, exercise, and medication. An orthopedist or neurosurgeon will help you decide if a back operation is necessary.

The Arthritis Foundation

OSTEOPOROSIS

Osteoporosis is a major underlying cause of bone fractures in postmenopausal women and older persons in general. This bone-thinning disease, for example, affects as many as half of

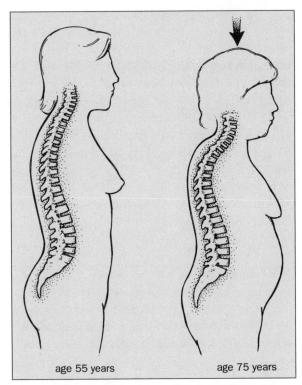

age 55 years   age 75 years

As bones lose their density and grow weaker with age, minuscule crush fractures within the vertebrae can dramatically alter a person's posture and height.

all women in the United States over 45 years of age and 90 percent of women over 75. It is the reason behind some familiar "signs" of aging that often begin in one's fifties or sixties—a loss of height over the years, an aching and curved back, or hips or wrists that break easily.

Osteoporosis has been called a "silent disease" because it develops with no symptoms for many years before the above signs begin to occur. Osteoporosis is difficult for doctors to diagnose early—before it causes problems.

However, there is good news. It is possible that osteoporosis and the fractures it causes can be prevented or at least delayed. Scientific evidence has suggested some measures women can take—with the support of their doctors—that may prevent or at least slow down the development of osteoporosis. These measures can be adopted whether a woman is in her thirties, fifties, or seventies. They can be helpful for men at risk for osteoporosis as well.

Osteoporosis literally means "porous bone." While the outer form of the bones does not change (unless there is a fracture), the bones have less substance and so are less dense. Osteoporosis is a common condition, affecting as many as 15 to 20 million individuals in the United States. It has been estimated to lead to 1.3 million bone fractures a year in people over 45 years of age, which is about 70 percent of all fractures occurring in this age group. Looked at in another way, each year about 1.7 percent of Americans between 45 and 64 years old and 2 percent of those age 65 and older break a bone because of osteoporosis.

In osteoporosis, bone mass decreases, causing bones to be more susceptible to fracture. A fall, blow, or lifting action that would not normally bruise or strain the average person can easily break one or more bones in someone with severe osteoporosis.

The spine, wrist, and hip are the most common sites of osteoporosis-related fractures, although the disease is generalized—that is, it can affect any bone of the body.

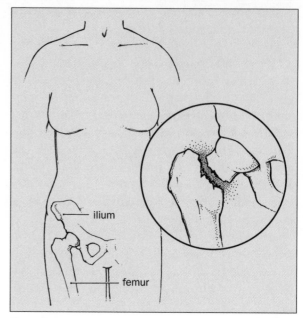

Bone fractures are a common consequence of osteoporosis. Adequate lifelong calcium intake is the best way to ensure strong bones later in life.

When the bones of the spinal column (the vertebrae) are weakened, a simple action like bending forward to make a bed or lifting a heavy roast pan out of the oven can be enough to cause a "crush fracture," or "spinal compression fracture." These vertebral crush fractures often cause back pain, decreased height, and a humped back or a "dowager's hump."

The occurrence of osteoporosis of the spine increases with age. One recent study of a group of about 2,000 women showed x-ray evidence of osteoporosis in the spine in about 29 percent of those age 45 to 54 years, 61 percent of those age 55 to 64, and 79 percent of those age 65 and older. Vertebral crush fractures are more common in women than men and generally occur in women between 55 and 75 years of age.

Wrist fractures also occur commonly among people with this disorder. For example, an otherwise healthy, vigorous woman in her fifties or sixties slips on ice, falls, reaches out to catch herself, and is taken to the emergency room with a broken wrist.

Osteoporosis is often the underlying cause of the broken hips suffered by more than 200,000 Americans over age 45 each year. A fall from a standing position can fracture a hip weakened by osteoporosis. In cases of severe osteoporosis, a change of posture or weight distribution alone can actually break the hip, and the fracture then causes a fall.

People who have hip fractures due to osteoporosis are generally older than people who suffer spinal fractures. There is more even distribution between women and men than with vertebral fractures, the rates for hip fractures being two to three times higher in women than in men.

WHO IS AT GREATEST RISK?

A number of risk factors for osteoporosis have been identified. These include the following.

- Being a woman. Osteoporosis—as evidenced by vertebral fractures—is estimated to be six to eight times more common in women than in men, partly because women have less bone mass to begin with. Furthermore, for several years after menopause, women also lose bone much more rapidly than men do, due to a fall in their bodies' production of estrogen.
- Early menopause. This is one of the strong predictors for the development of osteoporosis, especially if menopause is induced by surgery or other means that remove both ovaries or cause a sufficient drop in estrogen. Many experts define "early" menopause as menopause occurring before the age of 45.
- Being white, that is, Caucasian. White women are at higher risk than black women, and white men are at higher risk than black men. Some experts estimate that by age 65 a quarter of all white women have had one or more fractures related to osteoporosis. Oriental women are also thought to be at greater risk for the disease, but there are

not enough data to confirm this.
- A chronically low calcium intake.
- Lack of physical activity. However, exercising at an extreme level that halts menstruation in a young woman also may lead to bone loss.
- Being underweight. (This is not to suggest that being overweight is a good idea. Both overweight and underweight people are better off trying to attain their desirable weight.)

Other possible risk factors include:

- A family history of osteoporosis.
- Smoking cigarettes.
- Excessive use of alcohol. It is not known exactly how much alcohol is too much, in terms of osteoporosis, but alcoholics may be at risk for the disease.

Other factors often listed as increasing a person's risk of osteoporosis, although these are not well established by scientific studies, include:

- High intake of caffeine-containing foods such as coffee.
- Extremely high protein intake (to the extent that the diet is almost entirely protein).
- Phosphorus. Some people suggest avoiding eating large amounts of foods high in phosphorus and low in calcium such as red meats, cola drinks, brewer's yeast that does not have added calcium, and certain processed foods. Animal studies suggest that increases in phosphorus intake might speed bone loss; however, studies in humans show dietary phosphorus either promotes a positive calcium balance in the bones or has no effect.

WHAT CAUSES OSTEOPOROSIS?

Living bone contains a protein framework (the osteoid matrix) in which calcium salts are deposited. In fact, the bones and teeth contain about 99 percent of the calcium in the body. Calcium makes bone hard.

Bone, like many other tissues of the body, is constantly being rebuilt or "remodeled." Old bone is torn down, "resorbed," and replaced with new bone in much the same way that people remodel buildings by tearing out and replacing walls.

This process of bone resorption and remodeling serves two purposes: It keeps the skeleton well-tuned for its mechanical uses, and it helps to maintain the body's balance of certain essential minerals such as calcium. The body keeps a relatively constant level of calcium in the blood, because important biological activities such as contraction of muscles, beating of the heart, and clotting of blood require quite constant blood levels of calcium.

When the blood calcium level drops, more calcium is taken out of the bones to maintain the appropriate level. When the blood calcium level returns to normal, increased amounts of calcium are no longer taken from the bones.

As a person grows during youth, bones are metabolically active, and calcium is deposited into bone faster than it is taken out. The deposition of calcium into bone peaks at about 35 years of age in men and women. At the time of "peak bone mass" the bones are most dense and strong.

Some experts believe that the level of bone mass at this age may help determine whether a person may later lose enough bone to fracture easily. If a young woman achieves a high peak bone mass—possibly through increased calcium intake, moderate weight-bearing exercise, and other lifestyle choices—she may be less likely to develop osteoporosis later.

During a person's late thirties, after peak bone mass is attained, calcium begins to be lost from bones faster than it is replaced, and bones become less dense. This occurs naturally and gradually in both men and women. In addition, in general, as both women and men age, their bodies begin to absorb less calcium from food. This begins at about age 45 for women and age 60 for men.

Summarizing then, several complex factors influence the quantity and quality of bone throughout life, particularly after the age of 40. These include: level of adult peak bone mass; rates of bone loss due to menopause and due to aging; certain systemic hormones (such as calcitriol, an active form of vitamin D; parathyroid hormone; and calcitonin); substances produced by the bones themselves; diet (especially calcium intake); intestinal and kidney function; and physical forces that act on the bones such as those caused by body weight and exercise.

Given the complexity of the factors that influence bone, there may be many ways in which osteoporosis can develop. Current data point to two strong contributing factors: a drop in estrogen levels in women due to menopause (technically known as "estrogen deficiency") and a chronically low intake of calcium ("calcium deficiency").

Menopause

As a woman passes through menopause, her body's production of sex hormones declines and monthly bleeding—menstruation—gradually diminishes until it stops altogether. (If menopause occurs because of removal of the ovaries, the drop in estrogen is relatively sudden.) Hormones are chemical substances produced by glands to control activities of bodily organs. Estrogen, the female hormone, seems especially to influence bone substance by slowing or halting bone loss. It may also improve the absorption of dietary calcium by the intestine.

This role of estrogen makes biological sense. During the childbearing years, a woman needs a strong skeleton and a healthy reserve of calcium in case she becomes pregnant and later nurses children. After menopause, she no longer has the same need for this protective reserve of calcium. As her estrogen level drops, her bones start to contribute a larger share of calcium to meet the body's needs. (See also Menopause, page 415.)

Too Little Calcium in the Diet

Many scientists believe that a chronic shortage of dietary calcium is one important factor leading to osteoporosis. Each day, adults lose some calcium in the urine and feces and, to a lesser extent, through their skin. If these losses are not balanced by adequate amounts of calcium in the diet, "the body goes to the 'bank,'" as one expert put it, "and the bank, of course, is the skeleton." The bones begin to break down to supply the body's need for the mineral in maintaining the proper blood level of calcium.

Other Causes of Osteoporosis

Certain diseases or drugs can lead to bone loss. A doctor can evaluate a person who has one of these disorders or is taking one of these drugs and work with her to avoid osteoporosis. These include:

- Medications such as corticosteroids and heparin (an anticoagulant)
- Diseases such as hyperthyroidism, hyperparathyroidism, kidney disease, and certain forms of cancer (lymphoma, leukemia, and multiple myeloma)
- Impaired ability to absorb calcium from the intestine caused by diseases of the small intestine, liver, or pancreas
- Excessive excretion of calcium in the urine (idiopathic hypercalciuria)

WHAT ARE THE SYMPTOMS?

In most cases a patient is 50 to 70 years of age when osteoporosis is diagnosed. The disorder, however, can strike a woman as early as her mid-thirties. People with osteoporosis may have no symptoms until their bones become so weak that a sudden strain, bump, or fall causes a bone fracture. Then, of course, pain can be severe and can drastically curtail physical activity.

Crush fractures of the vertebrae can occur with or without causing pain. Thus, other clues to the presence of osteoporosis besides back pain are loss of height or curvature of the upper back. However, a chronic aching along the spine or, more often, pain from spasm in the muscles of the back may occur. With a partially collapsed spine, the muscles of the back must take a greater share of supporting the upper half of the body, so that these muscles may "complain" periodically.

Osteoporosis first may be discovered on an x-ray taken for some other purpose. In some cases, such x-rays may reveal that one or more weakened vertebrae have already been fractured. X-rays or other medical imaging methods can reveal that bones have weakened.

A person has to lose about a quarter of his or her bone mass before the loss can be detected on a regular x-ray. Unfortunately, by the time this much bone loss has occurred the bones already may be susceptible to breaking.

Scientists have developed new techniques to measure bone density, which might detect early bone loss, before fractures are likely to occur. These techniques are not available to some doctors. In one technique, called "photon absorptiometry" or "photon densitometry," rays like x-rays are passed through the skeleton and a machine measures how much these rays penetrate the bone (and therefore how dense the bones are).

Another technique is computed tomography (CT) scanning. It uses x-rays to measure bone density. Researchers are now adapting this technique to CT equipment already available in some hospitals.

While no blood or urine tests specifically diagnose osteoporosis, these tests may eliminate secondary causes of bone loss such as the disorders and medications listed before.

HOW CAN OSTEOPOROSIS BE PREVENTED AND TREATED?

In recent years, scientists have identified several measures that may help reduce the toll of osteoporosis. These measures are explained in the pages that follow. Estrogen replacement is the only one of these measures in which there is well-documented evidence of its effectiveness in the prevention of fractures from osteoporosis.

Although complete proof is lacking that the other measures—such as increased calcium intake—prevent bone loss leading to fractures, many scientists believe that the current data are sufficient to suggest that these measures be adopted.

Many of these measures can be taken throughout life to promote healthy bones. (Exceptions include estrogen replacement therapy for postmenopausal women and a newly approved drug, calcitonin, for the treatment of existing osteoporosis.) It is possible that young women could build a high peak bone mass to reduce the risk of developing osteoporosis. Middle-age and older women may be able to keep osteoporosis from occurring or progressing. Men too may lessen their risk of osteoporosis. All of these measures are best undertaken with the advice of a doctor

Estrogen Replacement Therapy

For women at risk of osteoporosis, a doctor may prescribe estrogen when the body's production of the hormone drops, that is, during and after menopause. Menopause occurs naturally around the age of 50, although it can occur when a woman is in her late thirties or into her early sixties. Menopause also will occur if the ovaries are removed by surgery.

Many experts feel that, in terms of its effects against osteoporosis, the benefits of estrogen replacement outweigh its risks. The decision to use estrogen, however, is one that should be made carefully by a woman and her doctor.

On the side of benefits, there is good evidence that low-dose estrogen is highly effective for the prevention and possibly treatment of osteoporosis in women. Estrogen reduces the amount of calcium taken out of bones and thus slows or halts postmenopausal bone loss. It cannot, however, restore bone mass to premenopausal levels. Studies have shown that women who have begun taking estrogen within a few years after the onset of menopause have fewer hip or wrist fractures and possibly fewer spinal fractures than women who do not take estrogen. Even when started as late as six years after menopause, estrogen therapy reduces further loss of bone.

There is also scientific evidence that estrogen replacement therapy confers protection against cardiovascular disease. It is thought to raise blood levels of a fraction of cholesterol known as "HDL" or high-density lipoprotein and to lower blood levels of "LDL" or low-density lipoprotein. Raised HDL levels and lowered LDL levels are associated with lower rates of heart and blood vessel disease.

On the risk side of the ledger, estrogen replacement therapy is thought to increase the risk of a type of cancer of the uterus known as endometrial cancer from one per 1,000 women to about four per 1,000 women. Endometrial cancer, fortunately, is relatively easy to detect and treat and is rarely fatal. It is not a problem for a woman who has had her uterus removed, of course. Estrogen is not linked to breast cancer, according to most studies. The therapy may increase the risk of blood clot formation (thrombosis).

In women on estrogen replacement therapy, periodic bleeding may resume. (Because estrogen therapy may cause the lining of the uterus to build up, it is often prescribed on an on-and-off basis—for example, 20 days on the drug, then 10 without it—so that the uterus lining can be shed during the days off the hormone.)

Estrogen may be combined with another female hormone, progestin, also called progestogen. (Progesterone is one form of progestin.) Progestins may reduce the risk of endometrial cancer. There is preliminary evidence that they may reduce bone loss.

There is little information on the long-term risks or benefits of estrogen combined with progestin in postmenopausal women. Studies on younger women taking progestins in birth control pills have shown an increased risk of high blood pressure and of disorders of the heart and blood vessels. Moreover, some progestins may blunt or do away with estrogen's protective effects against heart disease.

Until more data on the risks and benefits of estrogen replacement are available, doctors and patients may prefer to reserve estrogen (whether or not it is combined with a progestin), for situations in which there is a moderate to high risk of osteoporosis. Premature menopause—especially through surgical removal of the ovaries several years before the time of natural menopause—places a woman at high risk of osteoporosis. Postmenopausal women having risk factors other than an early menopause may also want to discuss estrogen therapy with their doctors. (The section on risk gives these other factors as: being white, having a low calcium intake, being inactive, having a slight build, and possibly heredity, cigarette smoking, and excessive use of alcohol.)

The preceding recommendations apply mainly to Caucasian women. Women of other races and their doctors might consider estrogen on a case-by-case basis. There is no good evidence that elderly women should be started on estrogen therapy to prevent osteoporosis.

Increased Calcium Intake

An intake of calcium of 1,000 to 1,500 mg (milligrams) per day—through diet or diet plus supplements—is thought to help protect against development of osteoporosis.

People, particularly women, should get plenty of calcium in their diets throughout life. Studies show that the usual intake of calcium for adult women (ages 25 to 74) in the

United States is 450 to 550 mg per day. This is well below the current Recommended Dietary Allowance (RDA) of 800 mg per day for women and men who are over 18 years old. Furthermore, studies cited by the National Institutes of Health Consensus Development Conference on Osteoporosis led the conference panel to offer the opinion that the RDA for calcium is too low, especially for post-menopausal women, and may well be too low for elderly men.

The panel recommended that women consume the following amounts of calcium daily.

- Premenopausal and older women receiving estrogen need about 1,000 mg of calcium per day for calcium balance, that is, to keep the amount of calcium in the bones constant.
- Postmenopausal women (that is, all women past the age of menopause) who are not on estrogen need about 1,500 mg of calcium per day.

In addition, men who increase their calcium intake may prevent age-related bone loss as well.

If the average American woman consumes an estimated 500 mg of calcium per day based on her current eating habits, then an additional 500 to 1,000 mg are needed; that is roughly the amount of calcium in two to four servings of milk or several servings of other calcium-rich foods. It can be helpful to consult a doctor, registered dietitian or nutritionist who can estimate the amount of calcium in a person's usual diet. Then he or she can suggest ways to increase calcium in the diet and can recommend calcium supplements, if necessary, to bring the daily intake up to 1,000 to 1,500 mg. Some sources of calcium are discussed in the information that follows.

Milk, other dairy products, fish, and dark green vegetables are the major dietary sources of calcium in this country. One eight-ounce glass of milk contains about 300 mg of calcium and a quart contains about 1,200 mg. Skim milk or low-fat milk, which actually contain a little more calcium than whole milk, are preferred to minimize fat intake. (The American diet is generally high in fat and efforts should be made to reduce fat intake. Consumption of low-fat dairy products reduces both fat and calories in the diet.)

In addition to milk itself, other milk products such as low-fat yogurt and nonfat dry milk are also high in calcium. Other calcium-rich foods include fish and shellfish such as oysters, shrimp, and canned sardines and salmon (when the edible bones are also consumed); and dark green vegetables such as collard, turnip, and mustard greens, kale, and broccoli. Spinach is not a good source of calcium because, although it is high in calcium and other nutrients, it contains substances (oxalates) that diminish absorption of calcium.

People who have difficulty digesting milk (as in lactase deficiency or lactose intolerance) might try eating yogurt or drinking milk that has been treated with the enzyme lactase (known as LactAid) so it can be digested. Some yogurts contain lactase naturally.

For some people, it may be difficult to reach the daily levels of calcium intake suggested previously without taking calcium supplements. Different formulations of the supplements contain different amounts of elemental calcium, so it is important to read the product label. For example, calcium carbonate is 40 percent calcium. That is, 100 mg of calcium carbonate contains 40 mg of calcium, or "elemental calcium." In the case of calcium lactate (at 13 percent calcium), 250 mg of the compound would contain about 34 mg of calcium.

Calcium supplements are often in the form of tablets. Chewable tablets and powders may be available. One source of calcium carbonate is oyster shells, so this compound is sometimes called "oyster shell calcium." Certain antacids contain calcium carbonate; in fact, one popular brand is virtually 100 percent calcium carbonate with only added sweeteners and flavorings. Other antacids with calcium carbonate also contain aluminum, which can hamper the intestine's ability to absorb calcium from food.

It is wise to consult a doctor to determine how much calcium you currently consume, whether you should take calcium supplements, and if so, what type. The number of calcium preparations on the market is growing steadily, and there is no one supplement that can be uniformly recommended. If you cannot get enough calcium in your diet and you must take supplements, here is some information to keep in mind.

- There is recent evidence that taking supplements between meals promotes better absorption. Some believe that it is useful to take calcium at bedtime because of increased calcium loss during sleep. (So, for example, someone who takes calcium twice a day might take it mid-morning and at night.)
- A recent study found that absorption of calcium from calcium carbonate is impaired in people with little or no stomach acid, which is common in people over 60. However, the scientists found that in these people absorption improved if the compound was taken with meals.
- Bone meal and dolomite should not be taken regularly. Although they are both high in calcium, they also tend to contain high amounts of lead and other toxic metals.
- Be alert to calcium supplements that have vitamin D added to them. Most people get enough of this vitamin in their diet and through sun exposure. Vitamin D becomes toxic at high doses.
- Avoid taking aluminum-containing antacids as a regular source of calcium.
- Drink a full glass of water when taking a calcium supplement. (In general, it is a good idea to drink several glasses of water each day.)

Levels of calcium intake greater than those recommended previously (that is, 1,000 to 1,500 mg per day) can cause kidney stones in susceptible people. Thus, people with a history of kidney stones should take calcium supplements only with a doctor's guidance. These people should be especially careful to drink plenty of water.

Normal Levels of Vitamin D

Vitamin D is required for optimal absorption of calcium in the intestine. People who get very little sunlight exposure are at risk of vitamin D deficiency. This particularly applies to older people who may be confined to a home or nursing facility.

Scientists recommend 400 I.U. (international units) of vitamin D each day. Most people get enough of this vitamin by being outside during the day and eating a normal diet. (Vitamin D is produced by the body naturally when a person is exposed to the sun.) Fifteen minutes to a half-hour of midday sunshine may meet the daily need for this vitamin. Food sources include vitamin D-fortified milk, vitamin-fortified cereals, egg yolks, saltwater fish, and liver.

The phrase "normal levels" is important here. Taking in high doses of vitamin D can have dangerous effects. No one needs to take more than the RDA per day without a doctor's guidance.

Moderate Weight-Bearing Exercise

Exercise may be an important part of both prevention and treatment programs for osteoporosis. It is clear that inactivity leads to bone loss. Research studies have shown that normal, healthy people who are bedridden for periods of time lose bone mineral rapidly. Studies have also revealed that astronauts living in the weightlessness of space lose bone mass.

Scientists believe that activity involving the muscles working against gravity such as walking or jogging will help to reduce bone loss.

The best type and amount of physical activity to prevent osteoporosis have not yet been established. However, a modest program of weight-bearing exercise is recommended for people of all ages, including middle-age and older women who want strong bones. Possibilities for "weight-bearing" exercises include: walking, hiking, racewalking, jogging, running, jumping rope, aerobic dancing, ballroom dancing, gymnastics, tennis, racquetball, squash, handball, rowing, weight training, basketball, volleyball, cross-country skiing, and to some extent, bicycling. Swimming and yoga are healthy activities, but are not generally thought to be weight-bearing. There are some cautions about exercise, of course. It is a good idea to consult a doctor before starting an exercise program, especially if there are heart, joint, or other problems or if a person has been sedentary for a long time. Exercise programs should also be started slowly and built up gradually. Exercising to the point of causing trauma to the bones should be avoided.

Doctors encourage patients with osteoporosis to remain as physically active as possible. It is important to avoid sudden strains from jumping or twisting and situations where a person might fall. Walking, however, is highly recommended. The worst thing to do is to give in to the disorder and take to one's bed or chair. Lack of activity will almost certainly do harm—both physically and psychologically.

New Modes of Treatment

Most of the measures described here are for the prevention, not the treatment, of osteoporosis. Treatment refers to methods of making more bone, rather than slowing down bone loss. The needs are great for drugs and techniques that can treat osteoporosis once it has occurred.

Several potential therapies for osteoporosis are being studied by researchers. In most cases, the effectiveness and safety of these therapies have not been fully established.

A new drug for osteoporosis was approved

by the Federal Food and Drug Administration in December 1984. This drug is calcitonin. Calcitonin occurs naturally in the body, as it is a hormone produced by the thyroid gland. It slows bone breakdown. The form that is sold by prescription is a synthetic form of calcitonin from salmon (also called calcitonin-salmon). As a treatment for osteoporosis, it is given by daily injection in conjunction with 1,500 mg of calcium and 400 I.U. per day of vitamin D.

Other agents under study include sodium fluoride; the hormone calcitriol (a form of vitamin D); anabolic steroids; thiazides (diuretics); biphosphonates; a biologically active fragment of parathyroid hormone; and "ADFR" (a complex series of drugs).

Prevention of Fractures

There are ways that people can make fractures less likely to occur, especially if their bones are already fragile. Minimizing hazards in the home can help, such as avoiding slippery floors and loose throw rugs, removing objects that might cause a fall, providing adequate lighting, and adding handles or nonslip bottoms to bathtubs. Railings on stairways inside and outside of the home can help.

It is also a good idea to avoid actions that stress the bones unduly. In particular, do not lift while bending forward. Lifting this way creates an unusual and unnecessary strain on the vertebral column. A person should carry the weight close to the body, squatting and lifting straight up, using the legs and not the back. If the spine is weak, it is wise to completely avoid lifting heavy objects.

The National Institute of Arthritis and Musculoskeletal and Skin Diseases

OSTEOARTHRITIS

Osteoarthritis is a disease that causes the breakdown of joint tissue, leading to joint pain and stiffness. It can affect any joint, but commonly occurs in the hips, knees, feet, and spine. It may also affect some finger joints, the joint at the base of the thumb, and the joint at the base of the big toe. It rarely affects the wrists, elbows, shoulders, ankles, or jaw, except as a result of injury or unusual stress.

Osteoarthritis is one of the oldest and most

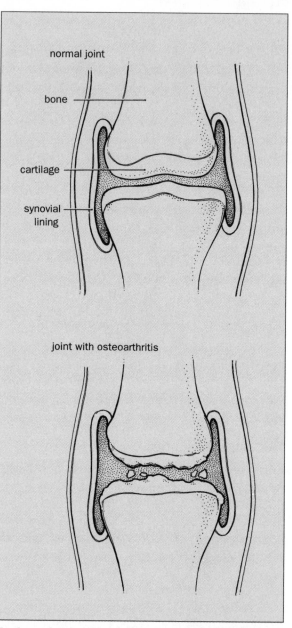

In the arthritic joint, the protective cartilage and synovial lining gradually erode, so that bone surfaces rub directly against each other and disintegrate.

common diseases of man. It probably affects almost every person over age 60 to some degree, but only some have it badly enough to notice any symptoms. Osteoarthritis is also known by many other names, such as degenerative joint disease, arthrosis, osteoarthrosis, or hypertrophic arthritis.

Although there is no cure for osteoarthritis, proper treatment can help relieve the symptoms and prevent or correct serious joint problems.

WHAT HAPPENS IN OSTEOARTHRITIS?

Osteoarthritis causes joint tissues to wear down. In healthy joints a firm, rubbery material called cartilage covers the end of each bone. Cartilage acts as a cushion, or shock absorber, between the bones. The bones of the joint are held together by ligaments and tendons, which act as strong, flexible cables that allow movement in the right directions.

All of these joint tissues are enclosed by a capsule. The capsule is lined by a thin material, called the synovial membrane. The membrane releases a slippery fluid, called synovial fluid, into the enclosed joint space. This liquid helps the joint tissues move smoothly and easily.

The breakdown of joint tissue caused by osteoarthritis occurs in several phases: (1) The smooth cartilage surface softens and becomes pitted and frayed. When this happens, the cartilage loses its elasticity and is more easily damaged by excess use or by injury. (2) With time, large sections of cartilage may be worn away completely. Without this "shock absorber" between the bones, the bones rub together and cause pain. (3) As the cartilage breaks down, the joint may lose its normal shape. The bone ends thicken and form bony growths, or spurs, where the ligaments and capsule attach to the bone. (4) Fluid-filled cysts may form in the bone near the joint. Bits of bone or cartilage may float loosely in the joint space. All these changes can create pain when the joint is moved.

If detected and treated at an early stage, some of the joint damage may be slowed down.

Symptoms

Osteoarthritis affects each joint differently. Osteoarthritis in the hands, for example, is different from osteoarthritis in the hips. No matter what joint it affects, the symptoms usually begin slowly and may not seem important. Most people feel mild aching and soreness, especially when they move. A few people develop constant nagging pain, even when they're resting.

General symptoms. Usually, the affected joint or joints hurt most after you've overused them or after long periods of remaining still. You will probably find it difficult to move the affected joints easily, but they usually will not become completely stiff. If you don't move and exercise the sore joints, the muscles surrounding the joints will become weaker and smaller in size. Because the weak muscles won't be able to support the joint as well, you may have increased joint pain. You may also notice that your coordination and posture may not be as good as they were before.

The pain of osteoarthritis usually occurs only in the joint or in the area around the joint. In rare cases, people feel pain far from the affected joint. This feeling is called referred pain. For example, it is possible to have osteoarthritis in your hip but feel referred pain in your thigh or near your knee.

In the hips. You may feel pain around the groin or inner thigh. Some people feel referred pain in the buttocks, knee, or along the side of the thigh. The pain may cause you to limp when you walk.

In the knees. You may feel joint tenderness in the knee area and pain when you move your knee. You may feel a "grating" or "catching" sensation in your joint when you move it. It may be painful to walk up or down stairs or hills. If the pain prevents you from moving or

OSTEOARTHRITIS VERSUS RHEUMATOID ARTHRITIS

Some people confuse osteoarthritis with rheumatoid arthritis. These diseases are different, but some people can have both conditions at the same time.

OSTEOARTHRITIS	RHEUMATOID ARTHRITIS
Usually begins after age 40	Usually begins between ages 25 and 50
Usually develops slowly, over many years	Often develops suddenly, within weeks or months
Often affects joints on only one side of body, at first	Usually affects same joint on both sides of body (e.g., both knees)
Usually doesn't cause redness, warmth, swelling (inflammation) of joint	Causes redness, warmth, and swelling of joints
Affects only certain joints; rarely affects elbows or shoulders	Affects many joints, including elbows and shoulders
Doesn't cause a general feeling of sickness	Often causes a general feeling of sickness, fatigue, weight loss, and fever

exercising your knee, the large muscles around the knee area will become weaker.

In the fingers. The breakdown of joint tissue in the fingers causes bony growths (spurs) to form in these joints. If spurs occur in the end joints of the fingers, they are called Heberden's nodes.

If they occur in the joints in the middle of the fingers they are called Bouchard's nodes.

Heberden's nodes appear most often in women with osteoarthritis and sometimes occur as early as age 40. They tend to run in families. Both Heberden's and Bouchard's nodes may appear first in one or a few fingers and then may develop in others. You may suddenly notice redness, swelling, tenderness, and aching in the affected joints. Your fingertips may be numb and may tingle. Although these nodes may make your finger joints painful, you'll probably still have good use of your hands. Some people don't feel any pain at all, and may never have serious problems in other joints.

In the feet. You may feel pain and tenderness in the large joint at the base of the big toe. Wearing tight shoes and high heels can make this pain worse.

In the spine. Breakdown of joint tissues in the spine may place extra pressure on the nerves in the spinal column. This may cause you to feel pain at the base of your head, in your neck, legs, or lower back, or down your arms. Some people also feel stiffness in the neck or lower back. You may also feel some weakness or numbness in your arms or legs, and may have difficulty using your arms or walking at times.

WHAT CAUSES OSTEOARTHRITIS?

Researchers now think there are several factors that lead to osteoarthritis, such as heredity, obesity, and overuse or injury to certain joints.

Heredity

A person born with bow legs or a dislocated hip may be more likely to develop osteoarthritis. Some scientists think people born with defective cartilage are more likely to develop osteoarthritis. Another theory is that it may occur in people born with slight defects that make their joints fit together incorrectly or move incorrectly. Such problems may not be noticeable during youth, but may gradually wear down the joints over time.

Obesity

There is increasing evidence that being obese (overweight) contributes to the development of osteoarthritis. Over time, a lot of extra weight is more likely to damage "weight-bearing" joints, such as the knees and hips.

Overuse or Injury

Some people may develop osteoarthritis due to joint injuries, overuse of injured joints, or the presence of a different kind of arthritis already in the joint.

WHO GETS OSTEOARTHRITIS?

Almost 16 million people in the United States have osteoarthritis. As people get older they are more likely to develop it, possibly because of the buildup of joint damage from injuries and stress over time.

Athletes who have injured joints during sports activities tend to be more likely to develop osteoarthritis. Football and soccer players, for instance, may be affected more often. Also, coal miners, foundry workers, and other workers who engage in manual labor that places a lot of stress on certain joints, may be more likely to develop osteoarthritis.

Most people don't feel the symptoms of osteoarthritis before age 40 unless they have injured or overused poorly fitting or damaged joints. Many people aren't bothered by osteoarthritis, even though x-rays show they have joint damage.

HOW IS IT DIAGNOSED?

To diagnose osteoarthritis, your doctor will ask you to explain your symptoms and describe possible physical stresses or injuries that may have led to your pain. A physical examination will be done, with close attention paid to your affected joints.

The doctor usually will be able to diagnose osteoarthritis based on your medical history and the physical examination. However, if many joints are affected or if certain joints are affected, your doctor may require some or all of the following tests. These tests will help make the diagnosis, determine how much joint damage has been done, and rule out other kinds of arthritis.

- *X-rays* can show bone and joint changes that are typical of osteoarthritis.
- *Joint aspiration*, an examination of fluid drained from affected joints, can help the doctor rule out other diseases.
- *Blood tests* may be used to rule out other diseases.

WHAT IS THE TREATMENT?

Presently, no known treatment can stop or reverse the process of osteoarthritis. A good treatment program may help you decrease joint pain and stiffness, and improve joint movement and function. Yet, it may or may not slow down the disease process. Your treatment program will be designed especially for you and should include a combination of:

- Joint protection
- Exercise
- Medication
- Heat and cold treatments
- Weight control
- Surgery, when necessary

Your treatment program will be based on how severe your disease is, which joints are affected, the nature of your symptoms and other medical problems, as well as your age, occupation, and your everyday activities. You will work in partnership with your doctor and other health professionals to make sure your program meets your needs.

Joint Protection

Joint protection means protecting painful joints from stresses and strains that can make them hurt more or cause further damage. This includes learning to perform daily activities in ways that will be less painful and stressful to your joints. Your doctor and therapist will show you what you'll need to do for your joints. They may suggest you do some or all of the following.

Reduce or avoid activities, such as jogging, high-impact aerobics, or task-related motions that increase or cause pain to your joints.

Use a cane, walker, or crutches, if your hips, knees, feet, or spine are severely affected. These devices will take some of the weight off the joints.

Use splints to rest and protect painful joints. Splints should be fitted by health professionals because they can actually do more harm than good if they fit improperly and if you don't learn the proper exercises to do when you're not wearing them.

Lose weight, if you are overweight, because extra weight adds more stress to your weight-bearing joints.

Use correct posture to avoid putting too much stress on many of your joints. Here are a few basic rules of good posture.

- Keep your back comfortably straight when you are lying down, sitting, standing, walking, or lifting.
- Use a firm mattress or bed board to help keep your posture correct while you sleep or rest in bed.
- Sit in straight-backed chairs which have arm rests, whenever possible, and try not to slump while sitting.
- Pull your stomach in and keep your back as straight as you can comfortably, while walking or sitting.
- Bend your knees rather than your back when lifting, if you have back problems but no arthritis in your knees.
- Avoid sitting for long periods of time. For instance, if you're watching TV or riding in a car, walk around every 30 to 60 minutes, if possible.
- Limit your lifting as much as possible, if you have osteoarthritis in your back or your knees.

- Use aids such as dollies or straps for sliding and moving objects.
- Ask others to help you with necessary lifting.

Exercise

Exercising regularly is extremely important in successfully controlling osteoarthritis. If you don't use your joints, they can become stiff and harder to move. As a result, the muscles can become weak. While improvement in your joints and muscles may seem slow, you will see results if you exercise regularly.

The goals of your exercise program are to:

- Keep your joints flexible.
- Strengthen the muscles that keep your joints stable.
- Protect diseased joints against further damaging stress.
- Reduce stiffness.
- Improve your posture.

Gentle exercises, such as swimming, a walking program, and pedaling a stationary bike, are less stressful on your joints and are good for your overall fitness. The Arthritis Foundation offers exercise programs that are specially designed for people with arthritis. Contact your local foundation chapter for information about programs in your area.

You may also have to do special exercises to help specific joints and muscles. Your therapist will show you how to do these exercises, which include moving your joints through their full range of motion, several times each day. To strengthen muscles, you may be shown how to tighten parts of your body without moving your joints and making the arthritis worse. You can do some of these exercises at home, but if you have an unusual amount of joint or muscle problems, you may be advised to see a physical therapist for help with special exercises.

Medication

Many different medicines are used to control the symptoms of osteoarthritis. Your doctor may have you try several types before you find the one that works best for you. The following are some of the medicines commonly used to treat osteoarthritis.

Nonsteroidal anti-inflammatory drugs, or NSAIDs (pronounced en-seds), include aspirin and aspirinlike drugs. They help reduce joint pain, stiffness, and swelling. You may have to take them every day, and may have to take several doses each day. One of the most common side effects is stomach upset or irritation. Your doctor may recommend you take a "coated" aspirin or take your medication with meals (not before meals) to help avoid irritating the stomach. There are many different types of NSAIDs, so your doctor may have you try several kinds before you find the one that works best and has the fewest side effects. In some cases, acetaminophen (Tylenol) may be used to relieve pain.

Corticosteroids are similar to cortisone, a natural body hormone. They may be injected into the joint to relieve pain and the swelling that sometimes occurs with osteoarthritis. These medicines also come in pill form, but this form is not used for osteoarthritis.

Heat and Cold Treatments

Heat and cold treatments are effective ways to temporarily relieve pain and soreness. To relax your muscles, your doctor may advise you to take a hot bath or shower in the morning just after you get out of bed. This is a time when many people find that their pain and stiffness is the worst. There are many other ways of applying heat treatment, such as with hot packs, heat lamps, electric pads, electric mitts, and paraffin wax. Cold treatments help numb the area, so you won't feel as much pain. Treatments include using cold compresses, ice cubes wrapped in towels, or a bag of frozen vegetables. Some people also find relief from creams or ointments that warm or numb the joint area. Ask your doctor or therapist which heat or cold methods are best for you.

Weight Control

Weight control is an important part of your treatment program. Extra pounds put even more stress on weight-bearing joints (hips, knees, back, and feet). This extra stress can lead to further joint pain and damage. Losing weight can also make you look better, have more energy, and feel healthier.

The formula to follow for losing weight is to eat fewer calories and increase your physical activity.

If you have another illness, such as diabetes or high blood pressure, work with your doctor to find the best weight-loss program for you. Here are some things you can do to control your weight.

- Eat more fish and poultry.
- Eat only lean red meat.
- Eat fresh fruits instead of baked goods for dessert.
- Limit butter, cream, lard, shortening, and margarine.
- Broil or bake food, rather than fry.
- Trim fat off meats; remove skin from poultry.
- Eat slowly and take smaller portions.
- Avoid seconds.
- Snack on fresh fruits and vegetables.

Surgery

Some people may need surgery on their joints to correct or prevent deformity, to relieve pain, and to improve overall movement. Joint operations are done by orthopedic surgeons (doctors who specialize in bone surgery), or other surgeons who specialize in hand operations. In the past several years, these operations have become very effective, and many people have benefited from joint repair or replacement. New operations are being developed that also appear promising.

Surgeons can replace or repair damaged joints with wear-resistant artificial joints made of metal and plastic. Today, there are man-made replacements available for all the major joints. Total hip and knee replacement operations have been in use for a longer time than other joint replacement procedures, and are among the most successful. Sometimes, surgical operations don't replace the whole joint. They may be needed just to remove damaged tissue and clear the way for smooth movement. This can often be done more easily now with a special instrument called an arthroscope. With this tool, the surgeon can look into the joint and perform operations through small incisions.

Some replacement joints are attached to the bones with a strong bone glue. More recently, new artificial joints that don't need this bone glue are being used. These joints may be of special value in younger people.

In general, surgery produces the best results when it is balanced with medications and a physical activity program.

COPING

Living and coping with any chronic disease is difficult. Your osteoarthritis may be mild and may only slightly affect your activities and emotions. On the other hand, there may be times when the pain or discomfort lead to depression, anger, and frustration. Emotional strain can also cause a loss of sleep, which can make you feel tired and run down.

Don't try to deny or ignore such feelings, thinking they will go away. Try to accept the truth about the disease and your feelings about it. This is often the best way to keep the problems in perspective.

Talk openly with your family, friends, and doctors about your concerns and stresses. You may also find it helpful to talk with a social worker, psychologist, or counselor at a family service agency. They are specially trained to help you understand and cope with the stress and emotional upsets that can often result from an illness.

The Arthritis Foundation

RHEUMATOID ARTHRITIS

Rheumatoid arthritis (RA) is a systemic disease—one that affects the entire body. It causes pain, stiffness, warmth, redness, and swelling—a process called inflammation—in the joints. It can also affect other parts of the body, including the muscles, lungs, heart, skin, blood vessels, nerves, and eyes. Other symptoms of RA include fatigue, weight loss, and a slight fever. In its most serious form, rheumatoid arthritis causes painful joint damage. But in its mild form, it causes less pain and damage.

Rheumatoid arthritis is one of the most common of the rheumatic diseases—diseases which cause aches, pains, and stiffness in tissues within or around joints. It is a chronic illness, meaning it may last throughout your lifetime. However, it can be managed through proper treatment programs. With proper treatment and possibly some changes in daily activities, most people with RA can lead a normal, productive life.

WHAT HAPPENS IN RHEUMATOID ARTHRITIS?

The many symptoms of rheumatoid arthritis are caused by a general process called inflammation. Inflammation in the joint is called synovitis, because the membrane (the synovium) lining the joint becomes inflamed. This causes the joint to appear swollen and to feel painful and warm. Over time, this destructive inflammation may damage the entire joint.

Symptoms

The course of rheumatoid arthritis varies from person to person. Early in the disease, you may notice general fatigue, soreness, stiffness, and aching. Later on, you may notice specific symptoms, such as those that follow.

Joint pain. RA usually starts as gradually developing joint and muscle stiffness. Although these symptoms usually develop over many weeks or months, they can also begin very suddenly. The pain usually occurs in the same joints on both sides of the body; that is, both hands, both feet, and so forth. Usually, you'll notice joint pain in your hands and feet, first. RA can also affect joints in the wrists, elbows, shoulders, neck, knees, hips, and ankles.

After a while, RA may cause joints to become bent or deformed. Fortunately, proper treatment can often prevent this process and can help correct it if it does occur.

Other general symptoms. In addition to joint and muscle pain, some people with RA may have a decreased appetite and lose weight, have a slight fever, and may be extremely fatigued. Also, lumps called rheumatoid nodules may form under the skin in areas that receive pressure, such as the back of the elbows. They come and go during the course of the illness and usually don't cause problems. However, they sometimes become sore or infected. Less commonly, RA may affect the heart or lungs, causing chest pain or difficulty breathing. It may cause dryness and mild pain in the eyes.

Rheumatoid arthritis is an illness of ups and downs. It is quite common—even if you have severe RA—to have periods in which the pain and stiffness decrease or even go away. This is called a remission, and may last weeks, months, or years.

Remissions may appear suddenly or gradually. You may also have periods, called flares, when the pain and stiffness become worse. Sometimes, RA may seem to go away completely. This happens to about one of every five people with RA—usually those who haven't had the disease very long. Although these people feel well, it still is possible for the RA to flare in the future.

WHAT CAUSES RHEUMATOID ARTHRITIS?

The cause of rheumatoid arthritis is not yet known. For years, researchers have looked without success for an infection caused by a virus or bacterium as the cause of RA. Researchers still suspect that something like a virus may trigger RA, but they don't think everyone who becomes infected with this "virus" will develop the illness. Scientists now believe that this unknown agent causes RA only in people who have a genetic, or inherited, tendency for the disease. One clue supporting this idea is that most people with RA have a certain genetic marker called HLA-DR4. It is a common marker and occurs in about one-fourth of the U.S. population. Most people with the HLA-DR4 marker will not get RA, but may develop it more easily than those who don't have the marker.

Some people notice their RA begins or gets worse after a disturbing emotional event, such as a death in the family, divorce, or other emotional strain or shock. While such events don't cause RA, they may seem to trigger it or make it worse.

WHO GETS RHEUMATOID ARTHRITIS?

About two million people in the United States have rheumatoid arthritis. It affects all races equally, but affects two to three times more women than men. The disease usually begins in middle age (forties or fifties), but it can start at any age.

HOW IS IT DIAGNOSED?

Because the symptoms of rheumatoid arthritis usually develop over a long period of time, it may take a while for your doctor to diagnose it. The diagnosis will not be based on one symptom or test alone, but on the overall pattern of the symptoms, your medical history, and the following tests.

Physical exam. The doctor will ask you about your symptoms and will look for signs of joint swelling, warmth, and tenderness characteristic of RA.

Blood tests. In addition to other blood and urine tests, the following blood tests may help determine if you have RA.

- *Rheumatoid factor.* An abnormal substance found in the blood of about 80 percent of adults with RA. It is also present in other diseases, so a positive test doesn't always indicate RA. It is possible for people without the rheumatoid factor to have RA.
- *Erythrocyte sedimentation rate* (called "sed rate" for short). A test which measures how fast red blood cells settle to the bottom of a thin tube. In people with chronic inflammation (including those with RA), the cells fall faster than normal. This test is an indicator of the activity of the disease.
- *Red blood cell count.* A test usually done during your first visit. It shows if you have anemia, a condition which often occurs along with RA and causes extreme tiredness.

Other tests. The doctor may also consider the following tests.

- *Joint aspiration.* A test in which the doctor drains fluid from swollen joints and examines it to make sure the arthritis is not due to an infection or some other cause.
- *Biopsy.* A test in which small bits of inflamed joint tissue or rheumatoid nodules are removed for examination with a microscope. This procedure may cause minor discomfort, but it is rarely used.
- *X-rays* may be used later in the disease to check the amount of damage in specific joints and to see if the illness is progressing.

WHAT IS THE TREATMENT?

Presently, no known treatment can stop or reverse the process of RA. Treatment involves some or all of the following: medication; exercise; rest; heat and cold applications; joint protection; surgery (when needed); managing stress and depression; physical and occupational therapy.

The goals of your treatment program are to reduce joint swelling, relieve pain and stiffness, and help you function as normally as possible. Your program will be designed by your doctor to meet your own needs, depending on: how severe your disease is, how long you've had it, which joints are affected, your general symptoms, other health problems and medications, as well as your age, occupation, and daily activities. Following a proper treatment program early in your illness may help control joint damage and prevent future problems.

You will get the best results from your treatment program if you stick with it at all times—even when you are feeling well.

Medication

The following medications are used to help control RA. Some work well for certain people but are less effective for others. Your doctor may have you try several medications in order to find the one that is the most effective and has the fewest side effects.

Nonsteroidal anti-inflammatory drugs, or NSAIDs, include aspirin and aspirinlike drugs. They reduce joint pain, stiffness, and swelling, usually within the first several days to weeks of taking them. They may be given in pill or liquid form. They are usually given in several doses every day, and you must continue taking them even when you don't have any symptoms. One of the most common side effects is stomach upset or irritation. Your doctor may recommend that you take "coated" aspirin and take your medication with meals to help avoid irritating the stomach. NSAIDs may also cause stomach ulcers in some people. Since it is possible to have an ulcer without having stomach pain, check with your doctor to be sure you know the signs and symptoms of ulcers. (If you are at risk for stomach ulcers, your doctor may prescribe other medicine to help treat or prevent them.)

There are many different types of NSAIDs, so your doctor may have you try several kinds before you find the one that works best and has the fewest side effects.

Corticosteroids are medications related to hydrocortisone, a natural body hormone. They are not the same as the steroids some athletes take. Corticosteroids are powerful and can cause serious side effects, so they are used only when the disease is active and has not responded to other medicines. When given over a long period of time, they are given in the smallest dose possible. Corticosteroids may also be used for short periods during severe flares.

Although corticosteroids can relieve joint pain and swelling to a great extent, they do not cure arthritis. If they are used in high doses for a long period of time, they can cause side effects such as thinning of the bones (osteoporosis). If you are taking corticosteroids, check with your doctor or pharmacist to be sure you understand the possible side effects for the dose you're taking. If you are taking these drugs over an extended period, you will need to be checked by your doctor on a regular basis for side effects. You might also want to wear a medical identification tag that states that you take corticosteroids. It could provide helpful information in case of an emergency.

Corticosteroids are sometimes injected directly into the affected joint. This reduces the possibility of developing some of the side effects just described. Although injections can bring short-term relief, they can actually cause joint damage if used too often.

Never reduce your dose of corticosteroid or stop taking it without first contacting your doctor. Stopping or suddenly reducing the drug could lead to serious health problems.

Slow-Acting Antirheumatic Drugs (SAARDs)

NSAIDs and corticosteroids provide fast relief from inflammation and pain, but they do not stop or slow down the disease process. Slow-acting antirheumatic drugs (SAARDs) work more slowly and, in some cases, can slow down the disease process. They usually provide relief within the first few months of taking them. Examples of SAARDs include gold salts, hydroxychloroquine, penicillamine, sulfasalazine, and immunosuppressive drugs.

Gold salts is a standard treatment which has been used for more than 50 years. Gold may be injected directly into the muscle or may be given in pill form. It may take up to six months to find out if this treatment will work for you. During this time, the doctor will watch for side effects, such as skin rashes, and will perform blood and urine tests to watch for problems in the kidneys and bone marrow (where the body makes new blood cells). With each person, it is a matter of trial to learn if gold works.

Hydroxychloroquine (Plaquenil) is given in pill form, usually twice per day. It usually begins working within 6 to 12 weeks after starting it. Most people tolerate this medicine easily, but it can cause side effects, such as stomach upset and skin rash. Rarely, it can cause muscle weakness or eye changes (which are usually reversible). If you are taking Plaquenil for many months, you should have your eyes checked regularly by an ophthalmologist, an eye doctor.

Penicillamine (Cuprimine, Depen) is given in pill form. It may take several months to determine if it will work. Side effects include kidney problems, anemia, fever, chills, skin rash, sores in the mouth, sore throat, stomach upset, muscle weakness, loss of taste, a higher risk for infections, and easy bruising or bleeding. Your doctor will watch closely for these side effects.

Sulfasalazine (Azulfidine) is used to treat other disorders, such as ulcerative colitis. Doctors have also found it useful for treating RA. It is given in pill form, usually two to four doses per day. It usually begins working within one to three months after starting it. Most people tolerate this medicine easily, but it can cause side effects, such as skin rash, stomach upset, or diarrhea. Since it is made from sulfa, you should not take it if you are allergic to sulfa drugs. Although it has been used for many years to treat RA, it is still pending approval by the Food and Drug Administration.

Immunosuppressive Drugs

Immunosuppressive drugs such as azathioprine (Imuran) and methotrexate (Rheumatrex) are powerful medicines sometimes used to treat RA. They work by affecting the growth and action of the immune system cells that cause joint pain and swelling. These drugs work over a long period of time. You may not notice much effect from the medicine for the first several weeks of treatment. Side effects may include loss of appetite, nausea, or stomach pain. Sometimes, more serious side effects may occur, such as anemia, higher risk for infection, and easier tendency to bleed or bruise. Because of these side effects, doctors try to keep the dose as low as possible by giving these drugs with other medicines that reduce pain and inflammation. You and your doctor must decide if the benefits of taking an immunosuppressive drug outweigh the risks.

Other Medications

Other medications may be used if you have RA along with other illnesses, or if the arthritis has caused problems in other organs. For example, antibiotics may be used to treat joint infections, and iron compounds may be given for anemia.

Exercise

Exercising regularly is extremely important when you have RA. Exercise helps keep your joints flexible, strengthens muscles that help keep your joints stable, and can help improve overall fitness. If you don't stretch and exercise your joints regularly, they can become stiff and difficult to move.

Check with your doctor before beginning an exercise program. It should include a combination of three types of exercise.

Range-of-motion exercises stretch your joints and help you move them as far as you can without causing severe pain. These exercises keep your joints from becoming stiff and bent in one position. Your doctor, physical therapist, or occupational therapist can plan an exercise program for you, based on your specific needs. Exercises can be done at home after you receive instructions. You may have to practice these exercises several times every day.

Muscle strengthening exercises strengthen muscles that surround your joints. Stronger muscles will provide more support to damaged or weak joints. To strengthen muscles without putting too much stress on your joints, you will be shown how to move parts of your body against gravity, water, or another kind of light force or pressure.

Endurance exercises strengthen your heart and improve your overall fitness. The best types for people with arthritis are those that don't stress your joints—for example, swimming and walking. Avoid exercises such as aerobics classes and jogging, because the constant pounding can further damage your joints. Water exercise in a heated pool is especially good if you have feet, knee, or hip problems.

Exercising should not hurt your joints too much. If your joints hurt, more than they normally do, two or more hours after exercising, then cut back on the amount of exercise. Here are some other tips to make exercising easier.

- Exercise at the same time, if possible. Make it a part of your daily routine.
- Warm up before exercising. Gently stretch your body and muscles.
- Use heat to relax muscles or joints before exercising.
- Exercise when your medication is at its peak action.

Rest

An important part of your treatment program is a balanced mixture of rest and exercise.

This means learning to pace yourself so you can complete tasks without getting too tired. At any one time, the balance depends on how severe your symptoms are. During flares, you'll need more rest and less exercise. When you're feeling better, you'll need less rest and more exercise.

In general, the idea of balancing rest with activity is to organize your activities and time so you can reduce the amount of effort needed to complete your daily tasks. Here are some ways to do this.

- Think ahead. Combine errands and tasks so you use the least amount of energy required to complete them.
- Plan time to rest every day. Alternate heavy and light activities. Your body is the best judge of how much rest you need on a given day.
- Pace your activities to reduce fatigue. If necessary, stop in the middle of a task and come back to it once you are well rested.
- Reorganize your storage systems at work and at home so that tools and gadgets for related tasks are within close reach.

Heat and Cold Applications

Heat application is an effective way to temporarily relieve pain and soreness. To relax your muscles, for example, you may want to take a hot bath or shower just after you get out of bed in the morning. This is a time when many people find that their pain and stiffness is the worst. There are many other ways of applying heat, such as with hot packs, heat lamps, electric pads, electric mitts, and paraffin wax.

Cold application reduces swelling and helps numb the area, so you won't feel as much pain. Methods include using cold compresses, ice cubes wrapped in towels, or a bag of frozen vegetables.

Some people also find relief from creams or ointments that warm or numb the joint area. Never use creams or ointments at the same time as other heat or cold methods, because the combination may burn your skin. Ask your doctor or therapist to suggest a heat or cold method that might work for you.

Joint Protection

Joint protection means learning to perform daily activities in ways which put the least stress on your joints. This may involve learning new ways to do things, or using assistive devices such as splints, a walker, or cane. Here are some basic guidelines for protecting your joints.

- Use large joints, whenever possible, to do a task. For example, use your hip instead of your hand to push open a door. Use your palm instead of just your fingers to open a jar.
- Spread your weight over several joints. For example, use both arms instead of one to lift objects.
- Use joints in their most "natural" or correct positions. Don't bend them awkwardly if you don't have to.
- Wear well-designed and properly fitted shoes. Your doctor or therapist can help you choose which shoes to wear. Wearing poorly designed or ill-fitting shoes may cause as much foot deformity and disability as does the illness itself.

Self-help devices are special tools that can help you with everyday activities such as bathing, dressing, and eating, or help you with many other jobs at home or work. Here are a few examples: long-handled reachers for removing clothes from the dryer or from a shelf; wide pencils and pens that are easy to grip; built-up handles on utensils; lightweight plastic dishes and cooking equipment that are easy to lift and carry.

These kinds of devices help you protect your joints. Ask an occupational therapist for advice about using these devices.

Splints are sometimes used at night or during the day to rest your joints, hold them in prop-

369

er positions, and keep the muscles around the joints from becoming too tight. The longer a joint stays bent, the more likely it may stay that way.

Your doctors or therapist may also recommend a cane, crutches, or a walker to help you walk. These aids help protect your knees, hips, ankles, and feet by taking some of your body weight off them while walking.

Surgery

Some people may need surgery to relieve pain, correct or prevent joint deformity, and to improve overall joint movement. Joint operations are done by orthopedic surgeons (doctors who specialize in bone surgery) or other surgeons. Surgeons can replace or repair damaged joints with wear-resistant artificial joints made from metal and plastic. Today, there are manmade replacements available for many of the major joints. Total hip and knee replacement operations have been in use for a longer time than other joint replacement procedures, and are among the most successful.

Some replacement joints are attached to the bones with a strong bone glue. More recently, new artificial joints that don't need this bone glue are being used. These joints may be of special value in younger people.

Sometimes, surgery may be needed just to remove damaged tissue in the joint so it can move more easily. This is often done with an arthroscope. With this tool, the surgeon can look into the joint and perform operations through small incisions.

Managing Stress and Depression

Living and coping with RA can be difficult. Your illness may be mild and may only slightly affect your activities and emotions. On the other hand, there may be times when the pain or discomfort lead to depression, anger, and frustration. Emotional strain can also cause a loss of sleep, which can make you feel tired and run down.

You may sometimes feel caught in a cycle of stress, depression, and pain—depression increases pain, pain causes more stress, stress causes more depression, and so on. Learning to manage stress and depression can help you feel better. So, you can see why it's an important part of your treatment plan.

Here are a few things that you can do to help yourself.

- Don't try to deny or ignore negative feelings, thinking they will go away. Try to accept the truth about the disease and your feelings about it. This is often the best way to keep the problems in perspective.
- Talk openly with your family, friends, and doctors about your concerns and stresses. You may also find it helpful to talk with a social worker, psychologist, or counselor at a family service agency. They are specially trained to help you understand and cope with the stress and emotional upsets that result from arthritis. They can help you identify problems and possible solutions.
- Get involved in other activities. Concentrating on something or someone else will give you a sense of satisfaction and pleasure and will help take your mind off pain and depression. Many Arthritis Foundation chapters sponsor support groups or clubs that enable people with arthritis to get together and discuss common problems and experiences of arthritis. Contact your local chapter for more information about these groups.
- Learn ways to relax—by practicing your favorite hobby, listening to music, or enjoying another activity you like. You can also learn special relaxation exercises, such as deep breathing, quiet meditation, or mental imagery.
- Learn as much as you can about your illness. The more you know, the more you'll feel in control of your life and your health.
- Work in partnership with your doctor and health care team. Write down a list of your

questions to take with you when you visit your doctor. If you don't understand something, ask about it. If you're having trouble following certain parts of your treatment program, discuss the problem and work out a solution.

- Don't be too hard on yourself. If you can't follow your complete treatment program some days, give yourself a break. Remember that tomorrow is a new day, and you can start again.   *The Arthritis Foundation*

FIBROMYALGIA

Fibromyalgia is a form of rheumatic disease. Like many other forms of rheumatic diseases, fibromyalgia is a chronic syndrome of pain that can come and go. It can affect a person's work habits and lifestyle.

Many of the 100 or so kinds of rheumatic diseases are characterized by arthritis which causes pain and swelling in the joints. With fibromyalgia, the pain is in the ligaments, tendons, and muscles. This can affect the way your joints function, and that's why you might think that fibromyalgia is in your joints.

However, fibromyalgia is not a form of arthritis. You need not worry about fibromyalgia causing deformities or permanent crippling.

Doctors originally thought that fibromyalgia was due to inflammation of the connective tissue within muscles. We now know that this is untrue, yet the term fibrositis (fibros = connective tissue; itis = inflammation) is still used. Terms such as fibromyalgia, fibromyositis, and muscular rheumatism are also used to describe the same condition.

WHO GETS FIBROMYALGIA?

Doctors are finding that fibromyalgia is a very common ailment. There are currently mil-

lions of Americans who have been diagnosed with it. Although anyone can get fibromyalgia, many more women have fibromyalgia than men—and most are between the ages of 20 and 50.

There is also increasing evidence that fibromyalgia can start in the teenage years. Some teenagers have symptoms just as severe as their middle-aged counterparts, while many people experience only occasional symptoms in their younger years that become more troublesome in later years.

WHAT CAUSES FIBROMYALGIA?

Although medical researchers and doctors don't know the exact causes of fibromyalgia, they have recognized a number of different conditions that are associated with it. These conditions are described in the following paragraphs.

Physically Unfit Muscles

There is increasing evidence that people with fibromyalgia have unfit or poorly developed muscles. (It is not yet known whether unfit muscles are the cause or the result of fibromyalgia.) Nonetheless, this theory does provide an important clue about treatment, because people who are able to engage in a regular exercise program usually have the most improvement in their symptoms.

The reason why exercise is so beneficial lies in the fact that your muscles are remarkable in their ability to adapt to specific training programs. On the other hand, underuse of your muscles leads to a "negative, detraining" effect, which results in unfit muscles. "Detrained" or unfit muscles are more likely to become injured or damaged from exercise. This sort of muscle damage is commonly called "microtrauma."

All of us have probably experienced the effects of muscle microtrauma after exercising too vigorously. When microtrauma occurs, you experience delayed muscle pain that may not appear until 24 to 48 hours after exercising, and may last six to seven days. In addition to the pain, increased fatigue occurs, resulting in a lack of desire to participate in further physical activity until energy has been restored.

It is common for anyone to experience the effects of microtrauma after too vigorous physical activity. Yet for people who have unfit muscles, these problems may develop after only slight exertion, such as routine day-to-day activities. Microtrauma may also result from overuse, or abuse, of certain muscles—such as poor posture or damage caused by a blow or fall.

Sleep Disturbances

Another interesting clue as to the cause of fibromyalgia comes from sleep laboratory studies. Tests of people with fibromyalgia often show a sleep disorder in which the deepest or most restful stage of sleep (stage IV) is disturbed or interrupted. Doctors refer to this disturbance as "alpha intrusion of stage IV sleep."

Sleep disturbances may be responsible, in part, for the low energy levels experienced by people with fibromyalgia. There is also evidence that continued sleep problems can lead to muscle pain. This combination of pain and fatigue often limits physical activity and endurance. The resulting lack of physical exercise can contribute to the overall symptoms of fibromyalgia. Current research indicates that stage IV sleep is also important in repairing tissue damage and feeling psychologically rested after sleep. As you can see, when this stage of sleep is reduced, it can contribute to other symptoms of fibromyalgia.

In fact, the inability to get a good night's sleep is considered by some to be a major factor contributing to the symptoms of fibromyalgia. In one study, volunteers who did not have fibromyalgia were subjected to artificial disturbance of their stage IV sleep. They developed pain and soreness in their muscles which were very similar to those of fibromyalgia.

Although pain itself and the psychological stress it may cause seem to be the most common causes of sleep disturbances in people with fibromyalgia, alcohol, caffeine, and nicotine can also contribute to sleep disturbances.

Stress

It was originally thought that the symptoms of fibromyalgia were caused by stress and worry, which caused additional muscle tension. Although recent studies of people with fibromyalgia do not prove that stress itself causes fibromyalgia, stress, anxiety, and fatigue can make your condition worse.

In fact, the pain and fatigue of fibromyalgia often cause stress and anxiety, which in turn can increase the pain and fatigue, thus creating a vicious cycle.

WHAT ARE THE SYMPTOMS OF FIBROMYALGIA?

Since fibromyalgia is not completely understood and symptoms often seem vague, it is sometimes difficult to describe symptoms to your friends and relatives. Even your doctor may have some initial difficulty getting a useful history. All people with fibromyalgia have two major problems: pain and fatigue.

Pain

The major symptom of fibromyalgia is pain. Most people feel the pain of fibromyalgia as aching, stiffness, and tenderness around joints, muscles, tendons, and ligaments. Pain may appear in one or more locations at the same time and also in many different parts of your body.

The pain is located within the muscles themselves, as well as at the points where ligaments attach muscles to bones. For reasons that are still unknown, if you have fibromyalgia, you will feel extreme tenderness over many of these locations. These sites of tenderness are called tender points (sometimes referred to as trigger points). The location of tender points is similar in all people with fibromyalgia and are, therefore, an important part of the diagnosis.

Sometimes, you'll notice that the symptoms of fibromyalgia are worse when you first wake up. But in most cases, the discomfort increases as the day goes on. The type of activities you do may be a factor. For example, if you sit slumped over a desk all day long, by the end of the day the pain may have gotten worse because of bad posture.

Fatigue

Fatigue is sometimes the most debilitating aspect of fibromyalgia. Some people experience fatigue as a lack of muscle endurance, while others describe the fatigue as an overall sense of lack of energy. Much of the fatigue is thought to result from a lack of restful sleep.

You may find it helpful to schedule a rest period during your day, if possible. A nap or time spent relaxing in bed may help you to face your activities more efficiently.

There's been much recent interest in the "chronic fatigue syndrome." This was once thought to be due to a persistent infection with the Epstein-Barr virus (the cause of infectious mononucleosis). This theory, however, has now been disproven and many people who had previously been diagnosed as having "chronic fatigue syndrome" are now known to have fibromyalgia.

Other Symptoms

Many people with fibromyalgia have other problems which often cause some confusion to their doctors. These include: Raynaud's Phenomenon (poor circulation to the hands or toes), tension headaches, migraine headaches, dizziness, tingling and numbness, an irritable bowel (abdominal bloating with alternating diarrhea and constipation), muscle tremors, bladder spasms, and blurred vision. While most instances of fibromyalgia-related blurred vision cause no permanent damage to eyesight, an ophthalmologist should be consulted if this symptom occurs.

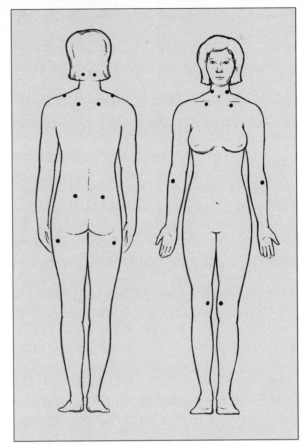

The dots indicate the locations of "tender points" common to fibromyalgia. Patients experience undue soreness when pressure is applied to these regions.

HOW IS FIBROMYALGIA DIAGNOSED?

There are no specific lab tests or x-rays that can detect fibromyalgia, at this time. Your doctor will base the diagnosis on your medical history, the identification of tender points, and the absence of other diseases. Describing the type of pain you feel and where it is located, as clearly as you can, may help your doctor diagnose the problem.

HOW IS FIBROMYALGIA TREATED?

There is presently no cure for fibromyalgia in the sense that your doctor could prescribe a medication or other type of treatment that will make your symptoms disappear forever.

However, the symptoms of fibromyalgia can be controlled and thus you should be able to maintain a productive lifestyle with only minor limitations.

Your doctor will discuss a combination of treatments that can help you improve your sleep, increase your physical fitness, and ease your pain and fatigue.

Improving Sleep

Improving the quality of your sleep will be a major part of your treatment plan. Certain medications such as amitriptyline (Elavil), cyclobenzaprine (Flexeril), and doxepin (Sinequan) are generally prescribed to promote stage IV sleep (the most restful stage of sleep). These medications are not sleeping pills. They are antidepressants, and antidepressants in low dose may help facilitate sleep and diminish chronic pain.

In fact, sleeping pills may make fibromyalgia worse by lowering the quality of sleep. If you are currently taking sleeping pills, tranquilizers, or narcotic analgesics (such as Dalmane, Darvon, Valium, or codeine), discuss discontinuing these medications with your doctor.

Improving sleep with medications so that you awaken feeling "refreshed," instead of tired, is just one part of your complete treatment plan.

There are many conditions that are commonly associated with a sleep disturbance, and it is important to control those factors. If you haven't already done so, it may help to limit or entirely omit caffeine, alcohol, and nicotine from your diet, since these have been proven to lower the quality of your sleep.

Exercise

Recent studies have shown that people can get a sustained benefit by participating in an aerobic exercise program. Aerobic exercise involves some activity that causes your pulse rate to increase and remain increased over an extended period of time. Usually 20 to 30 minutes of aerobic exercise is recommended.

Most people with fibromyalgia are reluctant to exercise because it initially causes more pain. But if your doctor or therapist works out an exercise program that starts out slowly and gradually becomes more challenging, the risk of muscle microtrauma will be significantly reduced, and your body will eventually be able to accept more vigorous exercise routines.

Low or nonimpact aerobic exercises are generally recommended. These include brisk walking, swimming, and the use of an exercycle. Exercises such as jogging, aerobic dancing, weight training, and racquet sports should be avoided until you have reached a good overall level of physical fitness.

Remember to gently stretch all your major muscle groups for about five minutes—both before and after—you exercise. Stretching helps reduce the chance of muscle injury. Consult your doctor before beginning aerobic activities and ask for a referral to a physical therapist who can teach you appropriate stretching exercises and help you get started on a nonimpact exercise program. Start your exercise program gradually. Then build up your routine as your body can tolerate more exercise.

Changing Your Work or Home Environment

Changing certain habits or physical arrangements in your daily routine may make a difference too. For example, pain in your arms, neck, or shoulders can be brought on by long hours of typing or entering data into a computer. If so, you may be able to relieve pain just by raising the height of your typewriter or computer table. A more comfortable mattress may help relieve aching muscles and reduce morning stiffness. If driving in heavy traffic causes your muscles to tighten, try using a backrest or try changing the way you sit in the car.

Dealing with Emotional Factors

Emotional factors may also affect your symptoms. Feelings are sometimes harder to pin down and understand than your physical symptoms, yet they may contribute to your symptoms.

It is important that your doctor be aware of the special stresses in your life. He may want you to undergo some standard psychological tests which will give your doctor more information about the ways you cope with stress. Do not be offended by this suggestion; everyone has stresses—including your doctor—and everyone reacts to stress in different ways.

If you are experiencing troublesome situations or feelings, both of which can make fibromyalgia worse by disturbing your sleep, you may benefit from psychological counseling to help you cope more effectively. Counseling sessions for the entire family can also be beneficial. They can help family members deal more effectively with stress and better understand each other's feelings. Some people have a mild depression that is contributing to their symptoms. Sometimes specific medications are needed to alleviate this type of depression.

Controlling Stress

Since stress and tension can contribute to your symptoms, it would be helpful for you to learn one or two relaxation techniques. Almost anyone can benefit from practicing relaxation techniques such as visual imagery, progressive muscle relaxation, biofeedback, yoga, or meditation.

Ask your doctor or physical therapist about relaxation techniques that might work for you, or take a stress management class. Most of all, recognize that help with the emotional aspects of your life may be a very important part of your treatment program.

Anti-Inflammatory Medication

The medications used to treat pain and inflammation for most other rheumatic diseases are not of great help in fibromyalgia. Aspirin and nonsteroidal anti-inflammatory drugs (NSAIDs), such as ibuprofen, do little to reduce pain. Even more powerful drugs, such as corticosteroids, do not seem to help the pain, stiffness, and fatigue associated with fibromyalgia.

Physical Therapy

Some short-term relief from your symptoms may be obtained by taking a hot bath, or by using hot packs or other forms of heat. In general, however, physical therapy is not indicated in the long-term management of fibromyalgia.

Taking an Active Part

In order for any of these treatments to be effective, you must take an active part. This includes becoming knowledgeable about fibromyalgia. With the growing awareness of the symptoms and diagnosis of fibromyalgia, many communities now have educational lectures given by doctors, as well as self-help groups.

It may be well worth your time and effort to find a doctor who is knowledgeable about fibromyalgia, and to choose a doctor with whom you feel comfortable.

Since all people respond differently to various treatments, what works for another person may or may not work for you. Therefore, it may take time and a trial of the different kinds of treatment before an effective combination can be worked out.

Even though you may have to modify some aspects of your lifestyle, deal with flare-ups from time to time, or add a few activities to your daily routine such as ways to relax and exercise, you, like most people with fibromyalgia, should be able to continue your normal activities.

With active involvement on your part, fibromyalgia can be controlled. Coping efficiently with the stresses and tensions of your life, maintaining a good level of physical fitness, and improving the quality of your sleep are the key ingredients to success.

The Arthritis Foundation

LOCALIZED PAIN SYNDROMES

Localized pain syndromes are conditions that cause pain, swelling, redness, and warmth (inflammation) in tissues that surround the joints. They can occur in many different parts of the body, including the shoulders, elbows, wrists, hands, hips, knees, feet, and chest. The most common syndromes include:

- *Bursitis*. Inflammation of the bursa, the small, fluid-filled sac that acts like a cushion between muscles and tendons, or between muscles and bones.
- *Tendinitis*. Inflammation of tendons, the fibrous cords that attach muscles to bones.
- *Myofascial pain*. Tender points (called "trigger" points) in muscles that cause pain when pressed or touched firmly.

These conditions often start suddenly. They usually stop within a few days or weeks, but sometimes may take longer to go away. Some people may have repeated attacks that occur in the same part of the body, or in another part. With proper treatment, most of these conditions usually do not cause lasting damage.

WHAT CAUSES THESE CONDITIONS?

These conditions result from one or a combination of the following.

- Overusing or injuring the joint or muscle may result from overdoing an activity or exercise that repeats the same movements over and over, including sports such as tennis, running, and ballet, or tasks such as typing or working on an assembly line.
- Improper body posture while lifting or moving objects, or during sports.
- Abnormal bone or muscle structures that are more easily injured than normal bone or muscle structures.

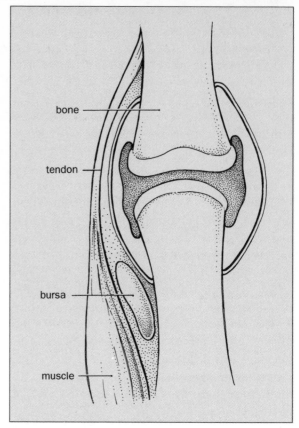

Bursitis is inflammation of the small, fluid-filled bursa inside the joint; tendinitis is inflammation of a tendon attaching a muscle to a bone.

Sometimes these conditions may also occur as a complication of another illness, such as rheumatoid arthritis.

WHO GETS THESE CONDITIONS?

Anyone can develop these conditions. They can occur in older people as a result of normal wear and tear over time. They also can affect younger people who are very active in sports, or whose work calls for doing the same movement over and over again.

WHAT ARE THE SYMPTOMS?

Pain is the main symptom of all these conditions. In some cases of bursitis and tendinitis, the pain can be so severe that you won't want to move the affected area. In severe cases you may not be able to move the area, due to swelling.

Myofascial pain differs from that in bursitis and tendinitis. It may feel like a knot or tender point deep within the muscle. When this area is pressed, you may feel pain at the tender spot and in nearby areas.

Other symptoms of these conditions depend upon the area of the body affected. The most common forms of bursitis, tendinitis, and myofascial pain, and their symptoms are described here. Treatments are described in a later section.

Shoulder

Rotator cuff tendinitis (impingement syndrome) is a very common cause of shoulder pain. The rotator cuff is a group of tendons and muscles in the shoulder joint that help rotate your arm.

Symptoms can occur in two ways: sudden, severe pain in the shoulder region; a recurring dull ache with difficulty raising and lowering your arm, pain at night from sleeping on the shoulder, tenderness in shoulder region, and sometimes a slight loss of movement.

This condition is thought to be caused by repeated stress or injury to the tendons.

Rotator cuff tear may result from severe injury to the shoulder or upper arm. It may also be caused by weakening of this area due to another condition, such as chronic tendinitis of the rotator cuff. Symptoms vary with the severity of the tear.

Symptoms include: muscle pain and weakness within hours to days of the injury that may last for many months; difficulty raising your arm beyond a horizontal position.

Frozen shoulder (adhesive capsulitis) causes pain, stiffness, and inability to move the shoulder. It is often due to injury, but may be associated with other medical conditions such as rheumatoid arthritis or diabetes. It is more common in women than in men, and often does not occur until age 40 or later.

Symptoms include: dull ache in upper, outer arm, with gradually increasing stiffness, followed by less severe pain, but total stiffness and inability to move your arm at the shoulder joint.

Most people with frozen shoulder recover fully within 12 to 18 months after the symptoms first begin. However, symptoms may last for several more months after recovery. Doctors sometimes refer to this recovery phase as "thawing."

Bicipital tendinitis usually occurs due to inflammation of or injury to the bicipital tendon. This tendon attaches the biceps muscle in the upper arm to the bone.

Symptoms include: severe pain in the front of the shoulder that often spreads down the upper arm and forearm.

Myofascial shoulder pain causes deep muscular pain between the neck and the shoulder blade. A common trigger point is located in the muscles around the shoulder blade, or between the shoulder blade and the spine.

Symptoms include: pain that shoots through your shoulder, down your arm, and into your hand when the trigger point in the shoulder is pressed; other trigger points that develop in the muscles between your neck and shoulder.

The trigger point in the shoulder often results from repeatedly reaching backward, such as when reaching to get a briefcase from the back seat of a car. Trigger points between the neck and shoulder can result from holding a telephone on your shoulder, keeping your head drooped forward for long periods of time while working or writing, or from sleeping with your head propped on the arm of a sofa or on thick pillows.

Sagging shoulder (thoracic outlet syndrome) is caused by nerves and blood vessels being pinched between the muscles and the bones.

This is more common in women than in men.

Symptoms include: pain, aching, numbness, or a sensation of swelling from your neck and shoulder down to your arms and hands.

The most common causes of sagging shoulder are heavy breasts, poor posture, frequently carrying heavy suitcases or a backpack, improper rest or work positions (such as sleeping or working with your arms above your head), or from having an extra rib (called a cervical rib).

Elbow

Tennis elbow doesn't happen only to tennis players, but also affects people who overuse their forearm muscles. It can be caused by activities such as gardening, throwing a heavy object, gripping and twisting hand tools, repeatedly moving your elbow, or clenching your hand too hard or too often.

Symptoms include: pain in your elbow when you lift heavy objects or shake hands with someone; tenderness along the outside of your elbow.

This condition usually goes away within several months of treatment.

Hand

Trigger finger is caused by inflammation of the tendons used to bend your fingers. It can affect any finger, including the thumb.

Symptoms include: after unclenching your fist, the affected finger remains bent—after a short time, the finger suddenly straightens (triggers); "bumps" in the palm of your hand that cause your finger(s) to temporarily "lock" in place; pain in the middle joints of some fingers.

This condition may cause no pain at all. It is usually caused by overuse or injury to the hand from gripping objects tightly and repeatedly. It may also occur in connection with other disorders, such as rheumatoid arthritis.

DeQuervain's wrist is usually caused by repeatedly pinching an object with your thumb while moving your wrist. Pain occurs in the thumb or wrist during activities that involve prolonged use of your hand, such as writing or pruning.

Symptoms include: pain, tenderness, and occasional swelling where the thumb meets the wrist.

Hip

Trochanteric bursitis is the inflammation of a bursa on the outer side of the hip. It is a common condition that often goes undiagnosed. It may start suddenly, but usually begins as gradual, mild aching over many months.

Symptoms include: aching along the outside of the hips and down the thigh; pain when climbing stairs, walking, sitting for a long period, or sleeping on your hip.

This condition usually affects middle-age and older persons, and affects women more often than men. In most cases, the cause is unknown. It may be due to constant, improper bending (bending without using your knees). It may also be caused by differences in the lengths of your legs and, if so, it is usually on the side of the longer leg. It may also occur in connection with other disorders, such as scoliosis and osteoarthritis in the back, hips, or knees.

Tailor's seat (weaver's bottom) is the inflammation in the bursa over the ischium, the bone in your "seat" (buttocks). It is caused by injury to this area or by repeatedly sitting or moving about on hard surfaces for long periods (as would a tailor or weaver).

Symptoms include: severe pain when sitting or lying down; pain that extends down the back of the thigh.

Knee

Housemaid's knee (prepatellar bursitis) is the inflammation of the bursa just in front of the kneecap. It is a common condition caused by frequent kneeling or by excess pressure on the knee.

Symptoms include: pain, heat, and swelling, in your kneecap.

Contact your doctor if your knee becomes red and swollen—it may be infected and could cause serious problems.

Clergyman's knee (infrapatellar bursitis) is similar to housemaid's knee except that it affects the area just below the kneecap.

Anserine bursitis occurs along the inner part of the knee. It usually occurs in middle-age or older women who are overweight and also have osteoarthritis in their knees.

Symptoms include: pain in the knee; increased knee pain when climbing stairs.

Myofascial knee pain sometimes occurs after sitting for a long time (such as after a long trip), due to the thigh muscles contracting or shortening.

Symptoms include: pain in front or behind the knee after sitting; stiffness in the quadriceps muscles (located on the front of the thigh), or the hamstring muscles (located on the back of the thigh).

Leg

Tennis leg happens when parts of a muscle in the calf region are suddenly torn. It often occurs while playing active sports, such as tennis.

Symptoms include: sharp, sudden pain, as if you had been kicked in the leg; pain when bending your ankle up or down; your leg may give out.

Ankle and Foot

Achilles tendinitis is caused by an injury, too much sports activity, or wearing shoes that do not fit properly and have a stiff heel. It can also be caused by other forms of arthritis, such as ankylosing spondylitis, Reiter's syndrome, gout, rheumatoid arthritis, and pseudogout syndrome.

Symptoms include: pain, swelling, and tenderness over the Achilles tendon (the strong cord located at the back of your ankle).

Achilles tendon rupture is a more severe condition than Achilles tendinitis. It is usually caused by injuring the Achilles tendon during sports or from a jump or fall.

Symptoms include: sudden pain and a "snapping" sound when the injury occurs; swelling at the back of your ankle; inability to move your ankle.

Calcaneal bursitis causes pain on the sole of the heel, especially when walking. It seems to be more common in older people who already have a bony heel spur and then injure the heel while playing sports or walking for long periods, or from obesity or shoes that do not fit properly.

Plantar fasciitis also causes pain on the sole of the heel, especially when walking.

HOW ARE THESE CONDITIONS DIAGNOSED?

Your doctor can usually make a diagnosis based on:

- A description of your recent activities, in order to find out what may have caused your condition.
- Your medical history, in order to determine if your problem is a sign of a more general condition.
- Physical examination, in order to locate the source of the pain.

There are no laboratory tests that confirm the presence of bursitis, tendinitis, or myofascial pain, but certain tests may be requested to rule out other diseases. X-rays may also be taken to look for problems with the tendons and to be sure no other problems are adding to your condition.

WHAT IS THE TREATMENT?

Your treatment program will be based upon your particular condition, your occupation, favorite sports and other activities, your age, and any other conditions you may have. Your treatment program may include a combination of the following:

Medicines

The two medicines usually used to treat these conditions are nonsteroidal anti-inflammatory drugs (NSAIDs) and corticosteroids.

Nonsteroidal anti-inflammatory drugs, or NSAIDs, help reduce pain and swelling. They are given in pill or liquid form, depending on the type you take. There are many types of NSAIDs: common examples include aspirin, ibuprofen (Advil, Motrin, etc.), and indomethacin (Indocin). You may have to try several types before you find the one that works best for you.

Common side effects include heartburn, constipation, diarrhea, nausea, dizziness, and easy bleeding. These usually do not cause severe problems.

NSAIDs may cause stomach bleeding or stomach ulcers in some people. This is a serious problem and should be treated right away. Sometimes ulcers have warning signs, but at other times they do not. Some warning signs are: heartburn or stomach cramps, nausea or vomiting for no reason, stomach pain that goes away after you eat food or take antacids, vomiting blood, and having black, tarry stools. If you have any of these signs, contact your doctor.

Corticosteroids are similar to hydrocortisone, a natural body hormone: they are not the same as steroids some athletes take. These medicines help reduce pain and swelling. To treat bursitis and tendinitis, these medicines are usually injected directly into the injured area. They can bring relief within a few days.

Heat and Cold Applications

Placing cold packs on the area right after you've injured it can help reduce swelling and pain. Here are some general tips for using cold packs.

- Place ice on the sore area three or four times a day. You can use ice packs, a frozen towel, or a plastic bag filled with ice cubes.
- Hold the pack over the area for about 20 minutes at a time, or until the area becomes numb or too painful.
- If the cold pack is too painful, wrap it in a towel.

For tendinitis of the wrist and thumb, trigger finger, or trigger thumb, your doctor may also recommend you massage the sore area with an ice cube.

If you treat an injury with ice first, replace the ice with heat after the first 48 hours. Here are some general tips for using heat.

- Use hot packs or a heating pad, or take a warm shower or bath.
- Ultrasound, a type of deep heat therapy, can be helpful when used along with other forms of physical therapy.

Be sure to ask your doctor or physical therapist which treatment is best for your condition.

Rest and Splints

Depending on your condition, you may have to rest the affected area for a period of time. You can also help relieve pain and aid the healing process by avoiding the activities that caused the problem for a while.

Splints, braces, or slings help rest your joints and keep them stable until the pain and swelling decrease. This may be especially helpful for tennis elbow, DeQuervain's wrist, rotator cuff tendinitis, rotator cuff tear, or myofascial shoulder pain.

Exercise

After the initial pain goes away, exercising the affected area will help you regain strength and flexibility. Exercise will also help prevent future injury to that area. Your doctor or physical therapist can teach you special exercises for your condition. If you need help with these exercises (until you can do them on your own), your doctor can refer you to a physical therapist or occupational therapist who can give you exercise treatments several times a week. You will obtain the most benefit from these exercises if you do them regularly, according to your doctor's instructions.

Massage

Deep friction massage, performed by an experienced physical therapist, may help ease some forms of tendinitis. However, any type of massage for these conditions should be prescribed by your doctor.

Surgery

Surgery is rarely necessary. It may sometimes be needed to treat a complete shoulder cuff tear or trigger finger.

HOW CAN FUTURE PROBLEMS BE PREVENTED?

In order to prevent further injuries, you should try to avoid or decrease activities that caused the problem. Here are some ways you can do this.

Shoulders

- Avoid activities that cause you to repeat the same arm movements over and over or that keep your arms raised over your head for long periods, for example, vacuuming, pushups, or sports that require you to move your arm in and out like a piston.
- Use good posture at all times. Hold your affected shoulder straight.
- Reduce the pain of rotator cuff tendinitis or impingement syndrome by keeping your elbow in close to your body whenever you need to raise your arm.

Elbows

- Avoid clenching your fist or gripping tools tightly with your hand.
- Avoid using your hands to push yourself up from a chair.

Wrists and Hands

- Build up tool handles, utensils, pencils and pens with tape or a foam rubber curler. With a built-up handle, you won't have to grip the handle tightly.
- Use your larger muscles whenever it is possible.
- Avoid doing the same hand movements for prolonged periods of time.
- Hold and carry objects with your palms open and flat.
- Interrupt handwork projects, from time to time, with other activities that do not stress your hands.
- Wear nylon stretch gloves if you clench your fists during sleep. Since clenched fists may be a sign of stress, talk to your doctor about ways to reduce stress.

Knees

- Use your feet to turn your body, rather than twisting your upper body.
- Avoid climbing stairs whenever possible.
- Place a portable toilet on the first floor of your home, if you do not have a bathroom on this floor.
- Use knee pads when kneeling on a hard surface or when gardening.
- Avoid sitting for more than 20 to 30 minutes at a time: get up and stretch.
- Ask your doctor or physical therapist to teach you leg strengthening exercises, such as "quad sets." These will strengthen your thigh muscles. Stronger thigh muscles will help support your knees.

Hips

- Bend with your knees, not with your hips and spine. This is especially important when doing routine activities such as making beds, picking up items from the floor, or getting into a low file drawer.
- Wear a shoe lift if one leg is longer than the other by more than five-eighths inch.

Feet

- Wear comfortable shoes that provide proper support. Wearing flat shoes or slippers can cause leg cramps or heel pain in some people.
- If you have bunions, wear shoes that are extra long or wide. This will help ease pressure on your toes.
- To find the right size shoe, measure your feet while standing. You may find that your shoe size changes as you get older.

The Arthritis Foundation

CARPAL TUNNEL SYNDROME

Carpal tunnel syndrome (or CTS) is a condition that can cause pain, tingling, numbness, and weakness in the fingers. CTS can begin suddenly or gradually. It often affects both hands. If not treated, it can lead to permanent nerve and muscle damage. With early diagnosis and treatment, however, there is an excellent chance of a complete recovery.

WHAT HAPPENS IN CTS?

The numbness and tingling of CTS happen when there is pressure on the median nerve. This nerve carries signals between your hand and brain. In the wrist, the median nerve and several tendons are surrounded by the carpal tunnel—a "tunnel" created by the wrist (carpal) bones and other tissue.

WHAT ARE THE SYMPTOMS?

If you have CTS, you might feel some or all of these symptoms:

- Pain, tingling, and numbness in the thumb, index, middle, and ring fingers
- Tingling in your entire hand

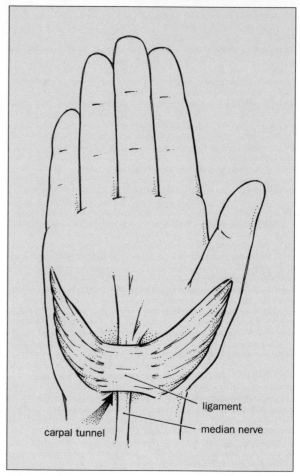

ligament

carpal tunnel — median nerve

Repeated pressure on the median nerve can result in carpal tunnel syndrome, which may be felt as pain, numbness, or tingling.

- Pain that shoots from the hand up the arm as far as the shoulder
- A swelling feeling in your fingers—even though they may not be visibly swollen

You may also notice that:

- Your symptoms are worse at night
- Your hands feel weak in the mornings
- You drop objects more than usual
- You have trouble grasping or pinching objects
- You have trouble using your hands for certain tasks, such as buttoning a shirt, writing with a pen, or opening a jar lid

- The muscles at the base of your thumb are smaller and weaker than they used to be

At first, the symptoms tend to come and go, and may not be very noticeable. Many people go for months without really being aware of them. Only when symptoms become troublesome do most people seek medical attention.

WHAT CAUSES CTS?

Anything that causes repeated pressure on the median nerve can lead to carpal tunnel syndrome. This includes the following.

Work activities and hobbies that keep the wrist bent for a long time, or that require pinching or gripping motions. Examples include:

- Typing or working at a computer keyboard
- Activities of hairdressers, carpenters, factory and farm workers, and mechanics
- Needlework or knitting
- Playing golf or tennis
- Paddling a canoe
- Holding a book

When CTS already exists, these activities can make it worse.

Injuries such as a blow to the front of the wrist. This may break one or more of the carpal bones and damage the median nerve.

Arthritis-related diseases such as rheumatoid arthritis and gout. These diseases cause pain and swelling in joints and other parts of the body. They can cause swelling of tissues in the carpal tunnel, causing pressure on the median nerve.

Other causes of CTS may include:

- Pregnancy or use of birth control pills (both may cause swelling in your hands)
- Diabetes
- A tumor on the median nerve
- Thyroid diseases
- Acromegaly, a rare disease of the pituitary gland
- Amyloidosis, a disease in which a protein substance collects in body organs

WHO GETS CTS?

Carpal tunnel syndrome can occur at any age, but usually affects people in their 40s or 50s. It is more common in women than in men.

HOW IS IT DIAGNOSED?

The doctor may perform one or all of the following tests to help diagnose CTS.

Tinel's sign test. The doctor will gently tap the front of your wrist. If this causes mild shooting pain in your hand or forearm, then you may have carpal tunnel syndrome.

Phalen's sign test. The doctor will ask you to bend your wrist down as far as it will go and to hold this position for one to three minutes. If you feel mild shooting pain, then you may have carpal tunnel syndrome.

Nerve conduction velocity (NCV) study. This measures the nerve's ability to send electrical impulses to the muscle. If the electrical impulses are slowed down in the carpal tunnel, then you probably have CTS.

X-rays of the hands and blood tests. These may be done to find out if there are any other medical problems that are causing CTS.

WHAT IS THE TREATMENT?

The goal of treatment is to relieve pain and prevent CTS from getting worse. The type of treatment you use depends on the severity of your CTS. It may include one or all of the following.

Splints

At first, a wrist splint may be used to keep the wrist in a straight position while you sleep. By wearing the splint only at night, you will be free to go about your usual daily activities. The splint helps reduce swelling that may be causing CTS.

An occupational therapist can make a splint that will meet your needs.

Medicines

Injections of corticosteroids (cortisonelike drugs) into the wrist can often reduce the swelling that causes pressure on the median nerve. These injections often bring significant relief for many people with CTS. Aspirin or other nonsteroidal anti-inflammatory drugs (NSAIDs) may also be used to reduce swelling and relieve pain.

Surgery

If medicines are not successful and you continue to have problems, surgery may be required to avoid permanent nerve or muscle damage. The procedure, called carpal tunnel release, relieves the pressure on the median nerve. This is usually a simple operation that can be done without having to stay overnight at the hospital.

After surgery, you'll probably have some use of your hand within a week or so. Usually, you'll regain full use of your hand about six weeks after surgery.

You may need wrist splints to support your wrist for a short time after surgery. You will also have to do exercises to strengthen your fingers and to keep your joints from becoming too stiff. If you have had CTS for a long time, you may need more exercises and physical therapy to regain full use of your hand and wrist.

Results from surgery are generally quite good if severe weakness has not developed. Most likely, you'll be able to resume your normal activities, but you should avoid activities that put too much stress on your wrist.

Work Changes

Adjusting your daily work activities may help relieve CTS. Here are some ways to do this.

- Rest your wrists and hands from time to time.
- Alternate tasks to reduce the pressure on your wrist.
- Delegate tasks that bother your hands to other co-workers or family members.
- Modify or change any daily activities, including hobbies, that put too much pressure on your wrist.

If you think your CTS may be due to activities at your job, talk to your doctor and your manager. They may be able to help you make some changes that will relieve the problem. This could include adjusting your work area (for example raising or lowering your desk so you can reach the computer keyboard more easily), or reducing the amount of time you spend at a particular task. An occupational therapist can help you find ways to modify your activities so they'll put less stress on your wrist.

The Arthritis Foundation

FOOT PROBLEMS

Every day, the average person takes about 10,000 steps; in a lifetime, you may walk 115,000 miles—the equivalent of four and a half strolls around the planet. Each one of those steps exerts a force even greater than your body weight on certain bones and muscles of your feet. Running triples that force. It's no wonder that this cumulative pounding, complicated by ill-fitting shoes and the natural changes that occur with aging, can conspire to cause aching feet.

Healthy feet are crucial for an active and independent lifestyle, but four out of five adults experience foot pain—and the great majority of them are over 50. Yet, according to a poll conducted by the Gallup Organization, 62 percent of Americans think foot pain is normal—which may be why the foot problems that tend to worsen with age are too often ignored. Left untreated, foot ailments can result

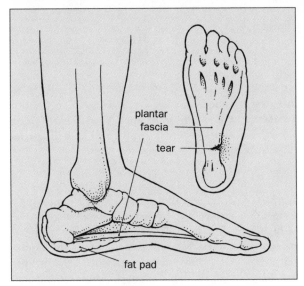

The plantar fascia runs from the heel bone to the underside of the toes. A tear can occur where this fibrous band connects to the heel, causing pain.

generally more difficult to care for.

The internal structure of your feet changes as well, as ligaments and tendons lose their elasticity, and muscle tone diminishes. This alters the shape of your feet so much that you may even have to switch shoe sizes. Usually, the feet become more splayed, necessitating shoes with larger forefoot space. Furthermore, foot problems can be caused or exacerbated by underlying conditions such as obesity, poor circulation, arthritis, and diabetes.

REGULAR FOOT CARE

It is all too easy to ignore your feet until they give you pain and call for attention. But periodic care of your feet can often prevent problems from occurring at all, or at least minimize their severity.

- Wash your feet every day in warm water. Dry them by blotting with a towel, rather than rubbing.
- Dust your feet lightly with hygienic foot powder or plain talc if they perspire a lot. Sprinkle powder into your shoes as well. Don't use cornstarch powder because it feeds fungus.
- Examine your feet for red spots, sores, or any unusual skin lesions. Diabetics should perform such inspections daily.
- Trim your nails shortly after you have taken a bath or shower, when they are softer. Cut straight across with a toenail clipper.

ACTIVE FOOT CARE

The best way to take care of your feet is to use them as intended: for walking. Regular walking and other exercise will improve circulation, increase flexibility, reduce fatigue, and encourage bone and muscle development.

Walking is crucial for maintaining the foot's overall condition. It improves strength, flexibility, and coordination in the supporting muscles of the shins and calves, and enhances

in altered gait and posture, which can progress to pain in the ankles, knees, hips, and lower back. However, pain in your feet is neither normal nor need it be tolerated. To counteract the effects of aging feet, it's important that you care for them properly, and seek professional care when problems occur.

HOW FEET AGE

As you get older, various changes in the feet combine to increase the likelihood of problems. The normal aging of the skin—which, for instance, causes it to become more easily dehydrated and lose its elasticity—may have more serious consequences on the feet than elsewhere because it makes them more susceptible to bacterial and fungal infections. Calluses, which can make walking painful, tend to develop on the weight-bearing points because the soles and heels lose fat and become less padded. As the skin on the top (the dorsum) of your feet thins, it is more easily bruised by tight-fitting or tight-laced shoes. The nails, too, become thicker, brittle, and

COMMON FOOT PROBLEMS AND TREATMENTS

	Foot Problem	*Self-Care/Products*
Bunion	Deformity at the big toe joint that causes the first joint to slant outward and rub against your shoe, leading to irritation, swelling, and inflammation (bursitis) of the joint.	Wear low-heeled shoes with plenty of extra space for toes. Do use donut-shaped bunion cushions or moleskin cut to size, which will take the pressure off the joint.
Calluses and Corns	A callus is a thickened pad of skin, usually on the weight-bearing portion of the sole, that results from chafing and pressure. A corn is a highly concentrated callus that occurs at a pressure point such as the top of the toe or under a toe joint. Either can become painful when they press on sensitive nerves in the surrounding skin, which may become red and inflamed.	Soak feet daily for at least five minutes in warm water to soften skin. Use a rough towel, callus file, or pumice stone to remove the dead tissue. Cover the area with a light pad or bandage. Do not use medicated corn or callus pads, salicylic acid or chemical corn removers. Do use an unmedicated circular pad with a hole for the corn or callus, or moleskin cut to size and shape, to relieve pressure.
Hammertoe	A permanently bent, clawlike deformity in which the middle joint of a toe (usually the second digit) is bent downward. As the toe contracts and the joint extends upward, inflammation occurs on the top of the joint where it rubs against your shoes. Over time, hammertoes may impair walking.	Wear shoes with resilient soles and enough forefoot room to protect the joints of the toes from irritation. Do use toe caps—padded sleeves that wrap around the joint and raise the toe tips.
Heel Pain	Inflammation around a heel spur (a hook of bony overgrowth at the bottom of the heel bone), plantar fasciitis (inflammation of a band of tissue that connects the heel bone to the toes), or simply the stress of multiple impacts on hard surfaces, can lead to redness, tenderness, or bruising in the heel or a burning sensation either directly under or just in front of the heel bone. Pain can occur after a long walk or without apparent reason, especially when you first arise in the morning.	Wear low-heeled (but not flat), supportive, and well-cushioned shoes. Regular calf-stretching exercises are usually the best prevention and treatment for the pain of a heel spur and plantar fasciitis. Do not use heel cups or cushions without consulting your podiatrist. If a precut variety is the wrong shape or size for your foot, it may do more harm than good.
Ingrown Toenail	A toenail edge that curves into the skin on the side of the toe, causing redness, swelling, and pain.	To prevent, cut nails straight across. Wear wide, roomy shoes. To treat, soak feet until the nail is soft. If this doesn't work, see a podiatrist. Do not use chemical "ingrown toenail relievers," which may remove healthy tissue as well.

What a Podiatrist May Do

Prescribe an orthotic—a custom-designed, molded plastic insert for your shoe that redistributes weight to take pressure off the big toe, supports the foot, and helps realign the toe. In severe cases, surgery (bunionectomy) may be needed.

Prescribe an orthotic, since the problem may be due to changes in the positions of the bones in the toes and forefoot region. Occasionally, surgery to remove a piece of bone or change the bone's position may be necessary to reduce these internal pressures.

Prescribe an orthotic (see bunion), which will not cure the problem, but can reposition the foot so that the muscles do not pull as hard on the toes. Surgery may be necessary in extreme cases.

Relieve inflammation with ibuprofen or other analgesics, or with steroid injections into the heel. May also prescribe an orthotic (see bunion). Will probably look for any underlying ailment, such as gout or arthritis, which may contribute to the problem. Surgery is rarely required.

Cut out edge of nail, possibly using a local anesthetic. If infected, your podiatrist will prescribe antibiotics.

circulation to the feet and legs. Try to schedule a brisk walk in your daily routine. Wear specially designed walking shoes, or ones that are flexible and provide good heel support. To fend off any injuries, warm up your muscles before walking.

Massaging your feet is a good way to relax them after an exercise session or just after a busy day. It also improves circulation to the skin and superficial tissues. You can massage your own feet, or have someone do it for you. Apply moisturizer to your hands, then gently stroke the entire foot, from the bottom of the shin to the end of the toes. Next, press on the ball of the foot and hold for 10 seconds. Press your thumbs into the heel of the foot and, moving in a circular motion, cover the sole from the heel to the ball. Now press your thumb into the spaces between the bones in the midfoot.

Conclude by gently pulling on each toe and holding it for 10 seconds. (If you are a diabetic, consult your doctor before doing foot massage.)

FINDING A FOOT SPECIALIST

When foot problems don't respond to home treatment, who to turn to depends in part on the nature of the problem. Orthopedists, for instance, will be able to help you with bone and joint disorders such as bunions and hammertoes. Few general physicians specialize in problems of the feet, although many are qualified to treat them.

The best all-around foot specialists are generally doctors of podiatric medicine (D.P.M.), or podiatrists. Although not M.D.s, they are medically trained, and can relate foot problems to overall health. They can prescribe medication and perform minor surgery, such as the removal of corns, calluses, and bunions. According to Bruce Lebowitz, D.P.M., director of the Podiatric Clinic at the Francis Scott Key Medical Center of Johns Hopkins, you should choose a podiatrist by asking for a referral from your primary-care physician or by contacting your local podiatry association. Most health insurance plans, including Medicare, cover certain podiatric services.

THE FOOT AND DIABETES

Foot care takes on crucial dimensions if you're a diabetic. Poor circulation to the extremities due to atherosclerosis of the large blood vessels as well as specific diabetic changes in the capillaries allow serious foot problems to develop more quickly in diabetics. Diabetic nerve damage can make such problems harder to detect, however, so that injuries and infections may go unnoticed for some time. Look for a persistent sensation of coldness, numbness, tingling, or burning. Other symptoms are dry and discolored skin, hair loss on your feet and legs, and muscle cramping or tightness.

Poor circulation can open the door for serious foot infections, skin ulceration, and other conditions. If you have diabetes, be especially vigilant about observing the aforementioned foot care pointers. In addition, it's very important for diabetics to wear comfortable shoes with plenty of support and room for their forefeet. To prevent cuts and bruises, don't go barefoot or wear sandals with thongs, even when you are at home. Inspect your feet daily for cuts, blisters, and scratches. Consult your doctor immediately if you develop an ingrown toenail, athlete's foot, a cut or sore that doesn't heal quickly, or persistent discoloration. Be sure to tell your podiatrist that you're a diabetic. (See also Diabetes Mellitus, page 230.)

COMMON FOOT PROBLEMS

The problems listed in the box on pages 386–387 are among the most common foot ailments of people over 50. Most cases can be treated with proper self-care. However, if pain persists or if the problem causes changes in your gait, consult a podiatrist. If surgery is recommended, be sure to seek a second opinion. Also, check with your insurance company to make sure which, if any, podiatric surgery is covered. *The Editors*

The Skin

As we grow older, many of the changes our bodies experience are seen and felt in our skin, the body's largest and most visible organ. It becomes drier, more wrinkled, and it may undergo changes in color. Spots and growths may form. Healing takes place more slowly.

Liver spots, cherry angiomas, moles, seborrheic keratoses, and senile purpura are to older folk what acne is to adolescents. Most of these skin problems merely present a cosmetic concern; others have the potential to be much more serious.

All of these skin problems are the function of two distinct aging processes: one is intrinsic chronological aging, a "program" that is set into motion at birth; the other is extrinsic photoaging, the wear and tear from all the environmental assaults encountered during a lifetime. Research shows that the latter process is enemy number one. Indeed, the world around us—with its diminishing ozone layer, multitude of pollutants, and ultraviolet radiation from sunlight—not only accentuates the sagging, wrinkling, and yellowing of skin that comes with age, but also causes injuries and irreversible changes of its own.

You can't reverse the aging process or undo childhood sunburns. However, you can and should be familiar with their resultant changes—benign, precancerous, and cancerous (see Skin Cancer, page 73)—both to dispel unwise complacency as well as reduce unnecessary anxiety. Even the most serious form of skin cancer, malignant melanoma, is almost always curable if detected and removed early. But count on yourself to do the checking, or to remind your doctor to do it. A recent survey of doctors by the American Cancer Society found that most doctors don't discuss the prevention of skin cancer unless you bring it up.

BENIGN SKIN CONDITIONS

These skin conditions will never become malignant; they can, however, be unsightly and even alarming when they first begin to appear.

LIVER SPOTS

Also called "age spots," these small, flat, evenly pigmented skin patches range in color from light brown to nearly black.

In spite of their name, these spots have nothing to do with the liver; they are simply patches where melanocytes (pigment cells) have proliferated and increased the production of pigment.

Liver spots appear almost exclusively on the face and the backs of hands.

CHERRY ANGIOMAS

Sometimes called "ruby spots," these clusters of dilated capillaries begin to appear at about age 40 and are present in 75 percent of people over 70. Developing singly or in groups,

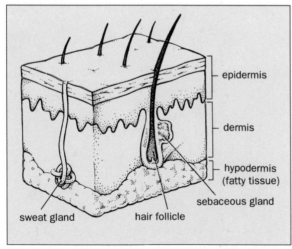

Skin has two main layers: the epidermis and dermis (with fatty tissue underneath). Cells on the surface are constantly shed and replaced by cells from below.

DRY SKIN AND SEBORRHEIC DERMATITIS

Dry Skin

As we age, the skin seems to become drier, which can result in flaky and itchy skin, especially in cold, dry, windy climates. Less severe cases of dry skin can be treated with a good moisturizer used after bathing while the skin is still damp. Bath oils, which have a limited effect, can cause the tub to be slippery, and should be avoided by older individuals.

Petrolatum, an ingredient used in many lotions, creams, and ointments, is an excellent moisturizer. Many moisturizers contain chemicals, such as urea, lactic acid, and ammonium lactate to help the skin hold water. Some of these chemicals can irritate the skin, however. Your dermatologist can help you to decide which formulation is best for you.

Bathing less often and using milder soaps or a soap substitute, or soaking in a tub of water without soap, can help relieve dry skin. During cold weather, soap should be confined to areas in which skin rubs against skin, such as armpits, genital areas, and between the toes. Hot water is more irritating to dry skin than cooler water. After bathing and drying off, a moisturizer such as petrolatum or lanolin should be applied to seal in moisture.

If dry skin continues to be a problem after following these guidelines, further investigation may be required.

Severe flaky, itchy, and cracked skin may be a sign of a more serious problem such as an allergy, psoriasis, or an internal condition such as liver or kidney disease, diabetes, or cancer.

Seborrheic Dermatitis

Seborrheic dermatitis is one of the most common skin disorders seen by dermatologists and is very common in older adults. It is cosmetically unpleasant and sometimes uncomfortable, but not serious. The signs of seborrheic dermatitis are redness and a greasy-looking scale on the skin. It usually affects areas of the skin with a high concentration of oil glands, such as the scalp, sides of the nose, eyebrows, eyelids, skin behind the ears, and the middle of the chest. It occasionally affects other areas such as the navel, breast, buttocks, and skin folds under the arms.

The cause of seborrheic dermatitis is not understood, but in older individuals it often accompanies diseases of the nervous system, such as Parkinson's disease, or a stressful medical problem such as a heart attack. Patients who have had long stays in hospitals or nursing homes also are more likely to develop the condition.

Seborrheic dermatitis often subsides on its own and can be successfully treated, but it tends to recur. There are several topical medications your dermatologist can prescribe, including a low-strength cortisone preparation.

The American Academy of Dermatology

these bumps—which range from pinhead-sized to a quarter inch or more in diameter—are most frequently noticed on the face, scalp, torso, neck, arms, and legs, but rarely on the hands or feet. On the lip, they often consist of a single, bluish-red, round nodule. Never try to puncture a cherry angioma, since it may bleed profusely.

SEBORRHEIC KERATOSES

These growths begin to appear after age 30, usually on the torso, face, or scalp. They start out small, as oval, waxy, flat-topped bumps that are flesh-colored or tan. Eventually growing to between a third of an inch to several inches, seborrheic keratoses become capped by a greasy, scaly, wartlike crust. Often, they are attached to the skin only at the center, giving them a pasted-on appearance, and sometimes they itch.

SENILE PURPURA

These irregularly shaped, vividly purple patches usually appear on the forearms and the backs of hands.

Caused by blood that has leaked through

PROTECTING YOUR SKIN WITH SUNSCREENS

For people over the age of 50, the advice is the same as it is for a teenager on the beach: Wear a sunscreen. The notion that we did the crucial damage to our skin when we were sunbathing youths—and so don't need to think about sun damage anymore—is simply not true. In fact, sun damage increases with age, says Dr. Antoinette Hood, associate professor of dermatology at Johns Hopkins. For one thing, older people have thinner skin, which increases vulnerability to environmental assaults. Also, they tend not to tan as readily because the skin's pigment cells, or melanocytes—the body's primary protective barrier against sunlight—disappear at a rate of 10 to 20 percent each decade.

Some recent research has suggested that people over the age of 50 should not protect themselves too thoroughly against the sun, lest they develop a vitamin D deficiency (the vitamin is synthesized when a certain compound is exposed to ultraviolet radiation). But rest assured, advises Dr. Warwick Morison, also a dermatologist at Johns Hopkins, you get enough sun in 15 or 20 minutes to meet your vitamin D needs. The research is applicable to people who are totally confined indoors—and the best advice for them is not to seek the sun for any presumed therapeutic benefits, but to take a vitamin D supplement.

Sunproofing

The Skin Cancer Foundation offers these tips for people of any age.
• Wear a hat, long-sleeved shirt, and long pants as much as you can outdoors. The tighter the weave, the better it will keep out the sun.
• Apply a sunscreen half an hour before you go out, so that it has time to penetrate the skin and provide optimum protection. Be sure to reapply it after you go swimming.
• Because perspiration will diminish its effectiveness, reapply a sunscreen every couple of hours.
• The fairer your skin, the higher the SPF (sun protection factor) you need. Use a sunscreen that indicates on the label it has an SPF of at least 15. An SPF tells you how long you may remain safely in the sun. If you normally burn after 10 minutes, for example, an SPF of 15 allows you to stay in the sun 15 times longer—150 minutes, or two and a half hours—before burning.
• Put sunscreen on with a liberal hand. Most people apply it so sparingly that they get only half the protection advertised.
• Don't forget to cover any bald spots.
• Consult your pharmacist or your physician to see if you are taking any drug that increases your skin's sensitivity to sunlight—such as certain diuretics, antihistamines, antidepressants, antibiotics, or oral hypoglycemics. You may need some extra protection.
• If one sunscreen irritates your skin, try another; there are dozens of good ones. Look for the Skin Cancer Foundation seal of recommendation on the label of any product you buy.
• Look for double protection. Recent research has demonstrated that ultraviolet B (UVB) rays are not the only ones that damage skin; longer-wave ultraviolet A rays can also cause harm, leading to premature aging and possible predisposition to skin cancer. Most sunscreens protect only against the sun's ultraviolet B rays. However, ultraviolet A rays also promote skin damage, although to a lesser degree. Some new products that protect against UVA and UVB rays are now available; consider using one of these, especially if you are very fair.

stretched and weakened capillaries and then spread through the dermis, the spots tend to fade after several weeks.

Although benign, you may find these conditions bothersome. If so, they can be safely removed, almost always under local anesthetic, with either electrosurgery, cryosurgery (freezing), laser surgery, traditional surgery, or chemical applications. Just which procedure is appropriate depends on the type of lesion, its size, and other factors that should be discussed with a dermatologist. *The Editors*

PRECANCEROUS SKIN CONDITIONS

More worrisome are skin changes that are potentially malignant—not only because skin cancers account for more than half of all malignancies in the United States each year, but because the changes that lead to cancer are often so insidious that they may be ignored until too late.

ACTINIC KERATOSES

Sometimes called "solar keratoses," these scaly growths almost always occur on sun-damaged skin. Their appearance varies, ranging from flesh-colored to pink to reddish-brown; from flat and smooth to slightly raised and rough. They sometimes have a conical, horn-like growth projecting from them. Most of the time, actinic keratoses develop after age 50. They grow slowly, over months or years, and unless they are removed, have as high as a 25 percent chance of becoming malignant. You can often feel actinic keratoses before they become visibly apparent.

DYSPLASTIC MOLES

Certain types of moles (known medically as "nevi") are noticeably different from the common moles that everyone has. Termed "dysplastic" (abnormally growing) nevi, they occur in about 5 percent of the population, especially among those who have an abun-

dance of moles (often over 100), compared to the 10 to 40 of the average adult. Furthermore, these people frequently develop new moles later in life, while most people hold steady with the ones they had in early adulthood. Self-checkups could help detect many cases that might otherwise develop into malignant melanoma at a point when they are still treatable. (See the box above for the types of changes for which you should be on the lookout.) If you do note changes, see a dermatologist, who may order a biopsy to determine if the mole is dysplastic. *The Editors*

MOLE INSPECTION— LEARNING YOUR ABCD'S

Mole inspection becomes simpler if you keep in mind the American Cancer Society's ABCD rule for distinguishing a normal mole or other skin blemish from an abnormal (dysplastic) one. (But remember, any mole, however small, is suspect, especially if it appears in an area of previous sunburn.)

Asymmetry. One half of the mole does not match the other.

Border. The edges are irregular—ragged, notched, or blurred.

Color. The color is not uniform, but may be differing shades of tan, brown, or black, sometimes with patches of red, white, or blue.

Diameter. The mole is larger than the size of a pencil eraser—about six millimeters or a quarter of an inch—or is increasing in size.

Health Problems of Men

A number of physiological changes occur with age—and some of them occur only in men. More than half of the men in their sixties and as many as 90 percent in their seventies or eighties have some symptoms of prostate enlargement; 30 percent of men age 65 have had recurrent episodes of impotence. While problems such as these may be difficult to talk about initially, help is there for the asking. Your physician can guide you in such matters—perhaps referring you to a urologist, the appropriate specialist for such problems.

The Editors

IMPOTENCE

Nearly every man will experience temporary impotence from time to time, due to such routine difficulties as fatigue or stress or acute illness. Some men, however, will be troubled and embarrassed by chronic impotence—the inability more often than not to achieve and sustain an erection for a long enough time to engage in sexual intercourse.

More than 10 million American men are chronically impotent. By the age of 55, 18 percent of men report the problem; by the age of 65, that figure increases to 30 percent; and by the age of 75, 55 percent of men report suffering from impotence.

Up until just a decade ago, more than 90 percent of all cases of impotence were blamed simply on emotional causes. During the past 10 years, however, doctors have come to believe that at least half, and perhaps as many as three-quarters, of all cases have a physiological basis as well. And in many cases, a man's potency can be restored by a combination of medical and psychological treatment.

An erection is caused by a complex neurological mechanism: a sensory stimulus—a touch, a sight, a scent—triggers a message that travels from the brain down the spinal cord to release a chemical messenger, which causes the corpora cavernosa—two rod-shaped bundles of spongy muscle that run along each side of the penis—to relax and fill with blood. As they fill, the corpora cavernosa expand and press against the veins that would normally drain blood from the penis. Thus engorged, the penis enlarges and stiffens.

CAUSES

Physiological

Impotence can result from faults in any part of this mechanism. Among the most common disrupters are medical problems such as diabetes, multiple sclerosis, Parkinson's disease, lower back problems, severe arthritis, liver or kidney disease, congestive heart failure, and extreme obesity; habits such as alcoholism, drug abuse, and, especially, smoking; injury to the spinal cord; certain surgical procedures; and the side effects of prescription medications—especially those for hypertension. (Drugs that are known to cause impotence include Aldomet, Catapres, propranolol, Ismelin, and thiazide; vasodilators and calcium channel blockers usually do not cause potency problems.) In addition, antihistamines taken for allergies and decongestants taken for colds may cause temporary impotence.

Although it was once thought that a low level of the male sex hormone testosterone would result in impotence, it now seems clear that a testosterone deficiency does not directly affect the physiology of an erection. It may, however, decrease sexual desire.

Psychological

Impotence can have solely emotional causes and, in that case, diagnosis can be difficult. Often a conversation with a physician will turn up reasons of fatigue, tension, or depression from overwork—or stress, anger, or other psychological interferences in an intimate relationship—that result in impotence.

If a man awakens at night or in the morning with a full, firm erection, it is unlikely that he has a significant medical problem, and the cause of his impotence is most likely psychological. If such erections don't seem to be occurring, there is a simple self-test—called a nocturnal penile tumescence test, or NPT—to sort out psychologically based from physiologically based impotence.

During a normal night's sleep, a man will have several erections that correspond to his REM dreaming time. If he puts a small roll of stamps around the penis, he can see in the morning whether the perforations have been broken. If they are, he can assume he has had an erection. A doctor can provide what is called a "snap gauge," which works more reliably for this test. But neither test is infallible. And, while the results may rule out physiological causes of impotence, it cannot dependably rule them in; for that, you will need further examination. These days there are a number of clinics and therapists who specialize in working through problems of impotence caused by psychological difficulties, and their success rates are generally very high.

WHAT CAN BE DONE

If a physiological cause is suspected, a doctor will test reflexes that would be affected by spinal cord problems. He will investigate whether the blood flow into the penis is adequate. Using ultrasound, he will determine both the diameter of the arteries and the amount of blood that flows through them into the penis. The adequacy of blood flow can also be tested by injecting the drug papaverine directly into the penis. Because papaverine relaxes smooth muscle, allowing a dilation of blood vessels, a good response to papaverine will usually rule out severe vascular problems.

Behavioral Changes

If there is reason to believe impotence is caused by smoking, alcohol, or drugs, the remedy is apparent. Cutting out smoking and drinking or changing medications will often cure the problem.

Some physicians will prescribe the drug yohimbine—long a constituent of folk remedies—to help men whose organic difficulties are minimal. It is thought that yohimbine may act on the arteries and other blood channels to enhance blood flow into the penis. In fact, there is no evidence at all that yohimbine does any good, but it does not do any harm, and since it evidently has no side effects, it seems worth a try.

Vacuum Device

Nearly all forms of impotence can be treated with a special vacuum device. The penis is put into an acrylic tube from which the air is pumped out. The resultant vacuum causes blood to flow into the penis; an erection is produced in three to five minutes. The device is then removed and a rubber band is slipped onto the base of the penis to keep the blood from flowing out and so hold the penis erect for a half hour. The sensory nerves that convey the sensation of intercourse and ejaculation are not affected by the device, although using it may initially seem cumbersome and embarrassing. But, with practice, the vacuum is effective for virtually all forms of impotence, and those who have used it generally report very high levels of sexual satisfaction. Such a vacuum device costs about $450.

Injections

If these comparatively simple remedies do not work, your physician may suggest injections of papaverine, not as a diagnostic measure but as a treatment option. Papaverine can be self-injected directly into the penis (with instructions from your physician) using a tiny syringe and needle. By dilating the blood vessels, the drug causes an erection that lasts for a half hour to 45 minutes. Papaverine has been known, however, to cause prolonged erections (priapism)—for as long as four to five hours—which can require immediate treatment to prevent permanent damage to the penis. Thus, papaverine should only be used where medical care is immediately available. In addition, researchers are still studying the question of whether long-term use of papaverine can cause scar tissue to form.

Implants

And, finally, ordinarily as a last resort, prosthetic devices can be surgically implanted in the penis. Some are simply rigid rods that are implanted in the corpora cavernosa as a substitute for the effect of blood flowing into these areas of spongy muscle. The rods are flexible and can be manually bent to be erect or to remain close to the body. Other implants are more complex inflatable devices, which are implanted along with fluid reservoirs and a tiny pump that can be manually operated to move the fluid from the reservoirs into the device and so make the prosthesis enlarge and stiffen. Penile implants are reliable, although —as with any mechanical device—they may break down, and surgery is required to make the repair.

Vascular Surgery

Some physicians may recommend vascular surgery to enhance the blood flow through the arteries into the corpora cavernosa, although such surgery is still considered experimental, and the results have been almost entirely unsatisfactory when it has been tried in men over the age of 50.

RESEARCH FOR THE FUTURE

Many men will find the notion of injecting themselves, having a surgical implant, or using a vacuum device too clumsy or distasteful—even though very high rates of satisfaction have been reported with all these treatments. The good news, however, is that research is increasingly being done on impotence. The search is on for treatments even more effective than those available at present. It may well be that surgical implants will lead the way to subtler, pacemakerlike devices—so that the somewhat awkward therapies of today will soon lead to treatments that are less intrusive but equally effective.

The Editors

PROSTATE ENLARGEMENT

The prostate is a walnut-sized gland that forms part of the male reproductive system. The gland is composed of two lobes, or regions, enclosed by an outer layer of tissue. The prostate is located in front of the rectum and just below the bladder, where urine is stored. The prostate also surrounds the urethra, the canal through which urine passes out of the body.

Scientists do not know all of the prostate's functions. One of its main roles, however, is to squeeze fluid into the urethra as sperm move through during sexual climax. This fluid, which helps make up semen, energizes the sperm and makes the vaginal canal less acidic.

BPH: A COMMON PART OF AGING

It is common for the prostate gland to become enlarged as a man ages. Doctors call the condition benign prostatic hyperplasia (BPH), or benign prostatic hypertrophy.

As a male matures, the prostate goes through two main periods of growth. The first occurs early in puberty, when the prostate doubles in size. At around age 25, the gland begins to grow again. It is this second growth phase that often results, years later, in BPH.

Though the prostate continues to grow during most of a man's life, the enlargement doesn't usually cause problems until late in life. BPH rarely causes symptoms before age

40, but more than half of men in their 60s and as many as 90 percent in their 70s and 80s have some symptoms of BPH.

As the prostate enlarges, the surrounding capsule stops it from expanding, causing the gland to press against the urethra like a clamp on a garden hose. As a result, the bladder wall becomes thicker and irritable. The bladder begins to contract even when it contains small amounts of urine, causing more frequent urination. As the bladder weakens, it loses the ability to empty itself, and urine remains behind. This narrowing of the urethra and partial emptying of the bladder cause many of the problems associated with BPH.

Many people feel uncomfortable talking about the prostate, since the gland plays a role in both sex and urination. However, prostate enlargement is as common a part of aging as gray hair. As life expectancy rises, so does the occurrence of BPH. In the United States alone, 350,000 operations take place each year for BPH.

It is not clear whether certain groups face a greater risk of getting BPH. Studies done over the years have suggested that BPH occurs more often among married men than single men and is more common in the United States and Europe than in other parts of the world. However, these findings have been debated, and no definite information on risk factors exists.

WHY BPH OCCURS

The cause of BPH is not well understood. For centuries, it has been known that BPH occurs mainly in older men and that it doesn't develop in males whose testes were removed before puberty. For this reason, some researchers believe that factors related to aging and the testes may spur the development of BPH.

Throughout their lives, men produce both testosterone, an important male hormone, and small amounts of estrogen, a female hormone. As men age, the amount of active testosterone in the blood decreases, leaving a higher proportion of estrogen. Studies done with animals have suggested that BPH may occur because the higher amount of estrogen within the gland increases the activity of substances that promote cell growth.

Another theory focuses on dihydrotestosterone (DHT), a substance derived from testosterone in the prostate, which may help to control its growth. Most animals lose their ability to produce DHT as they age. However, some research has indicated that even with a drop in the blood's testosterone level, older men continue to produce and accumulate high levels of DHT in the prostate. This accumulation of DHT may encourage the growth of cells. Scientists have also noted that men who do not produce DHT do not develop BPH.

Some researchers suggest that BPH may develop as a result of "instructions" given to cells early in life. According to this theory, BPH occurs because cells in one section of the gland follow these instructions and "reawaken" later in life. These "reawakened" cells then deliver signals to other cells in the gland, instructing them to grow or making them more sensitive to hormones that influence growth.

SYMPTOMS

Many symptoms of BPH are caused by obstruction of the urethra and gradual loss of bladder function, which results in incomplete emptying of the bladder. The symptoms of BPH vary, but the most common ones involve changes or problems with urination, such as:

- A hesitant, interrupted, weak stream
- Urgency and leaking or dribbling
- More frequent urination, especially at night

The size of the prostate does not always determine how severe the obstruction or the symptoms will be. Some men with greatly enlarged glands have little obstruction and few

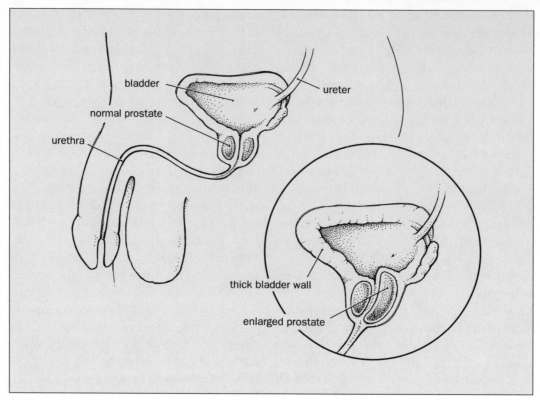

bladder

ureter

normal prostate

urethra

thick bladder wall

enlarged prostate

As the prostate enlarges, it may restrict urine flow, creating a frequent, urgent need to empty the bladder. Urine retention places excess demand upon the bladder wall, which can cause it to thicken.

symptoms while others, whose prostate glands are less enlarged, have more blockage and greater problems.

In some cases, a man may not know he has any obstruction until he suddenly finds himself unable to urinate at all. This condition, called acute urinary retention, may be triggered by taking over-the-counter cold or allergy medicines. Such medicines contain a decongestant drug, known as a sympathomimetic, which may, as a side effect, prevent the bladder opening from relaxing and allowing urine to empty. When partial obstruction is present, urinary retention can also be brought on by alcohol, cold temperatures, or a long period of immobility.

It is important to tell your doctor about urinary problems such as those just described. In 8 out of 10 cases, these symptoms suggest BPH, but they can also signal other, more serious conditions that require prompt treatment. These conditions can be ruled out only by a doctor's exam.

Severe BPH can also cause serious problems over time. Urine retention and strain on the bladder can lead to urinary tract infections, bladder or kidney damage, bladder stones, and incontinence. If the bladder is permanently damaged, treatment for BPH may be ineffective. When BPH is found in its earlier stages, there is a lower risk of developing such complications.

DIAGNOSIS

You may first notice symptoms of BPH yourself, or your doctor may find that your prostate is enlarged during a routine checkup. When BPH is suspected, you may be referred to a urologist, a doctor who specializes in problems of the urinary tract and the male reproductive system. A series of tests help the doctor identify the problem and decide whether surgery is needed. The tests vary from patient to patient, but the following are the most common.

Rectal exam. This is usually the first test done. The doctor inserts a gloved finger into the rectum and feels the part of the prostate next to the rectum. This gives the doctor a general idea of the size and condition of the gland.

Ultrasound. If there is a suspicion of prostate cancer, your doctor may recommend a test with rectal ultrasound. In this procedure, a probe inserted in the rectum directs sound waves at the prostate. The echo patterns of the sound waves form an image of the prostate gland on a display screen.

Urine flow study. Sometimes the doctor will ask a patient to urinate into a special device which measures how quickly the urine is flowing. A reduced flow often indicates obstruction caused by BPH.

Intravenous pyelogram (IVP). IVP is an x-ray of the urinary tract. A dye is injected into a vein, and the x-ray is taken. The dye makes the urine visible on the x-ray and shows any obstruction or blockage in the urinary tract.

Cystoscopy. In this exam, the doctor inserts a small tube through the opening of the urethra in the penis. (This procedure is done after a solution numbs the inside of the penis so all sensation is lost.) The tube, called a cystoscope, contains a lens and a light system, which help the doctor see the inside of the urethra and the bladder. This test allows the doctor to determine the size of the gland and identify the location and degree of the obstruction.

EARLY TREATMENT

Men who have BPH with symptoms usually need some kind of treatment at some time. However, a number of recent studies have questioned the need for early treatment when the gland is just mildly enlarged. These studies report that early treatment may not be needed because the symptoms of BPH clear up without treatment in as many as one-third of all mild cases. Instead of immediate treatment, they suggest regular checkups to watch for early problems. If the condition begins to pose a danger to the patient's health or causes a major inconvenience to him, treatment is usually recommended.

Since BPH may cause urinary tract infections, a doctor will usually clear up any infection with antibiotics before treating the BPH. Although the need for treatment is not usually urgent, doctors generally advise going ahead with treatment once the problems become bothersome or present a health risk. The following section describes the types of treatment that are most commonly used for BPH.

SURGICAL PROCEDURES

Most doctors recommend removal of the enlarged part of the prostate as the best long-range solution for patients with BPH. With surgery for BPH, only the enlarged tissue that is pressing against the urethra is removed; the rest of the inside tissue and the outside capsule are left intact. Surgery usually relieves the obstruction and incomplete emptying of the bladder caused by BPH.

Transurethral Surgery

In this type of surgery, no external incision is needed. After giving anesthesia, the surgeon reaches the prostate by inserting an instrument through the urethra.

A procedure called TURP (transurethral resection of the prostate) is used for 90 percent of all prostate surgeries done for BPH. With TURP, an instrument called a resectoscope is inserted through the penis. The resectoscope, which is about 12 inches long and one-half inch in diameter, contains a light, valves for controlling irrigating fluid, and an electrical loop that cuts tissue and seals blood vessels.

During the 90-minute operation, the surgeon uses the resectoscope's wire loop to remove the obstructing tissue one piece at a time. The pieces of tissue are carried by the fluid into the bladder and then flushed out at the end of the operation.

Although this procedure is delicate and requires a skilled surgeon, most doctors suggest using TURP whenever possible. Transurethral procedures are less traumatic than open forms of surgery and require a shorter recovery period.

Another surgical procedure is called transurethral incision of the prostate. Instead of removing tissue, as with TURP, this procedure widens the urethra by making a few small cuts in the bladder neck, where the urethra joins the bladder. Although some people believe that this procedure gives the same relief as TURP with less risk of side effects, its advantages and long-term side effects have not been clearly established.

Open Surgery

In the few cases when a transurethral procedure cannot be used, open surgery, which requires an external incision, may be used. Open surgery is often done when the gland is greatly enlarged, when there are complicating factors, or when the bladder has been damaged and needs to be repaired. The location of the enlargement within the gland and the patient's general health are considerations that help the surgeon decide which of the three open procedures to use.

With all of the open procedures, anesthesia is administered and an incision is made. Once the surgeon reaches the prostate capsule, he scoops out the enlarged tissue from inside the gland.

Laser Surgery

Some researchers are exploring the use of lasers to vaporize obstructing prostate tissue.

Early studies suggest that this method may be as effective as conventional surgery.

RECOVERY AFTER SURGERY

In the Hospital

Following surgery you will probably stay in the hospital from 3 to 10 days, depending on the type of surgery you had and how quickly you recover.

At the end of surgery, a special catheter is inserted through the opening of the penis to drain urine from the bladder into a collection bag. Called a Foley catheter, this device has a water-filled balloon on the end that is placed in the bladder, which keeps it in place.

This catheter is usually left in place for several days. Sometimes, the catheter causes recurring painful bladder spasms the day after surgery. These may be difficult to control, but they will eventually disappear.

You may also be given antibiotics while you are in the hospital. Many doctors start giving this medicine before or soon after surgery to prevent infection. However, some recent studies suggest that antibiotics may not be needed in every case, and your doctor may prefer to wait until an infection is present to give them.

After surgery, you will probably notice some blood or clots in your urine as the wound starts to heal. If your bladder is being irrigated (flushed with water), you may notice that your urine becomes red once the irrigation is stopped. Some bleeding is normal, and it should clear up by the time you leave the hospital. During your recovery, it is important to drink a lot of water (up to 8 cups a day) to help flush out the bladder and speed healing.

Do's and Don'ts

Take it easy the first few weeks after you get home. You may not have any pain, but you still have an incision that is healing—even with transurethral surgery, where the incision can't be seen. Since many people try to do too much at the beginning and then have a setback, it is a good idea to talk to your doctor before resuming your normal routine. During this initial period of recovery at home, avoid any straining or sudden movements that could tear the incision. The following are some guidelines.

- Continue drinking a lot of water to flush the bladder.
- Avoid straining when moving your bowel. Eat a balanced diet to prevent constipation, and take a laxative if you become constipated.
- Don't do any heavy lifting.
- Don't drive or operate machinery.

Getting Back to Normal

Even though you should feel much better by the time you leave the hospital, it will probably take a couple of months for you to heal completely. During the recovery period, you may experience some of the following common problems.

Problems urinating. You will probably notice that your urinary stream is stronger right after surgery, but it may take awhile before you can urinate completely normally again. After the catheter is removed, urine will pass over the surgical wound on the prostate, and you may initially have some discomfort or feel a sense of urgency when you urinate. This problem will gradually lessen, though, and after a couple of months you should be able to urinate less frequently and more easily.

Inability to control urination (incontinence). As the bladder returns to normal, you may have some temporary problems controlling urination, but long-term incontinence rarely occurs. Doctors find that the longer problems existed before surgery, the longer it will take for the bladder to regain its full function after the operation.

Bleeding. In the first few weeks after transurethral surgery, the scab inside the bladder may loosen, and blood may suddenly appear in the urine. Although this can be alarming, the bleeding usually stops with a short period of resting in bed and drinking fluids. However, if your urine is so red that it is difficult to see through or if it contains clots or if you feel discomfort, be sure to contact your doctor.

SEXUAL FUNCTION AFTER SURGERY

Many men worry about whether surgery for BPH will affect their ability to enjoy sex. Some sources state that sexual function is rarely affected, while others claim that it can cause problems in up to 30 percent of all cases. However, most doctors say that even though it takes awhile for sexual function to return fully, with time, most men are able to enjoy sex again.

Complete recovery of sexual function may take up to one year, lagging behind a person's general recovery. The exact length of time depends on how long BPH surgery was postponed despite symptoms and on the type of surgery that was done. Here is a summary of how surgery is likely to affect the following aspects of sexual function.

Erections

Most doctors agree that if you were potent (able to maintain an erection) shortly before surgery, you will probably be able to have erections afterward. Surgery rarely causes a loss of potency. But, surgery cannot usually restore potency that was lost before the operation.

Ejaculation

Although most men are able to continue having erections after surgery, a prostatectomy frequently makes them sterile (unable to father children) by causing a condition called "retrograde ejaculation" or "dry climax."

During sexual activity, sperm from the testicles enters the urethra near the opening of the bladder. Normally, a muscle blocks off the entrance to the bladder, and the semen is expelled through the penis. However, the coring action of prostate surgery cuts this muscle as it widens the neck of the bladder. Following surgery, the semen takes the path of least resistance and enters the wider opening to the bladder rather than being expelled through the penis. Later it is harmlessly flushed out with urine.

Orgasm

Most men find little or no difference in the sensation of orgasm, or sexual climax, before and after surgery. Although it may take some time to get used to retrograde ejaculation, you should eventually find sex as pleasurable after surgery as before.

Many people have found that concerns about sexual function can interfere with sex as much as the operation itself. Understanding the surgical procedure and talking over any worries with the doctor before surgery often help men regain sexual function earlier.

Many men also find it helpful to talk to a counselor during the adjustment period following BPH surgery.

ADDITIONAL TREATMENT

In the years after your surgery, it is important to continue having a rectal exam once a year and to have any symptoms checked by your doctor.

Since surgery for BPH leaves behind a good part of the gland, it is still possible for prostate problems, including BPH, to develop again. However, surgery usually offers relief from BPH for at least 15 years. Only 10 percent of the men who have surgery for BPH eventually need a second operation for enlargement. Usually these are men who had the first surgery at an early age.

Sometimes, scar tissue resulting from surgery requires treatment in the year after surgery. Rarely, the opening of the bladder becomes scarred and shrinks, causing obstruction. This problem may require a surgi-cal procedure similar to transurethral incision. More often, scar tissue may form in the urethra and cause narrowing. This problem can usually be solved during an office visit when the doctor stretches the urethra.

NONSURGICAL TREATMENT

Balloon Urethroplasty

In this procedure, a thin tube with a balloon is inserted into the opening of the penis and guided to the narrowed portion of the urethra, where the balloon is inflated. This action widens the urethra, easing the flow of urine.

Balloon urethroplasty is a simple procedure that can be done on an outpatient basis, so it may eventually offer men a safe alternative to surgery. Since the procedure doesn't actually remove the tissue causing the obstruction, more studies are needed to judge its long-range effectiveness.

Transurethral Hyperthermia

Researchers are also investigating a procedure that uses heat to shrink the prostate. During a series of treatments spread over several weeks, a doctor inserts a catheter containing a heating antenna into the urethra and then applies concentrated heat to the enlarged tissue, gradually shrinking it and relieving the obstruction. However, the long-range effectiveness of hyperthermia is not clear, and studies have indicated that the frequent insertion of a catheter and the use of heat can cause side effects such as irritation of the urethra, bleeding, or painful bladder spasms.

Medical Treatment

Over the years, many attempts have been made to find a way to shrink or at least stop the growth of the prostate without using surgery. Recently, scientists have developed several new medications, which are now being tested in clinical trials to determine whether they are safe and effective. Early results show that these medications can relieve the effects of BPH in some men, and, in some cases, slow down or stop the growth of the prostate. No medication, however, is currently approved for the treatment of BPH in the United States. Thus, surgery still remains the standard form of treatment.

BPH AND PROSTATE CANCER: NO APPARENT RELATION

Although some of the signs of BPH and prostate cancer are the same (see also Prostate Cancer, page 70), having BPH does not seem to increase the chances of getting prostate cancer. Nevertheless, a man who has BPH may have undetected prostate cancer at the same time or may develop prostate cancer in the future. For this reason, the National Cancer Institute and the American Cancer Society recommend that all men over the age of 40 have a rectal exam once a year to screen for prostate cancer.

After BPH surgery, the tissue removed is routinely checked for hidden cancer cells. In about 1 out of 10 cases, some cancer tissue is found, but often it is limited to a few cells of a nonaggressive type of cancer, and no treatment is needed.

The National Institute of Diabetes and
Digestive and Kidney Diseases

Health Problems of Women

Our entire body changes as we age—but for women, the most obvious and profound changes occur with the onset of menopause. Beyond this, certain other issues are of special concern to women over age 50. Questions about breast lumps, urinary incontinence, or vaginitis may be difficult to raise initially, but your family doctor, internist, or gynecologist can be a terrific resource in such matters.   *The Editors*

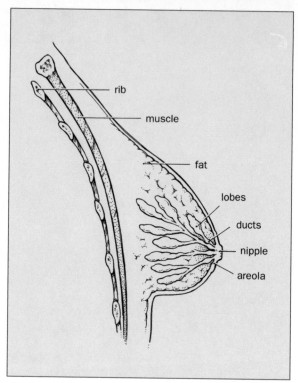

Regular breast self-exams can help a woman distinguish abnormal lumps from the lumps caused by ribs, muscles, lobes, and fat deposits in the breast.

BENIGN BREAST CONDITIONS

It's natural to be concerned if you've found a lump in your breast. But 80 percent of all breast lumps are benign, which means no cancer is present.

Most lumps are found by women themselves, either through regular breast self-exam or just by accident. Others are discovered during routine breast exams by a health professional and through mammograms, special x-rays of the breast.

About 20 percent of breast lumps are malignant (cancerous). However, if cancer is found at an early stage and treated promptly, the outlook is good. In fact, 85 to 95 percent of women with early breast cancer will be alive five years after diagnosis. Most of them will be free of breast cancer for the rest of their lives.

It is normal to be afraid when you find a lump in your breast. But don't let fear stop you from seeing a doctor right away if you think something is wrong. You will feel more confident about finding a breast lump early by:

- Having regular mammograms
- Having a regular breast exam by a health professional
- Doing a monthly breast self-exam (BSE), as illustrated on page 414

THE DIFFERENCE BETWEEN "LUMPY" BREASTS AND A LUMP IN THE BREAST

The breasts are made up of ducts, lobes, and fat. Under the breasts are muscles and ribs. These normal features may make the breasts feel "lumpy" or uneven.

In addition, many women have changes in their breasts that are related to their monthly menstrual cycle. Swelling, tenderness, and pain in the breasts may occur before and sometimes during the menstrual period. At the same time, one or more lumps or a feeling of increased "lumpiness" may appear in the breasts. These symptoms are caused by extra fluid collecting in the breast tissue, which is normal. If the "lumpiness" or lumps do not go away after the end of your period, it is important to see a doctor.

If you are past menopause and you find

any new lump or thickening in your breast, you should see your doctor.

PERFORMING A BREAST SELF-EXAM (BSE)

You are looking for a lump that stands out as different from the rest of your breast tissue. Many women are confused about BSE because their breasts generally feel "lumpy." Becoming more familiar with your breasts by doing BSE each month will help you tell the difference between your normal "lumpiness" and what may be a change.

Ask your doctor or other health professional to do a breast exam with you and to explain what you are feeling in your breasts. They can make sure you are doing BSE correctly and thoroughly, which will make you feel more confident.

DISCOVERING A BREAST LUMP

If you notice a lump in one breast, examine the other one. If both breasts feel the same, then what you feel is probably a normal part of your breast. You should, however, mention it to your doctor at your next visit.

If a lump of any size appears in either breast and does not go away after your menstrual period, see your doctor. The doctor may refer you to a specialist to discuss the need for further tests.

EVALUATING A BREAST LUMP

Your doctor can evaluate a lump by a number of different methods.

Palpation is a physical exam of the breast. The doctor examines each breast and underarm by feeling the tissue. Although a doctor can tell a lot by the way the lump feels, no one can be certain what a lump is just by palpation.

Aspiration, also called fine needle aspiration, can help the doctor discover whether the lump is a cyst (fluid-filled) or a solid mass of tissue. Aspiration is usually done in the doctor's office. First, the doctor uses a local anesthetic to numb the area. Then the doctor inserts a needle into the lump and tries to withdraw fluid. If it is a cyst, removing the fluid will collapse it. The fluid may be sent to a laboratory for testing to be sure no cancer cells are present. When the lump is solid, the doctor sometimes removes a sample of cells with the needle. These cells are then sent to a laboratory for analysis.

A mammogram is a type of x-ray that creates an image of the breast on film or paper. It can help determine whether a lump is benign or cancerous. In fact, it often can detect cancer in the breast before a lump can be felt. The National Cancer Institute (NCI) suggests that beginning at age 40, all women should have a mammogram every one to two years.

⚠ Breast specialists advise that a woman have a baseline (first) mammogram at age 35—and then, if no abnormalities are found, she need not have another one until the age of 40.

When a woman reaches the age of 50, she should have a mammogram each year. A doctor may also recommend a mammogram if any sign or symptom of breast cancer is found, regardless of age.

Several other methods also are being studied. None is now reliable enough to be used alone, but they may be helpful when combined with other methods.

- *Ultrasound* uses high-frequency sound waves to get an image of the breast and can help determine if a lump is a cyst or a solid mass. It is usually used along with palpation and mammography.
- *Diaphanography,* or transillumination, shines a light through the breast to show its inner features.
- *Thermography* measures the heat patterns in the breast to produce an image.

A biopsy is the only certain way to learn whether a breast lump or suspicious area seen on a mammogram is cancer. In a biopsy, the doctor surgically removes all or part of the lump and sends it to the laboratory for analysis. There are several biopsy methods that a doctor may use: needle biopsy, incisional biopsy, excisional biopsy, and mammographic localization with biopsy.

- *Needle biopsy.* Occasionally the doctor will do a needle biopsy to remove a small amount of tissue from the lump. A needle biopsy can be performed in the doctor's office. This is most often done when cancer is suspected and the doctor hopes to confirm the diagnosis immediately. If cancer is not found, a more thorough biopsy will follow. Once, it was thought that inserting a needle or cutting into a breast lump might cause cancer to spread. This is not true.
- *An incisional biopsy* is the surgical removal of a portion of a lump. This procedure is often used when the growth is very large. Again, if no cancer is found, a more thorough biopsy may follow to make sure the entire lump is free of cancer.
- *In an excisional biopsy* the doctor removes the entire lump. This is currently the "standard" biopsy procedure and the most thorough method of diagnosis. Incisional and excisional biopsies are usually done in the outpatient department of a hospital. Either a local or general anesthetic may be used.
- *Mammographic localization with biopsy* (also known as needle localization) is used for suspicious areas such as microcalcifications (tiny specks of calcium) that cannot be felt but can he seen on a mammogram. During this procedure, the breast is x-rayed and small needles are placed to outline the suspicious area for the surgeon, who then removes the tissue for biopsy. This can be done using a local anesthetic in the outpatient department of a hospital.

Your doctor may suggest one or more of these procedures to evaluate a lump or other change in your breast. The doctor may also suggest watching the suspicious area for a month or two. Because many lumps are caused by normal hormonal changes, this waiting period may provide additional information.

However, if you feel uncomfortable about waiting, speak with your doctor about your concerns. You also may want to get a second opinion, perhaps from a breast specialist or surgeon. Many cities have breast clinics where you can get a second opinion.

WHAT THE DOCTOR LEARNS FROM A BIOPSY

The biopsy can tell the doctor whether your lump is benign or malignant. If it is cancer, your doctor will talk with you about choices of treatments, and you may be advised to get a second opinion.

If no cancer is found, you may be told that the lump or suspicious area is the result of a fibrocystic condition, fibrocystic disease, benign breast disease, or one of many other conditions. Remember, 80 percent of all breast lumps are not cancer.

FIBROCYSTIC CONDITION, FIBROCYSTIC DISEASE, OR BENIGN BREAST DISEASE

Unfortunately, doctors do not agree on standard terms for benign breast changes. We prefer to use the term benign breast condition for those changes in a woman's breasts that are not cancerous. These include normal changes that occur during the menstrual cycle as well as benign lumps that can appear in the breast. If your doctor uses a different term, or one you do not understand, ask for an explanation.

Number of Women with a Benign Breast Condition

It is estimated that at least 50 percent of all women have irregular or "lumpy" breasts. In addition, many doctors believe that nearly all women have some benign breast changes beginning at age 30. A woman is more likely to have these breast changes if she has never had children, has had irregular menstrual cycles, has a family history of breast cancer, or is thin. Women who have had more than one child and women who are taking birth control pills have a reduced risk.

Symptoms of a Benign Breast Condition

Women may have increased "lumpiness" with tenderness, pain, and swelling just before their period begins. These symptoms lessen after the menstrual period, only to reappear the next month. Many women find that these symptoms disappear after menopause.

Benign breast lumps may appear at any time. Some cause pain, others don't. They may be large or small, soft or rubbery, fluid-filled or solid, and movable. In addition, some benign breast conditions may produce a discharge from the nipple.

Kinds of Benign Breast Conditions

Normal hormonal changes may cause a feeling of fullness in the breast, which goes away after the menstrual period. This condition is most common in women 35 to 50 years of age.

Cysts are fluid-filled sacs that often enlarge and become tender and painful just before the menstrual period. Cysts are found most often in women 35 to 50 years of age. They usually are found in both breasts. There may be many cysts of different sizes. Some cysts are so small that they can't be felt; others may be several inches across.

Fibroadenomas are solid, round, rubbery, and freely movable breast lumps. Usually they are painless. They appear most often in young women between 15 and 30 years of age. Fibroadenomas occur twice as often in black women as in others. They are benign but should be removed to be certain of the diagnosis. Fibroadenomas do not go away by

themselves and may enlarge during pregnancy and breast-feeding.

Lipomas are single, painless lumps that are sometimes found in older women. They are made up of fatty tissue and are slow-growing, soft, and movable. They can vary in size from a dime to a quarter. Lipomas should be removed or biopsied to make sure that they are not cancerous.

Intraductal papillomas are small wartlike growths in the lining of a duct near the nipple. They usually affect women between 45 and 50 years old and can produce bleeding from the nipple.

Mammary duct ectasia is an inflammation of the ducts that causes a thick, sticky, gray-to-green discharge from the nipple. Without treatment, the condition can become painful.

Mastitis (sometimes called "postpartum mastitis") is most often seen in women who are breast-feeding. It is an inflammatory condition in which the breast appears red and feels warm, tender, and lumpy.

Traumatic fat necrosis occasionally appears in older women and in women with very large breasts. The condition can result from a bruise or blow to the breast, although the woman might not remember the specific injury. The trauma causes the fat in the breast to form lumps that are painless, round, and firm. Sometimes the skin around them looks red or bruised. Again, a doctor should examine the area.

A word of caution: If you find a change in your breast, do not use these descriptions to try to diagnose it yourself. There is no substitute for a doctor's evaluation.

Treatment for a Benign Breast Condition

Treatment varies, depending on the type of condition a woman has. If you have a single lump, it is usually removed in the biopsy. Most cysts are aspirated, and if they don't disappear, they are removed by surgery. Although there is no treatment for normal monthly breast changes, some studies have looked at various ways of treating the uncomfortable symptoms. The results of those studies do not all agree. You may wish to discuss the following treatments with your doctor.

Change in diet. For a long time doctors thought that eliminating beverages and foods that contain caffeine such as coffee, tea, cola, and chocolate (all of which also contain a substance called methylxanthine) would reduce monthly breast pain and tenderness. Recent studies have been unable to prove that such a change in diet affects symptoms. However, women continue to report to doctors that when they stop drinking coffee or eating chocolate, the pain and swelling in their breasts is less.

Vitamin E is another treatment that has been suggested. It is generally accepted that taking this vitamin may help reduce the symptoms of breast pain and tenderness. You should speak with your doctor before taking vitamin E.

Antihormone treatment. Occasionally doctors will suggest an antihormone treatment (Danazol) when a woman has severe symptoms. Danazol may relieve pain and tenderness and decrease "lumpiness"; however, serious side effects are possible, and you should discuss all aspects of this treatment with your doctor if it is recommended.

PROPHYLACTIC MASTECTOMY

In cases where a woman's breasts are extremely difficult to examine, when there have been many biopsies or there are biopsy-proven tissue changes that place that woman in a high-risk category and there is a family history of breast cancer, a doctor may suggest a prophylactic mastectomy. In this surgery, both breasts are removed. Some women then choose to have breast reconstruction.

If your doctor suggests this treatment, you should consider getting a second opinion, preferably from a breast specialist. Remember that there is no reason to hurry into this decision. You should be comfortable with your choice and learn everything about the procedure, its possible side effects, and your risks of future problems. Prophylactic mastectomy is a controversial treatment, and many doctors prefer instead to schedule frequent exams to check for any breast changes.

INSURANCE COVERAGE

Talk with your doctor about your diagnosis and call your insurance company to ask about their coverage for benign breast conditions. Only a very small percentage of women with a benign breast condition are at greater risk of developing cancer. Despite this fact, some insurance companies have cancelled policies or raised premiums for women who have been diagnosed with "fibrocystic disease."

CAN BENIGN LUMPS TURN INTO CANCEROUS ONES?

Benign lumps do not turn into cancer. However, cancerous lumps can develop close to benign lumps and can be hidden on a mammogram. This is another reason why removal of a benign lump is usually recommended.

MICROCALCIFICATIONS

Microcalcifications are tiny specks of calcium in the tissue of the breast that are sometimes detected by a mammogram. These microcalcifications can be related to a benign breast condition or they can be an indication of breast cancer.

In some cases, microcalcifications are seen even when there is no lump present. The pattern and location of microcalcifications are factors that help the doctor determine if additional tests are needed.

NIPPLE DISCHARGE

You should see your doctor whenever you notice a spontaneous discharge from the nipple (when something comes out without the breast being squeezed). The fluid may be clear, milky, bloody, or even green. If you have a discharge when you do BSE, you should also check with your doctor.

Many conditions can cause a discharge. The doctor will take a sample of the discharge and send it to a laboratory to be analyzed. Occasionally, the doctor may order special tests to help in diagnosing the cause of the discharge. Your doctor can then recommend treatment.

DOES EVERY NEW LUMP NEED TO BE BIOPSIED?

Not necessarily. If a new lump appears, you cannot be sure that it is benign, even if you have had a benign lump removed in the past. Your doctor should evaluate it and decide whether a biopsy is needed.

Effects of a Breast Biopsy

Generally, a breast biopsy leaves only a minor scar, but this depends on the location and size of the lump and how deep it is in the breast. You should discuss the procedure with your doctor so you understand just what is going to be done and what the result is going to look like.

BENIGN BREAST CHANGE AND BREAST CANCER RISK

Most benign breast changes do not increase a woman's risk of getting breast cancer. Recent studies show that only certain, very specific breast changes, which are detected by biopsy, put a woman at higher risk of developing breast cancer. Most important, 70 percent of the women who have a breast biopsy for a benign condition are not at any increased risk of cancer. About 26 percent of breast biopsies show changes that slightly increase the risk of developing breast cancer, and only 4 percent show breast changes that moderately increase the woman's risk.

If your biopsy shows benign changes, discuss with your doctor what kind of changes were found and whether those changes increase your risk of developing breast cancer.

OTHER RISK FACTORS FOR BREAST CANCER

Age is a factor. The older you are, the greater your chance of getting breast cancer. About one in five women diagnosed with breast cancer has a family history of the disease. Other risk factors include having your first child after age 30, never being pregnant, getting your first period at an early age, or having a late menopause. Do not place too much faith in being "safe" if you have none of these risk factors—what puts you at risk for getting breast cancer is that you are a woman. The majority of women who are diagnosed with breast cancer do not fall into any special "high-risk" category.

BREAST SELF-EXAMINATION

Breast self-examination (BSE) should be done once a month so you become familiar with the usual appearance and feel of your breasts. Familiarity makes it easier to notice any changes in the breast from one month to another. Early discovery of a change from what is "normal" is the main idea behind BSE. The outlook is much better if you detect cancer in an early stage.

If you menstruate, the best time to do BSE is two or three days after your period ends, when your breasts are least likely to be tender or swollen. If you no longer menstruate, pick a day such as the first day of the month to remind yourself it is time to do BSE.

Here is one way to do BSE (as illustrated on the following page):

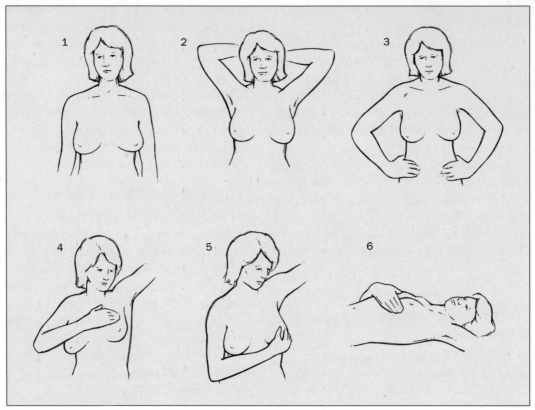

While regular mammograms are essential in the early detection of breast cancer, many lumps are detected during monthly breast self-exams. The text below explains each of the steps as shown here.

(1) Stand before a mirror. Inspect both breasts for anything unusual such as any discharge from the nipples or puckering, dimpling, or scaling of the skin.

The next two steps are designed to emphasize any change in the shape or contour of your breasts. As you do them, you should be able to feel your chest muscles tighten.

(2) Watching closely in the mirror, clasp your hands behind your head and press your hands forward.

(3) Next, press your hands firmly on your hips and bow slightly toward the mirror as you pull your shoulders and elbows forward.

Some women do the next part of the exam in the shower because fingers glide over soapy skin, making it easy to concentrate on the texture underneath.

(4) Raise your left arm. Use three or four fingers of your right hand to explore your left breast firmly, carefully, and thoroughly. Beginning at the outer edge, press the flat part of your fingers in small circles, moving the circles slowly around the breast. Gradually work toward the nipple. Be sure to cover the entire breast. Pay special attention to the area between the breast and the underarm, including the underarm itself. Feel for any unusual lump or mass under the skin.

(5) Gently squeeze the nipple and look for a discharge. (If you have any discharge during the month—whether or not it is during BSE—see your doctor.) Repeat steps 4 and 5 on your right breast.

(6) Steps 4 and 5 should be repeated lying down. Lie flat on your back with your left arm over your head and a pillow or folded towel under your left shoulder. This position flat-

tens the breast and makes it easier to examine. Use the same circular motion described earlier. Repeat the exam on your right breast.

The National Cancer Institute

MENOPAUSE

Menopause or "change of life" is the time in a woman's life when menstruation stops and the body no longer produces the monthly ovum, or egg, from which a baby could be formed. It usually occurs at about age 50, although it can occur as early as 45 or as late as 55. Menopause is usually considered finished when a woman has not menstruated for a year. Completion of menopause marks the end of the childbearing years.

Menopause is natural and takes place smoothly for most women. It is part of a gradual process sometimes called the climacteric, which begins about five years before menopause and may last about 10 years.

During the climacteric a woman's body produces decreasing amounts of the hormones estrogen and progesterone. This reduction in hormone production causes menstrual periods to stop.

Many women welcome menopause—no more periods, and after at least a year without a period to be sure it's safe, no more worry about pregnancy.

SURGICAL MENOPAUSE

Surgical procedures involving the ovaries and the uterus can affect how menopause takes place. When the uterus is removed (called a hysterectomy) and the ovaries remain, menstrual periods stop; meanwhile, other aspects of menopause occur in the same way and at the same age that they would occur naturally. When only one ovary is removed, menopause occurs normally. With the removal of both ovaries, complete menopause takes place abruptly, sometimes with intense effects.

THE REPRODUCTIVE CYCLE AND MENOPAUSE

During puberty increasing amounts of the female hormones estrogen and progesterone stimulate the reproductive system to mature and menstruation to begin. For more than 30 years of a woman's life (except during pregnancy) a monthly cycle takes place. The pituitary gland, located at the base of the brain, produces hormones that stimulate the ovary to release a new ovum, or egg cell, each month. The ovum produces the hormones estrogen and progesterone which cause the lining of the uterus to become thicker in order to receive and nourish a fertilized egg which could develop into a baby. If fertilization does not occur, estrogen and progesterone levels drop, the lining of the uterus breaks down, and menstruation occurs. Then the whole process begins again.

After age 35 estrogen and progesterone levels begin a very gradual decline. In the late forties this process accelerates and hormone levels eventually decrease so that the menstrual cycle becomes irregular or stops.

Following menopause the ovaries still produce some estrogen; other tissues and organs also produce hormones which are converted to estrogen.

THE SIGNS OF MENOPAUSE

The only sign of menopause for many women is the end of menstrual periods. They may stop suddenly or become irregular, with a lighter or heavier flow and with longer intervals between periods, until they eventually stop. About 80 percent of women experience mild or no signs of menopause; the other 20 percent report symptoms severe enough to seek medical attention.

Two other signs associated with menopause are hot flashes (which are often accompanied by sweating) and vaginal dryness. The fatigue, heart palpitations, or depression reported by some women during this time may be symptoms of menopause in some cases, but there is wide disagreement about this.

Hot Flashes

Hot flashes, or hot flushes, are one of the more common and earliest signs of menopause, sometimes beginning several years before other signs. They give a sudden feeling of warmth throughout the upper body or over all of the body. The face may become flushed, with red areas appearing on the chest, back, shoulders, and upper arms. This is often followed by perspiration and a cold clammy sensation as the body temperature readjusts. The process may last anywhere from a few seconds to a half hour or more.

Hot flashes may occur several times a day or only once a week. The sensations vary from woman to woman and from one episode to another. In most cases hot flashes are not severe and usually disappear after a few months, although in some women they can continue for several years. Sometimes hot flashes disturb sleep at night and may cause heavy perspiration.

Vaginal and Urinary Tract Changes

With age the walls of the vagina become thinner, less elastic, and drier. The vagina is then more vulnerable to infection. Also, these changes sometimes result in uncomfortable or painful sexual intercourse, although continuing regular sexual activity will reduce the possibility of problems developing.

As body tissues change with age some women experience urinary stress incontinence, which is the loss of a small quantity of urine when exercising, coughing, laughing, or performing other movements that put pressure on the bladder. As well as age changes, lack of physical exercise may also contribute to the condition. While inconti-

nence can be embarrassing, it is common and treatable—for example, certain exercises can strengthen the affected muscles or sometimes surgery is performed to cure it.

Some women are prone to urinary tract infections. These tend to recur but are easily treated with antibiotics or other measures. Preventive techniques include urinating after intercourse, not keeping the bladder over-full for long periods, drinking adequate amounts of fluids, and keeping the genital area very clean. It is important to see a doctor as soon as any symptoms appear, such as painful or frequent urination.

OSTEOPOROSIS

"Postmenopausal" osteoporosis is closely associated with menopause since it is caused in part by the decrease in estrogen that occurs with menopause. It is a major cause of bone fractures in older women. In women with this condition, bone mass slowly decreases over the years to produce thinner, more porous bone.

Osteoporotic bone is weaker than normal bone and fractures more easily. Common sites for fractures are the spine, wrists and forearms, and hips. Osteoporosis is sometimes called the "silent disease" because there are no symptoms during the early stages. Too often the condition is not recognized until it reaches an advanced stage when fractures are most likely to occur. (See also Osteoporosis, page 349.)

Once bone is lost it cannot be replaced, so an early prediction of which individuals are at high risk or have already developed mild osteoporosis is important. Unfortunately, accurate and inexpensive medical tests are not yet widely accessible.

The most accurate tests—single and dual photon absorptiometry and the computed tomography or CT scan—are expensive and usually available only at major medical and research centers.

Who Is Most Likely to Develop Osteoporosis?

In everyone the risk increases with age, but it is highest in white women after menopause—particularly in individuals who have an early or surgical menopause. Other people at high risk include those with fair skin (especially blonds and redheads), those whose diets are low in calcium, and those who are physically inactive, underweight, or smoke cigarettes. Women with a close relative (mother or sister) with the disease are also at high risk.

Prevention

Lifelong habits may be the best way to prevent osteoporosis. By practicing simple health measures, young women can prevent bone loss and older women who have already developed osteoporosis can slow down further bone loss. These measures include eating foods high in calcium, going outdoors for a short time every day (exposure to sunlight helps the body manufacture the vitamin D necessary for calcium absorption), and exercising regularly in activities that place stress on the weight-bearing bones (such as walking, jogging, or aerobics). In addition, for women most likely to develop osteoporosis, some doctors recommend the use of estrogen replacement therapy.

TREATMENT FOR MENOPAUSE

Menopause is a natural part of aging and does not necessarily require treatment. But if you experience great discomfort at this time, consult your physician.

Estrogen Replacement Therapy (ERT)

For severe symptoms of menopause (hot flashes, vaginal changes) and to prevent osteoporosis, many doctors prescribe estrogen replacement therapy, a synthetic estrogen which supplements the decreasing amounts of estrogen produced by the body. Estrogen in pill form is most often used for the prevention of osteoporosis; topically applied estrogen creams are used for severe vaginal symptoms.

Most recently, ERT has been offered not only to symptomatic women but to most menopausal women to prevent osteoporosis. The latest opinion is that ERT is beneficial for the majority of women who do not have specific contraindications.

Estrogen can be highly effective but it must be used with care. One reason for this caution is that roughly 10 percent of women who use estrogen experience side effects such as headaches, nausea, vaginal discharge, fluid retention, swollen breasts, and weight gain.

Who should not use ERT? Some women are not good candidates since estrogen can worsen certain conditions or increase the risk of complications. Persons who should avoid ERT are those who have had endometrial or breast cancer, stroke, migraine headaches, high blood pressure, blood clots, or other disorders related to the circulatory system.

Other conditions warrant that ERT be used with extra caution. These include exposure at birth to diethylstilbestrol (DES), obesity, a his-

---

ERT AND HRT

The terms ERT (estrogen replacement therapy) and HRT (hormone replacement therapy) are often used interchangeably. In fact, ERT only supplements the body's natural supply of estrogen; HRT supplements both estrogen and progestin, another female hormone—a combination that appears to reduce the risk of cancer of the endometrium, the lining of the uterus.

Many studies indicate that estrogen replacement therapy protects women against heart attacks. ERT may, however, increase the risk of cancer of the endometrium. For that reason, physicians today usually prescribe ERT for women who have had a hysterectomy, but HRT for women who have not had a hysterectomy.

The Editors

tory of cancer in the family, vaginal bleeding, and liver or gallbladder disease.

If you are at high risk of developing osteoporosis or have severe symptoms accompanying menopause, discuss the use of ERT with your doctor. To help ensure that ERT is safe for you, he or she should perform a thorough medical history and examination before prescribing treatment Then, as treatment proceeds, continue to see your physician for frequent follow-up examinations.

Stay informed. Research is being conducted at many universities and medical centers, and this research periodically results in new information that may bear on your treatment.

Other Treatments for Menopause

Several drugs are available to reduce hot flashes or to relieve other menopausal symptoms for women who cannot use ERT.

Some women report that certain vitamins are successful in reducing hot flashes or stress, although no scientific evidence supports these claims.

Doctors sometimes prescribe tranquilizers for women who are particularly tense, irritable, or nervous, but they are not recommended for symptoms specifically related to menopause. Tranquilizers are like other drugs; they can have side effects and should be used with care. Before turning to medication to reduce stress, many people first try exercise, an improved diet, or relaxation techniques.

MENTAL HEALTH AND MENOPAUSE

Most women have a healthy outlook throughout the menopause process and afterward feel "in their prime," glad to no longer be menstruating.

Mood changes may occur during menopause. Other symptoms commonly reported are fatigue, nervousness, excess sweating, breathlessness, headaches, sleeplessness, joint pain, depression, irritability, and impatience. These symptoms may be due in part to shift-ing hormonal balances or other factors such as heredity, general health, nutrition, medications, exercise, life events, and attitude. More research is needed on the role hormones play and how they interact with these other factors.

There is no specific mental disorder associated with menopause, and research shows that women experience no more depression during these years than at other times during life. Tension or depression can occur at any stage, but when these states occur during menopause, there is a tendency to blame the menopause process. Thus women with emotional problems are on occasion tagged "menopausal," sometimes long after menopause has taken place.

Important life changes often coincide with the menopause years: perhaps grown children are leaving home, aged parents need more attention and assistance, or a woman's life is taking on new directions. This is a time when many women think about growing older and the changes it will bring.

Developing positive attitudes toward menopause and aging is an important part of adjusting to life changes. As long as menopause is regarded as simply a normal life change and a woman goes on to participate in satisfying activities, coping with the transitions and body changes becomes easier. But viewing menopause as the end of a useful life only makes the transition difficult—so that if a crisis develops, such as a divorce or the need to care for parents who are ill, menopause is likely to seem an added burden.

Supportive friends and satisfying activities help ease any transition or crisis. Emotional support can come from a variety of sources: a friend, your husband, or relatives. Various types of support groups exist which can provide opportunities for you to talk with other people who are going through similar experiences. When coping is difficult, it may be useful to consult a gynecologist or seek the services of a social worker, psychologist, psychiatrist, or other mental health professional.

SEXUALITY AND MENOPAUSE

An active and fulfilling sex life can continue throughout menopause. While some physical responses slow with age, the capacity and need for sexual expression continues. Some women report that sex is more enjoyable after menopause, possibly because pregnancy is not a concern and there is more time and privacy when children are gone from home.

Although many women report no change in their sexual feelings or performance during and after menopause, certain physical changes may cause sexual problems. As the body produces less estrogen, for example, the walls of the vagina become smooth, drier, and less elastic, which may cause tiny sores on the vaginal wall, a burning or itching sensation, and uncomfortable intercourse. These physical changes can be treated successfully through a number of methods including vaginal lubricants and estrogen creams. The use of estrogen, however, depends on the nature of the problem and on whether the individual can tolerate estrogen.

Urine flows from the kidneys, through the ureters, to the bladder. Muscles surrounding the urethra normally stem the flow of urine until urination is initiated.

LOOKING AHEAD

No one has all the answers about menopause. Medical research is beginning to give us more information, but myths and negative attitudes remain deep-seated. Fortunately, more women are challenging stereotypes, gaining support from other women, learning about what takes place in their bodies, and taking more responsibility for their health.

The National Institute on Aging

URINARY INCONTINENCE

It's hard to imagine 5 million people keeping a secret. But experts estimate that's just how many older Americans suffer in secret—and, more often than not, needlessly—from urinary incontinence, or the involuntary loss of urine. And this shroud of secrecy is perpetuated by the manufacturers of adult diapers, who imply—erroneously—in their advertisements that urinary incontinence is a result of normal aging, and that diapers are the best recourse for the incontinent adult. In fact, incontinence is almost always treatable. As such, it requires an evaluation by a doctor and specific treatment, not a diaper. (Recently in New York State, two of the biggest manufacturers of adult diapers agreed to alter their advertising after the state's Attorney General demanded that the ads clearly state that incontinence should be treated by a doctor.)

A recent consensus conference of the National Institutes of Health concluded that there may be up to 10 million adult Americans, most of them older, who are incontinent. One study of a county in Michigan found that 38 percent of women and 19 percent of men over 60 suffered from incontinence. And these figures exclude nursing home residents. At least half of the 1.5 million Americans in nursing homes cannot control urination. In fact, incontinence is the second most common reason stated for admission to a nursing home—which, in part, explains why the national bill for the condition tops $10.3 billion each year. And, if left untreated, incontinence can lead to urinary tract infections, rashes, and other skin disorders. On a social level, embarrassment about odor and fear of being far from a restroom can make the incontinent person avoid outings, friends, and social activities.

Although incontinence is more prevalent among the older population, the condition is not, as myth would have it, an inevitable consequence of aging. Rather it is a symptom of some underlying disorder—and treatment for the conditions that cause incontinence can be highly successful.

A combination of techniques ranging from behavior modification to medication, and sometimes surgery, can cure or at least greatly improve the condition in 90 percent of sufferers. The first step to treatment, then, is acknowledging the problem and telling your physician about it.

CAUSES AND PROBLEMS

Control of urination, something continent people take for granted, is actually a complex synchronized process involving the kidneys, the ureters (the tubes connecting the kidneys to the bladder), the bladder itself, the urethra (the tube through which urine passes from the bladder to outside the body), and the muscles of the pelvic floor and abdominal wall.

The process of urination is coordinated by the central nervous system. Urine is produced by the kidneys, then passes into the bladder where it is stored. When the bladder, which is like a continually inflating and deflating balloon, reaches a certain degree of fullness, it signals nerves in the spinal cord. These nerves activate the voiding reflex, which causes the muscles of the bladder to contract and squeeze the urine into the urethra. However, the brain, in the toilet-training process of childhood, has learned to identify and control this reflex by tightening the muscles of the pelvic floor—a "sling" of muscles that support the bladder, urethra, and other pelvic organs—until the toilet is reached.

Disruption of nearly any part of this system can lead to incontinence. Underlying causes range from neurological problems that affect central nervous system control to anatomical abnormalities or an infection of the genital or urinary systems. Incontinence can begin suddenly (transient incontinence) or develop into a chronic condition (persistent incontinence).

Transient Incontinence

This is less common than the persistent type, and any sudden onset of incontinence should prompt a call to your physician. Most often, the problem is reversible. Common causes are infections of the genitourinary system, such as cystitis, urethritis, vaginitis; various medications, especially diuretics, sleeping pills, tranquilizers, and antidepressants; any illness that limits movement or causes confusion, such as a high fever; depression; and fecal impaction (a mass of stool in the rectum) that presses on the bladder.

Persistent Incontinence

This condition can be the outcome of untreated transient incontinence, or can gradually develop on its own. There are four patterns of persistent incontinence, although at least one-third of older patients have a combination of patterns simultaneously.

Urge incontinence is caused by difficulties suppressing the sense of bladder fullness and the subsequent urge to void. Usually, the bladder contracts involuntarily, causing such an uncontrollable need to release urine that the sufferer is unable to heed the voiding reflex in time to get to a toilet. People with urge incontinence are likely to have large-volume accidents. Central nervous system disturbances such as stroke or dementia, or a bladder problem such as a tumor can cause urge incontinence, although sometimes no underlying cause is found.

Stress incontinence is associated with problems of the urethra and the muscles of the pelvic floor. The kind of abdominal muscle contraction that occurs with sneezing, lifting, or coughing increases pressure on the bladder. In stress incontinence, the muscles surrounding the urethra are not able to resist the sudden increase in bladder pressure, so there is uncontrolled leakage of urine—usually a few drops, but occasionally a large amount. Stress incontinence is largely a women's problem, attributed to the strain of childbirth on the muscles of the pelvic floor, and the thinning of the pelvic floor muscles and other tissues in the vaginal area that can occur after estrogen levels drop following menopause.

Eighty-five percent of incontinence sufferers have stress or urge incontinence, or a combination pattern known as mixed incontinence. The two less common types of incontinence are overflow and functional.

Overflow incontinence occurs when the bladder cannot empty completely, usually due to a partial obstruction of the urethra or a drug that relaxes the bladder muscle. Even after urinating, the bladder remains full; if it becomes too full, urine leaks out through the urethra. The problem can also be caused by a dysfunction in the nerves controlling the bladder muscle or in the muscle itself, due to diabetes, injury, nervous system disorders, or drugs.

Functional incontinence develops when a person becomes unable to use the bathroom. This can be caused by a degenerative condition or illness that restricts movement, or unwillingness to use the toilet, as might occur with a psychiatric illness.

DIAGNOSTIC PROCEDURES

The most important step to the diagnosis, and subsequent treatment, of incontinence is to ask for help. Once you have informed your doctor of your problem, determining the underlying causes often only requires a simple examination that can usually be done by your internist, family physician, or gynecologist. The components of diagnosis are:

- *A detailed medical history.* Your doctor should ask very specific questions about your symptoms, including how frequently you urinate, the approximate volume of urine, how urgently you feel the need to urinate. Also, you should report all medications used.

- *Laboratory tests.* A urinalysis and culture should be performed, to check for infection or other possible diseases that might be contributing to the problem.

- *Physical examination.* Your doctor will probably do a manual rectal, genital, and abdominal exam to check for enlargement of the bladder or to identify other abnormalities that could cause incontinence.

- *Special tests.* Your doctor may perform a test to determine if the bladder is truly empty following urination. This procedure is usually done by catheterization of the bladder immediately after voiding. In a provoked full-bladder stress test, you will be asked to cough, bend over, or walk after the bladder has been filled to capacity through a catheter, to see if leakage occurs.

Most often, your medical history coupled with these procedures will be enough to determine what treatment you need. If not, or if the initial treatment plan doesn't relieve your symptoms, your physician should refer you to a specialist, usually a urologist.

THREE STEPS IN THE TREATMENT OF THE COMMON TYPES OF INCONTINENCE

Type	Behavioral Therapy	Drug Therapy	Surgery
Stress	• Muscle strengthening exercises • Biofeedback	• *Alpha adrenergic agonists* [drugs that increase sphincter strength]: pseudoephedrine, ephedrine, phenylpropanolamine (Ornade). • *Estrogens* [female hormones that increase sphincter and pelvic muscle strength].	• Vaginal sling operation (creation of a "hammock" under the urethra in order to support it). • Surgical tightening of the pelvic muscles and elevation of the bladder. • Implantation of an artificial urinary sphincter.
Urge	• Bladder training • Muscle strengthening exercises • Biofeedback	• *Anticholinergics and combination anticholinergics/antispasmodics* [drugs that reduce bladder contractions]: propantheline (ProBanthine), imipramine (Janamine, Tofranil), oxybutynin (Ditropan). • *Estrogens*	

TREATMENT OPTIONS

There are three types of treatment for urinary incontinence: behavior modification, medication, and surgery.

Generally, behavioral techniques are tried first, because they are the safest and, for many people, highly effective. Two methods are commonly used: bladder training, and exercises of the pelvic muscles (such as Kegel exercises) and bladder sphincter. Such treatments demand a commitment of time and practice. For example, Kegel exercises may need to be done for two to three months before they strengthen muscles enough to correct incontinence. Both Kegel exercises and bladder training can be done at home. Biofeedback uses sophisticated equipment that gives visual and auditory feedback to help patients identify and use their bladder-control muscles more effectively. It can thus be used to enhance bladder training and pelvic muscle exercises, and has led to complete control of incontinence in up to 25 percent of patients, and significant improvement in another 30 to 50 percent.

Also, there are a number of medications that may improve bladder control by relaxing the bladder, or by tightening the sphincter muscles and muscles of the pelvic floor. However, as with all medications, these drugs can have undesirable side effects, especially in those with other medical conditions.

Finally, surgery may be very effective for some cases of incontinence—especially pure stress incontinence in women.

The box above outlines treatment options for the two primary types of incontinence.

Several newer treatments are currently in the testing phase. For stress incontinence, the injection of collagen into the urethra is being tested as an alternative to surgery in several clinical trials around the country. The substance creates a tissuelike mass that strengthens the urethra and allows it to close fully. Also for stress incontinence, weighted vaginal cones designed to increase the effectiveness of muscle strengthening exercises are being evaluated. For urge incontinence, a new anti-spasmodic medication called Micturin, which only needs to be taken once a day, is in clinical trials.

Some of these new treatments are quite promising. However, until more long-term results on these devices and procedures are in, advertisements for a quick (and costly) fix for incontinence should be ignored as much as ads for adult diapers. "None of these newer treatments should yet be used, except in clinical trials," states Dr. John Burton, associate professor of geriatrics at Johns Hopkins. "Furthermore, the therapies currently in use are highly effective."

How to Treat Incontinence at Home

Two of the most effective methods of treating incontinence cost no money and can be done at home. Muscle strengthening exercises, such as Kegel exercises, increase the strength of the pelvic floor, which supports the base of the bladder and the bladder outlet sphincter. These exercises help with both stress and urge incontinence. To locate the proper muscles, when you are urinating, tighten up and try to stop the flow. Another technique is to tighten your anal sphincter—because of its proximity to the bladder sphincter, this helps identify muscles necessary for maintaining continence. Once you have located the correct muscles, you should practice the exercise regularly. Try to do between 15 and 20 squeezes three times a day; work up to holding each for 10 seconds. Practice during different activities, such as walking, sitting, or lying down.

Bladder training is effective for urge, stress, and mixed incontinence. Follow these steps:

- Schedule toileting every two hours, whether you have to go or not.
- Every other day, extend the interval between toileting by 30 minutes, aiming for four-hour intervals.
- If you have an urge to urinate in between your scheduled visits to the bathroom, stay still, relax, and use the muscle strengthening exercises described above. After the urge has passed, move slowly to a bathroom.
- Maintain the schedule whether you have accidents or not.
- Maintain the schedule when you are out of your home, but avoid drinking excess fluids before or while you are away from home.

The Editors

VAGINITIS

Vaginitis is an inflammation of the vagina: redness, swelling, and irritation of the vaginal tissues. It causes discharge, burning, itching, and odor. Infections of the vagina are most often the source of the problem, but other things that cause changes in the vagina can also result in vaginitis. The cause of vaginitis must be detected before it can be treated, and this often takes time. Although it is usually not serious, vaginitis can be stubbornly persistent and very uncomfortable.

Symptoms of vaginitis are a very common problem among women. Vaginitis usually affects women of childbearing age, but it can also affect young girls and older women. Some vaginal infections can be transmitted through sexual contact. These infections can affect male sexual partners of women who have the disease. Although men may show no symptoms, they can transmit such an infection. But it is not necessary to "catch" vaginitis—it can also occur without sexual contact.

Vaginitis does not pose major health problems, but it often does not go away on its own. Fortunately, medications can be very effective in treating and curing infections of the vagina. With proper treatment, according to your doctor's instructions, such infections are likely to disappear with no long-term effects. Other causes of vaginitis can also be eliminated once they are detected.

The following will help you identify some of the main causes and signs of vaginitis. It also describes the three most common types of vaginal infections as well as other causes of vaginitis. It gives suggestions for what you can do to avoid this irritating problem.

THE VAGINA

The vagina is the muscular tube leading to a woman's uterus. It is surrounded on the outside by the vulva, or external genital organs.

Vaginal Acidity

The normal vagina harbors some microscopic organisms, as does the rest of the body. Some of these organisms in the vagina break down substances in the vaginal secretions and produce an acidic environment in the vagina. The natural acid environment of the vagina keeps the number of potentially harmful organisms in check. However, any number of things can alter the vaginal acidity.

- Antibiotics prescribed for other diseases
- Douching too often
- Tampons irritating the vaginal walls
- Tight slacks
- Panties or panty hose without a cotton crotch
- Extra weight
- Diabetes
- Pregnancy
- Recent childbirth
- Birth control pills

A change in the acidity of the vagina can allow these potentially harmful organisms living in the vagina to grow rapidly. When this happens, they cause inflammation—redness, swelling, irritation—and abnormal discharge.

Not all types of vaginitis are caused by an upset in vaginal acidity, however. General resistance to infection can also be weakened by lack of sleep, poor diet, stress, or other illness. This lack of resistance can allow vaginal infections to thrive and cause inflammation. Some vaginal infections can be passed from one person to another during sexual intercourse.

Vaginal Discharge

A certain amount of discharge from the vagina is normal. Normal vaginal discharge helps to cleanse the vagina and keep it healthy. Between periods some women notice a discharge that is clear or cloudy and whitish. This normal discharge doesn't smell, itch, or burn. It also does not require any special care other than regular bathing.

Discharge caused by vaginitis is not normal. Identifying abnormal discharge is often a first step in identifying the problem. If you notice signs of abnormal discharge or itching, burning, or odor—see your doctor now.

INFORMING YOUR DOCTOR

You will need to work together with your doctor to detect the cause of the vaginitis. This often can take some time.

The doctor will need to know exactly which symptoms you have experienced. Because the physical makeup of the vaginal discharge helps in making a correct diagnosis, you should not douche or use vaginal medications just before visiting the doctor (one or two days before). He or she will examine the vagina and obtain a small sample of the vaginal discharge. This sample may be studied under a microscope or a culture may be taken so that the specific cause of the inflammation can be determined.

If the doctor detects an infection, proper medication can be prescribed. If the vaginitis has another cause, such as irritation from harsh douches, the source of the problem can be investigated.

VAGINAL INFECTIONS

Even though vaginitis is not a serious disease, the symptoms can be upsetting. Knowing the signs of vaginitis can lessen those fears and help a woman get to her doctor at the earliest stage of infection.

The following are descriptions of three common types of vaginal infections that can cause vaginitis.

Candidiasis

Candidiasis (also called fungus or yeast infection or moniliasis) is the most common type of vaginal infection that causes symptoms of irritation. It is often hard to get rid of, and recurrences are common.

Symptoms. Many women with this infection do not notice a discharge, but if it is present, it is usually described as an odorless, white, "cheesy" discharge. The main symptom of this type of inflammation is intense itching, burning, and redness of the vaginal tissues.

Causes. Candidiasis is caused by a fungus, like yeast. Although it can affect any woman, candidiasis is more frequent among women who are pregnant, diabetic, or obese. These conditions can alter the body's metabolic balance and vaginal acidity and promote the growth of the fungus.

The use of antibiotics and birth control pills also make a woman more prone to get this disorder. Antibiotics stimulate the growth of the fungus and eliminate certain protective bacteria. Birth control pills produce chemical changes in the vagina similar to those of pregnancy. In both cases, the fungus has a chance to overdevelop and cause inflammation.

Treatment. If the physical exam and lab tests reveal that candidiasis is present, your doctor will prescribe medication to destroy the fungus causing the problem. This may include vaginal suppositories or tablets or application of a cream or gel into the vagina. The medication may be somewhat messy—you may need to wear a sanitary napkin during treatment. Your doctor will advise you in detail about what is involved.

In most cases, candidiasis will be cured with treatment. However, the infection resists treatment in some women—especially pregnant and diabetic women—and a cure may take some time. Conditions that spur the growth of candidiasis will also have to be changed in order to get rid of the vaginal infection completely.

Bacterial Vaginosis

Bacterial vaginosis (formerly called Gardnerella vaginitis or nonspecific vaginitis) is a complex condition that is not understood well at present.

Symptoms. The predominant symptom of bacterial vaginosis is an increase in vaginal discharge. Often the discharge has an unpleasant or "fishy" odor. Redness and itching are rare; however, since bacterial vaginosis can occur with other types of infections, other symptoms may be present. You should see your doctor to determine the exact cause of the problem.

Causes. The cause of this infection is thought to be an overgrowth of several different types of organisms. Some of these are Gardnerella vaginalis, Mycoplasma species, and a recently discovered organism called Mobiluncus.

Treatment. Doctors usually recommend antibiotics taken by mouth for the treatment of bacterial vaginosis. A drug called metronidazole is an effective treatment. Sometimes drugs called ampicillin and amoxicillin may be used. It is not clear whether the infection can be transmitted through sexual intercourse. For this reason, your doctor may advise that your partner be treated as well.

Trichomoniasis

Trichomoniasis is the third most common type of vaginal infection. This condition affects the urinary tract as well as the vagina. As with a Gardnerella infection, both women and men can be infected.

Symptoms. A woman may have an irritating

discharge, frequently yellow-green in color. It may look frothy and have an offensive odor. The discharge can produce burning and itching, especially during urination. It also causes redness and swelling. Symptoms may be more severe just before and just after the menstrual period.

Causes. Trichomoniasis is caused by a protozoan—a one-cell organism much larger than bacteria. This type of vaginitis is usually transmitted sexually.

Treatment. Because trichomoniasis also affects the urinary tract, most doctors consider suppositories relatively ineffective in curing this condition. Metronidazole can cure almost all cases. A single large dose taken by mouth is usually effective. Sometimes smaller doses are taken over seven days. Doctors often recommend treatment for both sexual partners to avoid reinfection.

Metronidazole is effective and has relatively few complications. However, undesirable side effects (nausea, vomiting, darkening of urine) can occur and should be promptly reported to the doctor. In addition, anyone taking the drug should not drink alcohol during treatment—mixing this drug and alcohol can cause a violent reaction. Metronidazole is not recommended for use by pregnant women.

Treatment for Your Sexual Partner

Trichomoniasis is often shared by sexual partners. Successful treatment depends on getting rid of the infection in both—even though the partner may not show any symptoms. Unless both receive treatment at the same time, the infection can continue to recur.

Ideally, your partner should consult his doctor for examination and treatment. The important thing to remember is that he should be treated, even if he shows no signs of the infection. For this reason, your doctor may prescribe metronidazole for both of you. If so, your partner should contact his personal doctor before taking the medication—he needs to be sure there are no reasons for him not to take metronidazole. You and your partner should both feel free to talk about any questions or concerns with your doctor.

A Few Additional Words About Treatment

Medication depends on the type of infection—a drug used for candidiasis will not take care of trichomoniasis. Sometimes more than one type of infection is present and more than one method of treatment may have to be used.

If you are being treated for a vaginal infection, be sure to follow your doctor's instructions exactly—use any medication as directed. Even if the discharge disappears before the medication is finished, the infection may still be present. Also, if an infection does recur, go back to the doctor—it may be caused by different organisms and require different treatment.

Some doctors advise that you refrain from sex during treatment; others say you should use a condom to lessen the chance that you could become reinfected with the organisms. Each case is different, and your doctor will advise what is best for you.

OTHER CAUSES OF VAGINITIS

Vaginal inflammation is not always caused by infection. The vaginal area may have an adverse reaction to chemicals such as those used in feminine hygiene sprays or bubble baths. If injury to the vaginal walls occurs (for example, from improper tampon use), or if the outside organs are irritated by tight clothing or fabrics that don't "breathe," redness, swelling, and discharge can result. Synthetic hormones (such as birth control pills) can also alter the hormonal balance of the vagina and cause symptoms of vaginitis.

After a woman reaches menopause, the vaginal tissues are no longer stimulated by the female hormone estrogen from the ovaries. Tissue thins and becomes dry. The vagina is more prone to injury (from sexual intercourse, for example) and can more easily become irritated. Inflammation and discharge can develop. This is called atrophic vaginitis.

For atrophic vaginitis, your physician may recommend estrogen replacement therapy or the application of an estrogen cream or suppository directly to the vagina to thicken and help lubricate the tissues of the vagina. A water-soluble lubricant may also alleviate dryness, and sexual activity itself, aided by a lubricant, can improve circulation in the vagina and the elasticity of vaginal tissues.

WHAT YOU CAN DO

There are things you can do to help keep the vagina healthy. If you have recurrent vaginitis, keep in mind the following points.

- Avoid spreading bacteria from the rectum to the vagina. After a bowel movement, wipe front to back, away from the vagina.
- Clean the vulva thoroughly and keep the area as dry as possible.
- Avoid irritating agents—harsh soaps or detergents, feminine hygiene sprays, perfumed toilet paper, perfumed tampons.

- Avoid using tampons alone throughout your entire menstrual period.
- Thoroughly clean diaphragms and spermicide applicators.
- Avoid douching.
- Avoid tight jeans, panties, or panty hose without a cotton crotch, or other clothing that can trap moisture.
- Practice good general hygiene—it is important in keeping body tissue healthy to resist infection.
- Do not rely on home remedies. Home remedies or douches may appear to get rid of the problem but may only hide it.

Vaginitis affects many women at some time of their lives—perhaps one-third of all women in their childbearing years. It is unpleasant and aggravating, but it can be cured. Embarrassed silence should not keep anyone from seeing a doctor. Remember, treatment works best the earlier it is begun. With good medical care, a woman can quickly get back to her normal lifestyle without the worry of vaginitis.

The American College of Obstetricians and Gynecologists

Mental Health

The period of late adulthood generally brings with it quite a number of major life changes, including shifts in work status, social situation, and health. By age 65, for example, less than 20 percent of men, and even fewer women, are still in the work force. Not having to go to a job every morning after 40-some years of working is a relief for many—but, for some, it's hard to get used to. Learning to live on a fixed income during retirement can be stressful, too. Also in later years, some decline in physical health often sets in: Three out of four people over 65 have at least one chronic illness such as arthritis or heart disease. Furthermore, one out of every four persons over 65 lives alone. Feelings of loneliness are bound to occur after a spouse dies or when grown children move away.

Any of these major transitions can understandably affect our sense of emotional well-being. Depression, insomnia, or feelings of anxiety may develop. Fortunately, in the past several decades, more and more people have felt comfortable about seeking professional help in such circumstances. In many cases, emotional or psychiatric distress can be treated by your family physician. Appropriate therapy can significantly relieve such problems. Sometimes referral to a specialist is best.

The Editors

DEPRESSION

Everyone feels "blue" at certain times during his or her life. In fact, transitory feelings of sadness or discouragement are perfectly normal, especially during difficult times. But a person who cannot "snap out of it" or get over these feelings within two weeks may be suffering from the illness called depression.

Depression is one of the most common and treatable of all mental illnesses. In any six-month period, 9.4 million Americans suffer from this disease. One in four women and one in ten men can expect to develop it during their lifetime. Eighty to 90 percent of those who suffer from depression can be effectively treated.

Unfortunately, many fail to recognize the illness and get the treatment that would alleviate their suffering. They or their loved ones fail to notice a pattern and instead may attribute the physical symptoms to "the flu," the sleeping and eating problems to "stress," and the emotional problems to lack of sleep or improper eating.

But if people looked at all of these symptoms together and noticed that they occur over long periods of time, they might recognize them to be signs of depression.

WHAT IS DEPRESSION?

The term "depression" can be confusing since it's often used to describe normal emotional reactions. At the same time, the illness may be hard to recognize because its symptoms may be so easily attributed to other causes. People tend to deny the existence of depression by saying things like, "She has a right to be depressed! Look at what she's gone through." This attitude fails to recognize that people can go through tremendous hardships and stress without developing depression, and that those who do fall victim can and should seek treatment.

Nearly everyone suffering from depression has pervasive feelings of sadness. In addition, depressed people may feel helpless, hopeless, and irritable. For many victims of depression, these mental and physical feelings seem to follow them night and day, appear to have no end, and are not alleviated by happy events or good news. Some people are so disabled by feelings of despair that they cannot even build up the energy to call a doctor. If someone else calls for them, they may refuse to go because they are so hopeless that they think there's no point to it.

RECOGNIZING SYMPTOMS OF DEPRESSION

You should seek professional help if you or someone you know has had four or more of the following symptoms continually for more than two weeks.

• Noticeable change of appetite, with either significant weight loss not attributable to dieting or weight gain.

• Noticeable change in sleeping patterns, such as fitful sleep, inability to sleep, early morning awakening, or sleeping too much.

• Loss of interest and pleasure in activities formerly enjoyed.

• Loss of energy, fatigue.

• Feelings of worthlessness.

• Persistent feelings of hopelessness.

• Feelings of inappropriate guilt.

• Inability to concentrate or think, or inordinate difficulty making decisions.

• Recurring thoughts of death or suicide, wishing to die, or attempting suicide.

• Melancholia (defined as overwhelming feelings of sadness and grief), accompanied by waking at least two hours earlier than normal in the morning, feeling more depressed in the morning, and moving significantly more slowly.

• Disturbed thinking, a symptom developed by some severely depressed persons. For example, severely depressed people sometimes have beliefs not based in reality about physical disease, sinfulness, or poverty.

• Physical symptoms, such as stomachaches or headaches.

Family, friends, and co-workers offer advice, help, and comfort. But over time, they become frustrated with victims of depression because their efforts are to no avail. The person won't follow advice, refuses help, and denies the comfort. But persistence can pay off.

Many doctors think depression is the illness that underlies the majority of suicides in our country. Suicide is the eighth leading cause of death in America. One of the best strategies for preventing suicide is the early recognition and treatment of the depression that so often leads to self-destruction.

Depression can appear at any age. When it strikes late in life, its symptoms—including memory impairment, slowed speech, and slowed movement—may be mistaken for those of senility or stroke.

Scientists think that more than half of the people who have had one episode of major depression will have another at some point in their lives. Some victims have episodes separated by several years and others suffer several episodes of the disorder over a short period. Between episodes, they can function normally. However, 20 to 35 percent of the victims suffer chronic depression that prevents them from maintaining a normal routine.

Sadness at the loss of a loved one or over a divorce is normal, but these losses can also be the source of a depressive episode. In fact, most major environmental changes can trigger depression. Job promotions, moves to new areas, changes in living space—all can bring on depressive illness.

TYPES OF DEPRESSION

Depression strikes in several forms. When a psychiatrist makes a diagnosis of a patient's depressive illness, he may use a number of terms—such as bipolar, clinical, endogenous, major, melancholic, or unipolar—to describe it. These labels confuse many people who don't understand that they can overlap. People with depressive illness may also receive more than one diagnosis since the illness is often linked with other problems, such as alcoholism or other substance abuses, eating disorders, or anxiety disorders.

Clinical Depression

The term clinical depression means the depression is severe enough to require treatment. When a person is badly depressed during a single severe period, he or she can be said to have had an episode of clinical depression. More severe symptoms mark the period as an episode of major depression. Many mental health experts say the key to judging this gradation lies in the amount of change a person undergoes in his or her normal patterns along with a loss of interest and a lack of pleasure in them. An almost-daily tennis player, for instance, who began to break her court dates frequently, or a regular bridge player who lost interest in weekly games, might be said to be suffering with an episode of major depression. The more severe the depression, the more it is likely to affect its sufferer's life.

Dysthymia

While many people have single or infrequent episodes of severe depression, some suffer with recurrent or long-lasting depression. For these people, who seldom seem to be without at least a mild form of the illness, the diagnosis is dysthymia. A major depressive episode can hit the dysthymic person, too, causing double depression, a condition that demands careful treatment and close follow-up.

Bipolar Depression

In this type, the lows alternate with terrible highs in an often bewildering oscillation. Scientists now believe this up-and-down mood roller coaster is the product of an imbalance in the brain chemistry which can be treated successfully about 80 percent of the time with balance-restoring medications.

THEORIES ABOUT CAUSES

Medical research has contributed much to our understanding of depression. However, scientists do not know the exact mechanism that triggers depressive illness. Probably no single cause gives rise to the illness, and researchers are continuing the work of piecing the puzzle together.

Genetic Factors

Scientists now believe genetic factors play a role in some depressions. In 1987, researchers announced they had located genetic markers for susceptibility to manic-depressive disorder (bipolar affective disorder), a type of mood disorder characterized by swings between inappropriate "highs" and terrible "lows." (See Manic-Depressive Disorder, page 438.) Though they have not found the specific gene or genes for this illness, the existence of genetic markers brings scientists much closer to doing so. Moreover, researchers are much closer to understanding the biochemical reactions controlled by these genes that contribute to manic-depressive disorder.

This genetic research supports earlier studies reporting family links in depression. For example, if one identical twin suffers from depression or manic-depressive disorder, the other twin has a 70 percent chance of also having the illness. Other studies that looked at the rate of depression among adopted children supported this finding. Depressive illnesses among adoptive family members had little effect on a child's risk of depression; however, the disorder was three times more common among adopted children whose biological relatives suffered depression.

Chemical Imbalances

Additional research data indicate that people suffering from depression have imbalances of neurotransmitters, natural substances that allow brain cells to communicate with one another. Two transmitters implicated in depression are serotonin and norepinephrine. Scientists think a deficiency in serotonin may cause the sleep problems, irritability, and anxiety associated with depression. Likewise, a decreased amount of norepinephrine, which regulates alertness and arousal, may contribute to the fatigue and depressed mood of the illness.

Other body chemicals also may be altered

in depressed people. Among them is cortisol, a hormone that the body produces in response to stress, anger, or fear. In normal people the level of cortisol in the bloodstream peaks in the morning, then decreases as the day progresses. In depressed people, however, cortisol peaks earlier in the morning and does not level off or decrease in the afternoon or in the evening.

Researchers don't know if these imbalances cause the disease or if the illness gives rise to the imbalances. They do know that cortisol levels will increase in anyone who must live with long-term stress.

Other Factors

Other factors may also cause depression. For example, medications are known to cause some kinds of depression. About 30 years ago, physicians realized that some people taking reserpine, a medication for high blood pressure, developed symptoms of depression.

TREATMENTS

Depression is one of the most treatable mental illnesses. Between 80 and 90 percent of all depressed people respond to treatment. Along with the great strides made in understanding the causes of depression, scientists are closer to understanding how treatment of the illness works.

Before any treatment program begins, however, a complete evaluation is essential. Depression is a complex illness, and many factors in a depressed person's life may feed into his or her condition. For example, a number of prevalent illnesses (such as hypothyroidism or hypertension) and commonly used medications can bring on depression. An evaluation will reveal the presence of these conditions or medicines to the psychiatrist. The evaluation will also include a medical/psychiatric history that will outline the patient's physical and emotional background, and a mental status examination, to uncover changes in the patient's mood, thoughts, patterns of speech, and memory that are manifestations of depression.

The psychiatrist may also perform or order a physical exam for the patient to rule out undiagnosed medical problems that might lead to depressive illness.

Medication Therapy

Since the 1950s, physicians have learned much more about the effects of medication on depression. The effectiveness of a drug depends on a person's general health, weight, metabolism, and other characteristics unique to that patient. Medication must be used at an adequate dosage level and for a long enough time. Sometimes a psychiatrist will prescribe several medications, or will try a combination of medications to determine what works best. Generally, antidepressant drugs become fully effective within three to six weeks after a person begins taking them.

Physicians generally prescribe one of four major types of medication used to treat depression: heterocyclics, serotonin reuptake blockers, MAO inhibitors, and lithium.

Heterocyclics and serotonin reuptake blockers. The oldest of the heterocyclics, the tricyclics, and the serotonin reuptake blockers are most often prescribed for people whose depressions are characterized by fatigue; feelings of hopelessness, helplessness, and excessive guilt; inability to feel pleasure; and loss of appetite with resulting weight loss.

MAO inhibitors may be prescribed for people whose depressions are characterized by increased appetite; excessive sleepiness; and anxiety, phobic, and obsessive-compulsive symptoms in addition to the depression. These medications may also be prescribed for people whose depression has not been alleviated by other drugs.

Lithium is used for people who suffer from manic-depressive illness. It is also prescribed for people suffering from recurrent depression without mania.

Newer antidepressants have recently become available, and more are being developed. The newer drugs can help patients who either do not respond to the older tricyclics or have trouble with tricyclics' side effects.

Like medications for any other illness, antidepressants can have side effects. These may include dry mouth, blurred vision, drowsiness, lowered blood pressure, and constipation, and tend to lessen as the body adjusts to the medication.

Psychotherapies

Psychotherapy involves the verbal interaction between a trained professional and a patient with emotional or behavioral problems. The therapist applies techniques based on established psychological principles to help the patient gain insights about himself and thus change his maladaptive thoughts, feelings, and behavior. There are several forms of this "talk treatment" that have proven useful in helping the depressed person.

In the spring of 1986, scientists announced results of research into the effectiveness of short-term psychotherapy in treating depression. Their findings indicated that cognitive/behavioral therapy and interpersonal therapy were as effective as medications for depressed patients. Medications relieved the symptoms more quickly, but patients who received psychotherapy instead of medicine had as much relief from symptoms after 16 weeks.

The data from this study will help scientists better identify the depressed patients who will do best with psychotherapy alone and which patients may benefit from medications. In general, psychiatrists agree that severely depressed patients do best with a combination of medication and psychotherapy.

Interpersonal psychotherapy. This therapy is based on the theory that disturbed social and personal relationships can cause or precipitate depression. The illness, in turn, may make these relationships more problematic. The therapist helps the patient understand his or her illness and how depression and interpersonal conflicts are related.

Cognitive/behavioral therapy. This treatment approach is based on the theory that people's emotions are controlled by their views and opinions of the world. Depression results when patients constantly berate themselves, expect to fail, make inaccurate assessments of what others think of them, feel hopeless, and have a negative attitude toward the world and the future. The therapist uses various techniques of talk therapy and behavioral prescriptions to alleviate the negative thought patterns and beliefs.

Psychoanalysis. This therapy is based on the concept that depression is the result of past conflicts which patients have pushed into their unconscious. The therapist meets three to five times a week with the patient to identify and resolve the patient's past conflicts that have given rise to depression in later years.

Psychodynamic psychotherapy. Based on the principles of psychoanalysis, this therapy is less intense and often is provided once or twice a week over a shorter span of time. It is based on the premise that human behavior is determined by one's past experience, genetic endowment, and current reality. It recognizes the significant effects that emotions and unconscious motivation can have on behavior.

Electroconvulsive therapy (ECT). Scientists believe ECT works by affecting the same transmitter chemicals in the brain that are affected by medications. As more effective medications have been developed, the use of ECT for the treatment of depression has decreased. However, ECT is very effective for treating patients who cannot take medications due to heart conditions, old age, severe malnourishment, or for patients who do not respond to antidepressant medication. It can be a life-saving treatment technique that is considered when other therapies have failed or when a person is very likely to commit suicide.

Before ECT is administered, patients receive anesthesia and a muscle relaxant to protect them from physical harm and pain. Electrodes are placed on the head and a small amount of electricity is applied. This procedure is repeated two or three times a week until the patient improves or it becomes evident that further treatment will be ineffective.

Side effects of ECT are largely transitory. Some people may experience mild problems with memory of events that occurred within several months of the therapy.

In summary, medication or psychotherapy, or a combination of the two treatment methods, usually relieves symptoms of depression in weeks. Even the most severe forms of depression can respond to treatment rapidly.

The American Psychiatric Association

ANXIETY DISORDERS

Anxiety is as much a part of life as eating and sleeping. Under the right circumstances, anxiety is beneficial. It heightens alertness and readies the body for action. Faced with an unfamiliar challenge, a person is often spurred by anxiety to prepare for the upcoming event. For example, many people practice speeches and study for tests as a result of mild anxiety. Likewise, anxiety or fear is a protection from danger.

Fears are not normal, however, when they become overwhelming and interfere with daily living. They are symptoms of an anxiety disorder, the most common and most successfully treated form of mental illness.

As a group, anxiety disorders afflict 8.3 percent of Americans. Symptoms can be so severe that patients are almost totally disabled—too terrified to leave their homes, to enter the elevator that takes them to their offices, to attend parties, or to shop for food.

"Anxiety" is a word so commonly used that many people don't understand what it means in mental health care. Complicating matters is the fact that "anxiety" and "fear" are often used to describe the same thing. When the word "anxiety" is used to discuss a group of mental illnesses, it refers to an unpleasant and overriding mental tension that has no apparent identifiable cause. Fear, on the other hand, causes mental tension due to a specific, external reason, such as when your car skids out of control on ice.

THE DISORDERS

"Anxiety disorders" refers to a group of illnesses: generalized anxiety disorder, phobias, panic disorders, obsessive-compulsive disorders, and post-traumatic stress disorder. When people suffering from anxiety disorders talk about their condition, they often include these descriptions: shakiness; trembling; muscle aches; sweating; cold/clammy hands; dizziness; jitteriness; tension; fatigue; racing or pounding heart; dry mouth; numbness/tingling of hands, feet, or other body part; upset stomach; diarrhea; lump in throat; and high pulse and/or breathing rate.

In addition, people suffering from anxiety disorders are often apprehensive and worry that something bad may happen to themselves or loved ones. They often feel impatient, irritable, and easily distracted.

Phobias

This type of anxiety disorder afflicts between 5.1 and 12.5 percent of all Americans. People who suffer from this illness feel terror, dread, or panic when confronted with the feared object, situation, or activity.

Many have such an overwhelming desire to avoid the source of fear that it interferes with their jobs, family life, and social relationships. They may lose their jobs because they can't go to business lunches for fear of eating in front of others. They may quit a job in a high-rise office building to work on the ground floor because they fear elevators. They may become so fearful of leaving their homes that they live like hermits with their window shades down for added protection.

The following are common phobias.

Social phobia is the fear of situations in which the victim can be watched by others, such as public speaking, or in which the victim's behavior might prove embarrassing, such as eating in public, going to parties, or talking to strangers. It begins in late childhood or early adolescence.

Simple phobia is the fear of specific objects or situations that cause terror. The condition can begin at any age. Examples are fear of snakes, fear of flying, or fear of closed spaces.

Agoraphobia is the fear of being alone in a public place that has no escape hatch (such as a public bus or crowded store). This is the most disabling phobia because victims can become housebound.

Panic Disorders

Panic disorders afflict 1.2 million Americans. Victims suddenly suffer intense, overwhelming terror for no apparent reason. The fear is accompanied by at least four of the following symptoms: sweating; heart palpitations; hot or cold flashes; trembling; feelings of unreality; choking or smothering sensations; shortness of breath; chest discomfort; faintness; unsteadiness; tingling; fear of losing control, dying, or going crazy.

Often, people suffering a panic attack for the first time rush to the hospital, convinced they are having a heart attack.

Sufferers can't predict when the attacks will occur, although certain situations, such as driving a car, can become associated with

them if it was in those situations where the first attack occurred.

Obsessive-Compulsive Disorders

Obsessive-compulsive disorders (OCD) afflict 2.4 million Americans. Victims attempt to cope with their anxiety by associating it with obsessions, defined as repeated, unwanted thoughts, or through compulsive behaviors, defined as rituals that themselves get out of control. People who suffer from obsessive disorders do not automatically have compulsive behaviors. However, most people who go through compulsive, ritual behaviors also suffer from obsessions.

The key problem in OCD is the inability to feel certain about things, no matter how hard a person tries or how many times they may repeat actions to make sure. Victims of OCD are plagued with involuntary, persistent thoughts or impulses that are distasteful to them and that they feel will get out of control or cause harm to someone.

The most common obsessions focus on hurting others or violating socially acceptable behavior standards such as swearing or making sexual advances. They also can focus on religious or philosophical issues, which the patient never resolves.

People with compulsions go through senseless, repeated and ritualistic behaviors that are supposed to prevent or produce a future event. Sometimes the rituals themselves have nothing to do with that event. For example, patients may do things a certain number of times to get a desired result.

Examples of compulsive rituals include the following.

- *Cleaning,* which affects women more often than men. If victims come in contact with any dirt, they may spend hours washing and cleaning even to the point that their hands bleed. Often, people with this disorder also suffer from a complementary obsession such as worries over infection.

- *Repeating a behavior,* such as saying a loved one's name several times whenever that person comes up in conversation.
- *Checking,* which tends to affect men more than women. For example, victims check and recheck that doors are locked or electric switches, gas ovens, and water taps are turned off. Other patients will retrace a route they have driven to check that they did not hit a pedestrian or cause an accident without knowing it.

Obsessive-compulsive disorders often begin during the teens or early adulthood. Generally they are chronic and cause moderate to severe disability in their victims.

Post-Traumatic Stress Disorder (PTSD)

Often associated with war veterans, post-traumatic stress disorder can occur in anyone who has survived a severe and unusual physical or mental trauma.

People who have witnessed a midair collision or survived a life-threatening crime may develop this illness. The severity of the disorder increases if the trauma was unanticipated. For that reason, not all war veterans develop PTSD, despite prolonged and brutal combat. Soldiers expect a certain amount of violence. Rape victims, however, are unsuspecting of the attack on their lives.

People who suffer from PTSD re-experience the event that traumatized them in the following ways.

- Nightmares, night terrors, or flashbacks of the event. In rare cases, the person falls into a temporary dislocation from reality in which he relives the trauma. This can last for seconds or days.
- "Psychic numbing," or emotional anesthesia. Victims have decreased interest in or involvement with people or activities they once enjoyed.
- Excessive alertness and highly sharpened startle reaction. A car backfiring may cause

people once subjected to gunfire to instinctively drop to their stomachs.
- General anxiety, depression, inability to sleep, poor memory, difficulty concentrating or completing tasks, survivor's guilt.

THEORIES ABOUT CAUSES

Probably no single situation or condition causes anxiety disorders. Rather, physical and environmental triggers may combine to create a particular anxiety illness.

Biochemical Imbalances

Recent research suggests that biochemical imbalances are the culprits. Studies indicate, for instance, that infusions of certain chemicals can trigger panic attacks in some people. Scientists involved in this research believe that physicians treating anxiety disorders should work first to correct these biochemical imbalances. Though medication has a front-line role in this treatment, studies show that biochemical changes also come about as a result of the emotional, psychological, or behavioral changes produced through psychotherapy.

The Learning Theory

This theory says that anxiety is a learned behavior that can be unlearned. People who feel uncomfortable in a given situation or near a certain object will begin to avoid it. However, such avoidance can limit a patient's ability to live a normal life. Patients learn that their anxiety is reduced by persistently confronting the feared situation or object.

Psychoanalytic Theory

This theory suggests that anxiety stems from unconscious conflicts that arose from discomfort during infancy or childhood. For example, a person may carry the unconscious conflict of sexual feelings toward the parent of the opposite sex. Or the person may have developed problems from experiencing an illness, fright, or other emotionally laden event as a child. By this theory, anxiety can be resolved by identifying and resolving the unconscious conflict. The symptoms that symbolize the conflict would then disappear.

No doubt each of these theories is true to some extent. A person may develop or inherit a biological susceptibility to anxiety disorders. Events in childhood may lead to certain fears that, over time, develop into a full-blown anxiety disorder.

TREATMENTS

Generally psychiatrists treat anxiety disorders with a combination of psychotherapy and medication.

Medication

Psychiatrists use several types of medications to reduce the worst of their anxiety disorder patients' symptoms. The patient can then get the most benefit from a variety of psychotherapeutic techniques. Psychiatrists use three general classes of medication in their work with these patients: medications designed especially for anxiety disorders, antidepressants, and other medications.

The specially designed antianxiety medications include both benzodiazepines and nonbenzodiazepine antianxiety medicines. Psychiatrists also use antidepressants in treating anxiety disorders, including tricyclic antidepressants, monoamine oxidase (MAO) inhibitors and other antidepressant medications. Lastly, psychiatrists treat anxiety disorders with medicines that do not fit into either of the preceding categories, such as the beta-blockers and several medications used to treat psychoses.

Psychotherapy

With their symptoms lessened, anxiety disorder sufferers are better able to profit from various psychotherapies. Those with phobias and obsessive-compulsive disorders often are treated with behavior therapy. This involves exposing the patient to the feared object or situation under controlled circumstances, until fear lessens or disappears. After this treatment many phobia patients have long-term recovery.

Psychiatrists also use other psychotherapeutic techniques to help their patients deal with the consequences of their illness and any other problems that may exist side-by-side with and often hidden by it. Talking issues out and exploring their roots in psychodynamic psychotherapy can be crucial in some cases.

Before psychiatrists begin any form of treatment, they work carefully with their patients to custom tailor the treatment plan that includes the medications and psychotherapies that will answer each patient's needs. And there is good reason for optimism about treatment of even the most severe anxiety disorders. Medication helps about half of those suffering from obsessive-compulsive disorder. And research indicates that 90 percent of the phobic and obsessive-compulsive patients who can cooperate with the behavior therapist and conscientiously follow instructions will improve with that form of therapy. Studies have shown that while they are taking the medications, 60 to 80 percent of the patients who suffer from panic attacks do very well and up to 95 percent improve.

The American Psychiatric Association

MANIC-DEPRESSIVE DISORDER

Manic-depressive illness, known in medical terms as bipolar illness, is the most distinct and dramatic of the depressive or affective disorders. Unlike major depression, which can occur at any age, manic-depressive illness generally strikes before the age of 35. Nearly one in 100 people will suffer from the disorder at some time in their lives.

People with bipolar illness differ from those with other depressive disorders in that their moods swing from depression to mania, generally with periods of normal mood between the two extremes. The length of this cycle, from towering elation to near despair, varies from person to person.

SYMPTOMS

Manic Phase

When patients first suffer a manic phase, they feel a rather sudden onset of elation or euphoria that increases in a matter of days to a serious impairment. Symptoms of the manic phase include the following.

- *A mood that seems excessively good, euphoric, or expansive.* The patient feels "on top of the world," and nothing—bad news, horrifying event, or tragedy—will change his happiness. However, this euphoria can quickly change into irritability or anger. In either case, the mood is way out of bounds, given the situation and the individual's personality.
- *Expressions of unwarranted optimism and lack of judgment.* Self-confidence reaches the point of grandiose delusions in which the person thinks he has a special connection with God, celebrities, or political leaders. Or he may think that nothing—not even the laws of gravity—can stop him from accomplishing any task. As a result, he may think he can step off a building or out of a moving car without being hurt.
- *Hyperactivity and excessive plans or participation in numerous activities that have a good chance for painful results.* He becomes so enthusiastic about activities or involvements that he fails to recognize he hasn't enough time in the day for all of them. For example, he may book several meetings, parties, deadlines and other activities in a single day, thinking he can make all of them on time. Added to the expansive mood, mania also can result in reckless driving, spending sprees, foolish business investments, or sexual behavior unusual for the person.
- *Flight of ideas.* The person's thoughts race uncontrollably like a car without brakes careening down a mountain. When the person talks, his words come out in a non-stop rush of ideas that abruptly change from topic to topic. In its severe form, the loud, rapid speech becomes hard to interpret because the patient's thought processes become so totally disorganized and incoherent.
- *Decreased need for sleep,* allowing the patient to go with little or no sleep for days without feeling tired.
- *Distractibility* in which the patient's attention is easily diverted to inconsequential or unimportant details.
- *Sudden irritability, rage, or paranoia* when the person's grandiose plans are thwarted or his excessive social overtures are refused.

Untreated, the manic phase can last as long as three months. As it abates, the patient may have a period of normal mood and behavior. But eventually the depressive phase of the illness will set in. In some, depression occurs immediately or within the next few months. But with other patients there is a long interval before the next manic or depressive episode.

Depressive Phase

The depressive phase has the same symptoms as major or unipolar depression.

- Feelings of worthlessness, hopelessness, helplessness, total indifference, and/or inappropriate guilt; prolonged sadness or unexplained crying spells; jumpiness or irritability; withdrawal from formerly enjoyable activities, social contacts, work, or sex.
- Inability to concentrate or recall details.
- Thoughts of death or suicide attempts.

439

- Loss of appetite or noticeable increase in appetite; persistent fatigue and lethargy, insomnia, or noticeable increase in the amount of sleep needed.
- Aches and pains, constipation, or other physical ailments that cannot be otherwise explained.

THEORIES ABOUT CAUSES

Genetic Factors

Recent studies into the roots of bipolar illness have centered on genetic research. Scientists believe these studies will eventually help them identify the genetic culprits that cause manic-depressive illness in its various forms among different populations. This research will also help psychiatrists to understand the biochemical reactions that are controlled by these genes and that contribute to the disorder.

Close relatives of people suffering from bipolar illness are 10 to 20 times more likely to develop either depression or manic-depressive illness than the general population. In fact, between 80 and 90 percent of people suffering from manic-depressive disorder have relatives who suffer from some form of depression.

If one parent suffers from manic-depressive illness, a child has a 30 percent risk of suffering from a depressive disorder; if both parents suffer from manic-depressive illness, the children have a 75 percent chance of developing a depressive disorder.

Environmental Factors

Other studies hint that environmental factors may contribute to the illness. Psychoanalytic studies suggest that such environmental factors as difficult family relationships may aggravate manic-depressive illness.

Chemical Imbalances

Still other studies suggest that imbalances in the biochemistry controlling a person's mood could contribute to manic-depressive illness.

For example, people suffering from either manic-depressive disorder or major depression often respond to certain hormones or steroids in a way that indicates they have irregularities in their hormone production and release. Some research points to the possibility that bipolar patients' neurotransmitters—chemicals by which brain cells communicate—become imbalanced during various phases of the disease.

Finally, some people suffering from depressive illnesses have sleep patterns in which the dream phase begins earlier in the night than normal. These studies indicate that manic-depressive illness and major depression may be caused by biochemical imbalances. Such research also helps develop scientific theories about how medications work, and offers hope that psychiatrists some day will use laboratory tests to identify unipolar or bipolar illnesses.

DIAGNOSIS

Anyone who suspects they or a loved one suffers from manic-depressive illness should receive a complete medical evaluation to rule out any other mental or physical disorders. Many other physical and mental disorders can mimic manic-depressive illnesses. A person with symptoms of manic depression could be reacting to substances such as amphetamines or steroids or could suffer from thyroid, liver or kidney problems, or other illnesses, such as multiple sclerosis. A comprehensive medical and psychiatric evaluation by a qualified psychiatrist or other physician is vital to an accurate diagnosis. With this diagnosis a psychiatrist can then work with the patient to design the right treatment plan.

TREATMENT

Though manic-depressive disorder can become disabling, it is also among the most treatable of the mental illnesses. The combination of psychotherapy and medications returns the vast majority of manic-depressive patients to happy, functioning lives.

Medication

The most common medication, lithium carbonate, successfully reduces the number and intensity of manic episodes for 70 percent of those who take the medication. Twenty percent of those who use lithium become completely free of symptoms. Those who respond best to lithium are patients who have a family history of depressive illness and who have periods of relatively normal mood between their manic and depressive phases. In recent years, psychiatrists have also been successful with several medications—such as carbamazepine and valproic acid—in treating those for whom lithium is not effective.

Very effective in treating the manic phase, lithium also appears to prevent repeated episodes of depression. One theory for this is that in controlling the mania, lithium helps prevent the swing into depression.

Lithium works by bringing various neurotransmitters in the brain into balance. Scientists think the medication may affect the impact neurotransmitters have on the brain cells, thus altering moods.

Like all medications, lithium can have side effects and must be carefully monitored by a psychiatrist. The physician should measure the level of lithium in the patient's blood and determine how well the patient's kidneys and thyroid gland are working. Among the side effects are weight gain, excessive thirst and urination, stomach and intestinal irritation, hand tremors, and muscular weakness. If a patient overdoses on medication, it may cause confusion, delirium, seizures, coma, and may result, rarely, in death.

However, when properly monitored, lithium, sometimes used with other medications, has returned thousands of people to happy, functioning lives that would not be possible without medication.

Psychotherapy

Like all serious illnesses, manic-depressive disorders disrupt a person's self-esteem and relationships with others, especially with spouses and family. Without treatment, people with the illness may risk consequences such as financial and occupational disintegration, or even suicide. Because of these consequences of their illness, people under treatment for manic-depressive disorder also benefit from psychotherapy.

The patient and the psychiatrist work out the problems created by the disorder and re-establish the relationships and healthy self-image that have been shaken by the illness. In many cases, a patient needs the psychiatrist's support to ensure that he complies with the treatment plan.

Family members of manic-depressive patients also may benefit from professional care. This illness can cause serious disruptions of the family's life, as the stresses of living with a person suffering from manic depression are intense. Not only may family members learn coping strategies from the psychiatrist but they can also learn to be an active part of the treatment team.

The American Psychiatric Association

SLEEP DISORDERS

Like changes in hair color, vision, and other signs of aging, the "graying" of sleep usually develops gradually. Aging makes sleep more fragile even in extremely healthy older people.

Earlier in life, most of us fell asleep fast and could sleep through a thunderstorm. As we grow older, we may find it harder to settle down. Most of us awaken more often and take longer to fall back to sleep. The honk of a car horn or bark of a neighbor's dog down the street may be enough to rouse us. During the day, we doze off more easily, when watching TV, for example, or reading the newspaper.

Persistent trouble falling asleep at night is not, however, normal or inevitable at any age. Nor is frequently falling asleep in the daytime.

Normal age-related changes frequently mask recognition of sleep disorders that become more common with advancing years. Medical or psychiatric illnesses, particularly those involving pain or depression, go hand-in-hand with sleep disorders. Sleep specialists often cannot tell which comes first.

More than half of all people aged 65 and older experience disturbed sleep, according to a panel of experts convened by the National Institutes of Health in 1990 to develop consensus on the treatment of sleep disorders of older people. Insomnia is the most common problem.

The overuse of both prescription drugs and over-the-counter medications to aid sleep in older people worries physicians and other health professionals. While people over age 65 constitute about 13 percent of the American population, they consume more than 30 percent of prescription drugs and 40 percent of all sleeping pills. Yet recent studies show that some commonly used drugs may not work well in older people or may even make their sleep problems worse.

Such concerns fuel further research into how sleep changes as we grow older and how to improve both sleep and daytime alertness in the later years. Sleep experts say there are many steps you can take to improve your sleep and to maintain healthy, restful sleep as you grow older. New understanding also benefits those who need professional help.

WHAT HAPPENS TO SLEEP AS WE GET OLDER?

It's a myth that we need less sleep as we grow older. But it's a fact that most of us sleep less at a single stretch than we did when we were younger. Our bodies become less adept at sustaining sleep.

On the other hand, it's easier to nap during the daytime. Fortunately, we also often have more time to nap than we did in earlier years. Recent research suggests our bodies were designed for at least one afternoon nap a day. Only late in life, freed from constraints of a 9-to-5 work place and societal attitudes that frown on napping, can we let ourselves do what comes naturally.

As we grow older, we get less of the deeper stages of sleep and more of the lighter ones. We also awaken more often. We spend about the same amount of time in dreaming sleep during adulthood, well into old age.

Sleep laboratory studies show that the number of awakenings colors our perception of the quality of our sleep. People in their sixties and older awaken for a few seconds an astounding 150 times a night. By contrast, young adults awaken briefly about five times. Even though transient awakenings usually go unremembered in the morning, they may create the subjective impression of fitful nights. Moreover, most people over age 65 awaken more fully at least once a night for a trip to the bathroom.

WHAT PROBLEMS ARE MOST COMMON?

Some people focus on trouble with sleep, and others on trouble with mood or performance during the day.

Trouble Falling Asleep

Trouble falling asleep sometimes stems from simple, easily correctable causes, such as consuming caffeine or a heavy meal or exercising too late in the day. It may be the aftermath of hospitalization, recovery after surgery, or travel. It may flare up during times of worry or smolder under persistent stress.

In the quiet of the bedroom, some people find their minds race and worries overwhelm them. The solution here: Set aside another time as "worry" time, when you can write down both problems and possible solutions. At bedtime, focus on sleep-inducing situations. Imagine, for example, basking in the sun on a beach after lunch.

The hours we keep program our bodies for sleeping and waking at the same time the following day. If you still work, particularly if you frequently change your hours of work and sleep, you probably have noticed that it takes longer to adapt to schedule changes. The older we become, the harder it is for the body to adapt to irregular hours. If you travel frequently across time zones, you may find jet lag lasts longer than it used to.

If you lead a sedentary lifestyle, particularly if you have restricted mobility, you may doze more during the day than you suspect. People with insomnia prove less active during the day than those who are better sleepers. A 1988 Gallup survey found that active retirees had fewer sleep problems than those who were less active. Try to confine sleep to nighttime or nap time.

Sleep Apnea

Some people who feel lethargic during the day don't suspect that anything is wrong with their sleep. Or they may find sleep unsatisfactory without being able to pinpoint the nature of the problem. Disturbed breathing, known as sleep apnea, may trigger both day and night complaints. It disrupts sleep in varying degrees in an estimated one out of every four people aged 60 and over.

In some cases, disturbed breathing is obvious to bed partners or others. The sleeper snores raucously. The snoring reflects partial blockage of the airway during sleep. Snoring increases with age and usually is more of a nuisance to others than a medical problem.

A particular type of snoring, however, demands a visit to the doctor. Such snoring follows a crescendo pattern, with each breath becoming louder. It ends with a loud gasp before the pattern then repeats. Or it may involve loud snorts with gasping.

With each gasp, the person awakens, although usually too briefly to remember doing so in the morning. Some people with this problem, obstructive sleep apnea, awaken hundreds of times a night. As a result, they feel excessively drowsy during the daytime. Indeed, some sleep specialists think sleep apnea may contribute to difficulty thinking and concentrating during waking hours that is often blamed on dementia.

Weight loss and sleeping on one's side may be helpful. Severe obstructive sleep apnea may require surgery or use of mechanical devices that keep the airway open.

People with central sleep apnea may or may not snore excessively. When respiratory muscles fail to work properly, sleepers may sigh frequently or appear to breathe shallowly. In the morning, they may remember the frequent awakenings and complain of light and fragmented sleep. When this problem is severe, medication or use of oxygen may prove helpful.

Interrupted Sleep

Not only is the sleep process less robust as we get older, but we also are more likely to develop chronic medical illnesses that interfere with sleep. Asthma and other lung diseases, heart disease, and arthritis are notorious offenders. Pain, fever, itching, and coughing often contribute to insomnia. Many drugs that are necessary to treat these problems also disrupt sleep.

Talk with your doctor; sometimes adjusting the timing or amount of medication brings about substantial improvement. Paying attention to sleep habits and using relaxation techniques may help, too. Some people benefit from having sleeping pills on hand for occasional use when they feel desperate.

Early Awakening

Waking too early may represent a "rebound" from use of alcohol at bedtime or even from certain types of sleeping pills.

It also is a hallmark symptom of depression, a disorder that becomes more common as we grow older. Some people sink into depression gradually. Feeling blue eventually becomes a chronic way of living. Others focus on poor sleep, telling themselves and others, "Life would be much better if only I could get a decent night's sleep."

They also may not be eating regularly or may have lost their usual interest and pleasure in activities of daily life. Loss of a loved one commonly triggers insomnia and depression. Surveys show that more than three-quarters of the bereaved report trouble sleeping a month after the death of a spouse. One year later, half still report persistent sleep problems.

Often a concerned family member or friend may have to take the initiative in making an appointment with the doctor. Fortunately, most cases of depression respond well to a variety of drugs, along with counseling. Sleep improves as mood brightens.

Advanced Sleep Phase Syndrome (ASPS)

The tendency to be "early to bed and early to rise" increases as we grow older. Most of us adapt successfully. But some of us find that our bodies say, "It's bedtime," earlier than we desire, often well before 9 p.m.

Known as the advanced sleep phase syndrome or ASPS, this problem can wreak havoc with social life. Additionally, it's hard to find oneself awake for hours when most other people are still asleep.

Most people with ASPS try numerous strategies to help them stay up late. Even if they succeed in pushing bedtime later, however, they may not be able to sleep any later because their body clocks still awaken them in the early morning hours.

One solution is chronotherapy, literally, "time therapy." For ASPS, this involves following a schedule of prescribed bedtimes that move backwards around the clock in, for example, three-hour intervals every two days, until reaching the desired bedtime. Regular

hours from then on help maintain the new bedtime and wake time. With chronotherapy, a 65-year-old man moved his bedtime from 7 p.m. to 11 p.m. He then slept later in the morning, too.

A newer treatment, still under investigation, involves exposure in the evening to artificial lights several times brighter than ordinary room lights. Recent studies show such lights may shift both bedtime and arising time to later, more desirable, hours.

Periodic Limb Movements

Perhaps half of all people aged 65 and over experience twitching in the legs, and sometimes arms, during the night. These muscle jerks may occur infrequently or as often as once or twice each minute for an hour or two at a time. This disorder, known as periodic limb movements or PLM, seldom awakens the sleeper fully, but it understandably prevents sound sleep.

When it is mild, a person may be unaware of any impact on sleep or daytime functioning. When it is moderate, sleepers often complain of insomnia, reporting restless nights and waking to find bed sheets in disarray. When it is more severe, people often feel excessively sleepy during the day.

Many people with PLM during sleep experience "restless legs" when awake, a peculiar crawling sensation in calves or thighs that occurs when they are sitting or lying down. A variety of medications can ease these problems. Such behavior challenges the traditional view of sleep as a time of rest.

Dream Disturbances

Some people literally act out their dreams. They may crash into furniture, break windows, or fall down stairs, often injuring themselves and sometimes others as well.

Ordinarily the body lies virtually paralyzed during dreaming sleep (called REM sleep for the rapid eye movements that accompany it). But this normal paralysis vanishes in people

GUIDELINES FOR SLEEPING WELL

The following measures will help you to sleep well and feel alert during the day.

• *Get up about the same time every day, regardless of when you go to bed.* Recent research suggests that lingering in bed a short while in the morning eases the transition between sleep and waking and improves alertness in older people.

• *Go to bed only when sleepy.* Establish relaxing presleep rituals, such as a warm bath, light bedtime snack, or watching the news on TV.

• *Keep active.* Exercise regularly, and as vigorously as you can in the late afternoon. Two or three hours before bedtime, take a walk or do some simple stretching.

• *Organize your day.* Regular times for meals, taking medicines, performing chores, and other activities help keep inner clocks running smoothly. Spend time outdoors, particularly in the afternoon, when weather permits; recent studies suggest that regular exposure to bright light also helps synchronize body clocks. People with certain types of sleep and mood disorders may benefit from use of artificial lights several times brighter than ordinary room lights. A sleep specialist will tell you if this treatment is appropriate for you.

• *Avoid caffeine within six hours of bedtime.* Don't drink alcohol or smoke at bedtime.

• *Use alcohol sparingly, especially when sleepy.* Even a small dose of alcohol will have a much more potent effect when you are sleepy.

• *If you nap, try to nap at the same time each day.* Midafternoon is best for most people.

• *Use sleeping pills conservatively.* Most doctors seldom prescribe them for use every night or for longer than three weeks. Current recommendations call for taking a sleeping pill for a night or two, then skipping a night or two or longer if you sleep better. Don't take a sleeping pill after drinking alcohol.

with the REM sleep behavior disorder. Most are men over age 50, a finding that suggests aging plays a contributory role. Fortunately, the drug clonazepam improves sleep in people with this problem and eliminates the dream disturbances.

OTHER COMPLICATIONS

Seventy percent of care givers cite sleep disturbances, wandering, and confusion, sometimes called "sundowning," as a factor in their decision to institutionalize an elderly person. Most care givers report their charges' problems disrupt their own sleep, too.

Two-thirds of those living in long-term care facilities suffer sleep disturbances. In a nursing home or hospital, nocturnal problems typically continue or increase, prompting widespread use of tranquilizing drugs. The drugs in turn may contribute to further confusion and an increased likelihood of falls.

Some specialists in the field believe that sleep disorders, particularly those of breathing, may contribute to a significant proportion of reversible dementias. They urge family physicians, internists, and others to rule out sleep disorders when evaluating an elderly person afflicted with nocturnal symptoms.

WHEN TO SEE THE DOCTOR

If you sleep poorly for a month or more, or if you find that sleepiness during the day interferes with normal tasks, see your family doctor or internist or ask your doctor to refer you to a sleep disorders specialist. Your medical history, along with a physical exam and laboratory tests, such as those of hormone function, may help identify certain disorders. Ask your bed partner or other members of your household whether you snore loudly or kick or flail around. Let the doctor know.

When you make an appointment at a sleep center, you may be asked to log your sleep and waking patterns for a week or two before your visit. At the sleep center, expect a comprehensive physical and psychological exam.

You may be asked to spend a night or two having your sleep monitored, sometimes the only way to uncover a disorder that occurs only during sleep. Before you go to bed, technicians will position dime-sized sensors at various places on head and body to record brain waves, muscle activity, leg and arm movements, heart rhythms, breathing, and other bodily functions while you sleep. These monitoring devices cause little or no discomfort and will not hamper your movements during the night. Sleep specialists will compare the results from your night in the lab against norms for healthy people of all ages.

The specialists also may wish to study your sleep during the day by asking you to try to nap at two-hour intervals. The speed with which people fall asleep on this test, known as the multiple sleep latency test, documents the extent of daytime sleepiness.

Although evaluation at a sleep center may run $1,000 or more a night because of the many specialists involved, most medical insurance polices and Medicare cover this expense when it is medically indicated. Researchers are working to devise less costly alternatives, such as in-home sleep monitoring, now undergoing testing.

CAN SLEEPING PILLS HELP?

Although sleeping pills are used mostly by the elderly, and more often by women than men, they are tested mainly in young men. Doctors say many uncertainties remain about how sleeping pills and other drugs affect older people of both sexes. As we grow older, we metabolize and excrete drugs less efficiently than when we were younger. Because drugs stay in the body longer, their effects may last longer, too. Drowsiness—desirable at bedtime—is not welcome when you awaken to go to the bathroom during the night or when you drive a car the next day.

Ideally, a sleeping pill would help you fall asleep faster and awaken less often, with no "hangover" the next day. The most commonly prescribed sleeping pills, members of the benzodiazepine chemical family, come in both shorter- and longer-acting forms.

The shorter-acting drugs help induce and solidify sleep, but they usually wear off faster. The longer-acting drugs help maintain sleep through the night, but they sometimes cause sleepiness the next day. Your doctor will try to tailor the type of drug and the particular dose to your individual needs. Shorter-acting drugs commonly used to aid sleep include triazolam (Halcion) and temazepam (Restoril). A longer-acting drug is flurazepam (Dalmane).

Sleeping pills you can buy without a prescription, known as over-the-counter or OTC drugs, get their drowsiness-inducing effect from antihistamines. Like prescription sleep aids, they may cause sleepiness the next day. They require similar caution.

Warning: A complaint of insomnia sometimes signals disturbed breathing during sleep. If you have this problem, it may be a mistake to use sleeping pills. They may make interruptions in breathing occur more often and last longer. If you have more than occasional bad nights, see your doctor before using any drug for sleep.

Be wary of using multiple drugs. One 81-year-old woman entered the hospital for gallstone surgery. On learning that she had taken barbiturates nightly for years and felt "going to sleep" meant "taking a pill," her doctor switched her to a safer benzodiazepine. After she returned home, she became agitated and irritable. Another doctor prescribed a tranquilizer. Meanwhile, she continued a longtime habit, consumption of an evening vodka martini. The result: confusion, forgetfulness, and depression. Once doctors suspected that her medicines might be the culprit and stopped them, she rapidly returned to her former alert self.

The American Sleep Disorders Association

DIRECTORY TO THE AMERICAN MEDICAL CARE SYSTEM

CONTENTS

Using the Directory

Your own physician will doubtless be able to refer you to the care of a specialist if you need one. But if you have just moved into a new community and your previous physician had no recommendations for you, or if a friend recommends a physician to you, you might well consult the following list of medical specialty (and subspecialty) boards. These boards can refer you to a board certified physician in your area. You can also find out whether a physician is board certified by contacting the appropriate specialty board directly or by calling the American Board of Medical Specialties Verification Center at 800-776-2378. Descriptions of the specialties covered in the Directory are included after the list of boards.

Certification is not required for a licensed physician to practice a specialty. And certification by a medical specialty board is not a guarantee of excellence; in fact, there are many excellent physicians who are not board certified. But a board certified physician has taken and passed a written exam, thereby demonstrating a certain amount of knowledge to other specialists practicing in the same field.

The boards might refer you to a "board eligible" physician. Physicians who have met a board's requirements but have not yet passed the written test are called "board eligible." Those who have passed the test are called "board certified."

Another way to find a good physician is to ask for a referral from one of the Academic Medical Center Hospitals that are members of the Association of American Medical Colleges' Council of Teaching Hospitals. Look for these hospitals in the list of Teaching Hospitals by Disorder. The names of the Academic Medical Center Hospitals are printed in bold. Those with an asterisk are nonprofit and privately owned.

If you do not live close to one of these hospitals, you might ask the nearest one for the name of a physician who trained there and who now lives in or near your community.

The health information organizations listed in the Directory will sometimes make referrals, so you should also check with them.

MEDICAL SPECIALTY BOARDS WITH SUBSPECIALTIES

American Board of Allergy and Immunology
University City Science Center
3624 Market St.
Philadelphia, PA 19104
215-349-9466

American Board of Anesthesiology
100 Constitution Plaza
Hartford, CT 06103
203-522-9857
Subspecialties include:
Pain Management.

American Board of Colon and Rectal Surgery
20600 Eureka Rd., Suite 713
Taylor, MI 48180
313-282-9400

American Board of Dermatology
Henry Ford Hospital
2799 W. Grand Blvd.
Detroit, MI 48202
313-871-8739

American Board of Emergency Medicine
200 Woodland Pass, Suite D
East Lansing, MI 48823
517-332-4800

American Board of Family Practice
2228 Young Dr.
Lexington, KY 40505
606-269-5626
Subspecialties include:
Geriatric Medicine.

American Board of Internal Medicine
University City Science Center
3624 Market St.
Philadelphia, PA 19104
215-243-1500
Subspecialties include:
Cardiovascular Disease, Endocrinology and Metabolism, Gastroenterology, Geriatric Medicine, Hematology, Infectious Diseases, Medical Oncology, Nephrology, Pulmonary Disease, Rheumatology.

The American Board of Medical Specialties
One Rotary Center, Suite 805
Evanston, IL 60201-4889
708-491-9091

**American Board of
Neurological Surgery**
Smith Tower, 6550 Fannin St.
Suite 2139
Houston, TX 77030-2701
713-790-6015

**American Board of
Nuclear Medicine**
900 Veteran Ave., Rm. 12-200
Los Angeles, CA 90024-1786
310-825-6787

**American Board of Obstetrics
and Gynecology**
936 N. 34th St.
Seattle, WA 98056
206-547-4884
Subspecialties include:
Gynecologic Oncology.

American Board of Ophthalmology
111 Presidential Blvd., Suite 241
Bala Cynwyd, PA 19004
215-664-1175

**American Board of
Orthopaedic Surgery**
737 N. Michigan Ave.
Suite 1150
Chicago, IL 60611
312-664-9444
Subspecialties include:
Hand Surgery.

American Board of Otolaryngology
5615 Kirby Dr., Suite 936
Houston, TX 77005
713-528-6200

American Board of Pathology
PO Box 25915
5401 W. Kennedy Blvd.
Tampa, FL 33622-5915
813-286-2444
Subspecialties include:
Blood Banking/Transfusion Medicine.

**American Board of Physical
Medicine and Rehabilitation**
Nor'west Center, Suite 674
21 First St., SW
Rochester, MN 55902
507-282-1776

American Board of Plastic Surgery
7 Penn Center, Suite 400
1635 Market St.
Philadelphia, PA 19103-2204
215-587-9322
Subspecialties include:
Hand Surgery.

**American Board of
Preventive Medicine**
2222 Philadelphia Dr.
Dayton, OH 45406
513-278-6915

**American Board of Psychiatry
and Neurology**
500 Lake Cook Rd., Suite 335
Deerfield, IL 60015
708-945-7900
Subspecialties include:
Geriatric Psychiatry, Clinical
Neurophysiology.

American Board of Radiology
2301 W. Big Beaver Rd.
Suite 625
Troy, MI 48084
313-643-0300

American Board of Surgery
1617 John F. Kennedy Blvd.
Suite 860
Philadelphia, PA 19103-1847
215-568-4000
Subspecialties include:
Surgery of the Hand, General
Vascular Surgery.

**American Board of
Thoracic Surgery**
One Rotary Center, Suite 803
Evanston, IL 60201
708-475-1520

American Board of Urology
31700 Telegraph Rd., Suite 150
Bingham Farms, MI 48025
313-646-9720

DESCRIPTIONS OF THE MEDICAL SPECIALTIES

The basic training of a physician specialist includes four years of premedical education in a college or university, four years of medical school, and, after receiving the M.D. degree, at least three years of specialty training under supervision (called a "residency").

Specialists are doctors who concentrate on certain body systems, specific age groups, or on complex scientific techniques developed to diagnose or treat particular types of disorders. Specialties in medicine have developed because of the rapidly expanding body of knowledge about health and illness and the constantly evolving new treatment techniques for disease.

A subspecialist is a physician who has com-pleted training in a general medical specialty and then takes additional training in a more specific area of that specialty, called a "subspecialty." This training serves to increase the depth of knowledge of the specialist in that particular field.

Resident physicians dedicate themselves for three to seven years to full-time experience in a hospital or ambulatory care setting, caring for patients under the supervision of experienced teaching specialists. Educational conferences and research experience are also part of that training. A doctor in training to be a specialist is called a "resident," although the first year of residency used to be called an "internship."

In each state, the privilege to practice medicine is governed by state law and is not designed to recognize the knowledge and skills of a trained specialist. Specialty boards certify physicians only as having met certain published standards.

Allergy/Immunology

An allergist/immunologist is a certified internist or pediatrician expert in the evaluation, physical and laboratory diagnosis, and management of disorders potentially involving the immune system. Selected examples of such conditions include asthma, anaphylaxis, rhinitis, eczema, urticaria, and adverse reactions to drugs, foods, and insect stings as well as immune deficiency diseases (both acquired and congenital), defects in host defense, and problems related to autoimmune disease, organ transplantation, or malignancies of the immune system.

Anesthesiology

The anesthesiologist is a physician-specialist who, following medical school graduation and at least four years of postgraduate training, has the principal task of providing pain relief and maintenance, or restoration of a stable condition during and immediately following an operation or an obstetric or diagnostic procedure.

The anesthesiologist assesses the risk of the patient undergoing surgery and optimizes the patient's condition prior to, during, and after surgery.

Anesthesiologists direct resuscitation in the care of patients with cardiac or respiratory emergencies, including the provision of artificial ventilation.

Colon and Rectal Surgery

As a result of their extensive training and experience, colon and rectal surgeons develop the knowledge and skills necessary to diagnose and treat various diseases of the intestinal tract, colon, rectum, anal canal, and perianal area by medical and surgical means. They are also able to deal surgically with other organs and tissues (such as the liver, urinary, and female reproductive systems) involved with primary intestinal disease.

Dermatology

A dermatologist is a physician who has expertise in the diagnosis and treatment of pediatric and adult patients with benign and malignant disorders of the skin, mouth, external genitalia, hair, and nails, as well as a number of sexually transmitted diseases. Dermatologists have extensive training and experience in the diagnosis and treatment of skin cancers, melanomas, moles, and other tumors of the skin, contact dermatitis and other allergic and nonallergic disorders and in the recognition of the skin manifestations of systemic (including internal malignancy) and infectious diseases.

The dermatologist also has expertise in the management of cosmetic disorders of the skin such as hair loss and scars.

Internal Medicine

The general internist is a personal physician who provides long-term, comprehensive care in the office and the hospital, managing both common illnesses and complex problems for adolescents, adults, and the elderly. General internists are trained in the essentials of primary care internal medicine, which incorporates an understanding of disease prevention, wellness, substance abuse, mental health, and effective treatment of common problems of the eyes, ears, skin, nervous system, and reproductive organs.

Care by an internist is characterized by extensive knowledge and skill in diagnosis and treatment, by the humanistic qualities of integrity, support, sensitivity, and compassion, and by personal commitment to patients.

Well-trained internists are unique in their ability to deliver care with great professional expertise and often act as consultants to other specialists. Internists can subspecialize in the following areas:

Cardiovascular Disease: Cardiologists subspecialize in diseases of the heart, lungs, and blood vessels and manage complex cardiac conditions such as heart attacks and life-threatening abnormal heartbeat rhythms. They often perform complicated diagnostic procedures such as cardiac catheterization and consult with surgeons on heart surgery.

Endocrinology and Metabolism: The endocrinologist concentrates on disorders of the internal (endocrine) glands such as the thyroid and adrenal glands. Endocrinology also deals with disorders such as diabetes, metabolic and nutritional disorders, pituitary diseases, and menstrual and sexual problems.

Gastroenterology: The subspecialty of the digestive organs involves the stomach, bowels, liver, and gallbladder. The gastroenterologist treats conditions such as abdominal pain, ulcers, diarrhea, cancer, and jaundice. Gastroenterologists perform complex diagnostic and therapeutic procedures using lighted scopes to see internal organs.

Geriatric Medicine: The internist certified in geriatric medicine has special knowledge of the aging process and special skills in the diagnostic, therapeutic, preventive, and rehabilitative aspects of illness in the elderly. Geriatricians are trained to recognize the unusual presentations of illness and drug interactions. Some examples of common geriatric conditions are incontinence, falls, Parkinson's disease, Alzheimer's disease, and other dementias.

Hematology: Hematologists subspecialize in diseases of the blood, spleen, and lymph glands. They treat conditions such as anemia, clotting disorders, sickle cell disease, hemophilia, leukemia, and lymphoma. They perform special types of transfusions and biopsy the bone marrow for analysis.

Infectious Diseases: These subspecialists deal with infectious diseases of all types and in all organs. Conditions requiring selective use of antibiotics call for this special skill.

Medical Oncology: The medical oncologist specializes in the diagnosis and treatment of all types of cancer and other benign and malignant tumors. These subspecialists decide on and administer chemotherapy for malignancy as well as consult with surgeons and radiotherapists on other treatment for cancer.

Nephrology: The nephrologist is concerned with disorders of the kidneys, high blood pressure, fluid and mineral balance, dialysis of body wastes when the kidneys do not function, and consultation with surgeons about kidney transplantation.

Pulmonary Disease: Pulmonary disease is the subspecialty concerned with diseases of the lungs and airways. The pulmonologist diagnoses and treats pneumonia, cancer, pleurisy, asthma, occupational diseases, bronchitis, sleep disorders, emphysema, and other complex disorders of the lungs.

Rheumatology: The rheumatologist is concerned with diseases of the joints, muscles, bones, and tendons. The rheumatologist diagnoses and treats arthritis, back pain, muscle strains, common athletic injuries, and "collagen" diseases.

Neurological Surgery

Neurological surgery is a discipline of medicine and that specialty of surgery which deals with the diagnosis, evaluation, and treatment of disorders of the central, peripheral, and autonomic nervous systems, including their supporting structures and vascular supply; and the evaluation and treatment of pathological processes which modify function or activity of the nervous system, including the hypophysis.

Neurology

The neurologist is concerned with the diagnosis and treatment of all categories of disease or impaired function of the brain, spinal cord, peripheral nerves, muscles, and autonomic nervous system, as well as the blood vessels that relate to these structures.

Obstetrics and Gynecology

Obstetrician/gynecologists are physicians who, by virtue of satisfactory completion of a defined course of graduate medical education and appropriate certification, possess special knowledge, skills, and professional capability in the medical and surgical care of the female reproductive system and associated disorders, such that it distinguishes them from other physicians and enables them to serve as consultants to other physicians and as primary physicians for women.

Ophthalmology

Ophthalmologists have the knowledge and professional skills needed to provide comprehensive eye and vision care. They are the only practitioners medically trained to diagnose, monitor, and medically or surgically treat all eyelid and orbital problems affecting the eye and visual pathways and to diagnose, monitor, and treat all eye disorders. In so doing, they often prescribe vision services (glasses and contact lenses). The ophthalmologist also serves as a consultant to physicians and other professionals.

Orthopedic Surgery

Orthopedic surgery is the medical specialty that includes the preservation, investigation, and restoration of the form and function of the extremities, spine, and associated structures by medical, surgical, and physical means.

Otolaryngology

An otolaryngologist provides comprehensive medical and surgical care of patients with diseases and disorders that affect the ears, the respiratory and upper alimentary systems, and related structures—the head and neck in general.

Physical Medicine and Rehabilitation

Physical medicine and rehabilitation, also referred to as rehabilitation medicine, is the medical specialty concerned with diagnosing, evaluating, and treating patients with impairments and/or disabilities which involve musculoskeletal, neurologic, cardiovascular, or other body systems.

Psychiatry

A psychiatrist is a physician who specializes in the prevention, diagnosis, and treatment of mental, addictive, and emotional disorders, e.g., psychoses, depression, anxiety disorders, substance abuse disorders, developmental disabilities, sexual dysfunctions, adjustment reactions, etc.

Radiation Oncology

Radiation oncology is that branch of radiology which deals with the therapeutic applications of radiant energy and its modifiers and the study and management of disease, especially malignant tumors.

Surgery

A general surgeon is a specialist prepared to manage a broad spectrum of surgical conditions affecting almost any area of the body. The surgeon establishes the diagnosis and provides the preoperative, operative, and postoperative care to surgical patients and is usually responsible for the comprehensive management of the trauma victim and the critically ill.

Hand Surgery: A surgeon with special qualifications in the management of surgical disorders of the hand.

Vascular Surgery: A surgeon with special qualifications in the management of surgical disorders of the blood vessels, excluding

454

those immediately adjacent to the heart, lungs, or brain.

Thoracic Surgery

Thoracic surgery encompasses the operative, perioperative, and critical care of patients with pathologic conditions within the chest. Included is the surgical care of coronary artery disease, cancers of the lung, esophagus, and chest wall, abnormalities of the great vessels and heart valves, congenital abnormalities, tumors of the mediastinum, and diseases of the diaphragm.

Urology

A urologist is competent to manage benign and malignant medical and surgical disorders of the adrenal gland and of the genitourinary system. These subspecialists have comprehensive knowledge of, and skills in, endoscopic, percutaneous, and open surgery of congenital and acquired conditions of the reproductive and urinary systems and their contiguous structures.

Descriptions excerpted from Which Medical Specialist for You *by the American Board of Medical Specialties*
Revised 9/90

FINDING THE RIGHT HOSPITAL

Your doctor is your best resource for finding the right hospital. He is familiar with many of the hospitals in your community and will know about others through colleagues. If you do not have a regular doctor, talk to the physician who made your diagnosis. Ask her about the hospitals that she knows.

Where you go for treatment depends on your illness and the kind of surroundings that make you feel comfortable. Hospitals vary enormously in size and in the level of personalized care that they can deliver (the latter depends more on the nursing staff than anything else). Some treatments are well carried out in the setting of your community hospital, whereas others should be handled by the expertise of an Academic Medical Center Hospital.

If your illness does not require the cutting edge of technology or highly trained specialists, and if a doctor that you trust is affiliated with one, then you might consider a community hospital. This will make it easier for friends and family to visit often and will give you the reassurance of being close to home.

Expertise and experience of staff and the latest equipment for diagnostics and treatment are what recommend a large teaching hospital. For a physician to remain on the staff of a teaching hospital, she must be eminently qualified. And should she need consultation on an unusual problem, it is likely that one of the leading experts in the field is already on staff. Teaching hospitals treat a wide range of disorders every day, so their personnel are familiar with disorders or conditions that a small community hospital might only see a few times a year. Teaching hospitals also have much more experience in carrying out procedures done infrequently in a community hospital.

The research conducted at a teaching hospital can play an important role in the outcome of a patient's treatment. The same staff that will be treating you will, through their research, also have access to the latest in diagnostics, drugs, and treatments. But do not choose a hospital just because it does research. Keep in mind that research centers are funded for the quality of their research and not necessarily for the quality of their patient care.

The lists in the Directory provide a good place to start looking for a teaching hospital. Each hospital shown participates in either a Graduate Medical Education Program accredited by the Accreditation Council for Graduate Medical Education or an Advanced Dental Educational Program accredited by the American Dental Association's Commission on Dental Education. There are two ways to look: by location or by disorder. The list of Teaching Hospitals by State and City allows you simply to look up what hospitals are in your area. Under each listing you will find the hospital's name, address, phone number, and selected specialties for which it has a medical education program. For explanations of what each medical specialty covers, see page 451.

The list of Teaching Hospitals by Disorder will give you the names of the hospitals that have teaching programs related to the disorders covered in the Handbook. To guide you, the hospitals are arranged by state, then by name. Once you have located a hospital from this listing, you can find its address and phone number in the geographic listing. Because any number of teaching specialties could qualify a hospital for inclusion under one of the disorders, check the list of teaching specialties under the hospital's listing to see if it has the specific specialty that you need.

The Teaching Hospitals by Disorder section also identifies in bold type those hospitals that are among the 121 Academic Medical Center Hospitals in the United States. The Academic Medical Center Hospitals are designated by the Association of American Medical Colleges' Council of Teaching Hospitals. This means that the hospital must meet the following criteria: have a signed affiliation agreement with a medical school accredited by the Liaison Committee on Medical Education, be a non-Federal member of the council under either common ownership with a medical school or closely associated to one through its chiefs of service, and provide a short-stay, general hospital service.

An asterisk identifies the Academic Medical Center Hospitals that are nonprofit and privately owned, which, as a group, scored best on factors predicting good outcomes and had the lowest mortality rates per hospital stays in a recent study done by the New England Journal of Medicine.

Hospitals that are associated with treatment centers currently funded by the National Institutes of Health are marked by the symbol ▼ or † or ■ under certain disorders in the list of Teaching Hospitals by Disorder. Heart and liver transplant centers approved by Medicare are shown in italic type.

One final note: Remember that medical centers are often spread out over a wide area, so before you visit, call to get the exact location of the department you need.

FINDING A DENTAL CARE FACILITY

Chances are your dentist can provide all the care that you will ever need. But there might come a time when you will want a second opinion or might require a procedure unusual enough that your dentist would prefer to send you to a facility that has the extensive experience necessary for the best outcome.

Included in the list of Teaching Hospitals by State and City are those dental schools, hospitals, and organizations that run Advanced Dental Educational Programs accredited by the American Dental Association's Commission on Dental Education. These facilities will have "Dentistry" listed in their teaching specialties.

In the section called Health Information and Support Organizations by Disorder, you will find a listing of a number of organizations that you can contact for more information on your particular disorder. There are also dental certification boards included in the organizations list should you wish to find out whether a dentist has been board certified.

Before calling any of the dental education programs, talk to your dentist. She will probably already know the right place for you to go for the second opinion or procedure. If she has more than one name to choose from or if you wish to do some additional checking on your own, sit down with her and work out a list of questions that you should use when contacting these programs for more information. They should be aimed at finding out how much experience they have with your problem. Also, do not forget that, just as in medical surgery, there are other specialists that may be required in order to perform your procedure (such as anesthesiologists). Be sure to find out about their training too.

In general, your best bets are dental education programs that are affiliated with a den-tal or medical school. Although it is true that some good programs happen not to have such an affiliation, you will find that those that do have the widest experience in even uncommon dental disorders. The smaller programs tend to work in just a few specialties. When considering a small dental education program, check to see if its director is full-time and still actively practices dentistry. This makes it more likely that the program itself is up-to-date and professional.

Two notes on using this list: Hospitals with dental education programs have their main phone number listed, so when you call, ask for their dental education department. Also, remember that medical centers are often spread out over a wide area, so before you visit, call to get the exact location of the department you need.

FINDING A HEALTH INFORMATION ORGANIZATION

Health information organizations vary greatly in what services they can provide. The smallest can send you literature on a specific illness. The major ones can do everything from keeping you up-to-date on the latest progress in treatment, to making referrals to physicians or hospitals, to helping you locate a support group.

Because you want reliable health-related information, finding a good organization requires some careful checking. Start with your physician and ask him if he can recommend a health information organization for you to contact.

The Health Information and Support Organizations in the Directory are listed either by the disorders covered in the Handbook or in a "general" section. If you use the "by disorder" list and have trouble deciding which organization to call, start with the ones that provided material for the corresponding chapter in the Handbook. If they cannot help you directly, they should still be able to tell you who can.

The Federal Government provides a referral service called the Office of Disease Prevention and Health Promotion National Health Information Center at PO Box 1133, Washington, D.C. 20013-1133, phone: 800-336-4797 or 301-565-4167. Using their database, staff members can find a health information organization to help you, or they can answer questions about what a particular health information organization does.

Another way to find a health information organization is to ask for a referral from one of the listed Academic Medical Center Hospitals. Look for these hospitals under your disorder in the list of Teaching Hospitals by Disorder. The Academic Medical Center Hospitals are in bold. Those in bold with an asterisk are nonprofit and privately owned.

Sometimes medical treatment can only do so much. You may feel the need to address the personal aspect of your illness as well. Many people in difficult situations find that meeting with other people in the same predicament can be very helpful. Self-help or support groups can provide you with a sense of community, reinforcing the knowledge that you are not alone, that there are others who understand what you are feeling.

In the Health Information and Support Organizations section of the Directory, the organizations listed under "Support Groups" in Organizations by Disorder are nonprofit national support groups, without marketing ties to the health industry, that can provide you with information on how to contact one of their local offices. If you do not find a support group geared to your specific disorder in the "by disorder" lists, look in General Organizations under "National Self-Help Clearinghouses" or "Regional Self-Help Clearinghouses." These organizations operate at the state and national level and can tell you if there is a support group nearby that can help.

Just as in searching for a hospital or health information organization, check with your physician to see what she knows about the groups that you have found and whether she can suggest any. You might also try calling one of the health information organizations or Academic Medical Center Hospitals (these are the hospitals in bold type listed in the Teaching Hospitals by Disorder section). The Office of Disease Prevention and Health Promotion National Health Information Center can also provide you with information on support groups. They can be reached at PO Box 1133, Washington, D.C. 20013-1133, phone: 800-336-4797 or 301-565-4167.

One caveat: These groups are social entities. As a whole, they will have an agenda and a certain perspective on issues relating to their specialty. Keep this in mind when you contact a group. If you do not feel at ease with the people in the group, then there is no reason to stay. Remember, if you feel a certain way, there are bound to be countless others who feel exactly as you do, so the right group for you does exist.

Teaching Hospitals

To find a hospital in this section look under the state then city where it is located. Each listing shows the name of the hospital, its main address, its phone number, and selected medical specialties for which it has an education program.

To find a hospital that has medical education programs that correspond to one of the disorders covered in the Handbook, turn to page 514 for the list of Teaching Hospitals by Disorder.

ALABAMA

Birmingham

Baptist Medical Center-Montclair
800 Montclair Rd.
Birmingham, AL 35213
205-592-1000
Teaching Specialties:
Internal Medicine, Surgery.

Baptist Medical Center-Princeton
701 Princeton Ave., SW
Birmingham, AL 35211
205-783-3000
Teaching Specialties:
Internal Medicine, Surgery.

Carraway Methodist Medical Center
1600 N. 26th St.
Birmingham, AL 35234
205-226-6000
Teaching Specialties:
Anesthesiology, Internal Medicine, Obstetrics/Gynecology, Surgery.

Cooper Green Hospital
1515 6th Ave. S
Birmingham, AL 35233
205-934-7900
Teaching Specialties:
Anesthesiology, Internal Medicine, Obstetrics/Gynecology, Ophthalmology, Orthopedic Surgery, Surgery, Urology.

Eye Foundation Hospital
1720 University Blvd.
Birmingham, AL 35233
205-325-8100
Teaching Specialties:
Ophthalmology.

Lloyd Noland Hospital and Ambulatory Center
701 Lloyd Noland Parkway
Birmingham, AL 35064
205-783-5121
Teaching Specialties:
Surgery.

University of Alabama Hospitals
619 S. 19th St.
Birmingham, AL 35233
205-934-4011
Teaching Specialties:
Anesthesiology, Dermatology, Hand Surgery, Internal Medicine, Internal Medicine-Cardiovascular Disease, Internal Medicine-Endocrinology and Metabolism, Internal Medicine-Gastroenterology, Internal Medicine-Geriatric Medicine, Internal Medicine-Hematology, Internal Medicine-Infectious Diseases, Internal Medicine-Medi-

cal Oncology, Internal Medicine-Nephrology, Internal Medicine-Rheumatology, Neurological Surgery, Neurology, Obstetrics/Gynecology, Ophthalmology, Orthopedic Surgery, Otolaryngology, Physical Medicine and Rehabilitation, Psychiatry, Radiation Oncology, Surgery, Thoracic Surgery, Urology.

University of Alabama School of Dentistry
UAB Station
Birmingham, AL 35294
205-934-3000
Teaching Specialties:
Dentistry.

Mobile

University of South Alabama Medical Center
2451 Fillingim St.
Mobile, AL 36617
205-471-7000
Teaching Specialties:
Anesthesiology, Internal Medicine, Internal Medicine-Cardiovascular Disease, Internal Medicine-Hematology, Internal Medicine-Infectious Diseases, Internal Medicine-Medical Oncology, Neurology, Obstetrics/Gynecology, Ophthalmology, Orthopedic Surgery, Psychiatry, Surgery.

Montgomery

Baptist Medical Center
2105 E. South Blvd.
Montgomery, AL 36111
205-288-2100
Teaching Specialties:
Internal Medicine.

Humana Hospital-Montgomery
301 S. Ripley St.
Montgomery, AL 36104
205-269-8000
Teaching Specialties:
Internal Medicine.

Mt. Vernon

Searcy Hospital
PO Box 1001
Mt. Vernon, AL 36560
205-829-9411
Teaching Specialties:
Psychiatry.

ARIZONA

Phoenix

**Good Samaritan Regional
Medical Center**
1111 E. McDowell Rd.
Phoenix, AZ 85006
602-239-2000
Teaching Specialties:
Internal Medicine, Internal Medicine-Cardio-
vascular Disease, Obstetrics/Gynecology,
Psychiatry, Surgery.

Maricopa Medical Center
2601 W. Roosevelt St.
Phoenix, AZ 85008
602-267-5011
Teaching Specialties:
Anesthesiology, Internal Medicine, Neurolog-
ical Surgery, Obstetrics/Gynecology,
Orthopedic Surgery, Psychiatry, Surgery.

**St. Joseph's Hospital
and Medical Center**
350 W. Thomas Rd.
Phoenix, AZ 85013
602-285-3000
Teaching Specialties:
Internal Medicine, Obstetrics/Gynecology.

**St. Joseph's Hospital
and Medical Center**
Barrow Neurological Institute
350 W. Thomas Rd.
Phoenix, AZ 85013
602-285-3196

Teaching Specialties:
Neurological Surgery, Neurology.

Tucson

Carondelet St. Joseph's Hospital
1601 W. St. Mary's Rd.
Tucson, AZ 85732
602-296-3211
Teaching Specialties:
Ophthalmology.

Kino Community Hospital
2800 E. Ajo Way
Tucson, AZ 85713
602-573-2815
Teaching Specialties:
Dermatology, Internal Medicine, Internal
Medicine-Endocrinology and Metabolism,
Internal Medicine-Gastroenterology,
Obstetrics/Gynecology, Ophthalmology,
Psychiatry, Surgery.

Tucson Medical Center
5301 E. Grant Rd.
Tucson, AZ 85712
602-327-5461
Teaching Specialties:
Internal Medicine, Neurology, Surgery.

University Medical Center
1501 N. Campbell Ave.
Tucson, AZ 85724
602-694-0111
Teaching Specialties:
Anesthesiology, Dermatology, Internal
Medicine, Internal Medicine-Cardiovascular
Disease, Internal Medicine-Endocrinology
and Metabolism, Internal Medicine-Gastroen-
terology, Internal Medicine-Hematology,
Internal Medicine-Infectious Diseases,
Internal Medicine-Medical Oncology,
Internal Medicine-Nephrology, Internal
Medicine-Rheumatology, Neurology, Obstet-
rics/Gynecology, Ophthalmology, Orthope-
dic Surgery, Psychiatry, Radiation Oncology,
Surgery, Surgery-Vascular Surgery,
Thoracic Surgery, Urology.

ARKANSAS

Little Rock

Arkansas State Hospital
4313 W. Markham St.
Little Rock, AR 72205
501-686-9000
Teaching Specialties:
Psychiatry.

**Baptist Rehabilitation Institute
of Arkansas**
9601 Interstate 630, Exit 7
Little Rock, AR 72205

501-223-7578
Teaching Specialties:
Physical Medicine and Rehabilitation.

University Hospital of Arkansas
4301 W. Markham St.
Little Rock, AR 72205
501-686-7000
Teaching Specialties:
Anesthesiology, Dermatology, Internal
Medicine, Internal Medicine-Cardiovascular
Disease, Internal Medicine-Endocrinology
and Metabolism, Internal Medicine-Gastroen-
terology, Internal Medicine-Geriatric
Medicine, Internal Medicine-Hematology,
Internal Medicine-Infectious Diseases,
Internal Medicine-Medical Oncology, Inter-
nal Medicine-Nephrology, Internal Medicine-
Rheumatology, Neurological Surgery, Neurol-
ogy, Obstetrics/Gynecology, Ophthalmology,
Orthopedic Surgery, Otolaryngology, Physical
Medicine and Rehabilitation, Psychiatry,
Surgery, Surgery-Vascular Surgery,
Thoracic Surgery, Urology.

CALIFORNIA

Anaheim

Kaiser Foundation Hospital
441 N. Lakeview Ave.
Anaheim, CA 92807
714-978-4000
Teaching Specialties:
Internal Medicine-Geriatric Medicine,
Otolaryngology.

Bakersfield

Kern Medical Center
1830 Flower St.
Bakersfield, CA 93305
805-326-2000
Teaching Specialties:
Internal Medicine, Obstetrics/Gynecology,
Surgery.

Camarillo

**Camarillo State Hospital and
Development Center**
PO Box 6022, 1878 S. Lewis Rd.
Camarillo, CA 93011
805-484-3661
Teaching Specialties:
Psychiatry.

Culver City

Didi Hirsch Psychiatric Service
4760 S. Sepulveda Blvd.
Culver City, CA 90230
213-390-6612
Teaching Specialties:
Psychiatry.

Daly City

Seton Medical Center
1900 Sullivan Ave.
Daly City, CA 94015
415-992-4000
Teaching Specialties:
Orthopedic Surgery, Radiation Oncology.

Downey

**Los Angeles County-Rancho
Los Amigos Medical Center**
7601 E. Imperial Highway
Downey, CA 90242
213-940-7022
Teaching Specialties:
Internal Medicine-Infectious Diseases,
Orthopedic Surgery, Otolaryngology.

Duarte

**City of Hope National
Medical Center**
1500 E. Duarte Rd.
Duarte, CA 91010
818-359-8111
Teaching Specialties:
Radiation Oncology.

Fairfield

**Solano County Mental
Health Clinic**
1125 Missouri St., Suite 1000
Fairfield, CA 94533
707-421-6620
Teaching Specialties:
Psychiatry.

Fontana

Kaiser Foundation Hospital
9961 Sierra Ave.
Fontana, CA 92335
714-829-5000
Teaching Specialties:
Obstetrics/Gynecology, Surgery,
Thoracic Surgery.

Fresno

Valley Medical Center of Fresno
445 S. Cedar Ave.
Fresno, CA 93702
209-453-4000
Teaching Specialties:
Dentistry, Internal Medicine, Internal
Medicine-Cardiovascular Disease, Obstetrics/Gynecology, Psychiatry, Surgery.

Glendale

Glendale Adventist Medical Center
1509 Wilson Terrace
Glendale, CA 91206
818-409-8000
Teaching Specialties:
Obstetrics/Gynecology.

Greenbrae

Community Mental Health Services
250 Bonair Rd.
Greenbrae, CA 94904
415-499-6835
Teaching Specialties:
Psychiatry.

Hayward

Kaiser Foundation Hospital
27400 Hesperian Blvd.
Hayward, CA 94545
415-784-4000
Teaching Specialties:
Urology.

Inglewood

Centinela Hospital Medical Center
555 E. Hardy St.
Inglewood, CA 90307
213-673-4660
Teaching Specialties:
Orthopedic Surgery.

La Jolla

Green Hospital of Scripps Clinic
10666 N. Torrey Pines Rd.
La Jolla, CA 92037
619-455-9100
Teaching Specialties:
Allergy/Immunology, Internal Medicine,
Internal Medicine-Cardiovascular Disease,
Internal Medicine-Endocrinology and
Metabolism, Internal Medicine-Gastroenterology, Internal Medicine-Hematology, Internal
Medicine-Medical Oncology, Internal
Medicine-Rheumatology.

Loma Linda

**Loma Linda University
Medical Center**
PO Box 2000, 11234 Anderson St.
Loma Linda, CA 92354
714-824-4302
Teaching Specialties:
Anesthesiology, Dermatology, Hand Surgery,
Internal Medicine, Internal Medicine-Cardiovascular Disease, Internal Medicine-Gastroenterology, Internal Medicine-Nephrology, Internal Medicine-Rheumatology, Neurological
Surgery, Neurology, Obstetrics/Gynecology,
Ophthalmology, Orthopedic Surgery, Otolaryngology, Physical Medicine and Rehabilitation, Psychiatry, Radiation Oncology,
Surgery, Surgery-Vascular Surgery,
Thoracic Surgery, Urology.

**Loma Linda University
School of Dentistry**
Loma Linda, CA 92350
714-796-0141
Teaching Specialties:
Dentistry.

Long Beach

**Long Beach Memorial
Medical Center**
2801 Atlantic Ave.
Long Beach, CA 90806
213-595-2311
Teaching Specialties:
Internal Medicine, Internal Medicine-Cardiovascular Disease, Internal Medicine-Geriatric Medicine, Obstetrics/Gynecology,
Ophthalmology, Physical Medicine and Rehabilitation, Radiation Oncology, Surgery.

St. Mary Medical Center
1050 Linden Ave.
Long Beach, CA 90801
213-491-9000
Teaching Specialties:
Internal Medicine, Internal Medicine-Cardiovascular Disease, Surgery.

Los Angeles

**California Medical Center-
Los Angeles**
1401 S. Grand Ave.
Los Angeles, CA 90015
213-748-2411
Teaching Specialties:
Obstetrics/Gynecology, Radiation Oncology,
Surgery.

Cedars-Sinai Medical Center
PO Box 48750, 8700 Beverly Blvd.
Los Angeles, CA 90048
213-855-5000
Teaching Specialties:
Dentistry, Internal Medicine, Internal
Medicine-Cardiovascular Disease, Internal
Medicine-Endocrinology and Metabolism,
Internal Medicine-Gastroenterology, Internal
Medicine-Hematology, Internal Medicine-Infectious Diseases, Internal Medicine-Medical Oncology, Internal Medicine-Nephrology,
Internal Medicine-Rheumatology, Obstetrics/Gynecology, Physical Medicine and
Rehabilitation, Psychiatry, Surgery.

Century City Hospital
2070 Century Park E
Los Angeles, CA 90067

213-553-6211
Teaching Specialties:
Hand Surgery.

Hospital of the Good Samaritan
616 S. Witmer St.
Los Angeles, CA 90017
213-977-2121
Teaching Specialties:
Thoracic Surgery.

Kaiser Foundation Hospital
4867 Sunset Blvd.
Los Angeles, CA 90027
213-667-8100
Teaching Specialties:
Allergy/Immunology, Internal Medicine, Internal Medicine-Cardiovascular Disease, Internal Medicine-Gastroenterology, Internal Medicine-Hematology, Internal Medicine-Infectious Diseases, Internal Medicine-Nephrology, Neurology, Obstetrics/Gynecology, Radiation Oncology, Surgery, Urology.

Kaiser Foundation Hospital-West Los Angeles
6041 Cadillac Ave.
Los Angeles, CA 90034
213-857-2200
Teaching Specialties:
Internal Medicine.

Los Angeles County-King-Drew Medical Center
12021 S. Wilmington Ave.
Los Angeles, CA 90059
213-603-5201
Teaching Specialties:
Anesthesiology, Dentistry, Dermatology, Internal Medicine, Internal Medicine-Cardiovascular Disease, Internal Medicine-Gastroenterology, Internal Medicine-Infectious Diseases, Obstetrics/Gynecology, Ophthalmology, Orthopedic Surgery, Otolaryngology, Psychiatry, Surgery.

Los Angeles County-University of Southern California Medical Center
1200 N. State St.
Los Angeles, CA 90033
213-226-2622
Teaching Specialties:
Allergy/Immunology, Anesthesiology, Dentistry, Dermatology, Internal Medicine, Internal Medicine-Cardiovascular Disease, Internal Medicine-Endocrinology and Metabolism, Internal Medicine-Gastroenterology, Internal Medicine-Hematology, Internal Medicine-Infectious Diseases, Internal Medicine-Medical Oncology, Internal Medicine-Nephrology, Internal Medicine-Rheumatology, Neurological Surgery, Neurology, Obstetrics/Gynecology, Ophthalmology, Orthopedic Surgery,

Otolaryngology, Psychiatry, Radiation Oncology, Surgery, Thoracic Surgery, Urology.

Orthopaedic Hospital
2400 S. Flower St.
Los Angeles, CA 90060
213-742-1000
Teaching Specialties:
Orthopedic Surgery.

St. Vincent Medical Center
2131 W. 3rd St.
Los Angeles, CA 90057
213-484-7111
Teaching Specialties:
Internal Medicine-Cardiovascular Disease, Internal Medicine-Nephrology.

University of California at Los Angeles Medical Center
10833 LeConte Ave.
Los Angeles, CA 90024
310-825-9111
800-825-2631 physician referral
Teaching Specialties:
Allergy/Immunology, Anesthesiology, Dermatology, Hand Surgery, Internal Medicine, Internal Medicine-Cardiovascular Disease, Internal Medicine-Endocrinology and Metabolism, Internal Medicine-Gastroenterology, Internal Medicine-Geriatric Medicine, Internal Medicine-Hematology, Internal Medicine-Infectious Diseases, Internal Medicine-Medical Oncology, Internal Medicine-Nephrology, Internal Medicine-Rheumatology, Neurological Surgery, Neurology, Obstetrics/Gynecology, Orthopedic Surgery, Otolaryngology, Radiation Oncology, Surgery, Surgery-Vascular Surgery, Thoracic Surgery, Urology.

University of California at Los Angeles Medical Center
Jules Stein Eye Institute
800 Westwood Plaza
Los Angeles, CA 90024-7000
213-825-5000
Teaching Specialties:
Ophthalmology.

University of California at Los Angeles Neuropsychiatric Hospital
760 Westwood Plaza
Los Angeles, CA 90024
213-825-9548
Teaching Specialties:
Psychiatry.

University of California at Los Angeles School of Dentistry
Center for the Health Sciences
10833 LeConte Ave.

Los Angeles, CA 90024-1668
213-825-7354
Teaching Specialties:
Dentistry.

University of Southern California
The Kenneth Norris Jr. Cancer Hospital
1441 Eastlake Ave.
Los Angeles, CA 90033
213-224-6600
Teaching Specialties:
Radiation Oncology, Urology.

University of Southern California School of Dentistry
925 W. 34th St.,
University Park MC-0641
Los Angeles, CA 90089-0641
213-740-2800
Teaching Specialties:
Dentistry.

White Memorial Medical Center
1720 Brooklyn Ave.
Los Angeles, CA 90033
213-268-5000
Teaching Specialties:
Internal Medicine, Obstetrics/Gynecology, Ophthalmology, Urology.

Modesto

Scenic General Hospital
830 Scenic Dr.
Modesto, CA 95353
209-525-7000
Teaching Specialties:
Surgery.

Napa

Napa State Hospital
2100 Napa-Vallejo Highway
Napa, CA 94558
707-253-5454
Teaching Specialties:
Psychiatry.

Oakland

Highland General Hospital
1411 E. 31st St.
Oakland, CA 94602
415-437-4397
Teaching Specialties:
Dentistry, Internal Medicine, Neurology, Ophthalmology, Orthopedic Surgery, Surgery.

Kaiser Foundation Hospital
280 W. MacArthur Blvd.
Oakland, CA 94611

415-596-1000
Teaching Specialties:
Internal Medicine, Obstetrics/Gynecology,
Otolaryngology, Surgery.

Orange

St. Joseph Hospital
1100 W. Stewart Dr.
Orange, CA 92668
714-633-9111
Teaching Specialties:
Radiation Oncology.

**University of California
Irvine Medical Center**
101 The City Dr.
Orange, CA 92668
714-634-6011
Teaching Specialties:
Allergy/Immunology, Anesthesiology,
Dermatology, Internal Medicine, Internal
Medicine-Cardiovascular Disease, Internal
Medicine-Endocrinology and Metabolism,
Internal Medicine-Gastroenterology, Internal
Medicine-Geriatric Medicine, Internal
Medicine-Hematology, Internal Medicine-
Infectious Diseases, Internal Medicine-Medi-
cal Oncology, Internal Medicine-Nephrology,
Internal Medicine-Rheumatology, Neurologi-
cal Surgery, Neurology, Obstetrics/Gynecolo-
gy, Ophthalmology, Orthopedic Surgery,
Otolaryngology, Physical Medicine and
Rehabilitation, Psychiatry, Radiation
Oncology, Surgery, Urology.

Pasadena

Huntington Memorial Hospital
100 W. California Blvd.
Pasadena, CA 91109
818-397-5000
Teaching Specialties:
Internal Medicine, Neurological Surgery,
Surgery.

Reedley

Kings View Hospital
42675 Rd. 44
Reedley, CA 93654
209-638-2505
Teaching Specialties:
Psychiatry.

Riverside

Riverside General Hospital
University Medical Center
9851 Magnolia Ave.
Riverside, CA 92503
714-358-7100
Teaching Specialties:
Neurology, Obstetrics/Gynecology, Ophthal-
mology, Otolaryngology, Surgery.

Sacramento

Kaiser Foundation Hospital
2025 Morse Ave.
Sacramento, CA 95825
916-973-5000
Teaching Specialties:
Internal Medicine, Neurological Surgery,
Obstetrics/Gynecology, Orthopedic Surgery,
Surgery, Urology.

Sutter General Hospital
2801 L St.
Sacramento, CA 95816
916-454-2222
Teaching Specialties:
Obstetrics/Gynecology, Surgery.

Sutter Memorial Hospital
52nd & F Sts.
Sacramento, CA 95819
916-454-3333
Teaching Specialties:
Obstetrics/Gynecology, Surgery.

**University of California,
Davis Medical Center**
2315 Stockton Blvd.
Sacramento, CA 95817
916-734-2011
Teaching Specialties:
Allergy/Immunology, Anesthesiology,
Dermatology, Internal Medicine, Internal
Medicine-Cardiovascular Disease, Internal
Medicine-Endocrinology and Metabolism,
Internal Medicine-Gastroenterology, Internal
Medicine-Geriatric Medicine, Internal
Medicine-Hematology, Internal Medicine-
Infectious Diseases, Internal Medicine-Medi-
cal Oncology, Internal Medicine-Nephrology,
Internal Medicine-Rheumatology, Neurologi-
cal Surgery, Neurology, Obstetrics/Gynecolo-
gy, Ophthalmology, Orthopedic Surgery,
Otolaryngology, Physical Medicine and Reha-
bilitation, Psychiatry, Surgery, Urology.

San Bernardino

**San Bernardino County
Medical Center**
780 E. Gilbert St.
San Bernardino, CA 92415
714-387-8111
Teaching Specialties:
Anesthesiology, Hand Surgery, Obstetrics/
Gynecology, Orthopedic Surgery,
Otolaryngology, Surgery, Urology.

San Diego

Kaiser Foundation Hospital
4647 Zion Ave.
San Diego, CA 92120
619-528-5000
Teaching Specialties:

Neurological Surgery, Obstetrics/
Gynecology, Otolaryngology.

Mercy Hospital and Medical Center
4077 5th Ave.
San Diego, CA 92103
619-294-8111
Teaching Specialties:
Internal Medicine, Internal Medicine-
Cardiovascular Disease, Urology.

Sharp Memorial Hospital
7901 Frost St.
San Diego, CA 92123
619-541-3400
Teaching Specialties:
Internal Medicine-Cardiovascular Disease,
Thoracic Surgery.

**University of California
San Diego Medical Center**
225 Dickinson St.
San Diego, CA 92103
619-543-6222
Teaching Specialties:
Allergy/Immunology, Anesthesiology,
Dermatology, Internal Medicine, Internal
Medicine-Cardiovascular Disease, Internal
Medicine-Endocrinology and Metabolism,
Internal Medicine-Gastroenterology, Internal
Medicine-Geriatric Medicine, Internal
Medicine-Hematology, Internal Medicine-
Infectious Diseases, Internal Medicine-Medi-
cal Oncology, Internal Medicine-Nephrology,
Internal Medicine-Rheumatology, Neurologi-
cal Surgery, Neurology, Obstetrics/Gynecolo-
gy, Ophthalmology, Orthopedic Surgery,
Otolaryngology, Psychiatry, Surgery, Thoracic
Surgery, Urology.

San Francisco

California-Pacific Medical Center
Clay at Buchanan St.
San Francisco, CA 94115
415-563-4321
Teaching Specialties:
Internal Medicine, Internal Medicine-Cardio-
vascular Disease, Internal Medicine-Gastroen-
terology, Ophthalmology, Psychiatry.

Kaiser Foundation Hospital
2425 Geary Blvd.
San Francisco, CA 94115
415-929-4000
Teaching Specialties:
Internal Medicine, Obstetrics/Gynecology,
Orthopedic Surgery, Otolaryngology,
Surgery.

**Langley Porter Psychiatric
Hospital and Clinics**
401 Parnassus Ave.
San Francisco, CA 94143
415-476-7180

Teaching Specialties:
Psychiatry.

Mt. Zion Medical Center of University of California, San Francisco
1600 Divisadero St.
San Francisco, CA 94115
415-567-6600
Teaching Specialties:
Internal Medicine, Internal Medicine-Cardiovascular Disease, Internal Medicine-Geriatric Medicine, Internal Medicine-Infectious Diseases, Obstetrics/Gynecology, Orthopedic Surgery, Radiation Oncology.

San Francisco General Hospital and Medical Center
1001 Potrero Ave.
San Francisco, CA 94110
415-821-8200
Teaching Specialties:
Anesthesiology, Dermatology, Internal Medicine, Internal Medicine-Gastroenterology, Internal Medicine-Hematology, Internal Medicine-Infectious Diseases, Internal Medicine-Medical Oncology, Internal Medicine-Nephrology, Internal Medicine-Rheumatology, Neurological Surgery, Neurology, Obstetrics/Gynecology, Ophthalmology, Orthopedic Surgery, Otolaryngology, Psychiatry, Surgery, Urology.

St. Mary's Hospital and Medical Center
450 Stanyan St.
San Francisco, CA 94117
415-668-1000
Teaching Specialties:
Internal Medicine, Internal Medicine-Cardiovascular Disease, Orthopedic Surgery, Radiation Oncology.

University of California, San Francisco Medical Center
505 Parnassus Ave.
San Francisco, CA 94143
415-476-1000
Teaching Specialties:
Allergy/Immunology, Anesthesiology, Dermatology, Hand Surgery, Internal Medicine, Internal Medicine-Cardiovascular Disease, Internal Medicine-Endocrinology and Metabolism, Internal Medicine-Gastroenterology, Internal Medicine-Hematology, Internal Medicine-Infectious Diseases, Internal Medicine-Medical Oncology, Internal Medicine-Nephrology, Internal Medicine-Rheumatology, Neurological Surgery, Neurology, Obstetrics/Gynecology, Ophthalmology, Orthopedic Surgery, Otolaryngology, Psychiatry, Radiation Oncology, Surgery, Surgery-Vascular Surgery, Thoracic Surgery, Urology.

University of California, San Francisco School of Dentistry
Box 0430
San Francisco, CA 94143-0430
415-476-1323 dean's office
Teaching Specialties:
Dentistry.

University of the Pacific School of Dentistry
2155 Webster St.
San Francisco, CA 94115
415-929-6400
Teaching Specialties:
Dentistry.

San Jose

Santa Clara Valley Medical Center
675 E. Santa Clara St.
San Jose, CA 95128
408-299-5100
Teaching Specialties:
Anesthesiology, Dermatology, Internal Medicine, Internal Medicine-Endocrinology and Metabolism, Internal Medicine-Gastroenterology, Internal Medicine-Infectious Diseases, Internal Medicine-Rheumatology, Neurological Surgery, Neurology, Obstetrics/Gynecology, Ophthalmology, Orthopedic Surgery, Otolaryngology, Physical Medicine and Rehabilitation, Surgery, Urology.

San Mateo

San Mateo County General Hospital
222 W. 39th Ave.
San Mateo, CA 94403
415-573-2222
Teaching Specialties:
Psychiatry.

Santa Barbara

Sansum Medical Clinic
317 W. Pueblo St.
Santa Barbara, CA 93105
805-682-2621
Teaching Specialties:
Colon and Rectal Surgery.

Santa Barbara Cottage Hospital
Pueblo at Bath Sts.
Santa Barbara, CA 93102
805-682-7111
Teaching Specialties:
Colon and Rectal Surgery, Internal Medicine, Surgery.

Santa Clara

Kaiser Foundation Hospital
900 Kiely Blvd.

Santa Clara, CA 95051
408-236-6400
Teaching Specialties:
Internal Medicine, Obstetrics/Gynecology, Otolaryngology, Psychiatry, Surgery.

Stanford

Stanford University Hospital
300 Pasteur Dr.
Stanford, CA 94305
415-723-4000
Teaching Specialties:
Anesthesiology, Dermatology, Internal Medicine, Internal Medicine-Cardiovascular Disease, Internal Medicine-Endocrinology and Metabolism, Internal Medicine-Gastroenterology, Internal Medicine-Geriatric Medicine, Internal Medicine-Hematology, Internal Medicine-Infectious Diseases, Internal Medicine-Medical Oncology, Internal Medicine-Nephrology, Internal Medicine-Rheumatology, Neurological Surgery, Neurology, Obstetrics/Gynecology, Ophthalmology, Orthopedic Surgery, Otolaryngology, Physical Medicine and Rehabilitation, Psychiatry, Radiation Oncology, Surgery, Surgery-Vascular Surgery, Thoracic Surgery, Urology.

Stockton

San Joaquin General Hospital
PO Box 1020
Stockton, CA 95201
209-468-6000
Teaching Specialties:
Internal Medicine, Surgery.

Sylmar

Olive View Medical Center
14445 Olive View Dr.
Sylmar, CA 91342
818-364-1555
Teaching Specialties:
Internal Medicine, Internal Medicine-Endocrinology and Metabolism, Internal Medicine-Hematology, Obstetrics/Gynecology, Otolaryngology, Psychiatry, Surgery, Urology.

Torrance

Los Angeles County Harbor-University of California at Los Angeles Medical Center
1000 W. Carson St.
Torrance, CA 90509
213-533-2345
Teaching Specialties:
Allergy/Immunology, Anesthesiology, Dentistry, Dermatology, Internal Medicine, Internal Medicine-Cardiovascular Disease, Internal Medicine-Endocrinology and Metabolism, Internal Medicine-Gastroenterology, Internal Medicine-Hematology, Internal

Medicine-Infectious Diseases, Internal Medicine-Medical Oncology, Internal Medicine-Nephrology, Internal Medicine-Rheumatology, Neurological Surgery, Neurology, Obstetrics/Gynecology, Ophthalmology, Orthopedic Surgery, Psychiatry, Surgery, Urology.

Ventura

Ventura County Mental Health Center
300 N. Hillmont Ave.
Ventura, CA 93003
805-652-6737
805-652-6792 administration
Teaching Specialties:
Psychiatry.

Walnut Creek

Kaiser Foundation Hospital
1425 S. Main St.
Walnut Creek, CA 94596
415-295-4000
Teaching Specialties:
Urology.

COLORADO
Denver

Denver Health and Hospitals
777 Bannock St.
Denver, CO 80204-4507
303-893-6000
Teaching Specialties:
Anesthesiology, Dentistry, Dermatology, Internal Medicine, Internal Medicine-Cardiovascular Disease, Internal Medicine-Endocrinology and Metabolism, Internal Medicine-Gastroenterology, Internal Medicine-Hematology, Internal Medicine-Infectious Diseases, Internal Medicine-Medical Oncology, Internal Medicine-Nephrology, Neurological Surgery, Neurology, Obstetrics/Gynecology, Ophthalmology, Orthopedic Surgery, Otolaryngology, Psychiatry, Surgery, Urology.

National Jewish Center for Immunology and Respiratory Medicine
1400 Jackson St.
Denver, CO 80206
303-388-4461
Teaching Specialties:
Allergy/Immunology.

Presbyterian-Denver Hospital
1719 E. 19th Ave.
Denver, CO 80218
313-839-6100
Teaching Specialties:
Internal Medicine, Radiation Oncology.

Presbyterian-St. Luke's Medical Center
601 E. 19th Ave.
Denver, CO 80203
303-839-1000
Teaching Specialties:
Internal Medicine, Obstetrics/Gynecology, Radiation Oncology.

Rose Medical Center
4567 E. 9th Ave.
Denver, CO 80220
303-320-2121
Teaching Specialties:
Internal Medicine, Obstetrics/Gynecology, Surgery.

St. Joseph Hospital
1835 Franklin St.
Denver, CO 80218
303-837-7111
Teaching Specialties:
Dentistry, Internal Medicine, Obstetrics/Gynecology, Otolaryngology, Surgery.

University of Colorado Health Sciences Center
University Hospital
4200 E. 9th St.
Denver, CO 80262
303-399-1211
Teaching Specialties:
Allergy/Immunology, Anesthesiology, Dermatology, Internal Medicine, Internal Medicine-Cardiovascular Disease, Internal Medicine-Endocrinology and Metabolism, Internal Medicine-Gastroenterology, Internal Medicine-Geriatric Medicine, Internal Medicine-Hematology, Internal Medicine-Infectious Diseases, Internal Medicine-Medical Oncology, Internal Medicine-Nephrology, Internal Medicine-Rheumatology, Neurological Surgery, Neurology, Obstetrics/Gynecology, Ophthalmology, Orthopedic Surgery, Otolaryngology, Physical Medicine and Rehabilitation, Psychiatry, Surgery, Thoracic Surgery, Urology.

University of Colorado School of Dentistry
Box C-284, 4200 E. 9th Ave.
Denver, CO 80262
303-270-7901
Teaching Specialties:
Dentistry.

Englewood

Craig Hospital
3425 S. Clarkson St.
Englewood, CO 80110
303-789-8000
Teaching Specialties:
Physical Medicine and Rehabilitation.

CONNECTICUT
Bridgeport

Bridgeport Hospital
267 Grant St.
Bridgeport, CT 06610
203-384-3000
Teaching Specialties:
Internal Medicine, Internal Medicine-Cardiovascular Disease, Internal Medicine-Gastroenterology, Obstetrics/Gynecology, Surgery.

St. Vincent's Medical Center
2800 Main St.
Bridgeport, CT 06606
203-576-6000
Teaching Specialties:
Internal Medicine, Internal Medicine-Cardiovascular Disease.

Danbury

Danbury Hospital
24 Hospital Ave.
Danbury, CT 06810
203-797-7000
Teaching Specialties:
Dentistry, Internal Medicine, Obstetrics/Gynecology, Psychiatry.

Derby

Griffin Hospital
130 Division St.
Derby, CT 06418
203-735-7421
Teaching Specialties:
Internal Medicine, Internal Medicine-Gastroenterology, Surgery.

Farmington

University of Connecticut Health Center
John Dempsey Hospital
263 Farmington Ave.
Farmington, CT 06030
203-679-2000
Teaching Specialties:
Anesthesiology, Internal Medicine, Internal Medicine-Cardiovascular Disease, Internal Medicine-Endocrinology and Metabolism, Internal Medicine-Gastroenterology, Internal Medicine-Geriatric Medicine, Internal Medicine-Hematology, Internal Medicine-Infectious Diseases, Internal Medicine-Medical Oncology, Internal Medicine-Nephrology, Internal Medicine-Rheumatology, Neurological Surgery, Obstetrics/Gynecology, Orthopedic Surgery, Otolaryngology, Psychiatry, Surgery, Urology.

University of Connecticut School of Dental Medicine
263 Farmington Ave.
Farmington, CT 06030
203-679-2808
Teaching Specialties:
Dentistry.

Greenwich

Greenwich Hospital
5 Perryridge Rd.
Greenwich, CT 06830
203-863-3000
Teaching Specialties:
Internal Medicine, Psychiatry.

Hartford

Hartford Hospital
80 Seymour St.
Hartford, CT 06115
203-524-3011
Teaching Specialties:
Anesthesiology, Dentistry, Internal Medicine, Internal Medicine-Cardiovascular Disease, Internal Medicine-Infectious Diseases, Neurological Surgery, Obstetrics/Gynecology, Orthopedic Surgery, Otolaryngology, Psychiatry, Surgery, Urology.

Institute of Living
400 Washington St.
Hartford, CT 06106
203-241-8000
Teaching Specialties:
Psychiatry.

Mt. Sinai Hospital
500 Blue Hills Ave.
Hartford, CT 06112
203-242-4431
Teaching Specialties:
Dentistry, Internal Medicine, Internal Medicine-Cardiovascular Disease, Internal Medicine-Infectious Diseases, Obstetrics/Gynecology, Physical Medicine and Rehabilitation, Psychiatry, Surgery.

St. Francis Hospital and Medical Center
114 Woodland St.
Hartford, CT 06105
203-548-4000
Teaching Specialties:
Anesthesiology, Colon and Rectal Surgery, Dentistry, Internal Medicine, Obstetrics/Gynecology, Orthopedic Surgery, Otolaryngology, Psychiatry, Surgery, Urology.

Middletown

Connecticut Valley Hospital
Silver St.

Middletown, CT 06457
203-344-2666
Teaching Specialties:
Psychiatry.

New Britain

New Britain General Hospital
100 Grand St.
New Britain, CT 06050
203-224-5011
Teaching Specialties:
Internal Medicine, Obstetrics/Gynecology, Otolaryngology, Surgery, Urology.

New Haven

Connecticut Mental Health Center
34 Park St.
New Haven, CT 06519
203-789-7290
Teaching Specialties:
Psychiatry.

Hospital of St. Raphael
1450 Chapel St.
New Haven, CT 06511
203-789-3000
Teaching Specialties:
Dentistry, Internal Medicine, Internal Medicine-Cardiovascular Disease, Internal Medicine-Gastroenterology, Internal Medicine-Nephrology, Orthopedic Surgery, Otolaryngology, Psychiatry, Radiation Oncology, Surgery.

Yale-New Haven Hospital
20 York St.
New Haven, CT 06504
203-785-4242
Teaching Specialties:
Allergy/Immunology, Anesthesiology, Dentistry, Dermatology, Internal Medicine, Internal Medicine-Cardiovascular Disease, Internal Medicine-Endocrinology and Metabolism, Internal Medicine-Gastroenterology, Internal Medicine-Geriatric Medicine, Internal Medicine-Hematology, Internal Medicine-Infectious Diseases, Internal Medicine-Medical Oncology, Internal Medicine-Nephrology, Internal Medicine-Rheumatology, Neurological Surgery, Neurology, Obstetrics/Gynecology, Ophthalmology, Orthopedic Surgery, Otolaryngology, Psychiatry, Radiation Oncology, Surgery, Thoracic Surgery, Urology.

Yale Psychiatric Institute
184 Liberty St.
New Haven, CT 06519
203-785-7200
Teaching Specialties:
Psychiatry.

Norwalk

Norwalk Hospital
Maple St.
Norwalk, CT 06856
203-852-2000
Teaching Specialties:
Internal Medicine, Internal Medicine-Cardiovascular Disease, Internal Medicine-Gastroenterology, Psychiatry.

Norwich

Norwich Hospital
Route 12
Norwich, CT 06360
203-823-5261
Teaching Specialties:
Psychiatry.

University of Connecticut Health Center
Uncas on Thames Hospital
W. Thames St.
Norwich, CT 06360
203-823-4600
Teaching Specialties:
Radiation Oncology.

William W. Buckus Hospital
326 Washington St.
Norwich, CT 06360
203-889-8331
Teaching Specialties:
Psychiatry.

Southbury

Southbury Training School
Route 172
Southbury, CT 06488
203-264-8231
Teaching Specialties:
Dentistry.

Stamford

Stamford Hospital
Shelburne Rd. & W. Broad St.
Stamford, CT 06904
203-325-7000
Teaching Specialties:
Internal Medicine, Obstetrics/Gynecology, Psychiatry, Surgery.

Waterbury

St. Mary's Hospital
56 Franklin St.
Waterbury, CT 06706
203-574-6000
Teaching Specialties:
Dentistry, Internal Medicine, Surgery.

Waterbury Hospital
64 Robbins St.
Waterbury, CT 06721
203-573-6000
Teaching Specialties:
Dentistry, Internal Medicine, Internal
Medicine-Gastroenterology, Surgery, Urology.

DELAWARE

New Castle

Delaware State Hospital
Dupont Highway
New Castle, DE 19720
302-421-6011
Teaching Specialties:
Psychiatry.

Wilmington

Alfred I. Dupont Institute
1600 Rockland Rd.
Wilmington, DE 19803
302-651-4000
Teaching Specialties:
Orthopedic Surgery, Urology.

Medical Center of Delaware
501 W. 14th St.
Wilmington, DE 19899
302-733-1000
Teaching Specialties:
Dentistry, Internal Medicine, Neurology,
Obstetrics/Gynecology, Psychiatry, Surgery,
Thoracic Surgery.

DISTRICT OF
COLUMBIA

**District of Columbia
General Hospital**
19th St. & Massachusetts Ave., SE
Washington, DC 20003
203-675-7654
Teaching Specialties:
Allergy/Immunology, Internal Medicine,
Internal Medicine-Cardiovascular Disease,
Internal Medicine-Endocrinology and Metab-
olism, Internal Medicine-Gastroenterology,
Internal Medicine-Hematology, Internal
Medicine-Medical Oncology, Internal
Medicine-Nephrology, Internal Medicine-
Rheumatology, Neurology, Obstetrics/
Gynecology, Ophthalmology, Orthopedic
Surgery, Surgery, Urology.

**George Washington
University Hospital**
901 23rd St., NW
Washington, DC 20037
202-994-1000

Teaching Specialties:
Anesthesiology, Dermatology, Internal
Medicine, Internal Medicine-Cardiovascular
Disease, Internal Medicine-Endocrinology
and Metabolism, Internal Medicine-Gastroen-
terology, Internal Medicine-Geriatric
Medicine, Internal Medicine-Hematology,
Internal Medicine-Infectious Diseases, Inter-
nal Medicine-Medical Oncology, Internal
Medicine-Nephrology, Internal Medicine-
Rheumatology, Neurological Surgery, Neurol-
ogy, Obstetrics/Gynecology, Ophthalmology,
Orthopedic Surgery, Physical Medicine and
Rehabilitation, Psychiatry, Radiation Oncolo-
gy, Surgery, Thoracic Surgery, Urology.

Georgetown University Hospital
3800 Reservoir Rd., NW
Washington, DC 20007
202-687-5055
Teaching Specialties:
Allergy/Immunology, Anesthesiology, Den-
tistry, Internal Medicine, Internal Medicine-
Cardiovascular Disease, Internal Medicine-
Endocrinology and Metabolism, Internal
Medicine-Gastroenterology, Internal
Medicine-Hematology, Internal Medicine-
Infectious Diseases, Internal Medicine-Medi-
cal Oncology, Internal Medicine-Nephrology,
Internal Medicine-Rheumatology, Neurologi-
cal Surgery, Neurology, Obstetrics/Gynecolo-
gy, Ophthalmology, Orthopedic Surgery,
Otolaryngology, Physical Medicine and Reha-
bilitation, Psychiatry, Radiation Oncology,
Surgery, Urology.

**Greater Southeast
Community Hospital**
1310 Southern Ave., SE
Washington, DC 20032
202-574-6000
Teaching Specialties:
Internal Medicine, Obstetrics/Gynecology,
Orthopedic Surgery, Surgery.

**Howard University College
of Dentistry**
600 W. St., NW
Washington, DC 20059
202-806-0100
Teaching Specialties:
Dentistry.

Howard University Hospital
2041 Georgia Ave., NW
Washington, DC 20060
202-865-6100
Teaching Specialties:
Allergy/Immunology, Anesthesiology,
Dermatology, Internal Medicine, Internal
Medicine-Cardiovascular Disease, Internal
Medicine-Endocrinology and Metabolism,
Internal Medicine-Gastroenterology, Internal
Medicine-Hematology, Internal Medicine-
Infectious Diseases, Internal Medicine-Medi-
cal Oncology, Internal Medicine-Nephrology,

Internal Medicine-Rheumatology, Neurology,
Obstetrics/Gynecology, Ophthalmology,
Orthopedic Surgery, Psychiatry, Radiation
Oncology, Surgery, Urology.

National Rehabilitation Hospital
102 Irving St., NW
Washington, DC 20010
202-877-1000
Teaching Specialties:
Physical Medicine and Rehabilitation.

Providence Hospital
1150 Varnum St., NE
Washington, DC 20017
202-269-7000
Teaching Specialties:
Internal Medicine, Obstetrics/Gynecology,
Orthopedic Surgery.

Sibley Memorial Hospital
5255 Loughboro Rd.
Washington, DC 20016
202-537-4000
Teaching Specialties:
Orthopedic Surgery, Surgery, Urology.

St. Elizabeths Hospital
DC Commission on
Mental Health Services
2700 Martin Luther King, Jr. Ave., SE
Washington, DC 20032
202-373-7166
Teaching Specialties:
Dentistry, Psychiatry.

Washington Hospital Center
110 Irving St., NW
Washington, DC 20010
202-877-7000
Teaching Specialties:
Dentistry, Dermatology, Internal Medicine,
Internal Medicine-Cardiovascular Disease,
Internal Medicine-Infectious Diseases, Inter-
nal Medicine-Medical Oncology, Internal
Medicine-Rheumatology, Neurological
Surgery, Neurology, Obstetrics/Gynecology,
Ophthalmology, Orthopedic Surgery, Oto-
laryngology, Physical Medicine and Rehabili-
tation, Surgery, Thoracic Surgery, Urology.

FLORIDA

Coral Gables

Doctors' Hospital
5000 University Dr.
Coral Gables, FL 33146
305-666-2111
Teaching Specialties:
Orthopedic Surgery.

468

Fort Lauderdale

North Beach Hospital
2835 N. Ocean Blvd.
Fort Lauderdale, FL 33308
305-568-1000
Teaching Specialties:
Colon and Rectal Surgery.

Gainesville

**Shands Hospital at the
University of Florida**
1600 S.W. Archer Rd.
Gainesville, FL 32610
904-395-0111
Teaching Specialties:
Anesthesiology, Hand Surgery, Internal
Medicine, Internal Medicine-Cardiovascular
Disease, Internal Medicine-Endocrinology
and Metabolism, Internal Medicine-Gastroen-
terology, Internal Medicine-Geriatric
Medicine, Internal Medicine-Hematology,
Internal Medicine-Infectious Diseases, Inter-
nal Medicine-Medical Oncology, Internal
Medicine-Nephrology, Internal Medicine-
Rheumatology, Neurological Surgery, Neurol-
ogy, Obstetrics/Gynecology, Ophthalmology,
Orthopedic Surgery, Otolaryngology, Psychia-
try, Radiation Oncology, Surgery, Surgery-
Vascular Surgery, Thoracic Surgery, Urology.

**University of Florida College
of Dentistry**
PO Box 100405, J. Hillis Miller
Health Center
Gainesville, FL 32610-0405
904-392-2946
Teaching Specialties:
Dentistry.

Jacksonville

Baptist Medical Center
800 Prudential Dr.
Jacksonville, FL 32207
904-393-2000
Teaching Specialties:
Obstetrics/Gynecology.

University Medical Center
655 W. 8th St.
Jacksonville, FL 32209
904-549-5000
Teaching Specialties:
Dentistry, Internal Medicine, Internal
Medicine-Cardiovascular Disease, Internal
Medicine-Endocrinology and Metabolism,
Internal Medicine-Gastroenterology, Internal
Medicine-Hematology, Obstetrics/Gynecolo-
gy, Orthopedic Surgery, Surgery.

Miami

**Bascom Palmer Eye Institute-
Anne Bates Leach Eye Hospital**
900 N.W. 17th St.
Miami, FL 33136
305-326-6190
Teaching Specialties:
Ophthalmology.

**Dade County Dental
Research Clinic**
750 N.W. 20th St.
Miami, FL 33127
305-324-6070
Teaching Specialties:
Dentistry.

Jackson Memorial Hospital
1611 N.W. 12th Ave.
Miami, FL 33136
305-325-7429
Teaching Specialties:
Anesthesiology, Dentistry, Dermatology,
Hand Surgery, Internal Medicine, Internal
Medicine-Cardiovascular Disease, Internal
Medicine-Endocrinology and Metabolism,
Internal Medicine-Gastroenterology, Internal
Medicine-Geriatric Medicine, Internal Medi-
cine-Hematology, Internal Medicine-Infec-
tious Diseases, Internal Medicine-Medical On-
cology, Internal Medicine-Nephrology,
Internal Medicine-Rheumatology, Neurologi-
cal Surgery, Neurology, Obstetrics/Gynecolo-
gy, Ophthalmology, Orthopedic Surgery,
Otolaryngology, Psychiatry, Radiation Oncology, Surgery, Thoracic Surgery, Urology.

Miami Beach

Mt. Sinai Medical Center
4300 Alton Rd.
Miami Beach, FL 33140
305-674-2121
Teaching Specialties:
Anesthesiology, Dentistry, Dermatology,
Internal Medicine, Internal Medicine-Cardio-
vascular Disease, Internal Medicine-Gastroen-
terology, Internal Medicine-Infectious
Diseases, Neurological Surgery, Surgery,
Thoracic Surgery.

**South Shore Hospital
and Medical Center**
630 Alton Rd.
Miami Beach, FL 33139
305-672-2100
Teaching Specialties:
Internal Medicine-Geriatric Medicine.

Orlando

Florida Hospital Medical Center
601 Rollins St.
Orlando, FL 32803

407-896-6611
Teaching Specialties:
Colon and Rectal Surgery.

Orlando Regional Medical Center
1414 Kuhl Ave.
Orlando, FL 32806
407-841-5111
Teaching Specialties:
Colon and Rectal Surgery, Internal Medicine,
Obstetrics/Gynecology, Orthopedic Surgery,
Surgery.

Pensacola

Baptist Hospital
PO Box 17500
Pensacola, FL 32522
904-434-4011
Teaching Specialties:
Obstetrics/Gynecology.

Sacred Heart Hospital of Pensacola
5151 N. 9th Ave.
Pensacola, FL 32513
904-474-7000
Teaching Specialties:
Obstetrics/Gynecology.

St. Petersburg

Bayfront Medical Center
701 6th St. S
St. Petersburg, FL 33701
813-823-1234
Teaching Specialties:
Obstetrics/Gynecology.

Tampa

Tampa General Hospital
Davis Island
Tampa, FL 33606
813-251-7000
Teaching Specialties:
Anesthesiology, Dermatology, Internal
Medicine, Internal Medicine-Cardiovascular
Disease, Internal Medicine-Geriatric
Medicine, Internal Medicine-Infectious Dis-
eases, Internal Medicine-Nephrology, Inter-
nal Medicine-Rheumatology, Neurology, Ob-
stetrics/Gynecology, Ophthalmology,
Otolaryngology, Psychiatry, Surgery, Surgery-
Vascular Surgery, Urology.

University of South Florida
H. Lee Moffitt Cancer Center
12902 Magnolia Dr.
Tampa, FL 33682
813-972-4673
Teaching Specialties:
Anesthesiology, Internal Medicine-En-
docrinology and Metabolism, Internal
Medicine-Infectious Diseases, Internal
Medicine-Medical Oncology, Urology.

**University of South Florida
Psychiatry Center**
3515 E. Fletcher Ave.
Tampa, FL 33613
813-972-3000
Teaching Specialties:
Psychiatry.

Tarpon Springs

The Manors
1527 Riverside Dr.
Tarpon Springs, FL 34689
813-937-4211
Teaching Specialties:
Psychiatry.

GEORGIA

Atlanta

**Crawford Long Hospital
of Emory University**
550 Peachtree St., NE
Atlanta, GA 30365
404-686-4411
Teaching Specialties:
Internal Medicine, Neurological Surgery,
Obstetrics/Gynecology, Orthopedic Surgery,
Surgery, Thoracic Surgery.

Emory University Hospital
1364 Clifton Rd., NE
Atlanta, GA 30322
404-727-7021
Teaching Specialties:
Allergy/Immunology, Anesthesiology,
Dermatology, Internal Medicine, Internal
Medicine-Cardiovascular Disease, Internal
Medicine-Endocrinology and Metabolism,
Internal Medicine-Gastroenterology, Internal
Medicine-Hematology, Internal Medicine-
Infectious Diseases, Internal Medicine-Medi-
cal Oncology, Internal Medicine-Nephrology,
Internal Medicine-Rheumatology, Neurologi-
cal Surgery, Neurology, Obstetrics/Gynecolo-
gy, Ophthalmology, Orthopedic Surgery,
Otolaryngology, Physical Medicine and Reha-
bilitation, Psychiatry, Surgery, Surgery-Vascu-
lar Surgery, Thoracic Surgery, Urology.

**Emory University
School of Medicine**
1462 Clifton Rd., NE
Atlanta, GA 30322
404-727-6652 dean's office
404-727-6667 appointments
Teaching Specialties:
Dentistry.

Georgia Baptist Medical Center
300 Boulevard., NE
Atlanta, GA 30312

404-653-4000
Teaching Specialties:
Internal Medicine, Obstetrics/Gynecology,
Orthopedic Surgery, Surgery.

Grady Memorial Hospital
80 Butler St., SE
Atlanta, GA 30335
404-589-4307
Teaching Specialties:
Allergy/Immunology, Anesthesiology,
Dermatology, Internal Medicine, Internal
Medicine-Cardiovascular Disease, Internal
Medicine-Endocrinology and Metabolism,
Internal Medicine-Gastroenterology, Internal
Medicine-Hematology, Internal Medicine-
Infectious Diseases, Internal Medicine-Medi-
cal Oncology, Internal Medicine-Nephrology,
Internal Medicine-Rheumatology, Neurologi-
cal Surgery, Neurology, Obstetrics/Gynecolo-
gy, Ophthalmology, Orthopedic Surgery,
Otolaryngology, Physical Medicine and
Rehabilitation, Psychiatry, Surgery, Thoracic
Surgery, Urology.

HCA West Paces Ferry Hospital
3200 Howell Mill Rd., NW
Atlanta, GA 30327
404-351-0351
Teaching Specialties:
Psychiatry.

Piedmont Hospital
1968 Peachtree Rd., NW
Atlanta, GA 30309
404-350-2222
Teaching Specialties:
Surgery.

Augusta

Medical College of Georgia
Georgia Radiation Therapy Center
at Augusta
1120 15th St.
Augusta, GA 30912
404-721-2971
Teaching Specialties:
Radiation Oncology.

**Medical College of Georgia
Hospital and Clinics**
1120 15th St.
Augusta, GA 30912
404-721-0211
Teaching Specialties:
Allergy/Immunology, Anesthesiology,
Dermatology, Internal Medicine, Internal
Medicine-Cardiovascular Disease, Internal
Medicine-Endocrinology and Metabolism,
Internal Medicine-Gastroenterology, Internal
Medicine-Hematology, Internal Medicine-
Infectious Diseases, Internal Medicine-Medi-
cal Oncology, Internal Medicine-Nephrology,
Internal Medicine-Rheumatology, Neurologi-

cal Surgery, Neurology, Obstetrics/Gynecolo-
gy, Ophthalmology, Orthopedic Surgery,
Otolaryngology, Psychiatry, Radiation Oncology, Surgery, Thoracic Surgery, Urology.

**Medical College of Georgia
School of Dentistry**
Augusta, GA 30912
404-721-0211
Teaching Specialties:
Dentistry.

University Hospital
1350 Walton Way
Augusta, GA 30910
404-722-9011
Teaching Specialties:
Dermatology, Internal Medicine, Neurology,
Obstetrics/Gynecology, Orthopedic Surgery,
Surgery, Urology.

Columbus

**Hughston Sports Medicine
Hospital**
100 Frist Court
Columbus, GA 31995
404-576-2100
Teaching Specialties:
Orthopedic Surgery.

Decatur

**Georgia Regional Hospital
at Atlanta**
3073 Panthersville Rd.
Decatur, GA 30034
404-243-2100
Teaching Specialties:
Psychiatry.

Macon

Medical Center of Central Georgia
777 Hemlock St.
Macon, GA 31208
912-744-1000
Teaching Specialties:
Internal Medicine, Obstetrics/Gynecology,
Surgery.

Savannah

Memorial Medical Center
4700 Waters Ave.
Savannah, GA 31404
912-356-8000
Teaching Specialties:
Internal Medicine, Obstetrics/Gynecology,
Surgery.

Smyrna

Brawner Psychiatric Institute
3180 Atlanta St., SE
Smyrna, GA 30080
404-436-0081
Teaching Specialties:
Psychiatry.

Ridgeview Institute
3995 S. Cobb Dr.
Smyrna, GA 30080
404-434-4567
Teaching Specialties:
Psychiatry.

HAWAII
Honolulu

Kaiser Permanente Medical Center
3288 Moanalua Rd.
Honolulu, HI 96819
808-834-5333
Teaching Specialties:
Internal Medicine, Internal Medicine-
Geriatric Medicine, Surgery.

**Kapiolani Medical Center for
Women and Children**
1319 Punahou St.
Honolulu, HI 96826
808-973-8511
Teaching Specialties:
Obstetrics/Gynecology, Surgery.

Kuakini Medical Center
347 N. Kuakini St.
Honolulu, HI 96817
808-536-2236
Teaching Specialties:
Internal Medicine, Internal Medicine-
Geriatric Medicine, Surgery.

Queen's Medical Center
1301 Punchbowl St.
Honolulu, HI 96813
808-538-9011
Teaching Specialties:
Dentistry, Internal Medicine, Obstetrics/
Gynecology, Orthopedic Surgery, Psychiatry,
Surgery.

St. Francis Medical Center
2230 Liliha St.
Honolulu, HI 96817
808-547-6011
Teaching Specialties:
Internal Medicine, Psychiatry, Surgery.

Straub Clinic and Hospital
888 S. King St.

Honolulu, HI 96813
808-522-4000
Teaching Specialties:
Surgery.

IDAHO
Boise

St. Luke's Regional Medical Center
190 E. Bannock St.
Boise, ID 83712
208-386-2222
Teaching Specialties:
Internal Medicine-Geriatric Medicine.

ILLINOIS
Alton

**Southern Illinois University School
of Dental Medicine**
2800 College Ave.
Alton, IL 62002
618-463-3821
Teaching Specialties:
Dentistry.

Anna

**Choate Mental Health and
Developmental Center**
1000 N. Main St.
Anna, IL 62906
618-833-5161
Teaching Specialties:
Psychiatry.

Berwyn

MacNeal Hospital
3249 S. Oak Park Ave.
Berwyn, IL 60402
708-795-9100
Teaching Specialties:
Internal Medicine, Internal Medicine-
Cardiovascular Disease, Obstetrics/
Gynecology, Surgery.

Chicago

Columbus Hospital
2520 N. Lakeview Ave.
Chicago, IL 60614
312-883-7300
Teaching Specialties:
Internal Medicine, Obstetrics/Gynecology,
Radiation Oncology, Surgery.

Cook County Hospital
1835 W. Harrison St.
Chicago, IL 60612

312-633-6000
Teaching Specialties:
Anesthesiology, Colon and Rectal Surgery,
Dentistry, Dermatology, Internal Medicine,
Internal Medicine-Cardiovascular Disease,
Internal Medicine-Endocrinology and Me-
tabolism, Internal Medicine-Gastroenterol-
ogy, Internal Medicine-Hematology, Internal
Medicine-Infectious Diseases, Internal Medi-
cine-Medical Oncology, Internal Medicine-
Nephrology, Internal Medicine-Rheumatolo-
gy, Neurological Surgery, Neurology,
Obstetrics/Gynecology, Ophthalmology,
Orthopedic Surgery, Otolaryngology, Psychia-
try, Surgery, Thoracic Surgery, Urology.

Edgewater Medical Center
5700 N. Ashland Ave.
Chicago, IL 60660
312-878-6000
Teaching Specialties:
Internal Medicine.

Grant Hospital of Chicago
550 W. Webster Ave.
Chicago, IL 60614
312-883-2000
Teaching Specialties:
Internal Medicine.

Grant Hospital of Chicago
Max Samter Institute of
Allergy/Clinical Immunology
550 W. Webster Ave.
Chicago, IL 60614
312-883-2000 Grant Hospital
312-883-3655 Institute
Teaching Specialties:
Allergy/Immunology.

Humana Hospital-Michael Reese
Lake Shore Dr. at 31st St.
Chicago, IL 60616
312-791-2000
Teaching Specialties:
Anesthesiology, Internal Medicine, Internal
Medicine-Cardiovascular Disease, Internal
Medicine-Endocrinology and Metabolism,
Internal Medicine-Gastroenterology, Internal
Medicine-Infectious Diseases, Internal
Medicine-Medical Oncology, Internal Medi-
cine-Rheumatology, Neurology, Obstetrics/
Gynecology, Orthopedic Surgery, Physical
Medicine and Rehabilitation, Psychiatry, Ra-
diation Oncology, Surgery, Urology.

Hyde Park Hospital
5800 S. Stony Island Ave.
Chicago, IL 60637
312-643-9200
Teaching Specialties:
Surgery.

Illinois Masonic Medical Center
836 W. Wellington Ave.
Chicago, IL 60657
312-975-1600
Teaching Specialties:
Anesthesiology, Dentistry, Internal Medicine, Internal Medicine-Cardiovascular Disease, Internal Medicine-Rheumatology, Obstetrics/Gynecology, Surgery.

Illinois State Psychiatric Institute
1601 W. Taylor St.
Chicago, IL 60612
312-996-1000
Teaching Specialties:
Psychiatry.

Louis A. Weiss Memorial Hospital
4646 N. Marine Dr.
Chicago, IL 60640
312-878-8700
Teaching Specialties:
Internal Medicine, Otolaryngology, Surgery.

Lutheran General Hospital
1775 Dempster St.
Chicago, IL 60068
708-696-2210
Teaching Specialties:
Internal Medicine, Obstetrics/Gynecology, Orthopedic Surgery, Psychiatry, Surgery.

Martha Washington Hospital
4055 N. Western Ave.
Chicago, IL 60618
312-583-9000
Teaching Specialties:
Internal Medicine-Gastroenterology.

Mercy Hospital and Medical Center
Stevenson Expressway at King Dr.
Chicago, IL 60616
312-567-2000
Teaching Specialties:
Internal Medicine, Internal Medicine-Rheumatology, Obstetrics/Gynecology, Radiation Oncology, Surgery.

Mt. Sinai Hospital Medical Center of Chicago
California Ave. & 15th St.
Chicago, IL 60608
312-542-2000
Teaching Specialties:
Dentistry, Internal Medicine, Internal Medicine-Cardiovascular Disease, Internal Medicine-Gastroenterology, Internal Medicine-Geriatric Medicine, Internal Medicine-Hematology, Internal Medicine-Infectious Diseases, Internal Medicine-Medical Oncology, Internal Medicine-Nephrology, Obstetrics/Gynecology, Physical Medicine and Rehabilitation, Psychiatry, Surgery.

Northwestern Memorial Hospital
Superior St. & Fairbanks Court
Chicago, IL 60611
312-908-2000
Teaching Specialties:
Allergy/Immunology, Anesthesiology, Dermatology, Internal Medicine, Internal Medicine-Cardiovascular Disease, Internal Medicine-Endocrinology and Metabolism, Internal Medicine-Gastroenterology, Internal Medicine-Geriatric Medicine, Internal Medicine-Hematology, Internal Medicine-Infectious Diseases, Internal Medicine-Medical Oncology, Internal Medicine-Nephrology, Internal Medicine-Rheumatology, Neurological Surgery, Neurology, Ophthalmology, Orthopedic Surgery, Otolaryngology, Physical Medicine and Rehabilitation, Psychiatry, Radiation Oncology, Surgery, Surgery-Vascular Surgery, Thoracic Surgery, Urology.

Northwestern Memorial Hospital
Prentice Women's Hospital
Superior St. & Fairbanks Court
Chicago, IL 60611
312-908-2000
Teaching Specialties:
Obstetrics/Gynecology.

Northwestern University Dental School
240 E. Huron St.
Chicago, IL 60611-2972
312-908-5950
Teaching Specialties:
Dentistry.

Ravenswood Hospital Medical Center
4550 N. Winchester Ave.
Chicago, IL 60640
312-878-4300
Teaching Specialties:
Dentistry, Internal Medicine, Orthopedic Surgery.

Rehabilitation Institute of Chicago
345 E. Superior St.
Chicago, IL 60611
312-908-6000
Teaching Specialties:
Physical Medicine and Rehabilitation.

Resurrection Medical Center
7435 W. Talcott Ave.
Chicago, IL 60631
312-774-8000
Teaching Specialties:
Anesthesiology, Obstetrics/Gynecology, Surgery.

Rush-Presbyterian-St. Luke's Medical Center
1653 W. Congress Parkway
Chicago, IL 60612
312-942-5000
Teaching Specialties:
Anesthesiology, Dentistry, Dermatology, Internal Medicine, Internal Medicine-Cardiovascular Disease, Internal Medicine-Endocrinology and Metabolism, Internal Medicine-Gastroenterology, Internal Medicine-Geriatric Medicine, Internal Medicine-Hematology, Internal Medicine-Infectious Diseases, Internal Medicine-Medical Oncology, Internal Medicine-Nephrology, Internal Medicine-Rheumatology, Neurological Surgery, Neurology, Obstetrics/Gynecology, Ophthalmology, Orthopedic Surgery, Otolaryngology, Physical Medicine and Rehabilitation, Psychiatry, Radiation Oncology, Surgery, Surgery-Vascular Surgery, Thoracic Surgery, Urology.

Schwab Rehabilitation Center
1401 S. California Blvd.
Chicago, IL 60608
312-522-2010
Teaching Specialties:
Physical Medicine and Rehabilitation.

St. Cabrini Hospital
811 S. Lytle St.
Chicago, IL 60607
312-883-4300
Teaching Specialties:
Internal Medicine, Obstetrics/Gynecology, Radiation Oncology, Surgery.

St. Joseph Hospital and Health Care Center
2900 N. Lake Shore Dr.
Chicago, IL 60657
312-975-3000
Teaching Specialties:
Internal Medicine, Obstetrics/Gynecology.

University of Chicago Hospitals
PO Box 430, 5841 S. Maryland Ave.
Chicago, IL 60637
312-702-1000
Teaching Specialties:
Anesthesiology, Dentistry, Dermatology, Internal Medicine, Internal Medicine-Cardiovascular Disease, Internal Medicine-Endocrinology and Metabolism, Internal Medicine-Gastroenterology, Internal Medicine-Geriatric Medicine, Internal Medicine-Hematology, Internal Medicine-Infectious Diseases, Internal Medicine-Nephrology, Internal Medicine-Rheumatology, Neurological Surgery, Neurology, Obstetrics/Gynecology, Ophthalmology, Orthopedic Surgery, Otolaryngology, Psychiatry, Radiation Oncology, Surgery, Surgery-Vascular Surgery, Thoracic Surgery, Urology.

**University of Illinois at Chicago
College of Dentistry**
801 S. Paulina St.
Chicago, IL 60612
312-996-7520
Teaching Specialties:
Dentistry.

**University of Illinois
Hospital and Clinics**
1740 W. Taylor St.
Chicago, IL 60612
312-996-3900
Teaching Specialties:
Anesthesiology, Dermatology, Internal
Medicine, Internal Medicine-Cardiovascular
Disease, Internal Medicine-Endocrinology
and Metabolism, Internal Medicine-Gastroen-
terology, Internal Medicine-Geriatric
Medicine, Internal Medicine-Hematology, In-
ternal Medicine-Infectious Diseases, Internal
Medicine-Medical Oncology, Internal
Medicine-Nephrology, Internal Medicine-
Rheumatology, Neurological Surgery, Neurol-
ogy, Obstetrics/Gynecology, Orthopedic
Surgery, Otolaryngology, Physical Medicine
and Rehabilitation, Psychiatry, Radiation Oncology, Surgery, Thoracic Surgery, Urology.

**University of Illinois
Hospital and Clinics**
Illinois Eye and Ear Infirmary
1855 W. Taylor St.
Chicago, IL 60612
312-996-6500
Teaching Specialties:
Ophthalmology, Otolaryngology.

Decatur

Decatur Memorial Hospital
2300 N. Edward St.
Decatur, IL 62526
217-877-8121
Teaching Specialties:
Psychiatry.

Evanston

Evanston Hospital
2650 Ridge Ave.
Evanston, IL 60201
708-570-2000
Teaching Specialties:
Anesthesiology, Dentistry, Internal Medicine,
Internal Medicine-Gastroenterology, Internal
Medicine-Infectious Diseases, Neurological
Surgery, Neurology, Obstetrics/Gynecology,
Ophthalmology, Orthopedic Surgery, Oto-
laryngology, Psychiatry, Radiation Oncology,
Surgery, Thoracic Surgery.

Glenbrook Hospital
2100 Pfingsten Rd.

Evanston, IL 60025
708-729-8800
Teaching Specialties:
Internal Medicine-Infectious Diseases.

St. Francis Hospital of Evanston
355 Ridge Ave.
Evanston, IL 60202
708-492-4000
Teaching Specialties:
Internal Medicine, Internal Medicine-Cardio-
vascular Disease, Internal Medicine-Hematol-
ogy, Internal Medicine-Medical Oncology,
Obstetrics/Gynecology, Orthopedic Surgery,
Surgery.

Evergreen Park

**Little Company of Mary Hospital
and Health Care Centers**
2800 W. 95th St.
Evergreen Park, IL 60642
708-422-6200
Teaching Specialties:
Surgery.

Maywood

Loyola University of Chicago
Foster G. McGaw Hospital
2160 S. First Ave.
Maywood, IL 60153
708-216-3800
Teaching Specialties:
Anesthesiology, Dermatology, Internal
Medicine, Internal Medicine-Cardiovascular
Disease, Internal Medicine-Endocrinology
and Metabolism, Internal Medicine-Gastroen-
terology, Internal Medicine-Geriatric
Medicine, Internal Medicine-Hematology, In-
ternal Medicine-Infectious Diseases, Internal
Medicine-Nephrology, Internal Medicine-
Rheumatology, Neurological Surgery, Neurol-
ogy, Obstetrics/Gynecology, Ophthalmology,
Orthopedic Surgery, Otolaryngology, Physical
Medicine and Rehabilitation, Psychiatry,
Surgery, Surgery-Vascular Surgery, Thoracic
Surgery, Urology.

**Loyola University of Chicago
School of Dentistry**
2160 S. First Ave.
Maywood, IL 60153
708-216-4200
Teaching Specialties:
Dentistry.

Oak Forest

**Oak Forest Hospital of
Cook County**
15900 S. Cicero Ave.
Oak Forest, IL 60452
708-687-7200

Teaching Specialties:
Ophthalmology, Physical Medicine and Rehabilitation.

Oak Lawn

Christ Hospital and Medical Center
4440 W. 95th St.
Oak Lawn, IL 60453
708-425-8000
Teaching Specialties:
Internal Medicine, Internal Medicine-Cardiovascular Disease, Neurology, Obstetrics/Gy-
necology, Orthopedic Surgery, Surgery.

Oak Park

**West Suburban Hospital
Medical Center**
Erie at Austin Blvd.
Oak Park, IL 60302
708-383-6200
Teaching Specialties:
Internal Medicine.

Peoria

**Methodist Medical Center
of Illinois**
221 N.E. Glen Oak Ave.
Peoria, IL 61636
309-672-5522
Teaching Specialties:
Neurological Surgery, Neurology.

St. Francis Medical Center
530 N.E. Glen Oak Ave.
Peoria, IL 61637
309-655-2000
Teaching Specialties:
Internal Medicine, Neurological Surgery,
Neurology, Obstetrics/Gynecology, Surgery.

Springfield

**Andrew McFarland Mental
Health Center**
901 Southwind Rd.
Springfield, IL 62703
217-786-6994
Teaching Specialties:
Psychiatry.

Memorial Medical Center
800 N. Rutledge St.
Springfield, IL 62781
217-788-3000
Teaching Specialties:
Internal Medicine, Neurology, Obstetrics/Gy-
necology, Orthopedic Surgery, Otolaryngology, Psychiatry, Surgery, Surgery-Vascular
Surgery, Urology.

St. John's Hospital
800 E. Carpenter St.
Springfield, IL 62769
217-544-6464
Teaching Specialties:
Internal Medicine, Neurology, Obstetrics/Gynecology, Orthopedic Surgery, Otolaryngology, Psychiatry, Surgery, Surgery-Vascular Surgery, Urology.

Urbana

Carle Foundation Hospital
611 W. Park St.
Urbana, IL 61801
217-337-3311
Teaching Specialties:
Colon and Rectal Surgery, Dentistry, Internal Medicine.

Covenant Medical Center
1400 W. Park St.
Urbana, IL 61801
217-337-2500
Teaching Specialties:
Internal Medicine.

Wheaton

Marianjoy Rehabilitation Center
26 W. 171 Roosevelt Rd.
Wheaton, IL 60187
708-462-4000
Teaching Specialties:
Physical Medicine and Rehabilitation.

INDIANA

Fort Wayne

Lutheran Hospital of Indiana
3024 Fairfield Ave.
Fort Wayne, IN 46807
219-458-2001
Teaching Specialties:
Orthopedic Surgery.

Parkview Memorial Hospital
2200 Randallia Dr.
Fort Wayne, IN 46805
219-484-6636
Teaching Specialties:
Orthopedic Surgery.

St. Joseph Medical Center
700 Broadway
Fort Wayne, IN 46802
219-425-3000
Teaching Specialties:
Orthopedic Surgery.

Indianapolis

Indiana University Medical Center
926 W. Michigan St.
Indianapolis, IN 46202
317-274-5000
Teaching Specialties:
Anesthesiology, Dermatology, Internal Medicine, Internal Medicine-Cardiovascular Disease, Internal Medicine-Endocrinology and Metabolism, Internal Medicine-Gastroenterology, Internal Medicine-Geriatric Medicine, Internal Medicine-Hematology, Internal Medicine-Infectious Diseases, Internal Medicine-Medical Oncology, Internal Medicine-Nephrology, Internal Medicine-Rheumatology, Neurological Surgery, Neurology, Obstetrics/Gynecology, Ophthalmology, Orthopedic Surgery, Otolaryngology, Psychiatry, Radiation Oncology, Surgery, Thoracic Surgery, Urology.

Indiana University School of Dentistry
1121 W. Michigan St.
Indianapolis, IN 46202-5186
317-274-7957
Teaching Specialties:
Dentistry.

Larue D. Carter Memorial Hospital
1315 W. 10th St.
Indianapolis, IN 46202
317-634-8401
Teaching Specialties:
Psychiatry.

Methodist Hospital of Indiana
1701 N. Senate Blvd.
Indianapolis, IN 46202
317-929-2000
Teaching Specialties:
Internal Medicine, Internal Medicine-Cardiovascular Disease, Internal Medicine-Nephrology, Obstetrics/Gynecology, Ophthalmology, Orthopedic Surgery, Surgery, Urology.

St. Vincent Hospital and Health Care Center
2001 W. 86th St.
Indianapolis, IN 46240
317-871-2345
Teaching Specialties:
Internal Medicine, Obstetrics/Gynecology, Orthopedic Surgery.

William N. Wishard Memorial Hospital
1001 W. 10th St.
Indianapolis, IN 46202
317-639-6671
Teaching Specialties:
Anesthesiology, Dermatology, Internal Medicine, Internal Medicine-Geriatric

Medicine, Neurological Surgery, Neurology, Obstetrics/Gynecology, Ophthalmology, Orthopedic Surgery, Otolaryngology, Psychiatry, Radiation Oncology, Surgery, Urology.

Jeffersonville

Lifespring Mental Health Services
207 W. 13th St.
Jeffersonville, IN 47130
812-283-4491
Teaching Specialties:
Psychiatry.

Muncie

Ball Memorial Hospital
2401 University Ave.
Muncie, IN 47303
317-747-3111
Teaching Specialties:
Internal Medicine.

IOWA

Des Moines

Broadlawns Medical Center
18th St. & Hickman Rd.
Des Moines, IA 50314
515-282-2200
Teaching Specialties:
Surgery.

Iowa Methodist Medical Center
1200 Pleasant St.
Des Moines, IA 50309
515-283-6212
Teaching Specialties:
Internal Medicine, Surgery.

Mercy Hospital Medical Center
6th & University Ave.
Des Moines, IA 50314
515-247-3121
Teaching Specialties:
Surgery.

Iowa City

University of Iowa College of Dentistry
Iowa City, IA 52242
319-335-9650
Teaching Specialties:
Dentistry.

University of Iowa Hospitals and Clinics
650 Newton Rd.
Iowa City, IA 52242
319-356-1616
Teaching Specialties:

Allergy/Immunology, Anesthesiology, Dermatology, Hand Surgery, Internal Medicine, Internal Medicine-Cardiovascular Disease, Internal Medicine-Endocrinology and Metabolism, Internal Medicine-Gastroenterology, Internal Medicine-Geriatric Medicine, Internal Medicine-Hematology, Internal Medicine-Infectious Diseases, Internal Medicine-Medical Oncology, Internal Medicine-Nephrology, Internal Medicine-Rheumatology, Neurological Surgery, Neurology, Obstetrics/Gynecology, Ophthalmology, Orthopedic Surgery, Otolaryngology, Psychiatry, Radiation Oncology, Surgery, Surgery-Vascular Surgery, Thoracic Surgery, Urology.

KANSAS

Kansas City

Bethany Medical Center
51 N. 12th St.
Kansas City, KS 66102
913-281-8400
Teaching Specialties:
Internal Medicine.

Truman Medical Center-West
2301 Holmes St.
Kansas City, KS 64108
816-556-3000
Teaching Specialties:
Internal Medicine, Internal Medicine-Cardiovascular Disease, Internal Medicine-Gastroenterology, Internal Medicine-Hematology, Internal Medicine-Infectious Diseases, Internal Medicine-Medical Oncology, Obstetrics/Gynecology, Ophthalmology, Orthopedic Surgery, Surgery.

University of Kansas Hospital
39th & Rainbow Blvd.
Kansas City, KS 66103
913-588-5000
Teaching Specialties:
Allergy/Immunology, Anesthesiology, Dermatology, Internal Medicine, Internal Medicine-Cardiovascular Disease, Internal Medicine-Endocrinology and Metabolism, Internal Medicine-Gastroenterology, Internal Medicine-Geriatric Medicine, Internal Medicine-Hematology, Internal Medicine-Infectious Diseases, Internal Medicine-Medical Oncology, Internal Medicine-Nephrology, Internal Medicine-Rheumatology, Neurological Surgery, Neurology, Obstetrics/Gynecology, Ophthalmology, Orthopedic Surgery, Otolaryngology, Physical Medicine and Rehabilitation, Psychiatry, Radiation Oncology, Surgery, Surgery-Vascular Surgery, Thoracic Surgery, Urology.

Topeka

C.F. Menninger Memorial Hospital
5800 S.W. 6th St.
Topeka, KS 66601

913-273-7500
Teaching Specialties:
Psychiatry.

Stormont-Vail Regional Medical Center
1500 W. 10th St.
Topeka, KS 66604
913-354-6000
Teaching Specialties:
Internal Medicine.

Topeka State Hospital
2700 W. 6th St.
Topeka, KS 66606
913-296-4596
Teaching Specialties:
Psychiatry.

Wichita

HCA Wesley Medical Center
550 N. Hillside Ave.
Wichita, KS 67214
316-688-2468
Teaching Specialties:
Anesthesiology, Internal Medicine, Obstetrics/Gynecology, Orthopedic Surgery, Surgery.

St. Francis Regional Medical Center
929 N. St. Francis Ave.
Wichita, KS 67214
316-268-5000
Teaching Specialties:
Anesthesiology, Internal Medicine, Orthopedic Surgery, Surgery.

St. Joseph Medical Center
3600 E. Harry St.
Wichita, KS 67218
316-685-1111
Teaching Specialties:
Anesthesiology, Psychiatry.

KENTUCKY

Lexington

Cardinal Hill Hospital
2050 Versailles Rd.
Lexington, KY 40504
606-254-5701
Teaching Specialties:
Physical Medicine and Rehabilitation.

Central Baptist Hospital
1740 Nicholasville Rd.
Lexington, KY 40503
606-275-6100
Teaching Specialties:
Obstetrics/Gynecology.

St. Joseph Hospital
One St. Joseph Dr.
Lexington, KY 40504
606-278-3436
Teaching Specialties:
Urology.

University of Kentucky College of Dentistry
800 Rose St.
Lexington, KY 40536-0084
800-28-UKDMD
Teaching Specialties:
Dentistry.

University of Kentucky Hospital
Albert B. Chandler Medical Center
800 Rose St.
Lexington, KY 40526
606-233-5000
Teaching Specialties:
Anesthesiology, Internal Medicine, Internal Medicine-Cardiovascular Disease, Internal Medicine-Endocrinology and Metabolism, Internal Medicine-Gastroenterology, Internal Medicine-Geriatric Medicine, Internal Medicine-Hematology, Internal Medicine-Infectious Diseases, Internal Medicine-Medical Oncology, Internal Medicine-Nephrology, Internal Medicine-Rheumatology, Neurological Surgery, Neurology, Obstetrics/Gynecology, Ophthalmology, Orthopedic Surgery, Otolaryngology, Physical Medicine and Rehabilitation, Psychiatry, Radiation Oncology, Surgery, Surgery-Vascular Surgery, Thoracic Surgery, Urology.

Louisville

Frazier Rehabilitation Center
220 Abraham Flexner Way
Louisville, KY 40202
502-582-7400
Teaching Specialties:
Internal Medicine-Rheumatology, Physical Medicine and Rehabilitation.

Humana Hospital-University of Louisville
530 S. Jackson St.
Louisville, KY 40202
502-562-3000
Teaching Specialties:
Anesthesiology, Dermatology, Internal Medicine, Internal Medicine-Cardiovascular Disease, Internal Medicine-Endocrinology and Metabolism, Internal Medicine-Gastroenterology, Internal Medicine-Infectious Diseases, Internal Medicine-Nephrology, Internal Medicine-Rheumatology, Neurological Surgery, Neurology, Obstetrics/Gynecology, Ophthalmology, Orthopedic Surgery, Otolaryngology, Psychiatry, Radiation Oncology, Surgery, Thoracic Surgery, Urology.

Jewish Hospital
217 E. Chestnut St.
Louisville, KY 40202
502-587-4011
Teaching Specialties:
Orthopedic Surgery, Surgery,
Thoracic Surgery, Urology.

Methodist Evangelical Hospital
315 E. Broadway
Louisville, KY 40202
502-629-2000
Teaching Specialties:
Orthopedic Surgery.

Norton Hospital
200 E. Chestnut St.
Louisville, KY 40232
502-629-8000
Teaching Specialties:
Allergy/Immunology, Neurological Surgery,
Neurology, Obstetrics/Gynecology,
Orthopedic Surgery, Otolaryngology,
Psychiatry, Surgery, Urology.

**University of Louisville School
of Dentistry**
Louisville, KY 40292
502-588-5293
Teaching Specialties:
Dentistry.

L O U I S I A N A

Baton Rouge

Earl K. Long Memorial Hospital
5825 Airline Highway
Baton Rouge, LA 70805
504-356-3361
Teaching Specialties:
Internal Medicine, Obstetrics/Gynecology,
Orthopedic Surgery, Surgery.

Houma

South Louisiana Medical Center
1978 Industrial Blvd.
Houma, LA 70363
504-873-2200
Teaching Specialties:
Internal Medicine, Obstetrics/Gynecology,
Ophthalmology, Orthopedic Surgery,
Surgery, Urology.

Independence

Lallie Kemp Hospital
PO Box 70
Independence, LA 70443
504-878-9421
Teaching Specialties:
Obstetrics/Gynecology.

Lafayette

University Medical Center
2390 W. Congress St.
Lafayette, LA 70526
318-261-6000
Teaching Specialties:
Internal Medicine, Obstetrics/Gynecology,
Orthopedic Surgery, Surgery.

Lake Charles

**Dr. Walter Olin Moss Regional
Hospital**
1000 Walters St.
Lake Charles, LA 70605
318-477-3350
Teaching Specialties:
Obstetrics/Gynecology, Surgery.

Monroe

E.A. Conway Memorial Hospital
4864 Jackson St.
Monroe, LA 71201
318-388-7000
Teaching Specialties:
Obstetrics/Gynecology, Ophthalmology,
Surgery.

New Orleans

Eye, Ear, Nose and Throat Hospital
2626 Napoleon Ave.
New Orleans, LA 70115
504-896-1100
Teaching Specialties:
Ophthalmology, Otolaryngology.

Hotel Dieu Hospital
2021 Perdido St.
New Orleans, LA 70112
504-588-3000
Teaching Specialties:
Internal Medicine-Gastroenterology, Internal
Medicine-Infectious Diseases, Internal
Medicine-Medical Oncology, Internal
Medicine-Rheumatology, Neurology,
Ophthalmology, Orthopedic Surgery,
Surgery-Vascular Surgery, Urology.

Jo Ellen Smith Medical Center
4444 General Meyer Ave.
New Orleans, LA 70131
504-363-7011
Teaching Specialties:
Urology.

**Louisiana State University
Eye Center**
2020 Gravier St., Suite B
New Orleans, LA 70112
504-568-6700
Teaching Specialties:
Ophthalmology.

**Louisiana State University
School of Dentistry**
1100 Florida Ave.
New Orleans, LA 70119
504-947-9961
Teaching Specialties:
Dentistry.

**Medical Center of Louisiana
at New Orleans**
1532 Tulane Ave.
New Orleans, LA 70140
504-568-2311
Teaching Specialties:
Allergy/Immunology, Anesthesiology, Dentistry, Dermatology, Internal Medicine, Internal Medicine-Cardiovascular Disease, Internal Medicine-Endocrinology and Metabolism, Internal Medicine-Gastroenterology, Internal Medicine-Hematology, Internal Medicine-Infectious Diseases, Internal Medicine-Medical Oncology, Internal Medicine-Nephrology, Internal Medicine-Rheumatology, Neurological Surgery, Neurology, Obstetrics/Gynecology, Ophthalmology, Orthopedic Surgery, Otolaryngology, Physical Medicine and Rehabilitation, Psychiatry, Surgery, Surgery-Vascular Surgery, Thoracic Surgery, Urology.

**Medical Center of Louisiana
at New Orleans**
Louisiana Rehabilitation Institute
1532 Tulane Ave., L&M Bldg.
New Orleans, LA 70140
504-568-2200
Teaching Specialties:
Physical Medicine and Rehabilitation.

Ochsner Foundation Hospital
1516 Jefferson Highway
New Orleans, LA 70121
504-838-3000
Teaching Specialties:
Anesthesiology, Colon and Rectal Surgery, Dermatology, Internal Medicine, Internal Medicine-Cardiovascular Disease, Internal Medicine-Endocrinology and Metabolism, Internal Medicine-Gastroenterology, Internal Medicine-Infectious Diseases, Internal Medicine-Medical Oncology, Internal Medicine-Rheumatology, Neurology, Obstetrics/Gynecology, Ophthalmology, Orthopedic Surgery, Otolaryngology, Psychiatry, Surgery, Surgery-Vascular Surgery, Thoracic Surgery, Urology.

River Oaks Psychiatric Hospital
1525 River Oaks Rd., W
New Orleans, LA 70123
504-734-1740
Teaching Specialties:
Psychiatry.

Southern Baptist Hospital
2700 Napoleon Ave.
New Orleans, LA 70115
504-899-9311
Teaching Specialties:
Neurology.

Touro Infirmary
1401 Foucher St.
New Orleans, LA 70115
504-897-7011
Teaching Specialties:
Orthopedic Surgery, Psychiatry, Surgery.

**Tulane University Hospital
and Clinics**
1415 Tulane Ave.
New Orleans, LA 70112
504-588-5263
Teaching Specialties:
Allergy/Immunology, Anesthesiology, Dermatology, Internal Medicine, Internal Medicine-Cardiovascular Disease, Internal Medicine-Endocrinology and Metabolism, Internal Medicine-Gastroenterology, Internal Medicine-Hematology, Internal Medicine-Infectious Diseases, Internal Medicine Nephrology, Internal Medicine-Rheumatology, Neurological Surgery, Neurology, Obstetrics/Gynecology, Ophthalmology, Orthopedic Surgery, Otolaryngology, Psychiatry, Surgery, Surgery-Vascular Surgery, Thoracic Surgery, Urology.

Pineville

**Huey P. Long Regional
Medical Center**
Hospital Blvd.
Pineville, LA 71361
318-448-0811
Teaching Specialties:
Obstetrics/Gynecology, Orthopedic Surgery, Surgery, Urology.

Shreveport

Louisiana State University Hospital
PO Box 33932, 1541 Kings Highway
Shreveport, LA 71130
318-674-5000
Teaching Specialties:
Allergy/Immunology, Anesthesiology, Colon and Rectal Surgery, Internal Medicine, Internal Medicine-Cardiovascular Disease, Internal Medicine-Endocrinology and Metabolism, Internal Medicine-Gastroenterology, Internal Medicine-Hematology, Internal Medicine-Infectious Diseases, Internal Medicine-Medical Oncology, Internal Medicine-Nephrology, Internal Medicine-Rheumatology, Obstetrics/Gynecology, Ophthalmology, Orthopedic Surgery, Otolaryngology, Surgery, Urology.

Schumpert Medical Center
915 Margaret Pl.
Shreveport, LA 71101
318-227-4500
Teaching Specialties:
Colon and Rectal Surgery, Urology.

MAINE
Portland

Maine Medical Center
22 Bramhall St.
Portland, ME 04102
207-871-0111
Teaching Specialties:
Anesthesiology, Internal Medicine, Internal Medicine-Cardiovascular Disease, Internal Medicine-Endocrinology and Metabolism, Internal Medicine-Infectious Diseases, Internal Medicine-Nephrology, Obstetrics/Gynecology, Psychiatry, Surgery.

MARYLAND
Baltimore

Francis Scott Key Medical Center
4940 Eastern Ave.
Baltimore, MD 21224
410-550-0100
Teaching Specialties:
Anesthesiology, Internal Medicine, Internal Medicine-Gastroenterology, Internal Medicine-Geriatric Medicine, Internal Medicine-Nephrology, Neurological Surgery, Neurology, Obstetrics/Gynecology, Orthopedic Surgery, Otolaryngology, Psychiatry, Surgery, Urology.

Franklin Square Hospital Center
9000 Franklin Square
Baltimore, MD 21237
410-682-7000
Teaching Specialties:
Internal Medicine, Obstetrics/Gynecology, Psychiatry.

**Good Samaritan Hospital
of Maryland**
5601 Loch Raven Blvd.
Baltimore, MD 21239
410-323-2200
Teaching Specialties:
Allergy/Immunology, Dermatology, Internal Medicine, Orthopedic Surgery, Physical Medicine and Rehabilitation.

Greater Baltimore Medical Center
6701 N. Charles St.
Baltimore, MD 21204
410-828-2000
Teaching Specialties:

Colon and Rectal Surgery, Internal Medicine, Obstetrics/Gynecology, Ophthalmology, Otolaryngology.

Harbor Hospital Center
3001 S. Hanover St.
Baltimore, MD 21230
410-347-3200
Teaching Specialties:
Internal Medicine, Obstetrics/Gynecology.

**Homewood Hospital Center-
North Campus**
3100 Wyman Park Dr.
Baltimore, MD 21211
410-338-3000
Teaching Specialties:
Surgery.

James Lawrence Kernan Hospital
2200 N. Forest Park Ave.
Baltimore, MD 21207
410-448-2500
Teaching Specialties:
Orthopedic Surgery.

Johns Hopkins Hospital
600 N. Wolfe St.
Baltimore, MD 21205
410-955-5000
Teaching Specialties:
Allergy/Immunology, Anesthesiology, Dentistry, Dermatology, Internal Medicine, Internal Medicine-Cardiovascular Disease, Internal Medicine-Endocrinology and Metabolism, Internal Medicine-Gastroenterology, Internal Medicine-Geriatric Medicine, Internal Medicine-Hematology, Internal Medicine-Infectious Diseases, Internal Medicine-Medical Oncology, Internal Medicine-Nephrology, Internal Medicine-Rheumatology, Neurological Surgery, Neurology, Obstetrics/Gynecology, Orthopedic Surgery, Otolaryngology, Physical Medicine and Rehabilitation, Psychiatry, Radiation Oncology, Surgery, Thoracic Surgery, Urology.

Johns Hopkins Hospital
Wilmer Eye Institute
600 N. Wolfe St.
Baltimore, MD 21205
410-955-6275
Teaching Specialties:
Ophthalmology.

Maryland General Hospital
827 Linden Ave.
Baltimore, MD 21201
410-225-8000
Teaching Specialties:
Internal Medicine, Obstetrics/Gynecology, Ophthalmology, Otolaryngology, Surgery.

477

Mercy Medical Center
301 St. Paul Place
Baltimore, MD 21202
410-332-9000
Teaching Specialties:
Internal Medicine, Obstetrics/Gynecology,
Surgery.

Sheppard and Enoch Pratt Hospital
6501 N. Charles St.
Baltimore, MD 21204
410-938-3000
Teaching Specialties:
Psychiatry.

Sinai Hospital of Baltimore
2401 W. Belvedere Ave.
Baltimore, MD 21215
410-578-5678
Teaching Specialties:
Internal Medicine, Obstetrics/Gynecology,
Ophthalmology, Orthopedic Surgery,
Otolaryngology, Physical Medicine and
Rehabilitation, Surgery, Urology.

**St. Agnes Hospital of the
City of Baltimore**
900 Caton Ave.
Baltimore, MD 21229
410-368-6000
Teaching Specialties:
Internal Medicine, Orthopedic Surgery,
Surgery.

Union Memorial Hospital
201 E. University Parkway
Baltimore, MD 21218
410-554-2000
Teaching Specialties:
Internal Medicine, Obstetrics/Gynecology,
Orthopedic Surgery, Surgery.

**University of Maryland
at Baltimore**
Baltimore College of Dentistry
Dental School
666 W. Baltimore St.
Baltimore, MD 21201
410-328-7460
Teaching Specialties:
Dentistry.

**University of Maryland
Medical System**
22 S. Greene St.
Baltimore, MD 21201
410-328-8667
Teaching Specialties:
Anesthesiology, Dermatology, Internal
Medicine, Internal Medicine-Cardiovascular
Disease, Internal Medicine-Endocrinology
and Metabolism, Internal Medicine-Gastroen-

terology, Internal Medicine-Hematology,
Internal Medicine-Infectious Diseases, Inter-
nal Medicine-Medical Oncology, Internal
Medicine-Nephrology, Internal Medicine-
Rheumatology, Neurological Surgery, Neurol-
ogy, Obstetrics/Gynecology, Ophthalmology,
Orthopedic Surgery, Otolaryngology, Psychia-
try, Radiation Oncology, Surgery, Thoracic
Surgery, Urology.

Walter P. Carter Center
630 W. Fayette St.
Baltimore, MD 21201
410-528-2139
Teaching Specialties:
Psychiatry.

Bethesda

Suburban Hospital
8600 Old Georgetown Rd.
Bethesda, MD 20814
301-530-3100
Teaching Specialties:
Colon and Rectal Surgery.

Catonsville

Spring Grove Hospital Center
Wade Ave.
Catonsville, MD 21228
410-455-6000
Teaching Specialties:
Psychiatry.

Cheverly

Prince George's Hospital Center
3001 Hospital Dr.
Cheverly, MD 20785
301-618-2000
Teaching Specialties:
Dentistry, Internal Medicine, Internal
Medicine-Gastroenterology.

Crownsville

Crownsville Hospital Center
1400 General's Highway
Crownsville, MD 21032
410-987-6200
Teaching Specialties:
Psychiatry.

Silver Spring

**Holy Cross Hospital
of Silver Spring**
1500 Forest Glen Rd.
Silver Spring, MD 20910
301-905-0100
Teaching Specialties:
Obstetrics/Gynecology, Surgery.

Sykesville

Springfield Hospital Center
6655 Sykesville Rd.
Sykesville, MD 21784
410-795-2100
Teaching Specialties:
Psychiatry.

MASSACHUSETTS
Belmont

McLean Hospital
115 Mill St.
Belmont, MA 02178
800-333-0338
617-855-2000
Teaching Specialties:
Psychiatry.

Boston

Beth Israel Hospital
330 Brookline Ave.
Boston, MA 02215
617-735-2000
Teaching Specialties:
Anesthesiology, Dermatology, Internal
Medicine, Internal Medicine-Cardiovascular
Disease, Internal Medicine-Endocrinology
and Metabolism, Internal Medicine-Gastroen-
terology, Internal Medicine-Geriatric Medi-
cine, Internal Medicine-Hematology, Internal
Medicine-Infectious Diseases, Internal Medi-
cine-Medical Oncology, Internal Medicine-
Nephrology, Neurological Surgery, Neurolo-
gy, Obstetrics/Gynecology, Orthopedic
Surgery, Otolaryngology, Psychiatry,
Radiation Oncology, Surgery, Urology.

Boston City Hospital
818 Harrison Ave.
Boston, MA 02118
617-424-5000
Teaching Specialties:
Anesthesiology, Dentistry, Dermatology,
Internal Medicine, Internal Medicine-Cardio-
vascular Disease, Internal Medicine-Endo-
crinology and Metabolism, Internal Medicine-
Gastroenterology, Internal Medicine-Hema-
tology, Internal Medicine-Infectious Diseases,
Internal Medicine-Medical Oncology, Inter-
nal Medicine-Nephrology, Internal Medicine-
Rheumatology, Neurology, Obstetrics/Gyne-
cology, Ophthalmology, Orthopedic Surgery,
Otolaryngology, Psychiatry, Surgery, Surgery-
Vascular Surgery, Thoracic Surgery, Urology.

Boston University
Henry M. Goldman School
of Graduate Dentistry
100 E. Newton St.
Boston, MA 02118
617-638-4700

Teaching Specialties:
Dentistry.

Brigham and Women's Hospital
75 Francis St.
Boston, MA 02115
617-732-5500
Teaching Specialties:
Allergy/Immunology, Anesthesiology, Dentistry, Dermatology, Internal Medicine, Internal Medicine-Cardiovascular Disease, Internal Medicine-Endocrinology and Metabolism, Internal Medicine-Gastroenterology, Internal Medicine-Hematology, Internal Medicine-Infectious Diseases, Internal Medicine-Medical Oncology, Internal Medicine-Nephrology, Internal Medicine-Rheumatology, Neurological Surgery, Neurology, Obstetrics/Gynecology, Orthopedic Surgery, Radiation Oncology, Surgery, Surgery-Vascular Surgery, Thoracic Surgery, Urology.

Carney Hospital
2100 Dorchester Ave.
Boston, MA 02124
617-296-4000
Teaching Specialties:
Internal Medicine, Orthopedic Surgery, Surgery.

Dana-Farber Cancer Institute
44 Binney St.
Boston, MA 02115
617-732-3000
Teaching Specialties:
Radiation Oncology.

Dr. Solomon Carter Fuller Mental Health Center
85 E. Newton St.
Boston, MA 02118
617-266-8800
Teaching Specialties:
Psychiatry.

Erich Lindemann Mental Health Center
Government Center
Boston, MA 02114
617-727-7115
Teaching Specialties:
Psychiatry.

Faulkner Hospital
1153 Centre St.
Boston, MA 02130
617-522-5800
Teaching Specialties:
Internal Medicine, Internal Medicine-Gastroenterology, Psychiatry, Surgery.

Harvard School of Dental Medicine
188 Longwood Ave.
Boston, MA 02115

617-432-1405
Teaching Specialties:
Dentistry.

Jewish Memorial Hospital
59 Townsend St.
Boston, MA 02119
617-442-8760
Teaching Specialties:
Internal Medicine-Geriatric Medicine.

Joslin Diabetes Center, Inc.
One Joslin Place
Boston, MA 02215
617-732-2440
Fax: 617-732-2664
Teaching Specialties:
Internal Medicine-Endocrinology and Metabolism.

Lemuel Shattuck Hospital
170 Morton St.
Boston, MA 02130
617-522-8110
Teaching Specialties:
Internal Medicine-Gastroenterology, Psychiatry.

Lemuel Shattuck Hospital
Bay Cove Mental Health Center
170 Morton St.
Boston, MA 02130
617-522-8110
Teaching Specialties:
Psychiatry.

Massachusetts Eye and Ear Infirmary
243 Charles St.
Boston, MA 02114
617-523-7900
Teaching Specialties:
Ophthalmology, Otolaryngology.

Massachusetts General Hospital
55 Fruit St.
Boston, MA 02114
617-726-2000
Teaching Specialties:
Allergy/Immunology, Anesthesiology, Dentistry, Dermatology, Internal Medicine, Internal Medicine-Cardiovascular Disease, Internal Medicine-Endocrinology and Metabolism, Internal Medicine-Gastroenterology, Internal Medicine-Hematology, Internal Medicine-Infectious Diseases, Internal Medicine-Medical Oncology, Internal Medicine-Nephrology, Internal Medicine-Rheumatology, Neurological Surgery, Neurology, Obstetrics/Gynecology, Orthopedic Surgery, Psychiatry, Radiation Oncology, Surgery, Surgery-Vascular Surgery, Thoracic Surgery, Urology.

Massachusetts Mental Health Center
74 Fenwood Rd.
Boston, MA 02115
617-734-1300
Teaching Specialties:
Psychiatry.

New England Baptist Hospital
125 Parker Hill Ave.
Boston, MA 02120
617-738-5800
Teaching Specialties:
Orthopedic Surgery.

New England Deaconess Hospital
185 Pilgrim Rd.
Boston, MA 02215
617-732-7000
Teaching Specialties:
Internal Medicine, Internal Medicine-Cardiovascular Disease, Internal Medicine-Endocrinology and Metabolism, Internal Medicine-Gastroenterology, Internal Medicine-Hematology, Internal Medicine-Infectious Diseases, Internal Medicine-Medical Oncology, Neurology, Radiation Oncology, Surgery, Surgery-Vascular Surgery, Thoracic Surgery, Urology.

New England Medical Center
750 Washington St.
Boston, MA 02111
617-956-5000
Teaching Specialties:
Anesthesiology, Dermatology, Internal Medicine, Internal Medicine-Cardiovascular Disease, Internal Medicine-Endocrinology and Metabolism, Internal Medicine-Gastroenterology, Internal Medicine-Hematology, Internal Medicine-Infectious Diseases, Internal Medicine-Medical Oncology, Internal Medicine-Nephrology, Internal Medicine-Rheumatology, Neurological Surgery, Neurology, Obstetrics/Gynecology, Ophthalmology, Orthopedic Surgery, Otolaryngology, Physical Medicine and Rehabilitation, Psychiatry, Radiation Oncology, Surgery, Surgery-Vascular Surgery, Thoracic Surgery, Urology.

St. Elizabeth's Hospital of Boston
736 Cambridge St.
Boston, MA 02135
617-789-3000
Teaching Specialties:
Anesthesiology, Internal Medicine, Internal Medicine-Cardiovascular Disease, Internal Medicine-Gastroenterology, Internal Medicine-Hematology, Internal Medicine-Medical Oncology, Neurological Surgery, Orthopedic Surgery, Psychiatry, Surgery, Thoracic Surgery, Urology.

St. Margaret's Hospital for Women
90 Cushing Ave.,

Dorchester Station
Boston, MA 02125
617-436-8600
Teaching Specialties:
Obstetrics/Gynecology.

**Tufts University School
of Dental Medicine**
One Kneeland St.
Boston, MA 02111
617-956-5000
Teaching Specialties:
Dentistry.

University Hospital
88 E. Newton St.
Boston, MA 02118
617-638-6000
Teaching Specialties:
Anesthesiology, Dermatology, Internal
Medicine, Internal Medicine-Cardiovascular
Disease, Internal Medicine-Endocrinology
and Metabolism, Internal Medicine-Gastroen-
terology, Internal Medicine-Geriatric Medi-
cine, Internal Medicine-Hematology, Internal
Medicine-Infectious Diseases, Internal Medi-
cine-Medical Oncology, Internal Medicine-
Nephrology, Internal Medicine-Rheumatolo-
gy, Neurology, Ophthalmology, Orthopedic
Surgery, Otolaryngology, Physical Medicine
and Rehabilitation, Psychiatry, Surgery,
Surgery-Vascular Surgery, Thoracic Surgery,
Urology.

**West-Ros-Park Mental Health
Center**
Alternative House
591 Morton St., Cottage #1
Boston, MA 02124
617-325-6700
Teaching Specialties:
Psychiatry.

Brockton

Brockton Hospital
680 Centre St.
Brockton, MA 02402
508-941-7001
Teaching Specialties:
Surgery.

Cardinal Cushing General Hospital
235 N. Pearl St.
Brockton, MA 02401
508-588-4000
Teaching Specialties:
Surgery.

Burlington

Lahey Clinic Hospital
41 Mall Rd.
Burlington, MA 01805

617-273-5100
Teaching Specialties:
Colon and Rectal Surgery, Dermatology,
Internal Medicine-Cardiovascular Disease,
Internal Medicine-Endocrinology and Metab-
olism, Internal Medicine-Gastroenterology,
Neurology, Orthopedic Surgery, Otolaryngol-
ogy, Surgery, Thoracic Surgery, Urology.

Cambridge

Cambridge Hospital
1493 Cambridge St.
Cambridge, MA 02139
617-498-1000
Teaching Specialties:
Internal Medicine, Psychiatry.

Mt. Auburn Hospital
330 Mt. Auburn St.
Cambridge, MA 02238
617-492-3500
Teaching Specialties:
Internal Medicine, Surgery, Surgery-Vascular
Surgery, Thoracic Surgery.

Chelsea

**Lawrence F. Quigley
Memorial Hospital**
91 Crest Ave.
Chelsea, MA 02150
617-884-5660
Teaching Specialties:
Urology.

Framingham

Framingham Union Hospital
115 Lincoln St.
Framingham, MA 01701
508-879-7111
Teaching Specialties:
Internal Medicine, Obstetrics/Gynecology.

Hathorne

Danvers State Hospital
PO Box 50
Hathorne, MA 01937
508-774-5000
Teaching Specialties:
Psychiatry.

Hyannis

Cape Cod Hospital
27 Park St.
Hyannis, MA 02601
508-771-1800
Teaching Specialties:
Surgery.

Malden

Malden Hospital
Hospital Rd.
Malden, MA 02148
617-322-7560
Teaching Specialties:
Obstetrics/Gynecology.

Newton

Newton-Wellesley Hospital
2014 Washington St.
Newton, MA 02162
617-243-6000
Teaching Specialties:
Internal Medicine, Orthopedic Surgery,
Surgery.

Pittsfield

Berkshire Medical Center
725 North St.
Pittsfield, MA 01201
413-447-2000
Teaching Specialties:
Dentistry, Internal Medicine, Obstetrics/
Gynecology, Surgery.

Salem

Salem Hospital
81 Highland Ave.
Salem, MA 01970
508-741-1200
Teaching Specialties:
Internal Medicine.

Springfield

Baystate Medical Center
759 Chestnut St.
Springfield, MA 01199
413-784-0000
Teaching Specialties:
Anesthesiology, Internal Medicine, Internal
Medicine-Cardiovascular Disease, Internal
Medicine-Endocrinology and Metabolism,
Internal Medicine-Hematology, Internal
Medicine-Infectious Diseases, Internal
Medicine-Medical Oncology, Obstetrics/
Gynecology, Orthopedic Surgery, Surgery.

Stockbridge

Austen Riggs Center
Main St.
Stockbridge, MA 01262
413-298-5511
Teaching Specialties:
Psychiatry.

Stoughton

New England Sinai Hospital and Rehabilitation Center
150 York St.
Stoughton, MA 02072
617-364-4850
Teaching Specialties:
Physical Medicine and Rehabilitation.

Wellesley

Charles River Hospital
203 Grove St.
Wellesley, MA 02181
617-235-8400
Teaching Specialties:
Psychiatry.

Worcester

Medical Center of Central Massachusetts
119 Belmont St.
Worcester, MA 01605
508-856-9355
Teaching Specialties:
Internal Medicine, Internal Medicine-Geriatric Medicine, Obstetrics/Gynecology, Orthopedic Surgery, Surgery, Urology.

St. Vincent Hospital
25 Winthrop St.
Worcester, MA 01604
617-798-1234
Teaching Specialties:
Internal Medicine, Internal Medicine-Cardiovascular Disease, Neurology, Obstetrics/Gynecology, Orthopedic Surgery, Surgery, Thoracic Surgery.

University of Massachusetts Medical Center
55 Lake Ave. N
Worcester, MA 01655
508-856-0011
Teaching Specialties:
Anesthesiology, Internal Medicine, Internal Medicine-Cardiovascular Disease, Internal Medicine-Endocrinology and Metabolism, Internal Medicine-Gastroenterology, Internal Medicine-Geriatric Medicine, Internal Medicine-Hematology, Internal Medicine-Infectious Diseases, Internal Medicine-Medical Oncology, Internal Medicine-Nephrology, Internal Medicine-Rheumatology, Neurology, Obstetrics/Gynecology, Orthopedic Surgery, Psychiatry, Surgery, Surgery-Vascular Surgery, Thoracic Surgery, Urology.

Worcester Health and Hospitals Authority
26 Queen St.
Worcester, MA 01610

508-799-8000
Teaching Specialties:
Internal Medicine, Orthopedic Surgery, Surgery.

Worcester State Hospital
305 Belmont St.
Worcester, MA 01604
617-752-4681
Teaching Specialties:
Psychiatry.

MICHIGAN

Ann Arbor

St. Joseph Mercy Hospital
5301 E. Huron River Dr.
Ann Arbor, MI 48106
313-572-3456
Teaching Specialties:
Internal Medicine, Neurological Surgery, Obstetrics/Gynecology, Orthopedic Surgery, Surgery, Urology.

University of Michigan Hospitals
1500 E. Medical Center Dr.
Ann Arbor, MI 48109
313-936-4000
Teaching Specialties:
Allergy/Immunology, Anesthesiology, Dermatology, Internal Medicine, Internal Medicine-Cardiovascular Disease, Internal Medicine-Endocrinology and Metabolism, Internal Medicine-Gastroenterology, Internal Medicine-Geriatric Medicine, Internal Medicine-Hematology, Internal Medicine-Infectious Diseases, Internal Medicine-Medical Oncology, Internal Medicine-Nephrology, Internal Medicine-Rheumatology, Neurological Surgery, Neurology, Obstetrics/Gynecology, Ophthalmology, Orthopedic Surgery, Otolaryngology, Physical Medicine and Rehabilitation, Psychiatry, Radiation Oncology, Surgery, Surgery-Vascular Surgery, Thoracic Surgery, Urology.

University of Michigan School of Dentistry
Ann Arbor, MI 48109-1078
313-763-6933
Teaching Specialties:
Dentistry.

Dearborn

Oakwood Hospital
18101 Oakwood Blvd.
Dearborn, MI 48123
313-593-7000
Teaching Specialties:
Internal Medicine, Obstetrics/Gynecology, Orthopedic Surgery.

Detroit

Detroit-Macomb Hospital Corporation
Oral and Maxillofacial Surgery
7733 E. Jefferson
Detroit, MI 48214-2598
313-499-4190
Teaching Specialties:
Dentistry.

Detroit Psychiatric Institute
1151 Taylor St.
Detroit, MI 48202
313-874-7744
Teaching Specialties:
Psychiatry.

Detroit Receiving Hospital and University Health Center
4201 St. Antoine Blvd.
Detroit, MI 48201
313-745-3000
Teaching Specialties:
Allergy/Immunology, Dentistry, Dermatology, Internal Medicine, Internal Medicine-Cardiovascular Disease, Internal Medicine-Endocrinology and Metabolism, Internal Medicine-Gastroenterology, Internal Medicine-Hematology, Internal Medicine-Infectious Diseases, Internal Medicine-Medical Oncology, Internal Medicine-Nephrology, Internal Medicine-Rheumatology, Neurological Surgery, Neurology, Obstetrics/Gynecology, Ophthalmology, Orthopedic Surgery, Otolaryngology, Radiation Oncology, Surgery, Thoracic Surgery.

Grace Hospital
6071 W. Outer Dr.
Detroit, MI 48235
313-966-3300
Teaching Specialties:
Internal Medicine, Obstetrics/Gynecology, Ophthalmology, Orthopedic Surgery, Otolaryngology, Radiation Oncology, Surgery.

Harper Hospital
3990 John R. St.
Detroit, MI 48201
313-745-8040
Teaching Specialties:
Allergy/Immunology, Dermatology, Internal Medicine, Internal Medicine-Cardiovascular Disease, Internal Medicine-Endocrinology and Metabolism, Internal Medicine-Gastroenterology, Internal Medicine-Hematology, Internal Medicine-Infectious Diseases, Internal Medicine-Medical Oncology, Internal Medicine-Nephrology, Internal Medicine-Rheumatology, Neurological Surgery, Neurology, Obstetrics/Gynecology, Ophthalmology, Orthopedic Surgery, Otolaryngology, Psychiatry, Radiation Oncology, Surgery, Surgery-Vascular Surgery, Thoracic Surgery, Urology.

Henry Ford Hospital
2799 W. Grand Blvd.
Detroit, MI 48202
313-876-2600
Teaching Specialties:
Allergy/Immunology, Anesthesiology, Colon
and Rectal Surgery, Dentistry, Dermatology,
Internal Medicine, Internal Medicine-Cardiovascular Disease, Internal Medicine-Endocrinology and Metabolism, Internal Medicine-
Gastroenterology, Internal Medicine-Hematology, Internal Medicine-Infectious Diseases,
Internal Medicine-Medical Oncology, Internal Medicine-Nephrology, Internal Medicine-
Rheumatology, Neurological Surgery, Neurol-
ogy, Obstetrics/Gynecology, Ophthalmology,
Orthopedic Surgery, Otolaryngology, Psychiatry, Radiation Oncology, Surgery, Surgery-
Vascular Surgery, Urology.

Hutzel Hospital
4707 St. Antoine Blvd.
Detroit, MI 48201
313-745-7171
Teaching Specialties:
Internal Medicine-Rheumatology, Obstet-
rics/Gynecology, Otolaryngology, Surgery.

Lafayette Clinic
951 E. Lafayette
Detroit, MI 48207
313-256-9350
Teaching Specialties:
Psychiatry.

Rehabilitation Institute of Michigan
261 Mack Ave.
Detroit, MI 48201
313-745-1203
Teaching Specialties:
Physical Medicine and Rehabilitation.

Samaritan Health Center
5555 Conner Ave.
Detroit, MI 48213
313-579-4000
Teaching Specialties:
Surgery.

Sinai Hospital
6767 W. Outer Dr.
Detroit, MI 48235
313-493-6800
Teaching Specialties:
Anesthesiology, Dentistry, Internal Medicine,
Internal Medicine-Cardiovascular Disease,
Internal Medicine-Gastroenterology, Internal
Medicine-Rheumatology, Obstetrics/Gynecol-
ogy, Ophthalmology, Orthopedic Surgery,
Physical Medicine and Rehabilitation,
Psychiatry, Surgery.

**St. John Hospital and
Medical Center**

22101 Moross Rd.
Detroit, MI 48236
313-343-4000
Teaching Specialties:
Internal Medicine, Obstetrics/Gynecology,
Surgery.

University of Detroit
Mercy School of Dentistry
2985 E. Jefferson Ave.
Detroit, MI 48207
313-446-1800
Teaching Specialties:
Dentistry.

Flint

Hurley Medical Center
One Hurley Plaza
Flint, MI 48503
313-257-9000
Teaching Specialties:
Internal Medicine, Obstetrics/Gynecology,
Orthopedic Surgery.

McLaren Regional Medical Center
401 S. Ballenger Highway
Flint, MI 48532
313-762-2000
Teaching Specialties:
Internal Medicine, Orthopedic Surgery,
Surgery.

Grand Rapids

Blodgett Memorial Medical Center
1840 Wealthy St., SE
Grand Rapids, MI 49506
616-774-7444
Teaching Specialties:
Internal Medicine, Obstetrics/Gynecology,
Orthopedic Surgery, Surgery.

Butterworth Hospital
100 Michigan St., NE
Grand Rapids, MI 49503
616-774-1774
Teaching Specialties:
Internal Medicine, Obstetrics/Gynecology,
Orthopedic Surgery, Surgery.

Ferguson Hospital
72 Sheldon Blvd., SE
Grand Rapids, MI 49503
616-456-0202
Teaching Specialties:
Colon and Rectal Surgery.

**Kent Community Hospital
Complex**
750 Fuller Ave., NE
Grand Rapids, MI 49503
616-774-3300

Teaching Specialties:
Psychiatry.

Pine Rest Christian Hospital
300 68th St., SE
Grand Rapids, MI 49508
616-455-5000
Teaching Specialties:
Psychiatry.

St. Mary's Health Services
200 Jefferson St., SE
Grand Rapids, MI 49503
616-774-6090
Teaching Specialties:
Internal Medicine, Obstetrics/Gynecology,
Orthopedic Surgery, Psychiatry, Surgery.

Grosse Pointe

Bon Secours Hospital
468 Cadieux Rd.
Grosse Pointe, MI 48230
313-343-1000
Teaching Specialties:
Internal Medicine.

Kalamazoo

Borgess Medical Center
1521 Gull Rd.
Kalamazoo, MI 49001
616-383-7000
Teaching Specialties:
Internal Medicine, Orthopedic Surgery.

Bronson Methodist Hospital
252 E. Lovell St.
Kalamazoo, MI 49007
616-341-7654
Teaching Specialties:
Internal Medicine, Orthopedic Surgery.

Lansing

Ingham Medical Center
401 W. Greenlawn Ave.
Lansing, MI 48910
517-334-2121
Teaching Specialties:
Internal Medicine, Internal Medicine-
Gastroenterology, Surgery.

Sparrow Hospital
1215 E. Michigan Ave.
Lansing, MI 48909
517-483-2700
Teaching Specialties:
Internal Medicine, Obstetrics/Gynecology.

**St. Lawrence Hospital and
Healthcare Services**
1210 W. Saginaw St.

Lansing, MI 48915
517-372-3610
Teaching Specialties:
Internal Medicine, Internal Medicine-
Hematology, Psychiatry, Surgery.

Northville

Hawthorn Center
18471 Haggerty Rd.
Northville, MI 48167
313-349-3000
Teaching Specialties:
Psychiatry.

**Northville Regional
Psychiatric Hospital**
41001 W. Seven Mile Rd.
Northville, MI 48167
313-349-1800
Teaching Specialties:
Psychiatry.

Pontiac

Pontiac General Hospital
Seminole at W. Huron St.
Pontiac, MI 48341
313-857-7200
Teaching Specialties:
Obstetrics/Gynecology, Surgery.

St. Joseph Mercy Hospital
900 Woodward Ave.
Pontiac, MI 48341
313-858-3000
Teaching Specialties:
Internal Medicine, Obstetrics/Gynecology,
Surgery.

Royal Oak

William Beaumont Hospital
3601 W. 13 Mile Rd.
Royal Oak, MI 48073
313-551-5000
Teaching Specialties:
Colon and Rectal Surgery, Internal Medicine,
Internal Medicine-Cardiovascular Disease,
Internal Medicine-Gastroenterology, Internal
Medicine-Hematology, Internal Medicine-
Infectious Diseases, Internal Medicine-Medi-
cal Oncology, Obstetrics/Gynecology,
Ophthalmology, Orthopedic Surgery, Physi-
cal Medicine and Rehabilitation, Radiation
Oncology, Surgery, Urology.

Saginaw

Saginaw General Hospital
1447 N. Harrison St.
Saginaw, MI 48602
517-771-4000
Teaching Specialties:

Internal Medicine, Obstetrics/Gynecology,
Surgery.

St. Luke's Hospital
700 Cooper Ave.
Saginaw, MI 48602
517-771-6000
Teaching Specialties:
Internal Medicine, Surgery.

St. Mary's Medical Center
830 S. Jefferson Ave.
Saginaw, MI 48601
517-776-8000
Teaching Specialties:
Internal Medicine.

Southfield

Providence Hospital
16001 W. 9 Mile Rd.
Southfield, MI 48075
313-424-3000
Teaching Specialties:
Anesthesiology, Internal Medicine, Internal
Medicine-Cardiovascular Disease, Internal
Medicine-Gastroenterology, Obstetrics/
Gynecology, Orthopedic Surgery, Psychiatry,
Radiation Oncology, Surgery.

Westland

Westland Medical Center
2345 Merriman Rd.
Westland, MI 48185
313-467-2300
Teaching Specialties:
Ophthalmology.

MINNESOTA

Minneapolis

Abbott-Northwestern Hospital
800 E. 28th St.
Minneapolis, MN 55407
612-863-4000
Teaching Specialties:
Colon and Rectal Surgery, Internal Medicine.

Hennepin County Medical Center
701 Park Ave. S
Minneapolis, MN 55415
612-347-2121
Teaching Specialties:
Anesthesiology, Dentistry, Dermatology,
Internal Medicine, Internal Medicine-Cardio-
vascular Disease, Internal Medicine-Geriatric
Medicine, Internal Medicine-Nephrology,
Internal Medicine-Rheumatology, Neurologi-
cal Surgery, Neurology, Obstetrics/Gynecolo-
gy, Ophthalmology, Orthopedic Surgery,
Otolaryngology, Psychiatry, Surgery.

**Metropolitan-Mt. Sinai
Medical Center**
900 S. 8th St.
Minneapolis, MN 55404
612-347-4444
Teaching Specialties:
Colon and Rectal Surgery.

**University of Minnesota
Hospital and Clinic**
Harvard St. at E. River Rd.
Minneapolis, MN 55455
612-626-3000
Teaching Specialties:
Allergy/Immunology, Anesthesiology, Colon
and Rectal Surgery, Dermatology, Internal
Medicine, Internal Medicine-Cardiovascular
Disease, Internal Medicine-Endocrinology
and Metabolism, Internal Medicine-Gastroen-
terology, Internal Medicine-Geriatric
Medicine, Internal Medicine-Hematology,
Internal Medicine-Infectious Diseases, Inter-
nal Medicine-Medical Oncology, Internal
Medicine-Nephrology, Internal Medicine-
Rheumatology, Neurological Surgery, Neurol-
ogy, Obstetrics/Gynecology, Ophthalmology,
Orthopedic Surgery, Otolaryngology, Physical
Medicine and Rehabilitation, Psychiatry,
Radiation Oncology, Surgery, Thoracic
Surgery, Urology.

**University of Minnesota
School of Dentistry**
515 Delaware St., SE
Minneapolis, MN 55455
612-625-9982
Teaching Specialties:
Dentistry.

Moorhead

**Lakeland Mental Health
Center, Inc.**
810 4th Ave., S
Moorhead, MN 56560
218-233-7524
Teaching Specialties:
Psychiatry.

Rochester

Mayo Clinic and Foundation
200 S.W. First St.
Rochester, MN 55905
507-284-2511
Teaching Specialties:
Allergy/Immunology, Anesthesiology, Colon
and Rectal Surgery, Dentistry, Dermatology,
Hand Surgery, Internal Medicine, Internal
Medicine-Cardiovascular Disease, Internal
Medicine-Endocrinology and Metabolism,
Internal Medicine-Gastroenterology, Internal
Medicine-Geriatric Medicine, Internal Medi-
cine-Hematology, Internal Medicine-Infec-

tious Diseases, Internal Medicine-Medical Oncology, Internal Medicine-Nephrology, Internal Medicine-Rheumatology, Neurological
Surgery, Neurology, Obstetrics/Gynecology,
Ophthalmology, Orthopedic Surgery, Otolaryngology, Physical Medicine and Rehabilitation, Psychiatry, Surgery, Surgery-Vascular
Surgery, Thoracic Surgery, Urology.

Rochester Methodist Hospital
201 W. Center St.
Rochester, MN 55902
507-286-7890
Teaching Specialties:
Allergy/Immunology, Anesthesiology, Colon
and Rectal Surgery, Dermatology, Internal
Medicine, Internal Medicine-Cardiovascular
Disease, Internal Medicine-Endocrinology
and Metabolism, Internal Medicine-Gastroenterology, Internal Medicine-Geriatric Medicine, Internal Medicine-Hematology, Internal
Medicine-Infectious Diseases, Internal Medicine-Medical Oncology, Neurology, Obstet-
rics/Gynecology, Ophthalmology, Orthopedic Surgery, Otolaryngology, Surgery,
Surgery-Vascular Surgery, Thoracic Surgery,
Urology.

St. Marys Hospital
1216 Second St., SW
Rochester, MN 55902
507-255-5123
Teaching Specialties:
Allergy/Immunology, Anesthesiology, Colon
and Rectal Surgery, Dermatology, Internal
Medicine, Internal Medicine-Cardiovascular
Disease, Internal Medicine-Endocrinology
and Metabolism, Internal Medicine-Gastroen-
terology, Internal Medicine-Geriatric Medi-
cine, Internal Medicine-Hematology, Internal
Medicine-Infectious Diseases, Internal
Medicine-Medical Oncology, Neurological
Surgery, Neurology, Obstetrics/Gynecology,
Ophthalmology, Orthopedic Surgery, Oto-
laryngology, Physical Medicine and Rehabili-
tation, Psychiatry, Surgery, Surgery-Vascular
Surgery, Thoracic Surgery, Urology.

St. Paul

St. Paul-Ramsey Medical Center
640 Jackson St.
St. Paul, MN 55101
612-221-3456
Teaching Specialties:
Dermatology, Internal Medicine, Internal
Medicine-Geriatric Medicine, Neurology,
Obstetrics/Gynecology, Ophthalmology,
Otolaryngology, Psychiatry, Surgery, Thoracic
Surgery, Urology.

MISSISSIPPI
Jackson

Mississippi Baptist Medical Center
1225 N. State St.

Jackson, MS 39202
601-968-1000
Teaching Specialties:
Urology.

University of Mississippi Medical Center
University Hospitals and Clinics
2500 N. State St.
Jackson, MS 39216
601-984-4100
Teaching Specialties:
Anesthesiology, Internal Medicine, Internal
Medicine-Cardiovascular Disease, Internal
Medicine-Gastroenterology, Internal Medi-
cine-Hematology, Internal Medicine-Infec-
tious Diseases, Internal Medicine-Medical
Oncology, Internal Medicine-Nephrology,
Internal Medicine-Rheumatology, Neurologi-
cal Surgery, Neurology, Obstetrics/Gynecolo-
gy, Ophthalmology, Orthopedic Surgery,
Otolaryngology, Psychiatry, Surgery, Thoracic
Surgery, Urology.

University of Mississippi School of Dentistry
2500 N. State St.
Jackson, MS 39216-4505
601-984-6000
Teaching Specialties:
Dentistry.

Whitfield

Mississippi State Hospital
PO Box 157A
Whitfield, MS 39193
601-939-1221
Teaching Specialties:
Psychiatry.

MISSOURI
Chesterfield

St. Luke's Hospital
232 S. Woods Mill Rd.
Chesterfield, MO 63017
314-434-1500
Teaching Specialties:
Internal Medicine, Internal Medicine-
Cardiovascular Disease.

Columbia

Boone Hospital Center
1600 E. Broadway
Columbia, MO 65201
314-875-4545
Teaching Specialties:
Neurological Surgery.

Mid Missouri Mental Health Center
Three Hospital Dr.

Columbia, MO 65201
314-449-2511
Teaching Specialties:
Psychiatry.

University Hospital and Clinics
One Hospital Dr.
Columbia, MO 65212
314-882-4141
Teaching Specialties:
Anesthesiology, Dermatology, Internal
Medicine, Internal Medicine-Cardiovascular
Disease, Internal Medicine-Endocrinology
and Metabolism, Internal Medicine-Gastroen-
terology, Internal Medicine-Hematology,
Internal Medicine-Infectious Diseases, Inter-
nal Medicine-Medical Oncology, Internal
Medicine-Nephrology, Internal Medicine-
Rheumatology, Neurological Surgery, Neurol-
ogy, Obstetrics/Gynecology, Ophthalmology,
Orthopedic Surgery, Otolaryngology, Physical
Medicine and Rehabilitation, Psychiatry,
Surgery, Surgery-Vascular Surgery, Thoracic
Surgery, Urology.

University Hospital and Clinics
Howard A. Rusk Rehabilitation
Center
One Hospital Dr.
Columbia, MO 65212
314-882-3101
Teaching Specialties:
Physical Medicine and Rehabilitation.

Kansas City

Menorah Medical Center
4949 Rockhill Rd.
Kansas City, MO 64110
816-276-8000
Teaching Specialties:
Obstetrics/Gynecology, Surgery.

Research Medical Center
2316 E. Meyer Blvd.
Kansas City, MO 64132
816-276-4000
Teaching Specialties:
Internal Medicine-Infectious Diseases.

St. Luke's Hospital
44th St. and Wornall Rd.
Kansas City, MO 64111
816-932-2000
Teaching Specialties:
Anesthesiology, Internal Medicine,
Obstetrics/Gynecology, Orthopedic Surgery,
Surgery, Thoracic Surgery.

Trinity Lutheran Hospital
3030 Baltimore Ave.
Kansas City, MO 64108
816-751-4600
Teaching Specialties:

Internal Medicine-Hematology, Internal Medicine-Medical Oncology.

University of Missouri-Kansas City
School of Dentistry
650 E. 25th St.
Kansas City, MO 64108
816-235-2100
Teaching Specialties:
Dentistry.

Western Missouri Mental Health Center
600 E. 22nd St.
Kansas City, MO 64108
816-471-3000
Teaching Specialties:
Psychiatry.

St. Louis

Barnes Hospital
One Barnes Hospital Plaza
St. Louis, MO 63110
314-362-5000
Teaching Specialties:
Allergy/Immunology, Anesthesiology, Dermatology, Hand Surgery, Internal Medicine, Internal Medicine-Cardiovascular Disease, Internal Medicine-Endocrinology and Metabolism, Internal Medicine-Gastroenterology, Internal Medicine-Hematology, Internal Medicine-Infectious Diseases, Internal Medicine-Medical Oncology, Internal Medicine-Nephrology, Internal Medicine-Rheumatology, Neurological Surgery, Neurology, Obstetrics/Gynecology, Ophthalmology, Orthopedic Surgery, Otolaryngology, Psychiatry, Radiation Oncology, Surgery, Surgery-Vascular Surgery, Thoracic Surgery, Urology.

Bethesda Eye Institute
3655 Vista Ave.
St. Louis, MO 63110
314-577-8260
Teaching Specialties:
Ophthalmology.

Deaconess Hospital
6150 Oakland Ave.
St. Louis, MO 63139
314-768-3000
Teaching Specialties:
Internal Medicine, Obstetrics/Gynecology.

Jewish Hospital of St. Louis
216 S. Kingshighway Blvd.
St. Louis, MO 63110
314-454-7250
Teaching Specialties:
Colon and Rectal Surgery, Dentistry, Internal Medicine, Internal Medicine-Cardiovascular Disease, Internal Medicine-Endocrinology and Metabolism, Internal Medicine-Geriatric

Medicine, Internal Medicine-Nephrology, Obstetrics/Gynecology, Orthopedic Surgery, Otolaryngology, Physical Medicine and Rehabilitation, Psychiatry, Radiation Oncology, Surgery, Thoracic Surgery.

Malcolm Bliss Mental Health Center
5400 Arsenal St.
St. Louis, MO 63139
314-644-7800
Teaching Specialties:
Psychiatry.

Mallinckrodt Institute of Radiology
510 S. Kingshighway Blvd.
St. Louis, MO 63110
314-362-7120
Teaching Specialties:
Radiation Oncology.

St. John's Mercy Medical Center
615 S. New Ballas Rd.
St. Louis, MO 63141
314-569-6000
Teaching Specialties:
Dentistry, Internal Medicine, Obstetrics/Gynecology, Surgery, Surgery-Vascular Surgery, Urology.

St. Louis Regional Medical Center
5535 Delmar Blvd.
St. Louis, MO 63112
314-879-6308
Teaching Specialties:
Internal Medicine, Neurology, Obstetrics/Gynecology, Orthopedic Surgery, Otolaryngology.

St. Louis University Medical Center
3635 Vista at Grand Blvd.
St. Louis, MO 63110-0250
314-577-8000
Teaching Specialties:
Allergy/Immunology, Anesthesiology, Internal Medicine, Internal Medicine-Cardiovascular Disease, Internal Medicine-Endocrinology and Metabolism, Internal Medicine-Gastroenterology, Internal Medicine-Hematology, Internal Medicine-Infectious Diseases, Internal Medicine-Medical Oncology, Internal Medicine-Nephrology, Internal Medicine-Rheumatology, Neurological Surgery, Neurology, Obstetrics/Gynecology, Orthopedic Surgery, Otolaryngology, Psychiatry, Surgery, Surgery-Vascular Surgery, Thoracic Surgery, Urology.

St. Louis University Medical Center
Orthodontics Treatment
6556 Caroline St.
St. Louis, MO 63104
314-577-8181
Teaching Specialties:
Dentistry.

St. Mary's Health Center
6420 Clayton Rd.
St. Louis, MO 63117
314-768-8000
Teaching Specialties:
Internal Medicine, Internal Medicine-Gastroenterology, Obstetrics/Gynecology, Orthopedic Surgery, Surgery, Urology.

NEBRASKA
Lincoln

University of Nebraska Medical Center
College of Dentistry
40th & Holdrege Sts.
Lincoln, NE 68583-0740
402-472-1344
Teaching Specialties:
Dentistry.

Omaha

AMI St. Joseph Center for Mental Health
819 Dorcas St.
Omaha, NE 68108
402-449-4650
Teaching Specialties:
Psychiatry.

AMI St. Joseph Hospital
601 N. 30th St.
Omaha, NE 68131
402-449-4000
Teaching Specialties:
Allergy/Immunology, Colon and Rectal Surgery, Internal Medicine, Internal Medicine-Cardiovascular Disease, Internal Medicine-Infectious Diseases, Neurology, Obstetrics/Gynecology, Orthopedic Surgery, Surgery, Urology.

Archbishop Bergan Mercy Hospital
7500 Mercy Rd.
Omaha, NE 68124
402-398-6763
Teaching Specialties:
Obstetrics/Gynecology.

Bishop Clarkson Memorial Hospital
44th & Dewey Ave.
Omaha, NE 68105
402-559-2000
Teaching Specialties:
Internal Medicine.

Creighton University School of Dentistry
2500 California St.

Omaha, NE 68178
402-280-5060
Teaching Specialties:
Dentistry.

Methodist Hospital
8303 Dodge St.
Omaha, NE 68114
402-390-4000
Teaching Specialties:
Urology.

**University of Nebraska
Medical Center**
600 S. 42nd St.
Omaha, NE 68198
402-599-4000
Teaching Specialties:
Anesthesiology, Internal Medicine, Internal Medicine-Cardiovascular Disease, Internal Medicine-Gastroenterology, Internal Medicine-Geriatric Medicine, Internal Medicine-Hematology, Internal Medicine-Medical Oncology, Neurology, Obstetrics/Gynecology, Ophthalmology, Orthopedic Surgery, Otolaryngology, Psychiatry, Surgery, Urology.

NEVADA
Las Vegas

**University Medical Center
of Southern Nevada**
1800 W. Charleston Blvd.
Las Vegas, NV 89102
702-383-2000
Teaching Specialties:
Internal Medicine, Obstetrics/Gynecology, Surgery.

Women's Hospital
2025 E. Sahara Ave.
Las Vegas, NV 89150
702-735-7106
Teaching Specialties:
Obstetrics/Gynecology.

Reno

Washoe Medical Center
77 Pringle Way
Reno, NV 89520
702-328-4100
Teaching Specialties:
Internal Medicine.

NEW HAMPSHIRE
Concord

New Hampshire Hospital
105 Pleasant St.
Concord, NH 03301

603-271-5200
Teaching Specialties:
Psychiatry.

Hanover

**Dartmouth-Hitchcock
Medical Center**
Two Maynard St.
Hanover, NH 03756
603-650-5000
Teaching Specialties:
Anesthesiology, Dermatology, Internal Medicine, Internal Medicine-Cardiovascular Disease, Internal Medicine-Endocrinology and Metabolism, Internal Medicine-Gastroenterology, Internal Medicine-Hematology, Internal Medicine-Medical Oncology, Internal Medicine-Rheumatology, Neurological Surgery, Neurology, Orthopedic Surgery, Otolaryngology, Psychiatry, Surgery, Surgery-Vascular Surgery, Urology.

Mary Hitchcock Memorial Hospital
Two Maynard St.
Hanover, NH 03756
603-650-5000
Teaching Specialties:
Surgery-Vascular Surgery.

NEW JERSEY
Atlantic City

Atlantic City Medical Center
1925 Pacific Ave.
Atlantic City, NJ 08401
609-344-4081
Teaching Specialties:
Internal Medicine, Orthopedic Surgery.

Berlin

West Jersey Hospital-Berlin
Townsend Ave. & White Horse Pike
Berlin, NJ 08009
609-768-6000
Teaching Specialties:
Otolaryngology.

Blackwood

**Camden County Health
Services Center**
County House Rd.
Blackwood, NJ 08012
609-227-3000
Teaching Specialties:
Psychiatry.

Brown Mills

Deborah Heart and Lung Center
Trenton Rd.

Brown Mills, NJ 08015
609-893-6611
Teaching Specialties:
Thoracic Surgery.

Camden

**Cooper Hospital-University
Medical Center**
One Cooper Plaza
Camden, NJ 08103
609-342-2000
Teaching Specialties:
Internal Medicine, Internal Medicine-Cardiovascular Disease, Internal Medicine-Gastroenterology, Internal Medicine-Hematology, Internal Medicine-Infectious Diseases, Internal Medicine-Medical Oncology, Internal Medicine-Nephrology, Internal Medicine-Rheumatology, Obstetrics/Gynecology, Ophthalmology, Psychiatry, Radiation Oncology, Surgery.

West Jersey Hospital-Camden
Mt. Ephraim & Atlantic Aves.
Camden, NJ 08104
609-342-4500
Teaching Specialties:
Otolaryngology.

Edison

John F. Kennedy Medical Center
98 James St.
Edison, NJ 08818
908-632-1500
Teaching Specialties:
Colon and Rectal Surgery, Dentistry, Physical Medicine and Rehabilitation.

Elizabeth

St. Elizabeth Hospital
225 Williamson St.
Elizabeth, NJ 07207
908-527-5000
Teaching Specialties:
Internal Medicine.

Englewood

Englewood Hospital
350 Engle St.
Englewood, NJ 07631
201-894-3000
Teaching Specialties:
Dentistry, Internal Medicine, Obstetrics/Gynecology.

Hackensack

Hackensack Medical Center
30 Prospect Ave.
Hackensack, NJ 07601

201-441-2000
Teaching Specialties:
Anesthesiology, Dentistry, Internal Medicine, Internal Medicine-Cardiovascular Disease, Internal Medicine-Infectious Diseases, Obstetrics/Gynecology, Orthopedic Surgery, Psychiatry, Surgery, Surgery-Vascular Surgery, Urology.

Jersey City

Jersey City Medical Center
50 Baldwin Ave.
Jersey City, NJ 07304
201-915-2000
Teaching Specialties:
Dentistry, Internal Medicine, Internal Medicine-Cardiovascular Disease, Internal Medicine-Gastroenterology, Obstetrics/Gynecology, Ophthalmology, Orthopedic Surgery.

Livingston

St. Barnabas Medical Center
Old Short Hills Rd., #94
Livingston, NJ 07039
201-533-5000
Teaching Specialties:
Anesthesiology, Internal Medicine, Internal Medicine-Nephrology, Neurological Surgery, Obstetrics/Gynecology, Psychiatry, Radiation Oncology, Surgery.

Long Branch

Monmouth Medical Center
300 Second Ave.
Long Branch, NJ 07740
908-870-5209
Teaching Specialties:
Anesthesiology, Dentistry, Internal Medicine, Obstetrics/Gynecology, Orthopedic Surgery, Surgery.

Marlton

West Jersey Hospital-Marlton
Route 73 & Brick Rd.
Marlton, NJ 08053
609-596-3500
Teaching Specialties:
Otolaryngology.

Montclair

Mountainside Hospital
Bay & Highland Aves.
Montclair, NJ 07042
201-429-6000
Teaching Specialties:
Dentistry, Internal Medicine.

Morristown

Morristown Memorial Hospital
100 Madison Ave.

Morristown, NJ 07962
201-540-5000
Teaching Specialties:
Dentistry, Internal Medicine, Obstetrics/Gynecology, Surgery.

Neptune

Jersey Shore Medical Center
1945 Route 33
Neptune, NJ 07754
908-775-5500
Teaching Specialties:
Dentistry, Internal Medicine, Obstetrics/Gynecology, Surgery.

New Brunswick

Robert Wood Johnson University Hospital
One Robert Wood Johnson Place
New Brunswick, NJ 08901
201-828-3000
Teaching Specialties:
Anesthesiology, Dentistry, Internal Medicine, Internal Medicine-Cardiovascular Disease, Internal Medicine-Endocrinology and Metabolism, Internal Medicine-Gastroenterology, Internal Medicine-Hematology, Internal Medicine-Infectious Diseases, Internal Medicine-Medical Oncology, Internal Medicine-Nephrology, Internal Medicine-Rheumatology, Neurology, Obstetrics/Gynecology, Orthopedic Surgery, Surgery, Surgery-Vascular Surgery, Thoracic Surgery, Urology.

St. Peter's Medical Center
254 Easton Ave.
New Brunswick, NJ 08901
908-745-8600
Teaching Specialties:
Internal Medicine, Internal Medicine-Cardiovascular Disease, Internal Medicine-Endocrinology and Metabolism, Internal Medicine-Hematology, Internal Medicine-Infectious Diseases, Internal Medicine-Medical Oncology, Internal Medicine-Nephrology, Obstetrics/Gynecology, Orthopedic Surgery, Thoracic Surgery.

Newark

Newark Beth Israel Medical Center
201 Lyons Ave.
Newark, NJ 07112
201-926-7000
Teaching Specialties:
Dentistry, Internal Medicine, Internal Medicine-Cardiovascular Disease, Internal Medicine-Hematology, Internal Medicine-Medical Oncology, Internal Medicine-Nephrology, Internal Medicine-Rheumatology, Obstetrics/Gynecology, Surgery, Surgery-Vascular Surgery, Thoracic Surgery.

St. James Hospital of Newark
155 Jefferson St.
Newark, NJ 07105
201-589-1300
Teaching Specialties:
Obstetrics/Gynecology.

St. Michael's Medical Center
268 Dr. Martin Luther King, Jr. Blvd.
Newark, NJ 07102
201-877-5000
Teaching Specialties:
Internal Medicine, Internal Medicine-Cardiovascular Disease, Internal Medicine-Endocrinology and Metabolism, Internal Medicine-Gastroenterology, Internal Medicine-Hematology, Internal Medicine-Infectious Diseases, Internal Medicine-Medical Oncology, Internal Medicine-Rheumatology, Obstetrics/Gynecology, Surgery-Vascular Surgery, Thoracic Surgery.

United Hospitals Medical Center
15 S. 9th St.
Newark, NJ 07107
201-268-8000
Teaching Specialties:
Internal Medicine, Internal Medicine-Hematology, Internal Medicine-Medical Oncology, Ophthalmology, Orthopedic Surgery, Otolaryngology.

United Hospitals Medical Center
Newark Eye and Ear Infirmary
15 S. 9th St.
Newark, NJ 07107
201-268-8000
Teaching Specialties:
Ophthalmology, Otolaryngology.

United Hospitals Medical Center
Orthopedic Unit
15 S. 9th St.
Newark, NJ 07107
201-268-8000
Teaching Specialties:
Orthopedic Surgery.

University of Medicine and Dentistry of New Jersey
University Hospital
150 Bergen St.
Newark, NJ 07103
201-456-4300
Teaching Specialties:
Allergy/Immunology, Anesthesiology, Dermatology, Internal Medicine, Internal Medicine-Cardiovascular Disease, Internal Medicine-Endocrinology and Metabolism, Internal Medicine-Gastroenterology, Internal Medicine-Hematology, Internal Medicine-Infectious Diseases, Internal Medicine-Medi

cal Oncology, Internal Medicine-Nephrology, Internal Medicine-Rheumatology, Neurological Surgery, Neurology, Obstetrics/Gynecology, Ophthalmology, Orthopedic Surgery, Otolaryngology, Physical Medicine and Rehabilitation, Psychiatry, Surgery, Surgery-Vascular Surgery, Thoracic Surgery, Urology.

University of Medicine and Dentistry of New Jersey
New Jersey Dental School
110 Bergen St., University Heights
Newark, NJ 07103-2400
201-456-4300
Teaching Specialties:
Dentistry.

Orange

Hospital Center at Orange
188 S. Essex Ave.
Orange, NJ 07051
201-266-2000
Teaching Specialties:
Orthopedic Surgery.

Paramus

Bergen Pines County Hospital
E. Ridgewood Ave.
Paramus, NJ 07652
201-967-4000
Teaching Specialties:
Internal Medicine, Psychiatry.

Paterson

St. Joseph's Hospital and Medical Center
703 Main St.
Paterson, NJ 07503
201-977-2000
Teaching Specialties:
Anesthesiology, Dentistry, Internal Medicine, Internal Medicine-Gastroenterology, Internal Medicine-Hematology, Internal Medicine-Medical Oncology, Obstetrics/Gynecology, Orthopedic Surgery.

Perth Amboy

Raritan Bay Medical Center
Perth Amboy Div.
530 New Brunswick Ave.
Perth Amboy, NJ 08861
908-442-3700
Teaching Specialties:
Internal Medicine.

Piscataway

University of Medicine and Dentistry of New Jersey
Community Mental Health

Center at Piscataway
674 Hoes Lane
Piscataway, NJ 08854
908-463-4420
Teaching Specialties:
Psychiatry.

Plainfield

Muhlenberg Regional Medical Center
Park Ave. & Randolph Rd.
Plainfield, NJ 07061
201-668-2000
Teaching Specialties:
Colon and Rectal Surgery, Internal Medicine, Obstetrics/Gynecology, Surgery.

Princeton

Medical Center at Princeton
253 Witherspoon St.
Princeton, NJ 08540
609-497-4000
Teaching Specialties:
Internal Medicine, Surgery, Urology.

Scranton

Community Medical Center
1822 Mulberry St.
Scranton, NJ 18510
717-969-8000
Teaching Specialties:
Internal Medicine.

Summit

Overlook Hospital
99 Beauvoir Ave.
Summit, NJ 07902
201-522-2000
Teaching Specialties:
Dentistry, Internal Medicine, Psychiatry, Surgery.

Trenton

Greater Trenton Community Mental Health Center
132 N. Warren St.
Trenton, NJ 08607
609-396-6788
Teaching Specialties:
Psychiatry.

Helene Fuld Medical Center
750 Brunswick Ave.
Trenton, NJ 08638
609-394-6000
Teaching Specialties:
Internal Medicine.

St. Francis Medical Center
601 Hamilton Ave.
Trenton, NJ 08629
609-599-5000
Teaching Specialties:
Internal Medicine, Surgery.

Trenton Psychiatric Hospital
PO Box 7500
Trenton, NJ 08628
609-633-1500
Teaching Specialties:
Psychiatry.

Voorhees

West Jersey Hospital-Voorhees
101 Carnie Blvd.
Voorhees, NJ 08043
609-772-5000
Teaching Specialties:
Otolaryngology.

West Orange

Kessler Institute for Rehabilitation
1199 Pleasant Valley Way
West Orange, NJ 07052
201-731-3600
Teaching Specialties:
Physical Medicine and Rehabilitation.

Woodbury

Underwood-Memorial Hospital
509 N. Broad St.
Woodbury, NJ 08096
609-845-0100
Teaching Specialties:
Surgery.

NEW MEXICO
Albuquerque

Lovelace Medical Center
5400 Gibson Blvd.
Albuquerque, NM 87108
505-262-7000
Teaching Specialties:
Otolaryngology, Surgery, Urology.

University Hospital
2211 Lomas Blvd., NE
Albuquerque, NM 87106
505-843-2111
Teaching Specialties:
Dermatology, Internal Medicine, Internal Medicine-Cardiovascular Disease, Internal Medicine-Endocrinology and Metabolism, Internal Medicine-Gastroenterology, Internal Medicine-Hematology, Internal Medicine-Infectious Diseases, Internal Medicine-Medi-

cal Oncology, Internal Medicine-Nephrology, Internal Medicine-Rheumatology, Neurology, Obstetrics/Gynecology, Orthopedic Surgery, Otolaryngology, Psychiatry, Surgery, Thoracic Surgery, Urology.

University of New Mexico Mental Health Center
2600 Marble, NE
Albuquerque, NM 87131
505-843-2800
Teaching Specialties:
Psychiatry.

NEW YORK
Albany

Albany Medical Center Hospital
43 New Scotland Ave.
Albany, NY 12208
518-445-3125
Teaching Specialties:
Anesthesiology, Dentistry, Internal Medicine, Internal Medicine-Cardiovascular Disease, Internal Medicine-Endocrinology and Metabolism, Internal Medicine-Gastroenterology, Internal Medicine-Geriatric Medicine, Internal Medicine-Hematology, Internal Medicine-Infectious Diseases, Internal Medicine-Medical Oncology, Internal Medicine-Nephrology, Neurological Surgery, Neurology, Obstetrics/Gynecology, Ophthalmology, Orthopedic Surgery, Otolaryngology, Physical Medicine and Rehabilitation, Psychiatry, Surgery, Surgery-Vascular Surgery, Thoracic Surgery, Urology.

Capital District Psychiatric Center
75 New Scotland Ave.
Albany, NY 12208
518-447-9611
Teaching Specialties:
Psychiatry.

Child's Hospital
25 Hackett Blvd.
Albany, NY 12208
518-487-7200
Teaching Specialties:
Otolaryngology.

St. Peter's Hospital
315 S. Manning Blvd.
Albany, NY 12208
518-454-1550
Teaching Specialties:
Dentistry, Internal Medicine, Obstetrics/Gynecology, Orthopedic Surgery, Otolaryngology, Physical Medicine and Rehabilitation, Surgery.

Bronx

Bronx-Lebanon Hospital Center
1276 Fulton Ave.
Bronx, NY 10456
212-590-1800
Teaching Specialties:
Dentistry, Internal Medicine, Internal Medicine-Cardiovascular Disease, Internal Medicine-Gastroenterology, Internal Medicine-Hematology, Internal Medicine-Nephrology, Obstetrics/Gynecology, Ophthalmology, Orthopedic Surgery, Psychiatry, Surgery.

Bronx Municipal Hospital Center
Pelham Parkway & Eastchester Rd.
Bronx, NY 10461
212-918-8141
Teaching Specialties:
Allergy/Immunology, Anesthesiology, Dentistry, Dermatology, Internal Medicine, Internal Medicine-Cardiovascular Disease, Internal Medicine-Endocrinology and Metabolism, Internal Medicine-Gastroenterology, Internal Medicine-Hematology, Internal Medicine-Infectious Diseases, Internal Medicine-Medical Oncology, Internal Medicine-Nephrology, Internal Medicine-Rheumatology, Neurological Surgery, Neurology, Obstetrics/Gynecology, Ophthalmology, Orthopedic Surgery, Otolaryngology, Physical Medicine and Rehabilitation, Psychiatry, Surgery, Surgery-Vascular Surgery, Thoracic Surgery, Urology.

Bronx Psychiatric Center
1500 Waters Place
Bronx, NY 10461
212-931-0600
Teaching Specialties:
Psychiatry.

Lincoln Medical and Mental Health Center
234 E. 149th St.
Bronx, NY 10451
212-579-5000
Teaching Specialties:
Anesthesiology, Dentistry, Dermatology, Internal Medicine, Internal Medicine-Cardiovascular Disease, Internal Medicine-Endocrinology and Metabolism, Internal Medicine-Gastroenterology, Internal Medicine-Hematology, Internal Medicine-Infectious Diseases, Neurology, Obstetrics/Gynecology, Ophthalmology, Orthopedic Surgery, Otolaryngology, Physical Medicine and Rehabilitation, Psychiatry, Surgery, Urology.

Montefiore Medical Center
Henry and Lucy Moses Division
111 E. 210th St.
Bronx, NY 10467
212-920-4321
Teaching Specialties:
Anesthesiology, Dentistry, Dermatology,

Internal Medicine, Internal Medicine-Cardiovascular Disease, Internal Medicine-Endocrinology and Metabolism, Internal Medicine-Gastroenterology, Internal Medicine-Geriatric Medicine, Internal Medicine-Hematology, Internal Medicine-Infectious Diseases, Internal Medicine-Medical Oncology, Internal Medicine-Nephrology, Internal Medicine-Rheumatology, Neurological Surgery, Neurology, Obstetrics/Gynecology, Ophthalmology, Orthopedic Surgery, Otolaryngology, Physical Medicine and Rehabilitation, Psychiatry, Radiation Oncology, Surgery, Surgery-Vascular Surgery, Thoracic Surgery, Urology.

Montefiore Medical Center
Jack D. Weiler Hospital of the Albert Einstein College of Medicine
1825 Eastchester Rd.
Bronx, NY 10461
212-904-2000
Teaching Specialties:
Allergy/Immunology, Anesthesiology, Dermatology, Internal Medicine, Internal Medicine-Cardiovascular Disease, Internal Medicine-Endocrinology and Metabolism, Neurology, Obstetrics/Gynecology, Ophthalmology, Orthopedic Surgery, Otolaryngology, Physical Medicine and Rehabilitation, Radiation Oncology, Surgery, Surgery-Vascular Surgery, Thoracic Surgery, Urology.

North Central Bronx Hospital
3424 Kossuth Ave.
Bronx, NY 10467
212-519-5000
Teaching Specialties:
Dermatology, Internal Medicine, Internal Medicine-Endocrinology and Metabolism, Obstetrics/Gynecology, Ophthalmology, Orthopedic Surgery, Physical Medicine and Rehabilitation, Surgery, Surgery-Vascular Surgery, Urology.

Our Lady of Mercy Medical Center
600 E. 233rd St.
Bronx, NY 10466
212-920-9000
Teaching Specialties:
Dentistry, Internal Medicine, Internal Medicine-Cardiovascular Disease, Internal Medicine-Gastroenterology, Internal Medicine-Hematology, Internal Medicine-Nephrology, Obstetrics/Gynecology, Ophthalmology, Surgery, Urology.

St. Barnabas Hospital
183rd St. & Third Ave.
Bronx, NY 10457
212-960-6107
Teaching Specialties:
Dentistry, Internal Medicine.

Brooklyn

Brookdale Hospital Medical Center
Linden Blvd. & Brookdale Plaza
Brooklyn, NY 11212
718-240-5000
Teaching Specialties:
Anesthesiology, Dentistry, Internal Medicine, Internal Medicine-Endocrinology and Metabolism, Internal Medicine-Gastroenterology, Internal Medicine-Hematology, Internal Medicine-Medical Oncology, Internal Medicine-Nephrology, Obstetrics/Gynecology, Ophthalmology, Orthopedic Surgery, Otolaryngology, Psychiatry, Surgery, Urology.

Brooklyn Hospital Center
121 DeKalb Ave.
Brooklyn, NY 11201
718-403-8005
Teaching Specialties:
Dentistry, Internal Medicine, Internal Medicine-Cardiovascular Disease, Internal Medicine-Gastroenterology, Internal Medicine-Hematology, Internal Medicine-Medical Oncology, Obstetrics/Gynecology, Ophthalmology, Physical Medicine and Rehabilitation, Surgery.

Coney Island Hospital
2601 Ocean Parkway
Brooklyn, NY 11235
718-615-4000
Teaching Specialties:
Anesthesiology, Internal Medicine, Internal Medicine-Cardiovascular Disease, Internal Medicine-Endocrinology and Metabolism, Internal Medicine-Hematology, Internal Medicine-Rheumatology, Obstetrics/Gynecology, Ophthalmology, Orthopedic Surgery, Surgery, Urology.

Interfaith Medical Center
555 Prospect Place
Brooklyn, NY 11213
718-604-7000
Teaching Specialties:
Dentistry, Internal Medicine, Internal Medicine-Cardiovascular Disease, Internal Medicine-Endocrinology and Metabolism, Internal Medicine-Gastroenterology, Internal Medicine-Hematology, Internal Medicine-Medical Oncology, Internal Medicine-Nephrology, Obstetrics/Gynecology, Ophthalmology.

Kings County Hospital Center
451 Clarkson Ave.
Brooklyn, NY 11203
718-735-3101
Teaching Specialties:
Allergy/Immunology, Anesthesiology, Dentistry, Dermatology, Internal Medicine, Internal Medicine-Cardiovascular Disease, Internal Medicine-Endocrinology and Metabolism, Internal Medicine-Gastroenterology, Internal

Medicine-Hematology, Internal Medicine-Infectious Diseases, Internal Medicine-Medical Oncology, Internal Medicine-Nephrology, Internal Medicine-Rheumatology, Neurological Surgery, Neurology, Obstetrics/Gynecology, Ophthalmology, Orthopedic Surgery, Otolaryngology, Physical Medicine and Rehabilitation, Psychiatry, Radiation Oncology, Surgery, Thoracic Surgery, Urology.

Kingsboro Psychiatric Center
681 Clarkson Ave.
Brooklyn, NY 11203
212-735-1700
Teaching Specialties:
Psychiatry.

Kingsbrook Jewish Medical Center
585 Schenectady Ave.
Brooklyn, NY 11203
718-604-5000
Teaching Specialties:
Internal Medicine, Orthopedic Surgery, Physical Medicine and Rehabilitation.

Long Island College Hospital
340 Henry St.
Brooklyn, NY 11201
718-780-4651
Teaching Specialties:
Allergy/Immunology, Dentistry, Internal Medicine, Internal Medicine-Cardiovascular Disease, Internal Medicine-Gastroenterology, Internal Medicine-Hematology, Internal Medicine-Infectious Diseases, Internal Medicine-Medical Oncology, Internal Medicine-Nephrology, Internal Medicine-Rheumatology, Obstetrics/Gynecology, Ophthalmology, Orthopedic Surgery, Otolaryngology, Radiation Oncology, Surgery, Urology.

Lutheran Medical Center
150 55th St.
Brooklyn, NY 11220
718-630-7000
Teaching Specialties:
Dentistry, Internal Medicine, Obstetrics/Gynecology, Radiation Oncology.

Maimonides Medical Center
4802 10th Ave.
Brooklyn, NY 11219
718-283-6000
Teaching Specialties:
Anesthesiology, Dentistry, Internal Medicine, Internal Medicine-Cardiovascular Disease, Internal Medicine-Gastroenterology, Internal Medicine-Hematology, Internal Medicine-Infectious Diseases, Internal Medicine-Medical Oncology, Internal Medicine-Nephrology, Obstetrics/Gynecology, Ophthalmology, Orthopedic Surgery, Psychiatry, Surgery, Thoracic Surgery, Urology.

Methodist Hospital of Brooklyn
506 6th St.

Brooklyn, NY 11215
718-780-3000
Teaching Specialties:
Anesthesiology, Internal Medicine, Internal Medicine-Cardiovascular Disease, Internal Medicine-Hematology, Internal Medicine-Medical Oncology, Radiation Oncology, Surgery.

St. Mary's Hospital
170 Buffalo Ave.
Brooklyn, NY 11213
718-774-3600
Teaching Specialties:
Internal Medicine, Internal Medicine-Hematology, Internal Medicine-Medical Oncology, Obstetrics/Gynecology, Orthopedic Surgery, Surgery.

State University of New York Health Sciences Center at Brooklyn
University Hospital of Brooklyn
445 Lenox Rd.
Brooklyn, NY 11203
718-270-1000
Teaching Specialties:
Allergy/Immunology, Dermatology, Internal Medicine, Internal Medicine-Cardiovascular Disease, Internal Medicine-Endocrinology and Metabolism, Internal Medicine-Gastroenterology, Internal Medicine-Hematology, Internal Medicine-Infectious Diseases, Internal Medicine-Medical Oncology, Internal Medicine-Nephrology, Internal Medicine-Rheumatology, Neurological Surgery, Neurology, Obstetrics/Gynecology, Orthopedic Surgery, Otolaryngology, Psychiatry, Surgery, Thoracic Surgery, Urology.

Woodhull Medical and Mental Health Center
760 Broadway
Brooklyn, NY 11206
718-963-8000
Teaching Specialties:
Dentistry, Internal Medicine, Internal Medicine-Hematology, Internal Medicine-Medical Oncology, Surgery.

Wyckoff Heights Medical Center
374 Stockholm St.
Brooklyn, NY 11237
718-963-7102
Teaching Specialties:
Dentistry, Internal Medicine.

Buffalo

Buffalo General Hospital
100 High St.
Buffalo, NY 14203
716-845-5600
Teaching Specialties:
Allergy/Immunology, Anesthesiology, Colon

and Rectal Surgery, Dermatology, Internal Medicine, Internal Medicine-Cardiovascular Disease, Internal Medicine-Gastroenterology, Internal Medicine-Hematology, Neurological Surgery, Obstetrics/Gynecology, Ophthalmology, Orthopedic Surgery, Physical Medicine and Rehabilitation, Surgery, Thoracic Surgery, Urology.

Erie County Medical Center
462 Grider St.
Buffalo, NY 14215
716-898-4048
Teaching Specialties:
Anesthesiology, Dentistry, Dermatology, Hand Surgery, Internal Medicine, Internal Medicine-Cardiovascular Disease, Internal Medicine-Endocrinology and Metabolism, Internal Medicine-Gastroenterology, Internal Medicine-Hematology, Internal Medicine-Infectious Diseases, Internal Medicine-Nephrology, Internal Medicine-Rheumatology, Neurological Surgery, Neurology, Obstetrics/Gynecology, Ophthalmology, Orthopedic Surgery, Otolaryngology, Physical Medicine and Rehabilitation, Psychiatry, Surgery, Urology.

Mercy Hospital
565 Abbott Rd.
Buffalo, NY 14220
716-826-7000
Teaching Specialties:
Internal Medicine.

Millard Fillmore Hospitals
Three Gates Circle
Buffalo, NY 14209
716-887-4600
Teaching Specialties:
Anesthesiology, Dentistry, Hand Surgery, Internal Medicine, Internal Medicine-Cardiovascular Disease, Neurological Surgery, Obstetrics/Gynecology, Ophthalmology, Surgery, Thoracic Surgery.

Millard Fillmore Hospitals
Dent Neurological Institute
Three Gates Circle
Buffalo, NY 14209
716-887-4793
Teaching Specialties:
Neurology.

Roswell Park Cancer Institute
Elm & Carlton Sts.
Buffalo, NY 14263
716-845-2300
Teaching Specialties:
Dentistry, Internal Medicine-Gastroenterology, Internal Medicine-Medical Oncology, Thoracic Surgery, Urology.

Sisters of Charity Hospital of Buffalo
2157 Main St.
Buffalo, NY 14214
716-862-2000
Teaching Specialties:
Internal Medicine, Obstetrics/Gynecology, Otolaryngology.

State University of New York at Buffalo
School of Dental Medicine
325 Squire Hall
Buffalo, NY 14214
716-831-2383 Clinical Affairs
Teaching Specialties:
Dentistry.

Camden

Our Lady of Lourdes Medical Center
1600 Haddon Ave.
Camden, NY 08103
609-757-3500
Teaching Specialties:
Obstetrics/Gynecology.

Cooperstown

Mary Imogene Bassett Hospital
One Atwell Rd.
Cooperstown, NY 13326
607-547-3100
Teaching Specialties:
Internal Medicine, Surgery.

East Meadow

Nassau County Medical Center
2201 Hempstead Turnpike
East Meadow, NY 11554
516-542-0123
Teaching Specialties:
Allergy/Immunology, Anesthesiology, Dentistry, Internal Medicine, Internal Medicine-Cardiovascular Disease, Internal Medicine-Endocrinology and Metabolism, Internal Medicine-Gastroenterology, Internal Medicine-Hematology, Internal Medicine-Infectious Diseases, Internal Medicine-Medical Oncology, Internal Medicine-Nephrology, Neurology, Obstetrics/Gynecology, Ophthalmology, Orthopedic Surgery, Physical Medicine and Rehabilitation, Psychiatry, Surgery.

Elmhurst

St. John's Queens Hospital
90-02 Queens Blvd.
Elmhurst, NY 11373
718-457-1300
Teaching Specialties:

Internal Medicine, Obstetrics/Gynecology, Orthopedic Surgery.

Far Rockaway

Peninsula Hospital Center
51-15 Beach Channel Dr.
Far Rockaway, NY 11691
718-945-7100
Teaching Specialties:
Dentistry.

St. John's Episcopal Hospital-South Shore
327 Beach 19th St.
Far Rockaway, NY 11691
718-868-7000
Teaching Specialties:
Internal Medicine, Obstetrics/Gynecology.

Flushing

Booth Memorial Medical Center
Main St. at Booth Memorial Ave.
Flushing, NY 11355
718-670-1021
Teaching Specialties:
Dentistry, Internal Medicine, Internal Medicine-Gastroenterology, Internal Medicine-Infectious Diseases, Internal Medicine-Nephrology, Obstetrics/Gynecology, Surgery.

Elmhurst Hospital Center
79-01 Broadway
Flushing, NY 11373
718-830-1515
Teaching Specialties:
Anesthesiology, Dermatology, Internal Medicine, Internal Medicine-Cardiovascular Disease, Internal Medicine-Gastroenterology, Neurological Surgery, Obstetrics/Gynecology, Ophthalmology, Orthopedic Surgery, Otolaryngology, Physical Medicine and Rehabilitation, Psychiatry, Surgery, Surgery-Vascular Surgery, Urology.

Flushing Hospital Medical Center
45th Ave. at Parsons Blvd.
Flushing, NY 11355
718-670-5000
Teaching Specialties:
Dentistry, Internal Medicine, Obstetrics/Gynecology, Surgery.

Forest Hills

La Guardia Hospital
102-01 66th Rd.
Forest Hills, NY 11375
718-830-4000
Teaching Specialties:
Internal Medicine, Surgery, Urology.

Glen Oaks

Long Island Jewish Medical Center
Hillside Hospital
75-59 263rd St.
Glen Oaks, NY 11004
718-470-8000
Teaching Specialties:
Psychiatry.

Harrison

St. Vincent's Hospital and Medical Center of New York
Westchester Branch
240 North St.
Harrison, NY 10528
914-967-6500
Teaching Specialties:
Psychiatry.

Huntington

Huntington Hospital
270 Park Ave.
Huntington, NY 11743
516-351-2000
Teaching Specialties:
Surgery.

Jamaica

Catholic Medical Center of Brooklyn and Queens
88-25 153rd St.
Jamaica, NY 11432
718-657-6800
Teaching Specialties:
Dentistry.

Jamaica Hospital
89th Ave. & Van Wyck Expressway
Jamaica, NY 11418
718-262-6000
Teaching Specialties:
Dentistry, Internal Medicine, Internal Medicine-Cardiovascular Disease, Internal Medicine-Gastroenterology, Internal Medicine-Hematology, Obstetrics/Gynecology, Surgery.

Mary Immaculate Hospital
152-11 89th Ave.
Jamaica, NY 11432
718-291-3300
Teaching Specialties:
Internal Medicine, Internal Medicine-Cardiovascular Disease, Internal Medicine-Gastroenterology, Internal Medicine-Hematology, Internal Medicine-Infectious Diseases, Internal Medicine-Medical Oncology, Obstetrics/Gynecology, Ophthalmology, Orthopedic Surgery, Surgery.

Queens Hospital Center
82-68 164th St.
Jamaica, NY 11432
718-883-3000
Teaching Specialties:
Internal Medicine, Internal Medicine-Endocrinology and Metabolism, Neurology, Obstetrics/Gynecology, Ophthalmology, Orthopedic Surgery, Otolaryngology, Physical Medicine and Rehabilitation, Psychiatry, Surgery, Urology.

Johnson City

Wilson Memorial Hospital
33 Harrison St.
Johnson City, NY 13790
607-770-6726
Teaching Specialties:
Internal Medicine.

Manhasset

North Shore University Hospital
300 Community Dr.
Manhasset, NY 11030
516-562-0100
Teaching Specialties:
Allergy/Immunology, Dentistry, Internal Medicine, Internal Medicine-Cardiovascular Disease, Internal Medicine-Gastroenterology, Internal Medicine-Geriatric Medicine, Internal Medicine-Hematology, Internal Medicine-Infectious Diseases, Internal Medicine-Medical Oncology, Internal Medicine-Nephrology, Internal Medicine-Rheumatology, Neurology, Obstetrics/Gynecology, Ophthalmology, Psychiatry, Surgery.

Middletown

Middletown Psychiatric Center
141 Monhagen Ave.
Middletown, NY 10940
914-342-5511
Teaching Specialties:
Psychiatry.

Mineola

Winthrop-University Hospital
259 First St.
Mineola, NY 11501
516-663-0333
Teaching Specialties:
Internal Medicine, Internal Medicine-Cardiovascular Disease, Internal Medicine-Endocrinology and Metabolism, Internal Medicine-Gastroenterology, Internal Medicine-Hematology, Internal Medicine-Infectious Diseases, Internal Medicine-Medical Oncology, Internal Medicine-Nephrology, Obstetrics/Gynecology, Surgery.

New Hyde Park

Jewish Institute for Geriatric Care
271-11 76th Ave.
New Hyde Park, NY 11042
718-343-0074
516-358-2370
Teaching Specialties:
Physical Medicine and Rehabilitation.

Long Island Jewish Medical Center
New Hyde Park, NY 11042
718-470-7000
Teaching Specialties:
Allergy/Immunology, Anesthesiology, Dentistry, Internal Medicine, Internal Medicine-Cardiovascular Disease, Internal Medicine-Endocrinology and Metabolism, Internal Medicine-Gastroenterology, Internal Medicine-Geriatric Medicine, Internal Medicine-Hematology, Internal Medicine-Infectious Diseases, Internal Medicine-Medical Oncology, Internal Medicine-Nephrology, Internal Medicine-Rheumatology, Neurology, Obstetrics/Gynecology, Ophthalmology, Orthopedic Surgery, Otolaryngology, Physical Medicine and Rehabilitation, Psychiatry, Surgery, Surgery-Vascular Surgery, Thoracic Surgery, Urology.

New Rochelle

New Rochelle Hospital Medical Center
16 Guion Place
New Rochelle, NY 10802
914-632-5000
Teaching Specialties:
Internal Medicine, Surgery.

New York

Bellevue Hospital Center
27th St. & First Ave.
New York, NY 10016
212-561-4141
Teaching Specialties:
Anesthesiology, Dermatology, Internal Medicine, Internal Medicine-Cardiovascular Disease, Internal Medicine-Endocrinology and Metabolism, Internal Medicine-Gastroenterology, Internal Medicine-Hematology, Internal Medicine-Infectious Diseases, Internal Medicine-Medical Oncology, Internal Medicine-Nephrology, Internal Medicine-Rheumatology, Neurological Surgery, Neurology, Obstetrics/Gynecology, Ophthalmology, Orthopedic Surgery, Otolaryngology, Physical Medicine and Rehabilitation, Psychiatry, Radiation Oncology, Surgery, Surgery-Vascular Surgery, Thoracic Surgery, Urology.

Beth Israel Medical Center
First Ave. & 16th St.
New York, NY 10003
212-420-2873

Teaching Specialties:
Anesthesiology, Dentistry, Dermatology, Internal Medicine, Internal Medicine-Cardiovascular Disease, Internal Medicine-Endocrinology and Metabolism, Internal Medicine-Gastroenterology, Internal Medicine-Hematology, Internal Medicine-Infectious Diseases, Internal Medicine-Medical Oncology, Internal Medicine-Nephrology, Obstetrics/Gynecology, Ophthalmology, Physical Medicine and Rehabilitation, Psychiatry, Radiation Oncology, Surgery, Urology.

Cabrini Medical Center
227 E. 19th St.
New York, NY 10003
212-995-6000
Teaching Specialties:
Internal Medicine, Internal Medicine-Cardiovascular Disease, Internal Medicine-Gastroenterology, Internal Medicine-Hematology, Internal Medicine-Infectious Diseases, Internal Medicine-Medical Oncology, Internal Medicine-Rheumatology, Ophthalmology, Psychiatry, Surgery, Urology.

Coler Memorial Hospital
Franklin D. Roosevelt Island
New York, NY 10044
212-848-6000
Teaching Specialties:
Dentistry.

Columbia University School of Dental and Oral Surgery
630 W. 168th St.
New York, NY 10032
212-305-2500
Teaching Specialties:
Dentistry.

Goldwater Memorial Hospital
Franklin D. Roosevelt Island
New York, NY 10044
212-750-6800
Teaching Specialties:
Dentistry, Physical Medicine and Rehabilitation.

Harlem Hospital Center
506 Lenox Ave.
New York, NY 10037
212-491-1234
Teaching Specialties:
Dentistry, Internal Medicine, Internal Medicine-Cardiovascular Disease, Internal Medicine-Gastroenterology, Internal Medicine-Hematology, Internal Medicine-Infectious Diseases, Internal Medicine-Medical Oncology, Internal Medicine-Nephrology, Neurology, Obstetrics/Gynecology, Ophthalmology, Orthopedic Surgery, Psychiatry, Surgery.

Hospital for Joint Diseases Orthopedic Institute
301 E. 17th St.
New York, NY 10003
212-598-6000
Teaching Specialties:
Internal Medicine-Rheumatology, Orthopedic Surgery, Physical Medicine and Rehabilitation.

Hospital for Special Surgery
535 E. 70th St.
New York, NY 10021
212-606-1000
Teaching Specialties:
Hand Surgery, Orthopedic Surgery.

Lenox Hill Hospital
100 E. 77th St.
New York, NY 10021
212-439-2345
Teaching Specialties:
Dentistry, Internal Medicine, Internal Medicine-Cardiovascular Disease, Internal Medicine-Gastroenterology, Internal Medicine-Hematology, Internal Medicine-Infectious Diseases, Internal Medicine-Medical Oncology, Internal Medicine-Nephrology, Obstetrics/Gynecology, Ophthalmology, Orthopedic Surgery, Surgery, Urology.

Manhattan Eye, Ear and Throat Hospital
210 E. 64th St.
New York, NY 10021
212-838-9200
Teaching Specialties:
Ophthalmology, Otolaryngology.

Manhattan Psychiatric Center-Ward's Island
600 E. 125th St.
New York, NY 10035
212-369-0500
Teaching Specialties:
Psychiatry.

Memorial Sloan-Kettering Cancer Center
1275 York Ave.
New York, NY 10021
800-525-2225
212-639-2000
Teaching Specialties:
Anesthesiology, Dentistry, Internal Medicine, Internal Medicine-Cardiovascular Disease, Internal Medicine-Gastroenterology, Internal Medicine-Hematology, Internal Medicine-Infectious Diseases, Internal Medicine-Medical Oncology, Neurology, Otolaryngology, Physical Medicine and Rehabilitation, Radiation Oncology, Surgery, Thoracic Surgery, Urology.

Metropolitan Hospital Center
1901 First Ave.
New York, NY 10029
212-230-6262
Teaching Specialties:
Anesthesiology, Dentistry, Dermatology, Internal Medicine, Internal Medicine-Cardiovascular Disease, Internal Medicine-Gastroenterology, Internal Medicine-Hematology, Internal Medicine-Infectious Diseases, Internal Medicine-Nephrology, Internal Medicine-Rheumatology, Neurology, Obstetrics/Gynecology, Ophthalmology, Orthopedic Surgery, Physical Medicine and Rehabilitation, Psychiatry, Surgery, Urology.

Mt. Sinai Medical Center
One Gustave Levy Place
New York, NY 10029
212-241-6500
Teaching Specialties:
Allergy/Immunology, Anesthesiology, Dentistry, Dermatology, Internal Medicine, Internal Medicine-Cardiovascular Disease, Internal Medicine-Endocrinology and Metabolism, Internal Medicine-Gastroenterology, Internal Medicine-Geriatric Medicine, Internal Medicine-Hematology, Internal Medicine-Infectious Diseases, Internal Medicine-Medical Oncology, Internal Medicine-Nephrology, Internal Medicine-Rheumatology, Neurological Surgery, Neurology, Obstetrics/Gynecology, Ophthalmology, Orthopedic Surgery, Otolaryngology, Physical Medicine and Rehabilitation, Psychiatry, Surgery, Surgery-Vascular Surgery, Thoracic Surgery, Urology.

New York Eye and Ear Infirmary
310 E. 14th St.
New York, NY 10003
212-979-4000
Teaching Specialties:
Ophthalmology, Otolaryngology.

New York Hospital-Cornell Medical Center
525 E. 68th St.
New York, NY 10021
212-746-5454
Teaching Specialties:
Allergy/Immunology, Anesthesiology, Dentistry, Dermatology, Hand Surgery, Internal Medicine, Internal Medicine-Cardiovascular Disease, Internal Medicine-Endocrinology and Metabolism, Internal Medicine-Gastroenterology, Internal Medicine-Hematology, Internal Medicine-Infectious Diseases, Internal Medicine-Medical Oncology, Internal Medicine-Nephrology, Internal Medicine-Rheumatology, Neurological Surgery, Neurology, Obstetrics/Gynecology, Ophthalmology, Orthopedic Surgery, Otolaryngology, Physical Medicine and Rehabilitation, Psychiatry, Surgery, Thoracic Surgery, Urology.

New York Hospital
Payne Whitney Psychiatric Clinic
525 E. 68th St.
New York, NY 10021
212-746-5454
Teaching Specialties:
Psychiatry.

New York Infirmary-Beekman Downtown Hospital
170 William St.
New York, NY 10038
212-312-5000
Teaching Specialties:
Internal Medicine, Obstetrics/Gynecology.

New York State Psychiatric Institute
722 W. 168th St.
New York, NY 10032
212-960-2200
Teaching Specialties:
Psychiatry.

New York University College of Dentistry
345 E. 24th St.
New York, NY 10010-4099
212-998-9800
Teaching Specialties:
Dentistry.

New York University Medical Center
550 First Ave.
New York, NY 10016
212-263-7300
Teaching Specialties:
Anesthesiology, Dermatology, Internal Medicine, Neurological Surgery, Neurology, Obstetrics/Gynecology, Ophthalmology, Orthopedic Surgery, Otolaryngology, Psychiatry, Radiation Oncology, Surgery-Vascular Surgery, Thoracic Surgery, Urology.

New York University Medical Center
Rusk Institute
400 E. 34th St.
New York, NY 10016
212-263-6030
Teaching Specialties:
Physical Medicine and Rehabilitation.

North General Hospital
1919 Madison Ave.
New York, NY 10035
212-650-4000
Teaching Specialties:
Internal Medicine, Ophthalmology, Surgery.

Presbyterian Hospital in the City of New York
Columbia-Presbyterian Medical Center
622 W. 168th St.
New York, NY 10032
212-305-2500
Teaching Specialties:
Allergy/Immunology, Anesthesiology, Dermatology, Internal Medicine, Internal Medicine-Cardiovascular Disease, Internal Medicine-Endocrinology and Metabolism, Internal Medicine-Gastroenterology, Internal Medicine-Hematology, Internal Medicine-Infectious Diseases, Internal Medicine-Medical Oncology, Internal Medicine-Nephrology, Internal Medicine-Rheumatology, Neurological Surgery, Neurology, Obstetrics/Gynecology, Ophthalmology, Orthopedic Surgery, Otolaryngology, Physical Medicine and Rehabilitation, Psychiatry, Radiation Oncology, Surgery, Thoracic Surgery, Urology.

St. Luke's-Roosevelt Hospital Center
Roosevelt Division
428 W. 59th St.
New York, NY 10019
212-523-4000
Teaching Specialties:
Allergy/Immunology, Colon and Rectal Surgery, Internal Medicine, Internal Medicine-Gastroenterology, Internal Medicine-Hematology, Internal Medicine-Medical Oncology, Obstetrics/Gynecology, Otolaryngology, Surgery, Urology.

St. Luke's-Roosevelt Hospital Center
St. Luke's Division
Amsterdam Ave. & 114th St.
New York, NY 10025
212-523-4000
Teaching Specialties:
Anesthesiology, Dentistry, Dermatology, Hand Surgery, Internal Medicine, Internal Medicine-Cardiovascular Disease, Internal Medicine-Endocrinology and Metabolism, Internal Medicine-Gastroenterology, Internal Medicine-Hematology, Internal Medicine-Infectious Diseases, Internal Medicine-Medical Oncology, Internal Medicine-Nephrology, Internal Medicine-Rheumatology, Obstetrics/Gynecology, Ophthalmology, Orthopedic Surgery, Otolaryngology, Psychiatry, Urology.

St. Vincent's Hospital and Medical Center of New York
153 W. 11th St.
New York, NY 10011
212-790-7000
Teaching Specialties:
Anesthesiology, Internal Medicine, Internal

Medicine-Cardiovascular Disease, Internal Medicine-Gastroenterology, Internal Medicine-Hematology, Internal Medicine-Infectious Diseases, Internal Medicine-Medical Oncology, Internal Medicine-Nephrology, Internal Medicine-Rheumatology, Neurology, Obstetrics/Gynecology, Ophthalmology, Orthopedic Surgery, Otolaryngology, Physical Medicine and Rehabilitation, Psychiatry, Surgery.

Oceanside

South Nassau Communities Hospital
2445 Oceanside Rd.
Oceanside, NY 11570
516-763-2030
Teaching Specialties:
Surgery.

Port Jefferson

St. Charles Hospital and Rehabilitation Center
200 Belle Terre Rd.
Port Jefferson, NY 11777
516-474-6000
Teaching Specialties:
Dentistry, Orthopedic Surgery.

Queens Village

Creedmoor Psychiatric Center
80-45 Winchester Blvd.
Queens Village, NY 11427
718-464-7500
Teaching Specialties:
Psychiatry.

Rochester

Eastman Dental Center
625 Elmwood Ave.
Rochester, NY 14620
716-275-5051
Teaching Specialties:
Dentistry.

Genesee Hospital
224 Alexander St.
Rochester, NY 14607
716-263-6000
Teaching Specialties:
Dentistry, Internal Medicine, Obstetrics/Gynecology, Orthopedic Surgery, Otolaryngology, Surgery, Surgery-Vascular Surgery, Urology.

Highland Hospital of Rochester
1000 South Ave.
Rochester, NY 14620
716-473-2200
Teaching Specialties:

Internal Medicine, Obstetrics/Gynecology, Orthopedic Surgery, Surgery.

Monroe Community Hospital
435 E. Henrietta Rd.
Rochester, NY 14620
716-274-7100
Teaching Specialties:
Internal Medicine-Rheumatology, Physical Medicine and Rehabilitation.

Rochester General Hospital
1425 Portland Ave.
Rochester, NY 14621
716-338-4000
Teaching Specialties:
Internal Medicine, Internal Medicine-Hematology, Internal Medicine-Medical Oncology, Obstetrics/Gynecology, Orthopedic Surgery, Otolaryngology, Surgery, Surgery-Vascular Surgery, Thoracic Surgery, Urology.

St. Mary's Hospital
89 Genesee St.
Rochester, NY 14611
716-464-3000
Teaching Specialties:
Internal Medicine, Internal Medicine-Gastroenterology, Ophthalmology, Surgery.

Strong Memorial Hospital of the University of Rochester
601 Elmwood Ave.
Rochester, NY 14642
716-275-2121
Teaching Specialties:
Allergy/Immunology, Anesthesiology, Dentistry, Dermatology, Hand Surgery, Internal Medicine, Internal Medicine-Cardiovascular Disease, Internal Medicine-Endocrinology and Metabolism, Internal Medicine-Gastroenterology, Internal Medicine-Hematology, Internal Medicine-Infectious Diseases, Internal Medicine-Medical Oncology, Internal Medicine-Nephrology, Internal Medicine-Rheumatology, Neurological Surgery, Neurology, Obstetrics/Gynecology, Ophthalmology, Orthopedic Surgery, Otolaryngology, Physical Medicine and Rehabilitation, Psychiatry, Radiation Oncology, Surgery, Surgery-Vascular Surgery, Thoracic Surgery, Urology.

Rockville Centre

Mercy Hospital
1000 N. Village Ave.
Rockville Centre, NY 11570
516-255-0111
Teaching Specialties:
Obstetrics/Gynecology.

Schenectady

Ellis Hospital
1101 Nott St.

Schenectady, NY 12308
518-382-4124
Teaching Specialties:
Internal Medicine, Orthopedic Surgery.

St. Clare's Hospital of Schenectady
600 McClellan St.
Schenectady, NY 12304
518-382-2000
Teaching Specialties:
Dentistry.

Sunnyview Hospital and Rehabilitation Center
1270 Belmont Ave.
Schenectady, NY 12308
518-382-4523
Teaching Specialties:
Physical Medicine and Rehabilitation.

Staten Island

Bayley Seton Hospital
75 Vanderbilt Ave.
Staten Island, NY 10304
718-390-6000
Teaching Specialties:
Dermatology, Ophthalmology.

St. Vincent's Medical Center of Richmond
355 Bard Ave.
Staten Island, NY 10310
718-876-1234
Teaching Specialties:
Internal Medicine, Internal Medicine-Cardiovascular Disease, Obstetrics/Gynecology, Psychiatry, Surgery.

Staten Island University Hospital
475 Seaview Ave.
Staten Island, NY 10305
718-226-8966
Teaching Specialties:
Dentistry, Internal Medicine, Obstetrics/Gynecology, Surgery.

Stony Brook

State University of New York at Stony Brook
School of Dental Medicine
Health Sciences Center
Stony Brook, NY 11794-8700
516-632-8989
Teaching Specialties:
Dentistry.

State University of New York at Stony Brook University Hospital
Health Sciences Center
Stony Brook, NY 11794

516-689-8333
Teaching Specialties:
Allergy/Immunology, Anesthesiology, Dermatology, Internal Medicine, Internal Medicine-Cardiovascular Disease, Internal Medicine-Endocrinology and Metabolism, Internal Medicine-Gastroenterology, Internal Medicine-Hematology, Internal Medicine-Infectious Diseases, Internal Medicine-Medical Oncology, Internal Medicine-Nephrology, Internal Medicine-Rheumatology, Neurology, Obstetrics/Gynecology, Orthopedic Surgery, Psychiatry, Surgery, Surgery-Vascular Surgery.

Syracuse

Community-General Hospital of Greater Syracuse
Broad Rd.
Syracuse, NY 13215
315-492-5011
Teaching Specialties:
Otolaryngology, Surgery.

Crouse-Irving Memorial Hospital
736 Irving Ave.
Syracuse, NY 13210
315-470-7111
Teaching Specialties:
Anesthesiology, Internal Medicine, Internal Medicine-Infectious Diseases, Neurological Surgery, Neurology, Obstetrics/Gynecology, Ophthalmology, Orthopedic Surgery, Otolaryngology, Surgery, Thoracic Surgery, Urology.

Richard H. Hutchings Psychiatric Center
620 Madison St.
Syracuse, NY 13210
315-473-4980
Teaching Specialties:
Psychiatry.

St. Camillus Health and Rehabilitation Center
813 Fay Rd.
Syracuse, NY 13219-3098
315-488-2951
Teaching Specialties:
Physical Medicine and Rehabilitation.

St. Joseph's Hospital Health Center
301 Prospect Ave.
Syracuse, NY 13203
315-448-5111
Teaching Specialties:
Anesthesiology, Dentistry, Obstetrics/Gynecology, Otolaryngology, Urology.

State University of New York Health Science Center
University Hospital
750 E. Adams St.

Syracuse, NY 13210
315-464-5540
Teaching Specialties:
Anesthesiology, Dentistry, Internal Medicine, Internal Medicine-Cardiovascular Disease, Internal Medicine-Endocrinology and Metabolism, Internal Medicine-Gastroenterology, Internal Medicine-Hematology, Internal Medicine-Infectious Diseases, Internal Medicine-Medical Oncology, Internal Medicine-Nephrology, Internal Medicine-Rheumatology, Neurological Surgery, Neurology, Obstetrics/Gynecology, Ophthalmology, Orthopedic Surgery, Otolaryngology, Physical Medicine and Rehabilitation, Psychiatry, Radiation Oncology, Surgery, Thoracic Surgery, Urology.

Utica

St. Luke's Memorial Hospital Center
PO Box 479
Utica, NY 13503
315-798-6000
Teaching Specialties:
Dentistry.

Valhalla

Westchester County Medical Center
Valhalla Campus
Valhalla, NY 10595
914-285-7000
Teaching Specialties:
Anesthesiology, Dentistry, Dermatology, Internal Medicine, Internal Medicine-Cardiovascular Disease, Internal Medicine-Endocrinology and Metabolism, Internal Medicine-Gastroenterology, Internal Medicine-Geriatric Medicine, Internal Medicine-Hematology, Internal Medicine-Infectious Diseases, Internal Medicine-Medical Oncology, Internal Medicine-Nephrology, Internal Medicine-Rheumatology, Neurology, Obstetrics/Gynecology, Ophthalmology, Orthopedic Surgery, Physical Medicine and Rehabilitation, Psychiatry, Surgery, Urology.

West Haverstraw

Helen Hayes Hospital
Route 9W
West Haverstraw, NY 10993
914-947-3000
Teaching Specialties:
Orthopedic Surgery.

White Plains

New York Hospital
Westchester Division
21 Bloomingdale Rd.
White Plains, NY 10605
914-682-9100

Teaching Specialties:
Psychiatry.

NORTH CAROLINA
Chapel Hill

University of North Carolina at Chapel Hill
School of Dentistry
CB 7450, Brauer Hall
Chapel Hill, NC 27599-7450
919-966-1161
Teaching Specialties:
Dentistry.

University of North Carolina Hospitals
Manning Dr.
Chapel Hill, NC 27514
919-966-4131
Teaching Specialties:
Anesthesiology, Dermatology, Internal Medicine, Internal Medicine-Cardiovascular Disease, Internal Medicine-Endocrinology and Metabolism, Internal Medicine-Gastroenterology, Internal Medicine-Geriatric Medicine, Internal Medicine-Hematology, Internal Medicine-Infectious Diseases, Internal Medicine-Medical Oncology, Internal Medicine-Nephrology, Internal Medicine-Rheumatology, Neurological Surgery, Neurology, Obstetrics/Gynecology, Ophthalmology, Orthopedic Surgery, Otolaryngology, Psychiatry, Radiation Oncology, Surgery, Surgery-Vascular Surgery, Thoracic Surgery, Urology.

Charlotte

Carolinas Medical Center
1000 Blythe Blvd.
Charlotte, NC 28203
704-355-2000
Teaching Specialties:
Dentistry, Internal Medicine, Obstetrics/Gynecology, Orthopedic Surgery, Surgery, Surgery-Vascular Surgery, Thoracic Surgery.

Orthopaedic Hospital of Charlotte
1901 Randolph Rd.
Charlotte, NC 28207
704-375-6792
Teaching Specialties:
Orthopedic Surgery.

Durham

Duke University Medical Center
Durham, NC 27710
919-684-8111
Teaching Specialties:
Anesthesiology, Dermatology, Internal Medicine, Internal Medicine-Cardiovascular Disease, Internal Medicine-Endocrinology

and Metabolism, Internal Medicine-Gastroenterology, Internal Medicine-Geriatric Medicine, Internal Medicine-Hematology, Internal Medicine-Infectious Diseases, Internal Medicine-Medical Oncology, Internal Medicine-Nephrology, Internal Medicine-Rheumatology, Neurological Surgery, Neurology, Obstetrics/Gynecology, Ophthalmology, Orthopedic Surgery, Otolaryngology, Psychiatry, Radiation Oncology, Surgery, Thoracic Surgery, Urology.

Durham County General Hospital
3643 N. Roxboro St.
Durham, NC 27704
919-470-4000
Teaching Specialties:
Neurological Surgery, Orthopedic Surgery, Surgery.

McPherson Hospital
1110 W. Main St.
Durham, NC 27701
919-682-9341
Teaching Specialties:
Ophthalmology.

Goldsboro

Cherry Hospital
Caller Box 8000
Goldsboro, NC 27530
919-731-3202
Teaching Specialties:
Psychiatry.

Greensboro

Moses H. Cone Memorial Hospital
1200 N. Elm St.
Greensboro, NC 27401
919-379-3900
Teaching Specialties:
Internal Medicine.

Greenville

East Carolina University School of Medicine
Family Practice Center, Department of Dentistry
Greenville, NC 27858
919-551-4618
Teaching Specialties:
Dentistry.

Pitt County Memorial Hospital
2100 Stantonsburg Rd.
Greenville, NC 27835
919-551-4100
Teaching Specialties:
Allergy/Immunology, Internal Medicine, Internal Medicine-Cardiovascular Disease, Internal Medicine-Endocrinology and

Metabolism, Internal Medicine-Nephrology, Obstetrics/Gynecology, Psychiatry, Surgery.

Pitt County Mental Health Center
2310 Stantonsburg Rd.
Greenville, NC 27834
919-752-7151
Teaching Specialties:
Psychiatry.

Raleigh

Dorothea Dix Hospital
820 S. Boylan Ave.
Raleigh, NC 27603
919-733-5324
Teaching Specialties:
Psychiatry.

Wake Medical Center
3000 New Bern Ave.
Raleigh, NC 27610
919-250-8000
Teaching Specialties:
Obstetrics/Gynecology, Orthopedic Surgery, Surgery, Urology.

Wilmington

New Hanover Memorial Hospital
2131 S. 17th St.
Wilmington, NC 28401
919-343-7000
Teaching Specialties:
Internal Medicine, Obstetrics/Gynecology, Surgery.

Winston-Salem

Bowman Gray School of Medicine
Department of Dentistry
Medical Center Blvd.
Winston-Salem, NC 27157
919-748-2183
Teaching Specialties:
Dentistry.

Forsyth Memorial Hospital
3333 Silas Creek Parkway
Winston-Salem, NC 27103
919-760-5000
Teaching Specialties:
Obstetrics/Gynecology, Surgery, Urology.

North Carolina Baptist Hospital
300 S. Hawthorne Rd.
Winston-Salem, NC 27103
919-748-2011
Teaching Specialties:
Allergy/Immunology, Anesthesiology, Dermatology, Internal Medicine, Internal Medicine-Cardiovascular Disease, Internal Medicine-Gastroenterology, Internal Medicine-

Geriatric Medicine, Internal Medicine-Infectious Diseases, Internal Medicine-Medical Oncology, Internal Medicine-Nephrology, Internal Medicine-Rheumatology, Neurological Surgery, Neurology, Obstetrics/Gynecology, Ophthalmology, Orthopedic Surgery, Otolaryngology, Psychiatry, Radiation Oncology, Surgery, Thoracic Surgery, Urology.

NORTH DAKOTA

Fargo

Dakota Hospital
1720 S. University Dr.
Fargo, ND 58103
701-280-4100
Teaching Specialties:
Internal Medicine.

Southeast Human Services Center
15 N. Broadway
Fargo, ND 58102
701-237-4513
Teaching Specialties:
Psychiatry.

St. Luke's Hospitals-Meritcare
720 4th St., N
Fargo, ND 58122
701-234-6000
Teaching Specialties:
Internal Medicine, Psychiatry, Surgery.

Grand Forks

United Hospital
1200 S. Columbia Rd.
Grand Forks, ND 58206
701-780-5000
Teaching Specialties:
Surgery.

OHIO

Akron

Akron City Hospital
525 Market St.
Akron, OH 44309
216-375-3000
Teaching Specialties:
Internal Medicine, Obstetrics/Gynecology, Ophthalmology, Orthopedic Surgery, Surgery, Urology.

Akron General Medical Center
400 Wabash Ave.
Akron, OH 44307
216-384-6000
Teaching Specialties:
Internal Medicine, Obstetrics/Gynecology, Orthopedic Surgery, Psychiatry, Surgery, Urology.

St. Thomas Medical Center
444 N. Main St.
Akron, OH 44310
216-379-1111
Teaching Specialties:
Internal Medicine, Psychiatry.

Canton

Aultman Hospital
2600 6th St., SW
Canton, OH 44710
216-452-9911
Teaching Specialties:
Internal Medicine, Obstetrics/Gynecology.

Timken Mercy Medical Center
1320 Timken Mercy Dr., NW
Canton, OH 44708
216-489-1000
Teaching Specialties:
Internal Medicine.

Cincinnati

Bethesda Oak Hospital
619 Oak St.
Cincinnati, OH 45206
513-569-6111
Teaching Specialties:
Hand Surgery, Obstetrics/Gynecology, Orthopedic Surgery.

Christ Hospital
2139 Auburn Ave.
Cincinnati, OH 45219
513-369-2000
Teaching Specialties:
Internal Medicine, Neurological Surgery, Obstetrics/Gynecology, Surgery.

Good Samaritan Hospital
3217 Clifton Ave.
Cincinnati, OH 45220
513-872-1400
Teaching Specialties:
Internal Medicine, Neurological Surgery, Obstetrics/Gynecology, Orthopedic Surgery, Surgery, Surgery-Vascular Surgery.

Jewish Hospital of Cincinnati
3200 Burnet Ave.
Cincinnati, OH 45229
513-569-2000
Teaching Specialties:
Internal Medicine, Surgery.

Providence Hospital
2446 Kipling Ave.
Cincinnati, OH 45239
513-853-5000
Teaching Specialties:
Surgery.

University of Cincinnati Hospital
234 Goodman St.
Cincinnati, OH 45267
513-558-1000
Teaching Specialties:
Allergy/Immunology, Anesthesiology, Dentistry, Dermatology, Hand Surgery, Internal Medicine, Internal Medicine-Cardiovascular Disease, Internal Medicine-Endocrinology and Metabolism, Internal Medicine-Gastroenterology, Internal Medicine-Hematology, Internal Medicine-Infectious Diseases, Internal Medicine-Medical Oncology, Internal Medicine-Nephrology, Internal Medicine-Rheumatology, Neurological Surgery, Neurology, Obstetrics/Gynecology, Ophthalmology, Orthopedic Surgery, Otolaryngology, Physical Medicine and Rehabilitation, Psychiatry, Radiation Oncology, Surgery, Urology.

Cleveland

Case Western Reserve University School of Dentistry
2123 Abington Rd.
Cleveland, OH 44106
216-368-3200
Teaching Specialties:
Dentistry.

Cleveland Clinic Hospital
One Clinical Center,
9500 Euclid Ave.
Cleveland, OH 44195
800-223-2273
216-444-2200
Teaching Specialties:
Allergy/Immunology, Anesthesiology, Colon and Rectal Surgery, Dentistry, Dermatology, Internal Medicine, Internal Medicine-Cardiovascular Disease, Internal Medicine-Endocrinology and Metabolism, Internal Medicine-Gastroenterology, Internal Medicine-Geriatric Medicine, Internal Medicine-Hematology, Internal Medicine-Infectious Diseases, Internal Medicine-Medical Oncology, Internal Medicine-Nephrology, Internal Medicine-Rheumatology, Neurological Surgery, Neurology, Ophthalmology, Orthopedic Surgery, Otolaryngology, Psychiatry, Radiation Oncology, Surgery, Surgery-Vascular Surgery, Thoracic Surgery, Urology.

Cleveland Psychiatric Institute
1708 Aiken Ave.
Cleveland, OH 44109
216-661-6200
Teaching Specialties:
Psychiatry.

Cleveland Psychoanalytic Institute
11328 Euclid Ave.
Cleveland, OH 44106
216-229-5959

Teaching Specialties:
Psychiatry.

Fairview General Hospital
18101 Lorain Ave.
Cleveland, OH 44111
216-476-7000
Teaching Specialties:
Surgery.

Lutheran Medical Center
2609 Franklin Blvd.
Cleveland, OH 44113
216-696-4300
Teaching Specialties:
Internal Medicine, Surgery.

Meridia Huron Hospital
13951 Terrace Rd.
Cleveland, OH 44112
216-761-3300
Teaching Specialties:
Anesthesiology, Internal Medicine, Surgery.

MetroHealth Center for Rehabilitation
3395 Scranton Rd.
Cleveland, OH 44109
216-459-3473
216-459-4166
Teaching Specialties:
Internal Medicine-Endocrinology and Metabolism, Physical Medicine and Rehabilitation.

MetroHealth Medical Center
3395 Scranton Rd.
Cleveland, OH 44109
216-398-6000
Teaching Specialties:
Anesthesiology, Dentistry, Dermatology, Internal Medicine, Internal Medicine-Cardiovascular Disease, Internal Medicine-Endocrinology and Metabolism, Internal Medicine-Gastroenterology, Internal Medicine-Geriatric Medicine, Internal Medicine-Hematology, Internal Medicine-Infectious Diseases, Internal Medicine-Medical Oncology, Internal Medicine-Rheumatology, Neurological Surgery, Neurology, Obstetrics/Gynecology, Ophthalmology, Orthopedic Surgery, Otolaryngology, Physical Medicine and Rehabilitation, Psychiatry, Surgery, Thoracic Surgery, Urology.

Mt. Sinai Medical Center
One Mt. Sinai Dr.
Cleveland, OH 44106
216-421-4000
Teaching Specialties:
Dentistry, Internal Medicine, Obstetrics/Gynecology, Ophthalmology, Orthopedic Surgery, Psychiatry, Surgery.

St. Luke's Hospital
11311 Shaker Blvd.
Cleveland, OH 44104
216-368-7000
Teaching Specialties:
Dentistry, Internal Medicine, Obstetrics/Gynecology, Ophthalmology, Orthopedic Surgery, Surgery.

St. Vincent Charity Hospital and Health Center
2351 E. 22nd St.
Cleveland, OH 44115
216-861-6200
Teaching Specialties:
Internal Medicine, Ophthalmology.

University Hospitals of Cleveland
2074 Abington Rd.
Cleveland, OH 44106
216-844-1000
Teaching Specialties:
Anesthesiology, Dermatology, Internal Medicine, Internal Medicine-Cardiovascular Disease, Internal Medicine-Endocrinology and Metabolism, Internal Medicine-Gastroenterology, Internal Medicine-Geriatric Medicine, Internal Medicine-Hematology, Internal Medicine-Infectious Diseases, Internal Medicine-Medical Oncology, Internal Medicine-Nephrology, Internal Medicine-Rheumatology, Neurological Surgery, Neurology, Obstetrics/Gynecology, Ophthalmology, Orthopedic Surgery, Otolaryngology, Psychiatry, Radiation Oncology, Surgery, Thoracic Surgery, Urology.

Columbus

Grant Medical Center
111 S. Grant Ave.
Columbus, OH 43215
614-461-3232
Teaching Specialties:
Colon and Rectal Surgery, Internal Medicine-Gastroenterology, Obstetrics/Gynecology, Physical Medicine and Rehabilitation, Psychiatry, Surgery.

Mt. Carmel East Hospital
6001 E. Broad St.
Columbus, OH 43213
614-868-6000
Teaching Specialties:
Surgery.

Mt. Carmel Medical Center
793 W. State St.
Columbus, OH 43222
614-225-5000
Teaching Specialties:
Internal Medicine, Internal Medicine-Cardiovascular Disease, Obstetrics/Gynecology, Orthopedic Surgery, Physical Medicine and Rehabilitation, Psychiatry, Surgery.

**Ohio State University
College of Dentistry**
305 W.12th Ave.
Columbus, OH 43210
614-292-2401
Teaching Specialties:
Dentistry.

Ohio State University Hospitals
410 W. 10th Ave.
Columbus, OH 43210
614-293-8000
Teaching Specialties:
Anesthesiology, Dermatology, Hand Surgery, Internal Medicine, Internal Medicine-Cardiovascular Disease, Internal Medicine-Endocrinology and Metabolism, Internal Medicine-Gastroenterology, Internal Medicine-Hematology, Internal Medicine-Infectious Diseases, Internal Medicine-Medical Oncology, Internal Medicine-Nephrology, Neurological Surgery, Neurology, Obstetrics/Gynecology, Ophthalmology, Orthopedic Surgery, Otolaryngology, Physical Medicine and Rehabilitation, Psychiatry, Radiation Oncology, Surgery, Surgery-Vascular Surgery, Thoracic Surgery, Urology.

Riverside Methodist Hospitals
3535 Olentangy River Rd.
Columbus, OH 43214
614-261-5000
Teaching Specialties:
Hand Surgery, Internal Medicine, Neurological Surgery, Neurology, Obstetrics/Gynecology, Orthopedic Surgery, Physical Medicine and Rehabilitation, Psychiatry, Surgery, Urology.

Dayton

**Good Samaritan Hospital
and Health Center**
2222 Philadelphia Dr.
Dayton, OH 45406
513-278-2612
Teaching Specialties:
Dermatology, Internal Medicine, Internal Medicine-Cardiovascular Disease, Psychiatry, Surgery.

Miami Valley Hospital
One Wyoming St.
Dayton, OH 45409
513-223-6192
Teaching Specialties:
Dentistry, Internal Medicine, Obstetrics/Gynecology, Orthopedic Surgery, Surgery.

St. Elizabeth Medical Center
601 Edwin C. Moses Blvd.
Dayton, OH 45408
513-229-6000
Teaching Specialties:
Dermatology, Surgery.

Kettering

Kettering Medical Center
3535 Southern Blvd.
Kettering, OH 45429
513-298-4331
Teaching Specialties:
Internal Medicine, Psychiatry, Surgery.

Ravenna

Robinson Memorial Hospital
6847 N. Chestnut St.
Ravenna, OH 44266
216-297-0811
Teaching Specialties:
Surgery.

Toledo

Medical College of Ohio Hospital
3000 Arlington Ave.
Toledo, OH 43614
419-381-4172
Teaching Specialties:
Anesthesiology, Dentistry, Internal Medicine, Internal Medicine-Cardiovascular Disease, Internal Medicine-Endocrinology and Metabolism, Internal Medicine-Hematology, Internal Medicine-Infectious Diseases, Internal Medicine-Medical Oncology, Internal Medicine-Nephrology, Obstetrics/Gynecology, Orthopedic Surgery, Physical Medicine and Rehabilitation, Psychiatry, Surgery, Urology.

Mercy Hospital
2200 Jefferson Ave.
Toledo, OH 43624
419-259-1500
Teaching Specialties:
Internal Medicine-Endocrinology and Metabolism.

St. Vincent Medical Center
2213 Cherry St.
Toledo, OH 43608
419-321-3232
Teaching Specialties:
Internal Medicine, Internal Medicine-Hematology, Internal Medicine-Medical Oncology, Obstetrics/Gynecology, Orthopedic Surgery, Physical Medicine and Rehabilitation, Psychiatry, Surgery, Urology.

Toledo Hospital
2142 N. Cove Blvd.
Toledo, OH 43606
419-471-4218
Teaching Specialties:
Anesthesiology, Internal Medicine, Internal Medicine-Cardiovascular Disease, Obstetrics/Gynecology, Orthopedic Surgery, Physical Medicine and Rehabilitation, Surgery, Urology.

Toledo Mental Health Center
930 S. Detroit Ave.
Toledo, OH 43699
419-381-1881
Teaching Specialties:
Psychiatry.

Westerville

St. Ann's Hospital of Columbus
500 S. Cleveland Ave.
Westerville, OH 43081
614-898-4000
Teaching Specialties:
Obstetrics/Gynecology.

Worthington

Harding Hospital
445 E. Granville Rd.
Worthington, OH 43085
614-885-5381
Teaching Specialties:
Psychiatry.

Youngstown

**St. Elizabeth Hospital
Medical Center**
1044 Belmont Ave.
Youngstown, OH 44501
216-746-7211
Teaching Specialties:
Dentistry, Internal Medicine, Obstetrics/Gynecology, Surgery.

**Western Reserve Care System-
Northside Medical Center**
500 Gypsy Lane
Youngstown, OH 44501
216-747-1444
Teaching Specialties:
Anesthesiology, Internal Medicine, Surgery.

**Western Reserve Care System-
Southside Medical Center**
345 Oak Hill Ave.
Youngstown, OH 44501
216-747-0777
Teaching Specialties:
Anesthesiology, Dentistry, Internal Medicine, Surgery.

OKLAHOMA

Norman

Griffin Memorial Hospital
E. Main & Carter Sts.
Norman, OK 73070
405-321-4880
Teaching Specialties:
Psychiatry.

Oklahoma City

**Baptist Medical Center
of Oklahoma**
3300 N.W. Expressway
Oklahoma City, OK 73112
405-949-3011
Teaching Specialties:
Otolaryngology.

Bone and Joint Hospital
1111 N. Dewey Ave.
Oklahoma City, OK 73103
405-272-9671
Teaching Specialties:
Orthopedic Surgery.

Oklahoma Medical Center
800 N.E. 13th St.
Oklahoma City, OK 73104
405-271-3700
Teaching Specialties:
Anesthesiology, Dentistry, Dermatology,
Internal Medicine, Internal Medicine-Cardiovascular Disease, Internal Medicine-Endocrinology and Metabolism, Internal Medicine-
Gastroenterology, Internal Medicine-Hematology, Internal Medicine-Infectious Diseases,
Internal Medicine-Medical Oncology, Internal Medicine-Nephrology, Internal Medicine-
Rheumatology, Neurological Surgery, Obstet-
rics/Gynecology, Ophthalmology, Orthopedic Surgery, Otolaryngology, Psychiatry, Radiation Oncology, Surgery, Thoracic Surgery,
Urology.

Presbyterian Hospital
700 N.E. 13th St.
Oklahoma City, OK 73104
405-271-5100
Teaching Specialties:
Orthopedic Surgery, Surgery.

St. Anthony Hospital
1000 N. Lee St.
Oklahoma City, OK 73101
405-272-7000
Teaching Specialties:
Dentistry, Neurological Surgery.

**University of Oklahoma
College of Dentistry**
1001 N.E. Stanton L. Young
Oklahoma City, OK 73190
405-271-6326
Teaching Specialties:
Dentistry.

Tulsa

Hillcrest Medical Center
1120 S. Utica Ave.
Tulsa, OK 74104
918-584-1351

Teaching Specialties:
Internal Medicine, Obstetrics/Gynecology,
Psychiatry, Surgery.

St. Francis Hospital
6161 S. Yale Ave.
Tulsa, OK 74136
918-494-2200
Teaching Specialties:
Internal Medicine, Obstetrics/Gynecology,
Surgery.

St. John Medical Center
1923 S. Utica Ave.
Tulsa, OK 74104
918-744-2345
Teaching Specialties:
Internal Medicine, Obstetrics/Gynecology,
Surgery.

Tulsa Psychiatric Center
1620 E. 12th St.
Tulsa, OK 74120
918-582-2131
Teaching Specialties:
Psychiatry.

OREGON

Clackamas

Kaiser Sunnyside Medical Center
10200 S.E. Sunnyside Rd.
Clackamas, OR 97015
503-652-2880
Teaching Specialties:
Neurological Surgery.

Portland

**Emanuel Hospital and
Health Center**
2801 N. Gantenbein Ave.
Portland, OR 97227
503-280-3200
Teaching Specialties:
Internal Medicine, Obstetrics/Gynecology,
Orthopedic Surgery, Surgery.

**Good Samaritan Hospital
and Medical Center**
1015 N.W. 22nd Ave.
Portland, OR 97210
503-229-7711
Teaching Specialties:
Internal Medicine, Neurology, Obstetrics/
Gynecology, Ophthalmology, Surgery.

Oregon Health Sciences University
School of Dentistry
611 S.W. Campus Dr.
Portland, OR 97201

503-494-8850
Teaching Specialties:
Dentistry.

Oregon Health Sciences University
University Hospital
3181 S.W. Sam Jackson Park Rd.
Portland, OR 97201
503-494-8311
Teaching Specialties:
Anesthesiology, Dermatology, Internal
Medicine, Internal Medicine-Cardiovascular
Disease, Internal Medicine-Endocrinology
and Metabolism, Internal Medicine-Gastroenterology, Internal Medicine-Geriatric Medicine, Internal Medicine-Hematology, Internal
Medicine-Infectious Diseases, Internal Medicine-Medical Oncology, Internal Medicine-
Nephrology, Internal Medicine-Rheumatology, Neurological Surgery, Neurology, Obstet-
rics/Gynecology, Ophthalmology, Orthopedic Surgery, Otolaryngology, Psychiatry,
Radiation Oncology, Surgery, Surgery-Vascular Surgery, Thoracic Surgery, Urology.

Providence Medical Center
4805 N.E. Glisan St.
Portland, OR 97213
503-230-1111
Teaching Specialties:
Internal Medicine.

**St. Vincent Hospital and
Medical Center**
9205 S.W. Barnes Rd.
Portland, OR 97225
503-297-4411
Teaching Specialties:
Internal Medicine, Surgery.

PENNSYLVANIA

Abington

Abington Memorial Hospital
1200 York Rd.
Abington, PA 19001
215-576-2009
Teaching Specialties:
Dentistry, Internal Medicine, Obstetrics/
Gynecology, Orthopedic Surgery, Psychiatry,
Surgery, Urology.

Allentown

**The Allentown Hospital-
Lehigh Valley Hospital Center**
17th & Chew Sts.
Allentown, PA 18102
215-778-2300
Teaching Specialties:
Colon and Rectal Surgery, Dentistry,
Internal Medicine-Cardiovascular Disease,
Obstetrics/Gynecology, Surgery.

Sacred Heart Hospital
421 Chew St.
Allentown, PA 18102
215-776-4500
Teaching Specialties:
Dentistry.

Bethlehem

Muhlenberg Hospital Center
2545 Schoenersville Rd.
Bethlehem, PA 18017
215-861-2200
Teaching Specialties:
Dentistry.

St. Luke's Hospital
801 Ostrum St.
Bethlehem, PA 18015
215-954-4000
Teaching Specialties:
Internal Medicine, Obstetrics/Gynecology.

Bristol

Lower Bucks Hospital
501 Bath Rd.
Bristol, PA 19007
215-785-9200
Teaching Specialties:
Obstetrics/Gynecology.

Bryn Mawr

Bryn Mawr Hospital
130 S. Bryn Mawr Ave.
Bryn Mawr, PA 19010
215-526-3000
Teaching Specialties:
Internal Medicine, Orthopedic Surgery,
Surgery, Urology.

Danville

Geisinger Medical Center
N. Academy Ave.
Danville, PA 17822
717-271-5200
Teaching Specialties:
Anesthesiology, Dermatology, Internal
Medicine, Internal Medicine-Cardiovascular
Disease, Internal Medicine-Rheumatology,
Obstetrics/Gynecology, Ophthalmology,
Orthopedic Surgery, Otolaryngology,
Surgery, Urology.

Drexel Hill

**Delaware County
Memorial Hospital**
501 N. Lansdowne Ave.
Drexel Hill, PA 19026
215-284-8100

Teaching Specialties:
Orthopedic Surgery.

Easton

Easton Hospital
250 S. 21st St.
Easton, PA 18042
215-250-4000
Teaching Specialties:
Internal Medicine, Surgery.

Erie

Hamot Medical Center
201 State St.
Erie, PA 16550
814-870-6000
Teaching Specialties:
Colon and Rectal Surgery,
Orthopedic Surgery.

St. Vincent Health Center
232 W. 25th St.
Erie, PA 16544
814-452-5000
Teaching Specialties:
Colon and Rectal Surgery.

Fort Washington

Northwestern Institute
450 Bethlehem Pike
Fort Washington, PA 19034
215-641-5300
Teaching Specialties:
Psychiatry.

Harrisburg

Harrisburg Hospital
S. Front St.
Harrisburg, PA 17101
717-782-3131
Teaching Specialties:
Internal Medicine, Obstetrics/Gynecology,
Orthopedic Surgery, Surgery.

**Polyclinic Medical Center
of Harrisburg**
2601 N. Third St.
Harrisburg, PA 17110
717-782-2606
Teaching Specialties:
Internal Medicine, Orthopedic
Surgery, Surgery.

Hershey

Penn State University Hospital
Elizabethtown Hospital
500 University Dr.
Hershey, PA 17033

717-531-7320
Teaching Specialties:
Orthopedic Surgery.

Penn State University Hospital
The Milton S. Hershey Medical
Center
500 University Dr.
Hershey, PA 17033
717-531-8521
Teaching Specialties:
Anesthesiology, Dermatology, Internal Medi-
cine, Internal Medicine-Cardiovascular
Disease, Internal Medicine-Endocrinology
and Metabolism, Internal Medicine-Gastroen-
terology, Internal Medicine-Hematology, In-
ternal Medicine-Infectious Diseases, Internal
Medicine-Medical Oncology, Internal Medi-
cine-Nephrology, Neurology, Obstetrics/
Gynecology, Ophthalmology, Orthopedic
Surgery, Otolaryngology, Psychiatry, Surgery,
Surgery-Vascular Surgery, Thoracic Surgery,
Urology.

Johnstown

**Conemaugh Valley
Memorial Hospital**
1086 Franklin St.
Johnstown, PA 15905
814-533-9000
Teaching Specialties:
Internal Medicine, Surgery.

Lancaster

Lancaster General Hospital
555 N. Duke St.
Lancaster, PA 17603
717-299-5511
Teaching Specialties:
Urology.

McKeesport

McKeesport Hospital
1500 5th Ave.
McKeesport, PA 15132
412-664-2000
Teaching Specialties:
Internal Medicine, Surgery.

Norristown

Norristown State Hospital
1001 Sterigere St.
Norristown, PA 19401
215-270-1000
Teaching Specialties:
Psychiatry.

Sacred Heart Hospital
1430 DeKalb St.
Norristown, PA 19401

215-278-8200
Teaching Specialties:
Physical Medicine and Rehabilitation.

Philadelphia

Albert Einstein Medical Center
5501 Old York Rd.
Philadelphia, PA 19141
215-456-7890
Teaching Specialties:
Anesthesiology, Dentistry, Internal Medicine,
Internal Medicine-Cardiovascular Disease,
Internal Medicine-Gastroenterology, Internal
Medicine-Geriatric Medicine, Internal Medicine-Nephrology, Internal Medicine-Rheumatology, Neurology, Obstetrics/Gynecology,
Orthopedic Surgery, Physical Medicine and
Rehabilitation, Psychiatry, Radiation Oncology, Surgery.

American Oncologic Hospital-Fox Chase Cancer Center
7701 Burholme Ave.
Philadelphia, PA 19111
215-728-6900
Teaching Specialties:
Internal Medicine-Hematology, Internal
Medicine-Medical Oncology, Radiation
Oncology, Surgery.

Chestnut Hill Hospital
8835 Germantown Ave.
Philadelphia, PA 19118
215-248-8200
Teaching Specialties:
Obstetrics/Gynecology.

Episcopal Hospital
Front St. & Lehigh Ave.
Philadelphia, PA 19125
215-427-7000
Teaching Specialties:
Internal Medicine, Internal Medicine-Cardiovascular Disease, Otolaryngology, Surgery.

Frankford Hospital of the City of Philadelphia
Knights & Red Lion Rds.
Philadelphia, PA 19114
215-934-4000
Teaching Specialties:
Obstetrics/Gynecology, Surgery.

Friends Hospital
4641 Roosevelt Blvd.
Philadelphia, PA 19124
215-831-4600
Teaching Specialties:
Psychiatry.

Germantown Hospital and Medical Center
One Penn Blvd.

Philadelphia, PA 19144
215-951-8000
Teaching Specialties:
Internal Medicine, Obstetrics/Gynecology.

Graduate Hospital
19th & Lombard Sts.
Philadelphia, PA 19146
215-893-2000
Teaching Specialties:
Dentistry, Dermatology, Internal Medicine,
Internal Medicine-Cardiovascular Disease,
Internal Medicine-Gastroenterology, Physical
Medicine and Rehabilitation, Surgery.

Hahnemann University Hospital
Broad & Vine Sts.
Philadelphia, PA 19102
215-448-7700
Teaching Specialties:
Anesthesiology, Dentistry, Dermatology,
Internal Medicine, Internal Medicine-Cardiovascular Disease, Internal Medicine-Endocrinology and Metabolism, Internal Medicine-Gastroenterology, Internal Medicine-Hematology, Internal Medicine-Infectious Diseases,
Internal Medicine-Medical Oncology, Internal Medicine-Nephrology, Internal Medicine-Rheumatology, Neurological Surgery, Neurology, Obstetrics/Gynecology, Ophthalmology,
Orthopedic Surgery, Otolaryngology, Psychiatry, Radiation Oncology, Surgery, Surgery-Vascular Surgery, Thoracic Surgery.

Hospital of the Medical College of Pennsylvania
3300 Henry Ave.
Philadelphia, PA 19129
215-842-6000
Teaching Specialties:
Dentistry, Internal Medicine, Internal Medicine-Cardiovascular Disease, Internal
Medicine-Endocrinology and Metabolism,
Internal Medicine-Gastroenterology, Internal
Medicine-Hematology, Internal Medicine-Infectious Diseases, Internal Medicine-Medical Oncology, Internal Medicine-Nephrology,
Internal Medicine-Rheumatology, Neurology,
Obstetrics/Gynecology, Orthopedic Surgery,
Psychiatry, Surgery, Urology.

Hospital of the University of Pennsylvania
3400 Spruce St.
Philadelphia, PA 19104
215-662-4000
Teaching Specialties:
Allergy/Immunology, Anesthesiology, Dermatology, Hand Surgery, Internal Medicine,
Internal Medicine-Cardiovascular Disease,
Internal Medicine-Endocrinology and Metabolism, Internal Medicine-Gastroenterology,
Internal Medicine-Geriatric Medicine, Internal Medicine-Hematology, Internal Medicine-Infectious Diseases, Internal Medicine-Medical Oncology, Internal Medicine-Nephrology,

Internal Medicine-Rheumatology, Neurological Surgery, Neurology, Obstetrics/Gynecology, Orthopedic Surgery, Otolaryngology,
Physical Medicine and Rehabilitation, Psychiatry, Radiation Oncology, Surgery, Surgery-Vascular Surgery, Thoracic Surgery, Urology.

Mercy Catholic Medical Center
Fitzgerald Mercy Division
Lansdowne Ave. & Baily Rd.
Philadelphia, PA 19023
215-237-4000
Teaching Specialties:
Hand Surgery, Internal Medicine,
Psychiatry, Surgery.

Mercy Catholic Medical Center
Misericordia Division
54th St. & Cedar Ave.
Philadelphia, PA 19143
215-748-9000
Teaching Specialties:
Internal Medicine, Internal Medicine-Gastroenterology, Surgery.

Methodist Hospital
2301 S. Broad St.
Philadelphia, PA 19148
215-952-9000
Teaching Specialties:
Obstetrics/Gynecology, Orthopedic Surgery.

Moss Rehabilitation Hospital
12th St. & Tabor Rd.
Philadelphia, PA 19141
215-456-9900
Teaching Specialties:
Internal Medicine-Rheumatology, Orthopedic Surgery, Physical Medicine and
Rehabilitation.

Pennsylvania Hospital
800 Spruce St.
Philadelphia, PA 19107
215-829-3000
Teaching Specialties:
Dermatology, Internal Medicine, Internal
Medicine-Infectious Diseases, Neurological
Surgery, Neurology, Obstetrics/Gynecology,
Orthopedic Surgery, Otolaryngology, Psychiatry, Surgery, Urology.

Presbyterian Medical Center of Philadelphia
39th & Market Sts.
Philadelphia, PA 19104
215-662-8000
Teaching Specialties:
Internal Medicine, Internal Medicine-Cardiovascular Disease, Internal Medicine-Gastroenterology, Ophthalmology.

Scheie Eye Institute
51 N. 39th St.

Philadelphia, PA 19104
215-662-8100
Teaching Specialties:
Ophthalmology.

Temple University Hospital
Broad & Ontario Sts.
Philadelphia, PA 19140
215-221-2000
Teaching Specialties:
Anesthesiology, Internal Medicine, Internal Medicine-Cardiovascular Disease, Internal Medicine-Endocrinology and Metabolism, Internal Medicine-Gastroenterology, Internal Medicine-Hematology, Internal Medicine-Infectious Diseases, Internal Medicine-Medical Oncology, Internal Medicine-Nephrology, Internal Medicine-Rheumatology, Neurological Surgery, Neurology, Obstetrics/Gynecology, Ophthalmology, Orthopedic Surgery, Otolaryngology, Physical Medicine and Rehabilitation, Psychiatry, Surgery, Surgery-Vascular Surgery, Urology.

Temple University School of Dentistry
3223 N. Broad St.
Philadelphia, PA 19140
215-221-2803
Teaching Specialties:
Dentistry.

Thomas Jefferson University Hospital
111 S. 11th St.
Philadelphia, PA 19107
215-955-6000
Teaching Specialties:
Allergy/Immunology, Anesthesiology, Colon and Rectal Surgery, Dentistry, Dermatology, Hand Surgery, Internal Medicine, Internal Medicine-Cardiovascular Disease, Internal Medicine-Gastroenterology, Internal Medicine-Hematology, Internal Medicine-Infectious Diseases, Internal Medicine-Medical Oncology, Internal Medicine-Nephrology, Internal Medicine-Rheumatology, Neurological Surgery, Neurology, Obstetrics/Gynecology, Orthopedic Surgery, Otolaryngology, Physical Medicine and Rehabilitation, Psychiatry, Radiation Oncology, Surgery, Thoracic Surgery, Urology.

University of Pennsylvania School of Dental Medicine
4001 Spruce St.
Philadelphia, PA 19104
215-898-8961
Teaching Specialties:
Dentistry.

Wills Eye Hospital
900 Walnut St.
Philadelphia, PA 19107
215-928-3000

Teaching Specialties:
Ophthalmology.

Pittsburgh

Allegheny General Hospital
320 E. North Ave.
Pittsburgh, PA 15212
412-359-3131
Teaching Specialties:
Anesthesiology, Dentistry, Internal Medicine, Internal Medicine-Cardiovascular Disease, Internal Medicine-Gastroenterology, Internal Medicine-Medical Oncology, Obstetrics/Gynecology, Otolaryngology, Radiation Oncology, Surgery, Thoracic Surgery, Urology.

Harmarville Rehabilitation Center
PO Box 11460, Guys Run Rd.
Pittsburgh, PA 15238
412-781-5700
Teaching Specialties:
Physical Medicine and Rehabilitation.

Magee-Womens Hospital
300 Halket St.
Pittsburgh, PA 15213
412-647-1000
Teaching Specialties:
Anesthesiology, Obstetrics/Gynecology.

Mercy Hospital of Pittsburgh
1400 Locust St.
Pittsburgh, PA 15219
412-232-8111
Teaching Specialties:
Anesthesiology, Internal Medicine, Orthopedic Surgery, Physical Medicine and Rehabilitation, Surgery.

Montefiore University Hospital
3459 5th Ave.
Pittsburgh, PA 15213
412-648-6000
Teaching Specialties:
Anesthesiology, Dentistry, Internal Medicine, Internal Medicine-Cardiovascular Disease, Internal Medicine-Endocrinology and Metabolism, Internal Medicine-Gastroenterology, Internal Medicine-Hematology, Internal Medicine-Infectious Diseases, Internal Medicine-Medical Oncology, Internal Medicine-Nephrology, Neurological Surgery, Neurology, Orthopedic Surgery, Psychiatry, Surgery, Thoracic Surgery, Urology.

Montefiore University Hospital
Eye and Ear Hospital of Pittsburgh
230 Lothrop St.
Pittsburgh, PA 15213
412-648-6000
Teaching Specialties:
Otolaryngology.

Presbyterian University Hospital
DeSoto at O'Hara Sts.
Pittsburgh, PA 15213
412-647-3325
Teaching Specialties:
Anesthesiology, Dermatology, Internal Medicine, Internal Medicine-Cardiovascular Disease, Internal Medicine-Endocrinology and Metabolism, Internal Medicine-Gastroenterology, Internal Medicine-Geriatric Medicine, Internal Medicine-Hematology, Internal Medicine-Infectious Diseases, Internal Medicine-Medical Oncology, Internal Medicine-Nephrology, Internal Medicine-Rheumatology, Neurological Surgery, Neurology, Orthopedic Surgery, Physical Medicine and Rehabilitation, Psychiatry, Surgery, Thoracic Surgery, Urology.

Shadyside Hospital
5230 Centre Ave.
Pittsburgh, PA 15232
412-623-2010
Teaching Specialties:
Internal Medicine, Internal Medicine-Cardiovascular Disease, Internal Medicine-Endocrinology and Metabolism, Internal Medicine-Gastroenterology, Internal Medicine-Geriatric Medicine.

St. Francis Medical Center
45th St. off Penn Ave.
Pittsburgh, PA 15201
412-622-4343
Teaching Specialties:
Dentistry, Internal Medicine, Internal Medicine-Cardiovascular Disease, Ophthalmology, Physical Medicine and Rehabilitation, Psychiatry.

St. Margaret Memorial Hospital
815 Freeport Rd.
Pittsburgh, PA 15215
412-784-4000
Teaching Specialties:
Internal Medicine-Cardiovascular Disease, Orthopedic Surgery, Physical Medicine and Rehabilitation.

University of Pittsburgh School of Dental Medicine
C-333 Salk Hall, 3501 Terrace St.
Pittsburgh, PA 15261
412-648-8760
Teaching Specialties:
Dentistry.

Western Pennsylvania Hospital
4800 Friendship Ave.
Pittsburgh, PA 15224
412-578-5000
Teaching Specialties:
Anesthesiology, Internal Medicine, Internal Medicine-Cardiovascular Disease, Internal

Medicine-Gastroenterology, Obstetrics/
Gynecology, Surgery.

**Western Psychiatric Institute
and Clinic**
3811 O'Hara St.
Pittsburgh, PA 15213
412-624-3528
Teaching Specialties:
Psychiatry.

Reading

Community General Hospital
145 N. 6th St.
Reading, PA 19601
215-376-4881
Teaching Specialties:
Dentistry.

**Reading Hospital and
Medical Center**
6th Ave. & Spruce St.
Reading, PA 19603
215-378-6000
Teaching Specialties:
Internal Medicine, Obstetrics/
Gynecology, Surgery.

St. Joseph Hospital
12th & Walnut Sts.
Reading, PA 19603
215-378-2000
Teaching Specialties:
Dentistry.

Sayre

Robert Packer Hospital
Guthrie Square
Sayre, PA 18840
717-888-6666
Teaching Specialties:
Internal Medicine, Internal Medicine-
Gastroenterology, Surgery.

Scranton

Mercy Hospital of Scranton
746 Jefferson Ave.
Scranton, PA 18501
717-348-7100
Teaching Specialties:
Internal Medicine, Internal Medicine-
Gastroenterology.

Moses Taylor Hospital
700 Quincy Ave.
Scranton, PA 18510
717-963-2100
Teaching Specialties:
Internal Medicine.

Upland

Crozer-Chester Medical Center
One Medical Center Blvd.
Upland, PA 19013
215-447-2000
Teaching Specialties:
Internal Medicine, Internal Medicine-
Gastroenterology, Neurological Surgery,
Obstetrics/Gynecology, Psychiatry, Surgery.

Wynnewood

Lankenau Hospital
100 Lancaster Ave. W. of City Line
Wynnewood, PA 19096
215-645-2000
Teaching Specialties:
Internal Medicine, Internal Medicine-Cardio-
vascular Disease, Internal Medicine-Gastroen-
terology, Internal Medicine-Hematology,
Internal Medicine-Nephrology, Obstetrics/
Gynecology, Orthopedic Surgery, Surgery.

York

York Hospital
1001 S. George St.
York, PA 17405
717-771-2345
Teaching Specialties:
Dentistry, Internal Medicine, Obstetrics/
Gynecology, Surgery.

PUERTO RICO

Bayamon

**Hospital Universitario
Dr. Ramon Ruiz Arnau**
Ave. Laurel Santa Juanita
Bayamon, PR 00619
809-787-5151
Teaching Specialties:
Internal Medicine.

Caguas

Caguas Regional Hospital
Carretera Caguas A Cidra
Caguas, PR 00626
809-744-2500
Teaching Specialties:
Internal Medicine, Obstetrics/Gynecology.

Carolina

Hospital Dr. Federico Trilla
65th Infanteria, KM 8 3
Carolina, PR 00628
809-757-1800
Teaching Specialties:
Internal Medicine-Geriatric Medicine.

Mayaguez

**Dr. Ramon E. Betances Hospital-
Mayaguez Medical Center Branch**
Mayaguez, PR 00708
809-834-8686
Teaching Specialties:
Internal Medicine, Obstetrics/Gynecology,
Surgery.

Ponce

Hospital de Damas
Ponce by Pass
Ponce, PR 00731
809-840-8686
Teaching Specialties:
Internal Medicine, Internal Medicine-
Cardiovascular Disease, Surgery.

**Hospital Oncologico
Andres Grillasca**
Centro Medico de Ponce
Ponce, PR 00733
809-848-0800
Teaching Specialties:
Surgery.

Hospital San Lucas
Guadalupe St.
Ponce, PR 00731
809-840-4545
Teaching Specialties:
Internal Medicine, Internal Medicine-
Cardiovascular Disease.

Ponce Regional Hospital
Barrio Machuelo
Ponce, PR 00731
809-844-2080
Teaching Specialties:
Internal Medicine, Obstetrics/
Gynecology, Surgery.

Rio Piedras

San Juan Municipal Hospital
Apartado 21405
Rio Piedras, PR 00928
809-765-6728
Teaching Specialties:
Anesthesiology, Internal Medicine, Internal
Medicine-Cardiovascular Disease, Internal
Medicine-Endocrinology and Metabolism,
Internal Medicine-Gastroenterology, Internal
Medicine-Hematology, Internal Medicine-
Medical Oncology, Internal Medicine-
Rheumatology, Neurological Surgery, Neurol-
ogy, Obstetrics/Gynecology, Ophthalmology,
Orthopedic Surgery, Otolaryngology.

San German

Hospital de la Concepcion
41 Luna St.

San German, PR 00753
809-892-1860
Teaching Specialties:
Internal Medicine.

San Juan

Fundacion Hospital Metropolitan
PO Box 11981
San Juan, PR 00922
809-793-6200
Teaching Specialties:
Radiation Oncology.

Industrial Hospital
Puerto Rico Medical Center
San Juan, PR 00936
809-754-2500
Teaching Specialties:
Anesthesiology.

Puerto Rico Rehabilitation Center
Puerto Rico Medical Center
San Juan, PR 00935
809-765-3522
Teaching Specialties:
Physical Medicine and Rehabilitation.

University Hospital
Puerto Rico Medical Center
Rio Piedras Station
San Juan, PR 00935
809-754-3654
Teaching Specialties:
Anesthesiology, Dermatology, Internal Medicine, Internal Medicine-Cardiovascular Disease, Internal Medicine-Endocrinology and Metabolism, Internal Medicine-Gastroenterology, Internal Medicine-Geriatric Medicine, Internal Medicine-Hematology, Internal Medicine-Infectious Diseases, Internal Medicine-Medical Oncology, Internal Medicine-Nephrology, Internal Medicine-Rheumatology, Neurological Surgery, Neurology, Obstetrics/Gynecology, Ophthalmology, Orthopedic Surgery, Otolaryngology, Physical Medicine and Rehabilitation, Psychiatry, Radiation Oncology, Surgery, Urology.

**University of Puerto Rico
School of Dentistry**
GPO Box 5067,
Medical Sciences Campus
San Juan, PR 00936
809-758-2525
Teaching Specialties:
Dentistry.

RHODE ISLAND
East Providence

Emma Pendleton Bradley Hospital
1011 Veterans Memorial Parkway

East Providence, RI 02915
401-434-3400
Teaching Specialties:
Psychiatry.

Pawtucket

Memorial Hospital of Rhode Island
111 Brewster St.
Pawtucket, RI 02861
401-722-6000
Teaching Specialties:
Dermatology, Internal Medicine, Internal Medicine-Cardiovascular Disease, Internal Medicine-Geriatric Medicine, Internal Medicine-Hematology, Internal Medicine-Infectious Diseases, Internal Medicine-Medical Oncology.

Providence

Butler Hospital
345 Blackstone Blvd.
Providence, RI 02906
401-455-6200
Teaching Specialties:
Psychiatry.

Miriam Hospital
164 Summit Ave.
Providence, RI 02906
401-331-8500
Teaching Specialties:
Internal Medicine, Internal Medicine-Cardiovascular Disease, Internal Medicine-Hematology, Internal Medicine-Infectious Diseases, Internal Medicine-Medical Oncology, Psychiatry, Surgery.

Providence Center for Counseling and Psychiatric Services
520 Hope St.
Providence, RI 02906
401-274-2500
Teaching Specialties:
Psychiatry.

Rhode Island Hospital
593 Eddy St.
Providence, RI 02903
401-277-4000
Teaching Specialties:
Allergy/Immunology, Dermatology, Internal Medicine, Internal Medicine-Cardiovascular Disease, Internal Medicine-Endocrinology and Metabolism, Internal Medicine-Gastroenterology, Internal Medicine-Hematology, Internal Medicine-Infectious Diseases, Internal Medicine-Nephrology, Internal Medicine-Rheumatology, Neurological Surgery, Neurology, Obstetrics/Gynecology, Ophthalmology, Orthopedic Surgery, Psychiatry, Surgery, Urology.

Roger Williams Hospital
825 Chalkstone Ave.
Providence, RI 02908
401-456-2000
Teaching Specialties:
Dermatology, Internal Medicine, Internal Medicine-Cardiovascular Disease, Internal Medicine-Endocrinology and Metabolism, Internal Medicine-Gastroenterology, Internal Medicine-Geriatric Medicine, Internal Medicine-Hematology, Internal Medicine-Infectious Diseases, Internal Medicine-Medical Oncology, Internal Medicine-Nephrology, Internal Medicine-Rheumatology, Urology.

Women and Infants Hospital of Rhode Island
101 Dudley St.
Providence, RI 02905
401-274-1100
Teaching Specialties:
Obstetrics/Gynecology.

SOUTH CAROLINA
Charleston

Charleston Memorial Hospital
326 Calhoun St.
Charleston, SC 29401
803-577-0600
Teaching Specialties:
Internal Medicine, Internal Medicine-Nephrology, Obstetrics/Gynecology, Otolaryngology, Psychiatry, Surgery, Thoracic Surgery, Urology.

Medical University of South Carolina
College of Dental Medicine
171 Ashley Ave.
Charleston, SC 29425
803-792-3811
Teaching Specialties:
Dentistry.

Medical University of South Carolina
Medical Center of Medical University of South Carolina
171 Ashley Ave.
Charleston, SC 29425
803-792-7616
Teaching Specialties:
Anesthesiology, Dermatology, Internal Medicine, Internal Medicine-Cardiovascular Disease, Internal Medicine-Endocrinology and Metabolism, Internal Medicine-Gastroenterology, Internal Medicine-Hematology, Internal Medicine-Infectious Diseases, Internal Medicine-Medical Oncology, Internal Medicine-Nephrology, Internal Medicine-Rheumatology, Neurological Surgery, Neurology,

Obstetrics/Gynecology, Ophthalmology, Orthopedic Surgery, Otolaryngology, Psychiatry, Radiation Oncology, Surgery, Thoracic Surgery, Urology.

Columbia

Richland Memorial Hospital
5 Richland Medical Park
Columbia, SC 29203
803-765-7000
Teaching Specialties:
Anesthesiology, Dentistry, Internal Medicine, Internal Medicine-Cardiovascular Disease, Internal Medicine-Endocrinology and Metabolism, Internal Medicine-Gastroenterology, Internal Medicine-Medical Oncology, Obstetrics/Gynecology, Ophthalmology, Orthopedic Surgery, Surgery.

William S. Hall Psychiatric Institute
1800 Colonial Dr.
Columbia, SC 29202
803-734-7113
Teaching Specialties:
Psychiatry.

Greenville

Greenville Memorial Hospital
701 Grove Rd.
Greenville, SC 29605
803-455-7000
Teaching Specialties:
Internal Medicine, Obstetrics/Gynecology, Orthopedic Surgery, Surgery.

Spartanburg

Spartanburg Regional Medical Center
101 E. Wood St.
Spartanburg, SC 29303
803-591-6107
Teaching Specialties:
Surgery.

SOUTH DAKOTA
Sioux Falls

McKennan Hospital
800 E. 21st St.
Sioux Falls, SD 57105
605-339-8000
Teaching Specialties:
Internal Medicine, Psychiatry.

Sioux Valley Hospital
1100 S. Euclid Ave.
Sioux Falls, SD 57105
605-333-1000
Teaching Specialties:
Internal Medicine.

Southeastern Mental Health Center
2000 S. Summit Ave.
Sioux Falls, SD 57105
605-336-0510
Teaching Specialties:
Psychiatry.

TENNESSEE
Bristol

Bristol Regional Medical Center
209 Memorial Dr.
Bristol, TN 37620
615-968-1121
Teaching Specialties:
Internal Medicine.

Chattanooga

Erlanger Medical Center
975 E. Third Ave.
Chattanooga, TN 37403
615-778-7000
Teaching Specialties:
Internal Medicine, Obstetrics/Gynecology, Ophthalmology, Orthopedic Surgery, Surgery.

Willie D. Miller Eye Center
975 E. Third Ave.
Chattanooga, TN 37403
615-778-6011
Teaching Specialties:
Ophthalmology.

Johnson City

Johnson City Medical Center Hospital
400 State of Franklin Rd.
Johnson City, TN 37604
615-461-6111
Teaching Specialties:
Internal Medicine, Internal Medicine-Cardiovascular Disease, Internal Medicine-Gastroenterology, Internal Medicine-Medical Oncology, Psychiatry, Surgery.

Watauga Area Mental Health Center
109 W. Watauga Ave.
Johnson City, TN 37601
615-928-6545
Teaching Specialties:
Psychiatry.

Woodridge Hospital
403 State of Franklin Rd.
Johnson City, TN 37604
615-928-7111
Teaching Specialties:
Psychiatry.

Kingsport

Holston Valley Hospital and Medical Center
W. Ravine St.
Kingsport, TN 37662
615-246-3322
Teaching Specialties:
Internal Medicine, Surgery.

Knoxville

University of Tennessee Memorial Hospital
1924 Alcoa Highway
Knoxville, TN 37920
615-544-9000
Teaching Specialties:
Anesthesiology, Dentistry, Internal Medicine, Obstetrics/Gynecology, Surgery.

Memphis

Baptist Memorial Hospital
899 Madison Ave.
Memphis, TN 38146
901-522-5252
Teaching Specialties:
Allergy/Immunology, Dermatology, Internal Medicine, Internal Medicine-Endocrinology and Metabolism, Internal Medicine-Hematology, Internal Medicine-Medical Oncology, Internal Medicine-Rheumatology, Neurological Surgery, Neurology, Orthopedic Surgery, Surgery, Surgery-Vascular Surgery, Thoracic Surgery, Urology.

Memphis Mental Health Institute
865 Poplar Ave.
Memphis, TN 38174
901-524-1201
Teaching Specialties:
Psychiatry.

Methodist Hospitals of Memphis
Central Unit
1265 Union Ave.
Memphis, TN 38104
901-726-7000
Teaching Specialties:
Internal Medicine, Neurological Surgery, Ophthalmology, Otolaryngology, Surgery, Urology.

Regional Medical Center at Memphis
877 Jefferson Ave.
Memphis, TN 38103
901-575-7100
Teaching Specialties:
Anesthesiology, Dermatology, Internal Medicine, Internal Medicine-Cardiovascular Disease, Internal Medicine-Endocrinology and Metabolism, Internal Medicine-Gastroenterol-

ogy, Internal Medicine-Geriatric Medicine, Internal Medicine-Hematology, Internal Medicine-Infectious Diseases, Internal Medicine-Medical Oncology, Internal Medicine-Nephrology, Internal Medicine-Rheumatology, Neurological Surgery, Neurology, Obstetrics/Gynecology, Ophthalmology, Orthopedic Surgery, Otolaryngology, Psychiatry, Surgery, Thoracic Surgery, Urology.

University of Tennessee College of Dentistry

875 Union Ave.
Memphis, TN 38163
901-528-6241
Teaching Specialties:
Dentistry.

University of Tennessee Medical Center

951 Court Ave.
Memphis, TN 38103
901-577-4000
Teaching Specialties:
Allergy/Immunology, Anesthesiology, Dermatology, Internal Medicine, Neurology, Obstetrics/Gynecology, Otolaryngology, Psychiatry, Surgery, Thoracic Surgery.

Nashville

Baptist Hospital

2000 Church St.
Nashville, TN 37236
614-329-5555
Teaching Specialties:
Internal Medicine, Neurological Surgery, Obstetrics/Gynecology, Otolaryngology, Urology.

George W. Hubbard Hospital of Meharry Medical College

1005 D.B. Todd Blvd.
Nashville, TN 37208
615-327-5851
Teaching Specialties:
Internal Medicine, Psychiatry.

Meharry Medical College School of Dentistry

1005 D.B. Todd Blvd.
Nashville, TN 37208
615-327-6489
Teaching Specialties:
Dentistry.

Metropolitan Nashville General Hospital

72 Hermitage Ave.
Nashville, TN 37210
615-862-4490
Teaching Specialties:
Dermatology, Internal Medicine, Neurology,

Obstetrics/Gynecology, Orthopedic Surgery, Otolaryngology, Surgery, Urology.

Middle Tennessee Mental Health Institute

1501 Murfreesboro Rd.
Nashville, TN 37217
615-366-7616
Teaching Specialties:
Psychiatry.

St. Thomas Hospital

4220 Harding Rd.
Nashville, TN 37205
615-386-2111
Teaching Specialties:
Internal Medicine-Gastroenterology, Internal Medicine-Infectious Diseases, Internal Medicine-Medical Oncology, Internal Medicine-Rheumatology, Neurological Surgery, Surgery, Surgery-Vascular Surgery.

Vanderbilt University Hospital and Clinic

1161 21st Ave. S
Nashville, TN 37232
615-322-2415
Teaching Specialties:
Allergy/Immunology, Anesthesiology, Dentistry, Dermatology, Internal Medicine, Internal Medicine-Cardiovascular Disease, Internal Medicine-Endocrinology and Metabolism, Internal Medicine-Gastroenterology, Internal Medicine-Hematology, Internal Medicine-Infectious Diseases, Internal Medicine-Medical Oncology, Internal Medicine-Nephrology, Internal Medicine-Rheumatology, Neurological Surgery, Neurology, Obstetrics/Gynecology, Ophthalmology, Orthopedic Surgery, Otolaryngology, Psychiatry, Surgery, Surgery-Vascular Surgery, Thoracic Surgery, Urology.

Texas

Amarillo

The Don and Sybil Harrington Cancer Center

1500 Wallace Blvd.
Amarillo, TX 79106
800-274-4673
806-359-4673
Teaching Specialties:
Internal Medicine-Medical Oncology.

High Plains Baptist Hospital

1600 Wallace Blvd.
Amarillo, TX 79106
806-358-3151
Teaching Specialties:
Internal Medicine, Internal Medicine-Medical Oncology, Obstetrics/Gynecology.

Northwest Texas Hospital

1501 Coulter
Amarillo, TX 79106
806-354-1000
Teaching Specialties:
Internal Medicine, Internal Medicine-Medical Oncology, Obstetrics/Gynecology.

St. Anthony's Hospital

200 N.W. 7th
Amarillo, TX 79107
806-376-4411
Teaching Specialties:
Internal Medicine.

Austin

Austin State Hospital

4110 Guadalupe St.
Austin, TX 78751
512-452-0381
Teaching Specialties:
Psychiatry.

Austin-Travis County Mental Health Center

1430 Collier St.
Austin, TX 78764
512-447-4141
Teaching Specialties:
Psychiatry.

Brackenridge Hospital

601 E. 15th St.
Austin, TX 78701
512-476-6461
Teaching Specialties:
Internal Medicine, Obstetrics/Gynecology, Psychiatry.

Dallas

Baylor College of Dentistry

3302 Gaston Ave.
Dallas, TX 75246
214-828-8100
Teaching Specialties:
Dentistry.

Baylor Institute for Rehabilitation

3500 Gaston Ave.
Dallas, TX 75246
800-422-9567
214-826-7030
Teaching Specialties:
Physical Medicine and Rehabilitation.

Baylor University Medical Center

3500 Gaston Ave.
Dallas, TX 75246
214-820-0111
Teaching Specialties:

Colon and Rectal Surgery, Internal Medicine, Internal Medicine-Cardiovascular Disease, Internal Medicine-Gastroenterology, Internal Medicine-Infectious Diseases, Internal Medicine-Medical Oncology, Internal Medicine-Nephrology, Obstetrics/Gynecology, Orthopedic Surgery, Physical Medicine and Rehabilitation, Psychiatry, Surgery, Surgery-Vascular Surgery, Urology.

Dallas County Hospital District
Parkland Memorial Hospital
5201 Harry Hines Blvd.
Dallas, TX 75235
214-590-8000
Teaching Specialties:
Allergy/Immunology, Anesthesiology, Colon and Rectal Surgery, Dentistry, Dermatology, Internal Medicine, Internal Medicine-Cardiovascular Disease, Internal Medicine-Endocrinology and Metabolism, Internal Medicine-Gastroenterology, Internal Medicine-Hematology, Internal Medicine-Infectious Diseases, Internal Medicine-Medical Oncology, Internal Medicine-Nephrology, Internal Medicine-Rheumatology, Neurological Surgery, Neurology, Obstetrics/Gynecology, Ophthalmology, Orthopedic Surgery, Otolaryngology, Physical Medicine and Rehabilitation, Psychiatry, Surgery, Surgery-Vascular Surgery, Thoracic Surgery, Urology.

Methodist Medical Center
301 W. Colorado Blvd.
Dallas, TX 75208
214-944-8181
Teaching Specialties:
Internal Medicine, Obstetrics/Gynecology, Surgery.

Presbyterian Hospital of Dallas
8200 Walnut Hill Lane
Dallas, TX 75231
214-369-4111
Teaching Specialties:
Colon and Rectal Surgery, Internal Medicine, Psychiatry.

St. Paul Medical Center
5909 Harry Hines Blvd.
Dallas, TX 75235
214-879-1000
Teaching Specialties:
Internal Medicine, Neurological Surgery, Obstetrics/Gynecology, Otolaryngology, Surgery.

Timberlawn Psychiatric Hospital
4600 Samuell Blvd.
Dallas, TX 75228
214-381-7181
Teaching Specialties:
Psychiatry.

Zale-Lipshy University Hospital
5151 Harry Hines Blvd.

Dallas, TX 75235
214-590-3000
Teaching Specialties:
Dermatology, Neurological Surgery, Otolaryngology.

El Paso

R.E. Thomason General Hospital
4815 Alameda Ave.
El Paso, TX 79905
915-544-1200
Teaching Specialties:
Anesthesiology, Internal Medicine, Obstetrics/Gynecology, Orthopedic Surgery, Psychiatry, Surgery.

Fort Worth

Harris Methodist Fort Worth
1301 Pennsylvania Ave.
Fort Worth, TX 76104
817-882-2000
Teaching Specialties:
Obstetrics/Gynecology, Orthopedic Surgery.

Tarrant County Hospital District
John Peter Smith Hospital
1500 S. Main St.
Fort Worth, TX 76104
817-921-3431
Teaching Specialties:
Obstetrics/Gynecology, Orthopedic Surgery, Otolaryngology, Surgery.

Galveston

University of Texas Medical Branch Hospitals
301 University Blvd.
Galveston, TX 77550
409-761-1011
Teaching Specialties:
Allergy/Immunology, Anesthesiology, Dentistry, Dermatology, Internal Medicine, Internal Medicine-Cardiovascular Disease, Internal Medicine-Gastroenterology, Internal Medicine-Infectious Diseases, Internal Medicine-Medical Oncology, Internal Medicine-Nephrology, Internal Medicine-Rheumatology, Neurological Surgery, Neurology, Obstetrics/Gynecology, Ophthalmology, Orthopedic Surgery, Otolaryngology, Psychiatry, Radiation Oncology, Surgery, Thoracic Surgery, Urology.

Houston

Harris County Hospital District
Ben Taub General Hospital
1504 Taub Loop
Houston, TX 77030
713-793-2000
Teaching Specialties:

Anesthesiology, Dermatology, Internal Medicine, Internal Medicine-Cardiovascular Disease, Internal Medicine-Endocrinology and Metabolism, Internal Medicine-Gastroenterology, Internal Medicine-Hematology, Internal Medicine-Infectious Diseases, Internal Medicine-Medical Oncology, Internal Medicine-Nephrology, Internal Medicine-Rheumatology, Neurological Surgery, Neurology, Obstetrics/Gynecology, Ophthalmology, Orthopedic Surgery, Otolaryngology, Physical Medicine and Rehabilitation, Psychiatry, Radiation Oncology, Surgery, Surgery-Vascular Surgery, Thoracic Surgery, Urology.

Harris County Hospital District
Lyndon B. Johnson General Hospital
5656 Kelley St.
Houston, TX 77026
713-636-5000
Teaching Specialties:
Dermatology, Internal Medicine, Obstetrics/Gynecology, Otolaryngology, Physical Medicine and Rehabilitation, Surgery.

Harris County Psychiatric Center
2800 S. MacGregor Way
Houston, TX 77021
713-741-5000
Teaching Specialties:
Psychiatry.

Hermann Hospital
6411 Fannin St.
Houston, TX 77030
713-797-4011
Teaching Specialties:
Anesthesiology, Colon and Rectal Surgery, Dermatology, Internal Medicine, Internal Medicine-Cardiovascular Disease, Internal Medicine-Endocrinology and Metabolism, Internal Medicine-Gastroenterology, Internal Medicine-Hematology, Internal Medicine-Infectious Diseases, Internal Medicine-Nephrology, Internal Medicine-Rheumatology, Neurology, Obstetrics/Gynecology, Ophthalmology, Orthopedic Surgery, Otolaryngology, Psychiatry, Surgery, Thoracic Surgery, Urology.

The Institute for Rehabilitation and Research
1333 Moursund Ave.
Houston, TX 77030
800-447-3422
713-799-5000
Teaching Specialties:
Physical Medicine and Rehabilitation.

Methodist Hospital
6565 Fannin St.
Houston, TX 77030
713-790-3311
Teaching Specialties:

Anesthesiology, Dermatology, Internal Medicine, Internal Medicine-Cardiovascular Disease, Internal Medicine-Endocrinology and Metabolism, Internal Medicine-Gastroenterology, Internal Medicine-Hematology, Internal Medicine-Infectious Diseases, Internal Medicine-Medical Oncology, Internal Medicine-Nephrology, Neurological Surgery, Neurology, Ophthalmology, Orthopedic Surgery, Otolaryngology, Physical Medicine and Rehabilitation, Psychiatry, Radiation Oncology, Surgery, Surgery-Vascular Surgery, Thoracic Surgery, Urology.

St. Joseph Hospital
1919 LaBranch St.
Houston, TX 77002
713-757-1000
Teaching Specialties:
Internal Medicine, Obstetrics/Gynecology, Orthopedic Surgery, Surgery, Urology.

St. Luke's Episcopal Hospital
6720 Bertner Ave.
Houston, TX 77030
713-791-2011
Teaching Specialties:
Internal Medicine, Internal Medicine-Cardiovascular Disease, Ophthalmology, Physical Medicine and Rehabilitation, Surgery, Thoracic Surgery, Urology.

University of Texas Health Science Center at Houston
Dental Branch
PO Box 20068
Houston, TX 77225
713-792-4021
Teaching Specialties:
Dentistry.

University of Texas M.D. Anderson Cancer Center
1515 Holcombe Blvd.
Houston, TX 77030
713-792-2121
Teaching Specialties:
Dentistry, Dermatology, Internal Medicine-Rheumatology, Neurological Surgery, Psychiatry, Radiation Oncology, Surgery, Thoracic Surgery, Urology.

Lubbock

St. Mary of the Plains Hospital
4000 24th St.
Lubbock, TX 79410
806-796-6000
Teaching Specialties:
Orthopedic Surgery, Psychiatry.

University Medical Center
602 Indiana Ave.
Lubbock, TX 79417

806-743-3111
Teaching Specialties:
Anesthesiology, Dermatology, Internal Medicine, Internal Medicine-Cardiovascular Disease, Internal Medicine-Gastroenterology, Internal Medicine-Medical Oncology, Internal Medicine-Nephrology, Neurology, Obstetrics/Gynecology, Ophthalmology, Psychiatry, Surgery.

Odessa

Medical Center Hospital
500 W. 4th St.
Odessa, TX 79761
915-333-7111
Teaching Specialties:
Obstetrics/Gynecology.

San Antonio

Bexar County Hospital District
Medical Center Hospital
4502 Medical Dr.
San Antonio, TX 78229
512-694-3030
Teaching Specialties:
Anesthesiology, Dermatology, Internal Medicine, Internal Medicine-Cardiovascular Disease, Internal Medicine-Endocrinology and Metabolism, Internal Medicine-Gastroenterology, Internal Medicine-Geriatric Medicine, Internal Medicine-Hematology, Internal Medicine-Infectious Diseases, Internal Medicine-Medical Oncology, Internal Medicine-Nephrology, Internal Medicine-Rheumatology, Neurological Surgery, Neurology, Obstetrics/Gynecology, Ophthalmology, Orthopedic Surgery, Otolaryngology, Physical Medicine and Rehabilitation, Psychiatry, Radiation Oncology, Surgery, Thoracic Surgery, Urology.

Cancer Therapy and Research Center
4450 Medical Dr.
San Antonio, TX 78229
512-616-5500
Teaching Specialties:
Radiation Oncology.

Humana Hospital-San Antonio
8026 Floyd Curl Dr.
San Antonio, TX 78229
512-692-8110
Teaching Specialties:
Urology.

University of Texas Health Science Center at San Antonio
Dental School
7703 Floyd Curl Dr.
San Antonio, TX 78284-7906
512-567-3160

Teaching Specialties:
Dentistry.

Temple

Scott and White Memorial Hospital
2401 S. 31st St.
Temple, TX 76508
817-774-2111
Teaching Specialties:
Anesthesiology, Internal Medicine, Internal Medicine-Cardiovascular Disease, Internal Medicine-Endocrinology and Metabolism, Internal Medicine-Gastroenterology, Obstetrics/Gynecology, Ophthalmology, Orthopedic Surgery, Surgery, Urology.

Terrell

Terrell State Hospital
1200 E. Brin St.
Terrell, TX 75160
214-563-6452
Teaching Specialties:
Psychiatry.

UTAH

Salt Lake City

Holy Cross Hospital
1050 E. South Temple
Salt Lake City, UT 84102
801-350-4111
Teaching Specialties:
Orthopedic Surgery, Otolaryngology, Surgery.

LDS Hospital
8th Ave. & C St.
Salt Lake City, UT 84143
801-588-2000
Teaching Specialties:
Internal Medicine, Obstetrics/Gynecology, Orthopedic Surgery, Radiation Oncology, Surgery, Thoracic Surgery, Urology.

Salt Lake Valley Mental Health
2001 S. State St., Suite S2600
Salt Lake City, UT 84190
801-468-2360
Teaching Specialties:
Psychiatry.

University of Utah Hospital and Clinics
50 N. Medical Dr.
Salt Lake City, UT 84132
801-581-2121
Teaching Specialties:
Anesthesiology, Dentistry, Dermatology, Internal Medicine, Internal Medicine-Cardiovascular Disease, Internal Medicine-Endocrinology and Metabolism, Internal Medicine-

Gastroenterology, Internal Medicine-Geriatric Medicine, Internal Medicine-Hematology, Internal Medicine-Infectious Diseases, Internal Medicine-Medical Oncology, Internal Medicine-Nephrology, Internal Medicine-Rheumatology, Neurological Surgery, Neurology, Obstetrics/Gynecology, Ophthalmology, Orthopedic Surgery, Otolaryngology, Physical Medicine and Rehabilitation, Psychiatry, Radiation Oncology, Surgery, Thoracic Surgery, Urology.

Western Institute of Neuropsychiatry
501 Chipeta Way
Salt Lake City, UT 84108
801-583-2500
Teaching Specialties:
Psychiatry.

VERMONT
Brattleboro

Brattleboro Retreat
75 Linden St.
Brattleboro, VT 05301
802-257-7785
Teaching Specialties:
Psychiatry.

Burlington

Medical Center Hospital of Vermont
Colchester Ave.
Burlington, VT 05401
802-656-2345
Teaching Specialties:
Anesthesiology, Dentistry, Internal Medicine, Internal Medicine-Cardiovascular Disease, Internal Medicine-Endocrinology and Metabolism, Internal Medicine-Gastroenterology, Internal Medicine-Hematology, Internal Medicine-Infectious Diseases, Internal Medicine-Medical Oncology, Internal Medicine-Nephrology, Internal Medicine-Rheumatology, Neurological Surgery, Neurology, Obstetrics/Gynecology, Orthopedic Surgery, Otolaryngology, Psychiatry, Surgery, Urology.

Colchester

Fanny Allen Hospital
101 College Parkway
Colchester, VT 05446
802-654-1115
Teaching Specialties:
Urology.

VIRGINIA
Alexandria

Mt. Vernon Hospital
2501 Parker's Lane

Alexandria, VA 22306
703-664-7000
Teaching Specialties:
Internal Medicine, Physical Medicine and Rehabilitation.

Arlington

Arlington Hospital
4320 Seminary Rd.
Arlington, VA 22205
703-558-5000
Teaching Specialties:
Internal Medicine-Nephrology, Orthopedic Surgery, Surgery.

Charlottesville

University of Virginia Medical Center
Jefferson Park Ave.
Charlottesville, VA 22908
804-924-0211
Teaching Specialties:
Allergy/Immunology, Anesthesiology, Dentistry, Dermatology, Internal Medicine, Internal Medicine-Cardiovascular Disease, Internal Medicine-Endocrinology and Metabolism, Internal Medicine-Gastroenterology, Internal Medicine-Geriatric Medicine, Internal Medicine-Hematology, Internal Medicine-Infectious Diseases, Internal Medicine-Medical Oncology, Internal Medicine-Nephrology, Internal Medicine-Rheumatology, Neurological Surgery, Neurology, Obstetrics/Gynecology, Ophthalmology, Orthopedic Surgery, Otolaryngology, Physical Medicine and Rehabilitation, Psychiatry, Radiation Oncology, Surgery, Thoracic Surgery, Urology.

Danville

Memorial Hospital of Danville
142 S. Main St.
Danville, VA 24541
804-799-2100
Teaching Specialties:
Urology.

Falls Church

Fairfax Hospital
3300 Gallows Rd.
Falls Church, VA 22046
703-698-1110
Teaching Specialties:
Obstetrics/Gynecology, Orthopedic Surgery, Physical Medicine and Rehabilitation, Psychiatry, Surgery, Urology.

Newport News

Riverside Regional Medical Center
500 J. Clyde Morris Blvd.
Newport News, VA 23601

804-599-2000
Teaching Specialties:
Obstetrics/Gynecology.

Norfolk

Depaul Medical Center
150 Kingsley Lane
Norfolk, VA 23505
804-489-5000
Teaching Specialties:
Internal Medicine, Obstetrics/Gynecology, Surgery.

The Psychiatric Institute of the Medical College of Hampton Roads
721 Fairfax Ave.
Norfolk, VA 23501
804-446-5000
Teaching Specialties:
Psychiatry.

Sentara Leigh Hospital
830 Kempsville Rd.
Norfolk, VA 23502
804-466-6000
Teaching Specialties:
Internal Medicine, Orthopedic Surgery, Surgery, Urology.

Sentara Norfolk General Hospital
600 Gresham Dr.
Norfolk, VA 23507
804-628-3000
Teaching Specialties:
Internal Medicine, Neurological Surgery, Obstetrics/Gynecology, Ophthalmology, Orthopedic Surgery, Otolaryngology, Physical Medicine and Rehabilitation, Psychiatry, Radiation Oncology, Surgery, Surgery-Vascular Surgery, Urology.

Portsmouth

Maryview Medical Center
3636 High St.
Portsmouth, VA 23707
804-398-2200
Teaching Specialties:
Radiation Oncology.

Portsmouth General Hospital
850 Crawford Parkway
Portsmouth, VA 23704
804-398-4000
Teaching Specialties:
Obstetrics/Gynecology.

Richmond

Sheltering Arms Rehabilitation Hospital
1311 Palmyra Ave.

Richmond, VA 23227
804-254-6091
Teaching Specialties:
Physical Medicine and Rehabilitation.

Virginia Commonwealth University
Medical College of
Virginia Hospitals
401 N. 12th St.
Richmond, VA 23298
804-786-9000
Teaching Specialties:
Allergy/Immunology, Anesthesiology, Dermatology, Internal Medicine, Internal Medicine-Cardiovascular Disease, Internal Medicine-Endocrinology and Metabolism, Internal Medicine-Gastroenterology, Internal Medicine-Geriatric Medicine, Internal Medicine-Hematology, Internal Medicine-Infectious Diseases, Internal Medicine-Medical Oncology, Internal Medicine-Nephrology, Internal Medicine-Rheumatology, Neurological Surgery, Neurology, Obstetrics/Gynecology, Ophthalmology, Orthopedic Surgery, Otolaryngology, Physical Medicine and Rehabilitation, Psychiatry, Radiation Oncology, Surgery, Surgery-Vascular Surgery, Thoracic Surgery, Urology.

Virginia Commonwealth University
Medical College of Virginia
School of Dentistry
Box 566
Richmond, VA 23298
804-786-9190
Teaching Specialties:
Dentistry.

Roanoke

**Community Hospital
of Roanoke Valley**
101 Elm Ave., SE
Roanoke, VA 24029
703-985-8000
Teaching Specialties:
Internal Medicine.

Roanoke Memorial Hospitals
Belleview & Jefferson St.
Roanoke, VA 24014
703-981-7000
Teaching Specialties:
Internal Medicine, Internal Medicine-Cardiovascular Disease, Internal Medicine-Infectious Diseases, Obstetrics/Gynecology, Orthopedic Surgery, Otolaryngology, Surgery.

Virginia Beach

Virginia Beach General Hospital
1060 First Colonial Rd.
Virginia Beach, VA 23454
804-481-8000

Teaching Specialties:
Radiation Oncology.

WASHINGTON
Seattle

**Fred Hutchinson Cancer
Research Center**
1124 Columbia St.
Seattle, WA 98104
206-667-5000
Teaching Specialties:
Internal Medicine-Medical Oncology.

Harborview Medical Center
325 9th Ave.
Seattle, WA 98105
206-223-3000
Teaching Specialties:
Allergy/Immunology, Anesthesiology, Internal Medicine, Internal Medicine-Geriatric Medicine, Neurological Surgery, Neurology, Ophthalmology, Orthopedic Surgery, Physical Medicine and Rehabilitation, Psychiatry, Surgery, Thoracic Surgery, Urology.

Pacific Medical Center
1200 12th Ave. S
Seattle, WA 98144
206-326-4000
Teaching Specialties:
Internal Medicine, Surgery.

Providence Medical Center
500 17th Ave.
Seattle, WA 98122
206-320-2000
Teaching Specialties:
Internal Medicine, Surgery.

Swedish Hospital Medical Center
747 Summit Ave.
Seattle, WA 98104
206-386-6000
Teaching Specialties:
Internal Medicine, Obstetrics/Gynecology, Orthopedic Surgery, Surgery.

**University of Washington
Medical Center**
1959 N.E. Pacific St.
Seattle, WA 98195
206-548-3300
Teaching Specialties:
Allergy/Immunology, Anesthesiology, Dermatology, Internal Medicine, Internal Medicine-Cardiovascular Disease, Internal Medicine-Endocrinology and Metabolism, Internal Medicine-Gastroenterology, Internal Medicine-Hematology, Internal Medicine-Infectious Diseases, Internal Medicine-Medical Oncology, Internal Medicine-Nephrology,

Internal Medicine-Rheumatology, Neurological Surgery, Neurology, Obstetrics/Gynecology, Ophthalmology, Orthopedic Surgery, Otolaryngology, Physical Medicine and Rehabilitation, Psychiatry, Radiation Oncology, Surgery, Surgery-Vascular Surgery, Thoracic Surgery, Urology.

**University of Washington
School of Dentistry**
Health Sciences Bldg. SC 62
Seattle, WA 98195
206-543-5830
Teaching Specialties:
Dentistry.

Virginia Mason Medical Center
925 Seneca St.
Seattle, WA 98101
206-624-1144
Teaching Specialties:
Allergy/Immunology, Anesthesiology, Internal Medicine, Orthopedic Surgery, Surgery, Urology.

Spokane

Deaconess Medical Center-Spokane
800 W. 5th Ave.
Spokane, WA 99204
509-458-5800
Teaching Specialties:
Internal Medicine.

Sacred Heart Medical Center
W. 101 8th Ave.
Spokane, WA 99204
509-455-3131
Teaching Specialties:
Internal Medicine.

WEST VIRGINIA
Charleston

Charleston Area Medical Center
501 Morris St.
Charleston, WV 25326
304-348-5432
Teaching Specialties:
Psychiatry.

Charleston Area Medical Center
Memorial Division
3200 MacCorkle Ave., SE
Charleston, WV 25304
304-348-5432
Teaching Specialties:
Dentistry, Internal Medicine, Surgery.

Charleston Area Medical Center
Women and Children's
Hospital of West Virginia

800 Pennsylvania Ave.
Charleston, WV 25302
304-347-9200
Teaching Specialties:
Obstetrics/Gynecology.

Huntington

Cabell Huntington Hospital
1340 Hal Greer Blvd.
Huntington, WV 25701
304-526-2000
Teaching Specialties:
Internal Medicine, Internal Medicine-Cardiovascular Disease, Internal Medicine-Endocrinology and Metabolism, Internal Medicine-Infectious Diseases, Surgery.

St. Mary's Hospital
2900 First Ave.
Huntington, WV 25702
304-526-1234
Teaching Specialties:
Internal Medicine, Surgery.

Morgantown

Monongalia General Hospital
1200 J.D. Anderson Dr.
Morgantown, WV 26505
304-598-1212
Teaching Specialties:
Orthopedic Surgery, Thoracic Surgery.

West Virginia University Hospitals
Medical Center Dr.
Morgantown, WV 26506
304-598-4000
Teaching Specialties:
Anesthesiology, Dermatology, Internal Medicine, Internal Medicine-Cardiovascular Disease, Internal Medicine-Gastroenterology, Internal Medicine-Nephrology, Neurological Surgery, Neurology, Obstetrics/Gynecology, Ophthalmology, Orthopedic Surgery, Otolaryngology, Psychiatry, Surgery, Thoracic Surgery, Urology.

West Virginia University School of Dentistry
Health Sciences Center North
Morgantown, WV 26505
304-293-2459
Teaching Specialties:
Dentistry.

Wheeling

Ohio Valley Medical Center
2000 Eoff St.
Wheeling, WV 26003
304-234-0123
Teaching Specialties:

Internal Medicine, Obstetrics/Gynecology, Urology.

Wheeling Hospital
Medical Park
Wheeling, WV 26003
304-243-3000
Teaching Specialties:
Obstetrics/Gynecology.

WISCONSIN

La Crosse

Lutheran Hospital-La Crosse
1910 South Ave.
La Crosse, WI 54601
608-785-0530
Teaching Specialties:
Dentistry, Internal Medicine, Surgery, Urology.

Madison

Meriter Hospital
202 S. Park St.
Madison, WI 53715
608-267-6000
Teaching Specialties:
Dentistry, Neurological Surgery, Obstetrics/Gynecology, Orthopedic Surgery, Psychiatry, Surgery.

St. Marys Hospital Medical Center
707 S. Mills St.
Madison, WI 53715
608-251-6100
Teaching Specialties:
Obstetrics/Gynecology, Orthopedic Surgery, Surgery.

University of Wisconsin Hospital and Clinics
600 Highland Ave.
Madison, WI 53792
608-263-6400
Teaching Specialties:
Allergy/Immunology, Anesthesiology, Dermatology, Internal Medicine, Internal Medicine-Cardiovascular Disease, Internal Medicine-Endocrinology and Metabolism, Internal Medicine-Gastroenterology, Internal Medicine-Geriatric Medicine, Internal Medicine-Hematology, Internal Medicine-Infectious Diseases, Internal Medicine-Medical Oncology, Internal Medicine-Nephrology, Internal Medicine-Rheumatology, Neurological Surgery, Neurology, Obstetrics/Gynecology, Ophthalmology, Otolaryngology, Physical Medicine and Rehabilitation, Psychiatry, Radiation Oncology, Surgery, Thoracic Surgery, Urology.

Marshfield

St. Joseph's Hospital
611 St. Joseph Ave.
Marshfield, WI 54449
715-387-1713
Teaching Specialties:
Dermatology, Internal Medicine, Surgery.

Milwaukee

Columbia Hospital
2025 E. Newport Ave.
Milwaukee, WI 53211
414-961-3300
Teaching Specialties:
Orthopedic Surgery, Psychiatry.

Curative Rehabilitation Center
1000 N. 92nd St.
Milwaukee, WI 53226
414-259-1414
Teaching Specialties:
Physical Medicine and Rehabilitation.

Froedtert Memorial Lutheran Hospital
9200 W. Wisconsin Ave.
Milwaukee, WI 53226
414-259-3000
Teaching Specialties:
Allergy/Immunology, Dermatology, Internal Medicine, Internal Medicine-Gastroenterology, Internal Medicine-Infectious Diseases, Internal Medicine-Nephrology, Internal Medicine-Rheumatology, Neurological Surgery, Neurology, Orthopedic Surgery, Physical Medicine and Rehabilitation, Psychiatry, Surgery, Urology.

Marquette University School of Dentistry
604 N. 16th St.
Milwaukee, WI 53233
414-288-3532
Teaching Specialties:
Dentistry.

Medical College of Wisconsin
Department of Oral and Maxillofacial Surgery
9200 W. Wisconsin Ave.
Milwaukee, WI 53226
414-454-5760
Teaching Specialties:
Dentistry.

Milwaukee County Medical Complex
8700 W. Wisconsin Ave.
Milwaukee, WI 53226
414-257-7996
Teaching Specialties:

Allergy/Immunology, Anesthesiology, Dermatology, Internal Medicine, Internal Medicine-Cardiovascular Disease, Internal Medicine-Endocrinology and Metabolism, Internal Medicine-Gastroenterology, Internal Medicine-Hematology, Internal Medicine-Infectious Diseases, Internal Medicine-Medical Oncology, Internal Medicine-Nephrology, Internal Medicine-Rheumatology, Neurological Surgery, Neurology, Obstetrics/Gynecology, Ophthalmology, Orthopedic Surgery, Otolaryngology, Physical Medicine and Rehabilitation, Psychiatry, Radiation Oncology, Surgery, Surgery-Vascular Surgery, Thoracic Surgery, Urology.

Milwaukee Psychiatric Hospital
1220 Dewey Ave.
Milwaukee, WI 53213
414-258-2600
Teaching Specialties:
Psychiatry.

Sinai Samaritan Medical Center-Mt. Sinai Campus
945 N. 12th St.

Milwaukee, WI 53233
414-345-3400
Teaching Specialties:
Internal Medicine, Internal Medicine-Cardiovascular Disease, Obstetrics/Gynecology, Orthopedic Surgery, Psychiatry.

St. Joseph's Hospital
5000 W. Chambers St.
Milwaukee, WI 53210
414-447-2000
Teaching Specialties:
Orthopedic Surgery.

St. Luke's Medical Center
2900 W. Oklahoma Ave.
Milwaukee, WI 53215
414-649-6000
Teaching Specialties:
Otolaryngology, Physical Medicine and Rehabilitation, Thoracic Surgery.

Oshkosh

Mercy Medical Center
631 Hazel St.
Oshkosh, WI 54902
414-236-2000
Teaching Specialties:
Psychiatry.

Winnebago

Winnebago Mental Health Institute
PO Box 9
Winnebago, WI 54985
414-235-4910
Teaching Specialties:
Psychiatry.

To find a hospital with a teaching specialty of interest to you, turn to the appropriate disorder and look for your state. Because any number of teaching specialties could qualify a hospital for inclusion under one of these disorders, check the list of teaching specialties under the Teaching Hospitals by State and City listing (page 460) to see if the hospital has the specific specialty that you need.

Bold type indicates an Academic Medical Center Hospital.

Bold type with an asterisk indicates a private Academic Medical Center Hospital.

A ▼ or † or ■ indicates a hospital associated with a National Institutes of Health research center.

Italic type indicates Medicare-approved heart and liver transplant centers in The Heart and Blood Vessels and The Digestive System sections only.

Cancer

▼ indicates National Cancer Institute: Comprehensive, Clinical, or Consortium Cancer Center

ALABAMA

▼University of Alabama Hospitals, Birmingham

University of South Alabama Medical Center, Mobile

ARIZONA

▼*University Medical Center, Tucson

ARKANSAS

University Hospital of Arkansas, Little Rock

CALIFORNIA

California Medical Center-Los Angeles, Los Angeles

Cedars-Sinai Medical Center, Los Angeles

▼City of Hope National Medical Center, Duarte

Green Hospital of Scripps Clinic, La Jolla

Kaiser Foundation Hospital, Los Angeles

*Loma Linda University Medical Center, Loma Linda

Long Beach Memorial Medical Center, Long Beach

Los Angeles County Harbor-University of California at Los Angeles Medical Center, Torrance

Los Angeles County-University of Southern California Medical Center, Los Angeles

Mt. Zion Medical Center of University of California, San Francisco, San Francisco

San Francisco General Hospital and Medical Center, San Francisco

Seton Medical Center, Daly City

St. Joseph Hospital, Orange

St. Mary's Hospital and Medical Center, San Francisco

*Stanford University Hospital, Stanford

▼University of California at Los Angeles Medical Center, Los Angeles

University of California, Davis Medical Center, Sacramento

University of California Irvine Medical Center, Orange

▼University of California San Diego Medical Center, San Diego

University of California, San Francisco Medical Center, San Francisco

▼University of Southern California, The Kenneth Norris Jr. Cancer Hospital, Los Angeles

COLORADO

Denver Health and Hospitals, Denver

Presbyterian-Denver Hospital, Denver

Presbyterian-St. Luke's Medical Center, Denver

▼University of Colorado Health Sciences Center, University Hospital, Denver

CONNECTICUT

Hospital of St. Raphael, New Haven

University of Connecticut Health Center, John Dempsey Hospital, Farmington

University of Connecticut Health Center, Uncas on Thames Hospital, Norwich

▼*Yale-New Haven Hospital, New Haven

DISTRICT OF COLUMBIA

District of Columbia General Hospital, Washington

*George Washington University Hospital, Washington

▼*Georgetown University Hospital, Washington

*Howard University Hospital, Washington

Washington Hospital Center, Washington

FLORIDA

Jackson Memorial Hospital, Miami

*Shands Hospital at the University of Florida, Gainesville

University of South Florida, H. Lee Moffitt Cancer Center, Tampa

GEORGIA

*Emory University Hospital, Atlanta

Grady Memorial Hospital, Atlanta

Medical College of Georgia, Georgia Radiation Therapy Center at Augusta, Augusta

Medical College of Georgia Hospital and Clinics, Augusta

ILLINOIS

Columbus Hospital, Chicago

Cook County Hospital, Chicago

Evanston Hospital, Evanston

Humana Hospital-Michael Reese, Chicago

Mercy Hospital and Medical Center, Chicago

Mt. Sinai Hospital Medical Center of Chicago, Chicago

▼*Northwestern Memorial Hospital, Chicago

▼*Rush-Presbyterian-St. Luke's Medical Center, Chicago

St. Cabrini Hospital, Chicago

St. Francis Hospital of Evanston, Evanston

▼*University of Chicago Hospitals, Chicago

▼University of Illinois Hospital and Clinics, Chicago

INDIANA

Indiana University Medical Center, Indianapolis

William N. Wishard Memorial Hospital, Indianapolis

IOWA

University of Iowa Hospitals and Clinics, Iowa City

KANSAS

Truman Medical Center-West, Kansas City

University of Kansas Hospital, Kansas City

KENTUCKY

Humana Hospital-University of Louisville, Louisville

University of Kentucky Hospital, Albert B. Chandler Medical Center, Lexington

LOUISIANA

Hotel Dieu Hospital, New Orleans

Louisiana State University Hospital, Shreveport

Medical Center of Louisiana at New Orleans, New Orleans

Ochsner Foundation Hospital, New Orleans

MARYLAND

▼*Johns Hopkins Hospital, Baltimore

*University of Maryland Medical System, Baltimore

MASSACHUSETTS

Baystate Medical Center, Springfield

*Beth Israel Hospital, Boston

Boston City Hospital, Boston

*Brigham and Women's Hospital, Boston

▼Dana-Farber Cancer Institute, Boston

*Massachusetts General Hospital, Boston

New England Deaconess Hospital, Boston

*New England Medical Center, Boston

St. Elizabeth's Hospital of Boston, Boston

*University Hospital, Boston

University of Massachusetts Medical Center, Worcester

MICHIGAN

Detroit Receiving Hospital and University Health Center, Detroit

*Grace Hospital, Detroit

▼*Harper Hospital, Detroit

Henry Ford Hospital, Detroit

Providence Hospital, Southfield

▼University of Michigan Hospitals, Ann Arbor

William Beaumont Hospital, Royal Oak

MINNESOTA

▼Mayo Clinic and Foundation, Rochester

Rochester Methodist Hospital, Rochester

*St. Marys Hospital, Rochester

University of Minnesota Hospital and Clinic, Minneapolis

MISSISSIPPI

University of Mississippi Medical Center, University Hospitals and Clinics, Jackson

MISSOURI

*Barnes Hospital, St. Louis

Jewish Hospital of St. Louis, St. Louis

Mallinckrodt Institute of Radiology, St. Louis

*St. Louis University Medical Center, St. Louis

Trinity Lutheran Hospital, Kansas City

University Hospital and Clinics, Columbia

NEBRASKA

University of Nebraska Medical Center, Omaha

NEW HAMPSHIRE

▼Dartmouth-Hitchcock Medical Center, Hanover

NEW JERSEY

Cooper Hospital-University Medical Center, Camden

Newark Beth Israel Medical Center, Newark

*Robert Wood Johnson University Hospital, New Brunswick

St. Barnabas Medical Center, Livingston

St. Joseph's Hospital and Medical Center, Paterson

St. Michael's Medical Center, Newark

St. Peter's Medical Center, New Brunswick

United Hospitals Medical Center, Newark

University of Medicine and Dentistry of New Jersey, University Hospital, Newark

NEW MEXICO

University Hospital, Albuquerque

NEW YORK

*Albany Medical Center Hospital, Albany

Bellevue Hospital Center, New York

Beth Israel Medical Center, New York

Bronx Municipal Hospital Center, Bronx

Brookdale Hospital Medical Center, Brooklyn

Brooklyn Hospital Center, Brooklyn

Cabrini Medical Center, New York

Harlem Hospital Center, New York

Interfaith Medical Center, Brooklyn

Kings County Hospital Center, Brooklyn

Lenox Hill Hospital, New York

Long Island College Hospital, Brooklyn

Long Island Jewish Medical Center, New Hyde Park

Lutheran Medical Center, Brooklyn

Maimonides Medical Center, Brooklyn

Mary Immaculate Hospital, Jamaica

▼Memorial Sloan-Kettering Cancer Center, New York

Methodist Hospital of Brooklyn, Brooklyn

*Montefiore Medical Center, Henry and Lucy Moses Division, Bronx

▼Montefiore Medical Center, Jack D. Weiler Hospital of the Albert Einstein College of Medicine, Bronx

*Mt. Sinai Medical Center, New York

Nassau County Medical Center, East Meadow

*New York Hospital-Cornell Medical Center, New York

▼*New York University Medical Center, New York

North Shore University Hospital, Manhasset

▼*Presbyterian Hospital in the City of New York, Columbia-Presbyterian Medical Center, New York

▼Rochester General Hospital, Rochester

▼Roswell Park Cancer Institute, Buffalo

St. Luke's-Roosevelt Hospital Center, Roosevelt Division, New York

St. Luke's-Roosevelt Hospital Center, St. Luke's Division, New York

St. Mary's Hospital, Brooklyn

St. Vincent's Hospital and Medical Center of New York, New York

State University of New York at Stony Brook University Hospital, Stony Brook

State University of New York Health Science Center, University Hospital, Syracuse

State University of New York Health Sciences Center at Brooklyn, University Hospital of Brooklyn, Brooklyn

▼*Strong Memorial Hospital of the University of Rochester, Rochester

Westchester County Medical Center, Valhalla

Winthrop-University Hospital, Mineola

Woodhull Medical and Mental Health Center, Brooklyn

NORTH CAROLINA

▼*Duke University Medical Center, Durham

▼*North Carolina Baptist Hospital, Winston-Salem

▼University of North Carolina Hospitals, Chapel Hill

OHIO

Cleveland Clinic Hospital, Cleveland

Medical College of Ohio Hospital, Toledo

MetroHealth Medical Center, Cleveland

▼Ohio State University Hospitals, Columbus

St. Vincent Medical Center, Toledo

▼*University Hospitals of Cleveland, Cleveland

University of Cincinnati Hospital, Cincinnati

OKLAHOMA

Oklahoma Medical Center, Oklahoma City

OREGON

Oregon Health Sciences University, University Hospital, Portland

PENNSYLVANIA

Albert Einstein Medical Center, Philadelphia

***Allegheny General Hospital, Pittsburgh**

▼American Oncologic Hospital-Fox Chase Cancer Center, Philadelphia

***Hahnemann University Hospital, Philadelphia**

***Hospital of the Medical College of Pennsylvania, Philadelphia**

▼*Hospital of the University of Pennsylvania, Philadelphia**

▼Montefiore University Hospital, Pittsburgh

Penn State University Hospital, The Milton S. Hershey Medical Center, Hershey

▼*Presbyterian University Hospital, Pittsburgh**

***Temple University Hospital, Philadelphia**

***Thomas Jefferson University Hospital, Philadelphia**

PUERTO RICO

Fundacion Hospital Metropolitan, San Juan

San Juan Municipal Hospital, Rio Piedras

University Hospital, San Juan

RHODE ISLAND

Memorial Hospital of Rhode Island, Pawtucket

Miriam Hospital, Providence

▼Roger Williams Hospital, Providence

SOUTH CAROLINA

Medical University of South Carolina, Medical Center of Medical University of South Carolina, Charleston

Richland Memorial Hospital, Columbia

TENNESSEE

Baptist Memorial Hospital, Memphis

Johnson City Medical Center Hospital, Johnson City

Regional Medical Center at Memphis, Memphis

St. Thomas Hospital, Nashville

***Vanderbilt University Hospital and Clinic, Nashville**

TEXAS

Baylor University Medical Center, Dallas

Bexar County Hospital District, Medical Center Hospital, San Antonio

▼Cancer Therapy and Research Center, San Antonio

Dallas County Hospital District, Parkland Memorial Hospital, Dallas

The Don and Sybil Harrington Cancer Center, Amarillo

Harris County Hospital District, Ben Taub General Hospital, Houston

High Plains Baptist Hospital, Amarillo

***Methodist Hospital, Houston**

Northwest Texas Hospital, Amarillo

University Medical Center, Lubbock

▼University of Texas M.D. Anderson Cancer Center, Houston

University of Texas Medical Branch Hospitals, Galveston

UTAH

LDS Hospital, Salt Lake City

▼**University of Utah Hospital and Clinics, Salt Lake City**

VERMONT

▼***Medical Center Hospital of Vermont, Burlington**

VIRGINIA

Maryview Medical Center, Portsmouth

Sentara Norfolk General Hospital, Norfolk

University of Virginia Medical Center, Charlottesville

Virginia Beach General Hospital, Virginia Beach

▼**Virginia Commonwealth University, Medical College of**

Virginia Hospitals, Richmond

WASHINGTON

▼Fred Hutchinson Cancer Research Center, Seattle

University of Washington Medical Center, Seattle

WISCONSIN

Milwaukee County Medical Complex, Milwaukee

▼**University of Wisconsin Hospital and Clinics, Madison**

The Blood

■ indicates National Heart, Lung, and Blood Institute: Comprehensive Sickle Cell Center

ALABAMA

University of Alabama Hospitals, Birmingham

▼**University of South Alabama Medical Center, Mobile**

ARIZONA

***University Medical Center, Tucson**

ARKANSAS

University Hospital of Arkansas, Little Rock

CALIFORNIA

Cedars-Sinai Medical Center, Los Angeles

Green Hospital of Scripps Clinic, La Jolla

Kaiser Foundation Hospital, Los Angeles

Los Angeles County Harbor-University of California at Los Angeles Medical Center, Torrance

Los Angeles County-University of Southern California Medical Center, Los Angeles

Olive View Medical Center, Sylmar

▼**San Francisco General Hospital and Medical Center, San Francisco**

***Stanford University Hospital, Stanford**

University of California at
Los Angeles Medical Center,
Los Angeles

University of California, Davis
Medical Center, Sacramento

University of California Irvine
Medical Center, Orange

University of California San Diego
Medical Center, San Diego

University of California,
San Francisco Medical Center,
San Francisco

COLORADO

Denver Health and Hospitals,
Denver

University of Colorado Health
Sciences Center, University
Hospital, Denver

CONNECTICUT

University of Connecticut Health
Center, John Dempsey Hospital,
Farmington

*Yale-New Haven Hospital,
New Haven

DISTRICT OF COLUMBIA

District of Columbia General
Hospital, Washington

*George Washington University
Hospital, Washington

*Georgetown University Hospital,
Washington

*Howard University Hospital,
Washington

FLORIDA

Jackson Memorial Hospital, Miami

*Shands Hospital at the University
of Florida, Gainesville

University Medical Center,
Jacksonville

GEORGIA

*Emory University Hospital,
Atlanta

Grady Memorial Hospital, Atlanta

Medical College of Georgia
Hospital and Clinics, Augusta

ILLINOIS

Cook County Hospital, Chicago

*Loyola University of Chicago,
Foster G. McGaw Hospital,
Maywood

Mt. Sinai Hospital Medical Center
of Chicago, Chicago

*Northwestern Memorial Hospital,
Chicago

*Rush-Presbyterian-St. Luke's
Medical Center, Chicago

St. Francis Hospital of Evanston,
Evanston

*University of Chicago Hospitals,
Chicago

University of Illinois Hospital and
Clinics, Chicago

INDIANA

Indiana University Medical Center,
Indianapolis

IOWA

University of Iowa Hospitals and
Clinics, Iowa City

KANSAS

Truman Medical Center-West,
Kansas City

University of Kansas Hospital,
Kansas City

KENTUCKY

University of Kentucky Hospital,
Albert B. Chandler Medical Center,
Lexington

LOUISIANA

Louisiana State University
Hospital, Shreveport

Medical Center of Louisiana at
New Orleans, New Orleans

*Tulane University Hospital and
Clinics, New Orleans

MARYLAND

*Johns Hopkins Hospital,
Baltimore

*University of Maryland Medical
System, Baltimore

MASSACHUSETTS

Baystate Medical Center,
Springfield

*Beth Israel Hospital, Boston

▼Boston City Hospital, Boston

*Brigham and Women's Hospital,
Boston

*Massachusetts General Hospital,
Boston

New England Deaconess Hospital,
Boston

*New England Medical Center,
Boston

St. Elizabeth's Hospital of Boston,
Boston

*University Hospital, Boston

University of Massachusetts
Medical Center, Worcester

MICHIGAN

Detroit Receiving Hospital and
University Health Center, Detroit

*Harper Hospital, Detroit

Henry Ford Hospital, Detroit

St. Lawrence Hospital and
Healthcare Services, Lansing

University of Michigan Hospitals,
Ann Arbor

William Beaumont Hospital,
Royal Oak

MINNESOTA

Mayo Clinic and Foundation,
Rochester

Rochester Methodist Hospital,
Rochester

*St. Marys Hospital, Rochester

University of Minnesota Hospital
and Clinic, Minneapolis

MISSISSIPPI

University of Mississippi Medical
Center, University Hospitals and
Clinics, Jackson

MISSOURI

*Barnes Hospital, St. Louis

*St. Louis University Medical
Center, St. Louis

Trinity Lutheran Hospital,
Kansas City

University Hospital and Clinics, Columbia

NEBRASKA

University of Nebraska Medical Center, Omaha

NEW HAMPSHIRE

Dartmouth-Hitchcock Medical Center, Hanover

NEW JERSEY

Cooper Hospital-University Medical Center, Camden

Newark Beth Israel Medical Center, Newark

*Robert Wood Johnson University Hospital, New Brunswick

St. Joseph's Hospital and Medical Center, Paterson

St. Michael's Medical Center, Newark

St. Peter's Medical Center, New Brunswick

United Hospitals Medical Center, Newark

University of Medicine and Dentistry of New Jersey, University Hospital, Newark

NEW MEXICO

University Hospital, Albuquerque

NEW YORK

*Albany Medical Center Hospital, Albany

Bellevue Hospital Center, New York

Beth Israel Medical Center, New York

Bronx-Lebanon Hospital Center, Bronx

Bronx Municipal Hospital Center, Bronx

Brookdale Hospital Medical Center, Brooklyn

Brooklyn Hospital Center, Brooklyn

*Buffalo General Hospital, Buffalo

Cabrini Medical Center, New York

Coney Island Hospital, Brooklyn

Erie County Medical Center, Buffalo

Harlem Hospital Center, New York

Interfaith Medical Center, Brooklyn

Jamaica Hospital, Jamaica

Kings County Hospital Center, Brooklyn

Lenox Hill Hospital, New York

Lincoln Medical and Mental Health Center, Bronx

Long Island College Hospital, Brooklyn

Long Island Jewish Medical Center, New Hyde Park

Maimonides Medical Center, Brooklyn

Mary Immaculate Hospital, Jamaica

Memorial Sloan-Kettering Cancer Center, New York

Methodist Hospital of Brooklyn, Brooklyn

Metropolitan Hospital Center, New York

▼*Montefiore Medical Center, Henry and Lucy Moses Division, Bronx

*Mt. Sinai Medical Center, New York

Nassau County Medical Center, East Meadow

*New York Hospital-Cornell Medical Center, New York

North Shore University Hospital, Manhasset

Our Lady of Mercy Medical Center, Bronx

▼*Presbyterian Hospital in the City of New York, Columbia-Presbyterian Medical Center, New York

Rochester General Hospital, Rochester

St. Luke's-Roosevelt Hospital Center, Roosevelt Division, New York

St. Luke's-Roosevelt Hospital Center, St. Luke's Division, New York

St. Mary's Hospital, Brooklyn

St. Vincent's Hospital and Medical Center of New York, New York

State University of New York at Stony Brook University Hospital, Stony Brook

State University of New York Health Science Center, University Hospital, Syracuse

State University of New York Health Sciences Center at Brooklyn, University Hospital of Brooklyn, Brooklyn

*Strong Memorial Hospital of the University of Rochester, Rochester

Westchester County Medical Center, Valhalla

Winthrop-University Hospital, Mineola

Woodhull Medical and Mental Health Center, Brooklyn

NORTH CAROLINA

▼*Duke University Medical Center, Durham

University of North Carolina Hospitals, Chapel Hill

OHIO

Cleveland Clinic Hospital, Cleveland

Medical College of Ohio Hospital, Toledo

MetroHealth Medical Center, Cleveland

Ohio State University Hospitals, Columbus

St. Vincent Medical Center, Toledo

*University Hospitals of Cleveland, Cleveland

University of Cincinnati Hospital, Cincinnati

OKLAHOMA

Oklahoma Medical Center, Oklahoma City

OREGON

Oregon Health Sciences University, University Hospital, Portland

PENNSYLVANIA

American Oncologic Hospital-Fox Chase Cancer Center, Philadelphia

*Hahnemann University Hospital, Philadelphia

*Hospital of the Medical College of Pennsylvania, Philadelphia

*Hospital of the University of Pennsylvania, Philadelphia

Lankenau Hospital, Wynnewood

Montefiore University Hospital, Pittsburgh

Penn State University Hospital, The Milton S. Hershey Medical Center, Hershey

*Presbyterian University Hospital, Pittsburgh

*Temple University Hospital, Philadelphia

*Thomas Jefferson University Hospital, Philadelphia

PUERTO RICO

San Juan Municipal Hospital, Rio Piedras

University Hospital, San Juan

RHODE ISLAND

Memorial Hospital of Rhode Island, Pawtucket

Miriam Hospital, Providence

*Rhode Island Hospital, Providence

Roger Williams Hospital, Providence

SOUTH CAROLINA

Medical University of South Carolina, Medical Center of Medical University of South Carolina, Charleston

TENNESSEE

Baptist Memorial Hospital, Memphis

Regional Medical Center at Memphis, Memphis

*Vanderbilt University Hospital and Clinic, Nashville

TEXAS

Bexar County Hospital District, Medical Center Hospital, San Antonio

Dallas County Hospital District, Parkland Memorial Hospital, Dallas

Harris County Hospital District, Ben Taub General Hospital, Houston

*Hermann Hospital, Houston

*Methodist Hospital, Houston

UTAH

University of Utah Hospital and Clinics, Salt Lake City

VERMONT

*Medical Center Hospital of Vermont, Burlington

VIRGINIA

University of Virginia Medical Center, Charlottesville

Virginia Commonwealth University, Medical College of Virginia Hospitals, Richmond

WASHINGTON

University of Washington Medical Center, Seattle

WISCONSIN

Milwaukee County Medical Complex, Milwaukee

University of Wisconsin Hospital and Clinics, Madison

The Brain and Nervous System

▼ indicates National Institute on Aging: Alzheimer's Disease Center

† indicates National Institute of Neurological Disorders and Stroke: Epilepsy Clinical Research Center

■ indicates National Institute of Neurological Disorders and Stroke: Neuromuscular Clinical Research Center

ALABAMA

University of Alabama Hospitals, Birmingham

University of South Alabama Medical Center, Mobile

ARIZONA

Maricopa Medical Center, Phoenix

St. Joseph's Hospital and Medical Center, Barrow Neurological Institute, Phoenix

Tucson Medical Center, Tucson

*University Medical Center, Tucson

ARKANSAS

University Hospital of Arkansas, Little Rock

CALIFORNIA

Highland General Hospital, Oakland

Huntington Memorial Hospital, Pasadena

Kaiser Foundation Hospital, Los Angeles

Kaiser Foundation Hospital, Sacramento

Kaiser Foundation Hospital, San Diego

*Loma Linda University Medical Center, Loma Linda

Los Angeles County Harbor-University of California at Los Angeles Medical Center, Torrance

▼Los Angeles County-University of Southern California Medical Center, Los Angeles

Riverside General Hospital, University Medical Center, Riverside

San Francisco General Hospital and Medical Center, San Francisco

Santa Clara Valley Medical Center, San Jose

†*Stanford University Hospital, Stanford

†University of California at Los Angeles Medical Center, Los Angeles

University of California, Davis Medical Center, Sacramento

University of California Irvine Medical Center, Orange

▼University of California San Diego Medical Center, San Diego

University of California, San Francisco Medical Center, San Francisco

Denver Health and Hospitals, Denver

University of Colorado Health Sciences Center, University Hospital, Denver

CONNECTICUT

Hartford Hospital, Hartford

University of Connecticut Health Center, John Dempsey Hospital, Farmington

†*Yale-New Haven Hospital, New Haven

DELAWARE

Medical Center of Delaware, Wilmington

DISTRICT OF COLUMBIA

District of Columbia General Hospital, Washington

*George Washington University Hospital, Washington

*Georgetown University Hospital, Washington

*Howard University Hospital, Washington

Washington Hospital Center, Washington

FLORIDA

Jackson Memorial Hospital, Miami

Mt. Sinai Medical Center, Miami Beach

*Shands Hospital at the University of Florida, Gainesville

Tampa General Hospital, Tampa

GEORGIA

*Crawford Long Hospital of Emory University, Atlanta

*Emory University Hospital, Atlanta

Grady Memorial Hospital, Atlanta

Medical College of Georgia Hospital and Clinics, Augusta

University Hospital, Augusta

ILLINOIS

Christ Hospital and Medical Center, Oak Lawn

Cook County Hospital, Chicago

Evanston Hospital, Evanston

Humana Hospital-Michael Reese, Chicago

*Loyola University of Chicago, Foster G. McGaw Hospital, Maywood

▼Memorial Medical Center, Springfield

Methodist Medical Center of Illinois, Peoria

*Northwestern Memorial Hospital, Chicago

*Rush-Presbyterian-St. Luke's Medical Center, Chicago

St. Francis Medical Center, Peoria

▼St. John's Hospital, Springfield

*University of Chicago Hospitals, Chicago

University of Illinois Hospital and Clinics, Chicago

INDIANA

Indiana University Medical Center, Indianapolis

William N. Wishard Memorial Hospital, Indianapolis

IOWA

University of Iowa Hospitals and Clinics, Iowa City

KANSAS

University of Kansas Hospital, Kansas City

KENTUCKY

Humana Hospital-University of Louisville, Louisville

Norton Hospital, Louisville

▼University of Kentucky Hospital, Albert B. Chandler Medical Center, Lexington

LOUISIANA

Hotel Dieu Hospital, New Orleans

Medical Center of Louisiana at New Orleans, New Orleans

Ochsner Foundation Hospital, New Orleans

Southern Baptist Hospital, New Orleans

*Tulane University Hospital and Clinics, New Orleans

MARYLAND

Francis Scott Key Medical Center, Baltimore

▼*Johns Hopkins Hospital, Baltimore

*University of Maryland Medical System, Baltimore

MASSACHUSETTS

*Beth Israel Hospital, Boston

Boston City Hospital, Boston

*Brigham and Women's Hospital, Boston

Lahey Clinic Hospital, Burlington

▼*Massachusetts General Hospital, Boston

New England Deaconess Hospital, Boston

*New England Medical Center, Boston

St. Elizabeth's Hospital of Boston, Boston

St. Vincent Hospital, Worcester

*University Hospital, Boston

University of Massachusetts Medical Center, Worcester

MICHIGAN

Detroit Receiving Hospital and University Health Center, Detroit

*Harper Hospital, Detroit

Henry Ford Hospital, Detroit

St. Joseph Mercy Hospital, Ann Arbor

▼University of Michigan Hospitals, Ann Arbor

MINNESOTA

Hennepin County Medical Center, Minneapolis

▼■Mayo Clinic and Foundation, Rochester

Rochester Methodist Hospital, Rochester

*St. Marys Hospital, Rochester

St. Paul-Ramsey Medical Center, St. Paul

†University of Minnesota Hospital and Clinic, Minneapolis

MISSISSIPPI

University of Mississippi Medical Center, University Hospitals and Clinics, Jackson

MISSOURI

▼†*Barnes Hospital, St. Louis

Boone Hospital Center, Columbia

St. Louis Regional Medical Center, St. Louis

*St. Louis University Medical Center, St. Louis

University Hospital and Clinics, Columbia

NEBRASKA

AMI St. Joseph Hospital, Omaha

University of Nebraska Medical Center, Omaha

NEW HAMPSHIRE

Dartmouth-Hitchcock Medical Center, Hanover

NEW JERSEY

*Robert Wood Johnson University Hospital, New Brunswick

St. Barnabas Medical Center, Livingston

University of Medicine and Dentistry of New Jersey, University Hospital, Newark

NEW MEXICO

University Hospital, Albuquerque

NEW YORK

*Albany Medical Center Hospital, Albany

Bellevue Hospital Center, New York

Bronx Municipal Hospital Center, Bronx

*Buffalo General Hospital, Buffalo

Crouse-Irving Memorial Hospital, Syracuse

Elmhurst Hospital Center, Flushing

Erie County Medical Center, Buffalo

Harlem Hospital Center, New York

Kings County Hospital Center, Brooklyn

Lincoln Medical and Mental Health Center, Bronx

Long Island Jewish Medical Center, New Hyde Park

Memorial Sloan-Kettering Cancer Center, New York

Metropolitan Hospital Center, New York

Millard Fillmore Hospitals, Buffalo

Millard Fillmore Hospitals, Dent Neurological Institute, Buffalo

*Montefiore Medical Center, Henry and Lucy Moses Division, Bronx

Montefiore Medical Center, Jack D. Weiler Hospital of the Albert Einstein College of Medicine, Bronx

*Mt. Sinai Medical Center, New York

Nassau County Medical Center, East Meadow

*New York Hospital-Cornell Medical Center, New York

▼*New York University Medical Center, New York

North Shore University Hospital, Manhasset

▼■*Presbyterian Hospital in the City of New York, Columbia-Presbyterian Medical Center, New York

Queens Hospital Center, Jamaica

St. Vincent's Hospital and Medical Center of New York, New York

State University of New York at Stony Brook University Hospital, Stony Brook

State University of New York Health Science Center, University Hospital, Syracuse

State University of New York Health Sciences Center at Brooklyn, University Hospital of Brooklyn, Brooklyn

▼*Strong Memorial Hospital of the University of Rochester, Rochester

Westchester County Medical Center, Valhalla

NORTH CAROLINA

▼†*Duke University Medical Center, Durham

Durham County General Hospital, Durham

*North Carolina Baptist Hospital, Winston-Salem

University of North Carolina Hospitals, Chapel Hill

OHIO

Christ Hospital, Cincinnati

Cleveland Clinic Hospital, Cleveland

Good Samaritan Hospital, Cincinnati

MetroHealth Medical Center, Cleveland

Ohio State University Hospitals, Columbus

Riverside Methodist Hospitals, Columbus

▼*University Hospitals of Cleveland, Cleveland

University of Cincinnati Hospital, Cincinnati

OKLAHOMA

Oklahoma Medical Center, Oklahoma City

St. Anthony Hospital, Oklahoma City

OREGON

Good Samaritan Hospital and Medical Center, Portland

Kaiser Sunnyside Medical Center, Clackamas

▼Oregon Health Sciences University, University Hospital, Portland

PENNSYLVANIA

Albert Einstein Medical Center, Philadelphia

Crozer-Chester Medical Center, Upland

*Hahnemann University Hospital, Philadelphia

*Hospital of the Medical College of Pennsylvania, Philadelphia

■*Hospital of the University of Pennsylvania, Philadelphia

▼Montefiore University Hospital, Pittsburgh

Penn State University Hospital, The Milton S. Hershey Medical Center, Hershey

Pennsylvania Hospital, Philadelphia

▼*Presbyterian University Hospital, Pittsburgh

*Temple University Hospital, Philadelphia

*Thomas Jefferson University Hospital, Philadelphia

PUERTO RICO

San Juan Municipal Hospital, Rio Piedras

University Hospital, San Juan

RHODE ISLAND

*Rhode Island Hospital, Providence

SOUTH CAROLINA

Medical University of South Carolina, Medical Center of Medical University of South Carolina, Charleston

TENNESSEE

Baptist Hospital, Nashville

Baptist Memorial Hospital, Memphis

Methodist Hospitals of Memphis, Central Unit, Memphis

Metropolitan Nashville General Hospital, Nashville

Regional Medical Center at Memphis, Memphis

St. Thomas Hospital, Nashville

University of Tennessee Medical Center, Memphis

*Vanderbilt University Hospital and Clinic, Nashville

TEXAS

Bexar County Hospital District, Medical Center Hospital, San Antonio

Dallas County Hospital District, Parkland Memorial Hospital, Dallas

†Harris County Hospital District, Ben Taub General Hospital, Houston

*Hermann Hospital, Houston

▼†*Methodist Hospital, Houston

St. Paul Medical Center, Dallas

University Medical Center, Lubbock

University of Texas M.D. Anderson Cancer Center, Houston

University of Texas Medical Branch Hospitals, Galveston

Zale-Lipshy University Hospital, Dallas

UTAH

University of Utah Hospital and Clinics, Salt Lake City

VERMONT

*Medical Center Hospital of Vermont, Burlington

VIRGINIA

Sentara Norfolk General Hospital, Norfolk

University of Virginia Medical Center, Charlottesville

†Virginia Commonwealth University, Medical College of Virginia Hospitals, Richmond

WASHINGTON

Harborview Medical Center, Seattle

▼†University of Washington Medical Center, Seattle

WEST VIRGINIA

*West Virginia University Hospitals, Morgantown

WISCONSIN

*Froedtert Memorial Lutheran Hospital, Milwaukee

Meriter Hospital, Madison

Milwaukee County Medical Complex, Milwaukee

University of Wisconsin Hospital and Clinics, Madison

Dental and Oral Disorders

ALABAMA

University of Alabama School of Dentistry, Birmingham

CALIFORNIA

Cedars-Sinai Medical Center, Los Angeles

Highland General Hospital, Oakland

Loma Linda University School of Dentistry, Loma Linda

Los Angeles County Harbor-University of California at Los Angeles Medical Center, Torrance

Los Angeles County-King-Drew Medical Center, Los Angeles

Los Angeles County-University of Southern California Medical Center, Los Angeles

University of California at Los Angeles School of Dentistry, Center for the Health Sciences, Los Angeles

University of California, San Francisco School of Dentistry, San Francisco

University of Southern California School of Dentistry, Los Angeles

University of the Pacific School of Dentistry, San Francisco

Valley Medical Center of Fresno, Fresno

COLORADO

Denver Health and Hospitals, Denver

St. Joseph Hospital, Denver

University of Colorado School
of Dentistry, Denver

CONNECTICUT

Danbury Hospital, Danbury

Hartford Hospital, Hartford

Hospital of St. Raphael, New Haven

Mt. Sinai Hospital, Hartford

Southbury Training School,
Southbury

St. Francis Hospital and Medical
Center, Hartford

St. Mary's Hospital, Waterbury

University of Connecticut School
of Dental Medicine, Farmington

Waterbury Hospital, Waterbury

***Yale-New Haven Hospital,
New Haven**

DELAWARE

Medical Center of Delaware,
Wilmington

DISTRICT OF COLUMBIA

***Georgetown University Hospital,
Washington**

Howard University College of
Dentistry, Washington

St. Elizabeths Hospital, DC
Commission on Mental Health
Services, Washington

Washington Hospital Center,
Washington

FLORIDA

Dade County Dental Research
Clinic, Miami

Jackson Memorial Hospital, Miami

Mt. Sinai Medical Center,
Miami Beach

University Medical Center,
Jacksonville

University of Florida College
of Dentistry, Gainesville

GEORGIA

Emory University School
of Medicine, Atlanta

Medical College of Georgia School
of Dentistry, Augusta

HAWAII

Queen's Medical Center, Honolulu

ILLINOIS

Carle Foundation Hospital, Urbana

Cook County Hospital, Chicago

Evanston Hospital, Evanston

Illinois Masonic Medical Center,
Chicago

Loyola University of Chicago
School of Dentistry, Maywood

Mt. Sinai Hospital Medical Center
of Chicago, Chicago

Northwestern University
Dental School, Chicago

Ravenswood Hospital Medical
Center, Chicago

***Rush-Presbyterian-St. Luke's
Medical Center, Chicago**

Southern Illinois University School
of Dental Medicine, Alton

***University of Chicago Hospitals,
Chicago**

University of Illinois at Chicago
College of Dentistry, Chicago

INDIANA

Indiana University School of
Dentistry, Indianapolis

IOWA

University of Iowa College of
Dentistry, Iowa City

KENTUCKY

University of Kentucky College
of Dentistry, Lexington

University of Louisville School
of Dentistry, Louisville

LOUISIANA

Louisiana State University School
of Dentistry, New Orleans

**Medical Center of Louisiana at
New Orleans, New Orleans**

MARYLAND

***Johns Hopkins Hospital,
Baltimore**

Prince George's Hospital Center,
Cheverly

University of Maryland at Baltimore,
Baltimore College of Dentistry
Dental School, Baltimore

MASSACHUSETTS

Berkshire Medical Center, Pittsfield

Boston City Hospital, Boston

Boston University, Henry M.
Goldman School of Graduate
Dentistry, Boston

***Brigham and Women's Hospital,
Boston**

Harvard School of Dental
Medicine, Boston

***Massachusetts General Hospital,
Boston**

Tufts University School of Dental
Medicine, Boston

MICHIGAN

Detroit-Macomb Hospital
Corporation, Oral and Maxillofacial
Surgery, Detroit

Detroit Receiving Hospital and
University Health Center, Detroit

Henry Ford Hospital, Detroit

Sinai Hospital, Detroit

University of Detroit Mercy School
of Dentistry, Detroit

University of Michigan School
of Dentistry, Ann Arbor

MINNESOTA

Hennepin County Medical Center,
Minneapolis

Mayo Clinic and Foundation,
Rochester

University of Minnesota School
of Dentistry, Minneapolis

MISSISSIPPI

University of Mississippi School
of Dentistry, Jackson

MISSOURI

Jewish Hospital of St. Louis,
St. Louis

St. John's Mercy Medical Center,
St. Louis

St. Louis University Medical Center,
Orthodontics Treatment, St. Louis

University of Missouri-Kansas City School of Dentistry, Kansas City

NEBRASKA

Creighton University School of Dentistry, Omaha

University of Nebraska Medical Center, College of Dentistry, Lincoln

NEW JERSEY

Englewood Hospital, Englewood

Hackensack Medical Center, Hackensack

Jersey City Medical Center, Jersey City

Jersey Shore Medical Center, Neptune

John F. Kennedy Medical Center, Edison

Monmouth Medical Center, Long Branch

Morristown Memorial Hospital, Morristown

Mountainside Hospital, Montclair

Newark Beth Israel Medical Center, Newark

Overlook Hospital, Summit

*Robert Wood Johnson University Hospital, New Brunswick

St. Joseph's Hospital and Medical Center, Paterson

University of Medicine and Dentistry of New Jersey, New Jersey Dental School, Newark

NEW YORK

*Albany Medical Center Hospital, Albany

Beth Israel Medical Center, York

Booth Memorial Medical Center, Flushing

Bronx-Lebanon Hospital Center, Bronx

Bronx Municipal Hospital Center, Bronx

Brookdale Hospital Medical Center, Brooklyn

Brooklyn Hospital Center, Brooklyn

Catholic Medical Center of Brooklyn and Queens, Jamaica

Coler Memorial Hospital, New York

Columbia University School of Dental and Oral Surgery, New York

Eastman Dental Center, Rochester

Erie County Medical Center, Buffalo

Flushing Hospital Medical Center, Flushing

Genesee Hospital, Rochester

Goldwater Memorial Hospital, New York

Harlem Hospital Center, New York

Interfaith Medical Center, Brooklyn

Jamaica Hospital, Jamaica

Kings County Hospital Center, Brooklyn

Lenox Hill Hospital, New York

Lincoln Medical and Mental Health Center, Bronx

Long Island College Hospital, Brooklyn

Long Island Jewish Medical Center, New Hyde Park

Lutheran Medical Center, Brooklyn

Maimonides Medical Center, Brooklyn

Memorial Sloan-Kettering Cancer Center, New York

Metropolitan Hospital Center, New York

Millard Fillmore Hospitals, Buffalo

*Montefiore Medical Center, Henry and Lucy Moses Division, Bronx

*Mt. Sinai Medical Center, New York

Nassau County Medical Center, East Meadow

*New York Hospital-Cornell Medical Center, New York

New York University College of Dentistry, New York

North Shore University Hospital, Manhasset

Our Lady of Mercy Medical Center, Bronx

Peninsula Hospital Center, Far Rockaway

Roswell Park Cancer Institute, Buffalo

St. Barnabas Hospital, Bronx

St. Charles Hospital and Rehabilitation Center, Port Jefferson

St. Clare's Hospital of Schenectady, Schenectady

St. Joseph's Hospital Health Center, Syracuse

St. Luke's Memorial Hospital Center, Utica

St. Luke's-Roosevelt Hospital Center, St. Luke's Division, New York

St. Peter's Hospital, Albany

State University of New York at Buffalo, School of Dental Medicine, Buffalo

State University of New York at Stony Brook, School of Dental Medicine, Stony Brook

State University of New York Health Science Center, University Hospital, Syracuse

Staten Island University Hospital, Staten Island

*Strong Memorial Hospital of the University of Rochester, Rochester

Westchester County Medical Center, Valhalla

Woodhull Medical and Mental Health Center, Brooklyn

Wyckoff Heights Medical Center, Brooklyn

NORTH CAROLINA

Bowman Gray School of Medicine, Department of Dentistry, Winston-Salem

Carolinas Medical Center, Charlotte

East Carolina University School of Medicine, Family Practice Center, Department of Dentistry, Greenville

University of North Carolina at Chapel Hill, School of Dentistry, Chapel Hill

OHIO

Case Western Reserve University School of Dentistry, Cleveland

Cleveland Clinic Hospital, Cleveland

Medical College of Ohio Hospital, Toledo

MetroHealth Medical Center, Cleveland

Miami Valley Hospital, Dayton

Mt. Sinai Medical Center, Cleveland

Ohio State University College of Dentistry, Columbus

St. Elizabeth Hospital Medical Center, Youngstown

St. Luke's Hospital, Cleveland

University of Cincinnati Hospital, Cincinnati

Western Reserve Care System-Southside Medical Center, Youngstown

OKLAHOMA

Oklahoma Medical Center, Oklahoma City

St. Anthony Hospital, Oklahoma City

University of Oklahoma College of Dentistry, Oklahoma City

OREGON

Oregon Health Sciences University, School of Dentistry, Portland

PENNSYLVANIA

Abington Memorial Hospital, Abington

Albert Einstein Medical Center, Philadelphia

*Allegheny General Hospital, Pittsburgh

The Allentown Hospital-Lehigh Valley Hospital Center, Allentown

Community General Hospital, Reading

Graduate Hospital, Philadelphia

*Hahnemann University Hospital, Philadelphia

*Hospital of the Medical College of Pennsylvania, Philadelphia

Montefiore University Hospital, Pittsburgh

Muhlenberg Hospital Center, Bethlehem

Sacred Heart Hospital, Allentown

St. Francis Medical Center, Pittsburgh

St. Joseph Hospital, Reading

Temple University School of Dentistry, Philadelphia

*Thomas Jefferson University Hospital, Philadelphia

University of Pennsylvania School of Dental Medicine, Philadelphia

University of Pittsburgh School of Dental Medicine, Pittsburgh

York Hospital, York

PUERTO RICO

University of Puerto Rico School of Dentistry, San Juan

SOUTH CAROLINA

Medical University of South Carolina, College of Dental Medicine, Charleston

Richland Memorial Hospital, Columbia

TENNESSEE

Meharry Medical College School of Dentistry, Nashville

University of Tennessee College of Dentistry, Memphis

University of Tennessee Memorial Hospital, Knoxville

*Vanderbilt University Hospital and Clinic, Nashville

TEXAS

Baylor College of Dentistry, Dallas

Dallas County Hospital District, Parkland Memorial Hospital, Dallas

University of Texas Health Science Center at Houston, Dental Branch, Houston

University of Texas Health Science Center at San Antonio, Dental School, San Antonio

University of Texas M.D. Anderson Cancer Center, Houston

University of Texas Medical Branch Hospitals, Galveston

UTAH

University of Utah Hospital and Clinics, Salt Lake City

VERMONT

*Medical Center Hospital of Vermont, Burlington

VIRGINIA

University of Virginia Medical Center, Charlottesville

Virginia Commonwealth University, Medical College of Virginia, School of Dentistry, Richmond

WASHINGTON

University of Washington School of Dentistry, Seattle

WEST VIRGINIA

Charleston Area Medical Center, Memorial Division, Charleston

West Virginia University School of Dentistry, Morgantown

WISCONSIN

Lutheran Hospital-La Crosse, La Crosse

Marquette University School of Dentistry, Milwaukee

Medical College of Wisconsin, Department of Oral and Maxillofacial Surgery, Milwaukee

Meriter Hospital, Madison

The Digestive System

Italic type indicates Health Care Financing Administration: Medicare Liver Transplant Center

ALABAMA

University of Alabama Hospitals, Birmingham

ARIZONA

Kino Community Hospital, Tucson

*University Medical Center, Tucson

ARKANSAS

University Hospital of Arkansas, Little Rock

CALIFORNIA

California-Pacific Medical Center, San Francisco

Cedars-Sinai Medical Center, Los Angeles

Green Hospital of Scripps Clinic, La Jolla

Kaiser Foundation Hospital, Los Angeles

*Loma Linda University Medical Center, Loma Linda

Los Angeles County Harbor-University of California at Los Angeles Medical Center, Torrance

Los Angeles County-King-Drew Medical Center, Los Angeles

Los Angeles County-University of Southern California Medical Center, Los Angeles

San Francisco General Hospital and Medical Center, San Francisco

Sansum Medical Clinic, Santa Barbara

Santa Barbara Cottage Hospital, Santa Barbara

Santa Clara Valley Medical Center, San Jose

*Stanford University Hospital, Stanford

University of California at Los Angeles Medical Center, Los Angeles

University of California, Davis Medical Center, Sacramento

University of California Irvine Medical Center, Orange

University of California San Diego Medical Center, San Diego

University of California, San Francisco Medical Center, San Francisco

COLORADO

Denver Health and Hospitals, Denver

University of Colorado Health Sciences Center, University Hospital, Denver

CONNECTICUT

Bridgeport Hospital, Bridgeport

Griffin Hospital, Derby

Hospital of St. Raphael, New Haven

Norwalk Hospital, Norwalk

St. Francis Hospital and Medical Center, Hartford

University of Connecticut Health Center, John Dempsey Hospital, Farmington

Waterbury Hospital, Waterbury

*Yale-New Haven Hospital, New Haven

DISTRICT OF COLUMBIA

District of Columbia General Hospital, Washington

*George Washington University Hospital, Washington

*Georgetown University Hospital, Washington

*Howard University Hospital, Washington

FLORIDA

Florida Hospital Medical Center, Orlando

Jackson Memorial Hospital, Miami

Mt. Sinai Medical Center, Miami Beach

North Beach Hospital, Fort Lauderdale

Orlando Regional Medical Center, Orlando

*Shands Hospital at the University of Florida, Gainesville

University Medical Center, Jacksonville

GEORGIA

*Emory University Hospital, Atlanta

Grady Memorial Hospital, Atlanta

Medical College of Georgia Hospital and Clinics, Augusta

ILLINOIS

Carle Foundation Hospital, Urbana

Cook County Hospital, Chicago

Evanston Hospital, Evanston

Humana Hospital-Michael Reese, Chicago

*Loyola University of Chicago, Foster G. McGaw Hospital, Maywood

Martha Washington Hospital, Chicago

Mt. Sinai Hospital Medical Center of Chicago, Chicago

*Northwestern Memorial Hospital, Chicago

*Rush-Presbyterian-St. Luke's Medical Center, Chicago

*University of Chicago Hospitals, Chicago

University of Illinois Hospital and Clinics, Chicago

INDIANA

Indiana University Medical Center, Indianapolis

IOWA

University of Iowa Hospitals and Clinics, Iowa City

KANSAS

Truman Medical Center-West, Kansas City

University of Kansas Hospital, Kansas City

KENTUCKY

Humana Hospital-University of Louisville, Louisville

University of Kentucky Hospital, Albert B. Chandler Medical Center, Lexington

LOUISIANA

Hotel Dieu Hospital, New Orleans

Louisiana State University Hospital, Shreveport

Medical Center of Louisiana at New Orleans, New Orleans

Ochsner Foundation Hospital, New Orleans

Schumpert Medical Center, Shreveport

*Tulane University Hospital and Clinics, New Orleans

MARYLAND

Francis Scott Key Medical Center, Baltimore

Greater Baltimore Medical Center, Baltimore

*Johns Hopkins Hospital, Baltimore

Prince George's Hospital Center, Cheverly

Suburban Hospital, Bethesda

*University of Maryland Medical System, Baltimore

MASSACHUSETTS

*Beth Israel Hospital, Boston

Boston City Hospital, Boston

*Brigham and Women's Hospital, Boston

Faulkner Hospital, Boston

Lahey Clinic Hospital, Burlington

Lemuel Shattuck Hospital, Boston

*Massachusetts General Hospital, Boston

New England Deaconess Hospital, Boston

*New England Medical Center, Boston

St. Elizabeth's Hospital of Boston, Boston

*University Hospital, Boston

University of Massachusetts Medical Center, Worcester

MICHIGAN

Detroit Receiving Hospital and University Health Center, Detroit

Ferguson Hospital, Grand Rapids

*Harper Hospital, Detroit

Henry Ford Hospital, Detroit

Ingham Medical Center, Lansing

Providence Hospital, Southfield

Sinai Hospital, Detroit

University of Michigan Hospitals, Ann Arbor

William Beaumont Hospital, Royal Oak

MINNESOTA

Abbott-Northwestern Hospital, Minneapolis

Mayo Clinic and Foundation, Rochester

Metropolitan-Mt. Sinai Medical Center, Minneapolis

Rochester Methodist Hospital, Rochester

*St. Marys Hospital, Rochester

University of Minnesota Hospital and Clinic, Minneapolis

MISSISSIPPI

University of Mississippi Medical Center, University Hospitals and Clinics, Jackson

MISSOURI

*Barnes Hospital, St. Louis

Jewish Hospital of St. Louis, St. Louis

*St. Louis University Medical Center, St. Louis

St. Mary's Health Center, St. Louis

University Hospital and Clinics, Columbia

NEBRASKA

AMI St. Joseph Hospital, Omaha

University of Nebraska Medical Center, Omaha

NEW HAMPSHIRE

Dartmouth-Hitchcock Medical Center, Hanover

NEW JERSEY

Cooper Hospital-University Medical Center, Camden

Jersey City Medical Center, Jersey City

John F. Kennedy Medical Center, Edison

Muhlenberg Regional Medical Center, Plainfield

*Robert Wood Johnson University Hospital, New Brunswick

St. Joseph's Hospital and Medical Center, Paterson

St. Michael's Medical Center, Newark

University of Medicine and Dentistry of New Jersey, University Hospital, Newark

NEW MEXICO

University Hospital, Albuquerque

NEW YORK

*Albany Medical Center Hospital, Albany

Bellevue Hospital Center, New York

Beth Israel Medical Center, New York

Booth Memorial Medical Center, Flushing

Bronx-Lebanon Hospital Center, Bronx

Bronx Municipal Hospital Center, Bronx

Brookdale Hospital Medical Center, Brooklyn

Brooklyn Hospital Center, Brooklyn

*Buffalo General Hospital, Buffalo

Cabrini Medical Center, New York

Elmhurst Hospital Center, Flushing

Erie County Medical Center, Buffalo

Harlem Hospital Center, New York

Interfaith Medical Center, Brooklyn

Jamaica Hospital, Jamaica

Kings County Hospital Center, Brooklyn

Lenox Hill Hospital, New York

Lincoln Medical and Mental Health Center, Bronx

Long Island College Hospital, Brooklyn

Long Island Jewish Medical Center, New Hyde Park

Maimonides Medical Center, Brooklyn

Mary Immaculate Hospital, Jamaica

Memorial Sloan-Kettering Cancer Center, New York

Metropolitan Hospital Center, New York

*Montefiore Medical Center, Henry and Lucy Moses Division, Bronx

*Mt. Sinai Medical Center, New York

Nassau County Medical Center, East Meadow

*New York Hospital-Cornell Medical Center, New York

North Shore University Hospital, Manhasset

Our Lady of Mercy Medical Center, Bronx

*Presbyterian Hospital in the City of New York, Columbia-Presbyterian Medical Center, New York

Roswell Park Cancer Institute, Buffalo

St. Luke's-Roosevelt Hospital Center, Roosevelt Division, New York

St. Luke's-Roosevelt Hospital Center, St. Luke's Division, New York

St. Mary's Hospital, Rochester

St. Vincent's Hospital and Medical Center of New York, New York

State University of New York at Stony Brook University Hospital, Stony Brook

State University of New York Health Science Center, University Hospital, Syracuse

State University of New York Health Sciences Center at Brooklyn, University Hospital of Brooklyn, Brooklyn

*Strong Memorial Hospital of the University of Rochester, Rochester

Westchester County Medical Center, Valhalla

Winthrop-University Hospital, Mineola

NORTH CAROLINA

*Duke University Medical Center, Durham

*North Carolina Baptist Hospital, Winston-Salem

University of North Carolina Hospitals, Chapel Hill

OHIO

Cleveland Clinic Hospital, Cleveland

Grant Medical Center, Columbus

MetroHealth Medical Center, Cleveland

Ohio State University Hospitals, Columbus

*University Hospitals of Cleveland, Cleveland

University of Cincinnati Hospital, Cincinnati

OKLAHOMA

Oklahoma Medical Center, Oklahoma City

OREGON

Oregon Health Sciences University, University Hospital, Portland

PENNSYLVANIA

Albert Einstein Medical Center, Philadelphia

*Allegheny General Hospital, Pittsburgh

The Allentown Hospital-Lehigh Valley Hospital Center, Allentown

Crozer-Chester Medical Center, Upland

Graduate Hospital, Philadelphia

*Hahnemann University Hospital, Philadelphia

Hamot Medical Center, Erie

*Hospital of the Medical College of Pennsylvania, Philadelphia

*Hospital of the University of Pennsylvania, Philadelphia

Lankenau Hospital, Wynnewood

Mercy Catholic Medical Center, Misericordia Division, Philadelphia

Mercy Hospital of Scranton, Scranton

Montefiore University Hospital, Pittsburgh

Penn State University Hospital, The Milton S. Hershey Medical Center, Hershey

Presbyterian Medical Center of Philadelphia, Philadelphia

*Presbyterian University Hospital, Pittsburgh

Robert Packer Hospital, Sayre

Shadyside Hospital, Pittsburgh

St. Vincent Health Center, Erie

*Temple University Hospital, Philadelphia

*Thomas Jefferson University Hospital, Philadelphia

Western Pennsylvania Hospital, Pittsburgh

PUERTO RICO

San Juan Municipal Hospital, Rio Piedras

University Hospital, San Juan

RHODE ISLAND

*Rhode Island Hospital, Providence

Roger Williams Hospital, Providence

SOUTH CAROLINA

Medical University of South Carolina, Medical Center of Medical University of South Carolina, Charleston

Richland Memorial Hospital, Columbia

TENNESSEE

Johnson City Medical Center Hospital, Johnson City

Regional Medical Center at Memphis, Memphis

St. Thomas Hospital, Nashville

*Vanderbilt University Hospital and Clinic, Nashville

TEXAS

Baylor University Medical Center, Dallas

Bexar County Hospital District Medical Center Hospital, San Antonio

Dallas County Hospital District Parkland Memorial Hospital, Dallas

Harris County Hospital District, Ben Taub General Hospital, Houston

*Hermann Hospital, Houston

*Methodist Hospital, Houston

Presbyterian Hospital of Dallas, Dallas

*Scott and White Memorial Hospital, Temple

University Medical Center, Lubbock

University of Texas Medical Branch Hospitals, Galveston

UTAH

University of Utah Hospital and Clinics, Salt Lake City

VERMONT

*Medical Center Hospital of Vermont, Burlington

VIRGINIA

University of Virginia Medical Center, Charlottesville

Virginia Commonwealth University, Medical College of Virginia Hospitals, Richmond

WASHINGTON

University of Washington Medical Center, Seattle

WEST VIRGINIA

*West Virginia University Hospitals, Morgantown

WISCONSIN

*Froedtert Memorial Lutheran Hospital, Milwaukee

Milwaukee County Medical Complex, Milwaukee

University of Wisconsin Hospital and Clinics, Madison

The Ears, Nose, and Throat

ALABAMA

University of Alabama Hospitals, Birmingham

ARKANSAS

University Hospital of Arkansas, Little Rock

CALIFORNIA

Kaiser Foundation Hospital, Anaheim

Kaiser Foundation Hospital, Oakland

Kaiser Foundation Hospital, San Diego

Kaiser Foundation Hospital, San Francisco

Kaiser Foundation Hospital, Santa Clara

*Loma Linda University Medical Center, Loma Linda

Los Angeles County-King-Drew Medical Center, Los Angeles

Los Angeles County-Rancho Los Amigos Medical Center, Downey

Los Angeles County-University of Southern California Medical Center, Los Angeles

Olive View Medical Center, Sylmar

Riverside General Hospital, University Medical Center, Riverside

San Bernardino County Medical Center, San Bernardino

San Francisco General Hospital and Medical Center, San Francisco

Santa Clara Valley Medical Center, San Jose

*Stanford University Hospital, Stanford

University of California at Los Angeles Medical Center, Los Angeles

University of California, Davis Medical Center, Sacramento

University of California Irvine Medical Center, Orange

University of California San Diego Medical Center, San Diego

University of California, San Francisco Medical Center, San Francisco

COLORADO

Denver Health and Hospitals, Denver

St. Joseph Hospital, Denver

University of Colorado Health Sciences Center, University Hospital, Denver

CONNECTICUT

Hartford Hospital, Hartford

Hospital of St. Raphael, New Haven

New Britain General Hospital, New Britain

St. Francis Hospital and Medical Center, Hartford

University of Connecticut Health Center, John Dempsey Hospital, Farmington

*Yale-New Haven Hospital, New Haven

DISTRICT OF COLUMBIA

*Georgetown University Hospital, Washington

Washington Hospital Center, Washington

FLORIDA

Jackson Memorial Hospital, Miami

*Shands Hospital at the University of Florida, Gainesville

Tampa General Hospital, Tampa

GEORGIA

*Emory University Hospital, Atlanta

Grady Memorial Hospital, Atlanta

Medical College of Georgia Hospital and Clinics, Augusta

ILLINOIS

Cook County Hospital, Chicago

Evanston Hospital, Evanston

Louis A. Weiss Memorial Hospital, Chicago

*Loyola University of Chicago Foster G. McGaw Hospital, Maywood

Memorial Medical Center, Springfield

*Northwestern Memorial Hospital, Chicago

*Rush-Presbyterian-St. Luke's Medical Center, Chicago

St. John's Hospital, Springfield

*University of Chicago Hospitals, Chicago

University of Illinois Hospital and Clinics, Chicago

University of Illinois Hospital and Clinics, Illinois Eye and Ear Infirmary, Chicago

INDIANA

Indiana University Medical Center, Indianapolis

William N. Wishard Memorial Hospital, Indianapolis

IOWA

University of Iowa Hospitals and Clinics, Iowa City

KANSAS

University of Kansas Hospital, Kansas City

KENTUCKY

Humana Hospital-University of Louisville, Louisville

Norton Hospital, Louisville

University of Kentucky Hospital, Albert B. Chandler Medical Center, Lexington

LOUISIANA

Eye, Ear, Nose and Throat Hospital, New Orleans

Louisiana State University Hospital, Shreveport

Medical Center of Louisiana at New Orleans, New Orleans

Ochsner Foundation Hospital, New Orleans

***Tulane University Hospital and Clinics, New Orleans**

MARYLAND

Francis Scott Key Medical Center, Baltimore

Greater Baltimore Medical Center, Baltimore

***Johns Hopkins Hospital, Baltimore**

Maryland General Hospital, Baltimore

Sinai Hospital of Baltimore, Baltimore

***University of Maryland Medical System, Baltimore**

MASSACHUSETTS

***Beth Israel Hospital, Boston**

Boston City Hospital, Boston

Lahey Clinic Hospital, Burlington

Massachusetts Eye and Ear Infirmary, Boston

***New England Medical Center, Boston**

***University Hospital, Boston**

MICHIGAN

Detroit Receiving Hospital and University Health Center, Detroit

***Grace Hospital, Detroit**

***Harper Hospital, Detroit**

Henry Ford Hospital, Detroit

Hutzel Hospital, Detroit

University of Michigan Hospitals, Ann Arbor

MINNESOTA

Hennepin County Medical Center, Minneapolis

Mayo Clinic and Foundation, Rochester

Rochester Methodist Hospital, Rochester

***St. Marys Hospital, Rochester**

St. Paul-Ramsey Medical Center, St. Paul

University of Minnesota Hospital and Clinic, Minneapolis

MISSISSIPPI

University of Mississippi Medical Center, University Hospitals and Clinics, Jackson

MISSOURI

***Barnes Hospital, St. Louis**

Jewish Hospital of St. Louis, St. Louis

St. Louis Regional Medical Center, St. Louis

***St. Louis University Medical Center, St. Louis**

University Hospital and Clinics, Columbia

NEBRASKA

University of Nebraska Medical Center, Omaha

NEW HAMPSHIRE

Dartmouth-Hitchcock Medical Center, Hanover

NEW JERSEY

United Hospitals Medical Center, Newark

United Hospitals Medical Center, Newark Eye and Ear Infirmary, Newark

University of Medicine and Dentistry of New Jersey, University Hospital, Newark

West Jersey Hospital-Berlin, Berlin

West Jersey Hospital-Camden, Camden

West Jersey Hospital-Marlton, Marlton

West Jersey Hospital-Voorhees, Voorhees

NEW MEXICO

Lovelace Medical Center, Albuquerque

University Hospital, Albuquerque

NEW YORK

***Albany Medical Center Hospital, Albany**

Bellevue Hospital Center, New York

Bronx Municipal Hospital Center, Bronx

Brookdale Hospital Medical Center, Brooklyn

Child's Hospital, Albany

Community-General Hospital of Greater Syracuse, Syracuse

Crouse-Irving Memorial Hospital, Syracuse

Elmhurst Hospital Center, Flushing

Erie County Medical Center, Buffalo

Genesee Hospital, Rochester

Kings County Hospital Center, Brooklyn

Lincoln Medical and Mental Health Center, Bronx

Long Island College Hospital, Brooklyn

Long Island Jewish Medical Center, New Hyde Park

Manhattan Eye, Ear and Throat Hospital, New York

Memorial Sloan-Kettering Cancer Center, New York

*Montefiore Medical Center, Henry and Lucy Moses Division, Bronx

Montefiore Medical Center, Jack D. Weiler Hospital of the Albert Einstein College of Medicine, Bronx

*Mt. Sinai Medical Center, New York

New York Eye and Ear Infirmary, New York

*New York Hospital-Cornell Medical Center, New York

*New York University Medical Center, New York

*Presbyterian Hospital in the City of New York, Columbia-Presbyterian Medical Center, New York

Queens Hospital Center, Jamaica

Rochester General Hospital, Rochester

Sisters of Charity Hospital of Buffalo, Buffalo

St. Joseph's Hospital Health Center, Syracuse

St. Luke's-Roosevelt Hospital Center, Roosevelt Division, New York

St. Luke's-Roosevelt Hospital Center, St. Luke's Division, New York

St. Peter's Hospital, Albany

St. Vincent's Hospital and Medical Center of New York, New York

State University of New York Health Science Center, University Hospital, Syracuse

State University of New York Health Sciences Center at Brooklyn, University Hospital of Brooklyn, Brooklyn

*Strong Memorial Hospital of the University of Rochester, Rochester

NORTH CAROLINA

*Duke University Medical Center, Durham

*North Carolina Baptist Hospital, Winston-Salem

University of North Carolina Hospitals, Chapel Hill

OHIO

Cleveland Clinic Hospital, Cleveland

MetroHealth Medical Center, Cleveland

Ohio State University Hospitals, Columbus

*University Hospitals of Cleveland, Cleveland

University of Cincinnati Hospital, Cincinnati

OKLAHOMA

Baptist Medical Center of Oklahoma, Oklahoma City

Oklahoma Medical Center, Oklahoma City

OREGON

Oregon Health Sciences University, University Hospital, Portland

PENNSYLVANIA

*Allegheny General Hospital, Pittsburgh

Episcopal Hospital, Philadelphia

Geisinger Medical Center, Danville

*Hahnemann University Hospital, Philadelphia

*Hospital of the University of Pennsylvania, Philadelphia

Montefiore University Hospital, Eye and Ear Hospital of Pittsburgh, Pittsburgh

Penn State University Hospital, The Milton S. Hershey Medical Center, Hershey

Pennsylvania Hospital, Philadelphia

*Temple University Hospital, Philadelphia

*Thomas Jefferson University Hospital, Philadelphia

PUERTO RICO

San Juan Municipal Hospital, Rio Piedras

University Hospital, San Juan

SOUTH CAROLINA

Charleston Memorial Hospital, Charleston

Medical University of South Carolina, Medical Center of Medical University of South Carolina, Charleston

TENNESSEE

Baptist Hospital, Nashville

Methodist Hospitals of Memphis Central Unit, Memphis

Metropolitan Nashville General Hospital, Nashville

Regional Medical Center at Memphis, Memphis

University of Tennessee Medical Center, Memphis

*Vanderbilt University Hospital and Clinic, Nashville

TEXAS

Bexar County Hospital District, Medical Center Hospital, San Antonio

Dallas County Hospital District, Parkland Memorial Hospital, Dallas

Harris County Hospital District, Ben Taub General Hospital, Houston

Harris County Hospital District, Lyndon B. Johnson General Hospital, Houston

*Hermann Hospital, Houston

*Methodist Hospital, Houston

St. Paul Medical Center, Dallas

Tarrant County Hospital District, John Peter Smith Hospital, Fort Worth

University of Texas Medical Branch Hospitals, Galveston

Zale-Lipshy University Hospital, Dallas

UTAH

Holy Cross Hospital, Salt Lake City

University of Utah Hospital and Clinics, Salt Lake City

VERMONT

*Medical Center Hospital
of Vermont, Burlington

VIRGINIA

Roanoke Memorial Hospitals,
Roanoke

Sentara Norfolk General Hospital,
Norfolk

University of Virginia Medical
Center, Charlottesville

Virginia Commonwealth University,
Medical College of Virginia
Hospitals, Richmond

WASHINGTON

University of Washington
Medical Center, Seattle

WEST VIRGINIA

*West Virginia University
Hospitals, Morgantown

WISCONSIN

Milwaukee County Medical
Complex, Milwaukee

St. Luke's Medical Center,
Milwaukee

University of Wisconsin Hospital
and Clinics, Madison

The Endocrine System

■ indicates National Institute of Diabetes
and Digestive and Kidney Diseases: Diabetes
Control and Complications Trial Center

ALABAMA

University of Alabama Hospitals,
Birmingham

ARIZONA

Kino Community Hospital, Tucson

*University Medical Center,
Tucson

ARKANSAS

University Hospital of Arkansas,
Little Rock

CALIFORNIA

Cedars-Sinai Medical Center,
Los Angeles

Green Hospital of Scripps Clinic,
La Jolla

Los Angeles County Harbor-
University of California at Los
Angeles Medical Center, Torrance

Los Angeles County-University
of Southern California Medical
Center, Los Angeles

Olive View Medical Center, Sylmar

Santa Clara Valley Medical Center,
San Jose

*Stanford University Hospital,
Stanford

University of California at
Los Angeles Medical Center,
Los Angeles

University of California, Davis
Medical Center, Sacramento

University of California Irvine
Medical Center, Orange

▼University of California San
Diego Medical Center, San Diego

University of California,
San Francisco Medical Center,
San Francisco

COLORADO

Denver Health and Hospitals,
Denver

University of Colorado Health
Sciences Center, University
Hospital, Denver

CONNECTICUT

University of Connecticut Health
Center, John Dempsey Hospital,
Farmington

▼*Yale-New Haven Hospital,
New Haven

DISTRICT OF COLUMBIA

District of Columbia General
Hospital, Washington

*George Washington University
Hospital, Washington

*Georgetown University Hospital,
Washington

*Howard University Hospital,
Washington

FLORIDA

Jackson Memorial Hospital, Miami

*Shands Hospital at the University
of Florida, Gainesville

University Medical Center,
Jacksonville

University of South Florida, H. Lee
Moffitt Cancer Center, Tampa

GEORGIA

*Emory University Hospital,
Atlanta

Grady Memorial Hospital, Atlanta

Medical College of Georgia
Hospital and Clinics, Augusta

ILLINOIS

Cook County Hospital, Chicago

Humana Hospital-Michael Reese,
Chicago

*Loyola University of Chicago,
Foster G. McGaw Hospital,
Maywood

▼*Northwestern Memorial
Hospital, Chicago

*Rush-Presbyterian-St. Luke's
Medical Center, Chicago

*University of Chicago Hospitals,
Chicago

University of Illinois Hospital and
Clinics, Chicago

INDIANA

Indiana University Medical Center,
Indianapolis

IOWA

▼University of Iowa Hospitals
and Clinics, Iowa City

KANSAS

University of Kansas Hospital,
Kansas City

KENTUCKY

Humana Hospital-University
of Louisville, Louisville

University of Kentucky Hospital,
Albert B. Chandler Medical Center,
Lexington

LOUISIANA

Louisiana State University Hospital, Shreveport

Medical Center of Louisiana at New Orleans, New Orleans

Ochsner Foundation Hospital, New Orleans

*Tulane University Hospital and Clinics, New Orleans

MAINE

Maine Medical Center, Portland

MARYLAND

*Johns Hopkins Hospital, Baltimore

▼*University of Maryland Medical System, Baltimore

MASSACHUSETTS

Baystate Medical Center, Springfield

*Beth Israel Hospital, Boston

Boston City Hospital, Boston

*Brigham and Women's Hospital, Boston

▼Joslin Diabetes Center, Inc., Boston

Lahey Clinic Hospital, Burlington

▼*Massachusetts General Hospital, Boston

New England Deaconess Hospital, Boston

*New England Medical Center, Boston

*University Hospital, Boston

University of Massachusetts Medical Center, Worcester

MICHIGAN

Detroit Receiving Hospital and University Health Center, Detroit

*Harper Hospital, Detroit

▼Henry Ford Hospital, Detroit

▼University of Michigan Hospitals, Ann Arbor

MINNESOTA

▼Mayo Clinic and Foundation, Rochester

Rochester Methodist Hospital, Rochester

*St. Marys Hospital, Rochester

▼University of Minnesota Hospital and Clinic, Minneapolis

MISSOURI

*Barnes Hospital, St. Louis

Jewish Hospital of St. Louis, St. Louis

*St. Louis University Medical Center, St. Louis

▼University Hospital and Clinics, Columbia

NEW HAMPSHIRE

Dartmouth-Hitchcock Medical Center, Hanover

NEW JERSEY

*Robert Wood Johnson University Hospital, New Brunswick

St. Michael's Medical Center, Newark

St. Peter's Medical Center, New Brunswick

University of Medicine and Dentistry of New Jersey, University Hospital, Newark

NEW MEXICO

▼University Hospital, Albuquerque

NEW YORK

*Albany Medical Center Hospital, Albany

Bellevue Hospital Center, New York

Beth Israel Medical Center, New York

Bronx Municipal Hospital Center, Bronx

Brookdale Hospital Medical Center, Brooklyn

Coney Island Hospital, Brooklyn

Erie County Medical Center, Buffalo

Interfaith Medical Center, Brooklyn

Kings County Hospital Center, Brooklyn

Lincoln Medical and Mental Health Center, Bronx

Long Island Jewish Medical Center, New Hyde Park

*Montefiore Medical Center, Henry and Lucy Moses Division, Bronx

Montefiore Medical Center, Jack D. Weiler Hospital of the Albert Einstein College of Medicine, Bronx

*Mt. Sinai Medical Center, New York

Nassau County Medical Center, East Meadow

▼*New York Hospital-Cornell Medical Center, New York

North Central Bronx Hospital, Bronx

*Presbyterian Hospital in the City of New York, Columbia-Presbyterian Medical Center, New York

Queens Hospital Center, Jamaica

St. Luke's-Roosevelt Hospital Center, St. Luke's Division, New York

State University of New York at Stony Brook University Hospital, Stony Brook

State University of New York Health Science Center, University Hospital, Syracuse

State University of New York Health Sciences Center at Brooklyn, University Hospital of Brooklyn, Brooklyn

*Strong Memorial Hospital of the University of Rochester, Rochester

Westchester County Medical Center, Valhalla

Winthrop-University Hospital, Mineola

NORTH CAROLINA

*Duke University Medical Center, Durham

Pitt County Memorial Hospital, Greenville

University of North Carolina Hospitals, Chapel Hill

OHIO

Cleveland Clinic Hospital,
Cleveland

**Medical College of Ohio Hospital,
Toledo**

Mercy Hospital, Toledo

MetroHealth Center for
Rehabilitation, Cleveland

**MetroHealth Medical Center,
Cleveland**

**Ohio State University Hospitals,
Columbus**

***University Hospitals of Cleveland,
Cleveland**

**University of Cincinnati Hospital,
Cincinnati**

OKLAHOMA

**Oklahoma Medical Center,
Oklahoma City**

OREGON

**Oregon Health Sciences University,
University Hospital, Portland**

PENNSYLVANIA

***Hahnemann University Hospital,
Philadelphia**

***Hospital of the Medical College
of Pennsylvania, Philadelphia**

***Hospital of the University of
Pennsylvania, Philadelphia**

Montefiore University Hospital,
Pittsburgh

**Penn State University Hospital,
The Milton S. Hershey Medical
Center, Hershey**

***Presbyterian University Hospital,
Pittsburgh**

Shadyside Hospital, Pittsburgh

***Temple University Hospital,
Philadelphia**

PUERTO RICO

San Juan Municipal Hospital,
Rio Piedras

University Hospital, San Juan

RHODE ISLAND

***Rhode Island Hospital,
Providence**

Roger Williams Hospital,
Providence

SOUTH CAROLINA

**▼Medical University of South
Carolina, Medical Center of
Medical University of South
Carolina, Charleston**

Richland Memorial Hospital,
Columbia

TENNESSEE

Baptist Memorial Hospital,
Memphis

**Regional Medical Center
at Memphis, Memphis**

**▼*Vanderbilt University Hospital
and Clinic, Nashville**

TEXAS

**Bexar County Hospital District,
Medical Center Hospital,
San Antonio**

**▼Dallas County Hospital District,
Parkland Memorial Hospital,
Dallas**

Harris County Hospital District, Ben
Taub General Hospital, Houston

*Hermann Hospital, Houston

*Methodist Hospital, Houston

***Scott and White Memorial
Hospital, Temple**

UTAH

**University of Utah Hospital
and Clinics, Salt Lake City**

VERMONT

***Medical Center Hospital of
Vermont, Burlington**

VIRGINIA

**University of Virginia Medical
Center, Charlottesville**

**Virginia Commonwealth University,
Medical College of Virginia
Hospitals, Richmond**

WASHINGTON

**University of Washington Medical
Center, Seattle**

WEST VIRGINIA

Cabell Huntington Hospital,
Huntington

WISCONSIN

**Milwaukee County Medical
Complex, Milwaukee**

**University of Wisconsin Hospital
and Clinics, Madison**

The Eyes

ALABAMA

Cooper Green Hospital,
Birmingham

Eye Foundation Hospital,
Birmingham

**University of Alabama Hospitals,
Birmingham**

**University of South Alabama
Medical Center, Mobile**

ARIZONA

Carondelet St. Joseph's Hospital,
Tucson

Kino Community Hospital, Tucson

***University Medical Center,
Tucson**

ARKANSAS

**University Hospital of Arkansas,
Little Rock**

CALIFORNIA

California-Pacific Medical Center,
San Francisco

Highland General Hospital,
Oakland

***Loma Linda University Medical
Center, Loma Linda**

Long Beach Memorial Medical
Center, Long Beach

**Los Angeles County Harbor-
University of California at Los
Angeles Medical Center, Torrance**

Los Angeles County-King-Drew
Medical Center, Los Angeles

**Los Angeles County-University
of Southern California Medical
Center, Los Angeles**

Riverside General Hospital University Medical Center, Riverside

San Francisco General Hospital and Medical Center, San Francisco

Santa Clara Valley Medical Center, San Jose

*Stanford University Hospital, Stanford

University of California at Los Angeles Medical Center, Jules Stein Eye Institute, Los Angeles

University of California, Davis Medical Center, Sacramento

University of California Irvine Medical Center, Orange

University of California San Diego Medical Center, San Diego

University of California, San Francisco Medical Center, San Francisco

White Memorial Medical Center, Los Angeles

COLORADO

Denver Health and Hospitals, Denver

University of Colorado Health Sciences Center, University Hospital, Denver

CONNECTICUT

*Yale-New Haven Hospital, New Haven

DISTRICT OF COLUMBIA

District of Columbia General Hospital, Washington

*George Washington University Hospital, Washington

*Georgetown University Hospital, Washington

*Howard University Hospital, Washington

Washington Hospital Center, Washington

FLORIDA

Bascom Palmer Eye Institute-Anne Bates Leach Eye Hospital, Miami

Jackson Memorial Hospital, Miami

*Shands Hospital at the University of Florida, Gainesville

Tampa General Hospital, Tampa

GEORGIA

*Emory University Hospital, Atlanta

Grady Memorial Hospital, Atlanta

Medical College of Georgia Hospital and Clinics, Augusta

ILLINOIS

Cook County Hospital, Chicago

Evanston Hospital, Evanston

*Loyola University of Chicago, Foster G. McGaw Hospital, Maywood

*Northwestern Memorial Hospital, Chicago

Oak Forest Hospital of Cook County, Oak Forest

*Rush-Presbyterian-St. Luke's Medical Center, Chicago

*University of Chicago Hospitals, Chicago

University of Illinois Hospital and Clinics, Illinois Eye and Ear Infirmary, Chicago

INDIANA

Indiana University Medical Center, Indianapolis

Methodist Hospital of Indiana, Indianapolis

William N. Wishard Memorial Hospital, Indianapolis

IOWA

University of Iowa Hospitals and Clinics, Iowa City

KANSAS

Truman Medical Center-West, Kansas City

University of Kansas Hospital, Kansas City

KENTUCKY

Humana Hospital-University of Louisville, Louisville

University of Kentucky Hospital, Albert B. Chandler Medical Center, Lexington

LOUISIANA

E.A. Conway Memorial Hospital, Monroe

Eye, Ear, Nose and Throat Hospital, New Orleans

Hotel Dieu Hospital, New Orleans

Louisiana State University Eye Center, New Orleans

Louisiana State University Hospital, Shreveport

Medical Center of Louisiana at New Orleans, New Orleans

Ochsner Foundation Hospital, New Orleans

South Louisiana Medical Center, Houma

*Tulane University Hospital and Clinics, New Orleans

MARYLAND

Greater Baltimore Medical Center, Baltimore

Johns Hopkins Hospital Wilmer Eye Institute, Baltimore

Maryland General Hospital, Baltimore

Sinai Hospital of Baltimore, Baltimore

*University of Maryland Medical System, Baltimore

MASSACHUSETTS

Boston City Hospital, Boston

Massachusetts Eye and Ear Infirmary, Boston

*New England Medical Center, Boston

*University Hospital, Boston

MICHIGAN

Detroit Receiving Hospital and University Health Center, Detroit

*Grace Hospital, Detroit

*Harper Hospital, Detroit

Henry Ford Hospital, Detroit

Sinai Hospital, Detroit

University of Michigan Hospitals, Ann Arbor

Westland Medical Center, Westland

William Beaumont Hospital, Royal Oak

MINNESOTA

Hennepin County Medical Center, Minneapolis

Mayo Clinic and Foundation, Rochester

Rochester Methodist Hospital, Rochester

*St. Marys Hospital, Rochester

St. Paul-Ramsey Medical Center, St. Paul

University of Minnesota Hospital and Clinic, Minneapolis

MISSISSIPPI

University of Mississippi Medical Center, University Hospitals and Clinics, Jackson

MISSOURI

*Barnes Hospital, St. Louis

Bethesda Eye Institute, St. Louis

University Hospital and Clinics, Columbia

NEBRASKA

University of Nebraska Medical Center, Omaha

NEW JERSEY

Cooper Hospital-University Medical Center, Camden

Jersey City Medical Center, Jersey City

United Hospitals Medical Center, Newark

United Hospitals Medical Center, Newark Eye and Ear Infirmary, Newark

University of Medicine and Dentistry of New Jersey, University Hospital, Newark

NEW YORK

*Albany Medical Center Hospital, Albany

Bayley Seton Hospital, Staten Island

Bellevue Hospital Center, New York

Beth Israel Medical Center, New York

Bronx-Lebanon Hospital Center, Bronx

Bronx Municipal Hospital Center, Bronx

Brookdale Hospital Medical Center, Brooklyn

Brooklyn Hospital Center, Brooklyn

*Buffalo General Hospital, Buffalo

Cabrini Medical Center, New York

Coney Island Hospital, Brooklyn

Crouse-Irving Memorial Hospital, Syracuse

Elmhurst Hospital Center, Flushing

Erie County Medical Center, Buffalo

Harlem Hospital Center, New York

Interfaith Medical Center, Brooklyn

Kings County Hospital Center, Brooklyn

Lenox Hill Hospital, New York

Lincoln Medical and Mental Health Center, Bronx

Long Island College Hospital, Brooklyn

Long Island Jewish Medical Center, New Hyde Park

Maimonides Medical Center, Brooklyn

Manhattan Eye, Ear and Throat Hospital, New York

Mary Immaculate Hospital, Jamaica

Metropolitan Hospital Center, New York

Millard Fillmore Hospitals, Buffalo

*Montefiore Medical Center, Henry and Lucy Moses Division, Bronx

Montefiore Medical Center, Jack D. Weiler Hospital of the Albert Einstein College of Medicine, Bronx

*Mt. Sinai Medical Center, New York

Nassau County Medical Center, East Meadow

New York Eye and Ear Infirmary, New York

*New York Hospital-Cornell Medical Center, New York

*New York University Medical Center, New York

North Central Bronx Hospital, Bronx

North General Hospital, New York

North Shore University Hospital, Manhasset

Our Lady of Mercy Medical Center, Bronx

*Presbyterian Hospital in the City of New York, Columbia-Presbyterian Medical Center, New York

Queens Hospital Center, Jamaica

St. Luke's-Roosevelt Hospital Center, St. Luke's Division, New York

St. Mary's Hospital, Rochester

St. Vincent's Hospital and Medical Center of New York, New York

State University of New York Health Science Center, University Hospital, Syracuse

*Strong Memorial Hospital of the University of Rochester, Rochester

Westchester County Medical Center, Valhalla

NORTH CAROLINA

*Duke University Medical Center, Durham

McPherson Hospital, Durham

*North Carolina Baptist Hospital, Winston-Salem

University of North Carolina Hospitals, Chapel Hill

OHIO

Akron City Hospital, Akron

Cleveland Clinic Hospital, Cleveland

MetroHealth Medical Center, Cleveland

Mt. Sinai Medical Center, Cleveland

Ohio State University Hospitals, Columbus

St. Luke's Hospital, Cleveland

St. Vincent Charity Hospital and Health Center, Cleveland

*University Hospitals of Cleveland, Cleveland

University of Cincinnati Hospital, Cincinnati

OKLAHOMA

Oklahoma Medical Center, Oklahoma City

OREGON

Good Samaritan Hospital and Medical Center, Portland

Oregon Health Sciences University, University Hospital, Portland

PENNSYLVANIA

Geisinger Medical Center, Danville

*Hahnemann University Hospital, Philadelphia

Penn State University Hospital, The Milton S. Hershey Medical Center, Hershey

Presbyterian Medical Center of Philadelphia, Philadelphia

Scheie Eye Institute, Philadelphia

St. Francis Medical Center, Pittsburgh

*Temple University Hospital, Philadelphia

Wills Eye Hospital, Philadelphia

PUERTO RICO

San Juan Municipal Hospital, Rio Piedras

University Hospital, San Juan

RHODE ISLAND

*Rhode Island Hospital, Providence

SOUTH CAROLINA

Medical University of South Carolina, Medical Center of Medical University of South Carolina, Charleston

Richland Memorial Hospital, Columbia

TENNESSEE

Erlanger Medical Center, Chattanooga

Methodist Hospitals of Memphis Central Unit, Memphis

Regional Medical Center at Memphis, Memphis

*Vanderbilt University Hospital and Clinic, Nashville

Willie D. Miller Eye Center, Chattanooga

TEXAS

Bexar County Hospital District, Medical Center Hospital, San Antonio

Dallas County Hospital District, Parkland Memorial Hospital, Dallas

Harris County Hospital District, Ben Taub General Hospital, Houston

*Hermann Hospital, Houston

*Methodist Hospital, Houston

*Scott and White Memorial Hospital, Temple

St. Luke's Episcopal Hospital, Houston

University Medical Center, Lubbock

University of Texas Medical Branch Hospitals, Galveston

UTAH

University of Utah Hospital and Clinics, Salt Lake City

VIRGINIA

Sentara Norfolk General Hospital, Norfolk

University of Virginia Medical Center, Charlottesville

Virginia Commonwealth University, Medical College of Virginia Hospitals, Richmond

WASHINGTON

Harborview Medical Center, Seattle

University of Washington Medical Center, Seattle

WEST VIRGINIA

*West Virginia University Hospitals, Morgantown

WISCONSIN

Milwaukee County Medical Complex, Milwaukee

University of Wisconsin Hospital and Clinics, Madison

The Heart and Blood Vessels

Italic type indicates The Health Care Financing Administration: Medicare Heart Transplant Centers

▼ indicates National Institute of Neurological Disorders and Stroke: Stroke Clinical Research Center

ALABAMA

University of Alabama Hospitals, Birmingham

University of South Alabama Medical Center, Mobile

ARIZONA

Good Samaritan Regional Medical Center, Phoenix

*University Medical Center, Tucson

ARKANSAS

University Hospital of Arkansas, Little Rock

CALIFORNIA

California-Pacific Medical Center, San Francisco

Cedars-Sinai Medical Center, Los Angeles

Green Hospital of Scripps Clinic, La Jolla

Kaiser Foundation Hospital, Los Angeles

*Loma Linda University Medical Center, Loma Linda

Long Beach Memorial Medical Center, Long Beach

Los Angeles County Harbor-University of California at Los Angeles Medical Center, Torrance

Los Angeles County-King-Drew Medical Center, Los Angeles

Los Angeles County-University of Southern California Medical Center, Los Angeles

Mercy Hospital and Medical Center, San Diego

▼Mt. Zion Medical Center of University of California, San Francisco, San Francisco

Sharp Memorial Hospital, San Diego

St. Mary Medical Center, Long Beach

St. Mary's Hospital and Medical Center, San Francisco

St. Vincent Medical Center, Los Angeles

Stanford University Hospital, Stanford

▼*University of California at Los Angeles Medical Center, Los Angeles*

University of California, Davis Medical Center, Sacramento

University of California Irvine Medical Center, Orange

University of California San Diego Medical Center, San Diego

▼University of California, San Francisco Medical Center, San Francisco

Valley Medical Center of Fresno, Fresno

COLORADO

Denver Health and Hospitals, Denver

University of Colorado Health Sciences Center, University Hospital, Denver

CONNECTICUT

Bridgeport Hospital, Bridgeport

Hartford Hospital, Hartford

Hospital of St. Raphael, New Haven

Mt. Sinai Hospital, Hartford

Norwalk Hospital, Norwalk

St. Vincent's Medical Center, Bridgeport

University of Connecticut Health Center, John Dempsey Hospital, Farmington

Yale-New Haven Hospital, New Haven

DISTRICT OF COLUMBIA

District of Columbia General Hospital, Washington

*George Washington University Hospital, Washington

*Georgetown University Hospital, Washington

*Howard University Hospital, Washington

Washington Hospital Center, Washington

FLORIDA

▼Jackson Memorial Hospital, Miami

Mt. Sinai Medical Center, Miami Beach

Shands Hospital at the University of Florida, Gainesville

Tampa General Hospital, Tampa

University Medical Center, Jacksonville

GEORGIA

Emory University Hospital, Atlanta

Grady Memorial Hospital, Atlanta

Medical College of Georgia Hospital and Clinics, Augusta

ILLINOIS

Christ Hospital and Medical Center, Oak Lawn

Cook County Hospital, Chicago

Humana Hospital-Michael Reese, Chicago

Illinois Masonic Medical Center, Chicago

Loyola University of Chicago, Foster G. McGaw Hospital, Maywood

MacNeal Hospital, Berwyn

Memorial Medical Center, Springfield

Mt. Sinai Hospital Medical Center of Chicago, Chicago

*Northwestern Memorial Hospital, Chicago

*Rush-Presbyterian-St. Luke's Medical Center, Chicago

St. Francis Hospital of Evanston, Evanston

St. John's Hospital, Springfield

*University of Chicago Hospitals, Chicago

University of Illinois Hospital and Clinics, Chicago

INDIANA

Indiana University Medical Center, Indianapolis

Methodist Hospital of Indiana, Indianapolis

IOWA

▼University of Iowa Hospitals and Clinics, Iowa City

KANSAS

Truman Medical Center-West, Kansas City

University of Kansas Hospital, Kansas City

KENTUCKY

Humana Hospital-University of Louisville, Louisville

University of Kentucky Hospital, Albert B. Chandler Medical Center, Lexington

LOUISIANA

Hotel Dieu Hospital, New Orleans

Louisiana State University Hospital, Shreveport

Medical Center of Louisiana at New Orleans, New Orleans

Ochsner Foundation Hospital, New Orleans

*Tulane University Hospital and Clinics, New Orleans

MAINE

Maine Medical Center, Portland

MARYLAND

▼*Johns Hopkins Hospital, Baltimore*

▼*University of Maryland Medical System, Baltimore

MASSACHUSETTS

Baystate Medical Center, Springfield

*Beth Israel Hospital, Boston

Boston City Hospital, Boston

Brigham and Women's Hospital, Boston

Lahey Clinic Hospital, Burlington

▼***Massachusetts General Hospital, Boston***

Mt. Auburn Hospital, Cambridge

New England Deaconess Hospital, Boston

***New England Medical Center, Boston**

St. Elizabeth's Hospital of Boston, Boston

St. Vincent Hospital, Worcester

***University Hospital, Boston**

University of Massachusetts Medical Center, Worcester

MICHIGAN

Detroit Receiving Hospital and University Health Center, Detroit

***Harper Hospital, Detroit**

▼*Henry Ford Hospital, Detroit*

Providence Hospital, Southfield

Sinai Hospital, Detroit

University of Michigan Hospitals, Ann Arbor

William Beaumont Hospital, Royal Oak

MINNESOTA

Hennepin County Medical Center, Minneapolis

▼Mayo Clinic and Foundation, Rochester

Rochester Methodist Hospital, Rochester

***St. Marys Hospital, Rochester**

University of Minnesota Hospital and Clinic, Minneapolis

MISSISSIPPI

University of Mississippi Medical Center, University Hospitals and Clinics, Jackson

MISSOURI

▼***Barnes Hospital, St. Louis***

▼Jewish Hospital of St. Louis, St. Louis

St. John's Mercy Medical Center, St. Louis

***St. Louis University Medical Center, St. Louis**

St. Luke's Hospital, Chesterfield

University Hospital and Clinics, Columbia

NEBRASKA

AMI St. Joseph Hospital, Omaha

University of Nebraska Medical Center, Omaha

NEW HAMPSHIRE

Dartmouth-Hitchcock Medical Center, Hanover

***Mary Hitchcock Memorial Hospital, Hanover**

NEW JERSEY

Cooper Hospital-University Medical Center, Camden

Hackensack Medical Center, Hackensack

Jersey City Medical Center, Jersey City

Newark Beth Israel Medical Center, Newark

***Robert Wood Johnson University Hospital, New Brunswick**

St. Michael's Medical Center, Newark

St. Peter's Medical Center, New Brunswick

University of Medicine and Dentistry of New Jersey, University Hospital, Newark

NEW MEXICO

University Hospital, Albuquerque

NEW YORK

***Albany Medical Center Hospital, Albany**

Bellevue Hospital Center, New York

Beth Israel Medical Center, New York

Bronx-Lebanon Hospital Center, Bronx

Bronx Municipal Hospital Center, Bronx

Brooklyn Hospital Center, Brooklyn

***Buffalo General Hospital, Buffalo**

Cabrini Medical Center, New York

Coney Island Hospital, Brooklyn

Elmhurst Hospital Center, Flushing

Erie County Medical Center, Buffalo

Genesee Hospital, Rochester

Harlem Hospital Center, New York

Interfaith Medical Center, Brooklyn

Jamaica Hospital, Jamaica

Kings County Hospital Center, Brooklyn

Lenox Hill Hospital, New York

Lincoln Medical and Mental Health Center, Bronx

Long Island College Hospital, Brooklyn

Long Island Jewish Medical Center, New Hyde Park

Maimonides Medical Center, Brooklyn

Mary Immaculate Hospital, Jamaica

Memorial Sloan-Kettering Cancer Center, New York

Methodist Hospital of Brooklyn, Brooklyn

Metropolitan Hospital Center, New York

Millard Fillmore Hospitals, Buffalo

***Montefiore Medical Center, Henry and Lucy Moses Division, Bronx**

Montefiore Medical Center, Jack D. Weiler Hospital of the Albert Einstein College of Medicine, Bronx

***Mt. Sinai Medical Center, New York**

Nassau County Medical Center, East Meadow

▼***New York Hospital-Cornell Medical Center, New York**

***New York University Medical Center, New York**

North Central Bronx Hospital, Bronx

North Shore University Hospital, Manhasset

Our Lady of Mercy Medical Center, Bronx

Presbyterian Hospital in the City of New York, Columbia-Presbyterian Medical Center, New York

Rochester General Hospital, Rochester

St. Luke's-Roosevelt Hospital Center, St. Luke's Division, New York

St. Vincent's Hospital and Medical Center of New York, New York

St. Vincent's Medical Center of Richmond, Staten Island

State University of New York at Stony Brook University Hospital, Stony Brook

State University of New York Health Science Center, University Hospital, Syracuse

State University of New York Health Sciences Center at Brooklyn, University Hospital of Brooklyn, Brooklyn

***Strong Memorial Hospital of the University of Rochester, Rochester**

Westchester County Medical Center, Valhalla

Winthrop-University Hospital, Mineola

NORTH CAROLINA

Carolinas Medical Center, Charlotte

▼*Duke University Medical Center, Durham

▼*North Carolina Baptist Hospital, Winston-Salem

Pitt County Memorial Hospital, Greenville

University of North Carolina Hospitals, Chapel Hill

OHIO

Cleveland Clinic Hospital, Cleveland

Good Samaritan Hospital, Cincinnati

Good Samaritan Hospital and Health Center, Dayton

Medical College of Ohio Hospital, Toledo

MetroHealth Medical Center, Cleveland

Mt. Carmel Medical Center, Columbus

Ohio State University Hospitals, Columbus

Toledo Hospital, Toledo

***University Hospitals of Cleveland, Cleveland**

University of Cincinnati Hospital, Cincinnati

OKLAHOMA

Oklahoma Medical Center, Oklahoma City

OREGON

**▼*Oregon Health Sciences University, University Hospital, Portland*

PENNSYLVANIA

Albert Einstein Medical Center, Philadelphia

***Allegheny General Hospital, Pittsburgh**

The Allentown Hospital-Lehigh Valley Hospital Center, Allentown

Episcopal Hospital, Philadelphia

Geisinger Medical Center, Danville

Graduate Hospital, Philadelphia

***Hahnemann University Hospital, Philadelphia**

***Hospital of the Medical College of Pennsylvania, Philadelphia**

**▼*Hospital of the University of Pennsylvania, Philadelphia*

Lankenau Hospital, Wynnewood

Montefiore University Hospital, Pittsburgh

Penn State University Hospital, The Milton S. Hershey Medical Center, Hershey

Presbyterian Medical Center of Philadelphia, Philadelphia

***Presbyterian University Hospital, Pittsburgh**

Shadyside Hospital, Pittsburgh

St. Francis Medical Center, Pittsburgh

St. Margaret Memorial Hospital, Pittsburgh

***Temple University Hospital, Philadelphia*

***Thomas Jefferson University Hospital, Philadelphia**

Western Pennsylvania Hospital, Pittsburgh

PUERTO RICO

Hospital de Damas, Ponce

Hospital San Lucas, Ponce

San Juan Municipal Hospital, Rio Piedras

University Hospital, San Juan

RHODE ISLAND

Memorial Hospital of Rhode Island, Pawtucket

Miriam Hospital, Providence

***Rhode Island Hospital, Providence**

Roger Williams Hospital, Providence

SOUTH CAROLINA

Medical University of South Carolina, Medical Center of Medical University of South Carolina, Charleston

Richland Memorial Hospital, Columbia

TENNESSEE

Baptist Memorial Hospital, Memphis

Johnson City Medical Center Hospital, Johnson City

Regional Medical Center at Memphis, Memphis

St. Thomas Hospital, Nashville

Vanderbilt University Hospital and Clinic, Nashville

TEXAS

Baylor University Medical Center, Dallas

Bexar County Hospital District, Medical Center Hospital, San Antonio

Dallas County Hospital District, Parkland Memorial Hospital, Dallas

Harris County Hospital District, Ben Taub General Hospital, Houston

▼*Hermann Hospital, Houston

Methodist Hospital, Houston

*Scott and White Memorial Hospital, Temple

St. Luke's Episcopal Hospital, Houston

University Medical Center, Lubbock

University of Texas Medical Branch Hospitals, Galveston

UTAH

University of Utah Hospital and Clinics, Salt Lake City

VERMONT

*Medical Center Hospital of Vermont, Burlington

VIRGINIA

Roanoke Memorial Hospitals, Roanoke

Sentara Norfolk General Hospital, Norfolk

University of Virginia Medical Center, Charlottesville

Virginia Commonwealth University, Medical College of Virginia Hospitals, Richmond

WASHINGTON

University of Washington Medical Center, Seattle

WEST VIRGINIA

Cabell Huntington Hospital, Huntington

*West Virginia University Hospitals, Morgantown

WISCONSIN

Milwaukee County Medical Complex, Milwaukee

Sinai Samaritan Medical Center-Mt. Sinai Campus, Milwaukee

University of Wisconsin Hospital and Clinics, Madison

The Kidneys and Urinary Tract

ALABAMA

Cooper Green Hospital, Birmingham

University of Alabama Hospitals, Birmingham

ARIZONA

*University Medical Center, Tucson

ARKANSAS

University Hospital of Arkansas, Little Rock

CALIFORNIA

Cedars-Sinai Medical Center, Los Angeles

Kaiser Foundation Hospital, Hayward

Kaiser Foundation Hospital, Los Angeles

Kaiser Foundation Hospital, Sacramento

Kaiser Foundation Hospital, Walnut Creek

*Loma Linda University Medical Center, Loma Linda

Los Angeles County Harbor-University of California at Los Angeles Medical Center, Torrance

Los Angeles County-University of Southern California Medical Center, Los Angeles

Mercy Hospital and Medical Center, San Diego

Olive View Medical Center, Sylmar

San Bernardino County Medical Center, San Bernardino

San Francisco General Hospital and Medical Center, San Francisco

Santa Clara Valley Medical Center, San Jose

St. Vincent Medical Center, Los Angeles

*Stanford University Hospital, Stanford

University of California at Los Angeles Medical Center, Los Angeles

University of California, Davis Medical Center, Sacramento

University of California Irvine Medical Center, Orange

University of California San Diego Medical Center, San Diego

University of California, San Francisco Medical Center, San Francisco

University of Southern California, The Kenneth Norris Jr. Cancer Hospital, Los Angeles

White Memorial Medical Center, Los Angeles

COLORADO

Denver Health and Hospitals, Denver

University of Colorado Health Sciences Center, University Hospital, Denver

CONNECTICUT

Hartford Hospital, Hartford

Hospital of St. Raphael, New Haven

New Britain General Hospital, New Britain

St. Francis Hospital and Medical Center, Hartford

University of Connecticut Health Center, John Dempsey Hospital, Farmington

Waterbury Hospital, Waterbury

*Yale-New Haven Hospital, New Haven

DELAWARE

Alfred I. Dupont Institute, Wilmington

DISTRICT OF COLUMBIA

District of Columbia General Hospital, Washington

*George Washington University Hospital, Washington

*Georgetown University Hospital, Washington

*Howard University Hospital, Washington

Sibley Memorial Hospital, Washington

Washington Hospital Center, Washington

FLORIDA

Jackson Memorial Hospital, Miami

*Shands Hospital at the University of Florida, Gainesville

Tampa General Hospital, Tampa

University of South Florida, H. Lee Moffitt Cancer Center, Tampa

GEORGIA

*Emory University Hospital, Atlanta

Grady Memorial Hospital, Atlanta

Medical College of Georgia Hospital and Clinics, Augusta

University Hospital, Augusta

ILLINOIS

Cook County Hospital, Chicago

Humana Hospital-Michael Reese, Chicago

*Loyola University of Chicago, Foster G. McGaw Hospital, Maywood

Memorial Medical Center, Springfield

Mt. Sinai Hospital Medical Center of Chicago, Chicago

*Northwestern Memorial Hospital, Chicago

*Rush-Presbyterian-St. Luke's Medical Center, Chicago

St. John's Hospital, Springfield

*University of Chicago Hospitals, Chicago

University of Illinois Hospital and Clinics, Chicago

INDIANA

Indiana University Medical Center, Indianapolis

Methodist Hospital of Indiana, Indianapolis

William N. Wishard Memorial Hospital, Indianapolis

IOWA

University of Iowa Hospitals and Clinics, Iowa City

KANSAS

University of Kansas Hospital, Kansas City

KENTUCKY

Humana Hospital-University of Louisville, Louisville

Jewish Hospital, Louisville

Norton Hospital, Louisville

St. Joseph Hospital, Lexington

University of Kentucky Hospital, Albert B. Chandler Medical Center, Lexington

LOUISIANA

Hotel Dieu Hospital, New Orleans

Huey P. Long Regional Medical Center, Pineville

Jo Ellen Smith Medical Center, New Orleans

Louisiana State University Hospital, Shreveport

Medical Center of Louisiana at New Orleans, New Orleans

Ochsner Foundation Hospital, New Orleans

Schumpert Medical Center, Shreveport

South Louisiana Medical Center, Houma

*Tulane University Hospital and Clinics, New Orleans

MAINE

Maine Medical Center, Portland

MARYLAND

Francis Scott Key Medical Center, Baltimore

*Johns Hopkins Hospital, Baltimore

Sinai Hospital of Baltimore, Baltimore

*University of Maryland Medical System, Baltimore

MASSACHUSETTS

*Beth Israel Hospital, Boston

Boston City Hospital, Boston

*Brigham and Women's Hospital, Boston

Lahey Clinic Hospital, Burlington

Lawrence F. Quigley Memorial Hospital, Chelsea

*Massachusetts General Hospital, Boston

Medical Center of Central Massachusetts, Worcester

New England Deaconess Hospital, Boston

*New England Medical Center, Boston

St. Elizabeth's Hospital of Boston, Boston

*University Hospital, Boston

University of Massachusetts Medical Center, Worcester

MICHIGAN

Detroit Receiving Hospital and University Health Center, Detroit

*Harper Hospital, Detroit

Henry Ford Hospital, Detroit

St. Joseph Mercy Hospital, Ann Arbor

University of Michigan Hospitals, Ann Arbor

William Beaumont Hospital, Royal Oak

MINNESOTA

Hennepin County Medical Center, Minneapolis

Mayo Clinic and Foundation, Rochester

Rochester Methodist Hospital, Rochester

*St. Marys Hospital, Rochester

St. Paul-Ramsey Medical Center, St. Paul

University of Minnesota Hospital and Clinic, Minneapolis

MISSISSIPPI

Mississippi Baptist Medical Center, Jackson

University of Mississippi Medical Center, University Hospitals and Clinics, Jackson

MISSOURI

*Barnes Hospital, St. Louis

Jewish Hospital of St. Louis, St. Louis

St. John's Mercy Medical Center, St. Louis

*St. Louis University Medical Center, St. Louis

St. Mary's Health Center, St. Louis

University Hospital and Clinics,
Columbia

NEBRASKA

AMI St. Joseph Hospital, Omaha

Methodist Hospital, Omaha

**University of Nebraska Medical
Center, Omaha**

NEW HAMPSHIRE

Dartmouth-Hitchcock Medical
Center, Hanover

NEW JERSEY

Cooper Hospital-University
Medical Center, Camden

Hackensack Medical Center,
Hackensack

Medical Center at Princeton,
Princeton

Newark Beth Israel Medical Center,
Newark

***Robert Wood Johnson University
Hospital, New Brunswick**

St. Barnabas Medical Center,
Livingston

St. Peter's Medical Center,
New Brunswick

**University of Medicine and
Dentistry of New Jersey, University
Hospital, Newark**

NEW MEXICO

Lovelace Medical Center,
Albuquerque

University Hospital, Albuquerque

NEW YORK

***Albany Medical Center Hospital,
Albany**

**Bellevue Hospital Center,
New York**

Beth Israel Medical Center,
New York

Booth Memorial Medical Center,
Flushing

Bronx-Lebanon Hospital Center,
Bronx

Bronx Municipal Hospital Center,
Bronx

Brookdale Hospital Medical
Center, Brooklyn

*Buffalo General Hospital, Buffalo

Cabrini Medical Center, New York

Coney Island Hospital, Brooklyn

Crouse-Irving Memorial Hospital,
Syracuse

Elmhurst Hospital Center, Flushing

**Erie County Medical Center,
Buffalo**

Genesee Hospital, Rochester

Harlem Hospital Center, New York

Interfaith Medical Center,
Brooklyn

**Kings County Hospital Center,
Brooklyn**

La Guardia Hospital, Forest Hills

Lenox Hill Hospital, New York

Lincoln Medical and Mental
Health Center, Bronx

Long Island College Hospital,
Brooklyn

Long Island Jewish Medical Center,
New Hyde Park

Maimonides Medical Center,
Brooklyn

Memorial Sloan-Kettering Cancer
Center, New York

Metropolitan Hospital Center,
New York

***Montefiore Medical Center, Henry
and Lucy Moses Division, Bronx**

Montefiore Medical Center, Jack
D. Weiler Hospital of the Albert
Einstein College of Medicine,
Bronx

***Mt. Sinai Medical Center,
New York**

Nassau County Medical Center,
East Meadow

***New York Hospital-Cornell
Medical Center, New York**

***New York University Medical
Center, New York**

North Central Bronx Hospital,
Bronx

North Shore University Hospital,
Manhasset

Our Lady of Mercy Medical Center,
Bronx

***Presbyterian Hospital in
the City of New York, Columbia-
Presbyterian Medical Center,
New York**

Queens Hospital Center, Jamaica

Rochester General Hospital,
Rochester

Roswell Park Cancer Institute,
Buffalo

St. Joseph's Hospital Health
Center, Syracuse

St. Luke's-Roosevelt Hospital
Center, Roosevelt Division,
New York

St. Luke's-Roosevelt Hospital
Center, St. Luke's Division,
New York

St. Vincent's Hospital and Medical
Center of New York, New York

**State University of New York at
Stony Brook University Hospital,
Stony Brook**

**State University of New York
Health Science Center, University
Hospital, Syracuse**

**State University of New York
Health Sciences Center at Brooklyn,
University Hospital of Brooklyn,
Brooklyn**

***Strong Memorial Hospital of the
University of Rochester, Rochester**

**Westchester County Medical
Center, Valhalla**

Winthrop-University Hospital,
Mineola

NORTH CAROLINA

***Duke University Medical Center,
Durham**

Forsyth Memorial Hospital,
Winston-Salem

***North Carolina Baptist Hospital,
Winston-Salem**

**Pitt County Memorial Hospital,
Greenville**

**University of North Carolina
Hospitals, Chapel Hill**

Wake Medical Center, Raleigh

OHIO

Akron City Hospital, Akron

Akron General Medical Center,
Akron

Cleveland Clinic Hospital, Cleveland

Medical College of Ohio Hospital, Toledo

MetroHealth Medical Center, Cleveland

Ohio State University Hospitals, Columbus

Riverside Methodist Hospitals, Columbus

St. Vincent Medical Center, Toledo

Toledo Hospital, Toledo

*University Hospitals of Cleveland, Cleveland

University of Cincinnati Hospital, Cincinnati

OKLAHOMA

Oklahoma Medical Center, Oklahoma City

OREGON

Oregon Health Sciences University, University Hospital, Portland

PENNSYLVANIA

Abington Memorial Hospital, Abington

Albert Einstein Medical Center, Philadelphia

*Allegheny General Hospital, Pittsburgh

Bryn Mawr Hospital, Bryn Mawr

Geisinger Medical Center, Danville

*Hahnemann University Hospital, Philadelphia

*Hospital of the Medical College of Pennsylvania, Philadelphia

*Hospital of the University of Pennsylvania, Philadelphia

Lancaster General Hospital, Lancaster

Lankenau Hospital, Wynnewood

Montefiore University Hospital, Pittsburgh

Penn State University Hospital, The Milton S. Hershey Medical Center, Hershey

Pennsylvania Hospital, Philadelphia

*Presbyterian University Hospital, Pittsburgh

*Temple University Hospital, Philadelphia

*Thomas Jefferson University Hospital, Philadelphia

PUERTO RICO

University Hospital, San Juan

RHODE ISLAND

*Rhode Island Hospital, Providence

Roger Williams Hospital, Providence

SOUTH CAROLINA

Charleston Memorial Hospital, Charleston

Medical University of South Carolina, Medical Center of Medical University of South Carolina, Charleston

TENNESSEE

Baptist Hospital, Nashville

Baptist Memorial Hospital, Memphis

Methodist Hospitals of Memphis Central Unit, Memphis

Metropolitan Nashville General Hospital, Nashville

Regional Medical Center at Memphis, Memphis

*Vanderbilt University Hospital and Clinic, Nashville

TEXAS

Baylor University Medical Center, Dallas

Bexar County Hospital District, Medical Center Hospital, San Antonio

Dallas County Hospital District, Parkland Memorial Hospital, Dallas

Harris County Hospital District, Ben Taub General Hospital, Houston

*Hermann Hospital, Houston

Humana Hospital-San Antonio, San Antonio

*Methodist Hospital, Houston

*Scott and White Memorial Hospital, Temple

St. Joseph Hospital, Houston

St. Luke's Episcopal Hospital, Houston

University Medical Center, Lubbock

University of Texas M.D. Anderson Cancer Center, Houston

University of Texas Medical Branch Hospitals, Galveston

UTAH

LDS Hospital, Salt Lake City

University of Utah Hospital and Clinics, Salt Lake City

VERMONT

Fanny Allen Hospital, Colchester

*Medical Center Hospital of Vermont, Burlington

VIRGINIA

Arlington Hospital, Arlington

Fairfax Hospital, Falls Church

Memorial Hospital of Danville, Danville

Sentara Leigh Hospital, Norfolk

Sentara Norfolk General Hospital, Norfolk

University of Virginia Medical Center, Charlottesville

Virginia Commonwealth University, Medical College of Virginia Hospitals, Richmond

WASHINGTON

Harborview Medical Center, Seattle

University of Washington Medical Center, Seattle

Virginia Mason Medical Center, Seattle

WEST VIRGINIA

Ohio Valley Medical Center, Wheeling

*West Virginia University Hospitals, Morgantown

WISCONSIN

*Froedtert Memorial Lutheran Hospital, Milwaukee

Lutheran Hospital-La Crosse, La Crosse

Milwaukee County Medical Complex, Milwaukee

University of Wisconsin Hospital and Clinics, Madison

The Lungs and Respiratory System

ALABAMA

University of Alabama Hospitals, Birmingham

University of South Alabama Medical Center, Mobile

ARIZONA

Good Samaritan Regional Medical Center, Phoenix

*University Medical Center, Tucson

ARKANSAS

University Hospital of Arkansas, Little Rock

CALIFORNIA

Barlow Respiratory Hospital, Los Angeles

California-Pacific Medical Center, San Francisco

Cedars-Sinai Medical Center, Los Angeles

Hospital of the Good Samaritan, Los Angeles

Kaiser Foundation Hospital, Fontana

*Loma Linda University Medical Center, Loma Linda

Los Angeles County Harbor-University of California at Los Angeles Medical Center, Torrance

Los Angeles County-King-Drew Medical Center, Los Angeles

Los Angeles County-University of Southern California Medical Center, Los Angeles

Olive View Medical Center, Sylmar

Santa Clara Valley Medical Center, San Jose

Sharp Memorial Hospital, San Diego

St. Joseph Hospital, Orange

*Stanford University Hospital, Stanford

University of California at Los Angeles Medical Center, Los Angeles

University of California, Davis Medical Center, Sacramento

University of California Irvine Medical Center, Orange

University of California San Diego Medical Center, San Diego

University of California, San Francisco Medical Center, San Francisco

COLORADO

Denver Health and Hospitals, Denver

University of Colorado Health Sciences Center, University Hospital, Denver

CONNECTICUT

Mt. Sinai Hospital, Hartford

Norwalk Hospital, Norwalk

University of Connecticut Health Center, John Dempsey Hospital, Farmington

*Yale-New Haven Hospital, New Haven

DELAWARE

Medical Center of Delaware, Wilmington

DISTRICT OF COLUMBIA

District of Columbia General Hospital, Washington

*George Washington University Hospital, Washington

*Georgetown University Hospital, Washington

*Howard University Hospital, Washington

Washington Hospital Center, Washington

FLORIDA

Jackson Memorial Hospital, Miami

Mt. Sinai Medical Center, Miami Beach

*Shands Hospital at the University of Florida, Gainesville

Tampa General Hospital, Tampa

University of South Florida, H. Lee Moffitt Cancer Center, Tampa

GEORGIA

*Crawford Long Hospital of Emory University, Atlanta

*Emory University Hospital, Atlanta

Grady Memorial Hospital, Atlanta

Medical College of Georgia Hospital and Clinics, Augusta

ILLINOIS

Cook County Hospital, Chicago

Evanston Hospital, Evanston

Humana Hospital-Michael Reese, Chicago

*Loyola University of Chicago, Foster G. McGaw Hospital, Maywood

Mt. Sinai Hospital Medical Center of Chicago, Chicago

*Northwestern Memorial Hospital, Chicago

*Rush-Presbyterian-St. Luke's Medical Center, Chicago

*University of Chicago Hospitals, Chicago

University of Illinois Hospital and Clinics, Chicago

INDIANA

Indiana University Medical Center, Indianapolis

Methodist Hospital of Indiana, Indianapolis

IOWA

University of Iowa Hospitals and Clinics, Iowa City

KANSAS

Truman Medical Center-West, Kansas City

University of Kansas Hospital,
Kansas City

KENTUCKY

**Humana Hospital-University
of Louisville, Louisville**

Jewish Hospital, Louisville

**University of Kentucky Hospital,
Albert B. Chandler Medical Center,
Lexington**

LOUISIANA

Hotel Dieu Hospital, New Orleans

**Louisiana State University
Hospital, Shreveport**

**Medical Center of Louisiana at
New Orleans, New Orleans**

Ochsner Foundation Hospital,
New Orleans

Southern Baptist Hospital,
New Orleans

Touro Infirmary, New Orleans

***Tulane University Hospital
and Clinics, New Orleans**

MAINE

Maine Medical Center, Portland

MARYLAND

Francis Scott Key Medical Center,
Baltimore

***Johns Hopkins Hospital,
Baltimore**

***University of Maryland Medical
System, Baltimore**

MASSACHUSETTS

Boston City Hospital, Boston

***Brigham and Women's Hospital,
Boston**

Lahey Clinic Hospital, Burlington

***Massachusetts General Hospital,
Boston**

Mt. Auburn Hospital, Cambridge

New England Deaconess Hospital,
Boston

***New England Medical Center,
Boston**

St. Elizabeth's Hospital of Boston,
Boston

St. Vincent Hospital, Worcester

*University Hospital, Boston

**University of Massachusetts
Medical Center, Worcester**

MICHIGAN

Detroit Receiving Hospital and
University Health Center, Detroit

*Harper Hospital, Detroit

Henry Ford Hospital, Detroit

Ingham Medical Center, Lansing

Sinai Hospital, Detroit

**University of Michigan Hospitals,
Ann Arbor**

MINNESOTA

Mayo Clinic and Foundation,
Rochester

Rochester Methodist Hospital,
Rochester

*St. Marys Hospital, Rochester

St. Paul-Ramsey Medical Center,
St. Paul

**University of Minnesota Hospital
and Clinic, Minneapolis**

MISSISSIPPI

**University of Mississippi Medical
Center, University Hospitals and
Clinics, Jackson**

MISSOURI

*Barnes Hospital, St. Louis

Jewish Hospital of St. Louis,
St. Louis

***St. Louis University Medical
Center, St. Louis**

St. Luke's Hospital, Kansas City

St. Mary's Health Center, St. Louis

**University Hospital and Clinics,
Columbia**

NEBRASKA

AMI St. Joseph Hospital, Omaha

**University of Nebraska Medical
Center, Omaha**

NEW HAMPSHIRE

Dartmouth-Hitchcock Medical
Center, Hanover

NEW JERSEY

Community Medical Center,
Scranton

Cooper Hospital-University Medical
Center, Camden

Deborah Heart and Lung Center,
Brown Mills

Hackensack Medical Center,
Hackensack

Newark Beth Israel Medical Center,
Newark

***Robert Wood Johnson University
Hospital, New Brunswick**

St. Michael's Medical Center,
Newark

St. Peter's Medical Center,
New Brunswick

United Hospitals Medical Center,
Newark

**University of Medicine and
Dentistry of New Jersey, University
Hospital, Newark**

NEW MEXICO

University Hospital, Albuquerque

NEW YORK

***Albany Medical Center Hospital,
Albany**

**Bellevue Hospital Center,
New York**

Beth Israel Medical Center,
New York

Booth Memorial Medical Center,
Flushing

Bronx-Lebanon Hospital Center,
Bronx

Bronx Municipal Hospital Center,
Bronx

Brookdale Hospital Medical
Center, Brooklyn

Brooklyn Hospital Center,
Brooklyn

*Buffalo General Hospital, Buffalo

Cabrini Medical Center, New York

Coney Island Hospital, Brooklyn

Crouse-Irving Memorial Hospital,
Syracuse

Elmhurst Hospital Center, Flushing

**Erie County Medical Center,
Buffalo**

Harlem Hospital Center, New York

Interfaith Medical Center, Brooklyn

Kings County Hospital Center, Brooklyn

Lenox Hill Hospital, New York

Lincoln Medical and Mental Health Center, Bronx

Long Island College Hospital, Brooklyn

Long Island Jewish Medical Center, New Hyde Park

Maimonides Medical Center, Brooklyn

Mary Immaculate Hospital, Jamaica

Memorial Sloan-Kettering Cancer Center, New York

Methodist Hospital of Brooklyn, Brooklyn

Metropolitan Hospital Center, New York

Millard Fillmore Hospitals, Buffalo

*Montefiore Medical Center, Henry and Lucy Moses Division, Bronx

Montefiore Medical Center, Jack D. Weiler Hospital of the Albert Einstein College of Medicine, Bronx

*Mt. Sinai Medical Center, New York

Nassau County Medical Center, East Meadow

*New York Hospital-Cornell Medical Center, New York

*New York University Medical Center, New York

North Shore University Hospital, Manhasset

*Presbyterian Hospital in the City of New York, Columbia-Presbyterian Medical Center, New York

Rochester General Hospital, Rochester

Roswell Park Cancer Institute, Buffalo

St. Luke's-Roosevelt Hospital Center, Roosevelt Division, New York

St. Luke's-Roosevelt Hospital Center, St. Luke's Division, New York

St. Vincent's Hospital and Medical Center of New York, New York

State University of New York at Stony Brook University Hospital, Stony Brook

State University of New York Health Science Center, University Hospital, Syracuse

State University of New York Health Sciences Center at Brooklyn, University Hospital of Brooklyn, Brooklyn

*Strong Memorial Hospital of the University of Rochester, Rochester

Westchester County Medical Center, Valhalla

Winthrop-University Hospital, Mineola

NORTH CAROLINA

Carolinas Medical Center, Charlotte

*Duke University Medical Center, Durham

*North Carolina Baptist Hospital, Winston-Salem

Pitt County Memorial Hospital, Greenville

University of North Carolina Hospitals, Chapel Hill

OHIO

Cleveland Clinic Hospital, Cleveland

Medical College of Ohio Hospital, Toledo

MetroHealth Medical Center, Cleveland

Ohio State University Hospitals, Columbus

St. Vincent Medical Center, Toledo

Toledo Hospital, Toledo

*University Hospitals of Cleveland, Cleveland

University of Cincinnati Hospital, Cincinnati

OKLAHOMA

Oklahoma Medical Center, Oklahoma City

OREGON

Oregon Health Sciences University, University Hospital, Portland

PENNSYLVANIA

Albert Einstein Medical Center, Philadelphia

*Allegheny General Hospital, Pittsburgh

Crozer-Chester Medical Center, Upland

Geisinger Medical Center, Danville

Graduate Hospital, Philadelphia

*Hahnemann University Hospital, Philadelphia

*Hospital of the Medical College of Pennsylvania, Philadelphia

*Hospital of the University of Pennsylvania, Philadelphia

Montefiore University Hospital, Pittsburgh

Penn State University Hospital, The Milton S. Hershey Medical Center, Hershey

Presbyterian Medical Center of Philadelphia, Philadelphia

*Presbyterian University Hospital, Pittsburgh

*Temple University Hospital, Philadelphia

*Thomas Jefferson University Hospital, Philadelphia

Western Pennsylvania Hospital, Pittsburgh

PUERTO RICO

San Juan Municipal Hospital, Rio Piedras

University Hospital, San Juan

RHODE ISLAND

Memorial Hospital of Rhode Island, Pawtucket

Roger Williams Hospital, Providence

SOUTH CAROLINA

Charleston Memorial Hospital, Charleston

Medical University of South Carolina, Medical Center of

Medical University of South Carolina, Charleston

Richland Memorial Hospital, Columbia

TENNESSEE

Baptist Memorial Hospital, Memphis

Johnson City Medical Center Hospital, Johnson City

Regional Medical Center at Memphis, Memphis

University of Tennessee Medical Center, Memphis

*Vanderbilt University Hospital and Clinic, Nashville

TEXAS

Bexar County Hospital District, Medical Center Hospital, San Antonio

Dallas County Hospital District, Parkland Memorial Hospital, Dallas

Harris County Hospital District, Ben Taub General Hospital, Houston

*Hermann Hospital, Houston

*Methodist Hospital, Houston

*Scott and White Memorial Hospital, Temple

St. Luke's Episcopal Hospital, Houston

University of Texas M.D. Anderson Cancer Center, Houston

University of Texas Medical Branch Hospitals, Galveston

UTAH

LDS Hospital, Salt Lake City

University of Utah Hospital and Clinics, Salt Lake City

VERMONT

*Medical Center Hospital of Vermont, Burlington

VIRGINIA

Roanoke Memorial Hospitals, Roanoke

University of Virginia Medical Center, Charlottesville

Virginia Commonwealth University, Medical College of Virginia Hospitals, Richmond

WASHINGTON

Harborview Medical Center, Seattle

University of Washington Medical Center, Seattle

WEST VIRGINIA

Cabell Huntington Hospital, Huntington

Monongalia General Hospital, Morgantown

St. Mary's Hospital, Huntington

*West Virginia University Hospitals, Morgantown

WISCONSIN

*Froedtert Memorial Lutheran Hospital, Milwaukee

Milwaukee County Medical Complex, Milwaukee

St. Luke's Medical Center, Milwaukee

University of Wisconsin Hospital and Clinics, Madison

The Muscles and Bones

▼ indicates National Institute of Arthritis and Musculoskeletal and Skin Diseases: Multipurpose Arthritis and Musculoskeletal Diseases Center

ALABAMA

Cooper Green Hospital, Birmingham

▼University of Alabama Hospitals, Birmingham

University of South Alabama Medical Center, Mobile

ARIZONA

Maricopa Medical Center, Phoenix

*University Medical Center, Tucson

ARKANSAS

University Hospital of Arkansas, Little Rock

CALIFORNIA

Cedars-Sinai Medical Center, Los Angeles

Centinela Hospital Medical Center, Inglewood

Century City Hospital, Los Angeles

▼Green Hospital of Scripps Clinic, La Jolla

Highland General Hospital, Oakland

Kaiser Foundation Hospital, Sacramento

Kaiser Foundation Hospital, San Francisco

*Loma Linda University Medical Center, Loma Linda

Los Angeles County Harbor-University of California at Los Angeles Medical Center, Torrance

Los Angeles County-King-Drew Medical Center, Los Angeles

Los Angeles County-Rancho Los Amigos Medical Center, Downey

Los Angeles County-University of Southern California Medical Center, Los Angeles

Mt. Zion Medical Center of University of California, San Francisco, San Francisco

Orthopaedic Hospital, Los Angeles

San Bernardino County Medical Center, San Bernardino

San Francisco General Hospital and Medical Center, San Francisco

Santa Clara Valley Medical Center, San Jose

Seton Medical Center, Daly City

St. Mary's Hospital and Medical Center, San Francisco

▼*Stanford University Hospital, Stanford

▼University of California at Los Angeles Medical Center, Los Angeles

University of California, Davis Medical Center, Sacramento

University of California Irvine Medical Center, Orange

University of California San Diego Medical Center, San Diego

University of California, San Francisco Medical Center, San Francisco

COLORADO

Denver Health and Hospitals, Denver

University of Colorado Health Sciences Center, University Hospital, Denver

CONNECTICUT

Hartford Hospital, Hartford

Hospital of St. Raphael, New Haven

St. Francis Hospital and Medical Center, Hartford

▼University of Connecticut Health Center, John Dempsey Hospital, Farmington

*Yale-New Haven Hospital, New Haven

DELAWARE

Alfred I. Dupont Institute, Wilmington

DISTRICT OF COLUMBIA

District of Columbia General Hospital, Washington

*George Washington University Hospital, Washington

*Georgetown University Hospital, Washington

Greater Southeast Community Hospital, Washington

*Howard University Hospital, Washington

Providence Hospital, Washington

Sibley Memorial Hospital, Washington

Washington Hospital Center, Washington

FLORIDA

Doctors' Hospital, Coral Gables

Jackson Memorial Hospital, Miami

Orlando Regional Medical Center, Orlando

*Shands Hospital at the University of Florida, Gainesville

Tampa General Hospital, Tampa

University Medical Center, Jacksonville

GEORGIA

*Crawford Long Hospital of Emory University, Atlanta

*Emory University Hospital, Atlanta

Georgia Baptist Medical Center, Atlanta

Grady Memorial Hospital, Atlanta

Hughston Sports Medicine Hospital, Columbus

Medical College of Georgia Hospital and Clinics, Augusta

University Hospital, Augusta

HAWAII

Queen's Medical Center, Honolulu

ILLINOIS

Christ Hospital and Medical Center, Oak Lawn

Cook County Hospital, Chicago

Evanston Hospital, Evanston

Humana Hospital-Michael Reese, Chicago

Illinois Masonic Medical Center, Chicago

*Loyola University of Chicago, Foster G. McGaw Hospital, Maywood

Lutheran General Hospital, Chicago

Memorial Medical Center, Springfield

Mercy Hospital and Medical Center, Chicago

▼*Northwestern Memorial Hospital, Chicago

Ravenswood Hospital Medical Center, Chicago

*Rush-Presbyterian-St. Luke's Medical Center, Chicago

St. Francis Hospital of Evanston, Evanston

St. John's Hospital, Springfield

*University of Chicago Hospitals, Chicago

University of Illinois Hospital and Clinics, Chicago

INDIANA

▼Indiana University Medical Center, Indianapolis

Lutheran Hospital of Indiana, Fort Wayne

Methodist Hospital of Indiana, Indianapolis

Parkview Memorial Hospital, Fort Wayne

St. Joseph Medical Center, Fort Wayne

St. Vincent Hospital and Health Care Center, Indianapolis

William N. Wishard Memorial Hospital, Indianapolis

IOWA

University of Iowa Hospitals and Clinics, Iowa City

KANSAS

HCA Wesley Medical Center, Wichita

St. Francis Regional Medical Center, Wichita

Truman Medical Center-West, Kansas City

University of Kansas Hospital, Kansas City

KENTUCKY

Frazier Rehabilitation Center, Louisville

Humana Hospital-University of Louisville, Louisville

Jewish Hospital, Louisville

Methodist Evangelical Hospital, Louisville

Norton Hospital, Louisville

University of Kentucky Hospital, Albert B. Chandler Medical Center, Lexington

LOUISIANA

Earl K. Long Memorial Hospital, Baton Rouge

Hotel Dieu Hospital, New Orleans

Huey P. Long Regional Medical Center, Pineville

Louisiana State University Hospital, Shreveport

Medical Center of Louisiana at New Orleans, New Orleans

Ochsner Foundation Hospital, New Orleans

South Louisiana Medical Center, Houma

Touro Infirmary, New Orleans

*Tulane University Hospital and Clinics, New Orleans

University Medical Center, Lafayette

MARYLAND

Francis Scott Key Medical Center, Baltimore

Good Samaritan Hospital of Maryland, Baltimore

James Lawrence Kernan Hospital, Baltimore

*Johns Hopkins Hospital, Baltimore

Sinai Hospital of Baltimore, Baltimore

St. Agnes Hospital of the City of Baltimore, Baltimore

Union Memorial Hospital, Baltimore

*University of Maryland Medical System, Baltimore

MASSACHUSETTS

Baystate Medical Center, Springfield

*Beth Israel Hospital, Boston

▼Boston City Hospital, Boston

▼*Brigham and Women's Hospital, Boston

Carney Hospital, Boston

Lahey Clinic Hospital, Burlington

*Massachusetts General Hospital, Boston

Medical Center of Central Massachusetts, Worcester

New England Baptist Hospital, Boston

*New England Medical Center, Boston

Newton-Wellesley Hospital, Newton

St. Elizabeth's Hospital of Boston, Boston

St. Vincent Hospital, Worcester

▼*University Hospital, Boston

University of Massachusetts Medical Center, Worcester

Worcester Health and Hospitals Authority, Worcester

MICHIGAN

Blodgett Memorial Medical Center, Grand Rapids

Borgess Medical Center, Kalamazoo

Bronson Methodist Hospital, Kalamazoo

Butterworth Hospital, Grand Rapids

Detroit Receiving Hospital and University Health Center, Detroit

*Grace Hospital, Detroit

*Harper Hospital, Detroit

Henry Ford Hospital, Detroit

Hurley Medical Center, Flint

Hutzel Hospital, Detroit

McLaren Regional Medical Center, Flint

Oakwood Hospital, Dearborn

Providence Hospital, Southfield

Sinai Hospital, Detroit

St. Joseph Mercy Hospital, Ann Arbor

St. Mary's Health Services, Grand Rapids

▼University of Michigan Hospitals, Ann Arbor

William Beaumont Hospital, Royal Oak

MINNESOTA

Hennepin County Medical Center, Minneapolis

Mayo Clinic and Foundation, Rochester

Rochester Methodist Hospital, Rochester

*St. Marys Hospital, Rochester

University of Minnesota Hospital and Clinic, Minneapolis

MISSISSIPPI

University of Mississippi Medical Center, University Hospitals and Clinics, Jackson

MISSOURI

*Barnes Hospital, St. Louis

Jewish Hospital of St. Louis, St. Louis

St. Louis Regional Medical Center, St. Louis

*St. Louis University Medical Center, St. Louis

St. Luke's Hospital, Kansas City

St. Mary's Health Center, St. Louis

University Hospital and Clinics, Columbia

NEBRASKA

AMI St. Joseph Hospital, Omaha

University of Nebraska Medical Center, Omaha

NEW HAMPSHIRE

Dartmouth-Hitchcock Medical Center, Hanover

NEW JERSEY

Atlantic City Medical Center, Atlantic City

Cooper Hospital-University Medical Center, Camden

Hackensack Medical Center, Hackensack

Hospital Center at Orange, Orange

Jersey City Medical Center, Jersey City

Monmouth Medical Center, Long Branch

Newark Beth Israel Medical Center, Newark

*Robert Wood Johnson University Hospital, New Brunswick

St. Joseph's Hospital and Medical Center, Paterson

St. Michael's Medical Center, Newark

St. Peter's Medical Center, New Brunswick

United Hospitals Medical Center, Newark

United Hospitals Medical Center, Orthopedic Unit, Newark

University of Medicine and Dentistry of New Jersey, University Hospital, Newark

NEW MEXICO

University Hospital, Albuquerque

NEW YORK

*Albany Medical Center Hospital, Albany

Bellevue Hospital Center, New York

Bronx-Lebanon Hospital Center, Bronx

Bronx Municipal Hospital Center, Bronx

Brookdale Hospital Medical Center, Brooklyn

*Buffalo General Hospital, Buffalo

Cabrini Medical Center, New York

Coney Island Hospital, Brooklyn

Crouse-Irving Memorial Hospital, Syracuse

Ellis Hospital, Schenectady

Elmhurst Hospital Center, Flushing

Erie County Medical Center, Buffalo

Genesee Hospital, Rochester

Harlem Hospital Center, New York

Helen Hayes Hospital, West Haverstraw

Highland Hospital of Rochester, Rochester

Hospital for Joint Diseases Orthopedic Institute, New York

Hospital for Special Surgery, New York

Kings County Hospital Center, Brooklyn

Kingsbrook Jewish Medical Center, Brooklyn

Lenox Hill Hospital, New York

Lincoln Medical and Mental Health Center, Bronx

Long Island College Hospital, Brooklyn

Long Island Jewish Medical Center, New Hyde Park

Maimonides Medical Center, Brooklyn

Mary Immaculate Hospital, Jamaica

Metropolitan Hospital Center, New York

Millard Fillmore Hospitals, Buffalo

Monroe Community Hospital, Rochester

*Montefiore Medical Center, Henry and Lucy Moses Division, Bronx

Montefiore Medical Center, Jack D. Weiler Hospital of the Albert Einstein College of Medicine, Bronx

*Mt. Sinai Medical Center, New York

Nassau County Medical Center, East Meadow

▼*New York Hospital-Cornell Medical Center, New York

*New York University Medical Center, New York

North Central Bronx Hospital, Bronx

North Shore University Hospital, Manhasset

*Presbyterian Hospital in the City of New York, Columbia-Presbyterian Medical Center, New York

Queens Hospital Center, Jamaica

Rochester General Hospital, Rochester

St. Charles Hospital and Rehabilitation Center, Port Jefferson

St. John's Queens Hospital, Elmhurst

St. Luke's-Roosevelt Hospital Center, St. Luke's Division, New York

St. Mary's Hospital, Brooklyn

St. Peter's Hospital, Albany

St. Vincent's Hospital and Medical Center of New York, New York

State University of New York at Stony Brook University Hospital, Stony Brook

State University of New York Health Science Center, University Hospital, Syracuse

State University of New York Health Sciences Center at Brooklyn, University Hospital of Brooklyn, Brooklyn

*Strong Memorial Hospital of the University of Rochester, Rochester

Westchester County Medical Center, Valhalla

NORTH CAROLINA

Carolinas Medical Center, Charlotte

*Duke University Medical Center, Durham

Durham County General Hospital, Durham

*North Carolina Baptist Hospital, Winston-Salem

Orthopaedic Hospital of Charlotte, Charlotte

▼University of North Carolina Hospitals, Chapel Hill

Wake Medical Center, Raleigh

OHIO

Akron City Hospital, Akron

Akron General Medical Center, Akron

Bethesda Oak Hospital, Cincinnati

Cleveland Clinic Hospital, Cleveland

Good Samaritan Hospital, Cincinnati

Medical College of Ohio Hospital, Toledo

MetroHealth Medical Center, Cleveland

Miami Valley Hospital, Dayton

Mt. Carmel Medical Center, Columbus

Mt. Sinai Medical Center, Cleveland

Ohio State University Hospitals, Columbus

Riverside Methodist Hospitals, Columbus

St. Luke's Hospital, Cleveland

St. Vincent Medical Center, Toledo

Toledo Hospital, Toledo

▼*University Hospitals of Cleveland, Cleveland

University of Cincinnati Hospital, Cincinnati

OKLAHOMA

Bone and Joint Hospital, Oklahoma City

Oklahoma Medical Center, Oklahoma City

Presbyterian Hospital,
Oklahoma City

OREGON

Emanuel Hospital and Health
Center, Portland

**Oregon Health Sciences University,
University Hospital, Portland**

PENNSYLVANIA

Abington Memorial Hospital,
Abington

Albert Einstein Medical Center,
Philadelphia

Bryn Mawr Hospital, Bryn Mawr

Delaware County Memorial
Hospital, Drexel Hill

Geisinger Medical Center, Danville

***Hahnemann University Hospital,
Philadelphia**

Hamot Medical Center, Erie

Harrisburg Hospital, Harrisburg

***Hospital of the Medical College
of Pennsylvania, Philadelphia**

***Hospital of the University of
Pennsylvania, Philadelphia**

Lankenau Hospital, Wynnewood

Mercy Catholic Medical Center,
Fitzgerald Mercy Division,
Philadelphia

Mercy Hospital of Pittsburgh,
Pittsburgh

Methodist Hospital, Philadelphia

Montefiore University Hospital,
Pittsburgh

Moss Rehabilitation Hospital,
Philadelphia

Penn State University Hospital,
Elizabethtown Hospital, Hershey

**Penn State University Hospital,
The Milton S. Hershey Medical
Center, Hershey**

Pennsylvania Hospital,
Philadelphia

Polyclinic Medical Center of
Harrisburg, Harrisburg

***Presbyterian University Hospital,
Pittsburgh**

St. Margaret Memorial Hospital,
Pittsburgh

***Temple University Hospital,
Philadelphia**

***Thomas Jefferson University
Hospital, Philadelphia**

PUERTO RICO

San Juan Municipal Hospital,
Rio Piedras

University Hospital, San Juan

RHODE ISLAND

***Rhode Island Hospital,
Providence**

Roger Williams Hospital,
Providence

SOUTH CAROLINA

Greenville Memorial Hospital,
Greenville

**Medical University of South
Carolina, Medical Center of
Medical University of South
Carolina, Charleston**

Richland Memorial Hospital,
Columbia

TENNESSEE

Baptist Memorial Hospital,
Memphis

Erlanger Medical Center,
Chattanooga

Metropolitan Nashville General
Hospital, Nashville

**Regional Medical Center
at Memphis, Memphis**

St. Thomas Hospital, Nashville

***Vanderbilt University Hospital
and Clinic, Nashville**

TEXAS

Baylor University Medical Center,
Dallas

**Bexar County Hospital District,
Medical Center Hospital,
San Antonio**

**Dallas County Hospital District,
Parkland Memorial Hospital,
Dallas**

Harris County Hospital District, Ben
Taub General Hospital, Houston

Harris Methodist Fort Worth,
Fort Worth

*Hermann Hospital, Houston

*Methodist Hospital, Houston

R.E. Thomason General Hospital,
El Paso

***Scott and White Memorial
Hospital, Temple**

St. Joseph Hospital, Houston

St. Mary of the Plains Hospital,
Lubbock

Tarrant County Hospital District,
John Peter Smith Hospital,
Fort Worth

University of Texas M.D. Anderson
Cancer Center, Houston

**University of Texas Medical
Branch Hospitals, Galveston**

UTAH

Holy Cross Hospital, Salt Lake City

LDS Hospital, Salt Lake City

**University of Utah Hospital
and Clinics, Salt Lake City**

VERMONT

***Medical Center Hospital of
Vermont, Burlington**

VIRGINIA

Arlington Hospital, Arlington

Fairfax Hospital, Falls Church

Roanoke Memorial Hospitals,
Roanoke

Sentara Leigh Hospital, Norfolk

Sentara Norfolk General Hospital,
Norfolk

**University of Virginia Medical
Center, Charlottesville**

**Virginia Commonwealth University,
Medical College of Virginia
Hospitals, Richmond**

WASHINGTON

**Harborview Medical Center,
Seattle**

Swedish Hospital Medical Center,
Seattle

**University of Washington Medical
Center, Seattle**

Virginia Mason Medical Center,
Seattle

WEST VIRGINIA

Monongalia General Hospital, Morgantown

*West Virginia University Hospitals, Morgantown

WISCONSIN

Columbia Hospital, Milwaukee

*Froedtert Memorial Lutheran Hospital, Milwaukee

Meriter Hospital, Madison

Milwaukee County Medical Complex, Milwaukee

Sinai Samaritan Medical Center-Mt. Sinai Campus, Milwaukee

St. Joseph's Hospital, Milwaukee

St. Marys Hospital Medical Center, Madison

University of Wisconsin Hospital and Clinics, Madison

The Skin

ALABAMA

University of Alabama Hospitals, Birmingham

ARIZONA

Kino Community Hospital, Tucson

*University Medical Center, Tucson

ARKANSAS

University Hospital of Arkansas, Little Rock

CALIFORNIA

*Loma Linda University Medical Center, Loma Linda

Los Angeles County Harbor-University of California at Los Angeles Medical Center, Torrance

Los Angeles County-King-Drew Medical Center, Los Angeles

Los Angeles County-University of Southern California Medical Center, Los Angeles

San Francisco General Hospital and Medical Center, San Francisco

Santa Clara Valley Medical Center, San Jose

*Stanford University Hospital, Stanford

University of California at Los Angeles Medical Center, Los Angeles

University of California, Davis Medical Center, Sacramento

University of California Irvine Medical Center, Orange

University of California San Diego Medical Center, San Diego

University of California, San Francisco Medical Center, San Francisco

COLORADO

Denver Health and Hospitals, Denver

University of Colorado Health Sciences Center, University Hospital, Denver

CONNECTICUT

*Yale-New Haven Hospital, New Haven

DISTRICT OF COLUMBIA

*George Washington University Hospital, Washington

*Howard University Hospital, Washington

Washington Hospital Center, Washington

FLORIDA

Jackson Memorial Hospital, Miami

Mt. Sinai Medical Center, Miami Beach

Tampa General Hospital, Tampa

GEORGIA

*Emory University Hospital, Atlanta

Grady Memorial Hospital, Atlanta

Medical College of Georgia Hospital and Clinics, Augusta

University Hospital, Augusta

ILLINOIS

Cook County Hospital, Chicago

*Loyola University of Chicago, Foster G. McGaw Hospital, Maywood

*Northwestern Memorial Hospital, Chicago

*Rush-Presbyterian-St. Luke's Medical Center, Chicago

*University of Chicago Hospitals, Chicago

University of Illinois Hospital and Clinics, Chicago

INDIANA

Indiana University Medical Center, Indianapolis

William N. Wishard Memorial Hospital, Indianapolis

IOWA

University of Iowa Hospitals and Clinics, Iowa City

KANSAS

University of Kansas Hospital, Kansas City

KENTUCKY

Humana Hospital-University of Louisville, Louisville

LOUISIANA

Medical Center of Louisiana at New Orleans, New Orleans

Ochsner Foundation Hospital, New Orleans

*Tulane University Hospital and Clinics, New Orleans

MARYLAND

Good Samaritan Hospital of Maryland, Baltimore

*Johns Hopkins Hospital, Baltimore

*University of Maryland Medical System, Baltimore

MASSACHUSETTS

*Beth Israel Hospital, Boston

Boston City Hospital, Boston

*Brigham and Women's Hospital, Boston**

Lahey Clinic Hospital, Burlington

Massachusetts General Hospital, Boston

New England Medical Center, Boston

University Hospital, Boston

MICHIGAN

Detroit Receiving Hospital and University Health Center, Detroit

Harper Hospital, Detroit

Henry Ford Hospital, Detroit

University of Michigan Hospitals, Ann Arbor

MINNESOTA

Hennepin County Medical Center, Minneapolis

Mayo Clinic and Foundation, Rochester

Rochester Methodist Hospital, Rochester

St. Marys Hospital, Rochester

St. Paul-Ramsey Medical Center, St. Paul

University of Minnesota Hospital and Clinic, Minneapolis

MISSOURI

Barnes Hospital, St. Louis

University Hospital and Clinics, Columbia

NEW HAMPSHIRE

Dartmouth-Hitchcock Medical Center, Hanover

NEW JERSEY

University of Medicine and Dentistry of New Jersey, University Hospital, Newark

NEW MEXICO

University Hospital, Albuquerque

NEW YORK

Bayley Seton Hospital, Staten Island

Bellevue Hospital Center, New York

Beth Israel Medical Center, New York

Bronx Municipal Hospital Center, Bronx

Buffalo General Hospital, Buffalo

Elmhurst Hospital Center, Flushing

Erie County Medical Center, Buffalo

Kings County Hospital Center, Brooklyn

Lincoln Medical and Mental Health Center, Bronx

Metropolitan Hospital Center, New York

Montefiore Medical Center, Henry and Lucy Moses Division, Bronx

Montefiore Medical Center, Jack D. Weiler Hospital of the Albert Einstein College of Medicine, Bronx

Mt. Sinai Medical Center, New York

New York Hospital-Cornell Medical Center, New York

New York University Medical Center, New York

North Central Bronx Hospital, Bronx

Presbyterian Hospital in the City of New York, Columbia-Presbyterian Medical Center, New York

St. Luke's-Roosevelt Hospital Center, St. Luke's Division, New York

State University of New York at Stony Brook University Hospital, Stony Brook

State University of New York Health Sciences Center at Brooklyn, University Hospital of Brooklyn, Brooklyn

Strong Memorial Hospital of the University of Rochester, Rochester

Westchester County Medical Center, Valhalla

NORTH CAROLINA

Duke University Medical Center, Durham

North Carolina Baptist Hospital, Winston-Salem

University of North Carolina Hospitals, Chapel Hill

OHIO

Cleveland Clinic Hospital, Cleveland

Good Samaritan Hospital and Health Center, Dayton

MetroHealth Medical Center, Cleveland

Ohio State University Hospitals, Columbus

St. Elizabeth Medical Center, Dayton

University Hospitals of Cleveland, Cleveland

University of Cincinnati Hospital, Cincinnati

OKLAHOMA

Oklahoma Medical Center, Oklahoma City

OREGON

Oregon Health Sciences University, University Hospital, Portland

PENNSYLVANIA

Geisinger Medical Center, Danville

Graduate Hospital, Philadelphia

Hahnemann University Hospital, Philadelphia

Hospital of the University of Pennsylvania, Philadelphia

Penn State University Hospital, The Milton S. Hershey Medical Center, Hershey

Pennsylvania Hospital, Philadelphia

Presbyterian University Hospital, Pittsburgh

Thomas Jefferson University Hospital, Philadelphia

PUERTO RICO

University Hospital, San Juan

RHODE ISLAND

Memorial Hospital of Rhode Island, Pawtucket

*Rhode Island Hospital, Providence

Roger Williams Hospital, Providence

SOUTH CAROLINA

Medical University of South Carolina, Medical Center of Medical University of South Carolina, Charleston

TENNESSEE

Baptist Memorial Hospital, Memphis

Metropolitan Nashville General Hospital, Nashville

Regional Medical Center at Memphis, Memphis

University of Tennessee Medical Center, Memphis

*Vanderbilt University Hospital and Clinic, Nashville

TEXAS

Bexar County Hospital District, Medical Center Hospital, San Antonio

Dallas County Hospital District, Parkland Memorial Hospital, Dallas

Harris County Hospital District, Ben Taub General Hospital, Houston

Harris County Hospital District, Lyndon B. Johnson General Hospital, Houston

*Hermann Hospital, Houston

*Methodist Hospital, Houston

University Medical Center, Lubbock

University of Texas M.D. Anderson Cancer Center, Houston

University of Texas Medical Branch Hospitals, Galveston

Zale-Lipshy University Hospital, Dallas

UTAH

University of Utah Hospital and Clinics, Salt Lake City

VIRGINIA

University of Virginia Medical Center, Charlottesville

Virginia Commonwealth University, Medical College of Virginia Hospitals, Richmond

WASHINGTON

University of Washington Medical Center, Seattle

WEST VIRGINIA

*West Virginia University Hospitals, Morgantown

WISCONSIN

*Froedtert Memorial Lutheran Hospital, Milwaukee

Milwaukee County Medical Complex, Milwaukee

St. Joseph's Hospital, Marshfield

University of Wisconsin Hospital and Clinics, Madison

Health Problems of Men

ALABAMA

Cooper Green Hospital, Birmingham

University of Alabama Hospitals, Birmingham

ARIZONA

*University Medical Center, Tucson

ARKANSAS

University Hospital of Arkansas, Little Rock

CALIFORNIA

Kaiser Foundation Hospital, Hayward

Kaiser Foundation Hospital, Los Angeles

Kaiser Foundation Hospital, Sacramento

Kaiser Foundation Hospital, Walnut Creek

*Loma Linda University Medical Center, Loma Linda

Los Angeles County Harbor-University of California at Los Angeles Medical Center, Torrance

Los Angeles County-University of Southern California Medical Center, Los Angeles

Mercy Hospital and Medical Center, San Diego

Olive View Medical Center, Sylmar

San Bernardino County Medical Center, San Bernardino

San Francisco General Hospital and Medical Center, San Francisco

Santa Clara Valley Medical Center, San Jose

*Stanford University Hospital, Stanford

University of California at Los Angeles Medical Center, Los Angeles

University of California, Davis Medical Center, Sacramento

University of California Irvine Medical Center, Orange

University of California San Diego Medical Center, San Diego

University of California, San Francisco Medical Center, San Francisco

University of Southern California, The Kenneth Norris Jr. Cancer Hospital, Los Angeles

White Memorial Medical Center, Los Angeles

COLORADO

Denver Health and Hospitals, Denver

University of Colorado Health Sciences Center, University Hospital, Denver

CONNECTICUT

Hartford Hospital, Hartford

New Britain General Hospital, New Britain

St. Francis Hospital and Medical Center, Hartford

University of Connecticut Health Center, John Dempsey Hospital, Farmington

Waterbury Hospital, Waterbury

*Yale-New Haven Hospital, New Haven

DELAWARE
Alfred I. Dupont Institute,
Wilmington

DISTRICT OF COLUMBIA
District of Columbia General
Hospital, Washington

***George Washington University
Hospital, Washington**

***Georgetown University Hospital,
Washington**

***Howard University Hospital,
Washington**

Sibley Memorial Hospital,
Washington

Washington Hospital Center,
Washington

FLORIDA
Jackson Memorial Hospital, Miami

***Shands Hospital at the University
of Florida, Gainesville**

Tampa General Hospital, Tampa

University of South Florida, H. Lee
Moffitt Cancer Center, Tampa

GEORGIA
***Emory University Hospital,
Atlanta**

Grady Memorial Hospital, Atlanta

**Medical College of Georgia
Hospital and Clinics, Augusta**

University Hospital, Augusta

ILLINOIS
Cook County Hospital, Chicago

Humana Hospital-Michael Reese,
Chicago

***Loyola University of Chicago,
Foster G. McGaw Hospital,
Maywood**

Memorial Medical Center,
Springfield

***Northwestern Memorial Hospital,
Chicago**

***Rush-Presbyterian-St. Luke's
Medical Center, Chicago**

St. John's Hospital, Springfield

***University of Chicago Hospitals,
Chicago**

**University of Illinois Hospital
and Clinics, Chicago**

INDIANA
**Indiana University Medical Center,
Indianapolis**

Methodist Hospital of Indiana,
Indianapolis

**William N. Wishard Memorial
Hospital, Indianapolis**

IOWA
**University of Iowa Hospitals
and Clinics, Iowa City**

KANSAS
**University of Kansas Hospital,
Kansas City**

KENTUCKY
**Humana Hospital-University
of Louisville, Louisville**

Jewish Hospital, Louisville

Norton Hospital, Louisville

St. Joseph Hospital, Lexington

**University of Kentucky Hospital,
Albert B. Chandler Medical Center,
Lexington**

LOUISIANA
Hotel Dieu Hospital, New Orleans

Huey P. Long Regional Medical
Center, Pineville

Jo Ellen Smith Medical Center,
New Orleans

**Louisiana State University
Hospital, Shreveport**

**Medical Center of Louisiana at
New Orleans, New Orleans**

Ochsner Foundation Hospital,
New Orleans

Schumpert Medical Center,
Shreveport

South Louisiana Medical Center,
Houma

***Tulane University Hospital
and Clinics, New Orleans**

MARYLAND
Francis Scott Key Medical Center,
Baltimore

***Johns Hopkins Hospital,
Baltimore**

Sinai Hospital of Baltimore,
Baltimore

***University of Maryland Medical
System, Baltimore**

MASSACHUSETTS
*Beth Israel Hospital, Boston

Boston City Hospital, Boston

***Brigham and Women's Hospital,
Boston**

Lahey Clinic Hospital, Burlington

Lawrence F. Quigley Memorial
Hospital, Chelsea

***Massachusetts General Hospital,
Boston**

Medical Center of Central
Massachusetts, Worcester

New England Deaconess Hospital,
Boston

***New England Medical Center,
Boston**

St. Elizabeth's Hospital of Boston,
Boston

*University Hospital, Boston

**University of Massachusetts
Medical Center, Worcester**

MICHIGAN
*Harper Hospital, Detroit

Henry Ford Hospital, Detroit

St. Joseph Mercy Hospital,
Ann Arbor

**University of Michigan Hospitals,
Ann Arbor**

William Beaumont Hospital,
Royal Oak

MINNESOTA
Mayo Clinic and Foundation,
Rochester

Rochester Methodist Hospital,
Rochester

*St. Marys Hospital, Rochester

St. Paul-Ramsey Medical Center,
St. Paul

**University of Minnesota Hospital
and Clinic, Minneapolis**

MISSISSIPPI

Mississippi Baptist Medical Center, Jackson

University of Mississippi Medical Center, University Hospitals and Clinics, Jackson

MISSOURI

*Barnes Hospital, St. Louis

St. John's Mercy Medical Center, St. Louis

*St. Louis University Medical Center, St. Louis

St. Mary's Health Center, St. Louis

University Hospital and Clinics, Columbia

NEBRASKA

AMI St. Joseph Hospital, Omaha

Methodist Hospital, Omaha

University of Nebraska Medical Center, Omaha

NEW HAMPSHIRE

Dartmouth-Hitchcock Medical Center, Hanover

NEW JERSEY

Hackensack Medical Center, Hackensack

Medical Center at Princeton, Princeton

*Robert Wood Johnson University Hospital, New Brunswick

University of Medicine and Dentistry of New Jersey, University Hospital, Newark

NEW MEXICO

Lovelace Medical Center, Albuquerque

University Hospital, Albuquerque

NEW YORK

*Albany Medical Center Hospital, Albany

Bellevue Hospital Center, New York

Beth Israel Medical Center, New York

Bronx Municipal Hospital Center, Bronx

Brookdale Hospital Medical Center, Brooklyn

*Buffalo General Hospital, Buffalo

Cabrini Medical Center, New York

Coney Island Hospital, Brooklyn

Crouse-Irving Memorial Hospital, Syracuse

Elmhurst Hospital Center, Flushing

Erie County Medical Center, Buffalo

Genesee Hospital, Rochester

Kings County Hospital Center, Brooklyn

La Guardia Hospital, Forest Hills

Lenox Hill Hospital, New York

Lincoln Medical and Mental Health Center, Bronx

Long Island College Hospital, Brooklyn

Long Island Jewish Medical Center, New Hyde Park

Maimonides Medical Center, Brooklyn

Memorial Sloan-Kettering Cancer Center, New York

Metropolitan Hospital Center, New York

*Montefiore Medical Center, Henry and Lucy Moses Division, Bronx

Montefiore Medical Center, Jack D. Weiler Hospital of the Albert Einstein College of Medicine, Bronx

*Mt. Sinai Medical Center, New York

*New York Hospital-Cornell Medical Center, New York

*New York University Medical Center, New York

North Central Bronx Hospital, Bronx

Our Lady of Mercy Medical Center, Bronx

*Presbyterian Hospital in the City of New York, Columbia-Presbyterian Medical Center, New York

Queens Hospital Center, Jamaica

Rochester General Hospital, Rochester

Roswell Park Cancer Institute, Buffalo

St. Joseph's Hospital Health Center, Syracuse

St. Luke's-Roosevelt Hospital Center, Roosevelt Division, New York

St. Luke's-Roosevelt Hospital Center, St. Luke's Division, New York

State University of New York Health Science Center, University Hospital, Syracuse

State University of New York Health Sciences Center at Brooklyn, University Hospital of Brooklyn, Brooklyn

*Strong Memorial Hospital of the University of Rochester, Rochester

Westchester County Medical Center, Valhalla

NORTH CAROLINA

*Duke University Medical Center, Durham

Forsyth Memorial Hospital, Winston-Salem

*North Carolina Baptist Hospital, Winston-Salem

University of North Carolina Hospitals, Chapel Hill

Wake Medical Center, Raleigh

OHIO

Akron City Hospital, Akron

Akron General Medical Center, Akron

Cleveland Clinic Hospital, Cleveland

Medical College of Ohio Hospital, Toledo

MetroHealth Medical Center, Cleveland

Ohio State University Hospitals, Columbus

Riverside Methodist Hospitals, Columbus

St. Vincent Medical Center, Toledo

Toledo Hospital, Toledo

*University Hospitals of Cleveland, Cleveland

University of Cincinnati Hospital, Cincinnati

OKLAHOMA

Oklahoma Medical Center, Oklahoma City

OREGON

Oregon Health Sciences University, University Hospital, Portland

PENNSYLVANIA

Abington Memorial Hospital, Abington

*Allegheny General Hospital, Pittsburgh

Bryn Mawr Hospital, Bryn Mawr

Geisinger Medical Center, Danville

*Hospital of the Medical College of Pennsylvania, Philadelphia

*Hospital of the University of Pennsylvania, Philadelphia

Lancaster General Hospital, Lancaster

Montefiore University Hospital, Pittsburgh

Penn State University Hospital, The Milton S. Hershey Medical Center, Hershey

Pennsylvania Hospital, Philadelphia

*Presbyterian University Hospital, Pittsburgh

*Temple University Hospital, Philadelphia

*Thomas Jefferson University Hospital, Philadelphia

PUERTO RICO

University Hospital, San Juan

RHODE ISLAND

*Rhode Island Hospital, Providence

Roger Williams Hospital, Providence

SOUTH CAROLINA

Charleston Memorial Hospital, Charleston

Medical University of South Carolina, Medical Center of Medical University of South Carolina, Charleston

TENNESSEE

Baptist Hospital, Nashville

Baptist Memorial Hospital, Memphis

Methodist Hospitals of Memphis, Central Unit, Memphis

Metropolitan Nashville General Hospital, Nashville

Regional Medical Center at Memphis, Memphis

*Vanderbilt University Hospital and Clinic, Nashville

TEXAS

Baylor University Medical Center, Dallas

Bexar County Hospital District, Medical Center Hospital, San Antonio

Dallas County Hospital District, Parkland Memorial Hospital, Dallas

Harris County Hospital District, Ben Taub General Hospital, Houston

*Hermann Hospital, Houston

Humana Hospital-San Antonio, San Antonio

*Methodist Hospital, Houston

*Scott and White Memorial Hospital, Temple

St. Joseph Hospital, Houston

St. Luke's Episcopal Hospital, Houston

University of Texas M.D. Anderson Cancer Center, Houston

University of Texas Medical Branch Hospitals, Galveston

UTAH

LDS Hospital, Salt Lake City

University of Utah Hospital and Clinics, Salt Lake City

VERMONT

Fanny Allen Hospital, Colchester

*Medical Center Hospital of Vermont, Burlington

VIRGINIA

Fairfax Hospital, Falls Church

Memorial Hospital of Danville, Danville

Sentara Leigh Hospital, Norfolk

Sentara Norfolk General Hospital, Norfolk

University of Virginia Medical Center, Charlottesville

Virginia Commonwealth University, Medical College of Virginia Hospitals, Richmond

WASHINGTON

Harborview Medical Center, Seattle

University of Washington Medical Center, Seattle

Virginia Mason Medical Center, Seattle

WEST VIRGINIA

Ohio Valley Medical Center, Wheeling

*West Virginia University Hospitals, Morgantown

WISCONSIN

*Froedtert Memorial Lutheran Hospital, Milwaukee

Lutheran Hospital-La Crosse, La Crosse

Milwaukee County Medical Complex, Milwaukee

University of Wisconsin Hospital and Clinics, Madison

Health Problems of Women

ALABAMA

Carraway Methodist Medical Center, Birmingham

Cooper Green Hospital, Birmingham

University of Alabama Hospitals, Birmingham

University of South Alabama Medical Center, Mobile

ARIZONA

Good Samaritan Regional Medical Center, Phoenix

Kino Community Hospital, Tucson

Maricopa Medical Center, Phoenix

St. Joseph's Hospital and Medical Center, Phoenix

*University Medical Center, Tucson

ARKANSAS

University Hospital of Arkansas, Little Rock

CALIFORNIA

California Medical Center-Los Angeles, Los Angeles

Cedars-Sinai Medical Center, Los Angeles

Glendale Adventist Medical Center, Glendale

Kaiser Foundation Hospital, Fontana

Kaiser Foundation Hospital, Los Angeles

Kaiser Foundation Hospital, Oakland

Kaiser Foundation Hospital, Sacramento

Kaiser Foundation Hospital, San Diego

Kaiser Foundation Hospital, San Francisco

Kaiser Foundation Hospital, Santa Clara

Kern Medical Center, Bakersfield

*Loma Linda University Medical Center, Loma Linda

Long Beach Memorial Medical Center, Long Beach

Los Angeles County Harbor-University of California at Los Angeles Medical Center, Torrance

Los Angeles County-King-Drew Medical Center, Los Angeles

Los Angeles County-University of Southern California Medical Center, Los Angeles

Mt. Zion Medical Center of University of California, San Francisco, San Francisco

Olive View Medical Center, Sylmar

Riverside General Hospital, University Medical Center, Riverside

San Bernardino County Medical Center, San Bernardino

San Francisco General Hospital and Medical Center, San Francisco

Santa Clara Valley Medical Center, San Jose

*Stanford University Hospital, Stanford

Sutter General Hospital, Sacramento

Sutter Memorial Hospital, Sacramento

University of California at Los Angeles Medical Center, Los Angeles

University of California, Davis Medical Center, Sacramento

University of California Irvine Medical Center, Orange

University of California San Diego Medical Center, San Diego

University of California, San Francisco Medical Center, San Francisco

Valley Medical Center of Fresno, Fresno

White Memorial Medical Center, Los Angeles

COLORADO

Denver Health and Hospitals, Denver

Presbyterian-St. Luke's Medical Center, Denver

Rose Medical Center, Denver

St. Joseph Hospital, Denver

University of Colorado Health Sciences Center, University Hospital, Denver

CONNECTICUT

Bridgeport Hospital, Bridgeport

Danbury Hospital, Danbury

Hartford Hospital, Hartford

Mt. Sinai Hospital, Hartford

New Britain General Hospital, New Britain

St. Francis Hospital and Medical Center, Hartford

Stamford Hospital, Stamford

University of Connecticut Health Center, John Dempsey Hospital, Farmington

*Yale-New Haven Hospital, New Haven

DELAWARE

Medical Center of Delaware, Wilmington

DISTRICT OF COLUMBIA

District of Columbia General Hospital, Washington

*George Washington University Hospital, Washington

*Georgetown University Hospital, Washington

Greater Southeast Community Hospital, Washington

*Howard University Hospital, Washington

Providence Hospital, Washington

Washington Hospital Center, Washington

FLORIDA

Baptist Hospital, Pensacola

Baptist Medical Center, Jacksonville

Bayfront Medical Center, St. Petersburg

Jackson Memorial Hospital, Miami

Orlando Regional Medical Center, Orlando

Sacred Heart Hospital of Pensacola, Pensacola

*Shands Hospital at the University of Florida, Gainesville

Tampa General Hospital, Tampa

University Medical Center, Jacksonville

GEORGIA

*Crawford Long Hospital of Emory University, Atlanta

*Emory University Hospital, Atlanta

Georgia Baptist Medical Center, Atlanta

Grady Memorial Hospital, Atlanta

Medical Center of Central Georgia, Macon

Medical College of Georgia Hospital and Clinics, Augusta

Memorial Medical Center, Savannah

University Hospital, Augusta

HAWAII

Kapiolani Medical Center for Women and Children, Honolulu

Queen's Medical Center, Honolulu

ILLINOIS

Christ Hospital and Medical Center, Oak Lawn

Columbus Hospital, Chicago

Cook County Hospital, Chicago

Evanston Hospital, Evanston

Humana Hospital-Michael Reese, Chicago

Illinois Masonic Medical Center, Chicago

*Loyola University of Chicago, Foster G. McGaw Hospital, Maywood

Lutheran General Hospital, Chicago

MacNeal Hospital, Berwyn

Memorial Medical Center, Springfield

Mercy Hospital and Medical Center, Chicago

Mt. Sinai Hospital Medical Center of Chicago, Chicago

Northwestern Memorial Hospital, Prentice Women's Hospital, Chicago

Resurrection Medical Center, Chicago

*Rush-Presbyterian-St. Luke's Medical Center, Chicago

St. Cabrini Hospital, Chicago

St. Francis Hospital of Evanston, Evanston

St. Francis Medical Center, Peoria

St. John's Hospital, Springfield

St. Joseph Hospital and Health Care Center, Chicago

*University of Chicago Hospitals, Chicago

University of Illinois Hospital and Clinics, Chicago

INDIANA

Indiana University Medical Center, Indianapolis

Methodist Hospital of Indiana, Indianapolis

St. Vincent Hospital and Health Care Center, Indianapolis

William N. Wishard Memorial Hospital, Indianapolis

IOWA

University of Iowa Hospitals and Clinics, Iowa City

KANSAS

HCA Wesley Medical Center, Wichita

Truman Medical Center-West, Kansas City

University of Kansas Hospital, Kansas City

KENTUCKY

Central Baptist Hospital, Lexington

Humana Hospital-University of Louisville, Louisville

Norton Hospital, Louisville

University of Kentucky Hospital, Albert B. Chandler Medical Center, Lexington

LOUISIANA

Dr. Walter Olin Moss Regional Hospital, Lake Charles

E.A. Conway Memorial Hospital, Monroe

Earl K. Long Memorial Hospital, Baton Rouge

Huey P. Long Regional Medical Center, Pineville

Lallie Kemp Hospital, Independence

Louisiana State University Hospital, Shreveport

Medical Center of Louisiana at New Orleans, New Orleans

Ochsner Foundation Hospital, New Orleans

South Louisiana Medical Center, Houma

*Tulane University Hospital and Clinics, New Orleans

University Medical Center, Lafayette

MAINE

Maine Medical Center, Portland

MARYLAND

Francis Scott Key Medical Center, Baltimore

Franklin Square Hospital Center, Baltimore

Greater Baltimore Medical Center, Baltimore

Harbor Hospital Center, Baltimore

Holy Cross Hospital of Silver Spring, Silver Spring

*Johns Hopkins Hospital, Baltimore

Maryland General Hospital, Baltimore

Mercy Medical Center, Baltimore

Sinai Hospital of Baltimore, Baltimore

Union Memorial Hospital, Baltimore

*University of Maryland Medical System, Baltimore

MASSACHUSETTS

Baystate Medical Center, Springfield

Berkshire Medical Center, Pittsfield

*Beth Israel Hospital, Boston

Boston City Hospital, Boston

*Brigham and Women's Hospital, Boston

Framingham Union Hospital, Framingham

Malden Hospital, Malden

*Massachusetts General Hospital, Boston

Medical Center of Central Massachusetts, Worcester

*New England Medical Center, Boston

St. Margaret's Hospital for Women,
Boston

St. Vincent Hospital, Worcester

**University of Massachusetts
Medical Center, Worcester**

MICHIGAN

Blodgett Memorial Medical Center,
Grand Rapids

Butterworth Hospital,
Grand Rapids

Detroit Receiving Hospital and
University Health Center, Detroit

*Grace Hospital, Detroit

*Harper Hospital, Detroit

Henry Ford Hospital, Detroit

Hurley Medical Center, Flint

Hutzel Hospital, Detroit

Oakwood Hospital, Dearborn

Pontiac General Hospital, Pontiac

Providence Hospital, Southfield

Saginaw General Hospital, Saginaw

Sinai Hospital, Detroit

Sparrow Hospital, Lansing

St. John Hospital and Medical
Center, Detroit

St. Joseph Mercy Hospital,
Ann Arbor

St. Mary's Health Services,
Grand Rapids

**University of Michigan Hospitals,
Ann Arbor**

William Beaumont Hospital,
Royal Oak

MINNESOTA

Hennepin County Medical Center,
Minneapolis

Mayo Clinic and Foundation,
Rochester

Rochester Methodist Hospital,
Rochester

*St. Marys Hospital, Rochester

St. Paul-Ramsey Medical Center,
St. Paul

**University of Minnesota Hospital
and Clinic, Minneapolis**

MISSISSIPPI

**University of Mississippi Medical
Center, University Hospitals and
Clinics, Jackson**

MISSOURI

*Barnes Hospital, St. Louis

Deaconess Hospital, St. Louis

Jewish Hospital of St. Louis,
St. Louis

Menorah Medical Center,
Kansas City

St. John's Mercy Medical Center,
St. Louis

St. Louis Regional Medical Center,
St. Louis

***St. Louis University Medical
Center, St. Louis**

St. Luke's Hospital, Kansas City

St. Mary's Health Center, St. Louis

**University Hospital and Clinics,
Columbia**

NEBRASKA

AMI St. Joseph Hospital, Omaha

Archbishop Bergan Mercy
Hospital, Omaha

**University of Nebraska Medical
Center, Omaha**

NEVADA

University Medical Center of
Southern Nevada, Las Vegas

Women's Hospital, Las Vegas

NEW JERSEY

Cooper Hospital-University
Medical Center, Camden

Englewood Hospital, Englewood

Hackensack Medical Center,
Hackensack

Jersey City Medical Center,
Jersey City

Jersey Shore Medical Center,
Neptune

Monmouth Medical Center,
Long Branch

Morristown Memorial Hospital,
Morristown

Muhlenberg Regional Medical
Center, Plainfield

Newark Beth Israel Medical Center,
Newark

***Robert Wood Johnson University
Hospital, New Brunswick**

St. Barnabas Medical Center,
Livingston

St. James Hospital of Newark,
Newark

St. Joseph's Hospital and Medical
Center, Paterson

St. Michael's Medical Center,
Newark

St. Peter's Medical Center,
New Brunswick

**University of Medicine and
Dentistry of New Jersey, University
Hospital, Newark**

NEW MEXICO

University Hospital, Albuquerque

NEW YORK

***Albany Medical Center Hospital,
Albany**

**Bellevue Hospital Center,
New York**

Beth Israel Medical Center,
New York

Booth Memorial Medical Center,
Flushing

Bronx-Lebanon Hospital Center,
Bronx

Bronx Municipal Hospital Center,
Bronx

Brookdale Hospital Medical
Center, Brooklyn

Brooklyn Hospital Center,
Brooklyn

*Buffalo General Hospital, Buffalo

Coney Island Hospital, Brooklyn

Crouse-Irving Memorial Hospital,
Syracuse

Elmhurst Hospital Center, Flushing

**Erie County Medical Center,
Buffalo**

Flushing Hospital Medical Center,
Flushing

Genesee Hospital, Rochester

Harlem Hospital Center, New York

Highland Hospital of Rochester,
Rochester

Interfaith Medical Center, Brooklyn

Jamaica Hospital, Jamaica

Kings County Hospital Center, Brooklyn

Lenox Hill Hospital, New York

Lincoln Medical and Mental Health Center, Bronx

Long Island College Hospital, Brooklyn

Long Island Jewish Medical Center, New Hyde Park

Lutheran Medical Center, Brooklyn

Maimonides Medical Center, Brooklyn

Mary Immaculate Hospital, Jamaica

Mercy Hospital, Rockville Centre

Metropolitan Hospital Center, New York

Millard Fillmore Hospitals, Buffalo

*Montefiore Medical Center, Henry and Lucy Moses Division, Bronx

Montefiore Medical Center, Jack D. Weiler Hospital of the Albert Einstein College of Medicine, Bronx

*Mt. Sinai Medical Center, New York

Nassau County Medical Center, East Meadow

*New York Hospital-Cornell Medical Center, New York

New York Infirmary-Beekman Downtown Hospital, New York

*New York University Medical Center, New York

North Central Bronx Hospital, Bronx

North Shore University Hospital, Manhasset

Our Lady of Lourdes Medical Center, Camden

Our Lady of Mercy Medical Center, Bronx

*Presbyterian Hospital in the City of New York, Columbia-Presbyterian Medical Center, New York

Queens Hospital Center, Jamaica

Rochester General Hospital, Rochester

Sisters of Charity Hospital of Buffalo, Buffalo

St. John's Episcopal Hospital-South Shore, Far Rockaway

St. John's Queens Hospital, Elmhurst

St. Joseph's Hospital Health Center, Syracuse

St. Luke's-Roosevelt Hospital Center, Roosevelt Division, New York

St. Luke's-Roosevelt Hospital Center, St. Luke's Division, New York

St. Mary's Hospital, Brooklyn

St. Peter's Hospital, Albany

St. Vincent's Hospital and Medical Center of New York, New York

St. Vincent's Medical Center of Richmond, Staten Island

State University of New York at Stony Brook University Hospital, Stony Brook

State University of New York Health Science Center, University Hospital, Syracuse

State University of New York Health Sciences Center at Brooklyn, University Hospital of Brooklyn, Brooklyn

Staten Island University Hospital, Staten Island

*Strong Memorial Hospital of the University of Rochester, Rochester

Westchester County Medical Center, Valhalla

Winthrop-University Hospital, Mineola

NORTH CAROLINA

Carolinas Medical Center, Charlotte

*Duke University Medical Center, Durham

Forsyth Memorial Hospital, Winston-Salem

New Hanover Memorial Hospital, Wilmington

*North Carolina Baptist Hospital, Winston-Salem

Pitt County Memorial Hospital, Greenville

University of North Carolina Hospitals, Chapel Hill

Wake Medical Center, Raleigh

OHIO

Akron City Hospital, Akron

Akron General Medical Center, Akron

Aultman Hospital, Canton

Bethesda Oak Hospital, Cincinnati

Christ Hospital, Cincinnati

Good Samaritan Hospital, Cincinnati

Grant Medical Center, Columbus

Medical College of Ohio Hospital, Toledo

MetroHealth Medical Center, Cleveland

Miami Valley Hospital, Dayton

Mt. Carmel Medical Center, Columbus

Mt. Sinai Medical Center, Cleveland

Ohio State University Hospitals, Columbus

Riverside Methodist Hospitals, Columbus

St. Ann's Hospital of Columbus, Westerville

St. Elizabeth Hospital Medical Center, Youngstown

St. Luke's Hospital, Cleveland

St. Vincent Medical Center, Toledo

Toledo Hospital, Toledo

*University Hospitals of Cleveland, Cleveland

University of Cincinnati Hospital, Cincinnati

OKLAHOMA

Hillcrest Medical Center, Tulsa

Oklahoma Medical Center, Oklahoma City

St. Francis Hospital, Tulsa

St. John Medical Center, Tulsa

OREGON

Emanuel Hospital and Health Center, Portland

Good Samaritan Hospital and Medical Center, Portland

Oregon Health Sciences University, University Hospital, Portland

PENNSYLVANIA

Abington Memorial Hospital, Abington

Albert Einstein Medical Center, Philadelphia

*Allegheny General Hospital, Pittsburgh

The Allentown Hospital-Lehigh Valley Hospital Center, Allentown

Chestnut Hill Hospital, Philadelphia

Crozer-Chester Medical Center, Upland

Frankford Hospital of the City of Philadelphia, Philadelphia

Geisinger Medical Center, Danville

Germantown Hospital and Medical Center, Philadelphia

*Hahnemann University Hospital, Philadelphia

Harrisburg Hospital, Harrisburg

*Hospital of the Medical College of Pennsylvania, Philadelphia

*Hospital of the University of Pennsylvania, Philadelphia

Lankenau Hospital, Wynnewood

Lower Bucks Hospital, Bristol

Magee-Womens Hospital, Pittsburgh

Methodist Hospital, Philadelphia

Penn State University Hospital, The Milton S. Hershey Medical Center, Hershey

Pennsylvania Hospital, Philadelphia

Reading Hospital and Medical Center, Reading

St. Luke's Hospital, Bethlehem

*Temple University Hospital, Philadelphia

*Thomas Jefferson University Hospital, Philadelphia

Western Pennsylvania Hospital, Pittsburgh

York Hospital, York

PUERTO RICO

Caguas Regional Hospital, Caguas

Dr. Ramon E. Betances Hospital-Mayaguez Medical Center Branch, Mayaguez

Ponce Regional Hospital, Ponce

San Juan Municipal Hospital, Rio Piedras

University Hospital, San Juan

RHODE ISLAND

*Rhode Island Hospital, Providence

Women and Infants Hospital of Rhode Island, Providence

SOUTH CAROLINA

Charleston Memorial Hospital, Charleston

Greenville Memorial Hospital, Greenville

Medical University of South Carolina, Medical Center of Medical University of South Carolina, Charleston

Richland Memorial Hospital, Columbia

TENNESSEE

Baptist Hospital, Nashville

Erlanger Medical Center, Chattanooga

Metropolitan Nashville General Hospital, Nashville

Regional Medical Center at Memphis, Memphis

University of Tennessee Medical Center, Memphis

University of Tennessee Memorial Hospital, Knoxville

*Vanderbilt University Hospital and Clinic, Nashville

TEXAS

Baylor University Medical Center, Dallas

Bexar County Hospital District, Medical Center Hospital, San Antonio

Brackenridge Hospital, Austin

Dallas County Hospital District, Parkland Memorial Hospital, Dallas

Harris County Hospital District, Ben Taub General Hospital, Houston

Harris County Hospital District, Lyndon B. Johnson General Hospital, Houston

Harris Methodist Fort Worth, Fort Worth

*Hermann Hospital, Houston

High Plains Baptist Hospital, Amarillo

Medical Center Hospital, Odessa

Methodist Medical Center, Dallas

Northwest Texas Hospital, Amarillo

R.E. Thomason General Hospital, El Paso

*Scott and White Memorial Hospital, Temple

St. Joseph Hospital, Houston

St. Paul Medical Center, Dallas

Tarrant County Hospital District, John Peter Smith Hospital, Fort Worth

University Medical Center, Lubbock

University of Texas Medical Branch Hospitals, Galveston

UTAH

LDS Hospital, Salt Lake City

University of Utah Hospital and Clinics, Salt Lake City

VERMONT

*Medical Center Hospital of Vermont, Burlington

VIRGINIA

Depaul Medical Center, Norfolk

Fairfax Hospital, Falls Church

Portsmouth General Hospital, Portsmouth

Riverside Regional Medical Center, Newport News

Roanoke Memorial Hospitals, Roanoke

Sentara Norfolk General Hospital, Norfolk

University of Virginia Medical Center, Charlottesville

Virginia Commonwealth University, Medical College of Virginia Hospitals, Richmond

WASHINGTON

Swedish Hospital Medical Center, Seattle

University of Washington Medical Center, Seattle

WEST VIRGINIA

Charleston Area Medical Center, Women and Children's Hospital of West Virginia, Charleston

Ohio Valley Medical Center, Wheeling

*West Virginia University Hospitals, Morgantown

Wheeling Hospital, Wheeling

WISCONSIN

Meriter Hospital, Madison

Milwaukee County Medical Complex, Milwaukee

Sinai Samaritan Medical Center-Mt. Sinai Campus, Milwaukee

St. Marys Hospital Medical Center, Madison

University of Wisconsin Hospital and Clinics, Madison

Mental Health

ALABAMA

Searcy Hospital, Mt. Vernon

University of Alabama Hospitals, Birmingham

University of South Alabama Medical Center, Mobile

ARIZONA

Good Samaritan Regional Medical Center, Phoenix

Kino Community Hospital, Tucson

Maricopa Medical Center, Phoenix

*University Medical Center, Tucson

ARKANSAS

Arkansas State Hospital, Little Rock

University Hospital of Arkansas, Little Rock

CALIFORNIA

California-Pacific Medical Center, San Francisco

Camarillo State Hospital and Development Center, Camarillo

Cedars-Sinai Medical Center, Los Angeles

Community Mental Health Services, Greenbrae

Didi Hirsch Psychiatric Service, Culver City

Kaiser Foundation Hospital, Santa Clara

Kings View Hospital, Reedley

Langley Porter Psychiatric Hospital and Clinics, San Francisco

*Loma Linda University Medical Center, Loma Linda

Los Angeles County Harbor-University of California at Los Angeles Medical Center, Torrance

Los Angeles County-King-Drew Medical Center, Los Angeles

Los Angeles County-University of Southern California Medical Center, Los Angeles

Napa State Hospital, Napa

Olive View Medical Center, Sylmar

San Francisco General Hospital and Medical Center, San Francisco

San Mateo County General Hospital, San Mateo

Solano County Mental Health Clinic, Fairfield

*Stanford University Hospital, Stanford

University of California at Los Angeles Neuropsychiatric Hospital, Los Angeles

University of California, Davis Medical Center, Sacramento

University of California Irvine Medical Center, Orange

University of California San Diego Medical Center, San Diego

University of California, San Francisco Medical Center, San Francisco

Valley Medical Center of Fresno, Fresno

Ventura County Mental Health Center, Ventura

COLORADO

Denver Health and Hospitals, Denver

University of Colorado Health Sciences Center, University Hospital, Denver

CONNECTICUT

Connecticut Mental Health Center, New Haven

Connecticut Valley Hospital, Middletown

Danbury Hospital, Danbury

Greenwich Hospital, Greenwich

Hartford Hospital, Hartford

Hospital of St. Raphael, New Haven

Institute of Living, Hartford

Mt. Sinai Hospital, Hartford

Norwalk Hospital, Norwalk

Norwich Hospital, Norwich

St. Francis Hospital and Medical Center, Hartford

Stamford Hospital, Stamford

University of Connecticut Health Center, John Dempsey Hospital, Farmington

William W. Buckus Hospital, Norwich

*Yale-New Haven Hospital, New Haven

Yale Psychiatric Institute, New Haven

DELAWARE

Delaware State Hospital, New Castle

Medical Center of Delaware, Wilmington

DISTRICT OF COLUMBIA

*George Washington University Hospital, Washington

*Georgetown University Hospital, Washington

*Howard University Hospital, Washington

St. Elizabeths Hospital, DC Commission on Mental Health Services, Washington

FLORIDA

Jackson Memorial Hospital, Miami

The Manors, Tarpon Springs

*Shands Hospital at the University of Florida, Gainesville

Tampa General Hospital, Tampa

University of South Florida Psychiatry Center, Tampa

GEORGIA

Brawner Psychiatric Institute, Smyrna

*Emory University Hospital, Atlanta

Georgia Regional Hospital at Atlanta, Decatur

Grady Memorial Hospital, Atlanta

HCA West Paces Ferry Hospital, Atlanta

Medical College of Georgia Hospital and Clinics, Augusta

Ridgeview Institute, Smyrna

HAWAII

Queen's Medical Center, Honolulu

St. Francis Medical Center, Honolulu

ILLINOIS

Andrew McFarland Mental Health Center, Springfield

Choate Mental Health and Developmental Center, Anna

Cook County Hospital, Chicago

Decatur Memorial Hospital, Decatur

Evanston Hospital, Evanston

Humana Hospital-Michael Reese, Chicago

Illinois State Psychiatric Institute, Chicago

*Loyola University of Chicago, Foster G. McGaw Hospital, Maywood

Lutheran General Hospital, Chicago

Memorial Medical Center, Springfield

Mt. Sinai Hospital Medical Center of Chicago, Chicago

*Northwestern Memorial Hospital, Chicago

*Rush-Presbyterian-St. Luke's Medical Center, Chicago

St. John's Hospital, Springfield

*University of Chicago Hospitals, Chicago

University of Illinois Hospital and Clinics, Chicago

INDIANA

Indiana University Medical Center, Indianapolis

Larue D. Carter Memorial Hospital, Indianapolis

Lifespring Mental Health Services, Jeffersonville

William N. Wishard Memorial Hospital, Indianapolis

IOWA

University of Iowa Hospitals and Clinics, Iowa City

KANSAS

C.F. Menninger Memorial Hospital, Topeka

St. Joseph Medical Center, Wichita

Topeka State Hospital, Topeka

University of Kansas Hospital, Kansas City

KENTUCKY

Humana Hospital-University of Louisville, Louisville

Norton Hospital, Louisville

University of Kentucky Hospital, Albert B. Chandler Medical Center, Lexington

LOUISIANA

Medical Center of Louisiana at New Orleans, New Orleans

Ochsner Foundation Hospital, New Orleans

River Oaks Psychiatric Hospital, New Orleans

Touro Infirmary, New Orleans

*Tulane University Hospital and Clinics, New Orleans

MAINE

Maine Medical Center, Portland

MARYLAND

Crownsville Hospital Center, Crownsville

Francis Scott Key Medical Center, Baltimore

Franklin Square Hospital Center, Baltimore

*Johns Hopkins Hospital, Baltimore

Sheppard and Enoch Pratt Hospital, Baltimore

Spring Grove Hospital Center, Catonsville

Springfield Hospital Center, Sykesville

*University of Maryland Medical System, Baltimore

Walter P. Carter Center, Baltimore

MASSACHUSETTS

Austen Riggs Center, Stockbridge

*Beth Israel Hospital, Boston

Boston City Hospital, Boston

Cambridge Hospital, Cambridge

Charles River Hospital, Wellesley

Danvers State Hospital, Hathorne

Dr. Solomon Carter Fuller Mental Health Center, Boston

Erich Lindemann Mental Health Center, Boston

Faulkner Hospital, Boston

Lemuel Shattuck Hospital, Boston

Lemuel Shattuck Hospital, Bay Cove Mental Health Center, Boston

*Massachusetts General Hospital, Boston

Massachusetts Mental Health Center, Boston

McLean Hospital, Belmont

*New England Medical Center, Boston

St. Elizabeth's Hospital of Boston, Boston

*University Hospital, Boston

University of Massachusetts Medical Center, Worcester

West-Ros-Park Mental Health Center, Alternative House, Boston

Worcester State Hospital, Worcester

MICHIGAN

Detroit Psychiatric Institute, Detroit

*Harper Hospital, Detroit

Hawthorn Center, Northville

Henry Ford Hospital, Detroit

Kent Community Hospital Complex, Grand Rapids

Lafayette Clinic, Detroit

Northville Regional Psychiatric Hospital, Northville

Pine Rest Christian Hospital, Grand Rapids

Providence Hospital, Southfield

Sinai Hospital, Detroit

St. Lawrence Hospital and Healthcare Services, Lansing

St. Mary's Health Services, Grand Rapids

University of Michigan Hospitals, Ann Arbor

MINNESOTA

Hennepin County Medical Center, Minneapolis

Lakeland Mental Health Center, Inc., Moorhead

Mayo Clinic and Foundation, Rochester

*St. Marys Hospital, Rochester

St. Paul-Ramsey Medical Center, St. Paul

University of Minnesota Hospital and Clinic, Minneapolis

MISSISSIPPI

Mississippi State Hospital, Whitfield

University of Mississippi Medical Center, University Hospitals and Clinics, Jackson

MISSOURI

*Barnes Hospital, St. Louis

Jewish Hospital of St. Louis, St. Louis

Malcolm Bliss Mental Health Center, St. Louis

Mid Missouri Mental Health Center, Columbia

*St. Louis University Medical Center, St. Louis

University Hospital and Clinics, Columbia

Western Missouri Mental Health Center, Kansas City

NEBRASKA

AMI St. Joseph Center for Mental Health, Omaha

University of Nebraska Medical Center, Omaha

NEW HAMPSHIRE

Dartmouth-Hitchcock Medical Center, Hanover

New Hampshire Hospital, Concord

NEW JERSEY

Bergen Pines County Hospital, Paramus

Camden County Health Services Center, Blackwood

Cooper Hospital-University Medical Center, Camden

Greater Trenton Community Mental Health Center, Trenton

Hackensack Medical Center, Hackensack

Overlook Hospital, Summit

St. Barnabas Medical Center, Livingston

Trenton Psychiatric Hospital, Trenton

University of Medicine and Dentistry of New Jersey, University Hospital, Newark

University of Medicine and Dentistry of New Jersey, Community Mental Health Center at Piscataway, Piscataway

NEW MEXICO

University Hospital, Albuquerque

University of New Mexico Mental Health Center, Albuquerque

NEW YORK

*Albany Medical Center Hospital, Albany

Bellevue Hospital Center, New York

Beth Israel Medical Center, New York

Bronx-Lebanon Hospital Center, Bronx

Bronx Municipal Hospital Center, Bronx

Bronx Psychiatric Center, Bronx

Brookdale Hospital Medical Center, Brooklyn

Cabrini Medical Center, New York

Capital District Psychiatric Center, Albany

Creedmoor Psychiatric Center, Queens Village

Elmhurst Hospital Center, Flushing

Erie County Medical Center, Buffalo

Harlem Hospital Center, New York

Kings County Hospital Center, Brooklyn

Kingsboro Psychiatric Center, Brooklyn

Lincoln Medical and Mental Health Center, Bronx

Long Island Jewish Medical Center, New Hyde Park

Long Island Jewish Medical Center, Hillside Hospital, Glen Oaks

Maimonides Medical Center, Brooklyn

Manhattan Psychiatric Center-Ward's Island, New York

Metropolitan Hospital Center, New York

Middletown Psychiatric Center, Middletown

*Montefiore Medical Center, Henry and Lucy Moses Division, Bronx

*Mt. Sinai Medical Center, New York

Nassau County Medical Center,
East Meadow

***New York Hospital-Cornell
Medical Center, New York**

New York Hospital, Payne Whitney
Psychiatric Clinic, New York

New York Hospital, Westchester
Division, White Plains

New York State Psychiatric
Institute, New York

***New York University Medical
Center, New York**

North Shore University Hospital,
Manhasset

***Presbyterian Hospital in the
City of New York, Columbia-
Presbyterian Medical Center,
New York**

Queens Hospital Center, Jamaica

Richard H. Hutchings
Psychiatric Center, Syracuse

St. Luke's-Roosevelt Hospital
Center, St. Luke's Division,
New York

St. Vincent's Hospital and Medical
Center of New York, New York

St. Vincent's Hospital and Medical
Center of New York, Westchester
Branch, Harrison

St. Vincent's Medical Center of
Richmond, Staten Island

**State University of New York at
Stony Brook University Hospital,
Stony Brook**

**State University of New York
Health Science Center, University
Hospital, Syracuse**

**State University of New York
Health Sciences Center at Brooklyn,
University Hospital of Brooklyn,
Brooklyn**

***Strong Memorial Hospital of the
University of Rochester, Rochester**

**Westchester County Medical
Center, Valhalla**

NORTH CAROLINA

Cherry Hospital, Goldsboro

Dorothea Dix Hospital, Raleigh

***Duke University Medical Center,
Durham**

***North Carolina Baptist Hospital,
Winston-Salem**

**Pitt County Memorial Hospital,
Greenville**

Pitt County Mental Health Center,
Greenville

**University of North Carolina
Hospitals, Chapel Hill**

NORTH DAKOTA

Southeast Human Services Center,
Fargo

St. Luke's Hospitals-Meritcare,
Fargo

OHIO

Akron General Medical Center,
Akron

Cleveland Clinic Hospital,
Cleveland

Cleveland Psychiatric Institute,
Cleveland

Cleveland Psychoanalytic Institute,
Cleveland

Good Samaritan Hospital and
Health Center, Dayton

Grant Medical Center, Columbus

Harding Hospital, Worthington

Kettering Medical Center,
Kettering

**Medical College of Ohio Hospital,
Toledo**

**MetroHealth Medical Center,
Cleveland**

Mt. Carmel Medical Center,
Columbus

Mt. Sinai Medical Center,
Cleveland

**Ohio State University Hospitals,
Columbus**

Riverside Methodist Hospitals,
Columbus

St. Thomas Medical Center, Akron

St. Vincent Medical Center, Toledo

Toledo Mental Health Center,
Toledo

***University Hospitals of Cleveland,
Cleveland**

**University of Cincinnati Hospital,
Cincinnati**

OKLAHOMA

Griffin Memorial Hospital, Norman

Hillcrest Medical Center, Tulsa

**Oklahoma Medical Center,
Oklahoma City**

Tulsa Psychiatric Center, Tulsa

OREGON

**Oregon Health Sciences University,
University Hospital, Portland**

PENNSYLVANIA

Abington Memorial Hospital,
Abington

Albert Einstein Medical Center,
Philadelphia

Crozer-Chester Medical Center,
Upland

Friends Hospital, Philadelphia

***Hahnemann University Hospital,
Philadelphia**

***Hospital of the Medical College
of Pennsylvania, Philadelphia**

***Hospital of the University of
Pennsylvania, Philadelphia**

Mercy Catholic Medical Center,
Fitzgerald Mercy Division,
Philadelphia

Montefiore University Hospital,
Pittsburgh

Norristown State Hospital,
Norristown

Northwestern Institute,
Fort Washington

**Penn State University Hospital,
The Milton S. Hershey Medical
Center, Hershey**

Pennsylvania Hospital,
Philadelphia

***Presbyterian University Hospital,
Pittsburgh**

St. Francis Medical Center,
Pittsburgh

***Temple University Hospital,
Philadelphia**

***Thomas Jefferson University
Hospital, Philadelphia**

Western Psychiatric Institute
and Clinic, Pittsburgh

PUERTO RICO
University Hospital, San Juan

RHODE ISLAND
Butler Hospital, Providence

Emma Pendleton Bradley Hospital, East Providence

Miriam Hospital, Providence

Providence Center for Counseling and Psychiatric Services, Providence

*Rhode Island Hospital, Providence

SOUTH CAROLINA
Charleston Memorial Hospital, Charleston

Medical University of South Carolina, Medical Center of Medical University of South Carolina, Charleston

William S. Hall Psychiatric Institute, Columbia

SOUTH DAKOTA
McKennan Hospital, Sioux Falls

Southeastern Mental Health Center, Sioux Falls

TENNESSEE
*George W. Hubbard Hospital of Meharry Medical College, Nashville

Johnson City Medical Center Hospital, Johnson City

Memphis Mental Health Institute, Memphis

Middle Tennessee Mental Health Institute, Nashville

Regional Medical Center at Memphis, Memphis

University of Tennessee Medical Center, Memphis

*Vanderbilt University Hospital and Clinic, Nashville

Watauga Area Mental Health Center, Johnson City

Woodridge Hospital, Johnson City

TEXAS
Austin State Hospital, Austin

Austin-Travis County Mental Health Center, Austin

Baylor University Medical Center, Dallas

Bexar County Hospital District, Medical Center Hospital, San Antonio

Brackenridge Hospital, Austin

Dallas County Hospital District, Parkland Memorial Hospital, Dallas

Harris County Hospital District, Ben Taub General Hospital, Houston

Harris County Psychiatric Center, Houston

*Hermann Hospital, Houston

*Methodist Hospital, Houston

Presbyterian Hospital of Dallas, Dallas

R.E. Thomason General Hospital, El Paso

St. Mary of the Plains Hospital, Lubbock

Terrell State Hospital, Terrell

Timberlawn Psychiatric Hospital, Dallas

University Medical Center, Lubbock

University of Texas M.D. Anderson Cancer Center, Houston

University of Texas Medical Branch Hospitals, Galveston

UTAH
Salt Lake Valley Mental Health, Salt Lake City

University of Utah Hospital and Clinics, Salt Lake City

Western Institute of Neuropsychiatry, Salt Lake City

VERMONT
Brattleboro Retreat, Brattleboro

*Medical Center Hospital of Vermont, Burlington

VIRGINIA
Fairfax Hospital, Falls Church

The Psychiatric Institute of the Medical College of Hampton Roads, Norfolk

Sentara Norfolk General Hospital, Norfolk

University of Virginia Medical Center, Charlottesville

Virginia Commonwealth University, Medical College of Virginia Hospitals, Richmond

WASHINGTON
Harborview Medical Center, Seattle

University of Washington Medical Center, Seattle

WEST VIRGINIA
Charleston Area Medical Center, Charleston

*West Virginia University Hospitals, Morgantown

WISCONSIN
Columbia Hospital, Milwaukee

*Froedtert Memorial Lutheran Hospital, Milwaukee

Mercy Medical Center, Oshkosh

Meriter Hospital, Madison

Milwaukee County Medical Complex, Milwaukee

Milwaukee Psychiatric Hospital, Milwaukee

Sinai Samaritan Medical Center-Mt. Sinai Campus, Milwaukee

University of Wisconsin Hospital and Clinics, Madison

Winnebago Mental Health Institute, Winnebago

In talking to your friends and family about choosing the right hospital for the treatment of your disorder, you will no doubt hear of lists compiled by the popular press. To expand on the comprehensive lists of hospitals already presented in the Directory, we would like to share with you some of the results of two recent surveys—one put out by *U.S. News & World Report*, and the other from *The Best in Medicine*.

When reviewing these lists, remember that they are not definitive. The right hospital for you may not necessarily be among these names. As we said in the introduction to the Directory, choosing a hospital should be a decision made between you and your doctor. There will be very specific criteria that you will use to make your final selection, criteria that probably were not considered in compiling these lists. The methods used to conduct the surveys are not foolproof, and since doctors were polled for their opinions, the results are, of course, subjective.

What does make these surveys interesting is that they are able to do what no individual can, that is consult hundreds of physicians across the country about the hospitals that they feel are among the best in their specialty.

Because these hospitals enjoy good reputations among doctors, you may want to include them on your list of potential hospitals, but do not exclude others just because they are not listed here. By including these surveys in the Directory, we by no means endorse their methods or conclusions.

U.S. NEWS & WORLD REPORT SURVEY

The survey was designed and carried out after discussion with U.S. News editors and writers by the National Opinion Research Center, a social-science research group at the University of Chicago with a 50-year record of high-quality work. NORC's techniques produced a response rate of better than 64 percent (965 physicians).

To select knowledgeable specialists, NORC drew 138,000 names of board-certified doctors in the 15 specialties chosen from the American Medical Association's master file of more than 560,000 AMA members and non-members. NORC then selected a sample of about 100 physicians in each specialty from around the country, for a total of 1,501—one over because of the random sampling method used. NORC contacted them by mail and, if necessary, by fax and by phone. (The Directory includes 13 of the 15 specialties. These correspond to the disorders covered in the Handbook.)

Each physician was asked to name, in no special order, the five leading hospitals in his or her own specialty, regardless of location or expense, and was also asked to rate characteristics of high-quality hospital care. To test the notion that those at the top of their profession might have unrepresentative opinions, NORC also included questions to check "eliteness," defined by qualities such as holding an officer's position in a medical society. Tellingly, the 1 in 3 respondents who are among the most "elite" listed essentially the same hospitals as their less elite counterparts did. Neither did they rely more than less elite doctors on their own experience at one of the top hospitals. (Overall, 71 percent had direct experience with the hospital they listed first and no lower than 45 percent with any of the other four.) The confidential survey was conducted between April and May 1991.

The doctors named a total of 172 hospitals, many of them in more than one specialty, out of some 6,700 U.S. institutions. For the sake of credibility NORC established that in order to be named, the number of "best" citations that a hospital received had to be well above the mean (in statistical terms, one standard deviation above the mean). That produced lists of varying lengths, which could be presented as rankings. The percentage of doctors who named a given hospital is included next to its listing.

The Top Ten Hospitals

The following hospitals were on at least three of the specialty lists from U.S. News & World Report.

Johns Hopkins Hospital
Baltimore, MD
13 specialties

Mayo Clinic and Foundation
Rochester, MN
12 specialties

Massachusetts General Hospital
Boston, MA
9 specialties

University of California at Los Angeles Medical Center
Los Angeles, CA
9 specialties

Cleveland Clinic Hospital
Cleveland, OH
5 specialties

Brigham and Women's Hospital
Boston, MA
4 specialties

Memorial Sloan-Kettering Cancer Center
New York, NY
4 specialties

Duke University Medical Center
Durham, NC
3 specialties

Stanford University Hospital
Stanford, CA
3 specialties

University of California, San Francisco Medical Center
San Francisco, CA
3 specialties

The Best Hospitals by Specialty

Cancer

Memorial Sloan-Kettering Cancer Center New York, NY	63%
University of Texas M.D. Anderson Cancer Center Houston, TX	48%
Dana-Farber Cancer Institute Boston, MA	40.5%
Fred Hutchinson Cancer Research Center Seattle, WA	27.5%
Mayo Clinic and Foundation Rochester, MN	26.5%
Johns Hopkins Hospital Baltimore, MD	25.5%

Cardiology

Massachusetts General Hospital Boston, MA	48%
Mayo Clinic and Foundation Rochester, MN	42%
Cleveland Clinic Hospital Cleveland, OH	35.5%
Johns Hopkins Hospital Baltimore, MD	21.5%
Brigham and Women's Hospital Boston, MA	18%
Duke University Medical Center Durham, NC	16.5%
Emory University Hospital Atlanta, GA	16%
Stanford University Hospital Stanford, CA	15.5%
St. Luke's Episcopal Hospital (Texas Heart Institute) Houston, TX	15%

Endocrinology

Mayo Clinic and Foundation Rochester, MN	54.5%
Massachusetts General Hospital Boston, MA	50.5%
National Institutes of Health Bethesda, MD	30.5%
University of California, San Francisco Medical Center San Francisco, CA	25.5%
Johns Hopkins Hospital Baltimore, MD	17%
University of Washington Medical Center Seattle, WA	17%

Gastroenterology

Mayo Clinic and Foundation Rochester, MN	45%
Massachusetts General Hospital Boston, MA	24.5%
Cleveland Clinic Hospital Cleveland, OH	20.5%
University of California at Los Angeles Medical Center Los Angeles, CA	20.5%
Mount Sinai Medical Center New York, NY	16%
University of Chicago Hospitals Chicago, IL	15.5%
Johns Hopkins Hospital Baltimore, MD	14%

Gynecology

Mayo Clinic and Foundation
Rochester, MN   19.5%

University of Texas
M.D. Anderson Cancer Center
Houston, TX   19%

Johns Hopkins Hospital
Baltimore, MD   16%

Brigham and Women's Hospital
Boston, MA   15.5%

Memorial Sloan-Kettering
Cancer Center
New York, NY   14.5%

Duke University Medical Center
Durham, NC   13%

Los Angeles County-
University of Southern California
Medical Center
Los Angeles, CA   11.5%

Massachusetts General Hospital
Boston, MA   11.5%

Cleveland Clinic Hospital
Cleveland, OH   10.5%

Presbyterian Hospital in the
City of New York, Columbia-
Presbyterian Medical Center
New York, NY   10%

University of California at
Los Angeles Medical Center
Los Angeles, CA   9.5%

Neurology

Massachusetts General Hospital
Boston, MA   54.5%

Mayo Clinic and Foundation
Rochester, MN   54%

Johns Hopkins Hospital
Baltimore, MD   31.5%

Presbyterian Hospital in the City of
New York, Columbia-Presbyterian
Medical Center
New York, NY   26.5%

University of California,
San Francisco Medical Center
San Francisco, CA   23%

Cleveland Clinic Hospital
Cleveland, OH   19.5%

Ophthalmology

Johns Hopkins Hospital
Wilmer Eye Institute
Baltimore, MD   62%

Bascom Palmer Eye Institute-
Anne Bates Leach Eye Hospital
Miami, FL   59%

Wills Eye Hospital
Philadelphia, PA   49%

Massachusetts Eye and
Ear Infirmary
Boston, MA   48%

University of California at
Los Angeles Medical Center,
Jules Stein Eye Institute
Los Angeles, CA   33.5%

Orthopedics

Mayo Clinic and Foundation
Rochester, MN   45%

Massachusetts General Hospital
Boston, MA   33.5%

Hospital for Special Surgery
New York, NY   28.5%

University of California at
Los Angeles Medical Center
Los Angeles, CA   12.5%

Brigham and Women's Hospital
Boston, MA   9.5%

Otolaryngology

University of Iowa Hospitals
and Clinics
Iowa City, IA   27%

University of Michigan Hospitals
Ann Arbor, MI   19.5%

Barnes Hospital
St. Louis, MO   17.5%

Mayo Clinic and Foundation
Rochester, MN   17%

University of California at
Los Angeles Medical Center
Los Angeles, CA   16%

Johns Hopkins Hospital
Baltimore, MD   15.5%

Massachusetts Eye and
Ear Infirmary
Boston, MA   12.5%

Mount Sinai Medical Center
New York, NY   9.5%

Psychiatry

In a U.S. News & World Report survey, 66 psychiatrists selected the best hospitals for in-patient care, ignoring location and cost. Percentages reflect the doctors who named a given hospital. Clinics for substance abuse and eating disorders were excluded.

McLean Hospital
Belmont, MA   19%

Massachusetts General Hospital
Boston, MA   18%

New York Hospital-
Cornell Medical Center
New York, NY   15.5%

C.F. Menninger Memorial Hospital
Topeka, KS   13%

Institute of Living
Hartford, CT   10%

University of California at
Los Angeles Medical Center
Los Angeles, CA   9%

Sheppard and Enoch Pratt Hospital
Baltimore, MD   8.5%

Johns Hopkins Hospital
Baltimore, MD   6.5%

Mayo Clinic and Foundation
Rochester, MN   6.5%

Rehabilitation

Rehabilitation Institute of Chicago
Chicago, IL   54%

Craig Hospital
Englewood, CO   35.5%

Mayo Clinic and Foundation
Rochester, MN   32.5%

University of Washington
Medical Center
Seattle, WA   32%

Rusk Institute
New York, NY   27.5%

Baylor Institute for Rehabilitation
Dallas, TX   25.5%

The Institute for Rehabilitation
and Research
Houston, TX   21%

Rheumatology

Mayo Clinic and Foundation
Rochester, MN 49%

Brigham and Women's Hospital
Boston, MA 28%

Massachusetts General Hospital
Boston, MA 26%

Johns Hopkins Hospital
Baltimore, MA 23.5%

**University of California at
Los Angeles Medical Center**
Los Angeles, CA 20%

Stanford University Hospital
Stanford, CA 18.5%

Hospital for Special Surgery
New York, NY 17.5%

Urology

Johns Hopkins Hospital
Baltimore, MD 40%

Mayo Clinic and Foundation
Rochester, MN 30%

Cleveland Clinic Hospital
Cleveland, OH 27.5%

**Memorial Sloan-Kettering
Cancer Center**
New York, NY 21%

Stanford University Hospital
Stanford, CA 19.5%

Duke University Medical Center
Durham, NC 16.5%

**University of California at
Los Angeles Medical Center**
Los Angeles, CA 16.5%

© 1991, U.S. News & World Report

THE BEST IN MEDICINE SURVEY

Herbert J. Dietrich, M.D., and Virginia H. Biddle, the authors of the book *The Best in Medicine,* sent questionnaires to 10 representative doctors in each of 25 medical specialty categories. Each was asked to list 10 hospitals of outstanding excellence for his or her own specialty, excluding his or her own base of operation and regardless of location. The doctors were then asked to list three areas of specific expertise for each hospital chosen.

In addition, the authors personally interviewed a number of doctors who specialize in those fields about which more information was needed than the questionnaires could provide. They then consulted statistics pertaining to the postgraduate training programs of those medical institutions that are accredited by the Accreditation Council for Graduate Medical Education. Using the data from all these sources, they complied a list of approximately 20 medical centers of excellence for each category.

The 25 Best Medical Centers in the United States

The following hospitals scored high marks for at least eight departments in general medicine and surgery. The reader should remember that a center's exact position on the list is less important than the fact that these are peer institutions, with differences often reflected in the particular emphasis given to certain aspects of a specialty.

Mayo Clinic and Foundation
Rochester, MN

Massachusetts General Hospital
Boston, MA

University of Alabama Hospitals
Birmingham, AL

Johns Hopkins Hospital
Baltimore, MD

**Baylor College of Medicine
and Hospitals**
Houston, TX
(Principal affiliated Teaching Hospitals are Methodist Hospital and Harris County Hospital District-Ben Taub General Hospital.)

**University of Washington
Medical Center**
Seattle, WA

Cleveland Clinic Hospital
Cleveland, OH

**Hospital of the University
of Pennsylvania**
Philadelphia, PA

Duke University Medical Center
Durham, NC

**University of California,
San Francisco Medical Center**
San Francisco, CA

**New York Hospital-Cornell
Medical Center**
New York, NY

University of Michigan Hospitals
Ann Arbor, MI

Brigham and Women's Hospital
Boston, MA

Yale-New Haven Hospital
New Haven, CT

**Vanderbilt University Hospital
and Clinic**
Nashville, TN

University of Miami Affiliated Hospitals
Miami, FL
(Principal affiliated Teaching Hospital is Jackson Memorial Hospital.)

University of Minnesota Hospital and Clinic
Minneapolis, MN

University of Texas-Southwestern Medical Center
Dallas, TX
(Principal affiliated Teaching Hospital is Parkland Memorial Hospital.)

Northwestern Memorial Hospital
Chicago, IL

Barnes Hospital
St. Louis, MO

University of Pittsburgh Medical and Health Care Division
Pittsburgh, PA
(Principal affiliated Teaching Hospitals are Western Psychiatric Institute and Clinic, Montefiore University Hospital, and Presbyterian University Hospital.)

University of Colorado Health Sciences Center
Denver, CO

Stanford University Hospital
Stanford, CA

Presbyterian Hospital in the City of New York, Columbia-Presbyterian Medical Center
New York, NY

University of California at Los Angeles Medical Center
Los Angeles, CA

The Best Hospitals by Specialty

These are the specialties not covered by the U.S. News & World Report Survey.

Dermatology

ALABAMA
University of Alabama Hospitals
Birmingham

CALIFORNIA
Stanford University Hospital
Stanford

COLORADO
University of Colorado Health Sciences Center
Denver

CONNECTICUT
Yale-New Haven Hospital
New Haven

FLORIDA
Jackson Memorial Hospital
Miami

GEORGIA
Emory University Hospital
Atlanta

ILLINOIS
University of Illinois Hospital and Clinics
Chicago

MASSACHUSETTS
Massachusetts General Hospital
Boston

MICHIGAN
University of Michigan Hospitals
Ann Arbor

MINNESOTA
Mayo Clinic and Foundation
Rochester

NEW HAMPSHIRE
Dartmouth-Hitchcock Medical Center
Hanover

NEW YORK
New York Hospital-Cornell Medical Center
New York

Presbyterian Hospital in the City of New York, Columbia-Presbyterian Medical Center
New York

NORTH CAROLINA
Duke University Medical Center
Durham

OHIO
Cleveland Clinic Foundation
Cleveland

OKLAHOMA
University of Oklahoma Health Sciences Center
Oklahoma City
(Principal affiliated Teaching Hospitals are Oklahoma Medical Center and Presbyterian Hospital.)

PENNSYLVANIA
Hospital of the University of Pennsylvania
Philadelphia

TEXAS
University of Texas-Southwestern Medical Center
Dallas
(Principal affiliated Teaching Hospital is Parkland Memorial Hospital.)

Baylor College of Medicine and Hospitals
Houston
(Principal affiliated Teaching Hospitals are Methodist Hospital and Harris County Hospital District-Ben Taub General Hospital.)

VIRGINIA
Virginia Commonwealth University, Medical College of Virginia Hospitals
Richmond

Hematology

ALABAMA
University of Alabama Hospitals
Birmingham

CALIFORNIA
Green Hospital of Scripps Clinic
La Jolla

**University of California,
San Francisco Medical Center**
San Francisco

CONNECTICUT
Yale-New Haven Hospital
New Haven

DISTRICT OF COLUMBIA
**George Washington
University Hospital**
Washington

FLORIDA
**University of South Florida
Medical Center**
Tampa
*(Principal affiliated Teaching Hospital is
Tampa General Hospital.)*

**University of Miami
Affiliated Hospitals**
Miami
*(Principal affiliated Teaching Hospital is
Jackson Memorial Hospital.)*

ILLINOIS
**University of Illinois Hospital
and Clinics**
Chicago

MARYLAND
Johns Hopkins Hospital
Baltimore

MASSACHUSETTS
Brigham and Women's Hospital
Boston

New England Medical Center
Boston

Dana-Farber Cancer Institute
Boston

MINNESOTA
**University of Minnesota
Hospital and Clinic**
Minneapolis

MISSOURI
University Hospital and Clinics
Columbia

NEW YORK
**St. Luke's-Roosevelt Hospital
Center, St. Luke's Division**
New York

**State University of New York
Health Science Center,
University Hospital**
Syracuse

NORTH CAROLINA
**University of North Carolina
Hospitals**
Chapel Hill

Duke University Medical Center
Durham

PENNSYLVANIA
**Hospital of the University
of Pennsylvania**
Philadelphia

TEXAS
**University of Texas-Southwestern
Medical Center**
Dallas
*(Principal affiliated Teaching Hospital is
Parkland Memorial Hospital.)*

UTAH
**University of Utah Hospital
and Clinics**
Salt Lake City

Pulmonary Medicine

ALABAMA
University of Alabama Hospitals
Birmingham

ARKANSAS
University Hospital of Arkansas
Little Rock

CALIFORNIA
**University of California,
Davis Medical Center**
Sacramento

COLORADO
**University of Colorado Health
Sciences Center**
Denver

CONNECTICUT
**Yale-New Haven Hospital,
Winchester Chest Clinic**
New Haven

ILLINOIS
University of Chicago Hospitals
Chicago

INDIANA
Indiana University Medical Center
Indianapolis

MARYLAND
Johns Hopkins Hospital
Baltimore

MASSACHUSETTS
University Hospital
Boston

Brigham and Women's Hospital
Boston

MICHIGAN
University of Michigan Hospitals
Ann Arbor

MINNESOTA
Mayo Clinic and Foundation
Rochester

NEW YORK
Bellevue Hospital Center
New York

NORTH CAROLINA
Duke University Medical Center
Durham

PENNSYLVANIA

**Hospital of the University
of Pennsylvania**
Philadelphia

Presbyterian University Hospital
Pittsburgh

TENNESSEE

**Vanderbilt University Hospital
and Clinic**
Nashville

TEXAS

**Baylor College of Medicine
and Hospitals**
Houston
*(Principal affiliated Teaching Hospitals are
Methodist Hospital and Harris County Hos-
pital District-Ben Taub General Hospital.)*

**University of Texas-Southwestern
Medical Center**
Dallas
*(Principal affiliated Teaching Hospital is
Parkland Memorial Hospital.)*

UTAH

**University of Utah Hospital
and Clinics**
Salt Lake City

WASHINGTON

**University of Washington
Medical Center**
Seattle

Health Information and Support Organizations

The organizations in this section are listed first by disorder, then alphabetically according to whether they are a Health Information Organization or a Support Group. Each listing gives you the organization's name, address, and phone number.

If you cannot find an organization that covers your needs, turn to page 590 and look under the section called General Organizations.

Cancer

HEALTH INFORMATION ORGANIZATIONS

AMC Cancer Research Center
1600 Pierce St.
Denver, CO 80214
800-525-3777
303-233-6501 in CO

American Cancer Society, Inc.
1599 Clifton Rd., NE
Atlanta, GA 30329-4251
800-ACS-2345
404-320-3333

American College of Radiology
1891 Preston White Dr.
Reston, VA 22091
703-648-8900

Bloch Cancer Hot Line
4410 Main St.
Kansas City, MO 64111
816-932-8453

Cancer Research Institute, Inc.
133 E. 58th St.
New York, NY 10022
212-688-7515

Centers for Disease Control Office on Smoking and Health
Public Information Branch
Mail Stop K-50, 1600 Clifton Rd., NE
Atlanta, GA 30333
404-488-5705

Leukemia Society of America
733 Third Ave.
New York, NY 10017
212-573-8484

National Alliance of Breast Cancer Organizations
1180 Ave. of the Americas, 2nd Fl.
New York, NY 10036
212-719-0154

National Cancer Care Foundation, Inc./Cancer Care, Inc.
1180 Ave. of the Americas
New York, NY 10036
212-221-3300

National Cancer Institute
Public Inquiries Office
9000 Rockville Pike
Bldg. 31, Rm. 10A24
Bethesda, MD 20892
800-4-CANCER
301-496-5583

National Coalition for Cancer Survivorship
1010 Wayne Ave., Suite 300
Silver Spring, MD 20910
301-585-2616

Patient Advocates for Advanced Cancer Treatment
1143 Parmelee, NW
Grand Rapids, MI 49504
616-453-1477

Rose Kushner Breast Cancer Advisory Center
PO Box 224
Kensington, MD 20895
Please contact by mail.

The Skin Cancer Foundation
245 5th Ave., Suite 2402
New York, NY 10016
212-725-5176

United Ostomy Association
36 Executive Park, Suite 120
Irvine, CA 92714-6744
800-826-0826

Y-ME
National Organization for Breast Cancer Information and Support
18220 Harwood Ave.
Homewood, IL 60430
800-221-2141
708-799-8228 in IL

YWCA
ENCORE
726 Broadway
New York, NY 10003
212-614-2827
Fax: 212-677-9716

SUPPORT GROUPS

AMC Cancer Research Center
1600 Pierce St.
Denver, CO 80214
800-525-3777
303-233-6501 in CO

American Cancer Society, Inc.
1599 Clifton Rd., NE
Atlanta, GA 30329-4251
800-ACS-2345
404-320-3333

Cancer Guidance Institute
1323 Forbes Ave., Suite 200
Pittsburgh, PA 15219
412-261-2211

Cancer Lifeline
1191 Second Ave., Suite 680
Seattle, WA 98101
206-461-4542
800-255-5505 in WA

Cancer Support Network
802 E. Jefferson
Bloomington, IL 61701
309-829-2273

Cancer Wellness Center
9701 N. Kenton, Suite18
Skokie, IL 60076
708-982-9789 hotline
708-982-9689 office

**Intestinal Multiple Polyposis &
Colorectal Cancer (IMPACC)**
c/o Mrs. Dolores Boone
1008-101 Brinker Dr.
Hagerstown, MD 21740
301-791-7526

Let's Face It
PO Box 711
Concord, MA 01742
508-371-3186

Leukemia Society of America
733 Third Ave.
New York, NY 10017
212-573-8484

**National Alliance of Breast Cancer
Organizations**
1180 Ave. of the Americas, 2nd Fl.
New York, NY 10036
212-719-0154

**National Coalition for Cancer
Survivorship**
1010 Wayne Ave., Suite 300

Silver Spring, MD 20910
301-585-2616

**Patient Advocates for Advanced
Cancer Treatment**
1143 Parmelee, NW
Grand Rapids, MI 49504
616-453-1477

United Ostomy Association
36 Executive Park, Suite 120
Irvine, CA 92714-6744
800-826-0826

Y-ME
National Organization for Breast
Cancer Information and Support
18220 Harwood Ave.
Homewood, IL 60430
800-221-2141
708-799-8228 in IL

YWCA
ENCORE
726 Broadway
New York, NY 10003
212-614-2827
Fax: 212-677-9716

The Blood

HEALTH INFORMATION
ORGANIZATIONS

**International Center for Control
of Nutritional Anemia**
3901 Rainbow Blvd.
Kansas City, KS 66160
913-588-7037

**National Association for
Sickle Cell Disease**
3345 Wilshire Blvd., Suite 1106
Los Angeles, CA 90010-1880
800-421-8453
203-736-5455 in CA

**National Heart, Lung, and
Blood Institute**
Information Center
PO Box 30105
Bethesda, MD 20824-0105
301-951-3260

SUPPORT GROUPS

**National Association for
Sickle Cell Disease**
3345 Wilshire Blvd., Suite 1106

Los Angeles, CA 90010-1880
800-421-8453
203-736-5455 in CA

The Brain and
Nervous System

HEALTH INFORMATION
ORGANIZATIONS

Acoustic Neuroma Association
PO Box 12402
Atlanta, GA 30355
404-237-8023

**Alzheimer's Disease Education
and Referral Center**
PO Box 8250-JML
Silver Spring, MD 20907-8250
301-495-3311

Alzheimer's Association, Inc.
919 N. Michigan Ave., Suite 1000
Chicago, IL 60611-1676
800-272-3900
312-335-8700 office

The Alzheimer's Foundation
8177 S. Harvard, M/C-114
Tulsa, OK 74137
918-743-0098

**American Association of
Neurological Surgeons**
22 S. Washington St.
Park Ridge, IL 60068
708-692-9500
Fax: 708-692-2589

American Brain Tumor Association
3725 N. Talman Ave.
Chicago, IL 60618
800-886-2282 patient services
312-286-5571

**American Chronic Pain
Association, Inc.**
PO Box 850
Rocklin, CA 95677
916-632-0922

**American Council for
Headache Education**
875 Kings Highway, Suite 200
West Deptford, NJ 08096
800-255-ACHE
609-845-0322

American Parkinson's Disease Association
60 Bay St., Suite 401
Staten Island, NY 10301
800-223-2732

American Society of Anesthesiologists
515 Busse Highway
Park Ridge, IL 60068
708-825-5586

Brain Tumor Information Service
University of Chicago
5841 S. Maryland Ave., Rm. J331
Chicago, IL 60637
312-684-1400

Brain Tumor Society
258 Harvard St., Suite 308
Brookline, MA 02146
617-243-4229

Commission on Accreditation of Rehabilitation Facilities
101 N. Wilmot Rd., Suite 500
Tuscon, AZ 85711
602-748-1212
Fax: 602-571-1601

Epilepsy Foundation of America
4351 Garden City Dr., Suite 406
Landover, MD 20785
800-EFA-1000
301-459-3700

International Pain Foundation
909 N.E. 43rd St., Suite 306
Seattle, WA 98105
Please contact by mail.

International Tremor Foundation
360 W. Superior St.
Chicago, IL 60610
312-664-2344

National Ataxia Foundation
15500 Wayzata Blvd., Suite 750
Wayzata, MN 55391
612-473-7666

National Brain Tumor Foundation
323 Geary St., Suite 510
San Francisco, CA 94102
800-934-CURE
415-296-0404

National Foundation for Brain Research
1250 24th St., NW, Suite 300
Washington, DC 20037
202-293-5453

The National Head Injury Foundation, Inc.
1140 Connecticut Ave., NW
Suite 812
Washington, DC 20036
800-444-NHIF
202-296-6443

National Headache Foundation
5252 N. Western Ave.
Chicago, IL 60625
800-843-2256
312-878-7715

National Institute of Neurological Disorders and Stroke
Office of Scientific and Health Reports
PO Box 5801
Bethesda, MD 20824
800-352-9424
301-496-5751

National Parkinson Foundation
1501 N.W. 9th Ave.
Miami, FL 33136
800-327-4545
800-433-7022 in FL

National Spinal Cord Injury Association
600 W. Cummings Park, Suite 2000
Woburn, MA 01801
800-962-9629
617-935-2722

Parkinson Support Groups of America
11376 Cherry Hill Rd., Apt. 204
Beltsville, MD 20705
301-937-1545

Parkinson's Disease Foundation
650 W. 168th St.
New York, NY 10032
800-457-6676
212-923-4700

Parkinson's Educational Program USA
3900 Birch St., Suite 105
Newport Beach, CA 92660
800-344-7872
714-250-2975

United Parkinson Foundation
360 W. Superior St.
Chicago, IL 60610
312-664-2344

Vestibular Disorders Association
PO Box 4467

Portland, OR 97208-4467
503-229-7705 answering machine
Fax: 503-229-8064

SUPPORT GROUPS

Acoustic Neuroma Association
PO Box 12402
Atlanta, GA 30355
404-237-8023

Alzheimer's Association, Inc.
919 N. Michigan Ave., Suite 1000
Chicago, IL 60611-1676
800-272-3900
312-335-8700 office

The Alzheimer's Foundation
8177 S. Harvard, M/C-114
Tulsa, OK 74137
918-743-0098

American Chronic Pain Association, Inc.
PO Box 850
Rocklin, CA 95677
916-632-0922

American Council for Headache Education
875 Kings Highway, Suite 200
West Deptford, NJ 08096
800-255-ACHE
609-845-0322

American Paralysis Association
Spinal Cord Injury Hotline
2201 Argonne Dr.
Baltimore, MD 21218
800-526-3456

American Parkinson's Disease Association
60 Bay St., Suite 401
Staten Island, NY 10301
800-223-2732

Brain Tumor Information Service
University of Chicago
5841 S. Maryland Ave., Rm. J331
Chicago, IL 60637
312-684-1400

Brain Tumor Society
258 Harvard St., Suite 308
Brookline, MA 02146
617-243-4229

Chronic Pain Support Group
PO Box 148
Peninsula, OH 44264
216-657-2948

Epilepsy Foundation of America
4351 Garden City Dr., Suite 406
Landover, MD 20785
800-EFA-1000
301-459-3700

National Ataxia Foundation
15500 Wayzata Blvd., Suite 750
Wayzata, MN 55391
612-473-7666

National Brain Tumor Foundation
323 Geary St., Suite 510
San Francisco, CA 94102
800-934-CURE
415-296-0404

**The National Head Injury
Foundation, Inc.**
1140 Connecticut Ave., NW
Suite 812
Washington, DC 20036
800-444-NHIF
202-296-6443

National Parkinson Foundation
1501 N.W. 9th Ave.
Miami, FL 33136
800-327-4545
800-433-7022 in FL

**National Spinal Cord Injury
Association**
600 W. Cummings Park, Suite 2000
Woburn, MA 01801
800-962-9629
617-935-2722

**Parkinson Support Groups
of America**
11376 Cherry Hill Rd., Apt. 204
Beltsville, MD 20705
301-937-1545

Parkinson's Disease Foundation
650 W. 168th St.
New York, NY 10032
800-457-6676
212-923-4700

**Parkinson's Educational
Program USA**
3900 Birch St., Suite 105
Newport Beach, CA 92660
800-344-7872
714-250-2975

United Parkinson Foundation
360 W. Superior St.
Chicago, IL 60610
312-664-2344

Vestibular Disorders Association
PO Box 4467
Portland, OR 97208-4467
503-229-7705 answering machine
Fax: 503-229-8064

Dental and
Oral Disorders

HEALTH INFORMATION
ORGANIZATIONS

**American Association of
Endodontists**
211 E. Chicago Ave., Suite 1501
Chicago, IL 60611-2691
800-USA-ENDO

**American Association of Oral
and Maxillofacial Surgeons**
9700 W. Bryn Mawr Ave.
Rosemont, IL 60018
800-467-5268

American Board of Oral Pathology
5401 W. Kennedy Blvd., Suite 780
Tampa, FL 33609
813-286-2444

American Board of Orthodontics
225 S. Meramec, #310
St. Louis, MO 63105
314-727-5039

American Board of Periodontology
666 W. Baltimore St.
Baltimore, MD 21201
410-328-2432

American Board of Prosthodontics
PO Box 8437
Atlanta, GA 30306
404-876-2625
Written requests preferred.

American Dental Association
Department of Public Information
and Education
211 E. Chicago Ave.
Chicago, IL 60611
Please contact by mail.

**American Society for
Geriatric Dentistry**
211 E. Chicago Ave., Suite 1616
Chicago, IL 60611
Please contact by mail.

Centers for Disease Control
Division of Oral Health

1600 Clifton Rd., MS F10
Atlanta, GA 30333
404-488-4450

**National Institute of Dental
Research**
9000 Rockville Pike
Bldg. 31, Rm. 2C-35
Bethesda, MD 20892
301-496-4261

The Digestive System

HEALTH INFORMATION
ORGANIZATIONS

American Liver Foundation
1425 Pompton Ave.
Cedar Grove, NJ 07009
800-223-0179
201-256-2550
Fax: 201-256-3214

Center for Digestive Disorders
550 E. Washington St.
West Chicago, IL 60185
708-260-2685

**Center for Ulcer Research and
Education Foundation**
UCLA-CURE/VA Wadsworth
Bldg. 115, Rm. 115
Los Angeles, CA 90073
213-825-3187

**Crohn's & Colitis Foundation
of America, Inc.**
444 Park Ave. S
New York, NY 10016
800-343-3637
212-685-3440

**Digestive Disease National
Coalition**
711 Second St., NE, Suite 200
Washington, DC 20002
202-544-7497

**Gastro-Intestinal Research
Foundation**
70 E. Lake St., Suite 1015
Chicago, IL 60601
312-332-1350

**International Association for
Enterostomal Therapy**
2755 Bristal St.
Costa Mesa, CA 92626
800-228-4238

714-476-0268
Fax: 714-545-3643

Intestinal Disease Foundation, Inc.
1323 Forbes Ave., Suite 200
Pittsburgh, PA 15219
800-800-5776

National Digestive Diseases Information Clearinghouse
PO Box NDDIC
9000 Rockville Pike
Bethesda, MD 20892
Please contact by mail.

SUPPORT GROUPS

American Liver Foundation
1425 Pompton Ave.
Cedar Grove, NJ 07009
800-223-0179
201-256-2550
Fax: 201-256-3214

Center for Digestive Disorders
550 E. Washington St.
West Chicago, IL 60185
708-260-2685

Crohn's & Colitis Foundation of America, Inc.
444 Park Ave. S
New York, NY 10016
800-343-3637
212-685-3440

The Ears, Nose, and Throat

HEALTH INFORMATION ORGANIZATIONS

American Academy of Otolaryngology-Head and Neck Surgery
One Prince St.
Alexandria, VA 22314
703-836-4444
Fax: 703-683-5100

American Hearing Research Foundation
55 E. Washington St., Suite 2022
Chicago, IL 60602
312-726-9670

American Speech-Language-Hearing Association
10801 Rockville Pike

Rockville, MD 20852
800-638-8255
301-897-5700
Fax: 301-571-0457

American Tinnitus Association
PO Box 5
Portland, OR 97207
503-248-9985

Alexander Graham Bell Association for the Deaf, Inc.
3417 Volta Place, NW
Washington, DC 20007-2778
202-337-5220

Better Hearing Institute
PO Box 1840
Washington, DC 20013
800-327-9355

The Deafness Research Foundation
9 E. 38th St.
New York, NY 10016
800-535-3323

Dial a Hearing Test
PO Box 1880
Media, PA 19063
800-222-EARS
800-345-EARS in PA

Hearing Aid Helpline
20361 Middlebelt Rd.
Livonia, MI 48152
800-521-5247

National Association of the Deaf
814 Thayer Ave.
Silver Spring, MD 20910
301-587-1788
301-587-1789 TDD

National Information Center on Deafness
Gallaudet University
800 Florida Ave., NE
Washington, DC 20002
202-651-5051 voice
202-651-5052 TDD

National Institute on Deafness and Other Communication Disorders
9000 Rockville Pike
Bldg. 31, Rm. 3C-35
Bethesda, MD 20892
301-496-7243
301-402-0252 TDD
Fax: 301-402-0018

Self-Help for Hard of Hearing People, Inc.
7800 Wisconsin Ave.
Bethesda, MD 20814
301-657-2248 voice
301-657-2249 TDD

Vestibular Disorders Association
PO Box 4467
Portland, OR 97208-4467
503-229-7705 answering machine
Fax: 503-229-8064

SUPPORT GROUPS

American Academy of Otolaryngology-Head and Neck Surgery
One Prince St.
Alexandria, VA 22314
703-836-4444
Fax: 703-683-5100

American Hearing Research Foundation
55 E. Washington St., Suite 2022
Chicago, IL 60602
312-726-9670

American Tinnitus Association
PO Box 5
Portland, OR 97207
503-248-9985

Better Hearing Institute
PO Box 1840
Washington, DC 20013
800-327-9355

The Deafness Research Foundation
9 E. 38th St.
New York, NY 10016
800-535-3323

International Association of Laryngectomies
c/o American Cancer Society
1599-4251 Clifton Rd., NE
Atlanta, GA 30329
404-320-3333

National Information Center on Deafness
Gallaudet University
800 Florida Ave., NE
Washington, DC 20002
202-651-5051 voice
202-651-5052 TDD

Self-Help for Hard of Hearing People, Inc.
7800 Wisconsin Ave.
Bethesda, MD 20814
301-657-2248 voice
301-657-2249 TDD

Vestibular Disorders Association
PO Box 4467
Portland, OR 97208-4467
503-229-7705 answering machine
Fax: 503-229-8064

The Endocrine System

HEALTH INFORMATION ORGANIZATIONS

American Diabetes Association
1660 Duke St.
Alexandria, VA 22314
800-ADA-DISC
703-232-3472
Fax: 703-683-2890

American Dietetic Association
216 W. Jackson Blvd., Suite 800
Chicago, IL 60606
800-366-1655
312-899-0040

Joslin Diabetes Center, Inc.
One Joslin Place
Boston, MA 02215
617-732-2440
Fax: 617-732-2664

The National Agricultural Library
Food and Nutrition
Information Center
Rm. 304
Beltsville, MD 20705
301-504-5719
Fax: 301-504-5472

National Dairy Council
6300 N. River Rd.
Rosemont, IL 60018-4233
708-696-1860 ext. 220
Fax: 708-696-1033

National Diabetes Information Clearinghouse
Box NDIC, 9000 Rockville Pike
Bethesda, MD 20892
Please contact by mail.

National Federation of the Blind
Diabetics Division

811 Cherry St., Suite 9
Columbia, MO 65201
314-875-8911

The Thyroid Foundation of America, Inc.
Massachusetts General Hospital
Ruth Sleeper Hall, Rm. 350
Boston, MA 02114
617-726-8500
Fax: 617-726-4136

SUPPORT GROUPS

American Diabetes Association
1660 Duke St.
Alexandria, VA 22314
800-ADA-DISC
703-232-3472
Fax: 703-683-2890

The Thyroid Foundation of America, Inc.
Massachusetts General Hospital
Ruth Sleeper Hall, Rm. 350
Boston, MA 02114
617-726-8500
Fax: 617-726-4136

The Eyes

HEALTH INFORMATION ORGANIZATIONS

American Academy of Ophthalmology
Inquiry Clerk, 655 Beach St.
San Francisco, CA 94109
415-561-8500
Fax: 415-561-8567

American Council of the Blind
1155 15th St., NW, Suite 720
Washington, DC 20005
800-424-8666
202-467-5081
Fax: 202-467-5085

American Foundation for the Blind
15 W. 16th St.
New York, NY 10011
800-232-5463
212-620-2000
Fax: 212-620-2105

American Optometric Association
Communications Center
243 N. Lindbergh Blvd.

St. Louis, MO 63141
314-991-4100
Fax: 314-991-4101

Associated Services for the Blind
919 Walnut St.
Philadelphia, PA 19107
215-627-0600
Fax: 215-922-0692

Association for Macular Diseases, Inc.
210 E. 64th St.
New York, NY 10021
212-605-3719

Benign Essential Blepharospasm Research Foundation, Inc.
PO Box 12468
Beaumont, TX 77726-2468
409-832-0788

Eye Bank Association of America
1001 Connecticut Ave., NW
Suite 601
Washington, DC 20036
202-775-4999

Glaucoma Support Network
Foundation for
Glaucoma Research
490 Post St., Suite 830
San Francisco, CA 94102
415-986-3162

Guiding Eyes for the Blind, Inc.
611 Granite Springs Rd.
Yorktown Heights, NY 10598
914-245-4024

The Library of Congress
National Library Service for the
Blind and Physically Handicapped
1291 Taylor St., NW
Washington, DC 20542
800-424-8567
202-707-9275 reference

The Lighthouse National Center for Vision and Aging
800 Second Ave.
New York, NY 10017
800-334-5497 TDD
212-808-5544 TDD

National Association for the Visually Handicapped
22 W. 21st St., 6th Fl.
New York, NY 10010
212-889-3141

**National Eye Care Project
Help Line**
PO Box 429098
San Francisco, CA 94142-9098
800-222-EYES

National Eye Institute
Information Office
Bldg. 31, Rm. 6A-32
Bethesda, MD 20892
301-496-5248

**National Retinitis Pigmentosa
Foundation, Inc.**
1401 Mt. Royal Ave., 4th Fl.
Baltimore, MD 21217
800-683-5555

**The National Society to
Prevent Blindness**
500 E. Remington Rd.
Schaumburg, IL 60173
800-331-2020

Vision Foundation
818 Mt. Auburn St.
Watertown, MA 02172
617-926-4232

SUPPORT GROUPS

**American Academy of
Ophthalmology**
Inquiry Clerk, 655 Beach St.
San Francisco, CA 94109
415-561-8500
Fax: 415-561-8567

American Council of the Blind
1155 15th St., NW, Suite 720
Washington, DC 20005
800-424-8666
202-467-5081
Fax: 202-467-5085

American Foundation for the Blind
15 W. 16th St.
New York, NY 10011
800-232-5463
212-620-2000
Fax: 212-620-2105

**Association for Macular
Diseases, Inc.**
210 E. 64th St.
New York, NY 10021
212-605-3719

**Benign Essential Blepharospasm
Research Foundation, Inc.**
PO Box 12468

Beaumont, TX 77726-2468
409-832-0788

**Council of Citizens With
Low Vision**
International Organization
5707 Brockton Dr., Suite 302
Indianapolis, IN 46220-5481
800-733-2258
317-254-1185
Fax: 317-251-6588

Glaucoma Support Network
Foundation for
Glaucoma Research
490 Post St., Suite 830
San Francisco, CA 94102
415-986-3162

**The Lighthouse National Center
for Vision and Aging**
800 Second Ave.
New York, NY 10017
800-334-5497 TDD
212-808-5544 TDD

**National Association for the
Visually Handicapped**
22 W. 21st St., 6th Fl.
New York, NY 10010
212-889-3141

National Federation of the Blind
1800 Johnson St.
Baltimore, MD 21230
410-659-9314

**National Retinitis Pigmentosa
Foundation, Inc.**
1401 Mt. Royal Ave., 4th Fl.
Baltimore, MD 21217
800-683-5555

Vision Foundation
818 Mt. Auburn St.
Watertown, MA 02172
617-926-4232

*The Heart and
Blood Vessels*

HEALTH INFORMATION
ORGANIZATIONS

**American Association of
Neurological Surgeons**
22 S. Washington St.
Park Ridge, IL 60068

708-692-9500
Fax: 708-692-2589

American College of Cardiology
9111 Old Georgetown Rd.
Bethesda, MD 20814-1699
800-253-4636
301-897-5400
Fax: 301-897-9745

American Heart Association
7320 Greenville Ave.
Dallas, TX 75231-4599
214-373-6300
Fax: 214-706-1341

**American Occupational Therapy
Association, Inc.**
1383 Piccard Dr., Box 1725
Rockville, MD 20850
301-948-9626
Fax: 301-948-5529

American Paralysis Association
PO Box 187
Short Hills, NJ 07078
800-255-0292
201-379-2690

**American Physical Therapy
Association**
1111 N. Fairfax
Alexandria, VA 22314
703-684-2782
Fax: 703-684-7343

**Citizens for Public Action on Blood
Pressure and Cholesterol**
7200 Wisconsin Ave., Suite 1002
Bethesda, MD 20814
301-907-7790
Fax: 301-907-7792

**Commission on Accreditation
of Rehabilitation Facilities**
101 N. Wilmot Rd., Suite 500
Tuscon, AZ 85711
602-748-1212
Fax: 602-571-1601

Courage Stroke Network
3915 Golden Valley Rd.
Golden Valley, MN 55422
800-553-6321
612-520-0464

National Aphasia Association
PO Box 1887, Murray Hill Station
New York, NY 10156-0611
800-922-4NAA

**National Heart, Lung, and
Blood Institute**
Information Center
PO Box 30105
Bethesda, MD 20824-0105
301-951-3260

**National Institute of Neurological
Disorders and Stroke**
Office of Scientific and
Health Reports
PO Box 5801
Bethesda, MD 20824
800-352-9424
301-496-5751

**National Rehabilitation
Information Center**
8455 Colesville Rd., Suite 935
Silver Spring, MD 20910
800-34-NARIC voice/TDD
301-588-9284

National Stroke Association
300 E. Hampden Ave., Suite 240
Englewood , CO 80110-2654
800-787-6537
303-762-9922
Fax: 303-762-1190

**United States Department
of Education**
National Institute on Disability
and Rehabilitation Research
330 C St., SW, Rm. 3060
Washington, DC 20202-2572
202-732-1134

SUPPORT GROUPS

**Citizens for Public Action on Blood
Pressure and Cholesterol**
7200 Wisconsin Ave., Suite 1002
Bethesda, MD 20814
301-907-7790
Fax: 301-907-7792

Coronary Club, Inc.
9500 Euclid Ave., Rm. E4-15
Cleveland, OH 44195
216-444-3690

Courage Stroke Network
3915 Golden Valley Rd.
Golden Valley, MN 55422
800-553-6321
612-520-0464

Mended Hearts
7320 Greenville Ave.

Dallas, TX 75231-4599
214-706-1442

National Aphasia Association
PO Box 1887, Murray Hill Station
New York, NY 10156-0611
800-922-4NAA

**National Heart, Lung, and
Blood Institute**
Information Center
PO Box 30105
Bethesda, MD 20824-0105
301-951-3260

**National Rehabilitation
Information Center**
8455 Colesville Rd., Suite 935
Silver Spring, MD 20910
800-34-NARIC voice/TDD
301-588-9284

National Stroke Association
300 E. Hampden Ave., Suite 240
Englewood, CO 80110-2654
800-787-6537
303-762-9922
Fax: 303-762-1190

The Kidneys and Urinary Tract

HEALTH INFORMATION ORGANIZATIONS

**American Association of
Kidney Patients**
111 S. Parker St., Suite 405
Tampa, FL 33606
800-749-2257
813-251-0725
Fax: 813-254-3270

**American Foundation for
Urologic Disease**
1120 N. Charles St.
Baltimore, MD 21201
800-242-AFUD
301-727-2896
Fax: 301-783-1566

American Kidney Fund
6110 Executive Blvd., Suite 1010
Rockville, MD 20852
800-638-8299
301-881-3052
Fax: 301-881-0898

American Urological Association
1120 N. Charles St.
Baltimore, MD 21201
410-727-1100

Bladder Health Council
1120 N. Charles St.
Baltimore, MD 21201
410-727-2896

**The National Kidney and
Urologic Diseases Information
Clearinghouse**
PO Box NKUDIC
9000 Rockville Pike
Bethesda, MD 20892
Please contact by mail.

National Kidney Foundation
30 E. 33rd St.
New York, NY 10016
800-622-9010
212-889-2210
Fax: 212-689-9261

SUPPORT GROUPS

**American Association of
Kidney Patients**
111 S. Parker St., Suite 405
Tampa, FL 33606
800-749-2257
813-251-0725
Fax: 813-254-3270

**American Foundation for
Urologic Disease**
1120 N. Charles St.
Baltimore, MD 21201
800-242-AFUD
301-727-2896
Fax: 301-783-1566

American Kidney Fund
6110 Executive Blvd., Suite 1010
Rockville, MD 20852
800-638-8299
301-881-3052
Fax: 301-881-0898

**Transplant Recipients International
Organization**
244 N. Bellefield Ave.
Pittsburgh, PA 15213
412-687-2210
Fax: 412-687-7190

The Lungs and Respiratory System

HEALTH INFORMATION ORGANIZATIONS

American Academy of Allergy and Immunology
611 E. Wells St.
Milwaukee, WI 53202
800-822-2762
414-272-6071

American Allergy Association
PO Box 7273
Menlo Park, CA 94026
415-322-1663
Fax: 415-328-2295

American Lung Association
1740 Broadway
New York, NY 10019
212-315-8700
Fax: 212-265-5642

Asthma and Allergy Foundation of America
1125 15th St., NW, Suite 502
Washington, DC 20005
800-7ASTHMA
202-466-7643
Fax: 202-466-8940

Emphysema Anonymous, Inc.
PO Box 3224
Seminole, FL 34642
813-391-9977

National Heart, Lung, and Blood Institute
Information Center
PO Box 30105
Bethesda, MD 20824-0105
301-951-3260

National Institute of Allergy and Infectious Diseases
Bldg. 31, Rm. 7A-32
Bethesda, MD 20892
301-496-5717

National Jewish Center for Immunology and Respiratory Medicine
Lung Line
1400 Jackson St.
Denver, CO 80206
800-222-LUNG

SUPPORT GROUPS

American Academy of Allergy and Immunology
611 E. Wells St.
Milwaukee, WI 53202
800-822-2762
414-272-6071

American Allergy Association
PO Box 7273
Menlo Park, CA 94026
415-322-1663
Fax: 415-328-2295

American Lung Association
1740 Broadway
New York, NY 10019
212-315-8700
Fax: 212-265-5642

Asthma and Allergy Foundation of America
1125 15th St., NW, Suite 502
Washington, DC 20005
800-7ASTHMA
202-466-7643
Fax: 202-466-8940

Emphysema Anonymous, Inc.
PO Box 3224
Seminole, FL 34642
813-391-9977

The Muscles and Bones

HEALTH INFORMATION ORGANIZATIONS

American Academy of Orthopaedic Surgeons
222 S. Prospect Ave.
Park Ridge, IL 60068
800-346-AAOS
708-823-7186
Fax: 708-823-8125

American Lupus Society
3914 Del Amo Blvd., #922
Torrance, CA 90503
310-542-8891

American Podiatric Medical Association
9312 Old Georgetown Rd.
Bethesda, MD 20814-1621
800-FOOT CARE
Fax: 301-530-2752

Ankylosing Spondylitis Association
PO Box 5872
Sherman Oaks, CA 91413
800-777-8189
310-652-0609 in CA

Arthritis Foundation
PO Box 19000
Atlanta, GA 30326
800-283-7800
404-872-7100
Fax: 404-872-0457

National Arthritis and Musculoskeletal and Skin Diseases Information Clearinghouse
PO Box AMS, 9000 Rockville Pike
Bethesda, MD 20892
301-495-4484

National Osteoporosis Foundation
2100 M. St., NW, Suite 602
Washington, DC 20037
202-223-2226

Sjogren's Syndrome Foundation
382 Main St.
Port Washington, NY 11050
516-767-2866

SUPPORT GROUPS

American Lupus Society
3914 Del Amo Blvd., #922
Torrance, CA 90503
310-542-8891

Arthritis Foundation
PO Box 19000
Atlanta, GA 30326
800-283-7800
404-872-7100
Fax: 404-872-0457

National Osteoporosis Foundation
2100 M. St., NW, Suite 602
Washington, DC 20037
202-223-2226

The Skin

HEALTH INFORMATION ORGANIZATIONS

American Academy of Dermatology
PO Box 4014
Schaumburg, IL 60168-4014
708-330-0230
Fax: 708-330-0050

National Alopecia Areata Foundation
710 C St., Suite 11
San Rafael, CA 94901
415-456-4644

National Arthritis and Musculoskeletal and Skin Diseases Information Clearinghouse
PO Box AMS, 9000 Rockville Pike
Bethesda, MD 20892
301-495-4484

National Institute of Allergy and Infectious Diseases
Bldg. 31, Rm. 7A-32
Bethesda, MD 20892
301-496-5717

National Psoriasis Foundation
6443 S.W. Beaverton Highway
Suite 210
Portland, OR 97221
503-297-1545
Fax: 503-292-9341

Psoriasis Research Association
107 Vista del Grande
San Carlos, CA 94070
415-593-1394

The Skin Cancer Foundation
245 5th Ave., Suite 2402
New York, NY 10016
212-725-5176

SUPPORT GROUPS

American Academy of Dermatology
PO Box 4014
Schaumburg, IL 60168-4014
708-330-0230
Fax: 708-330-0050

National Alopecia Areata Foundation
710 C St., Suite 11
San Rafael, CA 94901
415-456-4644

National Psoriasis Foundation
6443 S.W. Beaverton Highway
Suite 210
Portland, OR 97221
503-297-1545
Fax: 503-292-9341

Health Problems of Men

HEALTH INFORMATION ORGANIZATIONS

American College of Surgeons
Office of Public Information
55 E. Erie St.
Chicago, IL 60611
312-664-4050

American Foundation for Urologic Disease
1120 N. Charles St.
Baltimore, MD 21201
800-242-AFUD
301-727-2896
Fax: 301-783-1566

American Urological Association
1120 N. Charles St.
Baltimore, MD 21201
410-727-1100

Bladder Health Council
1120 N. Charles St.
Baltimore, MD 21201
410-727-2896

Continence Restored, Inc.
785 Park Ave.
New York , NY 10021
212-879-3131 ask for
Anne Smith-Young

Help for Incontinent People
PO Box 544
Union, SC 29379
800-BLADDER
803-579-7900
Fax: 803-579-7902

Impotence Institute of America
119 S. Ruth St.
Maryville, TN 37801
800-669-1603
615-983-6064

International Association for Enterostomal Therapy
2755 Bristal St.
Costa Mesa, CA 92626
800-228-4238
714-476-0268
Fax: 714-545-3643

The Male Sexual Dysfunction Clinic
4940 Eastern Ave.
Baltimore, MD 21224
410-550-2329

The National Kidney and Urologic Diseases Information Clearinghouse
PO Box NKUDIC
9000 Rockville Pike
Bethesda, MD 20892
Please contact by mail.

Recovery of Male Potency
27211 Lahser Rd., Suite 208
Southfield, MI 48034
800-835-7667
313-357-1216

The Sexual Behaviors Consultation Unit
550 N. Broadway, Suite 114
Baltimore, MD 21205
410-955-6318

SUPPORT GROUPS

American Foundation for Urologic Disease
1120 N. Charles St.
Baltimore, MD 21201
800-242-AFUD
301-727-2896
Fax: 301-783-1566

Continence Restored, Inc.
785 Park Ave.
New York , NY 10021
212-879-3131 ask for
Anne Smith-Young

Help for Incontinent People
PO Box 544
Union, SC 29379
800-BLADDER
803-579-7900
Fax: 803-579-7902

Impotents Anonymous
119 S. Ruth St.
Maryville, TN 37801
615-983-6064

The Sexual Behaviors Consultation Unit
550 N. Broadway, Suite 114
Baltimore, MD 21205
410-955-6318

Health Problems of Women

HEALTH INFORMATION ORGANIZATIONS

American College of Obstetricians and Gynecologists
Resource Center
409 12th St., SW
Washington, DC 20024
202-638-5577
Fax: 202-484-5107

American College of Surgeons
Office of Public Information
55 E. Erie St.
Chicago, IL 60611
312-664-4050

American Urological Association
1120 N. Charles St.
Baltimore, MD 21201
410-727-1100

Center for Climacteric Studies
University of Florida
222 S.W. 36th Terrace, Suite C
Gainesville, FL 32607
904-372-5600
Fax: 904-376-3716

Continence Restored, Inc.
785 Park Ave.
New York , NY 10021
212-879-3131 ask for
Anne Smith-Young

Help for Incontinent People
PO Box 544
Union, SC 29379
800-BLADDER
803-579-7900
Fax: 803-579-7902

Hysterectomy Educational Resources, Inc.
422 Bryn Mawr Ave.
Bala Cynwyd, PA 19004
215-667-7757

International Association for Enterostomal Therapy
2755 Bristal St.
Costa Mesa, CA 92626
800-228-4238
714-476-0268
Fax: 714-545-3643

National Cancer Institute
Public Inquiries Office

9000 Rockville Pike
Bldg. 31, Rm. 10A24
Bethesda, MD 20892
800-4-CANCER
301-496-5583

National Women's Health Network
1325 G St., NW
Washington, DC 20005
202-347-1140
Fax: 202-347-1168

Women's Sports Foundation
342 Madison Ave., Suite 728
New York, NY 10173
800-227-3988
212-972-9170

SUPPORT GROUPS

Center for Climacteric Studies
University of Florida
222 S.W. 36th Terrace, Suite C
Gainesville, FL 32607
904-372-5600
Fax: 904-376-3716

Continence Restored, Inc.
785 Park Ave.
New York , NY 10021
212-879-3131 ask for
Anne Smith-Young

Help for Incontinent People
PO Box 544
Union, SC 29379
800-BLADDER
803-579-7900
Fax: 803-579-7902

Hysterectomy Educational Resources, Inc.
422 Bryn Mawr Ave.
Bala Cynwyd, PA 19004
215-667-7757

National Women's Health Network
1325 G St., NW
Washington, DC 20005
202-347-1140
Fax: 202-347-1168

Older Women's League
666 11th St., NW, Suite 700
Washington, DC 20001
202-783-6686
Fax: 202-638-2356

Mental Health

HEALTH INFORMATION ORGANIZATIONS

Al-Anon Family Group Headquarters
1372 Broadway
New York, NY 10018
800-356-9996
212-302-7240

American Mental Health Counselors Association
5999 Stevenson Ave.
Alexandria, VA 22304
800-326-2642
703-823-9800

American Narcolepsy Association
425 California St., Suite 201
San Francisco, CA 94104-6230
800-222-6085
415-788-4793

American Psychiatric Association
1400 K St., NW
Washington, DC 20005
202-682-6000
Fax: 202-789-2648

American Psychological Association
750 First St., NE
Washington, DC 20002
202-336-5500

American Sleep Apnea Association
PO Box 3893
Charlottesville, VA 22908
Please contact by mail.

The American Sleep Disorders Association
1610 14th St., NW, Suite 300
Rochester, MN 55901
507-287-6006
Fax: 507-287-6008

Depression and Related Affective Disorders Association
Johns Hopkins Hospital
600 N. Wolfe St., Meyer 3-181
Baltimore, MD 21205
410-955-4647

Depression Awareness Recognition & Treatment Program
5600 Fishers Lane
Rm. 1085, Parklawn Bldg.
Rockville, MD 20857

800-421-4211
301-443-4140

Emotions Anonymous
PO Box 4245
St. Paul, MN 55104
612-647-9712

**National Alliance for the
Mentally Ill**
2101 Wilson Blvd., Suite 302
Arlington, VA 22201
800-950-6264
703-524-7600

**National Association of Private
Psychiatric Hospitals**
1319 F St., NW, Suite 1000
Washington, DC 20004
202-393-6700

**National Council on Alcoholism
and Drug Dependence**
12 W. 21st St.
New York, NY 10010
212-206-6770

**National Depressive and
Manic-Depressive Association**
730 N. Franklin, Suite 501
Chicago, IL 60610
312-642-0049
Fax: 312-642-7243

National Institute of Mental Health
Mental Health Public Inquiries
5600 Fishers Lane, Rm. 15C-05
Rockville, MD 20857
301-443-4513 publications
Fax: 301-443-0008

National Mental Health Association
1021 Prince St.
Alexandria, VA 22314-2971
800-969-6977
703-684-7722
Fax: 703-684-5968

National Sleep Foundation
122 S. Robertson Blvd., Suite 201
Los Angeles, CA 90048
Please contact by mail.

Well Spouse Foundation
PO Box 28876
San Diego, CA 92198
619-673-9043

SUPPORT GROUPS

**Al-Anon Family Group
Headquarters**
1372 Broadway
New York, NY 10018
800-356-9996
212-302-7240

Alcoholics Anonymous
PO Box 459, Grand Central Station
New York, NY 10163
212-686-1100

American Narcolepsy Association
425 California St., Suite 201
San Francisco, CA 94104-6230
800-222-6085
415-788-4793

American Sleep Apnea Association
PO Box 3893
Charlottesville, VA 22908
Please contact by mail.

Council on Anxiety Disorders
PO Box 17011
Winston-Salem, NC 27116
919-722-7760

Emotional Health Anonymous
PO Box 429
Glendale, CA 91209
818-240-3215

Emotions Anonymous
PO Box 4245
St. Paul, MN 55104
612-647-9712

**National Alliance for the
Mentally Ill**
2101 Wilson Blvd., Suite 302
Arlington, VA 22201
800-950-6264
703-524-7600

**National Depressive and
Manic-Depressive Association**
730 N. Franklin, Suite 501
Chicago, IL 60610
312-642-0049
Fax: 312-642-7243

National Mental Health Association
1021 Prince St.
Alexandria, VA 22314-2971
800-969-6977
703-684-7722
Fax: 703-684-5968

**National Mental Health Consumer
Self-Help Clearinghouse**
311 S. Juniper St., Rm. 902
Philidelphia, PA 19107
800-688-4226
215-735-2481

Recoveries Anonymous
PO Box 1212
Hewitt Square Station
East Northport, NY 11731
516-261-1212

Recovery, Inc.
802 N. Dearborn St.
Chicago, IL 60610
312-337-5661

This section contains the General Health Information Organizations that do not easily fit under the disorders covered by the Handbook. They are ordered alphabetically, and each listing gives you the organization's name, address, and phone number. Also in this section are National and Regional Self-Help Clearinghouses, beginning on page 593.

To find a Health Information Organization by Disorder, turn to page 578.

GENERAL HEALTH INFORMATION ORGANIZATIONS

Aerobics and Fitness Foundation
15250 Ventura Blvd., Suite 310
Sherman Oaks, CA 91403
800-BE-FIT-86

Alcohol, Drug Abuse, and Mental Health Administration
Office of the Administrator
5600 Fishers Lane
Parklawn Bldg., Rm, 12-105
Rockville, MD 20857
301-443-4797

American Association of Retired Persons
601 E St., NW
Washington, DC 20049
202-434-2277

American Association of Retired Persons
Pharmacy Service
500 Montgomery St.
Alexandria, VA 22314
800-456-4636
703-684-0244

American College of Surgeons
Office of Public Information
55 E. Erie St.
Chicago, IL 60611
312-664-4050

American Dietetic Association
216 W. Jackson Blvd., Suite 800
Chicago, IL 60606
800-366-1655
312-899-0040

American Geriatrics Society
770 Lexington Ave., Suite 300
New York, NY 10021
212-308-1414

American Health Foundation
320 E. 43rd St.
New York, NY 10017
212-953-1900
Fax: 212-687-2339

American Hospital Association
840 N. Lake Shore Dr.
Chicago, IL 60611
800-242-2626
312-280-6000

American Lupus Society
3914 Del Amo Blvd., #922
Torrance, CA 90503
310-542-8891

American Medical Association
515 N. State St.
Chicago, IL 60610
800-262-3211
312-464-5000

American Nurses Association
2420 Pershing Rd.
Kansas City, MO 64108
800-444-5720
816-474-5720

American Red Cross
431 18th St., NW
Washington, DC 20006
202-737-8300

American Society of Internal Medicine
1101 Vermont Ave., NW
Suite 500
Washington, DC 20005-3457
800-338-ASIM
202-289-1700
Fax: 202-682-8659

American Society of Plastic and Reconstructive Surgical Surgeons
444 E. Algonquin Rd.
Arlington Heights, IL 60005
708-228-9900

American Society on Aging
833 Market St., Suite 512
San Francisco, CA 94103
415-882-2910

American Trauma Society
8903 Presidential Parkway
Suite 512
Upper Marlboro, MD 20772
800-556-7890
301-420-4189

Association of American Medical Colleges
2450 N St., NW
Washington, DC 20037
202-828-0400
Fax: 202-828-1125

Center for Medical Consumers
237 Thompson St.
New York, NY 10012
212-674-7105

Centers for Disease Control
Center for Chronic Disease Prevention and Health Promotion
1600 Clifton Rd., NE
Bldg. 1, SSB249, MS A 34
Atlanta, GA 30333
404-639-3492

Centers for Disease Control
Office of Public Affairs
1600 Clifton Rd., NE
Atlanta, GA 30333
404-639-3311
404-639-3534 publications

Choice in Dying
200 Varick St.
New York, NY 10014
212-246-6962

Community Health Accreditation Program, Inc.
350 Hudson St.
New York, NY 10014
800-669-1656
212-989-9393 ext. 242

Congress of the United States
Office of Technology Assessment
Washington, DC 20510-8025
202-228-6590
202-224-8996 publications

Consumer Health Information Research Institute
3521 Broadway
Kansas City, MO 64111
800-821-6671

Consumer Information Center
Pueblo, CO 81009
719-948-3334

Council of Better Business Bureaus
4200 Wilson Blvd., Suite 800
Arlington, VA 22203
703-276-0100

Department of Health and Human Services
Administration on Aging
330 Independence Ave., SW
Rm. 4646
Washington, DC 20201
202-619-0641

Department of Health and Human Services
Public Health Service
200 Independence Ave., SW
Rm. 717-H
Washington, DC 20201
202-245-6867

Food and Drug Administration
Center for Biologics Evaluation
and Research
8800 Rockville Pike
Bldg. 29-NIH Campus
Bethesda, MD 20852
301-295-8228

Food and Drug Administration
Center for Devices and
Radiological Health
1901 Chapman Ave.

Rockville, MD 20857
301-443-4190

Food and Drug Administration
Center for Drug Evaluation
and Research
5600 Fishers Lane
Rockville, MD 20857
301-295-8012

Food and Drug Administration
Office of Consumer Affairs
5600 Fishers Lane, HFE 88
Rockville, MD 20857
301-443-3170

Foundation for Hospice and Home Care
519 C St., NE
Washington, DC 20002
202-547-6586

The Gerontological Society of America
Information Service
1275 K St, NW, Suite 350
Washington, DC 20005-4006
202-842-1275
Fax: 202-842-1150

Gray Panthers Project Fund
1424 16th St., NW, Suite 602
Washington, DC 20036
202-387-3111

Health Care Financing Administration
200 Independence Ave., SW
Rm. 428-H
Washington, DC 20201
202-245-6145

Health Care Financing Administration
Office of Prepaid Health Care
330 Independence Ave., SW
Wilbur J. Cohen Bldg., Rm. 4360
Washington, DC 20201
202-619-0815
Fax: 202-619-2011

Health Resources and Services Administration
Office of the Administrator
5600 Fishers Lane
Parklawn Bldg., Rm. 14-05
Rockville, MD 20857
301-443-2216

Hospice Education Institute
Hospicelink
PO Box 713

5 Essex Square, Suite 3-B
Essex, CT 06426
800-331-1620
203-767-1620 in CT

Human Nutrition Information Service
6505 Belcrest Rd., Rm. 360
Hyattsville, MD 20782
301-436-8474

IBM National Support Center for Persons with Disabilities
PO Box 2150-HO6R1
Atlanta, GA 30301
800-426-2133

Joint Commission on Accreditation of Healthcare Organizations
Department of Corporate Relations
One Renaissance Blvd.
Oakbrook Terrace, IL 60181
708-916-5632
Fax: 708-916-5644

The Library of Congress
Science and Technology Division
101 Independence Ave., SE
Adams Bldg., 5th Fl.
Washington, DC 20540
202-707-5664

The Living Bank
PO Box 6725
Houston, TX 77265
800-528-2971
713-528-2971 in TX

The National Agricultural Library
Food and Nutrition Information
Center, Rm. 304
Beltsville, MD 20705
301-504-5719
Fax: 301-504-5472

National Association for Home Care
519 C St., NE
Washington, DC 20002
202-547-7424

National Association for Music Therapy
8455 Colesville Rd., Suite 930
Silver Spring, MD 20910
301-589-3300

National Association of Area Agencies on Aging
1112 16th St., NW, Suite 100

Washington, DC 20036
202-296-8130

**National Association of State
Units on Aging**
2033 K St., NW, Suite 304
Washington, DC 20006
202-785-0707

National Consumers League
815 15th St., NW, Suite 928
Washington, DC 20005
202-639-8140

**National Council Against Health
Fraud Resource Center**
3521 Broadway
Kansas City, MO 64111
800-821-6671

National Council of Senior Citizens
1331 F St., NW
Washington, DC 20004-1171
202-347-8800

National Council on Disability
800 Independence Ave., SW
Suite 814
Washington, DC 20591
202-267-3846

National Council on the Aging, Inc.
409 Third St., SW, 2nd Fl.
Washington, DC 20024
800-424-9046

National Council on the Aging, Inc.
National Institute of
Adult Day Care
409 Third St., SW, 2nd Fl.
Washington, DC 20024
202-479-6680

National Hospice Organization
1901 N. Moore St., Suite 901
Arlington, VA 22209
800-658-8898
703-243-5900

**National Information Center for
Orphan Drugs and Rare Diseases**
PO Box 1133
Washington, DC 20013-1133
800-456-3505
301-656-4167

**National Institute of General
Medical Sciences**
9000 Rockville Pike
Bldg. 31, Rm. 4A-52
Bethesda, MD 20892
301-496-7301

National Institute on Aging
Public Information Office
9000 Rockville Pike
Bldg. 31, Rm. 5C27
Bethesda, MD 20892
301-496-1752

National Institutes of Health
9000 Rockville Pike
Bethesda, MD 20892
301-496-4461
Fax: 301-496-0017

**National Interfaith Coalition
of Aging**
c/o NCA, 409 3rd St., SW, 2nd Fl.
Washington, DC 20024
202-479-6689

National League for Nursing
350 Hudson St.
New York, NY 10014
800-669-1656
212-989-9393

**National Organization for
Rare Disorders**
PO Box 8923
New Fairfield, CT 06812
800-447-6673
203-746-6518

**Office of Disease Prevention
and Health Promotion**
National Health Information
Center
PO Box 1133
Washington, DC 20013-1133
800-336-4797
301-565-4167 in MD

Office of Health Facilties
5600 Fishers Lane
Parklawn Bldg., Rm., 11-25
Rockville, MD 20857
800-638-0742 Hill-Burton Hospital
Free Care

**The President's Committee on
Employment of People with
Disabilities**
1331 F St., NW, Suite 300
Washington, DC 20004
202-376-6200
202-376-6205 TDD
Fax: 202-376-6219

**President's Council on Physical
Fitness and Sports**
701 Pennsylvania Ave., NW
Suite 250

Washington, DC 20004
202-272-3430

Sjogren's Syndrome Foundation
382 Main St.
Port Washington, NY 11050
516-767-2866

United Network for Organ Sharing
PO Box 13770
1100 Boulders Parkway, Suite 500
Richmond, VA 23225-8770
800-24-DONOR

United Scleroderma Foundation
PO Box 399
Watsonville, CA 95077-0399
800-722-HOPE
408-728-2202

**United States Department
of Education**
Clearinghouse on Disability
Information
Switzer Bldg., Rm. 3132
Washington, DC 20202-2524
202-732-1244

**United States Department
of Education**
National Institute on Disability
and Rehabilitation Research
330 C St., SW, Rm. 3060
Washington, DC 20202-2572
202-732-1134

**United States Government
Printing Office**
Washington, DC 20402-9325
202-783-3238 orders & information
202-275-3634 updates on
publications

United Way of America
701 N. Fairfax St.
Alexandria, VA 22314-2045
703-836-7100

Very Special Arts USA
The John F. Kennedy Center for
Performing Arts, Education Office
Washington, DC 20566
800-933-8721
202-737-0645 TDD

**Visiting Nurse Associations
of America**
3801 E. Florida Ave., Suite 206
Denver, CO 80210
800-426-2547

**Warren Grant Magnuson
Clinical Center**
Office of Clinical Center
Communications
9000 Rockville Pike
Bldg. 10, Rm. 1C-255
Bethesda, MD 20892
301-496-4891 referrals

NATIONAL SELF-HELP
CLEARINGHOUSES

American Self-Help Clearinghouse
St. Clare's Riverside Medical Center
Pocono Rd.
Denville, NJ 07834
201-625-9565

National Self-Help Clearinghouse
Graduate School and University
Center of the City University
of New York
25 W. 43rd St., Rm. 620
New York, NY 10036
212-642-2944

REGIONAL SELF-HELP
CLEARINGHOUSES

CALIFORNIA

Concord

**Mental Health Association
of Contra Costa County**
1070 Concord Ave., Suite 170
Concord, CA 94520
510-603-1212

Davis

**Mental Health Association
of Yolo County**
PO Box 447
Davis, CA 95617
916-756-8181

Fresno

**Fresno County Information
Referral Network**
2420 Mariposa St.
Fresno, CA 93721
209-488-3857

Self-Help Network
c/o Help in Emotional Trouble
PO Box 4282
Fresno, CA 93744

209-486-4703
209-485-1432 crisis hotline

Los Angeles

**University of California
Los Angeles**
California Self-Help Center
405 Hilgard Ave.
Los Angeles, CA 90024
800-222-LINK in CA
213-825-1799

Merced

**Mental Health Association
of Merced County**
480 E. 13th St.
Merced, CA 95340
209-723-8861

Sacramento

**Sacramento Self-Help
Clearinghouse**
8912 Volunteer Lane, Suite 210
Sacramento, CA 95826
916-368-3100

San Francisco

**San Francisco Self-Help
Clearinghouse**
2398 Pine St.
San Francisco, CA 94115
415-921-4044

CONNECTICUT

New Haven

**Self-Help Mutual Support Network
Consultation Center**
389 Whitney Ave.
New Haven, CT 06511
203-789-7645
Fax: 203-562-6355

FLORIDA

St. Petersburg

Hotline Information Referral
PO Box 13087
St. Petersburg, FL 33733
813-531-4664

ILLINOIS

Champaign

**Family Services of Champaign
County**

405 S. State St.
Champaign, IL 61820
217-352-0099
Fax: 217-352-9512

Evanston

Illinois Self-Help Center
1600 Dodge Ave., Suite S-122
Evanston, IL 60201
312-328-0470

INDIANA

Indianapolis

Information and Referral Network
1828 N. Meridian St.
Indianapolis, IN 46202
317-921-1305

IOWA

Fort Dodge

Iowa Self-Help Clearinghouse
PO Box 1151, 33 N. 12th St.
Fort Dodge, IA 50501
800-952-4777 in IA
515-576-5870

KANSAS

Wichita

Kansas Self-Help Network
Wichita State University
Campus Box 34
Wichita, KS 67208-1595
316-689-3843

MASSACHUSETTS

Amherst

**Massachusetts Clearinghouse of
Mutual Help Groups**
113 Skinner Hall, University of
Massachusetts
Amherst, MA 01003
413-545-2313
Fax: 413-545-4410

MICHIGAN

Benton Harbor

Center for Self-Help
Riverwood Center
PO Box 547, 1485 South M-139
Benton Harbor, MI 49022

800-336-0341
616-925-0585

Lansing

**Michigan Protection and
Advocacy Service**
Michigan Self-Help Clearinghouse
106 W. Allegan, Suite 210
Lansing, MI 48933
800-752-5858 in MI
517-484-7373

MINNESOTA

St. Paul

United Way
First Call for Help
166 E. 4th St., Suite 100
St. Paul, MN 55101-1448
612-224-1133

MISSOURI

Kansas City

**Greater Kansas City Mental
Health Association**
1009 Baltimore Ave., 5th Fl.
Kansas City, MO 64105
816-472-5000

St. Louis

**Mental Health Association
of St. Louis**
1905 S. Grand
St. Louis, MO 63104
314-773-1399
Fax: 314-773-5930

NEBRASKA

Lincoln

Self-Help Information Services
1601 Euclid Ave.
Lincoln, NE 68502
402-476-9668

NEW HAMPSHIRE

Concord

**New Hampshire Division of Mental
Health and Developmental Services**
105 Pleasant St.
State Office Park South
Concord, NH 03301
603-271-5060

NEW JERSEY

Denville

**New Jersey Self-Help
Clearinghouse**
St. Clare's Riverside Medical
Center, Pocono Rd.
Denville, NJ 07834
201-625-9565
800-367-6274 in NJ

NEW YORK

Albany

**New York State Council on
Children and Families**
New York State Self-Help
Clearinghouse
Empire State Plaza, Corning Tower
Albany, NY 12224
518-473-3652
Fax: 518-473-2570

Buffalo

**Mental Health Association
of Erie County**
Erie County Self-Help
Clearinghouse
999 Delaware Ave.
Buffalo, NY 14209
716-886-1242

Central Islip

New York Institute of Technology
Long Island Self-Help
Clearinghouse
Central Islip Campus
Central Islip, NY 11722
516-348-3030

Corning

Institute for Human Services
29 Denison Parkway, Suite B
Corning, NY 14830
800-346-2211 24-hour helpline
607-936-3725

Elmira

**Schuyler/Chemung Self-Help
Clearinghouse**
Economic Opportunity
Program, Inc.
318 Madison Ave.
Elmira, NY 14901
607-734-6174

Schuyline/Info Line
425 Pennsylvania Ave.
Elmira, NY 14904
800-348-0448
607-737-2077

Fulton

**Catholic Charities in Oswego
County**
365 W. First St.
Fulton, NY 13069
315-598-3980

Gloversville

**Fulton County Self-Help
Clearinghouse**
Family Counseling Center
113 Bleecker St.
Gloversville, NY 12078
518-725-4310

Goshen

**Mental Health Association
in Orange County, Inc.**
Tri-County Self-Help
Clearinghouse
223 Main St.
Goshen, NY 10924
914-294-9355

Ithaca

**Tompkins County Mental
Health Association**
301 S. Geneva St., G-8
Ithaca, NY 14850
607-273-9250

Kingston

**Mental Health Association
in Ulster County**
MHA Self-Help Clearinghouse
PO Box 2304
221 Tuyten Bridge Rd.
Kingston, NY 12401-0227
914-336-4747

Lockport

**Mental Health Association
in Niagara County, Inc.**
Niagara County Self-Help
Clearinghouse
151 East Ave.
Lockport, NY 14094
716-433-3780

Olean

**Cattaraugus County
Self-Help Clearinghouse**
Crossties
American Red Cross-
Olean Branch
528 N. Barry
Olean, NY 14760
716-372-5800

Plattsburgh

**Fulton County Self-Help
Clearinghouse**
CEF Crisis/Helpline
36 Brinkerhoff St.
Plattsburgh, NY 12901
518-561-2330

Pomona

**Mental Health Association
of Rockland**
Rockland County Self-Help
Clearinghouse and
Information Center
Sanatorium Rd., Bldg. F
Pomona, NY 10970
914-354-0200

Potsdam

**Reachout of St. Lawrence
County, Inc.**
PO Box 5051
Potsdam, NY 13676
315-265-2422

Poughkeepsie

**United Way of Dutchess
County, Inc.**
Dutchess County Self-Help
Clearinghouse
PO Box 832, 75 Market St.
Poughkeepsie, NY 12601
914-473-1500

Rochester

**Mental Health Association
of Rochester/Monroe**
Monroe County Self-Help
Clearinghouse
1100 University Ave.
Rochester, NY 14607
716-256-0590
Fax: 716-256-2732

Schenectady

**Human Services Planning Council
of Schenectady County, Inc.**
Schenectady County Self-Help
Clearinghouse
152 Barrett St., 2nd Fl.
Schenectady, NY 12305
518-374-2244

Syracuse

The Volunteer Center, Inc.
Onondaga County Self-Help
Clearinghouse
115 Jefferson St., Suite 400
Syracuse, NY 13202
315-474-7011
Fax: 315-479-6772

Utica

**Voluntary Action Center
of Greater Utica**
1644 Genesee St.
Utica, NY 13502
315-735-4463

White Plains

**Westchester Self-Help
Clearinghouse**
456 North St.
White Plains, NY 10605
914-949-6301

NORTH CAROLINA

Charlotte

Supportworks
1012 Kings Dr., Suite 923
Charlotte, NC 28283
704-331-9500

OHIO

Dayton

Ohio Self-Help Clearinghouse
Family Service Association
184 Salem Ave.
Dayton, OH 45406
513-222-9481
Fax: 513-222-3710

OREGON

Portland

**Northwest Regional Self-Help
Clearinghouse**

718 W. Burnside Ave.
Portland, OR 97209
503-222-5555

PENNSYLVANIA

Pittsburgh

**Self-Help Group Network
of the Pittsburgh Area**
1323 Forbes Ave., Suite 200
Pittsburgh, PA 15219
412-261-5363

Scranton

**Voluntary Action Center of
Northeast Pennsylvania**
Self-Help Information and
Networking Exchange
225 N. Washington Ave.
Park Plaza, Lower Level
Scranton, PA 18503
717-961-1234
Fax: 717-341-5816

SOUTH CAROLINA

West Columbia

The Support Group Network
Lexington Medical Center
2720 Sunset Blvd.
West Columbia, SC 29169
803-791-9227

TENNESSEE

Knoxville

**Mental Health Association
of Knox County**
Support Group Clearinghouse
6712 Kingston Pike, Suite 203
Knoxville, TN 37919
615-584-6736

TEXAS

Dallas

**Mental Health Association
of Dallas County**
Dallas Self-Help Clearinghouse
2929 Carlisle St.
Dallas, TX 75204-1058
214-871-2420

Fort Worth

Tarrant County Mental Health Association
Tarrant County Self-Help Clearinghouse
3136 W. 4th St.
Fort Worth, TX 76107
817-335-5405

Houston

Mental Health Association in Houston and Harris County
Houston Self-Help Clearinghouse
2211 Norfolk, Suite 810
Houston, TX 77098
713-523-8963

San Antonio

Mental Health Association in Greater San Antonio
Greater San Antonio Self-Help Clearinghouse
901 Northeast Loop 410, Suite 500
San Antonio, TX 78209
512-826-2288

VIRGINIA

Annadale

Mental Health Association of Northern Virginia
7630 Little River Turnpike
Suite 206
Annadale, VA 22003
703-642-0800

Self-Help Clearinghouse of Greater Washington
7630 Little River Turnpike
Annadale, VA 22003
703-941-5465

WASHINGTON

Olympia

Crisis Clinic/Thurston and Mason Counties
PO Box 2463
Olympia, WA 98507
800-627-2211
206-352-2211

ACKNOWLEDGMENTS

We wish to thank the following organizations who so generously gave us permission to reprint material from their publications. Grouped by Handbook chapter title, those publications are acknowledged below, preceded by the respective subject entry name as it appears in the Handbook:

CANCER

OVERVIEW—*What You Need To Know About Cancer,* revised August 1988, The National Cancer Institute.

BLADDER CANCER—*What You Need To Know About Bladder Cancer,* revised June 1989, reprinted October 1990, The National Cancer Institute.

BREAST CANCER—*What You Need To Know About Breast Cancer,* revised May 1989, reprinted October 1990, The National Cancer Institute.

CERVICAL CANCER—*What You Need To Know About Cancer of the Cervix,* revised April 1990, The National Cancer Institute.

COLORECTAL CANCER—*What You Need To Know About Cancer of the Colon and Rectum,* revised December 1987, reprinted November 1989, The National Cancer Institute.

HODGKIN'S DISEASE—*What You Need To Know About Hodgkin's Disease,* revised August 1988, reprinted November 1989, The National Cancer Institute.

KIDNEY CANCER—*What You Need To Know About Kidney Cancer,* revised June 1990, reprinted November 1990, The National Cancer Institute.

LEUKEMIA—*What You Need To Know About Leukemia,* reprinted October 1990, The National Cancer Institute.

LUNG CANCER—*What You Need To Know About Lung Cancer,* revised August 1987, reprinted November 1989, The National Cancer Institute.

MULTIPLE MYELOMA—*What You Need To Know About Multiple Myeloma,* reprinted August 1990, The National Cancer Institute.

NON-HODGKIN'S LYMPHOMAS—*What You Need To Know About Non-Hodgkin's Lymphomas,* revised November 1988, reprinted April 1990, The National Cancer Institute.

ORAL CANCERS—*What You Need To Know About Oral Cancers,* revised June 1989, printed November 1989, The National Cancer Institute.

OVARIAN CANCER—*What You Need To Know About Ovarian Cancer,* revised May 1990, printed October 1990, The National Cancer Institute.

PANCREATIC CANCER—*What You Need To Know About Cancer of the Pancreas,* revised October 1989, printed March 1990, The National Cancer Institute.

PROSTATE CANCER—*What You Need To Know About Prostate Cancer,* revised April 1990, The National Cancer Institute.

SKIN CANCER—*What You Need To Know About Skin Cancer,* revised August 1988, reprinted November 1989, The National Cancer Institute.

STOMACH CANCER—*What You Need To Know About Cancer of the Stomach,* reprinted February 1989, The National Cancer Institute.

UTERINE CANCER—*What You Need To Know About Cancer of the Uterus,* revised August 1988, The National Cancer Institute.

CHAPTER 2

THE BLOOD

VITAMIN AND MINERAL DEFICIENCY ANEMIAS—*The Johns Hopkins Medical Letter HEALTH AFTER 50,* Volume 2 Issue 12, © 1991 Medletter Associates.

SICKLE CELL ANEMIA—*Sickle Cell Anemia,* June 1990, The Warren Grant Magnuson Clinical Center.

THE BRAIN AND NERVOUS SYSTEM

DEMENTIA—*The Dementias: Hope Through Research,* printed 1983, The National Institute of Neurological Disorders and Stroke.

ALZHEIMER'S DISEASE—*Useful Information On Alzheimer's Disease,* printed 1990, The National Institute of Mental Health.

NORMAL CHANGES IN THE AGING BRAIN—*The Johns Hopkins Medical Letter HEALTH AFTER 50,* Volume 3 Issue 8, © 1991 Medletter Associates.

CHRONIC PAIN—*Chronic Pain: Hope Through Research,* November 1989, The National Institute of Neurological Disorders and Stroke.

HEADACHE—*Headache: Hope Through Research,* September 1984, The National Institute of Neurological Disorders and Stroke.

BRAIN TUMORS—*Brain Tumors: Hope Through Research,* December 1981, The National Institute of Neurological Disorders and Stroke.

DIZZINESS—*Dizziness: Hope Through Research,* September 1986, The National Institute of Neurological Disorders and Stroke.

EPILEPSY—*Epilepsy: Hope Through Research,* July 1981, The National Institute of Neurological Disorders and Stroke.

PARKINSON'S DISEASE—*Parkinson's Disease: Hope Through Research,* June 1983, The National Institute of Neurological Disorders and Stroke.

SHINGLES—*Shingles: Hope Through Research,* November 1981, The National Institute of Neurological Disorders and Stroke.

DENTAL AND ORAL DISORDERS

TOOTH DECAY—*Age Page: Taking Care of Your Teeth and Mouth,* revised October 1989, The National Institute on Aging.

PERIODONTAL DISEASE—*Periodontal (Gum) Disease,* The National Institute of Dental Research.

COSMETIC DENTAL OPTIONS—*The Johns Hopkins Medical Letter HEALTH AFTER 50,* Volume 2 Issue 3, © 1990 Medletter Associates.

DRY MOUTH (XEROSTOMIA)—*Dry Mouth (Xerostomia),* revised 1991, The National Institute of Dental Research.

DENTURES/DENTAL IMPLANTS—*The Johns Hopkins Medical Letter HEALTH AFTER 50,* Volume 1 Issues 7/1, © 1989 Medletter Associates.

THE DIGESTIVE SYSTEM

OVERVIEW—*Your Digestive System and How It Works,* March 1986, The National Institute of Diabetes and Digestive and Kidney Diseases.

HEARTBURN—*Heartburn,* April 1986, The National Institute of Diabetes and Digestive and Kidney Diseases.

HIATAL HERNIA—*What Is Hiatal Hernia?,* revised April 1990, The National Institute of Diabetes and Digestive and Kidney Diseases.

PEPTIC ULCER—*Peptic Ulcer,* September 1985, The National Institute of Diabetes and Digestive and Kidney Diseases.

PANCREATITIS—*Pancreatitis,* November 1991, The National Institute of Diabetes and Digestive and Kidney Diseases.

CIRRHOSIS OF THE LIVER—*Cirrhosis of the Liver,* reprinted October 1991, The National Institute of Diabetes and Digestive and Kidney Diseases.

VIRAL HEPATITIS—*Viral Hepatitis: Everybody's Problem?,* © The American Liver Foundation.

GALLSTONES—*Gallstones and Other Gallbladder Disorders: a National Health Problem,* May 1989, © The American Liver Foundation.

INFLAMMATORY BOWEL DISEASE—*Inflammatory Bowel Disease,* December 1985, The National Institute of Diabetes and Digestive and Kidney Diseases.

IRRITABLE BOWEL SYNDROME—*What Is Irritable Bowel Syndrome?,* reprinted October 1989, The National Institute of Diabetes and Digestive and Kidney Diseases.

DIVERTICULOSIS AND DIVERTICULITIS—*Diverticulosis and Diverticulitis,* October 1989, The National Institute of Diabetes and Digestive and Kidney Diseases.

CONSTIPATION—*What Is Constipation?,* reprinted February 1986, The National Institute of Diabetes and Digestive and Kidney Diseases.

DIARRHEA—*The Johns Hopkins Medical Letter HEALTH AFTER 50,* Volume 1 Issue 5, © 1989 Medletter Associates.

HEMORRHOIDS—*Hemorrhoids,* February 1991, The National Institute of Diabetes and Digestive and Kidney Diseases.

THE EARS, NOSE, AND THROAT

HEARING LOSS—*Hearing Loss,* January 1982, The National Institute of Neurological Disorders and Stroke.

SINUSITIS—*Sinus: Pain, Pressure, Drainage,* reprinted May 1990, © 1987 The American Academy of Otolaryngology–Head and Neck Surgery.

SMELL AND TASTE DISORDERS—*Smell and Taste Disorders,* reprinted March 1988, © 1986 The American Academy of Otolaryngology–Head and Neck Surgery.

SORE THROAT—*Sore Throats: Causes and Cures,* reprinted November 1990, © 1986 The American Academy of Otolaryngology–Head and Neck Surgery.

THE ENDOCRINE SYSTEM

DIABETES MELLITUS—*What You Need To Know About Diabetes,* reprinted December 1990, © 1984 The American Diabetes Association; *Basic Information Series,* Numbers 1-22, © 1988, 1989 The American Diabetes Association.

OBESITY—*Obesity and Energy Metabolism,* printed February 1984, The Warren Grant Magnuson Clinical Center.

LOSING WEIGHT AND KEEPING IT OFF—*The Johns Hopkins Medical Letter HEALTH AFTER 50,* Volume 3 Issue 3, © 1991 Medletter Associates.

THYROID DISEASE—*Thyroid Disease in the Elderly,* The Thyroid Foundation of America.

THE EYES

CATARACT—*Cataract: Clouding the Lens of Sight,* reprinted July 1991, © 1984 The American Academy of Ophthalmology.

GLAUCOMA—*Glaucoma: It Can Take Your Sight Away,* reviewed February 1988, reprinted February 1991, © 1984 The American Academy of Ophthalmology.

MACULAR DEGENERATION—*Macular Degeneration: Major Cause of Central Vision Loss,* reviewed October 1987, reprinted February 1991, © 1984 The American Academy of Ophthalmology.

THE BEST SUNGLASSES—*The Johns Hopkins Medical Letter HEALTH AFTER 50,* Volume 3 Issue 5, © 1991 Medletter Associates.

REFRACTIVE ERRORS—*Refractive Errors: Why You Need Glasses or Contact Lenses,* reprinted May 1988, © 1984 The American Academy of Ophthalmology.

AMAUROSIS FUGAX—*The Carotid Artery and the Eye,* © 1987 The American Academy of Ophthalmology.

FLOATERS AND FLASHES—*Floaters and Flashes: Should You Be Concerned?,* revised August 1990, reprinted July 1991, © 1985

The American Academy of
Ophthalmology.

THE HEART AND
BLOOD VESSELS

ATHEROSCLEROSIS—*1992 Heart and Stroke Facts,* © 1991 The American Heart Association.

HIGH BLOOD PRESSURE—*1992 Heart and Stroke Facts,* © 1991 The American Heart Association.

HEART ATTACK AND ANGINA—*1992 Heart and Stroke Facts,* © 1991 The American Heart Association.

STROKE—*1992 Heart and Stroke Facts,* © 1991 The American Heart Association.

CONGESTIVE HEART FAILURE—*1992 Heart and Stroke Facts,* © 1991 The American Heart Association.

PERIPHERAL VASCULAR DISEASE—*The Johns Hopkins Medical Letter HEALTH AFTER 50,* Volume 3 Issue 7, © 1991 Medletter Associates.

VARICOSE VEINS—*The Johns Hopkins Medical Letter HEALTH AFTER 50,* Volume 1 Issue 11, © 1990 Medletter Associates.

THE KIDNEYS
AND URINARY TRACT

OVERVIEW—*Your Kidneys: Master Chemists of the Body,* © 1989 The National Kidney Foundation.

DIALYSIS TREATMENTS—*Dialysis,* © 1989 The National Kidney Foundation.

URINARY TRACT INFECTIONS—*Understanding Urinary Tract Infections,* April 1988, The National Institute of Diabetes and Digestive and Kidney Diseases.

KIDNEY STONES—*About Kidney Stones,* © 1988, 1990 The National Kidney Foundation.

GLOMERULONEPHRITIS—*Glomerulonephritis,* April 1987, © 1987 The National Kidney Foundation.

THE LUNGS AND
RESPIRATORY SYSTEM

OVERVIEW—*How To Keep Your Lungs Healthy,* February 1990, © 1990 The American Lung Association.

ASTHMA—*Facts About Asthma,* November 1990, © 1990 The American Lung Association.

CHRONIC BRONCHITIS—*Facts About Chronic Bronchitis,* December 1989, © 1989 The American Lung Association.

EMPHYSEMA—*Facts About Emphysema,* January 1990, © 1990 The American Lung Association.

PNEUMONIA—*Facts About Pneumonia,* December 1990, © 1990 The American Lung Association.

INFLUENZA—*Facts About Influenza (Flu),* July 1991, © 1991 The American Lung Association.

THE MUSCLES AND BONES

BACK PAIN—*Back Pain,* © 1988 The Arthritis Foundation.

OSTEOPOROSIS—*Osteoporosis: Cause, Treatment, Prevention,* revised May 1986, The National Institute of Arthritis and Musculoskeletal and Skin Diseases.

OSTEOARTHRITIS—*Arthritis Information: Osteoarthritis,* June 1990, © 1986, 1990 The Arthritis Foundation.

RHEUMATOID ARTHRITIS—*Arthritis Information: Rheumatoid Arthritis,* July 1991, © 1983, 1987, 1990 The Arthritis Foundation.

FIBROMYALGIA—*Arthritis Information: Fibromyalgia (Fibrositis),* October 1989, © 1989 The Arthritis Foundation.

LOCALIZED PAIN SYNDROMES—*Arthritis Information: Bursitis, Tendinitis and Localized Pain Syndromes,* December 1990, © 1983, 1986, 1990 The Arthritis Foundation.

CARPAL TUNNEL SYNDROME—*Arthritis Information: Carpal Tunnel Syndrome,* May 1991, © 1987, 1991 The Arthritis Foundation.

FOOT PROBLEMS—*The Johns Hopkins Medical Letter HEALTH AFTER 50,* Volume 2 Issue 3, © 1990 Medletter Associates.

THE SKIN

BENIGN SKIN CONDITIONS—*The Johns Hopkins Medical Letter HEALTH AFTER 50,* Volume 2 Issue 4, © 1990 Medletter Associates.

DRY SKIN AND SEBORRHEIC DERMATITIS—*Lifelong Healthy Skin,* revised May 1988, © 1987 The American Academy of Dermatology.

PRECANCEROUS SKIN CONDITIONS—*The Johns Hopkins Medical Letter HEALTH AFTER 50,* Volumes 2/3 Issue 4, © 1990/1991 Medletter Associates.

MOLE INSPECTION—LEARNING YOUR ABCD'S—*The Johns Hopkins Medical Letter HEALTH AFTER 50,* Volume 2 Issue 4, © 1990 Medletter Associates.

HEALTH PROBLEMS OF MEN

IMPOTENCE—*The Johns Hopkins Medical Letter HEALTH AFTER 50,* Volume 2 Issue 1, © 1990 Medletter Associates.

PROSTATE ENLARGEMENT—*Prostate Enlargement: Benign Prostatic Hyperplasia,* April 1990, The National Institute of Diabetes and Digestive and Kidney Diseases.

CHAPTER 15

HEALTH PROBLEMS OF WOMEN

BENIGN BREAST CONDITIONS—*Questions and Answers about Breast Lumps,* revised May 1989, printed March 1990, The National Cancer Institute.

MENOPAUSE—*The Menopause Time of Life,* revised July 1986, The National Institute on Aging.

ACKNOWLEDGMENTS

URINARY INCONTINENCE—*The Johns Hopkins Medical Letter HEALTH AFTER 50,* Volume 3 Issue 3, © 1991 Medletter Associates.

VAGINITIS—*Vaginitis: Causes and Treatments,* revised September 1986, © June 1984 The American College of Obstetricians and Gynecologists.

MENTAL HEALTH

DEPRESSION—*Let's Talk Facts About Depression,* © 1988, 1989 The American Psychiatric Association.

ANXIETY DISORDERS—*Let's Talk Facts About Anxiety Disorders,* © 1988, 1990 The American Psychiatric Association.

MANIC-DEPRESSIVE DISORDER—*Let's Talk Facts About Manic-Depressive Disorders,* © 1988, 1990 The American Psychiatric Association.

SLEEP DISORDERS—*Sleep as We Grow Older,* © May 1990 The American Sleep Disorders Association.